Collins
Latin
Dictionary

D1380409

30130 139926959

HarperCollins Publishers
Westerhill Road
Bishopbriggs
Glasgow
G64 2QT
Great Britain

First Edition 1997

Latest Reprint 2004

© HarperCollins Publishers 1997

ISBN 0-00-719632-6

www.collins.co.uk

A catalogue record for this book is available
from the British Library

HarperCollins Publishers, Inc.
10 East 53rd Street, New York, NY 10022

ISBN 0-06-053690-x

Library of Congress Cataloging-in-
Publication Data has been applied for

www.harpercollins.com

First HarperCollins edition published 2003

Dictionary text typeset by Tradespools
Ltd, Somerset

Grammar text typeset by Latimer Trend
Ltd, Plymouth

Printed in Italy by Legoprint S.P.A.

Dictionary based on the Collins Latin Gem © 1957 by
Professor D. A. Kidd,
Canterbury University

Grammar text and dictionary supplements by
Mary Wade

Editorial coordinator
Joyce Littlejohn

Latin consultants
Ian Brookes
Denis Bruce
Michael D. Igoe

Series editor
Lorna Sinclair

Editorial management
Vivian Marr

CONTENTS

ABBREVIATIONS

adj	adjective	*MED*	medicine
abl	ablative	*MIL*	military
acc	accusative	*mod*	modern
adv	adverb	*n*	noun
AGR	agriculture	*NAUT*	nautical
ARCH	architecture	*neg*	negative
art	article	*nom*	nominative
ASTR	astronomy	*nt*	neuter
AUG	augury	*num*	numeral
COMM	business	*occ*	occasionally
CIRCS	circumstances	*p*	participle
compar	comparative	*pass*	passive
conj	conjunction	*perf*	perfect
cpd	compound	*perh*	perhaps
dat	dative	*pers*	person
defec	defective	*PHILOS*	philosophy
ECCL	ecclesiastical	*pl*	plural
esp	especially	*POL*	politics
excl	exclamatory	*ppa*	perfect participle active
f	feminine	*ppp*	perfect participle passive
fig	figurative	*prep*	preposition
fut	future	*pres*	present
gen	genitive	*pron*	pronoun
GEOG	geography	*prop*	properly
GRAM	grammar	*PROV*	proverb
impers	impersonal	*relat*	relative
imperf	imperfect	*RHET*	rhetoric
impv	imperative	*sg*	singular
indecl	indeclinable	*sim*	similarly
indic	indicative	*subj*	subjunctive
inf	informal	*superl*	superlative
infin	infinitive	*THEAT*	theatre
interj	interjection	*UNIV*	university
interrog	interrogative	*usu*	usually
LIT	literature	*vi*	intransitive verb
loc	locative	*voc*	vocative
m	masculine	*vt*	transitive verb
MATH	mathematics		

INTRODUCTION

Whether you are learning Latin for the first time or wish to "brush up" what you learned some time ago, this dictionary is designed to help you understand Latin and to express yourself in Latin, if you so wish.

HOW TO USE THE DICTIONARY

Entries are laid out as follows:

Headword

This is shown in **bold type**. On the Latin-English side all long vowels are shown by placing a ¯ above them. Latin nouns show the genitive singular form in bold. Latin verbs show the first person singular of the present indicative as the headword, followed by the infinitive, the first person singular of the perfect indicative and usually the past participle, all in bold type:

elegīa, -ae
elementum, -ī
ēlevō, āre
ēmātūrēscō, -ēscere, -uī

Part of Speech

Next comes the part of speech (noun, verb, adjective etc), shown in *italics*. Part of speech abbreviations used in the dictionary are shown in the abbreviations list (*p iv*). Where a word has more than one part of speech, each new part of speech is preceded by a black lozenge (♦). If a Latin headword is a preposition, the case taken by the preposition comes immediately after the part of speech, in *italics* and in brackets.

era, -ae *f*
ticklish *adj*
thunder *n* tonitrus *m* ♦ *vi* tonare, intonare.
ērgā *prep* (*with acc*) towards; against.

Meanings

Where a word or a part of speech has only one meaning, the translation comes immediately after the part of speech. However, many words have more than one meaning. Where the context is likely to show which translation is correct, variations in meaning are simply separated by a semi-colon. But usually there will also be an "indicator" in *italics* and in brackets. Some meanings relate to specific subject areas, for example religion, politics, military matters etc –

these indicators are in small italic capitals.

ēnsiger, -ī *adj* with his sword.
toy *n* crepundia *ntpl* ♦ *vi* ludere.
toll collector *n* exactor *m*; portitor *m*.
eō, -īre, īvī *and* **iī, itum** *vi* to go; (*MIL*) to march; (*time*) to pass; (*event*) to proceed, turn out.

Translations

Most words can be translated directly. On the English-Latin side, translations of nouns include the gender of the Latin noun in *italics*. However, sometimes a phrase is needed to show how a word is used, but in some cases a direct translation of a phrase would be meaningless: the symbol ~ in front of a translation shows that the translation is natural English, but does not mean word for word what the Latin means. Sometimes, even an approximate translation would not be very helpful (for place names, for example) – in these cases, an explanation in *italics* is given instead. In other cases, the user will need more information than simply the translation; in these cases, "indicators" are included in the translation(s), giving, for instance, the case required by a Latin verb or preposition or further details about a place or person.

thumb *n* pollex *m*; **have under one's ~** in potestate sua habere.
elephantomacha, -ae *m fighter mounted on an elephant.*
Erymanthus, -i *m* mountain range in Arcadia (*where Hercules killed the bear*).
thwart *vt* obstare (*dat*), officere (*dat*).

Pronunciation

Since Latin pronunciation is regular, once the basic rules have been learned (*see pp viii, ix*), the dictionary does not show phonetic transcriptions against each headword, but does show all long vowels.

Other Information

The dictionary also includes:

- a basic grammar section
- information about life in Roman times:
  – how government and the army were organized – how numbers and dates were calculated and expressed – family relationships – geographical names – major Roman authors – key events in Roman history – (*important historical and mythological characters and events are listed within the body of the main text*).
- a section on Latin poetry and scansion
- a list of Latin expressions commonly used in English today

LATIN ALPHABET

The Latin alphabet is the one which has been almost universally adopted by the modern languages of Europe and America. In the Classical period it had 23 letters, namely the English alphabet without letters **j**, **v** and **w**.

Letter *v*
The symbol **v** was the capital form of the letter **u**, but in a later age the small **v** came into use to represent the consonantal **u**, and as it is commonly so employed in modern editions of Latin authors, it has been retained as a distinct letter in this dictionary for convenience.

Letter *j*
The symbol **j** came to be used as the consonantal **i**, and is found in older editions of the Classics, but as it has been almost entirely discarded in modern texts, it is not used in this dictionary, and words found spelt with a **j** must therefore be looked up under **i**.

Letters *w, y, z*
The letter **w** may be seen in the Latinized forms of some modern names, *e.g.* **Westmonasterium**, Westminster. The letters **y** and **z** occur only in words of Greek origin.

ORTHOGRAPHY

Many Latin words which begin with a prefix can be spelled in two ways. The prefix can retain its original spelling, or it can be assimilated, changing a letter depending on the letter which follows it. Compare the following:

ad before **g, l, r** and **p**:

adpropinquare	appropinquare
adgredi	aggredi
adloquor	alloquor
adrogans	arrogans

ad is also often assimilated before **f** and **n**:

adfectus	affectus
adnexus	annexus

and **ad** is often shortened to **a** before **sc**:

adscendere	ascendere

in changes to **il** before **l**, to **im** before **m** or **p** and to **ir** before **r**.

con becomes **cor** when followed by another **r** and **col** when followed by **l**.

We have provided cross-references in the text to draw your attention to the alternative forms of words. Thus, although **arrogantia** does not appear in the Latin-English section, the cross-reference at **arr-** will point you to the entry for **adrogantia**, where the translation is given.

PRONUNCIATION

The ancient pronunciation of Latin has been established with a fair degree of certainty from the evidence of ancient authorities and inscriptions and inferences from the modern Romance languages. It is not possible, of course, to recapture the precise nuances of Classical Latin speech, but what follows is now generally accepted and generally understood as a reasonably accurate guide to the sounds of Latin as spoken by educated Romans during the two centuries from Cicero to Quintilian.

ACCENT

The Latin accent in the Classical period was a weak stress, perhaps with an element of pitch in it. It falls, as in English, on the second last syllable of the word, if that syllable is long, and on the third last syllable if the second last is short. Disyllabic words take the accent on the first syllable, unless they have already lost a final syllable, *e.g.* **illīc(e)**.

Inflected words are commonly learned with the accent wrongly placed on the last syllable, for convenience in memorizing the inflexions. But it is advisable to get the accent as well as the ending right.

The correct accent of other words can easily be found by noting carefully the quantity of the second last syllable and then accenting the word as in English, according to the rule given above. Thus **fuērunt** is accented on the second last syllable because the **e** is long, whereas **fuerant** is accented on the third last, because the **e** is short.

VOWELS

Vowels are pure and should not be diphthongized as in certain sounds of Southern English. They may be long or short. Throughout this Dictionary all vowels known or believed by the best authorities to be long are marked with a line above them; those unmarked are either known to be short or of uncertain quantity.

Short		Long	
agricolạ	rạt	rāmus	rạther
hederā	pẹn	avē	pạy
ītaque	kīn	cīvis	kееn
favor	rŏb	ampliō	rōbe
nebulā	full	lūna	fool

y is a Greek sound and is pronounced (both short and long) as **u** in French *ie* rue.

DIPHTHONGS

_ae_stas	tr_y_	
_au_diō	t_ow_n	
h_ei_	p_ayee_	
m_eu_s	_ay-oo_	*with the accent on first sound*
m_oe_cha	t_oy_	
t_ui_tus	L_oui_s	

CONSONANTS

_b_alneae	_b_a_b_y	
ab_s_tēmius	a_ps_e	
su_b_tractus	a_pt_	
_c_astra	_c_ar	
_ch_orda	sepul_ch_re	
inter_d_o	_d_og	
cōn_f_lō	_f_ortune	
in_g_redior	_g_o	
_h_abeō	_h_and	(*but faintly*)
_i_aceo	_y_es	(*consonantal i = j*)
_K_alendae	oa_k_	
conge_l_ō	_l_et	
co_m_es	_m_an	(*final m was hardly sounded and may have simply nasalized the preceding vowel*)
pā_n_is	_n_o	
pa_ng_o	fi_ng_er	
stu_p_eō	a_p_t	
ra_ph_anus	_p_ill	
exse_qu_or	_qu_ite	
suprē_m_us	_b_rae	(*Scottish*)
mā_gnus_	_s_i_s_ter	(*never as in rose*)
lae_t_us	_s_top	
_th_eātrum	_t_ake	
_v_apor	_w_in	
	(*and consonantal u*)	
de_x_tra	si_x_	(*ks, not gs*)
_z_ōna	_z_ero	

Double consonants lengthen the sound of the consonant.

Quick Reference Grammar

DECLENSIONS OF NOUNS

1st Declension

	mainly f		*m*	
SING				
Nom.	terra	crambē	Aenēās	Anchīsēs
Voc.	terra	crambē	Aenēā	Anchīsā, -ē
Acc.	terram	crambēn	Aenēam, -ān	Anchīsam, -ēn
Gen.	terrae	crambes	Aenēae	Anchīsae
Dat.	terrae	crambae	Aenēae	Anchīsae
Abl.	terra	cramba	Aenēā	Anchīsā

PLURAL		
Nom.	terrae	crambae
Voc.	terrae	crambae
Acc.	terrās	crambās
Gen.	terrārum	crambārum
Dat.	terrīs	crambīs
Abl.	terrīs	crambīs

2nd Declension

mainly m

SING					
Nom.	modus	Lūcius	Dēlos (*f*)	puer	liber
Voc.	mode	Lūcī	Dēle	puer	liber
Acc.	modum	Lūcium	Dēlon	puerum	librum
Gen.	modī	Lūcī	Dēlī	puerī	librī
Dat.	modō	Lūciō	Dēlō	puerō	librō
Abl.	modō	Lūciō	Dēlō	puerō	librō

PLURAL					
Nom.	modī			puerī	librī
Voc.	modī			puerī	librī
Acc.	modōs			puerōs	librōs
Gen.	modōrum			puerōrum	librōrum
Dat.	modīs			puerīs	librīs
Abl.	modīs			puerīs	librīs

nt

SING
Nom.	dōnum
Voc.	dōnum
Acc.	dōnum
Gen.	dōnī
Dat.	dōnō
Abl.	dōnō

PLURAL
Nom.	dōna
Voc.	dōna
Acc.	dōna
Gen.	dōnōrum
Dat.	dōnīs
Abl.	dōnīs

3rd Declension

Group I: *Vowel stems, with gen pl in* **-ium**

	m and f		*nt*	
SING				
Nom.	clādēs	nāvis	rēte	animal
Voc.	clādēs	nāvis	rēte	animal
Acc.	clādem	nāvem, -im	rēte	animal
Gen.	clādis	nāvis	rētis	animālīs
Dat.	clādī	nāvī	rētī	animālī
Abl.	clāde	nāve, -ī	rētī	animālī
PLURAL				
Nom.	clādēs	nāvēs	rētia	animālia
Voc.	clādēs	nāvēs	rētia	animālia
Acc.	clādēs, -īs	nāvēs, -īs	rētia	animālia
Gen.	clādium	nāvium	rētium	animālium
Dat.	clādibus	nāvibus	rētibus	animālibus
Abl.	clādibus	nāvibus	rētibus	animālibus

Group II: *Consonant stems, some with gen pl in* **-ium**, *some in* **-um** *and some in either. Monosyllabic nouns ending in two consonants (e.g.* **urbs** *below) regularly have* **-ium**.

	m and f			*f*	*nt*
SING					
Nom.	urbs	amāns	laus	aetās	os
Voc.	urbs	amāns	laus	aetās	os
Acc.	urbem	amantem	laudem	aetātem	os
Gen.	urbis	amantis	laudis	aetātis	ossis
Dat.	urbī	amantī	laudī	aetātī	ossī
Abl.	urbe	amante	laude	aetāte	osse
PLURAL					
Nom.	urbēs	amantēs	laudēs	aetātēs	ossa
Voc.	urbēs	amantēs	laudēs	aetātēs	ossa

Acc.	urbēs	amantēs	laudēs	aetātēs	ossa
Gen.	urbium	amantium,	laudum,	aetātum,	ossium
		-um	-ium	-ium	
Dat.	urbibus	amantibus	laudibus	aetātibus	ossibus
Abl.	urbibus	amantibus	laudibus	aetātibus	ossibus

Group III: *Consonant stems, with gen pl in* -um

	m and f			*nt*	
SING					
Nom.	mōs	ratiō	pater	nōmen	opus
Voc.	mōs	ratiō	pater	nōmen	opus
Acc.	mōrem	ratiōnem	patrem	nōmen	opus
Gen.	mōris	ratiōnis	patris	nōminis	operis
Dat.	mōrī	ratiōnī	patrī	nōminī	operī
Abl.	mōre	ratiōne	patre	nōmine	opere
PLURAL					
Nom.	mōrēs	ratiōnēs	patrēs	nōmina	opera
Voc.	mōrēs	ratiōnēs	patrēs	nōmina	opera
Acc.	mōrēs	ratiōnēs	patrēs	nōmina	opera
Gen.	mōrum	ratiōnum	patrum	nōminum	operum
Dat.	mōribus	ratiōnibus	patribus	nōminibus	operibus
Abl.	mōribus	ratiōnibus	patribus	nōminibus	operibus

Group IV: *Greek nouns*

	m		*f*		*nt*
SING					
Nom.	āēr	hērōs	Periclēs	Naias	poēma
Voc.	āēr	hērōs	Periclē	Naias	poēma
Acc.	āera	hērōa	{ Periclem,	Naiada	poēma
			Periclea		
Gen.	āeris	hērōis	Periclis, -ı	Naiadis, -os	poēmatis
Dat.	āerī	hērōī	Periclī	Naiadī	poēmatī
Abl.	āere	hērōe	Periclē	Naiade	poēmate
PLURAL					
Nom.	āeres	hērōes		Naiades	poēmata
Voc.	āeres	hērōes		Naiades	poēmata
Acc.	āeras	hērōas		Naiadas	poēmata
Gen.	āerum	hērōum		Naiadum	poēmatōrum
Dat.	āeribus	hērōibus		Naiadibus	poēmatīs
Abl.	āeribus	hērōibus		Naiadibus	poēmatīs

	4th Declension		**5th Declension**	
	mainly m	*nt*	*mainly f*	
SING				
Nom.	portus	genū	diēs	rēs
Voc.	portus	genū	diēs	rēs
Acc.	portum	genū	diem	rem
Gen.	portūs	genūs	diēī	reī
Dat.	portuī	genū	diēī	reī
Abl.	portū	genū	diē	rē
PLURAL				
Nom.	portūs	genua	diēs	rēs
Voc.	portūs	genua	diēs	rēs
Acc.	portūs	genua	diēs	rēs
Gen.	portuum	genuum	diērum	rērum
Dat.	portibus, -ubus	genibus, -ubus	diēbus	rēbus
Abl.	portibus, -ubus	genibus, -ubus	diēbus	rēbus

CONJUGATIONS OF VERBS

ACTIVE

PRESENT TENSE

	First parāre *prepare*	Second habēre *have*	Third sūmere *take*	Fourth audīre *hear*
Indicative				
SING				
1st pers	parō	habeō	sūmō	audiō
2nd pers	parās	habēs	sūmis	audīs
3rd pers	parat	habet	sūmit	audit
PLURAL				
1st pers	parāmus	habēmus	sūmimus	audīmus
2nd pers	parātis	habētis	sūmitis	audītīs
3rd pers	parant	habent	sūmunt	audiunt
Subjunctive				
SING				
1st pers	parem	habeam	sūmam	audiam
2nd pers	parēs	habeās	sūmās	audiās
3rd pers	paret	habeat	sūmat	audiat
PLURAL				
1st pers	parēmus	habeāmus	sūmāmus	audiāmus
2nd pers	parētis	habeātis	sūmātis	audiātis
3rd pers	parent	habeant	sūmant	audiant

IMPERFECT TENSE

Indicative

SING

1st pers	parābam	habēbam	sūmēbam	audiēbam
2nd pers	parābās	habēbās	sūmēbās	audiēbās
3rd pers	parābat	habēbat	sūmēbat	audiēbat

PLURAL

1st pers	parābāmus	habēbāmus	sūmēbāmus	audiēbāmus
2nd pers	parābātis	habēbātis	sūmēbātis	audiēbātis
3rd pers	parābant	habēbant	sūmēbant	audiēbant

Subjunctive

SING

1st pers	parārem	habērem	sūmerem	audīrem
2nd pers	parārēs	habērēs	sūmerēs	audīrēs
3rd pers	parāret	habēret	sūmeret	audīret

PLURAL

1st pers	parārēmus	habērēmus	sūmerēmus	audīrēmus
2nd pers	parārētis	habērētis	sūmerētis	audīrētis
3rd pers	parārent	habērent	sūmerent	audīrent

FUTURE TENSE

Indicative

SING

1st pers	parābō	habēbō	sūmam	audiam
2nd pers	parābis	habēbis	sūmēs	audiēs
3rd pers	parābit	habēbit	sūmet	audiet

PLURAL

1st pers	parābimus	habēbimus	sūmēmus	audiēmus
2nd pers	parābitis	habēbitis	sūmētis	audiētis
3rd pers	parābunt	habēbunt	sūment	audient

Subjunctive

SING

parātūrus, -a, -um			
habitūrus, -a, -um	sim	*or*	essem
sūmptūrus, -a, -um	sīs		essēs
audītūrus, -a, -um	sit		esset

PLURAL

parātūrī, -ae, -a			
habitūrī, -ae, -a	simus	*or*	essēmus
sūmptūrī, -ae, -a	sītis		essētis
audītūrī, -ae, -a	sint		essent

PERFECT TENSE

Indicative

SING				
1st pers	parāvī	habuī	sūmpsī	audīvī
2nd pers	parāvistī	habuistī	sūmpsistī	audīvistī
3rd pers	parāvit	habuit	sūmpsit	audīvit

PLURAL				
1st pers	parāvimus	habuimus	sūmpsimus	audīvimus
2nd pers	parāvistis	habuistis	sūmpsistis	audīvistis
3rd pers	parāvērunt, -e	habuērunt, -e	sūmpsērunt, -e	audīvērunt, -e

Subjunctive

SING				
1st pers	parāverim	habuerim	sūmpserim	audīverim
2nd pers	parāveris	habueris	sūmpseris	audīveris
3rd pers	parāverit	habuerit	sūmpserit	audīverit

PLURAL				
1st pers	parāverimus	habuerimus	sūmpserimus	audīverimus
2nd pers	parāveritis	habueritis	sūmpseritis	audīveritis
3rd pers	parāverint	habuerint	sūmpserint	audīverint

PLUPERFECT TENSE

Indicative

SING				
1st pers	parāveram	habueram	sūmpseram	audīveram
2nd pers	parāverās	habuerās	sūmpserās	audīverās
3rd pers	parāverat	habuerat	sūmpserat	audīverat

PLURAL				
1st pers	parāverāmus	habuerāmus	sūmpserāmus	audīverāmus
2nd pers	parāverātis	habuerātis	sūmpserātis	audīverātis
3rd pers	parāverant	habuerant	sūmpserant	audīverant

Subjunctive

SING				
1st pers	parāvissem	habuissem	sūmpsissem	audīvissem
2nd pers	parāvissēs	habuissēs	sūmpsissēs	audīvissēs
3rd pers	parāvisset	habuisset	sūmpsisset	audīvisset

PLURAL				
1st pers	parāvissēmus	habuissēmus	sūmpsissēmus	audīvissēmus
2nd pers	parāvissētis	habuissētis	sūmpsissētis	audīvissētis
3rd pers	parāvissent	habuissent	sūmpsissent	audīvissent

FUTURE PERFECT TENSE
Indicative

SING				
1st pers	parāverō	habuerō	sūmpserō	audīverō
2nd pers	parāveris	habueris	sūmpseris	audīveris
3rd pers	parāverit	habuerit	sūmpserit	audīverit

PLURAL				
1st pers	parāverimus	habuerimus	sūmpserimus	audīverimus
2nd pers	parāveritis	habueritis	sūmpseritis	audīveritis
3rd pers	parāverint	habuerint	sūmpserint	audīverint

IMPERATIVE
Present

SING	parā	habē	sūme	audī
PLURAL	parāte	habēte	sūmite	audīte

Future

SING				
2nd pers	parātō	habētō	sūmitō	audītō
3rd pers	parātō	habētō	sūmitō	audītō

PLURAL				
2nd pers	parātōte	habētōte	sūmitōte	audītōte
3rd pers	parantō	habentō	sūmuntō	audiuntō

INFINITIVE
Present

parāre	habēre	sūmere	audīre

Perfect

parāvisse	habuisse	sūmpsisse	audīvisse

Future

parātūrus,	-a, -um, esse
habitūrus,	-a, -um, esse
sūmptūrus,	-a, -um, esse
audītūrus,	-a, -um, esse

PASSIVE

PRESENT TENSE
Indicative

SING

1st pers	paror	habeor	sūmor	audior
2nd pers	parāris	habēris	sūmeris	audīris
3rd pers	parātur	habētur	sūmitur	audītur

PLURAL

1st pers	parāmur	habēmur	sūmimur	audīmur
2nd pers	parāminī	habēminī	sūmiminī	audīminī
3rd pers	parantur	habentur	sūmuntur	audiuntur

Subjunctive

SING

1st pers	parer	habear	sūmar	audiar
2nd pers	parēris	habeāris	sūmāris	audiāris
3rd pers	parētur	habeātur	sūmātur	audiātur

PLURAL

1st pers	parēmur	habeāmur	sūmāmur	audiāmur
2nd pers	parēminī	habeāminī	sūmāminī	audiāminī
3rd pers	parentur	habeantur	sūmantur	audiantur

IMPERFECT TENSE
Indicative

SING

1st pers	parābar	habēbar	sūmēbar	audiēbar
2nd pers	parābāris	habēbāris	sūmēbāris	audiēbāris
3rd pers	parābātur	habēbātur	sūmēbātur	audiēbātur

PLURAL

1st pers	parābāmur	habēbāmur	sūmēbāmur	audiēbāmur
2nd pers	parābāmini	habēbāmini	sūmēbāminī	audiēbāminī
3rd pers	parābāntur	habēbantur	sūmēbantur	audiēbantur

Subjunctive

SING

1st pers	parārer	habērer	sūmerer	audīrer
2nd pers	parārēris	habērēris	sūmerēris	audīrēris
3rd pers	parārētur	habērētur	sūmerētur	audīrētur

PLURAL				
1st pers	pararēmur	habērēmur	sūmerēmur	audīrēmur
2nd pers	pararēminī	habērēminī	sūmerēminī	audīrēminī
3rd pers	pararentur	habērentur	sūmerentur	audīrentur

FUTURE TENSE

Indicative

SING				
1st pers	parābor	habēbor	sūmar	audiar
2nd pers	parāberis	habēberis	sūmēris	audiēris
3rd pers	parābitur	habēbitur	sūmētur	audiētur

PLURAL				
1st pers	parābimur	habēbimur	sūmēmur	audiēmur
2nd pers	parābimini	habēbimini	sūmēminī	audiēminī
3rd pers	parābuntur	habēbuntur	sūmentur	audientur

PERFECT TENSE

Indicative

SING		PLURAL	
parātus, -a, -um	sum/es/est	parātī, -ae, -a	sumus/estis/sunt
habitus, -a, -um	sum/es/est	habītī, -ae, -a	sumus/estis/sunt
sūmptus, -a, -um	sum/es/est	sūmptī, -ae, -a	sumus/estis/sunt
audītus, -a, -um	sum/es/est	audītī, -ae, -a	sumus/estis/sunt

Subjunctive

SING		PLURAL	
parātus, -a, -um	sim/sīs/sit	parātī, -ae, -a	sīmus/sītis/sint
habitus, -a, -um	sim/sīs/sit	habītī, -ae, -a	sīmus/sītis/sint
sūmptus, -a, -um	sim/sīs/sit	sūmptī, -ae, -a	sīmus/sītis/sint
audītus, -a, -um	sim/sīs/sit	audītī, -ae, -a	sīmus/sītis/sint

PLUPERFECT TENSE

Indicative

SING		PLURAL	
parātus, -a, -um	eram/eras/erat	parātī, -ae, -a	eramus/eratis/erant
habitus, -a, -um	eram/eras/erat	habītī, -ae, -a	eramus/eratis/erant
sūmptus, -a, -um	eram/eras/erat	sūmptī, -ae, -a	eramus/eratis/erant
audītus, -a, -um	eram/eras/erat	audītī, -ae, -a	eramus/eratis/erant

Subjunctive

SING		PLURAL	
parātus, -a, -um	essem/essēs/esset	parātī, -ae, -a	essēmus/essētis/essent
habitus, -a, -um	essem/essēs/esset	habītī, -ae, -a	essēmus/essētis/essent
sūmptus, -a, -um	essem/essēs/esset	sūmptī, -ae, -a	essēmus/essētis/essent
audītus, -a, -um	essem/essēs/esset	audītī, -ae, -a	essēmus/essētis/essent

FUTURE PERFECT TENSE

Indicative

SING		PLURAL	
parātus, -a, -um	erō/eris/erit	parātī, -ae, -a	erimus/eritis/erunt
habitus, -a, -um	erō/eris/erit	habītī, -ae, -a	erimus/eritis/erunt
sūmptus, -a, -um	erō/eris/erit	sūmptī, -ae, -a	erimus/eritis/erunt
audītus, -a, -um	erō/eris/erit	audītī, -ae, -a	erimus/eritis/erunt

IMPERATIVE

Present

SING	parāre	habēre	sūmere	audīre
PLURAL	parāminī	habēminī	sūmiminī	audīminī

Future

SING				
2nd pers	parātor	habētor	sūmitor	audītor
3rd pers	parātor	habētor	sūmitor	audītor
PLURAL				
3rd pers	parantor	habentor	sūmuntor	audiuntor

INFINITIVE

Present

parārī	habērī	sūmī	audīrī

Perfect

parātus -a, -um, esse	habitus -a, -um, esse	sūmptus -a, -um, esse	audītus, -a, -um, esse

Future

parātum īrī	habitum īrī	sūmptum īrī	audītum īrī

VERBAL NOUNS AND ADJECTIVES

Present Participle Active

| parāns | habēns | sūmēns | audiēns |

Perfect Participle Passive

| parātus | habitus | sūmptus | audītus |

Future Participle Active

| parātūrus | habitūrus | sūmptūrus | audītūrus |

Gerund
(acc, gen, dat and abl)

| parandum, -ī, -ō | habendum, -ī, -ō | sūmendum, -ī, -ō | audiendum, -ī, -ō |

Gerundive

| parandus | habendus | sūmendus | audiendus |

Supines

| *1st* | parātum | habitum | sūmptum | audītum |
| *2nd* | parātū | habitū | sūmptū | audītū |

Note. *Some verbs of the 3rd conjugation have the present indicative ending in* **-io**; *e.g.* **capio**, *I capture.*

PRESENT TENSE

INDICATIVE		SUBJUNCTIVE	
Active	**Passive**	**Active**	**Passive**
capio	capior	capiam	capiar
capis	caperis	capiās	capiāris
capit	capitur	capiat	capiātur
capimus	capimur	capiāmus	capiāmur
capitis	capiminī	capiātis	capiāminī
capiunt	capiuntur	capiant	capiantur

IMPERFECT TENSE

| capiēbam *etc.* | capiēbar *etc.* | caperem *etc.* | caperer *etc.* |

FUTURE TENSE

| capiam | capiar |
| capiēs *etc.* | capiēris *etc.* |

INFINITIVE MOOD

| Present Active | capere |
| Present Passive | capī |

PRESENT IMPERATIVE

	Active			**Passive**
cape	capite	capere		capiminī

	PARTICIPLE	*GERUND*	*GERUNDIVE*
Pres.	capiēns	capiendum	capiendus, -a, um

In all other tenses and moods **capere** *is similar to* **sumere**.

IRREGULAR VERBS

	Esse *be*	**Posse** *be able*	**Velle** *wish*	**Ire** *go*

Present Indicative

SING

1st Pers	sum	possum	volō	eō
2nd Pers	es	potes	vīs	īs
3rd Pers	est	potest	vult, volt	it

PLURAL

1st Pers	sumus	possumus	volumus	īmus
2nd Pers	estis	potestis	vultis, voltis	ītis
3rd Pers	sunt	possunt	volunt	eunt

Present Subjunctive

SING

1st Pers	sim	possim	velim	eam
2nd Pers	sīs	possīs	velīs	eās
3rd Pers	sit	possit	velit	eat

PLURAL

1st Pers	sīmus	possīmus	velīmus	eāmus
2nd Pers	sītis	possītis	velītis	eātis
3rd Pers	sint	possint	velint	eant

Imperfect Indicative

| 1st Pers | eram | poteram | volēbam | ībam |

Imperfect Subjunctive

| 1st Pers | essem | possem | vellem | īrem |

Future Indicative

| 1st Pers | erō | poterō | volam | ībō |

Future Subjunctive

| 1st Pers | futūrus, -a, -um sim *or* essem | — | — | itūrus, -a, -um sim *or* essem |

Perfect Indicative

| 1st Pers | fuī | potuī | voluī | īvī, iī |

Perfect Subjunctive

| 1st Pers | fuerim | potuerim | voluerim | īverim, ierim |

Pluperfect Indicative

1st Pers	fueram	potueram	volueram	īveram, ieram

Pluperfect Subjunctive

1st Pers	fuissem	potuissem	voluissem	īvissem, iissem

Future Perfect Indicative

1st Pers	fuerō	potuerō	voluerō	īverō, ierō

Present Imperative

SING	es	—	—	ī
PLURAL	este	—	—	īte

Future Imperative

SING	estō	—	—	ītō
PLURAL	estōte	—	—	ītōte

Infinitives

PRES	esse	posse	velle	īre
PERF	fuisse	potuisse	voluisse	īvisse, iisse
FUT	futūrus, -a, -um, esse	—	—	itūrus, -a, -um, esse

Participles

PRES	—	—	—	iēns, euntis
FUT	futūrus	—	—	itūrus

Gerund and Supine

GERUND	—	—	—	eundum
SUPINE	—	—	—	itum

Latin-English

A, a

ā *prep (with abl)* from; after, since; by, in respect of; **ab epistulīs**, **ā manū** secretary; **ab hāc parte** on this side; **ab integrō** afresh; **ā nōbīs** on our side; **ā tergō** in the rear; **cōpiōsus ā frūmentō** rich in corn; **usque ab** ever since.

ā *interj* ah!

ab *prep see* **ā**.

abāctus *ppp of* **abigō**.

abacus, -ī *m* tray; sideboard; gaming board; panel; counting table.

abaliēnō, -āre, -āvī, -ātum *vt* to dispose of; to remove, estrange.

Abantiadēs *m* Acrisius *or* Perseus.

Abās, -antis *m* a king of Argos.

abavus, -ī *m* great-great-grandfather.

abbās, -ātis *m* abbot.

abbātia *f* abbey.

abbātissa *f* abbess.

Abdēra, -ōrum *or* **-ae** *ntpl or fs* a town in Thrace.

Abdērītānus *adj see n.*

Abdērītēs *m* Democritus *or* Protagoras.

abdicātiō, -ōnis *f* disowning, abdication.

abdicō, -āre, -āvī, -ātum *vt* to disown; to resign; **sē ~** abdicate.

abdīcō, -īcere, -īxī, -ictum *vt* (AUG) to be unfavourable to.

abditus *ppp of* **abdō**.

abdō, -ere, -idī, -itum *vt* to hide; to remove.

abdōmen, -inis *nt* paunch, belly; gluttony.

abdūcō, -ūcere, -ūxī, -uctum *vt* to lead away, take away; to seduce.

abductus *ppp of* **abdūcō**.

abecedārium, -iī *nt* alphabet.

abēgī *perf of* **abigō**.

abeō, -īre, -iī, -itum *vi* to go away, depart; to pass away; to be changed; to retire (*from an office*); **sīc ~** turn out like this.

abequitō, -āre, -āvī, -ātum *vi* to ride away.

aberrātiō, -ōnis *f* relief (*from trouble*).

aberrō, -āre, -āvī, -ātum *vi* to stray; to deviate; to have respite.

abfore *fut infin of* **absum**.

abfuī *perf of* **absum**.

abfutūrus *fut p of* **absum**.

abhinc *adv* since, ago.

abhorreō, -ēre, -uī *vi* to shrink from; to differ; to be inconsistent.

abiciō, -icere, -iēcī, -iectum *vt* to throw away, throw down; to abandon, degrade.

abiectus *ppp of* **abiciō** ♦ *adj* despondent; contemptible.

abiēgnus *adj* of fir.

abiēns, -euntis *pres p of* **abeō**.

abiēs, -etis *f* fir; ship.

abigō, -igere, -ēgī, -āctum *vt* to drive away.

abitus, -ūs *m* departure; exit.

abiūdicō, -āre, -āvī, -ātum *vt* to take away (*by judicial award*).

abiūnctus *ppp of* **abiungō**.

abiungō, -ungere, -ūnxī, -ūnctum *vt* to unyoke; to detach.

abiūrō, -āre, -āvī, -ātum *vt* to deny on oath.

ablātus *ppp of* **auferō**.

ablēgātiō, -ōnis *f* sending away.

ablēgō, -āre, -āvī, -ātum *vt* to send out of the way.

abligurriō, -īre, -īvī, -ītum *vt* to spend extravagantly.

ablocō, -āre, -āvī, -ātum *vt* to let (a house).

ablūdō, -dere, -sī, -sum *vi* to be unlike.

abluō, -uere, -uī, -ūtum *vt* to wash clean; to remove.

abnegō, -āre, -āvī, -ātum *vt* to refuse.

abnepōs, -ōtis *m* great-great-grandson.

abneptis *f* great-great-granddaughter.

abnoctō, -āre *vi* to stay out all night.

abnōrmis *adj* unorthodox.

abnuō, -uere, -uī, -ūtum *vt* to refuse; to deny.

aboleō, -ēre, -ēvī, -itum *vt* to abolish.

abolēscō, -ēscere, -ēvī *vi* to vanish.

abolitiō, -ōnis *f* cancelling.

abolla, -ae *f* greatcoat.

abōminātus *adj* accursed.

abōminor, -ārī, -ātus *vt* to deprecate; to detest.

Aborīginēs, -um *mpl* original inhabitants.

aborior, -īrī, -tus *vi* to miscarry.

abortiō, -ōnis *f* miscarriage.

abortīvus *adj* born prematurely.

abortus, -ūs *m* miscarriage.

abrādō, -dere, -sī, -sum *vt* to scrape off, shave.

abrāsus *ppp of* **abrādō**.

abreptus *ppp of* **abripiō**.

abripiō, -ipere, -ipuī, -eptum *vt* to drag away, carry off.

abrogātiō, -ōnis f repeal.
abrogō, -āre, -āvī, -ātum vt to annul.
abrotonum, -ī nt southernwood.
abrumpō, -umpere, -ūpī, -uptum vt to break off.
abruptus ppp of **abrumpō** ♦ adj steep; abrupt, disconnected.
abs etc see **ā**.
abscēdō, -ēdere, -essi, -essum vi to depart, withdraw; to cease.
abscīdō, -dere, -dī, -sum vt to cut off.
abscindō, -ndere, -dī, -ssum vt to tear off, cut off.
abscissus ppp of **abscindō**.
abscīsus ppp of **abscīdō** ♦ adj steep; abrupt.
abscondō, -ere, -ī and **idī, -itum** vt to conceal; to leave behind.
absēns, -entis pres p of **absum** ♦ adj absent.
absentia, -ae f absence.
absiliō, -īre, -iī and **uī** vi to spring away.
absimilis adj unlike.
absinthium, -ī and **iī** nt wormwood.
absis, -īdis f vault; (ECCL) chancel.
absistō, -istere, -titī vi to come away; to desist.
absolūte adv fully, unrestrictedly.
absolūtiō, -ōnis f acquittal; perfection.
absolūtus ppp of **absolvō** ♦ adj complete; (RHET) unqualified.
absolvō, -vere, -vī, -ūtum vt to release, set free; (law) to acquit; to bring to completion, finish off; to pay off, discharge.
absonus adj unmusical; incongruous; **~ ab** not in keeping with.
absorbeō, -bēre, -buī, -ptum vt to swallow up; to monopolize.
absp- etc see **asp-**.
absque prep (with abl) without, but for.
abstēmius adj temperate.
abstergeō, -gēre, -sī, -sum vt to wipe away; (fig) to banish.
absterreō, -ēre, -ui, -itum vt to scare away, deter.
abstinēns, -entis adj continent.
abstinenter adv with restraint.
abstinentia, -ae f restraint, self-control; fasting.
abstineō, -inēre, -inuī, -entum vt to withhold, keep off ♦ vi to abstain, refrain; **sē ~ refrain**.
abstitī perf of **absistō**.
abstō, -āre vi to stand aloof.
abstractus ppp of **abstrahō**.
abstrahō, -here, -xī, -ctum vt to drag away, remove; to divert.
abstrūdō, -dere, -sī, -sum vt to conceal.
abstrūsus ppp of **abstrūdō** ♦ adj deep, abstruse; reserved.
abstulī perf of **auferō**.
absum, abesse, āfuī vi to be away, absent, distant; to keep clear of; to be different; to be missing, fail to assist; **tantum abest ut** so far from; **haud multum āfuit quīn** I was (they were etc) within an ace of.
absūmō, -ere, -psī, -ptum vt to consume; to ruin, kill; (time) to spend.
absurdē adv out of tune; absurdly.
absurdus adj unmusical; senseless, absurd.
Absyrtus, -ī m brother of Medea.
abundāns, -antis adj overflowing; abundant; rich; abounding in.
abundanter adv copiously.
abundantia, -ae f abundance, plenty; wealth.
abundē adv abundantly, more than enough.
abundō, -āre, -āvī, -ātum vi to overflow; to abound, be rich in.
abūsiō, -ōnis f (RHET) catachresis.
abusque prep (with abl) all the way from.
abūtor, -tī, -sus vi (with abl) to use up; to misuse.
Abydēnus adj see n.
Abȳdos, Abȳdus, -ī m a town on Dardanelles.
ac etc see **atque**.
Acadēmia, -ae f Plato's Academy at Athens; Plato's philosophy; Cicero's villa.
Acadēmica ntpl Cicero's book on the Academic philosophy.
Acadēmus, -ī m an Athenian hero.
acalanthis, -dis f thistlefinch.
acanthus, -ī m bear's-breech.
Acarnānes, -um mpl the Acarnanians.
Acarnānia, -iae f a district of N.W. Greece.
Acarnānicus adj see n.
Acca Lārentia, -ae, -ae f Roman goddess.
accēdō, -ēdere, -essī, -essum vi to come, go to, approach; to attack; to be added; to agree with; (duty) to take up; **ad rem pūblicam ~** to enter politics; **prope ~ ad** to resemble; **~ēdit quod, hūc ~ēdit ut** moreover.
accelerō, -āre, -āvī, -ātum vt, vi to hasten.
accendō, -endere, -endī, -ēnsum vt to set on fire, light; to illuminate; (fig) to inflame, incite.
accēnseō, -ēre, -uī, -um vt to assign.
accēnsī mpl (MIL) supernumeraries.
accēnsus ppp of **accendō** and **accēnseō**.
accēnsus, -ī m officer attending a magistrate.
accentus, -ūs m accent.
accēpī perf of **accipiō**.
acceptiō, -ōnis f receiving.
acceptum nt credit side (of ledger); **in ~ referre** place to one's credit.
acceptus ppp of **accipiō** ♦ adj acceptable.
accersō etc see **arcessō**.
accessiō, -ōnis f coming, visiting; attack; increase, addition.
accessus, -ūs m approach, visit; flood tide; admittance, entrance.
Acciānus adj see **Accius**.
accīdō, -dere, -dī, -sum vt to fell, cut into; to eat up, impair.
accidō, -ere, -ī vi to fall (at, on); (senses) to strike; (usu misfortune) to befall, happen.
accingō, -gere, -xī, -ctum vt to gird on, arm; (fig) to make ready.
acciō, -īre, -īvī, -ītum vt to summon; to

procure.

accipiō, -ipere, -ēpī, -eptum *vt* to take, receive, accept; (*guest*) to treat; (*information*) to hear; to interpret, take as; to suffer; to approve.

accipiter, -ris *m* hawk.

accīsus *ppp of* **accīdō.**

accītus *ppp of* **acciō.**

accītus, -ūs *m* summons.

Accius, -ī *m* Roman tragic poet.

acclāmātiō, -ōnis *f* shout (*of approval or disapproval*).

acclāmō, -āre, -āvī, -ātum *vi* to cry out against; to hail.

acclārō, -āre, -āvī, -ātum *vt* to make known.

acclīnātus *adj* sloping.

acclīnis *adj* leaning against; inclined.

acclīnō, -āre, -āvī, -ātum *vt* to lean against; **sē ~** incline towards.

acclīvis *adj* uphill.

acclīvitās, -ātis *f* gradient.

accola, -ae *m* neighbour.

accolō, -olere, -oluī, -ultum *vt* to live near.

accommodātē *adv* suitably.

accommodātiō, -ōnis *f* fitting together; compliance.

accommodātus *adj* suited.

accommodō, -āre, -āvī, -ātum *vt* to fit, put on; to adjust, adapt, bring to; to apply; **sē ~** devote oneself.

accommodus *adj* suitable.

accrēdō, -ere, -idī, -itum *vi* to believe.

accrēscō, -ēscere, -ēvī, -ētum *vi* to increase, be added.

accrētiō, -ōnis *f* increasing.

accubitiō, -ōnis *f* reclining (*at meals*).

accubō, -āre *vi* to lie near; to recline (*at meals*).

accumbō, -mbere, -buī, -bitum *vi* to recline at table; **in sinū ~** sit next to.

accumulātē *adv* copiously.

accumulō, -āre, -āvī, -ātum *vt* to pile up, amass; to load.

accūrātē *adv* painstakingly.

accūrātiō, -ōnis *f* exactness.

accūrātus *adj* studied.

accūrō, -āre, -āvī, -ātum *vt* to attend to.

accurrō, -rrere, -currī *and* **rrī, -rsum** *vi* to hurry to.

accursus, -ūs *m* hurrying.

accūsābilis *adj* reprehensible.

accūsātiō, -ōnis *f* accusation.

accūsātor, -ōris *m* accuser, prosecutor.

accūsātōriē *adv* like an accuser.

accūsātōrius *adj* of the accuser.

accūsō, -āre, -āvī, -ātum *vt* to accuse, prosecute; to reproach; **ambitūs ~** prosecute for bribery.

acer, -is *nt* maple.

ācer, -ris *adj* sharp; (*sensation*) keen, pungent; (*emotion*) violent; (*mind*) shrewd; (*conduct*) eager, brave; hasty, fierce; (*circumstances*) severe.

acerbē *adv see* **acerbus.**

acerbitās, -ātis *f* bitterness; (*fig*) harshness, severity; sorrow.

acerbō, -āre, -āvī, -ātum *vt* to aggravate.

acerbus *adj* bitter, sour; harsh; (*fig*) premature; (*person*) rough, morose, violent; (*things*) troublesome, sad.

acernus *adj* of maple.

acerra, -ae *f* incense box.

acervātim *adv* in heaps.

acervō, -āre, -āvī, -ātum *vt* to pile up.

acervus, -ī *m* heap.

acēscō, -ere, acuī *vt* to turn sour.

Acestēs, -ae *m* a mythical Sicilian.

acētum, -ī *nt* vinegar; (*fig*) wit.

Achaemenēs, -is *m* first Persian king; type of Oriental wealth.

Achaeus *adj* Greek.

Achāia, -ae *f* a district in W. Greece; Greece; Roman province.

Achāicus *adj see* n.

Achātēs, -ae *m* companion of Aeneas.

Achelōius *adj see* n.

Achelōus, -ī *m* river in N.W. Greece; river god.

Acherōn, -ontis *m* river in Hades.

Acherūsius *adj see* **Acherōn.**

Achillēs, -is *m* Greek epic hero.

Achillēus *adj see* n.

Achīvus *adj* Greek.

Acidālia, -ae *f* Venus.

Acidālius *adj see* n.

acidus *adj* sour, tart; (*fig*) disagreeable.

aciēs, -ēī *f* sharp edge or point; (*eye*) sight, keen glance, pupil; (*mind*) power, apprehension; (*MIL*) line of troops, battle order, army, battle; (*fig*) debate; **prīma ~** van; **novissima ~** rearguard.

acīnacēs, -is *m* scimitar.

acinum, -ī *nt* berry, grape; fruit seed.

acinus, -ī *m* berry, grape; fruit seed.

acipēnser, -eris *m* sturgeon.

acipēnsis, -is *m* sturgeon.

aclys, -dis *f* javelin.

aconītum, -ī *nt* monkshood; poison.

acor, -ōris *m* sour taste.

acquiēscō, -ēscere, -ēvī, -ētum *vi* to rest, die; to find pleasure (in); to acquiesce.

acquīrō, -rere, -sīvī, -sītum *vt* to get in addition, acquire.

Acragās, -antis *m see* **Agrigentum.**

acrātophorum, -ī *nt* wine jar.

acrēdula, -ae *f* a bird (*unidentified*).

ācriculus *adj* peevish.

ācrimōnia, -ae *f* pungent taste; (*speech, action*) briskness, go.

Acrisiōniadēs, -ae *m* Perseus.

Acrisius, -ī *m* father of Danae.

Noun declensions and verb conjugations are shown on pp xiii to xxv. The present infinitive ending of a verb shows to which conjugation it belongs: **-āre** = 1st; **-ēre** = 2nd; **-ere** = 3rd and **-īre** = 4th. Irregular verbs are shown on p xxvi

ācriter *adv see* **ācer.**

ācroāma, -tis *nt* entertainment, entertainer.

ācroāsis, -is *f* public lecture.

Ācroceraunia, -ōrum *ntpl a promontory in N.W. Greece.*

Ācrocorinthus, -ī *f fortress of Corinth.*

acta, -ae *f* beach.

ācta, -ōrum *ntpl* public records, proceedings; ~ **diurna**, ~ **pūblica** daily gazette.

Actaeus *adj* Athenian.

āctiō, -ōnis *f* action, doing; official duties, negotiations; (*law*) action, suit, indictment, pleading, case, trial; (*RHET*) delivery; (*drama*) plot; ~ **grātiārum** expression of thanks; ~**ōnem intendere, īnstituere** bring an action.

āctitō, -āre, -āvī, -ātum *vt* to plead, act often.

Actium, -ī *and* **iī** *nt a town in N.W. Greece; Augustus's great victory.*

Actius, -iacus *adj see n.*

āctīvus *adj* of action, practical.

āctor, -ōris *m* driver, performer; (*law*) plaintiff, pleader; (*COMM*) agent; (*RHET*) orator; (*drama*) actor; ~ **pūblicus** manager of public property; ~ **summārum** cashier.

āctuāria *f* pinnace.

āctuāriolum, -ī *m* small barge.

āctuārius *adj* fast (ship).

āctuōsē *adv* actively.

āctuōsus *adj* very active.

āctus *ppp of* **agō.**

āctus, -ūs *m* moving, driving; right of way for cattle *or* vehicles; performance; (*drama*) playing a part, recital, act of a play.

āctūtum *adv* immediately.

acuī *perf of* **acēscō;** *perf of* **acuō.**

acula, -ae *f* small stream.

aculeātus *adj* prickly; (*words*) stinging; quibbling.

aculeus, -ī *m* sting, prickle barb; (*fig*) sting.

acūmen, -inis *nt* point, sting; (*fig*) shrewdness, ingenuity; trickery.

acuō, -uere, -uī, -ūtum *vt* to sharpen; to exercise; (*the mind*) to stimulate; to rouse (to action).

acus, -ūs *f* needle, pin; **acū pingere** embroider; **rem acū tangere** = hit the nail on the head.

acūtē *adv see* **acūtus.**

acūtulus *adj* rather subtle.

acūtus *adj* sharp, pointed; (*senses*) keen; (*sound*) high-pitched; severe; intelligent.

ad *prep* (*with acc*) to, towards, against; near, at; until; (*num*) about; with regard to, according to; for the purpose of, for; compared with; besides; **ad Castoris** to the temple of Castor; **ad dextram** on the right; **ad hōc** besides; **ad locum** on the spot; **ad manum** at hand; **ad rem** to the point; **ad summam** in short; **ad tempus** in time; **ad ūnum omnes** all without exception; **ad urbem esse** wait outside the city gates; **ad verbum** literally; **nīl ad** nothing to do with; **usque ad** right up to.

adāctiō, -ōnis *f* enforcing.

adāctus *ppp of* **adigō.**

adāctus, -ūs *m* snapping (*of teeth*).

adaequē *adv* equally.

adaequō, -āre, -āvī, -ātum *vt* to make equal, level; to equal, match ♦ *vi* to be equal.

adamantēus, adamantinus *adj see* **adamās.**

adamās, -antis *m* adamant, steel; diamond.

adamō, -āre, -āvī, -ātum *vt* to fall in love with.

adaperiō, -īre, -uī, -tum *vt* to throw open.

adapertilis *adj* openable.

adaquō, -āre, -āvī, -ātum *vt* (*plants, animals*) to water.

adaquor *vi* to fetch water.

adauctus, -ūs *m* growing.

adaugeō, -gēre, -xī, -ctum *vt* to aggravate; (*sacrifice*) to consecrate.

adaugēscō, -ere *vi* to grow bigger.

adbibō, -ere, -ī *vt* to drink; (*fig*) to drink in.

adbītō, -ere *vi* to come near.

adc- *etc see* **acc-.**

addecet, -ēre *vt* it becomes.

addēnseō, -ēre *vt* to close (ranks).

addīcō, -īcere, -īxī, -ictum *vi* (*AUG*) to be favourable ♦ *vt* (*law*) to award; (*auction*) to knock down; (*fig*) to sacrifice, devote.

addictiō, -ōnis *f* award (*at law*).

addictus *ppp of* **addīcō** ♦ *m* bondsman.

addiscō, -scere, -dicī *vt* to learn more.

additāmentum, -ī *nt* increase.

additus *ppp of* **addō.**

addō, -ere, -idī, -itum *vt* to add, put to, bring to; to impart; to increase; ~ **gradum** quicken pace; **~e quod** besides.

addoceō, -ēre, -uī, -tum *vt* to teach new.

addubitō, -āre, -āvī, -ātum *vi* to be in doubt ♦ *vt* to question.

addūcō, -ūcere, -ūxī, -uctum *vt* to take, bring to; to draw together, pull taut, wrinkle; (*fig*) to induce; (*pass*) to be led to believe.

adductus *ppp of* **addūcō** ♦ *adj* contracted; (*fig*) severe.

adedō, -edere, -ēdī, -ēsum *vt* to begin to eat; to eat up; to use up; to wear away.

adēmī *perf of* **adimō.**

ademptiō, -ōnis *f* taking away.

ademptus *ppp of* **adimō.**

adeō, -īre, -iī, -itum *vt, vi* to go to, approach; to address; to undertake, submit to, enter upon.

adeō *adv* so; (*after pron*) just; (*after conj, adv, adj: for emphasis*) indeed, very; (*adding an explanation*) for, in fact, thus; or rather; ~ **nōn... ut** so far from; **atque ~, sīve ~** or rather; **usque ~** so far, so long, so much.

adeps, -ipis *m/f* fat; corpulence.

adeptiō, -ōnis *f* attainment.

adeptus *ppa of* **adipīscor.**

adequitō, -āre, -āvī, -ātum *vi* to ride up (to).

adesdum come here!

adesse *infin of* **adsum.**

adēsus *ppp of* **adedō.**

adfābilis *adj* easy to talk to.

adfābilitās, -ātis *f* courtesy.

adfabrē *adv* ingeniously.

adfatim *adv* to one's satisfaction, enough, ad nauseam.

adfātur, -rī, -tus *vt (defec)* to speak to.

adfātus *ppa of* **adfātur**.

adfātus, -ūs *m* speaking to.

adfectātiō, -ōnis *f* aspiring; *(RHET)* affectation.

adfectātus *adj (RHET)* studied.

adfectiō, -ōnis *f* frame of mind, mood; disposition; goodwill; *(ASTRO)* relative position.

adfectō, -āre, -āvī, -ātum *vt* to aspire to, aim at; to try to win over; to make pretence of; **viam ~** to try to get to.

adfectus *ppp of* **adficiō** ♦ *adj* affected with, experienced *(abl)*; *(person)* disposed; *(things)* weakened; *(undertakings)* well-advanced.

adfectus, -ūs *m* disposition, mood; fondness; *(pl)* loved ones.

adferō, adferre, attulī, adlātum *and* **allātum** *vt* to bring, carry to; to bring to bear, use against; to bring news; *(explanation)* to bring forward; to contribute *(something useful)*.

adficiō, -icere, -ēcī, -ectum *vt* to affect; to endow, afflict with *(abl)*; **exsiliō ~** banish; **honōre ~** honour; *also used with other nouns to express the corresponding verbs*.

adfictus *ppp of* **adfingō**.

adfīgō, -gere, -xi, -xum *vt* to fasten, attach; to impress *(on the mind)*.

adfingō, -ngere, -nxī, -ctum *vt* to make, form *(as part of)*; to invent.

adfīnis, -is *m/f* neighbour; relation *(by marriage)* ♦ *adj* neighbouring; associated with *(dat or gen)*.

adfīnitās, -ātis *f* relationship *(by marriage)*.

adfirmātē *adv* with assurance.

adfirmātiō, -ōnis *f* declaration.

adfirmō, -āre, -āvī, -ātum *vt* to declare; to confirm.

adfīxus *ppp of* **adfīgō**.

adflātus, -ūs *m* breath, exhalation; *(fig)* inspiration.

adfleō, -ēre *vi* to weep (at).

adflīctātiō, -ōnis *f* suffering.

adflīctō, -āre, -āvī, -ātum *vt* to harass, distress.

adflīctor, -ōris *m* destroyer.

adflīctus *ppp of* **adflīgō** ♦ *adj* distressed, ruined; dejected; depraved.

adflīgō, -īgere, -īxī, -īctum *vt* to dash against, throw down; *(fig)* to impair, crush.

adflō, -āre, -āvī, -ātum *vt, vi* to blow on, breathe upon.

adfluēns, -entis *adj* rich (in).

adfluenter *adv* copiously.

adfluentia, -ae *f* abundance.

adfluō, -ere, -xī, -xum *vi* to flow; *(fig)* to flock in, abound in.

adfore *fut infin of* **adsum**.

adforem *imperf subj of* **adsum**.

adfuī *perf of* **adsum**.

adfulgeō, -gēre, -sī *vi* to shine on; to appear.

adfundō, -undere, -ūdī, -ūsum *vt* to pour in; to rush (troops) to.

adfūsus *adj* prostrate.

adfutūrus *fut p of* **adsum**.

adgemō, -ere *vi* to groan at.

adglomerō, -āre *vt* to add on.

adglūtinō, -āre *vt* to stick on.

adgravēscō, -ere *vi* to become worse.

adgravō, -āre, -āvī, -ātum *vt* to aggravate.

adgredior, -dī, -ssus *vt* to approach, accost; to attack; *(a task)* to undertake, take up.

adgregō, -āre, -āvī, -ātum *vt* to add, attach.

adgressiō, -ōnis *f* introductory remarks.

adgressus *ppa of* **adgredior**.

adhaereō, -rēre, -sī, -sum *vi* to stick to; *(fig)* to cling to, keep close to.

adhaerēscō, -ere *vi* to stick to *or* in; *(speech)* to falter.

adhaesiō, -ōnis *f* clinging.

adhaesus, -ūs *m* adhering.

adhibeō, -ēre, -uī, -itum *vt* to bring, put, add; to summon, consult, treat; to use, apply *(for some purpose)*.

adhinniō, -īre, -īvī, -ītum *vi* to neigh to; *(fig)* to go into raptures over.

adhortātiō, -ōnis *f* exhortation.

adhortātor, -ōris *m* encourager.

adhortor, -ārī, -ātus *vt* to encourage, urge.

adhūc *adv* so far; as yet, till now; still ~ **nōn** not yet.

adiaceō, -ēre, -uī *vi* to lie near, border on.

adiciō, -icere, -iēcī, -iectum *vt* to throw to; to add; to turn (mind, eyes) towards.

adiectiō, -ōnis *f* addition.

adiectus *ppp of* **adiciō**.

adiectus, -ūs *m* bringing close.

adigō, -igere, -ēgī, -āctum *vt* to drive (to); to compel; **iūs iūrandum ~** put on oath; **in verba ~** force to owe allegiance.

adimō, -imere, -ēmī, -emptum *vt* to take away (from *dat*).

adipātum *nt* pastry.

adipātus *adj* fatty; *(fig)* florid.

adipīscor, -ipīscī, -eptus *vt* to overtake; to attain, acquire.

aditus, -ūs *m* approach, access *(to a person)*; entrance; *(fig)* avenue.

adiūdicō, -āre, -āvī, -ātum *vt* to award *(in arbitration)*; to ascribe.

adiūmentum, -ī *nt* aid, means of support.

adiūncta *ntpl* collateral circumstances.

adiūnctiō, -ōnis *f* uniting; addition; *(RHET)* proviso; repetition.

Noun declensions and verb conjugations are shown on pp xiii to xxv. The present infinitive ending of a verb shows to which conjugation it belongs: -**āre** = 1st; -**ēre** = 2nd; -**ere** = 3rd and -**īre** = 4th. Irregular verbs are shown on p xxvi

adiūnctus *ppp of* **adiungō** ♦ *adj* connected.
adiungō, -ungere, -ūnxī, -ūnctum *vt* to yoke; to attach; (*suspicion etc*) to direct; (*remark*) to add.
adiūrō, -āre, -āvī, -ātum *vt*, *vi* to swear, swear by.
adiūtō, -āre, -āvī, -ātum *vt* to help.
adiūtor, -ōris *m* helper; (*MIL*) adjutant; (*POL*) official; (*THEAT*) supporting cast.
adiūtrīx, -rīcis *f see* **adiūtor**.
adiūtus *ppp of* **adiuvō**.
adiuvō, -uvāre, -ūvī, -ūtum *vt* to help; to encourage.
adj- *etc see* **adi-**.
adlābor, -bī, -psus *vi* to fall, move towards, come to.
adlabōrō, -āre, -āvī, -ātum *vi* to work hard; to improve by taking trouble.
adlacrimō, -āre, -āvī, -ātum *vi* to shed tears.
adlāpsus *ppa of* **adlābor**.
adlāpsus, -ūs *m* stealthy approach.
adlātrō, -āre, -āvī, -ātum *vt* to bark at; (*fig*) to revile.
adlātus *ppp of* **adferō**.
adlaudō, -āre, -āvī, -ātum *vt* to praise highly.
adlectō, -āre, -āvī, -ātum *vt* to entice.
adlēctus *ppp of* **adlegō**.
adlectus *ppp of* **adliciō**.
adlēgātī *mpl* deputies.
adlēgātiō, -ōnis *f* mission.
adlēgō, -āre, -āvī, -ātum *vt* to despatch, commission; to mention.
adlegō, -egere, -ēgī, -ēctum *vt* to elect.
adlevāmentum, -ī *nt* relief.
adlevātiō, -ōnis *f* easing.
adlevō, -āre, -āvī, -ātum *vt* to lift up; to comfort; to weaken.
adliciō, -icere, -exī, -ectum *vt* to attract.
adlīdō, -dere, -sī, -sum *vt* to dash (against); (*fig*) to hurt.
adligō, -āre, -āvī, -ātum *vt* to tie up, bandage; (*fig*) to bind, lay under an obligation.
adlinō, -inere, -ēvī, -itum *vt* to smear; (*fig*) to attach.
adlīsus *ppp of* **adlīdō**.
adlocūtiō, -ōnis *f* address; comforting words.
adlocūtus *ppa of* **adloquor**.
adloquium, -ī *and* **iī** *nt* talk; encouragement.
adloquor, -quī, -cūtus *vt* to speak to, address.
adlūdiō, -āre, -āvī, -ātum *vi* to play (with).
adlūdō, -dere, -sī, -sum *vi* to joke, play.
adluō, -ere, -ī *vt* to wash.
adluviēs, -ēī *f* pool left by flood water.
adluviō, -ōnis *f* alluvial land.
admātūrō, -āre, -āvī, -atum *vt* to hurry on.
admētior, -tīrī, -nsus *vt* to measure out.
adminiculor, -ārī, -ātus *vt* to prop.
adminiculum, -ī *nt* (*AGR*) stake; (*fig*) support.
administer, -rī *m* assistant.

administrātiō, -ōnis *f* services; management.
administrātor, -ōris *m* manager.
administrō, -āre, -āvī, -ātum *vt* to manage, govern.
admīrābilis *adj* wonderful, surprising.
admīrābilitās, -ātis *f* wonderfulness.
admīrābiliter *adv* admirably; paradoxically.
admīrātiō, -ōnis *f* wonder, surprise, admiration.
admīror, -ārī, -ātus *vt* to wonder at, admire; to be surprised at.
admīsceō, -scēre, -scuī, -xtum *vt* to mix in with, add to; (*fig*) to involve; **sē ~** interfere.
admissārius, -ī *and* **iī** *m* stallion.
admissum, -ī *nt* crime.
admissus *ppp of* **admittō**.
admittō, -ittere, -īsī, -issum *vt* to let in, admit; to set at a gallop; to allow; to commit (a crime); **equō ~issō** charging.
admixtiō, -ōnis *f* admixture.
admixtus *ppp of* **admisceō**.
admoderātē *adv* suitably.
admoderor, -ārī, -ātus *vt* to restrain.
admodum *adv* very, quite; fully; yes; (*with neg*) at all.
admoneō, -ēre, -uī, -itum *vt* to remind, suggest, advise, warn.
admonitiō, -ōnis *f* reminder, suggestion, admonition.
admonitor, -ōris *m* admonisher (*male*).
admonitrīx, -rīcis *f* admonisher (*female*).
admonitū at the suggestion, instance.
admordeō, -dēre, -sum *vt* to bite into; (*fig*) to cheat.
admorsus *ppp of* **admordeō**.
admōtiō, -ōnis *f* applying.
admōtus *ppp of* **admoveō**.
admoveo, -ovēre, -ōvī, -ōtum *vt* to move, bring up, apply; to lend (an ear), direct (the mind).
admurmurātiō, -ōnis *f* murmuring.
admurmurō, -āre, -āvī, -ātum *vi* to murmur (*of a crowd approving or disapproving*).
admutilō, -āre, -āvī, -ātum *vt* to clip close; (*fig*) to cheat.
adnectō, -ctere, -xuī, -xum *vt* to connect, tie.
adnexus, -ūs *m* connection.
adnīsus *ppp of* **adnītor**.
adnītor, -tī, -sus *and* **-xus** *vi* to lean on; to exert oneself.
adnīxus *ppp of* **adnītor**.
adnō, -āre *vt*, *vi* to swim to.
adnotō, -āre, -āvī, -ātum *vt* to comment on.
adnumerō, -āre, -āvī, -ātum *vt* to pay out; to reckon along with.
adnuō, -uere, -uī, -ūtum *vi* to nod; to assent, promise; to indicate.
adoleō, -olēre, -oluī, -ultum *vt* to burn; to pile with gifts.
adolēscen- *etc see* **adulēscen-**.
adolēscō, -ēscere, -ēvī *vi* to grow up, increase; to burn.

Adōnis, -is and **idis** m a beautiful youth loved by Venus.
adopertus adj covered.
adoptātiō, -ōnis f adopting.
adoptiō, -ōnis f adoption.
adoptīvus adj by adoption.
adoptō, -āre, -āvī, -ātum vt to choose; to adopt.
ador, -ōris and **oris** nt spelt.
adōreus adj see n.
adōrea f glory.
adorior, -īrī, -tus vt to accost; to attack; to set about.
adōrnō, -āre, -āvī, -ātum vt to get ready.
adōrō, -āre, -āvī, -ātum vt to entreat; to worship, revere.
adortus ppa of **adorior**.
adp- etc see **app-**.
adrādō, -dere, -sī, -sum vt to shave close.
Adrastus, -ī m a king of Argos.
adrāsus ppp of **adrādō**.
adrēctus ppp of **adrigō** ♦ adj steep.
adrēpō, -ere, -sī, -tum vi to creep, steal into.
adreptus ppp of **adripiō**.
Adria etc see **Hadria** etc.
adrīdeō, -dēre, -sī, -sum vt, vi to laugh, smile at; to please.
adrigō, -igere, -ēxī, -ēctum vt to raise; (fig) to rouse.
adripiō, -ipere, -ipuī, -eptum vt to seize; to appropriate; to take hold of; to learn quickly; (law) to arrest; to satirize.
adrōdō, -dere, -sī, -sum vt to gnaw, nibble at.
adrogāns, -antis adj arrogant, insolent.
adroganter adv see **adrogāns**.
adrogantia, -ae f arrogance, presumption, haughtiness.
adrogātiō, -ōnis f adoption.
adrogō, -āre, -āvī, -ātum vt to ask; to associate; to claim, assume; (fig) to award.
adsc- etc see **asc-**.
adsecla etc see **adsecula**.
adsectātiō, -ōnis f attendance.
adsectātor, -ōris m follower.
adsector, -ārī, -ātus vt to attend on, follow (esp a candidate).
adsecula, -ae m follower (derogatory).
adsēdī perf of **adsideō**; perf of **adsīdō**.
adsēnsiō, -ōnis f assent, applause; (PHILOS) acceptance of the evidence of the senses.
adsēnsor, -ōris m one in agreement.
adsēnsus ppa of **adsentior**.
adsēnsus, -ūs m assent, approval; echo; (PHILOS) acceptance of the evidence of the senses.
adsentātiō, -ōnis f flattery.
adsentātiuncula f trivial compliments.
adsentātor, -ōris m flatterer (male).
adsentātōriē adv ingratiatingly.

adsentātrīx, -rīcis f flatterer (female).
adsentiō, -entīre, -ēnsī, -ēnsum; -entior, -entīrī, -ēnsus vi to agree, approve.
adsentor, -ārī, -ātus vi to agree, flatter.
adsequor, -quī, -cūtus vt to overtake; to attain; to grasp (by understanding).
adserō, -ere, -uī, -tum vt (law) to declare free (usu with manū), liberate (a slave); to lay claim to, appropriate; ~ **in servitūtem** claim as a slave.
adserō, -erere, -ēvī, -itum vt to plant near.
adsertiō, -ōnis f declaration of status.
adsertor, -ōris m champion.
adserviō, -īre vi to assist.
adservō, -āre, -āvī, -ātum vt to watch carefully; to keep, preserve.
adsessiō, -ōnis f sitting beside.
adsessor, -ōris m counsellor.
adsessus, -ūs m sitting beside.
adsevēranter adv emphatically.
adsevērātiō, -ōnis f assertion; earnestness.
adsevērō, -āre, -āvī, -ātum vt to do in earnest; to assert strongly.
adsideō, -idēre, -ēdī, -essum vi to sit by; to attend, assist; to besiege; to resemble.
adsīdō, -īdere, -ēdī vi to sit down.
adsiduē adv continually.
adsiduitās, -ātis f constant attendance; continuance, frequent recurrence.
adsiduō adv continually.
adsiduus adj constantly in attendance, busy; continual, incessant.
adsiduus, -ī m taxpayer.
adsignātiō, -ōnis f allotment (of land).
adsignō, -āre, -āvī, -ātum vt to allot (esp land); to assign; to impute, attribute; to consign.
adsiliō, -ilīre, -iluī, -ultum vi to leap at or on to.
adsimilis adj like.
adsimiliter adv similarly.
adsimulātus adj similar; counterfeit.
adsimulō, -āre, -āvī, -ātum vt, vi to compare; to pretend, imitate.
adsistō, -istere, -titī vi to stand (by); to defend.
adsitus ppp of **adserō**.
adsoleō, -ēre vi to be usual.
adsonō, -āre vi to respond.
adsp- etc see **asp-**.
adsternō, -ere vt to prostrate.
adstipulātor, -ōris m supporter.
adstipulor, -ārī, -ātus vi to agree with.
adstitī perf of **adsistō**; perf of **adstō**.
adstō, -āre, -itī vi to stand near, stand up; to assist.
adstrepō, -ere vi to roar.
adstrictē adv concisely.
adstrictus ppp of **adstringō** ♦ adj tight, narrow; concise; stingy.

Noun declensions and verb conjugations are shown on pp xiii to xxv. The present infinitive ending of a verb shows to which conjugation it belongs: **-āre** = 1st; **-ēre** = 2nd; **-ere** = 3rd and **-īre** = 4th. Irregular verbs are shown on p xxvi

adstringō, -ngere, -nxī, -ctum *vt* to draw close, tighten; to bind, oblige; to abridge.

adstruō, -ere, -xī, -ctum *vt* to build on; to add.

adstupeō, -ēre *vi* to be astonished.

adsuēfaciō, -acere, -ēcī, -actum *vt* to accustom, train.

adsuēscō, -scere, -vī, -tum *vi* to accustom, train.

adsuētūdō, -inis *f* habit.

adsuētus *ppp of* **adsuēscō** ♦ *adj* customary.

adsultō, -āre, -āvī, -ātum *vi* to jump; to attack.

adsultus, -ūs *m* attack.

adsum, -esse, -fuī *vi* to be present; to support, assist (*esp at law*); to come; to appear before (a tribunal); **animō ~** pay attention; **iam aderō** I'll be back soon.

adsūmō, -ere, -psī, -ptum *vt* to take for oneself, receive; to take also.

adsūmptiō, -ōnis *f* taking up; (*logic*) minor premise.

adsūmptīvus *adj* (*law*) which takes its defence from extraneous circumstances.

adsūmptum, -ī *nt* epithet.

adsūmptus *ppp of* **adsūmō**.

adsuō, -ere *vt* to sew on.

adsurgō, -gere, -rēxī, -rēctum *vi* to rise, stand up; to swell, increase.

adt- *etc see* **att-**.

adulātiō, -ōnis *f* (*dogs*) fawning; servility.

adulātor, -ōris *m* sycophant.

adulātōrius *adj* flattering.

adulēscēns, -entis *m/f* young man *or* woman (*usu from 15 to 30 years*).

adulēscentia, -ae *f* youth (*age 15 to 30*).

adulēscentula, -ae *f* girl.

adulēscentulus, -ī *m* quite a young man.

adulō, -āre, -āvī, -ātum; adulor, -ārī, -ātus *vt, vi* to fawn upon, flatter, kowtow.

adulter, -ī *m*, **-a, -ae** *f* adulterer, adulteress ♦ *adj* adulterous.

adulterīnus *adj* forged.

adulterium, -ī *and* **iī** *nt* adultery.

adulterō, -āre, -āvī, -ātum *vt, vi* to commit adultery; to falsify.

adultus *ppp of* **adolēscō** ♦ *adj* adult, mature.

adumbrātim *adv* in outline.

adumbrātiō, -ōnis *f* sketch; semblance.

adumbrātus *adj* false.

adumbrō, -āre, -āvī, -ātum *vt* to sketch; to represent, copy.

aduncitās, -ātis *f* curvature.

aduncus *adj* hooked, curved.

adurgeō, -ēre *vt* to pursue closely.

adūrō, -rere, -ssī, -stum *vt* to burn; to freeze; (*fig*) to fire.

adusque *prep* (*with acc*) right up to ♦ *adv* entirely.

adūstus *ppp of* **adūrō** ♦ *adj* brown.

advectīcius *adj* imported.

advectō, -āre *vt* to carry frequently.

advectus *ppp of* **advehō**.

advectus, -ūs *m* bringing.

advehō, -here, -xī, -ctum *vt* to carry, convey; (*pass*) to ride.

advēlō, -āre *vt* to crown.

advena, -ae *m/f* stranger ♦ *adj* foreign.

adveniō, -enīre, -ēnī, -entum *vi* to arrive, come.

adventīcius *adj* foreign, extraneous; unearned.

adventō, -āre, -āvī, -ātum *vi* to come nearer and nearer, advance rapidly.

adventor, -ōris *m* visitor.

adventus, -ūs *m* arrival, approach.

adversāria *ntpl* daybook.

adversārius, -ī *and* **iī** *m* opponent ♦ *adj* opposing.

adversātrīx, -īcis *f* antagonist.

adversiō, -ōnis *f* turning (the attention).

adversor, -ārī, -ātus *vi* to oppose, resist.

adversum, -ī *nt* opposite; misfortune ♦ *prep* (+ *acc*) towards, against ♦ *adv* to meet.

adversus *ppp of* **advertō** ♦ *adj* opposite, in front; hostile; **~ō flūmine** upstream; **~ae rēs** misfortune ♦ *prep* (+ *acc*) towards, against ♦ *adv* to meet.

advertō, -tere, -tī, -sum *vt* to turn, direct towards; to call attention; **animum ~** notice, perceive; (*with* **ad**) to attend to; (*with* **in**) to punish.

advesperāscit, -scere, -vit *vi* it is getting dark.

advigilō, -āre *vi* to keep watch.

advocātiō, -ōnis *f* legal assistance, counsel.

advocātus, -ī *m* supporter in a lawsuit; advocate, counsel.

advocō, -āre, -āvī, -ātum *vt* to summon; (*law*) to call in the assistance of.

advolō, -āre, -āvī, -ātum *vi* to fly to, swoop down upon.

advolvō, -vere, -vī, -ūtum *vt* to roll to; to prostrate.

advor- *etc see* **adver-**.

adytum, -ī *nt* sanctuary.

Aeacidēs, -idae *m* Achilles; Pyrrhus.

Aeacus, -ī *m* father of Peleus, and judge of the dead.

Aeaea, -ae *f* Circe's island.

Aeaeus *adj* of Circe.

aedēs, -is *f* temple; (*pl*) house.

aedicula, -ae *f* shrine; small house, room.

aedificātiō, -ōnis *f* building.

aedificātiuncula, -ae *f* little house.

aedificātor, -ōris *m* builder.

aedificium, -ī *and* **iī** *nt* building.

aedificō, -āre, -āvī, -ātum *vt* to build, construct.

aedīlicius *adj* aedile's ♦ *m* ex-aedile.

aedīlis, -is *m* aedile.

aedīlitās, -ātis *f* aedileship.

aedis, -is *see* **aedēs**.

aeditumus, aedituus, -ī *m* temple-keeper.

Aeduī, -ōrum *mpl* a tribe of central Gaul.

Aeētēs, -ae *m* father of Medea.

Aegaeus *adj* Aegean ♦ *nt* Aegean Sea.
Aegātēs, -um *fpl islands off Sicily.*
aeger, -rī *adj* ill, sick; sorrowful; weak.
Aegīna, -ae *f a Greek island.*
Aegīnēta, -ae *m inhabitant of Aegīna.*
aegis, -dis *f shield of Jupiter or Athena,* aegis.
Aegisthus, -ī *m paramour of Clytemnestra.*
aegocerōs, -ōtis *m* Capricorn.
aegrē *adv* painfully; with displeasure; with difficulty; hardly; ~ **ferre** be annoyed.
aegrēscō, -ere *vi* to become ill; to be aggravated.
aegrimōnia, -ae *f* distress of mind.
aegritūdō, -inis *f* sickness; sorrow.
aegror, -ōris *m* illness.
aegrōtātiō, -ōnis *f* illness, disease.
aegrōtō, -āre, -āvī, -ātum *vi* to be ill.
aegrōtus *adj* ill, sick.
Aegyptius *adj see* n.
Aegyptus, -ī *f* Egypt ♦ *m brother of Danaus.*
aelinos, -ī *m* dirge.
Aemiliānus *adj esp Scipio, destroyer of Carthage.*
Aemilius, -ī *Roman family name;* **Via ~ia** *road in N. Italy.*
aemulātiō, -ōnis *f* rivalry (*good or bad*); jealousy.
aemulātor, -ōris *m* zealous imitator.
aemulor, -ārī, -ātus *vt* to rival, copy; to be jealous.
aemulus, -ī *m* rival ♦ *adj* rivalling; jealous.
Aeneadēs, -ae *m* Trojan; Roman.
Aenēās, -ae *m Trojan leader and hero of Virgil's epic.*
Aenēis, -idis *and* **idos** *f* Aeneid.
Aenēius *adj see* n.
aēneus *adj* of bronze.
aenigma, -tis *nt* riddle, mystery.
aēnum, -ī *nt* bronze vessel.
aēnus *adj* of bronze.
Aeolēs, -um *mpl* the Aeolians.
Aeolia *f* Lipari Island.
Aeolidēs *m a descendant of Aeolus.*
Aeolis, -idis *f* Aeolia (*N.W. of Asia Minor*).
Aeolis, -idis *f daughter of Aeolus.*
Aeolius *adj see* n.
Aeolus, -ī *m king of the winds.*
aequābilis *adj* equal; consistent, even; impartial.
aequābilitās, -ātis *f* uniformity; impartiality.
aequābiliter *adv* uniformly.
aequaevus *adj* of the same age.
aequālis *adj* equal, like; of the same age, contemporary; uniform.
aequālitās, -ātis *f* evenness; (*in politics, age*) equality, similarity.
aequāliter *adv* evenly.
aequanimitās, -ātis *f* goodwill; calmness.
aequātiō, -ōnis *f* equal distribution.
aeque *adv* equally; just as (*with* **ac, atque, et, quam**); justly.
Aequī, -ōrum *mpl a people of central Italy.*

Aequicus, Aequiculus *adj see* n.
Aequimaelium, -ī *and* **iī** *nt an open space in Rome.*
aequinoctiālis *adj see* n.
aequinoctium, -ī *and* **iī** *nt* equinox.
aequiperābilis *adj* comparable.
aequiperō, -āre, -āvī, -ātum *vt* to compare; to equal.
aequitās, -ātis *f* uniformity; fair dealing, equity; calmness of mind.
aequō, -āre, -āvī, -ātum *vt* to make equal, level; to compare; to equal; **solō ~** raze to the ground.
aequor, -is *nt* a level surface, sea.
aequoreus *adj* of the sea.
aequum, -i *nt* plain; justice.
aequus *adj* level, equal; favourable, friendly, fair, just; calm; **~ō animō** patiently; **~ō Marte** without deciding the issue; **~um est** it is reasonable; **ex ~ō** equally.
āēr, āeris *m* air, weather; mist.
aerāria *f* mine.
aerārium *nt* treasury.
aerārius *adj* of bronze; of money ♦ *m* a citizen of the lowest class at Rome; **tribūnī ~ī** paymasters; a wealthy middle class at Rome.
aerātus *adj* of bronze.
aereus *adj* of copper *or* bronze.
aerifer, -i *adj* carrying cymbals.
aeripēs, -edis *adj* bronze-footed.
āērius *adj* of the air; lofty.
aerūgō, -inis *f* rust; (*fig*) envy, avarice.
aerumna, -ae *f* trouble, hardship.
aerumnōsus *adj* wretched.
aes, aeris *nt* copper, bronze; money; (*pl*) objects made of copper *or* bronze (*esp statues, instruments, vessels; soldiers' pay*); ~ **aliēnum** debt; ~ **circumforāneum** borrowed money; ~ **grave** Roman coin, as.
Aeschylus, -ī *m Greek tragic poet.*
Aesculāpius, -ī *m god of medicine.*
aesculētum, -ī *nt* oak forest.
aesculeus *adj see* **aesculus.**
aesculus, -ī *f* durmast oak.
Aesōn, -onis *m father of Jason.*
Aesonidēs, -ae *m* Jason.
Aesōpius *adj see* n.
Aesōpus, -ī *m Greek writer of fables.*
aestās, -ātis *f* summer.
aestifer, -ī *adj* heat-bringing.
aestimātiō, -ōnis *f* valuation, assessment; **lītis ~** assessment of damages.
aestimātor, -ōris *m* valuer.
aestimō, -āre, -āvī, -ātum *vt* to value, estimate the value of; **māgnī ~** think highly of.
aestīva, -ōrum *ntpl* summer camp, campaign.
aestīvus *adj* summer.
aestuārium, -ī *and* **iī** *nt* tidal waters, estuary.
aestuō, -āre, -āvī, -ātum *vi* to boil, burn;

Noun declensions and verb conjugations are shown on pp xiii to xxv. The present infinitive ending of a verb shows to which conjugation it belongs: **-āre** = 1st; **-ēre** = 2nd; **-ere** = 3rd and **-īre** = 4th. Irregular verbs are shown on p xxvi

(*movement*) to heave, toss; (*fig*) to be excited; to waver.

aestuōsus *adj* very hot; agitated.

aestus, -ūs *m* heat; surge of the sea; tide; (*fig*) passion; hesitation.

aetās, -ātis *f* age, life; time.

aetātem *adv* for life.

aetātula, -ae *f* tender age.

aeternitās, -ātis *f* eternity.

aeternō, -āre *vt* to immortalize.

aeternus *adj* eternal, immortal; lasting; **in ~um** for ever.

aethēr, -eris *m* sky, heaven; air.

aetherius *adj* ethereal, heavenly; of air.

Aethiops, -is *adj* Ethiopian; (*fig*) stupid.

aethra, -ae *f* sky.

Aetna, -ae *f* Etna (*in Sicily*).

Aetnaeus, Aetnēnsis *adj see n.*

Aetōlia, -iae *f* a district of N. Greece.

Aetōlus, -icus *adj see n.*

aevitās, -ātis old form of **aetās.**

aevum, -ī *nt* age, lifetime; eternity; **in ~** for ever.

Āfer, -rī *adj* African.

āfore *fut infin of* **absum.**

Āfrānius, -ī *m* Latin comic poet.

Āfrica, -ae *f* Roman province (*now* Tunisia).

Āfricānae *fpl* panthers.

Āfricānus *adj* name of two Scipios.

Āfricus *adj* African ♦ *m* south-west wind.

āfuī, āfutūrus *perf, fut p of* **absum.**

Agamēmnōn, -onis *m* leader of Greeks against Troy.

Agamēmnonius *adj see n.*

Aganippē, -ēs *f* a spring on Helicon.

agāsō, -ōnis *m* ostler, footman.

age, agedum come on!, well then.

agellus, -ī *m* plot of land.

Agēnōr, -oris *m* father of Europa.

Agēnoreus *adj see n.*

Agēnoridēs, -ae *m* Cadmus; Perseus.

agēns, -entis *adj* (*RHET*) effective.

ager, -rī *m* land, field; countryside; territory.

agg- *etc see* **adg-.**

agger, -is *m* rampart; mound, embankment, any built-up mass.

aggerō, -āre, -āvī, -ātum *vt* to pile up; to increase.

aggerō, -rere, -ssi, -stum *vt* to carry, bring.

aggestus, -ūs *m* accumulation.

agilis *adj* mobile; nimble, busy.

agilitās, -ātis *f* mobility.

agitābilis *adj* light.

agitātiō, -ōnis *f* movement, activity.

agitātor, -ōris *m* driver, charioteer.

agitō, -āre, -āvī, -ātum *vt* (*animals*) to drive; to move, chase, agitate; (*fig*) to excite (to action); to persecute, ridicule; to keep (a ceremony) ♦ *vi* to live; to deliberate.

agmen, -inis *nt* forward movement, procession, train; army on the march; **~ claudere** bring up the rear; **novissimum ~** rearguard; **prīmum ~** van.

agna, -ae *f* ewe lamb; lamb (flesh).

agnāscor, -scī, -tus *vi* to be born after.

agnātus, -ī *m* relation (*by blood on father's side*).

agnellus, -ī *m* little lamb.

agnīnus *adj* of lamb.

agnitiō, -ōnis *f* recognition, knowledge.

agnitus *ppp of* **agnōscō.**

agnōmen, -inis *nt* an extra surname (*eg Africanus*).

agnōscō, -ōscere, -ōvī, -itum *vt* to recognize; to acknowledge, allow; to understand.

agnus, -ī *m* lamb.

agō, agere, ēgī, āctum *vt* to drive, lead; to plunder; to push forward, put forth; (*fig*) to move, rouse, persecute; to do, act, perform; (*time*) to pass, spend; (*undertakings*) to manage, wage; (*public speaking*) to plead, discuss; to negotiate, treat; (*THEAT*) to play, act the part of; **~ cum populō** address the people; **age** come on!, well then; **age age** all right!; **āctum est dē** it is all up with; **aliud ~** not attend; **animam ~** expire; **annum quartum ~** be three years old; **causam ~** plead a cause; **hōc age** pay attention; **id ~ ut** aim at; **lēge ~** go to law; **nīl agis** it's no use; **quid agis?** how are you?; **rēs agitur** interests are at stake; **sē ~** go, come.

agrāriī *mpl* the land reform party.

agrārius *adj* of public land; **lēx ~a** land law.

agrestis *adj* rustic; boorish, wild, barbarous ♦ *m* countryman.

agricola, -ae *m* countryman, farmer.

Agricola, -ae *m* a Roman governor of Britain; his biography by Tacitus.

Agrigentīnus *adj see n.*

Agrigentum, -ī *nt* a town in Sicily.

agripeta, -ae *m* landgrabber.

Agrippa, -ae *m* Roman surname (*esp Augustus's minister*).

Agrippīna, -ae *f* mother of Nero; **Colōnia ~a** or **~ēnsis** Cologne.

Agyīeus, -eī and **eos** *m* Apollo.

āh *interj* ah! (*in sorrow or joy*).

aha *interj* expressing reproof *or* laughter.

ahēn- *etc see* **aēn-.**

Āiāx, -ācis *m* Ajax (*name of two Greek heroes at Troy*).

āiō *vt* (*defec*) to say, speak; **ain tū?/ain vērō?** really?; **quid ais?** I say!

āla, -ae *f* wing; armpit; (*MIL*) wing of army.

alabaster, -rī *m* perfume box.

alacer, -ris *adj* brisk, cheerful.

alacritās, -ātis *f* promptness, liveliness; joy, rapture.

alapa, -ae *f* slap on the face; a slave's freedom.

ālāriī *mpl* allied troops.

ālārius *adj* (*MIL*) on the wing.

ālātus *adj* winged.

alauda, -ae *f* lark; name of a legion of Caesar's.

alāzōn, -onis *m* braggart.

Alba Longa, -ae, -ae *f* a Latin town (*precursor of Rome*).
Albānus *adj* Alban; **Lacus ~, Mōns ~** *lake and mountain near Alba Longa.*
albātus *adj* dressed in white.
albeō, -ēre *vi* to be white; to dawn.
albēscō, -ere *vi* to become white; to dawn.
albicō, -āre *vi* to be white.
albidus *adj* white.
Albiōn, -ōnis *f* ancient name for Britain.
albitūdō, -inis *f* whiteness.
Albula, -ae *f* old name for the Tiber.
albulus *adj* whitish.
album, -ī *nt* white; records.
Albunea, -ae *f* a spring at Tibur; a sulphur spring near Alban Lake.
albus *adj* white, bright.
Alcaeus, -ī *m* Greek lyric poet.
alcēdō, -inis *f* kingfisher.
alcēdōnia *ntpl* halcyon days.
alcēs, -is *f* elk.
Alcibiadēs, -is *m* brilliant Athenian politician.
Alcīdēs, -ae *m* Hercules.
Alcinous, -ī *m* king of Phaeacians in the Odyssey.
ālea, -ae *f* gambling, dice; (*fig*) chance, hazard; **iacta ~ est** the die is cast; **in ~am dare** to risk.
āleātor, -ōris *m* gambler.
āleātōrius *adj* in gambling.
ālec *etc see* **allēc.**
āleō, -ōnis *m* gambler.
āles, -itis *adj* winged; swift ♦ *m/f* bird; omen.
alēscō, -ere *vi* to grow up.
Alexander, -rī *m* a Greek name; Paris (*prince of Troy*); Alexander the Great (*king of Macedon*).
Alexandrēa (*later* **-īa**)**, -ēae** *f* Alexandria in Egypt.
alga, -ae *f* seaweed.
algeō, -gēre, -sī *vi* to feel cold; (*fig*) to be neglected.
algēscō, -ere *vi* to catch cold.
Algidus, -ī *m* mountain in Latium.
algidus *adj* cold.
algor, -ōris *m* cold.
algū *abl sg m* with cold.
aliā *adv* in another way.
aliās *adv* at another time; at one time … at another.
alibī *adv* elsewhere; otherwise; in one place … in another.
alicubī *adv* somewhere.
alicunde *adv* from somewhere.
alid *old form of* **aliud.**
aliēnātiō, -ōnis *f* transfer; estrangement.
aliēnigena, -ae *m* foreigner.
aliēnigenus *adj* foreign; heterogeneous.
aliēnō, -āre, -āvī, -ātum *vt* to transfer (property by sale); to alienate, estrange; (*mind*) to derange.

aliēnus *adj* of another, of others; alien, strange; (*with abl or ab*) unsuited to, different from; hostile ♦ *m* stranger.
āliger, -ī *adj* winged.
alimentārius *adj* about food.
alimentum, -ī *nt* nourishment, food; obligation of children to parents; (*fig*) support.
alimōnium, -i *and* **iī** *nt* nourishment.
aliō *adv* in another direction, elsewhere; one way … another way.
aliōquī, aliōquin *adv* otherwise, else; besides.
aliōrsum *adv* in another direction; differently.
ālipēs, -edis *adj* wing-footed; fleet.
alīptēs, -ae *m* sports trainer.
aliquā *adv* some way or other.
aliquam *adv*: **~ diū** for sometime; **~ multī** a considerable number.
aliquandō *adv* sometime, ever; sometimes; once, for once; now at last.
aliquantisper *adv* for a time.
aliquantō *adv* (*with comp*) somewhat.
aliquantulum *nt* a very little ♦ *adv* somewhat.
aliquantulus *adj* quite small.
aliquantum *adj* a good deal ♦ *adv* somewhat.
aliquantus *adj* considerable.
aliquātenus *adv* to some extent.
aliquī, -qua, -quod *adj* some, any; some other.
aliquid *adv* at all.
aliquis, -quid *pron* somebody, something; someone *or* something important.
aliquō *adv* to some place, somewhere else.
aliquot *adj* (*indecl*) some.
aliquotiēns *adv* several times.
aliter *adv* otherwise, differently; in one way … in another.
alitus *ppp of* **alō.**
ālium, -i *and* **iī** *nt* garlic.
aliunde *adv* from somewhere else.
alius, alia, aliud *adj* other, another; different; **alius … alius** some … others; **alius ex aliō** one after the other; **in alia omnia īre** oppose a measure; **nihil aliud quam** only.
all- *etc see* **adl-.**
allēc, -is *nt* fish pickle.
allex, -icis *m* big toe.
Allia, -ae *f* tributary of the Tiber (*scene of a great Roman defeat*).
Alliēnsis *adj see* **Allia.**
Allobrogēs, -um *mpl* a people of S.E. Gaul.
Allobrogicus *adj see n.*
almus *adj* nourishing; kindly.
alnus, -ī *f* alder.
alō, -ere, -uī, -tum *and* **-itum** *vt* to nourish, rear; to increase, promote.
Alpēs, -ium *fpl* Alps.
Alphēus, -ī *m* river of Olympia in S.W. Greece.
Alpīnus *adj see n.*

Noun declensions and verb conjugations are shown on pp xiii to xxv. The present infinitive ending of a verb shows to which conjugation it belongs: **-āre** = 1st; **-ēre** = 2nd; **-ere** = 3rd and **-īre** = 4th. Irregular verbs are shown on p xxvi

alsī *perf of* **algeō**.

alsius, alsus *adj* cold.

altāria, -ium *ntpl* altars, altar; altar top.

altē *adv* on high, from above; deep; from afar.

alter, -īus *adj* the one, the other (*of two*); second, the next; fellow man; different; ~ **ego,** ~ **īdem** a second self; **~um tantum** twice as much; **ūnus et ~** one or two.

altercātiō, -ōnis *f* dispute, debate.

altercor, -ārī, -ātus *vi* to wrangle, dispute; to cross-examine.

alternīs *adv* alternately.

alternō, -āre, -āvī, -ātum *vt* to do by turns, alternate.

alternus *adj* one after the other, alternate; elegiac (verses).

alteruter, -īusutrīus *adj* one or the other.

altilis *adj* fat (*esp fowls*).

altisonus *adj* sounding on high.

altitonāns, -antis *adj* thundering on high.

altitūdō, -inis *f* height, depth; (*fig*) sublimity, (*mind*) secrecy.

altivolāns, -antis *adj* soaring on high.

altor, -ōris *m* foster father.

altrīnsecus *adv* on the other side.

altrīx, -īcis *f* nourisher, foster mother.

altum, -ī *nt* heaven; sea (*usu out of sight of land*); **ex ~ō repetītus** far-fetched.

altus *adj* high, deep; (*fig*) noble; profound.

ālūcinor, -ārī, -ātus *vi* to talk wildly; (*mind*) to wander.

aluī *perf of* **alō**.

alumnus, -ī *m/f* foster child; pupil.

alūta, -ae *f* soft leather; shoe, purse, face patch.

alveārium, -ī *and* **iī** *nt* beehive.

alveolus, -ī *m* basin.

alveus, -eī *m* hollow; trough; (*ship*) hold; bath tub; riverbed.

alvus, -ī *f* bowels; womb; stomach.

amābilis *adj* lovely, lovable.

amābilitās, -ātis *f* charm.

amābiliter *adv see* **amābilis**.

Amalthēa, -ae *f* nymph or she-goat; **cornū ~ae** horn of plenty.

Amalthēum, -ī *nt* Atticus's library.

āmandātiō *f* sending away.

āmandō, -āre, -āvī, -ātum *vt* to send away.

amāns, -antis *adj* fond ♦ *m* lover.

amanter *adv* affectionately.

āmanuēnsis, -is *m* secretary.

amāracinum, -inī *nt* marjoram ointment.

amāracum, -ī *nt*, **amāracus, -ī** *m/f* sweet marjoram.

amārē *adv see* **amārus**.

amāritiēs, -ēī *f*, **amāritūdō, -inis** *f*, **amāror, -ōris** *m* bitterness.

amārus *adj* bitter; (*fig*) sad; ill-natured.

amāsius, -ī *and* **iī** *m* lover.

Amathūs, -ūntis *f* town in Cyprus.

Amathūsia *f* Venus.

amātiō, -ōnis *f* lovemaking.

amātor, -ōris *m* lover, paramour.

amātorculus *m* poor lover.

amātōriē *adv* amorously.

amātōrius *adj* of love, erotic.

amātrīx, -rīcis *f* mistress.

Amāzōn, -onis *f* Amazon, warrior woman.

Amāzonides *fpl* Amazons.

Amāzonius *adj see n*.

ambāctus, -ī *m* vassal.

ambāgēs, -is *f* windings; (*speech*) circumlocution, quibbling; enigma.

ambedō, -edere, -ēdī, -ēsum *vt* to consume.

ambēsus *ppp of* **ambedō**.

ambigō, -ere *vt, vi* to wander about; to be in doubt; to argue; to wrangle.

ambiguē *adv* doubtfully.

ambiguitās, -ātis *f* ambiguity.

ambiguus *adj* changeable, doubtful, unreliable; ambiguous.

ambiō, -īre, -īī, -ītum *vt* to go round, encircle; (*POL*) to canvass for votes; (*fig*) to court (for a favour).

ambitiō, -ōnis *f* canvassing for votes; currying favour; ambition.

ambitiōsē *adv* ostentatiously.

ambitiōsus *adj* winding; ostentatious, ambitious.

ambitus *ppp of* **ambiō**.

ambitus, -ūs *m* circuit, circumference; circumlocution; canvassing, bribery; **lēx de ~ū** a law against bribery.

ambō, ambae, ambō *num* both, two.

Ambracia, -ae *f* district of N.W. Greece.

Ambraciēnsis, -us *adj see n*.

ambrosia, -ae *f* food of the gods.

ambrosius *adj* divine.

ambūbāia, -ae *f* Syrian flute-girl.

ambulācrum, -ī *nt* avenue.

ambulātiō, -ōnis *f* walk, walking; walk (*place*).

ambulātiuncula *f* short walk.

ambulō, -āre, -āvī, -ātum *vi* to walk, go; to travel.

ambūrō, -rere, -ssī, -stum *vt* to burn up; to make frostbitten; (*fig*) to ruin.

ambūstus *ppp of* **ambūrō**.

amellus, -ī *m* Michaelmas daisy.

āmēns, -entis *adj* mad, frantic; stupid.

āmentia, -ae *f* madness; stupidity.

āmentum, -ī *nt* strap (for throwing javelin).

ames, -itis *m* fowler's pole.

amfr- *etc see* **anfr-**.

amīca, -ae *f* friend; mistress.

amiciō, -īre, -tus *vt* to clothe, cover.

amīciter, -ē *adv see* **amīcus**.

amīcitia, -ae *f* friendship; alliance.

amictus *ppp of* **amiciō**.

amictus, -ūs *m* (manner of) dress; clothing.

amiculum, -ī *nt* cloak.

amīculus, -ī *m* dear friend.

amīcus, -ī *m* friend ♦ *adj* friendly, fond.

āmissiō, -ōnis *f* loss.

āmissus *ppp of* **āmittō**.

amita, -ae *f* aunt (*on father's side*).

āmittō, -ittere, -īsī, -issum vt to let go, lose.
Ammōn, -is m Egyptian god identified with Jupiter.
Ammōniacus adj see n.
amnicola, -ae m/f sth growing by a river.
amniculus m brook.
amnicus adj see n.
amnis, -is m river.
amō, -āre, -āvī, -ātum vt to love, like; (colloq) to be obliged to; **ita mē dī ament!** ≈ bless my soul!; **amābō** please!
amoenitās, -ātis f delightfulness (esp of scenery).
amoenus adj delightful.
āmōlior, -īrī, -ītus vt to remove.
amōmum, -ī nt cardamom.
amor, -ōris m love; (fig) strong desire; term of endearment; Cupid; (pl) love affairs.
āmōtiō, -ōnis f removal.
āmōtus ppp of **āmoveō**.
āmoveō, -ovēre, -ōvī, -ōtum vt to remove; to banish.
amphibolia, -ae f ambiguity.
Amphīōn, -onis m musician and builder of Thebes.
Amphīonius adj see n.
amphitheātrum, -ī nt amphitheatre.
Amphitrītē, -ēs f sea goddess; the sea.
Amphitryō, -ōnis m husband of Alcmena.
Amphitryōniadēs m Hercules.
amphora, -ae f a two-handled jar; liquid measure; (NAUT) measure of tonnage.
Amphrysius adj of Apollo.
Amphrysus, -ī m river in Thessaly.
ample adv see **amplūs**.
amplector, -ctī, -xus vt to embrace, encircle; (mind) to grasp; (speech) to deal with; (fig) to cherish.
amplexor, -ārī, -ātus vt to embrace, love.
amplexus ppa of **amplector**.
amplexus, -ūs m embrace, encircling.
amplificātiō, -ōnis f enlargement; (RHET) a passage elaborated for effect.
amplificē adv splendidly.
amplificō, -āre, -āvī, -ātum vt to increase, enlarge; (RHET) to enlarge upon.
ampliō, -āre, -āvī, -ātum vt to enlarge; (law) to adjourn.
ampliter adv see **amplūs**.
amplitūdō, -inis f size; (fig) distinction; (RHET) fullness.
amplius adv more (esp amount or number), further, longer; ~ **ducentī** more than 200; ~ **nōn petere** take no further legal action; ~ **prōnūntiāre** adjourn a case.
amplūs adj large, spacious; great, abundant; powerful, splendid, eminent; (sup) distinguished.
ampulla, -ae f a two-handled flask; (fig) high-flown language.

ampullārius, -ārī m flask-maker.
ampullor, -ārī vi to use high-flown language.
amputātiō, -ōnis f pruning.
amputatus adj (RHET) disconnected.
amputō, -āre, -āvī, -ātum vt to cut off, prune; (fig) to lop off.
Amūlius, -ī m king of Alba Longa, grand-uncle of Romulus.
amurca, -ae f lees of olive oil.
amussitātus adj nicely adjusted.
Amӯclae, -ārum fpl town in S. Greece.
Amӯclaeus adj see n.
amygdalum, -ī nt almond.
amystis, -dis f emptying a cup at a draught.
an conj or; perhaps; (with single question) surely not; **haud sciō** ~ I feel sure.
Anacreōn, -ontis m Greek lyric poet.
anadēma, -tis nt headband.
anagnōstēs, -ae m reader.
anapaestum, -ī nt poem in anapaests.
anapaestus adj: ~ **pēs** anapaest.
anas, -tis f duck.
anaticula f duckling.
anatīnus adj see n.
anatocismus, -ī m compound interest.
Anaxagorās, -ae m early Greek philosopher.
Anaximander, -rī m early Greek philosopher.
anceps, -ipitis adj two-headed; double; wavering, doubtful; dangerous ♦ nt danger.
Anchīsēs, -ae m father of Aeneas.
Anchīsēus adj see n.
Anchīsiadēs m Aeneas.
ancīle, -is nt oval shield (esp one said to have fallen from heaven in Numa's reign).
ancilla, -ae f servant.
ancillāris adj of a young servant.
ancillula f young servant.
ancīsus adj cut round.
ancora, -ae f anchor.
ancorārius adj see n.
ancorāle, -is nt cable.
Ancus Marcius, -ī, -ī m 4th king of Rome.
Ancӯra, -ae f Ankara (capital of Galatia).
andabata, -ae m blindfold gladiator.
Andrius adj see **Andros**.
androgynē, -ēs f hermaphrodite.
androgynus, -ī m hermaphrodite.
Andromachē, -ēs f wife of Hector.
Andromeda, -ae f wife of Perseus; a constellation.
Andronicus, -ī m Livius (earliest Latin poet).
Andros (-us), -ī m Aegean island.
ānellus, -ī m little ring.
anēthum, -ī nt fennel.
ānfrāctus, -ūs m bend, orbit; roundabout way; (words) digression, prolixity.
angelus, -ī m angel.
angina, -ae f quinsy.
angiportum, -ī nt alley.
angiportus, -ūs m alley.

Noun declensions and verb conjugations are shown on pp xiii to xxv. The present infinitive ending of a verb shows to which conjugation it belongs: -**āre** = 1st; -**ēre** = 2nd; -**ere** = 3rd and -**īre** = 4th. Irregular verbs are shown on p xxvi

angō, -ere *vt* to throttle; (*fig*) to distress, torment.

angor, -ōris *m* suffocation; (*fig*) anguish, torment.

anguicomus *adj* with snakes for hair.

anguiculus, -ī *m* small snake.

anguifer, -ī *adj* snake-carrying.

anguigena, -ae *m* one born of serpents; Theban.

anguīlla, -ae *f* eel.

anguimanus *adj* with a trunk.

anguipēs, -edis *adj* serpent-footed.

anguis, -is *m/f* snake, serpent; (*constellation*) Draco.

Anguitenēns, -entis *m* Ophiuchus.

angulātus *adj* angular.

angulus, -ī *m* angle, corner; out-of-the-way place; **ad parēs ~ōs** at right angles.

angustē *adv* close, within narrow limits; concisely.

angustiae, -ārum *fpl* defile, strait; (*time*) shortness; (*means*) want; (*CIRCS*) difficulty; (*mind*) narrowness; (*words*) subtleties.

angusticlāvius *adj* wearing a narrow purple stripe.

angustō, -āre *vt* to make narrow.

angustum, -ī *nt* narrowness; danger.

angustus *adj* narrow, close; (*time*) short; (*means*) scanty; (*mind*) mean; (*argument*) subtle; (*CIRCS*) difficult.

anhēlitus, -ūs *m* panting; breath, exhalation.

anhēlō, -āre, -āvī, -ātum *vi* to breathe hard, pant; to exhale.

anhēlus *adj* panting.

anicula, -ae *f* poor old woman.

Aniēnsis, Aniēnus *adj* of the river Anio.

Aniēnus *m* Anio.

anīlis *adj* of an old woman.

anīlitās, -tātis *f* old age.

anīliter *adv* like an old woman.

anima, -ae *f* wind, air; breath; life; soul, mind; ghost, spirit; **~am agere, efflāre** expire; **~am comprimere** hold one's breath.

animadversiō, -ōnis *f* observation; censure, punishment.

animadversor, -ōris *m* observer.

animadvertō, -tere, -tī, -sum *vt* to pay attention to, notice; to realise; to censure, punish; **~ in** punish.

animal, -ālis *nt* animal; living creature.

animālis *adj* of air; animate.

animāns, -antis *m/f/nt* living creature; animal.

animātiō, -ōnis *f* being.

animātus *adj* disposed, in a certain frame of mind; courageous.

animō, -āre, -āvī, -ātum *vt* to animate; to give a certain temperament to.

animōsē *adv* boldly, eagerly.

animōsus *adj* airy; lifelike; courageous, proud.

animula, -ae *f* little soul.

animulus, -ī *m* darling.

animus, -ī *m* mind, soul; consciousness; reason, thought, opinion, imagination; heart, feelings, disposition; courage, spirit, pride, passion; will, purpose; term of endearment; **~ī** in mind, in heart; **~ī causā** for amusement; **~ō fingere** imagine; **~ō male est** I am fainting; **aequō ~ō esse** be patient, calm; **bonō ~ō esse** take courage; be well-disposed; **ex ~ō** sincerely; **ex ~ō effluere** be forgotten; **in ~ō habēre** purpose; **meō ~ō** in my opinion.

Aniō, -ēnis *m* tributary of the Tiber.

Anna Perenna, -ae, -ae *f* Roman popular goddess.

annālēs, -ium *mpl* annals, chronicle.

annālis *adj* of a year; **lēx ~** law prescribing ages for public offices.

anne *etc see* **an.**

anniculus *adj* a year old.

anniversārius *adj* annual.

annōn or not.

annōna, -ae *f* year's produce; grain; price of corn; the market.

annōsus *adj* aged.

annōtinus *adj* last year's.

annus, -ī *m* year; **~ māgnus** astronomical great year; **~ solidus** a full year.

annuus *adj* a year's; annual.

anquīrō, -rere, -sīvī, -sītum *vt* to search for; to make inquiries; (*law*) to institute an inquiry (**dē**) *or* prosecution (*abl or gen*).

ānsa, -ae *f* handle; (*fig*) opportunity.

ānsātus *adj* with a handle; (*comedy*) with arms akimbo.

ānser, -is *m* goose.

ānserīnus *adj* see *n.*

ante *prep* (*with acc*) before (*in time, place, comparison*) ♦ *adv* (*place*) in front; (*time*) before.

anteā *adv* before, formerly.

antecapiō, -apere, -ēpī, -eptum *vt* to take beforehand, anticipate.

antecēdō, -ēdere, -essī, -essum *vt* to precede; to surpass.

antecellō, -ere *vi* to excel, be superior.

anteceptus *ppp of* **antecapiō.**

antecessiō, -ōnis *f* preceding; antecedent cause.

antecessor, -ōris *m* forerunner.

antecursor, -ōris *m* forerunner, pioneer.

anteeō, -īre, -īī *vi* to precede, surpass.

anteferō, -ferre, -tulī, -lātum *vt* to carry before; to prefer; to anticipate.

antefīxus *adj* attached (in front) ♦ *ntpl* ornaments on roofs of buildings.

antegredior, -dī, -ssus *vt* to precede.

antehabeō, -ēre *vt* to prefer.

antehāc *adv* formerly, previously.

antelātus *ppp of* **anteferō.**

antelūcānus *adj* before dawn.

antemerīdiānus *adj* before noon.

antemittō, -ittere, -īsī, -issum *vt* to send on in front.

antenna, -ae *f* yardarm.

antepīlānī, -ōrum *mpl* (MIL) the front ranks.
antepōno, -ōnere, -osuī, -ositum *vt* to set before; to prefer.
antequam *conj* before.
Anterōs, -ōtis *m* avenger of slighted love.
antēs, -ium *mpl* rows.
antesignānus, -ī *m* (MIL) leader; (*pl*) defenders of the standards.
antestō, antistō, -āre, -ētī *vi* to excel, distinguish oneself.
antestor, -ārī, -ātus *vi* to call a witness.
anteveniō, -enīre, -ēnī, -entum *vt, vi* to anticipate; to surpass.
antevertō, -tere, -tī, -sum *vt* to precede; to anticipate; to prefer.
anticipātiō, -ōnis *f* foreknowledge.
anticipō, -āre, -āvī, -ātum *vt* to take before, anticipate.
antīcus *adj* in front.
Antigonē, -ēs *f* daughter of Oedipus.
Antigonus, -ī *m* name of Macedonian kings.
Antiochēnsis *adj see n.*
Antiochīa, -īae *f* Antioch (*capital of Syria*).
Antiochus, -ī *m* name of kings of Syria.
antīquārius, -ī *and* **īī** *m* antiquary.
antīquē *adv* in the old style.
antīquitās, -ātis *f* antiquity, the ancients; integrity.
antīquitus *adv* long ago, from ancient times.
antīquō, -āre, -āvī, -ātum *vt* to vote against (a bill).
antīquus *adj* ancient, former, old; good old-fashioned, honest, illustrious; **antīquior** more important; **antīquissimus** most important.
antistēs, -itis *m/f* high priest, chief priestess; (*fig*) master (*in any art*).
Antisthenēs, -is *and* **ae** *m* founder of Cynic philosophy.
antistita, -ae *f* chief priestess.
antistō *etc see* **antestō**.
antitheton, -ī *nt* (RHET) antithesis.
Antōnīnus, -ī *m* name of Roman emperors (*esp Pius and Marcus Aurelius*).
Antōnius, -ī *m* Roman name (*esp the famous orator, and Mark Antony*).
antrum, -ī *nt* cave, hollow.
ānulārius, -ī *m* ringmaker.
ānulātus *adj* with rings on.
ānulus, -ī *m* ring; equestrian rank.
ānus, -ī *m* rectum; ring.
anus, -ūs *f* old woman ♦ *adj* old.
ānxiē *adv see* **anxius**.
ānxietās, -ātis *f* anxiety, trouble (*of the mind*).
ānxifer, -ī *adj* disquieting.
ānxitūdō, -inis *f* anxiety.
ānxius *adj* (*mind*) troubled; disquieting.
Āones, -um *adj* Boeotian.
Āonia *f* part of Boeotia.
Āonius *adj* of Boeotia, of Helicon.

Aornos, -ī *m* lake Avernus.
apage *interj* away with!, go away!
apēliōtēs, -ae *m* east wind.
Apellēs, -is *m* Greek painter.
aper, -rī *m* boar.
aperiō, -īre, -uī, -tum *vt* to uncover, disclose, open; (*country*) to open up; (*fig*) to unfold, explain, reveal.
apertē *adv* clearly, openly.
apertum, -ī *nt* open space; **in ~ō esse** be well known; be easy.
apertus *ppp of* **aperiō** ♦ *adj* open, exposed; clear, manifest; (*person*) frank.
aperuī *perf of* **aperiō**.
apex, -icis *m* summit; crown, priest's cap; (*fig*) crown.
aphractus, -ī *f* a long open boat.
apiārius, -ī *and* **īī** *m* beekeeper.
Apīcius, -ī *m* Roman epicure.
apicula, -ae *f* little bee.
apis, -is *f* bee.
apīscor, -īscī, -tus *vt* to catch, get, attain.
apium, -ī *and* **īī** *nt* celery.
aplustre, -is *nt* decorated stern of a ship.
apoclētī, -ōrum *mpl* committee of the Aetolian League.
apodytērium, -ī *and* **īī** *nt* dressing room.
Apollināris, -ineus *adj:* **lūdī ~ināres** Roman games in July.
Apollō, -inis *m* Greek god of music, archery, prophecy, flocks and herds, and often identified with the sun.
apologus, -ī *m* narrative, fable.
apophorēta, -ōrum *ntpl* presents for guests to take home.
apoproēgmena, -ōrum *ntpl* (PHILOS) what is rejected.
apostolicus *adj see n.*
apostolus, -ī *m* (ECCL) apostle.
apothēca, -ae *f* storehouse, wine store.
apparātē *adv see* **apparātus**.
apparātiō, -ōnis *f* preparation.
apparātus *adj* ready, well-supplied, sumptuous.
apparātus, -ūs *m* preparation; equipment, munitions; pomp, ostentation.
appāreō, -ēre, -uī, -itum *vi* to come in sight, appear; to be seen, show oneself; to wait upon (*an official*); **~et** it is obvious.
appāritiō, -ōnis *f* service; domestic servants.
appāritor, -ōris *m* attendant.
apparō, -āre, -āvī, -ātum *vt* to prepare, provide.
appellātiō, -ōnis *f* accosting, appeal; title; pronunciation.
appellātor, -ōris *m* appellant.
appellitātus *adj* usually called.
appellō, -āre, -āvī, -ātum *vt* to speak to; to appeal to; (*for money*) to dun; (*law*) to sue; to call, name; to pronounce.

Noun declensions and verb conjugations are shown on pp xiii to xxv. The present infinitive ending of a verb shows to which conjugation it belongs: **-āre** = 1st; **-ēre** = 2nd; **-ere** = 3rd and **-īre** = 4th. Irregular verbs are shown on p xxvi

appellō, -ellere, -ulī, -ulsum _vt_ to drive, bring (to); (_NAUT_) to bring to land.
appendicula, -ae _f_ small addition.
appendix, -icis _f_ supplement.
appendō, -endere, -endī, -ensum _vt_ to weigh, pay.
appetēns, -entis _adj_ eager; greedy.
appetenter _adv see_ **appetēns.**
appetentia, -ae _f_ craving.
appetītiō, -ōnis _f_ grasping, craving.
appetītus _ppp of_ **appetō.**
appetītus, -ūs _m_ craving; natural desire (_as opposed to reason_).
appetō, -ere, -īvī, -ītum _vt_ to grasp, try to get at; to attack; to desire ♦ _vi_ to approach.
appingō, -ere _vt_ to paint (in); (_colloq_) to write more.
Appius, -ī _m_ Roman first name; **Via ~ia** main road from Rome to Capua and Brundisium.
applaudō, -dere, -sī, -sum _vt_ to strike, clap ♦ _vi_ to applaud.
applicātiō, -ōnis _f_ applying (_of the mind_); **iūs ~ōnis** the right of a patron to inherit a client's effects.
applicātus _and_ **itus** _ppp of_ **applicō.**
applicō, -āre, -āvī _and_ **uī, -ātum** _and_ **itum** _vt_ to attach, place close (to); (_NAUT_) to steer, bring to land; **sē, animum ~** devote self, attention (to).
applōrō, -āre _vt_ to deplore.
appōnō, -ōnere, -osuī, -ositum _vt_ to put (to, beside); (_meal_) to serve; to add, appoint; to reckon.
apporrēctus _adj_ stretched nearby.
apportō, -āre, -āvī, -ātum _vt_ to bring, carry (to).
apposcō, -ere _vt_ to demand also.
appositē _adv_ suitably.
appositus _ppp of_ **appōnō** ♦ _adj_ situated near; (_fig_) bordering on; suitable.
apposuī _perf of_ **appōnō.**
appōtus _adj_ drunk.
apprecor, -ārī, -ātus _vt_ to pray to.
apprehendō, -endere, -endī, -ēnsum _vt_ to take hold of; (_MIL_) to occupy; (_argument_) to bring forward.
apprīmē _adv_ especially.
apprimō, -imere, -essī, -essum _vt_ to press close.
approbātiō, -ōnis _f_ acquiescence; proof.
approbātor, -ōris _m_ approve.
approbē _adv_ very well.
approbō, -āre, -āvī, -ātum _vt_ to approve; to prove; to perform to someone's satisfaction.
apprōmittō, -ere _vt_ to promise also.
approperō, -āre, -āvī, -ātum _vt_ to hasten ♦ _vi_ to hurry up.
appropinquātiō, -ōnis _f_ approach.
appropinquō, -āre, -āvī, -ātum _vi_ to approach.
appugnō, -āre _vt_ to attack.
appulsus _ppp of_ **appellō.**
appulsus, -ūs _m_ landing; approach.

aprīcātiō, -ōnis _f_ basking.
aprīcor, -ārī _vi_ to bask.
aprīcus _adj_ sunny; basking; **in ~um prōferre** bring to light.
Aprīlis _adj_ April, of April.
aprūgnus _adj_ of the wild boar.
aps- _etc see_ **abs-.**
aptē _adv_ closely; suitably, rightly.
aptō, -āre, -āvī, -ātum _vt_ to fit, put on; (_fig_) to adapt; to prepare, equip.
aptus _adj_ attached, joined together, fitted (with); suitable.
apud _prep_ (_with acc_) **1.** (_with persons_) beside, by, with, at the house of, among, in the time of; (_speaking_) in the presence of, to; (_judgment_) in the opinion of; (_influence_) with; (_faith_) in; (_authors_) in. **2.** (_with places_) near, at, in; **est ~ mē** I have; **sum ~ mē** I am in my senses.
Āpūlia, -iae _f_ district of S.E. Italy.
Āpūlus _adj see n._
aput _prep see_ **apud.**
aqua, -ae _f_ water; **~ mihī haeret** I am in a fix; **~ intercus** dropsy; **~m adspergere** revive; **~m praebēre** entertain; **~m et terram petere** demand submission; **~ā et ignī interdīcere** outlaw.
aquae _fpl_ medicinal waters, spa.
aquaeductus, -ūs _m_ aqueduct; right of leading water.
aquāliculus _m_ belly.
aquālis, -is _m/f_ washbasin.
aquārius _adj_ of water ♦ _m_ water carrier, water inspector; a constellation.
aquāticus _adj_ aquatic; humid.
aquātilis _adj_ aquatic.
aquātiō, -ōnis _f_ fetching water; watering place.
aquātor, -ōris _m_ water carrier.
aquila, -ae _f_ eagle; standard of a legion; (_ARCH_) gable; a constellation; **~ae senectūs** a vigorous old age.
Aquileia, -ae _f_ town in N. Italy.
Aquileiēnsis _adj see n._
aquilifer, -ī _m_ chief standard-bearer.
aquilīnus _adj_ eagle's.
aquilō, -ōnis _m_ north wind; north.
aquilōnius _adj_ northerly.
aquilus _adj_ swarthy.
Aquīnās, ātis _adj see n._
Aquīnum, -ī _nt_ town in Latium.
Aquītānia, -iae _f_ district of S.W. Gaul.
Aquītānus _adj see n._
aquor, -ārī, -ātus _vi_ to fetch water.
aquōsus _adj_ humid, rainy.
aquula, -ae _f_ little stream.
āra, -ae _f_ altar; (_fig_) refuge; a constellation; **~ae et focī** hearth and home.
arabarchēs, -ae _m_ customs officer in Egypt.
Arabia, -iae _f_ Arabia.
Arabicē _adv_ with all the perfumes of Arabia.
Arabicus, Arabicius, Arabus _adj see n._
Arachnē, -s _f_ Lydian woman changed into a spider.

arānea, -ae f spider; cobweb.
arāneola f, **-olus** m small spider.
arāneōsus adj full of spiders' webs.
arāneum, -ī nt spider's web.
arāneus, -ī m spider ♦ adj of spiders.
Arar, -is m river Saône.
Arātēus adj see **Arātus.**
arātiō, -ōnis f ploughing, farming; arable land.
arātiuncula f small plot.
arātor -ōris m ploughman, farmer; (pl) cultivators of public land.
arātrum, -ī nt plough.
Arātus, -ī m Greek astronomical poet.
Araxēs, -is m river in Armenia.
arbiter, -rī m witness; arbiter, judge, umpire; controller; ~ **bibendī** president of a drinking party.
arbitra, -ae f witness.
arbitrāriō adv with some uncertainty.
arbitrārius adj uncertain.
arbitrātus, -ūs m decision; **meō ~ū** in my judgment.
arbitrium, -ī and **iī** nt decision (of an arbitrator), judgment; mastery, control.
arbitror, -ārī, -ātus vt, vi to be a witness of; to testify; to think, suppose.
arbor, (arbōs), -oris f tree; ship, mast, oar; ~ **īnfēlīx** gallows.
arboreus adj of trees, like a tree.
arbustum, -ī nt plantation, orchard; (pl) trees.
arbustus adj wooded.
arbuteus adj of the strawberry tree.
arbutum, -ī nt fruit of strawberry tree.
arbutus, -ī f strawberry tree.
arca, -ae f box; moneybox, purse; coffin; prison cell; **ex ~ā absolvere** pay cash.
Arcades, -um mpl Arcadians.
Arcadia, -iae f district of S. Greece.
Arcadicus, -ius adj see **Arcadia.**
arcānō adv privately.
arcānum, -ī nt secret, mystery.
arcānus adj secret; able to keep secrets.
arceō, -ēre, -uī, -tum vt to enclose; to keep off, prevent.
accessītū abl sg m at the summons.
accessītus ppp of **accessō** ♦ adj far-fetched.
accessō, -ere, -īvī, -ītum vt to send for, fetch; (law) to summon, accuse; (fig) to derive.
archetypus, -ī m original.
Archilochus, -ī m Greek iambic and elegiac poet.
archimagīrus, -ī m chief cook.
Archimēdēs, -is m famous mathematician of Syracuse.
archipīrāta, -ae m pirate chief.
architectōn, -onis m master builder; master in cunning.
architector, -ārī, -ātus vt to construct; (fig) to devise.
architectūra, -ae f architecture.

architectus, -ī m architect; (fig) author.
archōn, -ontis m Athenian magistrate.
Archytās, -ae m Pythagorean philosopher of Tarentum.
arcitenēns, -entis adj holding a bow ♦ m Apollo.
Arctophylax, -cis m (constellation) Bootes.
arctos, -ī f Great Bear, Little Bear; north, north wind; night.
Arctūrus, -ī m brightest star in Boōtes.
arctus etc see **artus** etc.
arcuī perf of **arceō.**
arcula, -ae f casket; (RHET) ornament.
arcuō, -āre, -āvī, -ātum vt to curve.
arcus, -ūs m bow; rainbow; arch, curve; (MATH) arc.
ardea, -ae f heron.
Ardea, -ae f town in Latium.
ardeliō, -ōnis m busybody.
ārdēns, -entis adj hot, glowing, fiery; (fig) eager, ardent.
ārdenter adv passionately.
ārdeō, -dēre, -sī, -sum vi to be on fire, burn, shine; (fig) to be fired, burn.
ārdēscō, -ere vi to catch fire, gleam; (fig) to become inflamed, wax hotter.
ārdor, -ōris m heat, brightness; (fig) ardour, passion.
arduum, -ī nt steep slope; difficulty.
arduus adj steep, high; difficult, troublesome.
ārea, -ae f vacant site, open space, playground; threshing-floor; (fig) scope (for effort).
ārefaciō, -acere, -ēcī, -actum vt to dry.
arēna etc see **harēna.**
ārēns, -entis adj arid; thirsty.
āreō, -ēre vi to be dry.
āreola, -ae f small open space.
Arēopagītēs m member of the court.
Arēopagus, -ī m Mars' Hill in Athens; a criminal court.
Arēs, -is m Greek god of war.
ārēscō, -ere vi to dry, dry up.
Arestoridēs, -ae m Argus.
aretālogus, -ī m braggart.
Arethūsa, -ae f spring near Syracuse.
Arethūsis adj Syracusan.
Argēī, -ōrum mpl sacred places in Rome; effigies thrown annually into the Tiber.
argentāria, -ae f bank, banking; silver mine.
argentārius adj of silver, of money ♦ m banker.
argentātus adj silver-plated; backed with money.
argenteus adj of silver, adorned with silver; silvery (in colour); of the silver age.
argentum, -ī nt silver, silver plate; money.
Argēus, -īvus, -olicus adj Argive; Greek.
Argīlētānus adj see n.
Argīlētum, -ī nt part of Rome (noted for

Noun declensions and verb conjugations are shown on pp xiii to xxv. The present infinitive ending of a verb shows to which conjugation it belongs: -**āre** = 1st; -**ēre** = 2nd; -**ere** = 3rd and -**īre** = 4th. Irregular verbs are shown on p xxvi

bookshops).

argilla, -ae *f* clay.

Argō, -ūs *f* Jason's ship.

Argolis, -olidis *f* district about Argos.

Argonautae, -ārum *mpl* Argonauts.

Argonauticus *adj see n.*

Argos *nt*, **-ī, -ōrum** *mpl* town in S.E. Greece.

Argōus *adj see* **Argō**.

argūmentātiō, -ōnis *f* adducing proofs.

argūmentor, -ārī, -ātus *vt, vi* to prove, adduce as proof; to conclude.

argūmentum, -ī *nt* evidence, proof; (*LIT*) subject matter, theme, plot (*of a play*); (*art*) subject, motif.

arguō, -uere, -uī, -ūtum *vt* to prove, make known; to accuse, blame, denounce.

Argus, -ī *m* monster with many eyes.

argūtē *adv* subtly.

argūtiae, -ārum *fpl* nimbleness, liveliness; wit, subtlety, slyness.

argūtor, -ārī, -ātus *vi* to chatter.

argūtulus *adj* rather subtle.

argūtus *adj* (*sight*) clear, distinct, graceful; (*sound*) clear, melodious, noisy; (*mind*) acute, witty, sly.

argyraspis, -dis *adj* silver-shielded.

Ariadna, -ae *f* daughter of Minos of Crete.

Ariadnaeus *adj see n.*

āridulus *adj* rather dry.

āridum, -ī *nt* dry land.

āridus *adj* dry, withered; meagre; (*style*) flat.

ariēs, -etis *m* ram; 1st sign of Zodiac; battering ram; beam used as a breakwater.

arietō, -āre *vt, vi* to butt, strike hard.

Ariōn, -onis *m* early Greek poet and musician.

Ariōnius *adj see n.*

arista, -ae *f* ear of corn.

Aristaeus, -ī *m* legendary founder of beekeeping.

Aristarchus, -ī *m* Alexandrian scholar; a severe critic.

Aristīdēs, -is *m* Athenian statesman noted for integrity.

Aristippēus *adj see n.*

Aristippus, -ī *m* Greek hedonist philosopher.

aristolochia, -ae *f* birthwort.

Aristophanēs, -is *m* Greek comic poet.

Aristophanēus, and īus *adj see n.*

Aristotelēs, -is *m* Aristotle (*founder of Peripatetic school of philosophy*).

Aristotelēus, and īus *adj see n.*

arithmētica, -ōrum *ntpl* arithmetic.

āritūdō, -inis *f* dryness.

Ariūsius *adj* of Ariusia in Chios.

arma, -ōrum *ntpl* armour, shield; arms, weapons (*of close combat only*); warfare, troops; (*fig*) defence, protection; implements, ship's gear.

armāmenta, -ōrum *ntpl* implements, ship's gear.

armāmentārium, -ī and iī *nt* arsenal.

armāriolum, -ī *nt* small chest.

armārium, -ī and iī *nt* chest, safe.

armātū *m abl* armour; **gravī ~** with heavy-armed troops.

armātūra, -ae *f* armour, equipment; **levis ~** light-armed troops.

armatus *adj* armed.

Armenia, -ae *f* Armenia.

Armeniaca, -acae *f* apricot tree.

Armeniacum, -acī *nt* apricot.

Armenius *adj see* **Armenia**.

armentālis *adj* of the herd.

armentārius, -ī and iī *m* cattle herd.

armentum, -ī *nt* cattle (*for ploughing*), herd (*cattle etc*).

armifer, -ī *adj* armed.

armiger, -ī *m* armour-bearer ♦ *adj* armed; productive of warriors.

armilla, -ae *f* bracelet.

armillātus *adj* wearing a bracelet.

armipotēns, -entis *adj* strong in battle.

armisonus *adj* resounding with arms.

armō, -āre, -āvī, -ātum *vt* to arm, equip; to rouse to arms (*against*).

armus, -ī *m* shoulder (*esp of animals*).

Arniēnsis *adj see* **Arnus**.

Arnus, -ī *m* river Arno.

arō, -āre, -āvī, -ātum *vt* to plough, cultivate; to live by farming; (*fig: sea, brow*) to furrow.

Arpīnās, -ātis *adj see n.*

Arpīnum, -ī *nt* town in Latium (*birthplace of Cicero*).

arquātus *adj* jaundiced.

arr- *etc see* **adr-**.

arrabō, -ōnis *m* earnest money.

ars, artis *f* skill (*in any craft*); the art (*of any profession*); science, theory; handbook; work of art; moral quality, virtue; artifice, fraud.

ārsī *perf of* **ārdeō**.

ārsus *ppp of* **ārdeō**.

artē *adv* closely, soundly, briefly.

artēria, -ae *f* windpipe; artery.

artēria, -ōrum *ntpl* trachea.

arthrīticus *adj* gouty.

articulātim *adv* joint by joint; (*speech*) distinctly.

articulō, -āre, -āvī, -ātum *vt* to articulate.

articulōsus *adj* minutely subdivided.

articulus, -ī *m* joint, knuckle; limb; (*words*) clause; (*time*) point, turning point; **in ipsō ~ō temporis** in the nick of time.

artifex, -icis *m* artist, craftsman, master; (*fig*) maker, author ♦ *adj* ingenious, artistic, artificial.

artificiōsē *adv* skilfully.

artificiōsus *adj* ingenious, artistic, artificial.

artificium, -ī and iī *nt* skill, workmanship; art, craft; theory, rule of an art; ingenuity, cunning.

artō, -āre *vt* to compress, curtail.

artolaganus, -ī *m* kind of cake.

artopta, -ae *m* baker; baking tin.

artus *adj* close, narrow, tight; (*sleep*) deep; (*fig*) strict, straitened.

artus, -ūs *m* joint; (*pl*) limbs, body; (*fig*) strength.

ārula, -ae *f* small altar.

arundō *etc see* **harundō** *etc.*

arvīna, -ae *f* grease.

arvum, -ī *nt* field; land, country, plain.

arvus *adj* ploughed.

arx, arcis *f* fortress, castle; height, summit; (*fig*) bulwark, stronghold; **arcem facere ē cloācā** make a mountain out of a molehill.

ās, assis *m* (*weight*) pound; (*coin*) bronze unit, of low value; (*inheritance*) the whole (*subdivided into 12 parts*); **ad assem** to the last farthing; **hērēs ex asse** sole heir.

Ascānius, -ī *m* son of Aeneas.

ascendō, -endere, -endī, -ēnsum *vt, vi* to go up, climb, embark; (*fig*) to rise.

ascēnsiō, -ōnis *f* ascent; (*fig*) sublimity.

ascēnsus, -ūs *m* ascent, rising; way up.

ascia, -ae *f* axe; mason's trowel.

asciō, -īre *vt* to admit.

ascīscō, -iscere, -īvī, -ītum *vt* to receive with approval; to admit (*to some kind of association*); to appropriate, adopt (*esp customs*); to arrogate to oneself.

ascītus *adj* acquired, alien.

Ascra, -ae *f* birthplace of Hesiod in Boeotia.

Ascraeus *adj* of Ascra; of Hesiod; of Helicon.

ascrībō, -bere, -psī, -ptum *vt* to add (*in writing*); to attribute, ascribe; to apply (*an illustration*); to enrol, include.

ascrīptīcius *adj* enrolled.

ascrīptiō, -ōnis *f* addition (*in writing*).

ascrīptīvus *adj* (MIL) supernumerary.

ascrīptor, -ōris *m* supporter.

ascrīptus *ppp of* **ascrībō**.

asella, -ae *f* young ass.

asellus, -ī *m* young ass.

Asia, -ae *f* Roman province; Asia Minor; Asia.

asīlus, -ī *m* gad fly.

asinus, -ī *m* ass; fool.

Asis, -dis *f* Asia.

Asius (Asiānus, Asiāticus) *adj see n.*

Asōpus, -ī *m* river in Boeotia.

asōtus, -ī *m* libertine.

asparagus, -ī *m* asparagus.

aspargō *etc see* **aspergō**.

aspectābilis *adj* visible.

aspectō, -āre *vt* to look at, gaze at; to pay heed to; (*places*) to face.

aspectus *ppp of* **aspiciō**.

aspectus, -ūs *m* look, sight; glance, sense of sight; aspect, appearance.

aspellō, -ere *vt* to drive away.

asper, -ī *adj* rough; (*taste*) bitter; (*sound*) harsh; (*weather*) severe; (*style*) rugged; (*person*) violent, exasperated, unkind, austere; (*animal*) savage; (*CIRCS*) difficult.

asperē *adv see adj.*

aspergō, -gere, -sī, -sum *vt* to scatter, sprinkle; to bespatter, besprinkle; **aquam ~** revive.

aspergō, -inis *f* sprinkling; spray.

asperitās, -ātis *f* roughness, unevenness, harshness, severity; (*fig*) ruggedness, fierceness; trouble, difficulty.

aspernātiō, -ōnis *f* disdain.

aspernor, -ārī, -ātus *vt* to reject, disdain.

asperō, -āre, -āvī, -ātum *vt* to roughen, sharpen; to exasperate.

aspersiō, -ōnis *f* sprinkling.

aspersus *ppp of* **aspergō**.

aspiciō, -icere, -exī, -ectum *vt* to catch sight of, look at; (*places*) to face; (*fig*) to examine, consider.

aspīrātiō, -ōnis *f* breathing (on); evaporation; pronouncing with an aspirate.

aspīrō, -āre, -āvī, -ātum *vi* to breathe, blow; to favour; to aspire, attain (to) ♦ *vt* to blow, instil.

aspis, -dis *f* asp.

asportātiō, -ōnis *f* removal.

asportō, -āre *vt* to carry off.

asprēta, -ōrum *ntpl* rough country.

ass- *etc see* **ads-**.

Assaracus, -ī *m* Trojan ancestor of Aeneas.

asser, -is *m* pole, stake.

assula, -ae *f* splinter.

assulātim *adv* in splinters.

āssum, -ī *nt* roast; (*pl*) sweating-bath.

āssus *adj* roasted.

Assyria, -ae *f* country in W. Asia.

Assyrius *adj* Assyrian; oriental.

ast *conj* (*laws*) and then; (*vows*) then; (*strong contrast*) and yet.

ast- *etc see* **adst-**.

Astraea, -ae *f* goddess of Justice.

Astraeus, -ī *m* father of winds; **~ī frātrēs** the winds.

astrologia, -ae *f* astronomy.

astrologus, -ī *m* astronomer; astrologer.

astrum, -ī *nt* star, heavenly body, constellation; a great height; heaven, immortality, glory.

astu *nt* (*indecl*) city (*esp Athens*).

astus, -ūs *m* cleverness, cunning.

astūtē *adv* cleverly.

astūtia, -ae *f* slyness, cunning.

astūtus *adj* artful, sly.

Astyanax, -ctis *m* son of Hector and Andromache.

asȳlum, -ī *nt* sanctuary.

asymbolus *adj* with no contribution.

at *conj* (*adversative*) but, on the other hand; (*objecting*) but it may be said; (*limiting*) at least, but at least; (*continuing*) then, thereupon; (*transitional*) now; (*with passionate appeals*) but oh!, look now!; **~ enim** yes, but; **~ tamen** nevertheless.

Atābulus, -ī *m* sirocco.

atat *interj* (*expressing fright, pain, surprise*) oh!

atavus, -ī *m* great-great-great-grandfather; ancestor.

Noun declensions and verb conjugations are shown on pp xiii to xxv. The present infinitive ending of a verb shows to which conjugation it belongs: **-āre** = 1st; **-ēre** = 2nd; **-ere** = 3rd and **-īre** = 4th. Irregular verbs are shown on p xxvi

Atella, -ae *f Oscan town in Campania.*
Atellānicus, Atellānius *adj see* n.
Atellānus *adj:* **fābula ~āna** *kind of comic show popular in Rome.*
āter, -rī *adj* black, dark; gloomy; dismal; malicious; **diēs ~rī** unlucky days.
Athamantēus *adj see* **Athamās.**
Athamantiadēs *m* Palaemon.
Athamantis *f* Helle.
Athamās, -antis *m* king of Thessaly (*who went mad*).
Athēnae, -ārum *fpl* Athens.
Athēnaeus, -iēnsis *adj see* n.
atheos, -ī *m* atheist.
athlēta, -ae *m* wrestler, athlete.
athlēticē *adv* athletically.
Athos (*dat* -ō, *acc* -ō, -on, -ōnem) *m* mount Athos in Macedonia.
Atlanticus *adj:* **mare ~anticum** Atlantic Ocean.
Atlantiadēs *m* Mercury.
Atlantis *f* lost Atlantic island; a Pleiad.
Atlās, -antis *m* giant supporting the sky; Atlas mountains.
atomus, -ī *m* atom.
atque (*before consonants* **ac**) *conj* (*connecting words*) and, and in fact; (*connecting clauses*) and moreover, and then, and so, and yet; (*in comparison*) as, than, to, from; **~ adeō** and that too; or rather; **~ nōn** and not rather; **~ sī** as if; **alius ~** different from; **contrā ~** opposite to; **īdem ~** same as; **plūs ~** more than.
atquī *conj* (*adversative*) and yet, nevertheless, yes but; (*confirming*) by all means; (*minor premise*) now; **~ sī** if now.
ātrāmentum, -ī *nt* ink; blacking.
ātrātus *adj* in mourning.
Atreus, -eī *m* son of Pelops (*king of Argos*).
Atrīdēs *m* Agamemnon; Menelaus.
ātriēnsis, -is *m* steward, major-domo.
ātriolum, -ī *nt* anteroom.
ātrium, -ī *and* **iī** *nt* hall, open central room in Roman house; forecourt of a temple; hall (*in other buildings*).
atrōcitās, -ātis *f* hideousness; (*mind*) brutality; (*PHILOS*) severity.
atrōciter *adv* savagely.
Atropos, -ī *f* one of the Fates.
atrōx, -ōcis *adj* hideous, dreadful; fierce, brutal, unyielding.
attāctus *ppp of* **attingō.**
attāctus, -ūs *m* contact.
attagēn, -is *m* heathcock.
Attalica *ntpl* garments of woven gold.
Attalicus *adj* of Attalus; of Pergamum; ornamented with gold cloth.
Attalus, -ī *m* king of Pergamum (*who bequeathed his kingdom to Rome*).
attamen *conj* nevertheless.
attat *etc see* **atat.**
attegia, -ae *f* hut.
attemperātē *adv* opportunely.
attempto *etc see* **attentō.**

attendō, -dere, -dī, -tum *vt* to direct (*the attention*); to attend to, notice.
attenē *adv* carefully.
attentiō, -ōnis *f* attentiveness.
attentō, -āre, -āvī, -ātum *vt* to test, try; (*loyalty*) to tamper with; to attack.
attentus *ppp of* **attendō ♦** *adj* attentive, intent; businesslike, careful (*esp about money*).
attentus *ppp of* **attineō.**
attenuātē *adv* simply.
attenuātus *adj* weak; (*style*) brief; refined; plain.
attenuō, -āre, -āvī, -ātum *vt* to weaken, reduce; to diminish; to humble.
atterō, -erere, -rīvī, -rītum *vt* to rub; to wear away; (*fig*) to impair, exhaust.
attestor, -ārī, -ātus *vt* to confirm.
attexō, -ere, -uī, -tum *vt* to weave on; (*fig*) to add on.
Atthis, -dis *f* Attica.
Attiānus *adj see* **Attius.**
Attica, -ae *f* district of Greece about Athens.
Atticē *adv* in the Athenian manner.
Atticissō *vi* to speak in the Athenian manner.
Atticus *adj* Attic, Athenian; (*RHET*) of a plain and direct style.
attigī *perf of* **attingō.**
attigō *see* **attingō.**
attineō, -inēre, -inuī, -entum *vt* to hold fast, detain; to guard; to reach for **♦** *vi* to concern, pertain, be of importance, avail.
attingō, -ingere, -igī, -āctum *vt* to touch; to strike, assault; to arrive at; to border on; to affect; to mention; to undertake; to concern, resemble.
Attis, -dis *m* Phrygian priest of Cybele.
Attius, -ī *m* Latin tragic poet.
attollō, -ere *vt* to lift up, erect; (*fig*) to exalt, extol.
attondeō, -ondēre, -ondī, -ōnsum *vt* to shear, prune, crop; (*fig*) to diminish; (*comedy*) to fleece.
attonitus *adj* thunderstruck, terrified, astonished; inspired.
attonō, -āre, -uī, -itum *vt* to stupefy.
attōnsus *ppp of* **attondeō.**
attorqueō, -ēre *vt* to hurl upwards.
attractus *ppp of* **attrahō.**
attraho, -here, -xī, -ctum *vt* to drag by force, attract; (*fig*) to draw, incite.
attrectō, -āre *vt* to touch, handle; to appropriate.
attrepidō, -āre *vi* to hobble along.
attribuō, -uere, -uī, -ūtum *vt* to assign, bestow; to add; to impute, attribute; to lay as a tax.
attribūtiō, -ōnis *f* (*money*) assignment; (*GRAM*) predicate.
attribūtum, -ī *nt* (*GRAM*) predicate.
attribūtus *ppp of* **attribuō ♦** *adj* subject.
attrītus *ppp of* **atterō ♦** *adj* worn; bruised; (*fig*) impudent.
attulī *perf of* **adferō.**

au *interj (expressing pain, surprise)* oh!
auceps, -upis *m* fowler; *(fig)* eavesdropper; a
pedantic critic.
auctārium, -ī *and* **iī** *nt* extra.
auctificus *adj* increasing.
auctiō, -ōnis *f* increase; auction sale.
auctiōnārius *adj* auction; **tabulae ~ae**
catalogues.
auctiōnor, -ārī, -ātus *vi* to hold an auction.
auctitō, -āre *vt* to greatly increase.
auctō, -āre *vt* to increase.
auctor, -ōris *m/f* **1.** *(originator: of families)*
progenitor; (: *of buildings*) founder; (: *of
deeds*) doer. **2.** *(composer: of writings*) author,
historian; (: *of knowledge*) investigator,
teacher; (: *of news*) informant. **3.** *(instigator:
of action*) adviser; (: *of measures*) promoter;
(: *of laws*) proposer, supporter; ratifier. **4.**
(person of influence: in public life) leader; (: *of
conduct*) model; (: *of guarantees*) witness,
bail; (: *of property*) seller; (: *of women and
minors*) guardian; (: *of others' welfare*)
champion; **mē ~ōre** at my suggestion.
auctōrāmentum, -ī *nt* contract; wages.
auctōrātus *adj* bound *(by a pledge)*; hired out
(for wages).
auctōritās, -ātis *f* **1.** source; lead,
responsibility. **2.** judgment; opinion; advice,
support; bidding, guidance; *(of senate)*
decree; *(of people)* will. **3.** power; *(person)*
influence, authority, prestige; *(things)*
importance, worth; *(conduct)* example;
(knowledge) warrant, document, authority;
(property) right of possession.
auctumn- *etc see* **autumn-**.
auctus *ppp of* **augeō** ♦ *adj* enlarged, great.
auctus, -ūs *m* growth, increase.
aucupium, -ī *and* **iī** *nt* fowling; birds caught;
(fig) hunting *(after)*, quibbling.
aucupō, -āre *vt* to watch for.
aucupor, -ārī, -ātus *vi* to go fowling ♦ *vt* to
chase; *(fig)* to try to catch.
audācia, -ae *f* daring, courage; audacity,
impudence; *(pl)* deeds of daring.
audācter, audāciter *adv see* **audāx**.
audāx, -ācis *adj* bold, daring; rash, audacious;
proud.
audēns, -entis *adj* bold, brave.
audenter *adv see* **audēns**.
audentia, -ae *f* boldness, courage.
audeō, -dēre, -sus *vt, vi* to dare, venture; to
be brave.
audiēns, -entis *m* hearer ♦ *adj* obedient.
audientia, -ae *f* hearing; **~m facere** gain a
hearing.
audiō, -īre, -īvī *and* **iī, -ītum** *vt* to hear; to
learn, be told; to be called; to listen, attend
to, study under (a teacher); to examine a
case; to agree with; to obey, heed; **bene/
male ~** have a good/bad reputation.

audītiō, -ōnis *f* listening; hearsay, news.
audītor, -ōris *m* hearer; pupil.
audītōrium, -ī *and* **iī** *nt* lecture room, law
court; audience.
audītus, -ūs *m* (sense of) hearing; a hearing;
rumour.
auferō, auferre, abstulī, ablātum *vt* to take
away, carry away; to mislead, lead into a
digression; to take by force, steal; to win,
obtain *(as the result of effort)*; **aufer** away
with!
Aufidus, -ō *m* river in Apulia.
aufugiō, -ugere, -ūgī *vi* to run away ♦ *vt* to
flee from.
Augeās, -ae *m* king of Elis *(whose stables
Hercules cleaned)*.
augeō, -gēre, -xī, -ctum *vt* to increase; to
enrich, bless (with); to praise, worship ♦ *vi*
to increase.
augēscō, -ere *vi* to begin to grow, increase.
augmen, -inis *nt* growth.
augur, -is *m/f* augur; prophet, interpreter.
augurāle, -is *nt* part of camp where auspices
were taken.
augurālis *adj* augur's.
augurātiō, -ōnis *f* soothsaying.
augurātō *adv* after taking auspices.
augurātus, -ūs *m* office of augur.
augurium, -ī *and* **iī** *nt* augury; an omen;
prophecy, interpretation; presentiment.
augurius *adj* of augurs.
augurō, -āre *vt, vi* to take auguries; to
consecrate by auguries; to forebode.
auguror, -ārī, -ātus *vt, vi* to take auguries; to
foretell by omens; to predict, conjecture.
Augusta, -ae *f* title of the emperor's wife,
mother, daughter *or* sister.
Augustālis *adj* of Augustus; **lūdī ~ēs** games in
October; **praefectus ~is** governor of Egypt;
sodālēs ~ēs priests of deified Augustus.
augustē *adv see* **augustus**.
augustus *adj* venerable, august, majestic.
Augustus, -ī *m* title given to C Octavius, first
Roman emperor, and so to his successors ♦ *adj*
imperial; *(month)* August, of August.
aula, -ae *f* courtyard of a Greek house; hall of a
Roman house; palace, royal court; courtiers;
royal power.
aula *etc see* **olla**.
aulaeum, -ī *nt* embroidered hangings,
canopy, covering; *(THEAT)* curtain.
aulicī, -ōrum *mpl* courtiers.
aulicus *adj* of the court.
Aulis, -idis *and* **is** *f* port in Boeotia from which the
Greeks sailed for Troy.
auloedus, -ī *m* singer accompanied by flute.
aura, -ae *f* breath of air, breeze, wind; air,
upper world; vapour, odour, sound, gleam;
(fig) winds *(of public favour)*, breeze *(of
prosperity)*, air *(of freedom)*, daylight *(of*

publicity).

aurāria, -ae *f* gold mine.

aurārius *adj* of gold.

aurātus *adj* gilt, ornamented with gold; gold.

Aurēlius, -ī *m* Roman name; **lēx ~ia** *law on the composition of juries*; **via ~ia** *main road running NW from Rome.*

aureolus *adj* gold; beautiful, splendid.

aureus *adj* gold, golden; gilded; (*fig*) beautiful splendid ♦ *m* gold coin.

aurichalcum, -ī *nt* a precious metal.

auricomus *adj* golden-leaved.

auricula, -ae *f* the external ear; ear.

aurifer, -ī *adj* gold-producing.

aurifex, -icis *m* goldsmith.

aurīga, -ae *m* charioteer, driver; groom; helmsman; a constellation.

aurigena, -ae *adj* gold-begotten.

auriger, -ī *adj* gilded.

aurigō, -āre *vi* to compete in the chariot race.

auris, -is *f* ear; (*RHET*) judgment; (*AGR*) earthboard (*of a plough*); **ad ~em admonēre** whisper; **in utramvis ~em dormīre** sleep soundly.

aurītulus, -ī *m* "Long-Ears".

aurītus *adj* long-eared; attentive.

aurōra, -ae *f* dawn, morning; *goddess of dawn*; the East.

aurum, -i *nt* gold; gold plate, jewellery, bit, fleece *etc*; money; lustre; the Golden Age.

auscultātiō, -ōnis *f* obedience.

auscultātor, -ōris *m* listener.

auscultō, -āre, -āvī, -ātum *vt* to listen to; to overhear ♦ *vi* (*of servants*) to wait at the door; to obey.

ausim *subj of* **audeō.**

Ausones, -um *mpl indigenous people of central Italy.*

Ausonia *f Italy.*

Ausonidae *mpl Italians.*

Ausonius, -is *adj Italian.*

auspex, -icis *m* augur, soothsayer; patron, commander; witness of a marriage contract.

auspicātō *adv* after taking auspices; at a lucky moment.

auspicātus *adj* consecrated; auspicious, lucky.

auspicium, -ī *and* **iī** *nt* augury, auspices; right of taking auspices; power, command; omen; **~ facere** give a sign.

auspicō, -āre *vi* to take the auspices.

auspicor, -ārī, -ātus *vi* to take the auspices; to make a beginning ♦ *vt* to begin, enter upon.

auster, -rī *m* south wind; south.

austērē *adv see* **austērus.**

austēritās, -ātis *f* severity.

austērus *adj* severe, serious; gloomy, irksome.

austrālis *adj* southern.

austrīnus *adj* from the south.

ausum, -ī *nt* enterprise.

ausus *ppa of* **audeō.**

aut *conj* or; either . . . or; or else *or* at least, or rather.

autem *conj* (*adversative*) but, on the other hand; (*in transitions, parentheses*) moreover, now, and; (*in dialogue*) indeed.

authepsa, -ae *f* stove.

autographus *adj* written with his own hand.

Autolycus, -ī *m* a robber.

automaton, -ī *nt* automaton.

automatus *adj* spontaneous.

Automedōn, -ontis *m* a charioteer.

autumnālis *adj* autumn, autumnal.

autumnus, -ī *m* autumn ♦ *adj* autumnal.

autumō, -āre *vt* to assert.

auxī *perf of* **augeō.**

auxilia, -iōrum *ntpl* auxiliary troops; military force.

auxiliāris *adj* helping, auxiliary; of the auxiliaries ♦ *mpl* auxiliary troops.

auxiliārius *adj* helping; auxiliary.

auxiliātor, -ōris *m* helper.

auxiliātus, -ūs *m* aid.

auxilior, -ārī, -ātus *vi* to aid, support.

auxilium, -ī *and* **iī** *nt* help, assistance.

avārē, avāiter *adv see* **avārus.**

avāritia, -ae *f* greed, selfishness.

avāritiēs, -ēī *f* avarice.

avārus *adj* greedy, covetous; eager.

avē, avēte, avētō *impv* hail!, farewell!

āvehō, -here, -xī, -ctum *vt* to carry away; (*pass*) to ride away.

āvellō, -ellere, -ellī *and* **ulsī (-olsī), -ulsum (-olsum)** *vt* to pull away, tear off; to take away (by force), remove.

avēna, -ae *f* oats; (*music*) reed, shepherd's pipe.

Aventīnum, -ī *nt* Aventine hill.

Aventīnus, -ī *m* Aventine hill in Rome ♦ *adj* of Aventine.

avēns, -entis *adj* eager.

aveō, -ēre *vt* to desire, long for.

Avernālis *adj* of lake Avernus.

Avernus, -ī *m* lake near Cumae (*said to be an entrance to the lower world*); the lower world ♦ *adj* birdless; of Avernus; infernal.

āverruncō, -āre *vt* to avert.

āversābilis *adj* abominable.

āversor, -ārī, -ātus *vi* to turn away ♦ *vt* to repulse, decline.

āversor, -ōris *m* embezzler.

āversūm, -ī *nt* back.

āversus *ppp of* **āvertō** ♦ *adj* in the rear, behind, backwards; hostile, averse.

āvertō, -tere, -tī, -sum *vt* to turn aside, avert; to divert; to embezzle; to estrange ♦ *vi* to withdraw.

avia, -ae *f* grandmother.

avia, -ōrum *ntpl* wilderness.

aviārium, -ī *nt* aviary, haunt of birds.

aviārius *adj* of birds.

avidē *adv see* **avidus.**

aviditās, -ātis *f* eagerness, longing; avarice.

avidus *adj* eager, covetous; avaricious; greedy; hungry; vast.

avis, -is *f* bird; omen; ~ **alba** a rarity.

avītus *adj* of a grandfather; ancestral.

āvius *adj* out of the way, lonely, untrodden; wandering, astray.

āvocāmentum, -ī *nt* relaxation.

āvocātiō, -ōnis *f* diversion.

āvocō, -āre *vt* to call off; to divert, distract; to amuse.

āvolō, -āre *vi* to fly away, hurry away; to depart, vanish.

āvolsus, avulsus *ppp of* **avellō**.

avunculus, -ī *m* uncle (*on mother's side*); ~ **māgnus** great-uncle.

avus, -ī *m* grandfather; ancestor.

Axenus, -ī *m* Black Sea.

axicia, axitia, -ae *f* scissors.

āxilla -ae *f* armpit.

axis, -is *m* axle, chariot; axis, pole, sky, clime; plank.

azȳmus *adj* unleavened.

B, b

babae *interj* (*expressing wonder or joy*) oho!

Babylōn, -ōnis *f* ancient city on the Euphrates.

Babylōnia *f* the country under Babylon.

Babylōnicus, (-)ōniēnsis *adj see n.*

Babylōnius *adj* Babylonian; Chaldaean, versed in astrology.

bāca, -ae *f* berry; olive; fruit; pearl.

bācātus *adj* of pearls.

bacca *etc see* **bāca**.

baccar, -is *nt* cyclamen.

Baccha, -ae *f* Bacchante.

Bacchānal, -ālis *nt* place consecrated to Bacchus; (*pl*) festival of Bacchus.

bacchātiō, -ōnis *f* revel.

Baccheus, -icus, -ius *adj see n.*

Bacchiadae, -ārum *mpl* kings of Corinth (*founders of Syracuse*).

bacchor, -ārī, -ātus *vi* to celebrate the festival of Bacchus; to revel, rave; to rage.

Bacchus, -ī *m* god of wine, vegetation, poetry, and religious ecstasy; vine, wine.

bācifer, -ī *adj* olive-bearing.

bacillum, -ī *nt* stick, lictor's staff.

Bactra, -ōrum *ntpl* capital of Bactria in central Asia (*now* Balkh).

Bactriāna *f* Bactria.

Bactriānus *and* **ius** *adj* Bactrian.

baculum, -ī *nt*, **-us, -ī** *m* stick, staff.

Baetica *f* Roman province (*now* Andalusia).

Baeticus *adj see* **Baetis**.

Baetis, -is *m* river in Spain (*now* Guadalquivir).

Bagrada, -ae *m* river in Africa (*now* Mejerdah).

Bāiae, -ārum *fpl* Roman spa on Bay of Naples.

Bāiānus *adj see n.*

bāiulō, -āre *vt* to carry (*something heavy*).

bāiulus, -ī *m* porter.

bālaena, -ae *f* whale.

balanus, -ī *f* balsam (*from an Arabian nut*); a shellfish.

balatrō, -ōnis *m* jester.

bālātus, -ūs *m* bleating.

balbus *adj* stammering.

balbūtiō, -īre *vt, vi* to stammer, speak indistinctly; (*fig*) to speak obscurely.

Baliārēs, -ium *fpl* Balearic islands.

Baliāris, Baliāricus *adj see n.*

balineum *etc see* **balneum** *etc.*

ballista, -ae *f* (*MIL*) catapult for shooting stones and other missiles; (*fig*) weapon.

ballistārium, -ī *and* **iī** *nt* catapult.

balneae, -ārum *fpl* bath, baths.

balneāria, -ōrum *ntpl* bathroom.

balneārius *adj* of the baths.

balneātor, -ōris *m* bath superintendent.

balneolum, -ī *nt* small bath.

balneum, -ī *nt* bath.

bālō, -āre *vi* to bleat.

balsamum, -ī *nt* balsam, balsam tree.

baltea, -ōrum *ntpl* belt (*esp swordbelt; woman's girdle; strapping*).

balteus, -ī *m* belt (*esp swordbelt; woman's girdle; strapping*).

Bandusia, -ae *f* spring near Horace's birthplace.

baptisma, -tis *nt* baptism.

baptizō, -āre *vt* (*ECCL*) to baptize.

barathrum, -ī *nt* abyss; the lower world; (*fig*) a greedy person.

barba, -ae *f* beard.

barbarē *adv* in a foreign language, in Latin; in an uncivilized way; roughly, cruelly.

barbaria, -ae, -ēs *acc,* and **-em** *f* a foreign country (*outside Greece or Italy*); (*words*) barbarism; (*manners*) rudeness, stupidity.

barbaricus *adj* foreign, outlandish; Italian.

barbarus *adj* foreign, barbarous; (*to a Greek*) Italian; rude, uncivilized; savage, barbarous ♦ *m* foreigner, barbarian.

barbātulus *adj* with a little beard.

barbātus *adj* bearded, adult; ancient (Romans); of philosophers.

barbiger, -ī *adj* bearded.

barbitos (*acc* **-on**) *m* lyre, lute.

barbula, -ae *f* little beard.

Barcās, -ae *m* ancestor of Hannibal.

Noun declensions and verb conjugations are shown on pp xiii to xxv. The present infinitive ending of a verb shows to which conjugation it belongs: **-āre** = 1st; **-ēre** = 2nd; **-ere** = 3rd and **-īre** = 4th. Irregular verbs are shown on p xxvi

Barcīnus *adj see n.*
bardus *adj* dull, stupid.
bardus, -ī *m* Gallic minstrel.
bārō, -ōnis *m* dunce.
barrus, -ī *m* elephant.
bascauda, -ae *f* basket (*for the table*).
bāsiātiō, -ōnis *f* kiss.
basilica, -ae *f* public building used as exchange and law court.
basilicē *adv* royally, in magnificent style.
basilicum, -ī *nt* regal robe.
basilicus *adj* royal, magnificent ♦ *m* highest throw at dice.
bāsiō, -āre *vt* to kiss.
basis, -is *f* pedestal, base.
bāsium, -ī and iī *nt* kiss.
Bassareus, -eī *m* Bacchus.
Batāvī, -ōrum *mpl* people of Batavia (*now* Holland).
batillum, -ī *nt* firepan.
Battiadēs, -ae *m* Callimachus.
bātuō, -ere, -ī *vt* to beat.
baubor, -ārī *vi* (*of dogs*) to howl.
Baucis, -idis *f* wife of Philemon.
beātē *adv see* **beātus**.
beātitās, -ātis *f* happiness.
beātitūdō, -inis *f* happiness.
beātus, -ī *m* the blessed man.
beātus *adj* happy; prosperous, well-off; rich, abundant.
Bēdriacēnsis *adj see n.*
Bēdriācum, -ī *nt* village in N. Italy.
Belgae, -ārum *mpl* people of N. Gaul (*now* Belgium).
Bēlīdēs, -īdae *m* Danaus, Aegyptus, Lynceus.
Bēlides, -um *fpl* Danaids.
bellāria, -ōrum *ntpl* dessert, confectionery.
bellātor, -ōris *m* warrior, fighter ♦ *adj* warlike.
bellātōrius *adj* aggressive.
bellātrīx, -īcis *f* warrioress ♦ *adj* warlike.
bellē *adv* well, nicely; ~ **habēre** be well (in health).
Bellerophōn, -ontis *m* slayer of Chimaera, rider of Pegasus.
Bellerophontēus *adj see n.*
bellicōsus *adj* warlike.
bellicus *adj* of war, military; ~um **canere** give the signal for marching or attack.
belliger, -ī *adj* martial.
belligerō, -āre, -āvī, -ātum *vi* to wage war.
bellipotēns, -entis *adj* strong in war.
bellō, -āre, -āvī, -ātum *vi* to fight, wage war.
Bellōna, -ae *f* goddess of war.
bellor, -ārī *vi* to fight.
bellulus *adj* pretty.
bellum, -ī *nt* war, warfare; battle; ~ **gerere** wage war; -ī **in** war.
bellus *adj* pretty, handsome; pleasant, nice.
bēlua, -ae *f* beast, monster (*esp large and fierce*); any animal; (*fig*) brute; ~ **Gaetula** India elephant.
bēluātus *adj* embroidered with animals.

bēluōsus *adj* full of monsters.
Bēlus, -ī *m* Baal; an oriental king.
Bēnācus, -ī *m* lake in N. Italy (*now* Garda).
bene *adv* (*compar* **melius**, *superl* **optimē**) well; correctly; profitably; very ♦ *interj* bravo!, good!; ~ **dīcere** speak well; speak well of, praise; ~ **emere** buy cheap; ~ **est tibi** you are well off; ~ **facere** do well; do good to; ~ **facis** thank you; **rem** ~ **gerere** be successful; ~ **sē habēre** have a good time; ~ **habet** all is well, it's all right; ~ **merērī dē** do a service to; ~ **partum** honestly acquired; ~ **tē!** your health!; ~ **vēndere** sell at a high price; ~ **vīvere** live a happy life.
benedīco, -īcere, -īxī, -ictum *vt* to speak well of, praise; (*ECCL*) to bless.
benedictiō, -ōnis *f* (*ECCL*) blessing.
beneficentia, -ae *f* kindness.
beneficiāriī, -ōrum *mpl* privileged soldiers.
beneficium, -ī and iī *nt* benefit, favour; (*POL, MIL*) promotion; ~ō **tuō** thanks to you.
beneficus *adj* generous, obliging.
Beneventānus *adj see n.*
Beneventum, -ī *nt* town in S. Italy (*now* Benevento).
benevolē *adv see* **benevolus**.
benevolēns, -entis *adj* kind-hearted.
benevolentia, -ae *f* goodwill, friendliness.
benevolus *adj* kindly, friendly; (*of servants*) devoted.
benīgnē *adv* willingly, courteously; generously; (*colloq*) no thank you; ~ **facere** do a favour.
benīgnitās, -ātis *f* kindness; liberality, bounty.
benīgnus *adj* kind, friendly; favourable; liberal, lavish; fruitful, bounteous.
beō, -āre, -āvī, -ātum *vt* to gladden, bless, enrich.
Berecyntia *f* Cybele.
Berecyntius *adj* of Berecyntus; of Cybele.
Berecyntus, -ī *m* mountain in Phrygia sacred to Cybele.
Berenīcē, -ēs *f* a queen of Egypt; **coma** ~**ēs** a constellation.
bēryllus, -ī *m* beryl.
bēs, bessis *m* two-thirds of the as; two-thirds.
bēstia, -ae *f* beast; wild animal for the arena.
bēstiārius *adj* of beasts ♦ *m* beast fighter in the arena.
bēstiola, -ae *f* small animal.
bēta, -ae *f* beet.
bēta *nt indecl* Greek letter beta.
bibī *perf of* **bibō**.
bibliopōla, -ae *m* bookseller.
bibliothēca, -ae, -ē, -ēs *f* library.
bibō, -ere, -ī *vt* to drink; to live on the banks of (*a river*); to drink in, absorb; (*fig*) to listen attentively, be imbued; ~ **aquas** be drowned; **Graecō mōre** ~ drink to one's health.
bibulus *adj* fond of drink, thirsty; (*things*) thirsty.
Bibulus, -ī *m* consul with Caesar in 59 BC.

biceps, -ipitis *adj* two-headed.
biclīnium, -ī *and* **iī** *nt* dining couch for two.
bicolor, -ōris *adj* two-coloured.
bicorniger, -ī *adj* two-horned.
bicornis *adj* two-horned, two-pronged; (*rivers*) two-mouthed.
bicorpor, -is *adj* two-bodied.
bidēns, -entis *adj* with two teeth *or* prongs ♦ *m* hoe ♦ *f* sheep (*or other sacrificial animal*).
bidental, -ālis *nt* a place struck by lightning.
biduum, -ī *nt* two days.
biennium -ī *and* **iī** *nt* two years.
bifāriam *adv* in two parts, twice.
bifer, -ī *adj* flowering twice a year.
bifidus *adj* split in two.
biforis *adj* double-doored; double.
bifōrmātus, bifōrmis *adj* with two forms.
bifrōns, -ontis *adj* two-headed.
bifurcus *adj* two-pronged, forked.
bīgae, -ārum *fpl* chariot and pair.
bigātus *adj* stamped with a chariot and pair.
biiugī, -ōrum *mpl* two horses yoked abreast; chariot with two horses.
biiugis, biiugus *adj* yoked.
bilībra, -ae *f* two pounds.
bilībris *adj* holding two pounds.
bilinguis *adj* double-tongued; bilingual; deceitful.
bīlis, -is *f* bile, gall; (*fig*) anger, displeasure; ~ ātra, nigra melancholy; madness.
bilīx, -īcis *adj* double-stranded.
bilūstris *adj* ten years.
bimaris *adj* between two seas.
bimarītus, -ī *m* bigamist.
bimāter, -ris *adj* having two mothers.
bimembris *adj* half man, half beast; (*pl*) Centaurs.
bimēstris *adj* of two months, two months old.
bīmulus *adj* only two years old.
bīmus *adj* two years old, for two years.
bīnī, bīnae, bīna *num* two each, two by two; a pair; (*with pl nouns having a meaning*) two.
binoctium, -ī *and* **iī** *nt* two nights.
binōminis *adj* with two names.
Biōn, -ōnis *m* satirical philosopher.
Biōnēus *adj* satirical.
bipalmis *adj* two spans long.
bipartītō *adv* in two parts, in two directions.
bipartītus *adj* divided in two.
bipatēns, -entis *adj* double-opening.
bipedālis *adj* two feet long broad *or* thick.
bipennifer, -ī *adj* wielding a battle-axe.
bipennis *adj* two-edged ♦ *f* battle-axe.
bipertītō *etc see* **bipartītō**.
bipēs, -edis *adj* two-footed ♦ *m* biped.
birēmis *adj* two-oared; with two banks of oars ♦ *f* two-oared skiff; galley with two banks of oars.
bis *adv* twice, double; ~ ad eundem make the same mistake twice; ~ diē, in diē twice a day;

~ tantō, tantum twice as much; ~ terque frequently; ~ terve seldom.
bissextus, -ī *m* intercalary day after 24th Feb.
Bistones, -um *mpl* people of Thrace.
Bistonis *f* Thracian woman, Bacchante.
Bistonius *adj* Thracian.
bisulcilingua, -ae *adj* fork-tongued, deceitful.
bisulcus *adj* cloven.
Bīthȳnia, -iae *f* province of Asia Minor.
Bīthȳnicus, Bīthȳnius, -us *adj see* **Bīthȳnia**.
bītō, -ere *vi* to go.
bitūmen, -inis *nt* bitumen, a kind of pitch.
bitūmineus *adj see* **bitūmen**.
bivium *nt* two ways.
bivius *adj* two-way.
blaesus *adj* lisping, indistinct.
blandē *adv see* **blandus**.
blandidicus *adj* fair-spoken.
blandiloquentia, -ae *f* attractive language.
blandiloquus, -entulus *adj* fair-spoken.
blandīmentum, -ī *nt* compliment, allurement.
blandior, -īrī, -ītus *vi* to coax, caress; to flatter, pay compliments; (*things*) to please, entice.
blanditia, -ae *f* caress, flattery; charm, allurement.
blandītim *adv* caressingly.
blandus *adj* smooth-tongued, flattering, fawning; charming, winsome.
blaterō, -āre *vi* to babble.
blatiō, -īre *vt* to babble.
blatta, -ae *f* cockroach.
blennus, -ī *m* idiot.
bliteus *adj* silly.
blitum, -ī *nt* kind of spinach.
boārius *adj* of cattle; **forum -um** *cattle market in* Rome.
Bodotria, -ae *f* Firth of Forth.
Boeōtarchēs *m* chief magistrate of Boeotia.
Boeōtia, -iae *f* district of central Greece.
Boeōtius, -us *adj see n.*
boiae, -ārum *fpl* collar.
Boiī, -ōrum *mpl* people of S.E. Gaul.
Boiohaemī, -ōrum *mpl* Bohemians.
bōlētus, -ī *m* mushroom.
bolus, -ī *m* (*dice*) throw; (*net*) cast; (*fig*) haul, piece of good luck; titbit.
bombus, -ī *m* booming, humming, buzzing.
bombȳcinus *adj* of silk.
bombȳx, -ȳcis *m* silkworm; silk.
Bona Dea, -ae, -ae *f* goddess worshipped by women.
bonitās, -ātis *f* goodness; honesty, integrity; kindness, affability.
Bonōnia, -ae *f* town in N. Italy (*now* Bologna).
Bonōniēnsis *adj see n.*
bonum, -ī *nt* a moral good; advantage, blessing; (*pl*) property; cuī ~ō? who was the

Noun declensions and verb conjugations are shown on pp xiii to xxv. The present infinitive ending of a verb shows to which conjugation it belongs: **-āre** = 1st; **-ēre** = 2nd; **-ere** = 3rd and **-īre** = 4th. Irregular verbs are shown on p xxvi

gainer?

bonus *adj* (*compar* **melior**, *superl* **optimus**) good; kind; brave; loyal; beneficial; lucky ♦ *mpl* upper class party, conservatives; ~**a aetās** prime of life; ~**ō animō** of good cheer; well-disposed; ~**ae artēs** integrity; culture, liberal education; ~ **a dicta** witticisms; ~**a fidēs** good faith; ~**ī mōrēs** morality; ~**ī nummī** genuine money; ~**a pars** large part; conservative party; ~**ae rēs** comforts, luxuries; prosperity; morality; ~**ā veniā** with kind permission; ~**a verba** words of good omen; well-chosen diction; ~**a vōx** loud voice.

boō, -āre *vi* to cry aloud.

Boōtēs, -ae *nt* constellation containing *Arcturus*.

Boreās, -ae *m* north wind; north.

Boreus *adj see n.*

Borysthenēs, -is *m* river Dnieper.

Borysthenidae *mpl dwellers near the Dnieper.*

Borysthenius *adj see* **Borysthenidae.**

bōs, bovis *m/f* ox, cow; kind of turbot; ~ **Lūca** elephant; **bovī clitellās impōnere** ≈ *put a round peg in a square hole.*

Bosporānus *adj see n.*

Bosporius *adj*: ~ **Cimmerius** *strait from Sea of Azov to Black Sea.*

Bosporus, -ī *m* strait from Black Sea to Sea of Marmora.

Boudicca, -ae *f* British queen (*falsely called* Boadicea).

bovārius *etc see* **boārius.**

Bovillae, -ārum *fpl* ancient Latin town.

Bovillānus *adj see n.*

bovillus *adj* of oxen.

brācae, -ārum *fpl* trousers.

brācātus *adj* trousered; barbarian (*esp of tribes beyond the Alps*).

bracchiālis *adj* of the arm.

bracchiolum, -ī *nt* dainty arm.

bracchium, -ī *and* **iī** *nt* arm, forearm; (*shellfish*) claw; (*tree*) branch; (*sea*) arm; (*NAUT*) yardarm; (*MIL*) outwork, mole; **levī, mollī bracchiō** casually.

bractea *etc see* **brattea.**

brassica, -ae *f* cabbage.

brattea, -ae *f* gold leaf.

bratteola, -ae *f* very fine gold leaf.

Brennus, -ī *m* Gallic chief who defeated the Romans.

brevī *adv* shortly, soon; briefly, in a few words.

brevia, -ium *ntpl* shoals.

breviārium, -ī *and* **iī** *nt* summary, statistical survey, official report.

breviculus *adj* shortish.

breviloquēns, -ēntis *adj* brief.

brevis *adj* short, small, shallow; brief, short-lived; concise.

brevitās, -ātis *f* shortness, smallness; brevity, conciseness.

breviter *adv* concisely.

Brigantēs, -um *mpl* British tribe in N. England.

Briganticus *adj see n.*

Brisēis, -idos *f* captive of Achilles.

Britannia, -iae *f* Britain; the British Isles.

Britannicus *m* son of emperor Claudius.

Britannus, (-icus) *adj see n.*

Bromius, -ī *and* **iī** *m* Bacchus.

brūma, -ae *f* winter solstice, midwinter; winter.

brūmālis *adj* of the winter solstice; wintry; ~ **flexus** tropic of Capricorn.

Brundisīnus *adj see n.*

Brundisium, -ī *and* **iī** *nt* port in S.E. Italy (*now* Brindisi).

Bruttiī, -ōrum *mpl* people of the toe of Italy.

Bruttius *adj see n.*

brūtus *adj* heavy, unwieldy; stupid, irrational.

Brūtus, -ī *m* liberator of Rome from kings; murderer of Caesar.

bubīle, -is *nt* stall.

būbo, -ōnis *m/f* owl.

būbula, -ae *f* beef.

bubulcitor, -ārī *vi* to drive oxen.

bubulcus, -ī *m* ploughman.

būbulus *adj* of cattle.

būcaeda, -ae *m* flogged slave.

bucca, -ae *f* cheek; mouth; ranter.

buccō, -ōnis *m* babbler.

buccula, -ae *f* visor.

bucculentus *adj* fat-cheeked.

būcerus *adj* horned.

būcina, -ae *f* shepherd's horn; military trumpet; night watch.

būcinātor, -ōris *m* trumpeter.

būcolica, -ōrum *ntpl* pastoral poetry.

būcula, -ae *f* young cow.

būfō, -ōnis *m* toad.

bulbus, -ī *m* bulb; onion.

būlē, -es *f* Greek senate.

būleuta *m* senator.

būleutērium *nt* senate house.

bulla, -ae *f* bubble; knob, stud; gold charm worn round the neck by children of noblemen.

bullātus *adj* wearing the bulla; still a child.

būmastus, -ī *f* kind of vine.

būris, -is *m* plough-beam.

Burrus old form of **Pyrrhus.**

Busīris, -idis *m* Egyptian king killed by Hercules.

bustirapus, -ī *m* graverobber.

bustuārius *adj* at a funeral.

bustum, -ī *nt* funeral place; tomb, grave.

buxifer, -ī *adj* famed for its box trees.

buxum, -ī *nt* boxwood; flute, top, comb, tablet.

buxus, -ī *f* box tree; flute.

Byzantium, -ī *and* **iī** *nt* city on Bosporus (*later* Constantinople, *now* Istanbul).

Byzantius *adj see n.*

C, c

caballīnus *adj* horse's.

caballus, -ī *m* horse.

cacātus *adj* impure.

cachinnātiō, -ōnis *f* loud laughter.

cachinnō, -āre *vi* to laugh, guffaw.

cachinnō, -ōnis *m* scoffer.

cachinnus, -ī *m* laugh, derisive laughter; (*waves*) splashing.

cacō, -āre *vi* to evacuate the bowels.

cacoēthes, -is *nt* (*fig*) itch.

cacula, -ae *m* soldier's slave.

cacūmen, -inis *nt* extremity, point, summit, treetop; (*fig*) height, limit.

cacūminō, -āre *vt* to make pointed.

Cācus, -ī *m* giant robber, son of Vulcan.

cadāver, -is *nt* corpse, carcass.

cadāverōsus *adj* ghastly.

Cadmēa, -ēae *f* fortress of Thebes.

Cadmēis, -ēidis *f* Agave; Ino; Semele.

Cadmēus, (-ēius) *adj* of Cadmus; Theban.

Cadmus, -ī *m* founder of Thebes.

cadō, -ere, cecidī, cāsum *vi* to fall; to droop, die, be killed; (ASTRO) to set; (*dice*) to be thrown; (*events*) to happen, turn out; (*money*) to be due; (*strength, speech, courage*) to diminish, cease, fail; (*wind, rage*) to subside; (*words*) to end; ~ **in** suit, agree with; come under; ~ **sub** be exposed to; **animīs** ~ be disheartened; **causā** ~ lose one's case.

cādūceātor, -ōris *m* officer with flag of truce.

cādūceus, -ī *m* herald's staff; Mercury's wand.

cādūcifer, -ī *adj* with herald's staff.

cadūcus *adj* falling, fallen; (*fig*) perishable, fleeting, vain; (*law*) without an heir ♦ *nt* property without an heir.

Cadurcī, -ōrum *mpl* Gallic tribe.

Cadurcum, -ī *nt* linen coverlet.

cadus, -ī *m* jar, flask (*esp for wine*); urn.

caecigenus *adj* born blind.

Caeciliānus *adj see n.*

Caecilius, -ī *m* Roman name (*esp early Latin comic poet*).

caecitās, -ātis *f* blindness.

caecō, -āre, -āvī, -ātum *vt* to blind; to make obscure.

Caecubum, -ī *nt* choice wine from the Ager Caecubus in S. Latium.

caecus *adj* blind; invisible, secret; dark, obscure; (*fig*) aimless, unknown, uncertain; **appāret ~ō** ≈ *it's as clear as daylight;* **domus ~a** a house with no windows; **~ā diē emere** buy on credit; **~um corpus** the back.

caedēs, -is *f* murder, massacre; gore; the slain.

caedō, -ere, cecīdī, caesum *vt* to cut; to strike; to kill, cut to pieces; (*animals*) to sacrifice.

caelāmen, -inis *nt* engraved work.

caelātor, -ōris *m* engraver.

caelātūra, -ae *f* engraving in bas-relief.

caelebs, -ibis *adj* unmarried (bachelor *or* widower); (*trees*) with no vine trained on.

caeles, -itis *adj* celestial ♦ *mpl* the gods.

caelestis, -is *adj* of the sky, heavenly; divine; glorious ♦ *mpl* the gods ♦ *ntpl* the heavenly bodies.

Caeliānus *adj see n.*

caelibātus, -ūs *m* celibacy.

caelicola, -ae *m* god.

caelifer, -ī *adj* supporting the sky.

Caelius, -ī *m* Roman name; Roman hill.

caelō, -āre, -āvī, -ātum *vt* to engrave (*in relief on metals*), carve (*on wood*); (*fig*) to compose.

caelum, -ī *nt* engraver's chisel.

caelum, -ī *nt* sky, heaven; air, climate, weather; (*fig*) height of success, glory; **~um ac terrās miscēre** create chaos; **ad ~um ferre** extol; **dē ~ō dēlāpsus** a messiah; **dē ~ō servāre** watch for omens; **dē ~ō tangī** be struck by lightning; **digitō ~um attingere** ≈ be in the seventh heaven; **in ~ō esse** be overjoyed.

caementum, -ī *nt* quarrystone, rubble.

caenōsus *adj* muddy.

caenum, -ī *nt* mud, filth.

caepa, -ae *f*, **caepe, -is** *nt* onion.

Caere *nt indecl* (*gen* -itis, *abl* -ēte) *f* ancient Etruscan town.

Caeres, -itis *and* **ētis** *adj:* **~ite cērā dignī** like the disfranchised masses.

caerimōnia, -ae *f* sanctity; veneration (*for gods*); religious usage, ritual.

caeruleus, caerulus *adj* blue, dark blue, dark green, dusky ♦ *ntpl* the sea.

Caesar, -is *m* Julius (*great Roman soldier, statesman, author*); Augustus; the emperor.

Caesareus, and iānus, and īnus *adj see n.*

caesariātus *adj* bushy-haired.

caesariēs, -ēī *f* hair.

caesīcius *adj* bluish.

caesim *adv* with the edge of the sword; (RHET) in short clauses.

caesius *adj* bluish grey, blue-eyed.

caespes, -itis *m* sod, turf; mass of roots.

caestus, -ūs *m* boxing glove.

caesus *ppp of* **caedō.**

caetra, -ae *f* targe.

caetrātus *adj* armed with a targe.

Caïcus, -ī *m* river in Asia Minor.

Cāiēta, -ae, -ē, -ēs *f* town in Latium.

Cāius *etc see* **Gaius.**

Calaber, -rī *adj* Calabrian.
Calabria *f* S.E. peninsula of Italy.
Calamis, -idis *m Greek sculptor.*
calamister, -rī *m*, **-rum, -rī** *nt* curling iron; (*RHET*) flourish.
calamistrātus *adj* curled; foppish.
calamitās, -ātis *f* disaster; (*MIL*) defeat; (*AGR*) damage, failure.
calamitōsē *adv see* **calamitōsus**.
calamitōsus *adj* disastrous, ruinous; blighted, unfortunate.
calamus, -ī *m* reed; stalk; pen, pipe, arrow, fishing rod.
calathiscus, -ī *m* small basket.
calathus, -ī *m* wicker basket; bowl, cup.
calātor, -ōris *m* servant.
calcāneum, -ī *nt* heel.
calcar, -āris *nt* spur.
calceāmentum, -ī *nt* shoe.
calceātus *ppp* shod.
calceolārius, -ī *and* **iī** *m* shoemaker.
calceolus, -ī *m* small shoe.
calceus, -ī *m* shoe.
Calchās, -antis *m Greek prophet at Troy.*
calcitrō, -āre *vi* to kick; (*fig*) to resist.
calcō, -āre, -āvī, -ātum *vt* to tread, trample on; (*fig*) to spurn.
calculus, -ī *m* pebble, stone; draughtsman, counting stone, reckoning, voting stone; **~um redūcere** take back a move; **~ōs subdūcere** compute; **ad ~ōs vocāre** subject to a reckoning.
caldārius *adj* with warm water.
caldus *etc see* **calidus**.
Calēdonia, -ae *f* the Scottish Highlands.
Calēdonius *adj see* n.
calefaciō, (calfaciō), -facere, -fēcī, -factum *vt* to warm, heat; (*fig*) to provoke, excite.
calefactō, -āre *vt* to warm.
Calendae *see* **Kalendae**.
Calēnus *adj* of Cales ♦ *nt* wine of Cales.
caleō, -ēre *vi* to be warm, be hot, glow; (*mind*) to be inflamed; (*things*) to be pursued with enthusiasm; to be fresh.
Calēs, -ium *fpl town in Campania.*
calēscō, -ere, -uī *vi* to get hot; (*fig*) to become inflamed.
calidē *adv* promptly.
calidus *adj* warm, hot; (*fig*) fiery, eager; hasty; prompt ♦ *f* warm water ♦ *nt* warm drink.
caliendrum, -ī *nt* headdress of hair.
caliga, -ae *f* soldier's boot.
caligātus *adj* heavily shod.
cālīginōsus *adj* misty, obscure.
cālīgō, -inis *f* mist, fog; dimness, darkness; (*mind*) obtuseness; (*CIRCS*) trouble.
cālīgō, -āre *vi* to be misty, be dim; to cause dizziness.
Caligula, -ae *m emperor Gaius.*
calix, -cis *m* wine cup; cooking pot.
calleō, -ēre *vi* to be thick-skinned; (*fig*) to be unfeeling; to be wise, be skilful ♦ *vt* to know, understand.

callidē *adv see* **callidus**.
calliditās, -ātis *f* skill; cunning.
callidus *adj* skilful, clever; crafty.
Callimachus, -ī *m Greek poet of Alexandria.*
Calliopē, -ēs, *and* **ēa, -ēae** *f Muse of epic poetry.*
callis, -is *m* footpath, mountain track; pass; hill pastures.
Callistō, -ūs *f daughter of Lycaon;* (*constellation*) Great Bear.
callōsus *adj* hard-skinned; solid.
callum, -ī *nt* hard *or* thick skin; firm flesh; (*fig*) callousness.
calō, -āre, -āvī, -ātum *vt* to convoke.
cālō, -ōnis *m* soldier's servant; drudge.
calor, -ōris *m* warmth, heat; (*fig*) passion, love.
Calpē, -ēs *f* Rock of Gibraltar.
Calpurniānus *adj see* n.
Calpurnius, -ī *m Roman name.*
caltha, -ae *f* marigold.
calthula, -ae *f* yellow dress.
caluī *perf of* **calēscō**.
calumnia, -ae *f* chicanery, sharp practice; subterfuge; misrepresentation; (*law*) dishonest accusation, blackmail; being convicted of malicious prosecution; **~am iūrāre** swear that an action is brought in good faith.
calumniātor, -ōris *m* legal trickster, slanderer.
calumnior, -ārī, -ātus *vt* to misrepresent, slander; (*law*) to bring an action in bad faith; **sē ~** deprecate oneself.
calva, -ae *f* bald head.
calvitium, -ī *and* **iī** *nt* baldness.
calvor, -ārī *vt* to deceive.
calvus *adj* bald.
calx, -cis *f* heel; foot; **~ce petere, ferīre** kick; **adversus stimulum ~cēs** ≈ *kicking against the pricks.*
calx, -cis *f* pebble; lime, chalk; finishing line, end; **ad carcerēs ā ~ce revocārī** have to begin all over again.
Calydōn, -ōnis *f town in Aetolia.*
Calydōnis *adj* Calydonian.
Calydōnius *f* Deianira; **~ōnius amnis** Achelous; **~ hērōs** Meleager; **~ōnia rēgna** Daunia in S. Italy.
Calypsō, -ūs (*acc* **-ō**) *f nymph who detained Ulysses in Ogygia.*
camēlīnus *adj* camel's.
camella, -ae *f* wine cup.
camēlus, -ī *m* camel.
Camēna, -ae *f* Muse; poetry.
camera, -ae *f* arched roof.
Camerīnum, -ī *nt town in Umbria.*
Camers, -tis, *and* **tīnus** *adj* of Camerinum.
Camillus, -ī *m* Roman hero (*who saved Rome from the Gauls*).
camīnus, -ī *m* furnace, fire; forge; **oleum addere ~ō** ≈ *add fuel to the flames.*
cammarus, -ī *m* lobster.

Campānia, -iae *f district of W. Italy.*
Campānicus, *and* **ius,** *and* **us** *adj* Campanian, Capuan.
campē, -ēs *f evasion.*
campester, -ris *adj* of the plain; of the Campus Martius ♦ *nt* loincloth ♦ *ntpl* level ground.
campus, -ī *m* plain; sports field; any level surface; (*fig*) theatre, arena (*of action, debate*); ~ **Martius** level ground by the Tiber (*used for assemblies, sports, military drills*).
Camulodūnum, -ī *nt* town of Trinobantes (*now* Colchester).
camur, -ī *adj* crooked.
canālis, -is *m* pipe, conduit, canal.
cancellī, -ōrum *mpl* grating, enclosure; barrier (*in public places*), bar of law court.
cancer, -rī *m* crab; (*constellation*) Cancer; south, tropical heat; (*MED*) cancer.
candefaciō, -ere *vt* to make dazzlingly white.
candēla, -ae *f* taper, tallow candle; waxed cord; ~**am appōnere valvīs** set the house on fire.
candēlābrum, -ī *nt* candlestick, chandelier, lampstand.
candēns, -entis *adj* dazzling white; white-hot.
candeō, -ēre *vi* to shine, be white; to be white-hot.
candēscō, -ere *vi* to become white; to grow white-hot.
candidātōrius *adj* of a candidate.
candidātus *adj* dressed in white ♦ *m* candidate for office.
candidē *adv* in white; sincerely.
candidulus *adj* pretty white.
candidus *adj* white, bright; radiant, beautiful; clothed in white; (*style*) clear; (*mind*) candid, frank; (*CIRCS*) happy; ~**a sententia** acquittal.
candor, -ōris *m* whiteness, brightness, beauty; (*fig*) brilliance, sincerity.
cānēns, -entis *adj* white.
cāneō, -ēre, -uī *vi* to be grey, be white.
cānescō, -ere *vi* to grow white; to grow old.
canīcula, -ae *f* bitch; Dog Star, Sirius.
canīnus *adj* dog's, canine; snarling, spiteful; ~ **littera** letter R.
canis, -is *m/f* dog, bitch; (*fig*) shameless *or* angry person; hanger-on; (*dice*) lowest throw; (*ASTRO*) Canis Major, Canis Minor; (*myth*) Cerberus.
canistrum, -ī *nt* wicker basket.
cānitiēs, -ēī *f* greyness; grey hair; old age.
canna, -ae *f* reed; pipe; gondola.
cannabis, -is *f* hemp.
Cannae, -ārum *fpl* village in Apulia (*scene of great Roman defeat by Hannibal*).
Cannēnsis *adj see n.*
canō, canere, cecinī *vt, vi* to sing; to play; to sing about, recite, celebrate; to prophesy; (*MIL*) to sound; (*birds*) to sing, crow.

canor, -ōris *m* song, tune, sound.
canōrus *adj* musical, melodious; singsong ♦ *nt* melodiousness.
Cantaber, -rī *m* Cantabrian.
Cantabria, -riae *f* district of N Spain.
Cantabricus *adj see n.*
cantāmen, -inis *nt* charm.
cantharis, -idis *f* beetle; Spanish fly.
cantharus, -ī *m* tankard.
canthērīnus *adj* of a horse.
canthērius, -ī *and* **iī** *m* gelding.
canticum, -ī *nt aria in Latin comedy*; song.
cantilēna, -ae *f* old song, gossip; ~**am eandem canere** keep harping on the same theme.
cantiō, -ōnis *f* song; charm.
cantitō, -āre, -āvī, -atum *vt* to sing *or* play often.
Cantium, -ī *and* **iī** *nt* Kent.
cantiunculae, -ārum *fpl* fascinating strains.
cantō, -āre, -āvī, -ātum *vt, vi* to sing; to play; to sing about, recite, celebrate; to proclaim, harp on; to use magic spells; to sound; to drawl.
cantor, -ōris *m*, **-rīx, -rīcis** *f* singer, musician, poet; actor.
cantus, -ūs *m* singing, playing, music; prophecy; magic spell.
cānus *adj* white, grey, hoary; old ♦ *mpl* grey hairs.
Canusīnus *adj see n.*
Canusium, -ī *nt* town in Apulia (*famous for wool*).
capācitās, -ātis *f* spaciousness.
capāx, -ācis *adj* capable of holding, spacious, roomy; capable, able, fit.
capēdō, -inis *f* sacrificial dish.
capēduncula *f* small dish.
capella, -ae *f* she-goat; (*ASTRO*) bright star in Auriga.
Capēna, -ae *f* old Etruscan town.
Capēnās, -us *adj*: **Porta ~a** *Roman gate leading to the Via Appia.*
caper, -rī *m* goat; odour of the armpits.
caperrō, -āre *vi* to wrinkle.
capessō, -ere, -īvī, -ītum *vt* to seize, take hold of, try to reach, make for; to take in hand, engage in; **rem pūblicam** ~ go in for politics.
capillātus *adj* long-haired; ancient.
capillus, -ī *m* hair (of head *or* beard); a hair.
capiō, -ere, cēpī, captum *vt* to take, seize; to catch, capture; (*MIL*) to occupy, take prisoner; (*NAUT*) to make, reach (*a goal*); (*fig*) to captivate, charm, cheat; (*pass*) to be maimed, lose the use of; to choose; (*appearance*) to assume; (*habit*) to cultivate; (*duty*) to undertake; (*ideas*) to conceive, form; (*feeling*) to experience; (*harm*) to suffer; to receive, get, inherit; to contain, hold; (*fig*) to bear; (*mind*) to grasp; **cōnsilium**

~ come to a decision; **impetum** ~ gather momentum; **initium** ~ start; **oculō capī** lose an eye; **mente captus** insane; **cupīdō eum cēpit** he felt a desire.

capis, -dis *f sacrificial bowl with one handle.*

capistrātus *adj* haltered.

capistrum, -ī *nt* halter, muzzle.

capital, -ālis *nt* capital crime.

capitālis *adj* mortal, deadly, dangerous; (*law*) capital; important, excellent.

capitō, -ōnis *m* bighead.

Capitōlīnus *adj* of the Capitol; of Jupiter.

Capitōlium, -ī *nt Roman hill with temple of Jupiter.*

capitulātim *adv* summarily.

capitulum, -ī *nt* small head; person, creature.

Cappadocia, -ae *f country of Asia Minor.*

capra, -ae *f* she-goat; odour of armpits; (*ASTRO*) Capella.

caprea, -ae *f* roe.

Capreae, -ārum *fpl* island of Capri.

capreolus, -ī *m* roebuck; (*pl*) crossbeams.

Capricornus, -ī *m* (*constellation*) Capricorn (*associated with midwinter*).

caprificus, -ī *f* wild fig tree.

caprigenus *adj* of goats.

caprimulgus, -ī *m* goatherd, rustic.

caprīnus *adj* of goats.

capripēs, -edis *adj* goat-footed.

capsa, -ae *f* box (*esp for papyrus rolls*).

capsō *archaic fut of* **capiō.**

capsula, -ae *f* small box; **dē ~ā tōtus** ≈ *out of a bandbox.*

Capta, -ae *f* Minerva.

captātiō, -ōnis *f* catching at.

captātor, -ōris *m* one who courts; legacy hunter.

captiō, -ōnis *f* fraud; disadvantage; (*argument*) fallacy, sophism.

captiōsē *adv see* **captiōsus.**

captiōsus *adj* deceptive; dangerous; captious.

captiuncula, -ae *f* quibble.

captīvitās, -ātis *f* captivity; capture.

captīvus *adj* captive, captured; of captives ♦ *m/f* prisoner of war.

captō, -āre, -āvī, -ātum *vt* to try to catch, chase; to try to win, court, watch for; to deceive, trap.

captus *ppp of* **capiō** ♦ *m* prisoner.

captus, -ūs *m* grasp, notion.

Capua, -ae *f* chief town of Campania.

capulāris *adj* due for a coffin.

capulus, -ī *m* coffin; handle, hilt.

caput, -itis *nt* head; top, extremity; (*rivers*) source; (*more rarely*) mouth; person, individual; life; civil rights; (*person*) chief, leader; (*towns*) capital; (*money*) principal; (*writing*) substance, chapter; principle, main point, the great thing; ~ **cēnae** main dish; **~itis accūsāre** charge with a capital offence; **~itis damnāre** condemn to death; **~itis dēminūtiō** loss of political rights; **~itis poena** capital punishment; **~ita cōnferre** confer in

secret; **in ~ita** per head; **suprā ~ut esse** be imminent.

Cār, -is *m* Carian.

carbaseus *adj* linen, canvas.

carbasus, -ī *f* (*pl* -**a,** -**ōrum** *nt*) Spanish flax, fine linen; garment, sail, curtain.

carbō, -ōnis *m* charcoal, embers.

carbōnārius, -ī *and* **iī** *m* charcoal burner.

carbunculus, -ī *m* small coal; precious stone.

carcer, -is *m* prison; jailbird; barrier, starting place (*for races*); **ad ~ēs ā calce revocārī** have to begin all over again.

carcerārius *adj* of a prison.

carchēsium, -ī *and* **iī** *nt* drinking cup; (*NAUT*) masthead.

cardiacus, -ī *m* dyspeptic.

cardō, -inis *m* hinge; (*ASTRO*) pole, axis, cardinal point; (*fig*) juncture, critical moment.

carduus, -ī *m* thistle.

cārē *adv see* **cārus.**

cārectum, -ī *nt* sedge.

cāreō, -ēre, -uī *vi* (*with abl*) to be free from, not have, be without; to abstain from, be absent from; to want, miss.

cārex, -icis *f* sedge.

Cāria, -ae *f* district of S.W. Asia Minor.

Cāricus *adj* Carian ♦ *f* dried fig.

cariēs (*acc* -**em,** *abl* -**ē**) *f* dry rot.

carīna, -ae *f* keel; ship.

Carīnae, -ārum *fpl district of Rome.*

carīnārius, -ī *and* **iī** *m* dyer of yellow.

cariōsus *adj* crumbling; (*fig*) withered.

cāris, -idis *f* kind of crab.

cāritās, -ātis *f* dearness, high price; esteem, affection.

carmen, -inis *nt* song, tune; poem, poetry, verse; prophecy; (*in law, religion*) formula; moral text.

Carmentālis *adj see n.*

Carmentis, -is, *and* **a, -ae** *f prophetess, mother of Evander.*

carnārium, -ī *and* **iī** *nt* fleshhook; larder.

Carneadēs, -is *m* Greek philosopher (*founder of the New Academy*).

Carneadēus *adj see n.*

carnifex, -icis *m* executioner, hangman; scoundrel; murderer.

carnificīna, -ae *f* execution; torture; **~am facere** to be an executioner.

carnificō, -āre *vt* to behead, mutilate.

carnuf- *etc see* **carnif-.**

carō, -nis *f* flesh.

cārō, -ere *vt* to card.

Carpathius *adj see n.*

Carpathus, -ī *f island between Crete and Rhodes.*

carpatina, -ae *f* leather shoe.

carpentum, -ī *nt* two-wheeled coach.

carpō, -ere, -sī, -tum *vt* to pick, pluck, gather; to tear off; to browse, graze on; (*wool*) to card; (*fig*) to enjoy, snatch; to carp at, slander; to weaken, wear down; to divide up; (*journey*) to go, travel.

carptim *adv* in parts; at different points; at
  different times.

carptor, -ōris *m* carver.

carptus *ppp of* **carpō.**

carrus, -ī *m* waggon.

Carthāginiēnsis *adj see n.*

Carthāgō, -inis *f* Carthage (*near Tunis*); ~
  Nova town in Spain (*now* Cartagena).

caruncula, -ae *f* piece of flesh.

cārus *adj* dear, costly; dear, beloved.

Carystēus *adj see n.*

Carystos, -ī *f* town in Euboea (*famous for
  marble*).

casa, -ae *f* cottage, hut.

cascus *adj* old.

cāseolus, -ī *m* small cheese.

cāseus, -ī *m* cheese.

casia, -ae *f* cinnamon; spurge laurel.

Caspius *adj* Caspian.

Cassandra, -ae *f* Trojan princess and
  prophetess, doomed never to be believed.

cassēs, -ium *mpl* net, snare; spider's web.

Cassiānus *adj see n.*

cassida, -ae *f* helmet.

Cassiepēa, -ae, Cassiopē, -ēs *f* mother of
  Andromeda; a constellation.

cassis, -idis *f* helmet.

Cassius, -ī *m* Roman family name.

cassō, -āre *vi* to shake.

cassus *adj* empty; devoid of, without (*abl*);
  vain, useless; ~ **lūmine** dead; **in ~um** in vain.

Castalia, -ae *f* spring on Parnassus, (*sacred to
  Apollo and the Muses*).

Castalides, -dum *fpl* Muses.

Castalius, -s *adj see n.*

castanea, -ae *f* chestnut tree; chestnut.

castē *adv see* **castus.**

castellānus *adj* of a fortress ♦ *mpl* garrison.

castellātim *adv* in different fortresses.

castellum, -ī *nt* fortress, castle; (*fig*) defence,
  refuge.

castēria, -ae *f* rowers' quarters.

castīgābilis *adj* punishable.

castīgātiō, -ōnis *f* correction, reproof.

castīgātor, -ōris *m* reprover.

castīgātus *adj* small, slender.

castīgō, -āre, -āvī, -ātum *vt* to correct,
  punish; to reprove; to restrain.

castimōnia, -ae *f* purity, morality; chastity,
  abstinence.

castitās, -ātis *f* chastity.

castor, -oris *m* beaver.

Castor, -oris *m* twin brother of Pollux (*patron
  of sailors*); star in Gemini.

castoreum, -ī *nt* odorous secretion of the beaver.

castra, -ōrum *ntpl* camp; day's march; army
  life; (*fig*) party, sect; ~ **movēre** strike camp;
  ~ **mūnīre** construct a camp; ~ **pōnere** pitch
  camp; **bīna** ~ two camps.

castrēnsis *adj* of the camp, military.

castrō, -āre *vt* to castrate; (*fig*) to weaken.

castrum, -ī *nt* fort.

castus *adj* clean, pure, chaste, innocent; holy,
  pious.

cāsū *adv* by chance.

casula, -ae *f* little cottage.

cāsus, -ūs *m* fall, downfall; event, chance,
  accident; misfortune, death; opportunity;
  (*time*) end; (*GRAM*) case.

Catadūpa, -ōrum *ntpl* Nile cataract near Syene.

catagraphus *adj* painted.

Catamītus, -ī *m* Ganymede.

cataphractēs, -ae *m* coat of mail.

cataphractus *adj* wearing mail.

cataplus, -ī *m* ship arriving.

catapulta, -ae *f* (*MIL*) catapult; (*fig*) missile.

catapultārius *adj* thrown by catapult.

cataracta, -ae *f* waterfall; sluice; drawbridge.

catasta, -ae *f* stage, scaffold.

catē *adv see* **catus.**

catēia, -ae *f* javelin.

catella, -ae *f* small chain.

catellus, -ī *m* puppy.

catēna, -ae *f* chain; fetter; (*fig*) bond,
  restraint; series.

catēnātus *adj* chained, fettered.

caterva, -ae *f* crowd, band; flock; (*MIL*) troop,
  body; (*THEAT*) company.

catervātim *adv* in companies.

cathedra, -ae *f* armchair, sedan chair;
  teacher's chair.

catholicus *adj* (*ECCL*) orthodox, universal.

Catilīna, -ae *m* Catiline (*conspirator suppressed
  by Cicero*).

Catilīnārius *adj see n.*

catillo, -āre *vt* to lick a plate.

catīllus, -ī *m* small dish.

catīnus, -ī *m* dish, pot.

Catō, -ōnis *m* famous censor and author,
  idealised as the pattern of an ancient Roman;
  famous Stoic and republican leader against
  Caesar.

Catōniānus *adj see n.*

Catōnīnī *mpl* Cato's supporters.

catōnium, -ī and iī *nt* the lower world.

Catulliānus *adj see n.*

Catullus, -ī *m* Latin lyric poet.

catulus, -ī *m* puppy; cub, young of other
  animals.

catus *adj* clever, wise; sly, cunning.

Caucasius *adj see n.*

Caucasus, -ī *m* Caucasus mountains.

cauda, -ae *f* tail; ~**am iactāre** fawn; ~**am
  trahere** be made a fool of.

caudeus *adj* wooden.

caudex, -icis *m* trunk; block of wood; book,
  ledger; (*fig*) blockhead.

caudicālis *adj* of woodcutting.

Caudīnus *adj see n.*

Noun declensions and verb conjugations are shown on pp xiii to xxv. The present infinitive ending of a verb shows
to which conjugation it belongs: **-āre** = 1st; **-ēre** = 2nd; **-ere** = 3rd and **-īre** = 4th. Irregular verbs are shown on p xxvi

Caudium, -ī *nt Samnite town.*
caulae, -ārum *fpl* opening; sheepfold.
caulis, -is *m* stalk; cabbage.
Cauneus *adj* Caunian.
Caunus, -ī *f town in Caria* ♦ *fpl* dried figs.
caupō, -ōnis *m* shopkeeper, innkeeper.
caupōna, -ae *f* shop, inn.
caupōnius *adj see n.*
caupōnor, -ārī *vt* to trade in.
caupōnula, -ae *f* tavern.
Caurus, -ī *m* north-west wind.
causa, -ae *f* cause, reason; purpose, sake; excuse, pretext; opportunity; connection, case, position; (*law*) case, suit; (*POL*) cause, party; (*RHET*) subject matter; **~am agere, ōrāre** plead a case; **~am dēfendere** speak for the defence; **~am dīcere** defend oneself; **~ā** for the sake of; **cum ~ā** with good reason; **quā dē ~ā** for this reason; **in ~ā esse** be responsible; **per ~am** under the pretext.
causārius *adj* (*MIL*) unfit for service.
causia, -ae *f* Macedonian hat.
causidicus, -ī *m* advocate.
causificor, -ārī *vi* to make a pretext.
causor, -ārī, -ātus *vt, vi* to pretend, make an excuse of.
caussa *etc see* **causa.**
causula, -ae *f* petty lawsuit; slight cause.
cautē *adv* carefully, cautiously; with security.
cautēla, -ae *f* caution.
cautēs, -is *f* rock, crag.
cautim *adv* warily.
cautiō, -ōnis *f* caution, wariness; (*law*) security, bond, bail; **mihi ~ est** I must take care; **mea ~ est** I must see to it.
cautor, -ōris *m* wary person; surety.
cautus *ppp of* **caveō** ♦ *adj* wary, provident; safe, secure.
cavaedium, -ī *and* **iī** *nt* inner court of a house.
cavea, -ae *f* cage, stall, coop, hive; (*THEAT*) auditorium; theatre; **prīma ~** upper class seats; **ultima ~** lower class seats.
caveō, -ēre, cāvī, cautum *vt* to beware of, guard against ♦ *vi* (*with ab or abl*) to be on one's guard against; (*with dat*) to look after; (*with nē*) to take care that ... not; (*with ut*) to take good care that; (*with subj or inf*) to take care not to, do not; (*law*) to stipulate, decree; (*COMM*) to get a guarantee, give a guarantee, stand security; **cavē!** look out!
caverna, -ae *f* hollow, cave, vault; (*NAUT*) hold.
cavilla, -ae *f* jeering.
cavillātiō, -ōnis *f* jeering, banter; sophistry.
cavillātor, -ōris *m* scoffer.
cavillor, -ārī, -ātus *vt* to scoff at ♦ *vi* to jeer, scoff; to quibble.
cavō, -āre, -āvī, -ātum *vt* to hollow, excavate.
cavus *adj* hollow, concave, vaulted; (*river*) deep-channelled ♦ *nt* cavity, hole.
Caystros, -us, -ī *m* river in Lydia (*famous for swans*).
-ce *demonstrative particle appended to pronouns and adverbs.*

Cēa, -ae *f* Aegean island (*birthplace of Simonides*).
cecidī *perf of* **cadō.**
cecidī *perf of* **caedō.**
cecinī *perf of* **canō.**
Cecropidēs, -idae *m* Theseus; Athenian.
Cecropis, -idis *f* Aglauros; Procne; Philomela; Athenian, Attic.
Cecropius *adj* Athenian ♦ *f* Athens.
Cecrops, -is *m ancient king of Athens.*
cēdō, -ere, cessī, cessum *vi* to go, walk; to depart, withdraw, retreat; to pass away, die; (*events*) to turn out; to be changed (into); to accrue (to); to yield, be inferior (to) ♦ *vt* to give up, concede, allow; **~ bonīs, possessiōne** make over property (to); **~ forō** go bankrupt; **~ locō** leave one's post; **~ memoriā** be forgotten.
cedo (*pl* **cette**) *impv* give me, bring here; tell me; let me; look at!
cedrus, -ī *f* cedar, perfumed juniper; cedar oil.
Celaenō, -ūs *f* a Harpy; a Pleiad.
cēlāta *ntpl* secrets.
celeber, -ris *adj* crowded, populous; honoured, famous; repeated.
celebrātiō, -ōnis *f* throng; celebration.
celebrātus *adj* full, much used; festive; famous.
celebritās, -ātis *f* crowd; celebration; fame.
celebrō, -āre, -āvī, -ātum *vt* to crowd, frequent; to repeat, practise; to celebrate, keep (*a festival*); to advertise, glorify.
celer, -is *adj* quick, swift, fast; hasty.
Celerēs, -um *mpl* royal bodyguard.
celeripēs, -edis *adj* swift-footed.
celeritās, -ātis *f* speed, quickness.
celeriter *adv see* **celer.**
celerō, -āre *vt* to quicken ♦ *vi* to make haste.
cella, -ae *f* granary, stall, cell; garret, hut, small room; sanctuary of a temple.
cellārius *adj* of the storeroom ♦ *m* steward.
cellula, -ae *f* little room.
cēlō, -āre, -āvī, -ātum *vt* to hide, conceal, keep secret; **id mē ~at** he keeps me in the dark about it.
celōx, -ōcis *adj* swift ♦ *f* fast ship, yacht.
celsus *adj* high, lofty; (*fig*) great, eminent; haughty.
Celtae, -ārum *mpl* Celts (*esp of central Gaul*) ♦ *nt* the Celtic nation.
Celtibērī, -ōrum *mpl* people of central Spain.
Celtibēria, -iae *f* Central Spain.
Celtibēricus *adj see n.*
Celticus *adj* Celtic.
cēna, -ae *f* dinner (*the principal Roman meal*); **inter ~am** at table.
cēnāculum, -ī *nt* dining-room; upper room, garret.
cēnāticus *adj* of dinner.
cēnātiō, -ōnis *f* dining-room.
cēnātus *ppa* having dined, after dinner ♦ *ppp* spent in feasting.

Cenchreae, -ārum *fpl* harbour of Corinth.
cēnitō, -āre *vi* to be accustomed to dine.
cēnō, -āre, -āvī, -ātum *vi* to dine ♦ *vt* to eat, dine on.
cēnseō, -ēre, -uī, -um *vt* (*census*) to assess, rate, take a census, make a property return; (*fig*) to estimate, appreciate, celebrate; (*senate or other body*) to decree, resolve; (*member*) to express an opinion, move, vote; to advise; to judge, think, suppose, consider; **cēnsuī ~endō** for census purposes.
cēnsiō, -ōnis *f* punishment; expression of opinion.
cēnsor, -ōris *m* censor; (*fig*) severe judge, critic.
cēnsōrius *adj* of the censors, to be dealt with by the censors; (*fig*) severe; **homō ~** an ex-censor.
cēnsūra, -ae *f* censorship; criticism.
cēnsus *ppp of* **cēnseō; capite ~ī** the poorest class of Roman citizens.
cēnsus, -ūs *m* register of Roman citizens and their property, census; registered property; wealth; **~um agere, habēre** hold a census; **sine ~ū** poor.
centaurēum, -ī *nt* centaury.
Centaurēus *adj see n.*
Centaurus, -ī *m* Centaur, half man half horse.
centēnī, -um *num* a hundred each, a hundred.
centēsimus *adj* hundredth ♦ *f* hundredth part; (*interest*) 1 per cent monthly (*12 per cent per annum*).
centiceps *adj* hundred-headed.
centiēns, -ēs *adv* a hundred times.
centimanus *adj* hundred-handed.
centō, -ōnis *m* patchwork; **~ōnēs sarcīre** ≈ *tell tall stories.*
centum *num* a hundred.
centumgeminus *adj* hundred-fold.
centumplex *adj* hundred-fold.
centumpondium, -ī *and* **iī** *nt* a hundred pounds.
centumvirālis *adj* of the centumviri.
centumvirī, -ōrum *mpl* a bench of judges who heard special civil cases in Rome.
centunculus, -ī *m* piece of patchwork, saddlecloth.
centuria, -ae *f* (*MIL*) company; (*POL*) century (*a division of the Roman people according to property*).
centuriātim *adv* by companies, by centuries.
centuriātus *adj* divided by centuries; **comitia ~a** assembly which voted by centuries.
centuriātus, -ūs *m* division into centuries; rank of centurion.
centuriō, -āre, -āvī, -ātum *vt* (*MIL*) to assign to companies; (*POL*) to divide by centuries.
centuriō, -ōnis *m* (*MIL*) captain, centurion.
centussis, -is *m* a hundred asses.
cēnula, -ae *f* little dinner.

Ceōs, acc -ō *see* **Cea.**
Cēphēis *f* Andromeda.
Cēphēius *adj* of Cepheus.
Cēphēus *adj* Ethiopian.
Cēpheus, -eī (*acc* -ea) *m* king of Ethiopia (*father of Andromeda*).
Cēphīsis *adj see n.*
Cēphīsius *m* Narcissus.
Cēphīsus, -ī *m* river in central Greece.
cēpī *perf of* **capiō.**
cēra, -ae *f* wax; honey cells; writing tablet, notebook; seal; portrait of an ancestor; **prīma ~** first page.
Ceramīcus, -ī *m* Athenian cemetery.
cērārium, -ī *and* **iī** *nt* seal-duty.
cerastēs, -ae *m* a horned serpent.
cerasus, -ī *f* cherry tree; cherry.
cērātus *adj* waxed.
Ceraunia, -ōrum *nt,* **Cerauniī** *m* mountains in Epirus.
Cerbereus *adj see n.*
Cerberus, -ī *m* three-headed watchdog of Hades.
cercopithēcus, -ī *m* monkey.
cercūrus, -ī *m* Cyprian type of ship.
cerdō, -ōnis *m* tradesman.
Cereālia, -ium *ntpl* festival of Ceres.
Cereālis *adj* of Ceres; of corn, of meal.
cerebrōsus *adj* hot-headed.
cerebrum, -ī *nt* brain; understanding; quick temper.
Cerēs, -eris *f* goddess of agriculture; (*fig*) grain, bread.
cēreus *adj* waxen; wax-coloured; (*fig*) supple, easily led ♦ *m* taper.
cēriāria, -ae *f* taper maker.
cērina, -ōrum *ntpl* wax-coloured clothes.
cērintha, -ae *f* honeywort.
cernō, -ere, -crēvī, crētum *vt* to see, discern; to understand, perceive; to decide, determine; (*law*) to decide to take up (an inheritance).
cernuus *adj* face downwards.
cērōma, -atis *nt* wrestlers' ointment.
cērōmaticus *adj* smeared with wax ointment.
cerrītus *adj* crazy.
certāmen, -inis *nt* contest, match; battle, combat; (*fig*) struggle, rivalry.
certātim *adv* emulously.
certātiō, -ōnis *f* contest; debate; rivalry.
certē *adv* assuredly, of course; at least.
certō *adv* certainly, really.
certō, -āre, -āvī, -ātum *vi* to contend, compete; (*MIL*) to fight it out; (*law*) to dispute; (*with inf*) to try hard.
certus *adj* determined, fixed, definite; reliable, unerring; sure, certain; **mihi ~um est** I have made up my mind; **~um scīre, prō ~ō habēre** know for certain, be sure; **~iōrem facere** inform.
cērula, -ae *f* piece of wax; **~ miniāta** red

Noun declensions and verb conjugations are shown on pp xiii to xxv. The present infinitive ending of a verb shows to which conjugation it belongs: **-āre** = 1st; **-ēre** = 2nd; **-ere** = 3rd and **-īre** = 4th. Irregular verbs are shown on p xxvi

pencil.

cērussa, -ae f white lead.

cērussātus adj painted with white lead.

cerva, -ae f hind, deer.

cervīcal, -ālis nt pillow.

cervīcula, -ae f slender neck.

cervīnus adj deer's.

cervīx, -īcis f neck; **in ~īcibus esse** be a burden (to), threaten.

cervus, -ī m stag, deer; (MIL) palisade.

cessātiō, -ōnis f delaying; inactivity, idleness.

cessātor, -ōris m idler.

cessī perf of **cēdō**.

cessiō, -ōnis f giving up.

cessō, -āre, -āvī, -ātum vi to be remiss, stop; to loiter, delay; to be idle, rest, do nothing; (land) to lie fallow; to err.

cestrosphendonē, -ēs f (MIL) engine for shooting stones.

cestus, -ī m girdle (esp of Venus).

cētārium, -ī and **iī** nt fishpond.

cētārius, -ī and **iī** m fishmonger.

cētera adv in other respects.

cēterī, -ōrum adj the rest, the others; (sg) the rest of.

cēterōquī, -n adv otherwise.

cēterum adv for the rest, otherwise; but for all that; besides.

Cethēgus, -ī m a conspirator with Catiline.

cētr- etc see **caetr-**.

cette etc see **cedo**.

cētus, -ī m (-ē ntpl) sea monster, whale.

ceu adv just as, as if.

Cēus adj see **Cēa**.

Cēyx, -ȳcis m husband of Alcyone, changed to a kingfisher.

Chalcidēnsis, (-discus) adj see n.

Chalcis, -dis f chief town of Euboea.

Chaldaeī, -aeōrum mpl Chaldeans; astrologers.

Chaldāicus adj see n.

chalybēius adj of steel.

Chalybes, -um mpl a people of Pontus (famous as ironworkers).

chalybs, -is m steel.

Chāones, -um mpl a people of Epirus.

Chāonia, -iae f Epirus.

Chāonius, -is adj see n.

Chaos (abl -ō) nt empty space, the lower world, chaos.

chara, -ae f an unidentified vegetable.

charistia, -ōrum ntpl a Roman family festival.

Charites, -um fpl the Graces.

Charōn, -ontis m Charon (ferryman of Hades).

charta, -ae f sheet of papyrus, paper; writing.

chartula, -ae f piece of paper.

Charybdis, -is f monster personifying a whirlpool in the Straits of Messina; (fig) peril.

Chattī, -ōrum mpl a people of central Germany.

Chēlae, -ārum fpl (ASTRO) the Claws (of Scorpio), Libra.

chelydrus, -ī m watersnake.

chelys (acc -yn) f tortoise; lyre.

cheragra, -ae f gout in the hands.

Cherronēsus, Chersonēsus, -ī f Gallipoli peninsula; Crimea.

chīliarchus, -ī m officer in charge of 1000 men; chancellor of Persia.

Chimaera, -ae f fire-breathing monster formed of lion, goat and serpent.

Chimaeriferus adj birthplace of Chimaera.

Chios, -ī f Aegean island (famous for wine).

Chīus adj Chian ♦ nt Chian wine; Chian cloth.

chīrographum, -ī nt handwriting; document.

Chīrōn, -ōnis m a learned Centaur (tutor of heroes).

chīronomos, -ī m/f, **chīronomōn, -untis** m mime actor.

chiūrūrgia, -ae f surgery; (fig) violent measures.

chlamydātus adj wearing a military cloak.

chlamys, -dis f Greek military cloak.

Choerilus, -ī m inferior Greek poet.

chorāgium, -i and **iī** nt producing of a chorus.

chorāgus, -ī m one who finances a chorus.

choraulēs, -ae m flute-player (accompanying a chorus).

chorda, -ae f string (of an instrument); rope.

chorēa, -ae f dance.

chorēus, -ī m trochee.

chorus, -ī m choral dance; chorus, choir of singers or dancers; band, troop.

Christiānismus, -ī m Christianity.

Christiānus adj Christian.

Christus, -ī m Christ.

Chrȳsēis, -ēidis f daughter of Chrȳsēs.

Chrȳsēs, -ae m priest of Apollo in the Iliad.

Chrȳsippēus adj see n.

Chrȳsippus, -ī m Stoic philosopher.

chrȳsolithos, -ī m/f topaz.

chrȳsos, -ī m gold.

cibārius adj food (in cpds); common ♦ ntpl rations.

cibātus, -ūs m food.

cibōrium, -ī and **iī** nt kind of drinking cup.

cibus, -ī m food, fodder, nourishment.

cicāda, -ae f cicada, cricket.

cicātrīcōsus adj scarred.

cicātrix, -īcis f scar; (plants) mark of an incision.

ciccus, -ī m pomegranate pip.

cicer, -is nt chickpea.

Cicerō, -ōnis m great Roman orator and author.

Cicerōniānus adj see n.

cichorēum, -ī nt chicory.

Cicōnes, -um mpl people of Thrace.

cicōnia, -ae f stork.

cicur, -is adj tame.

cicūta, -ae f hemlock; pipe.

cieō, ciēre, cīvī, citum vt to move, stir, rouse; to call, invoke; (fig) to give rise to, produce; **calcem ~** make a move (in chess).

Cilicia, -ae f country in S. Asia Minor (famous for piracy).

Ciliciēnsis, (-us) adj see n.

Cilix, -cis, -ssa *adj* Cilician ♦ *nt* goats' hair garment.
Cimbrī, -ōrum *mpl* people of N. Germany.
Cimbricus *adj see n.*
cīmex, -icis *m* bug.
Cimmeriī, -ōrum *mpl* people of the Crimea; mythical race in caves near Cumae.
Cimmerius *adj see n.*
cinaedius *adj* lewd.
cinaedus, -ī *m* sodomite; lewd dancer.
cincinnātus *adj* with curled hair.
Cincinnātus, -ī *m* ancient Roman dictator.
cincinnus, -ī *m* curled hair; (*fig*) rhetorical ornament.
Cincius, -ī *m* Roman tribune; Roman historian.
cincticulus, -ī *m* small girdle.
cinctus *ppp of* **cingō.**
cinctus, -ūs *m* girding; ~ **Gabīnus** *a ceremonial style of wearing the toga.*
cinctūtus *adj* girded.
cinefactus *adj* reduced to ashes.
cinerārius, -ī *and* **iī** *m* hair curler.
cingō, -gere, -xī, -ctum *vt* to surround, enclose; to gird, crown; (*MIL*) to besiege, fortify; to cover, escort; **ferrum ~or** I put on my sword.
cingula, -ae *f* girth (*of animals*).
cingulum, -ī *nt* belt.
cingulus, -ī *m* zone.
ciniflō, -ōnis *m* hair curler.
cinis, -eris *m* ashes; (*fig*) ruin.
Cinna, -ae *m* colleague of Marius; poet friend of Catullus.
cinnamōmum, cinnamum, -ī *nt* cinnamon.
cinxī *perf of* **cingō.**
Cinyphius *adj* of the Cinyps, river of N. Africa; African.
Cinyrās, -ae *m* father of Adonis.
Cinyrēius *adj see n.*
cippus, -ī *m* tombstone; (*pl*) palisade.
circā *adv* around, round about ♦ *prep* (*with acc*) (*place*) round, in the vicinity of, in; (*time, number*) about; with regard to.
Circaeus *adj see* **Circē.**
circamoerium, -ī *and* **iī** *nt* space on both sides of a wall.
Circē, -ēs *and* **ae** *f* goddess with magic powers living in Aeaea.
circēnsēs, -ium *mpl* the games.
circēnsis *adj* of the Circus.
circinō, -āre *vt* to circle through.
circinus, -ī *m* pair of compasses.
circiter *adv* (*time, number*) about ♦ *prep* (*with acc*) about, near.
circueō, circumeō, -ire, -īvī *and* **iī, -itum** *vt, vi* to go round, surround; (*MIL*) to encircle; to visit, go round canvassing; to deceive.
circuitiō, -ōnis *f* (*MIL*) rounds; (*speech*) evasiveness.
circuitus *ppp of* **circueō.**

circuitus, -ūs *m* revolution; way round, circuit; (*RHET*) period, periphrasis.
circulātor, -ōris *m* pedlar.
circulor, -ārī *vi* to collect in crowds.
circulus, -ī *m* circle; orbit; ring; social group.
circum *adv* round about ♦ *prep* (*with acc*) round, about; near; ~ **īnsulās mittere** send to the islands round about.
circumagō, -agere, -ēgī, -āctum *vt* to turn, move in a circle, wheel; (*pass: time*) to pass; (*: mind*) to be swayed.
circumarō, -āre *vt* to plough round.
circumcaesūra, -ae *f* outline.
circumcīdō, -dere, -dī, -sum *vt* to cut round, trim; to cut down, abridge.
circumcircā *adv* all round.
circumcīsus *ppp of* **circumcīdō** ♦ *adj* precipitous.
circumclūdō, -dere, -sī, -sum *vt* to shut in, hem in.
circumcolō, -ere *vt* to live round about.
circumcursō, -āre *vi* to run about.
circumdō, -are, -edī, -atum *vt* to put round; to surround, enclose.
circumdūcō, -ūcere, -ūxī, -uctum *vt* to lead round, draw round; to cheat; (*speech*) to prolong, drawl.
circumductus *ppp of* **circumdūcō.**
circumeō *etc see* **circueō.**
circumequitō, -āre *vt* to ride round.
circumferō, -ferre, -tulī, -lātum *vt* to carry round, pass round; to spread, broadcast; to purify; (*pass*) to revolve.
circumflectō, -ctere, -xī, -xum *vt* to wheel round.
circumflō, -āre *vt* (*fig*) to buffet.
circumfluō, -ere, -xī *vt, vi* to flow round; (*fig*) to overflow, abound.
circumfluus *adj* flowing round; surrounded (by water).
circumforāneus *adj* itinerant; (*money*) borrowed.
circumfundō, -undere, -ūdī, -ūsum *vt* to pour round, surround; (*fig*) to crowd round, overwhelm; (*pass*) to flow round.
circumgemō, -ere *vt* to growl round.
circumgestō, -āre *vt* to carry about.
circumgredior, -dī, -ssus *vt, vi* to make an encircling move, surround.
circumiaceō, -ēre *vi* to be adjacent.
circumiciō, -icere, -iēcī, -iectum *vt* to throw round, put round; to surround.
circumiecta *ntpl* neighbourhood.
circumiectus *adj* surrounding.
circumiectus, -ūs *m* enclosure; embrace.
circumit- *etc see* **circuit-.**
circumitiō, -ōnis *f see* **circuitiō.**
circumitus, -ūs *m see* **circuitus.**
circumlātus *ppp of* **circumferō.**
circumligō, -āre, -āvī, -ātum *vt* to tie to, bind

Noun declensions and verb conjugations are shown on pp xiii to xxv. The present infinitive ending of a verb shows to which conjugation it belongs: **-āre** = 1st; **-ēre** = 2nd; **-ere** = 3rd and **-īre** = 4th. Irregular verbs are shown on p xxvi

round.

circumlinō, -ere, -tum *vt* to smear all over, bedaub.

circumluō, -ere *vt* to wash.

circumluviō, -ōnis *f* alluvial land.

circummittō, -ittere, -īsī, -issum *vt* to send round.

circummoeniō (circummūniō), -īre, -īvī, -ītum *vt* to fortify.

circummūnītiō, -ōnis *f* investing.

circumpadānus *adj* of the Po valley.

circumpendeō, -ēre *vi* to hang round.

circumplaudō, -ere *vt* to applaud on all sides.

circumplector, -ctī, -xus *vt* to embrace, surround.

circumplicō, -āre, -āvī, -ātum *vt* to wind round.

circumpōnō, -pōnere, -posuī, -positum *vt* to put round.

circumpōtātiō, -ōnis *f* passing drinks round.

circumrētiō, -īre, -īvī, -ītum *vt* to ensnare.

circumrōdō, -rosī, -rodere *vt* to nibble round about; (*fig*) to slander.

circumsaepiō, -īre, -sī, -tum *vt* to fence round.

circumscindō, -ere *vt* to strip.

circumscrībō, -bere, -psī, -ptum *vt* to draw a line round; to mark the limits of; to restrict, circumscribe; to set aside; to defraud.

circumscriptē *adv* in periods.

circumscriptiō, -ōnis *f* circle, contour; fraud; (*RHET*) period.

circumscriptor, -ōris *m* defrauder.

circumscriptus *ppp of* **circumscrībō** ♦ *adj* restricted; (*RHET*) periodic.

circumsecō, -āre *vt* to cut round.

circumsedeō, -edēre, -ēdī, -essum *vt* to blockade, beset.

circumsēpiō *etc see* **circumsaepiō**.

circumsessiō, -ōnis *f* siege.

circumsessus *ppp of* **circumsedeō**.

circumsīdō, -ere *vt* to besiege.

circumsiliō, -īre *vi* to hop about; (*fig*) to be rampant.

circumsistō, -sistere, -stetī surround.

circumsonō, -āre *vi* to resound on all sides ♦ *vt* to fill with sound.

circumsonus *adj* noisy.

circumspectātrīx, -īcis *f* spy.

circumspectiō, -ōnis *f* caution.

circumspectō, -āre *vt, vi* to look all round, search anxiously, be on the lookout.

circumspectus *ppp of* **circumspiciō** ♦ *adj* carefully considered, cautious.

circumspectus, -ūs *m* consideration; view.

circumspiciō, -icere, -exī, -ectum *vi* to look all round; to be careful ♦ *vt* to survey; (*fig*) to consider, search for.

circumstantēs, -antium *mpl* bystanders.

circumstetī *perf of* **circumsistō**; *perf of* **circumstō**.

circumstō, -āre, -etī *vt, vi* to stand round; to

besiege; (*fig*) to encompass.

circumstrepō, -ere *vt* to make a clamour round.

circumsurgēns, -entis *pres p* rising on all sides.

circumtentus *adj* covered tightly.

circumterō, -ere *vt* to crowd round.

circumtextus *adj* embroidered round the edge.

circumtonō, -āre, -uī *vt* to thunder about.

circumvādō, -dere, -sī *vt* to assail on all sides.

circumvagus *adj* encircling.

circumvallō, -āre, -āvī, -ātum *vt* to blockade, beset.

circumvectiō, -ōnis *f* carrying about; (*sun*) revolution.

circumvector, -ārī *vi* to travel round, cruise round; (*fig*) describe.

circumvehor, -hī, -ctus *vt, vi* to ride round, sail round; (*fig*) to describe.

circumvēlō, -āre *vt* to envelop.

circumveniō, -enīre, -ēnī, -entum *vt* to surround, beset; to oppress; to cheat.

circumvertō, circumvortō, -ere *vt* to turn round.

circumvestiō, -īre *vt* to envelop.

circumvinciō, -īre *vt* to lash about.

circumvīsō, -ere *vt* to look at all round.

circumvolitō, -āre, -āvī, -ātum *vt, vi* to fly round; to hover around.

circumvolō, -āre *vt* to fly round.

circumvolvō, -vere *vt* to roll round.

circus, -ī *m* circle; the Circus Maximus (*famous Roman racecourse*); a racecourse.

Cirrha, -ae *f* town near Delphi (*sacred to Apollo*).

Cirrhaeus *adj see n.*

cirrus, -ī *m* curl of hair; fringe.

cis *prep* (*with acc*) on this side of; (*time*) within.

Cisalpīnus *adj* on the Italian side of the Alps, Cisalpine.

cisium, -ī *and* **iī** *nt* two-wheeled carriage.

Cissēis, -dis *f* Hecuba.

cista, -ae *f* box, casket; ballot box.

cistella, -ae *f* small box.

cistellātrīx, -īcis *f* keeper of the moneybox.

cistellula, -ae *f* little box.

cisterna, -ae *f* reservoir.

cistophorus, -ī *m* an Asiatic coin.

cistula, -ae *f* little box.

citātus *adj* quick, impetuous.

citerior (*sup* **-imus**) *adj* on this side, nearer.

Cithaerōn, -ōnis *m* mountain range between Attica and Boeotia.

cithara, -ae *f* lute.

citharista, -ae *m*, **citharistria, -ae** *f* lute player.

citharizō, -āre *vi* to play the lute.

citharoedus, -ī *m* a singer who accompanies himself on the lute.

citimus *adj* nearest.

citō (*com* **-ius**, *sup* **-issimē**) *adv* quickly, soon;

nōn ~ not easily.

citō, -āre, -āvī, -ātum *vt* to set in motion, rouse; to call (by name), appeal to, cite, mention.

citrā *adv* on this side, this way, not so far ♦ *prep* (*with acc*) on this side of, short of; (*time*) before, since; apart from; **~ quam** before.

citreus *adj* of citrus wood.

citrō *adv* hither, this way; **ultrō ~que** to and fro.

citrus, -ī *f* citrus tree; citron tree.

citus *ppp of* **cieō** ♦ *adj* quick.

cīvicus *adj* civic, civil; **corōna ~a** civic crown for saving a citizen's life in war.

cīvīlis *adj* of citizens, civil; political, civilian; courteous, democratic; **iūs ~e** civil rights; Civil Law; code of legal procedure.

cīvīlitās, -ātis *f* politics; politeness.

cīvīliter *adv* like citizens; courteously.

cīvis, -is *m/f* citizen, fellow citizen.

cīvitās, -ātis *f* citizenship; community state; city; **~āte dōnāre** naturalize.

clādēs, -is *f* damage, disaster, ruin; defeat; (*fig*) scourge; **dare ~em** make havoc.

clam *adv* secretly; unknown ♦ *prep* (*with acc*) unknown to; **~ mē habēre** keep from me.

clāmātor, -ōris *m* bawler.

clāmitātiō, -ōnis *f* bawling.

clāmitō, -āre, -āvī, -ātum *vt, vi* to bawl, screech, cry out.

clāmō, -āre, -āvī, -ātum *vt, vi* to shout, cry out; to call upon, proclaim.

clāmor, -ōris *m* shout, cry; acclamation.

clāmōsus *adj* noisy.

clanculum *adv* secretly ♦ *prep* (*with acc*) unknown to.

clandestīnō *adv see* **clandestīnus**.

clandestīnus *adj* secret.

clangor, -ōris *m* clang, noise.

clārē *adv* brightly, loudly, clearly, with distinction.

clāreō, -ēre *vi* to be bright, be clear; to be evident; to be renowned.

clārēscō, -ere, clāruī *vi* to brighten, sound clear; to become obvious; to become famous.

clārigātiō, -ōnis *f* formal ultimatum to an enemy; fine for trespass.

clārigō, -āre *vi* to deliver a formal ultimatum.

clārisonus *adj* loud and clear.

clāritās, -ātis *f* distinctness; (*RHET*) lucidity; celebrity.

clāritūdō, -inis *f* brightness; (*fig*) distinction.

Clarius *adj* of Claros ♦ *m* Apollo.

clārō, -āre *vt* to illuminate; to explain; to make famous.

Claros, -ī *f* town in Ionia (*famous for worship of Apollo*).

clārus *adj* (*sight*) bright; (*sound*) loud; (*mind*) clear; (*person*) distinguished; **~ intonāre**

thunder from a clear sky; **vir ~issimus** a courtesy title for eminent men.

classiārius *adj* naval ♦ *mpl* marines.

classicula, -ae *f* flotilla.

classicum, -ī *nt* battle-signal; trumpet.

classicus *adj* of the first class; naval ♦ *mpl* marines.

classis, -is *f* a political class; army; fleet.

clāthrī, -ōrum *mpl* cage.

clātrātus *adj* barred.

clātrī, -ōrum *mpl see* **clāthrī**.

claudeō, -ēre *vi* to limp; (*fig*) to be defective.

claudicātiō, -ōnis *f* limping.

claudicō, -āre *vi* to be lame; to waver, be defective.

Claudius, -ī *m* patrician family name (*esp Appius Claudius Caecus, famous censor*); *the Emperor Claudius*.

Claudius, -iānus, -iālis *adj see n.*

claudō, -dere, -sī, -sum *vt* to shut, close; to cut off, block; to conclude; to imprison, confine, blockade; **agmen ~** bring up the rear.

claudō, -ere *etc see* **claudeō**.

claudus *adj* lame, crippled; (*verse*) elegiac; (*fig*) wavering.

clausī *perf of* **claudō**.

claustra, -ōrum *ntpl* bar, bolt, lock; barrier, barricade, dam.

clausula, -ae *f* conclusion; (*RHET*) ending of a period.

clausum, -ī *nt* enclosure.

clausus *ppp of* **claudō**.

clāva, -ae *f* club, knotty branch; (*MIL*) foil.

clāvārium, -ī and iī *nt* money for buying shoe nails.

clāvātor, -ōris *m* cudgel-bearer.

clāvicula, -ae *f* vine tendril.

clāviger, -ī *m* (*Hercules*) club bearer; (*Janus*) key-bearer.

clāvis, -is *f* key.

clāvus, -ī *m* nail; tiller, rudder; purple stripe on the tunic (*broad for senators, narrow for equites*); **~um annī movēre** reckon the beginning of the year.

Cleanthēs, -is *m* Stoic philosopher.

clēmēns, -entis *adj* mild, gentle, merciful; (*weather, water*) mild, calm.

clēmenter *adv* gently, indulgently; gradually.

clēmentia, -ae *f* mildness, forbearance, mercy.

Cleopatra, -ae *f* queen of Egypt.

clepō, -ere, -sī, -tum *vt* to steal.

clepsydra, -ae *f* waterclock (*used for timing speakers*); **~am dare** give leave to speak; **~am petere** ask leave to speak.

clepta, -ae *m* thief.

cliēns, -entis *m* client, dependant; follower; vassal-state.

clienta, -ae *f* client.

Noun declensions and verb conjugations are shown on pp xiii to xxv. The present infinitive ending of a verb shows to which conjugation it belongs: **-āre** = 1st; **-ēre** = 2nd; **-ere** = 3rd and **-īre** = 4th. Irregular verbs are shown on p xxvi

clientēla, -ae f clientship, protection; clients.
clientulus, -ī m insignificant client.
clīnāmen, -inis nt swerve.
clīnātus adj inclined.
Cliō, -ūs f Muse of history.
clipeātus adj armed with a shield.
clipeus, -ī m, **-um, -ī** nt round bronze shield; disc; medallion on a metal base.
clitellae, -ārum fpl packsaddle, attribute of an ass.
clitellārius adj carrying packsaddles.
Clitumnus, -ī m river in Umbria.
clīvōsus adj hilly.
clīvus, -ī m slope, hill; ~ **sacer** part of the Via Sacra.
cloāca, -ae f sewer, drain.
Cloācīna, -ae f Venus.
Clōdius, -ī m Roman plebeian name (esp the tribune, enemy of Cicero).
Cloelia, -ae f Roman girl hostage (who escaped by swimming the Tiber).
Clōthō (acc -ō) f one of the Fates.
clueō, -ēre, -eor, -ērī vi to be called, be famed.
clūnis, -is m/f buttock.
clūrīnus adj of apes.
Clūsīnus adj see n.
Clūsium, -ī nt old Etruscan town (now Chiusi).
Clūsius, -ī m Janus.
Clytaemnēstra, -ae f wife of Agamemnon (whom she murdered).
Cnidius adj see n.
Cnidus, -ī f town in Caria (famous for worship of Venus).
coacervātiō, -ōnis f accumulation.
coacervō, -āre vt to heap, accumulate.
coacēscō, -ēscere, -uī vi to become sour.
coāctō, -āre vt to force.
coāctor, -ōris m collector (of money).
coāctōrēs agminis rearguard.
coāctum, -ī nt thick coverlet.
coāctus adj forced.
coāctus ppp of **cōgō**.
coāctus, -ūs m compulsion.
coaedificō, -āre, -ātum vt to build on.
coaequō, -āre, -āvī, -ātum vt to make equal, bring down to the same level.
coagmentātiō, -ōnis f combination.
coagmentō, -āre, -āvī, -ātum vt to glue, join together.
coagmentum, -ī nt joining, joint.
coāgulum, -ī nt rennet.
coalēscō, -ēscere, -uī, -itum vi to grow together; (fig) to agree together; to flourish.
coangustō, -āre vt to restrict.
coarct- etc see **coart-**.
coarguō, -ere, -ī vt to convict, prove conclusively.
coartātiō, -ōnis f crowding together.
coartō, -āre, -āvī, -ātum vt to compress, abridge.
coccineus, coccinus adj scarlet.
coccum, -ī nt scarlet.

cochlea, coclea, -ae f snail.
cocleāre, -is nt spoon.
cocles, -itis m man blind in one eye; surname of Horatius who defended the bridge.
coctilis adj baked; of bricks.
coctus ppp of **coquō ♦** adj (fig) well considered.
cocus etc see **coquus**.
Cōcȳtius adj see n.
Cōcȳtos, -us, -ī m river in the lower world.
cōda etc see **cauda**.
cōdex etc see **caudex**.
cōdicillī, -ōrum mpl letter, note, petition; codicil.
Codrus, -ī m last king of Athens.
coēgī perf of **cōgō**.
coel- etc see **cael-**.
coemō, -emere, -ēmī, -emptum vt to buy up.
coemptiō, -ōnis f a form of Roman marriage; mock sale of an estate.
coemptiōnālis adj used in a mock sale; worthless.
coen- etc see **caen-** or **cēn-**.
coeō, -īre, -īvī and **iī, -itum** vi to meet, assemble; to encounter; to combine, mate; (wounds) to close; to agree, conspire ♦ vt: ~ **societātem** make a compact.
coepiō, -ere, -ī, -tum vt, vi begin (esp in perf tenses); **rēs agī ~tae sunt** things began to be done; **coepisse** to have begun.
coeptō, -āre, -āvī, -ātum vt, vi to begin, attempt.
coeptum, -ī nt beginning, undertaking.
coeptus ppp of **coepiō**.
coeptus, -ūs m beginning.
coepulōnus, -ī m fellow-banqueter.
coerātor etc see **cūrātor**.
coerceō, -ēre, -uī, -itum vt to enclose; to confine, repress; (fig) to control, check, correct.
coercitiō, -ōnis f coercion, punishment.
coetus, coitus, -ūs m meeting, joining together; assembly, crowd.
cōgitātē adv deliberately.
cōgitātiō, -ōnis f thought, reflection; idea, plan; faculty of thought, imagination.
cōgitātus adj deliberate ♦ ntpl ideas.
cōgitō, -āre, -āvī, -ātum vt, vi to think, ponder, imagine; to feel disposed; to plan, intend.
cognātiō, -ōnis f relationship (by blood); kin, family; (fig) affinity, resemblance.
cognātus, -ī m, **-a, -ae** f relation ♦ adj related; (fig) connected, similar.
cognitiō, -ōnis f acquiring of knowledge, knowledge; idea, notion; (law) judicial inquiry; (comedy) recognition.
cognitor, -ōris m (law) attorney; witness of a person's identity; (fig) defender.
cognitus adj acknowledged.
cognitus ppp of **cognōscō**.
cognōmen, -inis nt surname; name.
cognōmentum, -ī nt surname, name.

cognōminis *adj* with the same name.

cognōminō, -āre, -āvī, -ātum *vt* to give a surname to; **verba ~āta** synonyms.

cognōscō, -ōscere, -ōvī, -itum *vt* to get to know, learn, understand; to know, recognize, identify; (*law*) to investigate; (*MIL*) to reconnoitre.

cōgō, -ere, coēgī, coāctum *vt* to collect, gather together; (*liquids*) to thicken, curdle; to contract, confine; to compel, force; to infer; **agmen ~** bring up the rear; **senātum ~** call a meeting of the senate.

cohaerentia, -ae *f* coherence.

cohaereō, -rēre, -sī, -sum *vi* to stick together, cohere; to cling to; (*fig*) to be consistent, harmonize; to agree, be consistent with.

cohaerēscō, -ere *vi* to stick together.

cohaesus *ppp of* **cohaereō**.

cohērēs, -ēdis *m/f* co-heir.

cohibeō, -ēre, -uī, -itum *vt* to hold together, encircle; to hinder, stop; (*fig*) to restrain, repress.

cohonestō, -āre *vt* to do honour to.

cohorrēscō, -ēscere, -uī *vi* to shudder all over.

cohors, -tis *f* courtyard; (*MIL*) cohort (*about 600 men*); retinue (*esp of the praetor in a province*); (*fig*) company.

cohortātiō, -ōnis *f* encouragement.

cohorticula, -ae *f* small cohort.

cohortor, -ārī, -ātus *vt* to encourage, urge.

coitiō, -ōnis *f* encounter; conspiracy.

coitus *etc see* **coetus**.

colaphus, -ī *m* blow with the fist, box.

Colchis, -idis *f* Medea's country (*at the E. end of the Black Sea*).

Colchis, -us, -icus *adj* Colchian.

cōleus *etc see* **culleus**.

cōlis *etc see* **caulis**.

collabāscō, -ere *vi* to waver also.

collabefactō, -āre *vt* to shake violently.

collabefīō, -fierī, -factus *vi* to be destroyed.

collābor, -bī, -psus *vi* to fall in ruin, collapse.

collacerātus *adj* torn to pieces.

collacrimātiō, -ōnis *f* weeping.

collactea, -ae *f* foster-sister.

collāpsus *ppa of* **collābor**.

collāre, -is *nt* neckband.

Collātia, -iae *f* ancient town near Rome ♦ *m* husband of Lucretia.

Collātīnus *adj* of Collatia.

collātiō, -ōnis *f* bringing together, combination; (*money*) contribution; (*RHET*) comparison; (*PHILOS*) analogy.

collātor, -ōris *m* contributor.

collātus *ppp of* **cōnferō**.

collaudātiō, -ōnis *f* praise.

collaudō, -āre, -āvī, -ātum *vt* to praise highly.

collaxō, -āre *vt* to make porous.

collēcta, -ae *f* money contribution.

collēctīcius *adj* hastily gathered.

collēctiō, -ōnis *f* gathering up; (*RHET*) recapitulation.

collēctus *ppp of* **colligō**.

collēctus, -ūs *m* accumulation.

collēga, -ae *m* colleague; associate.

collēgī *perf of* **colligō**.

collēgium, -ī *and* **iī** *nt* association in office; college, guild (*of magistrates, etc*).

collībertus, -ī *m* fellow freedman.

collibet, collubet, -uit *and* **itum est** *vi* it pleases.

collīdō, -dere, -sī, -sum *vt* to beat together, strike, bruise; (*fig*) to bring into conflict.

colligātiō, -ōnis *f* connection.

colligō, -āre, -āvī, -ātum *vt* to fasten, tie up; (*fig*) to combine; to restrain, check.

colligō, -igere, -ēgī, -ēctum *vt* to gather, collect; to compress, draw together; to check; (*fig*) to acquire; to think about; to infer, conclude; **animum, mentem ~** recover, rally; **sē ~** crouch; recover one's courage; **vāsa ~** (*MIL*) pack up.

Collīna Porta gate in N.E. of Rome.

collīneō, -āre *vt, vi* to aim straight.

collinō, -inere, -ēvī, -itum *vt* to besmear; (*fig*) to deface.

colliquefactus *adj* dissolved.

collis, -is *m* hill, slope.

collīsī *perf of* **collīdō**.

collīsus *ppp of* **collīdō**.

collitus *ppp of* **collinō**.

collocātiō, -ōnis *f* arrangement; giving in marriage.

collocō, -āre, -āvī, -ātum *vt* to place, station, arrange; to give in marriage; (*money*) to invest; (*fig*) to establish; to occupy, employ.

collocuplētō, -āre, -āvī *vt* to enrich.

collocūtiō, -ōnis *f* conversation.

colloquium, -ī *and* **iī** *nt* conversation, conference.

colloquor, -quī, -cūtus *vi* to converse, hold a conference ♦ *vt* to talk to.

collubet *etc see* **collibet**.

collūceō, -ēre *vi* to shine brightly; (*fig*) to be resplendent.

collūdō, -dere, -sī, -sum *vi* to play together *or* with; to practise collusion.

collum, -ī *nt* neck; **~ torquēre, obtorquēre, obstringere** arrest.

colluō, -uere, -uī, -ūtum *vt* to rinse, moisten.

collus *etc see* **collum**.

collūsiō, -ōnis *f* secret understanding.

collūsor, -ōris *m* playmate, fellow gambler.

collūstrō, -āre, -āvī, -ātum *vt* to light up; to survey.

colluviō, -ōnis, -ēs, -em, -ē *f* sweepings, filth; (*fig*) dregs, rabble.

Noun declensions and verb conjugations are shown on pp xiii to xxv. The present infinitive ending of a verb shows to which conjugation it belongs: **-āre** = 1st; **-ēre** = 2nd; **-ere** = 3rd and **-īre** = 4th. Irregular verbs are shown on p xxvi

collybus, -ī m money exchange, rate of exchange.

collȳra, -ae f vermicelli.

collȳricus adj see n.

collȳrium, -ī and **iī** nt eye lotion.

colō, -ere, -uī, cultum vt (AGR) to cultivate, work; (place) to live in; (human affairs) to cherish, protect, adorn; (qualities, pursuits) to cultivate, practise; (gods) to worship; (men) to honour, court; **vītam ~** live.

colocāsia, -ae f, **-a, -ōrum** ntpl Egyptian bean, caladium.

colōna, -ae f country-woman.

colōnia, -ae f settlement, colony; settlers.

colōnicus adj colonial.

colōnus, -ī m crofter, farmer; settler, colonist.

color (colōs), -ōris m colour; complexion; beauty, lustre; (fig) outward show; (RHET) style, tone; colourful excuse; **~ōrem mūtāre** blush, go pale; **homō nullīus ~ōris** an unknown person.

colōrātus adj healthily tanned.

colōrō, -āre, -āvī, -ātum vt to colour, tan; (fig) to give a colour to.

colossus, -ī m gigantic statue (esp that of Apollo at Rhodes).

colostra, colustra, -ae f beestings.

coluber, -rī m snake.

colubra, -ae f snake.

colubrifer, -ī adj snaky.

colubrīnus adj wily.

coluī perf of **colō.**

cōlum, -ī nt strainer.

columba, -ae f dove, pigeon.

columbar, -āris nt kind of collar.

columbārium, -ī and **iī** nt dovecote.

columbīnus adj pigeon's ♦ m little pigeon.

columbus, -ī m dove, cock-pigeon.

columella, -ae f small pillar.

columen, -inis nt height, summit; pillar; (fig) chief; prop.

columna, -ae f column, pillar; a pillory in the Forum Romanum; waterspout.

columnārium, -ī and **iī** nt pillar tax.

columnārius, -ī m criminal.

columnātus adj pillared.

colurnus adj made of hazel.

colus, -ī and **ūs** f (occ m) distaff.

colȳphia, -ōrum ntpl food of athletes.

coma, -ae f hair (of the head); foliage.

comāns, -antis adj hairy, plumed; leafy.

cōmarchus, -ī m burgomaster.

comātus adj long-haired; leafy; **Gallia ~** Transalpine Gaul.

combibō, -ere, -ī vt to drink to the full, absorb.

combibō, -ōnis m fellow-drinker.

combūrō, -rere, -ssī, -stum vt to burn up; (fig) to ruin.

combustus ppp of **combūrō.**

comedō, -ēsse, -ēdī, -ēsum and **-ēstum** vt to eat up, devour; (fig) to waste, squander; **sē ~**

pine away.

Cōmēnsis adj see **Cōmum.**

comes, -itis m/f companion, partner; attendant, follower; one of a magistrate's or emperor's retinue; (medieval title) count.

comēs, comēst pres tense of **comedō.**

comēstus, comēsus ppp of **comedō.**

comētēs, -ae m comet.

cōmicē adv in the manner of comedy.

cōmicus, -ī m comedy actor, comedy writer ♦ adj of comedy, comic.

cōmis adj courteous, friendly.

cōmissābundus adj carousing.

cōmissātiō, -ōnis f Bacchanalian revel.

cōmissātor, -ōris m reveller.

cōmissor, -ārī, -ātus vi to carouse, make merry.

cōmitās, -ātis f kindness, affability.

comitātus, -ūs m escort, retinue; company.

cōmiter adv see **cōmis.**

comitia, -iōrum ntpl assembly for the election of magistrates and other business (esp the ~ **centuriāta**); elections.

comitiālis adj of the elections; ~ **morbus** epilepsy.

comitiātus, -ūs m assembly at the elections.

comitium, -ī and **iī** nt place of assembly.

comitō, -āre, -āvī, -ātum vt to accompany.

comitor, -ārī, -ātus vt, vi to attend, follow.

commaculō, -āre, -āvī, -ātum vt to stain, defile.

commanipulāris, -is m soldier in the same company.

commeātus, -ūs m passage; leave, furlough; convoy (of troops or goods); (MIL) lines of communication, provisions, supplies.

commeditor, -ārī vt to practise.

commeminī, -isse vt, vi to remember perfectly.

commemorābilis adj memorable.

commemorātiō, -ōnis f recollection, recounting.

commemorō, -āre, -āvī, -ātum vt to recall, remind; to mention, relate.

commendābilis adj praiseworthy.

commendātīcius adj of recommendation or introduction.

commendātiō, -ōnis f recommendation; worth, excellence.

commendātor, -ōris m commender (male).

commendātrīx, -rīcis f commender (female).

commendātus adj approved, valued.

commendō, -āre, -āvī, -ātum vt to entrust, commit, commend (to one's care or charge); to recommend, set off to advantage.

commēnsus ppa of **commētior.**

commentāriolum, -ī nt short treatise.

commentārius, -ī and **iī** m, **-ium, -ī** and **iī** nt notebook; commentary, memoir; (law) brief.

commentātiō, -ōnis f studying, meditation.

commentīcius adj fictitious, imaginary; false.

commentor, -ārī, -ātus vt, vi to study, think

over, prepare carefully; to invent, compose, write.

commentor, -ōris *m* inventor.

commentum, -ī *nt* invention, fiction; contrivance.

commentus *ppa of* **comminīscor ♦** *adj* feigned, fictitious.

commeō, -āre *vi* to pass to and fro; to go *or* come often.

commercium, -ī *and* **iī** *nt* trade, commerce; right to trade; dealings, communication.

commercor, -ārī, -ātus *vt* to buy up.

commereō, -ēre, -uī, -itum; -eor, -ērī, -itus *vt* to deserve; to be guilty of.

commētior, -tīrī, -nsus *vt* to measure.

commētō, -āre *vi* to go often.

commictus *ppp of* **commingō**.

commigrō, -āre, -āvī, -ātum *vi* to remove, migrate.

commīlitium, -ī *and* **iī** *nt* service together.

commīlitō, -ōnis *m* fellow soldier.

comminātiō, -ōnis *f* threat.

commingō, -ingere, -īnxī, -ictum *vt* to pollute.

comminīscor, -ī, commentus *vt* to devise, contrive.

comminor, -ārī, -ātus *vt* to threaten.

comminuō, -uere, -uī, -ūtum *vt* to break up, smash; to diminish; to impair.

comminus *adv* hand to hand; near at hand.

commīsceō, -scēre, -scuī, -xtum *vt* to mix together, join together.

commiserātiō, -ōnis *f* (*RHET*) *passage intended to arouse pity.*

commiserēscō, -ere *vt* to pity.

commiseror, -ārī *vt* to bewail ♦ *vi* (*RHET*) to try to excite pity.

commissiō, -ōnis *f* start (*of a contest*).

commissum, -ī *nt* enterprise; offence, crime; secret.

commissūra, -ae *f* joint, connection.

commissus *ppp of* **committō**.

committō, -ittere, -īsī, -issum *vt* to join, connect, bring together; to begin, undertake; (*battle*) to join, engage in; (*offence*) to commit, be guilty of; (*punishment*) to incur, forfeit; to entrust, trust; **sē urbī ~** venture into the city.

commixtus *ppp of* **commisceō**.

commodē *adv* properly, well; aptly, opportunely; pleasantly.

commoditās, -ātis *f* convenience, ease, fitness; advantage; (*person*) kindliness; (*RHET*) apt expression.

commodō, -āre, -āvī, -ātum *vt* to adjust, adapt; to give, lend, oblige with; (*with dat*) to oblige.

commodulē, -um *adv* conveniently.

commodum, -ī *nt* convenience; advantage, interest; pay, salary; loan; **~ō tuō** at your

leisure; **~a vītae** the good things of life.

commodum *adv* opportunely; just.

commodus *adj* proper, fit, full; suitable, easy, opportune; (*person*) pleasant, obliging.

commōlior, -īrī *vt* to set in motion.

commonefaciō, -facere, -fēcī, -factum *vt* to remind, recall.

commoneō, -ēre, -uī, -itum *vt* to remind, impress upon.

commōnstrō, -āre *vt* to point out.

commorātiō, -ōnis *f* delay, residence; (*RHET*) dwelling (on a topic).

commoror, -ārī, -ātus *vi* to sojourn, wait; (*RHET*) to dwell ♦ *vt* to detain.

commōtiō, -ōnis *f* excitement.

commōtiuncula *f* slight indisposition.

commōtus *ppp of* **commoveō ♦** *adj* excited, emotional.

commoveō, -ovēre, -ōvī, -ōtum *vt* to set in motion, move, dislodge, agitate; (*mind*) to unsettle, shake, excite, move, affect; (*emotions*) to stir up, provoke.

commūne, -is *nt* common property; state; **in ~e** for a common end; equally; in general.

commūnicātiō, -ōnis *f* imparting; (*RHET*) *making the audience appear to take part in the discussion.*

commūnicō, -āre, -āvī, -ātum *vt* to share (by giving *or* receiving); to impart, communicate; **cōnsilia ~ cum** make common cause with.

commūniō, -īre, -īvī *and* **iī, -ītum** *vt* to build (a fortification); to fortify, strengthen.

commūniō, -ōnis *f* sharing in common, communion.

commūnis *adj* common, general, universal; (*person*) affable, democratic; **~ia loca** public places; **~ēs locī** general topics; **~is sēnsus** popular sentiment; **aliquid ~e habēre** have something in common.

commūnitās, -ātis *f* fellowship; sense of fellowship; affability.

commūniter *adv* in common, jointly.

commūnītiō, -ōnis *f* preparing the way.

commurmuror, -ārī, -ātus *vi* to mutter to oneself.

commūtābilis *adj* changeable.

commūtātiō, -iōnis *f* change.

commūtātus, -ūs *m* change.

commūtō, -āre, -āvī, -ātum *vt* to change, exchange, interchange.

cōmō, -ere, -psī, -ptum *vt* to arrange, dress, adorn.

cōmoedia, -ae *f* comedy.

cōmoedicē *adv* as in comedy.

cōmoedus, -ī *m* comic actor.

cōmōsus *adj* shaggy.

compāctiō, -ōnis *f* joining together.

compāctus *ppp of* **compingō**.

compāgēs, -is, -ō, -inis *f* joint, structure,

framework.

compār, -aris *m/f* comrade, husband, wife ♦ *adj* equal.

comparābilis *adj* comparable.

comparātē *adv* by bringing in a comparison.

comparātiō, -ōnis *f* comparison; (*ASTRO*) relative positions; agreement; preparation; procuring.

comparātīvus *adj* based on comparison.

compāreō, -ēre *vi* to be visible; to be present, be realised.

comparō, -āre, -āvī, -ātum *vt* to couple together, match; to compare; (*POL*) to agree (about respective duties); to prepare, provide; (*custom*) to establish; to procure, purchase, get.

compāscō, -ere *vt* to put (cattle) to graze in common.

compāscuus *adj* for common pasture.

compecīscor, -īscī, -tus *vi* to come to an agreement.

compectum, -tī *nt* agreement.

compediō, -īre, -ītum *vt* to fetter.

compēgī *perf of* **compingō**.

compellātiō, -ōnis *f* reprimand.

compellō, -āre, -āvī, -ātum *vt* to call, address; to reproach; (*law*) to arraign.

compellō, -ellere, -ulī, -ulsum *vt* to drive, bring together, concentrate; to impel, compel.

compendiārius *adj* short.

compendium, -ī *and* **iī** *nt* saving; abbreviating; short cut; **~ī facere** save; abridge; **~ī fierī** be brief.

compēnsātiō, -ōnis *f* (*fig*) compromise.

compēnsō, -āre, -āvī, -ātum *vt* to balance (against), make up for.

compercō, -cere, -sī *vt, vi* to save; to refrain.

comperendinātiō, -iōnis *f* adjournment for two days.

comperendinātus, -ūs *m* adjournment for two days.

comperendinō, -āre *vt* to adjourn for two days.

comperiō, -īre, -ī, -tum (*occ* **-ior**) *vt* to find out, learn; **~tus** detected; found guilty; **~tum habēre** know for certain.

compēs, -edis *f* fetter, bond.

compēscō, -ere, -uī *vt* to check, suppress.

competītor, -ōris *m*, **-rīx, -rīcis** *f* rival candidate.

competō, -ere, -īvī *and* **iī, -ītum** *vi* to coincide, agree; to be capable.

compīlātiō, -ōnis *f* plundering; compilation.

compīlō, -āre, -āvī, -ātum *vt* to pillage.

compingō, -ingere, -ēgī, -āctum *vt* to put together, compose; to lock up, hide away.

compitālia, -ium *and* **iōrum** *ntpl festival in honour of the Lares Compitales.*

compitālicius *adj* of the Compitalia.

compitālis *adj* of crossroads.

compitum, -ī *nt* crossroads.

complaceō, -ēre, -uī *and* **itus sum** *vi* to please (someone else) as well, please very much.

complānō, -āre *vt* to level, raze to the ground.

complector, -ctī, -xus *vt* to embrace, clasp; to enclose; (*speech, writing*) to deal with, comprise; (*mind*) to grasp, comprehend; to honour, be fond of.

complēmentum, -ī *nt* complement.

compleō, -ēre, -ēvī, -ētum *vt* to fill, fill up; (*MIL*) to man, make up the complement of; (*time, promise, duty*) to complete, fulfil, finish.

complētus *adj* perfect.

complexiō, -ōnis *f* combination; (*RHET*) period; (*logic*) conclusion of an argument; dilemma.

complexus, -ūs *m* embrace; (*fig*) affection, close combat; (*speech*) connection.

complicō, -āre *vt* to fold up.

complōrātiō, -iōnis *f*, **-us, -ūs** *m* loud lamentation.

complōrō, -āre, -āvī, -ātum *vt* to mourn for.

complūrēs, -ium *adj* several, very many.

complūriēns *adv* several times.

complūsculī, -ōrum *adj* quite a few.

compluvium, -ī *and* **iī** *nt* roof opening in a Roman house.

compōnō, -ōnere, -osuī, -ositum *vt* to put together, join; to compose, construct; to compare, contrast; to match, oppose; to put away, store up, stow; (*dead*) to lay out, inter; to allay, quieten, reconcile; to adjust, settle, arrange; to devise, prepare ♦ *vi* to make peace.

comportō, -āre *vt* to collect, bring in.

compos, -tis *adj* in control, in possession; sharing; **vōtī ~** having got one's wish.

compositē *adv* properly, in a polished manner.

compositiō, -ōnis *f* compounding, system; (*words*) arrangement; reconciliation; matching (of fighters).

compositor, -ōris *m* arranger.

compositūra, -ae *f* connection.

compositus *ppp of* **compōnō** ♦ *adj* orderly, regular; adapted, assumed, ready; calm, sedate; (*words*) compound; **compositō, ex compositō** as agreed.

compōtātiō, -ōnis *f* drinking party.

compōtiō, -īre *vt* to put in possession (of).

compōtor, -ōris *m*, **-rīx, -rīcis** *f* fellow drinker.

comprānsor, -ōris *m* fellow guest.

comprecātiō, -ōnis *f* public supplication.

comprecor, -ārī, -ātus *vt, vi* to pray to; to pray for.

comprehendō (comprendō), -endere, -endī, -ēnsum *vt* to grasp, catch; to seize, arrest, catch in the act; (*words*) to comprise, recount; (*thought*) to grasp, comprehend; to hold in affection; **numerō ~** count.

comprehēnsibilis *adj* conceivable.

comprehēnsiō, -ōnis *f* grasping, seizing;

perception, idea; (*RHET*) period.

comprehēnsus, comprēnsus *ppp of* **comprehendō.**

comprendō *etc see* **comprehendō.**

compressī *perf of* **comprimō.**

compressiō, -ōnis *f* embrace; (*RHET*) compression.

compressus *ppp of* **comprimō.**

compressus, -ūs *m* compression, embrace.

comprimō, -imere, -essī, -essum *vt* to squeeze, compress; to check, restrain; to suppress, withhold; **animam ~** hold one's breath; **~essīs manibus** with hands folded, idle.

comprobātiō, -ōnis *f* approval.

comprobātor, -ōris *m* supporter.

comprobō, -āre, -āvī, -ātum *vt* to prove, make good; to approve.

comprōmissum, -ī *nt* mutual agreement to abide by an arbitrator's decision.

comprōmittō, -ittere, -īsī, -issum *vt* to undertake to abide by an arbitrator's decision.

cōmpsī *perf of* **cōmō.**

cōmptus *ppp of* **cōmō** ♦ *adj* elegant.

cōmptus, -ūs *m* coiffure; union.

compulī *perf of* **compellō.**

compulsus *ppp of* **compellō.**

compungō, -ungere, -ūnxī, -ūnctum *vt* to prick, sting, tattoo.

computō, -āre, -āvī, -ātum *vt* to reckon, number.

Cōmum, -ī *nt* (*also* **Novum Cōmum**) town in N. Italy (*now* Como).

cōnāmen, -inis *nt* effort; support.

cōnāta, -ōrum *ntpl* undertaking, venture.

cōnātus, -ūs *m* effort; endeavour; inclination, impulse.

concaedēs, -ium *fpl* barricade of felled trees.

concalefaciō, -facere, -fēcī, -factum *vt* to warm well.

concaleō, -ēre *vi* to be hot.

concalēscō, -ēscere, -uī *vi* to become hot, glow.

concallēscō, -ēscere, -uī *vi* to become shrewd; to become unfeeling.

concastīgō, -āre *vt* to punish severely.

concavō, -āre *vt* to curve.

concavus *adj* hollow; vaulted, bent.

concēdō, -ēdere, -essī, -essum *vi* to withdraw, depart; to disappear, pass away, pass; to yield, submit, give precedence, comply ♦ *vt* to give up, cede; to grant, allow; to pardon, overlook.

concelebrō, -āre, -āvī, -ātum *vt* to frequent, fill, enliven; (*study*) to pursue eagerly; to celebrate; to make known.

concēnātiō, -ōnis *f* dining together.

concentiō, -ōnis *f* chorus.

concenturiō, -āre *vt* to marshal.

concentus, -ūs *m* chorus, concert; (*fig*) concord, harmony.

conceptiō, -ōnis *f* conception; drawing up legal formulae.

conceptīvus *adj* (*holidays*) movable.

conceptus *ppp of* **concipiō.**

conceptus, -ūs *m* conception.

concerpō, -ere, -sī, -tum *vt* to tear up; (*fig*) to abuse.

concertātiō, -ōnis *f* controversy.

concertātor, -ōris *m* rival.

concertātōrius *adj* controversial.

concertō, -āre, -āvī, -ātum *vi* to fight; to dispute.

concessiō, -ōnis *f* grant, permission; (*law*) pleading guilty and asking indulgence.

concessō, -āre *vi* to stop, loiter.

concessus *ppp of* **concēdō.**

concessus, -ūs *m* permission.

concha, -ae *f* mussel, oyster, murex; mussel shell, oyster shell, pearl; purple dye; trumpet, perfume dish.

conchis, -is *f* kind of bean.

conchīta, -ae *m* catcher of shellfish.

conchȳliātus *adj* purple.

conchȳlium, -ī *and* **iī** *nt* shellfish, oyster, murex; purple.

concidō, -ere, -ī *vi* to fall, collapse; to subside, fail, perish.

concīdō, -dere, -dī, -sum *vt* to cut up, cut to pieces, kill; (*fig*) to ruin, strike down; (*RHET*) to dismember, enfeeble.

concieō, -iēre, -īvī, -itum; conciō, -īre, -ītum *vt* to rouse, assemble; to stir up, shake; (*fig*) to rouse, provoke.

conciliābulum, -ī *nt* place for public gatherings.

conciliātiō, -ōnis *f* union; winning over (*friends, hearers*); (*PHILOS*) inclination.

conciliātor, -ōris *m* promoter.

conciliātrīx, -īcis *m*, **-īcula, -ae** *f* promoter, matchmaker.

conciliātus, -ūs *m* combination.

conciliātus *adj* beloved; favourable.

conciliō, -āre, -āvī, -ātum *vt* to unite; to win over, reconcile; to procure, purchase, bring about, promote.

concilium, -ī *and* **iī** *nt* gathering, meeting; council; (*things*) union.

concinnē *adv see* **concinnus.**

concinnitās, -ātis, -ūdō, -ūdinis *f* (*RHET*) rhythmical style.

concinnō, -āre, -āvī, -ātum *vt* to arrange; to bring about, produce; (*with adj*) to make.

concinnus *adj* symmetrical, beautiful; (*style*) polished, rhythmical; (*person*) elegant, courteous; (*things*) suited, pleasing.

concinō, -ere, -uī *vi* to sing, play, sound together; (*fig*) to agree, harmonize ♦ *vt* to sing about, celebrate, prophesy.

Noun declensions and verb conjugations are shown on pp xiii to xxv. The present infinitive ending of a verb shows to which conjugation it belongs: **-āre** = 1st; **-ēre** = 2nd; **-ere** = 3rd and **-īre** = 4th. Irregular verbs are shown on p xxvi

conciō *etc see* **concieō.**

concio- *etc see* **contio-.**

concipiō, -ipere, -ēpī, -eptum *vt* to take to oneself, absorb; (*women*) to conceive; (*senses*) to perceive; (*mind*) to conceive, imagine, understand; (*feelings, acts*) to harbour, foster, commit; (*words*) to draw up, intimate formally.

concīsiō, -ōnis *f* breaking up into short clauses.

concīsus *ppp of* **concīdō** ♦ *adj* broken up, concise.

concitātē *adv see* **concitātus.**

concitātiō, -ōnis *f* acceleration; (*mind*) excitement, passion; riot.

concitātor, -ōris *m* agitator.

concitātus *ppp of* **concitō** ♦ *adj* fast; excited.

concitō, -āre, -āvī, -ātum *vt* to move rapidly, bestir, hurl; to urge, rouse, impel; to stir up, occasion.

concitor, -ōris *m* instigator.

concitus, concītus *ppp of* **concieō;** *ppp of* **conciō.**

conclāmātiō, -ōnis *f* great shout.

conclāmitō, -āre *vi* to keep on shouting.

conclāmō, -āre, -āvī, -ātum *vt, vi* to shout, cry out; to call to help; (*MIL*) to give the signal; (*dead*) to call by name in mourning; **vāsa ~** give the order to pack up; **~ātum est** it's all over.

conclāve, -is *nt* room.

conclūdō, -dere, -sī, -sum *vt* to shut up, enclose; to include, comprise; to end, conclude, round off (*esp with a rhythmical cadence*); (*PHILOS*) to infer, demonstrate.

conclūsē *adv* with rhythmical cadences.

conclūsiō, -ōnis *f* (*MIL*) blockade; end, conclusion; (*RHET*) period, peroration; (*logic*) conclusion.

conclūsiuncula, -ae *f* quibble.

conclūsum, -ī *nt* logical conclusion.

conclūsus *ppp of* **conclūdō.**

concoctus *ppp of* **concoquō.**

concolor, -ōris *adj* of the same colour.

concomitātus *adj* escorted.

concoquō, -quere, -xī, -ctum *vt* to boil down; to digest; (*fig*) to put up with, stomach; (*thought*) to consider well, concoct.

concordia, -ae *f* friendship, concord, union; **goddess of Concord.**

concorditer *adv* amicably.

concordō, -āre *vi* to agree, be in harmony.

concors, -dis *adj* concordant, united, harmonious.

concrēbrēscō, -ēscere, -uī *vi* to gather strength.

concrēdō, -ere, -idī, -itum *vt* to entrust.

concremō, -āre, -āvī, -ātum *vt* to burn.

concrepō, -āre, -uī, -itum *vi* to rattle, creak, clash, snap (fingers) ♦ *vt* to beat.

concrēscō, -scere, -vī, -tum *vi* to harden, curdle, congeal, clot; to grow, take shape.

concrētiō, -ōnis *f* condensing; matter.

concrētum, -ī *nt* solid matter, hard frost.

concrētus *ppa of* **concrēscō** ♦ *adj* hard, thick, stiff, congealed; compounded.

concrīminor, -ārī, -ātus *vi* to bring a complaint.

concruciō, -āre *vt* to torture.

concubīna, -ae *f* (female) concubine.

concubīnātus, -ūs *m* concubinage.

concubīnus, -ī *m* (male) concubine.

concubitus, -ūs *m* reclining together (at table); sexual union.

concubius *adj*: **~iā nocte** during the first sleep ♦ *nt* the time of the first sleep.

conculcō, -āre *vt* to trample under foot, treat with contempt.

concumbō, -mbere, -buī, -bitum *vi* to lie together, lie with.

concupīscō, -īscere, -īvī, -ītum *vt* to covet, long for, aspire to.

concūrō, -āre *vt* to take care of.

concurrō, -rere, -rī, -sum *vi* to flock together, rush in; (*things*) to clash, meet; (*MIL*) to join battle, charge; (*events*) to happen at the same time, concur.

concursātiō, -ōnis *f* running together, rushing about; (*MIL*) skirmishing; (*dreams*) coherent design.

concursātor, -ōris *m* skirmisher.

concursiō, -ōnis *f* meeting, concourse; (*RHET*) repetition for emphasis.

concursō, -āre *vi* to collide; to rush about, travel about; (*MIL*) to skirmish ♦ *vt* to visit, go from place to place.

concursus, -ūs *m* concourse, gathering, collision; uproar; (*fig*) combination; (*MIL*) assault, charge.

concussī *perf of* **concutiō.**

concussus *ppp of* **concutiō.**

concussus, -ūs *m* shaking.

concutiō, -tere, -ssī, -ssum *vt* to strike, shake, shatter; (*weapons*) to hurl; (*power*) to disturb, impair; (*person*) to agitate, alarm; (*self*) to search, examine; to rouse.

condalium, -ī and iī *nt* slave's ring.

condecet, -ēre *vt impers* it becomes.

condecorō, -āre *vt* to enhance.

condemnātor, -ōris *m* accuser.

condemnō, -āre, -āvī, -ātum *vt* to condemn, sentence; to urge the conviction of; to blame, censure; **ambitūs ~** convict of bribery; **capitis ~** condemn to death; **vōtī ~ātus** obliged to fulfil a vow.

condēnsō, -āre, -eō, -ēre *vt* to compress, move close together.

condēnsus *adj* very dense, close, thick.

condiciō, -ōnis *f* arrangement, condition, terms; marriage contract, match; situation, position, circumstances; manner, mode; **eā ~ōne ut** on condition that; **sub ~ōne** conditionally; **hīs ~ōnibus** on these terms; **vītae ~** way of life.

condīcō, -īcere, -īxī, -ictum *vt, vi* to talk over, agree upon, promise; **ad cēnam ~** have a dinner engagement.

condidī *perf of* **condō**.

condignē *adv see* **condignus**.

condignus *adj* very worthy.

condīmentum, -ī *nt* spice, seasoning.

condiō, -īre, -īvī, -ītum *vt* to pickle, preserve, embalm; to season; (*fig*) to give zest to, temper.

condiscipulus, -ī *m* school-fellow.

condiscō, -scere, -dicī *vt* to learn thoroughly, learn by heart.

conditiō *etc see* **condiciō**.

condītiō, -ōnis *f* preserving, seasoning.

conditor, -ōris *m* founder, author, composer.

conditōrium, -ī *and* **iī** *nt* coffin, urn, tomb.

condītus *adj* savoury; (*fig*) polished.

conditus *ppp of* **condō**.

condītus *ppp of* **condiō**.

condō, -ere, -idī, -itum *vt* 1. (*build, found: arts*) to make, compose, write; (: *institutions*) to establish 2. (*put away for keeping, store up: fruit*) to preserve; (: *person*) to imprison; (: *dead*) to bury; (: *memory*) to lay up; (: *time*) to pass, bring to a close 3. (*put out of sight, conceal: eyes*) to close; (: *sword*) to sheathe, plunge; (: *troops*) to place in ambush.

condocefaciō, -ere *vt* to train.

condoceō, -ēre, -uī, -tum *vt* to train.

condolēscō, -ēscere, -uī *vi* to begin to ache, feel very sore.

condōnātiō, -ōnis *f* giving away.

condōnō, -āre, -āvī, -ātum *vt* to give, present, deliver up; (*debt*) to remit; (*offence*) to pardon, let off.

condormīscō, -īscere, -īvī *vi* to fall fast asleep.

condūcibilis *adj* expedient.

condūcō, -ūcere, -ūxī, -uctum *vt* to bring together, assemble, connect; to hire, rent, borrow; (*public work*) to undertake, get the contract for; (*taxes*) to farm ♦ *vi* to be of use, profit.

conductī, -ōrum *mpl* hirelings, mercenaries.

conductīcius *adj* hired.

conductiō, -ōnis *f* hiring, farming.

conductor, -ōris *m* hirer, tenant; contractor.

conductum, -ī *nt* anything hired *or* rented.

conductus *ppp of* **condūcō**.

conduplicō, -āre *vt* to double.

condūrō, -āre *vt* to make very hard.

condus, -ī *m* steward.

cōnectō, -ctere, -xuī, -xum *vt* to tie, fasten, link, join; (*logic*) to state a conclusion.

cōnexum, -ī *nt* logical inference.

cōnexus *ppp of* **cōnectō** ♦ *adj* connected; (*time*) following.

cōnexus, -ūs *m* combination.

cōnfābulor, -ārī, -ātus *vi* to talk (to), discuss.

cōnfarreātiō, -ōnis *f the most solemn of Roman marriage ceremonies.*

cōnfarreō, -āre, -ātum *vt* to marry by confarreatio.

cōnfātālis *adj* bound by the same destiny.

cōnfēcī *perf of* **cōnficiō**.

cōnfectiō, -ōnis *f* making, completion; (*food*) chewing.

cōnfector, -ōris *m* maker, finisher; destroyer.

cōnfectus *ppp of* **cōnficiō**.

cōnferciō, -cīre, -tum *vt* to stuff, cram, pack closely.

cōnferō, -ferre, -tulī, -lātum *vt* to gather together, collect; to contribute; to confer, talk over; (*MIL*) to oppose, engage in battle; to compare; (*words*) to condense; to direct, transfer; to transform (into), turn (to); to devote, bestow; to ascribe, assign, impute; (*time*) to postpone; **capita ~** put heads together, confer; **gradum ~ cum** walk beside; **sē ~** go, turn (to); **sermōnēs ~** converse; **signa ~** join battle.

cōnfertim *adv* in close order.

cōnfertus *ppp of* **cōnferciō** ♦ *adj* crowded, full; (*MIL*) in close order.

cōnfervēscō, -vēscere, -buī *vi* to boil up, grow hot.

cōnfessiō, -ōnis *f* acknowledgement, confession.

cōnfessus *ppa of* **cōnfiteor** ♦ *adj* acknowledged, certain; **in ~ō esse/in ~um venīre** be generally admitted.

cōnfestim *adv* immediately.

cōnficiō, -icere, -ēcī, -ectum *vt* to make, effect, complete, accomplish; to get together, procure; to wear out, exhaust, consume, destroy; (*COMM*) to settle; (*space*) to travel; (*time*) to pass, complete; (*PHILOS*) to be an active cause; (*logic*) to deduce; (*pass*) it follows.

cōnfictiō, -ōnis *f* fabrication.

cōnfictus *ppp of* **cōnfingō**.

cōnfīdēns, -entis *pres p of* **cōnfīdō** ♦ *adj* self-confident, bold, presumptuous.

cōnfīdenter *adv* fearlessly, insolently.

cōnfīdentia, -ae *f* confidence, self-confidence; impudence.

cōnfīdentiloquus *adj* outspoken.

cōnfīdō, -dere, -sus sum *vi* to trust, rely, be sure; **sibi ~** be confident.

cōnfīgō, -gere, -xī, -xum *vt* to fasten together; to pierce, shoot; (*fig*) to paralyse.

cōnfingō, -ingere, -inxī, -ictum *vt* to make, invent, pretend.

cōnfīnis *adj* adjoining; (*fig*) akin.

cōnfīnium, -ī *nt* common boundary; (*pl*) neighbours; (*fig*) close connection, borderland between.

cōnfiō, -fierī *occ pass of* **cōnficiō**.

cōnfirmātiō, -ōnis *f* establishing; (*person*) encouragement; (*fact*) verifying; (*RHET*) adducing of proofs.

cōnfirmātor, -ōris *m* guarantor (*of money*).

cōnfirmātus *adj* resolute; proved, certain.

cōnfirmō, -āre, -āvī, -ātum *vt* to strengthen, reinforce; (*decree*) to confirm, ratify; (*mind*) to encourage; (*fact*) to corroborate, prove, assert; **sē ~** recover; take courage.

cōnfiscō, -āre *vt* to keep in a chest; to confiscate.

cōnfisiō, -ōnis *f* assurance.

cōnfisus *ppa of* cōnfīdō.

cōnfiteor, -itērī, -essus *vt, vi* to confess, acknowledge; to reveal.

cōnfīxus *ppp of* cōnfīgō.

cōnflagrō, -āre, -āvī, -ātum *vi* to burn, be ablaze.

cōnflīctiō, -ōnis *f* conflict.

cōnflīctō, -āre, -āvī, -ātum *vt* to strike down, contend (with); (*pass*) to fight, be harassed, be afflicted.

cōnflīctus, -ūs *m* striking together.

cōnflīgō, -gere, -xī, -ctum *vt* to dash together; (*fig*) to contrast ♦ *vi* to fight, come into conflict.

cōnflō, -āre, -āvī, -ātum *vt* to ignite; (*passion*) to inflame; to melt down; (*fig*) to produce, procure, occasion.

cōnfluēns, -entis, -entēs, -entium *m* confluence of two rivers.

cōnfluō, -ere, -xī *vi* to flow together; (*fig*) to flock together, pour in.

cōnfodiō, -odere, -ōdī, -ossum *vt* to dig; to stab.

cōnfore *fut infin of* cōnsum.

cōnfōrmātiō, -ōnis *f* shape, form; (*words*) arrangement; (*voice*) expression; (*mind*) idea; (*RHET*) figure.

cōnfōrmō, -āre, -āvī, -ātum *vt* to shape, fashion.

cōnfossus *ppp of* cōnfodiō ♦ *adj* full of holes.

cōnfrāctus *ppa of* cōnfringō.

cōnfragōsus *adj* broken, rough; (*fig*) hard.

cōnfrēgī *pvrf of* cōnfringō.

cōnfremō, -ere, -uī *vi* to murmur aloud.

cōnfricō, -āre *vt* to rub well.

cōnfringō, -ingere, -ēgī, -āctum *vt* to break in pieces, wreck; (*fig*) to ruin.

cōnfugiō, -ugere, -ūgī *vi* to flee for help (to), take refuge (with); (*fig*) to have recourse (to).

cōnfugium, -ī *and* **iī** *nt* refuge.

cōnfundō, -undere, -ūdī, -ūsum *vt* to mix, mingle, join; to mix up, confuse, throw into disorder; (*mind*) to perplex, bewilder; to diffuse, spread over.

cōnfusē *adv* confusedly.

cōnfūsiō, -ōnis *f* combination; confusion, disorder; **ōris ~** going red in the face.

cōnfūsus *ppp of* cōnfundō ♦ *adj* confused, disorderly, troubled.

cōnfūtō, -āre, -āvī, -ātum *vt* to keep from boiling over; to repress; to silence, confute.

congelō, -āre, -āvī, -ātum *vt* to freeze, harden ♦ *vi* to freeze over, grow numb.

congeminō, -āre, -āvī, -ātum *vt* to double.

congemō, -ere, -uī *vi* to groan, sigh ♦ *vt* to lament.

conger, -rī *m* sea eel.

congeriēs, -ēī *f* heap, mass, accumulation.

congerō, -rere, -ssī, -stum *vt* to collect, accumulate, build; (*missiles*) to shower; (*speech*) to comprise; (*fig*) to heap (upon), ascribe.

congerō, -ōnis *m* thief.

congerrō, -ōnis *m* companion in revelry.

congestīcius *adj* piled up.

congestus *ppp of* congerō.

congestus, -ūs *m* accumulating; heap, mass.

congiālis *adj* holding a congius.

congiārium, -ī *and* **iī** *nt* gift of food to the people, gratuity to the army.

congius, -ī *and* **iī** *m* Roman liquid measure (*about 6 pints*).

conglaciō, -āre *vi* to freeze up.

conglīscō, -ere *vi* to blaze up.

conglobātiō, -ōnis *f* mustering.

conglobō, -āre, -āvī, -ātum *vt* to make round; to mass together.

conglomerō, -āre *vt* to roll up.

conglūtinātiō, -ōnis *f* gluing, cementing; (*fig*) combination.

conglūtinō, -āre, -āvī, -ātum *vt* to glue, cement; (*fig*) to join, weld together; to contrive.

congraecō, -āre *vt* to squander on luxury.

congrātulor, -ārī, -ātus *vi* to congratulate.

congredior, -dī, -ssus *vt, vi* to meet, accost; to contend, fight.

congregābilis *adj* gregarious.

congregātiō, -ōnis *f* union, society.

congregō, -āre, -āvī, -ātum *vt* to collect, assemble, unite.

congressiō, -ōnis *f* meeting, conference.

congressus *ppa of* congredior.

congressus, -ūs *m* meeting, association, union; encounter, fight.

congruēns, -entis *adj* suitable, consistent, proper; harmonious.

congruenter *adv* in conformity.

congruō, -ere, -ī *vi* to coincide; to correspond, suit; to agree, sympathize.

congruus *adj* agreeable.

coniciō, -icere, -iēcī, -iectum *vt* to throw together; to throw, hurl; to put, fling, drive, direct; to infer, conjecture; (*augury*) to interpret; **sē ~** rush, fly; devote oneself.

coniectiō, -ōnis *f* throwing; conjecture, interpretation.

coniectō, -āre *vt* to infer, conjecture, guess.

coniector, -ōris *m* (male) interpreter, diviner.

coniectrīx, -rīcis *f* (female) interpreter, diviner.

coniectūra, -ae *f* inference, conjecture, guess; interpretation.

coniectūrālis *adj* (*RHET*) involving a question of fact.

coniectus *ppp of* **coniciō.**
coniectus, -ūs *m* heap, mass, concourse;
throwing, throw, range; (*eyes, mind*) turning,
directing.
cōnifer, cōniger, -ī *adj* cone-bearing.
cōnītor, -tī, -sus *and* **-xus** *vi* to lean on; to
strive, struggle on; to labour.
coniugālis *adj* of marriage, conjugal.
coniugātiō, -ōnis *f* etymological
relationship.
coniugātor, -ōris *m* uniter.
coniugiālis *adj* marriage- (*in cpds*).
coniugium, -ī *and* **iī** *nt* union, marriage;
husband, wife.
coniugō, -āre *vt* to form (*a friendship*); **~āta
verba** words related etymologically.
coniūnctē *adv* jointly; on familiar terms;
(*logic*) hypothetically.
coniūnctim *adv* together, jointly.
coniūnctiō, -ōnis *f* union, connection,
association; (*minds*) sympathy, affinity;
(*GRAM*) conjunction.
coniūnctum, -ī *nt* (*RHET*) connection; (*PHILOS*)
inherent property (*of a body*).
coniūnctus *ppp of* **coniungō** ♦ *adj* near;
connected, agreeing, conforming; related,
friendly, intimate.
coniungō, -ūngere, -ūnxī, -ūnctum *vt* to
yoke, join together, connect; (*war*) to join
forces in; to unite in love, marriage,
friendship; to continue without a break.
coniūnx, -ugis *m/f* consort, wife, husband,
bride.
coniūrātī, -ōrum *mpl* conspirators.
coniūrātiō, -ōnis *f* conspiracy, plot; alliance.
coniūrātus *adj* (*MIL*) after taking the oath.
coniūrō, -āre, -āvī, -ātum *vi* to take an oath;
to conspire, plot.
coniux *etc see* **coniūnx.**
cōnīveō, -vēre, -vī *and* **xī** *vi* to shut the eyes,
blink; (*fig*) to be asleep; to connive at.
conj- *etc see* **coni-.**
conl- *etc see* **coll-.**
conm- *etc see* **comm-.**
conn- *etc see* **cōn-.**
Conōn, -is *m* Athenian commander; Greek
astronomer.
cōnōpēum (-eum), -ēī *nt* mosquito net.
cōnor, -ārī, -ātus *vt* to try, attempt, venture.
conp- *etc see* **comp-.**
conquassātiō, -ōnis *f* severe shaking.
conquassō, -āre, -ātum *vt* to shake, upset,
shatter.
conqueror, -rī, -stus *vt, vi* to complain
bitterly of, bewail.
conquestiō, -ōnis *f* complaining; (*RHET*)
appeal to pity.
conquestus *ppa of* **conqueror.**
conquestus, -ūs *m* outcry.
conquiēscō, -scere, -vī, -tum *vi* to rest, take

a respite; (*fig*) to be at peace, find recreation;
(*things*) to stop, be quiet.
conquīnīscō, -ere *vi* to cower, squat, stoop
down.
conquīrō, -rere, -sīvī, -sītum *vt* to search
for, collect.
conquīsītē *adv* carefully.
conquīsītiō, -ōnis *f* search; (*MIL*) levy.
conquīsītor, -ōris *m* recruiting officer;
(*THEATRE*) claqueur.
conquīsītus *ppp of* **conquīrō** ♦ *adj* select,
costly.
conr- *etc see* **corr-.**
cōnsaepiō, -īre, -sī, -tum *vt* to enclose, fence
round.
cōnsaeptum, -tī *nt* enclosure.
cōnsalūtātiō, -ōnis *f* mutual greeting.
cōnsalūtō, -āre, -āvī, -ātum *vt* to greet, hail.
cōnsānēscō, -ēscere, -uī *vi* to heal up.
cōnsanguineus *adj* brother, sister, kindred ♦
mpl relations.
cōnsanguinitās, -ātis *f* relationship.
cōnscelerātus *adj* wicked.
cōnscelerō, -āre, -āvī, -ātum *vt* to disgrace.
cōnscendō, -endere, -endī, -ēnsum *vt, vi* to
climb, mount, embark.
cōnscēnsiō, -ōnis *f* embarkation.
cōnscēnsus *ppp of* **cōnscendō.**
cōnscientia, -ae *f* joint knowledge, being in
the know; (sense of) consciousness; moral
sense, conscience, guilty conscience.
cōnscindō, -ndere, -dī, -ssum *vt* to tear to
pieces; (*fig*) to abuse.
cōnsciō, -īre *vt* to be conscious of guilt.
cōnscīscō, -scere, -vī *and* **iī, -ītum** *vt* to
decide on publicly; to inflict on oneself;
mortem (sibi) ~ commit suicide.
cōnscissus *ppp of* **cōnscindō.**
cōnscītus *ppp of* **cōnscīscō.**
cōnscius *adj* sharing knowledge, privy, in the
know; aware, conscious (of); conscious of
guilt ♦ *m/f* confederate, confidant.
cōnscreor, -ārī *vi* to clear the throat.
cōnscrībō, -bere, -psī, -ptum *vt* to enlist,
enrol; to write, compose, draw up,
prescribe.
cōnscrīptiō, -ōnis *f* document, draft.
cōnscrīptus *ppp of* **cōnscrībō; patrēs ~ī**
patrician and elected plebeian members;
senators.
cōnsecō, -āre, -uī, -tum *vt* to cut up.
cōnsecrātiō, -ōnis *f* consecration,
deification.
cōnsecrō, -āre, -āvī, -ātum *vt* to dedicate,
consecrate, deify; (*fig*) to devote; to
immortalise; **caput ~** doom to death.
cōnsectārius *adj* logical, consequent ♦ *ntpl*
inferences.
cōnsectātiō, -ōnis *f* pursuit.
cōnsectātrīx, -īcis *f* (*fig*) follower.

Noun declensions and verb conjugations are shown on pp xiii to xxv. The present infinitive ending of a verb shows
to which conjugation it belongs: **-āre** = 1st; **-ēre** = 2nd; **-ere** = 3rd and **-īre** = 4th. Irregular verbs are shown on p xxvi

cōnsectiō, -ōnis f cutting up.

cōnsector, -ārī, -ātus vt to follow, go after, try to gain; to emulate, imitate; to pursue, chase.

cōnsecūtiō, -ōnis f (PHILOS) consequences, effect; (RHET) sequence.

cōnsēdī perf of **cōnsīdō.**

cōnsenēscō, -ēscere, -uī vi to grow old, grow old together; (fig) to fade, pine, decay, become obsolete.

cōnsēnsiō, -ōnis f agreement, accord; conspiracy, plot.

cōnsēnsū adv unanimously.

cōnsēnsus ppp of **cōnsentiō.**

cōnsēnsus, -ūs m agreement, concord; conspiracy; (PHILOS) common sensation; (fig) harmony.

cōnsentāneus adj agreeing, in keeping with; **~um est** it is reasonable.

cōnsentiō, -entīre, -ēnsī, -ēnsum vi to agree, determine together; to plot, conspire; (PHILOS) to have common sensations; (fig) to harmonize, suit, be consistent (with); **bellum ~** vote for war.

cōnsequēns, -entis pres p of **cōnsequor** ♦ adj coherent, reasonable; logical, consequent ♦ nt consequence.

cōnsequor, -quī, -cūtus vt to follow, pursue; to overtake, reach; (time) to come after; (example) to follow, copy; (effect) to result, be the consequence of; (aim) to attain, get; (mind) to grasp, learn; (events) to happen to, come to; (standard) to equal, come up to; (speech) to do justice to.

cōnserō, -erere, -ēvī, -itum vt to sow, plant; (ground) to sow with, plant with; (fig) to cover, fill.

cōnserō, -ere, -uī, -tum vt to join, string together, twine; (MIL) to join battle; **manum/ manūs ~** engage in close combat; **ex iūre manum ~** lay claim to (in an action for possession).

cōnsertē adv connectedly.

cōnsertus ppp of **cōnserō.**

cōnserva, -ae f fellow slave.

cōnservātiō, -ōnis f preserving.

cōnservātor, -ōris m preserver.

cōnservitium, -ī and iī nt being fellow slaves.

cōnservō, -āre, -āvī, -ātum vt to preserve, save, keep.

cōnservus, -ī m fellow slave.

cōnsessor, -ōris m companion at table, fellow spectator; (law) assessor.

cōnsessus, -ūs m assembly; (law) court.

cōnsēvī perf of **cōnserō.**

cōnsīderātē adv cautiously, deliberately.

cōnsīderātiō, -ōnis f contemplation.

cōnsīderātus adj (person) circumspect; (things) well-considered.

cōnsīderō, -āre, -āvī, -ātum vt to look at, inspect; to contemplate.

cōnsīdō, -īdere, -ēdī, -essum vi to sit down, take seats; (courts) to be in session; (MIL) to take up a position; (residence) to settle; (places) to subside, sink; (fig) to sink, settle down, subside.

cōnsignō, -āre, -āvī, -ātum vt to seal, sign; to attest, vouch for; to record, register.

cōnsilēscō, -ere vi to calm down.

cōnsiliārius, -ī and iī m adviser, counsellor; spokesman ♦ adj counselling.

cōnsiliātor, -ōris m counsellor.

cōnsilior, -ārī, -ātus vi to consult; (with dat) to advise.

cōnsilium, -ī and iī nt deliberation, consultation; deliberating body, council; decision, purpose; plan, measure; stratagem; advice, counsel; judgement, insight, wisdom; **~ium capere, inīre** come to a decision, resolve; **~i esse** be an open question; **~iō** intentionally; **eō ~iō ut** with the intention of; **prīvātō ~iō** for one's own purposes.

cōnsimilis adj just like.

cōnsipiō, -ere vi to be in one's senses.

cōnsistō, -istere, -titī vi to stand, rest, take up a position; to consist (of), depend (on); to exist, be; (fig) to stand firm, endure; (liquid) to solidify, freeze; to stop, pause, halt, come to rest; (fig) to come to a standstill, come to an end.

cōnsitiō, -ōnis f sowing, planting.

cōnsitor, -ōris m sower, planter.

cōnsitus ppp of **cōnserō.**

cōnsōbrīnus, -ī m, **-a, -ae** f cousin.

cōnsociātiō, -ōnis f society.

cōnsociō, -āre, -āvī, -ātum vt to share, associate, unite.

cōnsōlābilis adj consolable.

cōnsōlātiō, -ōnis f comfort, encouragement, consolation.

cōnsōlātor, -ōris m comforter.

cōnsōlātōrius adj of consolation.

cōnsōlor, -ārī, -ātus vt to console, comfort, reassure; (things) to relieve, mitigate.

cōnsomniō, -āre vt to dream about.

cōnsonō, -āre, -uī vi to resound; (fig) to accord.

cōnsonus adj concordant; (fig) suitable.

cōnsōpiō, -īre, -ītum vt to put to sleep.

cōnsors, -tis adj sharing in common; (things) shared in common ♦ m/f partner, colleague.

cōnsortiō, -ōnis f partnership, fellowship.

cōnsortium, -ī and iī nt society, participation.

cōnspectus ppp of **cōnspiciō** ♦ adj visible; conspicuous.

cōnspectus, -ūs m look, view, sight; appearing on the scene; (fig) mental picture, survey; **in ~um venīre** come in sight, come near.

cōnspergō, -gere, -sī, -sum vt to besprinkle; (fig) to spangle.

cōnspiciendus adj noteworthy, distinguished.

cōnspiciō, -icere, -exī, -ectum vt to observe, catch sight of; to look at (esp with admiration),

contemplate; (*pass*) to attract attention, be
conspicuous, be notorious; (*mind*) to see,
perceive.

cōnspicor, -ārī, -ātus *vt* to observe, see,
catch sight of.

cōnspicuus *adj* visible; conspicuous,
distinguished.

cōnspīrātiō, -ōnis *f* concord, unanimity;
plotting, conspiracy.

cōnspīrō, -āre, -āvī, -ātum *vi* to agree, unite;
to plot, conspire; (*music*) to sound together.

cōnspōnsor, -ōris *m* co-guarantor.

cōnspuō, -ere *vt* to spit upon.

cōnspurcō, -āre *vt* to pollute.

cōnspūtō, -āre *vt* to spit upon (*with contempt*).

cōnstabiliō, -īre, -īvī, -itum *vt* to establish.

cōnstāns, -antis *pres p of* **cōnstō** ♦ *adj* steady,
stable, constant; consistent; faithful,
steadfast.

cōnstanter *adv* steadily, firmly, calmly;
consistently.

cōnstantia, -ae *f* steadiness, firmness;
consistency, harmony; self-possession,
constancy.

cōnsternātiō, -ōnis *f* disorder, tumult;
(*horses*) stampede; (*mind*) dismay, alarm.

cōnsternō, -ernere, -rāvī, -rātum *vt* to
spread, cover, thatch, pave; **~rāta nāvis**
decked ship.

cōnsternō, -āre, -āvī, -ātum *vt* to startle,
stampede; to alarm, throw into confusion.

cōnstīpō, -āre *vt* to crowd together.

cōnstitī *perf of* **cōnsistō**.

cōnstituō, -uere, -uī, -ūtum *vt* to put, place,
set down; (*MIL*) to station, post, halt; to
establish, build, create; to settle, arrange,
organize; to appoint, determine, fix; to
resolve, decide; **bene ~ūtum corpus** a good
constitution.

cōnstitūtiō, -ōnis *f* state, condition;
regulation, decree; definition, point at issue.

cōnstitūtum, -ūtī *nt* agreement.

cōnstō, -āre, -itī, -ātum *vi* to stand together;
to agree, correspond, tally; to stand firm,
remain constant; to exist, be; to consist (of),
be composed (of); (*facts*) to be established,
be well-known; (*COMM*) to cost; **sibi ~ be
consistent; **inter omnēs ~at** it is common
knowledge; **mihi ~at** I am determined; **ratiō
~at** the account is correct.

cōnstrātum, -ī *nt* flooring, deck.

cōnstrātus *ppp of* **cōnsternō**.

cōnstringō, -ingere, -inxī, -ictum *vt* to tie
up, bind, fetter; (*fig*) to restrain, restrict;
(*speech*) to compress, condense.

cōnstructiō, -ōnis *f* building up; (*words*)
arrangement, sequence.

cōnstruō, -ere, -xī, -ctum *vt* to heap up; to
build, construct.

cōnstuprātor, -ōris *m* debaucher.

cōnstuprō, -āre *vt* to debauch, rape.

cōnsuādeō, -ēre *vi* to advise strongly.

Cōnsuālia, -ium *ntpl festival of Consus*.

cōnsuāsor, -ōris *m* earnest adviser.

cōnsūdō, -āre *vi* to sweat profusely.

cōnsuēfaciō, -facere, -fēcī, -factum *vt* to
accustom.

cōnsuēscō, -scere, -vī, -tum *vt* to accustom,
inure ♦ *vi* to get accustomed; to cohabit
(with); (*perf tenses*) to be accustomed, be in
the habit of.

cōnsuētūdō, -inis *f* custom, habit;
familiarity, social intercourse; love affair;
(*language*) usage, idiom; **~ine/ex ~ine** as
usual; **epistulārum ~** correspondence.

cōnsuētus *ppp of* **cōnsuēscō** ♦ *adj* customary,
usual.

cōnsuēvī *perf of* **cōnsuēscō**.

cōnsul, -is *m* consul; **~ dēsignātus** consul
elect; **~ ōrdinārius** regular consul; **~
suffectus** *successor to a consul who has died
during his term of office*; **~ iterum/tertium**
consul for the second/third time; **~em
creāre, dīcere, facere** elect to the consulship;
L. Domitiō App. Claudiō ~ibus in the year 54
B.C.

cōnsulāris *adj* consular, consul's; of consular
rank ♦ *m* ex-consul.

cōnsulāriter *adv* in a manner worthy of a
consul.

cōnsulātus, -ūs *m* consulship; **~um petere**
stand for the consulship.

cōnsulō, -ere, -uī, -tum *vi* to deliberate, take
thought; (*with dat*) to look after, consult the
interests of; (*with dē or in*) to take measures
against, pass sentence on ♦ *vt* to consult, ask
advice of; to consider; to advise
(something); to decide; **bonī/optimī ~** take in
good part, be satisfied with.

cōnsultātiō, -ōnis *f* deliberation; inquiry;
case.

cōnsultē *adv* deliberately.

cōnsultō *adv* deliberately.

cōnsultō, -āre, -āvī, -ātum *vt, vi* to
deliberate, reflect; to consult; (*with dat*) to
consult the interests of.

cōnsultor, -ōris *m* counsellor; consulter;
client.

cōnsultrīx, -īcis *f* protectress.

cōnsultum, -ī *nt* decree (*esp of the Senate*);
consultation; response (*from an oracle*).

cōnsultus *ppp of* **cōnsulō** ♦ *adj* considered;
experienced, skilled ♦ *m* lawyer; **iūris ~us**
lawyer.

cōnsuluī *perf of* **cōnsulō**.

(cōnsum), futūrum, fore *vi* to be all right.

cōnsummātus *adj* perfect.

cōnsummō, -āre *vt* to sum up; to complete,
perfect.

cōnsūmō, -ere, -psī, -ptum *vt* to consume,

use up, eat up; to waste, squander; to exhaust, destroy, kill; to spend, devote.

cōnsūmptiō, -ōnis f wasting.

cōnsūmptor, -ōris m destroyer.

cōnsūmptus ppp of **cōnsūmō**.

cōnsuō, -uere, -uī, -ūtum vt to sew up; (fig) to contrive.

cōnsurgō, -gere, -rēxī, -rēctum vi to rise, stand up; to be roused (to); to spring up, start.

cōnsurrēctiō, -ōnis f standing up.

Cōnsus, -ī m ancient Roman god (connected with harvest).

cōnsusurrō, -āre vi to whisper together.

cōnsūtus ppp of **cōnsuō**.

contābefaciō, -ere vt to wear out.

contābēscō, -ēscere, -uī vi to waste away.

contabulātiō, -ōnis f flooring, storey.

contabulō, -āre, -āvī, -ātum vt to board over, build in storeys.

contāctus ppp of **contingō**.

contāctus, -ūs m touch, contact; contagion, infection.

contāgēs, -is f contact, touch.

contāgiō, -ōnis f, **contāgium, -ī** and **iī** nt contact; contagion, infection; (fig) contamination, bad example.

contāminātus adj impure, vicious.

contāminō, -āre, -āvī, -ātum vt to defile; (fig) to mar, spoil.

contechnor, -ārī, -ātus vi to think out plots.

contegō, -egere, -ēxī, -ēctum vt to cover up, cover over; to protect; to hide.

contemerō, -āre vt to defile.

contemnō, -nere, -psī, -ptum vt to think light of, have no fear of, despise, defy; to disparage.

contemplātiō, -ōnis f contemplation, surveying.

contemplātor, -ōris m observer.

contemplātus, -ūs m contemplation.

contemplō, -āre, -āvī, -ātum, -or, -ārī, -ātus vt to look at, observe, contemplate.

contempsī perf of **contemnō**.

contemptim adv contemptuously, slightingly.

contemptiō, -ōnis f disregard, scorn, despising.

contemptor, -ōris m (male) despiser, defiler.

contemptrīx, -rīcis f (female) despiser, defiler.

contemptus ppp of **contemnō** ♦ adj contemptible.

contemptus, -ūs m despising, scorn; being slighted; ~uī esse be despised.

contendō, -dere, -dī, -tum vt to stretch, draw, tighten; (instrument) to tune; (effort) to strain, exert; (argument) to assert, maintain; (comparison) to compare, contrast; (course) to direct ♦ vi to exert oneself, strive; to hurry; to journey, march; to contend, compete, fight; to entreat, solicit.

contentē adv (from **contendō**) earnestly, intensely.

contentē adv (from **contineō**) closely.

contentiō, -ōnis f straining, effort; striving (after); struggle, competition, dispute; comparison, contrast, antithesis.

contentus ppp of **contendō** ♦ adj strained, tense; (fig) intent.

contentus ppp of **contineō** ♦ adj content, satisfied.

conterminus adj bordering, neighbouring.

conterō, -erere, -rīvī, -rītum vt to grind, crumble; to wear out, waste; (time) to spend, pass; (fig) to obliterate.

conterreō, -ēre, -uī, -itum vt to terrify.

contestātus adj proved.

contestor, -ārī, -ātus vt to call to witness; lītem ~ open a lawsuit by calling witnesses.

contexō, -ere, -uī, -tum vt to weave, interweave; to devise, construct; (recital) to continue.

contextē adv in a connected fashion.

contextus adj connected.

contextus, -ūs m connection, coherence.

conticēscō (-īscō), -ēscere, -uī vi to become quiet, fall silent; (fig) to cease, abate.

contigī perf of **contingō**.

contignātiō, -ōnis f floor, storey.

contignō, -āre vt to floor.

contiguus adj adjoining, near; within reach.

continēns, -entis pres p of **contineō** ♦ adj bordering, adjacent; unbroken, continuous; (time) successive, continual, uninterrupted; (person) temperate, continent ♦ nt mainland, continent; essential point (in an argument).

continenter adv (place) in a row; (time) continuously; (person) temperately.

continentia, -ae f moderation, self-control.

contineō, -inēre, -inuī, -entum vt to hold, keep together; to confine, enclose; to contain, include, comprise; (pass) to consist of, rest on; to control, check, repress.

contingō, -ingere, -igī, -āctum vt to touch, take hold of, partake of; to be near, border on; to reach, come to; to contaminate; (mind) to touch, affect, concern ♦ vi to happen, succeed.

contingō, -ere vt to moisten, smear.

continuātiō, -ōnis f unbroken, succession, series; (RHET) period.

continuī perf of **continuō**.

continuō adv immediately, without delay; (argument) necessarily.

continuō, -āre, -āvī, -ātum vt to join together, make continuous, to continue without a break; **verba ~** form a sentence.

continuus adj joined (to); continuous, successive, uninterrupted; ~ā nocte the following night; **trīduum ~um** three days running.

cōntiō, -ōnis f public meeting; speech, address; rostrum; ~ōnem habēre hold a meeting; deliver an address; prō ~ōne in public.

cōntiōnābundus *adj* delivering a harangue, playing the demagogue.

cōntiōnālis *adj* suitable for a public meeting, demagogic.

cōntiōnārius *adj* fond of public meetings.

cōntiōnātor, -ōris *m* demagogue.

cōntiōnor, -ārī, -ātus *vi* to address a public meeting, harangue; to declare in public; to come to a meeting.

cōntiuncula, -ae *f* short speech.

contorqueō, -quēre, -sī, -tum *vt* to twist, turn; (*weapons*) to throw, brandish; (*words*) to deliver forcibly.

contortē *adv* intricately.

contortiō, -ōnis *f* intricacy.

contortor, -ōris *m* perverter.

contortulus *adj* somewhat complicated.

contortuplicātus *adj* very complicated.

contortus *ppp of* **contorqueō** ♦ *adj* vehement; intricate.

contrā *adv* (*place*) opposite, face to face; (*speech*) in reply; (*action*) to fight, in opposition, against someone; (*result, with* *esse*) adverse, unsuccessful; (*comparison*) the contrary, conversely, differently; (*argument*) on the contrary, on the other hand; ~ **atque, quam** contrary to what, otherwise than ♦ *prep* (*with acc*) facing, opposite to; against; contrary to, in violation of.

contractiō, -ōnis *f* contracting; shortening; despondency.

contractiuncula, -ae *f* slight despondency.

contractus *ppp of* **contrahō** ♦ *adj* contracted, narrow; short; in seclusion.

contrādīcō, -dīcere, -dīxī, -dictum (*usu two* *words*) *vt, vi* to oppose, object; (*law*) to be counsel for the other side.

contrādictiō, -ōnis *f* objection.

contrahō, -here, -xī, -ctum *vt* to draw together, assemble; to bring about, achieve; (*comm*) to contract, make a bargain; to shorten, narrow; to limit, depress; (*blame*) to incur; (*brow*) to wrinkle; (*sail*) to shorten; (*sky*) to overcast.

contrāriē *adv* differently.

contrārius *adj* opposite, from opposite; contrary; hostile, harmful ♦ *nt* opposite, reverse; **ex ~ō** on the contrary.

contrectābiliter *adv* so as to be felt.

contrectātiō, -ōnis *f* touching.

contrectō, -āre, -āvī, -ātum *vt* to touch, handle; (*fig*) to consider.

contremīscō, -īscere, -uī *vi* to tremble all over; (*fig*) to waver ♦ *vt* to be afraid of.

contremō, -ere *vi* to quake.

contribuō, -uere, -uī, -ūtum *vt* to bring together, join, incorporate.

contristō, -āre, -āvī, -ātum *vt* to sadden, darken, cloud.

contrītus *ppp of* **conterō** ♦ *adj* trite, well-worn.

contrōversia, -ae *f* dispute, argument, debate, controversy.

contrōversiōsus *adj* much disputed.

contrōversus *adj* disputed, questionable.

contrucīdō, -āre, -āvī, -ātum *vt* to massacre.

contrūdō, -dere, -sī, -sum *vt* to crowd together.

contruncō, -āre *vt* to hack to pieces.

contrūsus *ppp of* **contrūdō**.

contubernālis, -is *m/f* tent companion; junior officer serving with a general; (*fig*) companion, mate.

contubernium, -ī *and* **iī** *nt* service in the same tent, mess; service as junior officer with a general; common tent; slaves' home.

contueor, -ērī, -itus *vt* to look at, consider, observe.

contuitus, -ūs *m* observing, view.

contulī *perf of* **cōnferō**.

contumācia, -ae *f* obstinacy, defiance.

contumāciter *adv see* **contumāx**.

contumāx, -ācis *adj* stubborn, insolent, pig-headed.

contumēlia, -ae *f* (*verbal*) insult, libel, invective; (*physical*) assault, ill-treatment.

contumēliōsē *adv* insolently.

contumēliōsus *adj* insulting, outrageous.

contumulō, -āre *vt* to bury.

contundō, -undere, -udī, -ūsum *vt* to pound, beat, bruise; (*fig*) to suppress, destroy.

contuor *etc see* **contueor**.

conturbātiō, -ōnis *f* confusion, mental disorder.

conturbātus *adj* distracted, diseased.

conturbō, -āre, -āvī, -ātum *vt* to throw into confusion; (*mind*) to derange, disquiet; (*money*) to embarrass.

contus, -ī *m* pole.

contūsus *ppp of* **contundō**.

contūtus *see* **contuitus**.

cōnūbiālis *adj* conjugal.

cōnūbium, -ī *and* **iī** *nt* marriage; **iūs ~ī** right of intermarriage.

cōnus, -ī *m* cone; (*helmet*) apex.

convador, -ārī, -ātus *vt* (*law*) to bind over.

convalēscō, -ēscere, -uī *vi* to recover, get better; (*fig*) to grow stronger, improve.

convallis, -is *f* valley with hills on all sides.

convāsō, -āre *vt* to pack up.

convectō, -āre *vt* to bring home.

convector, -ōris *m* fellow passenger.

convehō, -here, -xī, -ctum *vt* to bring in, carry.

convellō, -ellere, -ellī, -ulsum *and* **olsum** *vt* to wrench, tear away; to break up; (*fig*) to destroy, overthrow; **signa ~** decamp.

convena, -ae *adj* meeting.

convenae, -ārum *m/f* crowd of strangers, refugees.

conveniēns, -entis *pres p of* **conveniō** ♦ *adj* harmonious, consistent; fit, appropriate.

convenienter *adv* in conformity (with), consistently; aptly.

convenientia, -ae *f* conformity, harmony.

conveniō, -enīre, -ēnī, -entum *vi* to meet, assemble; (*events*) to combine, coincide; (*person*) to agree, harmonize; (*things*) to fit, suit; (*impers*) to be suitable, be proper ♦ *vt* to speak to, interview.

conventīcium, -ī *and* **iī** *nt* payment for attendance at assemblies.

conventīcius *adj* visiting regularly.

conventiculum, -ī *nt* gathering; meeting place.

conventiō, -ōnis *f* agreement.

conventum, -ī *nt* agreement.

conventus *ppp of* **conveniō**.

conventus, -ūs *m* meeting; (*law*) local assizes; (*comm*) corporation; agreement; **~ūs agere** hold the assizes.

converrō, -rere, -rī, -sum *vt* to sweep up, brush together; (*comedy*) to give a good beating to.

conversātiō, -ōnis *f* associating (with).

conversiō, -ōnis *f* revolution, cycle; change over; (*RHET*) well-rounded period; verbal repetition at end of clauses.

conversō, -āre *vt* to turn round.

conversus *ppp of* **converrō**; *ppp of* **convertō**.

convertō, -tere, -tī, -sum *vt* to turn round, turn back; (*MIL*) to wheel; to turn, direct; to change, transform; (*writings*) to translate ♦ *vi* to return, turn, change.

convestiō, -īre, -īvī, -ītum *vt* to clothe, encompass.

convexus *adj* vaulted, rounded; hollow; sloping ♦ *nt* vault, hollow.

convīciātor, -ōris *m* slanderer.

convīcior, -ārī, -ātus *vt* to revile.

convīcium, -ī *and* **iī** *nt* loud noise, outcry; invective, abuse; reproof, protest.

convīctiō, -ōnis *f* companionship.

convīctor, -ōris *m* familiar friend.

convīctus *ppp of* **convincō**.

convīctus, -ūs *m* community life, intercourse; entertainment.

convincō, -incere, -īcī, -ictum *vt* to refute, convict, prove wrong; to prove, demonstrate.

convīsō, -ere *vt* to search, examine; to pervade.

convītium *see* **convīcium**.

convīva, -ae *m/f* guest.

convīvālis *adj* festive, convivial.

convīvātor, -ōris *m* host.

convīvium, -ī *and* **iī** *nt* banquet, entertainment; guests.

convīvor, -ārī, -ātus *vi* to feast together, carouse.

convocātiō, -ōnis *f* assembling.

convocō, -āre, -āvī, -ātum *vt* to call a meeting of, muster.

convolnerō *see* **convulnerō**.

convolō, -āre, -āvī, -ātum *vi* to flock together.

convolsus *see* **convulsus**.

convolvō, -vere, -vī, -ūtum *vt* to roll up, coil up; to intertwine.

convomō, -ere *vt* to vomit over.

convorrō *see* **converrō**.

convortō *see* **convertō**.

convulnerō, -āre *vt* to wound seriously.

convulsus *ppp of* **convellō**.

cooperiō, -īre, -uī, -tum *vt* to cover over, overwhelm.

cooptātiō, -ōnis *f* electing, nominating (of new members).

cooptō, -āre, -āvī, -ātum *vt* to elect (as a colleague).

coorior, -īrī, -tus *vi* to rise, appear; to break out, begin.

coortus, -ūs *m* originating.

cōpa, -ae *f* barmaid.

cophinus, -ī *m* basket.

cōpia, -ae *f* abundance, plenty, number; resources, wealth, prosperity; (*MIL, usu pl*) troops, force; (*words, thought*) richness, fulness, store; (*action*) opportunity, facility, means, access; **prō ~ā** according to one's resources, as good as possible considering.

cōpiolae, -ārum *fpl* small force.

cōpiōsē *adv* abundantly, fully, at great length.

cōpiōsus *adj* abounding, rich, plentiful; (*speech*) eloquent, fluent.

cōpis *adj* rich.

cōpula, -ae *f* rope, leash, grapnel; (*fig*) bond.

cōpulātiō, -ōnis *f* coupling, union.

cōpulātus *adj* connected, binding.

cōpulō, -āre, -āvī, -ātum *vt* to couple, join; (*fig*) to unite, associate.

coqua, -ae *f* cook.

coquīnō, -āre *vi* to be a cook.

coquīnus *adj* of cooking.

coquō, -quere, -xī, -ctum *vt* to cook, boil, bake; to parch, burn; (*fruit*) to ripen; (*stomach*) to digest; (*thought*) to plan, concoct; (*care*) to disquiet, disturb.

coquus (cocus), -ī *m* cook.

cor, cordis *nt* heart; (*feeling*) heart, soul; (*thought*) mind, judgement; **cordī esse** please, be agreeable.

cōram *adv* in one's presence; in person ♦ *prep* (*with abl*) in the presence of, before.

corbis, -is *m/f* basket.

corbīta, -ae *f* slow boat.

corbula, -ae *f* little basket.

corculum, -ī *nt* dear heart.

Corcȳra, -ae *f* island off W. coast of Greece (*now* Corfu).

Corcȳraeus *adj see n.*

cordātē *adv see* **cordātus**.

cordātus *adj* wise.

cordolium, -ī *and* **iī** *nt* sorrow.

Corfiniēnsis *adj see n.*

Corfinium, -ī *nt town in central Italy.*

coriandrum, -ī *nt* coriander.

Corinthiacus, -iēnsis, -ius *adj*: **~ium aes** Corinthian brass (*an alloy of gold, silver and copper*).

Corinthus, -ī *f* Corinth.

corium (corius *m*) **-ī** *and* **iī** *nt* hide, skin; leather, strap.

Cornēlia, -iae *f* mother of the Gracchi.

Cornēliānus, -ius *adj*: **lēgēs ~iae** Sulla's laws.

Cornēlius, -ī *m* famous Roman family name (*esp Scipios, Gracchi, Sulla*).

corneolus *adj* horny.

corneus *adj* of horn.

corneus *adj* of the cornel tree, of cornel wood.

cornicen, -inis *m* horn-blower.

cornīcula, -ae *f* little crow.

corniculārius, -ī *and* **iī** *m* adjutant.

corniculum, -ī *nt* a horn-shaped decoration.

corniger, -ī *adj* horned.

cornipēs, -edis *adj* horn-footed.

cornīx, -īcis *f* crow.

cornū, -ūs, -um, -ī *nt* horn; anything horn-shaped; (*army*) wing; (*bay*) arm; (*book*) roller-end; (*bow*) tip; (*helmet*) crest-socket; (*land*) tongue, spit; (*lyre*) arm; (*moon*) horn; (*place*) side; (*river*) branch; (*yardarm*) point; anything made of horn: bow, funnel, lantern; (*music*) horn; (*oil*) cruet; anything like horn; beak, hoof, wart; (*fig*) strength, courage; **~ cōpiae** Amalthea's horn, symbol of plenty.

cornum, -ī *nt* cornelian cherry.

cornum *see* **cornū.**

cornus, -ī *f* cornelian cherry tree; javelin.

corōlla, -ae *f* small garland.

corōllārium, -ī *and* **iī** *nt* garland for actors; present, gratuity.

corōna, -ae *f* garland, crown; (ASTRO) Corona Borealis; (*people*) gathering, bystanders; (MIL) cordon of besiegers *or* defenders; **sub ~ā vēndere, vēnīre** sell, be sold as slaves.

Corōnaeus, -ēus, -ēnsis *adj see* **Corōnēa.**

corōnārium aurum gold collected in the provinces for a victorious general.

Corōnēa, -eae *f* town in central Greece.

corōnō, -āre, -āvī, -ātum *vt* to put a garland on, crown; to encircle.

corporeus *adj* corporeal; of flesh.

corpulentus *adj* corpulent.

corpus, -oris *nt* body; substance, flesh; corpse; trunk, torso; person, individual; (*fig*) structure, corporation, body politic.

corpusculum, -ī *nt* particle; term of endearment.

corrādō, -dere, -sī, -sum *vt* to scrape together, procure.

correctiō, -ōnis *f* amending, improving.

corrēctor, -ōris *m* reformer, critic.

corrēctus *ppp of* **corrigō.**

corrēpō, -ere, -sī *vi* to creep, slink, cower.

correptē *adv* briefly.

correptus *ppp of* **corripiō.**

corrīdeō, -ēre *vi* to laugh aloud.

corrigia, -ae *f* shoelace.

corrigō, -igere, -ēxī, -ēctum *vt* to make straight; to put right, improve, correct.

corripiō, -ipere, -ipuī, -eptum *vt* to seize, carry off, get along quickly; (*speech*) to reprove, reproach, accuse; (*passion*) to seize upon, attack; (*time, words*) to cut short; **sē gradum, viam ~** hasten, rush.

corrōborō, -āre, -āvī, -ātum *vt* to make strong, invigorate.

corrōdō, -dere, -sī, -sum *vt* to nibble away.

corrogō, -āre *vt* to gather by requesting.

corrūgō, -āre *vt* to wrinkle.

corrumpō, -umpere, -ūpī, -uptum *vt* to break up, ruin, waste; to mar, adulterate, falsify; (*person*) to corrupt, seduce, bribe.

corruō, -ere, -ī *vi* to fall, collapse ♦ *vt* to overthrow, heap up.

corruptē *adv* perversely; in a lax manner.

corruptēla, -ae *f* corruption, bribery; seducer.

corruptiō, -ōnis *f* bribing, seducing; corrupt state.

corruptor, -ōris *m*, **-rīx, -rīcis** *f* corrupter, seducer.

corruptus *ppp of* **corrumpō** ♦ *adj* spoiled, corrupt, bad.

Corsus *adj* Corsican.

cortex, -icis *m/f* bark, rind; cork.

cortīna, -ae *f* kettle, cauldron; tripod of Apollo; (*fig*) vault, circle.

corulus, -ī *f* hazel.

Cōrus *see* **Caurus.**

coruscō, -āre *vt* to butt; to shake, brandish ♦ *vi* to flutter, flash, quiver.

coruscus *adj* tremulous, oscillating; shimmering, glittering.

corvus, -ī *m* raven; (MIL) grapnel.

Corybantēs, -ium *mpl* priests of Cybele.

Corybantius *adj see n.*

cōrycus, -ī *m* punchbag.

corylētum, -ī *nt* hazel copse.

corylus, -ī *f* hazel.

corymbifer *m* Bacchus.

corymbus, -ī *m* cluster (*esp of ivy berries*).

coryphaeus, -ī *m* leader.

cōrytos, -us, -ī *m* quiver.

cōs *f* hard rock, flint; grindstone.

Cōs, Coī *f* Aegean island (*famous for wine and weaving*) ♦ *nt* Coan wine ♦ *ntpl* Coan clothes.

cosmēta, -ae *m* master of the wardrobe.

costa, -ae *f* rib; side, wall.

costum, -ī *nt* an aromatic plant, perfume.

cothurnātus *adj* buskined, tragic.

cothurnus, -ī *m* buskin, hunting boot; tragedy, elevated style.

cotīd *see* **cottīd-.**

---

cōtis *f see* **cōs**.

cottabus, -ī *m* game of throwing drops of wine.

cottana, -ōrum *ntpl* Syrian figs.

cottīdiānō *adv* daily.

cottīdiānus *adj* daily; everyday, ordinary.

cottīdiē *adv* every day, daily.

coturnīx, -īcis *f* quail.

Cotyttia, -ōrum *ntpl festival of Thracian goddess Cotytto.*

Cōus *adj* Coan.

covinnārius, -ī *and* **iī** *m* chariot fighter.

covinnus, -ī *m* war chariot; coach.

coxa, -ae, coxendīx, -īcis *f* hip.

coxī *perf of* **coquō**.

crābrō, -ōnis *m* hornet.

crambē-, -ēs *f* cabbage; ~ **repetīta** stale repetitions.

Crantor, -oris *m Greek Academic philosopher.*

crāpula, -ae *f* intoxication, hangover.

crāpulārius *adj* for intoxication.

crās *adv* tomorrow.

crassē *adv* grossly, dimly.

Crassiānus *adj see* **Crassus**.

crassitūdō, -inis *f* thickness, density.

crassus *adj* thick, gross, dense; (*fig*) dull, stupid.

Crassus, -ī *m famous orator; wealthy politician, triumvir with Caesar and Pompey.*

crāstinum, -ī *nt* the morrow.

crāstinus *adj* of tomorrow; **diē ~ī** tomorrow.

crātēr, -is *m*, **-a, -ae** *f* bowl (*esp for mixing wine and water*); crater; a constellation.

crātis, -is *f* wickerwork, hurdle; (AGR) harrow; (MIL) faggots for lining trenches; (*shield*) ribs; (*fig*) frame, joints.

creātiō, -ōnis *f* election.

creātor, -ōris *m*, **-rīx, -rīcis** *f* creator, father, mother.

creātus *m* (*with abl*) son of.

crēber, -rī *adj* dense, thick, crowded; numerous, frequent; (*fig*) prolific, abundant.

crēbrēscō, -ēscere, -uī *vi* to increase, become frequent.

crēbritās, -ātis *f* frequency.

crēbrō *adv* repeatedly.

crēdibilis *adj* credible.

crēdibiliter *adv see* **crēdibilis**.

crēditor, -ōris *m* creditor.

crēditum, -itī *nt* loan.

crēdō, -ere, -idī, -itum *vt, vi* to entrust, lend; to trust, have confidence in; to believe; to think, suppose; **~erēs** one would have thought.

crēdulitās, -ātis *f* credulity.

crēdulus *adj* credulous, trusting.

cremō, -āre, -āvī, -ātum *vt* to burn, cremate.

Cremōna, -ae *f town in N. Italy.*

Cremōnēnsis *adj see n.*

cremor, -ōris *m* juice, broth.

creō, -āre, -āvī, -ātum *vt* to create, produce, beget; to elect (to an office); to cause, occasion.

creper, -ī *adj* dark; doubtful.

crepida, -ae *f* sandal; **nē sūtor suprā ~am** ≈ *let the cobbler stick to his last.*

crepidātus *adj* wearing sandals.

crepīdō, -inis *f* pedestal, base; bank, pier, dam.

crepidula, -ae *f* small sandal.

crepitācillum, -ī *nt* rattle.

crepitō, -āre *vi* to rattle, chatter, rustle, creak.

crepitus, -ūs *m* rattling, chattering, rustling, creaking.

crepō, -āre, -uī, -itum *vi* to rattle, creak, snap (fingers) ♦ *vt* to make rattle, clap; to chatter about.

crepundia, -ōrum *ntpl* rattle, babies' toys.

crepusculum, -ī *nt* twilight, dusk; darkness.

Crēs, -ētis *m* Cretan.

crēscō, -scere, -vī, -tum *vi* to arise, appear, be born; to grow up, thrive, increase, multiply; to prosper, be promoted, rise in the world.

Crēsius *adj* Cretan.

Crēssa, -ae *f* Cretan.

Crēta, -ae *f* Crete.

crēta, -ae *f* chalk; good mark.

Crētaeus *and* **-icus** *and* **-is, -idis** *adj see n.*

crētātus *adj* chalked; dressed in white.

Crētē *see* **Crēta**.

crēteus *adj* of chalk, of clay.

crētiō, -ōnis *f* declaration of accepting an inheritance.

crētōsus *adj* chalky, clayey.

crētula, -ae *f* white clay for sealing.

crētus *ppp of* **cernō** ♦ *ppa of* **crēscō** ♦ *adj* descended, born.

Creūsa, -ae *f wife of Jason; wife of Aeneas.*

crēvī *perf of* **cernō**; *perf of* **crēscō**.

crībrum, -ī *nt* sieve.

crīmen, -inis *nt* accusation, charge, reproach; guilt, crime; cause of offence; **esse in ~ine** stand accused.

crīminātiō, -ōnis *f* complaint, slander.

crīminātor, -ōris *m* accuser.

crīminō, -āre *vt* to accuse.

crīminor, -ārī, -ātus *dep* to accuse, impeach; (*things*) to complain of, charge with.

crīminōsē *adv* accusingly, slanderously.

crīminōsus *adj* reproachful, slanderous.

crīnālis *adj* for the hair, hair- (*in cpds*) ♦ *nt* hairpin.

crīnis, -is *m* hair; (*comet*) tail.

crīnītus *adj* long-haired; crested; **stēlla ~a** comet.

crīspāns, -antis *adj* wrinkled.

crīspō, -āre *vt* to curl, swing, wave.

crīspus *adj* curled; curly-headed; wrinkled; tremulous.

crista, -ae *f* cockscomb, crest; plume.

cristātus *adj* crested, plumed.

criticus, -ī *m* critic.

croceus *adj* of saffron, yellow.

crocinus *adj* yellow ♦ *nt* saffron oil.

crōciō, -īre *vi* to croak.
crocodīlus, -ī *m* crocodile.
crocōtārius *adj* of saffron clothes.
crocōtula, -ae *f* saffron dress.
crocus, -ī *m*, **-um, -ī** *nt* saffron; yellow.
Croesus, -ī *m* king of Lydia (*famed for wealth*).
crotalistria, -ae *f* castanet dancer.
crotalum, -ī *nt* rattle, castanet.
cruciābilitās, -ātis *f* torment.
cruciāmentum, -ī *nt* torture.
cruciātus, -ūs *m* torture; instrument of torture; (*fig*) ruin, misfortune.
cruciō, -āre, -āvī, -ātum *vt* to torture; to torment.
crūdēlis *adj* hard-hearted, cruel.
crūdēlitās, -ātis *f* cruelty, severity.
crūdēliter *adv see* **crūdēlis**.
crūdēscō, -ēscere, -uī *vi* to grow violent, grow worse.
crūditās, -ātis *f* indigestion.
crūdus *adj* bleeding; (*food*) raw, undigested; (*person*) dyspeptic; (*leather*) rawhide; (*fruit*) unripe; (*age*) immature, fresh; (*voice*) hoarse; (*fig*) unfeeling, cruel, merciless.
cruentō, -āre *vt* to stain with blood, wound.
cruentus *adj* bloody, gory; bloodthirsty, cruel; blood-red.
crumēna, -ae *f* purse; money.
crumilla, -ae *f* purse.
cruor, -ōris *m* blood; bloodshed.
cruppellāriī, -ōrum *mpl* mail-clad fighters.
crūrifragius, -ī *and* **iī** *m* one whose legs have been broken.
crūs, -ūris *nt* leg, shin.
crūsta, -ae *f* hard surface, crust; stucco, embossed *or* inlaid work.
crūstulum, -ī *nt* small pastry.
crūstum, -ī *nt* pastry.
crux, -ucis *f* gallows, cross; (*fig*) torment; **abī in malam ~cem** ≈ go and be hanged!
crypta, -ae *f* underground passage, grotto.
cryptoporticus, -ūs *f* covered walk.
crystallinus *adj* of crystal ♦ *ntpl* crystal vases.
crystallum, -ī *nt*, **-us, -ī** *m* crystal.
cubiculāris, cubiculārius *adj* of the bedroom ♦ *m* valet de chambre.
cubiculum, -ī *nt* bedroom.
cubīle, -is *nt* bed, couch; (*animals*) lair, nest; (*fig*) den.
cubital, -ālis *nt* cushion.
cubitālis *adj* a cubit long.
cubitō, -āre *vi* to lie (in bed).
cubitum, -ī *nt* elbow; cubit.
cubitus, -ūs *m* lying in bed.
cubō, -āre, -uī, -itum *vi* to lie in bed; to recline at table; (*places*) to lie on a slope.
cucullus, -ī *m* hood, cowl.
cucūlus, -ī *m* cuckoo.
cucumis, -eris *m* cucumber.
cucurbita, -ae *f* gourd; cupping glass.

cucurrī *perf of* **currō**.
cūdō, -ere *vt* to beat, thresh; (*metal*) to forge; (*money*) to coin.
cūiās, -tis *pron* of what country?, of what town?
cuicuimodī (*gen of* **quisquis** *and* **mōdus**) of whatever kind, whatever like.
cūius *pron* (*interrog*) whose?; (*rel*) whose.
culcita, -ae *f* mattress, pillow; eyepatch.
cūleus *see* **culleus**.
culex, -icis *m/f* gnat.
culīna, -ae *f* kitchen; food.
culleus, cūleus, -ī *m* leather bag for holding liquids; a fluid measure.
culmen, -inis *nt* stalk; top, roof, summit; (*fig*) height, acme.
culmus, -ī *m* stalk, straw.
culpa, -ae *f* blame, fault; mischief; **in ~ā sum, mea ~a est** I am at fault *or* to blame.
culpātus *adj* blameworthy.
culpitō, -āre *vt* to find fault with.
culpō, -āre, -āvī, -ātum *vt* to blame, reproach.
cultē *adv* in a refined manner.
cultellus, -ī *m* small knife.
culter, -rī *m* knife, razor.
cultiō, -ōnis *f* cultivation.
cultor, -ōris *m* cultivator, planter, farmer; inhabitant; supporter, upholder; worshipper.
cultrīx, -icis *f* inhabitant; (*fig*) nurse, fosterer.
cultūra, -ae *f* cultivation, agriculture; (*mind*) care, culture; (*person*) courting.
cultus *ppp of* **colō** ♦ *adj* cultivated; (*dress*) well-dressed; (*mind*) polished, cultured ♦ *ntpl* cultivated land.
cultus, -ūs *m* cultivation, care; (*mind*) training, culture; (*dress*) style, attire; (*way of life*) refinement, civilization; (*gods*) worship; (*men*) honouring.
culullus, -ī *m* goblet.
cūlus, -ī *m* buttocks.
cum *prep* (*with abl*) with; (*denoting accompaniment, resulting circumstances, means, dealings, comparison, possession*); **~ decimō** tenfold; **~ eō quod, ut** with the proviso that; **~ prīmīs** especially; **~ māgnā calamitāte cīvitātis** to the great misfortune of the community; **~ perīculō suō** at one's own peril.
cum *conj* (*time*) when, whenever, while, as, after, since; (*cause*) since, as, seeing that; (*concession*) although; (*condition*) if; (*contrast*) while, whereas; **multī annī sunt ~ in aere meō est** for many years now he has been in my debt; **aliquot sunt annī ~ vōs dēlēgī** it is now some years since I chose you; **~ māximē** just when; just then, just now; **~ prīmum** as soon as; **~ ... tum** not only ... but also; both ... and.

Noun declensions and verb conjugations are shown on pp xiii to xxv. The present infinitive ending of a verb shows to which conjugation it belongs: **-āre** = 1st; **-ēre** = 2nd; **-ere** = 3rd and **-īre** = 4th. Irregular verbs are shown on p xxvi

Cūmae, -ārum *fpl* town near Naples (*famous for its Sibyl*).

Cūmaeānum, -āni *nt Cicero's Cumaean residence.*

Cūmaeus, -ānus *adj see n.*

cumba, cymba, -ae *f* boat, skiff.

cumera, -ae *f* grain chest.

cumīnum, -ī *nt* cumin.

cumque (quomque) *adv* -ever, -soever; at any time.

cumulātē *adv* fully, abundantly.

cumulātus *adj* increased; complete.

cumulō, -āre, -āvī, -ātum *vt* to heap up; to amass, increase; to fill up, overload; (*fig*) to fill, overwhelm, crown, complete.

cumulus, -ī *m* heap, mass; crowning addition, summit.

cūnābula, -ōrum *ntpl* cradle.

cūnae, -ārum *fpl* cradle.

cunctābundus *adj* hesitant, dilatory.

cunctāns, -antis *adj* dilatory, reluctant; sluggish, tough.

cunctanter *adv* slowly.

cunctātiō, -ōnis *f* delaying, hesitation.

cunctātor, -ōris *m* loiterer; one given to cautious tactics (*esp Q Fabius Maximus*).

cunctor, -ārī, -ātus *vi* to linger, delay, hesitate; to move slowly.

cūnctus *adj* the whole of; (*pl*) all together, all.

cuneātim *adv* in the form of a wedge.

cuneātus *adj* wedge-shaped.

cuneus, -ī *m* wedge; (MIL) wedge-shaped formation of troops; (THEATRE) block of seats.

cunīculus, -ī *m* rabbit; underground passage; (MIL) mine.

cunque *see* **cumque.**

cūpa, -ae *f* vat, tun.

cupidē *adv* eagerly, passionately.

Cupīdineus *adj see* **Cupīdō.**

cupiditās, -ātis *f* desire, eagerness, enthusiasm; passion, lust; avarice, greed; ambition; partisanship.

cupīdō, -inis *f* desire, eagerness; passion, lust; greed.

Cupīdō, -inis *m* Cupid (*son of Venus*).

cupidus *adj* desirous, eager; fond, loving; passionate, lustful; greedy, ambitious; partial.

cupiēns, -entis *pres p of* **cupiō** ♦ *adj* eager, desirous.

cupienter *adv see* **cupiēns.**

cupiō, -ere, -īvī *and* **iī, -ītum** *vt* to wish, desire, long for; (*with dat*) to wish well.

cupītor, -ōris *m* desirer.

cupītus *ppp of* **cupiō.**

cuppēdia, -ae *f* fondness for delicacies.

cuppēdia, -ōrum *ntpl* delicacies.

cuppēdinārius, -ī *m* confectioner.

cuppēdō, -inis *f* longing, passion.

cuppes, -dis *adj* fond of delicacies.

cupressētum, -ī *nt* cypress grove.

cupresseus *adj* of cypress wood.

cupressifer, -ī *adj* cypress-bearing.

cupressus, -ī *f* cypress.

cūr *adv* why?; (*indirect*) why, the reason for.

cūra, -ae *f* care, trouble, pains (bestowed); anxiety, concern, sorrow (felt); attention (to), charge (of), concern (for); (MED) treatment, cure; (*writing*) work; (*law*) trusteeship; (*poet*) love; (*person*) mistress, guardian; **~ est** I am anxious; **~ae esse** be attended to, looked after.

cūrābilis *adj* troublesome.

cūralium, -ī *and* **iī** *nt* red coral.

cūrātē *adv* carefully.

cūrātiō, -ōnis *f* charge, management; office; treatment, healing.

cūrātor, -ōris *m* manager, overseer; (*law*) guardian.

cūrātūra, -ae *f* dieting.

cūrātus *adj* cared for; earnest, anxious.

curculiō, -ōnis *m* weevil.

curculiunculus, -ī *m* little weevil.

Curēnsis *adj see n.*

Curēs, -ium *mpl* ancient Sabine town.

Curētēs, -um *mpl attendants of Jupiter in Crete.*

Cūrētis, -idis *adj* Cretan.

cūria, -ae *f* earliest division of the Roman people; meeting-place of a curia; senate house; senate.

cūriālis, -is *m* member of a curia.

cūriātim *adv* by curiae.

cūriātus *adj* of the curiae; **comitia ~a** earliest Roman assembly.

cūriō, -ōnis *m* president of a curia; **~ māximus** head of all the curiae.

cūriō, -ōnis *adj* emaciated.

cūriōsē *adv* carefully; inquisitively.

cūriōsitās, -ātis *f* curiosity.

cūriōsus *adj* careful, thoughtful, painstaking; inquiring, inquisitive, officious; careworn.

curis, -ītis *f* spear.

cūrō, -āre, -āvī, -ātum *vt* to take care of, attend to; to bother about; (*with gerundive*) to get something done; (*with inf*) to take the trouble; (*with ut*) to see to it that; (*public life*) to be in charge of, administer; (MED) to treat, cure; (*money*) to pay, settle up; **aliud ~ā** never mind; **corpus/cutem ~** take it easy; **prōdigia ~** avert portents.

curriculum, -ī *nt* running, race; course, lap; (*fig*) career; **~ō** at full speed.

currō, -ere, cucurrī, cursum *vi* to run; to hasten, fly ♦ *vt* to run through, traverse; **~entem incitāre** ≈ *spur a willing horse.*

currus, -ūs *m* car, chariot; triumph; team of horses; ploughwheels.

cursim *adv* quickly, at the double.

cursitō, -āre *vi* to run about, fly hither and thither.

cursō, -āre *vi* to run about.

cursor, -ōris *m* runner, racer; courier.

cursūra, -ae *f* running.

cursus, -ūs *m* running, speed; passage, journey; course, direction; (*things*) movement, flow; (*fig*) rapidity, flow, progress; **~ honōrum** succession of magistracies; **~ rērum** course of events; **~um tenēre** keep on one's course; **~ū** at a run; **māgnō ~ū** at full speed.

curtō, -āre *vt* to shorten.

curtus *adj* short, broken off; incomplete.

curūlis *adj* official, curule; **aedīlis ~** patrician, aediile; **sella ~** magistrates' chair; **equī ~** horses provided for the games by the state.

curvāmen, -inis *nt* bend.

curvātūra, -ae *f* curve.

curvō, -āre, -āvī, -ātum *vt* to curve, bend, arch; (*fig*) to move.

curvus *adj* bent, curved, crooked; (*person*) aged; (*fig*) wrong.

cuspis, -dis *f* point; spear, javelin, trident, sting.

custōdēla, -ae *f* care, guard.

custōdia, -ae *f* watch, guard, care; (*person*) sentry, guard; (*place*) sentry's post, guardhouse; custody, confinement, prison; **lībera ~** confinement in one's own house.

custōdiō, -īre, -īvī *and* **iī, -ītum** *vt* to guard, defend; to hold in custody, keep watch on; to keep, preserve, observe.

custōs, -ōdis *m/f* guard, bodyguard, protector, protectress; jailer, warder; (MIL) sentry, spy; container.

cutīcula, -ae *f* skin.

cutis, -is *f* skin; **~em cūrāre** ≈ take it easy.

cyathissō, -āre *vi* to serve wine.

cyathus, -ī *m* wine ladle; (*measure*) one-twelfth of a pint.

cybaea, -ae *f* kind of merchant ship.

Cybēbē, Cybelē, -ēs *f* Phrygian mother-goddess, Magna Mater.

Cybelēius *adj see n.*

Cyclades, -um *fpl* group of Aegean islands.

cyclas, -adis *f* formal dress with a border.

cyclicus *adj* of the traditional epic stories.

Cyclōpius *adj see n.*

Cyclōps, -is *m* one-eyed giant (*esp* Polyphemus).

cycnēus *adj* of a swan, swan's.

cycnus, -ī *m* swan.

Cydōnius *adj* Cretan ♦ *ntpl* quinces.

cygnus *see* **cycnus.**

cylindrus, -ī *m* cylinder; roller.

Cyllēnē, -ēs *and* **ae** *f* mountain in Arcadia.

Cyllēnēus, -is, -ius *adj see n.*

Cyllēnius, -ī *m* Mercury.

cymba *see* **cumba.**

cymbalum, -ī *nt* cymbal.

cymbium, -ī *and* **iī** *nt* cup.

Cynicē *adv* like the Cynics.

Cynicus, -ī *m* a Cynic philosopher (*esp* Diogenes) ♦ *adj* Cynic.

cynocephalus, -ī *m* dog-headed ape.

Cynosūra, -ae *f* constellation of Ursa Minor.

Cynosūris, -idis *adj see n.*

Cynthia, -iae *f* Diana.

Cynthius, -ī *m* Apollo.

Cynthus, -ī *m* hill in Delos (*birthplace of Apollo and Diana*).

cyparissus, -ī *f* cypress.

Cypris, -idis *f* Venus.

Cyprius *adj* Cyprian; copper.

Cyprus, -ī *f* island of Cyprus (*famed for its copper and the worship of Venus*).

Cyrēnaeī, -aicī *mpl* followers of Aristippus.

Cyrēnaeus, -aicus, -ēnsis *adj see n.*

Cyrēnē, -ēs *f*, **-ae, -ārum** *fpl* town and province of N. Africa.

Cyrnēus *adj* Corsican.

Cȳrus, -ī *m* Persian king.

Cytaeis, -idis *f* Medea.

Cythēra, -ae *f* island S. of Greece (*famed for its worship of Venus*).

Cytherēa, -ēae *and* **-ēia, -ēiae** *and* **-ēis, -ēidis** *f* Venus.

Cytherēus, Cythēriacus *adj* Cytherean; of Venus.

cytisus, -ī *m/f* cytisus (*a kind of clover*).

Cyzicēnus *adj see* **Cyzicum.**

Cyzicum, -ī *nt*, **-us, -os, -ī** *f* town on Sea of Marmora.

D, d

Dācī, -ōrum *mpl* Dacians, a people on the lower Danube.

Dācia, -iae *f* the country of the Dācī (*now Romania*).

Dācicus, -icī *m* gold coin of Domitian's reign.

dactylicus *adj* dactylic.

dactylus, -ī *m* dactyl.

Daedalēus *adj see n.*

daedalus *adj* artistic, skilful in creating; skilfully made, variegated.

Daedalus, -ī *m* mythical Athenian craftsman and inventor.

Dalmatae, -ārum *mpl* Dalmatians (*a people on the East coast of the Adriatic*).

Dalmatia, -iae *f* Dalmatia.

Dalmaticus *adj see n.*

dāma, -ae *f* deer; venison.

Damascēnus *adj see n.*

Damascus, -ī *f* Damascus.

damma *f see* **dama.**

damnātiō, -ōnis *f* condemnation.

damnātōrius *adj* condemnatory.

damnātus *adj* criminal; miserable.

damnificus *adj* pernicious.

Noun declensions and verb conjugations are shown on pp xiii to xxv. The present infinitive ending of a verb shows to which conjugation it belongs: **-āre** = 1st; **-ēre** = 2nd; **-ere** = 3rd and **-īre** = 4th. Irregular verbs are shown on p xxvi

damnō, -āre, -āvī, -ātum *vt* to condemn, sentence; to procure the conviction of; (*heirs*) to oblige; to censure; **capitis/capite ~** condemn to death; **māiestātis, dē māiestāte ~** condemn for treason; **vōtī ~** oblige to fulfil a vow.

damnōsē *adv* ruinously.

damnōsus *adj* harmful, ruinous; spendthrift; wronged.

damnum, -ī *nt* loss, harm, damage; (*law*) fine, damages; **~ facere** suffer loss.

Danaē, -ēs *f* mother of Perseus.

Danaēius *adj* see n.

Danaī, -ōrum *and* **um** *mpl* the Greeks.

Danaides, -idum *fpl* daughters of Danaus.

Danaus, -ī *m* king of Argos and father of 50 daughters.

Danaus *adj* Greek.

danista, -ae *m* moneylender.

danisticus *adj* moneylending.

danō *see* **dō.**

Dānuvius, -ī *m* upper Danube.

Daphnē, -ēs *f* nymph changed into a laurel tree.

Daphnis, -idis (*acc* **-im** *and* **-in**) *m* mythical Sicilian shepherd.

dapinō, -āre *vt* to serve (food).

daps, dapis *f* religious feast; meal, banquet.

dapsilis *adj* sumptuous, abundant.

Dardania, -iae *f* Troy.

Dardanidēs, -idae *m* Trojan (*esp Aeneas*).

Dardanus, -ī *m* son of Jupiter and ancestor of Trojan kings.

Dardanus, -ius, -is, -idis *adj* Trojan.

Darēus, -ī *m* Persian king.

datārius *adj* to give away.

datātim *adv* passing from one to the other.

datiō, -ōnis *f* right to give away; (*laws*) making.

datō, -āre *vt* to be in the habit of giving.

dator, -ōris *m* giver; (*sport*) bowler.

Daulias, -adis *adj* see n.

Daulis, -dis *f* town in central Greece (*noted for the story of Procne and Philomela*).

Daunias, -iadis *f* Apulia.

Daunius *adj* Rutulian; Italian.

Daunus, -ī *m* legendary king of Apulia (*ancestor of Turnus*).

dē *prep* (*with abl: movement*) down from, from; (*origin*) from, of, out of; (*time*) immediately after, in; (*thought, talk, action*) about, concerning; (*reason*) for, because of; (*imitation*) after, in accordance with; **~ industriā** on purpose; **~ integrō** afresh; **~ nocte** during the night; **diem ~ diē** from day to day.

dea, -ae *f* goddess.

dealbō, -āre *vt* to whitewash, plaster.

deambulātiō, -ōnis *f* walk.

deambulō, -āre, -āvī, -ātum *vi* to go for a walk.

deamō, -āre, -āvī, -ātum *vt* to be in love with; to be much obliged to.

dearmātus *adj* disarmed.

deartuō, -āre, -āvī, -ātum *vt* to dismember, ruin.

deasciō, -āre *vt* to smooth with an axe; (*fig*) to cheat.

dēbacchor, -ārī, -ātus *vi* to rage furiously.

dēbellātor, -ōris *m* conqueror.

dēbellō, -āre, -āvī, -ātum *vi* to bring a war to an end ♦ *vt* to subdue; to fight out.

dēbeō, -ēre, -uī, -itum *vt* to owe; (*with inf*) to be bound, ought, should, must; to have to thank for, be indebted for; (*pass*) to be destined.

dēbilis *adj* frail, weak, crippled.

dēbilitās, -ātis *f* weakness, infirmity.

dēbilitātiō, -ōnis *f* weakening.

dēbilitō, -āre, -āvī, -ātum *vt* to cripple, disable; (*fig*) to paralyse, unnerve.

dēbitiō, -ōnis *f* owing.

dēbitor, -ōris *m* debtor.

dēbitum, -ī *nt* debt.

dēblaterō, -āre *vt* to blab.

dēcantō, -āre, -āvī, -ātum *vt* to keep on repeating ♦ *vi* to stop singing.

dēcēdō, -ēdere, -essī, -essum *vi* to withdraw, depart; to retire from a province (*after term of office*); to abate, cease, die; (*rights*) to give up, forgo; (*fig*) to go wrong, swerve (from duty); **dē viā ~** get out of the way.

decem *num* ten.

December, -ris *adj* of December ♦ *m* December.

decempeda, -ae *f* ten-foot rule.

decempedātor, -ōris *m* surveyor.

decemplex, -icis *adj* tenfold.

decemprīmī, -ōrum *mpl* civic chiefs of Italian towns.

decemscalmus *adj* ten-oared.

decemvirālis *adj* of the decemviri.

decemvirātus, -ūs *m* office of decemvir.

decemvirī, -ōrum *and* **um** *mpl* commission of ten men (*for public or religious duties*).

decennis *adj* ten years'.

decēns, -entis *adj* seemly, proper; comely, handsome.

decenter *adv* with propriety.

decentia, -ae *f* comeliness.

dēceptus *ppp of* **dēcipiō.**

dēcernō, -ernere, -rēvī, -rētum *vt* to decide, determine; to decree; to fight it out, decide the issue.

dēcerpō, -ere, -sī, -tum *vt* to pluck off, gather; (*fig*) to derive, enjoy.

dēcertātiō, -ōnis *f* deciding the issue.

dēcertō, -āre, -āvī, -ātum *vi* to fight it out, decide the issue.

dēcessiō, -ōnis *f* departure; retirement (from a province); deduction, disappearance.

dēcessor, -ōris *m* retiring magistrate.

dēcessus, -ūs *m* retirement (from a province); death; (*tide*) ebbing.

decet, -ēre, -uīt *vt, vi* it becomes, suits; it is

right, proper.

decidō, -ere, -ī vi to fall down, fall off; to die; (fig) to fail, come down.

dēcīdō, -dere, -dī, -sum vt to cut off; to settle, put an end to.

deciēns, deciēs adv ten times.

decimus, decumus adj tenth; **cum ~ō** tenfold; **~um** for the tenth time.

dēcipiō, -ipere, -ēpī, -eptum vt to ensnare; to deceive, beguile, disappoint.

dēcīsiō, -ōnis f settlement.

dēcīsus ppp of **dēcīdō**.

Decius, -ī m Roman plebeian name (esp P Decius Mus, father and son, who devoted their lives in battle).

Decius, -iānus adj see n.

dēclāmātiō, -ōnis f loud talking; rhetorical exercise on a given theme.

dēclāmātor, -ōris m apprentice in public speaking.

dēclāmātōrius adj rhetorical.

dēclāmitō, -āre vi to practise rhetoric; to bluster ♦ vt to practise pleading.

dēclāmō, -āre, -āvī, -ātum vi to practise public speaking, declaim; to bluster.

dēclārātiō, -ōnis f expression, making known.

dēclārō, -āre, -āvī, -ātum vt to make known; to proclaim, announce, reveal, express, demonstrate.

dēclīnātiō, -ōnis f swerving; avoidance; (RHET) digression; (GRAM) inflection.

dēclīnō, -āre, -āvī, -ātum vt to turn aside, deflect; (eyes) to close; to evade, shun ♦ vi to turn aside, swerve; to digress.

dēclive nt slope, decline.

dēclīvis adj sloping, steep, downhill.

dēclīvitās, -ātis f sloping ground.

dēcocta, -ae f a cold drink.

dēcoctor, -ōris m bankrupt.

dēcoctus ppp of **dēcoquō** ♦ adj (style) ripe, elaborated.

dēcōlō, -āre vi to run out; (fig) to fail.

dēcolor, -ōris adj discoloured, faded; **~ aetās** a degenerate age.

dēcolōrātiō, -ōnis f discolouring.

dēcolōrō, -āre, -āvī, -ātum vt to discolour, deface.

dēcoquō, -quere, -xī, -ctum vt to boil down; to cook ♦ vi to go bankrupt.

decor, -ōris m comeliness, ornament, beauty.

decorē adv becomingly, beautifully.

decorō, -āre, -āvī, -ātum vt to adorn, embellish; (fig) to distinguish, honour.

decōrum, -ī nt propriety.

decōrus adj becoming, proper; beautiful, noble; adorned.

dēcrepitus adj decrepit.

dēcrēscō, -scere, -vī, -tum vi to decrease, wane, wear away; to disappear.

dēcrētum, -ī nt decree, resolution; (PHILOS) doctrine.

dēcrētus ppp of **dēcernō**.

dēcrēvī perf of **dēcernō**; perf of **dēcrēscō**.

decuma, -ae f tithe; provincial land tax; largess.

decumāna, -ae f wife of a tithe-collector.

decumānus adj paying tithes; (MIL) of the 10th cohort or legion ♦ m collector of tithes; **~ī, ~ōrum** mpl men of the 10th legion; **porta ~a** main gate of a Roman camp.

decumātēs, -ium adj pl subject to tithes.

dēcumbō, -mbere, -buī vi to lie down; to recline at table; to fall (in fight).

decumus see **decimus**.

decuria, -ae f group of ten; panel of judges; social club.

decuriātiō, -ōnis f, **decuriātus, -ūs** m dividing into decuriae.

decuriō, -āre, -āvī, -ātum vt to divide into decuriae or groups.

decuriō, -ōnis m head of a decuria; (MIL) cavalry officer; senator of a provincial town or colony.

dēcurrō, -rrere, -currī and **rrī, -rsum** vt, vi to run down, hurry, flow, sail down; to traverse; (MIL) to parade, charge; (time) to pass through; (fig) to have recourse to.

dēcursiō, -ōnis f military manoeuvre.

dēcursus ppp of **dēcurrō**.

dēcursus, -ūs m descent, downrush; (MIL) manoeuvre, attack; (time) career.

dēcurtātus adj mutilated.

decus, -oris nt ornament, glory, beauty; honour, virtue; (pl) heroic deeds.

dēcussō, -āre vt to divide crosswise.

dēcutiō, -tere, -ssī, -ssum vt to strike down, shake off.

dēdecet, -ēre, -uit vt it is unbecoming to, is a disgrace to.

dēdecorō, -āre vt to disgrace.

dēdecōrus adj dishonourable.

dēdecus, -oris nt disgrace, shame; vice, crime.

dedī perf of **dō**.

dēdicātiō, -ōnis f consecration.

dēdicō, -āre, -āvī, -ātum vt to consecrate, dedicate; to declare (property in a census return).

dēdidī perf of **dēdō**.

dēdignor, -ārī, -ātus vt to scorn, reject.

dēdiscō, -scere, -dicī vt to unlearn, forget.

dēditīcius, -ī and **iī** m one who has capitulated.

dēditiō, -ōnis f surrender, capitulation.

dēditus ppp of **dēdō** ♦ adj addicted, devoted; **~ā operā** intentionally.

dēdō, -ere, -idī, -itum vt to give up, yield, surrender; to devote.

dēdoceō, -ēre vt to teach not to.

dēdoleō, -ēre, -uī vi to cease grieving.

Noun declensions and verb conjugations are shown on pp xiii to xxv. The present infinitive ending of a verb shows to which conjugation it belongs: **-āre** = 1st; **-ēre** = 2nd; **-ere** = 3rd and **-īre** = 4th. Irregular verbs are shown on p xxvi

dēdūcō, -ūcere, -ūxī, -uctum _vt_ to bring down, lead away, deflect; (_MIL_) to lead, withdraw; (_bride_) to bring home; (_colony_) to settle; (_hair_) to comb out; (_important person_) to escort; (_law_) to evict, bring to trial; (_money_) to subtract; (_sail_) to unfurl; (_ship_) to launch; (_thread_) to spin out; (_writing_) to compose; (_fig_) to bring, reduce, divert, derive.

dēductiō, -ōnis _f_ leading off; settling a colony; reduction; eviction; inference.

dēductor, -ōris _m_ escort.

dēductus _ppp of_ **dēdūcō ♦** _adj_ finely spun.

deerrō, -āre, -āvī, -ātum _vi_ to go astray.

deesse _infin of_ **dēsum.**

dēfaecō, -āre, -āvī, -ātum _vt_ to clean; (_fig_) to make clear, set at ease.

dēfatīgātiō, -ōnis _f_ tiring out; weariness.

dēfatīgō, -āre, -āvī, -ātum _vt_ to tire out, exhaust.

dēfatīscor _etc see_ **dēfetīscor.**

dēfectiō, -ōnis _f_ desertion; failure, faintness; (_ASTRO_) eclipse.

dēfector, -ōris _m_ deserter, rebel.

dēfectus _ppp of_ **dēficiō ♦** _adj_ weak, failing.

dēfectus, -ūs _m_ failure; eclipse.

dēfendō, -dere, -dī, -sum _vt_ to avert, repel; to defend, protect; (_law_) to speak in defence, urge, maintain; (_THEATRE_) to play (a part); **crīmen ~** answer an accusation.

dēfēnsiō, -ōnis _f_ defence, speech in defence.

dēfēnsitō, -āre _vt_ to defend often.

dēfēnsō, -āre _vt_ to defend.

dēfēnsor, -ōris _m_ averter; defender, protector, guard.

dēferō, -ferre, -tulī, -lātum _vt_ to bring down, bring, carry; to bear away; (_power, honour_) to offer, confer; (_information_) to report; (_law_) to inform against, indict; to recommend (for public services); **ad cōnsilium ~** take into consideration.

dēfervēscō, -vēscere, -vī _and_ **buī** _vi_ to cool down, calm down.

dēfessus _adj_ tired, exhausted.

dēfetīgō _etc see_ **dēfatīgō.**

dēfetīscor, -tīscī, -ssus _vi_ to grow weary.

dēficiō, -icere, -ēcī, -ectum _vt, vi_ to desert, forsake, fail; to be lacking, run short, cease; (_ASTRO_) to be eclipsed; **animō ~** lose heart.

dēfīgō, -gere, -xī, -xum _vt_ to fix firmly; to drive in, thrust; (_eyes, mind_) to concentrate; (_fig_) to stupefy, astound; (_magic_) to bewitch.

dēfingō, -ere _vt_ to make, portray.

dēfīniō, -īre, -īvī, -ītum _vt_ to mark the limit of, limit; to define, prescribe; to restrict; to terminate.

dēfīnītē _adv_ precisely.

dēfīnītiō, -ōnis _f_ limiting, prescribing, definition.

dēfīnītīvus _adj_ explanatory.

dēfīnītus _adj_ precise.

dēfīō, -ierī _vi_ to fail.

dēflagrātiō, -ōnis _f_ conflagration.

dēflagrō, -āre, -āvī, -ātum _vi_ to be burned down, perish; to cool down, abate **♦** _vt_ to burn down.

dēflectō, -ctere, -xī, -xum _vt_ to bend down, turn aside; (_fig_) to pervert **♦** _vi_ to turn aside, deviate.

dēfleō, -ēre, -ēvī, -ētum _vt_ to lament bitterly, bewail **♦** _vi_ to weep bitterly.

dēflexus _ppp of_ **dēflectō.**

dēflōrēscō, -ēscere, -uī _vi_ to shed blooms; (_fig_) to fade.

dēfluō, -ere, -xī, -xum _vi_ to flow down, float down; to fall, drop, droop; (_fig_) to come from be derived; to flow past; (_fig_) to pass away, fail.

dēfodiō, -ōdere, -ōdī, -ossum _vt_ to dig, dig out; to bury; (_fig_) to hide away.

dēfore _fut infin of_ **dēsum.**

dēfōrmis _adj_ misshapen, disfigured, ugly; shapeless; (_fig_) disgraceful, disgusting.

dēfōrmitās, -ātis _f_ deformity, hideousness; baseness.

dēfōrmō, -āre, -āvī, -ātum _vt_ to form, sketch; to deform, disfigure; to describe; to mar, disgrace.

dēfossus _ppp of_ **dēfodiō.**

dēfraudō, -āre _vt_ to cheat, defraud; **genium ~** deny oneself.

dēfrēnātus _adj_ unbridled.

dēfricō, -āre, -uī, -ātum _and_ **tum** _vt_ to rub down; (_fig_) to satirize.

dēfringō, -ingere, -ēgī, -āctum _vt_ to break off, break down.

dēfrūdō _etc see_ **dēfraudō.**

dēfrutum, -ī _nt_ new wine boiled down.

dēfugiō, -ugere, -ūgī _vt_ to run away from, shirk **♦** _vi_ to flee.

dēfuī _perf of_ **dēsum.**

dēfūnctus _ppa of_ **dēfungor ♦** _adj_ discharged; dead.

dēfundō, -undere, -ūdī, -ūsum _vt_ to pour out.

dēfungor, -ungī, -ūnctus _vi_ (_with abl_) to discharge, have done with; to die.

dēfutūrus _fut p of_ **dēsum.**

dēgener, -is _adj_ degenerate, unworthy, base.

dēgenerātum, -ātī _nt_ degenerate character.

dēgenerō, -āre, -āvī, -ātum _vi_ to degenerate, deteriorate **♦** _vt_ to disgrace.

dēgerō, -ere _vt_ to carry off.

dēgō, -ere, -ī _vt_ (_time_) to pass, spend; (_war_) wage **♦** _vi_ to live.

dēgrandinat it is hailing heavily.

dēgravō, -āre _vt_ to weigh down, overpower.

dēgredior, -dī, -ssus _vi_ to march down, descend, dismount.

dēgrunniō, -īre _vi_ to grunt hard.

dēgustō, -āre _vt_ to taste, touch; (_fig_) to try, experience.

dehinc _adv_ from here; from now, henceforth; then, next.

dehīscō, -ere _vi_ to gape, yawn.

dehonestāmentum, -ī _nt_ disfigurement.

dehonestō, -āre vt to disgrace.

dehortor, -ārī, -ātus vt to dissuade, discourage.

Dēianīra, -ae f wife of Hercules.

dēiciō, -icere, -iēcī, -iectum vt to throw down, hurl, fell; to overthrow, kill; (eyes) to lower, avert; (law) to evict; (MIL) to dislodge; (ship) to drive off its course; (hopes, honours) to foil, disappoint.

dēiectiō, -ōnis f eviction.

dēiectus ppp of **dēiciō** ♦ adj low-lying; disheartened.

dēiectus, -ūs m felling; steep slope.

dēierō, -āre, -āvī, -ātum vi to swear solemnly.

dein etc see **deinde**.

deinceps adv successively, in order.

deinde, dein adv from there, next; then, thereafter; next in order.

Dēiotarus, -ī m king of Galatia (defended by Cicero).

Dēiphobus, -ī m son of Priam (second husband of Helen).

dēiungō, -ere vt to sever.

dēiuvō, -āre vt to fail to help.

dej- etc see **dei-**.

dēlābor, -bī, -psus vi to fall down, fly down, sink; (fig) to come down, fall into.

dēlacerō, -āre vt to tear to pieces.

dēlāmentor, -ārī vt to mourn bitterly for.

dēlāpsus ppa of **dēlābor**.

dēlassō, -āre vt to tire out.

dēlātiō, -ōnis f accusing, informing.

dēlātor, -ōris m informer, denouncer.

dēlectābilis adj enjoyable.

dēlectāmentum, -ī nt amusement.

dēlectātiō, -ōnis f delight.

dēlectō, -āre vt to charm, delight, amuse.

dēlectus ppp of **dēligō**.

dēlēctus, -ūs m choice; see also **dīlēctus**.

dēlēgātiō, -ōnis f assignment.

dēlēgī perf of **dēligō**.

dēlēgō, -āre, -āvī, -ātum vt to assign, transfer, make over; to ascribe.

dēlēnificus adj charming.

dēlēnīmentum, -ī nt solace, allurement.

dēlēniō, -īre, -īvī, -ītum vt to soothe, solace; to seduce, win over.

dēlēnītor, -ōris m cajoler.

dēleō, -ēre, -ēvī, -ētum vt to destroy, annihilate; to efface, blot out.

Dēlia, -ae f Diana.

Dēliacus adj of Delos.

dēlīberābundus adj deliberating.

dēlīberātiō, -ōnis f deliberating, consideration.

dēlīberātīvus adj deliberative.

dēlīberātor, -ōris m consulter.

dēlīberātus adj determined.

dēlīberō, -āre, -āvī, -ātum vt, vi to consider,

deliberate, consult; to resolve, determine; **~ārī potest** it is in doubt.

dēlībō, -āre, -āvī, -ātum vt to taste, sip; to pick, gather; to detract from, mar.

dēlibrō, -āre vt to strip the bark off.

dēlibuō, -uere, -uī, -ūtum vt to smear, steep.

dēlicātē adv luxuriously.

dēlicātus adj delightful; tender, soft; voluptuous, spoiled, effeminate; fastidious.

dēliciae, -ārum fpl delight, pleasure; whimsicalities, sport; (person) sweetheart, darling.

dēliciolae, -ārum fpl darling.

dēlicium, -ī and **iī** nt favourite.

dēlicō, -āre vt to explain.

dēlictum, -ī nt offence, wrong.

dēlicuus adj lacking.

dēligō, -igere, -ēgī, -ēctum vt to select, gather; to set aside.

dēligō, -āre, -āvī, -ātum vt to tie up, make fast.

dēlingō, -ere vt to have a lick of.

dēlīni- etc see **dēlēni-**.

dēlinquō, -inquere, -īquī, -ictum vi to fail, offend, do wrong.

dēliquēscō, -quēscere, -cuī vi to melt away; (fig) to pine away.

dēliquiō, -ōnis f lack.

dēlīrāmentum, -ī nt nonsense.

dēlīrātiō, -ōnis f dotage.

dēlīrō, -āre vi to be crazy, drivel.

dēlīrus adj crazy.

dēlitēscō, -ēscere, -uī vi to hide away, lurk; (fig) to skulk, take shelter under.

dēlītigō, -āre vi to scold.

Dēlius, -iacus adj see n.

Delmatae see **Dalmatae**.

Dēlos, -ī f sacred Aegean island (birthplace of Apollo and Diana).

Delphī, -ōrum mpl town in central Greece (famous for its oracle of Apollo); the Delphians.

Delphicus adj see n.

delphīnus, -ī and **delphīn, -is** m dolphin.

Deltōton, -ī nt (constellation) Triangulum.

dēlubrum, -ī nt sanctuary, temple.

dēluctō, -āre, -or, -ārī vi to wrestle.

dēlūdificō, -āre vt to make fun of.

dēlūdō, -dere, -sī, -sum vt to dupe, delude.

dēlumbis adj feeble.

dēlumbō, -āre vt to enervate.

dēmadēscō, -ēscere, -uī vi to be drenched.

dēmandō, -āre vt to entrust, commit.

dēmarchus, -ī m demarch (chief of a village in Attica).

dēmēns, -entis adj mad, foolish.

dēmēnsum, -ī nt ration.

dēmēnsus ppa of **dēmētior**.

dementer adv see **dēmēns**.

dēmentia, -ae f madness, folly.

dēmentiō, -īre vi to rave.

dēmereō, -ēre, -uī, -itum, -eor, -ērī vt to earn, deserve; to do a service to.

dēmergō, -gere, -sī, -sum vt to submerge, plunge, sink; (fig) to overwhelm.

dēmessus ppp of dēmetō.

dēmētior, -tīrī, -nsus vt to measure out.

dēmetō, -tere, -ssuī, -ssum vt to reap, harvest; to cut off.

dēmigrātiō, -ōnis f emigration.

dēmigrō, -āre vi to move, emigrate.

dēminuō, -uere, -uī, -ūtum vt to make smaller, lessen, detract from; capite ~ deprive of citizenship.

dēminūtiō, -ōnis f decrease, lessening; (law) right to transfer property; capitis ~ loss of political rights.

dēmīror, -ārī, -ātus vt to marvel at, wonder.

dēmissē adv modestly, meanly.

dēmissīcius adj flowing.

dēmissiō, -ōnis f letting down; (fig) dejection.

dēmissus ppp of dēmittō ♦ adj low-lying; drooping; humble, unassuming; dejected; (origin) descended.

dēmītigō, -āre vt to make milder.

dēmittō, -ittere, -īsī, -issum vt to let down, lower, sink; to send down, plunge; (beard) to grow; (ship) to bring to land; (troops) to move down; (fig) to cast down, dishearten, reduce, impress; sē ~ stoop; descend; be disheartened.

dēmiūrgus, -ī m chief magistrate in a Greek state.

dēmō, -ere, -psī, -ptum vt to take away, subtract.

Dēmocriticus, -ius, -ēus adj see n.

Dēmocritus, -ī m Greek philosopher (author of the atomic theory).

dēmōlior, -īrī vt to pull down, destroy.

dēmōlītiō, -ōnis f pulling down.

dēmōnstrātiō, -ōnis f pointing out, explanation.

dēmōnstrātīvus adj (RHET) for display.

dēmōnstrātor, -ōris m indicator.

dēmōnstrō, -āre, -āvī, -ātum vt to point out; to explain, represent, prove.

dēmorior, -ī, -tuus vi to die, pass away ♦ vt to be in love with.

dēmoror, -ārī, -ātus vi to wait ♦ vt to detain, delay.

dēmortuus ppa of dēmorior.

Dēmosthenēs, -is m greatest Athenian orator.

dēmoveō, -ovēre, -ōvī, -ōtum vt to remove, turn aside, dislodge.

dēmpsī perf of dēmō.

dēmptus ppp of dēmō.

dēmūgītus adj filled with lowing.

dēmulceō, -cēre, -sī vt to stroke.

dēmum adv (time) at last, not till; (emphasis) just, precisely; ibi ~ just there; modo ~ only now; nunc ~ now at last; post ~ not till after; tum ~ only then.

dēmurmurō, -āre vt to mumble through.

dēmūtātiō, -ōnis f change.

dēmūtō, -āre vt to change, make worse ♦ vi to change one's mind.

dēnārius, -ī and iī m Roman silver coin.

dēnārrō, -āre vt to relate fully.

dēnāsō, -āre vt to take the nose off.

dēnatō, -āre vi to swim down.

dēnegō, -āre, -āvī, ātum vt to deny, refuse, reject ♦ vi to say no.

dēnī, -ōrum adj ten each, in tens; ten; tenth.

dēnicālis adj for purifying after a death.

dēnique adv at last, finally; (enumerating) lastly, next; (summing up) in short, briefly; (emphasis) just, precisely.

dēnōminō, -āre vt to designate.

dēnōrmō, -āre vt to make irregular.

dēnotō, -āre, -āvī, -ātum vt to point out, specify; to observe.

dēns, dentis m tooth; ivory; prong, fluke.

dēnsē adv repeatedly.

dēnsō, -āre, -āvī, -ātum, dēnseō, -ēre vt to thicken; (ranks) to close.

dēnsus adj thick, dense, close; frequent; (style) concise.

dentālia, -ium ntpl ploughbeam.

dentātus adj toothed; (paper) polished.

dentiō, -īre vi to cut one's teeth; (teeth) to grow.

dēnūbō, -bere, -psī, -ptum vi to marry, marry beneath one.

dēnūdō, -āre, -āvī, -ātum vt to bare, strip; (fig) to disclose.

dēnūntiātiō, -ōnis f intimation, warning.

dēnūntiō, -āre, -āvī, -ātum vt to intimate, give notice of, declare; to threaten, warn; (law) to summon as witness.

dēnuō adv afresh, again, once more.

deonerō, -āre vt to unload.

deorsum, deorsus adv downwards.

deōsculor, -ārī vt to kiss warmly.

dēpacīscor etc see dēpecīscor.

dēpāctus adj driven in firmly.

dēpāscō, -scere, -vī, -stum, -scor, -scī vt to feed on, eat up; (fig) to devour, destroy, prune away.

dēpecīscor, -īscī, -tus vt to bargain for, agree about.

dēpectō, -ctere, -xum vt to comb; (comedy) to flog.

dēpectus ppa of dēpecīscor.

dēpeculātor, -ōris m embezzler.

dēpeculor, -ārī, -ātus vt to plunder.

dēpellō, -ellere, -ulī, -ulsum vt to expel, remove, cast down; (MIL) to dislodge; (infants) to wean; (fig) to deter, avert.

dēpendeō, -ēre vi to hang down, hang from; to depend on; to be derived.

dēpendō, -endere, -endī, -ēnsum vt to weigh, pay up.

dēperdō, -ere, -idī, -itum vt to lose completely, destroy, ruin.

dēpereō, -īre, -iī vi to perish, be completely destroyed; to be undone ♦ vt to be hopelessly in love with.

dēpexus *ppp of* **dēpectō**.

dēpingō, -ingere, -inxī, -ictum *vt* to paint; (*fig*) to portray, describe.

dēplangō, -gere, -xī *vt* to bewail frantically.

dēplexus *adj* grasping.

dēplōrābundus *adj* weeping bitterly.

dēplōrō, -āre, -āvī, -ātum *vi* to weep bitterly ♦ *vt* to bewail bitterly, mourn; to despair of.

dēpluit, -ere *vi* to rain down.

dēpōnō, -ōnere, -osuī, -ositum *vt* to lay down; to set aside, put away, get rid of; to wager; to deposit, entrust, commit to the care of; (*fig*) to give up.

dēpopulātiō, -ōnis *f* ravaging.

dēpopulātor, -ōris *m* marauder.

dēpopulor, -ārī, -ātus; -ō, -āre *vt* to ravage, devastate; (*fig*) to waste, destroy.

dēportō, -āre, -āvī, -ātum *vt* to carry down, carry off; to bring home (from a province); (*law*) to banish for life; (*fig*) to win.

dēposcō, -scere, -poscī *vt* to demand, require, claim.

dēpositum, -ī *nt* trust, deposit.

dēpositus *ppp of* **dēpōnō** ♦ *adj* dying, dead, despaired of.

dēprāvātē *adv* perversely.

dēprāvātiō, -ōnis *f* distorting.

dēprāvō, -āre, -āvī, -ātum *vt* to distort; (*fig*) to pervert, corrupt.

dēprecābundus *adj* imploring.

dēprecātiō, -ōnis *f* averting by prayer; imprecation, invocation; plea for indulgence.

dēprecātor, -ōris *m* intercessor.

dēprecor, -ārī, -ātus *vt* to avert (by prayer); to deprecate, intercede for.

dēprehendō, dēprendō, -endere, -endī, -ēnsum *vt* to catch, intercept; to overtake, surprise; to catch in the act, detect; (*fig*) to perceive, discover.

dēprehēnsiō, -ōnis *f* detection.

dēprehēnsus, dēprēnsus *ppp of* **dēprehendō**.

dēpressī *perf of* **dēprimō**.

dēpressus *ppp of* **dēprimō** ♦ *adj* low.

dēprimō, -imere, -essī, -essum *vt* to press down, weigh down; to dig deep; (*ship*) to sink; (*fig*) to suppress, keep down.

dēproelior, -ārī *vi* to fight it out.

dēprōmō, -ere, psī, -ptum *vt* to fetch, bring out, produce.

dēproperō, -āre *vi* to hurry up ♦ *vt* to hurry and make.

depsō, -ere *vt* to knead.

dēpudet, -ēre, -uit *v impers* not to be ashamed.

dēpūgis *adj* thin-buttocked.

dēpugnō, -āre, -āvī, -ātum *vi* to fight it out, fight hard.

dēpulī *perf of* **dēpellō**.

dēpulsiō, -ōnis *f* averting; defence.

dēpulsō, -āre *vt* to push out of the way.

dēpulsor, -ōris *m* repeller.

dēpulsus *ppp of* **dēpellō**.

dēpūrgō, -āre *vt* to clean.

dēputō, -āre *vt* to prune; to consider, reckon.

dēpȳgis *etc see* **dēpūgis**.

dēque *adv* down.

dērēctā, -ē, -ō *adv* straight.

dērēctus *ppp of* **dērigō** ♦ *adj* straight, upright, at right angles; straightforward.

dērelictiō, -ōnis *f* disregarding.

dērelinquō, -inquere, -īquī, -ictum *vt* to abandon, forsake.

dērepente *adv* suddenly.

dērēpō, -ere *vi* to creep down.

dēreptus *ppp of* **dēripiō**.

dērīdeō, -dēre, -sī, -sum *vt* to laugh at, deride.

dērīdiculum, -ī *nt* mockery, absurdity; object of derision.

dērīdiculus *adj* laughable.

dērigēscō, -ēscere, -uī *vi* to stiffen, curdle.

dērigō, -igere, -ēxī, -ēctum *vt* to turn, aim, direct; (*fig*) to regulate.

dēripiō, -ipere, -ipuī, -eptum *vt* to tear off, pull down.

dērīsor, -ōris *m* scoffer.

dērīsus *ppp of* **dērīdeō**.

dērīsus, -ūs *m* scorn, derision.

dērīvātiō, -ōnis *f* diverting.

dērīvō, -āre, -āvī, -ātum *vt* to lead off, draw off.

dērogō, -āre *vt* (*law*) to propose to amend; (*fig*) to detract from.

dērōsus *adj* gnawed away.

dēruncinō, -āre *vt* to plane off; (*comedy*) to cheat.

dēruō, -ere, -ī *vt* to demolish.

dēruptus *adj* steep ♦ *ntpl* precipice.

dēsaeviō, -īre *vi* to rage furiously; to cease raging.

dēscendō, -endere, -endī, -ēnsum *vi* to come down, go down, descend, dismount; (*MIL*) to march down; (*things*) to fall, sink, penetrate; (*fig*) to stoop (to), lower oneself.

dēscēnsiō, -ōnis *f* going down.

dēscēnsus, -ūs *m* way down.

dēscīscō, -īscere, -īvī *and* **iī, -ītum** *vi* to desert, revolt; to deviate, part company.

dēscrībō, -bere, -psī, -ptum *vt* to copy out; to draw, sketch; to describe; *see also* **dīscrībō**.

dēscrīptiō, -ōnis *f* copy; drawing, diagram; description.

dēscrīptus *ppp of* **dēscrībō**; *see also* **dīscrīptus**.

dēsecō, -āre, -uī, -tum *vt* to cut off.

dēserō, -ere, -uī, -tum *vt* to desert, abandon, forsake; (*bail*) to forfeit.

dēsertor, -ōris *m* deserter.

dēsertus *ppp of* **dēserō** ♦ *adj* desert,

uninhabited ♦ *ntpl* deserts.

dēserviō, -īre *vi* to be a slave (to), serve.

dēses, -idis *adj* idle, inactive.

dēsiccō, -āre *vt* to dry, drain.

dēsideō, -idēre, -ēdī *vi* to sit idle.

dēsīderābilis *adj* desirable.

dēsīderātiō, -ōnis *f* missing.

dēsīderium, -ī *and* **iī** *nt* longing, sense of loss; want; petition; **mē ~ tenet urbis** I miss Rome.

dēsīderō, -āre, -āvī, -ātum *vt* to feel the want of, miss; to long for, desire; (*casualties*) to lose.

dēsidia, -ae *f* idleness, apathy.

dēsidiōsē *adv* idly.

dēsidiōsus *adj* lazy, idle; relaxing.

dēsīdō, -īdere, -ēdī *vi* to sink, settle down; (*fig*) to deteriorate.

dēsignātiō, -ōnis *f* specifying; election (of magistrates).

dēsignātor *etc see* **dissignātor**.

dēsignātus *adj* elect.

dēsignō, -āre, -āvī, -ātum *vt* to trace out; to indicate, define; (*POL*) to elect; (*art*) to depict.

dēsiī *perf of* **dēsinō**.

dēsiliō, -īlīre, -iluī, -ultum *vi* to jump down, alight.

dēsinō, -nere, -ī *vt* to leave off, abandon ♦ *vi* to stop, desist; to end (in).

dēsipiēns, -ientis *adj* silly.

dēsipientia, -ae *f* folly.

dēsipiō, -ere *vi* to be stupid, play the fool.

dēsistō, -istere, -titī, -titum *vi* to stop, leave off, desist.

dēsitus *ppp of* **dēsinō**.

dēsōlō, -āre, -āvī, -ātum *vt* to leave desolate, abandon.

dēspectō, -āre *vt* to look down on, command a view of; to despise.

dēspectus *ppp of* **dēspiciō** ♦ *adj* contemptible.

dēspectus, -ūs *m* view, prospect.

dēspēranter *adv* despairingly.

dēspērātiō, -ōnis *f* despair.

dēspērātus *adj* despaired of, hopeless; desperate, reckless.

dēspērō, -āre, -āvī, -ātum *vt, vi* to despair, give up hope of.

dēspexī *perf of* **dēspiciō**.

dēspicātiō, -ōnis *f* contempt.

despicātus *adj* despised, contemptible.

dēspicātus, -ūs *m* contempt.

dēspicientia, -ae *f* contempt.

dēspiciō, -icere, -exī, -ectum *vt* to look down on; to despise ♦ *vi* to look down.

dēspoliātor, -ōris *m* robber.

dēspoliō, -āre *vt* to rob, plunder.

dēspondeō, -ondēre, -ondī *and* **opondī, -ōnsum** *vt* to pledge, promise; to betroth; to devote; to give up, despair of; **animum ~** despair.

dēspūmō, -āre *vt* to skim off.

dēspuō, -ere *vi* to spit on the ground ♦ *vt* to reject.

dēsquāmō, -āre *vt* to scale, peel.

dēstillō, -āre *vi* to drop down ♦ *vt* to distil.

dēstimulō, -āre *vt* to run through.

dēstinātiō, -ōnis *f* resolution, appointment.

dēstinātus *adj* fixed, decided.

dēstinō, -āre, -āvī, -ātum *vt* to make fast; to appoint, determine, resolve; (*archery*) to aim at; (*fig*) to intend to buy ♦ *nt* mark; intention; **~ātum est mihi** I have decided.

dēstitī *perf of* **dēsistō**.

dēstituō, -uere, -uī, -ūtum *vt* to set apart, place; to forsake, leave in the lurch.

dēstitūtiō, -ōnis *f* defaulting.

dēstitūtus *ppp of* **dēstituō**.

dēstrictus *ppp of* **dēstringō** ♦ *adj* severe.

dēstringō, -ingere, -inxī, -ictum *vt* (*leaves*) to strip; (*body*) to rub down; (*sword*) to draw; to graze, skim; (*fig*) to censure.

dēstruō, -ere, -xī, -ctum *vt* to demolish; to destroy.

dēsubitō *adv* all of a sudden.

dēsūdāscō, -ere *vi* to sweat all over.

dēsūdō, -āre *vi* to exert oneself.

dēsuēfactus *adj* unaccustomed.

dēsuētūdō, -inis *f* disuse.

dēsuētus *adj* unaccustomed, unused.

dēsultor, -ōris *m* circus rider; (*fig*) fickle lover.

dēsultūra, -ae *f* jumping down.

dēsum, deesse, -fuī *vi* to be missing, fail, fail in one's duty.

dēsūmō, -ere, -psī, -ptum *vt* to select.

dēsuper *adv* from above.

dēsurgō, -ere *vi* to rise.

dētegō, -egere, -ēxī, -ēctum *vt* to uncover, disclose; (*fig*) to reveal, detect.

dētendō, -endere, -ēnsum *vt* (*tent*) to strike.

dētentus *ppp of* **dētineō**.

dētergō, -gere, -sī, -sum *vt* to wipe away, clear away; to clean; to break off.

dēterior, -ōris *adj* lower; inferior, worse.

dēterius *adv* worse.

dēterminātiō, -ōnis *f* boundary, end.

dēterminō, -āre, -āvī, -ātum *vt* to bound, limit; to settle.

dēterō, -erere, -rīvī, -rītum *vt* to rub, wear away; (*style*) to polish; (*fig*) to weaken.

dēterreō, -ēre, -uī, -itum *vt* to frighten away; to deter, discourage, prevent.

dētersus *ppp of* **dētergeō**.

dētestābilis *adj* abominable.

dētestātiō, -ōnis *f* execration, curse; averting.

dētestor, -ārī, -ātus *vt* to invoke, invoke against; to curse, execrate; to avert, deprecate.

dētexō, -ere, -uī, -tum *vt* to weave, finish weaving; (*comedy*) to steal; (*fig*) to describe.

dētineō, -inēre, -inuī, -entum *vt* to hold back, detain; to keep occupied.

dētondeō, -ondēre, -ondī, -ōnsum *vt* to shear off, strip.

dētonō, -āre, -uī *vi* to cease thundering.

dētorqueō, -quēre, -sī, -tum *vt* to turn aside,

direct; to distort, misrepresent.

dētractātiō, -ōnis f declining.

dētractātor, -ōris m disparager.

dētractiō, -ōnis f removal, departure.

dētractō etc see **dētrectō**.

dētractus ppp of **dētrahō**.

dētrahō, -here, -xī, -ctum vt to draw off, take away, pull down; to withdraw, force to leave; to detract, disparage.

dētrectō, -āre, -āvī, -ātum vt to decline, shirk; to detract from, disparage.

dētrīmentōsus adj harmful.

dētrīmentum, -ī nt loss, harm; (MIL) defeat; ~ **capere** suffer harm.

dētrītus ppp of **dēterō**.

dētrūdō, -dere, -sī, -sum vt to push down, thrust away; to dislodge, evict; to postpone; (fig) to force.

dētruncō, -āre, -āvī, -ātum vt to cut off, behead, mutilate.

dētrūsus ppp of **dētrūdō**.

dēturbō, -āre, -āvī, -ātum vt to dash down, pull down; (fig) to cast down, deprive.

Deucaliōn, -ōnis m son of Prometheus (survivor of the Flood).

Deucaliōnēus adj see **Deucaliōn**.

deūnx, -cis m eleven twelfths.

deūrō, -rere, -ssī, -stum vt to burn up; to frost.

deus, -ī (voc deus, pl dī, deos, deum, dīs) m god; **dī meliōra!** Heaven forbid!; **dī tē ament!** bless you!

deūstus ppp of **deūrō**.

deūtor, -ī vi to maltreat.

dēvāstō, -āre vt to lay waste.

dēvehō, -here, -xī, -ctum vt to carry down, convey; (pass) to ride down, sail down.

dēvellō, -ellere, -ellī and **olsī, -ulsum** vt to pluck, pull out.

dēvēlō, -āre vt to unveil.

dēveneror, -ārī vt to worship; to avert by prayers.

dēveniō, -enīre, -ēnī, -entum vi to come, reach, fall into.

dēverberō, -āre, -āvī, -ātum vt to thrash soundly.

dēversor, -ārī vi to lodge, stay (as guest).

dēversor, -ōris m guest.

dēversōriolum, -ī nt small lodging.

dēversōrium, -ī and **iī** nt inn, lodging.

dēversōrius adj for lodging.

dēverticulum, -ī nt by-road, by-pass; digression; lodging place; (fig) refuge.

dēvertō, -tere, -tī, -sum vi to turn aside, put up; to have recourse to; to digress.

dēvertor, -tī, versus vi see **dēvertō**.

dēvexus adj sloping, going down, steep.

dēvinciō, -cīre, -xī, -ctum vt to tie up; (fig) to bind, lay under an obligation.

dēvincō, -incere, -īcī, -ictum vt to defeat

completely, win the day.

dēvītātiō, -ōnis f avoiding.

dēvītō, -āre vt to avoid.

dēvius adj out of the way, devious; (person) solitary, wandering off the beaten track; (fig) inconstant.

dēvocō, -āre, -āvī, -ātum vt to call down, fetch; to entice away.

dēvolō, -āre vi to fly down.

dēvolvō, -vere, -vī, -ūtum vt to roll down, fall; (wool) to spin off.

dēvorō, -āre, -āvī, -ātum vt to swallow, gulp down; to engulf, devour; (money) to squander; (tears) to repress; (trouble) to endure patiently.

dēvors-, dēvort- see **dēvers-, dēvert-**.

dēvortia, -ōrum ntpl byways.

dēvōtiō, -ōnis f devoting; (magic) spell.

dēvōtō, -āre vt to bewitch.

dēvōtus ppp of **dēvoveō** ♦ adj faithful; accursed.

dēvoveō, -ovēre, -ōvī, -ōtum vt to devote, vow, dedicate; to give up; to curse; to bewitch.

dēvulsus ppp of **dēvellō**.

dextella, -ae f little right hand.

dexter, -erī and **rī** adj right, right-hand; handy, skilful; favourable.

dexteritās, -ātis f adroitness.

dextra f right hand, right-hand side; hand; pledge of friendship.

dextrā prep (with acc) on the right of.

dextrē (compar -erius) adv adroitly.

dextrōrsum, -rsus, -vorsum adv to the right.

dī pl of **deus**.

diabathrārius, -ī and **iī** m slipper maker.

diabolus, -ī m devil.

diāconus, -ī m (ECCL) deacon.

diadēma, -tis nt royal headband, diadem.

diaeta, -ae f diet; living room.

dialectica, -ae, -ē, -ēs f dialectic, logic ♦ ntpl logical questions.

dialecticē adv dialectically.

dialecticus adj dialectical ♦ m logician.

Diālis adj of Jupiter ♦ m high priest of Jupiter.

dialogus, -ī m dialogue, conversation.

Diāna, -ae f virgin goddess of hunting (also identified with the moon and Hecate, and patroness of childbirth).

Diānius adj of Diana ♦ nt sanctuary of Diana.

diāria, -ōrum ntpl daily allowance of food or pay.

dibaphus, -ī f Roman state robe.

dica, -ae f lawsuit.

dicācitās, -ātis f raillery, repartee.

dicāculus adj pert.

dicātiō, -ōnis f declaration of citizenship.

dicāx, -ācis adj witty, smart.

dichorēus, -ī m double trochee.

diciō, -ōnis f power, sway, authority.

dicis causā for the sake of appearance.
dicō, -āre, -āvī, -ātum vt to dedicate,
  consecrate; to deify; to devote, give over.
dīcō, -cere, -xī, dictum vt to say, tell; to
  mention, mean, call, name; to pronounce;
  (_RHET_) to speak, deliver; (_law_) to plead;
  (_poetry_) to describe, celebrate; (_official_) to
  appoint; (_time, place_) to settle, fix ♦ vi to
  speak (in public); **causam ~** plead; **iūs ~**
  deliver judgment; **sententiam ~** vote; **~cō**
  namely; **~xī** I have finished; **dictum factum**
  no sooner said than done.
dicrotum, -ī nt bireme.
Dictaeus adj Cretan.
dictamnus, -ī f dittany (_a kind of wild
  marjoram_).
dictāta, -ōrum ntpl lessons, rules.
dictātor, -ōris m dictator.
dictātōrius adj dictator's.
dictātūra, -ae f dictatorship.
Dictē, -ēs f mountain in Crete (_where Jupiter
  was brought up_).
dictiō, -ōnis f speaking, declaring; style,
  expression, oratory; (_oracle_) response.
dictitō, -āre vt to keep saying, assert; to plead
  often.
dictō, -āre, -āvī, -ātum vt to say repeatedly;
  to dictate; to compose.
dictum, -ī nt saying, word; proverb; bon mot,
  witticism; command.
dictus ppa of **dīcō**.
Dictynna, -ae f Britomartis; Diana.
Dictynnaeus adj see n.
didicī perf of **discō**.
dīdō, -ere, -idī, -itum vt to distribute,
  broadcast.
Dīdō, -ūs and **-ōnis** (_acc_ -ō) f Queen of Carthage.
dīdūcō, -ūcere, -ūxī, -uctum vt to separate,
  split, open up; (_MIL_) to disperse; (_fig_) to part,
  divide.
diēcula, -ae f one little day.
diērēctus adj crucified; **abī ~** go and be
  hanged.
diēs, -ēī m/f day; set day (_usu fem_); a day's
  journey; (_fig_) time; **~ meus** my birthday; **~em
  dīcere** impeach; **~em obīre** die; **~em dē ~ō,
  ~em ex ~ē** from day to day; **in ~em** to a later
  day; for today; **in ~ēs** daily.
Diēspiter, -ris m Jupiter.
diffāmō, -āre, -āvī, -ātum vt to divulge; to
  malign.
differentia, -ae f difference, diversity;
  species.
differitās, -ātis f difference.
differō, -erre, distulī, dīlātum vt to disperse;
  to divulge, publish; (_fig_) to distract, disquiet;
  (_time_) to put off, delay ♦ vi to differ, be
  distinguished.
differtus adj stuffed, crammed.
difficilis adj difficult; (_person_) awkward, surly.
difficiliter adv with difficulty.
difficultās, -ātis f difficulty, distress,
  hardship; surliness.

difficulter adv with difficulty.
diffīdēns, -entis adj nervous.
diffīdenter adv without confidence.
diffīdentia, -ae f mistrust, diffidence.
diffīdō, -dere, -sus vi to distrust, despair.
diffindō, -ndere, -dī, -ssum vt to split, open
  up; (_fig_) to break off.
diffingō, -ere vt to remake.
diffissus ppp of **diffindō**.
diffīsus ppa of **diffīdō**.
diffiteor, -ērī vt to disown.
diffluēns, -entis adj (_RHET_) loose.
diffluō, -ere vi to flow away; to melt away; (_fig_)
  to wallow.
diffringō, -ere vt to shatter.
diffugiō, -ugere, -ūgī vi to disperse,
  disappear.
diffugium, -ī and **ī ī** nt dispersion.
diffunditō, -āre vt to pour out, waste.
diffundō, -undere, -ūdī, -ūsum vt to pour
  off; to spread, diffuse; to cheer, gladden.
diffūsē adv expansively.
diffūsilis adj diffusive.
diffūsus ppp of **diffundō** ♦ adj spreading;
  (_writing_) loose.
Dīgentia, -ae f tributary of the Anio (_near
  Horace's villa_).
dīgerō, -rere, -ssī, -stum vt to divide,
  distribute; to arrange, set out; to interpret.
dīgestiō, -ōnis f (_RHET_) enumeration.
dīgestus ppp of **dīgerō**.
digitulus, -ī m little finger.
digitus, -ī m finger; toe; inch; (_pl_) skill in
  counting; **~um porrigere, prōferre** take the
  slightest trouble; **~um trānsversum nōn
  discēdere** not swerve a finger's breadth;
  attingere caelum ~ō reach the height of
  happiness; **licērī ~ō** bid at an auction;
  mōnstrārī ~ō be a celebrity; **extrēmī, summī
  ~ī** the fingertips; **concrepāre ~īs** snap the
  fingers.
dīgladior, -ārī vi to fight fiercely.
dignātiō, -ōnis f honour, dignity.
dignē adv see **dignus**.
dignitās, -ātis f worth, worthiness; dignity,
  rank, position; political office.
dignō, -āre vt to think worthy.
dignor, -ārī vt to think worthy; to deign.
dīgnōscō, -ere vt to distinguish.
dignus adj worth, worthy; (_things_) fitting,
  proper.
dīgredior, -dī, -ssus vi to separate, part; to
  deviate, digress.
dīgressiō, -ōnis f parting; deviation,
  digression.
dīgressus ppa of **dīgredior**.
dīgressus, -ūs m parting.
dīiūdicātiō, -ōnis f decision.
dīiūdicō, -āre vt to decide; to discriminate.
dīiun- etc see **disiun-**.
dīlābor, -bī, -psus vi to dissolve,
  disintegrate; to flow away; (_troops_) to
  disperse; (_fig_) to decay, vanish.

dīlacerō, -āre vt to tear to pieces.

dīlāminō, -āre vt to split in two.

dīlaniō, -āre, -āvī, -ātum vt to tear to shreds.

dīlapidō, -āre vt to demolish.

dīlāpsus ppa of **dīlābor**.

dīlargior, -īrī vt to give away liberally.

dīlātiō, -ōnis f putting off, adjournment.

dīlātō, -āre, -āvī, -ātum vt to expand; (pronunciation) to broaden.

dīlātor, -ōris m procrastinator.

dīlātus ppp of **differō**.

dīlaudō, -āre vt to praise extravagantly.

dīlēctus ppp of **dīligō** ♦ adj beloved.

dīlēctus, -ūs m selection, picking; (MIL) levy; **~um habēre** hold a levy, recruit.

dīlēxī perf of **dīligō**.

dīligēns, -entis adj painstaking, conscientious, attentive (to); thrifty.

dīligenter adv see **dīligēns**.

dīligentia, -ae f carefulness, attentiveness; thrift.

dīligō, -igere, -ēxī, -ēctum vt to prize especially, esteem, love.

dīlōrīcō, -āre vt to tear open.

dīlūceō, -ēre vi to be evident.

dīlūcēscit, -cēscere, -xit vi to dawn, begin to grow light.

dīlūcidē adv see **dīlūcidus**.

dīlūcidus adj clear, distinct.

dīlūculum, -ī nt dawn.

dīlūdium, -ī and **iī** nt interval.

dīluō, -uere, -uī, -ūtum vt to wash away, dissolve, dilute; to explain; (fig) to weaken, do away with.

dīluviēs, -iēī f, **-ium, -ī** and **iī** nt flood, deluge.

dīluviō, -āre vt to inundate.

dīmānō, -āre vi to spread abroad.

dīmēnsiō, -ōnis f measuring.

dīmēnsus adj measured.

dīmētior, -tīrī, -nsus vt to measure out.

dīmētō, -āre, -or, -ārī vt to mark out.

dīmicātiō, -ōnis f fighting, struggle.

dīmicō, -āre, -āvī, -ātum vi to fight, struggle, contend.

dīmidiātus adj half, halved.

dīmidius adj half ♦ nt half.

dīmissiō, -ōnis f sending away; discharging.

dīmissus ppp of **dīmittō**.

dīmittō, -ittere, -īsī, -issum vt to send away, send round; to let go, lay down; (meeting) to dismiss; (MIL) to disband, detach; (fig) to abandon, forsake.

dimminuō, -ere vt to dash to pieces.

dīmoveō, -ovēre, -ōvī, -ōtum vt to part, separate; to disperse; to entice away.

Dindymēnē, -ēnēs f Cybele.

Dindymus, -ī m mountain in Mysia (sacred to Cybele).

dīnōscō see **dignōscō**.

dīnumerātiō, -ōnis f reckoning up.

dīnumerō, -āre vt to count, reckon up; to pay out.

diōbolāris adj costing two obols.

dioecēsis, -is f district; (ECCL) diocese.

dioecētēs, -ae m treasurer.

Diogenēs, -is m famous Cynic philosopher; a Stoic philosopher.

Diomēdēs, -is m Greek hero at the Trojan War.

Diomēdēus adj see n.

Diōnaeus adj see **Diōnē**.

Diōnē, -ēs and **-a, -ae** f mother of Venus; Venus.

Dionȳsius, -ī m tyrant of Syracuse.

Dionȳsus, -ī m Bacchus; **-ia, -iōrum** ntpl Greek festival of Bacchus.

diōta, -ae f a two-handled wine jar.

diplōma, -tis nt letter of recommendation.

Dipylon, -ī nt Athenian gate.

Dircaeus adj Boeotian.

Dircē, -ēs f famous spring in Boeotia.

dīrēctus ppp of **dīrigō** ♦ adj straight; straightforward, simple; see also **dērēctus**.

dīrēmī perf of **dirimō**.

dīremptus ppp of **dirimō**.

dīremptus, -ūs m separation.

dīreptiō, -ōnis f plundering.

dīreptor, -ōris m plunderer.

dīreptus ppp of **dīripiō**.

dīrēxī perf of **dīrigō**.

dīribeō, -ēre vt to sort out (votes taken from ballot-boxes).

dīribitiō, -ōnis f sorting.

dīribitor, -ōris m ballot-sorter.

dīrigō, -igere, -ēxī, -ēctum vt to put in line, arrange; see also **dērigō**.

dirimō, -imere, -ēmī, -emptum vt to part, divide; to interrupt, break off; to put an end to.

dīripiō, -ipere, -ipuī, -eptum vt to tear in pieces; to plunder, ravage; to seize; (fig) to distract.

dīritās, -ātis f mischief, cruelty.

dīrumpō, disrumpō, -umpere, -ūpī, -uptum vt to burst, break in pieces; (fig) to break off; (pass) to burst (with passion).

dīruō, -ere, -ī, -tum vt to demolish; to scatter; **aere ~tus** having one's pay stopped.

dīruptus ppp of **dīrumpō**.

dīrus adj ominous, fearful; (pers) dread, terrible ♦ fpl bad luck; the Furies ♦ ntpl terrors.

dīrutus ppp of **dīruō** ♦ adj bankrupt.

dīs, dītis adj rich.

Dīs, Dītis m Pluto.

discēdō, -ēdere, -essī, -essum vi to go away, depart; to part, disperse; (MIL) to march away; (result of battle) to come off; (POL) to go over (to a different policy); to pass away, disappear; to leave out of consideration; **ab signīs ~** break the ranks; **victor ~** come off best.

disceptātiō, -ōnis *f* discussion, debate.
disceptātor, -ōris *m*, **-rīx, -rīcis** *f* arbitrator.
disceptō, -āre *vt* to debate, discuss; (*law*) to decide.
discernō, -ernere, -rēvī, -rētum *vt* to divide, separate; to distinguish between.
discerpō, -ere, -sī, -tum *vt* to tear apart, disperse; (*fig*) to revile.
discessiō, -ōnis *f* separation, departure; (*senate*) division.
discessus, -ūs *m* parting; departure; marching away.
discidium, -i *and* **ii** *nt* disintegration; separation, divorce; discord.
discīdō, -ere *vt* to cut in pieces.
discinctus *ppp of* **discingō ♦** *adj* ungirt; negligent; dissolute.
discindō, -ndere, -dī, -ssum *vt* to tear up, cut open.
discingō, -gere, -xī, -ctum *vt* to ungird.
disciplīna, -ae *f* teaching, instruction; learning, science, school, system; training, discipline; habits.
discipulus, -ī *m*, **-a, -ae** *f* pupil, apprentice.
discissus *ppp of* **discindō**.
disclūdō, -dere, -sī, -sum *vt* to keep apart, separate out.
discō, -ere, didicī *vt* to learn, be taught, be told.
discolor, -ōris *adj* of a different colour; variegated; different.
discondūcit it is not worthwhile.
disconveniō, -īre *vi* to disagree, be inconsistent.
discordābilis *adj* disagreeing.
discordia, -ae *f* discord, disagreement.
discordiōsus *adj* seditious.
discordō, -āre *vi* to disagree, quarrel; to be unlike.
discors, -dis *adj* discordant, at variance; inconsistent.
discrepantia, -ae *f* disagreement.
discrepātiō, -ōnis *f* dispute.
discrepitō, -āre *vi* to be quite different.
discrepō, -āre, -uī *vi* to be out of tune; to disagree, differ; to be disputed.
discrētus *ppp of* **discernō**.
dīscrībō, -bere, -psī, -ptum *vt* to distribute, apportion, classify.
discrīmen, -inis *nt* interval, dividing line; distinction, difference; turning point, critical moment; crisis, danger.
discrīminō, -āre *vt* to divide.
dīscrīptē *adv* in good order.
dīscrīptiō, -ōnis *f* apportioning, distributing.
dīscrīptus *ppp of* **dīscrībō ♦** *adj* secluded; well-arranged.
discruciō, -āre *vt* to torture; (*fig*) to torment, trouble.
discumbō, -mbere, -buī, -bitum *vi* to recline at table; to go to bed.
discupiō, -ere *vi* to long.
discurrō, -rrere, -currī *and* **rrī, -rsum** *vi* to run about, run different ways.
discursus, -ūs *m* running hither and thither.
discus, -ī *m* quoit.
discussus *ppp of* **discutiō**.
discutiō, -tere, -ssī, -ssum *vt* to dash to pieces, smash; to scatter; to dispel.
disertē, -im *adv* distinctly; eloquently.
disertus *adj* fluent, eloquent; explicit.
disiciō, -icere, -iēcī, -iectum *vt* to scatter, cast asunder; to break up, destroy; (*MIL*) to rout.
disiectō, -āre *vt* to toss about.
disiectus *ppp of* **disiciō**.
disiectus, -ūs *m* scattering.
disiūnctiō, -ōnis *f* separation, differing; (*logic*) statement of alternatives; (*RHET*) a sequence of short co-ordinate clauses.
disiūnctius *adv* rather in the manner of a dilemma.
disiūnctus *ppp of* **disiungō ♦** *adj* distinct, distant, removed; (*speech*) disjointed; (*logic*) opposite.
disiungō, -ungere, -ūnxī, -ūnctum *vt* to unyoke; to separate, remove.
dispālēscō, -ere *vi* to be noised abroad.
dispandō, -āndere, -ānsum *and* **-essum** *vt* to spread out.
dispār, -aris *adj* unlike, unequal.
disparilis *adj* dissimilar.
disparō, -āre, -āvī, -ātum *vt* to segregate.
dispart- *etc see* **dispert-**.
dispectus *ppp of* **dispiciō**.
dispellō, -ellere, -ulī, -ulsum *vt* to scatter, dispel.
dispendium, -ī *and* **ii** *nt* expense, loss.
dispennō *etc see* **dispandō**.
dispēnsātiō, -ōnis *f* management, stewardship.
dispēnsātor, -ōris *m* steward, treasurer.
dispēnsō, -āre, -āvī, -ātum *vi* to weigh out, pay out; to manage, distribute; (*fig*) to regulate.
dispercutiō, -ere *vt* to dash out.
disperdō, -ere, -idī, -itum *vt* to ruin, squander.
dispereō, -īre, -iī *vi* to go to ruin, be undone.
dispergō, -gere, -sī, -sum *vt* to disperse, spread over, space out.
dispersē *adv* here and there.
dispersus *ppp of* **dispergō**.
dispertiō, -īre, -īvī, -ītum; -ior, -īrī *vt* to apportion, distribute.
dispertītiō, -ōnis *f* division.
dispessus *ppp of* **dispandō**.
dispiciō, -icere, -exī, -ectum *vt* to see clearly, see through; to distinguish, discern; (*fig*) to consider.
displiceō, -ēre *vi* (*with dat*) to displease; **sibi ~** be in a bad humour.
displōdō, -dere, -sum *vt* to burst with a crash.
dispōnō, -ōnere, -osuī, -ositum *vt* to set out, arrange; (*MIL*) to station.

dispositē adv methodically.
dispositiō, -ōnis f arrangement.
dispositūra, -ae f arrangement.
dispositus ppp of **dispōnō** ♦ adj orderly.
dispositus, -ūs m arranging.
dispudet, -ēre, -uit v impers to be very ashamed.
dispulsus ppp of **dispellō**.
disputātiō, -ōnis f argument.
disputātor, -ōris m debater.
disputō, -āre, -āvī, -ātum vt to calculate; to examine, discuss.
disquīrō, -ere vt to investigate.
disquīsītiō, -ōnis f inquiry.
disrumpō etc see **dīrumpō**.
dissaepiō, -īre, -sī, -tum vt to fence off, separate off.
dissaeptum, -ī nt partition.
dissāvior, -ārī vt to kiss passionately.
dissēdī perf of **dissideō**.
dissēminō, -āre vt to sow, broadcast.
dissēnsiō, -ōnis f disagreement, conflict.
dissēnsus, -ūs m dissension.
dissentāneus adj contrary.
dissentiō, -entīre, -ēnsī, -ēnsum vi to disagree, differ; to be unlike, be inconsistent.
dissēp- etc see **dissaep-**.
disserēnō, -āre vi to clear up.
disserō, -erere, -ēvī, -itum vt to sow, plant at intervals.
disserō, -ere, -uī, -tum vt to set out in order, arrange; to examine, discuss.
disserpō, -ere vi to spread imperceptibly.
dissertō, -āre vt to discuss, dispute.
dissideō, -idēre, -ēdī, -essum vi to be distant; to disagree, quarrel; to differ, be unlike, be uneven.
dissignātiō, -ōnis f arrangement.
dissignātor, -ōris m master of ceremonies; undertaker.
dissignō, -āre vt to arrange, regulate; see also **dēsignō**.
dissiliō, -īre, -uī vi to fly apart, break up.
dissimilis adj unlike, different.
dissimiliter adv differently.
dissimilitūdō, -inis f unlikeness.
dissimulanter adv secretly.
dissimulantia, -ae f dissembling.
dissimulātiō, -ōnis f disguising, dissembling; Socratic irony.
dissimulātor, -ōris m dissembler.
dissimulō, -āre, -āvī, -ātum vt to dissemble, conceal, pretend that ... not, ignore.
dissipābilis adj diffusible.
dissipātiō, -ōnis f scattering, dispersing.
dissipō, dissupō, -āre, -āvī, -ātum vt to scatter, disperse; to spread, broadcast; to squander, destroy; (MIL) to put to flight.
dissitus ppp of **disserō**.

dissociābilis adj disuniting; incompatible.
dissociātiō, -ōnis f separation.
dissociō, -āre, -āvī, -ātum vt to disunite, estrange.
dissolūbilis adj dissoluble.
dissolūtē adv loosely, negligently.
dissolūtiō, -ōnis f breaking up, destruction; looseness; (law) refutation; (person) weakness.
dissolūtum, -ī nt asyndeton.
dissolūtus ppp of **dissolvō** ♦ adj loose; lax, careless; licentious.
dissolvō, -vere, -vī, -ūtum vt to unloose, dissolve; to destroy, abolish; to refute; to pay up, discharge (debt); to free, release.
dissonus adj discordant, jarring, disagreeing, different.
dissors, -tis adj not shared.
dissuādeō, -dēre, -sī, -sum vt to advise against, oppose.
dissuāsiō, -ōnis f advising against.
dissuāsor, -ōris m opposer.
dissultō, -āre vi to fly asunder.
dissuō, -ere vt to undo, open up.
dissupō etc see **dissipō**.
distaedet, -ēre v impers to weary, disgust.
distantia, -ae f diversity.
distendō (-nō), -dere, -dī, -tum vt to stretch out, swell.
distentus ppp of **distendō** ♦ adj full ♦ ppp of **distineō** ♦ adj busy.
disterminō, -āre vt to divide, limit.
distichon, -ī nt couplet.
distinctē adv distinctly, lucidly.
distinctiō, -ōnis f differentiating, difference; (GRAM) punctuation; (RHET) distinction between words.
distinctus ppp of **distinguō** ♦ adj separate, distinct; ornamented, set off; lucid.
distinctus, -ūs m difference.
distineō, -inēre, -inuī, -entum vt to keep apart, divide; to distract; to detain, occupy; to prevent.
distinguō, -guere, -xī, -ctum vt to divide, distinguish, discriminate; to punctuate; to adorn, set off.
distō, -āre vi to be apart, be distant; to be different.
distorqueō, -quēre, -sī, -tum vt to twist, distort.
distortiō, -ōnis f contortion.
distortus ppp of **distorqueō** ♦ adj deformed.
distractiō, -ōnis f parting, variance.
distractus ppp of **distrahō** ♦ adj separate.
distrahō, -here, -xī, -ctum vt to tear apart, separate, estrange; to sell piecemeal, retail; (mind) to distract, perplex; **aciem ~** break up a formation; **contrōversiās ~** end a dispute; **vōcēs ~** leave a hiatus.
distribuō, -uere, -uī, -ūtum vt to distribute,

divide.

distribūtē *adv* methodically.

distribūtiō, -ōnis *f* distribution, division.

districtus *ppp of* **distringō** ♦ *adj* busy, occupied; perplexed; severe.

distringō, -ngere, -nxī, -ctum *vt* to draw apart; to engage, distract; (*MIL*) to create a diversion against.

distruncō, -āre *vt* to cut in two.

distulī *perf of* **differō**.

disturbō, -āre, -āvī, -ātum *vt* to throw into confusion; to demolish; to frustrate, ruin.

dītēscō, -ere *vi* to grow rich.

dīthyrambicus *adj* dithyrambic.

dīthyrambus, -ī *m* dithyramb.

dītiae, -ārum *fpl* wealth.

dītiō *etc see* **diciō**.

dītō, -āre *vt* to enrich.

diū (*comp* **diūtius,** *sup* **diūtissimē**) *adv* long, a long time; long ago; by day.

diurnum, -ī *nt* day-book; **ācta ~a** Roman daily gazette.

diurnus *adj* daily, for a day; by day, day- (*in cpds*).

dīus *adj* divine, noble.

diūtinē *adv* long.

diūtinus *adj* long, lasting.

diūtissimē, -ius *etc see* **diū**.

diūturnitās, -ātis *f* long time, long duration.

diūturnus *adj* long, lasting.

dīva, -ae *f* goddess.

dīvāricō, -āre *vt* to spread.

dīvellō, -ellere, -ellī, -ulsum *vt* to tear apart, tear in pieces; (*fig*) to tear away, separate, estrange.

dīvēndō, -ere, -itum *vt* to sell in lots.

dīverberō, -āre *vt* to divide, cleave.

dīverbium, -ī *and* **iī** *nt* (*comedy*) passage in dialogue.

dīversē *adv* in different directions, variously.

dīversitās, -ātis *f* contradiction, disagreement, difference.

dīversus, dīvorsus *ppp of* **dīvertō** ♦ *adj* in different directions, apart; different; remote; opposite, conflicting; hostile ♦ *mpl* individuals.

dīvertō, -tere, -tī, -sum *vi* to turn away; differ.

dīves, -itis *adj* rich.

dīvexō, -āre *vt* to pillage.

dīvidia, -ae *f* worry, concern.

dīvidō, -idere, -īsī, -īsum *vt* to divide, break open; to distribute, apportion; to separate, keep apart; to distinguish; (*jewel*) to set off; **sententiam ~** *take the vote separately on the parts of a motion*.

dīviduus *adj* divisible; divided.

dīvīnātiō, -ōnis *f* foreseeing the future, divination; (*law*) inquiry to select the most suitable prosecutor.

dīvīnē *adv* by divine influence; prophetically; admirably.

dīvīnitās, -ātis *f* divinity; divination; divine quality.

dīvīnitus *adv* from heaven, by divine influence; excellently.

dīvīnō, -āre, -āvī, -ātum *vt* to foresee, prophesy.

dīvīnus *adj* divine, of the gods; prophetic; superhuman, excellent ♦ *m* soothsayer ♦ *nt* sacrifice; oath; **rēs ~a** religious service, sacrifice; **~a hūmānaque** all things in heaven and earth; **~ī crēdere** believe on oath.

dīvīsī *perf of* **dīvīdō**.

dīvīsiō, -ōnis *f* division; distribution.

dīvīsor, -ōris *m* distributor; bribery agent.

dīvīsus *ppp of* **dīvīdō** ♦ *adj* separate.

dīvīsus, -ūs *m* division.

dīvitiae, -ārum *fpl* wealth; (*fig*) richness.

dīvor- *etc see* **dīver-**.

dīvortium, -ī *and* **iī** *nt* separation; divorce (by consent); road fork, watershed.

dīvulgātus *adj* widespread.

dīvulgō, -āre, -āvī, -ātum *vt* to publish, make public.

dīvulsus *ppp of* **dīvellō**.

dīvum, -ī *nt* sky; **sub ~ō** in the open air.

dīvus *adj* divine; deified ♦ *m* god.

dīxī *perf of* **dīcō**.

dō, dare, dedī, datum *vt* to give; to permit, grant; to put, bring, cause, make; to give up, devote; to tell; to impute; **fābulam ~** produce a play; **in fugam ~** put to flight; **litterās ~** post a letter; **manūs ~** surrender; **nōmen ~** enlist; **operam ~** take pains, do one's best; **poenās ~** pay the penalty; **vēla ~** set sail; **verba ~** cheat.

doceō, -ēre, -uī, -tum *vt* to teach; to inform, tell; **fābulam ~** produce a play.

dochmius, -ī *and* **iī** *m* dochmiac foot.

docilis *adj* easily trained, docile.

docilitās, -ātis *f* aptness for being taught.

doctē *adv* skilfully, cleverly.

doctor, -ōris *m* teacher, instructor.

doctrīna, -ae *f* instruction, education, learning; science.

doctus *ppp of* **doceō** ♦ *adj* learned, skilled; cunning, clever.

documentum, -ī *nt* lesson, example, proof.

Dōdōna, -ae *f* town in Epirus (*famous for its oracle of Jupiter*).

Dōdōnaeus, -is, -idis *adj see* **Dōdōna**.

dōdrāns, -antis *m* three-fourths.

dogma, -tis *nt* philosophical doctrine.

dolābra, -ae *f* pickaxe.

dolēns, -entis *pres p of* **doleō** ♦ *adj* painful.

dolenter *adv* sorrowfully.

doleō, -ēre, -uī, -itum *vt, vi* to be in pain, be sore; to grieve, lament, be sorry (for); to pain; **cui ~et meminit** ≈ *once bitten, twice shy*.

dōliāris *adj* tubby.

dōliolum, -ī *nt* small cask.

dōlium, -ī *and* **iī** *nt* large wine jar.

dolō, -āre, -āvī, -ātum *vt* to hew, shape with an axe.

dolō, -ōnis *m* pike; sting; fore-topsail.

Dolopes, -um *mpl people of Thessaly.*

Dolopia, -iae *f the country of the people of Thessaly.*

dolor, -ōris *m* pain, pang; sorrow, trouble; indignation, resentment; (*RHET*) pathos.

dolōsē *adv see* **dolōsus.**

dolōsus *adj* deceitful, crafty.

dolus, -ī *m* deceit, guile, trick; ~ **malus** wilful fraud.

domābilis *adj* tameable.

domesticus *adj* domestic, household; personal, private; of one's own country, internal ♦ *mpl* members of a household; **bellum ~** civil war.

domī *adv* at home.

domicilium, -ī *and* **iī** *nt* dwelling.

domina, -ae *f* mistress, lady of the house; wife, mistress; (*fig*) lady.

domināns, -antis *pres p of* **dominor** ♦ *adj* (*words*) literal ♦ *m* tyrant.

dominātiō, -ōnis *f* mastery, tyranny.

dominātor, -ōris *m* lord.

dominātrīx, -rīcis *f* queen.

dominātus, -ūs *m* mastery, sovereignty.

dominicus *adj* (*ECCL*) the Lord's.

dominium, -ī *and* **iī** *nt* absolute ownership; feast.

dominor, -ārī, -ātus *vi* to rule, be master; (*fig*) to lord it.

dominus, -ī *m* master, lord; owner; host; despot; (*ECCL*) the Lord.

Domitiānus *adj m Roman Emperor.*

Domitius, -ī *m* Roman plebeian name (*esp with surname Ahenobarbus*).

domitō, -āre *vt* to break in.

domitor, -ōris *m*, **-rīx, -rīcis** *f* tamer; conqueror.

domitus *ppp of* **domō.**

domitus, -ūs *m* taming.

domō, -āre, -uī, -itum *vt* to tame, break in; to conquer.

domus, -ūs *and* **ī** *f* house (*esp in town*); home, native place; family; (*PHILOS*) sect; **~ī** at home; in peace; **~ī habēre** have plenty of one's own, have plenty of; **~um** home(wards); **~ō** from home.

dōnābilis *adj* deserving a present.

dōnārium, -ī *and* **iī** *nt* offering; altar, temple.

dōnātiō, -ōnis *f* presenting.

dōnātīvum, -ī *nt* largess, gratuity.

dōnec (dōnicum, dōnique) *conj* until; while, as long as.

dōnō, -āre, -āvī, -ātum *vt* to present, bestow; to remit, condone (for another's sake); (*fig*) to sacrifice.

dōnum, -ī *nt* gift; offering.

dorcas, -dis *f* gazelle.

Dōrēs, -um *mpl* Dorians (*mostly the Greeks of the Peloponnese*).

Dōricus *adj* Dorian; Greek.

Dōris, -dis *f* a sea nymph; the sea.

dormiō, -īre, -īvī, -ītum *vi* to sleep, be asleep.

dormītātor, -ōris *m* dreamer.

dormītō, -āre *vi* to be drowsy, nod.

dorsum, -ī *nt* back; mountain ridge.

dōs, dōtis *f* dowry; (*fig*) gift, talent.

Dossēnus, -ī *m* hunchback, clown.

dōtālis *adj* dowry (*in cpds*), dotal.

dōtātus *adj* richly endowed.

dōtō, -āre *vt* to endow.

drachma (drachuma), -ae *f a Greek silver coin.*

dracō, -ōnis *m* serpent, dragon; (*ASTRO*) Draco.

dracōnigena, -ae *adj* sprung from dragon's teeth.

drāpeta, -ae *m* runaway slave.

Drepanum, -ī, -a, -ōrum *nt town in W. Sicily.*

dromas, -dis *m* dromedary.

dromos, -ī *m* racecourse at Sparta.

Druidēs, -um, -ae, -ārum *mpl* Druids.

Drūsiānus *adj see* **Drūsus.**

Drūsus, -ī *m* Roman surname (*esp famous commander in Germany under Augustus*).

Dryades, -um *fpl* woodnymphs, Dryads.

Dryopes, -um *mpl a people of Epirus.*

dubiē *adv* doubtfully.

dubitābilis *adj* doubtful.

dubitanter *adv* doubtingly, hesitatingly.

dubitātiō, -ōnis *f* wavering, uncertainty, doubting; hesitancy, irresolution; (*RHET*) misgiving.

dubitō, -āre, -āvī, -ātum *vt, vi* to waver, be in doubt, wonder, doubt; to hesitate, stop to think.

dubium *nt* doubt.

dubius *adj* wavering, uncertain; doubtful, indecisive; precarious; irresolute ♦ *nt* doubt; **in ~um vocāre** call in question; **in ~um venīre** be called in question; **sine ~ō, haud ~ē** undoubtedly.

ducēnī, -ōrum *adj* 200 each.

ducentēsima, -ae *f* one-half per cent.

ducentī, -ōrum *num* two hundred.

ducentiēs, -iēns *adv* 200 times.

dūcō, -cere, -xī, ductum *vt* to lead, guide, bring, take; to draw, draw out; to reckon, consider; (*MIL*) to lead, march, command; (*breath*) to inhale; (*ceremony*) to conduct; (*changed aspect*) to take on, receive; (*dance*) to perform; (*drink*) to quaff; (*metal*) to shape, beat out; (*mind*) to attract, induce, deceive; (*oars*) to pull; (*origin*) to derive, trace; (*time*) to prolong, put off, pass; (*udders*) to milk; (*wool*) to spin; (*a work*) to construct, compose, make; (*COMM*) to calculate; **īlia ~** become broken-winded; **in numerō hostium ~** regard as an enemy; **ōs ~** make faces; **parvī ~** think little of; **ratiōnem ~** have regard for; **uxōrem ~** marry.

ductim *adv* in streams.

ductitō, -āre *vt* to lead on, deceive; to marry.

ductō, -āre vt to lead, draw; to take home; to cheat.

ductor, -ōris m leader, commander; guide, pilot.

ductus ppp of **dūcō**.

ductus, -ūs m drawing, drawing off; form; command, generalship.

dūdum adv a little while ago, just now; for long; **haud ~** not long ago; **iam ~ adsum** I have been here a long time; **quam ~** how long.

duellum etc see **bellum**.

Duillius, -ī m consul who defeated the Carthaginians at sea.

duim pres subj of **dō**.

dulce, -iter adv see **dulcis**.

dulcēdō, -inis f sweetness; pleasantness, charm.

dulcēscō, -ere vi to become sweet.

dulciculus adj rather sweet.

dulcifer, -ī adj sweet.

dulcis adj sweet; pleasant, lovely; kind, dear.

dulcitūdō, -inis f sweetness.

dūlicē adv like a slave.

Dūlichium, -ī nt island in the Ionian Sea near Ithaca.

Dūlichius adj of Dulichium; of Ulysses.

dum conj while, as long as; provided that, if only; until ♦ adv (enclitic) now, a moment; (with neg) yet.

dūmētum, -ī nt thicket, thornbushes.

dummodo conj provided that.

dūmōsus adj thorny.

dumtaxat adv at least; only, merely.

dūmus, -ī m thornbush.

duo, duae, duo num two.

duodeciēns, -ēs adv twelve times.

duodecim num twelve.

duodecimus adj twelfth.

duodēnī, -ōrum adj twelve each, in dozens.

duodēquadrāgēsimus adj thirty-eighth.

duodēquadrāgintā num thirty-eight.

duodēquīnquāgēsimus adj forty-eighth.

duodētrīciēns adv twenty-eight times.

duodētrīgintā num twenty-eight.

duodēvīcēnī adj eighteen each.

duodēvīgintī num eighteen.

duoetvīcēsimānī, -ānōrum mpl soldiers of the 22nd legion.

duoetvīcēsimus adj twenty-second.

duovirī, duumvirī, -ōrum mpl a board of two men; colonial magistrates; **~ nāvālēs** naval commissioners (for supply and repair); **~ sacrōrum** keepers of the Sibylline Books.

duplex, -icis adj double, twofold; both; (person) false.

duplicārius, -ī and **iī** m soldier receiving double pay.

dupliciter adv doubly, on two accounts.

duplicō, -āre, -āvī, -ātum vt to double, increase; to bend.

duplus adj double, twice as much ♦ nt double ♦ f double the price.

dupondius, -ī and **iī** m coin worth two asses.

dūrābilis adj lasting.

dūrāmen, -inis nt hardness.

dūrateus adj wooden.

dūrē, -iter adv stiffly; hardily; harshly, roughly.

dūrēscō, -ēscere, -uī vi to harden.

dūritās, -ātis f harshness.

dūritia, -ae, -ēs, -em f hardness; hardiness; severity; want of feeling.

dūrō, -āre, -āvī, -ātum vt to harden, stiffen; to make hardy, inure; (mind) to dull ♦ vi to harden; to be patient, endure; to hold out, last; (mind) to be steeled.

dūrus adj hard, harsh, rough; hardy, tough; rude, uncultured; (character) severe, unfeeling, impudent, miserly; (circs) hard, cruel.

duumvirī etc see **duovirī**.

dux, ducis m leader, guide; chief, head; (MIL) commander, general.

dūxī perf of **dūcō**.

Dymantis, -antidis f Hecuba.

Dymās, -antis m father of Hecuba.

dynamis, -is f plenty.

dynastēs, -ae m ruler, prince.

Dyrrhachīnus adj see n.

Dyrrhachium (Dyrrachium), -ī nt Adriatic port (now Durazzo).

E, e

ē prep see **ex**.

ea f pron she, it ♦ adj see **is**.

eā adv there, that way.

eādem adv the same way; at the same time.

eadem f adj see **idem**.

eāīdem, eapse f of **ipse**.

eapse f of **ipse**.

eātenus adv so far.

ebenus etc see **hebenus**.

ēbibō, -ere, -ī vt to drink up, drain; to squander; to absorb.

ēblandior, -īrī vt to coax out, obtain by flattery; **~ītus** obtained by flattery.

Eborācum, -ī nt York.

ēbrietās, ātis f drunkenness.

ēbriolus adj tipsy.

ēbriōsitās, -ātis f addiction to drink.

ēbriōsus adj drunkard; (berry) juicy.

ēbrius adj drunk; full; (fig) intoxicated.

ēbulliō, -īre vi to bubble up ♦ vt to brag about.

ebulus, -ī m, **-um, -ī** nt danewort, dwarf elder.

ebur, -is nt ivory; ivory work.

Eburācum, -ī nt York.

eburātus adj inlaid with ivory.

eburneolus adj of ivory.

eburneus, eburnus adj of ivory; ivory-white.

ēcastor interj by Castor!

ecce adv look!, here is!, there is!; lo and behold!; **~a, ~am, ~illam, ~istam** here she is!; **~um, ~illum** here he is!; **~ōs, ~ās** here they are!

eccerē interj there now!

eccheuma, -tis nt pouring out.

ecclēsia, -ae f a Greek assembly; (ECCL) congregation, church.

eccum etc see **ecce**.

ecdicus, -ī m civic lawyer.

ecf- see **eff-**.

echidna, -ae f viper; **~ Lernaea** hydra.

echīnus, -ī m sea-urchin; hedgehog; a rinsing bowl.

Echīōn, -onis m Theban hero.

Echīonidēs m Pentheus.

Echīonius adj Theban.

Echō, -us f wood nymph; echo.

ecloga, -ae f selection; eclogue.

ecquandō adv ever.

ecquī, -ae, -od adj interrog any.

ecquid, -ī adv whether.

ecquis, -id pron interrog anyone, anything.

ecquō adv anywhere.

eculeus, -ī m foal; rack.

edācitās, -ātis f gluttony.

edāx, -ācis adj gluttonous; (fig) devouring, carking.

ēdentō, -āre vt to knock the teeth out of.

ēdentulus adj toothless; old.

edepol interj by Pollux, indeed.

ēdī perf of **edō**.

ēdīcō, -īcere, -īxī, -ictum vt to declare; to decree, publish an edict.

ēdictiō, -ōnis f decree.

ēdictō, -āre vt to proclaim.

ēdictum, -ī nt proclamation, edict (esp a praetor's).

ēdidī perf of **edō**.

ēdiscō, -ere, ēdidicī vt to learn well, learn by heart.

ēdisserō, -ere, -uī, -tum vt to explain in detail.

ēdissertō, -āre vt to explain fully.

ēditīcius adj chosen by the plaintiff.

ēditiō, -ōnis f publishing, edition; statement; (law) designation of a suit.

ēditus ppp of **ēdō** ♦ adj high; descended ♦ nt height; order.

edō, edere and **ēsse, ēdī, ēsum** vt to eat; (fig) to devour.

ēdō, -ere, -idī, -itum vt to put forth, discharge; to emit; to give birth to, produce; (speech) to declare, relate, utter; (action) to cause, perform; (book) to publish; (POL) to

promulgate; **lūdōs ~** put on a show; **tribūs ~** nominate tribes of jurors.

ēdoceō, -ere, -uī, -ctum vt to instruct clearly, teach thoroughly.

ēdomō, -āre, -uī, -itum vt to conquer, overcome.

Ēdōnus adj Thracian.

ēdormiō, -īre vi to have a good sleep ♦ vt to sleep off.

ēdormīscō, -ere vt to sleep off.

ēducātiō, -ōnis f bringing up, rearing.

ēducātor, -ōris m foster father, tutor.

ēducātrīx, -īcis f nurse.

ēducō, -āre, -āvī, -ātum vt to bring up, rear, train; to produce.

ēdūcō, -ūcere, -ūxī, -uctum vt to draw out, bring away; to raise up, erect; (law) to summon; (MIL) to lead out, march out; (ship) to put to sea; (young) to hatch, rear, train.

edūlis adj edible.

ēdūrō, -āre vi to last out.

ēdūrus adj very hard.

effarciō etc see **efferciō**.

effātus ppa of **effor** ♦ adj solemnly pronounced, declared ♦ nt axiom; (pl) predictions.

effectiō, -ōnis f performing; efficient cause.

effector, -ōris m, **-rīx, -rīcis** f producer, author.

effectus ppp of **efficiō**.

effectus, -ūs m completion, performance; effect.

effēminātē adv see **effēminātus**.

effēminātus adj effeminate.

effēminō, -āre, -āvī, -ātum vt to make a woman of; to enervate.

efferātus adj savage.

efferciō, -cīre, -tum vt to cram full.

efferitās, -ātis f wildness.

efferō, -āre, -āvī, -ātum vt to make wild; (fig) to exasperate.

efferō (ecferō), -re, extulī, ēlātum vt to bring out, carry out; to lift up, raise; (dead) to carry to the grave; (emotion) to transport; (honour) to exalt; (news) to spread abroad; (soil) to produce; (trouble) to endure to the end; **sē ~** rise; be conceited.

effertus ppp of **efferciō** ♦ adj full, bulging.

efferus adj savage.

effervēscō, -vēscere, -buī vi to boil over; (fig) to rage.

effervō, -ere vi to boil up.

effētus adj exhausted.

efficācitās, -ātis f power.

efficāciter adv effectually.

efficāx, -ācis adj capable, effective.

efficiēns, -entis pres p of **efficiō** ♦ adj effective, efficient.

efficienter adv efficiently.

efficientia, -ae f power, efficacy.

efficiō, -icere, -ēcī, -ectum vt to make,

Noun declensions and verb conjugations are shown on pp xiii to xxv. The present infinitive ending of a verb shows to which conjugation it belongs: **-āre** = 1st; **-ēre** = 2nd; **-ere** = 3rd and **-īre** = 4th. Irregular verbs are shown on p xxvi

accomplish; to cause, bring about; (*numbers*)
to amount to; (*soil*) to yield; (*theory*) to make
out, try to prove.

effictus *ppp of* **effingō.**

effigiēs, -ēī, -a, -ae *f* likeness, copy; ghost;
portrait, statue; (*fig*) image, ideal.

effingō, -ngere, -nxī, -ctum *vt* to form,
fashion; to portray, represent; to wipe clean;
to fondle.

efflāgitātiō, -ōnis *f* urgent demand.

efflāgitātus, -ūs *m* urgent request.

efflāgitō, -āre *vt* to demand urgently.

efflictim *adv* desperately.

efflictō, -āre *vt* to strike dead.

effligō, -gere, -xī, -ctum *vt* to exterminate.

efflō, -āre, -āvī, -ātum *vt* to breathe out, blow
out ♦ *vi* to billow out; **animam ~ expire.**

efflōrēscō, -ēscere, -uī *vi* to blossom forth.

effluō, -ere, -xī *vi* to run out, issue, emanate;
(*fig*) to pass away, vanish; (*rumour*) to get
known; **ex animō ~ become forgotten.**

effluvium, -ī *and* **iī** *nt* outlet.

effodiō, -odere, -ōdī, -ossum *vt* to dig up;
(*eyes*) to gouge out; (*house*) to ransack.

effor, -ārī, -ātus *vt* to speak, utter; (*augury*) to
ordain; (*logic*) to state a proposition.

effossus *ppp of* **effodiō.**

effrēnātē *adv see* **effrēnātus.**

effrēnātiō, -ōnis *f* impetuousness.

effrēnātus *adj* unbridled, violent, unruly.

effrēnus *adj* unbridled.

effringō, -ingere, -ēgī, -āctum *vt* to break
open, smash.

effugiō, -ugere, -ūgī *vi* to run away, escape ♦
vt to flee from, escape; to escape the notice
of.

effugium, -ī *and* **iī** *nt* flight, escape; means of
escape.

effulgeō, -gēre, -sī *vi* to shine out, blaze.

effultus *adj* supported.

effundō, -undere, -ūdī, -ūsum *vt* to pour
forth, pour out; (*crops*) to produce in
abundance; (*missiles*) to shoot; (*rider*) to
throw; (*speech*) to give vent to; (*effort*) to
waste; (*money*) to squander; (*reins*) to let go;
sē ~, ~undī rush out; indulge (in).

effūsē *adv* far and wide; lavishly,
extravagantly.

effūsiō, -ōnis *f* pouring out, rushing out;
profusion, extravagance; exuberance.

effūsus *ppp of* **effundō** ♦ *adj* vast, extensive;
loose, straggling; lavish, extravagant.

effūtiō, -īre *vt* to blab, chatter.

ēgelidus *adj* mild, cool.

egēns, -entis *pres p of* **egeō** ♦ *adj* needy.

egēnus *adj* destitute.

egeō, -ēre, -uī *vi* to be in want; (*with abl or gen*)
to need, want.

Egeria, -ae *f* nymph who taught Numa.

ēgerō, -rere, -ssī, -stum *vt* to carry out; to
discharge, emit.

egestās, -ātis *f* want, poverty.

ēgestus *ppp of* **ēgerō.**

ēgī *perf of* **agō.**

ego *pron* I; **~met** I (*emphatic*).

ēgredior, -dī, -ssus *vi* to go out, come out; to
go up, climb; (*MIL*) to march out; (*NAUT*) to
disembark, put to sea; (*speech*) to digress ♦
vt to go beyond, quit; (*fig*) to overstep,
surpass.

ēgregiē *adv* uncommonly well, singularly.

ēgregius *adj* outstanding, surpassing;
distinguished, illustrious.

ēgressus *ppa of* **ēgredior.**

ēgressus, -ūs *m* departure; way out;
digression; (*NAUT*) landing; (*river*) mouth.

eguī *perf of* **egeō.**

ēgurgitō, -āre *vt* to lavish.

ehem *interj* (*expressing surprise*) ha!, so!

ēheu *interj* (*expressing pain*) alas!

eho *interj* (*expressing rebuke*) look here!

eī *dat of* **is.**

ei *interj* (*expressing alarm*) oh!

eia *interj* (*expressing delight, playful
remonstrance, encouragement*) aha!, come
now!, come on!

ēiaculor, -ārī *vt* to shoot out.

ēiciō, -icere, -iēcī, -iectum *vt* to throw out,
drive out, put out; (*joint*) to dislocate; (*mind*)
to banish; (*NAUT*) to bring to land, run
aground, wreck; (*rider*) to throw; (*speech*) to
utter; (*THEAT*) to hiss off; **sē ~ rush out, break
out.**

ēiectāmenta, -ōrum *ntpl* refuse.

ēiectiō, -ōnis *f* banishment.

ēiectō, -āre *vt* to throw up.

ēiectus *ppp of* **ēiciō** ♦ *adj* shipwrecked.

ēiectus, -ūs *m* emitting.

ēierō, ēiūrō, -āre *vt* to abjure, reject on oath,
forswear; (*office*) to resign; **bonam cōpiam ~
declare oneself bankrupt.**

ēiulātiō, -ōnis *f*, **ēiulātus, -ūs** *m* wailing.

ēiulō, -āre *vi* to wail, lament.

ēius *pron* his, her, its; **~modī** such.

ej- *etc see* **ei-.**

ēlābor, -bī, -psus *vi* to glide away, slip off; to
escape, get off; to pass away.

ēlabōrātus *adj* studied.

ēlabōrō, -āre, -āvī, -ātum *vi* to exert oneself,
take great pains ♦ *vt* to work out, elaborate.

ēlāmentābilis *adj* very mournful.

ēlanguēscō, -ēscere, -ī *vi* to grow faint; to
relax.

ēlāpsus *ppa of* **ēlābor.**

ēlātē *adv* proudly.

ēlātiō, -ōnis *f* ecstasy, exaltation.

ēlātrō, -āre *vt* to bark out.

ēlātus *ppp of* **efferō** ♦ *adj* high; exalted.

ēlavō, -avāre, -āvī, -autum *and* **-ōtum** *vt* to
wash clean; (*comedy*) to rob.

Elea, -ae *f* town in S. Italy (*birthplace of
Parmenides*).

Eleātēs, -āticus *adj see n.*

ēlecebra, -ae *f* snare.

ēlēctē *adv* choicely.

ēlēctilis *adj* choice.

ēlectiō, -ōnis *f* choice, option.
ēlectō, -āre *vt* to coax out.
ēlectō, -āre *vt* to select.
Ēlectra, -ae *f* a Pleiad (*daughter of Atlas; sister of Orestes*).
ēlectrum, -ī *nt* amber; an alloy of gold and silver.
ēlēctus *ppp of* **ēligō ♦** *adj* select, choice.
ēlēctus, -ūs *m* choice.
ēlegāns, -antis *adj* tasteful, refined, elegant; fastidious; (*things*) fine, choice.
ēleganter *adv* with good taste.
ēlegantia, -ae *f* taste, finesse, elegance; fastidiousness.
ēlēgī *perf of* **ēligō.**
elegī, -ōrum *mpl* elegiac verses.
elegīa, -ae *f* elegy.
Eleleides, -eidum *fpl* Bacchantes.
Eleleus, -eī *m* Bacchus.
elementum, -ī *nt* element; (*pl*) first principles, rudiments; beginnings; letters (*of alphabet*).
elenchus, -ī *m* a pear-shaped pearl.
elephantomacha, -ae *m* fighter mounted on an elephant.
elephantus, -ī, elephās, -antis *m* elephant; ivory.
Ēlēus, -ius, -ias *adj* Elean; Olympian.
Eleusīn, -is *f* Eleusis (*Attic town famous for its mysteries of Demeter*).
Eleusīus *adj see* **Eleusīn.**
eleutheria, -ae *f* liberty.
ēlevō, -āre *vt* to lift, raise; to alleviate; to make light of, lessen, disparage.
ēliciō, -ere, -uī, -itum *vt* to lure out, draw out; (*god*) to call down; (*spirit*) to conjure up; (*fig*) to elicit, draw.
ēlīdō, -dere, -sī, -sum *vt* to dash out, squeeze out; to drive out; to crush, destroy.
ēligō, -igere, -ēgī, -ēctum *vt* to pick, pluck out; to choose.
ēlīminō, -āre *vt* to carry outside.
ēlīmō, -āre *vt* to file; (*fig*) to perfect.
ēlinguis *adj* speechless; not eloquent.
ēlinguō, -āre *vt* to tear the tongue out of.
Ēlis, -idis *f* district and town in W. Peloponnese (*famous for Olympia*).
Elissa, -ae *f* Dido.
ēlīsus *ppp of* **ēlīdō.**
ēlixus *adj* boiled.
elleborōsus *adj* quite mad.
elleborus, -ī *m*, **-um, -ī** *nt* hellebore.
ellum, ellam there he (she) is!
ēlocō, -āre *vt* to lease, farm out.
ēlocūtiō, -ōnis *f* delivery, style.
ēlocūtus *ppa of* **ēloquor.**
ēlogium, -ī *and* **iī** *nt* short saying; inscription; (*will*) clause.
ēloquēns, -entis *adj* eloquent.
ēloquenter *adv see adj.*

ēloquentia, -ae *f* eloquence.
ēloquium, -ī *and* **iī** *nt* eloquence.
ēloquor, -quī, -cūtus *vt, vi* to speak out, speak eloquently.
ēlūceō, -cēre, -xī *vi* to shine out, glitter.
ēluctor, -ārī, -ātus *vi* to struggle, force a way out **♦** *vt* to struggle out of, surmount.
ēlūcubrō, -āre, -or, -ārī, -ātus *vt* to compose by lamplight.
ēlūdificor, -ārī, -ātus *vt* to cheat, play up.
ēlūdō, -dere, -sī, -sum *vt* to parry, ward off, foil; to win off at play; to outplay, outmanoeuvre; to cheat, make fun of **♦** *vi* to finish one's sport.
ēlūgeō, -gēre, -xī *vt* to mourn for.
ēlumbis *adj* feeble.
ēluō, -uere, -uī, -ūtum *vt* to wash clean; (*money*) to squander; (*fig*) to wash away, get rid of.
ēlūsus *ppp of* **ēlūdō.**
ēlūtus *ppp of* **ēluō ♦** *adj* insipid.
ēluviēs, -em -ē *f* discharge; overflowing.
ēluviō, -ōnis *f* deluge.
Ēlysium, -ī *nt* Elysium.
Ēlysius *adj* Elysian.
em *interj* there you are!
ēmancipātiō, -ōnis *f* giving a son his independence; conveyance of property.
ēmancipō, -āre *vt* to declare independent; to transfer, give up, sell.
ēmānō, -āre, -āvī, -ātum *vi* to flow out; to spring (from); (*news*) to leak out, become known.
Ēmathia, -ae *f* district of Macedonia; Macedonia, Thessaly.
Ēmathius *adj* Macedonian, Pharsalian; **~des, ~dum** *fpl* Muses.
ēmātūrēscō, -ēscere, -uī *vi* to soften.
emāx, -ācis *adj* fond of buying.
emblēma, -tis *nt* inlaid work, mosaic.
embolium, -ī *and* **iī** *nt* interlude.
ēmendābilis *adj* corrigible.
ēmendātē *adv see* **ēmendātor.**
ēmendātiō, -ōnis *f* correction.
ēmendātor, -ōris *m*, **-rīx, -rīcis** *f* corrector.
ēmendātus *adj* faultless.
ēmendō, -āre, -āvī, -ātum *vt* to correct, improve.
ēmēnsus *ppa of* **ēmētior ♦** *adj* traversed.
ēmentior, -īrī, -ītus *vi* to tell lies **♦** *vt* to pretend, fabricate; **~ītus** pretended.
ēmercor, -ārī *vt* to purchase.
ēmereō, -ēre, -uī, -itum, -eor, -ērī *vt* to earn fully, deserve; to lay under an obligation; to complete one's term of service.
ēmergō, -gere, -sī, -sum *vt* to raise out; (*fig*) to extricate **♦** *vi* to rise, come up, emerge; (*fig*) to get clear, extricate oneself; (*impers*) it becomes evident.
ēmeritus *ppa of* **ēmereor ♦** *adj* superannuated,

Noun declensions and verb conjugations are shown on pp xiii to xxv. The present infinitive ending of a verb shows to which conjugation it belongs: **-āre** = 1st; **-ēre** = 2nd; **-ere** = 3rd and **-īre** = 4th. Irregular verbs are shown on p xxvi

worn-out ♦ _m_ veteran.
ēmersus _ppp of_ **ēmergō.**
emetica, -ae _f_ emetic.
ēmētior, -tīrī, -nsus _vt_ to measure out; to traverse, pass over; (_time_) to live through; (_fig_) to impart.
ēmetō, -ere _vt_ to harvest.
ēmī _perf of_ **emō.**
ēmicō, -āre, -uī, -ātum _vi_ to dart out, dash out, flash out; (_fig_) to shine.
ēmigrō, -āre, -āvī, -ātum _vi_ to remove, depart.
ēminēns, -entis _pres p of_ **ēmineō** ♦ _adj_ high, projecting; (_fig_) distinguished, eminent.
ēminentia, -ae _f_ prominence; (_painting_) light.
ēmineō, -ēre, -uī _vi_ to stand out, project; to be prominent, be conspicuous, distinguish oneself.
ēminor, -ārī _vi_ to threaten.
ēminus _adv_ at _or_ from a distance.
ēmīror, -ārī _vt_ to marvel at.
ēmissārium, -ī _and_ **iī** _nt_ outlet.
ēmissārius, -ī _and_ **iī** _m_ scout.
ēmissīcius _adj_ prying.
ēmissiō, -ōnis _f_ letting go, discharge.
ēmissus _ppp of_ **ēmittō.**
ēmissus, -ūs _m_ emission.
ēmittō, -ittere, -īsī, -issum _vt_ to send out, let out; to let go, let slip; (_missile_) to discharge; (_person_) to release, free; (_sound_) to utter; (_writing_) to publish.
emō, -ere, ēmī, emptum _vt_ to buy, procure; to win over; **bene** ~ buy cheap; **male** ~ buy dear; **in diem** ~ buy on credit.
ēmoderor, -ārī _vt_ to give expression to.
ēmodulor, -ārī _vt_ to sing through.
ēmōlior, -īrī _vt_ to accomplish.
ēmolliō, -īre, -iī, -ītum _vt_ to soften; to mollify; to enervate.
ēmolumentum, -ī _nt_ profit, advantage.
ēmoneō, -ēre _vt_ to strongly advise.
ēmorior, -ī, -tuus _vi_ to die; (_fig_) to pass away.
ēmortuālis _adj_ of death.
ēmoveō, -ovēre, -ōvī, -ōtum _vt_ to remove, drive away.
Empedoclēs, -is _m_ Sicilian philosopher.
Empedoclēus _adj see n._
empīricus, -ī _m_ empirical doctor.
emporium, -ī _and_ **iī** _nt_ market, market town.
emptiō, -ōnis _f_ buying; a purchase.
emptitō, -āre _vt_ to often buy.
emptor, -ōris _m_ purchaser.
emptus _ppp of_ **emō.**
ēmulgeō, -ēre _vt_ to drain.
ēmunctus _ppp of_ **ēmungō** ♦ _adj_ discriminating.
ēmungō, -gere, -xī, -ctum _vt_ to blow the nose of; (_comedy_) to cheat.
ēmūniō, -īre, -īvī, -ītum _vt_ to strengthen, secure; to build up; to make roads through.
ēn _interj_ (_drawing attention_) look!, see!; (_excited question_) really, indeed; (_command_) come now!

ēnārrābilis _adj_ describable.
ēnārrō, -āre, -āvī, -ātum _vt_ to describe in detail.
ēnāscor, -scī, -tus _vi_ to sprout, grow.
ēnatō, -āre _vi_ to swim ashore; (_fig_) to escape.
ēnātus _ppa of_ **ēnāscor.**
ēnāvigō, -āre _vi_ to sail clear, clear ♦ _vt_ to sail over.
Enceladus, -ī _m_ giant under Etna.
endromis, -dis _f_ sports wrap.
Endymiōn, -ōnis _m_ a beautiful youth loved by the Moon, and doomed to lasting sleep.
ēnecō, -āre, -uī _and_ **-āvī, -tum** _and_ **ātum** _vt_ to kill; to wear out; to torment.
ēnervātus _adj_ limp.
ēnervis _adj_ enfeebled.
ēnervō, -āre, -āvī, -ātum _vt_ to weaken, unman.
ēnicō _etc see_ **ēnecō.**
enim _conj_ (_affirming_) yes, truly, in fact; (_explaining_) for, for instance, of course; **at** ~ but it will be objected; **quid** ~ well?; **sed** ~ but actually.
enimvērō _conj_ certainly, yes indeed.
Enīpeus, -eī _m_ river in Thessaly.
ēnīsus _ppa of_ **ēnītor.**
ēniteō, -ēre, -uī _vi_ to shine, brighten up; (_fig_) to be brilliant, distinguish oneself.
ēnitēscō, -ēscere, -uī _vi_ to shine, be brilliant.
ēnītor, -tī, -sus _and_ **xus** _vi_ to struggle up, climb; to strive, make a great effort ♦ _vt_ to give birth to; to climb.
ēnīxē _adv_ earnestly.
ēnīxus _ppa of_ **ēnītor** ♦ _adj_ strenuous.
Enniānus _adj see n._
Ennius, -ī _m_ greatest of the early Latin poets.
Ennosigaeus, -ī _m_ Earthshaker, Neptune.
ēnō, -āre, -āvī _vi_ to swim out, swim ashore; to fly away.
ēnōdātē _adv_ lucidly.
ēnōdātiō, -ōnis _f_ unravelling.
ēnōdis _adj_ free from knots; plain.
ēnōdō, -āre, -āvī, -ātum _vt_ to elucidate.
ēnōrmis _adj_ irregular; immense.
ēnōtēscō, -ēscere, -uī _vi_ to get known.
ēnotō, -āre _vt_ to make a note of.
ēnsiculus, -ī _m_ little sword.
ēnsiger, -ī _adj_ with his sword.
ēnsis, -is _m_ sword.
enthȳmēma, -tis _nt_ argument.
ēnūbō, -bere, -psī _vi_ to marry out of one's station; to marry and go away.
ēnucleātē _adv_ plainly.
ēnucleātus _adj_ (_style_) straightforward; (_votes_) honest.
ēnucleō, -āre _vt_ to elucidate.
ēnumerātiō, -ōnis _f_ enumeration; (_RHET_) recapitulation.
ēnumerō, -āre _vt_ to count up; to pay out; to relate.
ēnūntiātiō, -ōnis _f_ proposition.
ēnūntiātum, -ī _nt_ proposition.
ēnūntiō, -āre _vt_ to disclose, report; to

express; to pronounce.

ēnūptiō, -ōnis *f* marrying out of one's station.

ēnūtriō, -īre *vt* to feed, bring up.

eō, īre, īvī and **iī, itum** *vi* to go; (*MIL*) to march; (*time*) to pass; (*event*) to proceed, turn out; **in alia omnia ~** vote against a bill; **in sententiam ~** support a motion; **sīc eat** so may he fare!; **ī** (*mocking*) go on!

eō *adv* (*place*) thither, there; (*purpose*) with a view to; (*degree*) so far, to such a pitch; (*time*) so long; (*cause*) on that account, for the reason; (*with compar*) the; **accēdit eō** besides; **rēs erat eō locī** such was the state of affairs; **eō magis** all the more.

eōdem *adv* to the same place, purpose *or* person; **~ locī** in the same place.

Ēōs *f* dawn ♦ *m* morning star; Oriental.

Ēous *adj* at dawn, eastern.

Epamīnōndās, -ae *m* Theban general.

epāstus *adj* eaten up.

ephēbus, -ī *m* youth (*18 to 20*).

ephēmeris, -idis *f* diary.

Ephesius *adj see n.*

Ephesus, -ī *f* Ionian town in Asia Minor.

ephippiātus *adj* riding a saddled horse.

ephippium, -ī and **iī** *nt* saddle.

ephorus, -ī *m* a Spartan magistrate, ephor.

Ephyra, -ae, -ē, -ēs *f* Corinth.

Ephyrēius *adj see* **Ephyra**.

Epicharmus, -ī *m* Greek philosopher and comic poet.

epichysis, -is *f* kind of jug.

epicōpus *adj* rowing.

Epicūrēus, epicus *adj* epic.

Epicūrus, -ī *m* famous Greek philosopher.

Epidaurius *adj see n.*

Epidaurus, -ī *f* town in E. Peloponnese.

epidīcticus *adj* (*RHET*) for display.

epigramma, -tis *nt* inscription; epigram.

epilogus, -ī *m* peroration.

epimēnia, -ōrum *ntpl* a month's rations.

Epimēthis, -dis *f* Pyrrha (*daughter of Epimetheus*).

epirēdium, -ī and **iī** *nt* trace.

Ēpīrōtēs, -ōtae *m* native of Epirus.

Ēpīrōticus, -ēnsis *adj see n.*

Ēpīrus, -os, -ī *f* district of N.W. Greece.

episcopus, -ī *m* bishop.

epistolium, -ī and **iī** *nt* short note.

epistula, -ae *f* letter; **ab ~īs** secretary.

epitaphium, -ī and **iī** *nt* funeral oration.

epithēca, -ae *f* addition.

epitoma, -ae, -ē, -ēs *f* abridgement.

epitȳrum, -ī *nt* olive salad.

epops, -is *m* hoopoe.

epos (*pl* -**ē**) *nt* epic.

ēpōtō, -āre, -āvī, -um *vt* to drink up, drain; to waste in drink; to absorb.

epulae, -ārum *fpl* dishes; feast, banquet.

epulāris *adj* at a banquet.

epulō, -ōnis *m* guest at a feast; priest in charge of religious banquets.

epulor, -ārī, -ātus *vi* to be at a feast ♦ *vt* to feast on.

epulum, -ī *nt* banquet.

equa, -ae *f* mare.

eques, -itis *m* horseman, trooper; (*pl*) cavalry; knight, member of the equestrian order.

equester, -ris *adj* equestrian; cavalry- (*in cpds*).

equidem *adv* (*affirming*) indeed, of course, for my part; (*concessive*) to be sure.

equīnus *adj* horse's.

equīria, -ōrum *ntpl* horseraces.

equitātus, -ūs *m* cavalry.

equitō, -āre *vi* to ride.

equuleus *etc see* **eculeus**.

equulus, -ī *m* colt.

equus, -ī *m* horse; (*ASTRO*) Pegasus; **~ bipēs** seahorse; **~ō merēre** serve in the cavalry; **~īs virīsque** with might and main.

era, -ae *f* mistress (of the house); (*goddess*) Lady.

ērādīcō, -āre *vt* to root out, destroy.

ērādō, -dere, -sī, -sum *vt* to erase, obliterate.

Eratō *f* Muse of lyric poetry.

Eratosthenēs, -is *m* famous Alexandrian geographer.

Erebēus *adj see n.*

Erebus, -ī *m* god of darkness; the lower world.

Erechtheus, -eī *m* legendary king of Athens.

Erechthēus *adj see n.*

Erechthīdae *mpl* Athenians

Erechthis, -idis *f* Orithyia; Procris.

ērēctus *ppp of* **ērigō** ♦ *adj* upright, lofty; noble, haughty; alert, tense; resolute.

ērēpō, -ere, -sī *vi* to creep out, clamber up ♦ *vt* to crawl over, climb.

ēreptiō, -ōnis *f* seizure, robbery.

ēreptor, -ōris *m* robber.

ēreptus *ppp of* **ēripiō**.

ergā *prep* (*with acc*) towards; against.

ergastulum, -ī *nt* prison (*esp for slaves*); (*pl*) convicts.

ergō *adv* therefore, consequently; (*questions, commands*) then, so; (*resuming*) well then; (*with gen*) for the sake of, because of.

Erichthonius, -ī *m* a king of Troy; a king of Athens ♦ *adj* Trojan; Athenian.

ēricius, -ī and **iī** *m* hedgehog; (*MIL*) beam with iron spikes.

Ēridanus, -ī *m* mythical name of river Po.

erifuga, -ae *m* runaway slave.

ērigō, -igere, -ēxī, -ēctum *vt* to make upright, raise up, erect; to excite; to encourage.

Ērigonē, -ēs *f* (*constellation*) Virgo.

Ērigonēius *adj see n.*

Noun declensions and verb conjugations are shown on pp xiii to xxv. The present infinitive ending of a verb shows to which conjugation it belongs: **-āre** = 1st; **-ēre** = 2nd; **-ere** = 3rd and **-īre** = 4th. Irregular verbs are shown on p xxvi

erīlis *adj* the master's, the mistress's.

Erīnȳs, -yos *f* Fury; (*fig*) curse, frenzy.

Eriphȳla, -ae *f* mother of Alcmaeon (*who killed her*).

ēripiō, -ipere, -ipuī, -eptum *vt* to tear away, pull away, take by force; to rob; to rescue; **sē ~** escape.

ērogātiō, -ōnis *f* paying out.

ērogitō, -āre *vt* to enquire.

ērogō, -āre, -āvī, -ātum *vt* to pay out, expend; to bequeath.

errābundus *adj* wandering.

errāticus *adj* roving, shifting.

errātiō, -ōnis *f* wandering, roving.

errātum, -ī *nt* mistake, error.

errātus, -ūs *m* wandering.

errō, -āre, -āvī, -ātum *vi* to wander, stray, lose one's way; to waver; to make a mistake, err ♦ *vt* to traverse; **stēllae ~antēs** planets.

errō, -ōnis *m* vagabond.

error, -ōris *m* wandering; meander, maze; uncertainty; error, mistake, delusion; deception.

ērubēscō, -ēscere, -uī *vi* to blush; to feel ashamed ♦ *vt* to blush for, be ashamed of; to respect.

ērūca, -ae *f* colewort.

ēructō, -āre *vt* to belch, vomit; to talk drunkenly about; to throw up.

ērudiō, -īre, -īī, -ītum *vt* to educate, instruct.

ērudītē *adv* learnedly.

ērudītiō, -ōnis *f* education, instruction; learning, knowledge.

ērudītulus *adj* somewhat skilled.

ērudītus *ppp of* **ērudiō** ♦ *adj* learned, educated, accomplished.

ērumpō, -umpere, -ūpī, -uptum *vt* to break open; to make break out ♦ *vi* to burst out, break through; to end (in).

ēruō, -ere, -ī, -tum *vt* to uproot, tear out; to demolish, destroy; to elicit, draw out; to rescue.

ēruptiō, -ōnis *f* eruption; (*MIL*) sally.

ēruptus *ppp of* **ērumpō**.

erus, -ī *m* master (of the house); owner.

ērutus *ppp of* **ēruō**.

ervum, -ī *nt* vetch.

Erycīnus *adj* of Eryx; of Venus; Sicilian ♦ *f* Venus.

Erymanthius, -is *adj see n.*

Erymanthus and -ī *m* mountain range in Arcadia, (*where Hercules killed the bear*).

Eryx, -cis *m* town and mountain in the extreme W. of Sicily.

esca, -ae *f* food, tit-bits; bait.

escārius *adj* of food; of bait ♦ *ntpl* dishes.

ēscendō, -endere, -endī, -ēnsum *vi* to climb up, go up ♦ *vt* to mount.

ēscēnsiō, -ōnis *f* raid (from the coast); disembarkation.

esculentus *adj* edible, tasty.

Esquiliae, -iārum *fpl* Esquiline hill in Rome.

Esquilīnus *adj* Esquiline ♦ *f* Esquiline gate.

essedārius, -ī and iī *m* chariot fighter.

essedum, -ī *nt* war chariot.

essitō, -āre *vt* to usually eat.

ēst *pres of* **edō**.

ēstrīx, -īcis *f* glutton.

ēsuriālis *adj* of hunger.

ēsuriō, -īre, -ītum *vi* to be hungry ♦ *vt* to hunger for.

ēsurītiō, -ōnis *f* hunger.

ēsus *ppp of* **edō**.

et *conj* and; (*repeated*) both ... and; (*adding emphasis*) in fact, yes; (*comparing*) as, than ♦ *adv* also, too; even.

etenim *conj* (*adding an explanation*) and as a matter of fact, in fact.

etēsiae, -ārum *fpl* Etesian winds.

etēsius *adj see n.*

ēthologus, -ī *m* mimic.

etiam *adv* also, besides; (*emphatic*) even, actually; (*affirming*) yes, certainly; (*indignant*) really!; (*time*) still, as yet; again; **~ atque ~** again and again; **~ cavēs!** do be careful!; **nihil ~** nothing at all.

etiamdum *adv* still, as yet.

etiamnum, etiamnunc *adv* still, till now, till then; besides.

etiamsī *conj* even if, although.

etiamtum, etiamtunc *adv* till then, still.

Etrūria, -ae *f* district of Italy north of Rome.

Etruscus *adj* Etruscan.

etsī *conj* even if, though; and yet.

etymologia, -ae *f* etymology.

eu *interj* well done!, bravo!

Euan *m* Bacchus.

Euander and rus, -rī *m* Evander (*ancient king on the site of Rome*).

Euandrius *adj see n.*

euax *interj* hurrah!

Euboea, -oeae *f* Greek island.

Euboicus *adj* Euboean.

euge, eugepae *interj* bravo!, cheers!

Euhan *m* Bacchus.

euhāns, -antis *adj* shouting the Bacchic cry.

Euhias *f* Bacchante.

Euhius, -ī *m* Bacchus.

euhoe *interj* ecstatic cry of Bacchic revellers.

Euius, -ī *m* Bacchus.

Eumenides, -um *fpl* Furies.

eunūchus, -ī *m* eunuch.

Euphrātēs, -is *m* river Euphrates.

Eupolis, -dis *m* Athenian comic poet.

Eurīpidēs, -is *m* Athenian tragic poet.

Eurīpidēus *adj see n.*

Eurīpus, -ī *m* strait between Euboea and mainland; a channel, conduit.

Eurōpa, -ae and ē, -ēs *f* mythical princess of Tyre (*who was carried by a bull to Crete*); continent of Europe.

Eurōpaeus *adj see n.*

Eurōtās, -ae *m* river of Sparta.

Euroüs *adj* eastern.

Eurus, -ī *m* east wind; south-east wind.

Eurydicē, -ēs *f* wife of Orpheus.

Eurystheus, -eī m king of Mycenae (who imposed the labours on Hercules).

euschēmē adv gracefully.

Euterpē, -ēs f Muse of music.

Euxīnus m the Black (Sea).

ēvādō, -dere, -sī, -sum vi to come out; to climb up; to escape; to turn out, result, come true ♦ vt to pass, mount; to escape from.

ēvagor, -ārī, -ātus vi (MIL) to manoeuvre; (fig) to spread ♦ vt to stray beyond.

ēvalēscō, -escere, -uī vi to grow, increase; to be able; to come into vogue.

Ēvander etc see **Euander.**

ēvānēscō, -escere, -uī vi to vanish, die away, lose effect.

ēvangelium, -ī and iī nt (ECCL) Gospel.

ēvānidus adj vanishing.

ēvāsī perf of **ēvādō.**

ēvastō, -āre vt to devastate.

ēvehō, -here, -xī, -ctum vt to carry out; to raise up, exalt; to spread abroad; (pass) to ride, sail, move out.

ēvellō, -ellere, -ellī, -ulsum vt to tear out, pull out; to eradicate.

ēveniō, -enīre, -ēnī, -entum vi to come out; to turn out, result; to come to pass, happen, befall.

ēventum, -ī nt result, issue; occurrence, event; fortune, experience.

ēventus, -ūs m result, issue; success; fortune, fate.

ēverberō, -āre vt to beat violently.

ēverriculum, -ī nt dragnet.

ēverrō, -rere, -rī, -sum vt to sweep out, clean out.

ēversiō, -ōnis f overthrow, destruction.

ēversor, -ōris m destroyer.

ēversus ppp of **ēverrō;** ppp of **ēvertō.**

ēvertō, -tere, -tī, -sum vt to turn out, eject; to turn up, overturn; to overthrow, ruin, destroy.

ēvestīgātus adj tracked down.

ēvictus ppp of **ēvincō.**

ēvidēns, -entis adj visible, plain, evident.

ēvidenter adv see **ēvidēns.**

ēvidentia, -ae f distinctness.

ēvigilō, -āre, -āvī, -ātum vi to be wide awake ♦ vt to compose carefully.

ēvīlēscō, -ere vi to become worthless.

ēvinciō, -cīre, -xī, -ctum vt to garland, crown.

ēvinco, -incere, -īcī, -ictum vt to overcome, conquer; to prevail over; to prove.

ēvirō, -āre vt to castrate.

ēviscerō, -āre vt to disembowel, tear to pieces.

ēvītābilis adj avoidable.

ēvītō, -āre, -āvī, -ātum vt to avoid, clear.

ēvocātī, -ōrum mpl veteran volunteers.

ēvocātor, -ōris m enlister.

ēvocō, -āre, -āvī, -ātum vt to call out, summon; to challenge; to call up; to call forth, evoke.

ēvolō, -āre, -āvī, -ātum vi to fly out, fly away; to rush out; (fig) to rise, soar.

ēvolūtiō, -ōnis f unrolling (a book).

ēvolvō, -vere, -vī, -ūtum vt to roll out, roll along; to unroll, unfold; (book) to open, read; (fig) to disclose, unravel, disentangle.

ēvomō, -ere, -uī, -itum vt to vomit up, disgorge.

ēvulgō, -āre, -āvī, -ātum vt to divulge, make public.

ēvulsiō, -ōnis f pulling out.

ēvulsus ppp of **ēvellō.**

ex, ē prep (with abl) (place) out of, from, down from; (person) from; (time) after, immediately after, since; (change) from being; (source, material) of; (cause) by reason of, through; (conformity) in accordance with; **ex itinere** on the march; **ex parte** in part; **ex quō** since; **ex rē, ex ūsū** for the good of; **ē rē pūblicā** constitutionally; **ex sententiā** to one's liking; **aliud ex aliō** one thing after another; **ūnus ex** one of.

exacerbō, -āre vt to exasperate.

exāctiō, -ōnis f expulsion; supervision; tax; (debts) calling in.

exāctor, -ōris m expeller; superintendent; tax collector.

exāctus ppp of **exigō** ♦ adj precise, exact.

exacuō, -uere, -uī, -ūtum vt to sharpen; (fig) to quicken, inflame.

exadversum, -us adv, prep (with acc) right opposite.

exaedificātiō, -ōnis f construction.

exaedificō, -āre vt to build up; to finish the building of.

exaequātiō, -ōnis f levelling.

exaequō, -āre, -āvī, -ātum vt to level out; to compensate; to put on an equal footing; to equal.

exaestuō, -āre vi to boil up.

exaggerātiō, -ōnis f exaltation.

exaggerō, -āre, -āvī, -ātum vt to pile up; (fig) to heighten, enhance.

exagitātor, -ōris m critic.

exagitō, -āre, -āvī, -ātum vt to disturb, harass; to scold, censure; to excite, incite.

exagōga, -ae f export.

exalbēscō, -ēscere, -uī vi to turn quite pale.

exāmen, -inis nt swarm, crowd; tongue of a balance; examining.

examinō, -āre, -āvī, -ātum vt to weigh; to consider, test.

examussim adv exactly, perfectly.

exanclō, -āre vt to drain; to endure to the end.

exanimālis adj dead; deadly.

exanimātiō, -ōnis f panic.

exanimis adj lifeless, breathless; terrified.

Noun declensions and verb conjugations are shown on pp xiii to xxv. The present infinitive ending of a verb shows to which conjugation it belongs: **-āre** = 1st; **-ēre** = 2nd; **-ere** = 3rd and **-īre** = 4th. Irregular verbs are shown on p xxvi

exanimō, -āre, -āvī, -ātum *vt* to wind; to kill; to terrify, agitate; (*pass*) to be out of breath.
exanimus *see* **exanimis**.
exārdēscō, -dēscere, -sī, -sum *vi* to catch fire, blaze up; (*fig*) to be inflamed, break out.
exārēscō, -ēscere, -uī *vi* to dry, dry up.
exarmō, -āre *vt* to disarm.
exarō, -āre, -āvi, -ātum *vt* to plough up; to cultivate, produce; (*brow*) to furrow; (*writing*) to pen.
exārsī *perf of* **exārdēscō**.
exasciātus *adj* hewn out.
exasperō, -āre, -āvī, -ātum *vt* to roughen; (*fig*) to provoke.
exauctōrō, -āre, -āvī, -ātum *vt* (*MIL*) to discharge, release; to cashier.
exaudiō, -īre, -īvī, -ītum *vt* to hear clearly; to listen to; to obey.
exaugeō, -ēre *vt* to increase.
exaugurātiō, -ōnis *f* desecrating.
exaugurō, -āre *vt* to desecrate.
exauspicō, -āre *vi* to take an omen.
exbibō *etc see* **ēbibō**.
excaecō, -āre *vt* to blind; (*river*) to block up.
excandēscentia, -ae *f* growing anger.
excandēscō, -ēscere, -uī *vi* to burn, be inflamed.
excantō, -āre *vt* to charm out, spirit away.
excarnificō, -āre *vt* to tear to pieces.
excavō, -āre *vt* to hollow out.
excēdō, -ēdere, -essī, -essum *vi* to go out, go away; to die, disappear; to advance, proceed (to); to digress ♦ *vt* to leave; to overstep, exceed.
excellēns, -entis *pres p of* **excellō** ♦ *adj* outstanding, excellent.
excellenter *adv see* **excellēns**.
excellentia, -ae *f* superiority, excellence.
excellō, -ere *vi* to be eminent, excel.
excelsē *adv* loftily.
excelsitās, -ātis *f* loftiness.
excelsum, -ī *nt* height.
excelsus *adj* high, elevated; eminent, illustrious.
exceptiō, -ōnis *f* exception, restriction; (*law*) objection.
exceptō, -āre *vt* to catch, take out.
exceptus *ppp of* **excipiō**.
excernō, -ernere, -rēvī, -rētum *vt* to sift out, separate.
excerpō, -ere, -sī, -tum *vt* to take out; to select, copy out extracts; to leave out, omit.
excessus, -ūs *m* departure, death.
excetra, -ae *f* snake.
excidiō, -ōnis *f* destruction.
excidium, -ī *and* **iī** *nt* overthrow, destruction.
excidō, -ere, -ī *vi* to fall out, fall; (*speech*) to slip out, escape; (*memory*) to get forgotten, escape; (*person*) to fail, lose; (*things*) to disappear, be lost.
excīdō, -dere, -dī, -sum *vt* to cut off, hew out, fell; to raze; (*fig*) to banish.
excieō *vt see* **exciō**.

exciō, -īre, -īvī *and* **iī, -itum** *and* **ītum** *vt* to call out, rouse, summon; to occasion, produce; to excite.
excipiō, -ipere, -ēpī, -eptum *vt* to take out, remove; to exempt, make an exception of, mention specifically; to take up, catch, intercept, overhear; to receive, welcome, entertain; to come next to, follow after, succeed.
excīsiō, -ōnis *f* destroying.
excīsus *ppp of* **excīdō**.
excitātus *adj* loud, strong.
excitō, -āre, -āvī, -ātum *vt* to rouse, wake up, summon; to raise, build; to call on (to stand up); (*fig*) to encourage, revive, excite.
excitus, excītus *ppp of* **exciō**.
exclāmātiō, -ōnis *f* exclamation.
exclāmō, -āre, -āvī, -ātum *vi* to cry out, shout ♦ *vt* to exclaim, call.
exclūdō, -dere, -sī, -sum *vt* to shut out, exclude; to shut off, keep off; (*egg*) to hatch out; (*eye*) to knock out; (*fig*) to prevent, except.
exclūsiō, -ōnis *f* shutting out.
exclūsus *ppp of* **exclūdō**.
excoctus *ppp of* **excoquō**.
excōgitātiō, -ōnis *f* thinking out, devising.
excōgitō, -āre, -āvī, -ātum *vt* to think out, contrive.
excolō, -olere, -oluī, -ultum *vt* to work carefully; to perfect, refine.
excoquō, -quere, -xī, -ctum *vt* to boil away; to remove with heat, make with heat; to dry up.
excors, -dis *adj* senseless, stupid.
excrēmentum, -ī *nt* excretion.
excreō *etc see* **exscreō**.
excrēscō, -scere, -vī, -tum *vi* to grow, rise up.
excrētus *ppp of* **excernō**.
excruciō, -āre, -āvī, -ātum *vt* to torture, torment.
excubiae, -ārum *fpl* keeping guard, watch; sentry.
excubitor, -ōris *m* sentry.
excubō, -āre, -uī, -itum *vi* to sleep out of doors; to keep watch; (*fig*) to be on the alert.
excūdō, -dere, -dī, -sum *vt* to strike out, hammer out; (*egg*) to hatch; (*fig*) to make, compose.
exculcō, -āre *vt* to beat, tramp down.
excultus *ppp of* **excolō**.
excurrō, -rrere, -currī *and* **rrī, -rsum** *vi* to run out, hurry out; to make an excursion; (*MIL*) to make a sortie; (*place*) to extend, project; (*fig*) to expand.
excursiō, -ōnis *f* raid, sortie; (*gesture*) stepping forward; (*fig*) outset.
excursor, -ōris *m* scout.
excursus, -ūs *m* excursion, raid, charge.
excūsābilis *adj* excusable.
excūsātē *adv* excusably.
excūsātiō, -ōnis *f* excuse, plea.

excūsō, -āre, -āvī, -ātum *vt* to excuse; to apologize for; to plead as an excuse.
excussus *ppp of* **excutiō**.
excūsus *ppp of* **excūdō**.
excutiō, -tere, -ssī, -ssum *vt* to shake out, shake off; to knock out, drive out, cast off; (*fig*) to discard, banish; to examine, inspect.
exdorsuō, -āre *vt* to fillet.
exec- *etc see* **exsec-**.
exedō, -ēsse, -ēdī, -ēsum *vt* to eat up; to wear away, destroy; (*feelings*) to prey on.
exedra, -ae *f* hall, lecture room.
exedrium, -ī *and* **iī** *nt* sitting room.
exēmī *perf of* **eximō**.
exemplar, -āris *nt* copy; likeness; model, ideal.
exemplārēs *mpl* copies.
exemplum, -ī *nt* copy; example, sample, precedent, pattern; purport, nature; warning, object lesson; **~ dare** set an example; **~ī causā, gratiā** for instance.
exemptus *ppp of* **eximō**.
exenterō, -āre *vt* (*comedy*) to empty, clean out; to torture.
exeō, -īre, -iī, -itum *vi* to go out, leave; to come out, issue; (*MIL*) to march out; (*time*) to expire; to spring up, rise ♦ *vt* to pass beyond; to avoid; **~ ex potestāte** lose control.
exeq- *etc see* **exseq-**.
exerceō, -ēre, -uī, -itum *vt* to keep busy, supervise; (*ground*) to work, cultivate; (*MIL*) to drill, exercise; (*mind*) to engage, employ; (*occupation*) to practise, follow, carry on; (*trouble*) to worry, harass; **sē ~** practise, exercise.
exercitātiō, -ōnis *f* practice, exercise, experience.
exercitātus *adj* practised, trained, versed; troubled.
exercitium, -ī *and* **iī** *nt* exercising.
exercitō, -āre *vt* to exercise.
exercitor, -ōris *m* trainer.
exercitus *ppp of* **exerceō** ♦ *adj* disciplined; troubled; troublesome.
exercitus, -ūs *m* army (*esp the infantry*); assembly; troop, flock; exercise.
exerō *etc see* **exserō**.
exēsor, -ōris *m* corroder.
exēsus *ppp of* **exedō**.
exhālātiō, -ōnis *f* vapour.
exhālō, -āre *vt* to exhale, breathe out ♦ *vi* to steam; to expire.
exhauriō, -rīre, -sī, -stum *vt* to drain off; to empty; to take away, remove; (*fig*) to exhaust, finish; (*trouble*) to undergo, endure to the end.
exhērēdō, -āre *vt* to disinherit.
exhērēs, -ēdis *adj* disinherited.
exhibeō, -ere, -uī, -itum *vt* to hold out, produce (in public); to display, show; to

cause, occasion.
exhilarātus *adj* delighted.
exhorrēscō, -ēscere, -uī *vi* to be terrified ♦ *vt* to be terrified at.
exhortātiō, -ōnis *f* encouragement.
exhortor -ārī, -ātus *vt* to encourage.
exigō, -igere, -ēgī, -āctum *vt* to drive out, thrust; (*payment*) to exact, enforce; to demand, claim; (*goods*) to dispose of; (*time*) to pass, complete; (*work*) to finish; (*news*) to ascertain; to test, examine, consider.
exiguē *adv* briefly, slightly, hardly.
exiguitās, -ātis *f* smallness, meagreness.
exiguus *adj* small, short, meagre ♦ *nt* a little bit.
exiliō *etc see* **exsiliō**.
exīlis *adj* thin, small, meagre; poor; (*style*) flat, insipid.
exīlitās, -ātis *f* thinness, meagreness.
exīliter *adv* feebly.
exilium *etc see* **exsilium**.
exim *see* **exinde**.
eximiē *adv* exceptionally.
eximius *adj* exempt; select; distinguished, exceptional.
eximō, -imere, -ēmī, -emptum *vt* to take out, remove; to release, free; to exempt; (*time*) to waste; (*fig*) to banish.
exin *see* **exinde**.
exināniō, -īre, -iī, -ītum *vt* to empty; to pillage.
exinde *adv* (*place*) from there, next; (*time*) then, thereafter, next; (*measure*) accordingly.
exīstimātiō, -ōnis *f* opinion, judgment; reputation, character; (*money*) credit.
exīstimātor, -ōris *m* judge, critic.
exīstimō, -āre, -āvī, -ātum *vt* to value, estimate, judge, think, consider.
existō *etc see* **exsistō**.
exīstumō *vt see* **exīstimō**.
exitiābilis *adj* deadly, fatal.
exitiālis *adj* deadly.
exitiōsus *adj* pernicious, fatal.
exitium, -ī *and* **iī** *nt* destruction, ruin.
exitus, -ūs *m* departure; way out, outlet; conclusion, end; death; outcome, result.
exlēx, -ēgis *adj* above the law, lawless.
exoculō, -āre *vt* to knock the eyes out of.
exodium, -ī *and* **iī** *nt* afterpiece.
exolēscō, -scere, -vī, -tum *vi* to decay, become obsolete.
exolētus *adj* full-grown.
exonerō, -āre, -āvī, -ātum *vt* to unload, discharge; (*fig*) to relieve, exonerate.
exoptātus *adj* welcome.
exoptō, -āre, -āvī, -ātum *vt* to long for, desire.
exōrābilis *adj* sympathetic.
exōrātor, -ōris *m* successful pleader.

Noun declensions and verb conjugations are shown on pp xiii to xxv. The present infinitive ending of a verb shows to which conjugation it belongs: **-āre** = 1st; **-ēre** = 2nd; **-ere** = 3rd and **-īre** = 4th. Irregular verbs are shown on p xxvi

exōrdior, -dīrī, -sus *vt* to lay the warp; to begin.

exōrdium, -ī *and* **iī** *nt* beginning; (*RHET*) introductory section.

exorior, -īrī, -tus *vi* to spring up, come out, rise; to arise, appear, start.

exōrnātiō, -ōnis *f* embellishment.

exōrnātor, -ōris *m* embellisher.

exōrnō, -āre, -āvī, -ātum *vt* to equip, fit out; to embellish, adorn.

exōrō, -āre, -āvī, -ātum *vt* to prevail upon, persuade; to obtain, win by entreaty.

exōrsus *ppa of* **exōrdior** ♦ *adj* begun ♦ *ntpl* preamble.

exōrsus, -ūs *m* beginning.

exortus *ppa of* **exorior**.

exortus, -ūs *m* rising; east.

exos, -ossis *adj* boneless.

exōsculor, -ārī, -ātus *vt* to kiss fondly.

exossō, -āre *vt* to bone.

exōstra, -ae *f* stage mechanism; (*fig*) public.

exōsus *adj* detesting.

exōticus *adj* foreign.

expallēscō, -ēscere, -uī *vi* to turn pale, be afraid.

expalpō, -āre *vt* to coax out.

expandō, -ere *vt* to unfold.

expatrō, -āre *vt* to squander.

expavēscō, -ere, expāvī *vi* to be terrified ♦ *vt* to dread.

expect- *etc see* **exspect-**.

expediō, -īre, -īvī *and* **iī, -ītum** *vt* to free, extricate, disentangle; to prepare, clear (for action); to put right, settle; to explain, relate; (*impers*) it is useful, expedient.

expedītē *adv* readily, freely.

expedītiō, -ōnis *f* (*MIL*) expedition, enterprise.

expedītus *ppp of* **expediō** ♦ *adj* light-armed; ready, prompt; at hand ♦ *m* light-armed soldier; in **~ō esse, habēre** be, have in readiness.

expellō, -ellere, -ulī, -ulsum *vt* to drive away, eject, expel; to remove, repudiate.

expendō, -endere, -endī, -ēnsum *vt* to weigh out; to pay out; (*penalty*) to suffer; (*mind*) to ponder, consider, judge.

expēnsum, -ī *nt* payment, expenditure.

expergēfaciō, -facere, -fēcī, -factum *vt* to rouse, excite.

expergīscor, -gīscī, -rēctus *vi* to wake up; to bestir oneself.

expergō, -ere, -ī, -itum *vt* to awaken.

experiēns, -entis *pres p of* **experior** ♦ *adj* enterprising.

experientia, -ae *f* experiment; endeavour; experience, practice.

experīmentum, -ī *nt* proof, test; experience.

experior, -īrī, -tus *vt* to test, make trial of; to attempt, experience; (*law*) to go to law; (*perf tenses*) to know from experience.

experrēctus *ppa of* **expergīscor**.

expers, -tis *adj* having no part in, not sharing; free from, without.

expertus *ppa of* **experior** ♦ *adj* proved, tried; experienced.

expetessō, -ere *vt* to desire.

expetō, -ere, -īvī *and* **iī, -ītum** *vt* to aim at, tend towards; to desire, covet; to attack; to demand, require ♦ *vi* to befall, happen.

expiātiō, -ōnis *f* atonement.

expictus *ppp of* **expingō**.

expīlātiō, -ōnis *f* pillaging.

expīlātor, -ōris *m* plunderer.

expīlō, -āre, -āvī, -ātum *vt* to rob, plunder.

expingō, -ingere, -inxī, -ictum *vt* to portray.

expiō, -āre, -āvī, -ātum *vt* to purify; to atone for, make amends for; to avert (evil).

expīrō *etc see* **exspīrō**.

expiscor, -ārī, -ātus *vt* to try to find out, ferret out.

explānātē *adv see* **explānātus**.

explānātiō, -ōnis *f* explanation.

explānātor, -ōris *m* interpreter.

explānātus *adj* distinct.

explānō, -āre, -āvī, -ātum *vt* to state clearly, explain; to pronounce clearly.

explaudō *etc see* **explōdō**.

explēmentum, -ī *nt* filling.

expleō, -ēre, -ēvī, -ētum *vt* to fill up; to complete; (*desire*) to satisfy, appease; (*duty*) to perform, discharge; (*loss*) to make good; (*time*) to fulfil, complete.

explētiō, -ōnis *f* satisfying.

explētus *ppp of* **expleō** ♦ *adj* complete.

explicātē *adv* plainly.

explicātiō, -ōnis *f* uncoiling; expounding; analyzing.

explicātor, -ōris *m*, **-rīx, -rīcis** *f* expounder.

explicātus *adj* spread out; plain, clear.

explicātus, -ūs *m* explanation.

explicitus *adj* easy.

explicō, -āre, -āvī *and* **uī, -ātum** *and* **itum** *vt* to unfold, undo, spread out; (*book*) to open; (*MIL*) to deploy, extend; (*difficulty*) to put in order, settle; (*speech*) to develop, explain; to set free.

explōdō, -dere, -sī, -sum *vt* to hiss off, drive away; (*fig*) to reject.

explōrātē *adv* with certainty.

explōrātiō, -ōnis *f* spying.

explōrātor, -ōris *m* spy, scout.

explōrātus *adj* certain, sure.

explōrō, -āre, -āvī, -ātum *vt* to investigate, reconnoitre; to ascertain; to put to the test.

explōsī *perf of* **explōdō**.

explōsiō, -ōnis *f* driving off (the stage).

explōsus *ppp of* **explōdō**.

expoliō, -īre, -īvī, -ītum *vt* to smooth off, polish; (*fig*) to refine, embellish.

expolītiō, -ōnis *f* smoothing off; polish, finish.

expōnō, -ōnere, -osuī, -ositum *vt* to set out, put out; (*child*) to expose; (*NAUT*) to disembark; (*money*) to offer; (*fig*) to set forth, expose, display; (*speech*) to explain, expound.

exporrigō, -igere, -ēxī, -ēctum vt to extend, smooth out.

exportātiō, -ōnis f exporting.

exportō, -āre, -āvī, -ātum vt to carry out, export.

exposcō, -ere, expoposcī vt to implore, pray for; to demand.

expositīcius adj foundling.

expositiō, -ōnis f narration, explanation.

expositus ppp of **expōnō** ♦ adj open, affable; vulgar.

expostulātiō, -ōnis f complaint

expostulō, -āre, -āvī, -ātum vt to demand urgently; to complain of, expostulate.

expōtus ppp of **ēpōtō**.

expressus ppp of **exprimō** ♦ adj distinct, prominent.

exprimō, -imere, -essī, -essum vt to squeeze out, force out; to press up; (fig) to extort, wrest; (art) to mould, model; (words) to imitate, portray, translate, pronounce.

exprobrātiō, -ōnis f reproach.

exprobrō, -āre, -āvī, -ātum vt to reproach, cast up.

exprōmō, -ere, -psī, -ptum vt to bring out, fetch out; (acts) to exhibit, practise; (feelings) to give vent to; (speech) to disclose, state.

expugnābilis adj capable of being taken by storm.

expugnācior, -ōris adj more effective.

expugnātiō, -ōnis f storming, assault.

expugnātor, -ōris m stormer.

expugnō, -āre, -āvī, -ātum vt to storm, reduce; to conquer; (fig) to overcome, extort.

expulī perf of **expellō**.

expulsiō, -ōnis f expulsion.

expulsor, -ōris m expeller.

expulsus ppp of **expellō**.

expultrīx, -īcis f expeller.

expungō, -ungere, -ūnxī, -ūnctum vt to prick out, cancel.

expūrgātiō, -ōnis f excuse.

expūrgō, -āre vt to purify; to justify.

exputō, -āre vt to consider, comprehend.

exquīrō, -rere, -sīvī, -sītum vt to search out, investigate; to inquire; to devise.

exquīsītē adv with particular care.

exquīsītus ppp of **exquīrō** ♦ adj well thought out, choice.

exsaeviō, -īre vi to cease raging.

exsanguis adj bloodless, pale; feeble.

exsarciō, -cīre, -tum vt to repair.

exsatiō, -āre vt to satiate, satisfy.

exsaturābilis adj appeasable.

exsaturō, -āre vt to satiate.

exsce- etc see **esce-**.

exscindō, -ndere, -dī, -ssum vt to extirpate.

exscreō, -āre vt to cough up.

exscrībō, -bere, -psī, -ptum vt to copy out; to note down.

exsculpō, -ere, -sī, -tum vt to carve out; to erase; (fig) to extort.

exsecō, -āre, -uī, -tum vt to cut out; to castrate.

exsecrābilis adj cursing, deadly.

exsecrātiō, -ōnis f curse; solemn oath.

exsecrātus adj accursed.

exsecror, -ārī, -ātus vt to curse; to take an oath.

exsectiō, -ōnis f cutting out.

exsecūtiō, -ōnis f management; discussion.

exsecūtus ppa of **exsequor**.

exsequiae, -ārum fpl funeral, funeral rites.

exsequiālis adj funeral.

exsequor, -quī, -cūtus vt to follow, pursue; to follow to the grave; (duty) to carry out, accomplish; (speech) to describe, relate; (suffering) to undergo; (wrong) to avenge, punish.

exserciō vt see **exsarciō**.

exserō, -ere, -uī, -tum vt to put out, stretch out; to reveal.

exsertō, -āre vt to stretch out repeatedly.

exsertus ppp of **exserō** ♦ adj protruding.

exsībilō, -āre vt to hiss off.

exsiccātus adj (style) uninteresting.

exsiccō, -āre, -āvī, -ātum vt to dry up; to drain.

exsicō etc see **exsecō**.

exsignō, -āre vt to write down in detail.

exsiliō, -īre, -uī vi to jump up, spring out; to start.

exsilium, -ī and **iī** nt banishment, exile; retreat.

exsistō, -istere, -titī, -titum vi to emerge, appear; to arise, spring (from); to be, exist.

exsolvō, -vere, -vī, -ūtum vt to undo, loosen, open; to release, free; to get rid of, throw off; (debt, promise) to discharge, fulfil, pay up; (words) to explain.

exsomnis adj sleepless, watchful.

exsorbeō, -ēre, -uī vt to suck, drain; to devour, endure.

exsors, -tis adj chosen, special; free from.

exspargō etc see **exspergō**.

exspatior, -ārī, -ātus vi to go off the course.

exspectābilis adj to be expected.

exspectātiō, -ōnis f waiting, expectation.

exspectātus adj looked for, welcome.

exspectō, -āre, -āvī, -ātum vt to wait for, till; to see; to expect; to hope for, dread; to require.

exspergō, -gere, -sum vt to scatter; to diffuse.

exspēs adj despairing.

exspīrātiō, -ōnis f exhalation.

exspīrō, -āre, -āvī, -ātum vt to breathe out, exhale; to emit ♦ vi to rush out; to expire, come to an end.

exsplendēscō, -ere *vi* to shine.

exspoliō, -āre *vt* to pillage.

exspuō, -uere, -uī, -ūtum *vt* to spit out, eject; (*fig*) to banish.

externō, -āre *vt* to terrify.

exstillō, -āre *vi* to drip.

exstimulātor, -ōris *m* instigator.

exstimulō, -āre *vt* to goad on; to excite.

exstīnctiō, -ōnis *f* annihilation.

exstīnctor, -ōris *m* extinguisher; destroyer.

exstinguō, -guere, -xī, -ctum *vt* to put out, extinguish; to kill, destroy, abolish.

exstirpō, -āre *vt* to root out, eradicate.

exstitī *perf of* **exsistō**.

exstō, -āre *vi* to stand out, project; to be conspicuous, be visible; to be extant, exist, be.

exstrūctiō, -ōnis *f* erection.

exstruō, -ere, -xī, -ctum *vt* to heap up; to build up, construct.

exsūdō, -āre *vi* to come out in sweat ♦ *vt* (*fig*) to toil through.

exsūgō, -gere, -xī, -ctum *vt* to suck out.

exsul, -is *m/f* exile.

exsulō, -āre, -āvī, -ātum *vi* to be an exile.

exsultātiō, -ōnis *f* great rejoicing.

exsultim *adv* friskily.

exsultō, -āre, -āvī, -ātum *vi* to jump up, prance; (*fig*) to exult, run riot, boast; (*speech*) to range at will.

exsuperābilis *adj* superable.

exsuperantia, -ae *f* superiority.

exsuperō, -āre, -āvī, -ātum *vi* to mount up; to gain the upper hand, excel ♦ *vt* to go over; to surpass; to overpower.

exsurdō, -āre *vt* to deafen; (*fig*) to dull.

exsurgō, -gere, -rēxī, -rēctum *vi* to rise, stand up; to recover.

exsuscitō, -āre *vt* to wake up; (*fire*) to fan; (*mind*) to excite.

exta, -ōrum *ntpl* internal organs.

extābēscō, -ēscere, -uī *vi* to waste away; to vanish.

extāris *adj* sacrificial.

extemplō *adv* immediately, on the spur of the moment; **quom ~** as soon as.

extemporālis *adj* extempore.

extempulō *see* **extemplō**.

extendō, -dere, -dī, -tum *and* **extēnsum** *vt* to stretch out, spread, extend; to enlarge, increase; (*time*) to prolong; **sē ~** exert oneself; **īre per ~tum fūnem** walk the tightrope.

extēnsus *ppp of* **extendō**.

extentō, -āre *vt* to strain, exert.

extentus *ppp of* **extendō** ♦ *adj* broad.

extenuātiō, -ōnis *f* (*RHET*) diminution.

extenuō, -āre, -āvī, -ātum *vt* to thin out, rarefy; to diminish, weaken.

exter *adj* from outside; foreign.

exterebrō, -āre *vt* to bore out; to extort.

extergeō, -gēre, -sī, -sum *vt* to wipe off,

clean; to plunder.

exterior, -ōris *adj* outer, exterior.

exterius *adv* on the outside.

exterminō, -āre *vt* to drive out, banish; (*fig*) to put aside.

externus *adj* outward, external; foreign, strange.

exterō, -erere, -rīvī, -rītum *vt* to rub out, wear away.

exterreō, -ēre, -uī, -itum *vt* to frighten.

extersus *ppp of* **extergeō**.

exterus *see* **exter**.

extexō, -ere *vt* to unweave; (*fig*) to cheat.

extimēscō, -ēscere, -uī *vi* to be very frightened ♦ *vt* to be very afraid of.

extimus *adj* outermost, farthest.

extin- *etc see* **exstin-**.

extispex, -icis *m* diviner.

extollō, -ere *vt* to lift up, raise; (*fig*) to exalt, beautify; (*time*) to defer.

extorqueō, -quēre, -sī, -tum *vt* to wrench out, wrest; to dislocate; (*fig*) to obtain by force, extort.

extorris *adj* banished, in exile.

extortor, -ōris *m* extorter.

extortus *ppp of* **extorqueō**.

extrā *adv* outside; **~ quam** except that, unless ♦ *prep* (*with acc*) outside, beyond; free from; except.

extrahō, -here, -xī, -ctum *vt* to draw out, pull out; to extricate, rescue; to remove; (*time*) to prolong, waste.

extrāneus, -ī *m* stranger ♦ *adj* external, foreign.

extraōrdinārius *adj* special, unusual.

extrārius *adj* external; unrelated ♦ *m* stranger.

extrēmitās, -ātis *f* extremity, end.

extrēmum, -ī *nt* end; **ad ~** at last.

extrēmum *adv* for the last time.

extrēmus *adj* outermost, extreme; last; utmost, greatest, meanest.

extrīcō, -āre, -āvī, -ātum *vt* to disentangle, extricate; to clear up.

extrīnsecus *adv* from outside, from abroad; on the outside.

extrītus *ppp of* **exterō**.

extrūdō, -dere, -sī, -sum *vt* to drive out; to keep out; (*sale*) to push.

extulī *perf of* **efferō**.

extumeō, -ēre *vi* to swell up.

extundō, -undere, -udī, -ūsum *vt* to beat out, hammer out; (*comedy*) to extort; (*fig*) to form, compose.

exturbō, -āre, -āvī, -ātum *vt* to drive out, throw out, knock out; (*wife*) to put away; (*fig*) to banish, disturb.

exūberō, -āre *vi* to abound.

exul *etc see* **exsul**.

exulcerō, -āre, -āvī, -ātum *vt* to aggravate.

exululō, -āre *vi* to howl wildly ♦ *vt* to invoke with cries.

exūnctus *ppp of* **exungō**.

exundō, -āre *vi* to overflow; to be washed up.

exungō, -ere *vt* to anoint liberally.

exuō, -uere, -uī, -ūtum *vt* to draw out, put off; to lay aside; to strip.

exūrō, -rere, -ssī, -stum *vt* to burn up; to dry up; to burn out; (*fig*) to inflame.

exūstiō, -ōnis *f* conflagration.

exūtus *ppp of* **exuō.**

exuviae, -ārum *fpl* clothing, arms; hide; spoils.

F, f

faba, -ae *f* bean.

fabālis *adj* bean- (*in cpds*).

fābella, -ae *f* short story, fable; play.

faber, -rī *m* craftsman (*in metal, stone, wood*), tradesman, smith; (*MIL*) artisan; ~ **ferrārius** blacksmith; ~ **tignārius** carpenter ♦ *adj* skilful.

Fabius, -ī *m* Roman family name (*esp Q F Maximus Cunctator, dictator against Hannibal*).

Fabius, -iānus *adj see n.*

fabrē *adv* skilfully.

fabrēfaciō, -facere, -fēcī, -factum *vt* to make, build, forge.

fabrica, -ae *f* art, trade; work of art; workshop; (*comedy*) trick.

fabricātiō, -ōnis *f* structure.

fabricātor, -ōris *m* artificer.

Fabricius, -ī *m* Roman family name (*esp C F Luscinus, incorruptible commander against Pyrrhus*).

Fabricius, -iānus *adj see n.*

fabricō, -āre; -or, -ārī, -ātus *vt* to make, build, forge.

fabrīlis *adj* artificer's ♦ *ntpl* tools.

fābula, -ae *f* story; common talk; play, drama; fable; ~**ae!** nonsense!; **lupus in ~ā** ≈ *talk of the devil!*

fābulor, -ārī, -ātus *vi* to talk, converse ♦ *vt* to say, invent.

fābulōsus *adj* legendary.

facessō, -ere, -īvī, -ītum *vt* to perform, carry out; to cause (trouble) ♦ *vi* to go away, retire.

facētē *adv* humorously; brilliantly.

facētiae, -ārum *fpl* wit, clever talk, humour.

facētus *adj* witty, humorous; fine, genteel, elegant.

faciēs, -ēī *f* form, shape; face, looks; appearance, aspect, character.

facile *adv* easily; unquestionably; readily; pleasantly.

facilis *adj* easy; well-suited; ready, quick; (*person*) good-natured, approachable; (*fortune*) prosperous.

facilitās, -ātis *f* ease, readiness; (*speech*) fluency; (*person*) good nature, affability.

facinorōsus *adj* criminal.

facinus, -oris *nt* deed, action; crime.

faciō, -ere, fēcī, factum (*imp* **fac**, *pass* **fīō**) *vt* to make, create, compose, cause; to do, perform; (*profession*) to practise; (*property*) to put under; (*value*) to regard, think of; (*words*) to represent, pretend, suppose ♦ *vi* to do, act; (*religion*) to offer sacrifice; (*with* **ad** *or dat*) to be of use; **cōpiam ~** afford an opportunity; **damnum ~** suffer loss; **metum ~** excite fear; **proelium ~** join battle; **rem ~** make money; **verba ~** talk; **māgnī ~** think highly of; **quid tibi faciam?** how am I to answer you?; **quid tē faciam?** what am I to do with you?; **fac sciam** let me know; **fac potuisse** suppose one could have.

factiō, -ōnis *f* making, doing; group, party, faction (*esp in politics and chariot racing*).

factiōsus *adj* factious, oligarchical.

factitō, -āre, -āvī, -ātum *vt* to keep making or doing; to practise; to declare (to be).

factor, -ōris *m* (*sport*) batsman.

factum, -ī *nt* deed, exploit.

factus *ppp of* **faciō.**

facula, -ae *f* little torch.

facultās, -ātis *f* means, opportunity; ability; abundance, supply, resources.

fācundē *adv see* **fācundus.**

fācundia, -ae *f* eloquence.

fācundus *adj* fluent, eloquent.

faeceus *adj* impure.

faecula, -ae *f* wine lees.

faenebris *adj* of usury.

faenerātiō, -ōnis *f* usury.

faenerātō *adv* with interest.

faenerātor, -ōris *m* moneylender.

faenerō, -āre; -or, -ārī, -ātus *vt* to lend at interest; to ruin with usury; (*fig*) to trade in.

faenīlia, -um *ntpl* hayloft.

faenum, -ī *nt* hay; ~ **habet in cornū** he is dangerous.

faenus, -oris *nt* interest; capital lent at interest; (*fig*) profit, advantage.

faenusculum, -ī *nt* a little interest.

Faesulae, -ārum *fpl* town in Etruria (*now Fiesole*).

Faesulānus *adj see n.*

faex, faecis *f* sediment, lees; brine (of pickles); (*fig*) dregs.

fāgineus, fāginus *adj* of beech.

fāgus, -ī *f* beech.

fala, -ae *f* siege tower, used in assaults; (*Circus*) pillar.

Noun declensions and verb conjugations are shown on pp xiii to xxv. The present infinitive ending of a verb shows to which conjugation it belongs: **-āre** = 1st; **-ēre** = 2nd; **-ere** = 3rd and **-īre** = 4th. Irregular verbs are shown on p xxvi

falārica, -ae *f* a missile, firebrand.
falcārius, -ī *and* **iī** *m* sicklemaker.
falcātus *adj* scythed; sickle-shaped.
falcifer, -ī *adj* scythe-carrying.
Falernus *adj* Falernian (*of a district in N. Campania famous for its wine*) ♦ *nt* Falernian wine.
Faliscī, -ōrum *mpl* a people of S.E. Etruria (*with chief town Falerii*).
Faliscus *adj see* n.
fallācia, -ae *f* trick, deception.
fallāciter *adv see* **fallāx**.
fallāx, -ācis *adj* deceitful, deceptive.
fallō, -lere, fefellī, -sum *vt* to deceive, cheat, beguile; to disappoint, fail, betray; (*promise*) to break; to escape the notice of, be unknown to; (*pass*) to be mistaken; **mē ~lit** I am mistaken; I do not know.
falsē *adv* wrongly, by mistake; fraudulently.
falsidicus *adj* lying.
falsificus *adj* deceiving.
falsiiūrius *adj* perjurious.
falsiloquus *adj* lying.
falsiparēns, -entis *adj* with a pretended father.
falsō *adv see* **falsē**.
falsus *ppp of* **fallō** ♦ *adj* false, mistaken; deceitful; forged, falsified; sham, fictitious ♦ *nt* falsehood, error.
falx, falcis *f* sickle, scythe; pruning hook; (*MIL*) siege hook.
fāma, -ae *f* talk, rumour, tradition; public opinion; reputation, fame; infamy.
famēlicus *adj* hungry.
famēs, -is *f* hunger; famine; (*fig*) greed; (*RHET*) poverty of expression.
fāmigerātiō, -ōnis *f* rumour.
fāmigerātor, -ōris *m* telltale.
familia, -ae *f* domestics, slaves of a household; family property, estate; family, house; school, sect; **pater ~ās** master of a household; **~am dūcere** be head of a sect, company *etc*.
familiāris *adj* domestic, household, family; intimate, friendly; (*entrails*) relating to the sacrificer ♦ *m* servant; friend.
familiāritās, -ātis *f* intimacy, friendship.
familiāriter *adv* on friendly terms.
fāmōsus *adj* celebrated; infamous; slanderous.
famula, -ae *f* maidservant, handmaid.
famulāris *adj* of servants.
famulātus, -ūs *m* slavery.
famulor, -ārī *vi* to serve.
famulus, -ī *m* servant, attendant ♦ *adj* serviceable.
fānāticus *adj* inspired; frantic, frenzied.
fandī *gerund of* **for**.
fandum, -ī *nt* right.
fānum, -ī *nt* sanctuary temple.
fār, farris *nt* spelt; corn; meal.
farciō, -cīre, -sī, -tum *vt* to stuff, fill full.
farīna, -ae *f* meal, flour.

farrāgō, -inis *f* mash, hotch-potch; medley.
farrātus *adj* of corn; filled with corn.
farsī *perf of* **farciō**.
fartem, -im *f acc* filling; mincemeat.
fartor, -ōris *m* fattener, poulterer.
fartus *ppp of* **farciō**.
fās *nt* divine law; right; **~ est** it is lawful, possible.
fascia, -ae *f* band, bandage; streak of cloud.
fasciculus, -ī *m* bundle, packet.
fascinō, -āre *vt* to bewitch, (*esp with the evil eye*).
fascinum, -ī *nt*, **-us, -ī** *m* charm.
fasciola, -ae *f* small bandage.
fascis, -is *m* bundle, faggot; soldier's pack, burden; (*pl*) rods and axe carried before the highest magistrates; high office (*esp the consulship*).
fassus *ppa of* **fateor**.
fāstī, -ōrum *mpl* register of days for legal and public business; calendar; registers of magistrates and other public records.
fastīdiō, -īre, -iī, -ītum *vt* to loathe, dislike, despise ♦ *vi* to feel squeamish, be disgusted; to be disdainful.
fastīdiōsē *adv* squeamishly; disdainfully.
fastīdiōsus *adj* squeamish, disgusted; fastidious, nice; disagreeable.
fastīdium, -ī *and* **iī** *nt* squeamishness, distaste; disgust, aversion; disdain, pride.
fastīgātē *adv* in a sloping position.
fastīgātus *adj* sloping up *or* down.
fastīgium, -ī *and* **iī** *nt* gable, pediment; slope; height, depth; top, summit; (*fig*) highest degree, acme, dignity; (*speech*) main headings.
fāstus *adj* lawful for public business.
fastus, -ūs *m* disdain, pride.
Fāta *ntpl* the Fates.
fātālis *adj* fateful, destined; fatal, deadly.
fātāliter *adv* by fate.
fateor, -tērī, -ssus *vt* to confess, acknowledge; to reveal, bear witness to.
fāticanus, -inus *adj* prophetic.
fātidicus *adj* prophetic ♦ *m* prophet.
fātifer, -ī *adj* deadly.
fatīgātiō, -ōnis *f* weariness.
fatīgō, -āre, -āvī, -ātum *vt* to tire, exhaust; to worry, importune; to wear down, torment.
fātiloqua, -ae *f* prophetess.
fatīscō, -ere; -or, -ī *vi* to crack, split; (*fig*) to become exhausted.
fatuitās, -ātis *f* silliness.
fātum, -ī *nt* divine word, oracle; fate, destiny; divine will; misfortune, doom, death; **~ō obīre** die a natural death.
fātur, fātus *3rd pers, ppa of* **for.**
fatuus *adj* silly; unwieldy ♦ *m* fool.
faucēs, -ium *fpl* throat; pass, narrow channel, chasm; (*fig*) jaws.
Faunus, -ī *m* father of Latinus (*god of forests and herdsmen, identified with Pan*); (*pl*) woodland spirits, Fauns.

fauste *adv see* **faustus.**

faustitās, -ātis *f* good fortune, fertility.

faustus *adj* auspicious, lucky.

fautor, -ōris *m* supporter, patron.

fautrix, -īcis *f* protectress.

favea, -ae *f* pet slave.

faveō, -ēre, fāvī, fautum *vi* (*with dat*) to favour, befriend, support; **~ linguīs** keep silence.

favilla, -ae *f* embers, ashes; (*fig*) spark.

favitor *etc see* **fautor.**

Favōnius, -ī *m* west wind, zephyr.

favor, -ōris *m* favour, support; applause.

favōrābilis *adj* in favour; pleasing.

favus, -ī *m* honeycomb.

fax, facis *f* torch, wedding torch, funeral torch; marriage, death; (ASTRO) meteor; (*fig*) flame, fire, instigator; guide; **facem praeferre** act as guide.

faxim, faxō *old subj and fut of* **faciō.**

febrīcula, -ae *f* slight fever.

febris, -is *f* fever.

Februārius, -ī *m* February ♦ *adj* of February.

februum, -ī *nt* purification; **Februa** *pl festival of purification in February.*

fēcī *perf of* **faciō.**

fēcunditās, -ātis *f* fertility; (*style*) exuberance.

fēcundō, -āre *vt* to fertilise.

fēcundus *adj* fertile, fruitful; fertilising; (*fig*) abundant, rich, prolific.

fefellī *perf of* **fallō.**

fel, fellis *nt* gall bladder, bile; poison; (*fig*) animosity.

fēlēs, -is *f* cat.

fēlicitās, -ātis *f* happiness, good luck.

fēliciter *adv* abundantly; favourably; happily.

fēlix, -īcis *adj* fruitful; auspicious, favourable; fortunate, successful.

fēmella, -ae *f* girl.

fēmina, -ae *f* female, woman.

fēmineus *adj* woman's, of women; unmanly.

femur, -oris and inis *nt* thigh.

fēn- *etc see* **faen-.**

fenestra, -ae *f* window; (*fig*) loophole.

fera, -ae *f* wild beast.

ferācius *adv* more fruitfully.

fērālis *adj* funereal; of the Feralia; deadly ♦ *ntpl festival of the dead in February.*

ferāx, -ācis *adj* fruitful, productive.

ferbuī *perf of* **ferveō.**

ferculum, -ī *nt* litter, barrow; dish, course.

ferē *adv* almost, nearly, about; quite, just; usually, generally, as a rule; (*with neg*) hardly; **nihil ~** hardly anything.

ferentārius, -ī *and* **iī** *m* a light-armed soldier.

Feretrius, -ī *m* an epithet of Jupiter.

feretrum, -ī *nt* bier.

fēriae, -ārum *fpl* festival, holidays; (*fig*) peace, rest.

fēriātus *adj* on holiday, idle.

ferīnus *adj* of wild beasts ♦ *f* game.

feriō, -īre *vt* to strike, hit; to kill, sacrifice; (*comedy*) to cheat; **foedus ~** conclude a treaty.

feritās, -ātis *f* wildness, savagery.

fermē *see* **ferē.**

fermentum, -ī *nt* yeast; beer; (*fig*) passion, vexation.

ferō, ferre, tulī, lātum *vt* to carry, bring, bear; to bring forth, produce; to move, stir, raise; to carry off, sweep away, plunder; (*pass*) to rush, hurry, fly, flow, drift; (*road*) to lead; (*trouble*) to endure, suffer, sustain; (*feelings*) to exhibit, show; (*speech*) to talk about, give out, celebrate; (*bookkeeping*) to enter; (CIRCS) to allow, require; **sē ~** rush, move; profess to be, boast; **condiciōnem, lēgem ~** propose terms, a law; **iūdicem ~** sue; **sententiam, suffrāgium ~** vote; **signa ~** march; attack; **aegrē, graviter ~** be annoyed at; **laudibus ~** extol; **in oculīs ~** be very fond of; **prae sē ~** show, declare; **fertur, ferunt** it is said, they say; **ut mea fert opīniō** in my opinion.

ferōcia, -ae *f* courage; spirit; pride, presumption.

ferōcitās, -ātis *f* high spirits, aggressiveness; presumption.

ferōciter *adv* bravely; insolently.

Fērōnia, -ae *f* old Italian goddess.

ferōx, -ōcis *adj* warlike, spirited, daring; proud, insolent.

ferrāmentum, -ī *nt* tool, implement.

ferrārius *adj* of iron; **faber ~** blacksmith ♦ *f* iron-mine, iron-works.

ferrātus *adj* ironclad, ironshod ♦ *mpl* men in armour.

ferreus *adj* of iron, iron; (*fig*) hard, cruel; strong, unyielding.

ferrūgineus *adj* rust-coloured, dark.

ferrūgō, -inis *f* rust; dark colour; gloom.

ferrum, -ī *nt* iron; sword; any iron implement; force of arms; **~ et ignis** devastation.

fertilis *adj* fertile, productive; fertilising.

fertilitās, -ātis *f* fertility.

ferula, -ae *f* fennel; staff, rod.

ferus *adj* wild; uncivilised, cruel ♦ *m* beast.

fervēfaciō, -ere, -tum *vt* to boil.

fervēns, -entis *pres p of* **ferveō** ♦ *adj* hot; raging; (*fig*) impetuous, furious.

ferventer *adv* hotly.

ferveō, -vēre, -buī *vi* to boil, burn; (*fig*) to rage, bustle, be agitated.

fervēscō, -ere *vi* to boil up, grow hot.

fervidus *adj* hot, raging; (*fig*) fiery, violent.

fervō, -vere, -vī *vi see* **ferveō.**

fervor, -ōris *m* seething; heat; (*fig*) ardour, passion.

Fescennīnus *adj* Fescennine (*a kind of ribald*

song, perhaps from Fescennium in Etruria).

fessus _adj_ tired, worn out.

festīnanter _adv_ hastily.

festīnātiō, -ōnis _f_ haste, hurry.

festīnō, -āre _vi_ to hurry, be quick ♦ _vt_ to hasten, accelerate.

festīnus _adj_ hasty, quick.

fēstīvē _adv_ gaily; humorously.

fēstīvitās, -ātis _f_ gaiety, merriment; humour, fun.

fēstīvus _adj_ gay, jolly; delightful; (_speech_) humorous.

festūca, -ae _f_ rod (_with which slaves were manumitted_).

fēstus _adj_ festal, on holiday ♦ _nt_ holiday; feast.

fētiālis, -is _m_ priest who carried out the ritual in making war and peace.

fētūra, -ae _f_ breeding; brood.

fētus _adj_ pregnant; newly delivered; (_fig_) productive, full of.

fētus, -ūs _m_ breeding, bearing, producing; brood, young; fruit, produce; (_fig_) production.

fiber, -rī _m_ beaver.

fibra, -ae _f_ fibre; section of lung _or_ liver; entrails.

fībula, -ae _f_ clasp, brooch; clamp.

fīcedula, -ae _f_ fig pecker.

fictē _adv_ falsely.

fictilis _adj_ clay, earthen ♦ _nt_ jar; clay figure.

fictor, -ōris _m_ sculptor; maker, inventor.

fictrīx, -īcis _f_ maker.

fictūra, -ae _f_ shaping, invention.

fictus _ppp of_ **fingō** ♦ _adj_ false, fictitious ♦ _nt_ falsehood.

fīculnus _adj_ of the fig tree.

fīcus, -ī _and_ **ūs** _f_ fig tree; fig.

fidēle _adv_ faithfully, surely, firmly.

fidēlia, -ae _f_ pot, pail; **dē eādem ~ā duōs parietēs dealbāre** ≈ kill two birds with one stone.

fidēlis _adj_ faithful, loyal; trustworthy, sure.

fidēlitās, -ātis _f_ faithfulness, loyalty.

fidēliter _adv_ faithfully, surely, firmly.

Fīdēnae, -ārum _fpl_ ancient Latin town.

Fīdēnās, -ātis _adj see n._

fīdēns, -entis _pres p of_ **fīdō** ♦ _adj_ bold, resolute.

fīdenter _adv see_ **fīdens.**

fīdentia, -ae _f_ self-confidence.

fidēs, -ēī _f_ trust, faith, belief; trustworthiness, honour, loyalty, truth; promise, assurance, word; guarantee, safe-conduct, protection; (_COMM_) credit; (_law_) good faith; **~ mala** dishonesty; **rēs ~que** entire resources; **~em facere** convince; **~em servāre ergā** keep faith with; **dī vostram ~em!** for Heaven's sake!; **ex fidē bonā** in good faith.

fidēs, -is _f_ (_usu pl_) stringed instrument, lyre, lute; (_ASTRO_) Lyra.

fidī _perf of_ **findō.**

fidicen, -inis _m_ musician; lyric poet.

fidicina, -ae _f_ music girl.

fidicula, -ae _f_ small lute.

Fidius, -ī _m_ an epithet of Jupiter.

fīdō, -dere, -sus _vi_ (_with dat or abl_) to trust, rely on.

fīdūcia, -ae _f_ confidence, assurance; self-confidence; (_law_) trust, security.

fidūciārius _adj_ to be held in trust.

fīdus _adj_ trusty, reliable; sure, safe.

fīgō, -gere, -xī, -xum _vt_ to fix, fasten, attach; to drive in, pierce; (_speech_) to taunt.

figulāris _adj_ a potter's.

figulus, -ī _m_ potter; builder.

figūra, -ae _f_ shape, form; nature, kind; phantom; (_RHET_) figure of speech.

figūrō, -āre _vt_ to form, shape.

fīlātim _adv_ thread by thread.

fīlia, -ae _f_ daughter.

fīlicātus _adj_ with fern patterns.

fīliola, -ae _f_ little daughter.

fīliolus, -ī _m_ little son.

fīlius, -ī _and_ **iī** _m_ son; **terrae ~** a nobody.

filix, -cis _f_ fern.

fīlum, -ī _nt_ thread; band of wool, fillet; string, shred, wick; contour, shape; (_speech_) texture, quality.

fimbriae, -ārum _fpl_ fringe, end.

fimus, -ī _m_ dung; dirt.

findō, -ndere, -dī, -ssum _vt_ to split, divide; to burst.

fingō, -ere, finxī, fictum _vt_ to form, shape, make; to mould, model; to dress, arrange; to train; (_mind, speech_) to imagine, suppose, represent, sketch; to invent, fabricate; **vultum ~** compose the features.

fīniō, -īre, -īvī, -ītum _vt_ to bound, limit; to restrain; to prescribe, define, determine; to end, finish, complete ♦ _vi_ to finish, die.

fīnis, -is _m_ (_occ f_) boundary, border; (_pl_) territory; bound, limit; end; death; highest point, summit; aim, purpose; **~ bonōrum** the chief good; **quem ad ~em?** how long?; **~e genūs** up to the knee.

fīnītē _adv_ within limits.

fīnitimus _adj_ neighbouring, adjoining; akin, like ♦ _mpl_ neighbours.

fīnītor, -ōris _m_ surveyor.

fīnitumus _adj see_ **fīnitimus.**

fīnītus _ppp of_ **fīniō** ♦ _adj_ (_RHET_) well-rounded.

finxī _perf of_ **fingō.**

fīō, fierī, factus _vi_ to become, arise; to be made, be done; to happen; **quī fit ut?** how is it that?; **ut fit** as usually happens; **quid mē fīet?** what will become of me?

firmāmen, -inis _nt_ support.

firmāmentum, -ī _nt_ support, strengthening; (_fig_) mainstay.

firmātor, -ōris _m_ establisher.

firmē _adv_ powerfully, steadily.

firmitās, -ātis _f_ firmness, strength; steadfastness, stamina.

firmiter _adv see_ **firmē.**

firmitūdō, -inis _f_ strength, stability.

firmō, -āre, -āvī, -ātum _vt_ to strengthen, support, fortify; (_mind_) to encourage, steady; (*fact*) to confirm, prove, assert.

firmus *adj* strong, stable, firm; (*fig*) powerful, constant, sure, true.

fiscella, -ae *f* wicker basket.

fiscina, -ae *f* wicker basket.

fiscus, -ī *m* purse, moneybox; public exchequer; imperial treasury, the emperor's privy purse.

fissilis *adj* easy to split.

fissiō, -ōnis *f* dividing.

fissum, -ī *nt* slit, fissure.

fissus *ppp of* **findō**.

fistūca, -ae *f* rammer.

fistula, -ae *f* pipe, tube; panpipes; (*MED*) ulcer.

fistulātor, -ōris *m* panpipe player.

fīsus *ppa of* **fīdō**.

fīxī *perf of* **fīgō**.

fīxus *ppp of* **fīgō** ♦ *adj* fixed, fast, permanent.

flābellifera, -ae *f* fanbearer.

flābellum, -ī *nt* fan.

flābilis *adj* airy.

flābra, -ōrum *ntpl* blasts, gusts; wind.

flacceō, -ēre *vi* to flag, lose heart.

flaccēscō, -ere *vi* to flag, droop.

flaccidus *adj* flabby, feeble.

flaccus *adj* flap-eared.

Flaccus, -ī *m* surname of Horace.

flagellō, -āre *vt* to whip, lash.

flagellum, -ī *nt* whip, lash; strap, thong; (*vine*) shoot; (*polyp*) arm; (*feelings*) sting.

flāgitātiō, -ōnis *f* demand.

flāgitātor, -ōris *m* demander, dun.

flāgitiōsē *adv* infamously.

flāgitiōsus *adj* disgraceful, profligate.

flāgitium, -ī *and* **iī** *nt* offence, disgrace, shame; scoundrel.

flāgitō, -āre, -āvī, -ātum *vt* to demand, importune, dun; (*law*) to summon.

flagrāns, -antis *pres p of* **flagrō** ♦ *adj* hot, blazing; brilliant; passionate.

flagranter *adv* passionately.

flagrantia, -ae *f* blazing; (*fig*) shame.

flagrō, -āre *vi* to blaze, burn, be on fire; (*feelings*) to be excited, be inflamed; (*ill-will*) to be the victim of.

flagrum, -ī *nt* whip, lash.

flāmen, -inis *m* priest of a particular deity.

flāmen, -inis *nt* blast, gale, wind.

flāminica, -ae *f* wife of a priest.

Flāminīnus, -ī *m* Roman surname (*esp the conqueror of Philip V of Macedon*).

flāminium, -ī *and* **iī** *nt* priesthood.

Flāminius, -ī *m* Roman family name (*esp the consul defeated by Hannibal*).

Flāminius, -iānus *adj*: **Via ~ia** *road from Rome N.E. to Ariminum*.

flamma, -ae *f* flame, fire; torch, star; fiery colour; (*fig*) passion; danger, disaster.

flammeolum, -ī *nt* bridal veil.

flammēscō, -ere *vi* to become fiery.

flammeus *adj* fiery, blazing; flame-coloured ♦ *nt* bridal veil.

flammifer, -ī *adj* fiery.

flammō, -āre, -āvī, -ātum *vi* to blaze ♦ *vt* to set on fire, burn; (*fig*) to inflame, incense.

flammula, -ae *f* little flame.

flātus, -ūs *m* blowing, breath; breeze; (*fig*) arrogance.

flāvēns, -entis *adj* yellow, golden.

flāvēscō, -ere *vi* to turn yellow.

Flāviānus *adj see n.*

Flāvius, -ī *m* Roman family name (*esp the emperors Vespasian, Titus and Domitian*).

flāvus *adj* yellow, golden.

flēbilis *adj* lamentable; tearful, mournful.

flēbiliter *adv see* **flēbilis**.

flectō, -ctere, -xī, -xum *vt* to bend, turn; to turn aside, wheel; (*promontory*) to round; (*mind*) to direct, persuade, dissuade ♦ *vi* to turn, march.

fleō, -ēre, -ēvī, -ētum *vi* to weep, cry ♦ *vt* to lament, mourn for.

flētus, -ūs *m* weeping, tears.

flexanimus *adj* moving.

flexī *perf of* **flectō**.

flexibilis *adj* pliant, flexible; fickle.

flexilis *adj* pliant.

flexiloquus *adj* ambiguous.

flexiō, -ōnis *f* bending, winding, (*voice*) modulation.

flexipēs, -edis *adj* twining.

flexuōsus *adj* tortuous.

flexūra, -ae *f* bending.

flexus *ppp of* **flectō** ♦ *adj* winding.

flexus, -ūs *m* winding, bending; change.

flīctus, -ūs *m* collision.

flō, -āre, -āvī, -ātum *vt, vi* to blow; (*money*) to coin.

floccus, -ī *m* bit of wool; triviality; ~**ī nōn faciō** ≈ *I don't care a straw for.*

Flōra, -ae *f* goddess of flowers.

Flōrālis *adj see n.*

flōrēns, -entis *pres p of* **flōreō** ♦ *adj* in bloom; bright; prosperous, flourishing.

flōreō, -ēre, -uī *vi* to blossom, flower; (*age*) to be in one's prime; (*wine*) to froth; (*fig*) to flourish, prosper; (*places*) to be gay with.

flōrēscō, -ere *vi* to begin to flower; to grow prosperous.

flōreus *adj* of flowers, flowery.

flōridulus *adj* pretty, little.

flōridus *adj* of flowers, flowery; fresh, pretty; (*style*) florid, ornate.

flōrifer, -ī *adj* flowery.

flōrilegus *adj* flower-sipping.

flōrus *adj* beautiful.

flōs, -ōris *m* flower, blossom; (*wine*) bouquet; (*age*) prime, heyday; (*youth*) downy beard, youthful innocence; (*fig*) crown, glory; (*speech*) ornament.

Noun declensions and verb conjugations are shown on pp xiii to xxv. The present infinitive ending of a verb shows to which conjugation it belongs: **-āre** = 1st; **-ēre** = 2nd; **-ere** = 3rd and **-īre** = 4th. Irregular verbs are shown on p xxvi

flōsculus, -ī *m* little flower; (*fig*) pride, ornament.

flūctifragus *adj* surging.

flūctuātiō, -ōnis *f* wavering.

flūctuō, -āre *vi* to toss, wave; (*fig*) to rage, swell, waver.

flūctuōsus *adj* stormy.

flūctus, -ūs *m* wave; flowing, flood; (*fig*) disturbance; **~ūs** (*pl*) **in simpulō** ≈ *a storm in a teacup.*

fluēns, -entis *pres p of* **fluō ♦** *adj* lax, loose, enervated; (*speech*) fluent.

fluenta, -ōrum *ntpl* stream, flood.

fluenter *adv* in a flowing manner.

fluentisonus *adj* wave-echoing.

fluidus *adj* flowing, fluid; lax, soft; relaxing.

fluitō, -āre *vi* to flow, float about; to wave, flap, move unsteadily; (*fig*) to waver.

flūmen, -inis *nt* stream, river; (*fig*) flood, flow, fluency; **adversō ~ine** upstream; **secundō ~ine** downstream.

flūmineus *adj* river- (*in cpds*).

fluō, -ere, -xī, -xum *vi* to flow; to overflow, drip; (*fig*) to fall in, fall away, vanish; (*speech*) to run evenly; (*CIRCS*) to proceed, tend.

flūtō *etc see* **fluitō**.

fluviālis *adj* river- (*in cpds*).

fluviātilis *adj* river- (*in cpds*).

flūvidus *etc see* **fluidus**.

fluvius, -ī *and* **iī** *m* river, stream.

fluxi *perf of* **fluō**.

fluxus *adj* flowing, loose, leaky; (*person*) lax, dissolute; (*thing*) frail, fleeting, unreliable.

fōcāle, -is *nt* scarf.

foculus, -ī *m* stove, fire.

focus, -ī *m* hearth, fireplace; pyre, altar; (*fig*) home.

fodicō, -āre *vt* to nudge, jog.

fodiō, -ere, fōdī, fossum *vt* to dig; to prick, stab; (*fig*) to goad.

foedē *adv see* **foedus**.

foederātus *adj* confederated.

foedifragus *adj* perfidious.

foeditās, -ātis *f* foulness, hideousness.

foedō, -āre, -āvī, -ātum *vt* to mar, disfigure; to disgrace, sully.

foedus *adj* foul, hideous, revolting; vile, disgraceful.

foedus, -eris *nt* treaty, league; agreement, compact; law.

foen- *etc see* **faen-**.

foeteō, -ēre *vi* to stink.

foetidus *adj* stinking.

foetor, -ōris *m* stench.

foetu- *etc see* **fētu-**.

foliātum, -ī *nt* nard oil.

folium, -ī *and* **iī** *nt* leaf.

folliculus, -ī *m* small bag; eggshell.

follis, -is *m* bellows; punchball; purse.

fōmentum, -ī *nt* poultice, bandage; (*fig*) alleviation.

fōmes, -itis *m* tinder, kindling.

fōns, fontis *m* spring, source; water; (*fig*) origin, fountainhead.

fontānus *adj* spring- (*in cpds*).

fonticulus, -ī *m* little spring.

for, fārī, fātus *vt, vi* to speak, utter.

forābilis *adj* penetrable.

forāmen, -inis *nt* hole, opening.

forās *adv* out, outside.

forceps, -ipis *m/f* tongs, forceps.

forda, -ae *f* cow in calf.

fore, forem *fut infin, imperf subj of* **sum**.

forēnsis *adj* public, forensic; of the marketplace.

foris, -is *f* (*usu pl*) door; (*fig*) opening, entrance.

forīs *adv* out of doors, outside, abroad; from outside, from abroad; **~ cēnāre** dine out.

fōrma, -ae *f* form, shape, appearance; mould, stamp, last; (*person*) beauty; (*fig*) idea, nature, kind.

fōrmāmentum, -ī *nt* shape.

fōrmātūra, -ae *f* shaping.

Formiae, -ārum *fpl* town in S. Latium.

Formiānus *adj* of Formiae **♦** *nt* villa at Formiae.

formīca, -ae *f* ant.

formīcinus *adj* crawling.

formīdābilis *adj* terrifying.

formīdō, -āre, -āvī, -ātum *vt, vi* to fear, be terrified.

formīdō, -inis *f* terror, awe, horror; scarecrow.

formīdolōsē *adv see* **formīdolōsus**.

formīdolōsus *adj* fearful, terrifying; afraid.

fōrmō, -āre, -āvī, -ātum *vt* to shape, fashion, form.

fōrmōsitās, -ātis *f* beauty.

fōrmōsus *adj* beautiful, handsome.

fōrmula, -ae *f* rule, regulation; (*law*) procedure, formula; (*PHILOS*) principle.

fornācula, -ae *f* small oven.

fornāx, -ācis *f* furnace, oven, kiln.

fornicātus *adj* arched.

fornix, -icis *m* arch, vault; brothel.

forō, -āre *vt* to pierce.

Foroiūliēnsis *adj see* **Forum Iuli**.

fors, fortis *f* chance, luck **♦** *adv* perchance; **~te** by chance, as it happened; perhaps; **nē ~te** in case; **sī ~te** if perhaps; in the hope that.

forsan, forsit, forsitan *adv* perhaps.

fortasse, -is *adv* perhaps, possibly; (*irony*) very likely.

forticulus *adj* quite brave.

fortis *adj* strong, sturdy; brave, manly, resolute.

fortiter *adv* vigorously; bravely.

fortitūdō, -inis *f* courage, resolution; strength.

fortuītō *adv* by chance.

fortuītus *adj* casual, accidental.

fortūna, -ae *f* chance, luck, fortune; good luck, success; misfortune; circumstances, lot; (*pl*) possessions; **~ae fīlius** Fortune's

favourite; ~**am habēre** be successful.
fortūnātē *adv see* **fortūnātus.**
fortūnātus *adj* happy, lucky; well off, rich,
blessed.
fortūnō, -āre *vt* to bless, prosper.
forulī, -ōrum *mpl* bookcase.
forum, -ī *nt* public place, market; market
town; *Roman Forum between the Palatine and
Capitol*; public affairs, law courts, business;
~ **boārium** cattle market; ~ **olitōrium**
vegetable market; ~ **piscātorium** fish
market; ~ **agere** hold an assize; ~ **attingere**
enter public life; **cēdere** ~**ō** go bankrupt; **utī**
~**ō** take advantage of a situation.
Forum Iūli colony in S. Gaul (*now* Fréjus).
forus, -ī *m* gangway; block of seats; (*bees*) cell
frame.
fossa, -ae *f* ditch, trench.
fossiō, -ōnis *f* digging.
fossor, -ōris *m* digger.
fossus *ppp of* **fodiō.**
fōtus *ppp of* **foveō.**
fovea, -ae *f* pit, pitfall.
foveō, -ēre, fōvī, fōtum *vt* to warm, keep
warm; (*MED*) to foment; to fondle, keep; (*fig*)
to cherish, love, foster, pamper, encourage;
castra ~ remain in camp.
frāctus *ppp of* **frangō** ♦ *adj* weak, faint.
frāga, -ōrum *ntpl* strawberries.
fragilis *adj* brittle, fragile; frail, fleeting.
fragilitās, -ātis *f* frailness.
fragmen, -inis *nt* (*pl*) fragments, ruins,
wreck.
fragmentum, -ī *nt* fragment, remnant.
fragor, -ōris *m* crash, din; disintegration.
fragōsus *adj* crashing, roaring, breakable;
rough.
frāgrāns, -antis *adj* fragrant.
framea, -ae *f* German spear.
frangō, -angere, -ēgī, -āctum *vt* to break,
shatter, wreck; to crush, grind; (*fig*) to break
down, weaken, humble; (*emotion*) to touch,
move; **cervīcem** ~ strangle.
frāter, -ris *m* brother; cousin; (*fig*) friend, ally.
frāterculus, -ī *m* brother.
frāternē *adv* like a brother.
frāternitās, -ātis *f* brotherhood.
frāternus *adj* brotherly, a brother's, fraternal.
frātricīda, -ae *m* fratricide.
fraudātiō, -ōnis *f* deceit, fraud.
fraudātor, -ōris *m* swindler.
fraudō, -āre, -āvī, -ātum *vt* to cheat, defraud;
to steal, cancel.
fraudulentus *adj* deceitful, fraudulent.
fraus, -audis *f* deceit, fraud; delusion, error;
offence, wrong; injury, damage; **lēgī** ~**dem**
facere evade the law; **in** ~**dem incidere** be
disappointed; **sine** ~**de** without harm.
fraxineus, fraxinus *adj* of ash.
fraxinus, -ī *f* ash tree; ashen spear.

Fregellae, -ārum *fpl* town in S. Latium.
Fregellānus *adj see n.*
frēgī *perf of* **frangō.**
fremebundus *adj* roaring.
fremitus, -ūs *m* roaring, snorting, noise.
fremō, -ere, -uī, -itum *vi* to roar, snort,
grumble ♦ *vt* to shout for, complain.
fremor, -ōris *m* murmuring.
frendō, -ere *vi* to gnash the teeth.
frēnō, -āre, -āvī, -ātum *vt* to bridle; (*fig*) to
curb, restrain.
frēnum, -ī *nt* (*pl* -**a**, -**ōrum** *nt*, -**ī**, -**ōrum** *m*)
bridle, bit; (*fig*) curb, check; ~**ōs dare** give
vent to; ~**um mordēre** ≈ *take the bit between
one's teeth.*
frequēns, -entis *adj* crowded, numerous,
populous; regular, repeated, frequent; ~
senatus a crowded meeting of the senate.
frequentātiō, -ōnis *f* accumulation.
frequenter *adv* in large numbers; repeatedly,
often.
frequentia, -ae *f* full attendance, throng,
crowd.
frequentō, -āre, -āvī, -ātum *vt* to crowd,
populate; to visit repeatedly, frequent; to
repeat; (*festival*) to celebrate, keep.
fretēnsis *adj* of the Straits of Messina.
fretum, -ī *nt* strait; sea; (*fig*) violence; ~
Siciliēnse Straits of Messina.
fretus, -ūs *m* strait.
frētus *adj* relying, confident.
fricō, -āre, -uī, -tum *vt* to rub, rub down.
frictus *ppp of* **frigō.**
frīgefactō, -āre *vt* to cool.
frīgeō, -ēre *vi* to be cold; (*fig*) to be lifeless,
flag; to be coldly received, fall flat.
frīgerāns *adj* cooling.
frīgēscō, -ere *vi* to grow cold; to become
inactive.
frīgida, -ae *f* cold water.
frīgidē *adv* feebly.
frīgidulus *adj* rather cold, faint.
frīgidus *adj* cold, cool; chilling; (*fig*) dull,
torpid; (*words*) flat, uninteresting.
frīgō, -gere, -xī, -ctum *vt* to roast, fry.
frīgus, -oris *nt* cold; cold weather, winter;
death; (*fig*) dullness, inactivity; coldness,
indifference.
friguttiō, -īre *vi* to stammer.
friō, -āre *vt* to crumble.
fritillus, -ī *m* dice box.
frīvolus *adj* empty, paltry.
frīxī *perf of* **frigō.**
frondātor, -ōris *m* vinedresser, pruner.
frondeō, -ēre *vi* to be in leaf.
frondēscō, -ere *vi* to become leafy, shoot.
frondeus *adj* leafy.
frondifer, -ī *adj* leafy.
frondōsus *adj* leafy.
frōns, -ondis *f* leaf, foliage; garland of leaves.

Noun declensions and verb conjugations are shown on pp xiii to xxv. The present infinitive ending of a verb shows
to which conjugation it belongs: **-āre** = 1st; **-ēre** = 2nd; **-ere** = 3rd and **-īre** = 4th. Irregular verbs are shown on p xxvi

frōns, -ontis f forehead, brow; front, facade; (fig) look, appearance, exterior; **~ontem contrahere** frown; **ā ~onte** in front; **in ~onte** in breadth.

frontālia, -um ntpl frontlet.

frontō, -ōnis m a broad-browed man.

frūctuārius adj productive; paid for out of produce.

fructuōsus adj productive; profitable.

frūctus ppa of **fruor**.

frūctus, -ūs m enjoyment; revenue, income; produce, fruit; (fig) consequence, reward; **~uī esse** be an asset (to); **~um percipere** reap the fruits (of).

frūgālis adj thrifty, worthy.

frūgālitās, -ātis f thriftiness, restraint.

frūgāliter adv temperately.

frūgēs etc see **frūx**.

frūgī adj (indecl) frugal, temperate, honest; useful.

frūgifer, -ī adj fruitful, fertile.

frūgiferēns, -entis adj fruitful.

frūgilegus adj food-gatherering.

frūgiparus adj fruitful.

frūmentārius adj of corn, corn- (in cpds) ♦ m corn dealer; **lēx ~a** law about the distribution of corn; **rēs ~a** commissariat.

frūmentātiō, -ōnis f foraging.

frūmentātor, -ōris m corn merchant, forager.

frūmentor, -ārī, -ātus vi to go foraging.

frūmentum, -ī nt corn, grain, (pl) crops.

frūnīscor, -ī vt to enjoy.

fruor, -uī, -ūctus vt, vi (usu with abl) to enjoy, enjoy the company of; (law) to have the use and enjoyment of.

frūstillātim adv in little bits.

frūstrā adv in vain, for nothing; groundlessly; in error; **~ esse** be deceived; **~ habēre** foil.

frūstrāmen, -inis nt deception.

frūstrātiō, -ōnis f deception, frustration.

frūstrō, -āre; -or, -ārī, -ātus vt to deceive, trick.

frūstulentus adj full of crumbs.

frūstum, -ī nt bit, scrap.

frutex, -icis m bush, shrub; (comedy) blockhead.

fruticētum, -ī nt thicket.

fruticor, -ārī vi to sprout.

fruticōsus adj bushy.

frūx, -ūgis f, **-ūgēs, -ūgum** fruits of the earth, produce; (fig) reward, success; virtue; **sē ad ~ūgem bonam recipere** reform.

fuam old pres subj of **sum**.

fūcātus adj counterfeit, artificial.

fūcō, -āre, -āvī, -ātum vt to paint, dye (esp red).

fūcōsus adj spurious.

fūcus, -ī m red dye, rouge; bee glue; (fig) deceit, pretence.

fūcus, -ī m drone.

fūdī perf of **fundō**.

fuga, -ae f flight, rout; banishment; speed, swift passing; refuge; (fig) avoidance, escape; **~am facere, in ~am dare** put to flight.

fugācius adv more timidly.

fugāx, -ācis adj timorous, shy, fugitive; swift, transient; (with gen) avoiding.

fūgī perf of **fugiō**.

fugiēns, -entis pres p of **fugiō** ♦ adj fleeting, dying; averse (to).

fugiō, -ere, fūgī, -itum vi to flee, run away, escape; to go into exile; (fig) to vanish, pass swiftly ♦ vt to flee from, escape from; to shun, avoid; (fig) to escape, escape notice of; **~e quaerere** do not ask; **mē ~it** I do not notice or know.

fugitīvus, -ī m runaway slave, truant, deserter ♦ adj fugitive.

fugitō, -āre vt to flee from, shun.

fugō, -āre, -āvī, -ātum vt to put to flight; to banish; to rebuff.

fulcīmen, -inis nt support.

fulciō, -cīre, -sī, -tum vt to prop, support; to strengthen, secure; (fig) to sustain, bolster up.

fulcrum, -ī nt bedpost; couch.

fulgeō, -gēre, -sī vi to flash, lighten; to shine; (fig) to be illustrious.

fulgidus adj flashing.

fulgō etc see **fulgeō**.

fulgor, -ōris m lightning; flash, brightness; (fig) splendour.

fulgur, -is nt lightning; thunderbolt; splendour.

fulgurālis adj on lightning as an omen.

fulgurātor, -ōris m interpreter of lightning.

fulgurītus adj struck by lightning.

fulgurō, -āre vi to lighten.

fulica, -ae f coot.

fūlīgō, -inis f soot; black paint.

fulix, -cis f see **fulica**.

fullō, -ōnis m fuller.

fullōnius adj fuller's.

fulmen, -inis nt thunderbolt; (fig) disaster.

fulmenta, -ae f heel of a shoe.

fulmineus adj of lightning; (fig) deadly.

fulminō, -āre vi to lighten; (fig) to threaten.

fulsī perf of **fulciō**; perf of **fulgeō**.

fultūra, -ae f support.

fultus ppp of **fulciō**.

Fulvia, -iae f wife of M. Antony.

Fulvius, -ī m Roman family name.

fulvus adj yellow, tawny, dun.

fūmeus adj smoking.

fūmidus adj smoky, smoking.

fūmifer, -ī adj smoking.

fūmificō, -āre vi to burn incense.

fūmificus adj steaming.

fūmō, -āre vi to smoke, steam.

fūmōsus adj smoky, smoked.

fūmus, -ī m smoke, steam.

fūnāle, -is nt cord; wax torch; chandelier.

fūnambulus, -ī m tightrope walker.

fūnctiō, -ōnis f performance.

fūnctus ppa of **fungor**.

fūnda, -ae f sling; dragnet.
fundāmen, -inis nt foundation.
fundāmentum, -ī nt foundation; **~a agere,
    iacere** lay the foundations.
Fundānus adj see **Fundī.**
fundātor, -ōris m founder.
Fundī, -ōrum mpl coast town in Latium.
funditō, -āre vt to sling.
funditor, -ōris m slinger.
funditus adv utterly, completely; at the
    bottom.
fundō, -āre, -āvī, -ātum vt to found; to
    secure; (fig) to establish, make secure.
fundō, -ere, fūdī, fūsum vt to pour, shed,
    spill; (metal) to cast; (solids) to hurl, scatter,
    shower; (MIL) to rout; (crops) to produce in
    abundance; (speech) to utter; (fig) to spread,
    extend.
fundus, -ī m bottom; farm, estate; (law)
    authorizer.
fūnebris adj funeral- (in cpds); murderous.
fūnerātus adj killed.
fūnereus adj funeral- (in cpds); fatal.
fūnestō, -āre vt to pollute with murder,
    desecrate.
fūnestus adj deadly, fatal; sorrowful, in
    mourning.
fungīnus adj of a mushroom.
fungor, -gī, fūnctus vt, vi (usu with abl) to
    perform, discharge, do; to be acted on.
fungus, -ī m mushroom, fungus; (candle) clot
    on the wick.
fūniculus, -ī m cord.
fūnis, -is m rope, rigging; **~em dūcere** be the
    master.
fūnus, -eris nt funeral; death; corpse; ruin,
    destruction.
fūr, fūris m thief; slave.
fūrācissimē adv most thievishly.
fūrāx, -ācis adj thieving.
furca, -ae f fork; fork-shaped pole; pillory.
furcifer, -ī m gallows rogue.
furcilla, -ae f little fork.
furcillō, -āre vt to prop up.
furcula, -ae f forked prop; **~ae Caudīnae** Pass
    of Caudium.
furenter adv furiously.
furfur, -is m bran; scurf.
Furia, -ae f Fury, avenging spirit; madness,
    frenzy, rage.
furiālis adj of the Furies; frantic, fearful;
    infuriating.
furiāliter adv madly.
furibundus adj mad, frenzied.
furiō, -āre, -āvī, -ātum vt to madden.
furiōsē adv in a frenzy.
furiōsus adj mad, frantic.
furnus, -ī m oven.
furō, -ere vi to rave, rage, be mad, be crazy.
fūror, -ārī, -ātus vt to steal; to pillage; to
    impersonate.
furor, -ōris m madness, frenzy, passion.
fūrtificus adj thievish.
fūrtim adv by stealth, secretly.
fūrtīvē adv secretly.
fūrtīvus adj stolen; secret, furtive.
fūrtō adv secretly.
fūrtum, -ī nt theft, robbery; (pl) stolen goods;
    (fig) trick, intrigue.
fūrunculus, -ī m pilferer.
furvus adj black, dark.
fuscina, -ae f trident.
fuscō, -āre vt to blacken.
fuscus adj dark, swarthy; (voice) husky,
    muffled.
fūsē adv diffusely.
fūsilis adj molten, softened.
fūsiō, -ōnis f outpouring.
fūstis, -is m stick, club, cudgel; (MIL) beating to
    death.
fūstuārium, -ī and iī nt beating to death.
fūsus ppp of **fundō** ♦ adj broad, diffuse;
    copious.
fūsus, -ī m spindle.
futtile adv in vain.
futtilis adj brittle; worthless.
futtilitās, -ātis f futility.
futūrum, -ī nt future.
futūrus fut p of **sum** ♦ adj future, coming.

G, g

Gabiī, -iōrum mpl ancient town in Latium.
Gabinius, -ī m Roman family name (esp Aulus,
    tribune 67 B.C.).
Gabinius, -iānus adj: **lēx ~ia** law giving Pompey
    command against the pirates.
Gabīnus adj see **Gabiī.**
Gādēs, -ium fpl town in Spain (now Cadiz).
Gāditānus adj see n.
gaesum, -ī nt Gallic javelin.
Gaetūlī, -ōrum mpl African people N of Sahara.
Gaetūlus, -icus adj Gaetulian; African.
Gāius, -ī m Roman praenomen (esp emperor
    Caligula).
Gāius, -ia m/f (wedding ceremony) bridegroom,
    bride.
Galatae, -ārum mpl Galatians of Asia Minor.
Galatia, -iae f Galatia.
Galba, -ae m Roman surname (esp emperor
    68–9).
galbaneus adj of galbanum, a Syrian plant.

Noun declensions and verb conjugations are shown on pp xiii to xxv. The present infinitive ending of a verb shows
to which conjugation it belongs: **-āre** = 1st; **-ēre** = 2nd; **-ere** = 3rd and **-īre** = 4th. Irregular verbs are shown on p xxvi

galbinus *adj* greenish-yellow ♦ *ntpl* pale green clothes.

galea, -ae *f* helmet.

galeātus *adj* helmeted.

galērītus *adj* rustic.

galērum, -ī *nt*, **-us, -ī** *m* leather hood, cap; wig.

galla, -ae *f* oak apple.

Gallī, -ōrum *mpl* Gauls (*people of what is now France and N. Italy*).

Gallia, -iae *f* Gaul.

Gallicānus *adj* of Italian Gaul.

Gallicus *adj* Gallic ♦ *f* a Gallic shoe.

gallīna, -ae *f* hen; ~**ae albae fīlius** fortune's favourite.

gallīnāceus *adj* of poultry.

gallīnārius, -ī *and* **iī** *m* poultry farmer.

Gallograecī, -ōrum *mpl* Galatians.

Gallograecia, -iae *f* Galatia.

gallus, -ī *m* cock.

Gallus, -ī *m* Gaul; Roman surname (*esp the lyric poet; priest of Cybele*).

ganēa, -ae *f* low eating house.

ganeō, -ōnis *m* profligate.

ganeum, -ī *nt* low eating house.

Gangaridae, -ārum *mpl* a people on the Ganges.

Gangēs, -is *m* river Ganges.

Gangēticus *adj* see n.

ganniō, -īre *vi* to yelp; (*fig*) to grumble.

gannītus, -ūs *m* yelping.

Ganymēdēs, -is *m* Ganymede, (*cup bearer in Olympus*).

Garamantes, -um *mpl* N. African tribe.

Garamantis, -idis *adj* see n.

Gargānus, -ī *m* mountain in E. Italy.

garriō, -īre *vi* to chatter.

garrulitās, -ātis *f* chattering.

garrulus *adj* talkative, babbling.

garum, -ī *nt* fish sauce.

Garumna, -ae *f* river Garonne.

gaudeō, -ēre, gāvīsus *vt, vi* to rejoice, be pleased, delight (in); **in sē, in sinū ~** be secretly pleased.

gaudium, -ī *and* **iī** *nt* joy, delight, enjoyment.

gaulus, -ī *m* bucket.

gausape, -is *nt*, **-a, -ōrum** *pl* a woollen cloth, frieze.

gāvīsus *ppa of* **gaudeō**.

gāza, -ae *f* treasure, riches.

gelidē *adv* feebly.

gelidus *adj* cold, frosty; stiff, numb; chilling ♦ *f* cold water.

gelō, -āre *vt* to freeze.

Gelōnī, -ōrum *mpl* Scythian tribe (*now Ukraine*).

gelū, -ūs *nt* frost, cold; chill.

gemebundus *adj* groaning.

gemellipara, -ae *f* mother of twins.

gemellus *adj* twin, double; alike ♦ *m* twin.

geminātiō, -ōnis *f* doubling.

geminō, -āre, -āvī, -ātum *vt* to double, bring together; to repeat ♦ *vi* to be double.

geminus *adj* twin, double, both; similar ♦ *mpl* twins (*esp Castor and Pollux*).

gemitus, -ūs *m* groan, sigh; moaning sound.

gemma, -ae *f* bud, precious stone, jewel; jewelled cup, signet.

gemmātus *adj* bejewelled.

gemmeus *adj* jewelled; sparkling.

gemmifer, -ī *adj* gem-producing.

gemmō, -āre *vi* to bud, sprout; to sparkle.

gemō, -ere, -uī, -itum *vi* to sigh, groan, moan ♦ *vt* to bewail.

Gemōniae, -ārum *fpl* steps in Rome on which bodies of criminals were thrown.

genae, -ārum *fpl* cheeks; eyes, eye sockets.

geneālogus, -ī *m* genealogist.

gener, -ī *m* son-in-law.

generālis *adj* of the species; universal.

generāliter *adv* generally.

generāscō, -ere *vi* to be produced.

generātim *adv* by species, in classes; in general.

generātor, -ōris *m* producer.

generō, -āre, -āvī, -ātum *vt* to breed, procreate.

generōsus *adj* high-born, noble; well-stocked; generous, chivalrous; (*things*) noble, honourable.

genesis, -is *f* birth; horoscope.

genethliacon, -ī *nt* birthday poem.

genetīvus *adj* native, inborn.

genetrīx, -īcis *f* mother.

geniālis *adj* nuptial; joyful, genial.

geniāliter *adv* merrily.

geniculātus *adj* jointed.

genista, -ae *f* broom.

genitābilis *adj* productive.

genitālis *adj* fruitful, generative; of birth.

genitāliter *adv* fruitfully.

genitor, -ōris *m* father, creator.

genitus *ppp of* **gignō**.

genius, -ī *and* **iī** *m* guardian spirit; enjoyment, inclination; talent; ~**iō indulgēre** enjoy oneself.

gēns, gentis *f* clan, family, stock, race; tribe, people, nation; descendant; (*pl*) foreign peoples; **minimē gentium** by no means; **ubi gentium** where in the world.

genticus *adj* national.

gentīlicius *adj* family.

gentīlis *adj* family, hereditary; national ♦ *m* kinsman.

gentīlitās, -ātis *f* clan relationship.

genū, -ūs *nt* knee.

genuālia, -um *ntpl* garters.

genuī *perf of* **gignō**.

genuīnus *adj* natural.

genuīnus *adj* of the cheek ♦ *mpl* back teeth.

genus, -eris *nt* birth, descent, noble birth, descendant; race; kind, class, species, respect, way; (*logic*) genus, general term; **id ~** of that kind; **in omnī ~ere** in all respects.

geōgraphia, -ae *f* geography.

geōmetrēs, -ae *m* geometer.

geōmetria, -ae f geometry.
geōmetricus adj geometrical ♦ ntpl geometry.
germānē adv sincerely.
Germānī, -ōrum mpl Germans.
Germānia, -iae f Germany.
Germānicus adj, m cognomen of Nero Claudius Drusus and his son.
germānitās, -ātis f brotherhood, sisterhood; relation of sister colonies.
germānus adj of the same parents, full (brother, sister); genuine, true ♦ m full brother ♦ f full sister.
germen, -inis nt bud, shoot; embryo; (fig) germ.
gerō, -rere, -ssī, -stum vt to carry, wear; to bring; (plants) to bear, produce; (feelings) to entertain, show; (activity) to conduct, manage, administer, wage; (time) spend; **mōrem ~** comply, humour; **persōnam ~** play a part; **sē ~** behave; **sē medium ~** be neutral; **prae sē ~** exhibit; **rēs ~stae** exploits.
gerō, -ōnis nt carrier.
gerrae, -ārum fpl trifles, nonsense.
gerrō, -ōnis m idler.
gerulus, -ī m carrier.
Gēryōn, -onis m mythical three-bodied king killed by Hercules.
gessī perf of **gerō**.
gestāmen, -inis nt arms, ornaments, burden; litter, carriage.
gestiō, -ōnis f performance.
gestiō, -īre vi to jump for joy, be excited; to be very eager.
gestitō, -āre vt to always wear or carry.
gestō, -āre vt to carry about, usually wear; to fondle; to blab; (pass) to go for a ride, drive, sail.
gestor, -ōris m telltale.
gestus ppp of **gerō**.
gestus, -ūs m posture, gesture; gesticulation.
Getae, -ārum mpl Thracian tribe on the lower Danube.
Geticus adj Getan, Thracian.
gibbus, -ī m hump.
Gigantes, -um mpl Giants, sons of Earth.
Gigantēus adj see n.
gignō, -ere, genuī, genitum vt to beget, bear, produce; to cause.
gilvus adj pale yellow, dun.
gingīva, -ae f gum.
glaber, -rī adj smooth, bald ♦ m favourite slave.
glaciālis adj icy.
glaciēs, -ēī f ice.
glaciō, -āre vt to freeze.
gladiātor, -ōris m gladiator; (pl) gladiatorial show.
gladiātōrius adj of gladiators ♦ nt gladiators' pay.
gladiātūra, -ae f gladiator's profession.

gladius, -ī and iī m sword; (fig) murder, death; **~ium stringere** draw the sword; **suō sibi ~iō iugulāre** ≈ beat at his own game.
glaeba, -ae f sod, clod of earth; soil; lump.
glaebula, -ae f small lump; small holding.
glaesum etc see **glēsum**.
glandifer, -ī adj acorn-bearing.
glandium, -ī and iī nt glandule (in meat).
glāns, -andis f acorn, nut; bullet.
glārea, -ae f gravel.
glāreōsus adj gravelly.
glaucūma, -ae f cataract; **~am ob oculōs obicere** ≈ throw dust in the eyes of.
glaucus adj bluish grey.
glēba etc see **glaeba**.
glēsum, -ī nt amber.
glīs, -īris m dormouse.
glīscō, -ere vi to grow, swell, blaze up.
globōsus adj spherical.
globus, -ī m ball, sphere; (MIL) troop; mass, crowd, cluster.
glōmerāmen, -inis nt bell.
glomerō, -āre, -āvī, -ātum vt to form into a ball, gather, accumulate.
glomus, -eris nt ball of thread, clue.
glōria, -ae f glory, fame; ambition, pride, boasting; (pl) glorious deeds.
glōriātiō, -ōnis f boasting.
glōriola, -ae f a little glory.
glōrior, -ārī, -ātus vt, vi to boast, pride oneself.
glōriōsē adv see **glōriōsus**.
glōriōsus adj famous, glorious; boastful.
glūten, -inis nt glue.
glūtinātor, -ōris m bookbinder.
gluttiō, -īre vt to gulp down.
gnāruris, gnārus adj knowing, expert; known.
gnātus see **nātus**.
gnāvus see **nāvus**.
Gnōsius and iacus and ias adj of Cnossos, Cretan.
Gnōsis, -idis f Ariadne.
Gnōsus, -ī f Cnossos (ancient capital of Crete) ♦ f Ariadne.
gōbiō, -ōnis, gōbius, -ī and iī m gudgeon.
Gorgiās, -ae m Sicilian sophist and teacher of rhetoric.
Gorgō, -ōnis f mythical monster capable of turning men to stone, Medusa.
Gorgoneus adj: **equus ~** Pegasus; **lacus ~** Hippocrene.
Gortȳna, -ae f Cretan town.
Gortȳnius, -iacus adj Gortynian, Cretan.
gōrȳtos, -ī m quiver.
grabātus, -ī m camp bed, low couch.
Gracchānus adj see n.
Gracchus, -ī m Roman surname (esp the famous tribunes Tiberius and Gaius).
gracilis adj slender, slight, meagre, poor;

Noun declensions and verb conjugations are shown on pp xiii to xxv. The present infinitive ending of a verb shows to which conjugation it belongs: **-āre** = 1st; **-ēre** = 2nd; **-ere** = 3rd and **-īre** = 4th. Irregular verbs are shown on p xxvi

(*style*) plain.

gracilitās, -ātis *f* slimness, leanness; (*style*) simplicity.

grāculus, -ī *m* jackdaw.

gradātim *adv* step by step, gradually.

gradātiō, -ōnis *f* (*RHET*) climax.

gradior, -adī, -essus *vi* to step, walk.

Grādīvus, -ī *m* Mars.

gradus, -ūs *m* step, pace; stage, step towards; firm stand, position, standing; (*pl*) stair, steps; (*hair*) braid; (*MATH*) degree; (*fig*) degree, rank; **citātō, plēnō ~ū** at the double; **suspēnsō ~ū** on tiptoe; **dē ~ū deicī** be disconcerted.

Graecē *adv* in Greek.

Graecia, -iae *f* Greece; **Māgna ~** S. Italy.

graecissō, -āre *vi* to ape the Greeks.

graecor, -ārī *vi* to live like Greeks.

Graeculus *adj* (*contemptuous*) Greek.

Graecus *adj* Greek.

Grāiugena, -ae *m* Greek.

Grāius *adj* Greek.

grallātor, -ōris *m* stiltwalker.

grāmen, -inis *nt* grass; herb.

grāmineus *adj* grassy; of cane.

grammaticus *adj* literary, grammatical ♦ *m* teacher of literature and language ♦ *f/ntpl* grammar, literature, philology.

grānāria, -ōrum *ntpl* granary.

grandaevus *adj* aged, very old.

grandēscō, -ere *vi* to grow.

grandiculus *adj* quite big.

grandifer, -ī *adj* productive.

grandiloquus, -ī *m* grand speaker; boaster.

grandinat, -āre *vi* it hails.

grandis *adj* large, great, tall; old; strong; (*style*) grand, sublime; **~ nātū** old.

granditās, -ātis *f* grandeur.

grandō, -inis *f* hail.

grānifer, -ī *adj* grain-carrying.

grānum, -ī *nt* seed, grain.

graphicē *adv* nicely.

graphicus *adj* fine, masterly.

graphium, -ī *and* **iī** *nt* stilus, pen.

grassātor, -ōris *m* vagabond; robber, footpad.

grassor, -ārī, -ātus *vi* to walk about, prowl, loiter; (*action*) to proceed; (*fig*) to attack, rage against.

grātē *adv* with pleasure; gratefully.

grātēs *fpl* thanks.

grātia, -ae *f* charm, grace; favour, influence, regard, friendship; kindness, service; gratitude, thanks; **~am facere** excuse; **~am referre** return a favour; **in ~am redīre cum** be reconciled to; **~ās agere** thank; **~ās habēre** feel grateful; **~ā** (*with gen*) for the sake of; **eā ~ā** on that account; **~īs** for nothing.

Grātiae, -ārum *fpl* the three Graces.

grātificātiō, -ōnis *f* obligingness.

grātificor, -ārī *vi* to do a favour, oblige ♦ *vt* to make a present of.

gratiīs, grātīs *adv* for nothing.

grātiōsus *adj* in favour, popular; obliging.

grātor, -ārī, -ātus *vi* to rejoice, congratulate.

grātuītō *adv* for nothing.

grātuītus *adj* free, gratuitous.

grātulābundus *adj* congratulating.

grātulātiō, -ōnis *f* rejoicing; congratulation; public thanksgiving.

grātulor, -ārī, -ātus *vt, vi* to congratulate; to give thanks.

grātus *adj* pleasing, welcome, dear; grateful, thankful; (*acts*) deserving thanks; **~um facere** do a favour.

gravātē *adv* reluctantly, grudgingly.

gravātim *adv* unwillingly.

gravēdinōsus *adj* liable to colds.

gravēdō, -inis *f* cold in the head.

graveolēns, -entis *adj* strong-smelling.

gravēscō, -ere *vi* to become heavy; to grow worse.

graviditās, -ātis *f* pregnancy.

gravidō, -āre *vt* to impregnate.

gravidus *adj* pregnant; loaded, full.

gravis *adj* heavy; loaded, pregnant; (*smell*) strong, offensive; (*sound*) deep, bass; (*body*) sick; (*food*) indigestible; (*fig*) oppressive, painful, severe; important, influential, dignified.

gravitās, -ātis *f* weight, severity, sickness; importance, dignity, seriousness; **annōnae ~** high price of corn.

graviter *adv* heavily; strongly, deeply; severely, seriously, violently; gravely, with dignity; **~ ferre** be vexed at.

gravō, -āre *vt* to load, weigh down; to oppress, aggravate.

gravor, -ārī *vt, vi* to feel annoyed, object to, disdain.

gregālis *adj* of the herd, common ♦ *m* comrade.

gregārius *adj* common; (*MIL*) private.

gregātim *adv* in crowds.

gremium, -ī *nt* bosom, lap.

gressus *ppa of* **gradior**.

gressus, -ūs *m* step; course.

grex, -egis *m* flock, herd; company, troop.

grunniō, -īre *vi* to grunt.

grunnītus, -ūs *m* grunting.

grūs, -uis *f* crane.

grȳps, -ȳpis *m* griffin.

gubernāclum (gubernāculum), -ī *nt* rudder, tiller; helm, government.

gubernātiō, -ōnis *f* steering, management.

gubernātor, -ōris *m* steersman, pilot, governor.

gubernātrīx, -īcis *f* directress.

gubernō, -āre, -āvī, -ātum *vt* to steer, pilot; to manage, govern.

gula, -ae *f* gullet, throat; gluttony, palate.

gulōsus *adj* dainty.

gurges, -itis *m* abyss, deep water, flood; (*person*) spendthrift.

gurguliō, -ōnis *f* gullet, windpipe.

gurgustium, -ī *and* **iī** *nt* hovel, shack.

gustātus, -ūs *m* sense of taste; flavour.
gustō, -āre, -āvī, -ātum *vt* to taste; to have a snack; (*fig*) to enjoy, overhear; **prīmīs labrīs ~ have** a superficial knowledge of.
gustus, -ūs *m* tasting; preliminary dish.
gutta, -ae *f* drop; spot, speck.
guttātim *adv* drop by drop.
guttur, -is *nt* throat, gluttony.
gūtus, -ī *m* flask.
Gyās, -ae *m* giant with a hundred arms.
Gȳgaeus *adj* see n.
Gȳgēs, -is *and* **ae** *m* king of Lydia (*famed for his magic ring*).
gymnasiarchus, -ī *m* master of a gymnasium.
gymnasium, -ī *and* **iī** *nt* sports ground, school.
gymnasticus *adj* gymnastic.
gymnicus *adj* gymnastic.
gynaecēum, -ēī *and* **īum, -ī** *nt* women's quarters.
gypsātus *adj* coated with plaster.
gypsum, -ī *nt* plaster of Paris; a plaster figure.
gȳrus, -ī *m* circle, coil, ring; course.

H, h

ha *interj* (*expressing joy or laughter*) hurrah!, ha ha!
habēna, -ae *f* strap; (*pl*) reins; (*fig*) control; **~ās dare, immittere** allow to run freely.
habeō, -ēre, -uī, -itum *vt* to have, hold; to keep, contain, possess; (*fact*) to know; (*with infin*) to be in a position to; (*person*) to treat, regard, consider; (*action*) to make, hold, carry out ♦ *vi* to have possessions;
ōrātiōnem ~ make a speech; **in animō ~** intend; **prō certō ~** be sure; **sē ~** find oneself, be; **sibi, sēcum ~** keep to oneself; (*fight*) **~et a** hit!; **bene ~et** it is well; **sīc ~et** so it is; **sīc ~ētō** be sure of this.
habilis *adj* manageable, handy; suitable, nimble, expert.
habilitās, -ātis *f* aptitude.
habitābilis *adj* habitable.
habitātiō, -ōnis *f* dwelling, house.
habitātor, -ōris *m* tenant, inhabitant.
habitō, -āre, -āvī, -ātum *vt* to inhabit ♦ *vi* to live, dwell; to remain, be always (in).
habitūdō, -inis *f* condition.
habitus *ppp of* **habeō** ♦ *adj* stout; in a humour.
habitus, -ūs *m* condition, appearance; dress;

character, quality; disposition, feeling.
hāc *adv* this way.
hāctenus *adv* thus far, so far; till now.
Hadria, -ae *f* town in N. Italy; Adriatic Sea.
Hadriānus, -ānī *m* emperor Hadrian.
Hadriāticus *and* **acus** *adj of emperor Hadrian*.
haedilia, -ae *f* little kid.
haedinus *adj* kid's.
haedulus, -ī *m* little kid.
haedus, -ī *m* kid; (ASTRO, *usu pl*) the Kids (*a cluster in Auriga*).
Haemonia, -ae *f* Thessaly.
Haemonius *adj* Thessalian.
Haemus, -ī *m* mountain range in Thrace.
haereō, -rēre, -sī, -sum *vi* to cling, stick, be attached; (*nearness*) to stay close, hang on; (*continuance*) to linger, remain (at); (*stoppage*) to stick fast, come to a standstill, be at a loss.
haerēscō, -ere *vi* to adhere.
haeresis, -is *f* sect.
haesī *perf of* **haereō**.
haesitantia, -ae *f* stammering.
haesitātiō, -ōnis *f* stammering; indecision.
haesitō, -āre *vi* to get stuck; to stammer; to hesitate, be uncertain.
hahae, hahahae *see* **ha**.
hālitus, -ūs *m* breath, vapour.
hallex, -icis *m* big toe.
hallūc- *see* **ālūc-**.
hālō, -āre *vi* to be fragrant ♦ *vt* to exhale.
hāluc *etc see* **ālūc**.
halyaeetos, -ī *m* osprey.
hama, -ae *f* water bucket.
Hamādryas, -adis *f* woodnymph.
hāmātilis *adj* with hooks.
hāmātus *adj* hooked.
Hamilcar, -is *m* father of Hannibal.
hāmus, -ī *m* hook; talons.
Hannibal, -is *m* famous Carthaginian general in 2nd Punic War.
hara, -ae *f* stye, pen.
harēna, -ae *f* sand; desert, seashore; arena (*in the amphitheatre*).
harēnōsus *adj* sandy.
hariola, -ae *f*, **hariolus, -ī** *m* soothsayer.
hariolor, -ārī *vi* to prophesy; to talk nonsense.
harmonia, -ae *f* concord, melody; (*fig*) harmony.
harpagō, -āre *vt* to steal.
harpagō, -ōnis *m* grappling hook; (*person*) robber.
harpē, -ēs *f* scimitar.
Harpȳiae, -ārum *fpl* Harpies (*mythical monsters, half woman, half bird*).
harundifer, -ī *adj* reed-crowned.
harundineus *adj* reedy.
harundinōsus *adj* abounding in reeds.
harundō, -inis *f* reed, cane; fishing rod; shaft, arrow; (*fowling*) limed twig; (*music*) pipe,

---

Noun declensions and verb conjugations are shown on pp xiii to xxv. The present infinitive ending of a verb shows to which conjugation it belongs: **-āre** = 1st; **-ēre** = 2nd; **-ere** = 3rd and **-īre** = 4th. Irregular verbs are shown on p xxvi

flute; (*toy*) hobbyhorse; (*weaving*) comb; (*writing*) pen.

haruspex, -icis *m* diviner (*from entrails*); prophet.

haruspica, -ae *f* soothsayer.

haruspicīnus *adj* of divination by entrails ♦ *f* art of such divination.

haruspicium, -ī *and* **iī** *nt* divination.

Hasdrubal, -is *m* brother of Hannibal.

hasta, -ae *f* spear, pike; sign of an auction sale; **sub ~ā vēndere** put up for auction.

hastātus *adj* armed with a spear ♦ *mpl* first line of Roman army in battle; **prīmus ~** 1st company of hastati.

hastīle, -is *nt* shaft, spear, javelin; vine prop.

hau, haud *adv* not, not at all.

hauddum *adv* not yet.

haudquāquam *adv* not at all, not by any means.

hauriō, -rīre, -sī, -stum *vt* to draw, draw off, derive; to drain, empty, exhaust; to take in, drink, swallow, devour.

haustus *ppp of* **hauriō.**

haustus, -ūs *m* drawing (water); drinking; drink, draught.

haut *etc see* **haud.**

hebdomas, -dis *f* week.

Hēbē, -ēs *f* goddess of youth (*cup bearer to the gods*).

hebenus, -ī *f* ebony.

hebeō, -ēre *vi* to be blunt, dull, sluggish.

hebes, -tis *adj* blunt, dull, sluggish; obtuse, stupid.

hebēscō, -ere *vi* to grow dim *or* dull.

hebetō, -āre *vt* to blunt, dull, dim.

Hebrus, -ī *m* Thracian river (*now* Maritza).

Hecatē, -ēs *f* goddess of magic (*and often identified with Diana*).

Hecatēius, -eis *adj see n.*

hecatombē, -ēs *f* hecatomb.

Hector, -is *m* son of Priam (*chief warrior of the Trojans against the Greeks*).

Hectoreus *adj* of Hector; Trojan.

Hecuba, -ae *and* **ē, -ēs** *f* wife of Priam.

hedera, -ae *f* ivy.

hederiger, -ī *adj* wearing ivy.

hederōsus *adj* covered with ivy.

hēdychrum, -ī *nt* a cosmetic perfume.

hei, heia *etc see* **ei, eia.**

Helena, -ae *and* **ē, -ēs** *f* Helen (*wife of Menelaus, abducted by Paris*).

Helenus, -ī *m* son of Priam (*with prophetic powers*).

Hēliades, -um *fpl* daughters of the Sun (*changed to poplars or alders, and their tears to amber*).

Helicē, -ēs *f* the Great Bear.

Helicōn, -ōnis *m* mountain in Greece sacred to Apollo and the Muses.

Helicōniades, -um *fpl* the Muses.

Helicōnius *adj see* **Helicōn.**

Hellas, -dis *f* Greece.

Hellē, -ēs *f* mythical Greek princess (*carried by the golden-fleeced ram, and drowned in the Hellespont*).

Hellēspontius, -iacus *adj see n.*

Hellēspontus, -ī *m* Hellespont (*now* Dardanelles).

helluō, -ōnis *m* glutton.

helluor, -ārī *vi* to be a glutton.

helvella, -ae *f* a savoury herb.

Helvētiī, -ōrum *mpl* people of E. Gaul (*now* Switzerland).

Helvētius, -cus *adj see n.*

hem *interj* (*expressing surprise*) eh?, well well!

hēmerodromus, -ī *m* express courier.

hēmicillus, -ī *m* mule.

hēmicyclium, -ī *and* **iī** *nt* semicircle with seats.

hēmīna, -ae *f* half a pint.

hendecasyllabī, -ōrum *mpl* hendecasyllabics, verses of eleven syllables.

heptēris, -is *f* ship with seven banks of oars.

hera *etc see* **era.**

Hēra, -ae *f* Greek goddess identified with Juno.

Hēraclītus, -ī *m* early Greek philosopher.

Hēraea, -aeōrum *ntpl* festival of Hera.

herba, -ae *f* blade, young plant; grass, herb, weed.

herbēscō, -ere *vi* to grow into blades.

herbeus *adj* grass-green.

herbidus *adj* grassy.

herbifer, -ī *adj* grassy.

herbōsus *adj* grassy, made of turf; made of herbs.

herbula, -ae *f* little herb.

hercīscō, -ere *vt* to divide an inheritance.

hercle *interj* by Hercules!

herctum, -ī *nt* inheritance.

Hercule *interj* by Hercules!

Herculēs, -is *and* **ī** *m* mythical Greek hero, later deified.

Herculeus *adj*: **arbor ~** poplar; **urbs ~** Herculaneum.

here *etc see* **herī.**

hērēditārius *adj* inherited; about an inheritance.

hērēditās, -ātis *f* inheritance; **~ sine sacrīs** a gift without awkward obligations.

hērēdium, -ī *and* **iī** *nt* inherited estate.

hērēs, -ēdis *m/f* heir, heiress; (*fig*) master, successor.

herī *adv* yesterday.

herīlis *etc see* **erilis.**

Hermēs, -ae *m* Greek god identified with Mercury; Hermes pillar.

Hernicī, -ōrum *mpl* people of central Italy.

Hernicus *adj see n.*

Hērodotus, -ī *m* first Greek historian.

hērōicus *adj* heroic, epic.

hērōīna, -ae *f* demigoddess.

hērōis, -dis *f* demigoddess.

hērōs, -is *m* demigod, hero.

hērōus *adj* heroic, epic.

herus *etc see* **erus.**

Hēsiodēus, -ius *adj see n.*
Hēsiodus, -ī *m* Hesiod (*Greek didactic poet*).
Hesperia, -iae *f* Italy; Spain.
Hesperides, -idum *fpl keepers of a garden in the far West.*
Hesperius, -is *adj* western.
Hesperus, -ī *m* evening star.
hesternus *adj* of yesterday.
heu *interj* (*expressing dismay or pain*) oh!, alas!
heus *interj* (*calling attention*) ho!, hallo!
hexameter, -rī *m* hexameter verse.
hexēris, -is *f* ship with six banks of oars.
hiātus, -ūs *m* opening, abyss; open mouth, gaping; (*GRAM*) hiatus.
Hibērēs, -um *mpl* Spaniards.
Hibēria, -iae *f* Spain.
hīberna, -ōrum *ntpl* winter quarters.
hībernācula, -ōrum *ntpl* winter tents.
Hibernia, -ae *f* Ireland.
hībernō, -āre *vi* to winter, remain in winter quarters.
hībernus *adj* winter, wintry.
Hibērus, -icus *adj* Spanish.
Hibērus, -ī *m* river Ebro.
hibīscum, -ī *nt* marsh mallow.
hibrida, hybrida, -ae *m/f* mongrel, half-breed.
hīc, haec, hōc *pron, adj* this; he, she, it; my, the latter, the present; **hīc homō** I; **hōc magis** the more; **hōc est** that is.
hīc *adv* here; herein; (*time*) at this point.
hīce, haece, hōce *emphatic forms of* **hīc, haec, hōc.**
hīcine, haecine, hōcine *emphatic forms of* **hīc, haec, hōc.**
hiemālis *adj* winter, stormy.
hiemō, -āre *vi* to pass the winter; to be wintry, stormy.
hiems, (hiemps), -is *f* winter; stormy weather, cold.
Hierōnymus, -ī *m* Jerome.
Hierosolyma, -ōrum *ntpl* Jerusalem.
Hierosolymārius *adj see n.*
hietō, -āre *vi* to yawn.
hilare *adv see* **hilaris.**
hilaris *adj* cheerful, merry.
hilaritās, -ātis *f* cheerfulness.
hilaritūdō, -inis *f* merriment.
hilarō, -āre *vt* to cheer, gladden.
hilarulus *adj* a gay little thing.
hilarus *etc see* **hilaris.**
hīllae, -ārum *fpl* smoked sausage.
Hīlōtae, -ārum *mpl* Helots (*of Sparta*).
hīlum, -ī *nt* something, a whit.
hinc *adv* from here, hence; on this side; from this source, for this reason; (*time*) henceforth.
hinniō, -īre *vi* to neigh.
hinnītus, -ūs *m* neighing.
hinnuleus, -ī *m* fawn.

hiō, -āre *vi* to be open, gape, yawn; (*speech*) to be disconnected, leave a hiatus ♦ *vt* to sing.
hippagōgī, -ōrum *fpl* cavalry transports.
hippocentaurus, -ī *m* centaur.
hippodromos, -ī *m* racecourse.
Hippolytus, -ī *m* son of Theseus (*slandered by stepmother Phaedra*).
hippomanes, -is *nt* mare's fluid; membrane on foal's forehead.
Hippōnactēus *adj* of Hipponax ♦ *m* iambic verse used by Hipponax.
Hippōnax, -ctis *m* Greek satirist.
hippotoxotae, -ārum *mpl* mounted archers.
hīra, -ae *f* the empty gut.
hircīnus *adj* of a goat.
hircōsus *adj* goatish.
hircus, -ī *m* he-goat; goatish smell.
hirnea, -ae *f* jug.
hirq- *etc see* **hirc-.**
hirsūtus *adj* shaggy, bristly; uncouth.
hirtus *adj* hairy, shaggy; rude.
hirūdō, -inis *f* leech.
hirundinīnus *adj* swallows'.
hirundō, -inis *f* swallow.
hīscō, -ere *vi* to gape; to open the mouth ♦ *vt* to utter.
Hispānia, -iae *f* Spain.
Hispāniēnsis, -us *adj* Spanish.
hispidus *adj* hairy, rough.
Hister, -rī *m* lower Danube.
historia, -ae *f* history, inquiry; story.
historicus *adj* historical ♦ *m* historian.
histricus *adj* of the stage.
histriō, -ōnis *m* actor.
histriōnālis *adj* of an actor.
histriōnia, -ae *f* acting.
hiulcē *adv* with hiatus.
hiulcō, -āre *vt* to split open.
hiulcus *adj* gaping, open; (*speech*) with hiatus.
hodiē *adv* today; nowadays, now; up to the present.
hodiernus *adj* today's.
holitor, -ōris *m* market gardener.
holitōrius *adj* for market gardeners.
holus, -eris *nt* vegetables.
holusculum, -ī *nt* small cabbage.
Homēricus *adj see n.*
Homērus, -ī *m* Greek epic poet, Homer.
homicīda, -ae *m* killer, murderer.
homicīdium, -ī and iī *nt* murder.
homō, -inis *m/f* human being, man; (*pl*) people, the world; (*derogatory*) fellow, creature; **inter ~inēs esse** be alive; see the world.
homullus, -ī, homunciō, -ōnis, homunculus, -ī *m* little man, poor creature, mortal.
honestās, -ātis *f* good character, honourable reputation; sense of honour, integrity;

(*things*) beauty.

honestē *adv* decently, virtuously.

honestō, -āre *vt* to honour, dignify, embellish.

honestus *adj* honoured, respectable; honourable, virtuous; (*appearance*) handsome ♦ *m* gentleman ♦ *nt* virtue, good; beauty.

honor, -ōris *m* honour, esteem; public office, position, preferment; award, tribute, offering; ornament, beauty; ~**ōris causā** out of respect; for the sake of; ~**ōrem praefārī** apologize for a remark.

honōrābilis *adj* a mark of respect.

honōrārius *adj* done out of respect, honorary.

honōrātē *adv* honourably.

honōrātus *adj* esteemed, distinguished; in high office; complimentary.

honōrificē *adv* in complimentary terms.

honōrificus *adj* complimentary.

honōrō, -āre, -āvī, -ātum *vt* to do honour to, embellish.

honōrus *adj* complimentary.

honōs *etc see* **honor.**

hōra, -ae *f* hour; time, season; (*pl*) clock; **in ~ās** hourly; **in ~am vīvere** ≈ *live from hand to mouth.*

hōraeum, -ī *nt* pickle.

Horātius, -ī *m* Roman family name (*esp the defender of Rome against Porsenna); the lyric poet Horace.*

Horātius *adj see n.*

hordeum, -ī *nt* barley.

horia, -ae *f* fishing smack.

hōrnō *adv* this year.

hōrnōtinus *adj* this year's.

hōrnus *adj* this year's.

hōrologium, -ī and iī *nt* clock.

horrendus *adj* fearful, terrible; awesome.

horrēns, -entis *pres p of* **horreō** ♦ *adj* bristling, shaggy.

horreō, -ēre, -uī *vi* to stand stiff, bristle; to shiver, shudder, tremble ♦ *vt* to dread; to be afraid, be amazed.

horrēscō, -ere *vi* to stand on end, become rough; to begin to quake; to start, be terrified ♦ *vt* to dread.

horreum, -ī *nt* barn, granary, store.

horribilis *adj* terrifying; amazing.

horridē *adv see* **horridus.**

horridulus *adj* protruding a little; unkempt; (*fig*) uncouth.

horridus *adj* bristling, shaggy, rough, rugged; shivering; (*manners*) rude, uncouth; frightening.

horrifer, -ī *adj* chilling; terrifying.

horrificē *adv* in awesome manner.

horrificō, -āre *vt* to ruffle; to terrify.

horrificus *adj* terrifying.

horrisonus *adj* dread-sounding.

horror, -ōris *m* bristling; shivering, ague; terror, fright, awe, a terror.

hōrsum *adv* this way.

hortāmen, -inis *nt* encouragement.

hortāmentum, -ī *nt* encouragement.

hortātiō, -ōnis *f* harangue, encouragement.

hortātor, -ōris *m* encourager.

hortātus, -ūs *m* encouragement.

Hortēnsius, -ī *m* Roman family name (*esp an orator in Cicero's time*).

hortor, -ārī, -ātus *vt* to urge, encourage, exhort, harangue.

hortulus, -ī *m* little garden.

hortus, -ī *m* garden; (*pl*) park.

hospes, -itis *m*, **hospita, -ae** *f* host, hostess; guest, friend; stranger, foreigner ♦ *adj* strange.

hospitālis *adj* host's, guest's; hospitable.

hospitālitās, -ātis *f* hospitality.

hospitāliter *adv* hospitably.

hospitium, -ī and iī *nt* hospitality, friendship; lodging, inn.

hostia, -ae *f* victim, sacrifice.

hostiātus *adj* provided with victims.

hosticus *adj* hostile; strange ♦ *nt* enemy territory.

hostīlis *adj* of the enemy, hostile.

hostīliter *adv* in hostile manner.

hostīmentum, -ī *nt* recompense.

hostiō, -īre *vt* to requite.

hostis, -is *m/f* enemy.

hūc *adv* hither, here; to this, to such a pitch; ~ **illūc** hither and thither.

hui *interj* (*expressing surprise*) ho!, my word!

hūiusmodī such.

hūmānē, -iter *adv* humanly; gently, politely.

hūmānitās, -ātis *f* human nature, mankind; humanity, kindness, courtesy; culture, refinement.

hūmānitus *adv* in accordance with human nature; kindly.

hūmānus *adj* human, humane, kind, courteous; cultured, refined, well-educated; ~**ō māior** superhuman.

humātiō, -ōnis *f* burying.

hūme-, hūmi- *see* **ūme-, ūmi-.**

humilis *adj* low, low-lying, shallow; (*condition*) lowly, humble, poor; (*language*) commonplace; (*mind*) mean, base.

humilitās, -ātis *f* low position, smallness, shallowness; lowliness, insignificance; meanness, baseness.

humiliter *adv* meanly, humbly.

humō, -āre, -āvī, -ātum *vt* to bury.

humus, -ī *f* earth, ground; land; ~**ī** on the ground.

hyacinthinus *adj* of the hyacinthus.

hyacinthus, -ī *m* iris, lily.

Hyades, -um *fpl* Hyads (*a group of stars in Taurus*).

hyaena, -ae *f* hyena.

hyalus, -ī *m* glass.

Hybla, -ae *f* mountain in Sicily (*famous for bees*).

Hyblaeus *adj see n.*

hybrida *etc see* **hibrida.**

Hydaspēs, -is *m* tributary of river Indus (*now* Jelum).

Hydra, -ae *f* hydra (*a mythical dragon with seven heads*).

hydraulus, -ī *m* water organ.

hydria, -ae *f* ewer.

Hydrochous, -ī *m* Aquarius.

hydrōpicus *adj* suffering from dropsy.

hydrōps, -is *m* dropsy.

hydrus, -ī *m* serpent.

Hylās, -ae *m* a youth loved by Hercules.

Hymēn, -enis, Hymenaeus, -ī *m* god of marriage; wedding song; wedding.

Hymettius *adj see n.*

Hymettus, -ī *m* mountain near Athens (*famous for honey and marble*).

Hypanis, -is *m* river of Sarmatia (*now* Bug).

Hyperboreī, -ōrum *mpl* fabulous people in the far North.

Hyperboreus *adj see n.*

Hyperīōn, -onis *m* father of the Sun; the Sun.

hypodidasculus, -ī *m* assistant teacher.

hypomnēma, -tis *nt* memorandum.

Hyrcānī, -ōrum *mpl* people on the Caspian Sea.

Hyrcānus *adj* Hyrcanian.

I, i

Iacchus, -ī *m* Bacchus; wine.

iaceō, -ēre, -uī *vi* to lie; to be ill, lie dead; (*places*) to be situated, be flat *or* low-lying, be in ruins; (*dress*) to hang loose; (*fig*) to be inactive, be downhearted; (*things*) to be dormant, neglected, despised.

iaciō, -ere, iēcī, iactum *vt* to throw; to lay, build; (*seed*) to sow; (*speech*) to cast, let fall, mention.

iactāns, -antis *pres p of* **iactō** ♦ *adj* boastful.

iactanter *adv* ostentatiously.

iactantia, -ae *f* boasting, ostentation.

iactātiō, -ōnis *f* tossing, gesticulation; boasting, ostentation; ~ **populāris** publicity.

iactātus, -ūs *m* waving.

iactitō, -āre *vt* to mention, bandy.

iactō, -āre, -āvī, -ātum *vt* to throw, scatter; to shake, toss about; (*mind*) to disquiet; (*ideas*) to consider, discuss, mention; (*speech*) to boast of; **sē ~** waver, fluctuate; to behave ostentatiously, be officious.

iactūra, -ae *f* throwing overboard; loss, sacrifice.

iactus *ppp of* **iaciō**.

iactus, -ūs *m* throwing, throw; **intrā tēlī iactum** within spear's range.

iacuī *perf of* **iaceō**.

iaculābilis *adj* missile.

iaculātor, -ōris *m* thrower, shooter; light-armed soldier.

iaculātrīx, -īcis *f* huntress.

iaculor, -ārī, -ātus *vt* to throw, hurl, shoot; to throw the javelin; to shoot at, hit; (*fig*) to aim at, attack.

iaculum, -ī *nt* javelin; fishing net.

iāien- *etc see* **iēn-**.

iam *adv* (*past*) already, by then; (*present*) now, already; (*future*) directly, very soon; (*emphasis*) indeed, precisely; (*inference*) therefore, then surely; (*transition*) moreover, next; **iam dūdum** for a long time, long ago; immediately; **iam iam** right now, any moment now; **non ~** no longer; **iam ... iam** at one time ... at another; **iam nunc** just now; **iam prīdem** long ago, for a long time; **iam tum** even at that time; **sī iam** supposing for the purpose of argument.

iambēus *adj* iambic.

iambus, -ī *m* iambic foot; iambic poetry.

lānālis *adj see* **lānus**.

lāniculum, -ī *nt* Roman hill across the Tiber.

iānitor, -ōris *m* doorkeeper, porter.

iānua, -ae *f* door; entrance; (*fig*) key.

lānuārius *adj* of January ♦ *m* January.

lānus, -ī *m* god of gateways and beginnings; archway, arcade.

lapetīonidēs, -ae *m* Atlas.

lapetus, -ī *m* a Titan (*father of Atlas and Prometheus*).

lāpyx, -gis *adj* Iapygian; Apulian ♦ *m* west-north-west wind from Apulia.

lāsōn, -onis *m* Jason (*leader of Argonauts, husband of Medea*).

lāsonius *adj see n.*

iaspis, -dis *f* jasper.

lbēr- *etc see* **Hībēr-**.

ibi *adv* there; then; in this, at it.

ibīdem *adv* in the same place; at that very moment.

lbis, -is *and* **idis** *f* ibis.

Icarium, -ī *nt* Icarian Sea.

Icarius *adj see n.*

Icarus, -ī *m* son of Daedalus (*drowned in the Aegean*).

īcō, -ere, -ī, ictum *vt* to strike; **foedus ~** make a treaty.

ictericus *adj* jaundiced.

ictis, -dis *f* weasel.

ictus *ppp of* **īcō**.

ictus, -ūs *m* stroke, blow; wound; (*metre*) beat.

Īda, -ae, -ē, -ēs *f* mountain in Crete; mountain near Troy.

Īdaeus *adj* Cretan; Trojan.

idcircō *adv* for that reason; for the purpose.

Noun declensions and verb conjugations are shown on pp xiii to xxv. The present infinitive ending of a verb shows to which conjugation it belongs: **-āre** = 1st; **-ēre** = 2nd; **-ere** = 3rd and **-īre** = 4th. Irregular verbs are shown on p xxvi

īdem, eadem, idem *pron* the same; also, likewise.

identidem *adv* repeatedly, again and again.

ideō *adv* therefore, for this reason, that is why.

idiōta, -ae *m* ignorant person, layman.

īdōlon, -ī *nt* apparition.

idōneē *adv see* **idōneus**.

idōneus *adj* fit, proper, suitable, sufficient.

Īdūs, -uum *fpl* Ides (*the 15th March, May, July, October, the 13th of other months*).

iēcī *perf of* **iaciō**.

iecur, -oris *and* **inoris** *nt* liver; (*fig*) passion.

iecusculum, -ī *nt* small liver.

iēiūniōsus *adj* hungry.

iēiūnitās, -ātis *f* fasting; (*fig*) meagreness.

iēiūnium, -ī *and* **iī** *nt* fast; hunger; leanness.

iēiūnus *adj* fasting, hungry; (*things*) barren, poor, meagre; (*style*) feeble.

iēntāculum, -ī *nt* breakfast.

igitur *adv* therefore, then, so.

ignārus *adj* ignorant, unaware; unknown.

ignāvē, -iter *adv* without energy.

ignāvia, -ae *f* idleness, laziness; cowardice.

ignāvus *adj* idle, lazy, listless; cowardly; relaxing.

ignēscō, -ere *vi* to take fire, burn.

igneus *adj* burning, fiery.

igniculus, -ī *m* spark; (*fig*) fire, vehemence.

ignifer, -ī *adj* fiery.

ignigena, -ae *m* the fireborn (Bacchus).

ignipēs, -edis *adj* fiery-footed.

ignipotēns, -entis *adj* fire-working (Vulcan).

ignis, -is *m* fire, a fire; firebrand, lightning; brightness, redness; (*fig*) passion, love.

ignōbilis *adj* unknown, obscure; low-born.

ignōbilitās, -ātis *f* obscurity; low birth.

ignōminia, -ae *f* dishonour, disgrace.

ignōminiōsus *adj* (*person*) degraded, disgraced; (*things*) shameful.

ignōrābilis *adj* unknown.

ignōrantia, -ae *f* ignorance.

ignōrātiō, -ōnis *f* ignorance.

ignōrō, -āre, -āvī, -ātum *vt* to not know, be unacquainted with; to disregard.

ignōscō, -scere, -vī, -tum *vt, vi* to forgive, pardon.

ignōtus *adj* unknown; low-born; ignorant.

īlex, -icis *f* holm oak.

īlia, -um *ntpl* groin; entrails; ~ **dūcere** become broken-winded.

Īlia, -ae *f* mother of Romulus and Remus.

Īliadēs, -adae *m* son of Ilia; Trojan.

Īlias, -dis *f* the Iliad; a Trojan woman.

īlicet *adv* it's all over, let us go; immediately.

īlicō *adv* on the spot; instantly.

īlignus *adj* of holm oak.

Īlithyia, -ae *f* Greek goddess of childbirth.

Īlium, -on, -ī *nt*, **-os, -ī** *f* Troy.

Īlius, -acus *adj* Trojan.

illā *adv* that way.

illābefactus *adj* unbroken.

illābor, -bī, -psus *vi* to flow into, fall down.

illabōrō, -āre *vi* to work (at).

illāc *adv* that way.

illacessītus *adj* unprovoked.

illacrimābilis *adj* unwept; inexorable.

illacrimō, -āre; -or, -ārī *vi* to weep over, lament; to weep.

illaesus *adj* unhurt.

illaetābilis *adj* cheerless.

illāpsus *ppa of* **illābor**.

illaqueō, -āre *vt* to ensnare.

illātus *ppp of* **īnferō**.

illaudātus *adj* wicked.

ille, -a, -ud *pron and adj* that, that one; he, she, it; the famous; the former, the other; **ex ~ō** since then.

illecebra, -ae *f* attraction, lure, bait, decoy bird.

illecebrōsus *adj* seductive.

illectus *ppp of* **illiciō**.

illēctus *adj* unread.

illepidē *adv see* **illepidus**.

illepidus *adj* inelegant, churlish.

illex, -icis *m/f* lure.

illēx, -ēgis *adj* lawless.

illexī *perf of* **illiciō**.

illībātus *adj* unimpaired.

illīberālis *adj* ungenerous, mean, disobliging.

illīberālitās, -ātis *f* meanness.

illīberāliter *adv see* **illīberālis**.

illic, -aec, -ūc *pron* he, she, it; that.

illīc *adv* there, yonder; in that matter.

illiciō, -icere, -exī, -ectum *vt* to seduce, decoy, mislead.

illicitātor, -ōris *m* sham bidder (at an auction).

illicitus *adj* unlawful.

illīdō, -dere, -sī, -sum *vt* to strike, dash against.

illigō, -āre, -āvī, -ātum *vt* to fasten on, attach; to connect; to impede, encumber, oblige.

illim *adv* from there.

illīmis *adj* clear.

illinc *adv* from there; on that side.

illinō, -inere, -ēvī, -itum *vt* to smear over, cover, bedaub.

illiquefactus *adj* melted.

illīsī *perf of* **illīdō**.

illisus *ppp of* **illīdō**.

illitterātus *adj* uneducated, uncultured.

illitus *ppp of* **illinō**.

illō *adv* (to) there; to that end.

illōtus *adj* dirty.

illūc *adv* (to) there; to that; to him/her.

illūceō, -ēre *vi* to blaze.

illūcēscō, -cēscere, -xī *vi* to become light, dawn.

illūdō, -dere, -sī, -sum *vt, vi* to play, amuse oneself; to abuse; to jeer at, ridicule.

illūminātē *adv* luminously.

illūminō, -āre, -āvī, -ātum *vt* to light up; to enlighten; to embellish.

illūsiō, -ōnis *f* irony.

illūstris *adj* bright, clear; distinct, manifest;

distinguished, illustrious.
illūstrō, -āre, -āvī, -ātum vt to illuminate; to make clear, explain; to make famous.
illūsus ppp of **illūdō**.
illuviēs, -ēī f dirt, filth; floods.
Illyria, -ae f, **-cum, -cī** nt Illyria.
Illyricus, -us adj see **Illyricum**.
Illyriī, -ōrum mpl people E. of the Adriatic.
Ilva, -ae f Italian island (now Elba).
imāginārius adj fancied.
imāginātiō, -ōnis f fancy.
imāginor, -ārī, vt to picture to oneself.
imāgō, -inis f likeness, picture, statue; portrait of ancestor; apparition, ghost; echo, mental picture, idea; (fig) semblance, mere shadow; (RHET) comparison.
imbēcillē adv faintly.
imbēcillitās, -ātis f weakness, helplessness.
imbēcillus adj weak, frail; helpless.
imbellis adj non-combatant; peaceful; cowardly.
imber, -ris m rain, heavy shower; water; (fig) stream, shower.
imberbis, imberbus adj beardless.
imbibō, -ere, -ī vt (mind) to conceive; to resolve.
imbrex, -icis f tile.
imbricus adj rainy.
imbrifer, -ī adj rainy.
imbuō, -uere, -uī, -ūtum vt to wet, steep, dip; (fig) to taint, fill; to inspire, accustom, train; to begin, be the first to explore.
imitābilis adj imitable.
imitāmen, -inis nt imitation; likeness.
imitāmenta, -ōrum ntpl pretence.
imitātiō, -ōnis f imitation.
imitātor,-ōris m, **-rīx,-rīcis** f imitator.
imitātus adj copied.
imitor, -ārī, -ātus vt to copy, portray; to imitate, act like.
immadēscō, -ēscere, -uī vi to become wet.
immāne adv savagely.
immānis adj enormous, vast; monstrous, savage, frightful.
immānitās, -ātis f vastness; savageness, barbarism.
immānsuētus adj wild.
immātūritās, -ātis f over-eagerness.
immātūrus adj untimely.
immedicābilis adj incurable.
immemor, -is adj unmindful, forgetful, negligent.
immemorābilis adj indescribable, not worth mentioning.
immemorātus adj hitherto untold.
immēnsitās, -ātis f immensity.
immēnsum, -ī nt infinity, vast extent ♦ adv exceedingly.
immēnsus adj immeasurable, vast, unending.
immerēns, -entis adj undeserving.

immergō, -gere, -sī, -sum vt to plunge, immerse.
immeritō adv unjustly.
immeritus adj undeserving, innocent; undeserved.
immērsābilis adj never foundering.
immērsus ppp of **immergō**.
immētātus adj unmeasured.
immigrō, -āre, -āvī, -ātum vi to move (into).
immineō, -ēre, -uī vi to overhang, project; to be near, adjoin, impend; to threaten, be a menace to; to long for, grasp at.
imminuō, -uere, -uī, -ūtum vt to lessen, shorten; to impair; to encroach on, ruin.
imminūtiō, -ōnis f mutilation; (RHET) understatement.
immisceō, -scēre, -scuī, -xtum vt to intermingle, blend; **sē ~** join, meddle with.
immiserābilis adj unpitied.
immisericorditer adv unmercifully.
immisericors, -dis adj pitiless.
immissiō, -ōnis f letting grow.
immissus ppp of **immittō**.
immītis adj unripe; severe, inexorable.
immittō, -ittere, -īsī, -issum vt to let in, put in; to graft on; to let go, let loose, let grow; to launch, throw; to incite, set on.
immīxtus ppp of **immisceō**.
immo adv (correcting preceding words) no, yes; on the contrary, or rather; **~ sī** ah, if only.
immōbilis adj motionless; immovable.
immoderātē adv extravagantly.
immoderātiō, -ōnis f excess.
immoderātus adj limitless; excessive, unbridled.
immodestē adv extravagantly.
immodestia, -ae f license.
immodestus adj immoderate.
immodicē adv see **immodicus**.
immodicus adj excessive, extravagant, unruly.
immodulātus adj unrhythmical.
immolātiō, -ōnis f sacrifice.
immolātor, -ōris m sacrificer.
immōlītus adj erected.
immolō, -āre, -āvī, -ātum vt to sacrifice; to slay.
immorior, -ī, -tuus vi to die upon; to waste away.
immorsus adj bitten; (fig) stimulated.
immortālis adj immortal, everlasting.
immortālitās, -ātis f immortality; lasting fame.
immortāliter adv infinitely.
immōtus adj motionless, unmoved, immovable.
immūgiō, -īre, -iī vi to roar (in).
immulgeō, -ēre vt to milk.
immundus adj unclean, dirty.
immūniō, -īre, -īvī vt to strengthen.

immūnis adj with no public obligations, untaxed, free from office; exempt, free (from).

immūnitās, -ātis f exemption, immunity, privilege.

immūnītus adj undefended; (roads) unmetalled.

immurmurō, -āre vi to murmur (at).

immūtābilis adj unalterable.

immūtābilitās, -ātis f immutability.

immūtātiō, -ōnis f exchange; (RHET) metonymy.

immūtātus adj unchanged.

immūtō, -āre, -āvī, -ātum vt to change; (words) to substitute by metonymy.

impācātus adj aggressive.

impāctus ppp of **impingō**.

impār, -aris adj unequal, uneven, unlike; no match for, inferior; (metre) elegiac.

imparātus adj unprepared, unprovided.

impariter adv unequally.

impāstus adj hungry.

impatiēns, -entis adj unable to endure, impatient.

impatienter adv intolerably.

impatientia, -ae f want of endurance.

impavidē adv see **impavidus**.

impavidus adj fearless, undaunted.

impedīmentum, -ī nt hindrance, obstacle; (pl) baggage, luggage, supply train.

impediō, -īre, -īvī and iī, -ītum vt to hinder, entangle; to encircle; (fig) to embarrass, obstruct, prevent.

impedītiō, -ōnis f obstruction.

impedītus adj (MIL) hampered with baggage, in difficulties; (place) difficult, impassable; (mind) busy, obsessed.

impēgī perf of **impingō**.

impellō, -ellere, -ulī, -ulsum vt to strike, drive; to set in motion, impel, shoot; to incite, urge on; (fig) to overthrow, ruin.

impendeō, -ēre vi to overhang; to be imminent, threaten.

impendiō adv very much.

impendium, -ī and iī nt expense, outlay; interest on a loan.

impendō, -endere, -endī, -ēnsum vt to weigh out, pay out, spend; (fig) to devote.

impenetrābilis adj impenetrable.

impēnsa, -ae f expense, outlay.

impēnsē adv very much; earnestly.

impēnsus ppp of **impendō** ♦ adj (cost) high, dear; (fig) great, earnest.

imperātor, -ōris m commander-in-chief, general; emperor; chief, master.

imperātōrius adj of a general; imperial.

imperātum, -ī nt order.

imperceptus adj unknown.

impercussus adj noiseless.

imperditus adj not slain.

imperfectus adj unfinished, imperfect.

imperfossus adj not stabbed.

imperiōsus adj powerful, imperial; tyrannical.

imperītē adv awkwardly.

imperītia, -ae f inexperience.

imperītō, -āre vt, vi to rule, command.

imperītus adj inexperienced, ignorant.

imperium, -ī and **iī** nt command, order; mastery, sovereignty, power; military command, supreme authority; empire; (pl) those in command, the authorities.

impermissus adj unlawful.

imperō, -āre, -āvī, -ātum vt, vi to order, command; to requisition, demand; to rule, govern, control; to be emperor.

imperterritus adj undaunted.

impertiō, -īre, -īvī and **iī, -ītum** vt to share, communicate, impart.

imperturbātus adj unruffled.

impervius adj impassable.

impetibilis adj intolerable.

impetis (gen), **-e** (abl) m force; extent.

impetrābilis adj attainable; successful.

impetrātiō, -ōnis f favour.

impetriō, -īre vt to succeed with the auspices.

impetrō, -āre, -āvī, -ātum vt to achieve; to obtain, secure (a request).

impetus, -ūs m attack, onset; charge; rapid motion, rush; (mind) impulse, passion.

impexus adj unkempt.

impiē adv wickedly.

impietās, -ātis f impiety, disloyalty, unfilial conduct.

impiger, -rī adj active, energetic.

impigrē adv see adj.

impigritās, -ātis f energy.

impingō, -ingere, -ēgī, -āctum vt to dash, force against; to force upon; (fig) to bring against, drive.

impiō, -āre vt to make sinful.

impius adj (to gods) impious; (to parents) undutiful; (to country) disloyal; wicked, unscrupulous.

implācābilis adj implacable.

implācābiliter adv see adj.

implācātus adj unappeased.

implacidus adj savage.

impleō, -ēre, -ēvī, -ētum vt to fill; to satisfy; (time, number) to make up, complete; (duty) to discharge, fulfil.

implexus adj entwined; involved.

implicātiō, -ōnis f entanglement.

implicātus adj complicated, confused.

implicītē adv intricately.

implicō, -āre, -āvī and **uī, -ātum** and **itum** vt to entwine, enfold, clasp; (fig) to entangle, involve; to connect closely, join.

implōrātiō, -ōnis f beseeching.

implōrō, -āre, -āvī, -ātum vt to invoke, entreat, appeal to.

implūmis adj unfledged.

impluō, -ere vi to rain upon.

impluvium, -ī and **iī** nt roof-opening of the Roman atrium; rain basin in the atrium.

impolītē adv without ornament.

impolītus *adj* unpolished, inelegant.
impollūtus *adj* unstained.
impōnō, -ōnere, -osuī, -ositum *vt* to put in, lay on, place; to embark; (*fig*) to impose, inflict, assign; to put in charge; (*tax*) to impose; (*with dat*) to impose upon, cheat.
importō, -āre, -āvī, -ātum *vt* to bring in, import; (*fig*) to bring upon, introduce.
importūnē *adv see adj*.
importūnitās, -ātis *f* insolence, ill nature.
importūnus *adj* unsuitable; troublesome; ill-natured, uncivil, bullying.
importuōsus *adj* without a harbour.
impos, -tis *adj* not master (of).
impositus, impostus *ppp of* **impōnō**.
impotēns, -entis *adj* powerless, weak; with no control over; headstrong, violent.
impotenter *adv* weakly; violently.
impotentia, -ae *f* poverty; want of self-control, violence.
impraesentiārum *adv* at present.
imprānsus *adj* fasting, without breakfast.
imprecor, -ārī *vt* to invoke.
impressiō, -ōnis *f* (*MIL*) thrust, raid; (*mind*) impression; (*speech*) emphasis; (*rhythm*) beat.
impressus *ppp of* **imprimō**.
imprīmīs *adv* especially.
imprimō, -imere, -essī, -essum *vt* to press upon, impress, imprint, stamp.
improbātiō, -ōnis *f* blame.
improbē *adv* badly, wrongly; persistently.
improbitās, -ātis *f* badness, dishonesty.
improbō, -āre, -āvī, -ātum *vt* to disapprove, condemn, reject.
improbulus *adj* a little presumptuous.
improbus *adj* bad, inferior (in quality); wicked, perverse, cruel; unruly, persistent, rebellious.
imprōcērus *adj* undersized.
imprōdictus *adj* not postponed.
imprōmptus *adj* unready, slow.
improperātus *adj* lingering.
improsper, -ī *adj* unsuccessful.
improsperē *adv* unfortunately.
imprōvidē *adv see adj*.
imprōvidus *adj* unforeseeing, thoughtless.
imprōvīsus *adj* unexpected; ~ō, de ~ō, ex ~ō unexpectedly.
imprūdēns, -entis *adj* unforeseeing, not expecting; ignorant, unaware.
imprūdenter *adv* thoughtlessly, unawares.
imprūdentia, -ae *f* thoughtlessness; ignorance; aimlessness.
impūbēs, -eris *and* **is** *adj* youthful; chaste.
impudēns, -entis *adj* shameless, impudent.
impudenter *adv see adj*.
impudentia, -ae *f* impudence.
impudīcitia, -ae *f* lewdness.
impudīcus *adj* shameless; immodest.

impugnātiō, -ōnis *f* assault.
impugnō, -āre, -āvī, -ātum *vt* to attack; (*fig*) to oppose, impugn.
impulī *perf of* **impellō**.
impulsiō, -ōnis *f* pressure; (*mind*) impulse.
impulsor, -ōris *m* instigator.
impulsus *ppp of* **impellō**.
impulsus, -ūs *m* push, pressure, impulse; (*fig*) instigation.
impūne *adv* safely, with impunity.
impūnitās, -ātis *f* impunity.
impūnītē *adv* with impunity.
impūnītus *adj* unpunished.
impūrātus *adj* vile.
impūrē *adv see adj*.
impūritās, -ātis *f* uncleanness.
impūrus *adj* unclean; infamous, vile.
imputātus *adj* unpruned.
imputō, -āre, -āvī, -ātum *vt* to put to one's account; to ascribe, credit, impute.
īmulus *adj* little tip of.
īmus *adj* lowest, deepest, bottom of; last.
in *prep* (*with abl*) in, on, at; among; in the case of; (*time*) during; (*with acc*) into, on to, to, towards; against; (*time*) for, till; (*purpose*) for; ~ armīs under arms; ~ equō on horseback; ~ eō esse ut be in the position of; be on the point of; ~ hōrās hourly; ~ modum in the manner of; ~ rem of use; ~ universum in general.
inaccēssus *adj* unapproachable.
inacēscō, -ere *vi* to turn sour.
Īnachidēs, -idae *m* Perseus; Epaphus.
Īnachis, -idis *f* Io.
Īnachius *adj* of Inachus, Argive, Greek.
Īnachus, -ī *m* first king of Argos.
inadsuētus *adj* unaccustomed.
inadūstus *adj* unsinged.
inaedificō, -āre, -āvī, -ātum *vt* to build on, erect; to wall up, block up.
inaequābilis *adj* uneven.
inaequālis *adj* uneven; unequal; capricious.
inaequāliter *adv see adj*.
inaequātus *adj* unequal.
inaequō, -āre *vt* to level up.
inaestimābilis *adj* incalculable; invaluable; valueless.
inaestuō, -āre *vi* to rage in.
inamābilis *adj* hateful.
inamārēscō, -ere *vi* to become bitter.
inambitiōsus *adj* unambitious.
inambulātiō, -ōnis *f* walking about.
inambulō, -āre *vi* to walk up and down.
inamoenus *adj* disagreeable.
inanimus *adj* lifeless, inanimate.
ināniō, -īre *vt* to make empty.
inānis *adj* empty, void; poor, unsubstantial; useless, worthless, vain, idle ♦ *nt* (*PHILOS*) space; (*fig*) vanity.
inānitās, -ātis *f* empty space; inanity.

Noun declensions and verb conjugations are shown on pp xiii to xxv. The present infinitive ending of a verb shows to which conjugation it belongs: **-āre** = 1st; **-ēre** = 2nd; **-ere** = 3rd and **-īre** = 4th. Irregular verbs are shown on p xxvi

ināniter *adv* idly, vainly.

inarātus *adj* fallow.

inārdēscō, -dēscere, -sī *vi* to be kindled, flare up.

inass- *etc see* **inads-**.

inattenuātus *adj* undiminished.

inaudāx, -ācis *adj* timorous.

inaudiō, -īre *vt* to hear of, learn.

inaudītus *adj* unheard of, unusual; without a hearing.

inaugurātō *adv* after taking the auspices.

inaugurō, -āre *vi* to take auspices ♦ *vt* to consecrate, inaugurate.

inaurēs, -ium *fpl* earrings.

inaurō, -āre, -āvi, -ātum *vt* to gild; (*fig*) to enrich.

inauspicātō *adv* without taking the auspices.

inauspicātus *adj* done without auspices.

inausus *adj* unattempted.

incaeduus *adj* uncut.

incalēscō, -ēscere, -uī *vi* to grow hot; (*fig*) to warm, glow.

incalfaciō, -ere *vt* to heat.

incallidē *adv* unskilfully.

incallidus *adj* stupid, simple.

incandēscō, -ēscere, -uī *vi* to become hot; to turn white.

incānēscō, -ēscere, -uī *vi* to grow grey.

incantātus *adj* enchanted.

incānus *adj* grey.

incassum *adv* in vain.

incastīgātus *adj* unrebuked.

incautē *adv* negligently.

incautus *adj* careless, heedless; unforeseen, unguarded.

incēdō, -ēdere, -ēssī, -ēssum *vi* to walk, parade, march; (MIL) to advance; (*feelings*) to come upon.

incelebrātus *adj* not made known.

incēnātus *adj* supperless.

incendiārius, -ī *and* **iī** *m* incendiary.

incendium, -ī *and* **iī** *nt* fire, conflagration; heat; (*fig*) fire, vehemence, passion.

incendō, -ere, -ī, incēnsum *vt* to set fire to, burn; to light, brighten; (*fig*) to inflame, rouse, incense.

incēnsiō, -ōnis *f* burning.

incēnsus *ppp of* **incendō**.

incēnsus *adj* not registered.

incēpī *perf of* **incipiō**.

inceptiō, -ōnis *f* undertaking.

inceptō, -āre *vt* to begin, attempt.

inceptor, -ōris *m* originator.

inceptum, -ī *nt* beginning, undertaking, attempt.

inceptus *ppp of* **incipiō**.

incērō, -āre *vt* to cover with wax.

incertō *adv* not for certain.

incertus *adj* uncertain, doubtful, unsteady ♦ *nt* uncertainty.

incēssō, -ere, -īvī *vt* to attack; (*fig*) to assail.

incēssus, -ūs *m* gait, pace, tramp; invasion; approach.

incestē *adv see adj*.

incestō, -āre *vt* to pollute, dishonour.

incestus *adj* sinful; unchaste, incestuous ♦ *nt* incest.

incestus, -ūs *m* incest.

incho- *etc see* **incoh-**.

incidō, -idere, -idī, -āsum *vi* to fall upon, fall into; to meet, fall in with, come across; to befall, occur, happen; **in mentem ~** occur to one.

incīdō, -dere, -dī, -sum *vt* to cut open; to cut up; to engrave, inscribe; to interrupt, cut short.

incīle, -is *nt* ditch.

incīlō, -āre *vt* to rebuke.

incingō, -gere, -xī, -ctum *vt* to gird, wreathe; to surround.

incinō, -ere *vt* to sing, play.

incipiō, -ipere, -ēpī, -eptum *vt, vi* to begin.

incipissō, -ere *vt* to begin.

incīsē *adv* in short clauses.

incīsim *adv* in short clauses.

incīsiō, -ōnis *f* clause.

incīsum, -ī *nt* clause.

incīsus *ppp of* **incīdō**.

incitāmentum, -ī *nt* incentive.

incitātē *adv* impetuously.

incitātiō, -ōnis *f* inciting; rapidity.

incitātus *ppp of* **incitō** ♦ *adj* swift, rapid; **equō ~ō** at a gallop.

incitō, -āre, -āvī, -ātum *vt* to urge on, rush; to rouse, encourage, excite; to inspire; to increase; **sē ~** rush; **currentem ~** ≈ *spur a willing horse*.

incitus *adj* swift.

incitus *adj* immovable; **ad ~ās, ~a redigere** bring to a standstill.

inclāmō, -āre *vt, vi* to call out, cry out to; to scold, abuse.

inclārēscō, -ēscere, -uī *vi* to become famous.

inclēmēns, -entis *adj* severe.

inclēmenter *adv* harshly.

inclēmentia, -ae *f* severity.

inclīnātiō, -ōnis *f* leaning, slope; (*fig*) tendency, inclination, bias; (CIRCS) change; (*voice*) modulation.

inclīnātus *adj* inclined, prone; falling; (*voice*) deep.

inclīnō, -āre, -āvī, -ātum *vt* to bend, turn; to turn back; (*fig*) to incline, direct, transfer; to change ♦ *vi* to bend, sink; (MIL) to give way; (*fig*) to change, deteriorate; to incline, tend, turn in favour.

inclitus *etc see* **inclutus**.

inclūdō, -dere, -sī, -sum *vt* to shut in, keep in, enclose; to obstruct, block; (*fig*) to include; (*time*) to close, end.

inclūsiō, -ōnis *f* imprisonment.

inclūsus *ppp of* **inclūdō**.

inclutus *adj* famous, glorious.

incoctus *ppp of* **incoquō**.

incoctus *adj* uncooked, raw.

incōgitābilis *adj* thoughtless.

incōgitāns, -antis *adj* thoughtless.
incōgitantia, -ae *f* thoughtlessness.
incōgitō, -āre *vt* to contrive.
incognitus *adj* unknown, unrecognised; (*law*) untried.
incohātus *adj* unfinished.
incohō, -āre, -āvī, -ātum *vt* to begin, start.
incola, -ae *f* inhabitant, resident.
incolō, -ere, -uī *vt* to live in, inhabit ♦ *vi* to live, reside.
incolumis *adj* safe and sound, unharmed.
incolumitās, -ātis *f* safety.
incomitātus *adj* unaccompanied.
incommendātus *adj* unprotected.
incommodē *adv* inconveniently, unfortunately.
incommoditās, -ātis *f* inconvenience, disadvantage.
incommodō, -āre *vi* to be inconvenient, annoy.
incommodum, -ī *nt* inconvenience, disadvantage, misfortune.
incommodus *adj* inconvenient, troublesome.
incommūtābilis *adj* unchangeable.
incompertus *adj* unknown.
incompositē *adv see adj.*
incompositus *adj* in disorder, irregular.
incōmptus *adj* undressed, inelegant.
inconcessus *adj* forbidden.
inconciliō, -āre *vt* to win over (by guile); to trick, inveigle, embarrass.
inconcinnus *adj* inartistic, awkward.
inconcussus *adj* unshaken, stable.
inconditē *adv* confusedly.
inconditus *adj* undisciplined, not organised; (*language*) artless.
incōnsīderātē *adv see adj.*
incōnsīderātus *adj* thoughtless, ill-advised.
incōnsōlābilis *adj* incurable.
incōnstāns, -antis *adj* fickle, inconsistent.
incōnstanter *adv* inconsistently.
incōnstantia, -ae *f* fickleness, inconsistency.
incōnsultē *adv* indiscreetly.
incōnsultū without consulting.
incōnsultus *adj* indiscreet, ill-advised; unanswered; not consulted.
incōnsūmptus *adj* unconsumed.
incontāminātus *adj* untainted.
incontentus *adj* untuned.
incontinēns, -entis *adj* intemperate.
incontinenter *adv* without self-control.
incontinentia, -ae *f* lack of self-control.
inconveniēns, -entis *adj* ill-matched.
incoquō, -quere, -xī, -ctum *vt* to boil; to dye.
incorrēctus *adj* unrevised.
incorruptē *adv* justly.
incorruptus *adj* unspoiled; uncorrupted, genuine.
incrēbrēscō, incrēbēscō, -ēscere, -uī *vi* to increase, grow, spread.

incrēdibilis *adj* incredible, extraordinary.
incrēdibiliter *adv see adj.*
incrēdulus *adj* incredulous.
incrēmentum, -ī *nt* growth, increase; addition; offspring.
increpitō, -āre *vt* to rebuke; to challenge.
increpō, -āre, -uī, -itum *vi* to make a noise, sound; (*news*) to be noised abroad ♦ *vt* to cause to make a noise; to exclaim against, rebuke.
incrēscō, -scere, -vī *vi* to grow in, increase.
incrētus *adj* sifted in.
incruentātus *adj* unstained with blood.
incruentus *adj* bloodless, without bloodshed.
incrūstō, -āre *vt* to encrust.
incubō, -āre, -uī, -itum *vi* to lie in or on; (*fig*) to brood over.
incubuī *perf of* **incubō**; *perf of* **incumbō**.
inculcō, -āre, -āvī, -ātum *vt* to force in; to force upon, impress on.
inculpātus *adj* blameless.
incultē *adv* uncouthly.
incultus *adj* uncultivated; (*fig*) neglected, uneducated, rude.
incultus, -ūs *m* neglect, squalor.
incumbō, -mbere, -buī, -bitum *vi* to lean, recline on; to fall upon, throw oneself upon; to oppress, lie heavily upon; (*fig*) to devote attention to, take pains with; to incline.
incūnābula, -ōrum *ntpl* swaddling clothes; (*fig*) cradle, infancy, birthplace, origin.
incūrātus *adj* neglected.
incūria, -ae *f* negligence.
incūriōsē *adv* carelessly.
incūriōsus *adj* careless, indifferent.
incurrō, -rrere, -rrī *and* **curri, -rsum** *vi* to run into, rush, attack; to invade; to meet with, get involved in; (*events*) to occur, coincide.
incursiō, -ōnis *f* attack; invasion, raid; collision.
incursō, -āre *vt, vi* to run into, assault; to frequently invade; (*fig*) to meet, strike.
incursus, -ūs *m* assault, striking; (*mind*) impulse.
incurvō, -āre *vt* to bend, crook.
incurvus *adj* bent, crooked.
incūs, -ūdis *f* anvil.
incūsātiō, -ōnis *f* blaming.
incūsō, -āre, -āvī, -ātum *vt* to find fault with, accuse.
incussī *perf of* **incutiō**.
incussus *ppp of* **incutiō**.
incussus, -ūs *m* shock.
incustōdītus *adj* unguarded, unconcealed.
incūsus *adj* forged.
incutiō, -tere, -ssī, -ssum *vt* to strike, dash against; to throw; (*fig*) to strike into, inspire with.
indāgātiō, -ōnis *f* search.
indāgātor, -ōris *m* explorer.

Noun declensions and verb conjugations are shown on pp xiii to xxv. The present infinitive ending of a verb shows to which conjugation it belongs: -**āre** = 1st; -**ēre** = 2nd; -**ere** = 3rd and -**īre** = 4th. Irregular verbs are shown on p xxvi

indāgātrīx, -rīcis *f* female explorer.
indāgō, -āre *vt* to track down; (*fig*) to trace, investigate.
indāgō, -inis *f* (*hunt*) drive, encirclement.
indaudiō *etc see* **inaudiō**.
inde *adv* from there, from that, from them; on that side; from then, ever since; after that, then.
indēbitus *adj* not due.
indēclīnātus *adj* constant.
indecor, -is *adj* dishonourable, a disgrace.
indecōrē *adv* indecently.
indecorō, -āre *vt* to disgrace.
indecōrus *adj* unbecoming, unsightly.
indēfēnsus *adj* undefended.
indēfessus *adj* unwearied, tireless.
indēflētus *adj* unwept.
indēiectus *adj* undemolished.
indēlēbilis *adj* imperishable.
indēlībātus *adj* unimpaired.
indemnātus *adj* unconvicted.
indēplōrātus *adj* unlamented.
indēprēnsus *adj* undetected.
indeptus *ppa of* **indipīscor**.
indēsertus *adj* unforsaken.
indēstrictus *adj* unscathed.
indētōnsus *adj* unshorn.
indēvītātus *adj* unerring.
index, -icis *m* forefinger; witness, informer; (*book, art*) title, inscription; (*stone*) touchstone; (*fig*) indication, pointer, sign.
India, -iae *f* India.
indicātiō, -ōnis *f* value.
indīcente mē without my telling.
indicium, -ī *and* **iī** *nt* information, evidence; reward for information; indication, sign, proof; **~ profitērī, offerre** ≈ *turn King's evidence*; **~ postulāre, dare** ask, grant permission to give evidence.
indicō, -āre, -āvī, -ātum *vt* to point out; to disclose, betray; to give information, give evidence; to put a price on.
indīcō, -īcere, -īxī, -ictum *vt* to declare, proclaim, appoint.
indictus *ppp of* **indīcō**.
indictus *adj* not said, unsung; **causā ~ā** without a hearing.
Indicus *adj see n.*
indidem *adv* from the same place *or* thing.
indidī *perf of* **indō**.
indifferēns, -entis *adj* neither good nor bad.
indigena, -ae *m* native ♦ *adj* native.
indigēns, -entis *adj* needy.
indigentia, -ae *f* need; craving.
indigeō, -ēre, -uī *vi* (*with abl*) to need, want, require; to crave.
indiges, -etis *m* national deity.
indīgestus *adj* confused.
indignābundus *adj* enraged.
indignāns, -antis *adj* indignant.
indignātiō, -ōnis *f* indignation.
indignē *adv* unworthily; indignantly.
indignitās, -ātis *f* unworthiness, enormity;

insulting treatment; indignation.
indignor, -ārī, -ātus *vt* to be displeased with, be angry at.
indignus *adj* unworthy, undeserving; shameful, severe; undeserved.
indigus *adj* in want.
indīligēns, -entis *adj* careless.
indīligenter *adv see adj.*
indīligentia, -ae *f* carelessness.
indipīscor, -ī, indeptus *vt* to obtain, get, reach.
indīreptus *adj* unplundered.
indiscrētus *adj* closely connected, indiscriminate, indistinguishable.
indisertē *adv* without eloquence.
indisertus *adj* not eloquent.
indispositus *adj* disorderly.
indissolūbilis *adj* imperishable.
indistinctus *adj* confused, obscure.
inditus *ppp of* **indō**.
indīviduus *adj* indivisible; inseparable ♦ *nt* atom.
indō, -ere, -idī, -itum *vt* to put in *or* on; to introduce; to impart, impose.
indocilis *adj* difficult to teach, hard to learn; untaught.
indoctē *adv* unskilfully.
indoctus *adj* untrained, illiterate, ignorant.
indolentia, -ae *f* freedom from pain.
indolēs, -is *f* nature, character, talents.
indolēscō, -ēscere, -uī *vi* to feel sorry.
indomitus *adj* untamed, wild; ungovernable.
indormiō, -īre *vi* to sleep on; to be careless.
indōtātus *adj* with no dowry; unhonoured; (*fig*) unadorned.
indubitō, -āre *vi* to begin to doubt.
indubius *adj* undoubted.
indūcō, -ūcere, -ūxī, -uctum *vt* to bring in, lead on; to introduce; to overlay, cover over; (*fig*) to move, persuade, seduce; (*book-keeping*) to enter; (*dress*) to put on; (*public show*) to exhibit; (*writing*) to erase; **animum, in animum ~** determine, imagine.
inductiō, -ōnis *f* leading, bringing on; (*mind*) purpose, intention; (*logic*) induction.
inductus *ppp of* **indūcō**.
indugredior *etc see* **ingredior**.
induī *perf of* **induō**.
indulgēns, -entis *pres p of* **indulgeō** ♦ *adj* indulgent, kind.
indulgenter *adv* indulgently.
indulgentia, -ae *f* indulgence, gentleness.
indulgeō, -gēre, -sī *vi* (*with dat*) to be kind to, indulge, give way to; to indulge in ♦ *vt* to concede; **sibi ~** take liberties.
induō, -uere, -uī, -ūtum *vt* (*dress*) to put on; (*fig*) to assume, entangle.
indup- *etc see* **imp-**.
indūrēscō, -ēscere, -uī *vi* to harden.
indūrō, -āre *vt* to harden.
Indus, -ī *m* Indian; Ethiopian; mahout.
Indus *adj see n.*
industria, -ae *f* diligence; **dē, ex ~ā** on

purpose.

industriē *adv see* **industrius.**

industrius *adj* diligent, painstaking.

indūtiae, -ārum *fpl* truce, armistice.

indūtus *ppp of* **induō.**

indūtus, -ūs *m* wearing.

induviae, -ārum *fpl* clothes.

indūxī *perf of* **indūcō.**

inēbriō, -āre *vt* to intoxicate; (*fig*) to saturate.

inedia, -ae *f* starvation.

inēditus *adj* unpublished.

inēlegāns, -antis *adj* tasteless.

inēleganter *adv* without taste.

inēluctābilis *adj* inescapable.

inēmorior, -ī *vi* to die in.

inemptus *adj* unpurchased.

inēnārrābilis *adj* indescribable.

inēnōdābilis *adj* inexplicable.

ineō, -īre, -īvī *and* **iī, -itum** *vi* to go in, come in;
to begin ♦ *vt* to enter; to begin, enter upon,
form, undertake; **cōnsilium ~** form a plan;
grātiam ~ win favour; **numerum ~**
enumerate; **ratiōnem ~** calculate, consider,
contrive; **suffrāgium ~** vote; **viam ~** find out a
way.

ineptē *adv see adj.*

ineptia, -ae *f* stupidity; (*pl*) nonsense.

ineptiō, -īre *vi* to play the fool.

ineptus *adj* unsuitable; silly, tactless, absurd.

inermis, inermus *adj* unarmed, defenceless;
harmless.

inerrāns, -antis *adj* fixed.

inerrō, -āre *vi* to wander about in.

iners, -tis *adj* unskilful; inactive, indolent,
timid; insipid.

inertia, -ae *f* lack of skill; idleness, laziness.

inērudītus *adj* uneducated.

inescō, -āre *vt* to entice, deceive.

inēvectus *adj* mounted.

inēvītābilis *adj* inescapable.

inexcītus *adj* peaceful.

inexcūsābilis *adj* with no excuse.

inexercitātus *adj* untrained.

inexhaustus *adj* unexhausted.

inexōrābilis *adj* inexorable; (*things*) severe.

inexperrēctus *adj* unawakened.

inexpertus *adj* inexperienced; untried.

inexpiābilis *adj* inexpiable; implacable.

inexplēbilis *adj* insatiable.

inexplētus *adj* incessant.

inexplicābilis *adj* inexplicable; impracticable,
unending.

inexplōrātō *adv* without making a
reconnaissance.

inexplōrātus *adj* unreconnoitred.

inexpugnābilis *adj* impregnable, safe.

inexspectātus *adj* unexpected.

inexstinctus *adj* unextinguished; insatiable,
imperishable.

inexsuperābilis *adj* insurmountable.

inextrīcābilis *adj* inextricable.

īnfabrē *adv* unskilfully.

īnfabricātus *adj* unfashioned.

infacētus *adj* not witty, crude.

īnfācundus *adj* ineloquent.

īnfāmia, -ae *f* disgrace, scandal.

īnfāmis *adj* infamous, disreputable.

īnfāmō, -āre, -āvī, -ātum *vt* to disgrace,
bring into disrepute.

īnfandus *adj* unspeakable, atrocious.

īnfāns, -antis *adj* mute, speechless; young,
infant; tongue-tied; childish ♦ *m/f* infant,
child.

īnfantia, -ae *f* inability to speak; infancy; lack
of eloquence.

īnfatuō, -āre *vt* to make a fool of.

īnfaustus *adj* unlucky.

īnfector, -ōris *m* dyer.

īnfectus *ppp of* **īnficiō.**

īnfectus *adj* undone, unfinished; **rē ~ā** without
achieving one's purpose.

īnfēcunditās, -ātis *f* infertility.

īnfēcundus *adj* unfruitful.

īnfēlīcitās, -ātis *f* misfortune.

īnfēlīciter *adv see adj.*

īnfēlīcō, -āre *vt* to make unhappy.

īnfēlīx, -īcis *adj* unfruitful; unhappy, unlucky.

īnfēnsē *adv* aggressively.

īnfēnsō, -āre *vt* to make dangerous, make
hostile.

īnfēnsus *adj* hostile, dangerous.

īnferciō, -īre *vt* to cram in.

īnferiae, -ārum *fpl* offerings to the dead.

īnferior, -ōris *compar of* **īnferus.**

īnferius *compar of* **īnfrā.**

īnfernē *adv* below.

īnfernus *adj* beneath; of the lower world,
infernal ♦ *mpl* the shades ♦ *ntpl* the lower
world.

īnferō, -re, intulī, illātum *vt* to carry in,
bring to, put on; to move forward; (*fig*) to
introduce, cause; (*book-keeping*) to enter;
(*logic*) to infer; **bellum ~** make war (on);
pedem ~ advance; **sē ~** repair, rush, strut
about; **signa ~** attack, charge.

īnferus (*compar* **~ior,** *superl* **īnfimus**) *adj* lower,
below ♦ *mpl* the dead, the lower world ♦
compar lower; later; inferior ♦ *superl* lowest,
bottom of; meanest, humblest.

īnfervēscō, -vēscere, -buī *vi* to boil.

īnfestē *adv* aggressively.

īnfestō, -āre *vt* to attack.

īnfestus *adj* unsafe; dangerous, aggressive.

īnficet- *see* **īnfacēt-.**

īnficiō, -icere, -ēcī, -ectum *vt* to dip, dye,
discolour; to taint, infect; (*fig*) to instruct,
corrupt, poison.

īnfidēlis *adj* faithless.

īnfidēlitās, -ātis *f* disloyalty.

īnfidēliter *adv* treacherously.

Noun declensions and verb conjugations are shown on pp xiii to xxv. The present infinitive ending of a verb shows
to which conjugation it belongs: **-āre** = 1st; **-ēre** = 2nd; **-ere** = 3rd and **-īre** = 4th. Irregular verbs are shown on p xxvi

infīdus *adj* unsafe, treacherous.

infīgō, -gere, -xī, -xum *vt* to thrust, drive in; (*fig*) to impress, imprint.

infimus *superl of* **īnferus**.

īnfindō, -ere *vt* to cut into, plough.

īnfinitās, -ātis *f* boundless extent, infinity.

īnfinītē *adv* without end.

īnfinītiō, -ōnis *f* infinity.

īnfinītus *adj* boundless, endless, infinite; indefinite.

īnfirmātiō, -ōnis *f* invalidating, refuting.

īnfirmē *adv* feebly.

īnfirmitās, -ātis *f* weakness; infirmity, sickness.

īnfirmō, -āre *vt* to weaken; to invalidate, refute.

īnfirmus *adj* weak, indisposed; weak-minded; (*things*) trivial.

īnfit *vi* (*defec*) begins.

īnfitiālis *adj* negative.

īnfitiās eō deny.

īnfitiātiō, -ōnis *f* denial.

īnfitiātor, -ōris *m* denier (of a debt).

īnfitior, -ārī, -ātus *vt* to deny, repudiate.

īnfixus *ppp of* **īnfigō**.

īnflammātiō, -ōnis *f* (*fig*) exciting.

īnflammō, -āre, -āvī, -ātum *vt* to set on fire, light; (*fig*) to inflame, rouse.

īnflātē *adv* pompously.

īnflātiō, -ōnis *f* flatulence.

īnflātus, -ūs *m* blow; inspiration ♦ *adj* blown up, swollen; (*fig*) puffed up, conceited; (*style*) turgid.

īnflectō, -ctere, -xī, -xum *vt* to bend, curve; to change; (*voice*) to modulate; (*fig*) to affect, move.

īnflētus *adj* unwept.

īnflexiō, -ōnis *f* bending.

īnflexus *ppp of* **īnflectō**.

īnflīgō, -gere, -xī, -ctum *vt* to dash against, strike; to inflict.

īnflō, -āre, -āvī, -ātum *vt* to blow, inflate; (*fig*) to inspire, puff up.

īnfluō, -ere, -xī, -xum *vi* to flow in; (*fig*) to stream, pour in.

īnfodiō, -odere, -ōdī, -ossum *vt* to dig in, bury.

īnfōrmātiō, -ōnis *f* sketch, idea.

īnfōrmis *adj* shapeless; hideous.

īnfōrmō, -āre, -āvī, -ātum *vt* to shape, fashion; to sketch; to educate.

īnfortūnātus *adj* unfortunate.

īnfortūnium, -ī *and* **ī ī** *nt* misfortune.

īnfossus *ppp of* **īnfodiō**.

īnfrā (*compar* **īnferius**) *adv* underneath, below ♦ *compar* lower down ♦ *prep* (*with acc*) below, beneath, under; later than.

īnfrāctiō, -ōnis *f* weakening.

īnfrāctus *ppp of* **īnfringō**.

īnfragilis *adj* strong.

īnfremō, -ere, -uī *vi* to growl.

īnfrēnātus *ppp of* **īnfrēnō**.

īnfrēnātus *adj* without a bridle.

īnfrendō, -ere *vi* to gnash.

īnfrēnis, -us *adj* unbridled.

īnfrēnō, -āre, -āvī, -ātum *vt* to put a bridle on, harness; (*fig*) to curb.

īnfrequēns, -entis *adj* not crowded, infrequent; badly attended.

īnfrequentia, -ae *f* small number; emptiness.

īnfringō, -ingere, -ēgī, -āctum *vt* to break, bruise; (*fig*) to weaken, break down, exhaust.

īnfrōns, -ondis *adj* leafless.

īnfūcātus *adj* showy.

īnfula, -ae *f* woollen band, fillet, badge of honour.

īnfumus *etc see* **infimus**.

īnfundō, -undere, -ūdī, -ūsum *vt* to pour in *or* on; to serve; (*fig*) to spread.

īnfuscō, -āre *vt* to darken; to spoil, tarnish.

īnfūsus *ppp of* **īnfundō**.

ingeminō, -āre *vt* to redouble ♦ *vi* to be redoubled.

ingemīscō, -īscere, -uī *vi* to groan, sigh ♦ *vt* to sigh over.

ingemō, -ere, -uī *vt*, *vi* to sigh for, mourn.

ingenerō, -āre, -āvī, -ātum *vt* to engender, produce, create.

ingeniātus *adj* with a natural talent.

ingeniōsē *adv* cleverly.

ingeniōsus *adj* talented, clever; (*things*) naturally suited.

ingenitus *ppp of* **ingignō** ♦ *adj* inborn, natural.

ingenium, -ī *and* **i ī** *nt* nature; (*disposition*) bent character; (*intellect*) ability, talent, genius; (*person*) genius.

ingēns, -entis *adj* huge, mighty, great.

ingenuē *adv* liberally, frankly.

ingenuitās, -ātis *f* noble birth, noble character.

ingenuus *adj* native, innate; free-born; noble, frank; delicate.

ingerō, -rere, -ssī, -stum *vt* to carry in; to heap on; to throw, hurl; (*fig*) to press, obtrude.

ingignō, -ignere, -enuī, -enitum *vt* to engender, implant.

inglōrius *adj* inglorious.

ingluviēs, -ēī *f* maw; gluttony.

ingrātē *adv* unwillingly; ungratefully.

ingrātiīs, ingrātīs *adv* against one's will.

ingrātus *adj* disagreeable, unwelcome; ungrateful, thankless.

ingravēscō, -ere *vi* to grow heavy, become worse, increase.

ingravō, -āre *vt* to weigh heavily on; to aggravate.

ingredior, -dī, -ssus *vt*, *vi* to go in, enter; to walk, march; to enter upon, engage in; to commence, begin to speak.

ingressiō, -ōnis *f* entrance; beginning; pace.

ingressus, -ūs *m* entrance; (*MIL*) inroad; beginning; walking, gait.

ingruō, -ere, -ī *vi* to fall upon, assail.

inguen, -inis *nt* groin.

ingurgitō, -āre *vt* to pour in; **sē ~** gorge

oneself; (*fig*) to be absorbed in.

ingustātus *adj* untasted.

inhabilis *adj* unwieldy, awkward; unfit.

inhabitābilis *adj* uninhabitable.

inhabitō, -āre *vt* to inhabit.

inhaereō, -rēre, -sī, -sum *vi* to stick in, cling to; to adhere, be closely connected with; to be always in.

inhaerēscō, -ere *vi* to take hold, cling fast.

inhālō, -āre *vt* to breathe on.

inhibeō, -ēre, -uī, -itum *vt* to check, restrain, use, practise; ~ **rēmīs/nāvem** back water.

inhibitiō, -ōnis *f* backing water.

inhiō, -āre *vi* to gape ♦ *vt* to gape at, covet.

inhonestē *adv see adj.*

inhonestō, -āre *vt* to dishonour.

inhonestus *adj* dishonourable, inglorious; ugly.

inhonōrātus *adj* unhonoured; unrewarded.

inhonōrus *adj* defaced.

inhorreō, -ēre, -uī *vt* to stand erect, bristle.

inhorrēscō, -ēscere, -uī *vi* to bristle up; to shiver, shudder, tremble.

inhospitālis *adj* inhospitable.

inhospitālitās, -ātis *f* inhospitality.

inhospitus *adj* inhospitable.

inhūmānē *adv* savagely; uncivilly.

inhūmānitās, -ātis *f* barbarity; discourtesy, churlishness, meanness.

inhūmāniter *adv* = **inhūmānē**.

inhūmānus *adj* savage, brutal; ill-bred, uncivil, uncultured.

inhumātus *adj* unburied.

inibi *adv* there, therein; about to happen.

iniciō, -icere, -iēcī, -iectum *vt* to throw into, put on; (*fig*) to inspire, cause; (*speech*) to hint, mention; **manum ~** take possession.

iniectus, -ūs *m* putting in, throwing over.

inimīcē *adv* hostilely.

inimīcitia, -ae *f* enmity.

inimīcō, -āre *vt* to make enemies.

inimīcus *adj* unfriendly, hostile; injurious ♦ *m/f* enemy; ~**issimus** greatest enemy.

inīquē *adv* unequally, unjustly.

inīquitās, -ātis *f* unevenness; difficulty; injustice, unfair demands.

inīquus *adj* unequal, uneven; adverse, unfavourable, injurious; unfair, unjust; excessive; impatient, discontented ♦ *m* enemy.

initiō, -āre *vt* to initiate.

initium, -ī *and* **iī** *nt* beginning; (*pl*) elements, first principles; holy rites, mysteries.

initus *ppp of* **ineō.**

initus, -ūs *m* approach; beginning.

iniūcundē *adv see adj.*

iniūcunditās, -ātis *f* unpleasantness.

iniūcundus *adj* unpleasant.

iniungō, -ungere, -ūnxī, -ūnctum *vt* to join, attach; (*fig*) to impose, inflict.

iniūrātus *adj* unsworn.

iniūria, -ae *f* wrong, injury, injustice; insult, outrage; severity, revenge; unjust possession; ~**ā** unjustly.

iniūriōsē *adv* wrongfully.

iniūriōsus *adj* unjust, wrongful; harmful.

iniūrius *adj* wrong, unjust.

iniūssū without orders (from).

iniūssus *adj* unbidden.

iniūstē *adv see adj.*

iniūstitia, -ae *f* injustice, severity.

iniūstus *adj* unjust, wrong; excessive, severe.

inl- *etc see* **ill-.**

inm- *etc see* **imm-.**

innābilis *adj* that none may swim.

innāscor, -scī, -tus *vi* to be born in, grow up in.

innatō, -āre *vt* to swim in, float on; to swim, flow into.

innātus *ppa of* **innāscor** ♦ *adj* innate, natural.

innāvigābilis *adj* unnavigable.

innectō, -ctere, -xuī, -xum *vt* to tie, fasten together, entwine; (*fig*) to connect; to contrive.

innītor, -tī, -xus *and* **sus** *vi* to rest, lean on; to depend.

innō, -āre *vi* to swim in, float on, sail on.

innocēns, -entis *adj* harmless; innocent; upright, unselfish.

innocenter *adv* blamelessly.

innocentia, -ae *f* innocence; integrity, unselfishness.

innocuē *adv* innocently.

innocuus *adj* harmless; innocent; unharmed.

innōtēscō, -ēscere, -uī *vi* to become known.

innovō, -āre *vt* to renew; **sē ~** return.

innoxius *adj* harmless, safe; innocent; unharmed.

innuba, -ae *adj* unmarried.

innūbilus *adj* cloudless.

innūbō, -bere, -psī *vi* to marry into.

innumerābilis *adj* countless.

innumerābilitās, -ātis *f* countless number.

innumerābiliter *adv* innumerably.

innumerālis *adj* numberless.

innumerus *adj* countless.

innuō, -ere, -ī *vi* to give a nod.

innūpta, -ae *adj* unmarried.

Īnō, -ūs *f daughter of Cadmus.*

inoblītus *adj* unforgetful.

inobrutus *adj* not overwhelmed.

inobservābilis *adj* unnoticed.

inobservātus *adj* unobserved.

inoffēnsus *adj* without hindrance, uninterrupted.

inofficiōsus *adj* irresponsible; disobliging.

inolēns, -entis *adj* odourless.

inolēscō, -scere, -vī *vi* to grow in.

inōminātus *adj* inauspicious.

inopia, -ae *f* want, scarcity, poverty,

helplessness.

inopīnāns, -antis *adj* unaware.

inopīnātō *adv* unexpectedly.

inopīnātus *adj* unexpected; off one's guard.

inopīnus *adj* unexpected.

inopiōsus *adj* in want.

inops, -is *adj* destitute, poor, in need (of); helpless, weak; (*speech*) poor in ideas.

inōrātus *adj* unpleaded.

inōrdinātus *adj* disordered, irregular.

inōrnātus *adj* unadorned, plain; uncelebrated.

Inōus *adj see* **n**.

inp- *etc see* **imp -**.

inquam *vt* (*defec*) to say; (*emphatic*) I repeat, maintain.

inquiēs, -ētis *adj* restless.

inquiētō, -āre *vt* to unsettle, make difficult.

inquiētus *adj* restless, unsettled.

inquilīnus, -ī *m* inhabitant, tenant.

inquinātē *adv* filthily.

inquinātus *adj* filthy, impure.

inquinō, -āre, -āvī, -ātum *vt* to defile, stain, contaminate.

inquīrō, -rere, -sīvī, -sītum *vt* to search for, inquire into; (*law*) to collect evidence.

inquīsītiō, -ōnis *f* searching, inquiry; (*law*) inquisition.

inquīsītor, -ōris *m* searcher, spy; investigator.

inquīsītus *ppp of* **inquīrō**.

inquīsītus *adj* not investigated.

inr- *etc see* **irr-**.

īnsalūtātus *adj* ungreeted.

īnsānābilis *adj* incurable.

īnsānē *adv* madly.

īnsānia, -ae *f* madness; folly, mania, poetic rapture.

īnsāniō, -īre, -īvī, -ītum *vi* to be mad, rave; to rage; to be inspired.

īnsānitās, -ātis *f* unhealthiness.

īnsānum *adv* (*slang*) frightfully.

īnsānus *adj* mad; frantic, furious; outrageous.

īnsatiābilis *adj* insatiable; never cloying.

īnsatiābiliter *adv see adj*.

īnsatietās, -ātis *f* insatiateness.

īnsaturābilis *adj* insatiable.

īnsaturābiliter *adv see adj*.

īnscendō, -endere, -endī, -ēnsum *vt, vi* to climb up, mount, embark.

īnscēnsiō, -ōnis *f* going on board.

īnscēnsus *ppp of* **īnscendō**.

īnsciēns, -entis *adj* unaware; stupid.

īnscienter *adv* ignorantly.

īnscientia, -ae *f* ignorance, inexperience; neglect.

īnscītē *adv* clumsily.

īnscītia, -ae *f* ignorance, stupidity, inattention.

īnscītus *adj* ignorant, stupid.

īnscius *adj* unaware, ignorant.

īnscrībō, -bere, -psī, -ptum *vt* to write on, inscribe; to ascribe, assign; (*book*) to entitle; (*for sale*) to advertise.

īnscrīptiō, -ōnis *f* inscribing, title.

īnscrīptus *ppp of* **īnscrībō**.

īnsculpō, -ere, -sī, -tum *vt* to carve in, engrave on.

īnsectātiō, -ōnis *f* hot pursuit; (*words*) abusing, persecution.

īnsectātor, -ōris *m* persecutor.

īnsector, -ārī, -ātus; -ō, -āre *vt* to pursue, attack, criticise.

īnsectus *adj* notched.

īnsēdābiliter *adv* incessantly.

īnsēdī *perf of* **īnsīdō**.

īnsenēscō, -ēscere, -uī *vi* to grow old in.

īnsēnsilis *adj* imperceptible.

īnsepultus *adj* unburied.

īnsequēns, -entis *pres p of* **īnsequor** ♦ *adj* the following.

īnsequor, -quī, -cūtus *vt* to follow, pursue hotly; to proceed; (*time*) to come after, come next; (*fig*) to attack, persecute.

īnserō, -erere, -ēvī, -itum *vt* to graft; (*fig*) to implant.

īnserō, -ere, -uī, -tum *vt* to let in, insert; to introduce, mingle, involve.

īnsertō, -āre *vt* to put in.

īnsertus *ppp of* **īnserō**.

īnserviō, -īre, -iī, -ītum *vt, vi* to be a slave (to); to be devoted, submissive (to).

īnsessus *ppp of* **īnsīdō**.

īnsībilō, -āre *vi* to whistle in.

īnsideō, -ēre *vi* to sit on *or* in; to remain fixed ♦ *vt* to hold, occupy.

īnsidiae, -ārum *fpl* ambush; (*fig*) trap, trickery.

īnsidiātor, -ōris *nt* soldier in ambush; (*fig*) waylayer, plotter.

īnsidior, -ārī, -ātus *vi* to lie in ambush; (*with dat*) to lie in wait for, plot against.

īnsidiōsē *adv* insidiously.

īnsidiōsus *adj* artful, treacherous.

īnsīdō, -īdere, -ēdī, -ēssum *vi* to settle on; (*fig*) to become fixed, rooted in ♦ *vt* to occupy.

īnsigne, -is *nt* distinguishing mark, badge, decoration; (*pl*) insignia, honours; (*speech*) purple passages.

īnsigniō, -īre *vt* to distinguish.

īnsignis *adj* distinguished, conspicuous.

īnsignītē *adv* remarkably.

īnsigniter *adv* markedly.

īnsilia, -um *ntpl* treadle (of a loom).

īnsiliō, -īre, -uī *vi* to jump into *or* onto.

īnsimulātiō, -ōnis *f* accusation.

īnsimulō, -āre, -āvī, -ātum *vt* to charge, accuse, allege (*esp falsely*).

īnsincērus *adj* adulterated.

īnsinuātiō, -ōnis *f* ingratiating.

īnsinuō, -āre, -āvī, -ātum *vt* to bring in, introduce stealthily ♦ *vi* to creep in, worm one's way in, penetrate; **sē ~** ingratiate oneself; to make one's way into.

īnsipiēns, -entis *adj* senseless, foolish.

īnsipienter *adv* foolishly.

īnsipientia, -ae *f* folly.

īnsistō, -istere, -titī *vi* to stand on, step on; to stand firm, halt, pause; to tread on the heels, press on, pursue; to enter upon, apply oneself to, begin; to persist, continue.

īnsitiō, -ōnis *f* grafting; grafting time.

īnsitīvus *adj* grafted; (*fig*) spurious.

īnsitor, -ōris *m* grafter.

īnsitus *ppp of* **īnserō** ♦ *adj* innate; incorporated.

īnsociābilis *adj* incompatible.

īnsōlābiliter *adv* unconsolably.

īnsolēns, -entis *adj* unusual, unaccustomed; excessive, extravagant, insolent.

īnsolenter *adv* unusually; immoderately, insolently.

īnsolentia, -ae *f* inexperience, novelty, strangeness; excess, insolence.

īnsolēscō, -ere *vi* to become insolent, elated.

īnsolidus *adj* soft.

īnsolitus *adj* unaccustomed, unusual.

īnsomnia, -ae *f* sleeplessness.

īnsomnis *adj* sleepless.

īnsomnium, -ī *and* **iī** *nt* dream.

īnsonō, -āre, -uī *vi* to resound, sound; to make a noise.

īnsōns, -ontis *adj* innocent; harmless.

īnsōpītus *adj* sleepless.

īnspectō, -āre *vt* to look at.

īnspectus *ppp of* **īnspiciō**.

īnspērāns, -antis *adj* not expecting.

īnspērātus *adj* unexpected; ~ō, ex ~ō unexpectedly.

īnspergō, -gere, -sī, -sum *vt* to sprinkle on.

īnspiciō, -icere, -exī, -ectum *vt* to look into; to examine, inspect; (MIL) to review; (*mind*) to consider, get to know.

īnspīcō, -āre *vt* to sharpen.

īnspīrō, -āre, -āvī, -ātum *vt, vi* to blow on, breathe into.

īnspoliātus *adj* unpillaged.

īnspūtō, -āre *vt* to spit on.

īnstābilis *adj* unsteady, not firm; (*fig*) inconstant.

īnstāns, -antis *pres p of* **īnstō** ♦ *adj* present; urgent, threatening.

īnstanter *adv* vehemently.

īnstantia, -ae *f* presence; vehemence.

īnstar *nt* (*indecl*) likeness, appearance; as good as, worth.

īnstaurātiō, -ōnis *f* renewal.

īnstaurātīvus *adj* renewed.

īnstaurō, -āre, -āvī, -ātum *vt* to renew, restore; to celebrate; to requite.

īnsternō, -ernere, -rāvī, -rātum *vt* to spread over, cover.

īnstigātor, -ōris *m* instigator.

īnstigātrīx, -rīcis *f* female instigator.

īnstigō, -āre *vt* to goad, incite, instigate.

īnstillō, -āre *vt* to drop on, instil.

īnstimulātor, -ōris *m* instigator.

īnstimulō, -āre *vt* to urge on.

īnstinctor, -ōris *m* instigator.

īnstinctus *adj* incited, inspired.

īnstinctus, -ūs *m* impulse, inspiration.

īnstipulor, -ārī, -ātus *vi* to bargain for.

īnstita, -ae *f* flounce of a lady's tunic.

īnstitī *perf of* **īnsistō**.

īnstitiō, -ōnis *f* stopping.

īnstitor, -ōris *m* pedlar.

īnstituō, -uere, -uī, -ūtum *vt* to set, implant; to set up, establish, build, appoint; to marshal, arrange, organize; to teach, educate; to undertake, resolve on.

īnstitūtiō, -ōnis *f* custom; arrangement; education; (*pl*) principles of education.

īnstitūtum, -ī *nt* way of life, tradition, law; stipulation, agreement; purpose; (*pl*) principles.

īnstō, -āre, -itī *vi* to stand on or in; to be close, be hard on the heels of, pursue; (*events*) to approach, impend; (*fig*) to press on, work hard at; (*speech*) to insist, urge.

īnstrātus *ppp of* **īnsternō**.

īnstrēnuus *adj* languid, slow.

īnstrepō, -ere *vi* to creak.

īnstructiō, -ōnis *f* building; setting out.

īnstructius *adv* in better style.

īnstructor, -ōris *m* preparer.

īnstructus *ppp of* **īnstruō** ♦ *adj* provided, equipped; prepared, versed.

īnstructus, -ūs *m* equipment.

īnstrūmentum, -ī *nt* tool, instrument; equipment, furniture, stock; (*fig*) means, provision; dress, embellishment.

īnstruō, -ere, -xī, -ctum *vt* to erect, build up; (MIL) to marshal, array; to equip, provide, prepare; (*fig*) to teach, train.

īnsuāsum, -ī *nt* a dark colour.

īnsuāvis *adj* disagreeable.

īnsūdō, -āre *vi* to perspire on.

īnsuēfactus *adj* accustomed.

īnsuēscō, -scere, -vī, -tum *vt* to train, accustom ♦ *vi* to become accustomed.

īnsuētus *ppp of* **īnsuēscō**.

īnsuētus *adj* unaccustomed, unused; unusual.

īnsula, -ae *f* island; block of houses.

īnsulānus, -ī *m* islander.

īnsulsē *adv see adj*.

īnsulsitās, -ātis *f* lack of taste, absurdity.

īnsulsus *adj* tasteless, absurd, dull.

īnsultō, -āre *vt, vi* to jump on, leap in; (*fig*) to exult, taunt, insult.

īnsultūra, -ae *f* jumping on.

īnsum, inesse, īnfuī *vi* to be in or on; to belong to.

īnsūmō, -ere, -psī, -ptum *vt* to spend, devote.

īnsuō, -uere, -uī, -ūtum *vt* to sew in, sew up in.

īnsuper *adv* above, on top; besides; over and above; (*prep with abl*) besides.

īnsuperābilis *adj* unconquerable, impassable.

īnsurgō, -gere, -rēxī, -rēctum *vi* to stand up, rise to; to rise, grow, swell; to rise against.

īnsusurrō, -āre *vt, vi* to whisper.

īnsūtus *ppp of* **īnsuō**.

intābēscō, -ēscere, -uī *vi* to melt away, waste away.

intāctilis *adj* intangible.

intāctus *adj* untouched, intact; untried; undefiled, chaste.

intāminātus *adj* unsullied.

intēctus *ppp of* **integō**.

intēctus *adj* uncovered, unclad; frank.

integellus *adj* fairly whole *or* pure.

integer, -rī *adj* whole, complete, unimpaired, intact; sound, fresh, new; (*mind*) unbiassed, free; (*character*) virtuous, pure, upright; (*decision*) undecided, open; **in ~rum restituere** restore to a former state; **ab, dē, ex ~rō** afresh; **~rum est mihi** I am at liberty (to).

integō, -egere, -ēxī, -ēctum *vt* to cover over; to protect.

integrāscō, -ere *vi* to begin all over again.

integrātiō, -ōnis *f* renewing.

integrē *adv* entirely; honestly; correctly.

integritās, -ātis *f* completeness, soundness, integrity, honesty; (*language*) correctness.

integrō, -āre *vt* to renew, replenish, repair; (*mind*) to refresh.

integumentum, -ī *nt* cover, covering, shelter.

intellēctus *ppp of* **intellegō**.

intellēctus, -ūs *m* understanding; (*word*) meaning.

intellegēns, -entis *pres p of* **intellegō ♦** *adj* intelligent, a connoisseur.

intellegenter *adv* intelligently.

intellegentia, -ae *f* discernment, understanding; taste.

intellegō, -egere, -ēxī, -ēctum *vt* to understand, perceive, realize; to be a connoisseur.

intemerātus *adj* pure, undefiled.

intemperāns, -antis *adj* immoderate, extravagant; incontinent.

intemperanter *adv* extravagantly.

intemperantia, -ae *f* excess, extravagance; arrogance.

intemperātē *adv* dissolutely.

intemperātus *adj* excessive.

intemperiae, -ārum *fpl* inclemency; madness.

intemperiēs, -ēī *f* inclemency, storm; (*fig*) fury.

intempestīvē *adv* inopportunely.

intempestīvus *adj* unseasonable, untimely.

intempestus *adj* (*night*) the dead of; unhealthy.

intemptātus *adj* untried.

intendō, -dere, -dī, -tum *vt* to stretch out, strain, spread; (*weapon*) to aim; (*tent*) to pitch; (*attention, course*) to direct, turn; (*fact*) to increase, exaggerate; (*speech*) to maintain; (*trouble*) to threaten ♦ *vi* to make for, intend; **animō ~** purpose; **sē ~** exert oneself.

intentē *adv* strictly.

intentiō, -ōnis *f* straining, tension; (*mind*) exertion, attention; (*law*) accusation.

intentō, -āre *vt* to stretch out, aim; (*fig*) to threaten with, attack.

intentus *ppp of* **intendō ♦** *adj* taut; attentive, intent; strict; (*speech*) vigorous.

intentus, -ūs *m* stretching out.

intepeō, -ēre *vi* to be warm.

intepēscō, -ēscere, -uī *vi* to be warmed.

inter *prep* (*with acc*) between, among, during, in the course of; in spite of; **~ haec** meanwhile; **~ manūs** within reach; **~ nōs** confidentially; **~ sē** mutually, one another; **~ sīcāriōs** in the murder court; **~ viam** on the way.

interāmenta, -ōrum *ntpl* ship's timbers.

interaptus *adj* joined together.

interārēscō, -ere *vi* to wither away.

interbibō, -ere *vi* to drink up.

interbītō, -ere *vi* to fall through.

intercalāris *adj* intercalary.

intercalārius *adj* intercalary.

intercalō, -āre *vt* to intercalate.

intercapēdō, -inis *f* interruption, respite.

intercēdō, -ēdere, -ēssī, -ēssum *vi* to come between, intervene; to occur; to become surety; to interfere, obstruct; (*tribune*) to protest, veto.

interceptiō, -ōnis *f* taking away.

interceptor, -ōris *m* embezzler.

interceptus *ppp of* **intercipiō**.

intercessiō, -ōnis *f* (*law*) becoming surety; (*tribune*) veto.

intercessor, -ōris *m* mediator, surety; interposer of the veto; obstructor.

intercidō, -ere, -ī *vi* to fall short; to happen in the meantime; to get lost, become obsolete, be forgotten.

intercīdō, -dere, -dī, -sum *vt* to cut through, sever.

intercinō, -ere *vt* to sing between.

intercipiō, -ipere, -ēpī, -eptum *vt* to intercept; to embezzle, steal; to cut off, obstruct.

intercīsē *adv* piecemeal.

intercīsus *ppp of* **intercīdō**.

interclūdō, -dere, -sī, -sum *vt* to cut off, block, shut off, prevent; **animam ~** suffocate.

interclūsiō, -ōnis *f* stoppage.

interclūsus *ppp of* **interclūdō**.

intercolumnium, -ī *and* **iī** *nt* space between two pillars.

intercurrō, -ere *vi* to mingle with; to intercede; to hurry in the meantime.

intercursō, -āre *vi* to crisscross; to attack

between the lines.

intercursus, -ūs *m* intervention.

intercus, -tis *adj*: **aqua ~** dropsy.

interdīcō, -īcere, -ixī, -ictum *vt, vi* to forbid, interdict; (*praetor*) to make a provisional order; **aquā et ignī ~** banish.

interdictiō, -ōnis *f* prohibiting, banishment.

interdictum, -ī *nt* prohibition; provisional order (by a praetor).

interdiū *adv* by day.

interdō, -are *vt* to make at intervals; to distribute; **nōn ~uim** I wouldn't care.

interductus, -ūs *m* punctuation.

interdum *adv* now and then, occasionally.

intereā *adv* meanwhile, in the meantime; nevertheless.

interēmī *perf of* **interimō**.

interemptus *ppp of* **interimō**.

intereō, -īre, -iī, -itum *vi* to be lost, perish, die.

interequitō, -āre *vt, vi* to ride between.

interesse *infin of* **intersum**.

interfātiō, -ōnis *f* interruption.

interfātur, -ārī, -ātus *vi* to interrupt.

interfectiō, -ōnis *f* killing.

interfector, -ōris *m* murderer.

interfectrīx, -rīcis *f* murderess.

interfectus *ppp of* **interficiō**.

interficiō, -icere, -ēcī, -ectum *vt* to kill, destroy.

interfīō, -ierī *vi* to pass away.

interfluō, -ere, -xī *vt, vi* to flow between.

interfodiō, -ere *vt* to pierce.

interfugiō, -ere *vi* to flee among.

interfuī *perf of* **intersum**.

interfulgeō, -ēre *vi* to shine amongst.

interfūsus *ppp* lying between; marked here and there.

interiaceō, -ēre *vi* to lie between.

interibi *adv* in the meantime.

intericiō, -icere, -iēcī, -iectum *vt* to put amongst or between, interpose, mingle; **annō ~iectō** after a year.

interiectus, -ūs *m* coming in between; interval.

interiī *perf of* **intereō**.

interim *adv* meanwhile, in the meantime; sometimes; all the same.

interimō, -imere, -ēmī, -emptum *vt* to abolish, destroy, kill.

interior, -ōris *adj* inner, interior; nearer, on the near side; secret, private; more intimate, more profound.

interitiō, -ōnis *f* ruin.

interitus, -ūs *m* destruction, ruin, death.

interiūnctus *adj* joined together.

interius *adv* inwardly; too short.

interlābor, -ī *vi* to glide between.

interlegō, -ere *vt* to pick here and there.

interlinō, -inere, -ēvī, -itum *vt* to smear in

parts; to erase here and there.

interloquor, -quī, -cūtus *vi* to interrupt.

interlūceō, -cēre, -xī *vi* to shine through, be clearly seen.

interlūnia, -ōrum *ntpl* new moon.

interluō, -ere *vt* to wash, flow between.

intermēnstruus *adj* of the new moon ♦ *nt* new moon.

interminātus *ppa of* **interminor** ♦ *adj* forbidden.

interminātus *adj* endless.

interminor, -ārī, -ātus *vi* to threaten; to forbid threateningly.

intermisceō, -scēre, -scuī, -xtum *vt* to mix, intermingle.

intermissiō, -ōnis *f* interruption.

intermittō, -ittere, -īsī, -issum *vt* to break off; to interrupt; to omit, neglect; to allow to elapse ♦ *vi* to cease, pause.

intermixtus *ppp of* **intermisceō**.

intermorior, -ī, -tuus *vi* to die suddenly.

intermortuus *adj* falling unconscious.

intermundia, -ōrum *ntpl* space between worlds.

intermūrālis *adj* between two walls.

internātus *adj* growing among.

internecīnus *adj* murderous, of extermination.

interneciō, -ōnis *f* massacre, extermination.

internecīvus *adj* = **internecīnus**.

internectō, -ere *vt* to enclasp.

internōdia, -ōrum *ntpl* space between joints.

internōscō, -scere, -vī, -tum *vt* to distinguish between.

internūntia, -iae *f* messenger, mediator, go-between.

internūntiō, -āre *vi* to exchange messages.

internūntius, -ī and iī *m* messenger, mediator, go-between.

internus *adj* internal, civil ♦ *ntpl* domestic affairs.

interō, -erere, -rīvī, -rītum *vt* to rub in; (*fig*) to concoct.

interpellātiō, -ōnis *f* interruption.

interpellātor, -ōris *m* interrupter.

interpellō, -āre, -āvī, -ātum *vt* to interrupt; to disturb, obstruct.

interpolis *adj* made up.

interpolō, -āre *vt* to renovate, do up; (*writing*) to falsify.

interpōnō, -ōnere, -osuī, -ositum *vt* to put between *or* amongst, insert; (*time*) to allow to elapse; (*person*) to introduce, admit; (*pretext etc*) to put forward, interpose; **fidem ~** pledge one's word; **sē ~** interfere, become involved.

interpositiō, -ōnis *f* introduction.

interpositus *ppp of* **interpōnō**.

interpositus, -ūs *m* obstruction.

interpres, -tis *m/f* agent, negotiator;

Noun declensions and verb conjugations are shown on pp xiii to xxv. The present infinitive ending of a verb shows to which conjugation it belongs: **-āre** = 1st; **-ēre** = 2nd; **-ere** = 3rd and **-īre** = 4th. Irregular verbs are shown on p xxvi

interpreter, explainer, translator.
interpretātiō, -ōnis *f* interpretation,
exposition, meaning.
interpretātus *adj* translated.
interpretor, -ārī, -ātus *vt* to interpret,
explain, translate, understand.
interprimō, -imere, -essī, -essum *vt* to
squeeze.
interpūnctiō, -ōnis *f* punctuation.
interpūnctus *adj* well-divided ♦ *ntpl*
punctuation.
interquiēscō, -scere, -vī *vi* to rest awhile.
interrēgnum, -ī *nt* regency, interregnum;
interval between consuls.
interrēx, -ēgis *m* regent; deputy consul.
interritus *adj* undaunted, unafraid.
interrogātiō, -ōnis *f* question; (*law*) cross-
examination; (*logic*) syllogism.
interrogātiuncula, -ae *f* short argument.
interrogō, -āre, -āvī, -ātum *vt* to ask, put a
question; (*law*) to cross-examine, bring to
trial.
interrumpō, -umpere, -ūpī, -uptum *vt* to
break up, sever; (*fig*) to break off, interrupt.
interruptē *adv* interruptedly.
intersaepiō, -īre, -sī, -tum *vt* to shut off,
close.
interscindō, -ndere, -dī, -ssum *vt* to cut off,
break down.
interserō, -erere, -ēvī, -itum *vt* to plant at
intervals.
interserō, -ere, -uī, -tum *vt* to interpose.
intersitus *ppp of* **interserō**.
interspīrātiō, -ōnis *f* pause for breath.
interstinguō, -guere, -ctum *vt* to mark, spot;
to extinguish.
interstringō, -ere *vt* to strangle.
intersum, -esse, -fuī *vi* to be between; to be
amongst, be present at; (*time*) to elapse; ~est
there is a difference; it is of importance, it
concerns, it matters; **meā ~est** it is
important for me.
intertextus *adj* interwoven.
intertrahō, -here, -xī *vt* to take away.
intertrīmentum, -ī *nt* wastage; loss, damage.
interturbātiō, -ōnis *f* confusion.
intervallum, -ī *nt* space, distance, interval;
(*time*) pause, interval, respite; difference.
intervellō, -ere *vt* to pluck out; to tear apart.
interveniō, -enīre, -ēnī, -entum *vi* to come
on the scene, intervene; to interfere (with),
interrupt; to happen, occur.
interventor, -ōris *m* intruder.
interventus, -ūs *m* appearance, intervention;
occurrence.
intervertō, -tere, -tī, -sum *vt* to embezzle; to
rob, cheat.
intervīsō, -ere, -ī, -um *vt* to have a look at,
look and see; to visit occasionally.
intervolitō, -āre *vi* to fly about, amongst.
intervomō, -ere *vt* to throw up (amongst).
intervortō *vt see* **intervertō**.
intestābilis *adj* infamous, wicked.

intestātō *adv* without making a will.
intestātus *adj* intestate; not convicted by
witnesses.
intestīnus *adj* internal ♦ *nt and ntpl* intestines,
entrails.
intexō, -ere, -uī, -tum *vt* to inweave,
embroider, interlace.
intibum, -ī *nt* endive.
intimē *adv* most intimately, cordially.
intimus *adj* innermost; deepest, secret;
intimate ♦ *m* most intimate friend.
intingō (**intinguō**), **-gere, -xī, -ctum** *vt* to
dip in.
intolerābilis *adj* unbearable; irresistible.
intolerandus *adj* intolerable.
intolerāns, -antis *adj* impatient; unbearable.
intoleranter *adv* excessively.
intolerantia, -ae *f* insolence.
intonō, -āre, -uī, -ātum *vi* to thunder,
thunder out.
intōnsus *adj* unshorn, unshaven; long-haired,
bearded; uncouth.
intorqueō, -quēre, -sī, -tum *vt* to twist, wrap
round; to hurl at.
intortus *ppp of* **intorqueō** ♦ *adj* twisted, curled;
confused.
intrā *adv* inside, within ♦ *prep* (*with acc*) inside,
within; (*time*) within, during; (*amount*) less
than, within the limits of.
intrābilis *adj* navigable.
intractābilis *adj* formidable.
intractātus *adj* not broken in; unattempted.
intremīscō, -īscere, -uī *vi* to begin to shake.
intremō, -ere *vi* to tremble.
intrepidē *adv see adj*.
intrepidus *adj* calm, brave; undisturbed.
intrīcō, -āre *vt* to entangle.
intrīnsecus *adv* on the inside.
intrītus *adj* not worn out.
intrīvī *perf of* **interō**.
intrō *adv* inside, in.
intrō, -āre, -āvī, -ātum *vt, vi* to go in, enter; to
penetrate.
intrōdūcō, -ūcere, -ūxī, -uctum *vt* to bring
in, introduce, escort in; to institute.
intrōductiō, -ōnis *f* bringing in.
intrōeō, -īre, -iī, -itum *vi* to go into, enter.
intrōferō, -ferre, -tulī, -lātum *vt* to carry
inside.
intrōgredior, -dī, -ssus *vi* to step inside.
intrōitus, -ūs *m* entrance; beginning.
intrōlātus *ppp of* **intrōferō**.
intrōmittō, -ittere, -īsī, -issus *vt* to let in,
admit.
intrōrsum, intrōrsus *adv* inwards, inside.
intrōrumpō, -ere *vi* to break into.
intrōspectō, -āre *vt* to look in at.
intrōspiciō, -icere, -exī, -ectum *vt* to look
inside; to look at, examine.
intubum *etc see* **intibum**.
intueor, -ērī, -itus *vt* to look at, watch; to
contemplate, consider; to admire.
intumēscō, -ēscere, -uī *vi* to begin to swell,

rise; to increase; to become angry.

intumulātus *adj* unburied.

intuor *etc see* **intueor**.

inturbidus *adj* undisturbed; quiet.

intus *adv* inside, within, in; from within.

intūtus *adj* unsafe; unguarded.

inula, -ae *f* elecampane.

inultus *adj* unavenged; unpunished.

inumbrō, -āre *vt* to shade; to cover.

inundō, -āre, -āvī, -ātum *vt, vi* to overflow, flood.

inunguō, -unguere, -ūnxī, -ūnctum *vt* to anoint.

inurbānē *adv see adj.*

inurbānus *adj* rustic, unmannerly, unpolished.

inurgeō, -ēre *vi* to push, butt.

inūrō, -rere, -ssī, -stum *vt* to brand; (*fig*) to brand, inflict.

inūsitātē *adv* strangely.

inūsitātus *adj* unusual, extraordinary.

inūstus *ppp of* **inūrō**.

inūtilis *adj* useless; harmful.

inūtilitās, -ātis *f* uselessness, harmfulness.

inūtiliter *adv* unprofitably.

invādō, -dere, -sī, -sum *vt, vi* to get in, make one's way in; to enter upon; to fall upon, attack, invade; to seize, take possession of.

invalēscō, -ēscere, -uī *vi* to grow stronger.

invalidus *adj* weak; inadequate.

invāsī *perf of* **invādō**.

invectiō, -ōnis *f* importing; invective.

invectus *ppp of* **invehō**.

invehō, -here, -xī, -ctum *vt* to carry in, bring in; **sē** ~ attack.

invehor, -hī, -ctus *vi* to ride, drive, sail in or into, enter; to attack; to inveigh against.

invēndibilis *adj* unsaleable.

inveniō, -enīre, -ēnī, -entum *vt* to find, come upon; to find out, discover; to invent, contrive; to win, get.

inventiō, -ōnis *f* invention; (*RHET*) compiling the subject-matter.

inventor, -ōris *m* inventor, discoverer.

inventrīx, -rīcis *f* inventor, discoverer.

inventus *ppp of* **inveniō** ♦ *nt* invention, discovery.

invenustus *adj* unattractive; unlucky in love.

inverēcundus *adj* immodest, shameless.

invergō, -ere *vt* to pour upon.

inversiō, -ōnis *f* transposition; irony.

inversus *ppp of* **invertō** ♦ *adj* upside down, inside out; perverted.

invertō, -tere, -tī, -sum *vt* to turn over, invert; to change, pervert.

invesperāscit, -ere *vi* it is dusk.

investīgātiō, -ōnis *f* search.

investīgātor, -ōris *m* investigator.

investīgō, -āre, -āvī, -ātum *vt* to follow the trail of; (*fig*) to track down, find out.

inveterāscō, -scere, -vī *vi* to grow old (in); to become established, fixed, inveterate; to grow obsolete.

inveterātiō, -ōnis *f* chronic illness.

inveterātus *adj* of long standing, inveterate.

invexī *perf of* **invehō**.

invicem *adv* in turns, alternately; mutually, each other.

invictus *adj* unbeaten; unconquerable.

invidentia, -ae *f* envy.

invideō, -idēre, -īdī, -īsum *vt, vi* to cast an evil eye on; (*with dat*) to envy, grudge; to begrudge.

invidia, -ae *f* envy, jealousy, ill-will; unpopularity.

invidiōsē *adv* spitefully.

invidiōsus *adj* envious, spiteful; enviable; invidious, hateful.

invidus *adj* envious, jealous, hostile.

invigilō, -āre *vi* to be awake over; to watch over, be intent on.

inviolābilis *adj* invulnerable; inviolable.

inviolātē *adv* inviolately.

inviolātus *adj* unhurt; inviolable.

invīsitātus *adj* unseen, unknown, strange.

invīsō, -ere, -ī, -um *vt* to go and see, visit, have a look at; to inspect.

invīsus *adj* hateful, detested; hostile.

invīsus *adj* unseen.

invītāmentum, -ī *nt* attraction, inducement.

invītātiō, -ōnis *f* invitation; entertainment.

invītātus, -ūs *m* invitation.

invītē *adv* unwillingly.

invītō, -āre, -āvī, -ātum *vt* to invite; to treat, entertain; to summon; to attract, induce.

invītus *adj* against one's will, reluctant.

invius *adj* trackless, impassable; inaccessible.

invocātus *ppp of* **invocō**.

invocātus *adj* unbidden, uninvited.

invocō, -āre, -āvī, -ātum *vt* to call upon, invoke; to appeal to; to call.

involātus, -ūs *m* flight.

involitō, -āre *vi* to play upon.

involō, -āre *vi* to fly at, pounce on, attack.

involūcre, -is *nt* napkin.

involūcrum, -ī *nt* covering, case.

involūtus *ppp of* **involvō** ♦ *adj* complicated.

involvō, -vere, -vī, -ūtum *vt* to roll on; to wrap up, envelop, entangle.

involvolus, -ī *m* caterpillar.

invulnerātus *adj* unwounded.

iō *interj* (*joy*) hurrah!; (*pain*) oh!; (*calling*) ho there!

Iōannēs, -is *m* John.

iocātiō, -ōnis *f* joke.

iocor, -ārī, -ātus *vt, vi* to joke, jest.

iocōsē *adv* jestingly.

iocōsus *adj* humorous, playful.

ioculāris *adj* laughable, funny ♦ *ntpl* jokes.

ioculārius *adj* ludicrous.

ioculātor, -ōris m jester.
ioculor, -ārī vi to joke.
ioculus, -ī m a bit of fun.
iocus, -ī m (pl -a, -ōrum nt) joke, jest; **extrā
~um** joking apart; **per ~um** for fun.
Iōnes, -um mpl Ionians.
Iōnia, -iae f Ionia, coastal district of Asia Minor.
Iōnium, -ī nt Ionian Sea, W. of Greece.
Iōnius, -icus adj Ionian.
iōta nt (indecl) Greek letter I.
Iovis gen of **Iuppiter**.
Īphianasse, -ae f Iphigenia.
Īphigenīa, -ae f daughter of Agamemnon
(who sacrificed her at Aulis to Diana).
ipse, -a, -um, -īus prep self, himself etc; in
person, for one's own part, of one's own
accord, by oneself; just, precisely, very; the
master, the host.
ipsissimus his very own self; **nunc ~um** right
now.
īra, -ae f anger, rage; object of indignation.
īrācundē adv angrily.
īrācundia, -ae f irascibility, quick temper;
rage, resentment.
īrācundus adj irascible, choleric; resentful.
īrāscor, -ī vi to be angry, get furious.
īrātē adv see adj.
īrātus adj angry, furious.
īre infin of **eō**.
Iris, -dis (acc -m) f messenger of the gods; the
rainbow.
īrōnīa, -ae f irony.
irrāsus adj unshaven.
irraucēscō, -cēscere, -sī vi to become hoarse.
irredivīvus adj irreparable.
irreligātus adj not tied.
irreligiōsē adv see adj.
irreligiōsus adj impious.
irremeābilis adj from which there is no
returning.
irreparābilis adj irretrievable.
irrepertus adj undiscovered.
irrēpō, -ere, -sī vi to steal into, insinuate
oneself into.
irreprehēnsus adj blameless.
irrequiētus adj restless.
irresectus adj unpared.
irresolūtus adj not slackened.
irrētiō, -īre, -īī, -ītum vt to ensnare, entangle.
irretortus adj not turned back.
irreverentia, -ae f disrespect.
irrevocābilis adj irrevocable; implacable.
irrevocātus adj without an encore.
irrīdeō, -dēre, -sī, -sum vi to laugh, joke ♦ vt
to laugh at, ridicule.
irrīdiculē adv unwittily.
irrīdiculum, -ī nt laughing stock.
irrigātiō, -ōnis f irrigation.
irrigō, -āre, -āvī, -ātum vt to water, irrigate;
to inundate; (fig) to shed over, flood, refresh.
irriguus adj well-watered, swampy;
refreshing.
irrīsiō, -ōnis f ridicule, mockery.

irrīsor, -ōris m scoffer.
irrīsus ppp of **irrīdeō**.
irrīsus, -ūs m derision.
irrītābilis adj excitable.
irrītāmen, -inis nt excitement, provocation.
irrītātiō, -ōnis f incitement, irritation.
irrītō, -āre, -āvī, -ātum vt to provoke, incite,
enrage.
irritus adj invalid, null and void; useless, vain,
ineffective; (person) unsuccessful; **ad ~um
cadere** come to nothing.
irrogātiō, -ōnis f imposing.
irrogō, -āre vt to propose (a measure) against;
to impose.
irrōrō, -āre vt to bedew.
irrumpō, -umpere, -ūpī, -uptum vt, vi to
rush in, break in; to intrude, invade.
irruō, -ere, -ī vi to force a way in, rush in,
attack; (speech) to make a blunder.
irruptiō, -ōnis f invasion, raid.
irruptus ppp of **irrumpō**.
irruptus adj unbroken.
is, ea, id pron he, she, it; this, that, the; such;
nōn is sum quī I am not the man to; **id** (with
vi) for this reason; **id quod** what; **ad id**
hitherto; for the purpose; besides; **in eō est**
it has come to this; one is on the point of; it
depends on this.
Ismara, -ōrum ntpl, **-us, -ī** m Mt Ismarus in
Thrace.
Ismarius adj Thracian.
Isocratēs, -is m Athenian orator and teacher of
rhetoric.
istāc adv that way.
iste, -a, -ud, -īus pron that of yours; (law) your
client, the plaintiff, the defendant;
(contemptuous) the fellow; that, such.
Isthmius adj, ntpl the Isthmian Games.
Isthmus (-os), -ī m Isthmus of Corinth.
istic, -aec, -uc and **oc** pron that of yours, that.
istīc adv there; in this, on this occasion.
istinc adv from there; of that.
istiusmodī such, of that kind.
istō, istōc adv to you, there, yonder.
istōrsum adv in that direction.
istūc adv (to) there, to that.
ita adv thus, so; as follows; yes; accordingly;
itane really?; **nōn ita** not so very; **ita ut** just
as; **ita ... ut** so, to such an extent that; on
condition that; only in so far as; **ita ... ut nōn**
without; **ut ... ita** just as ... so; although ...
nevertheless.
Italī, -ōrum mpl Italians.
Italia, -iae f Italy.
Italicus, -is, -us adj Italian.
itaque conj and so, therefore, accordingly.
item adv likewise, also.
iter, -ineris nt way, journey, march; a day's
journey or march; route, road, passage; (fig)
way, course; **~ mihi est** I have to go to; **~ dare**
grant a right of way; **~ facere** to journey,
march, travel; **ex, in ~inere** on the way, on
the march; **māgnīs ~ineribus** by forced

marches.

iterātiō, -ōnis f repetition.

iterō, -āre, -āvī, -ātum vt to repeat, renew; to plough again.

iterum adv again, a second time; ~ **atque** ~ repeatedly.

Ithaca, -ae, -ē, -ēs f island W. of Greece (home of Ulysses).

Ithacēnsis, -us adj Ithacan.

Ithacus, -ī m Ulysses.

itidem adv in the same way, similarly.

itiō, -ōnis f going.

itō, -āre vi to go.

itus, -ūs m going, movement, departure.

iuba, -ae f mane; crest.

Iuba, -ae m king of Numidia (supporter of Pompey).

iubar, -is nt brightness, light.

iubātus adj crested.

iubeō, -bēre, -ssī, -ssum vt to order, command, tell; (greeting) to bid; (MED) to prescribe; (POL) to decree, ratify, appoint.

iūcundē adv agreeably.

iūcunditās, -ātis f delight, enjoyment.

iūcundus adj delightful, pleasing.

Iūdaea, -ae f Judaea, Palestine.

Iūdaeus, -ī m Jew.

Iūdaeus, Iūdaicus adj Jewish.

iūdex, -icis m judge; (pl) panel of jurors; (fig) critic.

iūdicātiō, -ōnis f judicial inquiry; opinion.

iūdicātum, -ī nt judgment, precedent.

iūdicātus, -ūs m office of judge.

iūdiciālis adj judicial, forensic.

iūdiciārius adj judiciary.

iūdicium, -ī and iī nt trial; court of justice; sentence; judgment, opinion; discernment, taste, tact; **in ~ vocāre, ~ō arcessere** sue, summon.

iūdicō, -āre, -āvī, -ātum vt to judge, examine, sentence, condemn; to form an opinion of, decide; to declare.

iugālis adj yoked together; nuptial.

iugātiō, -ōnis f training (of a vine).

iūgerum, -ī nt a land measure (240 x 120 feet).

iūgis adj perpetual, never-failing.

iūglāns, -andis f walnut tree.

iugō, -āre, -āvī, -ātum vt to couple, marry.

iugōsus adj hilly.

Iugulae, -ārum fpl Orion's Belt.

iugulō, -āre, -āvī, -ātum vt to cut the throat of, kill, murder.

iugulus, -ī m, **-um, -ī** nt throat.

iugum, -ī nt (animals) yoke, collar; pair, team; (MIL) yoke of subjugation; (mountain) ridge, height, summit; (ASTRO) Libra; (loom) crossbeam; (ship) thwart; (fig) yoke, bond.

Iugurtha, -ae m king of Numidia (rebel against Rome).

Iugurthīnus adj see n.

Iūlēus adj of Iulus; of Caesar; of July.

Iūlius, -ī m Roman family name (esp Caesar); (month) July.

Iūlius, -iānus adj see n.

Iūlus, -ī m son of Aeneas, Ascanius.

iūmentum, -ī nt beast of burden, packhorse.

iunceus adj of rushes; slender.

iuncōsus adj rushy.

iūnctiō, -ōnis f union.

iūnctūra, -ae f joint; combination; relationship.

iūnctus ppp of **iungō** ♦ adj connected, attached.

iuncus, -ī m rush.

iungō, -gere, iūnxī, iūnctum vt to join together, unite; to yoke, harness; to mate; (river) to span, bridge; (fig) to bring together, connect, associate; (agreement) to make; (words) to compound.

iūnior, -ōris adj younger.

iūniperus, -ī f juniper.

Iūnius, -ī m Roman family name; (month) June.

Iūnius adj of June.

Iūnō, -ōnis f Roman goddess wife of Jupiter, patroness of women and marriage.

Iūnōnālis adj see n.

Iūnōnicola, -ae m worshipper of Juno.

Iūnōnigena, -ae m Vulcan.

Iūnōnius adj = **Iūnōnālis.**

Iuppiter, Iovis m Jupiter (king of the gods, god of sky and weather); ~ **Stygius** Pluto; **sub Iove** in the open air.

iūrātor, -ōris m sworn judge.

iūrecōnsultus etc see **iūriscōnsultus.**

iūreiūrō, -āre vi to swear.

iūreperītus etc see **iūrisperītus.**

iūrgium, -ī and iī nt quarrel, brawl.

iūrgō, -āre vi to quarrel, squabble ♦ vt to scold.

iūridiciālis adj of law, juridical.

iūriscōnsultus, -ī m lawyer.

iūrisdictiō, -ōnis f administration of justice; authority.

iūrisperītus adj versed in the law.

iūrō, -āre, -āvī, -ātum vi, vt to swear, take an oath; to conspire; **in nōmen ~** swear allegiance to; **in verba ~** take a prescribed form of oath; **~ātus** having sworn, under oath.

iūs, iūris nt broth, soup.

iūs, iūris nt law, right, justice; law court; jurisdiction, authority; ~ **gentium** international law; ~ **pūblicum** constitutional law; **summum** ~ the strict letter of the law; ~ **dīcere** administer justice; **suī iūris** independent; **iūre** rightly, justly.

iūsiūrandum, iūrisiūrandī nt oath.

iussī perf of **iubeō.**

iussū abl m by order.

iussus ppp of **iubeō** ♦ nt order, command, prescription.

iūstē *adv* duly, rightly.
iūstificus *adj* just dealing.
iūstitia, -ae *f* justice, uprightness, fairness.
iūstitium, -ī *and* iī *nt* cessation of legal
   business.
iūstus *adj* just, fair; lawful, right; regular,
   proper ♦ *nt* right ♦ *ntpl* rights; formalities,
   obsequies.
iūtus *ppp of* iuvō.
iuvenālis *adj* youthful ♦ *ntpl* youthful games.
Iuvenālis, -is *m* Juvenal (*Roman satirist*).
iuvenāliter *adv* vigorously, impetuously.
iuvenca, -ae *f* heifer; girl.
iuvencus, -ī *m* bullock; young man ♦ *adj*
   young.
iuvenēscō, -ēscere, -uī *vi* to grow up; to grow
   young again.
iuvenīlis *adj* youthful.
iuvenīliter *adv see adj*.
iuvenis *adj* young ♦ *m/f* young man *or* woman
   (*20-45 years*), man, warrior.
iuvenor, -ārī *vi* to behave indiscreetly.
iuventa, -ae *f* youth.
iuventās, -ātis *f* youth.
iuventūs, -ūtis *f* youth, manhood; men,
   soldiers.
iuvō, -āre, iūvī, iūtum *vt* to help, be of use to;
   to please, delight; **-at mē** I am glad.
iuxtā *adv* near by, close; alike, just the same ♦
   prep (*with acc*) close to, hard by; next to; very
   like, next door to; **~ ac, cum, quam** just the
   same as.
iuxtim *adv* near; equally.
īvī *perf of* eō.
Ixīōn, -onis *m* Lapith king (*bound to a revolving
   wheel in Tartarus*).
Ixīoneus *adj see n*.
Ixīonidae, -ārum *mpl* Centaurs.
Ixīonidēs, -ae *m* Pirithous.

J, j

J *see* I.

K, k

Kalendae, -ārum *fpl* Kalends, first day of
   each month.
Karthāgō *see* Carthāgō.

L, l

labāscō, -ere *vi* to totter, waver.
lābēcula, -ae *f* aspersion.
labefaciō, -facere, -fēcī, -factum (*pass* -fīō,
   -fierī) *vt* to shake; (*fig*) to weaken, ruin.
labefactō, -āre, -āvī, -ātum *vt* to shake; (*fig*)
   to weaken, destroy.
labellum, -ī *nt* lip.
lābellum, -ī *nt* small basin.
Laberius, -ī *m* Roman family name (*esp a
   writer of mimes*).
lābēs, -is *f* sinking, fall; ruin, destruction.
lābēs, -is *f* spot, blemish; disgrace, stigma;
   (*person*) blot.
labia, -iae *f* lip.
Labiēnus, -ī *m* Roman surname (*esp Caesar's
   officer who went over to Pompey*).
labiōsus *adj* large-lipped.
labium, -ī *and* iī *nt* lip.
labō, -āre *vi* to totter, be unsteady, give way;
   to waver, hesitate, collapse.
lābor, -bī, -psus *vi* to slide, glide; to sink, fall;
   to slip away, pass away; (*fig*) to fade,
   decline, perish; to be disappointed, make a
   mistake.
labor (-ōs), -ōris *m* effort, exertion, labour;
   work, task; hardship, suffering, distress;
   (*ASTRO*) eclipse.
labōrifer, -ī *adj* sore afflicted.
labōriōsē *adv* laboriously, with difficulty.
labōriōsus *adj* troublesome, difficult;
   industrious.
labōrō, -āre, -āvī, -ātum *vi* to work, toil, take
   pains; to suffer, be troubled (with), be in
   distress; to be anxious, worried ♦ *vt* to work
   out, make, produce.
labōs *etc see* labor.
labrum, -ī *nt* lip; edge, rim; **primīs ~īs gustāre**
   acquire a smattering of.
lābrum, -ī *nt* tub, vat; bath.
lābrusca, -ae *f* wild vine.
lābruscum, -ī *nt* wild grape.

labyrinthēus *adj* labyrinthine.
labyrinthus, -ī *m* labyrinth, maze (*esp that of Cnossos in Crete*).
lac, lactis *nt* milk.
Lacaena, -ae *f* Spartan woman ♦ *adj* Spartan.
Lacedaemōn (-ō), -onis (*acc* -ona) *f* Sparta.
Lacedaemonius *adj* Spartan.
lacer, -ī *adj* torn, mangled, lacerated; tearing.
lacerātiō, -ōnis *f* tearing.
lacerna, -ae *f* cloak (*worn in cold weather*).
lacernātus *adj* cloaked.
lacerō, -āre, -āvī, -ātum *vt* to tear, lacerate, mangle; (*ship*) to wreck; (*speech*) to slander, abuse; (*feeling*) to torture, distress; (*goods, time*) to waste, destroy.
lacerta, -ae *f* lizard; a seafish.
lacertōsus *adj* brawny.
lacertus, -ī *m* upper arm, arm; (*pl*) brawn, muscle.
lacertus, -ī *m* lizard; a sea fish.
lacessō, -ere, -īvī *and* **iī, -ītum** *vt* to strike, provoke, challenge; (*fig*) to incite, exasperate.
Lachesis, -is *f* one of the Fates.
lacinia, -ae *f* flap, corner (*of dress*).
Lacīnium, -ī *nt* promontory in S. Italy, with a temple of Juno.
Lacīnius *adj see n.*
Lacō (-ōn), -ōnis *m* Spartan; Spartan dog.
Lacōnicus *adj* Spartan ♦ *nt* sweating bath.
lacrima, -ae *f* tear; (*plant*) gumdrop.
lacrimābilis *adj* mournful.
lacrimābundus *adj* bursting into tears.
lacrimō, -āre, -āvī, -ātum *vt, vi* to weep, weep for.
lacrimōsus *adj* tearful; lamentable.
lacrimula, -ae *f* tear, crocodile tear.
lacrum- *etc see* **lacrim-**.
lactāns, -antis *adj* giving milk; sucking.
lactātiō, -ōnis *f* allurement.
lactēns, -entis *adj* sucking; milky, juicy.
lacteolus *adj* milk-white.
lactēs, -ium *fpl* guts, small intestines.
lactēscō, -ere *vi* to turn to milk.
lacteus *adj* milky, milk-white.
lactō, -āre *vt* to dupe, wheedle.
lactūca, -ae *f* lettuce.
lacūna, -ae *f* hole, pit; pool, pond; (*fig*) deficiency.
lacūnar, -āris *nt* panel ceiling.
lacūnō, -āre *vt* to panel.
lacūnōsus *adj* sunken.
lacus, -ūs *m* vat, tank; lake; reservoir, cistern.
laedō, -dere, -sī, -sum *vt* to hurt, strike, wound; (*fig*) to offend, annoy, break.
Laelius, -ī *m* Roman family name (*esp the friend of Scipio*).
laena, -ae *f* a lined cloak.
Lāērtēs, -ae *m* father of Ulysses.
Lāērtiadēs *m* Ulysses.

Lāērtius *adj see n.*
laesī *perf of* **laedō**.
laesiō, -ōnis *f* attack.
Laestrygonēs, -um *mpl* fabulous cannibals of Campania, founders of Formiae.
Laestrygonius *adj see n.*
laesus *ppp of* **laedō**.
laetābilis *adj* joyful.
laetē *adv* gladly.
laetificō, -āre *vt* to gladden.
laetificus *adj* glad, joyful.
laetitia, -ae *f* joy, delight, exuberance.
laetor, -ārī, -ātus *vi* to rejoice, be glad.
laetus *adj* glad, cheerful; delighting (in); pleasing, welcome; (*growth*) fertile, rich; (*style*) exuberant.
laevē *adv* awkwardly.
laevus *adj* left; stupid; ill-omened, unfortunate; (*augury*) lucky, favourable ♦ *f* left hand.
laganum, -ī *nt* a kind of oilcake.
lagēos, -ī *f* a Greek vine.
lagoena, -ae *f* flagon.
lagōis, -idis *f* a kind of grouse.
lagōna, -ae *f* flagon.
Lāiadēs, -ae *m* Oedipus.
Lāius, -ī *m* father of Oedipus.
lallō, -āre *vi* to sing a lullaby.
lāma, -ae *f* bog.
lamberō, -āre *vt* to tear to pieces.
lambō, -ere, -ī *vt* to lick, touch; (*river*) to wash.
lāmenta, -ōrum *ntpl* lamentation.
lāmentābilis *adj* mournful, sorrowful.
lāmentārius *adj* sorrowful.
lāmentātiō, -ōnis *f* weeping, lamentation.
lāmentor, -ārī, -ātus *vi* to weep, lament ♦ *vt* to weep for, bewail.
lamia, -ae *f* witch.
lāmina (lammina, lāmna), -ae *f* plate, leaf (*of metal, wood*); blade; coin.
lampas, -dis *f* torch; brightness, day.
Lamus, -ī *m* Laestrygonian king.
lāna, -ae *f* wool.
lānārius, -ī *and* **iī** *m* wool-worker.
lānātus *adj* woolly.
lancea, -ae *f* spear, lance.
lancinō, -āre *vt* to tear up; to squander.
lāneus *adj* woollen.
languefaciō, -ere *vt* to make weary.
languēo, -ēre *vi* to be weary, be weak, droop; to be idle, dull.
languēscō, -ēscere, -uī *vi* to grow faint, droop.
languidē *adv see adj.*
languidulus *adj* languid.
languidus *adj* faint, languid, sluggish; listless, feeble.
languor, -ōris *m* faintness, fatigue, weakness; dullness, apathy.
laniātus, -ūs *m* mangling; (*mind*) anguish.

Noun declensions and verb conjugations are shown on pp xiii to xxv. The present infinitive ending of a verb shows to which conjugation it belongs: **-āre** = 1st; **-ēre** = 2nd; **-ere** = 3rd and **-īre** = 4th. Irregular verbs are shown on p xxvi

laniēna, -ae *f* butcher's shop.
lānificium, -ī *and* **iī** *nt* wool-working.
lānificus *adj* wool-working.
lāniger, -ī *adj* fleecy ♦ *m/f* ram, sheep.
laniō, -āre, -āvī, -ātum *vt* to tear to pieces, mangle.
lanista, -ae *m* trainer of gladiators, fencing master; (*fig*) agitator.
lānitium, -ī *and* **iī** *nt* woolgrowing.
lanius, -ī *and* **iī** *m* butcher.
lanterna, -ae *f* lamp.
lanternārius, -ī *and* **iī** *m* guide.
lānūgō, -inis *f* down, woolliness.
Lānuvīnus *adj see n.*
Lānuvium, -ī *nt* Latin town on the Appian Way.
lānx, lancis *f* dish, platter; (*balance*) scale.
Lāomedōn, -ontis *m* king of Troy (*father of Priam*).
Lāomedontēus *adj and* **ontiadēs, -ae** *m* son of Lāomedōn; (*pl*) Trojans.
Lāomedontius *adj* Trojan.
lapathum, -ī *nt,* **-us, -ī** *f* sorrel.
lapicīda, -ae *m* stonecutter.
lapicīdīnae, -ārum *fpl* quarries.
lapidārius *adj* stone- (*in cpds*).
lapidātiō, -ōnis *f* throwing of stones.
lapidātor, -ōris *m* stone thrower.
lapideus *adj* of stones, stone- (*in cpds*).
lapidō, -āre *vt* to stone ♦ *vi* to rain stones.
lapidōsus *adj* stony; hard as stone.
lapillus, -ī *m* stone, pebble; precious stone, mosaic piece.
lapis, -dis *m* stone; milestone, boundary stone, tombstone; precious stone; marble; auctioneer's stand; (*abuse*) blockhead; **bis ad eundem (offendere)** ≈ *make the same mistake twice*; **Juppiter ~** the Jupiter stone.
Lapithae, -ārum *and* **-um** *mpl* Lapiths (*mythical people of Thessaly*).
Lapithaeus, -ēius *adj see n.*
lappa, -ae *f* goosegrass.
lāpsiō, -ōnis *f* tendency.
lāpsō, -āre *vi* to slip, stumble.
lāpsus *ppa of* **lābor**.
lāpsus, -ūs *m* fall, slide, course, flight; error, failure.
laqueāria, -ium *ntpl* panelled ceiling.
laqueātus *adj* panelled, with a panelled ceiling.
laqueus, -ī *m* noose, snare, halter; (*fig*) trap.
Lār, Laris *m* tutelary deity, household god; hearth, home.
lārdum *etc see* **lāridum**.
largē *adv* plentifully, generously, very much.
largificus *adj* bountiful.
largifluus *adj* copious.
largiloquus *adj* talkative.
largior, -īrī, -ītus *vt* to give freely, lavish; to bestow, confer ♦ *vi* to give largesses.
largitās, -ātis *f* liberality, abundance.
largiter *adv* = **large**.
largītiō, -ōnis *f* giving freely, distributing; bribery.

largītor, -ōris *m* liberal giver, dispenser; spendthrift; briber.
largus *adj* copious, ample; liberal, bountiful.
lāridum, -ī *nt* bacon fat.
Lārissa (Lārīsa), -ae *f* town in Thessaly.
Lārissaeus, -ēnsis *adj see n.*
Lārius, -ī *m* lake Como.
larix, -cis *f* larch.
larva, -ae *f* ghost; mask.
larvātus *adj* bewitched.
lasanum, -ī *nt* pot.
lasārpīcifer, -ī *adj* producing asafoetida.
lascīvia, -ae *f* playfulness; impudence, lewdness.
lascīviō, -īre *vi* to frolic, frisk; to run wild, be irresponsible.
lascīvus *adj* playful, frisky; impudent, lustful.
laserpīcium, -ī *and* **iī** *nt* silphium.
lassitūdō, -inis *f* fatigue, heaviness.
lassō, -āre, *vt* to tire, fatigue.
lassulus *adj* rather weary.
lassus *adj* tired, exhausted.
lātē *adv* widely, extensively; **longē ~que** far and wide, everywhere.
latebra, -ae *f* hiding place, retreat; (*fig*) loophole, pretext.
latebricola, -ae *adj* low-living.
latebrōsē *adv* in hiding.
latebrōsus *adj* secret, full of coverts; porous.
latēns, -entis *pres p of* **lateō** ♦ *adj* hidden, secret.
latenter *adv* in secret.
lateō, -ēre, -uī *vi* to lie hid, lurk, skulk; to be in safety, live a retired life; to be unknown, escape notice.
later, -is *m* brick, tile; **~em lavāre** ≈ *waste one's time.*
laterāmen, -inis *nt* earthenware.
laterculus, -ī *m* small brick, tile; kind of cake.
latericius *adj* of bricks ♦ *nt* brickwork.
lāterna *etc see* **lanterna**.
latēscō, -ere *vi* to hide oneself.
latex, -icis *m* water; any other liquid.
Latiar, -iaris *nt* festival of Jupiter Latiaris.
Latiaris *adj* Latin.
latibulum, -ī *nt* hiding place, den, lair.
lāticlāvius *adj* with a broad purple stripe ♦ *m* senator, patrician.
lātifundium, -ī *and* **iī** *nt* large estate.
Latīnē *adv* in Latin, into Latin; **~ loquī** speak Latin, speak plainly, speak correctly; **~ reddere** translate into Latin.
Latīnitās, -ātis *f* good Latin, Latinity; Latin rights.
Latīnus *adj* Latin ♦ *m legendary king of the Laurentians.*
lātiō, -ōnis *f* bringing; proposing.
latitō, -āre *vi* to hide away, lurk, keep out of the way.
lātitūdō, -inis *f* breadth, width; size; broad pronunciation.
Latium, -ī *nt* district of Italy including Rome; Latin rights.

Latius = Latiaris, Latinus.
Lātōis, -idis *f* Diana.
Lātōis , -ius *adj see n.*
lātom- *etc see* **lautum-**.
Lātōna, -ae *f mother of Apollo and Diana.*
Lātōnigenae, -ārum *pl* Apollo and Diana.
Lātōnius *adj, f* Diana.
lātor, -ōris *m* proposer.
Lātōus *adj* of Latona ♦ *m* Apollo.
lātrātor, -ōris *m* barker.
lātrātus, -ūs *m* barking.
lātrō, -āre *vi* to bark; to rant, roar ♦ *vt* to bark at; to clamour for.
latrō, -ōnis *m* mercenary soldier; bandit, brigand; (*chess*) man.
latrōcinium, -ī and iī *nt* highway robbery, piracy.
latrōcinor, -āri, -ātus *vi* to serve as a mercenary; to be a brigand *or* pirate.
latrunculus, -ī *m* brigand; (*chess*) man.
lātumiae *etc see* **lautumiae.**
lātus *ppp of* **ferō.**
lātus *adj* broad, wide; extensive; (*pronunciation*) broad; (*style*) diffuse.
latus, -eris *nt* side, flank; lungs; body; ~ **dare** expose oneself; ~ **tegere** walk beside; **~eris dolor** pleurisy; **ab ~ere** on the flank.
latusculum, -ī *nt* little side.
laudābilis *adj* praiseworthy.
laudābiliter *adv* laudably.
laudātiō, -ōnis *f* commendation, eulogy; panegyric, testimonial.
laudātor, -ōris *m*, **-rīx, -rīcis** *f* praiser, eulogizer; speaker of a funeral oration.
laudātus *adj* excellent.
laudō, -āre, -āvī, -ātum *vt* to praise, commend, approve; to pronounce a funeral oration over; to quote, name.
laurea, -ae *f* bay tree; crown of bay; triumph.
laureātus *adj* crowned with bay; (*despatches*) victorious.
Laurentēs, -um *mpl* Laurentians (*people of ancient Latium*).
Laurentius *adj see n.*
laureola, -ae *f* triumph.
laureus *adj* of bay.
lauricomus *adj* bay-covered.
lauriger, -ī *adj* crowned with bay.
laurus, -ī *f* bay tree; bay crown; victory, triumph.
laus, laudis *f* praise, approval; glory, fame; praiseworthy act, merit, worth.
lautē *adv* elegantly, splendidly; excellently.
lautia, -ōrum *ntpl* State banquet.
lautitia, -ae *f* luxury.
lautumiae, -ārum *fpl* stone quarry; prison.
lautus *ppp of* **lavō** ♦ *adj* neat, elegant, sumptuous; fine, grand, distinguished.
lavābrum, -ī *nt* bath.
lavātiō, -ōnis *f* washing, bath; bathing gear.

Lāvīnium, -ī *nt town of ancient Latium.*
Lāvīnius *adj see n.*
lavō, -āre, lāvī, lautum (lavātum *and* **lōtum)** *vt* to wash, bathe; to wet, soak, wash away.
laxāmentum, -ī *nt* respite, relaxation.
laxē *adv* loosely, freely.
laxitās, -ātis *f* roominess.
laxō, -āre, -āvī, -ātum *vt* to extend, open out; to undo; to slacken; (*fig*) to release, relieve; to relax, abate ♦ *vi* (*price*) to fall off.
laxus *adj* wide, loose, roomy; (*time*) deferred; (*fig*) free, easy.
lea, -ae *f* lioness.
leaena, -ae *f* lioness.
Lēander, -rī *m* Hero's lover (*who swam the Hellespont*).
lebēs, -ētis *m* basin, pan, cauldron.
lectīca, -ae *f* litter, sedan chair.
lectīcārius, -ī *and* **iī** *m* litter-bearer.
lectīcula, -ae *f* small litter; bier.
lectiō, -ōnis *f* selecting; reading, calling the roll.
lectisterniātor, -ōris *m* arranger of couches.
lectisternium, -ī *and* **iī** *nt* religious feast.
lectitō, -āre *vt* to read frequently.
lectiuncula, -ae *f* light reading.
lēctor, -ōris *m* reader.
lectulus, -ī *m* couch, bed.
lectus, -ī *m* couch, bed; bier.
lēctus *ppp of* **legō** ♦ *adj* picked; choice, excellent.
Lēda, -ae *and* **ē, -ēs** *f* mother of Castor, Pollux, Helen and Clytemnestra.
Lēdaeus *adj see n.*
lēgātiō, -ōnis *f* mission, embassy; members of a mission; (MIL) staff appointment, command of a legion; **lībera ~** free commission (to visit provinces); **vōtīva ~** free commission for paying a vow in a province.
lēgātor, -ōris *m* testator.
lēgātum, -ī *nt* legacy, bequest.
lēgātus, -ī *m* delegate, ambassador; deputy, lieutenant; commander (of a legion).
lēgifer, -ī *adj* law-giving.
legiō, -ōnis *f* legion (*up to 6000 men*); (*pl*) troops, army.
legiōnārius *adj* legionary.
lēgirupa, -ae; -iō, -iōnis *m* lawbreaker.
lēgitimē *adv* lawfully, properly.
lēgitimus *adj* lawful, legal; right, proper.
legiuncula, -ae *f* small legion.
lēgō, -āre, -āvī, -ātum *vt* to send, charge, commission; to appoint as deputy or lieutenant; (*will*) to leave, bequeath.
legō, -ere, lēgī, lēctum *vt* to gather, pick; to choose, select; (*sail*) to furl; (*places*) to traverse, pass, coast along; (*view*) to scan; (*writing*) to read, recite; **senātum ~** call the

roll of the senate.

lēgulēius, -ī _and_ **iī** _m_ pettifogging lawyer.

legūmen, -inis _nt_ pulse, bean.

lembus, -ī _m_ pinnace, cutter.

Lemnias _f_ Lemnian woman.

Lemnicola, -ae _m_ Vulcan.

lēmniscātus _adj_ beribboned.

lēmniscus, -ī _m_ ribbon (_hanging from a victor's crown_).

Lēmnius _adj see n._

Lēmnos (-us), -ī _f_ Aegean island, abode of Vulcan.

Lemurēs, -um _mpl_ ghosts.

lēna, -ae _f_ procuress; seductress.

Lēnaeus _adj_ Bacchic ♦ _m_ Bacchus.

lēnīmen, -inis _nt_ solace, comfort.

lēnīmentum, -ī _nt_ sop.

lēniō, -īre, -īvī _and_ **iī, -ītum** _vt_ to soften, soothe, heal, calm.

lēnis _adj_ soft, smooth, mild, gentle, calm.

lēnitās, -ātis _f_ softness, smoothness, mildness, tenderness.

lēniter _adv_ softly, gently; moderately, half-heartedly.

lēnitūdō, -inis _f_ smoothness, mildness.

lēnō, -ōnis _m_ pander, brothel keeper; go-between.

lēnōcinium, -ī _and_ **iī** _nt_ pandering; allurement; meretricious ornament.

lēnōcinor, -ārī, -ātus _vi_ to pay court to; to promote.

lēnōnius _adj_ pander's.

lēns, lentis _f_ lentil.

lentē _adv_ slowly; calmly, coolly.

lentēscō, -ere _vi_ to become sticky, soften; to relax.

lentīscifer, -ī _adj_ bearing mastic trees.

lentīscus, -ī _f_ mastic tree.

lentitūdō, -inis _f_ slowness, dullness, apathy.

lentō, -āre _vt_ to bend.

lentulus _adj_ rather slow.

lentus _adj_ sticky, sluggish; pliant; slow, lasting, lingering; (_person_) calm, at ease, indifferent.

lēnunculus, -ī _m_ skiff.

leō, -ōnis _m_ lion.

Leōnidās, -ae _m_ Spartan king who fell at Thermopylae.

leōnīnus _adj_ lion's.

Leontīnī, -ōrum _mpl_ town in Sicily.

Leontīnus _adj see n._

lepas, -dis _f_ limpet.

lepidē _adv_ neatly, charmingly; (_reply_) very well, splendidly.

lepidus _adj_ pleasant, charming, neat, witty.

lepōs (lepor), -ōris _m_ pleasantness, charm; wit.

lepus, -oris _m_ hare.

lepusculus, -ī _m_ young hare.

Lerna, -ae _and_ **ē, -ēs** _f_ marsh near Argos (_where Hercules killed the Hydra_).

Lernaeus _adj_ Lernaean.

Lesbias, -iadis _f_ Lesbian woman.

Lesbis, Lesbius _adj see n._

Lesbos (-us), -ī _f_ Aegean island (_home of Alcaeus and Sappho_).

Lesbous _f_ Lesbian woman.

lētālis _adj_ deadly.

Lēthaeus _adj_ of Lethe; infernal; soporific.

lēthargicus, -ī _m_ lethargic person.

lēthargus, -ī _m_ drowsiness.

Lēthē, -ēs _f_ river in the lower world, which caused forgetfulness.

lētifer, -ī _adj_ fatal.

lētō, -āre _vt_ to kill.

lētum, -ī _nt_ death; destruction.

Leucadius _adj see n._

Leucas, -dis _and_ **dia, -diae** _f_ island off W. Greece.

Leucothea, -ae, -ē, -ēs _f_ Ino (_a sea goddess_).

Leuctra, -ōrum _ntpl_ battlefield in Boeotia.

Leuctricus _adj see n._

levāmen, -inis _nt_ alleviation, comfort.

levāmentum, -ī _nt_ mitigation, consolation.

levātiō, -ōnis _f_ relief; diminishing.

lēvī _perf of_ **linō**.

leviculus _adj_ rather vain.

levidēnsis _adj_ slight.

levipēs, -edis _adj_ light-footed.

levis _adj_ (_weight_) light; (_MIL_) light-armed; (_fig_) easy, gentle; (_importance_) slight, trivial; (_motion_) nimble, fleet; (_character_) fickle, unreliable.

lēvis _adj_ smooth; (_youth_) beardless, delicate.

levisomnus _adj_ light-sleeping.

levitās, -ātis _f_ lightness; nimbleness; fickleness, frivolity.

lēvitās, -ātis _f_ smoothness; fluency.

leviter _adv_ lightly; slightly; easily.

levō, -āre _vt_ to lighten, ease; (_fig_) to alleviate, lessen; to comfort, relieve; to impair; (_danger_) to avert; **sē ~** rise.

lēvō, -āre _vt_ to smooth, polish.

lēvor, -ōris _m_ smoothness.

lēx, lēgis _f_ law, statute; bill; rule, principle; contract, condition; **lēgem ferre** propose a bill; **lēgem perferre** carry a motion; **lēge agere** proceed according to law; **sine lēge** out of control.

lībāmen, -inis _nt_ offering, libation.

lībāmentum, -ī _nt_ offering, libation.

lībātiō, -ōnis _f_ libation.

lībella, -ae _f_ small coin, as; level; **ad ~am** exactly; **ex ~ā** sole heir.

libellus, -ī _m_ small book; notebook, diary, letter; notice, programme, handbill; petition, complaint; lampoon.

libēns, -entis _adj_ willing, glad.

libenter _adv_ willingly, with pleasure.

liber, -rī _m_ inner bark (of a tree); book; register.

Līber, -ī _m_ Italian god of fertility (_identified with Bacchus_).

līber, -ī _adj_ free, open, unrestricted, undisturbed; (_with abl_) free from; (_speech_) frank; (_POL_) free, not slave, democratic.

Libera, -ae f Proserpine; Ariadne.

Liberālia, -ālium ntpl festival of Liber in March.

liberālis adj of freedom, of free citizens, gentlemanly, honourable; generous, liberal; handsome.

liberālitās, -ātis f courtesy, kindness; generosity; bounty.

liberāliter adv courteously, nobly; generously.

liberātiō, -ōnis f delivery, freeing; (law) acquittal.

liberātor, -ōris m liberator, deliverer.

liberē adv freely, frankly, boldly.

liberī, -ōrum mpl children.

liberō, -āre, -āvī, -ātum vt to free, set free, release; to exempt; (law) to acquit; (slave) to give freedom to; **fidem ~** keep one's promise; **nōmina ~** cancel debts.

liberta, -ae f freedwoman.

libertās, -ātis f freedom, liberty; status of a freeman; (POL) independence; freedom of speech, outspokenness.

libertīnus adj of a freedman, freed ♦ m freedman ♦ f freedwoman.

libertus, -ī m freedman.

libet (lubet), -ēre, -uit and **itum est** vi (impers) it pleases; **mihi ~** I like; **ut ~** as you please.

libīdinōsē adv wilfully.

libīdinōsus adj wilful, arbitrary, extravagant; sensual, lustful.

libīdō (lubīdō), -inis f desire, passion; wilfulness, caprice; lust.

libita, -ōrum ntpl pleasure, fancy.

Libitīna, -ae f goddess of burials.

libō, -āre, -āvī, -ātum vt to taste, sip, touch; to pour (a libation), offer; to extract, take out; to impair.

libra, -ae f pound; balance, pair of scales; **ad ~am** of equal size.

librāmentum, -ī nt level surface, weight (to give balance or movement); (water) fall.

librāria, -ae f head spinner.

librāriolus, -ī m copyist.

librārium, -ī and **iī** nt bookcase.

librārius adj of books ♦ m copyist.

librātus adj level; powerful.

librīlis adj weighing a pound.

libritor, -ōris m slinger.

librō, -āre, -āvī, -ātum vt to poise, hold balanced; to swing, hurl.

libum, -ī nt cake.

Liburna, -ae f a fast galley, frigate.

Liburnī, -ōrum mpl people of Illyria.

Liburnus adj Liburnian.

Libya, -ae, -ē, -ēs f Africa.

Libycus adj African.

Libyes, -um mpl Libyans, people in N. Africa.

Libyssus, Libystinus, Libystis adj = **Libycus**.

licēns, -entis adj free, bold, unrestricted.

licenter adv freely, lawlessly.

licentia, -ae f freedom, license; lawlessness, licentiousness.

liceō, -ēre, -uī vi to be for sale, value at.

liceor, -ērī, -itus vt, vi to bid (at an auction), bid for.

licet, -ēre, -uit and **itum est** vi (impers) it is permitted, it is lawful; (reply) all right ♦ conj although; **mihi ~** I may.

Licinius, -ī m Roman family name (esp with surname Crassus).

Licinius adj see n.

licitātiō, -ōnis f bidding (at a sale).

licitor, -ārī vi to make a bid.

licitus adj lawful.

licium, -ī and **iī** nt thread.

lictor, -ōris m lictor (an attendant with fasces preceding a magistrate).

licuī perf of **liceō**; perf of **liquēscō**.

liēn, -ēnis m spleen.

ligāmen, -inis nt band, bandage.

ligāmentum, -ī nt bandage.

Liger, -is m river Loire.

lignārius, -ī and **iī** m carpenter.

lignātiō, -ōnis f fetching wood.

lignātor, -ōris m woodcutter.

ligneolus adj wooden.

ligneus adj wooden.

lignor, -ārī vi to fetch wood.

lignum, -ī nt wood, firewood, timber; **in silvam ~a ferre** ≈ carry coals to Newcastle.

ligō, -āre, -āvī, -ātum vt to tie up, bandage; (fig) to unite.

ligō, -ōnis m mattock, hoe.

ligula, -ae f shoestrap.

Ligur, -ris m/f Ligurian.

Liguria, -riae f district of N.W. Italy.

ligūriō (ligurriō), -īre vt to lick; to eat daintily; (fig) to feast on, lust after.

ligūrītiō, -ōnis f daintiness.

Ligus, -ris m/f Ligurian.

Ligusticus, -stīnus adj see n.

ligustrum, -ī nt privet.

lilium, -ī and **iī** nt lily; (MIL) spiked pit.

līma, -ae f file; (fig) revision.

līmātius adv more elegantly.

līmātulus adj refined.

līmāx, -ācis f slug, snail.

limbus, -ī m fringe, hem.

līmen, -inis nt threshold, lintel; doorway, entrance; house, home; (fig) beginning.

līmes, -itis m path between fields, boundary; path, track, way; frontier, boundary line.

līmō, -āre, -āvī, -ātum vt to file; (fig) to polish, refine; to file down, investigate carefully; to take away from.

līmōsus adj muddy.

limpidus adj clear, limpid.

līmus adj sidelong, askance.

līmus, -ī m mud, slime, dirt.

līmus, -ī m ceremonial apron.

līnea, -ae *f* line, string; plumbline; boundary; **ad ~am, rectā ~ā** vertically; **extrēmā ~ā amāre** love at a distance.

līneāmentum, -ī *nt* line; feature; outline.

līneus *adj* flaxen, linen.

lingō, -ere *vt* to lick.

lingua, -ae *f* tongue; speech, language; tongue of land; **~ Latīna** Latin.

lingula, -ae *f* tongue of land.

līniger, -ī *adj* linen-clad.

linō, -ere, lēvī, litum *vt* to daub, smear; to overlay; (*writing*) to rub out; (*fig*) to befoul.

linquō, -ere, līquī *vt* to leave, quit; to give up, let alone; (*pass*) to faint, swoon; **~itur ut it** remains to.

linteātus *adj* canvas.

linteō, -ōnis *m* linen weaver.

linter, -ris *f* boat; trough.

linteum, -ī *nt* linen cloth, canvas; sail.

linteus *adj* linen.

lintriculus, -ī *m* small boat.

līnum, -ī *nt* flax; linen; thread, line, rope; net.

Lipara, -ae, -ē, -ēs *f* island N. of Sicily (*now* Lipari).

Liparaeus, -ēnsis *adj see n.*

lippiō, -īre *vi* to have sore eyes.

lippitūdō, -inis *f* inflammation of the eyes.

lippus *adj* blear-eyed, with sore eyes; (*fig*) blind.

liquefaciō, -facere, -fēcī, -factum (*pass* -fīō) *vt* to melt, dissolve; to decompose; (*fig*) to enervate.

liquēns, -entis *adj* fluid, clear.

liquēscō, -ere, licuī *vi* to melt; to clear; (*fig*) to grow soft, waste away.

liquet, -ēre, licuit *vi* (*impers*) it is clear, it is evident; **nōn ~** not proven.

līquī *perf of* **linquō.**

liquidō *adv* clearly.

liquidus *adj* fluid, liquid, flowing; clear, transparent, pure; (*mind*) calm, serene ♦ *nt* liquid water.

liquō, -āre *vt* to melt; to strain.

liquor, -ī *vi* to flow; (*fig*) to waste away.

liquor, -ōris *m* fluidity; liquid, the sea.

Līris, -is *m* river between Latium and Campania.

līs, lītis *f* quarrel, dispute; lawsuit; matter in dispute; **lītem aestimāre** assess damages.

litātiō, -ōnis *f* favourable sacrifice.

lītera *etc see* **littera.**

lītigātor, -ōris *m* litigant.

lītigiōsus *adj* quarrelsome, contentious; disputed.

lītigium, -ī *and* **iī** *nt* quarrel.

lītigō, -āre *vi* to quarrel; to go to law.

litō, -āre, -āvī, -ātum *vi* to offer an acceptable sacrifice, obtain favourable omens; (*with dat*) to propitiate ♦ *vt* to offer successfully.

lītorālis *adj* of the shore.

lītoreus *adj* of the shore.

littera, -ae *f* letter (of the alphabet).

litterae, -ārum *fpl* writing; letter, dispatch;

document, ordinance; literature; learning, scholarship; **~ās discere** learn to read and write; **homō trium ~ārum** thief (*of fur*); **sine ~īs** uncultured.

litterārius *adj* of reading and writing.

litterātē *adv* in clear letters; literally.

litterātor, -ōris *m* grammarian.

litterātūra, -ae *f* writing, alphabet.

litterātus *adj* with letters on it, branded; educated, learned.

litterula, -ae *f* small letter; short note; (*pl*) studies.

litūra, -ae *f* correction, erasure, blot.

litus *ppp of* **linō.**

lītus, -oris *nt* shore, beach, coast; bank; **~ arāre** labour in vain.

lituus, -ī *m* augur's staff; trumpet; (*fig*) starter.

līvēns, -entis *pres p of* **līveō** ♦ *adj* bluish, black and blue.

līveō, -ēre *vi* to be black and blue; to envy.

līvēscō, -ere *vi* to turn black and blue.

Līviānus *adj* = **Līvius.**

līvidulus *adj* a little jealous.

līvidus *adj* bluish, black and blue; envious, malicious.

Līvius, -ī Roman family name (*esp the first Latin poet*); *the famous historian, Livy.*

Līvius *adj see n.*

līvor, -ōris *m* bluish colour; envy, malice.

lixa, -ae *m* sutler, camp-follower.

locātiō, -ōnis *f* leasing; lease, contract.

locātōrius *adj* concerned with leases.

locitō, -āre *vt* to let frequently.

locō, -āre, -āvī, -ātum *vt* to place, put; to give in marriage; to let, lease, hire out; to contract for; (*money*) to invest.

loculus, -ī *m* little place; (*pl*) satchel, purse.

locuplēs, -ētis *adj* rich, opulent; reliable, responsible.

locuplētō, -āre *vt* to enrich.

locus, -ī *m* (*pl* -ī *m and* -a *nt*) place, site, locality region; (*MIL*) post; (*theatre*) seat; (*book*) passage; (*speech*) topic, subject, argument; (*fig*) room, occasion; situation, state; rank, position; **~ī** individual spots; **~a** regions, ground; **~ī commūnēs** general arguments; **~ō** (*with gen*) instead of; **in ~ō** opportunely; **eō ~ī** in the position; **intereā ~ī** meanwhile.

lōcusta, -ae *f* locust.

locūtiō, -ōnis *f* speech; pronunciation.

locūtus *ppa of* **loquor.**

lōdīx, -īcis *f* blanket.

logica, -ōrum *ntpl* logic.

logos (-us), -ī *m* word; idle talk; witticism.

lōlīg- *etc see* **lollīg-.**

lolium, -ī *and* **iī** *nt* darnel.

lollīgō, -inis *f* cuttlefish.

lōmentum, -ī *nt* face cream.

Londinium, -ī *nt* London.

longaevus *adj* aged.

longē *adv* far, far off; (*time*) long; (*compar*) by far, very much; **~ esse** be far away, of no avail; ~ **latēque** everywhere.

longinquitās, -ātis f length; distance; duration.

longinquus adj distant, remote; foreign, strange; lasting, wearisome; (hope) long deferred.

longitūdō, -inis f length; duration; **in ~inem** lengthwise.

longiusculus adj rather long.

longulē adv rather far.

longulus adj rather long.

longurius, -ī and **iī** m long pole.

longus adj long; vast; (time) long, protracted, tedious; (hope) far-reaching; **~a nāvis** warship; **~um est** it would be tedious; **nē ~um faciam** ≈ to cut a long story short.

loquācitās, -ātis f talkativeness.

loquāciter adv see adj.

loquāculus adj somewhat talkative.

loquāx, -ācis adj talkative, chattering.

loquella, -ae f language, words.

loquor, -quī, cūtus vt, vi to speak, talk, say; to talk about, mention; (fig) to indicate; **rēs ~quitur ipsa** the facts speak for themselves.

lōrārius, -ī and **iī** m flogger.

lōrātus adj strapped.

lōreus adj of leather strips.

lōrīca, -ae f breastplate; parapet.

lōrīcātus adj mailed.

lōripēs, -edis adj bandylegged.

lōrum, -ī nt strap; whip, lash; leather charm; (pl) reins.

lōtos (-us), -ī f lotus.

lōtus ppp of **lavō**.

lubēns see **libēns**.

lubentia, -ae f pleasure.

lubet, lubīdō see **libet, libīdō**.

lūbricō, -āre vt to make slippery.

lūbricus adj slippery, slimy; gliding, fleeting; (fig) dangerous, hazardous.

Lūca bōs f elephant.

Lūcānia, -iae f district of S. Italy.

Lūcanica f kind of sausage.

Lūcānus adj Lucanian ♦ m the epic poet Lucan.

lūcar, -āris nt forest tax.

lucellum, -ī nt small gain.

lūceō, -cēre, -xī vi to shine, be light; (impers) to dawn, be daylight; (fig) to shine, be clear; **meridiē nōn ~cēre** ≈ (argue) that black is white.

Lūcerēs, -um mpl a Roman patrician tribe.

Lūceria, -iae f town in Apulia.

Lūcerīnus adj see n.

lucerna, -ae f lamp; (fig) ≈ midnight oil.

lūcēscō, -ere vi to begin to shine, get light, dawn.

lūcidē adv clearly.

lūcidus adj bright, clear; (fig) lucid.

lūcifer, -ī adj light-bringing ♦ m morning star, Venus; day.

lūcifugus adj shunning the light.

Lūcīlius, -ī m Roman family name (esp the first Latin satirist).

Lūcīna, -ae f goddess of childbirth.

lūcīscō etc see **lūcēscō**.

Lucmō (Lucumō), -ōnis m Etruscan prince or priest.

Lucrētia, -iae f wife of Collatinus, ravished by Tarquin.

Lucrētius, -ī m Roman family name (esp the philosophic poet).

lucrifuga, -ae m non-profiteer.

Lucrīnēnsis adj see n.

Lucrīnus, -ī m lake near Baiae (famous for oysters).

lucror, -ārī, -ātus vt to gain, win, acquire.

lucrōsus adj profitable.

lucrum, -ī nt profit, gain; greed; wealth; **~ī facere** gain, get the credit of; **~ō esse** be of advantage; **in ~īs pōnere** count as gain.

luctāmen, -inis nt struggle, exertion.

luctātiō, -ōnis f wrestling; fight, contest.

luctātor, -ōris m wrestler.

lūctificus adj baleful.

lūctisonus adj mournful.

luctor, -ārī, -ātus vi to wrestle; to struggle, fight.

lūctuōsus adj sorrowful, lamentable.

lūctus, -ūs m mourning, lamentation; mourning (dress).

lūcubrātiō, -ōnis f work by lamplight, nocturnal study.

lūcubrō, -āre, -āvī, -ātum vi to work by night ♦ vt to compose by night.

lūculentē adv splendidly, right.

lūculenter adv very well.

lūculentus adj bright; (fig) brilliant, excellent, rich, fine.

Lūcullus, -ī m Roman surname (esp the conqueror of Mithridates).

lūcus, -ī m grove; wood.

lūdia, -ae f woman gladiator.

lūdibrium, -ī and **iī** nt mockery, derision; laughing stock; sport, play; **~iō habēre** make fun of.

lūdibundus adj playful; safely, easily.

lūdicer, -rī adj playful; theatrical.

lūdicrum, -ī nt public show, play; sport.

lūdificātiō, -ōnis f ridicule; tricking.

lūdificātor, -ōris m mocker.

lūdificō, -āre; -or, -ārī, -ātus vt to make a fool of, ridicule; to delude, thwart.

lūdiō, -ōnis m actor.

lūdius, -ī and **iī** m actor; gladiator.

lūdō, -dere, -sī, -sum vi to play; to sport, frolic; to dally, make love ♦ vt to play at; to amuse oneself with; to mimic, imitate; to ridicule, mock; to delude.

lūdus, -ī m game, sport, play; (pl) public spectacle, games; school; (fig) child's play; fun, jest; (love) dalliance; **~um dare** humour;

~ōs facere put on a public show; make fun of.

luella, -ae *f* atonement.

luēs, -is *f* plague, pest; misfortune.

Lugdūnēnsis *adj see n.*

Lugdūnum, -ī *nt* town in E. Gaul (*now* Lyons).

lūgeō, -gēre, -xī *vt, vi* to mourn; to be in mourning.

lūgubris *adj* mourning; disastrous; (*sound*) plaintive ♦ *ntpl* mourning dress.

lumbī, -ōrum *mpl* loins.

lumbrīcus, -ī *m* worm.

lūmen, -inis *m* light; lamp, torch; day; eye; life; (*fig*) ornament, glory; clarity.

lūmināre, -is *nt* window.

lūminōsus *adj* brilliant.

lūna, -ae *f* moon; month; crescent.

lūnāris *adj* of the moon.

lūnātus *adj* crescent-shaped.

lūnō, -āre *vt* to bend into a crescent.

luō, -ere, -ī *vt* to pay; to atone for; to avert by expiation.

lupa, -ae *f* she-wolf; prostitute.

lupānar, -āris *nt* brothel.

lupātus *adj* toothed ♦ *m and ntpl* curb.

Lupercal, -ālis *nt* a grotto sacred to Pan.

Lupercālia, -ālium *ntpl* festival of Pan in February.

Lupercus, -ī *m* Pan; priest of Pan.

lupīnum, -ī *nt* lupin; sham money, counters.

lupīnus *adj* wolf's.

lupīnus, -ī *m* lupin; sham money, counters.

lupus, -ī *m* wolf; (*fish*) pike; toothed bit; grapnel; ~ **in fābulā** ≈ talk of the devil.

lūridus *adj* pale yellow, ghastly pallid.

lūror, -ōris *m* yellowness.

lūscinia, -ae *f* nightingale.

luscitiōsus *adj* purblind.

luscus *adj* one-eyed.

lūsiō, -ōnis *f* play.

Lūsitānia, -iae *f* part of W. Spain (*including what is now* Portugal).

Lūsitānus *adj see n.*

lūsitō, -āre *vi* to play.

lūsor, -ōris *m* player; humorous writer.

lūstrālis *adj* lustral, propitiatory; quinquennial.

lūstrātiō, -ōnis *f* purification; roving.

lūstrō, -āre, -āvī, -ātum *vt* to purify; (*motion*) to go round, encircle, traverse; (*MIL*) to review; (*eyes*) to scan, survey; (*mind*) to consider; (*light*) to illuminate.

lustror, -ārī *vi* to frequent brothels.

lustrum, -ī *nt* den, lair; (*pl*) wild country; (*fig*) brothels; debauchery.

lūstrum, -ī *nt* purificatory sacrifice; (*time*) five years.

lūsus *ppp of* lūdō.

lūsus, -ūs *m* play, game, sport; dalliance.

lūteolus *adj* yellow.

Lutetia, -ae *f* town in N. Gaul (*now* Paris).

lūteus *adj* yellow, orange.

luteus *adj* of clay; muddy, dirty, (*fig*) vile.

lutitō, -āre *vt* to throw mud at.

lutulentus *adj* muddy, filthy; (*fig*) foul.

lūtum, -ī *nt* dyer's weed; yellow.

lutum, -ī *nt* mud, mire; clay.

lūx, lūcis *f* light; daylight; day; life; (*fig*) public view; glory, encouragement, enlightenment; **lūce** in the daytime; **prīmā lūce** at daybreak; **lūce carentēs** the dead.

lūxī *perf of* lūceō; *perf of* lūgeō.

luxor, -ārī *vi* to live riotously.

luxuria, -ae, -ēs, -ēī *f* rankness, profusion; extravagance, luxury.

luxuriō, -āre, -or, -ārī *vi* to grow to excess, be luxuriant; (*fig*) to be exuberant, run riot.

luxuriōsē *adv* voluptuously.

luxuriōsus *adj* luxuriant; excessive, extravagant; voluptuous.

luxus, -ūs *m* excess, debauchery, pomp.

Lyaeus, -ī *m* Bacchus; wine.

Lycaeus, -ī *m* mountain in Arcadia (*sacred to* Pan).

Lycāōn, -onis *m* father of Callisto, the Great Bear.

Lycāonius *adj see n.*

Lycēum (Lycīum), -ī *nt* Aristotle's school at Athens.

lychnūchus, -ī *m* lampstand.

lychnus, -ī *m* lamp.

Lycia, -ae *f* country in S.W. Asia Minor.

Lycius *adj* Lycian.

Lyctius *adj* Cretan.

Lycurgus, -ī *m* Thracian king killed by Bacchus; Spartan lawgiver; Athenian orator.

Lȳdia, -iae *f* country of Asia Minor.

Lȳdius *adj* Lydian; Etruscan.

Lȳdus, -ī *m* Lydian.

lympha, -ae *f* water.

lymphāticus *adj* crazy, frantic.

lymphātus *adj* distracted.

Lynceus, -eī *m* keen-sighted Argonaut.

lynx, lyncis *m/f* lynx.

lyra, -ae *f* lyre; lyric poetry.

lyricus *adj* of the lyre, lyrical.

Lysiās, -ae *m* Athenian orator.

M, m

Macedō, -onis *m* Macedonian.

Macedonia *f* Macedonia.

Macedonicus, -onius *adj see n.*

macellum, -ī *nt* market.

maceō, -ēre *vi* to be lean.

macer, -rī *adj* lean, meagre; poor.

māceria, -ae *f* wall.

mācerō, -āre *vt* to soften; (*body*) to enervate; (*mind*) to distress.

macēscō, -ere vi to grow thin.
machaera, -ae f sword.
machaerophorus, -ī m soldier armed with a
sword.
Machāōn, -onis m legendary Greek surgeon.
Machāonius adj see n.
māchina, -ae f machine, engine; (fig) scheme,
trick.
māchināmentum, -ī nt engine.
māchinātiō, -ōnis f mechanism, machine;
(fig) contrivance.
māchinātor, -ōris m engineer; (fig) contriver.
māchinor, -ārī, -ātus vt to devise, contrive;
(fig) to plot, scheme.
maciēs, -ēī f leanness, meagreness; poorness.
macilentus adj thin.
macrēscō, -ere vi to grow thin.
macritūdō, -inis f leanness.
macrocollum, -ī nt large size of paper.
mactābilis adj deadly.
mactātus, -ūs m sacrifice.
macte blessed; well done!
mactō, -āre, -āvī, -ātum vt to sacrifice; to
punish, kill.
mactō, -āre vt to glorify.
macula, -ae f spot, stain; (net) mesh; (fig)
blemish, fault.
maculō, -āre, -āvī, -ātum vt to stain, defile.
maculōsus adj dappled, mottled; stained,
polluted.
madefaciō, -facere, -fēcī, -factum (pass -fīō,
-fierī) vt to wet, soak.
madeō, -ēre vi to be wet, be drenched; to be
boiled soft; (comedy) to be drunk; (fig) to be
steeped in.
madēscō, -ere vi to get wet, become moist.
madidus adj wet, soaked; sodden; drunk.
madulsa, -ae m drunkard.
Maeander (-ros), -rī m a winding river of Asia
Minor; winding, wandering.
Maecēnās, -ātis m friend of Augustus, patron of
poets.
maena, -ae f sprat.
Maenala, -ōrum ntpl mountain range in Arcadia.
Maenalis, -ius adj of Maenalus; Arcadian.
Maenalus (-os), -ī m Maenala.
Maenas, -dis f Bacchante.
Maeniānum nt balcony.
Maenius, -ī m Roman family name; ~ia columna
whipping post in the Forum.
Maeonia, -ae f Lydia.
Maeonidēs, -dae m Homer.
Maeonius, -s adj Lydian; Homeric; Etruscan.
Maeōticus, -us adj Scythian, Maeotic.
Maeōtis, -dis f Sea of Azov.
maereō, -ēre vi to mourn, be sad.
maeror, -ōris m mourning, sorrow, sadness.
maestiter adv see adj.
maestitia, -ae f sadness, melancholy.
maestus adj sad, sorrowful; gloomy;
mourning.
māgālia, -um ntpl huts.
mage etc see **magis**.
magicus adj magical.
magis (mage) adv more; eō ~ the more, all the
more.
magister, -rī m master, chief, director;
(school) teacher; (fig) instigator; ~ equitum
chief of cavalry, second in command to a
dictator; ~ mōrum censor; ~ sacrōrum chief
priest.
magisterium, -ī and **iī** nt presidency,
tutorship.
magistra, -ae f mistress, instructress.
magistrātus, -ūs m magistracy, office;
magistrate, official.
magnanimitās, -ātis f greatness.
māgnanimus adj great, brave.
Magnēs, -ētis m Magnesian; magnet.
Magnēsia f district of Thessaly.
Magnēsius, -ēssus, -ētis adj see n.
magnidicus adj boastful.
magnificē adv grandly; pompously.
magnificentia, -ae f greatness, grandeur;
pomposity.
magnificō, -āre vt to esteem highly.
magnificus (compar **-entior** superl **-entissimus**)
adj great, grand, splendid; pompous.
magniloquentia, -ae f elevated language;
pomposity.
magniloquus adj boastful.
magnitūdō, -inis f greatness, size, large
amount; dignity.
magnopere adv greatly, very much.
magnus (compar **māior** superl **māximus**) adj
great, large, big, tall; (voice) loud; (age)
advanced; (value) high, dear; (fig) grand,
noble, important; **avunculus ~** great-uncle;
~a loquī boast; **~ī aestimāre** think highly of;
~ī esse be highly esteemed; **~ō stāre** cost
dear; **~ō opere** very much.
magus, -ī m wise man; magician ♦ adj magic.
Māia, -ae f mother of Mercury.
māiestās, -ātis f greatness, dignity, majesty;
treason; **~ātem laedere, minuere** offend
against the sovereignty of; **lēx ~ātis** law
against treason.
māior, -ōris compar of **magnus**; ~ **nātū** older,
elder.
māiōrēs, -ōrum mpl ancestors; **in ~us**
crēdere/ferre exaggerate.
Māius, -ī m May ♦ adj of May.
māiusculus adj somewhat greater; a little
older.
māla, -ae f cheek, jaw.
malacia, -ae f dead calm.
malacus adj soft.
male (compar **pēius**, superl **pessimē**) adv badly,
wrongly, unfortunately; not; (with words
having bad sense) very much; **~ est animō** I

feel ill; ~ **sānus** insane; ~ **dīcere** abuse, curse; ~ **facere** harm.
maledicē *adv* abusively.
maledictiō, -ōnis *f* abuse.
maledictum, -ī *nt* curse.
maledicus *adj* scurrilous.
malefactum, -ī *nt* wrong.
Ꞌᵐᵃˡᵉᶠⁱᶜē *adv see adj.*
Ꞌ**maleficium, -ī** *and* **iī** *nt* misdeed, wrong, mischief.
maleficus *adj* wicked ♦ *m* criminal.
malesuādus *adj* seductive.
malevolēns, -entis *adj* spiteful.
malevolentia, -ae *f* ill-will.
malevolus *adj* ill-disposed, malicious.
mālifer, -ī *adj* apple-growing.
malīgnē *adv* spitefully; grudgingly.
malīgnitās, -ātis *f* malice; stinginess.
malīgnus *adj* unkind, ill-natured, spiteful; stingy; (*soil*) unfruitful; (*fig*) small, scanty.
malitia, -ae *f* badness, malice; roguishness.
malitiōsē *adv see adj.*
malitiōsus *adj* wicked, crafty.
maliv- *etc see* **malev-**.
mālle *infin of* **mālō**.
malleolus, -ī *m* hammer; (*MIL*) fire-brand.
malleus, -ī *m* hammer, mallet, maul.
mālō, -le, -uī *vt* to prefer; would rather.
malobathrum, -ī *nt* an oriental perfume.
māluī *perf of* **mālō**.
mālum, -ī *nt* apple, fruit.
malum, -ī *nt* evil, wrong, harm, misfortune; (*interj*) mischief.
mālus, -ī *f* apple tree.
mālus, -ī *m* mast, pole.
malus (*compar* **pēior** *superl* **pessimus**) *adj* bad, evil, harmful; unlucky; ugly; **ī in ~am rem** go to hell!
malva, -ae *f* mallow.
Māmers, -tis *m* Mars.
Māmertīnī, -ōrum *mpl mercenary troops who occupied Messana.*
mamma, -ae *f* breast; teat.
mammilla, -ae *f* breast.
mānābilis *adj* penetrating.
manceps, -ipis *m* purchaser; contractor.
mancipium, -ī *and* **iī** *nt* formal purchase; property; slave.
mancipō, -āre *vt* to sell, deliver up.
mancup- *etc see* **mancip-**.
mancus *adj* crippled.
mandātum, -ī *nt* commission, command; (*law*) contract.
mandātus, -ūs *m* command.
mandō, -āre, -āvī, -ātum *vt* to entrust, commit; to commission, command.
mandō, -ere, -ī, mānsum *vt* to chew, eat, devour.
mandra, -ae *f* drove of cattle.
mandūcus, -ī *m* masked figure of a glutton.
māne *nt* (*indecl*) morning ♦ *adv* in the morning, early.
maneō, -ēre, mānsī, mānsum *vi* to remain;

to stay, stop; to last, abide, continue ♦ *vt* to wait for, await; **in condiciōne** ~ abide by an agreement.
Mānēs, -ium *mpl* ghosts, shades of the dead; the lower world; bodily remains.
mangō, -ōnis *m* dealer.
manicae, -ārum *fpl* sleeves, gloves; handcuffs.
manicātus *adj* with long sleeves.
manicula, -ae *f* little hand.
manifestō, -āre *vt* to disclose.
manifestō *adv* clearly, evidently.
manifestus *adj* clear, obvious; convicted, caught.
manipl- *etc see* **manipul-**.
manipulāris *adj* of a company ♦ *m* private (in the ranks); fellow soldier.
manipulātim *adv* by companies.
manipulus, -ī *m* bundle (*esp of hay*); (*MIL*) company.
Manlius, -iānus *adj see n.*
Manlius, -ī *m* Roman family name (*esp the saviour of the Capitol from the Gauls*); a severe disciplinarian.
mannus, -ī *m* Gallic horse.
mānō, -āre, -āvī, -ātum *vi* to flow, drip, stream; (*fig*) to spread, emanate.
mānsī *perf of* **maneō**.
mānsiō, -ōnis *f* remaining, stay.
mānsitō, -āre *vi* to stay on.
mānsuēfaciō, -facere, -fēcī, -factum (*pass* -**fīō, -fierī**) *vt* to tame.
mānsuēscō, -scere, -vī, -tum *vt* to tame ♦ *vi* to grow tame, grow mild.
mānsuētē *adv see adj.*
mānsuētūdō, -inis *f* tameness; gentleness.
mānsuētus *ppp of* **mānsuēscō** ♦ *adj* tame; mild, gentle.
mānsus *ppp of* **mandō**; *ppp of* **maneō**.
mantēle, -is *nt* napkin, towel.
mantēlum, -ī *nt* cloak.
mantica, -ae *f* knapsack.
manticinor, -ārī, -ātus *vi* to be a prophet.
mantō, -āre *vi* to remain, wait.
Mantua, -ae *f* birthplace of Vergil in N. Italy.
manuālis *adj* for the hand.
manubiae, -ārum *fpl money from sale of booty.*
manūbrium, -ī *and* **iī** *nt* handle, haft.
manuleātus *adj* with long sleeves.
manūmissiō, -ōnis *f* emancipation (of a slave).
manūmittō, -ittere, -īsī, -issum *vt* to emancipate, make free.
manupretium, -ī *and* **iī** *nt* pay, wages, reward.
manus, -ūs *f* hand; corps, band, company; (*elephant*) trunk; (*art*) touch; (*work*) handiwork, handwriting; (*war*) force, valour, hand to hand fighting; (*fig*) power; ~ **extrēma** finishing touch; ~ **ferrea** grappling iron; ~**um dare** give up, yield; ~**ū** artificially; ~**ū mittere** emancipate; **ad ~um** at hand; **in ~ū** obvious; subject; **in ~ūs venīre** come to hand; **in ~ibus** well known; at hand; **in ~ibus habēre** be

engaged on; fondle; **per ~ūs** forcibly; **per ~ūs trādere** hand down.

mapālia, -um *ntpl* huts.

mappa, -ae *f* napkin, cloth.

Marathōn, -ōnis *f* Attic village famous for Persian defeat.

Marathōnius *adj see n.*

Marcellia, -iōrum *ntpl* festival of the Marcelli.

Marcellus, -ī *m* Roman surname (*esp* the captor of Syracuse).

marceō, -ēre *vi* to droop, be faint.

marcēscō, -ere *vi* to waste away, grow feeble.

Marciānus *adj see n.*

marcidus *adj* withered; enervated.

Marcius, -ī *m* Roman family name (*esp Ancus, fourth king*).

Marcius *adj see n.*

mare, -is *nt* sea; **~ nostrum** Mediterranean; **~ inferum** Tyrrhenian Sea; **~ superum** Adriatic.

Mareōticus *adj* Mareotic; Egyptian.

margarīta, -ae *f* pearl.

marginō, -āre *vt* to put a border *or* kerb on.

margō, -inis *m/f* edge, border, boundary; **~ cēnae** side dishes.

Mariānus *adj see n.*

Marīca, -ae *f* nymph of Minturnae.

marīnus *adj* of the sea.

marītālis *adj* marriage- (*in cpds*).

maritimus *adj* of the sea, maritime, coastal ♦ *ntpl* coastal area.

marītō, -āre *vt* to marry.

marītus, -ī *m* husband ♦ *adj* nuptial.

Marius, -ī *m* Roman family name (*esp* the victor over Jugurtha and the Teutons).

Marius *adj see n.*

marmor, -is *nt* marble; statue, tablet; sea.

marmoreus *adj* of marble; like marble.

Marō, -ōnis *m* surname of Vergil.

marra, -ae *f* kind of hoe.

Mars, Martis *m* god of war, father of Romulus; war, conflict; planet Mars; **aequō Marte** on equal terms; **suō Marte** by one's own exertions.

Marsī, -ōrum *mpl* people of central Italy, famous as fighters.

Marsicus, -us *adj* Marsian.

marsuppium, -ī and iī *nt* purse.

Mārtiālis *adj* of Mars.

Mārticola, -ae *m* worshipper of Mars.

Mārtigena, -ae *m* son of Mars.

Mārtius *adj* of Mars; of March; warlike.

mās, maris *m* male, man ♦ *adj* male; manly.

māsculus *adj* male, masculine; manly.

Masinissa, -ae *m* king of Numidia.

massa, -ae *f* lump, mass.

Massicum, -ī *nt* Massic wine.

Massicus, -ī *m* mountain in Campania, famous for vines.

Massilia, -ae *f* Greek colony in Gaul (*now* Marseilles).

Massiliēnsis *adj see n.*

mastīgia, -ae *nt* scoundrel.

mastrūca, -ae *f* sheepskin.

mastrūcātus *adj* wearing sheepskin.

matara, -ae *and* **is, -is** *f* Celtic javelin.

matelliō, -ōnis *m* pot.

māter, -ris *f* mother; **Māgna ~** Cybele.

mātercula, -ae *f* poor mother.

māteria, -ae; -ēs, -ēī *f* matter, substance; wood, timber; (*fig*) subject matter, theme; occasion, opportunity; (*person*) ability, character.

māteriārius, -ī and iī *m* timber merchant.

māteriātus *adj* timbered.

māteriēs *etc see* **māteria**.

māterior, -ārī *vi* to fetch wood.

māternus *adj* mother's.

mātertera, -ae *f* aunt (maternal).

mathēmaticus, -ī *m* mathematician; astrologer.

mātricīda, -ae *m* matricide.

mātricīdium, -ī and iī *nt* a mother's murder.

mātrimōnium, -ī and iī *nt* marriage.

mātrimus *adj* whose mother is still alive.

mātrōna, -ae *f* married woman, matron, lady.

mātrōnālis *adj* a married woman's.

matula, -ae *f* pot.

mātūrē *adv* at the right time; early, promptly.

mātūrēscō, -ēscere, -uī *vi* to ripen.

mātūritās, -ātis *f* ripeness; (*fig*) maturity, perfection, height.

mātūrō, -āre, -āvī, -ātum *vt* to bring to maturity; to hasten, be too hasty with ♦ *vi* to make haste.

mātūrus *adj* ripe, mature; timely, seasonable; early.

Mātūta, -ae *f* goddess of dawn.

mātūtīnus *adj* morning, early.

Mauritānia, -ae *f* Mauretania (*now* Morocco).

Maurus, -ī *m* Moor ♦ *adj* Moorish, African.

Maurūsius *adj see n.*

Māvors, -tis *m* Mars.

Māvortius *adj see n.*

maxilla, -ae *f* jaw.

maximē *adv* most, very much, especially; precisely, just; certainly, yes; **cum ~** just as; **quam ~** as much as possible.

maximitās, -ātis *f* great size.

maximus *superl of* **magnus**.

māxum- *etc see* **māxim-**.

māzonomus, -ī *m* dish.

meāpte my own.

meātus, -ūs *m* movement, course.

mēcastor *interj* by Castor!

mēcum with me.

meddix tuticus *m* senior Oscan magistrate.

Mēdēa, -ae *f* Colchian wife of Jason, expert in magic.

Noun declensions and verb conjugations are shown on pp xiii to xxv. The present infinitive ending of a verb shows to which conjugation it belongs: **-āre** = 1st; **-ēre** = 2nd; **-ere** = 3rd and **-īre** = 4th. Irregular verbs are shown on p xxvi

Mēdēis *adj* magical.
medentēs, -entum *mpl* doctors.
medeor, -ērī *vi* (*with dat*) to heal, remedy.
mediastīnus, -ī *m* drudge.
mēdica, -ae *f* lucern (*kind of clover*).
medicābilis *adj* curable.
medicāmen, -inis *nt* drug, medicine;
  cosmetic; (*fig*) remedy.
medicāmentum, -ī *nt* drug, medicine; potion,
  poison; (*fig*) relief; embellishment.
medicātus, -ūs *m* charm.
medicīna, -ae *f* medicine; cure; (*fig*) remedy,
  relief.
medicō, -āre, -āvī, -ātum *vt* to cure; to steep,
  dye.
medicor, -ārī *vt, vi* to cure.
medicus *adj* healing ♦ *m* doctor.
medietās, -ātis *f* mean.
medimnum, -ī *nt*, **-us, -ī** *m* bushel.
mediocris *adj* middling, moderate, average.
mediocritās, -ātis *f* mean, moderation;
  mediocrity.
mediocriter *adv* moderately, not particularly;
  calmly.
Mediolānēnsis *adj see n.*
Mediolānum, -ī *nt* town in N. Italy (*now
  Milan*).
meditāmentum, -ī *nt* preparation, drill.
meditātiō, -ōnis *f* thinking about;
  preparation, practice.
meditātus *adj* studied.
mediterrāneus *adj* inland.
meditor, -ārī, -ātus *vt, vi* to think over,
  contemplate, reflect; to practise, study.
medius *adj* middle, the middle of;
  intermediate; intervening; middling,
  moderate; neutral ♦ *nt* middle; public ♦ *m*
  mediator; ~um complectī clasp round the
  waist; ~um sē gerere be neutral; ~ō midway;
  ~ō temporis meanwhile; in ~um for the
  common good; in ~um prōferre publish; dē
  ~ō tollere do away with; ē ~ō abīre die,
  disappear; in ~ō esse be public; in ~ō positus
  open to all; in ~ō relinquere leave undecided.
medius fidius *interj* by Heaven!
medix *etc see* **meddix**.
medulla, -ae *f* marrow, pith.
medullitus *adv* from the heart.
medullula, -ae *f* marrow.
Mēdus, -ī *m* Mede, Persian.
Mēdus *adj see n.*
Medūsa, -ae *f* Gorgon, whose look turned
  everything to stone.
Medūsaeus *adj*: ~ equus Pegasus.
Megalēnsia (Megalēsia), -um *ntpl festival of
  Cybele in April.*
Megara, -ae *f*, **-ōrum** *ntpl town in Greece near
  the Isthmus.*
Megarēus and **icus** *adj* Megarean.
megistānes, -um *mpl* grandees.
mehercle, mehercule, mehercules *interj* by
  Hercules!
mēiō, -ere *vi* to make water.

mel, mellis *nt* honey.
melancholicus *adj* melancholy.
melē *pl* melos.
Meleager (-ros), -rī *m prince of Calydon.*
melicus *adj* musical; lyrical.
melilōtos, -ī *f* kind of clover.
melimēla, -ōrum *ntpl* honey apples.
Mēlīnum, -ī *nt* Melian white.
melior, -ōris *adj* better.
melisphyllum, -ī *nt* balm.
Melita, -ae *f* Malta.
Melitēnsis *adj* Maltese.
melius *nt* melior ♦ *adv* better.
meliusculē *adv* fairly well.
meliusculus *adj* rather better.
mellifer, -ī *adj* honey-making.
mellītus *adj* honeyed; sweet.
melos, -ī *nt* tune, song.
Melpomenē, -ēs *f Muse of tragedy.*
membrāna, -ae *f* skin, membrane, slough;
  parchment.
membrānula, -ae *f* piece of parchment.
membrātim *adv* limb by limb; piecemeal; in
  short sentences.
membrum, -ī *nt* limb, member; part, division;
  clause.
mēmet *emphatic form of* **mē**.
meminī, -isse *vi* (*with gen*) to remember,
  think of; to mention.
Memnōn, -onis *m Ethiopian king, killed at Troy.*
Memnonius *adj see n.*
memor, -is *adj* mindful, remembering; in
  memory (of).
memorābilis *adj* memorable, remarkable.
memorandus *adj* noteworthy.
memorātus, -ūs *m* mention.
memorātus *adj* famed.
memoria, -ae *f* memory, remembrance; time,
  lifetime; history; **haec** ~ our day; ~ae
  prōdere hand down to posterity; **post
  hominum** ~am since the beginning of
  history.
memoriola, -ae *f* weak memory.
memoriter *adv* from memory; accurately.
memorō, -āre, -āvī, -ātum *vt* to mention,
  say, speak.
Memphis, -is and **idos** *f town in middle Egypt.*
Memphītēs and **ītis** and **īticus** *adj* of
  Memphis; Egyptian.
Menander (-ros), -rī *m Greek writer of comedy.*
Menandrēus *adj see n.*
menda, -ae *f* fault.
mendācium, -ī and **iī** *nt* lie.
mendāciunculum, -ī *nt* fib.
mendāx, -ācis *adj* lying; deceptive, unreal ♦
  m liar.
mendīcitās, -ātis *f* beggary.
mendīcō, -āre, -or, -ārī, *vi* to beg, go begging.
mendīcus *adj* beggarly, poor ♦ *m* beggar.
mendōsē *adv see adj.*
mendōsus *adj* faulty; wrong, mistaken.
mendum, -ī *nt* fault, blunder.
Menelāēus *adj see n.*

Menelāus, -ī m *brother of Agamemnon, husband of Helen.*

Menoetiadēs, -ae m *Patroclus.*

mēns, mentis f mind, understanding; feelings, heart; idea, plan, purpose; courage; **venit in mentem** it occurs; **mente captus** insane; **eā mente ut** with the intention of.

mēnsa, -ae f table; meal, course; counter, bank; **secunda ~** dessert.

mēnsārius, -ī *and* **iī** m banker.

mēnsiō, -ōnis f *(metre)* quantity.

mēnsis, -is m month.

mēnsor, -ōris m measurer, surveyor.

mēnstruālis *adj* for a month.

mēnstruus *adj* monthly; for a month ♦ *nt* a month's provisions.

mēnsula, -ae f little table.

mēnsūra, -ae f measure, measurement; standard, standing; amount, size, capacity.

mēnsus *ppa of* **mētior.**

menta, -ae f mint.

Menteus *adj see n.*

mentiēns, -ientis m fallacy.

mentiō, -ōnis f mention, hint.

mentior, -īrī, -ītus *vi* to lie, deceive ♦ *vt* to say falsely; to feign, imitate.

mentītus *adj* lying, false.

Mentor, -is m artist in metalwork; ornamental cup.

mentum, -ī *nt* chin.

meō, -āre *vi* to go, pass.

mephītis, -is f noxious vapour, malaria.

merācus *adj* pure.

mercābilis *adj* buyable.

mercātor, -ōris m merchant, dealer.

mercātūra, -ae f commerce; purchase; goods.

mercātus, -ūs m trade, traffic; market, fair.

mercēdula, -ae f poor wages, small rent.

mercēnārius *adj* hired, mercenary ♦ *m* servant.

mercēs, -ēdis f pay, wages, fee; bribe; rent; *(fig)* reward, retribution, cost.

mercimōnium, -ī *and* **iī** *nt* wares, goods.

mercor, -ārī, -ātus *vt* to trade in, purchase.

Mercurius, -ī m *messenger of the gods, god of trade, thieves, speech and the lyre;* **stēlla ~ī** planet Mercury.

Mercuriālis *adj see n.*

merda, -ae f dung.

merenda, -ae f lunch.

mereō, -ēre, -uī; -eor, -ērī, -itus *vt, vi* to deserve; to earn, win, acquire; *(MIL)* to serve; **bene ~ dē** do a service to, serve well; **~ equō** serve in the cavalry.

meretrīcius *adj* a harlot's.

meretrīcula, -ae f pretty harlot.

meretrīx, -īcis f harlot.

mergae, -ārum *fpl* pitchfork.

merges, -itis f sheaf.

mergō, -gere, -sī, -sum *vt* to dip, immerse, sink; *(fig)* to bury, plunge, drown.

mergus, -ī m *(bird)* diver.

merīdiānus *adj* midday; southerly.

merīdiātiō, -ōnis f siesta.

merīdiēs, -ēī f midday, noon; south.

merīdiō, -āre *vi* to take a siesta.

meritō, -āre *vt* to learn.

meritō *adv* deservedly.

meritōrius *adj* money-earning ♦ *ntpl* lodgings.

meritum, -ī *nt* service, kindness, merit; blame.

meritus *ppp of* **mereō** ♦ *adj* deserved, just.

merops, -is f bee-eater.

mersī *perf of* **mergō.**

mersō, -āre *vt* to immerse, plunge; to overwhelm.

mersus *ppp of* **mergō.**

merula, -ae f blackbird.

merum, -ī *nt* wine.

merus *adj* pure, undiluted; bare, mere.

merx, mercis f goods, wares.

Messalla, -ae m *Roman surname (esp ~ Corvīnus Augustan orator, soldier and literary patron).*

Messallīna, -īnae f *wife of emperor Claudius; wife of Nero.*

Messāna, -ae f *Sicilian town (now Messina).*

messis, -is f harvest.

messor, -ōris m reaper.

messōrius *adj* a reaper's.

messuī *perf of* **metō.**

messus *ppp of* **metō.**

mēta, -ae f *pillar at each end of the Circus course;* turning point, winning post; *(fig)* goal, end, limit.

metallum, -ī *nt* mine, quarry; metal.

mētātor, -ōris m surveyor.

Metaurus, -ī m *river in Umbria, famous for the defeat of Hasdrubal.*

Metellus, -ī m *Roman surname (esp the commander against Jugurtha).*

Mēthymna, -ae f *town in Lesbos.*

Mēthymnaeus *adj see n.*

mētior, -tīrī, -nsus *vt* to measure, measure out; to traverse; *(fig)* to estimate, judge.

metō, -tere, -ssuī, -ssum *vt* to reap, gather; to mow, cut down.

mētor, -ārī, -ātus *vt* to measure off, lay out.

metrēta, -ae f liquid measure *(about 9 gallons).*

metuculōsus *adj* frightful.

metuō, -uere, -uī, -ūtum *vt* to fear, be apprehensive.

metus, -ūs m fear, alarm, anxiety.

meus *adj* my, mine.

mī *dat of* **ego;** *voc and mpl of* **meus.**

mīca, -ae f crumb, grain.

micō, -āre, -uī *vi* to quiver, flicker, beat, flash, sparkle.

Midās, -ae m *Phrygian king whose touch turned*

everything to gold.
migrātiō, -ōnis *f* removal, change.
migrō, -āre, -āvī, -ātum *vi* to remove, change, pass away ♦ *vt* to transport, transgress.
mīles, -itis *m* soldier, infantryman; army troops.
Mīlēsius *adj see n.*
Mīlētus, -tī *f* town in Asia Minor.
mīlia, -um *ntpl* thousands; ~ **passuum** miles.
mīliārium (milliārium), -ī *and* **iī** *nt* milestone.
mīlitāris *adj* military, a soldier's.
mīlitāriter *adv* in a soldierly fashion.
mīlitia, -ae *f* military service, war; the army; ~**ae** on service; **domī ~aeque** at home and abroad.
mīlitō, -āre *vi* to serve, be a soldier.
mīlium, -ī *and* **iī** *nt* millet.
mīlle, *(pl* ~**ia)** *num* a thousand; ~ **passūs** a mile.
mīllensimus, -ēsimus *adj* thousandth.
mīllia *etc see* **mīlia.**
mīlliārium *etc see* **mīliārium.**
mīlliēns, -ēs *adv* a thousand times.
Milō, -ōnis *m tribune who killed Clodius and was defended by Cicero.*
Milōniānus *adj see n.*
Miltiadēs, -is *m Athenian general, victor at Marathon.*
mīluīnus *adj* resembling a kite; rapacious.
mīluus (mīlvus), -ī *m* kite; gurnard.
mīma, -ae *f* actress.
Mimallonis, -dis *f* Bacchante.
mīmicē *adv see adj.*
mīmicus *adj* farcical.
Mimnermus, -ī *m Greek elegiac poet.*
mīmula, -ae *f* actress.
mīmus, -ī *m* actor; mime, farce.
mina, -ae *f Greek silver coin.*
mināciter *adv see adj.*
minae, -ārum *fpl* threats; (*wall*) pinnacles.
minanter *adv* threateningly.
minātiō, -ōnis *f* threat.
mināx, -ācis *adj* threatening; projecting.
Minerva, -ae *f goddess of wisdom and arts, esp weaving;* (*fig*) talent, genius; working in wool; **sūs ~am** ≈ *"teach your grandmother!"*
miniānus *adj* red-leaded.
miniātulus *adj* painted red.
minimē *adv* least, very little; (*reply*) no, not at all.
minimus *adj* least, smallest, very small; youngest.
miniō, -āre, -āvī, -ātum *vt* to colour red.
minister, -rī *m*, ~**ra,** ~**rae** *f* attendant, servant; helper, agent, tool.
ministerium, -ī *and* **iī** *nt* service, office, duty; retinue.
ministrātor, -ōris *m*, ~**rīx,** ~**rīcis** *f* assistant, handmaid.
ministrō, -āre *vt* to serve, supply; to manage.
minitābundus *adj* threatening.
minitor, -ārī, -ō, -āre *vt, vi* to threaten.
minium, -ī *and* **iī** *nt* vermilion, red lead.

Mīnōis, -idis *f* Ariadne.
Mīnōius, -us *adj see n.*
minor, -ārī, -ātus *vt, vi* to threaten; to project.
minor, -ōris *adj* smaller, less, inferior; younger; (*pl*) descendants.
Mīnōs, -is *m king of Crete, judge in the lower world.*
Mīnōtaurus, -ī *m monster of the Cretan labyrinth, half bull, half man.*
Minturnae, -ārum *fpl town in S. Latium.*
Minturnēnsis *adj see n.*
minum- *etc see* **minim-.**
minuō, -uere, -uī, -ūtum *vt* to make smaller, lessen; to chop up; to reduce, weaken ♦ *vi* (*tide*) to ebb.
minus *nt* minor ♦ *adv* less; not, not at all; **quō ~** (*prevent*) from.
minusculus *adj* smallish.
minūtal, -ālis *nt* mince.
minūtātim *adv* bit by bit.
minūtē *adv* in a petty manner.
minūtus *ppp of* **minuō** ♦ *adj* small; paltry.
mīrābilis *adj* wonderful, extraordinary.
mīrābiliter *adv see adj.*
mīrābundus *adj* astonished.
mīrāculum, -ī *nt* marvel, wonder; amazement.
mīrandus *adj* wonderful.
mīrātiō, -ōnis *f* wonder.
mīrātor, -ōris *m* admirer.
mīrātrīx, -īcis *adj* admiring.
mīrē *adv see adj.*
mīrificē *adv see adj.*
mīrificus *adj* wonderful.
mirmillō *see* **murmillō.**
mīror, -ārī, -ātus *vt* to wonder at, be surprised at, admire ♦ *vi* to wonder, be surprised.
mīrus *adj* wonderful, strange; ~**um quam,** quantum extraordinarily.
miscellānea, -ōrum *ntpl* (*food*) hotchpotch.
misceō, -scēre, -scuī, -xtum *vt* to mix, mingle, blend; to join, combine; to confuse, embroil.
misellus *adj* poor little.
Mīsēnēnsis *adj see n.*
Mīsēnum, -ī *nt promontory and harbour near Naples.*
miser, -ī *adj* wretched, poor, pitiful, sorry.
miserābilis *adj* pitiable, sad, plaintive.
miserābiliter *adv see adj.*
miserandus *adj* deplorable.
miserātiō, -ōnis *f* pity, compassion, pathos.
miserē *adv see adj.*
misereō, -ēre, -uī, -eor, -ērī, -itus *vt, vi* (*with gen*) to pity, sympathize with; ~**et mē** I pity, I am sorry.
miserēscō, -ere *vi* to feel pity.
miseria, -ae *f* misery, trouble, distress.
misericordia, -ae *f* pity, sympathy, mercy.
misericors, -dis *adj* sympathetic, merciful.
miseriter *adv* sadly.
miseror, -ārī, -ātus *vt* to deplore; to pity.

nīsī *perf of* **mittō.**

nissa, -ae *f (ECCL)* mass.

nissilis *adj* missile.

nissiō, -ōnis *f* sending; release; *(MIL)* discharge; *(gladiators)* quarter; *(events)* end; **sine ~ōne** to the death.

nissitō, -āre *vt* to send repeatedly.

nissus *ppp of* **mittō.**

nissus, -ūs *m* sending; throwing; **~ sagittae** bowshot.

nitella, -ae *f* turban.

nītēscō, -ere *vi* to ripen; to grow mild.

Mithridātēs, -is *m king of Pontus, defeated by Pompey.*

Mithridātēus, -icus *adj see n.*

nītigātiō, -ōnis *f* soothing.

nītigō, -āre, -āvī, -ātum *vt* to ripen, soften; to calm, pacify.

nītis *adj* ripe, mellow; soft, mild; gentle.

nitra, -ae *f* turban.

nittō, -ere, mīsī, missum *vt* to send, dispatch; to throw, hurl; to let go, dismiss; to emit, utter; *(news)* to send word; *(gift)* to bestow; *(event)* to end; *(speech)* to omit, stop; **sanguinem ~** bleed ; **ad cēnam ~** invite to dinner; **missum facere** forgo.

mītulus, -ī *m* mussel.

mixtim *adv* promiscuously.

mixtūra, -ae *f* mingling.

Mnēmosynē, -ēs *f mother of the Muses.*

mnēmosynon, -ī *nt* souvenir.

nōbilis *adj* movable; nimble, fleet; excitable, fickle.

mōbilitās, -ātis *f* agility, rapidity; fickleness.

mōbiliter *adv* rapidly.

mōbilitō, -āre *vt* to make rapid.

moderābilis *adj* moderate.

moderāmen, -inis *nt* control; government.

moderanter *adv* with control.

moderātē *adv* with restraint.

moderātim *adv* gradually.

moderātiō, -ōnis *f* control, government; moderation; rules.

moderātor, -ōris *m* controller, governor.

moderātrīx, -īcis *f* mistress, controller.

moderātus *adj* restrained, orderly.

moderor, -ārī, -ātus *vt, vi (with dat)* to restrain, check; *(with acc)* to manage, govern, guide.

modestē *adv* with moderation; humbly.

modestia, -ae *f* temperate behaviour, discipline; humility.

modestus *adj* sober, restrained; well-behaved, disciplined; modest, unassuming.

modiālis *adj* holding a peck.

modicē *adv* moderately; slightly.

modicus *adj* moderate; middling, small, mean.

modificātus *adj* measured.

modius, -ī *and* **iī** *m* corn measure, peck.

modo *adv* only; at all, in any way; *(with imp)* just; *(time)* just now, a moment ago, in a moment ♦ *conj* if only; **nōn ~** not only; **non ~ ... sed** not only ... but also ...; **~ nōn** all but, almost; **~ ... ~** sometimes ... sometimes; **~ ... tum** at first ... then.

modulātē *adv* melodiously.

modulātor, -ōris *m* musician.

modulātus *adj* played, measured.

modulor, -ārī, - ātus *vt* to modulate, play, sing.

modulus, -ī *m* measure.

modus, -ī *m* measure; size; metre, music; way, method; limit, end; **ēius ~ī** such; **~ō, in, ~um** like.

moecha, -ae *f* adulteress.

moechor, -ārī *vi* to commit adultery.

moechus, -ī *m* adulterer.

moenera *etc see* **mūnus.**

moenia, -um *ntpl* defences, walls; town, stronghold.

moeniō *etc see* **mūniō.**

Moesī, -ōrum *mpl people on lower Danube (now Bulgaria).*

mola, -ae *f* millstone, mill; grains of spelt.

molāris, -is *m* millstone; *(tooth)* molar.

mōlēs, -is *f* mass, bulk, pile; dam, pier, massive structure; *(fig)* greatness, weight, effort, trouble.

molestē *adv see adj.*

molestia, -ae *f* trouble, annoyance, worry; *(style)* affectation.

molestus *adj* irksome, annoying; *(style)* laboured.

mōlīmen, -inis *nt* exertion, labour; importance.

mōlīmentum, -ī *nt* great effort.

mōlior, -īrī, -ītus *vt* to labour at, work, build; to wield, move, heave; to undertake, devise, occasion ♦ *vi* to exert oneself, struggle.

mōlītiō, -ōnis *f* laborious work.

mōlītor, -ōris *m* builder.

mollēscō, -ere *vi* to soften, become effeminate.

molliculus *adj* tender.

molliō, -īre, -īvī, -ītum *vt* to soften, make supple; to mitigate, make easier; to demoralize.

mollis *adj* soft, supple; tender, gentle; *(character)* sensitive, weak, unmanly; *(poetry)* amatory; *(opinion)* changeable; *(slope)* easy.

molliter *adv* softly, gently; calmly; voluptuously.

mollitia, -ae, -ēs, -ēī *f* softness, suppleness; tenderness, weakness, effeminacy.

mollitūdō, -inis *f* softness; susceptibility.

molō, -ere *vt* to grind.

Molossī, -ōrum *mpl Molossians, people in Epirus.*

Molossicus, -us *adj see n.*

Molossis, -idis *f country of the Molossians.*

Molossus, -ī m Molossian hound.
mōly, -os nt a magic herb.
mōmen, -inis nt movement, momentum.
mōmentum, -ī nt movement; change; (_time_) short space, moment; (_fig_) cause, influence, importance; **nullīus ~ī** unimportant.
momordī perf of **mordeō**.
Mona, -ae f Isle of Man; Anglesey.
monachus, -ī m monk.
monēdula, -ae f jackdaw.
moneō, -ēre, -uī, -itum vt to remind, advise, warn; to instruct, foretell.
monēris, -is f galley with one bank of oars.
monērula etc see **monēdula**.
monēta, -ae f mint; money; stamp.
monīle, -is nt necklace, collar.
monim- etc see **monum-**.
monitiō, -ōnis f admonishing.
monitor, -ōris m admonisher; prompter; teacher.
monitum, -ī nt warning; prophecy.
monitus, -ūs m admonition; warning.
monogrammus adj shadowy.
monopodium, -ī and **iī** nt table with one leg.
mōns, montis m mountain.
mōnstrātor, -ōris m shower, inventor.
mōnstrātus adj distinguished.
mōnstrē adv see adj.
mōnstrō, -āre, -āvī, -ātum vt to point out, show; to inform, instruct; to appoint; to denounce.
mōnstrum, -ī nt portent, marvel; monster.
mōnstruōsus adj unnatural.
montānus adj mountainous; mountain- (_in cpds_), highland.
monticola, -ae m highlander.
montivagus adj mountain-roving.
montuōsus, montōsus adj mountainous.
monumentum, -ī nt memorial, monument; record.
Mopsopius adj Athenian.
mora, -ae f delay, pause; hindrance; space of time, sojourn; **~am facere** put off.
mora, -ae f division of the Spartan army.
mōrālis adj moral.
mōrātor, -ōris m delayer.
mōrātus adj mannered, of a nature; (_writing_) in character.
morbidus adj unwholesome.
morbus, -ī m illness, disease; distress.
mordāciter adv see adj.
mordāx, -ācis adj biting, sharp, pungent; (_fig_) snarling, carking.
mordeō, -dēre, momordī, -sum vt to bite; to bite into, grip; (_cold_) to nip; (_words_) to sting, hurt, mortify.
mordicus adv with a bite; (_fig_) doggedly.
mōrēs pl of **mōs**.
morētum, -ī nt salad.
moribundus adj dying, mortal; deadly.
mōrigeror, -ārī, -ātus vi (_with dat_) to gratify, humour.
mōrigerus adj obliging, obedient.

morior, -ī, -tuus vi to die; to decay, fade.
moritūrus fut p of **morior**.
mōrologus adj foolish.
moror, -ārī, -ātus vi to delay, stay, loiter ♦ vt to detain, retard; to entertain; (_with neg_) to heed, object; **nihil, nīl ~** have no objection to; to not care for; to withdraw a charge against.
mōrōsē adv see adj.
mōrōsitās, -ātis f peevishness.
mōrōsus adj peevish, difficult.
Morpheus, -eos m god of dreams.
mors, mortis f death; corpse; **mortem sibi cōnscīscere** commit suicide; **mortis poena** capital punishment.
morsiuncula, -ae f little kiss.
morsus ppp of **mordeō** ♦ ntpl little bits.
morsus, -ūs m bite; grip; (_fig_) sting, vexation.
mortālis adj mortal; transient; man-made ♦ m human being.
mortālitās, -ātis f mortality, death.
mortārium, -ī and **iī** nt mortar.
mortifer, -ī adj fatal.
mortuus ppa of **morior** ♦ adj dead ♦ m dead man.
mōrum, -ī nt blackberry, mulberry.
mōrus, -ī f black mulberry tree.
mōrus adj foolish ♦ m fool.
mōs, mōris m nature, manner; humour, mood; custom, practice, law; (_pl_) behaviour, character, morals; **~ māiōrum** national tradition; **mōrem gerere** oblige, humour; **mōre, in mōrem** like.
Mosa, -ae m river Meuse.
Mōsēs, -is m Moses.
mōtiō, -ōnis f motion.
mōtō, -āre vt to keep moving.
mōtus ppp of **moveō**.
mōtus, -ūs m movement; dance, gesture; (_mind_) impulse, emotion; (_POL_) rising, rebellion; **terrae ~** earthquake.
movēns, -entis pres p of **moveō** ♦ adj movable ♦ ntpl motives.
moveō, -ēre, mōvī, mōtum vt to move, set in motion; to disturb; to change; to dislodge, expel; to occasion, begin; (_opinion_) to shake; (_mind_) to affect, influence, provoke ♦ vi to move; **castra ~** strike camp; **sē ~** budge; to dance.
mox adv presently, soon, later on; next.
Mōysēs see **Mōsēs**.
mūcidus adj snivelling; mouldy.
Mūcius, -ī m Roman family name (_esp Scaevola, who burned his right hand before Porsena_).
mūcrō, -ōnis m point, edge; sword.
mūcus, -ī m mucus.
mūgilis, -is m mullet.
muginor, -ārī vi to hesitate.
mūgiō, -īre vi to bellow, groan.
mūgītus, -ūs m lowing, roaring.
mūla, -ae f she-mule.
mulceō, -cēre, -sī, -sum vt to stroke, caress;

to soothe, alleviate, delight.

Mulciber, -is *and* **ī** *m* Vulcan.

mulcō, -āre, -āvī, -ātum *vt* to beat, ill-treat, damage.

mulctra, -ae *f*, **-ārium, -ārī,** *and* **āriī, -um, -ī** *nt* milkpail.

mulgeō, -ēre, mulsī *vt* to milk.

muliebris *adj* woman's, feminine; effeminate.

muliebriter *adv* like a woman; effeminately.

mulier, -is *f* woman; wife.

mulierārius *adj* woman's.

muliercula, -ae *f* girl.

mulierōsitās, -ātis *f* fondness for women.

mulierōsus *adj* fond of women.

mūlīnus *adj* mulish.

mūliō, -ōnis *m* mule driver.

mūliōnius *adj* mule driver's.

mullus, -ī *m* red mullet.

mulsī *perf of* **mulceō**; *perf of* **mulgeō**.

mulsus *ppp of* **mulceō**.

mulsus *adj* honeyed, sweet ♦ *nt* honey-wine, mead.

multa, -ae *f* penalty, fine; loss.

multangulus *adj* many-angled.

multātīcius *adj* fine- (*in cpds*).

multātiō, -ōnis *f* fining.

multēsimus *adj* very small.

multicavus *adj* many-holed.

multicia, -ōrum *ntpl* transparent garments.

multifāriam *adv* in many places.

multifidus *adj* divided into many parts.

multifōrmis *adj* of many forms.

multiforus *adj* many-holed.

multigeneris, -us *adj* of many kinds.

multiiugis, -us *adj* yoked together; complex.

multiloquium, -ī *and* **iī** *nt* talkativeness.

multiloquus *adj* talkative.

multimodīs *adv* variously.

multiplex, -icis *adj* with many folds, tortuous; many-sided, manifold, various; (*comparison*) far greater; (*character*) fickle, sly.

multiplicō, -āre, -āvī, -ātum *vt* to multiply, enlarge.

multipotēns, -entis *adj* very powerful.

multitūdō, -inis *f* great number, multitude, crowd.

multivolus *adj* longing for much.

multō *adv* much, far, by far; (*time*) long.

multō, -āre, -āvī, -ātum *vt* to punish, fine.

multum *adv* much, very, frequently.

multus (*compar* **plūs** *super* **plūrimus**) *adj* much, many; (*speech*) lengthy, tedious; (*time*) late; **~ā nocte** late at night; **nē ~a ≈ to cut a long story short.**

mūlus, -ī *m* mule.

Mulvius *adj* Mulvian (*a Tiber bridge above Rome*).

mundānus, -ī *m* world citizen.

munditia, -ae, -ēs, -ēī *f* cleanness; neatness; elegance.

mundus *adj* clean, neat, elegant; **in ~ō esse** be in readiness.

mundus, -ī *m* toilet gear; universe, world, heavens; mankind.

mūnerigerulus, -ī *m* bringer of presents.

mūnerō, -āre, -or, -ārī *vt* to present, reward.

mūnia, -ōrum *ntpl* official duties.

mūniceps, -ipis *m/f* citizen (*of a municipium*), fellow-citizen.

mūnicipālis *adj* provincial.

mūnicipium, -ī *and* **iī** *nt* provincial town, burgh.

mūnificē *adv see adj.*

mūnificentia, -ae *f* liberality.

mūnificō, -āre *vt* to treat generously.

mūnificus *adj* liberal.

mūnīmen, -inis *nt* defence.

mūnīmentum, -ī *nt* defencework, protection.

mūniō, -īre, -īī, -ītum *vt* to fortify, secure, strengthen; (*road*) to build; (*fig*) to protect.

mūnis *adj* ready to oblige.

mūnītiō, -ōnis *f* building; fortification; (*river*) bridging.

mūnītō, -āre *vt* (*road*) to open up.

mūnītor, -ōris *m* sapper, builder.

mūnus, -eris *nt* service, duty; gift; public show; entertainment; tax; (*funeral*) tribute; (*book*) work.

mūnusculum, -ī *nt* small present.

mūraena, -ae *f* a fish.

mūrālis *adj* wall- (*in cpds*), mural, for fighting from *or* attacking walls.

mūrex, -icis *m* purple-fish; purple dye, purple; jagged rock.

muria, -ae *f* brine.

murmillō, -ōnis *m* kind of gladiator.

murmur, -is *nt* murmur, hum, rumbling, roaring.

murmurillum, -ī *nt* low murmur.

murmurō, -āre *vi* to murmur, rumble; to grumble.

murra, -ae *f* myrrh.

murreus *adj* perfumed; made of the stone called murra.

murrina, -ae *f* myrrh wine.

murrina, -ōrum *ntpl* murrine vases.

murt- *etc see* **myrt-.**

mūrus, -ī *m* wall; dam; defence.

mūs, mūris *m/f* mouse, rat.

Mūsa, -ae *f* goddess inspiring an art; poem; (*pl*) studies.

mūsaeus *adj* poetic, musical.

musca, -ae *f* fly.

mūscipula, -ae *f*, **-um, -ī** *nt* mousetrap.

mūscōsus *adj* mossy.

mūsculus, -ī *m* mouse; muscle; (MIL) shed.

mūscus, -ī *m* moss.

mūsicē *adv* very pleasantly.

mūsicus *adj* of music, of poetry ♦ *m* musician ♦ *f* music, culture ♦ *ntpl* music.

mussitō, -āre *vi* to say nothing; to mutter ♦ *vt* to bear in silence.

mussō, -āre *vt, vi* to say nothing, brood over; to mutter, murmur.

mustāceum, -ī *nt*, **-us, -ī** *m* wedding cake.

mūstēla, -ae *f* weasel.

mustum, -ī *nt* unfermented wine, must; vintage.

mūtābilis *adj* changeable, fickle.

mūtābilitās, -ātis *f* fickleness.

mūtātiō, -ōnis *f* change, alteration; exchange.

mutilō, -āre, -āvī, -ātum *vt* to cut off, maim; to diminish.

mutilus *adj* maimed.

Mutina, -ae *f town in N. Italy* (*now* Modena).

Mutinēnsis *adj see n.*

mūtiō *etc see* **muttiō.**

mūtō, -āre, -āvī, -ātum *vt* to shift; to change, alter; to exchange, barter ♦ *vi* to change; **~āta verba** figurative language.

muttiō, -īre *vi* to mutter, mumble.

mūtuātiō, -ōnis *f* borrowing.

mūtuē *adv* mutually, in turns.

mūtuitō, -āre *vt* to try to borrow.

mūtuō *adv* = **mūtuē.**

mūtuor, -ārī, -ātus *vt* to borrow.

mūtus *adj* dumb, mute; silent, still.

mūtuum, -ī *nt* loan.

mūtuus *adj* borrowed, lent; mutual, reciprocal; **~um dare** lend; **~um sūmere** borrow; **~um facere** return like for like.

Mycēnae, -ārum *fpl Agamemnon's capital in S. Greece.*

Mycēnaeus, -ēnsis *adj*, **-is, -idis** *f* Iphigenia.

Mygdonius *adj* Phrygian.

myoparō, -ōnis *m* pirate galley.

myrīca, -ae *f* tamarisk.

Myrmidones, -um *mpl followers of Achilles.*

Myrōn, -ōnis *m famous Greek sculptor.*

myropōla, -ae *m* perfumer.

myropōlium, -ī *and* **iī** *nt* perfumer's shop.

myrothēcium, -ī *and* **iī** *nt* perfume-box.

myrrh- *etc see* **murr-.**

myrtētum, -ī *nt* myrtlegrove.

myrteus *adj* myrtle- (*in cpds*).

Myrtōum mare *Sea N.W. of Crete.*

myrtum, -ī *nt* myrtle-berry.

myrtus, -ī *and* **ūs** *f* myrtle.

Mȳsia, -iae *f country of Asia Minor.*

Mȳsius, -us *adj see n.*

mysta, -ae *m* priest of mysteries.

mystagōgus, -ī *m* initiator.

mystērium, -ī *and* **iī** *nt* secret religion, mystery; secret.

mysticus *adj* mystic.

Mytilēnae, -ārum *fpl*; **-ē, -es** *f* capital of Lesbos.

Mytilēnaeus *adj see n.*

Mytilēnēnsis *adj see n.*

N, n

nablium, -ī *and* **iī** *nt* kind of harp.

nactus *ppa of* **nancīscor.**

nae *etc see* **nē.**

naenia *etc see* **nēnia.**

Naeviānus *adj see n.*

Naevius, -ī *m early Latin poet.*

naevus, -ī *m* mole (on the body).

Nāias, -adis *and* **s, -dis** *f* water nymph, Naiad.

Nāicus *adj see n.*

nam *conj* (*explaining*) for; (*illustrating*) for example; (*transitional*) now; (*interrog*) but; (*enclitic*) an emphatic particle.

namque *conj* for, for indeed, for example.

nancīscor, -ī, nactus *and* **nanctus** *vt* to obtain, get; to come upon, find.

nānus, -ī *m* dwarf.

Napaeae, -ārum *fpl* dell nymphs.

nāpus, -ī *m* turnip.

Narbō, -ōnis *m town in S. Gaul.*

Narbōnēnsis *adj see n.*

narcissus, -ī *m* narcissus.

nardus, -ī *f*, **-um, -ī** *nt* nard, nard oil.

nāris, -is *f* nostril; (*pl*) nose; (*fig*) sagacity, scorn.

nārrābilis *adj* to be told.

nārrātiō, -ōnis *f* narrative.

nārrātor, -ōris *m* storyteller, historian.

nārrātus, -ūs *m* narrative.

nārrō, -āre, -āvī, -ātum *vt* to tell, relate, say; **male ~** bring bad news.

narthēcium, -ī *and* **iī** *nt* medicine chest.

nāscor, -scī, -tus *vi* to be born; to originate, grow, be produced.

Nāsō, -ōnis *m surname of Ovid.*

nassa, -ae *f* wicker basket for catching fish; (*fig*) snare.

nasturtium, -ī *and* **iī** *nt* cress.

nāsus, -ī *m* nose.

nāsūtē *adv* sarcastically.

nāsūtus *adj* big-nosed; satirical.

nāta, -ae *f* daughter.

nātālicius *adj* of one's birthday, natal ♦ *f* birthday party.

nātālis *adj* of birth, natal ♦ *m* birthday ♦ *mpl* birth, origin.

nātātiō, -ōnis *f* swimming.

natātor, -ōris *m* swimmer.

nātiō, -ōnis *f* tribe, race; breed, class.

natis, -is *f* (*usu pl*) buttocks.

nātīvus *adj* created; inborn, native, natural.

natō, -āre *vi* to swim, float; to flow, overflow; (*eyes*) to swim, fail; (*fig*) to waver.

nātrīx, -īcis *f* watersnake.

nātū *abl m* by birth, in age; **grandis ~, māgnō ~** quite old; **māior ~** older; **māximus ~** oldest.

nātūra, -ae f birth; nature, quality, character; natural order of things; the physical world; (*physics*) element; **rērum ~** Nature.

nātūrālis adj by birth; by nature, natural.

nātūrāliter adv by nature.

nātus ppa of **nāscor** ♦ m son ♦ adj born, made (for); old, of age; **prō, ē rē nātā** under the circumstances, as things are; **annōs vīgintī ~ 20** years old.

nauarchus, -ī m captain.

naucī: nōn esse, facere, habēre to be worthless, consider worthless.

nauclēricus adj skipper's.

nauclērus, -ī m skipper.

naufragium, -ī and iī nt shipwreck, wreck; **~ facere** be shipwrecked.

naufragus adj shipwrecked, wrecked; (*sea*) dangerous to shipping ♦ m shipwrecked man; (*fig*) ruined man.

naulum, -ī nt fare.

naumachia, -ae f mock sea fight.

nausea, -ae f seasickness.

nauseō, -āre vi to be sick; (*fig*) to disgust.

nauseola, -ae f squeamishness.

nauta, (nāvita), -ae m sailor, mariner.

nauticus adj nautical, sailors' ♦ mpl seamen.

nāvālis adj naval, of ships ♦ nt and ntpl dockyard; rigging.

nāvicula, -ae f boat.

nāviculāria, -ae f shipping business.

nāviculārius, -ī and iī m ship-owner.

nāvifragus adj dangerous.

nāvigābilis adj navigable.

nāvigātiō, -ōnis f voyage.

nāviger, -ī adj ship-carrying.

nāvigium, -ī and iī nt vessel, ship.

nāvigō, -āre, -āvī, -ātum vi to sail, put to sea ♦ vt to sail across, navigate.

nāvis, -is f ship; **~ longa** warship; **~ mercātōria** merchantman; **~ onerāria** transport; **~ praetōria** flagship; **~em dēdūcere** launch; **~em solvere** set sail; **~em statuere** heave to; **~em subdūcere** beach; **~ibus atque quadrīgīs** with might and main.

nāvita etc see **nauta**.

nāvitās, -ātis f energy.

nāviter adv energetically; absolutely.

nāvō, -āre vt to perform energetically; **operam ~** be energetic; to come to the assistance (of).

nāvus adj energetic.

Naxos, -ī f Aegean island (*famous for wines and the story of Ariadne*).

nē interj truly, indeed.

nē adv not ♦ conj that not, lest; (*fear*) that; (*purpose*) so that ... not, to avoid, to prevent.

-ne enclitic (*introducing a question*).

Neāpolis, -is f Naples.

Neāpolītānus adj see n.

nebula, -ae f mist, vapour, cloud.

nebulō, -ōnis m idler, good-for-nothing.

nebulōsus adj misty, cloudy.

nec etc see **neque**.

necdum adv and not yet.

necessāriē, -ō adv of necessity, unavoidably.

necessārius adj necessary, inevitable; indispensable; (*kin*) related ♦ m/f relative ♦ ntpl necessities.

necesse adj (*indecl*) necessary, inevitable; needful.

necessitās, -ātis f necessity, compulsion; requirement, want; relationship, connection.

necessitūdō, -inis f necessity, need, want; connection; friendship (*pl*) relatives.

necessum etc see **necesse**.

necne adv or not.

necnōn adv also, besides.

necō, -āre, -āvī, -ātum vt to kill, murder.

necopīnāns, -antis adj unaware.

necopīnātō adv see adj.

necopīnātus adj unexpected.

necopīnus adj unexpected; unsuspecting.

nectar, -is nt nectar (*the drink of the gods*).

nectareus adj of nectar.

nectō, -ctere, -xī and xuī, -xum vt to tie, fasten, connect; to weave; (*fig*) to bind, enslave (*esp for debt*); to contrive, frame.

nēcubi conj so that nowhere.

nēcunde conj so that from nowhere.

nēdum adv much less, much more.

nefandus adj abominable, impious.

nefāriē adv see adj.

nefārius adj heinous, criminal.

nefās nt (*indecl*) wickedness, sin, wrong ♦ interj horror!, shame!

nefāstus adj wicked; unlucky; (*days*) closed to public business.

negātiō, -ōnis f denial.

negitō, -āre vt to deny, refuse.

neglēctiō, -ōnis f neglect.

neglēctus ppp of **neglegō**.

neglēctus, -ūs m neglecting.

neglegēns, -entis pres p of **neglegō** ♦ adj careless, indifferent.

neglegenter adv carelessly.

neglegentia, -ae f carelessness, neglect, coldness.

neglegō, -egere, -ēxī, -ēctum vt to neglect, not care for; to slight, disregard; to overlook.

negō, -āre, -āvī, -ātum vt, vi to say no; to say not, deny; to refuse, decline.

negōtiālis adj business- (*in cpds*).

negōtiāns, -antis m businessman.

negōtiātiō, -ōnis f banking business.

negōtiātor, -ōris m businessman, banker.

negōtiolum, -ī nt trivial matter.

negōtior, -ārī, -ātus vi to do business, trade.

negōtiōsus adj busy.

negōtium, -ī *and* **iī** *nt* business, work; trouble; matter, thing; **quid est ~i?** what is the matter?

Nēlēius *adj see n.*

Nēleus, -eī *m* father of Nestor.

Nēlēus *adj see n.*

Nemea, -ae *f* town in S. Greece, where Hercules killed the lion.

Nemea, -ōrum *ntpl* Nemean Games.

Nemeaeus *adj* Nemean.

nēmō, -inis *m/f* no one, nobody ♦ *adj* no; **~ nōn** everybody; **nōn ~** many; **~ ūnus** not a soul.

nemorālis *adj* sylvan.

nemorēnsis *adj* of the grove.

nemoricultrīx, -īcis *f* forest dweller.

nemorivagus *adj* forest-roving.

nemorōsus *adj* well-wooded; leafy.

nempe *adv* (confirming) surely, of course, certainly; (in questions) do you mean?

nemus, -ōris *nt* wood, grove.

nēnia, -ae *f* dirge; incantation; song, nursery rhyme.

neō, nēre, nēvī, nētum *vt* to spin; to weave.

Neoptolemus, -ī *m* Pyrrhus (son of Achilles).

nepa, -ae *f* scorpion.

nepōs, -ōtis *m* grandson; descendant; spendthrift.

nepōtīnus, -ī *m* little grandson.

neptis, -is *f* granddaughter.

Neptūnius *adj:* **~ hērōs** Theseus.

Neptūnus, -ī *m* Neptune (god of the sea); sea.

nēquam *adj* (indecl) worthless, bad.

nēquāquam *adv* not at all, by no means.

neque, nec *adv* not ♦ *conj* and not, but not; neither, nor; **~ ... et** not only not ... but also.

nequeō, -īre, -īvī, -ītum *vi* to be unable, cannot.

nēquīquam *adv* fruitlessly, for nothing; without good reason.

nēquior, nēquissimus *compar, superl of* **nēquam.**

nēquiter *adv* worthlessly, wrongly.

nēquitia, -ae, -ēs *f* worthlessness, badness.

Nērēis, -eidis *f* Nereid, sea nymph.

Nērēius *adj see n.*

Nēreus, -eī *m* a sea god; the sea.

Nērītius *adj* of Neritos; Ithacan.

Nēritos, -ī *m* island near Ithaca.

Nerō, -ōnis *m* Roman surname (esp the emperor).

Nerōniānus *adj see n.*

nervōsē *adv* vigorously.

nervōsus *adj* sinewy, vigorous.

nervulī, -ōrum *mpl* energy.

nervus, -ī *m* sinew; string; fetter, prison; (shield) leather; (pl) strength, vigour, energy.

nesciō, -īre, -īvī *and* **iī, -ītum** *vt* to not know, be ignorant of; to be unable; **~ quis, quid** somebody, something; **~ an** probably.

nescius *adj* ignorant, unaware; unable; unknown.

Nestor, -oris *m* Greek leader at Troy (famous for his great age and wisdom).

neu *etc see* **nēve.**

neuter, -rī *adj* neither; neuter.

neutiquam *adv* by no means, certainly not.

neutrō *adv* neither way.

nēve, neu *conj* and not; neither, nor.

nēvī *perf of* **neō.**

nex, necis *f* murder, death.

nexilis *adj* tied together.

nexum, -ī *nt* personal enslavement.

nexus *ppp of* **nectō.**

nexus, -ūs *m* entwining, grip; (law) bond, obligation, (esp enslavement for debt).

nī *adv* not ♦ *conj* if not, unless; that not; **quid nī?** why not?

nīcētērium, -ī *and* **iī** *nt* prize.

nictō, -āre *vi* to wink.

nīdāmentum, -ī *nt* nest.

nīdor, -ōris *m* steam, smell.

nīdulus, -ī *m* little nest.

nīdus, -ī *m* nest; (pl) nestlings; (fig) home.

niger, -rī *adj* black, dark; dismal, ill-omened; (character) bad.

nigrāns, -antis *adj* black, dusky.

nigrēscō, -ere *vi* to blacken, grow dark.

nigrō, -āre *vi* to be black.

nigror, -ōris *m* blackness.

nihil, nīl *nt* (indecl) nothing ♦ *adv* not; **~ ad nōs** it has nothing to do with us; **~ est** it's no use; **~ est quod** there is no reason why; **~ nisi** nothing but, only; **~ nōn** everything; **nōn ~** something.

nihilum, -ī *nt* nothing; **~ī esse** be worthless; **~ō minus** none the less.

nīl, nīlum *see* **nihil, nihilum.**

Nīliacus *adj* of the Nile; Egyptian.

Nīlus, -ī *m* Nile; conduit.

nimbifer, -ī *adj* stormy.

nimbōsus *adj* stormy.

nimbus, -ī *m* cloud, rain, storm.

nimiō *adv* much, far.

nīmīrum *adv* certainly, of course.

nimis *adv* too much, very much; **nōn ~** not very.

nimium *adv* too, too much; very, very much.

nimius *adj* too great, excessive; very great ♦ *nt* excess.

ningit, ninguit, -ere *vi* it snows.

ninguēs, -ium *fpl* snow.

Nioba, -ae, -ē, -ēs *f* daughter of Tantalus (changed to a weeping rock).

Niobēus *adj see n.*

Nīreus, -eī *and* **eos** *m* handsomest of the Greeks at Troy.

Nīsaeus, -ēius *adj see n.*

Nīsēis, -edis *f* Scylla.

nisi *conj* if not, unless; except, but.

nīsus *ppa of* **nītor.**

nīsus, -ūs *m* pressure, effort; striving, soaring.

Nīsus, -ī *m* father of Scylla.

nītēdula, -ae *f* dormouse.

nitēns, -entis *pres p of* **niteō** ♦ *adj* bright;

brilliant, beautiful.

niteō, -ēre *vi* to shine, gleam; to be sleek, be greasy; to thrive, look beautiful.

nitēscō, -ere, nituī *vi* to brighten, shine, glow.

nitidiusculē *adv* rather more finely.

nitidiusculus *adj* a little shinier.

nitidē *adv* magnificently.

nitidus *adj* bright, shining; sleek; blooming; smart, spruce; (*speech*) refined.

nitor, -ōris *m* brightness, sheen; sleekness, beauty; neatness, elegance.

nītor, -tī, -sus *and* **xus** *vi* to rest on, lean on; to press, stand firmly; to press forward, climb; to exert oneself, strive, labour; to depend on.

nitrum, -ī *nt* soda.

nivālis *adj* snowy.

niveus *adj* of snow, snowy, snow-white.

nivōsus *adj* snowy.

nix, nivis *f* snow.

nīxor, -ārī *vi* to rest on; to struggle.

nīxus *ppp of* **nītor**.

nīxus, -ūs *m* pressure; labour.

nō, nāre, nāvī *vi* to swim, float; to sail, fly.

nōbilis *adj* known, noted, famous, notorious; noble, high-born; excellent.

nōbilitās, -ātis *f* fame; noble birth; the nobility; excellence.

nōbilitō, -āre, -āvī, -ātum *vt* to make famous *or* notorious.

nocēns, -entis *pres p of* **noceō** ♦ *adj* harmful; criminal, guilty.

noceō, -ēre, -uī, -itum *vi* (*with dat*) to harm, hurt.

nocīvus *adj* injurious.

noctifer, -ī *m* evening star.

noctilūca, -ae *f* moon.

noctivagus *adj* night-wandering.

noctū *adv* by night.

noctua, -ae *f* owl.

noctuābundus *adj* travelling by night.

nocturnus *adj* night- (*in cpds*), nocturnal.

nōdō, -āre, -āvī, -ātum *vt* to knot, tie.

nōdōsus *adj* knotty.

nōdus, -ī *m* knot; knob; girdle; (*fig*) bond, difficulty.

nōlō, -le, -uī *vt, vi* to not wish, be unwilling, refuse; ~**ī**, ~**īte** do not.

Nomas, -dis *m/f* nomad; Numidian.

nōmen, -inis *nt* name; title; (*COMM*) demand, debt; (*GRAM*) noun; (*fig*) reputation, fame; account, pretext; ~ **dare profitērī** enlist; ~ **dēferre** accuse; ~**ina facere** enter the items of a debt.

nōmenclātor, -ōris *m* slave who told his master the names of people.

nōminātim *adv* by name, one by one.

nōminātiō, -ōnis *f* nomination.

nōminitō, -āre *vt* to usually name.

nōminō, -āre, -āvī, -ātum *vt* to name, call; to mention; to make famous; to nominate; to accuse, denounce.

nomisma, -tis *nt* coin.

nōn *adv* not; no.

Nōnae, -ārum *fpl* Nones (*7th day of March, May, July, October, 5th of other months*).

nōnāgēsimus *adj* ninetieth.

nōnāgiēns, -ēs *adv* ninety times.

nōnāgintā *num* ninety.

nōnānus *adj* of the ninth legion.

nōndum *adv* not yet.

nōngentī, -ōrum *num* nine hundred.

nonna, -ae *f* nun.

nōnne *adv* do not?, is not? *etc.*; (*indirect*) whether not.

nōnnullus *adj* some.

nōnnunquam *adv* sometimes.

nōnus *adj* ninth ♦ *f* ninth hour.

nōnusdecimus *adj* nineteenth.

Nōricum, -ī *nt* country between the Danube and the Alps.

Nōricus *adj see* n.

nōrma, -ae *f* rule.

nōs *pron* we, us; I, me.

nōscitō, -āre *vt* to know, recognise; to observe, examine.

nōscō, -scere, -vī, -tum *vt* to get to know, learn; to examine; to recognise, allow; (*perf*) to know.

nōsmet *pron* (*emphatic*) *see* **nōs**.

noster, -rī *adj* our, ours; for us; my; (*with names*) my dear, good old ♦ *m* our friend ♦ *mpl* our side, our troops; ~**rī, ~rum** of us.

nostrās, -ātis *adj* of our country, native.

nota, -ae *f* mark, sign, note; (*writing*) note, letter; (*pl*) memoranda, shorthand, secret writing; (*books*) critical mark, punctuation; (*wine, etc*) brand, quality; (*gesture*) sign; (*fig*) sign, token; (*censor's*) black mark; (*fig*) stigma, disgrace.

notābilis *adj* remarkable; notorious.

notābiliter *adv* perceptibly.

notārius, -ī *and* **iī** *m* shorthand writer; secretary.

notātiō, -ōnis *f* marking; choice; observation; (*censor*) stigmatizing; (*words*) etymology.

nōtēscō, -ere, nōtuī *vi* to become known.

nothus *adj* bastard; counterfeit.

nōtiō, -ōnis *f* (*law*) cognisance, investigation; (*PHILOS*) idea.

nōtitia, -ae, -ēs, -ēī *f* fame; acquaintance; (*PHILOS*) idea, preconception.

notō, -āre, -āvī, -ātum *vt* to mark, write; to denote; to observe; to brand, stigmatize.

nōtuī *perf of* **nōtēscō**.

nōtus *ppp of* **nōscō** ♦ *adj* known, familiar; notorious ♦ *mpl* acquaintances.

Notus (-os), -ī *m* south wind.

novācula, -ae *f* razor.

Noun declensions and verb conjugations are shown on pp xiii to xxv. The present infinitive ending of a verb shows to which conjugation it belongs: **-āre** = 1st; **-ēre** = 2nd; **-ere** = 3rd and **-īre** = 4th. Irregular verbs are shown on p xxvi

novālis, -is f, **-e, -is** nt fallow land; field; crops.
novātrīx, -īcis f renewer.
novē adv unusually.
novellus adj young, fresh, new.
novem num nine.
November, -ris adj of November ♦ m November.
novendecim num nineteen.
novendiālis adj nine days'; on the ninth day.
novēnī, -ōrum adj in nines; nine.
Novēnsilēs, -ium mpl new gods.
noverca, -ae f stepmother.
novercālis adj stepmother's.
nōvī perf of **nōscō**.
novīcius adj new.
noviēns, -ēs adv nine times.
novissimē adv lately; last of all.
novissimus adj latest, last, rear.
novitās, -ātis f newness, novelty; strangeness.
novō, -āre, -āvī, -ātum vt to renew, refresh; to change; (words) to coin; **rēs ~** effect a revolution.
novus adj new, young, fresh, recent; strange, unusual; inexperienced; **~ homō** upstart, first of his family to hold curule office; **~ae rēs** revolution; **~ae tabulae** cancellation of debts; **quid ~ī** what news?
nox, noctis f night; darkness, obscurity; **nocte, noctū** by night; **dē nocte** during the night.
noxa, -ae f hurt, harm; offence, guilt; punishment.
noxia, -ae f harm, damage; guilt, fault.
noxius adj harmful; guilty.
nūbēcula, -ae f cloudy look.
nūbēs, -is f cloud; (fig) gloom; veil.
nūbifer, -ī adj cloud-capped; cloudy.
nūbigena, -ae m cloudborn, Centaur.
nūbilis adj marriageable.
nūbilus adj cloudy; gloomy, sad ♦ ntpl clouds.
nūbō, -bere, -psī, -ptum vi (women) to be married.
nucleus, -ī m nut, kernel.
nūdius day since, days ago; **~ tertius** the day before yesterday.
nūdō, -āre, -āvī, -ātum vt to bare, strip, expose; (MIL) to leave exposed; to plunder; (fig) to disclose, betray.
nūdus adj naked, bare; exposed, defenceless; wearing only a tunic; (fig) destitute, poor; mere; unembellished, undisguised; **vestīmenta dētrahere ~ō ≈** draw blood from a stone.
nūgae, -ārum fpl nonsense, trifles; (person) waster.
nūgātor, -ōris m silly creature, liar.
nūgātōrius adj futile.
nūgāx, -ācis adj frivolous.
nūgor, -ārī, -ātus vi to talk nonsense; to cheat.
nullus, -īus (dat -ī) adj no, none; not, not at all; non-existent, of no account ♦ m/f nobody.

num interrog particle surely not? (indirect) whether, if.
Numa, -ae m second king of Rome.
nūmen, -inis nt nod, will; divine will, power; divinity, god.
numerābilis adj easy to count.
numerātus adj in cash ♦ nt ready money.
numerō, -āre, -āvī, -ātum vt to count, number; (money) to pay out; (fig) to reckon, consider as.
numerō adv just now, quickly, too soon.
numerōsē adv rhythmically.
numerōsus adj populous; rhythmical.
numerus, -ī m number; many, numbers; (MIL) troop; (fig) a cipher; (pl) mathematics; rank, category, regard; rhythm, metre, verse; **in ~ō esse, habērī** be reckoned as; **nullō ~ō** of no account.
Numida adj see n.
Numidae, -ārum mpl Numidians (people of N. Africa).
Numidia, -iae f the country of the Numidians.
Numidicus adj see n.
Numitor, -ōris m king of Alba (grandfather of Romulus).
nummārius adj money- (in cpds), financial; mercenary.
nummātus adj moneyed.
nummulī, -ōrum mpl some money, cash.
nummus, -ī m coin, money, cash; (Roman coin) sestertius; (Greek coin) two-drachma piece.
numnam, numne see num.
numquam adv never; **~ nōn** always; **nōn ~** sometimes.
numquid (question) do you? does he? etc; (indirect) whether.
nunc adv now; at present, nowadays; but as it is; **~ ... ~** at one time ... at another.
nuncupātiō, -ōnis f pronouncing.
nuncupō, -āre, -āvī, -ātum vt to call, name; to pronounce formally.
nūndinae, -ārum fpl market day; market; trade.
nūndinātiō, -ōnis f trading.
nūndinor, -ārī vi to trade, traffic; to flock together ♦ vt to buy.
nūndinum, -ī nt market time; **trīnum ~** 17 days.
nunq- etc see numq-.
nūntiātiō, -ōnis f announcing.
nūntiō, -āre, -āvī, -ātum vt to announce, report, tell.
nūntius adj informative, speaking ♦ m messenger; message, news; injunction; notice of divorce ♦ nt message.
nūper adv recently, lately.
nūpsī perf of **nūbō**.
nūpta, -ae f bride, wife.
nūptiae, -ārum fpl wedding, marriage.
nūptiālis adj wedding- (in cpds), nuptial.
nurus, -ūs f daughter-in-law; young woman.
nūsquam adv nowhere; in nothing, for nothing.

nūtō, -āre *vi* to nod; to sway, totter, falter.
nūtrīcius, -ī *m* tutor.
nūtrīcō, -āre, -or, -ārī *vt* to nourish, sustain.
nūtrīcula, -ae *f* nurse.
nūtrīmen, -inis *nt* nourishment.
nūtrīmentum, -ī *nt* nourishment, support.
nūtriō, -īre, -īvī, -ītum *vt* to suckle, nourish, rear, nurse.
nūtrīx, -īcis *f* nurse, foster mother.
nūtus, -ūs *m* nod; will, command; (*physics*) gravity.
nux, nucis *f* nut; nut tree, almond tree.
Nyctēis, -idis *f* Antiopa.
nympha, -ae, -ē, -ēs *f* bride; nymph; water.
Nysa, -ae *f* birthplace of Bacchus.
Nysaeus, -ēis, -ius *adj see n.*

O, o

ō *interj* (*expressing joy, surprise, pain, etc*) oh!; (*with voc*) O!
ob *prep* (*with acc*) in front of; for, on account of, for the sake of; **quam ~ rem** accordingly.
obaerātus *adj* in debt ♦ *m* debtor.
obambulō, -āre *vi* to walk past, prowl about.
obarmō, -āre *vt* to arm (against).
obarō, -āre *vt* to plough up.
obc- *etc see* **occ-**.
obdō, -ere, -idī, -itum *vt* to shut; to expose.
obdormīscō, -īscere, -īvī *vi* to fall asleep ♦ *vt* to sleep off.
obdūcō, -ūcere, -ūxī, -uctum *vt* to draw over, cover; to bring up; (*drink*) to swallow; (*time*) to pass.
obductō, -āre *vt* to bring as a rival.
obductus *ppp of* **obdūcō**.
obdūrēscō, -ēscere, -uī *vi* to harden; to become obdurate.
obdūrō, -āre *vi* to persist, stand firm.
obduticō, -ōnis *f* veiling.
obeō, -īre, -īvī, *and* **iī, -itum** *vi* to go to, meet; to die; (*ASTRO*) to set ♦ *vt* to visit, travel over; to survey, go over; to envelop; (*duty*) to engage in, perform; (*time*) to meet; **diem ~ die**; (*law*) to appear on the appointed day.
obequitō, -āre *vi* to ride up to.
oberrō, -āre *vi* to ramble about; to make a mistake.
obēsus *adj* fat, plump; coarse.
ōbex, -icis *m/f* bolt, bar, barrier.
obf- *etc see* **off-**.
obg- *etc see* **ogg-**.

obhaerēscō, -rēscere, -sī *vi* to stick fast.
obiaceō, -ēre *vi* to lie over against.
obiciō, -icere, -iēcī, -iectum *vt* to throw to, set before; (*defence*) to put up, throw against; (*fig*) to expose, give up; (*speech*) to taunt, reproach.
obiectātiō, -ōnis *f* reproach.
obiectō, -āre *vt* to throw against; to expose, sacrifice; to reproach; (*hint*) to let on.
obiectus *ppp of* **obiciō** ♦ *adj* opposite, in front of; exposed ♦ *ntpl* accusations.
obiectus, -ūs *m* putting in the way, interposing.
obirātus *adj* angered.
obiter *adv* on the way; incidentally.
obitus *ppp of* **obeō**.
obitus, -ūs *m* death, ruin; (*ASTRO*) setting; visit.
obiūrgātiō, -ōnis *f* reprimand.
obiūrgātor, -ōris *m* reprover.
obiūrgātōrius *adj* reproachful.
obiūrgitō, -āre *vt* to keep on reproaching.
obiūrgō, -āre, -āvī, -ātum *vt* to scold, rebuke; to deter by reproof.
oblanguēscō, -ēscere, -uī *vi* to become feeble.
oblātrātrīx, -īcis *f* nagging woman.
oblātus *ppp of* **offerō**.
oblectāmentum, -ī *nt* amusement.
oblectātiō, -ōnis *f* delight.
oblectō, -āre, -āvī, -ātum *vt* to delight, amuse, entertain; to detain; (*time*) to spend pleasantly; **sē ~** enjoy oneself.
oblīdō, -dere, -sī, -sum *vt* to crush, strangle.
obligātiō, -ōnis *f* pledge.
obligō, -āre, -āvī, -ātum *vt* to tie up, bandage; to put under an obligation, embarrass; (*law*) to render liable, make guilty; to mortgage.
oblīmō, -āre *vt* to cover with mud.
oblinō, -inere, -ēvī, -itum *vt* to smear over; to defile; (*fig*) to overload.
oblīquē *adv* sideways; indirectly.
oblīquō, -āre *vt* to turn aside, veer.
oblīquus *adj* slanting, downhill; from the side, sideways; (*look*) askance, envious; (*speech*) indirect.
oblīsus *ppp of* **oblīdō**.
oblitēscō, -ere *vi* to hide away.
oblitterō, -āre, -āvī, -ātum *vt* to erase, cancel; (*fig*) to consign to oblivion.
oblitus *ppp of* **oblinō**.
oblītus *ppa of* **oblīvīscor**.
oblīviō, -ōnis *f* oblivion, forgetfulness.
oblīviōsus *adj* forgetful.
oblīvīscor, -vīscī, -tus *vt, vi* to forget.
oblīvium, -ī *and* **iī** *nt* forgetfulness, oblivion.
oblocūtor, -ōris *m* contradicter.
oblongus *adj* oblong.
obloquor, -quī, -cūtus *vi* to contradict, interrupt; to abuse; (*music*) to accompany.

Noun declensions and verb conjugations are shown on pp xiii to xxv. The present infinitive ending of a verb shows to which conjugation it belongs: **-āre** = 1st; **-ēre** = 2nd; **-ere** = 3rd and **-īre** = 4th. Irregular verbs are shown on p xxvi

obluctor, -ārī *vi* to struggle against.
obmōlior, -īrī *vt* to throw up (*as a defence*).
obmurmurō, -āre *vi* to roar in answer.
obmūtēscō, -ēscere, -uī *vi* to become silent; to cease.
obnātus *adj* growing on.
obnītor, -tī, -xus *vi* to push against, struggle; to stand firm, resist.
obnīxē *adv* resolutely.
obnīxus *ppa of* **obnītor ♦** *adj* steadfast.
obnoxiē *adv* slavishly.
obnoxiōsus *adj* submissive.
obnoxius *adj* liable, addicted; culpable; submissive, slavish; under obligation, indebted; exposed (to danger).
obnūbō, -bere, -psī, -ptum *vt* to veil, cover.
obnūntiātiō, -ōnis *f* announcement of an adverse omen.
obnūntiō, -āre *vt* to announce an adverse omen.
oboediēns, -entis *pres p of* **oboediō ♦** *adj* obedient.
oboedienter *adv* readily.
oboedientia, -ae *f* obedience.
oboediō, -īre *vi* to listen; to obey, be subject to.
oboleō, -ēre, -uī *vt* to smell of.
oborior, -īrī, -tus *vi* to arise, spring up.
obp- *etc see* **opp-**.
obrēpō, -ere, -sī, -tum *vt, vi* to creep up to, steal upon, surprise; to cheat.
obrētiō, -īre *vt* to entangle.
obrigēscō, -ēscere, -uī *vi* to stiffen.
obrogō, -āre, -āvī, -ātum *vt* to invalidate (*by making a new law*).
obruō, -ere, -ī, -tum *vt* to cover over, bury, sink; to overwhelm, overpower ♦ *vi* to fall to ruin.
obrussa, -ae *f* test, touchstone.
obrutus *ppp of* **obruō**.
obsaepiō, -īre, -sī, -tum *vt* to block, close.
obsaturō, -āre *vt* to sate, glut.
obscaen- *etc see* **obscen-**.
obscēnē *adv* indecently.
obscēnitās, -ātis *f* indecency.
obscēnus *adj* filthy; indecent; ominous.
obscūrātiō, -ōnis *f* darkening, disappearance.
obscūrē *adv* secretly.
obscūritās, -ātis *f* darkness; (*fig*) uncertainty; (*rank*) lowliness.
obscūrō, -āre, -āvī, -ātum *vt* to darken; to conceal, suppress; (*speech*) to obscure; (*pass*) to become obsolete.
obscūrus *adj* dark, shady, hidden; (*fig*) obscure, indistinct; unknown, ignoble; (*character*) reserved.
obsecrātiō, -ōnis *f* entreaty; public prayer.
obsecrō, -āre *vt* to implore, appeal to.
obsecundō, -āre *vi* to comply with, back up.
obsēdī *perf of* **obsideō**.
obsēp- *etc see* **obsaep-**.
obsequēns, -entis *pres p of* **obsequor ♦** *adj*

compliant; (*gods*) gracious.
obsequenter *adv* compliantly.
obsequentia, -ae *f* complaisance.
obsequiōsus *adj* complaisant.
obsequium, -ī *and* **iī** *nt* compliance, indulgence; obedience, allegiance.
obsequor, -quī, -cūtus *vi* to comply with, yield to, indulge.
obserō, -āre *vt* to bar, close.
obserō, -erere, -ēvī, -itum *vt* to sow, plant; to cover thickly.
observāns, -antis *pres p of* **observō ♦** *adj* attentive, respectful.
observantia, -ae *f* respect.
observātiō, -ōnis *f* watching; caution.
observitō, -āre *vt* to observe carefully.
observō, -āre, -āvī, -ātum *vt* to watch, watch for; to guard; (*laws*) to keep, comply with; (*person*) to pay respect to.
obses, -idis *m/f* hostage; guarantee.
obsessiō, -ōnis *f* blockade.
obsessor, -ōris *m* frequenter; besieger.
obsessus *ppp of* **obsideō**.
obsideō, -idēre, -ēdī, -essum *vt* to sit at, frequent; (*MIL*) to blockade, besiege; to block, fill, take up; to guard, watch for ♦ *vi* to sit.
obsidiō, -ōnis *f* siege, blockade; (*fig*) imminent danger.
obsidium, -ī *and* **iī** *nt* siege, blockade; hostageship.
obsīdō, -ere *vt* to besiege, occupy.
obsignātor, -ōris *m* sealer; witness.
obsignō, -āre, -āvī, -ātum *vt* to seal up; to sign and seal; (*fig*) to stamp.
obsistō, -istere, -titī, -titum *vi* to put oneself in the way, resist.
obsitus *ppp of* **obserō**.
obsolefīō, -fierī *vi* to wear out, become degraded.
obsolēscō, -scere, -vī, -tum *vi* to wear out, become out of date.
obsolētius *adv* more shabbily.
obsolētus *ppa of* **obsolēscō ♦** *adj* worn out, shabby; obsolete; (*fig*) ordinary, mean.
obsōnātor, -ōris *m* caterer.
obsōnātus, -ūs *m* marketing.
obsōnium, -ī *and* **iī** *nt* food eaten with bread, (*usu fish*).
obsōnō, -āre, -or, -ārī *vi* to cater, buy provisions; to provide a meal.
obsonō, -āre *vi* to interrupt.
obsorbeō, -ēre *vt* to swallow, bolt.
obstantia, -ium *ntpl* obstructions.
obstetrīx, -īcis *f* midwife.
obstinātiō, -ōnis *f* determination, stubbornness.
obstinātē *adv* firmly, obstinately.
obstinātus *adj* firm, resolute; stubborn.
obstinō, -āre *vi* to be determined, persist.
obstipēscō *etc see* **obstupēscō**.
obstīpus *adj* bent, bowed, drawn back.
obstitī *perf of* **obsistō**; *perf of* **obstō**.
obstō, -āre, -itī *vi* to stand in the way; to

obstruct, prevent.

obstrepō, -ere, -uī, -itum vi to make a noise; to shout against, cry down, molest ♦ vt to drown (in noise); to fill with noise.

obstrictus ppp of **obstringō**.

obstringō, -ingere, -inxī, -ictum vt to bind up, tie round; (fig) to confine, hamper; to lay under an obligation.

obstructiō, -ōnis f barrier.

obstructus ppp of **obstruō**.

obstrūdō (obtrūdō), -dere, -sī, -sum vt to force on to; to gulp down.

obstruō, -ere, -xī, -ctum vt to build up against, block; to shut, hinder.

obstupefaciō, -facere, -fēcī, -factum (pass **-fīō, -fierī**) vt to astound, paralyse.

obstupēscō, -ēscere, -uī vi to be astounded, paralysed.

obstupidus adj stupefied.

obsum, -esse, -fuī vi to be against, harm.

obsuō, -uere, -uī, -ūtum vt to sew on, sew up.

obsurdēscō, -ēscere, -uī vi to grow deaf; to turn a deaf ear.

obsūtus ppp of **obsuō**.

obtegō, -egere, -ēxī, -ēctum vt to cover over; to conceal.

obtemperātiō, -ōnis f obedience.

obtemperō, -āre, -āvī, -ātum vi (with dat) to comply with, obey.

obtendō, -dere, -dī, -tum vt to spread over, stretch over against; to conceal; to make a pretext of.

obtentus ppp of **obtendō**; ppp of **obtineō**.

obtentus, -ūs m screen; pretext.

obterō, -erere, -rīvī, -rītum vt to trample on, crush; to disparage.

obtestātiō, -ōnis f adjuring; supplication.

obtestor, -ārī, -ātus vt to call to witness; to entreat.

obtexō, -ere, -uī vt to overspread.

obticeō, -ēre vi to be silent.

obticēscō, -ēscere, -uī vi to be struck dumb.

obtigī perf of **obtingō**.

obtigō see **obtegō**.

obtineō, -inēre, -inuī, -entum vt to hold, possess; to maintain; to gain, obtain ♦ vi to prevail, continue.

obtingō, -ngere, -gī vi to fall to one's lot; to happen.

obtorpēscō, -ēscere, -uī vi to become numb, lose feeling.

obtorqueō, -quēre, -sī, -tum vt to twist about, wrench.

obtrectātiō, -ōnis f disparagement.

obtrectātor, -ōris m disparager.

obtrectō, -āre vt, vi to detract, disparage.

obtrītus ppp of **obterō**.

obtrūdō etc see **obstrūdō**.

obtruncō, -āre vt to cut down, slaughter.

obtueor, -ērī, -or, -ī vt to gaze at, see clearly.

obtulī perf of **offerō**.

obtundō, -undere, -udī, -ūsum and **-ūnsum** vt to beat, thump; to blunt; (speech) to deafen, annoy.

obturbō, -āre vt to throw into confusion; to bother, distract.

obturgēscō, -ere vi to swell up.

obtūrō, -āre vt to stop up, close.

obtūsus, obtūnsus ppp of **obtundō** ♦ adj blunt; (fig) dulled, blurred, unfeeling.

obtūtus, -ūs m gaze.

obumbrō, -āre vt to shade, darken; (fig) to cloak, screen.

obuncus adj hooked.

obūstus adj burnt, hardened in fire.

obvallātus adj fortified.

obveniō, -enīre, -ēnī, -entum vi to come up; to fall to; to occur.

obversor, -ārī vi to move about before; (visions) to hover.

obversus ppp of **obvertō** ♦ adj turned towards ♦ mpl enemy.

obvertō, -tere, -tī, -sum vt to direct towards, turn against.

obviam adv to meet, against; ~ ire to go to meet.

obvius adj in the way, to meet; opposite, against; at hand, accessible; exposed.

obvolvō, -vere, -vī, -ūtum vt to wrap up, muffle up; (fig) to cloak.

occaecō, -āre, -āvī, -ātum vt to blind, obscure, conceal; to benumb.

occallēscō, -ēscere, -uī vi to grow a thick skin; to become hardened.

occanō, -ere vi to sound the attack.

occāsiō, -ōnis f opportunity, convenient time; (MIL) surprise.

occāsiuncula, -ae f opportunity.

occāsus, -ūs m setting; west; downfall, ruin.

occātiō, -ōnis f harrowing.

occātor, -ōris m harrower.

occēdō, -ere vi to go up to.

occentō, -āre vt, vi to serenade; to sing a lampoon.

occēpī perf of **occipiō**.

occepsō archaic fut of **occipiō**.

occeptō, -āre vt to begin.

occidēns, -entis pres p of **occidō** ♦ m west.

occīdiō, -ōnis f massacre; ~ōne occīdere annihilate.

occīdō, -dere, -dī, -sum vt to fell; to cut down, kill; to pester.

occidō, -idere, -idī, -āsum vi to fall; to set; to die, perish, be ruined.

occiduus adj setting; western; failing.

occinō, -ere, -uī vi to sing inauspiciously.

occipiō, -ipere, -ēpī, -eptum vt, vi to begin.

occipitium, -ī and **iī** nt back of the head.

occīsiō, -ōnis f massacre.

occīsor, -ōris m killer.

occīsus _ppp of_ **occīdō.**

occlāmitō, -āre _vi_ to bawl.

occlūdō, -dere, -sī, -sum _vt_ to shut up; to stop.

occō, -āre _vt_ to harrow.

occubō, -āre _vi_ to lie.

occulcō, -āre _vt_ to trample down.

occulō, -ere, -uī, -tum _vt_ to cover over, hide.

occultātiō, -ōnis _f_ concealment.

occultātor, -ōris _m_ hider.

occultē _adv_ secretly.

occultō, -āre, -āvī, -ātum _vt_ to conceal, secrete.

occultus _ppp of_ **occulō** ◆ _adj_ hidden, secret; (_person_) reserved, secretive ◆ _nt_ secret, hiding.

occumbō, -mbere, -buī, -bitum _vi_ to fall, die.

occupātiō, -ōnis _f_ taking possession; business; engagement.

occupātus _adj_ occupied, busy.

occupō, -āre, -āvī, -ātum _vt_ to take possession of, seize; to occupy, take up; to surprise, anticipate; (_money_) to lend, invest.

occurrō, -rere, -rī, -sum _vi_ to run up to, meet; to attack; to fall in with; to hurry to; (_fig_) to obviate, counteract; (_words_) to object; (_thought_) to occur, suggest itself.

occursātiō, -ōnis _f_ fussy welcome.

occursō, -āre _vi_ to run to meet, meet; to oppose; (_thought_) to occur.

occursus, -ūs _m_ meeting.

Ōceanītis, -ītidis _f_ daughter of Ocean.

Ōceanus, -ī _m_ Ocean, a stream encircling the earth; the Atlantic.

ocellus, -ī _m_ eye; darling, gem.

ōcior, -ōris _adj_ quicker, swifter.

ōcius _adv_ more quickly; sooner, rather; quickly.

ocrea, -ae _f_ greave.

ocreātus _adj_ greaved.

Octāviānus _adj_ of Octavius ◆ _m_ Octavian (_a surname of Augustus_).

Octāvius, -ī _m_ Roman family name (_esp the emperor Augustus; his father_).

octāvum _adv_ for the eighth time.

octāvus _adj_ eighth ◆ _f_ eighth hour.

octāvusdecimus _adj_ eighteenth.

octiēns, -ēs _adv_ eight times.

octingentēsimus _adj_ eight hundredth.

octingentī, -ōrum _num_ eight hundred.

octipēs, -edis _adj_ eight-footed.

octō _num_ eight.

Octōber, -ris _adj_ of October ◆ _m_ October.

octōgēnī, -ōrum _adj_ eighty each.

octōgēsimus _adj_ eightieth.

octōgiēns, -ēs _adv_ eighty times.

octōgintā _num_ eighty.

octōiugis _adj_ eight together.

octōnī, -ōrum _adj_ eight at a time, eight each.

octōphoros _adj_ (_litter_) carried by eight bearers.

octuplicātus _adj_ multiplied by eight.

octuplus _adj_ eightfold.

octussis, -is _m_ eight asses.

oculātus _adj_ with eyes; visible; **~ā diē vēndere** sell for cash.

oculus, -ī _m_ eye; sight; (_plant_) bud; (_fig_) darling, jewel; **~ōs adicere ad** glance at, covet; **ante ~ōs pōnere** imagine; **ex ~īs** out of sight; **esse in ~īs** be in view; be a favourite.

ōdī, -isse _vt_ to hate, dislike.

odiōsē _adv see adj._

odiōsus _adj_ odious, unpleasant.

odium, -ī _and_ **iī** _nt_ hatred, dislike, displeasure; insolence; **~iō esse** be hateful, be disliked.

odor (-ōs), -ōris _m_ smell, perfume, stench; (_fig_) inkling, suggestion.

odōrātiō, -ōnis _f_ smelling.

odōrātus _adj_ fragrant, perfumed.

odōrātus, -ūs _m_ sense of smell; smelling.

odōrifer, -ī _adj_ fragrant; perfume-producing.

odōrō, -āre _vt_ to perfume.

odōror, -ārī, -ātus _vt_ to smell, smell out; (_fig_) to search out; to aspire to; to get a smattering of.

odōrus _adj_ fragrant; keen-scented.

odōs _etc see_ **odor.**

Odrysius _adj_ Thracian.

Odyssēa, -ae _f_ Odyssey.

Oeagrius _adj_ Thracian.

Oebalia, -iae _f_ Tarentum.

Oebalidēs, -idae _m_ Castor, Pollux.

Oebalis, -idis _f_ Helen.

Oebalius _adj_ Spartan.

Oebalus, -ī _m_ king of Sparta.

Oedipūs, -odis _and_ **ī** _m_ king of Thebes; solver of riddles.

oenophorum, -ī _nt_ wine basket.

Oenopia, -ae _f_ Aegina.

Oenotria, -ae _f_ S.E. Italy.

Oenotrius _adj_ Italian.

oestrus, -ī _m_ gadfly; (_fig_) frenzy.

Oeta, -ae, -ē, -ēs _f_ mountain range in Thessaly, associated with Hercules.

Oetaeus _adj see n._

ofella, -ae _f_ morsel.

offa, -ae _f_ pellet, lump; swelling.

offectus _ppp of_ **officiō.**

offendō, -endere, -endī, -ēnsum _vt_ to hit; to hit on, come upon; to offend, blunder; to take offence; to fail, come to grief.

offēnsa, -ae _f_ displeasure, enmity; offence, injury.

offēnsiō, -ōnis _f_ stumbling; stumbling block; misfortune, indisposition; offence, displeasure.

offēnsiuncula, -ae _f_ slight displeasure; slight check.

offēnsō, -āre _vt, vi_ to dash against.

offēnsus _ppp of_ **offendō** ◆ _adj_ offensive; displeased ◆ _nt_ offence.

offēnsus, -ūs _m_ shock; offence.

offerō, -re, obtulī, oblātum _vt_ to present, show; to bring forward, offer; to expose; to cause, inflict; **sē ~** encounter.

offerumenta, -ae f present.
officīna, -ae f workshop factory.
officiō, -icere, -ēcī, -ectum vi to obstruct; to interfere with; to hurt, prejudice.
officiōsē adv courteously.
officiōsus adj obliging; dutiful.
officium, -ī and **iī** nt service, attention; ceremonial; duty, sense of duty; official duty, function.
offīgō, -ere vt to fasten, drive in.
offirmātus adj determined.
offirmō, -āre vt, vi to persevere in.
offlectō, -ere vt to turn about.
offrēnātus adj checked.
offūcia, -ae f (cosmetic) paint; (fig) trick.
offulgeō, -gēre, -sī vi to shine on.
offundō, -undere, -ūdī, -ūsum vt to pour out to; to pour over; to spread; to cover, fill.
offūsus ppp of **offundō**.
ogganniō, -īre vi to growl at.
oggerō, -ere vt to bring, give.
Ōgygius adj Theban.
oh interj (expressing surprise, joy, grief) oh!
ohē interj (expressing surfeit) stop!, enough!
oi interj (expressing complaint, weeping) oh!, oh dear!
oiei interj (lamenting) oh dear!
Oīleus, -eī m father of the less famous Ajax.
olea, -ae f olive; olive tree.
oleāginus adj of the olive tree.
oleārius adj oil- (in cpds) ♦ m oil seller.
oleaster, -rī m wild olive.
olēns, -entis pres p of **oleō** ♦ adj fragrant; stinking, musty.
oleō, -ēre, -uī vt, vi to smell, smell of; (fig) to betray.
oleum, -ī nt olive oil, oil; wrestling school; **~ et operam perdere** waste time and trouble.
olfaciō, -facere, -fēcī, -factum vt to smell, scent.
olfactō, -āre vt to smell at.
olidus adj smelling, rank.
ōlim adv once, once upon a time; at the time, at times; for a good while; one day (in the future).
olit- etc see **holit-**.
olīva, -ae f olive, olive tree; olive branch, olive staff.
olīvētum, -ī nt olive grove.
olīvifer, -ī adj olive-bearing.
olīvum, -ī nt oil; wrestling school; perfume.
olla, -ae f pot, jar.
olle, ollus etc see **ille**.
olor, -ōris m swan.
olōrinus adj swan's.
olus etc see **holus**.
Olympia, -ae f site of the Greek games in Elis.
Olympia, -ōrum ntpl Olympic Games.
Olympiacus adj = **Olympicus**.
Olympias, -adis f Olympiad, period of four years.
Olympicus, -us adj Olympic.
Olympionīcēs, -ae m Olympic winner.
Olympus, -ī m mountain in N. Greece, abode of the gods; heaven.
omāsum, -ī nt tripe; paunch.
ōmen, -inis nt omen, sign; solemnity.
ōmentum, -ī nt bowels.
ōminor, -ārī, -ātus vt to forebode, prophesy.
ōmissus ppp of **ōmittō** ♦ adj remiss.
ōmittō, -ittere, -īsī, -issum vt to let go; to leave off, give up; to disregard, overlook; (speech) to pass over, omit.
omnifer, -ī adj all-sustaining.
omnigenus adj of all kinds.
omnimodīs adv wholly.
omnīnō adv entirely, altogether, at all; in general; (concession) to be sure, yes; (number) in all, just; **~ nōn** not at all.
omniparēns, -entis adj mother of all.
omnipotēns, -entis adj almighty.
omnis adj all, every, any; every kind of; the whole of ♦ nt the universe ♦ mpl everybody ♦ ntpl everything.
omnituēns, -entis adj all-seeing.
omnivagus adj roving everywhere.
omnivolus adj willing everything.
onager, -rī m wild ass.
onerārius adj (beast) of burden; (ship) transport.
onerō, -āre, -āvī, -ātum vt to load, burden; (fig) to overload, oppress; to aggravate.
onerōsus adj heavy, burdensome, irksome.
onus, -eris nt load, burden, cargo; (fig) charge, difficulty.
onustus adj loaded, burdened; (fig) filled.
onyx, -chis m/f onyx; onyx box.
opācitās, -ātis f shade.
opācō, -āre vt to shade.
opācus adj shady; dark.
ope abl of **ops**.
opella, -ae f light work, small service.
opera, -ae f exertion, work; service; care, attention; leisure, time; (person) workman, hired rough; **~am dare** pay attention; do one's best; **~ae pretium** worth while; **~ā meā** thanks to me.
operārius adj working ♦ m workman.
operculum, -ī nt cover, lid.
operīmentum, -ī nt covering.
operiō, -īre, -uī, -tum vt to cover; to close; (fig) to overwhelm, conceal.
operor, -ārī, -ātus vi to work, take pains, be occupied.
operōsē adv painstakingly.
operōsus adj active, industrious; laborious, elaborate.
opertus ppp of **operiō** ♦ adj covered, hidden ♦ nt secret.
opēs pl of **ops**.

Noun declensions and verb conjugations are shown on pp xiii to xxv. The present infinitive ending of a verb shows to which conjugation it belongs: **-āre** = 1st; **-ēre** = 2nd; **-ere** = 3rd and **-īre** = 4th. Irregular verbs are shown on p xxvi

opicus *adj* barbarous, boorish.
opifer, -ī *adj* helping.
opifex, -icis *m/f* maker; craftsman, artisan.
ōpiliō, -ōnis *m* shepherd.
opīmitās, -ātis *f* abundance.
opīmus *adj* rich, fruitful, fat; copious,
sumptuous; (*style*) overloaded; **spolia ~a**
*spoils of an enemy commander killed by a
Roman general.*
opīnābilis *adj* conjectural.
opīnātiō, -ōnis *f* conjecture.
opīnātor, -ōris *m* conjecturer.
opīnātus, -ūs *m* supposition.
opīniō, -ōnis *f* opinion, conjecture, belief;
reputation, esteem; rumour; **contrā, praeter
~ōnem** contrary to expectation.
opīniōsus *adj* dogmatic.
opīnor, -ārī, -ātus *vi* to think, suppose,
imagine ♦ *adj* imagined.
opiparē *adv see adj.*
opiparus *adj* rich, sumptuous.
opitulor, -ārī, -ātus *vi* (*with dat*) to help.
oportet, -ēre, -uit *vt* (*impers*) ought, should.
oppēdō, -ere *vi* to insult.
opperior, -īrī, -tus *vt, vi* to wait, wait for.
oppetō, -ere, -īvī, -ītum *vt* to encounter; to
die.
oppidānus *adj* provincial ♦ *mpl* townsfolk.
oppidō *adv* quite, completely, exactly.
oppidulum, -ī *nt* small town.
oppidum, -ī *nt* town.
oppignerō, -āre *vt* to pledge.
oppīlō, -āre *vt* to stop up.
oppleō, -ēre, -ēvī, -ētum *vt* to fill, choke up.
oppōnō, -ōnere, -osuī, -ositum *vt* to put
against, set before; to expose; to present;
(*argument*) to adduce, reply, oppose;
(*property*) to pledge, mortgage.
opportūnitās, -ātis *f* suitableness,
advantage; good opportunity.
opportūnē *adv* opportunely.
opportūnus *adj* suitable, opportune; useful;
exposed.
oppositiō, -ōnis *f* opposing.
oppositus *ppp of* **oppōnō** ♦ *adj* against,
opposite.
oppositus, -ūs *m* opposing.
oppsuī *perf of* **oppōnō.**
oppressiō, -ōnis *f* violence; seizure;
overthrow.
oppressus *ppp of* **opprimō.**
oppressus, -ūs *m* pressure.
opprimō, -imere, -essī, -essum *vt* to press
down, crush; to press together, close; to
suppress, overwhelm, overthrow; to
surprise, seize.
opprobrium, -ī *and* **iī** *nt* reproach, disgrace,
scandal.
opprobrō, -āre *vt* to taunt.
oppugnātiō, -ōnis *f* attack, assault.
oppugnātor, -ōris *m* assailant.
oppugnō, -āre, -āvī, -ātum *vt* to attack,
assault.

ops, -opis *f* power, strength; help.
Ops goddess of plenty.
ops- *etc see* **obs-.**
optābilis *adj* desirable.
optātiō, -ōnis *f* wish.
optātus *adj* longed for ♦ *nt* wish; **~ātō**
according to one's wish.
optimās, -ātis *adj* aristocratic ♦ *mpl* the
nobility.
optimē *adv* best, very well; just in time.
optimus *adj* best, very good; excellent; **~ō iūre**
deservedly.
optiō, -ōnis *f* choice ♦ *m* assistant.
optīvus *adj* chosen.
optō, -āre, -āvī, -ātum *vt* to choose; to wish
for.
optum- *etc see* **optim-.**
opulēns, -entis *adj* rich.
opulentia, -ae *f* wealth; power.
opulentō, -āre *vt* to enrich.
opulentē, -er *adv* sumptuously.
opulentus *adj* rich, sumptuous, powerful.
opum *fpl* resources, wealth.
opus, -eris *nt* work, workmanship; (*art*) work,
building, book; (*MIL*) siege work; (*colloq*)
business; (*with* **esse**) need; **virō ~ est** a man is
needed; **māgnō ~ere** much, greatly.
opusculum, -ī *nt* little work.
ōra, -ae *f* edge, boundary; coast; country,
region; (*NAUT*) hawser.
ōrāculum, -ī *nt* oracle, prophecy.
ōrātē *adv see adj.*
ōrātiō, -ōnis *f* speech, language; a speech,
oration; eloquence; prose; emperor's
message; **~ōnem habēre** deliver a speech.
ōrātiuncula, -ae *f* short speech.
ōrātor, -ōris *m* speaker, spokesman, orator.
ōrātōrius *adj* oratorical.
ōrātrīx, -īcis *f* suppliant.
ōrātus, -ūs *m* request.
orbātor, -ōris *m* bereaver.
orbiculātus *adj* round.
orbis, -is *m* circle, ring, disc, orbit; world;
(*movement*) cycle, rotation; (*style*) rounding
off; **~ lacteus** Milky Way; **~ signifer** Zodiac; **~
fortūnae** wheel of Fortune; **~ terrārum** the
earth, world; **in ~em cōnsistere** form a
circle; **in ~em īre** go the rounds.
orbita, -ae *f* rut, track, path.
orbitās, -ātis *f* childlessness, orphanhood,
widowhood.
orbitōsus *adj* full of ruts.
orbō, -āre, -āvī, -ātum *vt* to bereave, orphan,
make childless.
orbus *adj* bereaved, orphan, childless;
destitute.
orca, -ae *f* vat.
orchas, -dis *f* kind of olive.
orchēstra, -ae *f* senatorial seats (in the
theatre).
Orcus, -ī *m* Pluto; the lower world; death.
ōrdinārius *adj* regular.
ōrdinātim *adv* in order, properly.

ōrdinātiō, -ōnis f orderly arrangement.

ōrdinātus adj appointed.

ōrdinō, -āre, -āvī, -ātum vt to arrange, regulate, set in order.

ōrdior, -dīrī, -sus vt, vi to begin, undertake.

ōrdō, -inis m line, row, series; order, regularity, arrangement; (MIL) rank, line, company, (pl) captains; (building) course, layer; (seats) row; (POL) class, order, station; **ex ~ine** in order, in one's turn; one after the other; **extrā ~inem** irregularly, unusually.

Orēas, -dis f mountain nymph.

Orestēs, -is and **ae** m son of Agamemnon, whom he avenged by killing his mother.

Orestēus adj see n.

orexis, -is f appetite.

organum, -ī nt instrument, organ.

orgia, -ōrum ntpl Bacchic revels; orgies.

orichalcum, -ī nt copper ore, brass.

ōricilla, -ae f lobe.

oriēns, -entis pres p of **orior ♦** m morning; east.

orīgō, -inis f beginning, source; ancestry, descent; founder.

Orīōn, -onis and **ōnis** m mythical hunter and constellation.

orior, -īrī, -tus vi to rise; to spring, descend.

oriundus adj descended, sprung.

ōrnāmentum, -ī nt equipment, dress; ornament, decoration; distinction, pride of.

ōrnātē adv elegantly.

ōrnātus ppp of **ōrnō ♦** adj equipped, furnished; embellished, excellent.

ōrnātus, -ūs m preparation; dress, equipment; embellishment.

ōrnō, -āre, -āvī, -ātum vt to fit out, equip, dress, prepare; to adorn, embellish, honour.

ornus, -ī f manna ash.

ōrō, -āre, -āvī, -ātum vt to speak, plead; to beg, entreat; to pray.

Orontēs, -is and **ī** m river of Syria.

Orontēus adj Syrian.

Orpheus, -eī and **eos** (acc -ea) m legendary Thracian singer, who went down to Hades for Eurydice.

Orphēus, -icus adj see n.

ōrsus ppp of **ōrdior ♦** ntpl beginning; utterance.

ōrsus, -ūs m beginning.

ortus ppp of **orior ♦** adj born, descended.

ortus, -ūs m rising; east; origin, source.

Ortygia, -ae and **ē, -ēs** f Delos.

Ortygius adj see n.

oryx, -gis m gazelle.

oryza, -ae f rice.

os, ossis nt bone; (fig) very soul.

ōs, ōris nt mouth; face; entrance, opening; effrontery; **ūnō ōre** unanimously; **in ōre esse** be talked about; **quō ōre redībō** how shall I have the face to go back?

oscen, -inis m bird of omen.

ōscillum, -ī nt little mask.

ōscitāns, -antis pres p of **ōscitō ♦** adj listless, drowsy.

ōscitanter adv half-heartedly.

ōscitō, -āre; -or, -ārī vi to yawn, be drowsy.

ōsculātiō, -ōnis f kissing.

ōsculor, -ārī, -ātus vt to kiss; to make a fuss of.

ōsculum, -ī nt sweet mouth; kiss.

Oscus adj Oscan.

Osīris, -is and **idis** m Egyptian god, husband of Isis.

Ossa, -ae f mountain in Thessaly.

osseus adj bony.

ossifraga, -ae f osprey.

ostendō, -dere, -dī, -tum vt to hold out, show, display; to expose; to disclose, reveal; (speech) to say, make known.

ostentātiō, -ōnis f display; showing off; ostentation; pretence.

ostentātor, -ōris m displayer, boaster.

ostentō, -āre vt to hold out, proffer, exhibit; to show off, boast of; to make known, indicate.

ostentum, -ī nt portent.

ostentus ppp of **ostendō**.

ostentus, -ūs m display, appearance; proof.

Ostia, -ae f, **-ōrum** ntpl port at the Tiber mouth.

ōstiārium, -ī and **iī** nt door tax.

ōstiātim adv from door to door.

Ōstiēnsis adj see n.

ōstium, -ī and **iī** nt door; entrance, mouth.

ostrea, -ae f oyster.

ostreōsus adj rich in oysters.

ostreum, -ī nt oyster.

ostrifer, -ī adj oyster-producing.

ostrīnus adj purple.

ostrum, -ī nt purple; purple dress or coverings.

ōsus, ōsūrus ppa and fut p of **ōdī**.

Othō, -ōnis m author of a law giving theatre seats to Equites; Roman emperor after Galba.

Othōniānus adj see n.

ōtiolum, -ī nt bit of leisure.

ōtior, -ārī vi to have a holiday, be idle.

ōtiōsē adv leisurely; quietly; fearlessly.

ōtiōsus adj at leisure, free; out of public affairs; neutral, indifferent; quiet, unexcited; (things) free, idle ♦ m private citizen, civilian.

ōtium, -ī and **iī** nt leisure, time (for), idleness, retirement; peace, quiet.

ovātiō, -ōnis f minor triumph.

ovīle, -is nt sheep fold, goat fold.

ovillus adj of sheep.

ovis, -is f sheep.

ovō, -āre vi to rejoice; to celebrate a minor triumph.

ōvum, -ī nt egg.

Noun declensions and verb conjugations are shown on pp xiii to xxv. The present infinitive ending of a verb shows to which conjugation it belongs: **-āre** = 1st; **-ēre** = 2nd; **-ere** = 3rd and **-īre** = 4th. Irregular verbs are shown on p xxvi

P, p

pābulātiō, -ōnis f foraging.
pābulātor, -ōris m forager.
pābulor, -ārī vi to forage.
pābulum, -ī nt food, fodder.
pācālis adj of peace.
pācātus adj peaceful, tranquil ♦ nt friendly country.
Pachȳnum, -ī nt S.E. point of Sicily (now Cape Passaro).
pācifer, -ī adj peace-bringing.
pācificātiō, -ōnis f peacemaking.
pācificātor, -ōris m peacemaker.
pācificātōrius adj peacemaking.
pācificō, -āre vi to make a peace ♦ vt to appease.
pācificus adj peacemaking.
pacīscor, -īscī, -tus vi to make a bargain, agree ♦ vt to stipulate for; to barter.
pācō, -āre, -āvī, -ātum vt to pacify, subdue.
pactiō, -ōnis f bargain, agreement, contract; collusion; (words) formula.
Pactōlus, -ī m river of Lydia (famous for its gold).
pactor, -ōris m negotiator.
pactum, -ī nt agreement, contract.
pactus ppa of pacīscor ♦ adj agreed, settled; betrothed.
Pācuvius, -ī m Latin tragic poet.
Padus, -ī m river Po.
paeān, -ānis m healer, epithet of Apollo; hymn of praise, shout of joy; (metre) paeon.
paedagōgus, -ī m slave who took children to school.
paedor, -ōris m filth.
paelex, -icis f mistress, concubine.
paelicātus, -ūs m concubinage.
Paelignī, -ōrum mpl people of central Italy.
Paelignus adj see n.
paene adv almost, nearly.
paenīnsula, -ae f peninsula.
paenitendus adj regrettable.
paenitentia, -ae f repentance.
paenitet, -ēre, -uit vt, vi (impers) to repent, regret, be sorry; to be dissatisfied; an ~et is it not enough?
paenula, -ae f travelling cloak.
paenulātus adj wearing a cloak.
paeōn, -ōnis m metrical foot of one long and three short syllables.
paeōnius adj healing.
Paestānus adj see n.
Paestum, -ī nt town in S. Italy.
paetulus adj with a slight cast in the eye.
paetus adj with a cast in the eye.
pāgānus adj rural ♦ m villager, yokel.

pāgātim adv in every village.
pāgella, -ae f small page.
pāgina, -ae f (book) page, leaf.
pāginula, -ae f small page.
pāgus, -ī m village, country district; canton.
pāla, -ae f spade; (ring) bezel.
palaestra, -ae f wrestling school, gymnasium; exercise, wrestling; (RHET) exercise, training.
palaestricē adv in gymnastic fashion.
palaestricus adj of the wrestling school.
palaestrīta, -ae m head of a wrestling school.
palam adv openly, publicly, well-known ♦ prep (with abl) in the presence of.
Palātīnus adj Palatine; imperial.
Palātium, -ī nt Palatine Hill in Rome; palace.
palātum, -ī nt palate; taste, judgment.
palea, -ae f chaff.
paleāria, -ium ntpl dewlap.
Palēs, -is f goddess of shepherds.
Palīlis adj of Pales ♦ ntpl festival of Pales.
palimpsēstus, -ī m palimpsest.
Palinūrus, -ī m pilot of Aeneas; promontory in S. Italy.
paliūrus, -ī m Christ's thorn.
palla, -ae f woman's robe; tragic costume.
Palladium, -dī nt image of Pallas.
Palladius adj of Pallas.
Pallantēus adj see n.
Pallas, -dis and dos f Athene, Minerva; oil; olive tree.
Pallās, -antis m ancestor or son of Evander.
pallēns, -entis pres p of palleō ♦ adj pale; greenish.
palleō, -ēre, -uī vi to be pale or yellow; to fade; to be anxious.
pallēscō, -escere, -uī vi to turn pale, turn yellow.
palliātus adj wearing a Greek cloak.
pallidulus adj palish.
pallidus adj pale, pallid, greenish; in love.
palliolum, -ī nt small cloak, cape, hood.
pallium, -ī and iī nt coverlet; Greek cloak.
pallor, -ōris m paleness, fading; fear.
palma, -ae f (hand) palm, hand; (oar) blade; (tree) palm, date; branch; (fig) prize, victory, glory.
palmāris adj excellent.
palmārius adj prizewinning.
palmātus adj palm-embroidered.
palmes, -itis m pruned shoot, branch.
palmētum, -ī nt palm grove.
palmifer, -ī adj palm-bearing.
palmōsus adj palm-clad.
palmula, -ae f oar blade.
pālor, -ārī, -ātus vi to wander about, straggle.
palpātiō, -ōnis f flatteries.
palpātor, -ōris m flatterer.
palpebra, -ae f eyelid.
palpitō, -āre vi to throb, writhe.
palpō, -āre; -or, -ārī vt to stroke; to coax, flatter.
palpus, -ī m coaxing.

paludāmentum, -ī nt military cloak.
paludātus adj in a general's cloak.
paludōsus adj marshy.
palumbēs, -is m/f wood pigeon.
pālus, -ī m stake, pale.
palūs, -ūdis f marsh, pool, lake.
palūster, -ris adj marshy.
pampineus adj of vineshoots.
pampinus, -ī m vineshoot.
Pān, -ānos (acc -āna) m Greek god of shepherds, hills and woods, esp associated with Arcadia.
panacēa, -ae f a herb supposed to cure all diseases.
Panaetius, -ī m Stoic philosopher.
Panchāaeus adj see n.
Panchāaius adj see n.
Panchāia, -iae f part of Arabia.
panchrēstus adj good for everything.
pancratium, -ī and **iī** nt all-in boxing and wrestling match.
pandiculor, -āre vi to stretch oneself.
Pandīōn, -onis m king of Athens, father of Procne and Philomela.
Pandīonius adj see n.
pandō, -ere, -ī, pānsum and **passum** vt to spread out, stretch, extend; to open; (fig) to disclose, explain.
pandus adj curved, bent.
pangō, -ere, panxī and **pepigī, pāctum** vt to drive in, fasten; to make, compose; to agree, settle.
pānicula, -ae f tuft.
pānicum, -ī nt Italian millet.
pānis, -is m bread, loaf.
Pāniscus, -ī m little Pan.
panniculus, -ī m rag.
Pannonia, -ae f country on the middle Danube.
Pannonius adj see n.
pannōsus adj ragged.
pannus, -ī m piece of cloth, rag, patch.
Panormus, -ī f town in Sicily (now Palermo).
pānsa adj splayfoot.
pānsus ppp of **pandō**.
panthēra, -ae f panther.
Panthoīdēs, -ae m Euphorbus.
Panthūs, -ī m priest of Apollo at Troy.
panticēs, -um mpl bowels; sausages.
panxī perf of **pangō**.
papae interj (expressing wonder) ooh!
pāpas, -ae m tutor.
papāver, -is nt poppy.
papāvereus adj see n.
Paphius adj see n.
Paphos, -ī f town in Cyprus, sacred to Venus.
pāpiliō, -ōnis m butterfly.
papilla, -ae f teat, nipple; breast.
pappus, -ī m woolly seed.
papula, -ae f pimple.
papȳrifer, -ī adj papyrus-bearing.
papȳrum, -ī nt papyrus; paper.

papȳrus, -ī m/f papyrus; paper.
pār, paris adj equal, like; a match for; proper, right ♦ m peer, partner, companion ♦ nt pair;
pār parī respondēre return like for like;
parēs cum paribus facillimē congregantur ≈ birds of a feather flock together; **lūdere pār impār** play at evens and odds.
parābilis adj easy to get.
parasīta, -ae f woman parasite.
parasītaster, -rī m sorry parasite.
parasīticus adj of a parasite.
parasītus, -ī m parasite, sponger.
parātē adv with preparation; carefully; promptly.
parātiō, -ōnis f trying to get.
paratragoedō, -āre vi to talk theatrically.
parātus ppp of **parō** ♦ adj ready; equipped; experienced.
parātus, -ūs m preparation, equipment.
Parca, -ae f Fate.
parcē adv frugally; moderately.
parcō, -ere, pepercī, -sum vt, vi (with dat) to spare, economize; to refrain from, forgo; (with inf) to forbear, stop.
parcus adj sparing, thrifty; niggardly, scanty; chary.
pardus, -ī m panther.
pārēns, -entis pres p of **pāreō** ♦ adj obedient ♦ mpl subjects.
parēns, -entis m/f parent, father, mother; ancestor; founder.
parentālis adj parental ♦ ntpl festival in honour of dead ancestors and relatives.
parentō, -āre vi to sacrifice in honour of dead parents or relatives; to avenge (with the death of another).
pāreō, -ēre, -uī, -itum vi to be visible, be evident; (with dat) to obey, submit to, comply with; **~et** it is proved.
pariēs, -etis m wall.
parietinae, -ārum fpl ruins.
Parīlia, -ium ntpl festival of Pales.
parīlis adj equal.
pariō, -ere, peperī, -tum vt to give birth to; to produce, create, cause; to procure.
Paris, -idis m son of Priam (abductor of Helen).
pariter adv equally, alike; at the same time, together.
paritō, -āre vt to get ready.
Parius adj see **Paros**.
parma, -ae f shield, buckler.
parmātus adj armed with a buckler.
parmula, -ae f little shield.
Parnāsis, -idis adj Parnassian.
Parnāsius adj = **Parnāsis**.
Parnāsus, -ī m mount Parnassus in central Greece, sacred to the Muses.
parō, -āre, -āvī, -ātum vt to prepare, get ready, provide; to intend, set about; to procure, get, buy; to arrange.

Noun declensions and verb conjugations are shown on pp xiii to xxv. The present infinitive ending of a verb shows to which conjugation it belongs: **-āre** = 1st; **-ēre** = 2nd; **-ere** = 3rd and **-īre** = 4th. Irregular verbs are shown on p xxvi

parocha, -ae *f* provision of necessaries (*to officials travelling*).

parochus, -ī *m* purveyor; host.

paropsis, -dis *f* dish.

Paros, -ī *f* Aegean island (*famous for white marble*).

parra, -ae *f* owl.

Parrhasis, -idis, -ius *adj* Arcadian.

parricīda, -ae *m* parricide, assassin; traitor.

parricīdium, -ī *and* **iī** parricide, murder; high treason.

pars, -tis *f* part, share, fraction; party, side; direction; respect, degree; (*with pl verb*) some; (*pl*) stage part, role; duty, function; **māgna ~** the majority; **māgnam ~tem** largely; **in eam ~tem** in that direction, on that side, in that sense; **nullā ~te** not at all; **omnī ~te** entirely; **ex ~te** partly; **ex alterā ~te** on the other hand; **ex māgnā ~te** to a large extent; **prō ~te** to the best of one's ability; **~tēs agere** play a part; **duae ~tēs** two-thirds; **trēs ~tēs** three-fourths; **multīs ~ibus** a great deal.

parsimōnia, -ae *f* thrift, frugality.

parthenicē, -ēs *f* a plant.

Parthenopē, -ēs *f* old name of Naples.

Parthenopēius *adj see n.*

Parthī, -ōrum *mpl* Parthians (*Rome's great enemy in the East*).

Parthicus, -us *adj see n.*

particeps, -ipis *adj* sharing, partaking ♦ *m* partner.

participō, -āre *vt* to share, impart, inform.

particula, -ae *f* particle.

partim *adv* partly, in part; mostly; some ... others.

partiō, -īre, -īvī, -ītum; -ior, -īrī *vt* to share, distribute, divide.

partītē *adv* methodically.

partītiō, -ōnis *f* distribution, division.

parturiō, -īre *vi* to be in labour; (*fig*) to be anxious ♦ *vt* to teem with, be ready to produce; (*mind*) to brood over.

partus *ppp of* **pariō** ♦ *ntpl* possessions.

partus, -ūs *m* birth; young.

parum *adv* too little, not enough; not very, scarcely.

parumper *adv* for a little while.

parvitās, -ātis *f* smallness.

parvulus, parvolus *adj* very small, slight; quite young ♦ *m* child.

parvus (*comp* **minor** *superl* **minimus**) *adj* small, little, slight; (*time*) short; (*age*) young; **~ī esse** be of little value.

Pascha, -ae *f* Easter.

pāscō, -scere, -vī, -stum *vt* to feed, put to graze; to keep, foster; (*fig*) to feast, cherish ♦ *vi* to graze, browse.

pāscuus *adj* for pasture ♦ *nt* pasture.

Pāsiphaē, -ēs *f* wife of Minos (*mother of the Minotaur*).

passer, -is *m* sparrow; (*fish*) plaice; **~ marīnus** ostrich.

passerculus, -ī *m* little sparrow.

passim *adv* here and there, at random; indiscriminately.

passum, -ī *nt* raisin wine.

passus *ppp of* **pandō** ♦ *adj* spread out, dishevelled; dried.

passus *ppa of* **patior**.

passus, -ūs *m* step, pace; footstep; **mille ~ūs** mile; **mīlia ~uum** miles.

pastillus, -ī *m* lozenge.

pāstor, -ōris *m* shepherd.

pāstōrālis *adj* shepherd's, pastoral.

pāstōricius, pāstōrius *adj* shepherd's.

pāstus *ppp of* **pāscō**.

pāstus, -ūs *m* pasture, food.

Patara, -ae *f* town in Lycia (*with oracle of Apollo*).

Pataraeus *and* **eus** *adj see n.*

Patavīnus *adj see n.*

Patavium, -ī *nt* birthplace of Livy (*now Padua*).

patefaciō, -facere, -fēcī, -factum (*pass* **-fīō, -fierī**) *vt* to open, open up; to disclose.

patefactiō, -ōnis *f* disclosing.

patefiō *etc see* **patefaciō**.

patella, -ae *f* small dish, plate.

patēns, -entis *pres p of* **pateō** ♦ *adj* open, accessible, exposed; broad; evident.

patenter *adv* clearly.

pateō, -ēre, -uī *vi* to be open, accessible, exposed; to extend; to be evident, known.

pater, -ris *m* father; (*pl*) forefathers; senators.

patera, -ae *f* dish, saucer, bowl.

paterfamiliās, patrisfamiliās *m* master of the house.

paternus *adj* father's, paternal; native.

patēscō, -ere *vi* to open out; to extend; to become evident.

patibilis *adj* endurable; sensitive.

patibulātus *adj* pilloried.

patibulum, -ī *nt* fork-shaped yoke, pillory.

patiēns, -entis *pres p of* **patior** ♦ *adj* able to endure; patient; unyielding.

patienter *adv* patiently.

patientia, -ae *f* endurance, stamina; forbearance; submissiveness.

patina, -ae *f* dish, pan.

patior, -tī, -ssus *vt* to suffer, experience; to submit to; to allow, put up with; **facile ~** be well pleased with; **aegrē ~** be displeased with.

Patrae, -ārum *fpl* Greek seaport (*now* Patras).

patrātor, -ōris *m* doer.

patrātus *adj*: **pater ~** officiating priest.

Patrēnsis *adj see n.*

patria, -ae *f* native land, native town, home.

patricius *adj* patrician ♦ *m* aristocrat.

patrimōnium, -ī *and* **iī** *nt* inheritance, patrimony.

patrimus *adj* having a father living.

patrissō, -āre *vi* to take after one's father.

patrītus *adj* of one's father.

patrius *adj* father's; hereditary, native.

patrō, -āre, -āvī, -ātum *vt* to achieve, execute, complete.

patrōcinium, -ī and **iī** *nt* patronage, advocacy, defence.

patrōcinor, -ārī *vi* (*with dat*) to defend, support.

patrōna, -ae *f* patron goddess; protectress, safeguard.

patrōnus, -ī *m* patron, protector; (*law*) advocate, counsel.

patruēlis *adj* cousin's ♦ *m* cousin.

patruus, -ī *m* (paternal) uncle ♦ *adj* uncle's.

patulus *adj* open; spreading, broad.

paucitās, -ātis *f* small number, scarcity.

pauculus *adj* very few.

paucus *adj* few, little ♦ *mpl* a few, the select few ♦ *ntpl* a few words.

paulātim *adv* little by little, gradually.

paulisper *adv* for a little while.

Paullus, -ī *m* = **Paulus.**

paulō *adv* a little, somewhat.

paululus *adj* very little ♦ *nt* a little bit.

paulum *adv* = **paulō.**

paulus *adj* little.

Paulus, -ī *m* Roman surname (*esp victor of Pydna*).

pauper, -is *adj* poor; meagre ♦ *mpl* the poor.

pauperculus *adj* poor.

pauperiēs, -ēī *f* poverty.

pauperō, -āre *vt* to impoverish; to rob.

paupertās, -ātis *f* poverty, moderate means.

pausa, -ae *f* stop, end.

pauxillātim *adv* bit by bit.

pauxillulus *adj* very little.

pauxillus *adj* little.

pavefactus *adj* frightened.

paveō, -ēre, -āvī *vi* to be terrified, quake ♦ *vt* to dread, be scared of.

pavēscō, -ere *vt, vi* to become alarmed (at).

pāvī *perf of* **pāscō.**

pavidē *adv* in a panic.

pavidus *adj* quaking, terrified.

pavīmentātus *adj* paved.

pavīmentum, -ī *nt* pavement, floor.

paviō, -īre *vt* to strike.

pavitō, -āre *vi* to be very frightened; to shiver.

pāvō, -ōnis *m* peacock.

pavor, -ōris *m* terror, panic.

pāx, pācis *f* peace; (*gods*) grace; (*mind*) serenity ♦ *interj* enough!; **pāce tuā** by your leave.

peccātum, -ī *nt* mistake, fault, sin.

peccō, -āre, -āvī, -ātum *vi* to make a mistake, go wrong, offend.

pecorōsus *adj* rich in cattle.

pecten, -inis *m* comb; (*fish*) scallop; (*loom*) reed; (*lyre*) plectrum.

pectō, -ctere, -xī, -xum *vt* to comb.

pectus, -oris *nt* breast; heart, feeling; mind, thought.

pecū *nt* flock of sheep; (*pl*) pastures.

pecuārius *adj* of cattle ♦ *m* cattle breeder ♦ *ntpl* herds.

peculātor, -ōris *m* embezzler.

pecūlātus, -ūs *m* embezzlement.

pecūliāris *adj* one's own; special.

pecūliātus *adj* provided with money.

pecūliōsus *adj* with private property.

pecūlium, -ī and **iī** *nt* small savings, private property.

pecūnia, -ae *f* property; money.

pecūniārius *adj* of money.

pecūniōsus *adj* moneyed, well-off.

pecus, -oris *nt* cattle, herd, flock; animal.

pecus, -udis *f* sheep, head of cattle, beast.

pedālis *adj* a foot long.

pedārius *adj* (*senator*) without full rights.

pedes, -itis *m* foot soldier, infantry ♦ *adj* on foot.

pedester, -ris *adj* on foot, pedestrian; infantry- (*in cpds*); on land; (*writing*) in prose, prosaic.

pedetemptim *adv* step by step, cautiously.

pedica, -ae *f* fetter, snare.

pedis, -is *m* louse.

pedisequa, -ae *f* handmaid.

pedisequus, -ī *m* attendant, lackey.

peditātus, -ūs *m* infantry.

pedum, -ī *nt* crook.

Pēgaseus and **is, -idis** *adj* Pegasean.

Pēgasus, -ī *m* mythical winged horse (*associated with the Muses*).

pēgma, -tis *nt* bookcase; stage elevator.

pēierō, -āre *vi* to perjure oneself.

pēior, -ōris *compar of* **malus.**

pēius *adv* worse.

pelagius *adj* of the sea.

pelagus, -ī (*pl* -ē) *nt* sea, open sea.

pelamys, -dis *f* young tunny fish.

Pelasgī, -ōrum *mpl* Greeks.

Pelasgias and **is** and **us** *adj* Grecian.

Pēleus, -eī and **eos** (*acc* -ea) *m* king of Thessaly (*father of Achilles*).

Peliās, -ae *m* uncle of Jason.

Pēlias and **iacus** and **ius** *adj see* **Pēlion.**

Pēlīdēs, -īdae *m* Achilles; Neoptolemus.

Pēlion, -ī *nt* mountain in Thessaly.

Pella, -ae, -ē, -ēs *f* town of Macedonia (*birthplace of Alexander*).

pellācia, -ae *f* attraction.

Pellaeus *adj* of Pella; Alexandrian; Egyptian.

pellāx, -ācis *adj* seductive.

pellēctiō, -ōnis *f* reading through.

pellectus *ppp of* **pelliciō.**

pellegō *etc see* **perlegō.**

pelliciō, -icere, -exī, -ectum *vt* to entice, inveigle.

pellicula, -ae *f* skin, fleece.

pelliō, -ōnis *m* furrier.

Noun declensions and verb conjugations are shown on pp xiii to xxv. The present infinitive ending of a verb shows to which conjugation it belongs: **-āre** = 1st; **-ēre** = 2nd; **-ere** = 3rd and **-īre** = 4th. Irregular verbs are shown on p xxvi

pellis, -is *f* skin, hide; leather, felt; tent.

pellītus *adj* wearing skins, with leather coats.

pellō, -ere, pepulī, pulsum *vt* to push, knock, drive; to drive off, rout, expel; (*lyre*) to play; (*mind*) to touch, affect; (*feeling*) to banish.

pellūc- *etc see* **perlūc-**.

Pelopēis *and* **ēius** *and* **ēus** *adj see n.*

Pelopidae, -idārum *mpl* house of Pelops.

Pelopōias *adj see n.*

Peloponnēsiacus, -ius *adj see n.*

Peloponnēsus, -ī *f* Peloponnese, S. Greece.

Pelops, -is *m* son of Tantalus (*grandfather of Agamemnon*).

pelōris, -idis *f* a large mussel.

pelta, -ae *f* light shield.

peltastae, -ārum *mpl* peltasts.

peltātus *adj* armed with the pelta.

Pēlūsiacus *adj see n.*

Pēlūsium, -ī *nt Eygptian town at the E. mouth of the Nile.*

Pēlūsius *adj see n.*

pelvis, -is *f* basin.

penārius *adj* provision- (*in cpds*).

Penātēs, -ium *mpl* spirits of the larder, household gods; home.

penātiger, -ī *adj* carrying his home gods.

pendeō, -ēre, pependī *vi* to hang; to overhang, hover; to hang down, be flabby; (*fig*) to depend; to gaze, listen attentively; (*mind*) to be in suspense, be undecided.

pendō, -ere, pependī, pēnsum *vt* to weigh; to pay; (*fig*) to ponder, value ♦ *vi* to weigh.

pendulus *adj* hanging; in doubt.

Pēnēēis *and* **ēius** *and* **ēus** *adj see n.*

Pēnelopē, ēs *and* **a, -ae** *f* wife of Ulysses (*famed for her constancy*).

Pēnelopēus *adj see n.*

penes *prep* (*with acc*) in the power or possession of; in the house of, with.

penetrābilis *adj* penetrable; piercing.

penetrālis *adj* penetrating; inner, inmost ♦ *ntpl* inner room, interior, sanctuary; remote parts.

penetrō, -āre, -āvī, -ātum *vt, vi* to put into, penetrate, enter.

Pēnēus, -ī *m* chief river of Thessaly.

pēnicillus, -ī *m* painter's brush, pencil.

pēniculus, -ī *m* brush; sponge.

pēnis, -is *m* penis.

penitē *adj* inwardly.

penitus *adv* inside, deep within; deeply, from the depths; utterly, thoroughly.

penna, pinna, -ae *f* feather, wing; flight.

pennātus *adj* winged.

penniger, -ī *adj* feathered.

pennipotēns, -entis *adj* winged.

pennula, -ae *f* little wing.

pēnsilis *adj* hanging, pendent.

pēnsiō, -ōnis *f* payment, instalment.

pēnsitō, -āre *vt* to pay; to consider.

pēnsō, -āre, -āvī, -ātum *vt* to weight out; to compensate, repay; to consider, judge.

pēnsum, -ī *nt* spinner's work; task, duty; weight, value; **~ī esse** be of importance; **~ī habēre** care at all about.

pēnsus *ppp of* **pendō**.

pentēris, -is *f* quinquereme.

Pentheus, -eī *and* **eos** *m* king of Thebes (*killed by Bacchantes*).

pēnūria, -ae *f* want, need.

penus, -ūs *and* **ī** *m/f*, **-um, -ī, -us, -oris** *nt* provisions, store of food.

pependī *perf of* **pendeō**; *perf of* **pendō**.

pepercī *perf of* **parcō**.

peperī *perf of* **pariō**.

pepigī *perf of* **pangō**.

peplum, -ī *nt*, **-us, -ī** *m* state robe of Athena.

pepulī *perf of* **pellō**.

per *prep* (*with acc: space*) through, all over; (: *time*) throughout, during; (: *means*) by, by means of; (: *cause*) by reason of, for the sake of; **~ īram** in anger; **~ manūs** from hand to hand; **~ mē** as far as I am concerned; **~ vim** forcibly; **~ ego tē deōs ōrō** in Heaven's name I beg you.

pēra, -ae *f* bag.

perabsurdus *adj* very absurd.

peraccommodātus *adj* very convenient.

perācer, -ris *adj* very sharp.

peracerbus *adj* very sour.

peracēscō, -ēscere, -uī *vi* to get vexed.

perāctiō, -ōnis *f* last act.

perāctus *ppp of* **peragō**.

peracūtē *adv* very acutely.

peracūtus *adj* very sharp, very clear.

peradulēscēns, -entis *adj* very young.

peraequē *adv* quite equally, uniformly.

peragitātus *adj* harried.

peragō, -agere, -ēgī, -āctum *vt* to carry through, complete; to pass through, pierce; to disturb; (*law*) to prosecute to a conviction; (*words*) to go over, describe.

peragrātiō, -ōnis *f* travelling.

peragrō, -āre, -āvī, -ātum *vt* to travel through, traverse.

peramāns, -antis *adj* very fond.

peramanter *adv* devotedly.

perambulō, -āre *vt* to walk through, traverse.

peramoenus *adj* very pleasant.

peramplus *adj* very large.

perangustē *adv see adj.*

perangustus *adj* very narrow.

perantīquus *adj* very old.

perappositus *adj* very suitable.

perarduus *adj* very difficult.

perargūtus *adj* very witty.

perarō, -āre *vt* to furrow; to write (on wax).

perattentē *adv see adj.*

perattentus *adj* very attentive.

peraudiendus *adj* to be heard to the end.

perbacchor, -ārī *vt* to carouse through.

perbeātus *adj* very happy.

perbellē *adv* very nicely.

perbene *adv* very well.

perbenevolus *adj* very friendly.

perbenignē *adv* very kindly.

perbibō, -ere, -ī *vt* to drink up, imbibe.
perbītō, -ere *vi* to perish.
perblandus *adj* very charming.
perbonus *adj* very good.
perbrevis *adj* very short.
perbreviter *adv* very briefly.
perca, -ae *f* perch.
percalefactus *adj* quite hot.
percalēscō, -ēscere, -uī *vi* to become quite hot.
percallēscō, -ēscere, -uī *vi* to become quite hardened ♦ *vt* to become thoroughly versed in.
percārus *adj* very dear.
percautus *adj* very cautious.
percelebrō, -āre *vt* to talk much of.
perceler, -is *adj* very quick.
perceleriter *adv see adj.*
percellō, -ellere, -ulī, -ulsum *vt* to knock down, upset; to strike; (*fig*) to ruin, overthrow; to discourage, unnerve.
percēnseō, -ēre, -uī *vt* to count over; (*place*) to travel through; (*fig*) to review.
perceptiō, -ōnis *f* harvesting; understanding, idea.
perceptus *ppp of* **percipiō.**
percieō, -iēre, -iō, -īre *vt* to rouse, excite.
percipiō, -ipere, -ēpī, -eptum *vt* to take, get hold of; to gather in; (*senses*) to feel; (*mind*) to learn, grasp, understand.
percitus *ppp of* **percieō** ♦ *adj* roused, excited; excitable.
percoctus *ppp of* **percoquō.**
percōlō, -āre *vt* to filter through.
percolō, -olere, -oluī, -ultum *vt* to embellish; to honour.
percōmis *adj* very friendly.
percommodē *adv* very conveniently.
percommodus *adj* very suitable.
percontātiō, -ōnis *f* asking questions.
percontātor, -ōris *m* inquisitive person.
percontor, -ārī, -ātus *vt* to question, inquire.
percontumāx, -ācis *adj* very obstinate.
percoquō, -quere, -xī, -ctum *vt* to cook thoroughly, heat, scorch, ripen.
percrēbēscō, percrēbrēscō, -ēscere, -uī *vi* to be spread abroad.
percrepō, -āre, -uī *vi* to resound.
perculī *perf of* **percellō.**
perculsus *ppp of* **percellō.**
percultus *ppp of* **percolō.**
percunct- *etc see* **percont-.**
percupidus *adj* very fond.
percupiō, -ere *vi* to wish very much.
percūriōsus *adj* very inquisitive.
percūrō, -āre *vt* to heal completely.
percurrō, -rrere, -currī *and* **rrī, -rsum** *vt* to run through, hurry over; (*fig*) to run over, look over ♦ *vi* to run along; to pass.
percursātiō, -ōnis *f* travelling through.

percursiō, -ōnis *f* running over.
percursō, -āre *vi* to rove about.
percursus *ppp of* **percurrō.**
percussiō, -ōnis *f* beating; (*fingers*) snapping; (*music*) time.
percussor, -ōris *m* assassin.
percussus *ppp of* **percutiō.**
percussus, -ūs *m* striking.
percutiō, -tere, -ssī, -ssum *vt* to strike, beat; to strike through, kill; (*feeling*) to shock, impress, move; (*colloq*) to trick.
perdēlīrus *adj* quite crazy.
perdidī *perf of* **perdō.**
perdifficilis *adj* very difficult.
perdifficiliter *adv* with great difficulty.
perdignus *adj* most worthy.
perdīligēns, -entis *adj* very diligent.
perdīligenter *adv see adj.*
perdiscō, -scere, -dicī *vt* to learn by heart.
perdisertē *adv* very eloquently.
perditē *adv* desperately; recklessly.
perditor, -ōris *m* destroyer.
perditus *ppp of* **perdō** ♦ *adj* desperate, ruined; abandoned, profligate.
perdiū *adv* for a very long time.
perdiūturnus *adj* protracted.
perdīves, -itis *adj* very rich.
perdix, -īcis *m/f* partridge.
perdō, -ere, -idī, -itum *vt* to destroy, ruin; to squander, waste; to lose; **dī tē ~uint** curse you!
perdoceō, -ēre, -uī, -tum *vt* to teach thoroughly.
perdolēscō, -ēscere, -uī *vi* to take it to heart.
perdomō, -āre, -uī, -itum *vt* to subjugate, tame completely.
perdormīscō, -ere *vi* to sleep on.
perdūcō, -ūcere, -ūxī, -uctum *vt* to bring, guide to; to induce, seduce; to spread over; to prolong, continue.
perductō, -āre *vt* to guide.
perductor, -ōris *m* guide; pander.
perductus *ppp of* **perdūcō.**
perduelliō, -ōnis *f* treason.
perduellis, -is *m* enemy.
perduint *archaic subj of* **perdō.**
perdūrō, -āre *vi* to endure, hold out.
peredō, -edere, -ēdī, -ēsum *vt* to consume, devour.
peregrē *adv* away from home, abroad; from abroad.
peregrīnābundus *adj* travelling.
peregrīnātiō, -ōnis *f* living abroad, travel.
peregrīnātor, -ōris *m* traveller.
peregrīnitās, -ātis *f* foreign manners.
peregrīnor, -ārī, -ātus *vi* to be abroad, travel; to be a stranger.
peregrīnus *adj* foreign, strange ♦ *m* foreigner, alien.
perēlegāns, -antis *adj* very polished.

Noun declensions and verb conjugations are shown on pp xiii to xxv. The present infinitive ending of a verb shows to which conjugation it belongs: **-āre** = 1st; **-ēre** = 2nd; **-ere** = 3rd and **-īre** = 4th. Irregular verbs are shown on p xxvi

perēleganter *adv* in a very polished manner.
perēloquēns, -entis *adj* very eloquent.
perēmī *perf of* **perimō**.
peremnia, -ium *ntpl* auspices taken on crossing a river.
peremptus *ppp of* **perimō**.
perendiē *adv* the day after tomorrow.
perendinus *adj* (the day) after tomorrow.
perennis *adj* perpetual, unfailing.
perennitās, -ātis *f* continuance.
perennō, -āre *vi* to last a long time.
pereō, -īre, -iī, -itum *vi* to be lost, pass away, perish, die; (*fig*) to be wasted, be in love, be undone.
perequitō, -āre *vt, vi* to ride up and down.
pererrō, -āre, -āvī, -ātum *vt* to roam over, cover.
perērudītus *adj* very learned.
perēsus *ppp of* **peredō**.
perexcelsus *adj* very high.
perexiguē *adv* very meagrely.
perexiguus *adj* very small, very short.
perfacētē *adv* very wittily.
perfacētus *adj* very witty.
perfacilē *adv* very easily.
perfacilis *adj* very easy; very courteous.
perfamiliāris *adj* very intimate ♦ *m* very close friend.
perfectē *adv* fully.
perfectiō, -ōnis *f* completion, perfection.
perfector, -ōris *m* perfecter.
perfectus *ppp of* **perficiō** ♦ *adj* complete, perfect.
perferō, -ferre, -tulī, -lātum *vt* to carry through, bring, convey; to bear, endure, put up with; (*work*) to finish, bring to completion; (*law*) to get passed; (*message*) to bring news.
perficiō, -icere, -ēcī, -ectum *vt* to carry out, finish, complete; to perfect; to cause, make.
perficus *adj* perfecting.
perfidēlis *adj* very loyal.
perfidia, -ae *f* treachery, dishonesty.
perfidiōsē *adv see adj.*
perfidiōsus *adj* treacherous, dishonest.
perfidus *adj* treacherous, faithless.
perfīgō, -gere, -xī, -xum *vt* to pierce.
perflābilis *adj* that can be blown through.
perflāgitiōsus *adj* very wicked.
perflō, -āre *vt* to blow through, blow over.
perfluctuō, -āre *vt* to flood through.
perfluō, -ere, -xī *vi* to run out, leak.
perfodiō, -odere, -ōdī, -ossum *vt* to dig through, excavate, pierce.
perforō, -āre, -āvī, -ātum *vt* to bore through, pierce.
perfortiter *adv* very bravely.
perfossor, -ōris *m*: ~ **parietum** burglar.
perfossus *ppp of* **perfodiō**.
perfrāctus *ppp of* **perfringō**.
perfrēgī *perf of* **perfringō**.
perfremō, -ere *vi* to snort along.
perfrequēns, -entis *adj* much frequented.
perfricō, -āre, -uī, -tum *and* **ātum** *vt* to rub all

over; **ōs** ~ put on a bold face.
perfrīgefaciō, -ere *vt* to make shudder.
perfrīgēscō, -gēscere, -xī *vi* to catch a bad cold.
perfrīgidus *adj* very cold.
perfringō, -ingere, -ēgī, -āctum *vt* to break through, fracture, wreck; (*fig*) to violate; to affect powerfully.
perfrīxī *perf of* **perfrīgēscō**.
perfrūctus *ppa of* **perfruor**.
perfruor, -uī, -ūctus *vi* (*with abl*) to enjoy to the full; to fulfil.
perfuga, -ae *m* deserter.
perfugiō, -ugere, -ūgī *vi* to flee for refuge, desert to.
perfugium, -ī *and* **ī** *nt* refuge, shelter.
perfūnctiō, -ōnis *f* performing.
perfūnctus *ppa of* **perfungor**.
perfundō, -undere, -ūdī, -ūsum *vt* to pour over, drench, besprinkle; to dye; (*fig*) to flood, fill.
perfungor, -gī, perfūnctus *vi* (*with abl*) to perform, discharge; to undergo.
perfurō, -ere *vi* to rage furiously.
perfūsus *ppp of* **perfundō**.
Pergama, -ōrum *ntpl* Troy.
Pergamēnus *adj see n.*
Pergameus *adj* Trojan.
Pergamum, -ī *nt* town in Mysia (*famous for its library*).
pergaudeō, -ēre *vi* to be very glad.
pergō, -gere, -rēxī, -rēctum *vi* to proceed, go on, continue ♦ *vt* to go on with, continue.
pergraecor, -ārī *vi* to have a good time.
pergrandis *adj* very large; very old.
pergraphicus *adj* very artful.
pergrātus *adj* very pleasant.
pergravis *adj* very weighty.
pergraviter *adv* very seriously.
pergula, -ae *f* balcony; school; brothel.
perhibeō, -ēre, -uī, -itum *vt* to assert, call, cite.
perhīlum *adv* very little.
perhonōrificē *adv* very respectfully.
perhonōrificus *adj* very complimentary.
perhorrēscō, -ēscere, -uī *vi* to shiver, tremble violently ♦ *vt* to have a horror of.
perhorridus *adj* quite horrible.
perhūmāniter *adv see adj.*
perhūmānus *adj* very polite.
Periclēs, -is *and* **ī** *m* famous Athenian statesman and orator.
perīclitātiō, -ōnis *f* experiment.
perīclitor, -ārī, -ātus *vt* to test, try; to risk, endanger ♦ *vi* to attempt, venture; to run a risk, be in danger.
perīculōsē *adv see adj.*
perīculōsus *adj* dangerous, hazardous.
perīculum (perīclum), -ī *nt* danger, risk; trial, attempt; (*law*) lawsuit, writ.
peridōneus *adj* very suitable.
periī *perf of* **pereō**.
perillūstris *adj* very notable; highly honoured.

perimbēcillus *adj* very weak.

perimō, -imere, -ēmī, -emptum *vt* to destroy, prevent, kill.

perincommodē *adv see adj.*

perincommodus *adj* very inconvenient.

perinde *adv* just as, exactly as.

perindulgēns, -entis *adj* very tender.

perīnfirmus *adj* very feeble.

peringeniōsus *adj* very clever.

perinīquus *adj* very unfair; very discontented.

perinsignis *adj* very conspicuous.

perinvītus *adj* very unwilling.

periodus, -ī *f* sentence, period.

Peripatēticī, -ōrum *mpl* Peripatetics (*followers of Aristotle*).

peripetasmata, -um *ntpl* curtains.

perīrātus *adj* very angry.

periscelis, -dis *f* anklet.

peristrōma, -atis *nt* coverlet.

peristylum, -ī *nt* colonnade, peristyle.

perītē *adv* expertly.

perītia, -ae *f* practical knowledge, skill.

perītus *adj* experienced, skilled, expert.

periūcundē *adv see adj.*

periūcundus *adj* very enjoyable.

periūrium, -ī and iī *nt* perjury.

periūrō *see* **pēierō.**

periūrus *adj* perjured, lying.

perlābor, -bī, -psus *vi* to glide along *or* through, move on.

perlaetus *adj* very glad.

perlāpsus *ppa of* **perlābor.**

perlātē *adv* very extensively.

perlateō, -ēre *vi* to lie quite hidden.

perlātus *ppp of* **perferō.**

perlegō, -egere, -ēgī, -ēctum *vt* to survey; to read through.

perlevis *adj* very slight.

perleviter *adv see adj.*

perlibēns, -entis *adj* very willing.

perlibenter *adv see adj.*

perlīberālis *adj* very genteel.

perlīberāliter *adv* very liberally.

perlibet, -ēre *vi* (*impers*) (I) should very much like.

perliciō *etc see* **pelliciō.**

perlitō, -āre, -āvī, -ātum *vi* to sacrifice with auspicious results.

perlongē *adv* very far.

perlongus *adj* very long, very tedious.

perlub- *etc see* **perlib-.**

perlūceō, -cēre, -xī *vi* to shine through, be transparent; (*fig*) to be quite intelligible.

perlūcidulus *adj* transparent.

perlūcidus *adj* transparent; very bright.

perlūctuōsus *adj* very mournful.

perluō, -ere *vt* to wash thoroughly; (*pass*) to bathe.

perlūstrō, -āre *vt* to traverse; (*fig*) to survey.

permāgnus *adj* very big, very great.

permānanter *adv* by flowing through.

permānāscō, -ere *vi* to penetrate.

permaneō, -anēre, -ānsī, -ānsum *vi* to last, persist, endure to the end.

permānō, -āre, -āvī, -ātum *vi* to flow *or* ooze through, penetrate.

permānsiō, -ōnis *f* continuing, persisting.

permarīnus *adj* of seafaring.

permātūrēscō, -ēscere, -uī *vi* to ripen fully.

permediocris *adj* very moderate.

permēnsus *ppa of* **permētior.**

permeō, -āre *vt, vi* to pass through, penetrate.

permētior, -tīrī, -nsus *vt* to measure out; to traverse.

permīrus *adj* very wonderful.

permisceō, -scēre, -scuī, -xtum *vt* to mingle, intermingle; to throw into confusion.

permissiō, -ōnis *f* unconditional surrender; permission.

permissus *ppp of* **permittō.**

permissus, -ūs *m* leave, permission.

permitiālis *adj* destructive.

permitiēs, -ēī *f* ruin.

permittō, -ittere, -īsī, -issum *vt* to let go, let pass; to hurl; to give up, entrust, concede; to allow, permit.

permixtē *adv see adj.*

permixtiō, -ōnis *f* mixture; disturbance.

permixtus *ppp of* **permisceō** ♦ *adj* promiscuous, disordered.

permodestus *adj* very moderate.

permolestē *adv* with much annoyance.

permolestus *adj* very troublesome.

permōtiō, -ōnis *f* excitement; emotion.

permōtus *ppp of* **permoveō.**

permoveō, -ovēre, -ōvī, -ōtum *vt* to stir violently; (*fig*) to influence, induce; to excite, move deeply.

permulceō, -cēre, -sī, -sum *vt* to stroke, caress; (*fig*) to charm, flatter; to soothe, appease.

permulsus *ppp of* **permulceō.**

permultus *adj* very much, very many.

permūniō, -īre, -īvī, -ītum *vt* to finish fortifying; to fortify strongly.

permūtātiō, -ōnis *f* change, exchange.

permūtō, -āre, -āvī, -ātum *vt* to change completely; to exchange; (*money*) to remit by bill of exchange.

perna, -ae *f* ham.

pernecessārius *adj* very necessary; very closely related.

pernecesse *adj* indispensable.

pernegō, -āre *vi* to deny flatly.

perniciābilis *adj* ruinous.

perniciēs, -ēī *f* destruction, ruin, death.

perniciōsē *adv see adj.*

perniciōsus *adj* ruinous.

pernīcitās, -ātis *f* agility, swiftness.
perniciter *adv* nimbly.
pernimius *adj* much too much.
pernīx, -īcis *adj* nimble, agile, swift.
pernōbilis *adj* very famous.
pernoctō, -āre *vi* to stay all night.
pernōscō, -scere, -vī, -tum *vt* to examine thoroughly; to become fully acquainted with, know thoroughly.
pernōtēscō, -ēscere, -uī *vi* to become generally known.
pernōtus *ppp of* **pernōscō**.
pernox, -octis *adj* all night long.
pernumerō, -āre *vt* to count up.
pērō, -ōnis *m* rawhide boot.
perobscūrus *adj* very obscure.
perodiōsus *adj* very troublesome.
perofficiōsē *adv* very attentively.
peroleō, -ēre *vi* to give off a strong smell.
peropportūnē *adv* very opportunely.
peropportūnus *adj* very timely.
peroptātō *adv* very much to one's wish.
peropus est it is most essential.
perōrātiō, -ōnis *f* peroration.
perōrnātus *adj* very ornate.
perōrnō, -āre *vt* to give great distinction to.
perōrō, -āre, -āvī, -ātum *vt* to plead at length; (*speech*) to bring to a close; to conclude.
perōsus *adj* detesting.
perpācō, -āre *vt* to quieten completely.
perparcē *adv* very stingily.
perparvulus *adj* very tiny.
perparvus *adj* very small.
perpāstus *adj* well fed.
perpauculus *adj* very very few.
perpaucus *adj* very little, very few.
perpaulum, -ī *nt* a very little.
perpauper, -is *adj* very poor.
perpauxillum, -ī *nt* a very little.
perpellō, -ellere, -ulī, -ulsum *vt* to urge, force, influence.
perpendiculum, -ī *nt* plumbline; ad ~ perpendicularly.
perpendō, -endere, -endī, -ēnsum *vt* to weigh carefully, judge.
perperam *adv* wrongly, falsely.
perpes, -etis *adj* continuous.
perpessiō, -ōnis *f* suffering, enduring.
perpessus *ppa of* **perpetior**.
perpetior, -tī, -ssus *vt* to endure patiently, allow.
perpetrō, -āre, -āvī, -ātum *vt* to perform, carry out.
perpetuitās, -ātis *f* continuity, uninterrupted duration.
perpetuō *adv* without interruption, forever, utterly.
perpetuō, -āre *vt* to perpetuate, preserve.
perpetuus *adj* continuous, entire; universal; in ~um forever.
perplaceō, -ēre *vi* to please greatly.
perplexē *adv* obscurely.

perplexor, -ārī *vi* to cause confusion.
perplexus *adj* confused, intricate, obscure.
perplicātus *adj* interlaced.
perpluō, -ere *vi* to let the rain through, leak.
perpoliō, -īre, -īvī, -ītum *vt* to polish thoroughly.
perpolītus *adj* finished, refined.
perpopulor, -ārī, -ātus *vt* to ravage completely.
perpōtātiō, -ōnis *f* drinking bout.
perpōtō, -āre *vi* to drink continuously ♦ *vt* to drink off.
perprimō, -ere *vt* to lie on.
perpugnāx, -ācis *adj* very pugnacious.
perpulcher, -rī *adj* very beautiful.
perpulī *perf of* **perpellō**.
perpūrgō, -āre, -āvī, -ātum *vt* to make quite clean; to explain.
perpusillus *adj* very little.
perquam *adv* very, extremely.
perquīrō, -rere, -sīvī, -sītum *vt* to search for, inquire after; to examine carefully.
perquīsītius *adv* more accurately.
perrārō *adv* very seldom.
perrārus *adj* very uncommon.
perreconditus *adj* very abstruse.
perrēpō, -ere *vt* to crawl over.
perrēptō, -āre, -āvī, -ātum *vt, vi* to creep about *or* through.
perrēxī *perf of* **pergō**.
perrīdiculē *adv see adj*.
perrīdiculus *adj* very laughable.
perrogātiō, -ōnis *f* passing (of a law).
perrogō, -āre *vt* to ask one after another.
perrumpō, -umpere, -ūpī, -uptum *vt, vi* to break through, force a way through; (*fig*) to break down.
perruptus *ppp of* **perrumpō**.
Persae, -ārum *mpl* Persians.
persaepe *adv* very often.
persalsē *adv see adj*.
persalsus *adj* very witty.
persalūtātiō, -ōnis *f* greeting everyone in turn.
persalūtō, -āre *vt* to greet in turn.
persanctē *adv* most solemnly.
persapiēns, -entis *adj* very wise.
persapienter *adv see adj*.
perscienter *adv* very discreetly.
perscindō, -ndere, -dī, -ssum *vt* to tear apart.
perscītus *adj* very smart.
perscrībō, -bere, -psī, -ptum *vt* to write in full; to describe, report; (*record*) to enter; (*money*) to make over in writing.
perscrīptiō, -ōnis *f* entry; assignment.
perscrīptor, -ōris *m* writer.
perscrīptus *ppp of* **perscrībō**.
perscrūtor, -ārī, -ātus *vt* to search, examine thoroughly.
persecō, -āre, -uī, -tum *vt* to dissect; to do away with.
persector, -ārī *vt* to investigate.

persecūtiō, -ōnis *f* (*law*) prosecution.
persecūtus *ppa of* **persequor.**
persedeō, -edēre, -ēdī, -essum *vi* to remain sitting.
persegnis *adj* very slow.
Perseïus *adj see* **Perseus.**
persentiō, -entīre, -ēnsī *vt* to see clearly; to feel deeply.
persentīscō, -ere *vi* to begin to see; to begin to feel.
Persephonē, -ēs *f* Proserpine.
persequor, -quī, -cūtus *vt* to follow all the way; to pursue, chase, hunt after; to overtake; (*pattern*) to be a follower of, copy; (*enemy*) to proceed against, take revenge on; (*action*) to perform, carry out; (*words*) to write down, describe.
Persēs, -ae *m* last king of Macedonia.
Persēs, -ae *m* Persian.
Perseus, -eī *and* **eos** (*acc* **-ea**) *m* son of Danaë (*killer of Medusa, rescuer of Andromeda*).
Persēus *adj see* **n.**
persevērāns, -antis *pres p of* **persevērō** ♦ *adj* persistent.
persevēranter *adv see* **adj.**
persevērantia, -ae *f* persistence.
persevērō, -āre, -āvī, -ātum *vi* to persist ♦ *vt* to persist in.
persevērus *adj* very strict.
Persicus *adj* Persian; of Perses.
Persicum *nt* peach.
persīdō, -īdere, -ēdī, -essum *vi* to sink down into.
persignō, -āre *vt* to record.
persimilis *adj* very like.
persimplex, -icis *adj* very simple.
Persis, -idis *f* Persia.
persistō, -istere, -titī *vi* to persist.
persōlus *adj* one and only.
persolūtus *ppp of* **persolvō.**
persolvō, -vere, -vī, -ūtum *vt* to pay, pay up; to explain.
persōna, -ae *f* mask; character, part; person, personality.
persōnātus *adj* masked; in an assumed character.
personō, -āre, -uī, -itum *vi* to resound, ring (with); to play ♦ *vt* to make resound; to cry aloud.
perspectē *adv* intelligently.
perspectō, -āre *vt* to have a look through.
perspectus *ppp of* **perspiciō** ♦ *adj* well-known.
perspeculor, -ārī *vt* to reconnoitre.
perspergō, -gere, -sī, -sum *vt* to besprinkle.
perspicāx, -ācis *adj* sharp, shrewd.
perspicientia, -ae *f* full understanding.
perspiciō, -icere, -exī, -ectum *vt* to see through; to examine, observe.
perspicuē *adv* clearly.
perspicuitās, -ātis *f* clarity.

perspicuus *adj* transparent; clear, evident.
persternō, -ernere, -rāvī, -rātum *vt* to pave all over.
perstimulō, -āre *vt* to rouse violently.
perstitī *perf of* **persistō**; *perf of* **perstō.**
perstō, -āre, -itī, -ātum *vi* to stand fast; to last; to continue, persist.
perstrātus *ppp of* **persternō.**
perstrepō, -ere *vi* to make a lot of noise.
perstrictus *ppp of* **perstringō.**
perstringō, -ingere, -inxī, -ictum *vt* to graze, touch lightly; (*words*) to touch on, belittle, censure; (*senses*) to dull, deaden.
perstudiōsē *adv* very eagerly.
perstudiōsus *adj* very fond.
persuādeō, -dēre, -sī, -sum *vi* (*with dat*) to convince, persuade; ~**sum habeō, mihi ~sum est** I am convinced.
persuāsiō, -ōnis *f* convincing.
persuāsus, -ūs *m* persuasion.
persubtīlis *adj* very fine.
persultō, -āre *vt, vi* to prance about, frisk over.
pertaedet, -dēre, -sum est *vt* (*impers*) to be weary of, be sick of.
pertegō, -egere, -ēxī, -ēctum *vt* to cover over.
pertemptō, -āre *vt* to test carefully; to consider well; to pervade, seize.
pertendō, -ere, -ī *vi* to push on, persist ♦ *vt* to go on with.
pertenuis *adj* very small, very slight.
perterebrō, -āre *vt* to bore through.
pertergeō, -gēre, -sī, -sum *vt* to wipe over; to touch lightly.
perterrefaciō, -ere *vt* to scare thoroughly.
perterreō, -ēre, -uī, -itum *vt* to frighten thoroughly.
perterricrepus *adj* with a terrifying crash.
perterritus *adj* terrified.
pertexō, -ere, -uī, -tum *vt* to accomplish.
pertica, -ae *f* pole, staff.
pertimefactus *adj* very frightened.
pertimēscō, -ēscere, -uī *vt, vi* to be very alarmed, be very afraid of.
pertinācia, -ae *f* perseverance, stubbornness.
pertināciter *adv see* **adj.**
pertināx, -ācis *adj* very tenacious; unyielding, stubborn.
pertineō, -ēre, -uī *vi* to extend, reach; to tend, lead to, concern; to apply, pertain, belong; **quod ~et ad** as far as concerns.
pertingō, -ere *vi* to extend.
pertolerō, -āre *vt* to endure to the end.
pertorqueō, -ēre *vt* to distort.
pertractātē *adv* in a hackneyed fashion.
pertractātiō, -ōnis *f* handling.
pertractō, -āre *vt* to handle, feel all over; (*fig*) to treat, study.
pertractus *ppp of* **pertrahō.**

---

pertrahō, -here, -xī, -ctum *vt* to drag across, take forcibly; to entice.

pertrect- *etc see* **pertract-**.

pertristis *adj* very sad, very morose.

pertulī *perf of* **perferō**.

pertumultuōsē *adv* very excitedly.

pertundō, -undere, -udī, -ūsum *vt* to perforate.

perturbātē *adv* in confusion.

perturbātiō, -ōnis *f* confusion, disturbance; emotion.

perturbātrīx, -īcis *f* disturber.

perturbātus *ppp of* **perturbō** ♦ *adj* troubled; alarmed.

perturbō, -āre, -āvī, -ātum *vt* to throw into disorder, upset, alarm.

perturpis *adj* scandalous.

pertūsus *ppp of* **pertundō** ♦ *adj* in holes, leaky.

perungō, -ungere, -ūnxī, -ūnctum *vt* to smear all over.

perurbānus *adj* very refined; over-fine.

perūrō, -rere, -ssi, -stum *vt* to burn up, scorch; to inflame, chafe; to freeze, nip.

Perusia, -iae *f* Etruscan town (*now* Perugia).

Perusīnus *adj see* n.

perūstus *ppp of* **perūrō**.

perūtilis *adj* very useful.

pervādō, -dere, -sī, -sum *vt, vi* to pass through, spread through; to penetrate, reach.

pervagātus *adj* widespread, well-known; general.

pervagor, -ārī, -ātus *vi* to range, rove about; to extend, spread ♦ *vt* to pervade.

pervagus *adj* roving.

pervariē *adv* very diversely.

pervastō, -āre, -āvī, -ātum *vt* to devastate.

pervāsus *ppp of* **pervādō**.

pervectus *ppp of* **pervehō**.

pervehō, -here, -xī, -ctum *vt* to carry, convey, bring through; (*pass*) to ride, drive, sail through; to attain.

pervellō, -ere, -ī *vt* to pull, twitch, pinch; to stimulate; to disparage.

perveniō, -enīre, -ēnī, -entum *vi* to come to, arrive, reach; to attain to.

pervēnor, -ārī *vi* to chase through.

perversē *adv* perversely.

perversitās, -ātis *f* perverseness.

perversus (pervorsus) *ppp of* **pervertō** ♦ *adj* awry, squint; wrong, perverse.

pervertō, -tere, -tī, -sum *vt* to overturn, upset; to overthrow, undo; (*speech*) to confute.

pervesperī *adv* very late.

pervestīgātiō, -ōnis *f* thorough search.

pervestīgō, -āre, -āvī, -ātum *vt* to track down; to investigate.

pervetus, -eris *adj* very old.

pervetustus *adj* antiquated.

pervicācia, -ae *f* obstinacy; firmness.

pervicāciter *adv see adj.*

pervicāx, -ācis *adj* obstinate, wilful; dogged.

pervictus *ppp of* **pervincō**.

pervideō, -idēre, -īdī, -īsum *vt* to look over, survey; to consider; to discern.

pervigeō, -ēre, -uī *vi* to continue to flourish.

pervigil, -is *adj* awake, watchful.

pervigilātiō, -ōnis *f* vigil.

pervigilium, -ī *and* **iī** *nt* vigil.

pervigilō, -āre, -āvī, -ātum *vt, vi* to stay awake all night, keep vigil.

pervīlis *adj* very cheap.

pervincō, -incere, -īcī, -ictum *vt, vi* to conquer completely; to outdo, surpass; to prevail upon, effect; (*argument*) to carry a point, maintain, prove.

pervīvō, -ere *vi* to survive.

pervius *adj* passable, accessible.

pervolgō *etc see* **pervulgō**.

pervolitō, -āre *vt, vi* to fly about.

pervolō, -āre, -āvī, -ātum *vt, vi* to fly through *or* over, fly to.

pervolō, -elle, -oluī *vi* to wish very much.

pervolūtō, -āre *vt* (*books*) to read through.

pervolvō, -vere, -vī, -ūtum *vt* to tumble about; (*book*) to read through; (*pass*) to be very busy (with).

pervor- *etc see* **perver-**.

pervulgātus *adj* very common.

pervulgō, -āre, -āvī, -ātum *vt* to make public, impart; to haunt.

pēs, pedis *m* foot; (*length*) foot; (*verse*) foot, metre; (*sailrope*) sheet; **pedem cōnferre** come to close quarters; **pedem referre** go back; **ante pedēs** self-evident; **pedibus** on foot, by land; **pedibus īre in sententiam** take sides; **pedibus aequīs** (*NAUT*) with the wind right aft; **servus ā pedibus** footman.

pessimē *superl of* **male**.

pessimus *superl of* **malus**.

pessulus, -ī *m* bolt.

pessum *adv* to the ground, to the bottom; ~ **dare** put an end to, ruin, destroy; ~ **īre** sink, perish.

pestifer, -ī *adj* pestilential; baleful, destructive.

pestilēns, -entis *adj* unhealthy; destructive.

pestilentia, -ae *f* plague, pest; unhealthiness.

pestilitās, -ātis *f* plague.

pestis, -is *f* plague, pest; ruin, destruction.

petasātus *adj* wearing the petasus.

petasunculus, -ī *m* small leg of pork.

petasus, -ī *m* broadbrimmed hat.

petessō, -ere *vt* to be eager for.

petītiō, -ōnis *f* thrust, attack; request, application; (*office*) candidature, standing for; (*law*) civil suit, right of claim.

petītor, -ōris *m* candidate; plaintiff.

petīturiō, -īre *vt* to long to be a candidate.

petītus *ppp of* **petō**.

petītus, -ūs *m* falling to.

petō, -ere, -īvī *and* **iī, -ītum** *vt* to aim at, attack; (*place*) to make for, go to; to seek, look for, demand, ask; to go and fetch; (*law*) to sue; (*love*) to court; (*office*) to stand for.

petorritum, -ī nt carriage.

petrō, -ōnis m yokel.

Petrōnius, -ī m arbiter of fashion under Nero.

petulāns, -antis adj pert, impudent, lascivious.

petulanter adv see adj.

petulantia, -ae f pertness, impudence.

petulcus adj butting.

pexus ppp of **pectō**.

Phaeāccius and cus, -x adj Phaeacian.

Phaeāces, -cum mpl fabulous islanders in the Odyssey.

Phaedra, -ae f stepmother of Hippolytus.

Phaedrus, -ī m pupil of Socrates; writer of Latin fables.

Phaethōn, -ontis m son of the Sun (killed while driving his father's chariot).

Phaethonteus adj see n.

Phaethontiades, -um fpl sisters of Phaethon.

phalangae, -ārum fpl wooden rollers.

phalangītae, -ārum mpl soldiers of a phalanx.

phalanx, -gis f phalanx; troops, battle order.

Phalaris, -dis m tyrant of Agrigentum.

phalerae, -ārum fpl medallions, badges; (horse) trappings.

phalerātus adj wearing medallions; ornamented.

Phalēreus, -icus adj see n.

Phalērum, -ī nt harbour of Athens.

pharetra, -ae f quiver.

pharetrātus adj wearing a quiver.

Pharius adj see n.

pharmaceutria, -ae f sorceress.

pharmacopōla, -ae m quack doctor.

Pharsālicus, -ius adj see n.

Pharsālus (-os), -ī f town in Thessaly (where Caesar defeated Pompey).

Pharus (-os), -ī f island off Alexandria with a famous lighthouse; lighthouse.

phasēlus, -ī m/f French beans; (boat) pinnace.

Phāsiacus adj Colchian.

Phāsiānus, -āna m/f pheasant.

Phāsis, -dis and dos m river of Colchis.

Phāsis adj see n.

phasma, -tis nt ghost.

Pherae, -ārum fpl town in Thessaly (home of Admetus).

Pheraeus adj see n.

phiala, -ae f saucer.

Phīdiacus adj see n.

Phīdiās, -ae m famous Athenian sculptor.

philēma, -tis nt kiss.

Philippī, -ōrum mpl town in Macedonia (where Brutus and Cassius were defeated).

Philippēus adj see n.

Philippicae fpl Cicero's speeches against Antony.

Philippicus adj see n.

Philippus, -ī m king of Macedonia; gold coin.

philitia, (phīditia), -ōrum ntpl public meals at Sparta.

Philō (-ōn), -ōnis m Academic philosopher (teacher of Cicero).

Philoctētēs, -ae m Greek archer who gave Hercules poisoned arrows.

philologia, -ae f study of literature.

philologus adj scholarly, literary.

Philomēla, -ae f sister of Procne; nightingale.

philosophē adv see adj.

philosophia, -ae f philosophy.

philosophor, -ārī, -ātus vi to philosophize.

philosophus, -ī m philosopher ♦ adj philosophical.

philtrum, -ī nt love potion.

philyra, -ae f inner bark of the lime tree.

phīmus, -ī m dice box.

Phlegethōn, -ontis m a river of Hades.

Phlegethontis adj see n.

Phlīāsius adj see n.

Phlīūs, -ūntis f town in Peloponnese.

phōca, -ae f seal.

Phōcaicus adj see n.

Phōcēus adj see n.

Phōcis, -idis f country of central Greece.

Phōcius adj see n.

Phoebas, -adis f prophetess.

Phoebē, -ēs f Diana, the moon.

Phoebēius, -ēus adj see n.

Phoebigena, -ae m son of Phoebus, Aesculapius.

Phoebus, -ī m Apollo; the sun.

Phoenīcē, -cēs f Phoenicia.

Phoenīces, -cum mpl Phoenicians.

phoenīcopterus, -ī m flamingo.

Phoenīssus adj Phoenician ♦ f Dido.

Phoenix, -īcis m friend of Achilles.

phoenīx, -īcis m phoenix.

Phorcis, -idos = **Phorcȳnis**.

Phorcus, -ī m son of Neptune (father of Medusa).

Phorcȳnis, -ȳnidos f Medusa.

Phraātēs, -ae m king of Parthia.

phrenēsis, -is f delirium.

phrenēticus adj mad, delirious.

Phrixēus adj see n.

Phrixus, -ī m Helle's brother (who took the ram with the golden fleece to Colchis).

Phryges, -um mpl Phrygians; Trojans.

Phrygia, -iae f Phrygia (country of Asia Minor); Troy.

Phrygius adj Phrygian, Trojan.

Phthīa, -ae f home of Achilles in Thessaly.

Phthīōta, -ōtēs, -ōtae m native of Phthia.

phthisis f consumption.

Phthīus adj see n.

phy interj bah!

phylaca, -ae f prison.

phylarchus, -ī m chieftain.

physica, -ae and ē, -ēs f physics.

physicē adv scientifically.

Noun declensions and verb conjugations are shown on pp xiii to xxv. The present infinitive ending of a verb shows to which conjugation it belongs: **-āre** = 1st; **-ēre** = 2nd; **-ere** = 3rd and **-īre** = 4th. Irregular verbs are shown on p xxvi

physicus *adj* of physics, natural ♦ *m* natural philosopher ♦ *ntpl* physics.
physiognōmōn, -onis *m* physiognomist.
physiologia, -ae *f* natural philosophy, science.
piābilis *adj* expiable.
piāculāris *adj* atoning ♦ *ntpl* sin offerings.
piāculum, -ī *nt* sin offering; victim; atonement, punishment; sin, guilt.
piāmen, -inis *nt* atonement.
pīca, -ae *f* magpie.
picāria, -ae *f* pitch hut.
picea, -ae *f* pine.
Picēns, -entis *adj* = **Picēnus**.
Picēnum, -ēnī *nt* Picenum.
Picēnus *adj* of Picenum in E. Italy.
piceus *adj* pitch black; of pitch.
pictor, -ōris *m* painter.
pictūra, -ae *f* painting; picture.
pictūrātus *adj* painted; embroidered.
pictus *ppp of* **pingō** ♦ *adj* coloured, tattooed; (*style*) ornate; (*fear*) unreal.
pīcus, -ī *m* woodpecker.
piē *adv* religiously, dutifully.
Pīeris, -dis *f* Muse.
Pīerius *adj* of the Muses, poetic.
pietās, -ātis *f* sense of duty (*to gods, family, country*), piety, filial affection, love, patriotism.
piger, -rī *adj* reluctant, slack, slow; numbing, dull.
piget, -ēre, -uit *vt* (*impers*) to be annoyed, dislike; to regret, repent.
pigmentārius, -ī *and* **iī** *m* dealer in paints.
pigmentum, -ī *nt* paint, cosmetic; (*style*) colouring.
pignerātor, -ōris *m* mortgagee.
pignerō, -āre *vt* to pawn, mortgage.
pigneror, -ārī, -ātus *vt* to claim, accept.
pignus, -oris *and* **eris** *nt* pledge, pawn, security; wager, stake; (*fig*) assurance, token; (*pl*) children, dear ones.
pigritia, -ae, -ēs, -ēī *f* sluggishness, indolence.
pigrō, -āre, -or, -ārī *vi* to be slow, be slack.
pīla, -ae *f* mortar.
pīla, -ae *f* pillar; pier.
pila, -ae *f* ball, ball game.
pīlānus, -ī *m* soldier of the third line.
pīlātus *adj* armed with javelins.
pilentum, -ī *nt* carriage.
pilleātus *adj* wearing the felt cap.
pilleolus, -ī *m* skullcap.
pilleum, -ī *nt*, **pilleus, -ī** *m* felt cap presented to freed slaves; (*fig*) liberty.
pilōsus *adj* hairy.
pīlum, -ī *nt* javelin.
pīlus, -ī *m* division of triarii; **prīmus ~** chief centurion.
pilus, -ī *m* hair; a whit.
Pimplēa, -ae *and* **is, -idis** *f* Muse.
Pimplēus *adj* of the Muses.
Pindaricus *adj see n.*

Pindarus, -ī *m* Pindar (*Greek lyric poet*).
Pindus, -ī *m* mountain range in Thessaly.
pīnētum, -ī *nt* pine wood.
pīneus *adj* pine- (*in cpds*).
pingō, -ere, pinxī, pictum *vt* to paint, embroider; to colour; (*fig*) to embellish, decorate.
pinguēscō, -ere *vi* to grow fat, become fertile.
pinguis *adj* fat, rich, fertile; (*mind*) gross, dull; (*ease*) comfortable, calm; (*weather*) thick ♦ *nt* grease.
pīnifer, -ī, pīniger, -ī *adj* pine-clad.
pinna, -ae *f* feather; wing, arrow; battlement; (*fish*) fin.
pinnātus *adj* feathered, winged.
pinniger, -ī *adj* winged; finny.
pinnipēs, -edis *adj* wing-footed.
pinnirapus, -ī *m* plume-snatcher.
pinnula, -ae *f* little wing.
pīnotērēs, -ae *m* hermit crab.
pīnsō, -ere *vt* to beat, pound.
pīnus, -ūs *and* **ī** *f* stone pine, Scots fir; ship, torch, wreath.
pinxī *perf of* **pingō**.
piō, -āre *vt* to propitiate, worship; to atone for, avert; to avenge.
piper, -is *nt* pepper.
pipilō, -āre *vi* to chirp.
Pīraea, -ōrum *ntpl* Piraeus (*port of Athens*).
Pīraeeus *and* **us, -ī** *m* main port of Athens.
Pīraeus *adj see n.*
pīrāta, -ae *m* pirate.
pīrāticus *adj* pirate ♦ *f* piracy.
Pīrēnē, -ēs *f* spring in Corinth.
Pīrēnis, -idis *adj see n.*
Pīrithous, -ī *m* king of the Lapiths.
pirum, -ī *nt* pear.
pirus, -ī *f* pear tree.
Pīsa, -ae *f* Greek town near the Olympic Games site.
Pīsae, -ārum *fpl* town in Etruria (*now* Pisa).
Pīsaeus *adj see n.*
Pīsānus *adj see n.*
piscārius *adj* fish- (*in cpds*), fishing- (*in cpds*).
piscātor, -ōris *m* fisherman.
piscātōrius *adj* fishing- (*in cpds*).
piscātus, -ūs *m* fishing; fish; catch, haul.
pisciculus, -ī *m* little fish.
piscīna, -ae *f* fishpond; swimming pool.
piscīnārius, -ī *and* **iī** *m* person keen on fish ponds.
piscis -is *m* fish; (*ASTRO*) Pisces.
piscor, -ārī, -ātus *vi* to fish.
piscōsus *adj* full of fish.
pisculentus *adj* full of fish.
Pīsistratidae, -idārum *mpl* sons of Pisistratus.
Pīsistratus, -ī *m* tyrant of Athens.
pistillum, -ī *nt* pestle.
pistor, -ōris *m* miller; baker.
pistrilla, -ae *f* little mortar.
pīstrīnum, -ī *nt* mill, bakery; drudgery.
pistris, -is *and* **īx, -īcis** *f* sea monster, whale;

swift ship.

pithēcium, -ī *and* **iī** *nt* little ape.

pītuīta, -ae *f* phlegm; catarrh, cold in the head.

pītuītōsus *adj* phlegmatic.

pius *adj* dutiful, conscientious; godly, holy; filial, affectionate; patriotic; good, upright ♦ *mpl* the blessed dead.

pix, picis *f* pitch.

plācābilis *adj* easily appeased.

plācābilitās, -ātis *f* readiness to condone.

plācāmen, -inis, plācāmentum, -ī *nt* peace-offering.

plācātē *adv* calmly.

plācātiō, -ōnis *f* propitiating.

plācātus *ppp of* **plācō** ♦ *adj* calm, quiet, reconciled.

placenta, -ae *f* cake.

Placentia, -iae *f* town in N. Italy (*now* Piacenza).

Placentīnus *adj see n.*

placeō, -ēre, -uī, -itum *vi* (*with dat*) to please, satisfy; **~et** it seems good, it is agreed, resolved; **mihi ~eō** I am pleased with myself.

placidē *adv* peacefully, gently.

placidus *adj* calm, quiet, gentle.

placitum,-ī *nt* principle, belief.

placitus *ppa of* **placeō** ♦ *adj* pleasing; agreed on.

plācō, -āre, -āvī, -ātum *vt* to calm, appease, reconcile.

plāga, -ae *f* blow, stroke, wound.

plaga, -ae *f* region, zone.

plaga, -ae *f* hunting net, snare, trap.

plagiārius, -ī *and* **iī** *m* plunderer, kidnapper.

plāgigerulus *adj* much flogged.

plāgōsus *adj* fond of punishing.

plagula, -ae *f* curtain.

planctus, -ūs *m* beating the breast, lamentation.

plānē *adv* plainly, clearly; completely, quite; certainly.

plangō, -gere, -xī, -ctum *vt, vi* to beat noisily; to beat in grief; to lament loudly, bewail.

plangor, -ōris *m* beating; loud lamentation.

plānipēs, -edis *m* ballet dancer.

plānitās, -ātis *f* perspicuity.

plānitiēs, -ēī, (-a, -ae) *f* level ground, plain.

planta, -ae *f* shoot, slip; sole, foot.

plantāria, -ium *ntpl* slips, young trees.

plānus *adj* level, flat; plain, clear ♦ *nt* level ground; **dē ~ō** easily.

plānus, -ī *m* impostor.

platalea, -ae *f* spoonbill.

platea, -ae *f* street.

Platō, -ōnis *m* Plato (*founder of the Academic school of philosophy*).

Platōnicus *adj see n.*

plaudō, -dere, -sī, -sum *vt* to clap, beat, stamp ♦ *vi* to clap, applaud; to approve, be

pleased with.

plausibilis *adj* praiseworthy.

plausor, -ōris *m* applauder.

plaustrum, -ī *nt* waggon, cart; (*ASTRO*) Great Bear; **~ percellere** *upset the applecart.*

plausus *ppp of* **plaudō.**

plausus, -ūs *m* flapping; clapping, applause.

Plautīnus *adj see n.*

Plautus, -ī *m* early Latin comic poet.

plēbēcula, -ae *f* rabble.

plēbēius *adj* plebeian; common, low.

plēbicola, -ae *m* friend of the people.

plēbīscītum, -ī *nt* decree of the people.

plēbs (plēbēs), -is *f* common people, plebeians; lower classes, masses.

plēctō, -ere *vt* to punish.

plēctrum, -ī *nt* plectrum; lyre, lyric poetry.

Plēias, -dis *f* Pleiad; (*pl*) the Seven Sisters.

plēnē *adv* fully, entirely.

plēnus *adj* full, filled; (*fig*) sated; (*age*) mature; (*amount*) complete; (*body*) stout, plump; (*female*) pregnant; (*matter*) solid; (*style*) copious; (*voice*) loud; **ad ~um** abundantly.

plērumque *adv* generally, mostly.

plērusque *adj* a large part, most; (*pl*) the majority, the most; very many.

plexus *adj* plaited, interwoven.

Plīas *see* **Plēias.**

plicātrīx, -īcis *f* clothes folder.

plicō, -āre, -āvī *and* **uī, -ātum** *and* **itum** *vt* to fold, coil.

Plīnius, -ī *m* Roman family name (*esp Pliny the Elder, who died in the eruption of Vesuvius*); Pliny the Younger, writer of letters.

plōrātus, -ūs *m* wailing.

plōrō, -āre, -āvī, -ātum *vi* to wail, lament ♦ *vt* to weep for, bewail.

plōstellum, -ī *nt* cart.

ploxenum, -ī *nt* cart box.

pluit, -ere, -ī *vi* (*impers*) it is raining.

plūma, -ae *f* soft feather, down.

plumbeus *adj* of lead; (*fig*) heavy, dull, worthless.

plumbum, -ī *nt* lead; bullet, pipe, ruler; **~ album** tin.

plūmeus *adj* down, downy.

plūmipēs, -edis *adj* feather-footed.

plūmōsus *adj* feathered.

plūrimus *superl of* **multus.**

plūs, -ūris *compar of* **multus** ♦ *adv* more.

plūsculus *adj* a little more.

pluteus, -ī *m* shelter, penthouse; parapet; couch; bookcase.

Plūtō, -ōnis *m* king of the lower world.

Plūtōnius *adj see n.*

pluvia, -ae *f* rain.

pluviālis *adj* rainy.

pluvius *adj* rainy, rain- (*in cpds*).

pōcillum, -ī *nt* small cup.

pōculum, -ī *nt* cup; drink, potion.

podagra, -ae f gout.
podagrōsus adj gouty.
podium, -ī and **iī** nt balcony.
poēma, -tis nt poem.
poena, -ae f penalty, punishment; **poenas dare** to be punished.
Poenī, -ōrum mpl Carthaginians.
Poenus, Pūnicus adj Punic.
poēsis, -is f poetry, poem.
poēta, -ae m poet.
poēticē adv poetically.
poēticus adj poetic ♦ f poetry.
poētria, -ae f poetess.
pol interj by Pollux!, truly.
polenta, -ae f pearl barley.
poliō, -īre, -īvī, -ītum vt to polish; to improve, put in good order.
polītē adv elegantly.
polītīa, -ae f Plato's Republic.
politicus adj political.
polītus adj polished, refined, cultured.
pollen, -inis nt fine flour, meal.
pollēns, -entis pres p of **polleō** ♦ adj powerful, strong.
pollentia, -ae f power.
polleō, -ēre vi to be strong, be powerful.
pollex, -icis m thumb.
polliceor, -ērī, -itus vt to promise, offer.
pollicitātiō, -ōnis f promise.
pollicitor, -ārī, -ātus vt to promise.
pollicitum, -ī nt promise.
Polliō, -ōnis m Roman surname (esp C. Asinius, soldier, statesman and literary patron under Augustus).
pollis, -inis m/f see **pollen**.
pollūcibiliter adv sumptuously.
pollūctus adj offered up ♦ nt offering.
polluō, -uere, -uī, -ūtum vt to defile, pollute, dishonour.
Pollūx, -ūcis m twin brother of Castor (famous as a boxer).
polus, -ī m pole, North pole; sky.
Polyhymnia, -ae f a Muse.
Polyphēmus, -ī m one-eyed Cyclops.
pōlypus, -ī m polypus.
pōmārium, -ī and **iī** nt orchard.
pōmārius, -ī and **iī** m fruiterer.
pōmerīdiānus adj afternoon.
pōmērium, -ī and **iī** nt free space round the city boundary.
pōmifer, -ī adj fruitful.
pōmoerium see **pōmērium**.
pōmōsus adj full of fruit.
pompa, -ae f procession; retinue, train; ostentation.
Pompeiānus adj see n.
Pompeiī, -ōrum mpl Campanian town buried by an eruption of Vesuvius.
Pompeius, -ī m Roman family name (esp Pompey the Great).
Pompeius, -ānus adj see n.
Pompilius, -ī m Numa (second king of Rome).
Pompilius adj see n.

Pomptīnus adj Pomptine (name of marshy district in S. Latium).
pōmum, -ī nt fruit; fruit tree.
pōmus, -ī f fruit tree.
ponderō, -āre vt to weigh; to consider, reflect on.
ponderōsus adj heavy, weighty.
pondō adv in weight; pounds.
pondus, -eris nt weight; mass, burden; (fig) importance, authority; (character) firmness; (pl) balance.
pōne adv behind.
pōnō, -ere, posuī, positum vt to put, place, lay, set; to lay down, lay aside; (fig) to regard, reckon; (art) to make, build; (camp) to pitch; (corpse) to lay out, bury; (example) to take; (food) to serve; (hair) to arrange; (hope) to base, stake; (hypothesis) to suppose, assume; (institution) to lay down, ordain; (money) to invest; (sea) to calm; (theme) to propose; (time) to spend, devote; (tree) to plant; (wager) to put down ♦ vi (wind) to abate.
pōns, pontis m bridge; drawbridge; (ship) gangway, deck.
ponticulus, -ī m small bridge.
Ponticus adj see **Pontus**.
pontifex, -icis m high priest, pontiff.
pontificālis adj pontifical.
pontificātus, -ūs m high priesthood.
pontificius adj pontiff's.
pontō, -ōnis m ferryboat.
pontus, -ī m sea.
Pontus, -ī m Black Sea; kingdom of Mithridates in Asia Minor.
popa, -ae m minor priest.
popanum, -ī nt sacrificial cake.
popellus, -ī m mob.
popīna, -ae f eating house, restaurant.
popīnō, -ōnis m glutton.
popl- etc see **pūbl-**.
poples, -itis m knee.
poposcī perf of **poscō**.
poppysma, -tis nt clicking of the tongue.
populābilis adj destroyable.
populābundus adj ravaging.
populāris adj of, from, for the people; popular, democratic; native ♦ m fellow countryman ♦ mpl the people's party, the democrats.
populāritās, -ātis f courting popular favour.
populāriter adv vulgarly; democratically.
populātiō, -ōnis f plundering; plunder.
populātor, -ōris m ravager.
pōpuleus adj poplar- (in cpds).
pōpulifer, -ī adj rich in poplars.
populor, -ārī, -ātus; -ō, -āre vt to ravage, plunder; to destroy, ruin.
populus, -ī m people, nation; populace, the public; large crowds; district.
pōpulus, -ī f poplar tree.
porca, -ae f sow.
porcella, -ae f, **-us, -ī** m little pig.

porcīna, -ae f pork.
porcīnārius, -ī and **iī** m pork seller.
Porcius, -ī m family name of Cato.
Porcius adj see n.
porculus, -ī m porker.
porcus, -ī m pig, hog.
porgō etc see **porrigō**.
Porphyriōn, -ōnis m a Giant.
porrēctiō, -ōnis f extending.
porrēctus ppp of **porrigō** ♦ adj long, protracted; dead.
porrēxī perf of **porrigō**.
porriciō, -ere vt to make an offering of; **inter caesa et porrēcta** ≈ at the eleventh hour.
porrigō, -igere, -ēxī, -ēctum vt to stretch, spread out, extend; to offer, hold out.
porrīgō, -inis f scurf, dandruff.
porrō adv forward, a long way off; (time) in future, long ago; (sequence) next, moreover, in turn.
porrum, -ī nt leek.
Porsena, Porsenna, Porsinna, -ae f king of Clusium in Etruria.
porta, -ae f gate; entrance, outlet.
portātiō, -ōnis f carrying.
portendō, -dere, -dī, -tum vt to denote, predict.
portentificus adj marvellous.
portentōsus adj unnatural.
portentum, -ī nt omen, unnatural happening; monstrosity, monster; (story) marvel.
porthmeus, -eī and **eos** m ferryman.
porticula, -ae f small gallery.
porticus, -ūs m portico, colonnade; (MIL) gallery; (PHILOS) Stoicism.
portiō, -ōnis f share, instalment; **prō ~ōne** proportionally.
portitor, -ōris m customs officer.
portitor, -ōris m ferryman.
portō, -āre, -āvī, -ātum vt to carry, convey, bring.
portōrium, -ī and **iī** nt customs duty, tax.
portula, -ae f small gate.
portuōsus adj well-off for harbours.
portus, -ūs m harbour, port; (fig) safety, haven.
pōsca, -ae f a vinegar drink.
poscō, -ere, poposcī vt to ask, require, demand; to call on.
Posīdōnius, -ī m Stoic philosopher (teacher of Cicero).
positiō, -ōnis f position, climate.
positor, -ōris m builder.
positūra, -ae f position; formation.
positus ppp of **pōnō** ♦ adj situated.
posse infin of **possum**.
possēdī perf of **possideō**; perf of **possīdō**.
possessiō, -ōnis f seizing; occupation; possession, property.
possessiuncula, -ae f small estate.

possessor, -ōris m occupier, possessor.
possessus ppp of **possideō** and **possīdō**.
possideō, -idēre, -ēdī, -essum vt to hold, occupy; to have, possess.
possīdō, -idere, -ēdī, -essum vt to take possession of.
possum, -sse, -tuī vi to be able, can; to have power, avail.
post adv (place) behind; (time) after; (sequence) next ♦ prep (with acc) behind; after, since; **paulō ~** soon after; **~ urbem conditam** since the foundation of the city.
posteā adv afterwards, thereafter; next, then; **~ quam** conj after.
posterior, -ōris adj later, next; inferior, less important.
posteritās, -ātis f posterity, the future.
posterius adv later.
posterus adj next, following ♦ mpl posterity.
postferō, -re vt to put after, sacrifice.
postgenitī, -ōrum mpl later generations.
posthabeō, -ēre, -uī, -itum vt to put after, neglect.
posthāc adv hereafter, in future.
postibi adv then, after that.
postīculum, -ī nt small back building.
postīcus adj back- (in cpds), hind- (in cpds) ♦ nt back door.
postideā adv after that.
postillā adv afterwards.
postis, -is m doorpost, door.
postlīminium, -ī and **iī** nt right of recovery.
postmerīdiānus adj in the afternoon.
postmodo, postmodum adv shortly, presently.
postpōnō, -ōnere, -osuī, -ositum vt to put after, disregard.
postputō, -āre vt to consider less important.
postquam conj after, when.
postrēmō adv finally.
postrēmus adj last, rear; lowest, worst.
postrīdiē adv next day, the day after.
postscaenium, -ī and **iī** nt behind the scenes.
postscrībō, -ere vt to write after.
postulātiō, -ōnis f demand, claim; complaint.
postulātum, -ī nt demand, claim.
postulātus, -ūs m claim.
postulō, -āre, -āvī, -ātum vt to demand, claim; (law) to summon, prosecute; to apply for a writ (to prosecute).
postumus adj last, last-born.
postus etc see **positus**.
posuī perf of **pōnō**.
pōtātiō, -ōnis f drinking.
pōtātor, -ōris m toper.
pote etc see **potis**.
potēns, -entis adj able, capable; powerful, strong, potent; master of, ruling over; successful in carrying out.
potentātus, -ūs m political power.

---

potenter *adv* powerfully; competently.
potentia, -ae *f* power, force, efficacy; tyranny.
potērium, -ī *and* **iī** *nt* goblet.
potesse *archaic infin of* **possum.**
potestās, -ātis *f* power, ability; control, sovereignty, authority; opportunity; permission; (*person*) magistrate; (*things*) property; **~ātem suī facere** allow access to oneself.
potin can (you)?, is it possible?
pōtiō, -ōnis *f* drink, draught, philtre.
potiō, -īre *vt* to put into the power of.
potior, -īrī, -ītus *vi* (*with gen and abl*) to take possession of, get hold of, acquire; to be master of.
potior, -ōris *adj* better, preferable.
potis *adj* (*indecl*) able; possible.
potissimum *adv* especially.
potissimus *adj* chief, most important.
pōtitō, -āre *vt* to drink much.
potius *adv* rather, more.
pōtō, -āre, -āvī, -ātum *and* **um** *vt* to drink.
pōtor, -ōris *m* drinker.
pōtrīx, -īcis *f* woman tippler.
potuī *perf of* **possum.**
pōtulenta, -ōrum *ntpl* drinks.
pōtus *ppp of* **pōtō** ♦ *adj* drunk.
pōtus, -ūs *m* drink.
prae *adv* in front, before; in comparison ♦ *prep* (*with abl*) in front of; compared with; (*cause*) because of, for; **~ sē** openly; **~ sē ferre** display; **~ manū** to hand.
praeacūtus *adj* pointed.
praealtus *adj* very high, very deep.
praebeō, -ēre, -uī, -itum *vt* to hold out, proffer; to give, supply; to show, represent; **sē ~** behave, prove.
praebibō, -ere, -ī *vt* to toast.
praebitor, -ōris *m* purveyor.
praecalidus *adj* very hot.
praecānus *adj* prematurely grey.
praecautus *ppp of* **praecaveō.**
praecaveō, -avēre, -āvī, -autum *vt* to guard against ♦ *vi* to beware, take precautions.
praecēdō, -dere, -ssī, -ssum *vt* to go before; to surpass ♦ *vi* to lead the way; to excel.
praecellō, -ere *vi* to excel, be distinguished ♦ *vt* to surpass.
praecelsus *adj* very high.
praecentiō, -ōnis *f* prelude.
praecentō, -āre *vi* to sing an incantation for.
praeceps, -ipitis *adj* head first, headlong; going down, precipitous; rapid, violent, hasty; inclined (to); dangerous ♦ *nt* edge of an abyss, precipice; danger ♦ *adv* headlong; into danger.
praeceptiō, -ōnis *f* previous notion; precept.
praeceptor, -ōris *m* teacher.
praeceptrīx, -rīcis *f* teacher.
praeceptum, -ī *nt* maxim, precept; order.
praeceptus *ppp of* **praecipiō.**
praecerpō, -ere, -sī, -tum *vt* to gather prematurely; to forestall.
praecīdō, -dere, -dī, -sum *vt* to cut off, damage; (*fig*) to cut short, put an end to.
praecinctus *ppp of* **praecingō.**
praecingō, -ingere, -inxī, -inctum *vt* to gird in front; to surround.
praecinō, -inere, -inuī, -entum *vt* to play before; to chant a spell ♦ *vt* to predict.
praecipiō, -ipere, -ēpī, -ēptum *vt* to take beforehand, get in advance; to anticipate; to teach, admonish, order.
praecipitanter *adv* at full speed.
praecipitem *acc of* **praeceps.**
praecipitō, -āre, -āvī, -ātum *vt* to throw down, throw away, hasten; (*fig*) to remove, carry away, ruin ♦ *vi* to rush headlong, fall; to be hasty.
praecipuē *adv* especially, chiefly.
praecipuus *adj* special; principal, outstanding.
praecīsē *adv* briefly, absolutely.
praecīsus *ppp of* **praecīdō** ♦ *adj* steep.
praeclārē *adv* very clearly; excellently.
praeclārus *adj* very bright; beautiful, splendid; distinguished, noble.
praeclūdō, -dere, -sī, -sum *vt* to close, shut against; to close to, impede.
praecō, -ōnis *m* crier, herald; auctioneer.
praecōgitō, -āre *vt* to premeditate.
praecognitus *adj* foreseen.
praecolō, -olere, -oluī, -ultum *vt* to cultivate early.
praecompositus *adj* studied.
praecōnium, -ī *and* **iī** *nt* office of a crier; advertisement; commendation.
praecōnius *adj* of a public crier.
praecōnsūmō, -ere, -ptum *vt* to use up beforehand.
praecontrectō, -āre *vt* to consider beforehand.
praecordia, -ōrum *ntpl* midriff; stomach; breast, heart; mind.
praecorrumpō, -umpere, -ūpī, -uptum *vt* to bribe beforehand.
praecox, -cis *adj* early, premature.
praecultus *ppp of* **praecolō.**
praecurrentia, -ium *ntpl* antecedents.
praecurrō, -rrere, -currī *and* **rrī, -rsum** *vi* to hurry on before, precede; to excel ♦ *vt* to anticipate; to surpass.
praecursiō, -ōnis *f* previous occurrence; (*RHET*) preparation.
praecursor, -ōris *m* advance guard; scout.
praecutiō, -ere *vt* to brandish before.
praeda, -ae *f* booty, plunder; (*animal*) prey; (*fig*) gain.
praedābundus *adj* plundering.
praedamnō, -āre *vt* to condemn beforehand.
praedātiō, -ōnis *f* plundering.
praedātor, -ōris *m* plunderer.
praedātōrius *adj* marauding.
praedēlassō, -āre *vt* to weaken beforehand.
praedēstinō, -āre *vt* to predetermine.

praediātor, -ōris m buyer of landed estates.
praediātōrius adj relating to the sale of
estates.
praedicābilis adj laudatory.
praedicātiō, -ōnis f proclamation;
commendation.
praedicātor, -ōris m eulogist.
praedicō, -āre, -āvī, -ātum vt to proclaim,
make public; to declare; to praise, boast.
praedīcō, -īcere, -īxī, -ictum vt to mention
beforehand, prearrange; to foretell; to
warn, command.
praedictiō, -ōnis f foretelling.
praedictum, -ī nt prediction; command;
prearrangement.
praedictus ppp of **praedīcō.**
praediolum, -ī nt small estate.
praediscō, -ere vt to learn beforehand.
praedispositus adj arranged beforehand.
praeditus adj endowed, provided.
praedium, -ī and **iī** nt estate.
praedīves, -itis adj very rich.
praedō, -ōnis m robber, pirate.
praedor, -ārī, -ātus vt, vi to plunder, rob; (fig)
to profit.
praedūcō, -ūcere, -ūxī, -uctum vt to draw in
front.
praedulcis adj very sweet.
praedūrus adj very hard, very tough.
praeēmineō, -ēre vt to surpass.
praeeō, -īre, -īvī and **iī, -itum** vi to lead the
way, go first; (formula) to dictate, recite first
♦ vt to precede, outstrip.
praeesse infin of **praesum.**
praefātiō, -ōnis f formula; preface.
praefātus ppa of **praefor.**
praefectūra, -ae f superintendence;
governorship; Italian town governed by Roman
edicts, prefecture; district, province.
praefectus ppp of **praeficiō** ♦ m overseer,
director, governor, commander; ~ **classis**
admiral; ~ **legiōnis** colonel; ~ **urbis** or **urbī**
city prefect (of Rome).
praeferō, -ferre, -tulī, -lātum vt to carry in
front, hold out; to prefer; to show, display; to
anticipate; (pass) to hurry past, outflank.
praeferōx, -ōcis adj very impetuous, very
insolent.
praefervidus adj very hot.
praefestīnō, -āre vi to be too hasty; to hurry
past.
praefica, -ae f hired mourner.
praeficiō, -icere, -ēcī, -ectum vt to put in
charge, give command over.
praefīdēns, -entis adj over-confident.
praefīgō, -gere, -xī, -xum vt to fasten in
front, set up before; to tip, point; to transfix.
praefīniō, -īre, -īvī and **iī, -ītum** vt to
determine, prescribe.
praefīscinē, -ī adv without offence.

praeflōrō, -āre vt to tarnish.
praefluō, -ere vt, vi to flow past.
praefocō, -āre vt to choke.
praefodiō, -odere, -ōdī vt to dig in front of;
to bury beforehand.
praefor, -ārī, -ātus vt, vi to say in advance,
preface; to pray beforehand; to predict.
praefrāctē adv resolutely.
praefrāctus ppp of **praefringō** ♦ adj abrupt;
stern.
praefrīgidus adj very cold.
praefringō, -ingere, -ēgī, -āctum vt to break
off, shiver.
praefuī perf of **praesum.**
praefulciō, -cīre, -sī, -tum vt to prop up; to
use as a prop.
praefulgeō, -ulgēre, -ulsī vt to shine
conspicuously; to outshine.
praegelidus adj very cold.
praegestiō, -īre vi to be very eager.
praegnāns, -antis adj pregnant; full.
praegracilis adj very slim.
praegrandis adj very large, very great.
praegravis adj very heavy; very wearisome.
praegravō, -āre vt to weigh down; to eclipse.
praegredior, -dī, -ssus vt, vi to go before; to
go past; to surpass.
praegressiō, -ōnis f precession, precedence.
praegustātor, -ōris m taster.
praegustō, -āre vt to taste beforehand.
praehibeō, -ēre vt to offer, give.
praeiaceō, -ēre vt to lie in front of.
praeiūdicium, -ī and **iī** nt precedent, example;
prejudgment.
praeiūdicō, -āre, -āvī, -ātum vt to prejudge,
decide beforehand.
praeiuvō, -āre vt to give previous assistance
to.
praelabor, -bī, -psus vt, vi to move past, move
along.
praelambō, -ere vt to lick first.
praelātus ppp of **praeferō.**
praelegō, -ere vt to coast along.
praeligō, -āre vt to bind, tie up.
praelongus adj very long, very tall.
praeloquor, -quī, -cūtus vi to speak first.
praelūceō, -cēre, -xī vi to light, shine; to
outshine.
praelūstris adj very magnificent.
praemandāta ntpl warrant of arrest.
praemandō, -āre, -āvī, -ātum vt to bespeak.
praemātūrē adv too soon.
praemātūrus adj too early, premature.
praemedicātus adj protected by charms.
praemeditātiō, -ōnis f thinking over the
future.
praemeditātus adj premeditated.
praemeditor, -ārī, -ātus vt to think over,
practise.
praemetuenter adv anxiously.

praemetuō, -ere *vi* to be anxious ♦ *vt* to fear the future.

praemissus *ppp of* **praemittō**.

praemittō, -ittere, -īsī, -issum *vt* to send in advance.

praemium, -ī *and* **iī** *nt* prize, reward.

praemolestia, -ae *f* apprehension.

praemōlior, -īrī *vt* to prepare thoroughly.

praemoneō, -ēre, -uī, -itum *vt* to forewarn, foreshadow.

praemonitus, -ūs *m* premonition.

praemōnstrātor, -ōris *m* guide.

praemōnstrō, -āre *vt* to guide; to predict.

praemordeō, -ēre *vt* to bite off; to pilfer.

praemorior, -ī, -tuus *vi* to die too soon.

praemūniō, -īre, -īvī, -ītum *vt* to fortify, strengthen, secure.

praemūnītiō, -ōnis *f* (*RHET*) preparation.

praenārrō, -āre *vt* to tell beforehand.

praenatō, -āre *vt* to flow past.

Praeneste, -is *nt/f* Latin town (*now* Palestrina).

Praenestīnus *adj see n.*

praeniteō, -ēre, -uī *vi* to seem more attractive.

praenōmen, -inis *nt* first name.

praenōscō, -ere *vt* to foreknow.

praenōtiō, -ōnis *f* preconceived idea.

praenūbilus *adj* very gloomy.

praenūntia, -iae *f* harbinger.

praenūntiō, -āre *vt* to foretell.

praenūntius, -ī *and* **iī** *m* harbinger.

praeoccupō, -āre, -āvī, -ātum *vt* to take first, anticipate.

praeolit mihi I get a hint of.

praeoptō, -āre, -āvī, -ātum *vt* to choose rather, prefer.

praepandō, -ere *vt* to spread out; to expound.

praeparātiō, -ōnis *f* preparation.

praeparō, -āre, -āvī, -ātum *vt* to prepare, prepare for; **ex ~ātō** by arrangement.

praepediō, -īre, -īvī, -ītum *vt* to shackle, tether; to hamper.

praependeō, -ēre *vi* to hang down in front.

praepes, -etis *adj* swift, winged; of good omen ♦ *f* bird.

praepilātus *adj* tipped with a ball.

praepinguis *adj* very rich.

praepolleō, -ēre *vi* to be very powerful, be superior.

praeponderō, -āre *vt* to outweigh.

praepōnō, -ōnere, -osuī, -ositum *vt* to put first, place in front; to put in charge, appoint commander; to prefer.

praeportō, -āre *vt* to carry before.

praepositiō, -ōnis *f* preference; (*GRAM*) preposition.

praepositus *ppp of* **praepōnō** ♦ *m* overseer, commander.

praepossum, -sse, -tuī *vi* to gain the upper hand.

praeposterē *adv* the wrong way round.

praeposterus *adj* inverted, perverted; absurd.

praepotēns, -entis *adj* very powerful.

praeproperanter *adv* too hastily.

praeproperē *adv* too hastily.

praeproperus *adj* overhasty, rash.

praepūtium, -ī *and* **iī** *nt* foreskin.

praequam *adv* compared with.

praequestus *adj* complaining beforehand.

praeradiō, -āre *vt* to outshine.

praerapidus *adj* very swift.

praereptus *ppp of* **praeripiō**.

praerigēscō, -ēscere, -uī *vi* to become very stiff.

praeripiō, -ipere, -ipuī, -eptum *vt* to take before, forestall; to carry off prematurely; to frustrate.

praerōdō, -dere, -sum *vt* to bite the end of, nibble off.

praerogātīva, -ae *f* tribe or century with the first vote, the first vote; previous election; omen, sure token.

praerogātīvus *adj* voting first.

praerōsus *ppp of* **praerōdō**.

praerumpō, -umpere, -ūpī, -uptum *vt* to break off.

praeruptus *ppp of* **praerumpō** ♦ *adj* steep, abrupt; headstrong.

praes, -aedis *m* surety; property of a surety.

praesaep- *etc see* **praesēp-**.

praesāgiō, -īre *vt* to have a presentiment of, forebode.

praesāgītiō, -ōnis *f* foreboding.

praesāgium, -ī *and* **iī** *nt* presentiment; prediction.

praesāgus *adj* foreboding, prophetic.

praesciō, -īre, -iī *vt* to know before.

praescīscō, -ere *vt* to find out beforehand.

praescius *adj* foreknowing.

praescrībō, -bere, -psī, -ptum *vt* to write first; to direct, command; to dictate, describe; to put forward as a pretext.

praescrīptiō, -ōnis *f* preface, heading; order, rule; pretext.

praescrīptum, -ī *nt* order, rule.

praescrīptus *ppp of* **praescrībō**.

praesecō, -āre, -uī, -tum *and* **-ātum** *vt* to cut off, pare.

praesēns, -entis *adj* present, in person; (*things*) immediate, ready, prompt; (*mind*) resolute; (*gods*) propitious ♦ *ntpl* present state of affairs; **in ~ēns** for the present; **~in rē ~entī** on the spot.

praesēnsiō, -ōnis *f* foreboding; preconception.

praesēnsus *ppp of* **praesentiō**.

praesentārius *adj* instant, ready.

praesentia, -ae *f* presence; effectiveness.

praesentiō, -entīre, -ēnsī, -ēnsum *vt* to presage, have a foreboding of.

praesēpe, -is *nt*, **-ēs, -is** *f* stable, fold, pen; hovel; hive.

praesēpiō, -īre, -sī, -tum *vt* to barricade.

praesēpis *f* = **praesēpe**.

praesertim *adv* especially.

praeserviō, -īre *vi* to serve as a slave.

praeses, -idis *m* guardian, protector; chief, ruler.

praesideō, -idēre, -ēdī *vi* to guard, defend; to preside over, direct.

praesidiārius *adj* garrison-.

praesidium, -ī *and* **iī** *nt* defence, protection; support, assistance; guard, garrison, convoy; defended position, entrenchment.

praesignificō, -āre *vt* to foreshadow.

praesignis *adj* conspicuous.

praesonō, -āre, -uī *vi* to sound before.

praespargō, -ere *vt* to strew before.

praestābilis *adj* outstanding; preferable.

praestāns, -antis *pres p of* **praestō** ♦ *adj* outstanding, pre-eminent.

praestantia, -ae *f* pre-eminence.

praestes, -itis *adj* presiding, guardian.

praestīgiae, -ārum *fpl* illusion, sleight of hand.

praestīgiātor, -ōris *m*, **-rīx, -rīcis** *f* conjurer, cheat.

praestinō, -āre *vt* to buy.

praestitī *perf of* **praestō**.

praestituō, -uere, -uī, -ūtum *vt* to prearrange, prescribe.

praestitus *ppp of* **praestō**.

praestō *adv* at hand, ready.

praestō, -āre, -itī, -itum *and* **ātum** *vi* to be outstanding, be superior; (*impers*) it is better ♦ *vt* to excel; to be responsible for, answer for; (*duty*) to discharge, perform; (*quality*) to show, prove; (*things*) to give, offer, provide; **sē ~** behave, prove.

praestōlor, -ārī, -ātus *vt, vi* to wait for, expect.

praestrictus *ppp of* **praestringō**.

praestringō, -ingere, -inxī, -ictum *vt* to squeeze; to blunt, dull; (*eyes*) to dazzle.

praestruō, -ere, -xī, -ctum *vt* to block up; to build beforehand.

praesul, -is *m/f* public dancer.

praesultātor, -ōris *m* public dancer.

praesultō, -āre *vi* to dance before.

praesum, -esse, -fuī *vi* (*with dat*) to be at the head of, be in command of; to take the lead; to protect.

praesūmō, -ere, -psī, -ptum *vt* to take first; to anticipate; to take for granted.

praesūtus *adj* sewn over at the point.

praetemptō, -āre *vt* to feel for, grope for; to test in advance.

praetendō, -dere, -dī, -tum *vt* to hold out, put before, spread in front of; to give as an excuse, allege.

praetentō *etc see* **praetemptō**.

praetentus *ppp of* **praetendō** ♦ *adj* lying over against.

praetepeō, -ēre, -uī *vi* to glow before.

praeter *adv* beyond; excepting ♦ *prep* (*with acc*) past, along; except, besides; beyond, more than, in addition to, contrary to.

praeteragō, -ere *vt* to drive past.

praeterbitō, -ere *vt, vi* to pass by.

praeterdūcō, -ere *vt* to lead past.

praetereā *adv* besides; moreover; henceforth.

praetereō, -īre, -iī, -itum *vi* to go past ♦ *vt* to pass, overtake; to escape, escape the notice of; to omit, leave out, forget, neglect; to reject, exclude; to surpass; to transgress.

praeterequitāns, -antis *adj* riding past.

praeterfluō, -ere *vt, vi* to flow past.

praetergredior, -dī, -ssus *vt* to pass, march past; to surpass.

praeterhāc *adv* further, more.

praeteritus *ppp of* **praetereō** ♦ *adj* past, gone by ♦ *ntpl* the past.

praeterlābor, -bī, -psus *vt* to flow past, move past ♦ *vi* to slip away.

praeterlātus *adj* driving, flying past.

praetermeō, -āre *vi* to pass by.

praetermissiō, -ōnis *f* omission, passing over.

praetermittō, -ittere, -īsī, -issum *vt* to let pass; to omit, neglect; to make no mention of; to overlook.

praeterquam *adv* except, besides.

praetervectiō, -ōnis *f* passing by.

praetervehor, -hī, -ctus *vt, vi* to ride past, sail past; to march past; to pass by, pass over.

praetervolō, -āre *vt, vi* to fly past; to escape.

praetexō, -ere, -uī, -tum *vt* to border, fringe; to adorn; to pretend, disguise.

praetextātus *adj* wearing the toga praetexta, under age.

praetextus *ppp of* **praetexō** ♦ *adj* wearing the toga praetexta ♦ *f* toga with a purple border; Roman tragedy ♦ *nt* pretext.

praetextus, -ūs *m* splendour; pretence.

praetimeō, -ēre *vi* to be afraid in advance.

praetinctus *adj* dipped beforehand.

praetor, -ōris *m* chief magistrate, commander; praetor; propraetor, governor.

praetōriānus *adj* of the emperor's bodyguard.

praetōrium, -ī *and* **iī** *nt* general's tent, camp headquarters; governor's residence; council of war; palace, grand building; emperor's bodyguard.

praetōrius *adj* praetor's, praetorian; of a propraetor; of the emperor's bodyguard ♦ *m* ex-praetor; **~ia cohors** bodyguard of general *or* emperor; **porta ~ia** camp gate facing the enemy.

praetorqueō, -ēre *vt* to strangle first.

praetrepidāns, -antis *adj* very impatient.

praetruncō, -āre *vt* to cut off.

praetulī *perf of* **praeferō**.

praetūra, -ae *f* praetorship.

Noun declensions and verb conjugations are shown on pp xiii to xxv. The present infinitive ending of a verb shows to which conjugation it belongs: **-āre** = 1st; **-ēre** = 2nd; **-ere** = 3rd and **-īre** = 4th. Irregular verbs are shown on p xxvi

praeumbrāns, -antis *adj* obscuring.
praeūstus *adj* hardened at the point; frostbitten.
praeut *adv* compared with.
praevaleō, -ēre, -uī *vi* to be very powerful, have most influence, prevail.
praevalidus *adj* very strong, very powerful; too strong.
praevāricātiō, -ōnis *f* collusion.
praevāricātor, -ōris *m* advocate guilty of collusion.
praevāricor, -ārī, -ātus *vi* (*with dat*) to favour by collusion.
praevehor, -hī, -ctus *vi* to ride, fly in front, flow past.
praeveniō, -enīre, -ēnī, -entum *vt, vi* to come before; to anticipate, prevent.
praeverrō, -ere *vt* to sweep before.
praevertō, -ere, -ī; -or, -ī *vt* to put first, prefer; to turn to first, attend first to; to oustrip; to anticipate, frustrate, prepossess.
praevideō, -idēre, -īdī, -īsum *vt* to foresee.
praevitiō, -āre *vt* to taint beforehand.
praevius *adj* leading the way.
praevolō, -āre *vi* to fly in front.
pragmaticus *adj* of affairs ♦ *m* legal expert.
prandeō, -ēre, -ī *vi* to take lunch ♦ *vt* to eat.
prandium, -ī *and* **iī** *nt* lunch.
prānsor, -ōris *m* guest at lunch.
prānsus *adj* having lunched, fed.
prasinus *adj* green.
prātēnsis *adj* meadow.
prātulum, -ī *nt* small meadow.
prātum, -ī *nt* meadow; grass.
prāvē *adv* wrongly, badly.
prāvitās, -ātis *f* irregularity; perverseness, depravity.
prāvus *adj* crooked, deformed; perverse, bad, wicked.
Prāxitelēs, -is *m* famous Greek sculptor.
Prāxitelius *adj see* n.
precāriō *adv* by request.
precārius *adj* obtained by entreaty.
precātiō, -ōnis *f* prayer.
precātor, -ōris *m* intercessor.
preces *pl of* **prex.**
preciae, -ārum *fpl* kind of vine.
precor, -ārī, -ātus *vt, vi* to pray, beg, entreat; to wish (well), curse.
prehendō, -endere, -endī, -ēnsum *vt* to take hold of, catch; to seize, detain; to surprise; (*eye*) to take in; (*mind*) to grasp.
prehēnsō *etc see* **prēnsō.**
prehēnsus *ppp of* **prehendō.**
prēlum, -ī *nt* wine press, oil press.
premō, -mere, -ssī, -ssum *vt* to press, squeeze; to press together, compress; (*eyes*) to close; (*reins*) to tighten; (*trees*) to prune; to press upon, lie, sit, stand on, cover, conceal, surpass; to press hard on, follow closely; (*coast*) to hug; to press down, lower, burden; (*fig*) to overcome, rule; (*words*) to disparage; to press in, sink, stamp, plant; to press back,

repress, check, stop.
prendō *etc see* **prehendō.**
prēnsātiō, -ōnis *f* canvassing.
prēnsō (prehēnsō), -āre, -āvī, -ātum *vt* to clutch at, take hold of, buttonhole.
prēnsus *ppp of* **prehendō.**
presbyter, -ī *m* (*ECCL*) elder.
pressē *adv* concisely, accurately, simply.
pressī *perf of* **premō.**
pressiō, -ōnis *f* fulcrum.
pressō, -āre *vt* to press.
pressus *ppp of* **premō** ♦ *adj* (*style*) concise, compressed; (*pace*) slow; (*voice*) subdued.
pressus, -ūs *m* pressure.
prēster, -ēris *m* waterspout.
pretiōsē *adv* expensively.
pretiōsus *adj* valuable, expensive; extravagant.
pretium, -ī *and* **iī** *nt* price, value; worth; money, fee, reward; **māgnī ~ī, in ~iō** valuable; **operae ~** worth while.
prex, -ecis *f* request, entreaty; prayer; good wish; curse.
Priamēis, -ēidis *f* Cassandra.
Priamēius *adj see* **Priamus.**
Priamidēs, -idae *m* son of Priam.
Priamus, -ī *m* king of Troy.
Priāpus, -ī *m* god of fertility and of gardens.
prīdem *adv* long ago, long.
prīdiē *adv* the day before.
prīmaevus *adj* youthful.
prīmānī, -ōrum *mpl* soldiers of the 1st legion.
prīmārius *adj* principal, first-rate.
prīmigenus *adj* original.
prīmipīlāris, -is *m* chief centurion.
prīmipīlus, -ī *m* chief centurion.
prīmitiae, -ārum *fpl* first fruits.
prīmitus *adv* originally.
prīmō *adv* at first; firstly.
prīmōrdium, -ī *and* **iī** *nt* beginning; **~ia rērum** atoms.
prīmōris *adj* first, foremost, tip of; principal ♦ *mpl* nobles; (*MIL*) front line.
prīmulum *adv* first.
prīmulus *adj* very first.
prīmum *adv* first, to begin with, in the first place; for the first time; **cum, ubi, ut ~** as soon as; **quam ~** as soon as possible; **~ dum** in the first place.
prīmus *adj* first, foremost, tip of; earliest; principal, most eminent; **~ veniō** I am the first to come; **prīma lūx** dawn, daylight; **~ō mēnse** at the beginning of the month; **~īs digitīs** with the fingertips; **~ās agere** play the leading part; **~ās dare** give first place to; **in ~īs** in the front line; especially.
prīnceps, -ipis *adj* first, in front, chief, most eminent ♦ *m* leader, chief; first citizen, emperor; (*MIL*) company, captain, captaincy ♦ *pl* (*MIL*) the second line.
prīncipālis *adj* original; chief; the emperor's.
prīncipātus, -ūs *m* first place; post of commander-in-chief; emperorship.

prīncipiālis *adj* from the beginning.
prīncipium, -ī *and* **iī** *nt* beginning, origin; first to vote ♦ *pl* first principles; (*MIL*) front line; camp headquarters.
prior, -ōris (*nt* **-us**) *adj* former, previous, first; better, preferable ♦ *mpl* forefathers.
prīscē *adv* strictly.
prīscus *adj* former, ancient, old-fashioned.
prīstinus *adj* former, original; of yesterday.
prius *adv* previously, before; in former times; ~ **quam** before, sooner than.
prīvātim *adv* individually, privately; at home.
prīvātiō, -ōnis *f* removal.
prīvātus *adj* individual, private; not in public office ♦ *m* private citizen.
Prīvernās, -ātis *adj see n.*
Prīvernum, -ī *nt* old Latin town.
prīvīgna, -ae *f* stepdaughter.
prīvīgnus, -ī *m* stepson; *pl* stepchildren.
prīvilēgium, -ī *and* **iī** *nt* law in favour of *or* against an individual.
prīvō, -āre, -āvī, -ātum *vt* to deprive, rob; to free.
prīvus *adj* single, one each; own, private.
prō *adv* (*with* **ut** *and* **quam**) in proportion (as) ♦ *prep* (*with abl*) in front of, on the front of; for, on behalf of, instead of, in return for; as, as good as; according to, in proportion to, by virtue of; ~ **eō ac** just as; ~ **eō quod** just because; ~ **eō quantum, ut** in proportion as.
prō *interj* (*expressing wonder or sorrow*) O!, alas!
proāgorus, -ī *m* chief magistrate (*in Sicilian towns*).
proavītus *adj* ancestral.
proavus, -ī *m* great-grandfather, ancestor.
probābilis *adj* laudable; credible, probable.
probābilitās, -ātis *f* credibility.
probābiliter *adv* credibly.
probātiō, -ōnis *f* approval; testing.
probātor, -ōris *m* approver.
probātus *adj* tried, excellent; acceptable.
probē *adv* well, properly; thoroughly, well done!
probitās, -ātis *f* goodness, honesty.
probō, -āre, -āvī, -ātum *vt* to approve, approve of; to appraise; to recommend; to prove, show.
probrōsus *adj* abusive; disgraceful.
probrum, -ī *nt* abuse, reproach; disgrace; infamy, unchastity.
probus *adj* good, excellent; honest, upright.
procācitās, -ātis *f* impudence.
procāciter *adv* insolently.
procāx, -ācis *adj* bold, forward, insolent.
prōcēdō, -ēdere, -essī, -essum *vi* to go forward, advance; to go out, come forth; (*time*) to go on, continue; (*fig*) to make progress, get on; (*events*) to turn out, succeed.
procella, -ae *f* hurricane, storm; (*MIL*) charge.

procellōsus *adj* stormy.
procer, -is *m* chief, noble, prince.
prōcēritās, -ātis *f* height; length.
prōcērus *adj* tall; long.
prōcessiō, -ōnis *f* advance.
prōcessus, -ūs *m* advance, progress.
prōcidō, -ere, -ī *vi* to fall forwards, fall down.
prōcinctus, -ūs *m* readiness (for action).
prōclāmātor, -ōris *m* bawler.
prōclāmō, -āre *vi* to cry out.
prōclīnātus *adj* tottering.
prōclīnō, -āre *vt* to bend.
prōclīvē *adv* downwards; easily.
prōclīvis, -us *adj* downhill, steep; (*mind*) prone, willing; (*act*) easy; **in ~ī** easy.
prōclīvitās, -ātis *f* descent; tendency.
prōclīvus *etc see* **prōclīvis**.
Procnē, -ēs *f* wife of Tereus (*changed to a swallow*); swallow.
prōcōnsul, -is *m* proconsul, governor.
prōcōnsulāris *adj* proconsular.
prōcōnsulātus, -ūs *m* proconsulship.
prōcrāstinātiō, -ōnis *f* procrastination.
prōcrāstinō, -āre *vt* to put off from day to day.
prōcreātiō, -ōnis *f* begetting.
prōcreātor, -ōris *m* creator, parent.
prōcreātrīx, -īcis *f* mother.
prōcreō, -āre *vt* to beget, produce.
prōcrēscō, -ere *vi* to be produced, grow up.
Procrūstēs, -ae *m* Attic highwayman (*who tortured victims on a bed*).
prōcubō, -āre *vi* to lie on the ground.
prōcūdō, -dere, -dī, -sum *vt* to forge; to produce.
procul *adv* at a distance, far, from afar.
prōculcō, -āre *vt* to trample down.
prōcumbō, -mbere, -buī, -bitum *vi* to fall forwards, bend over; to sink down, be broken down.
prōcūrātiō, -ōnis *f* management; (*religion*) expiation.
prōcūrātor, -ōris *m* administrator, financial agent; (*province*) governor.
prōcūrātrīx, -īcis *f* governess.
prōcūrō, -āre, -āvī, -ātum *vt* to take care of, manage; to expiate ♦ *vi* to be a procurator.
prōcurrō, -rrere, -currī *and* **rrī, -rsum** *vi* to rush forward; to jut out.
prōcursātiō, -ōnis *f* charge.
prōcursātor, -ōris *m* skirmisher.
prōcursō, -āre *vi* to make a sally.
prōcursus, -ūs *m* charge.
prōcurvus *adj* curving forwards.
procus, -ī *m* nobleman.
procus, -ī *m* wooer, suitor.
Procyōn, -ōnis *m* Lesser Dog Star.
prōdeambulō, -āre *vi* to go out for a walk.
prōdeō, -īre, -iī, -itum *vi* to come out, come forward, appear; to go ahead, advance; to

project.

prōdesse _infin of_ **prōsum**.

prōdīcō, -īcere, -īxī, -ictum _vt_ to appoint, adjourn.

prōdictātor, -ōris _m_ vice-dictator.

prōdige _adv_ extravagantly.

prōdigentia, -ae _f_ profusion.

prōdigiāliter _adv_ unnaturally.

prōdigiōsus _adj_ unnatural, marvellous.

prōdigium, -ī _and_ **iī** _nt_ portent; unnatural deed; monster.

prōdigō, -igere, -ēgī, -āctum _vt_ to squander.

prōdigus _adj_ wasteful; lavish, generous.

prōditiō, -ōnis _f_ betrayal.

prōditor, -ōris _m_ traitor.

prōditus _ppp of_ **prōdō**.

prōdō, -ere, -idī, -itum _vt_ to bring forth, produce; to make known, publish; to betray, give up; (_tradition_) to hand down.

prōdoceō, -ēre _vt_ to preach.

prodromus, -ī _m_ forerunner.

prōdūcō, -ūcere, -ūxī, -uctum _vt_ to bring forward, bring out; to conduct; to drag in front; to draw out, extend; (_acting_) to perform; (_child_) to beget, bring up; (_fact_) to bring to light; (_innovation_) to introduce; (_rank_) to promote; (_slave_) to put up for sale; (_time_) to prolong, protract, put off; (_tree_) to cultivate; (_vowel_) to lengthen.

prōductē _adv_ long.

prōductiō, -ōnis _f_ lengthening.

prōductō, -āre _vt_ to spin out.

prōductus _ppp of_ **prōdūcō** ♦ _adj_ lengthened, long.

proēgmenon, -ī _nt_ a preferred thing.

proeliātor, -ōris _m_ fighter.

proelior, -ārī, -ātus _vi_ to fight, join battle.

proelium, -ī _and_ **iī** _nt_ battle, conflict.

profānō, -āre _vt_ to desecrate.

profānus _adj_ unholy, common; impious; ill-omened.

profātus _ppa of_ **profor**.

profectiō, -ōnis _f_ departure; source.

profectō _adv_ really, certainly.

profectus _ppa of_ **proficīscor**.

prōfectus _ppp of_ **prōficiō**.

prōfectus, -ūs _m_ growth, progress, profit.

prōferō, -ferre, -tulī, -lātum _vt_ to bring forward, forth or out; to extend, enlarge; (_time_) to prolong, defer; (_instance_) to mention, quote; (_knowledge_) to publish, reveal; **pedem ~** proceed; **signa ~** advance.

professiō, -ōnis _f_ declaration; public register; profession.

professor, -ōris _m_ teacher.

professōrius _adj_ authoritative.

professus _ppa of_ **profiteor**.

profēstus _adj_ not holiday, working.

prōficiō, -icere, -ēcī, -ectum _vi_ to make progress, profit; to be of use.

proficīscor, -icīscī, -ectus _vi_ to set out, start; to originate, proceed.

profiteor, -itērī, -essus _vt_ to declare,

profess; to make an official return of; to promise, volunteer.

prōflīgātor, -ōris _m_ spendthrift.

prōflīgātus _adj_ dissolute.

prōflīgō, -āre, -āvī, -ātum _vt_ to dash to the ground; to destroy, overthrow; to bring almost to an end; to degrade.

prōflō, -āre _vt_ to breathe out.

prōfluēns, -entis _pres p of_ **prōfluō** ♦ _adj_ flowing; fluent ♦ _f_ running water.

prōfluenter _adv_ easily.

prōfluentia, -ae _f_ fluency.

prōfluō, -ere, -xī _vi_ to flow on, flow out; (_fig_) to proceed.

prōfluvium, -ī _and_ **iī** _nt_ flowing.

profor, -ārī, -ātus _vi_ to speak, give utterance.

profugiō, -ugere, -ūgī _vi_ to flee, escape; to take refuge (with) ♦ _vt_ to flee from.

profugus _adj_ fugitive; exiled; nomadic.

prōfuī _perf of_ **prōsum**.

profundō, -undere, -ūdī, -ūsum _vt_ to pour out, shed; to bring forth, produce; to prostrate; to squander; **sē ~** burst forth, rush out.

profundus _adj_ deep, vast, high; infernal; (_fig_) profound, immoderate ♦ _nt_ depths, abyss.

profūsē _adv_ in disorder, extravagantly.

profūsus _ppp of_ **profundō** ♦ _adj_ lavish; excessive.

prōgener, -ī _m_ grandson-in-law.

prōgenerō, -āre _vt_ to beget.

prōgeniēs, -ēī _f_ descent; offspring, descendants.

prōgenitor, -ōris _m_ ancestor.

prōgignō, -ignere, -enuī, -enitum _vt_ to beget, produce.

prōgnātus _adj_ born, descended ♦ _m_ son, descendant.

Prognē _see_ **Procnē**.

prognōstica, -ōrum _ntpl_ weather signs.

prōgredior, -dī, -ssus _vi_ to go forward, advance; to go out.

prōgressiō, -ōnis _f_ advancing, increase; (_RHET_) climax.

prōgressus _ppa of_ **prōgredior**.

prōgressus, -ūs _m_ advance, progress; (_events_) march.

prōh _see_ **prō** _interj_.

prohibeō, -ēre, -uī, -itum _vt_ to hinder, prevent; to keep away, protect; to forbid.

prohibitiō, -ōnis _f_ forbidding.

prōiciō, -icere, -iēcī, -iectum _vt_ to throw down, fling forwards; to banish; (_building_) to make project; (_fig_) to discard, renounce; to forsake; (_words_) to blurt out; (_time_) to defer; **sē ~** rush forward, run into danger; to fall prostrate.

prōiectiō, -ōnis _f_ forward stretch.

prōiectus _ppp of_ **prōiciō** ♦ _adj_ projecting, prominent; abject, useless; downcast; addicted (to).

prōiectus, -ūs _m_ jutting out.

proinde, proin _adv_ consequently, therefore;

just (as).

prōlābor, -bī, -psus *vi* to slide, move forward; to fall down; (*fig*) to go on, come to; to slip out; to fail, fall, sink into ruin.

prōlāpsiō, -ōnis *f* falling.

prōlāpsus *ppa of* **prōlābor.**

prōlātiō, -ōnis *f* extension; postponement; adducing.

prōlātō, -āre *vt* to extend; to postpone.

prōlātus *ppp of* **prōferō.**

prōlectō, -āre *vt* to entice.

prōlēs, -is *f* offspring; child; descendants, race.

prōlētārius, -ī *and* **iī** *m* citizen of the lowest class.

prōliciō, -cere, -xī *vt* to entice.

prōlixē *adv* fully, copiously, willingly.

prōlixus *adj* long, wide, spreading; (*person*) obliging; (*CIRCS*) favourable.

prōlogus, -ī *m* prologue.

prōloquor, -quī, -cūtus *vt* to speak out.

prōlubium, -ī *and* **iī** *nt* inclination.

prōlūdō, -dere, -sī, -sum *vi* to practise.

prōluō, -uere, -uī, -ūtum *vt* to wash out, wash away.

prōlūsiō, -ōnis *f* prelude.

prōluviēs, -ēī *f* flood; excrement.

prōmereō, -ēre, -uī; prōmereor, -ērī, -itus *vt* to deserve, earn.

prōmeritum, -ī *nt* desert, merit, guilt.

Promētheus, -eī *and* **eos** *m* demigod who stole fire from the gods.

Promēthēus *adj see n.*

prōminēns, -entis *pres p of* **prōmineō** ♦ *adj* projecting ♦ *nt* headland, spur.

prōmineō, -ēre, -uī *vi* to jut out, overhang; to extend.

prōmiscam, -ē, -uē *adv* indiscriminately.

prōmiscuus (prōmiscus) *adj* indiscriminate, in common; ordinary; open to all.

prōmīsī *perf of* **prōmittō.**

prōmissiō, -ōnis *f* promise.

prōmissor, -ōris *m* promiser.

prōmissum, -ī *nt* promise.

prōmissus *ppp of* **prōmittō** ♦ *adj* long.

prōmittō, -ittere, -īsī, -issum *vt* to let grow; to promise, give promise of.

prōmō, -ere, -psī, -ptum *vt* to bring out, produce; to disclose.

prōmont- *etc see* **prōmunt-.**

prōmōtus *ppp of* **prōmoveō** ♦ *ntpl* preferable things.

prōmoveō, -ovēre, -ōvī, -ōtum *vt* to move forward, advance; to enlarge; to postpone; to disclose.

prōmpsī *perf of* **prōmō.**

prōmptē *adv* readily; easily.

prōmptō, -āre *vt* to distribute.

prōmptū *abl m:* in ~ at hand, in readiness; obvious, in evidence; easy.

prōmptus *ppp of* **prōmō** ♦ *adj* at hand, ready; prompt, resolute; easy.

prōmulgātiō, -ōnis *f* promulgating.

prōmulgō, -āre, -āvī, -ātum *vt* to make public, publish.

prōmulsis, -idis *f* hors d'oeuvre.

prōmunturium, -ī *and* **iī** *nt* headland, promontory, ridge.

prōmus, -ī *m* cellarer, butler.

prōmūtuus *adj* as a loan in advance.

prōnepōs, -ōtis *m* great-grandson.

pronoea, -ae *f* providence.

prōnōmen, -inis *nt* pronoun.

prōnuba, -ae *f* matron attending a bride.

prōnūntiātiō, -ōnis *f* declaration; (*RHET*) delivery; (*logic*) proposition.

prōnūntiātor, -ōris *m* narrator.

prōnūntiātum, -ātī *nt* proposition.

prōnūntiō, -āre, -āvī, -ātum *vt* to declare publicly, announce; to recite, deliver; to narrate; to nominate.

prōnurus, -ūs *f* granddaughter-in-law.

prōnus *adj* leaning forward; headlong, downwards; sloping, sinking; (*fig*) inclined, disposed, favourable; easy.

prooemium, -ī *and* **iī** *nt* prelude, preface.

propāgātiō, -ōnis *f* propagating; extension.

propāgātor, -ōris *m* enlarger.

propāgō, -āre, -āvī, -ātum *vt* to propagate; to extend; to prolong.

propāgō, -inis *f* (*plant*) layer, slip; (*men*) offspring, posterity.

prōpalam *adv* openly, known.

prōpatulum, -ī *nt* open space.

prōpatulus *adj* open.

prope *adv* (*comp* **propius,** *superl* **proximē**) near; nearly ♦ *prep* (*with acc*) near, not far from.

propediem *adv* very soon.

prōpellō, -ellere, -ulī, -ulsum *vt* to drive, push forward, impel; to drive away, keep off.

propemodum, -o *adv* almost.

prōpendeō, -endēre, -endī, -ēnsum *vi* to hang down; to preponderate; to be disposed (to).

propēnsē *adv* willingly.

propēnsiō, -ōnis *f* inclination.

propēnsus *adj* inclining; inclined, well-disposed; important.

properanter *adv* hastily, quickly.

properantia, -ae *f* haste.

properātiō, -ōnis *f* haste.

properātō *adv* quickly.

properātus *adj* speedy.

properē *adv* quickly.

properipēs, -edis *adj* swiftfooted.

properō, -āre, -āvī, -ātum *vt* to hasten, do with haste ♦ *vi* to make haste, hurry.

Propertius, -ī *m* Latin elegiac poet.

properus *adj* quick, hurrying.

Noun declensions and verb conjugations are shown on pp xiii to xxv. The present infinitive ending of a verb shows to which conjugation it belongs: **-āre** = 1st; **-ēre** = 2nd; **-ere** = 3rd and **-īre** = 4th. Irregular verbs are shown on p xxvi

prōpexus *adj* combed forward.
propīnō, -āre *vt* to drink as a toast; to pass on (a cup).
propinquitās, -ātis *f* nearness; relationship, friendship.
propinquō, -āre *vi* to approach ♦ *vt* to hasten.
propinquus *adj* near, neighbouring; related ♦ *mf* relation ♦ *nt* neighbourhood.
propior, -ōris *adj* nearer; more closely related, more like; (*time*) more recent.
propitiō, -āre *vt* to appease.
propitius *adj* favourable, gracious.
propius *adv* nearer, more closely.
propōla, -ae *f* retailer.
prōpolluō, -ere *vt* to defile further.
prōpōnō, -ōnere, -osuī, -ositum *vt* to set forth, display; to publish, declare; to propose, resolve; to imagine; to expose; (*logic*) to state the first premise; **ante oculōs** ~ picture to oneself.
Propontiacus *adj see n.*
Propontis, -idis *and* **idos** *f* Sea of Marmora.
prōporrō *adv* furthermore; utterly.
prōportiō, -ōnis *f* symmetry, analogy.
prōpositiō, -ōnis *f* purpose; theme; (*logic*) first premise.
prōpositum, -ī *nt* plan, purpose; theme; (*logic*) first premise.
prōpositus *ppp of* **prōpōnō**.
prōpraetor, -ōris *m* propraetor, governor; vice-praetor.
propriē *adv* properly, strictly; particularly.
proprietās, -ātis *f* peculiarity, property.
proprītim *adv* properly.
proprius *adj* one's own, peculiar; personal, characteristic; permanent; (*words*) literal, regular.
propter *adv* near by ♦ *prep* (*with acc*) near, beside; on account of; by means of.
proptereā *adv* therefore.
prōpudium, -ī *and* **iī** *nt* shameful act; villain.
prōpugnāculum, -ī *nt* bulwark, tower; defence.
prōpugnātiō, -ōnis *f* defence.
prōpugnātor, -ōris *m* defender, champion.
prōpugnō, -āre *vi* to make a sortie; to fight in defence.
prōpulsātiō, -ōnis *f* repulse.
prōpulsō, -āre, -āvī, -ātum *vt* to repel, avert.
prōpulsus *ppp of* **prōpellō**.
Propylaea, -ōrum *ntpl* gateway to the Acropolis of Athens.
prō quaestōre *m* proquaestor.
prōquam *conj* according as.
prōra, -ae *f* prow, bows; ship.
prōrēpō, -ere, -sī, -tum *vi* to crawl out.
prōrēta -ae *m* man at the prow.
prōreus, -eī *m* man at the prow.
prōripiō, -ipere, -ipuī, -eptum *vt* to drag out; to hurry away; **sē** ~ rush out, run away.
prōrogātiō, -ōnis *f* extension; deferring.
prōrogō, -āre, -āvī, -ātum *vt* to extend, prolong, continue; to defer.

prōrsum *adv* forwards; absolutely.
prōrsus *adv* forwards; absolutely; in short.
prōrumpō, -umpere, -ūpī, -uptum *vt* to fling out; (*pass*) to rush forth ♦ *vi* to break out, burst forth.
prōruō, -ere, -ī, -tum *vt* to throw down, demolish ♦ *vi* to rush forth.
prōruptus *ppp of* **prōrumpō**.
prōsāpia, -ae *f* lineage.
proscaenium, -ī *and* **iī** *nt* stage.
proscindō, -ndere, -dī, -ssum *vt* to plough up; (*fig*) to revile.
prōscrībō, -bere, -psī, -ptum *vt* to publish in writing; to advertise; to confiscate; to proscribe, outlaw.
prōscrīptiō, -ōnis *f* advertisement; proscription.
prōscrīpturiō, -īre *vi* to want to have a proscription.
prōscrīptus *ppp of* **prōscrībō** ♦ *m* outlaw.
prōsecō, -āre, -uī, -tum *vt* to cut off (for sacrifice).
prōsēminō, -āre *vt* to scatter; to propagate.
prōsentiō, -entīre, -ēnsī *vt* to see beforehand.
prōsequor, -quī, -cūtus *vt* to attend, escort; to pursue, attack; to honour (with); (*words*) to proceed with, continue.
Proserpina, -ae *f* Proserpine (*daughter of Ceres and wife of Pluto*).
proseucha, -ae *f* place of prayer.
prōsiliō, -īre, -uī *vi* to jump up, spring forward; to burst out, spurt.
prōsocer, -ī *m* wife's grandfather.
prōspectō, -āre *vt* to look out at, view; to look forward to, await; (*place*) to look towards.
prōspectus *ppp of* **prōspiciō**.
prōspectus, -ūs *m* sight, view, prospect; gaze.
prōspeculor, -ārī *vi* to look out, reconnoitre ♦ *vt* to watch for.
prosper, prosperus *adj* favourable, successful.
prosperē *adv see adj.*
prosperitās, -ātis *f* good fortune.
prosperō, -āre *vt* to make successful, prosper.
prosperus *etc see* **prosper**.
prōspicientia, -ae *f* foresight.
prōspiciō, -icere, -exī, -ectum *vi* to look out, watch; to see to, take precautions ♦ *vt* to descry, watch for; to foresee; to provide; (*place*) to command a view of.
prōsternō, -ernere, -rāvī, -rātum *vt* to throw in front, prostrate; to overthrow, ruin; **sē** ~ fall prostrate; to demean oneself.
prōstibulum, -ī *nt* prostitute.
prōstituō, -uere, -uī, -ūtum *vt* to put up for sale, prostitute.
prōstō, -āre, -itī *vi* to project; to be on sale; to prostitute oneself.
prōstrātus *ppp of* **prōsternō**.
prōsubigō, -ere *vt* to dig up.

prōsum, -desse, -fuī vi (with dat) to be useful to, benefit.

Prōtagorās, -ae m Greek sophist (native of Abdera).

prōtēctus ppp of **prōtegō**.

prōtegō, -egere, -ēxī, -ēctum vt to cover over, put a projecting roof on; (fig) to shield, protect.

prōtēlō, -āre vt to drive off.

prōtēlum, -ī nt team of oxen; (fig) succession.

prōtendō, -dere, -dī, -tum vt to stretch out, extend.

prōtentus ppp of **prōtendō**.

prōterō, -erere, -rīvī, -rītum vt to trample down, crush; to overthrow.

prōterreō, -ēre, -uī, -itum vt to scare away.

protervē adv insolently; boldly.

protervitās, -ātis f forwardness, insolence.

protervus adj forward, insolent, violent.

Prōtesilāēus adj see n.

Prōtesilāus, -ī m first Greek killed at Troy.

Prōteus, -eī and **eos** m seagod with power to assume many forms.

prothȳmē adv gladly.

prōtinam adv immediately.

prōtinus adv forward, onward; continuously; right away, forthwith.

prōtollō, -ere vt to stretch out; to put off.

prōtractus ppp of **prōtrahō**.

prōtrahō, -here, -xī, -ctum vt to draw on (to); to drag out; to bring to light, reveal.

prōtrītus ppp of **prōterō**.

prōtrūdō, -dere, -sī, -sum vt to thrust forward, push out; to postpone.

prōtulī perf of **prōferō**.

prōturbō, -āre, -āvī, -ātum vt to drive off; to overthrow.

prout conj according as.

prōvectus ppp of **prōvehō** ♦ adj advanced.

prōvehō, -here, -xī, -ctum vt to carry along, transport; to promote, advance, bring to; (speech) to prolong; (pass) to drive, ride, sail on.

prōveniō, -enīre, -ēnī, -entum vi to come out, appear; to arise, grow; to go on, prosper, succeed.

prōventus, -ūs m increase; result, success.

prōverbium, -ī and **iī** nt saying, proverb.

prōvidēns, -entis pres p of **prōvideō** ♦ adj prudent.

prōvidenter adv with foresight.

prōvidentia, -ae f foresight, forethought.

prōvideō, -idēre, -īdī, -īsum vi to see ahead; to take care, make provision ♦ vt to foresee; to look after, provide for; to obviate.

prōvidus adj foreseeing, cautious, prudent; provident.

prōvincia, -ae f sphere of action, duty, province.

prōvinciālis adj provincial ♦ mpl provincials.

prōvīsiō, -ōnis f foresight; precaution.

prōvīsō adv with forethought.

prōvīsō, -ere vi to go and see.

prōvīsor, -ōris m foreseer; provider.

prōvīsus ppp of **prōvideō**.

prōvīsus, -ūs m looking forward; foreseeing; providing providence.

prōvīvō, -vere, -xī vi to live on.

prōvocātiō, -ōnis f challenge; appeal.

prōvocātor, -ōris m kind of gladiator.

prōvocō, -āre, -āvī, -ātum vt to challenge, call out; to provoke; to bring about ♦ vi to appeal.

prōvolō, -āre vi to fly out, rush out.

prōvolvō, -vere, -vī, -ūtum vt to roll forward, tumble over; (pass) to fall down, humble oneself, be ruined; sē ~ wallow.

prōvomō, -ere vt to belch forth.

proximē adv next, nearest; (time) just before or after; (with acc) next to, very close to, very like.

proximitās, -ātis f nearness; near relationship; similarity.

proximus adj nearest, next; (time) previous, last, following, next; most akin, most like ♦ m next of kin ♦ nt next door.

proxum etc see **proxim-**.

prūdēns, -entis adj foreseeing, aware; wise, prudent, circumspect; skilled, versed (in).

prūdenter adv prudently; skilfully.

prūdentia, -ae f prudence, discretion; knowledge.

pruīna, -ae f hoar frost.

pruīnōsus adj frosty.

prūna, -ae f live coal.

prūnitius adj of plum tree wood.

prūnum, -ī nt plum.

prūnus, -ī f plum tree.

prūriō, -īre vi to itch.

prytanēum, -ī nt Greek town hall.

prytanis, -is m Greek chief magistrate.

psallō, -ere vi to play the lyre or lute.

psaltērium, -ī and **iī** nt kind of lute.

psaltria, -ae f girl musician.

psecas, -adis f slave who perfumed the lady's hair.

psēphisma, -tis nt decree of the people.

Pseudocatō, -ōnis m sham Cato.

pseudomenos, -ī m sophistical argument.

pseudothyrum, -ī nt back door.

psithius adj psithian (kind of Greek vine).

psittacus, -ī m parrot.

psychomantēum (-īum), -ī nt place of necromancy.

-pte enclitic (to pronouns) self, own.

ptisanārium, -ī and **iī** nt gruel.

Ptolemaeēus, -us adj see n.

Ptolemaeus, -ī m Ptolemy (name of Egyptian kings).

pūbēns, -entis adj full-grown; (plant) juicy.

pūbertās, -ātis *f* manhood; signs of puberty.
pūbēs (pūber), -eris *adj* grown up, adult;
(*plant*) downy.
pūbēs, -is *f* hair at age of puberty; groin;
youth, men, people.
pūbēscō, -ēscere, -uī *vi* to grow to manhood,
become mature; to become clothed.
pūblicānus *adj* of public revenue ♦ *m* tax
farmer.
pūblicātiō, -ōnis *f* confiscation.
pūblicē *adv* by *or* for the State, at the public
expense; all together.
pūblicitus *adv* at the public expense; in
public.
pūblicō, -āre, -āvī, -ātum *vt* to confiscate; to
make public.
Pūblicola, -ae *m* P. Valerius (*an early Roman
consul*).
pūblicum, -ī *nt* State revenue; State territory;
public.
pūblicus *adj* of the State, public, common ♦ *m*
public official; **~a causa** criminal trial; **rēs ~a**
the State; **dē ~ō** at the public expense; **in ~ō**
in public.
Pūblius, -ī Roman first name.
pudendus *adj* shameful.
pudēns, -entis *adj* bashful, modest.
pudenter *adv* modestly.
pudet, -ēre, -uit *and* **itum est** *vt* (*impers*) to
shame, be ashamed.
pudibundus *adj* modest.
pudīcē *adv* see *adj*.
pudīcitia, -ae *f* modesty, chastity.
pudīcus *adj* modest, chaste.
pudor, -ōris *m* shame, modesty, sense of
honour; disgrace.
puella, -ae *f* girl; sweetheart, young wife.
puellāris *adj* girlish, youthful.
puellula, -ae *f* little girl.
puellus, -ī *m* little boy.
puer, -ī *m* boy, child; son; slave.
puerīlis *adj* boyish, child's; childish, trivial.
puerīliter *adv* like a child; childishly.
pueritia, -ae *f* childhood, youth.
puerperium, -ī *and* **iī** *nt* childbirth.
puerperus *adj* to help childbirth ♦ *f* woman in
labour.
puertia *etc see* **pueritia.**
puerulus, -ī *m* little boy, slave.
pugil, -is *m* boxer.
pugilātiō, -iōnis *f*, **-us, -ūs** *m* boxing.
pugillāris *adj* that can be held in the hand ♦
mpl, ntpl writing tablets.
pugillātōrius *adj*: **follis ~** punchball.
pugiō, -ōnis *m* dirk, dagger.
pugiunculus, -ī *m* small dagger.
pugna, -ae *f* fight, battle.
pugnācitās, -ātis *f* fondness for a fight.
pugnāciter *adv* aggressively.
pugnāculum, -ī *nt* fortress.
pugnātor, -ōris *m* fighter.
pugnāx, -ācis *adj* fond of a fight, aggressive;
obstinate.

pugneus *adj* with the fist.
pugnō, -āre, -āvī, -ātum *vi* to fight; to
disagree; to struggle; **sēcum ~** be
inconsistent; **~ātum est** the battle was
fought.
pugnus, -ī *m* fist.
pulchellus *adj* pretty little.
pulcher, -rī *adj* beautiful, handsome; fine,
glorious.
pulchrē *adv* excellently; well done!
pulchritūdō, -inis *f* beauty, excellence.
pūlēium, pūlegium, -ī *and* **iī** *nt* pennyroyal.
pūlex, -icis *m* flea.
pullārius, -ī *and* **iī** *m* keeper of the sacred
chickens.
pullātus *adj* dressed in black.
pullulō, -āre *vi* to sprout.
pullus, -ī *m* young (of animals), chicken.
pullus *adj* dark-grey; mournful ♦ *nt* dark grey
clothes.
pulmentārium, -ārī *and* **-āriī, -um, -ī** *nt*
relish; food.
pulmō, -ōnis *m* lung.
pulmōneus *adj* of the lungs.
pulpa, -ae *f* fleshy part.
pulpāmentum, -ī *nt* tit-bits.
pulpitum, -ī *nt* platform, stage.
puls, pultis *f* porridge.
pulsātiō, -ōnis *f* beating.
pulsō, -āre, -āvī, -ātum *vt* to batter, knock,
strike.
pulsus *ppp of* **pellō.**
pulsus, -ūs *m* push, beat, blow; impulse.
pultiphagus, -ī *m* porridge eater.
pultō, -āre *vt* to beat, knock at.
pulvereus *adj* of dust, dusty, fine as dust;
raising dust.
pulverulentus *adj* dusty; laborious.
pulvillus, -ī *m* small cushion.
pulvīnar, -āris *nt* sacred couch; seat of
honour.
pulvīnus, -ī *m* cushion, pillow.
pulvis, -eris *m* dust, powder; arena; effort.
pulvisculus, -ī *m* fine dust.
pūmex, -icis *m* pumice stone; stone, rock.
pūmiceus *adj* of soft stone.
pūmicō, -āre *vt* to smooth with pumice stone.
pūmiliō, -ōnis *m/f* dwarf, pygmy.
pūnctim *adv* with the point.
pūnctum, -ī *nt* point, dot; vote; (*time*) moment;
(*speech*) short section.
pūnctus *ppp of* **pungō.**
pungō, -ere, pupugī, pūnctum *vt* to prick,
sting, pierce; (*fig*) to vex.
Pūnicānus *adj* in the Carthaginian style.
Pūnicē *adv* in Punic.
pūniceus *adj* reddish, purple.
Pūnicum, -ī *nt* pomegranate.
Pūnicus *adj* Punic, Carthaginian; purple-red.
pūniō (poeniō), -īre, -ior, -īrī *vt* to punish; to
avenge.
pūnītor, -ōris *m* avenger.
pūpa, -ae *f* doll.

pūpilla, -ae *f* ward; (*eye*) pupil.
pūpillāris *adj* of a ward, of an orphan.
pūpillus, -ī *m* orphan, ward.
puppis, -is *f* after part of a ship, stern; ship.
pupugī *perf of* **pungō**.
pūpula, -ae *f* (*eye*) pupil.
pūpulus, -ī *m* little boy.
pūrē *adv* cleanly, brightly; plainly, simply,
    purely, chastely.
pūrgāmen, -inis *nt* sweepings, dirt; means of
    expiation.
pūrgāmentum, -ī *nt* refuse, dirt.
pūrgātiō, -ōnis *f* purging; justification.
pūrgō, -āre, -āvī, -ātum *vt* to cleanse, purge,
    clear away; to exculpate, justify; to purify.
pūriter *adv* cleanly, purely.
purpura, -ae *f* purple-fish, purple; purple
    cloth; finery, royalty.
purpurātus *adj* wearing purple ♦ *m* courtier.
purpureus *adj* red, purple, black; wearing
    purple; bright, radiant.
purpurissum, -ī *nt* kind of rouge.
pūrus *adj* clear, unadulterated, free from
    obstruction *or* admixture; pure, clean; plain,
    unadorned; (*moral*) pure, chaste ♦ *nt* clear
    sky.
pūs, pūris *nt* pus; (*fig*) malice.
pusillus *adj* very little; petty, paltry.
pūsiō, -ōnis *m* little boy.
pūstula, -ae *f* pimple, blister.
putāmen, -inis *nt* peeling, shell, husk.
putātiō, -ōnis *f* pruning.
putātor, -ōris *m* pruner.
puteal, -ālis *nt* low wall round a well *or* sacred
    place.
puteālis *adj* well- (*in cpds*).
puteō, -ēre *vi* to stink.
Puteolānus *adj see n.*
Puteolī, -ōrum *mpl* town on the Campanian
    coast.
puter, putris, -ris *adj* rotten, decaying;
    crumbling, flabby.
putēscō, -ēscere, -uī *vi* to become rotten.
puteus, -ī *m* well; pit.
pūtidē *adv see* **pūtidus**.
pūtidiusculus *adj* somewhat nauseating.
pūtidus *adj* rotten, stinking; (*speech*) affected,
    nauseating.
putō, -āre, -āvī, -ātum *vt* to think, suppose;
    to think over; to reckon, count; (*money*) to
    settle; (*tree*) to prune.
pūtor, -ōris *m* stench.
putrefaciō, -facere, -fēcī, -factum *vt* to
    make rotten; to make crumble.
putrēscō, -ere *vi* to rot, moulder.
putridus *adj* rotten, decayed; withered.
putris *etc see* **puter**.
putus *adj* perfectly pure.
putus, -ī *m* boy.
pycta, -ēs, -ae *m* boxer.

Pydna, -ae *f* town in Macedonia.
Pydnaeus *adj see n.*
pȳga, -ae *f* buttocks.
Pygmaeus *adj* Pygmy.
Pyladēs, -ae *and* **is** *m* friend of Orestes.
Pyladēus *adj see n.*
Pylae, -ārum *fpl* Thermopylae.
Pylaicus *adj see n.*
Pylius *adj see n.*
Pylos, -ī *f* Pylus (Peloponnesian town, home of
    Nestor).
pyra, -ae *f* funeral pyre.
Pȳramaeus *adj see* **Pȳramus**.
pȳramis, -idis *f* pyramid.
Pȳramus, -ī *m* lover of Thisbe.
Pȳrēnē, -ēs *f* Pyrenees.
pyrethrum, -ī *nt* Spanish camomile.
Pyrgēnsis *adj see* **Pyrgī**.
Pyrgī, -ōrum *mpl* ancient town in Etruria.
pyrōpus, -ī *m* bronze.
Pyrrha, -ae *and* **ē, -ēs** *f* wife of Deucalion.
Pyrrhaeus *adj see n.*
Pyrrhō, -ōnis *m* Greek philosopher (*founder of
    the Sceptics*).
Pyrrhōnēus *adj see n.*
Pyrrhus, -ī *m* son of Achilles; king of Epirus,
    enemy of Rome.
Pȳthagorās, -ae *m* Greek philosopher who
    founded a school in S. Italy.
Pȳthagorēus, -icus *adj* Pythagorean.
Pȳthius, -icus *adj* Pythian, Delphic ♦ *m* Apollo
    ♦ *f* priestess of Apollo ♦ *ntpl* Pythian Games.
Pȳthō, -ūs *f* Delphi.
Pȳthōn, -ōnis *m* serpent killed by Apollo.
pȳtisma, -tis *nt* what is spit out.
pȳtissō, -āre *vi* to spit out wine.
pyxis, -dis *f* small box, toilet box.

Q, q

quā *adv* where, which way; whereby; as far as;
    partly . . . partly.
quācumque *adv* wherever; anyhow.
quādam: ~ tenus *adv* only so far.
quadra, -ae *f* square; morsel; table.
quadrāgēnī, -ōrum *adj* forty each.
quadrāgēsimus *adj* fortieth ♦ *f* 2 ½ per cent
    tax.
quadrāgiēns, -ēs *adv* forty times.
quadrāgintā *num* forty.
quadrāns, -antis *m* quarter; (*coin*) quarter as.
quadrantārius *adj* of a quarter.

Noun declensions and verb conjugations are shown on pp xiii to xxv. The present infinitive ending of a verb shows
to which conjugation it belongs: **-āre** = 1st; **-ēre** = 2nd; **-ere** = 3rd and **-īre** = 4th. Irregular verbs are shown on p xxvi

quadrātum, -ī nt square; (_ASTRO_) quadrature.
quadrātus ppp of **quadrō** ♦ adj square; **~ō agmine** in battle order.
quadriduum, -ī nt four days.
quadriennium, -ī and **iī** nt four years.
quadrifāriam adv in four parts.
quadrifidus adj split in four.
quadrīgae, -ārum fpl team of four; chariot.
quadrīgārius, -ī and **iī** m chariot racer.
quadrīgātus adj stamped with a chariot.
quadrīgulae, -ārum fpl little four horse team.
quadriiugī, -ōrum mpl team of four.
quadriiugis, -us adj of a team of four.
quadrilībris adj weighing four pounds.
quadrīmulus adj four years old.
quadrīmus adj four years old.
quadringēnārius adj of four hundred each.
quadringēnī, -ōrum adj four hundred each.
quadringentēsimus adj four-hundredth.
quadringentī, -ōrum num four hundred.
quadringentiēns, -ēs adv four hundred times.
quadripertītus adj fourfold.
quadrirēmis, -is f quadrireme.
quadrivium, -ī and **iī** nt crossroads.
quadrō, -āre vt to make square; to complete ♦ vi to square, fit, agree.
quadrum, -ī nt square.
quadrupedāns, -antis adj galloping.
quadrupēs, -edis adj four-footed, on all fours ♦ m/f quadruped.
quadruplātor, -ōris m informer, twister.
quadruplex, -icis adj four-fold.
quadruplum, -ī nt four times as much.
quaeritō, -āre vt to search diligently for; to earn (a living); to keep on asking.
quaerō, -rere, -sīvī and **siī, -sītum** vt to look for, search for; to seek, try to get; to acquire, earn; (_plan_) to think out, work out; (_question_) to ask, make inquiries; (_law_) to investigate; (_with infin_) to try, wish; **quid ~ris?** in short; **sī ~ris/~rimus** to tell the truth.
quaesītiō, -ōnis f inquisition.
quaesītor, -ōris m investigator, judge.
quaesītus ppp of **quaerō** ♦ adj special; far-fetched ♦ nt question ♦ ntpl gains.
quaesīvī perf of **quaerō**.
quaesō, -ere vt to ask, beg.
quaesticulus, -ī m slight profit.
quaestiō, -ōnis f seeking, questioning; investigation, research; criminal trial; court; **servum in ~ōnem ferre** take a slave for questioning by torture; **~ōnēs perpetuae** standing courts.
quaestiuncula, -ae f trifling question.
quaestor, -ōris m quaestor, treasury official.
quaestōrius adj of a quaestor ♦ m ex-quaestor ♦ nt quaestor's tent or residence.
quaestuōsus adj lucrative, productive; money-making; wealthy.
quaestūra, -ae f quaestorship; public money.
quaestus, -ūs m profit, advantage; money-making, occupation; **~uī habēre** make money

out of; **~um facere** make a living.
quālibet adv anywhere; anyhow.
quālis adj (_interrog_) what kind of?; (_relat_) such as, even as.
quāliscumque adj of whatever kind; any, whatever.
qualiscunque adj = **qualiscumque**.
quālitās, -ātis f quality, nature.
quāliter adv just as.
quālubet adv anywhere; anyhow.
quālus, -ī m wicker basket.
quam adv (_interrog, excl_) how?, how much?; (_comparison_) as, than; (_with superl_) as … as possible; (_emphatic_) very; **dīmidium ~ quod** half of what; **quīntō diē ~** four days after.
quamdiū adv how long?; as long as.
quamlibet, quamlubet adv as much as you like, however.
quamobrem adv (_interrog_) why?; (_relat_) why ♦ conj therefore.
quamquam conj although; and yet.
quamvīs adv however, ever so ♦ conj however much, although.
quānam adv what way.
quandō adv (_interrog_) when?; (_relat_) when; (_with sī, nē, num_) ever ♦ conj when; since.
quandōcumque, quandocunque adv whenever, as often as; some day.
quandōque adv whenever; some day ♦ conj seeing that.
quandō quidem conj seeing that, since.
quanquam etc see **quamquam**.
quantillus adj how little, how much.
quantopere adv how much; (_after_ **tantopere**) as.
quantulus adj how little, how small.
quantuluscumque adj however small, however trifling.
quantum adv how much; as much as; **~cumque** as much as ever; **~libet** however much; **~vīs** as much as you like; although.
quantus adj how great; so great as, such as; **~ī** how dear, how highly; **~ō** (_with compar_) how much; the; **in ~um** as far as.
quantuscumque adj however great, whatever size.
quantuslibet adj as great as you like.
quantus quantus adj however great.
quantusvīs adj however great.
quāpropter adv why; and therefore.
quāquā adv whatever way.
quārē adv how, why; whereby; and therefore.
quartadecumānī, -ōrum mpl men of the fourteenth legion.
quartānus adj every four days ♦ f quartan fever ♦ mpl men of the fourth legion.
quartārius, -ī and **iī** m quarter pint.
quartus adj fourth; **quartum/quartō** for the fourth time.
quartusdecimus adj fourteenth.
quasi adv as if; as it were; (_numbers_) about.
quasillus, -ī m, **-um, -ī** nt wool basket.
quassātiō, -ōnis f shaking.

quassō, -āre, -āvī, -ātum *vt* to shake, toss; to shatter, damage.

quassus *ppp of* **quatiō** ♦ *adj* broken.

quatefaciō, -facere, -fēcī *vt* to shake, give a jolt to.

quātenus *adv* (*interrog*) how far?; how long?; (*relat*) as far as; in so far as, since.

quater *adv* four times; ~ **deciēs** fourteen times.

quaternī, -ōrum *adj* four each, in fours.

quatiō, -tere, -ssum *vt* to shake, disturb, brandish; to strike, shatter; (*fig*) to agitate, harass.

quattuor *num* four.

quattuordecim *num* fourteen.

quattuorvirātus, -ūs *m* membership of quattuorviri.

quattuorvirī, -ōrum *mpl* board of four officials.

-que *conj* and; both . . . and; (*after neg*) but.

quemadmodum *adv* (*interrog*) how?; (*relat*) just as.

queō, -īre, -īvī *and* **iī, -itum** *vi* to be able to, can.

quercētum, -ī *nt* oak forest.

querceus *adj* of oak.

quercus, -ūs *f* oak; garland of oak leaves; acorn.

querēla, querella, -ae *f* complaint; plaintive sound.

queribundus *adj* complaining.

querimōnia, -ae *f* complaint; elegy.

queritor, -ārī *vi* to complain much.

quernus *adj* oak- (*in cpds*).

queror, -rī, -stus *vt, vi* to complain, lament; (*birds*) to sing.

querquetulānus *adj* of oakwoods.

querulus *adj* complaining; plaintive, warbling.

questus *ppa of* **queror**.

questus, -ūs *m* complaint, lament.

quī, quae, quod *pron* (*interrog*) what?, which?; (*relat*) who, which, that; what; and this, he, etc.; (*with sī, nisi, nē, num*) any.

quī *adv* (*interrog*) how?; (*relat*) with which, whereby; (*indef*) somehow; (*excl*) indeed.

quia *conj* because; ~**nam** why?

quicquam *nt see* **quisquam**.

quicque *nt see* **quisque**.

quicquid *nt see* **quisquis**.

quīcum with whom, with which.

quīcumque, quīcunque *pron* whoever, whatever, all that; every possible.

quid *nt see* **quis** ♦ *adv* why?

quīdam, quaedam, quoddam *pron* a certain, a sort of, a . . . .

quiddam *nt* something.

quidem *adv* (*emphatic*) in fact; (*qualifying*) at any rate; (*conceding*) it is true; (*alluding*) for instance; nē . . . ~ not even.

quidlibet *nt* anything.

quidnam *nt see* **quisnam**.

quidnī *adv* why not?

quidpiam *nt* = **quispiam**.

quidquam *nt* = **quisquam**.

quidquid *nt* = **quisquis**.

quiēs, -ētis *f* rest, peace, quiet; sleep, dream, death; neutrality; lair.

quiēscō, -scere, -vī, -tum *vi* to rest, keep quiet; to be at peace, keep neutral; to sleep; (*with acc and infin*) to stand by and see; (*with infin*) to cease.

quiētē *adv* peacefully, quietly.

quiētus *ppa of* **quiēscō** ♦ *adj* at rest; peaceful, neutral; calm, quiet, asleep.

quīlibet, quaelibet, quodlibet *pron* any, anyone at all.

quīn *adv* (*interrog*) why not?; (*correcting*) indeed, rather ♦ *conj* who not; but that, but, without; (*preventing*) from; (*doubting*) that.

quīnam, quaenam, quodnam *pron* which?, what?

Quīnct- *etc see* **Quīnt-**.

quīncūnx, -ūncis *m* five-twelfths; number five on a dice; in ~**ūncem dispositī** arranged in oblique lines.

quīndeciēns, -ēs *adv* fifteen times.

quīndecim *num* fifteen; ~ **prīmī** fifteen chief magistrates.

quīndecimvirālis *adj* of the council of fifteen.

quīndecimvirī, -ōrum *mpl* council of fifteen.

quīngēnī, -ōrum *adj* five hundred each.

quīngentēsimus *adj* five-hundredth.

quīngentī, -ōrum *num* five hundred.

quīngentiēns, -ēs *adv* five hundred times.

quīnī, -ōrum *adj* five each; five; ~ **dēnī** fifteen each; ~ **vīcēnī** twenty-five each.

quīnquāgēnī, -ōrum *adj* fifty each.

quīnquāgēsimus *adj* fiftieth ♦ *f* 2 per cent tax.

quīnquāgintā *num* fifty.

Quīnquātria, -iōrum *and* **ium** *ntpl* festival of Minerva.

Quīnquātrūs, -uum *fpl* festival of Minerva.

quīnque *num* five.

quīnquennālis *adj* quinquennial; lasting five years.

quīnquennis *adj* five years old; quinquennial.

quīnquennium, -ī *and* **iī** *nt* five years.

quīnquepartītus *adj* fivefold.

quīnqueprīmī, -ōrum *mpl* five leading men.

quīnquerēmis *adj* five-banked ♦ *f* quinquereme.

quīnquevirātus, -ūs *m* membership of the board of five.

quīnquevirī, -ōrum *mpl* board of five.

quīnquiēns, -ēs *adv* five times.

quīnquiplicō, -āre *vt* to multiply by five.

quīntadecimānī, -ōrum *mpl* men of the fifteenth legion.

quīntānus *adj* of the fifth ♦ *f* street in a camp

Noun declensions and verb conjugations are shown on pp xiii to xxv. The present infinitive ending of a verb shows to which conjugation it belongs: **-āre** = 1st; **-ēre** = 2nd; **-ere** = 3rd and **-īre** = 4th. Irregular verbs are shown on p xxvi

between the 5th and 6th maniples ♦ *mpl* men of the fifth legion.

Quintiliānus, -ī *m* Quintilian (*famous teacher of rhetoric in Rome*).

Quintīlis *adj* of July.

quintum, -ō *adv* for the fifth time.

Quintus, -ī *m* Roman first name.

quintus *adj* fifth.

quintusdecimus *adj* fifteenth.

quippe *adv* (*affirming*) certainly, of course ♦ *conj* (*explaining*) for in fact, because, since; ~ **quī** since I, he *etc*.

quippiam *etc see* **quispiam**.

quippinī *adv* certainly.

Quirīnālis *adj* of Romulus; Quirinal (*hill*).

Quirīnus, -ī *m* Romulus ♦ *adj* of Romulus.

Quiris, -ītis *m* inhabitant of Cures; Roman citizen; citizen.

quirītātiō, -ōnis *f* shriek.

Quirītēs *pl* inhabitants of Cures; Roman citizens.

quirītō, -āre *vi* to cry out, wail.

quis, quid *pron* who?, what?; (*indef*) anyone, anything.

quīs *poetic form of* **quibus**.

quisnam, quaenam, quidnam *pron* who?, what?

quispiam, quaepiam, quodpiam *and* **quidpiam** *pron* some, some one, something.

quisquam, quaequam, quicquam *and* **quidquam** *pron* any, anyone, anything; **nec ~** and no one.

quisque, quaeque, quodque *pron* each, every, every one; **quidque, quicque** everything; **decimus ~** every tenth; **optimus ~** all the best; **prīmus ~** the first possible.

quisquiliae, -ārum *fpl* refuse, rubbish.

quisquis, quaequae, quodquod, quidquid *and* **quicquid** *pron* whoever, whatever, all.

quīvīs, quaevīs, quodvīs, quidvīs *pron* any you please, anyone, anything.

quīvīscumque, quaevīscumque, quodvīscumque *pron* any whatsoever.

quō *adv* (*interrog*) where?; whither?; for what purpose?, what for?; (*relat*) where, to which (place), to whom; (*with compar*) the (more); (*with sī*) anywhere ♦ *conj* (*with subj*) in order that; **nōn ~** not that.

quoad *adv* how far?; how long? ♦ *conj* as far as, as long as; until.

quōcircā *conj* therefore.

quōcumque *adv* whithersoever.

quod *conj* as for, in that, that; because; why; **~ sī** but if.

quōdam modo *adv* in a way.

quoi, quōius *old forms of* **cui, cūius**.

quōlibet *adv* anywhere, in any direction.

quom *etc see* **cum** *conj*.

quōminus *conj* that not; (*preventing*) from.

quōmodo *adv* (*interrog*) how?; (*relat*) just as; **~cumque** howsoever; **~nam** how?

quōnam *adv* where, where to?

quondam *adv* once, formerly; sometimes;

(*fut*) one day.

quōniam *conj* since, seeing that.

quōpiam *adv* anywhere.

quōquam *adv* anywhere.

quoque *adv* also, too.

quōquō *adv* to whatever place, wherever.

quōquō modo *adv* howsoever.

quōquō versus, -um *adv* in every direction.

quōrsus, quōrsum *adv* where to?, in what direction?; what for?, to what end?

quot *adj* how many; as many as, every.

quotannīs *adv* every year.

quotcumque *adj* however many.

quotēnī, -ōrum *adj* how many.

quotīd- *etc see* **cottīd-**.

quotiēns, -ēs *adv* how often?; (*relat*) as often as.

quotiēnscumque *adv* however often.

quotquot *adj* however many.

quotumus *adj* which number?, what date?.

quotus *adj* what number, how many; **~ quisque** how few; **~a hōra** what time.

quotuscumque *adj* whatever number, however big.

quōusque *adv* how long, till when; how far.

quōvīs *adv* anywhere.

quum *etc see* **cum** *conj*.

R, r

rabidē *adv* furiously.

rabidus *adj* raving, mad; impetuous.

rabiēs, -em, -ē *f* madness, rage, fury.

rabiō, -ere *vi* to rave.

rabiōsē *adv* wildly.

rabiōsulus *adj* somewhat rabid.

rabiōsus *adj* furious, mad.

rabula, -ae *m* wrangling lawyer.

racēmifer, -ī *adj* clustered.

racēmus, -ī *m* stalk of a cluster; bunch of grapes; grape.

radiātus *adj* radiant.

rādīcitus *adv* by the roots; utterly.

rādīcula, -ae *f* small root.

radiō, -āre *vt* to irradiate ♦ *vi* to radiate, shine.

radius, -i *and* **iī** *m* stick, rod; (*light*) beam, ray; (*loom*) shuttle; (*MATH*) rod for drawing figures, radius of a circle; (*plant*) long olive; (*wheel*) spoke.

rādīx, -īcis *f* root; radish; (*hill*) foot; (*fig*) foundation, origin.

rādō, -dere, -sī, -sum *vt* to scrape, shave, scratch; to erase; to touch in passing, graze, pass along.

raeda, -ae *f* four-wheeled carriage.

raedārius, -ī and **iī** m driver.

Raetī, -ōrum mpl Alpine people between Italy and Germany.

Raetia, -iae f country of the Raetī.

Raeticus and **ius** and **us** adj see n.

rāmālia, -ium ntpl twigs, brushwood.

rāmentum, -ī nt shavings, chips.

rāmeus adj of branches.

rāmex, -icis m rupture, blood vessels of the lungs.

Ramnēnsēs, Ramnēs, -ium mpl one of the original Roman tribes; a century of equites.

rāmōsus adj branching.

rāmulus, -ī m twig, sprig.

rāmus, -ī m branch, bough.

rāna, -ae f frog; frogfish.

rancēns, -entis adj putrid.

rancidulus adj rancid.

rancidus adj rank, rancid; disgusting.

rānunculus, -ī m tadpole.

rapācida, -ae m son of a thief.

rapācitās, -ātis f greed.

rapāx, -ācis adj greedy, grasping, ravenous.

raphanus, -ī m radish.

rapidē adv swiftly, hurriedly.

rapiditās, -ātis f rapidity.

rapidus adj tearing, devouring; swift, rapid; hasty, impetuous.

rapīna, -ae f pillage, robbery; booty, prey.

rapiō, -ere, -uī, -tum vt to tear, snatch, carry off; to seize, plunder; to hurry, seize quickly.

raptim adv hastily, violently.

raptiō, -ōnis f abduction.

raptō, -āre, -āvī, -ātum vt to seize and carry off, drag away, move quickly; to plunder, lay waste; (passion) to agitate.

raptor, -ōris m plunderer, robber, ravisher.

raptus ppp of **rapiō** ♦ nt plunder.

raptus, -ūs m carrying off, abduction; plundering.

rāpulum, -ī nt small turnip.

rāpum, -ī nt turnip.

rārēfaciō, -facere, -fēcī, -factum (pass -fīō, -fierī) vt to rarefy.

rārēscō, -ere vi to become rarefied, grow thin; to open out.

rāritās, -ātis f porousness, open texture; thinness, fewness.

rārō, -ē adv seldom.

rārus adj porous, open in texture; thin, scanty; scattered, straggling, here and there; (MIL) in open order; few, infrequent; uncommon, rare.

rāsī perf of **rādō**.

rāsilis adj smooth, polished.

rāstrum, -ī nt hoe, mattock.

rāsus ppp of **rādō**.

ratiō, -ōnis f 1. (reckoning of) account, calculation; list, register; affair, business.

2. (relation) respect, consideration; procedure, method, system, way, kind.

3. (reason) reasoning, thought; cause, motive; science, knowledge, philosophy; ~ atque ūsus theory and practice; ~ est it is reasonable; **Stōicōrum** ~ Stoicism; **~ōnem dūcere, inīre** calculate; **~ōnem habēre** take account of, have to do with, consider; **~ōnem reddere** give an account of; **cum ~ōne** reasonably; **meae ~ōnēs** my interests; **ā ~ōnibus** accountant.

ratiōcinātiō, -ōnis f reasoning; syllogism.

ratiōcinātīvus adj syllogistic.

ratiōcinātor, -ōris m accountant.

ratiōcinor, -ārī, -ātus vt, vi to calculate; to consider; to argue, infer.

ratiōnālis adj rational; syllogistic.

ratis, -is f raft; boat.

ratiuncula, -ae f small calculation; slight reason; petty syllogism.

ratus ppa of **reor** ♦ adj fixed, settled, sure; valid; **prō ~ā (parte)** proportionally; **~um dūcere, facere, habēre** ratify.

raucisonus adj hoarse.

raucus adj hoarse; harsh, strident.

raudus, -eris nt copper coin.

raudusculum, -ī nt bit of money.

Ravenna, -ae f port in N.E. Italy.

Ravennās, -ātis adj see n.

rāvis, -im f hoarseness.

rāvus adj grey, tawny.

rea, -ae f defendant, culprit.

reāpse adv in fact, actually.

Reāte, -is nt ancient Sabine town.

Reātīnus adj see n.

rebelliō, -ōnis f revolt.

rebellātrīx, -īcis f rebellious.

rebelliō, -ōnis f revolt.

rebellis adj rebellious ♦ mpl rebels.

rebellium, -ī and **iī** nt revolt.

rebellō, -āre vi to revolt.

rebītō, -ere vi to return.

reboō, -āre vi to re-echo ♦ vt to make resound.

recalcitrō, -āre vi to kick back.

recaleō, -ēre vi to be warm again.

recalēscō, -ere vi to grow warm again.

recalfaciō, -facere, -fēcī vt to warm again.

recalvus adj bald in front.

recandēscō, -ēscere, -uī vi to whiten (in response to); to glow.

recantō, -āre, -āvī, -ātum vt to recant; to charm away.

reccidī perf of **recidō**.

recēdō, -ēdere, -essī, -essum vi to move back, withdraw, depart; (place) to recede; (head) to be severed.

recellō, -ere vi to spring back.

recēns, -entis adj fresh, young, recent; (writer) modern; (with ab) immediately after ♦ adv newly, just.

recēnseō, -ēre, -uī, -um *vt* to count; to review.

recēnsiō, -ōnis *f* revision.

recēnsus *ppp of* **recēnseō**.

recēpī *perf of* **recipiō**.

receptāculum, -ī *nt* receptacle, reservoir; refuge, shelter.

receptō, -āre *vt* to take back; to admit, harbour; to tug hard at.

receptor, -ōris *m* (male) receiver, shelterer.

receptrīx, -īcis *f* (female) receiver, shelterer.

receptum, -ī *nt* obligation.

receptus *ppp of* **recipiō**.

receptus, -ūs *m* withdrawal; retreat; return; refuge; **~uī canere** sound the retreat.

recessī *perf of* **recēdō**.

recessim *adv* backwards.

recessus, -ūs *m* retreat, departure; recess, secluded spot; (*tide*) ebb.

recidīvus *adj* resurrected; recurring.

recidō, -idere, -cidī, -āsum *vi* to fall back; to recoil, relapse; (*fig*) to fall, descend.

recīdō, -dere, -dī, -sum *vt* to cut back, cut off.

recingō, -gere, -ctum *vt* to ungird, loose.

recinō, -ere *vt, vi* to re-echo, repeat; to sound a warning.

reciper- *etc see* **recuper-**.

recipiō, -ipere, -ēpī, -eptum *vt* to take back, retake; to get back, regain, rescue; to accept, admit; (*MIL*) to occupy; (*duty*) to undertake; (*promise*) to pledge, guarantee; **sē ~** withdraw, retreat; **nōmen ~** receive notice of a prosecution.

reciprocō, -āre *vt* to move to and fro; (*ship*) to bring round to another tack; (*proposition*) to reverse ♦ *vi* (*tide*) to rise and fall.

reciprocus *adj* ebbing.

recīsus *ppp of* **recīdō**.

recitātiō, -ōnis *f* reading aloud, recital.

recitātor, -ōris *m* reader, reciter.

recitō, -āre, -āvī, -ātum *vt* to read out, recite.

reclāmātiō, -ōnis *f* outcry (*of disapproval*).

reclāmitō, -āre *vi* to cry out against.

reclāmō, -āre *vi* to cry out, protest; to reverberate.

reclīnis *adj* leaning back.

reclīnō, -āre, -āvī, -ātum *vt* to lean back.

reclūdō, -dere, -sī, -sum *vt* to open up; to disclose.

reclūsus *ppp of* **reclūdō**.

recoctus *ppp of* **recoquō**.

recōgitō, -āre *vi* to think over, reflect.

recognitiō, -ōnis *f* review.

recognōscō, -ōscere, -ōvī, -itum *vt* to recollect; to examine, review.

recolligō, -igere, -ēgī, -ēctum *vt* to gather up; (*fig*) to recover, reconcile.

recolō, -olere, -oluī, -ultum *vt* to recultivate; to resume; to reflect on, contemplate; to revisit.

recommīnīscor, -ī *vi* to recollect.

recompositus *adj* rearranged.

reconciliātiō, -ōnis *f* restoration, reconciliation.

reconciliō, -āre, -āvī, -ātum *vt* to win back again, restore, reconcile.

reconcinnō, -āre *vt* to repair.

reconditus *ppp of* **recondō** ♦ *adj* hidden, secluded; abstruse, profound; (*disposition*) reserved.

recondō, -ere, -idī, -itum *vt* to store away, stow; to hide away, bury.

reconflō, -āre *vt* to rekindle.

recoquō, -quere, -xī, -ctum *vt* to cook again, boil again; to forge again, recast; (*fig*) to rejuvenate.

recordātiō, -ōnis *f* recollection.

recordor, -ārī, -ātus *vt, vi* to recall, remember; to ponder over.

recreō, -āre, -āvī, -ātum *vt* to remake, reproduce; to revive, refresh.

recrepō, -āre *vt, vi* to ring, re-echo.

recrēscō, -scere, -vī *vi* to grow again.

recrūdēscō, -ēscere, -uī *vi* (*wound*) to open again; (*war*) to break out again.

rēctā *adv* straight forward, right on.

rēctē *adv* straight; correctly, properly, well; quite; (*inf*) good, all right, no thank you.

rēctiō, -ōnis *f* government.

rēctor, -ōris *m* guide, driver, helmsman; governor, master.

rēctum, -ī *nt* right, virtue.

rēctus *ppp of* **regō** ♦ *adj* straight; upright, steep; right, correct, proper; (*moral*) good, virtuous.

recubō, -āre *vi* to lie, recline.

recultus *ppp of* **recolō**.

recumbō, -mbere, -buī *vi* to lie down, recline; to fall, sink down.

recuperātiō, -ōnis *f* recovery.

recuperātor, -ōris *m* recapturer; (*pl*) *board of justices who tried civil cases requiring a quick decision, esp cases involving foreigners.*

recuperātōrius *adj* of the recuperatores.

recuperō, -āre, -āvī, -ātum *vt* to get back, recover, recapture.

recūrō, -āre *vt* to restore.

recurrō, -ere, -ī *vi* to run back; to return, recur; to revert.

recursō, -āre *vi* to keep coming back, keep recurring.

recursus, -ūs *m* return, retreat.

recurvō, -āre *vt* to bend back, curve.

recurvus *adj* bent, curved.

recūsātiō, -ōnis *f* refusal, declining; (*law*) objection, counterplea.

recūsō, -āre, -āvī, -ātum *vt* to refuse, decline, be reluctant; (*law*) to object, plead in defence.

recussus *adj* reverberating.

redāctus *ppp of* **redigō**.

redambulō, -āre *vi* to come back.

redamō, -āre *vt* to love in return.

redārdēscō, -ere *vi* to blaze up again.

redarguō, -ere, -ī *vt* to refute, contradict.
redauspicō, -āre *vi* to take auspices for going back.
redditus *ppp of* **reddō**.
reddō, -ere, -idī, -itum *vt* to give back, return, restore; to give in, response, repay; to give up, deliver, pay; (*copy*) to represent, reproduce; (*speech*) to report, repeat, recite, reply; to translate; (*with adj*) to make; **iūdicium ~** fix the date for a trial; **iūs ~** administer justice.
redēgī *perf of* **redigō**.
redēmī *perf of* **redimō**.
redemptiō, -ōnis *f* ransoming; bribing; (*revenue*) farming.
redemptō, -āre *vt* to ransom.
redemptor, -ōris *m* contractor.
redemptūra, -ae *f* contracting.
redemptus *ppp of* **redimō**.
redeō, -īre, -iī, -itum *vi* to go back, come back, return; (*speech*) to revert; (*money*) to come in; (*CIRCS*) to be reduced to, come to.
redhālō, -āre *vt* to exhale.
redhibeō, -ēre *vt* to take back.
redigō, -igere, -ēgī, -āctum *vt* to drive back, bring back; (*money*) to collect, raise; (*to a condition*) to reduce, bring; (*number*) to reduce; **ad irritum ~** make useless.
rediī *perf of* **redeō**.
redimīculum, -ī *nt* band.
redimiō, -īre, -iī, -ītum *vt* to bind, crown, encircle.
redimō, -imere, -ēmī, -emptum *vt* to buy back; to ransom, redeem; to release, rescue; (*good*) to procure; (*evil*) to avert; (*fault*) to make amends for; (*COMM*) to undertake by contract, hire.
redintegrō, -āre, -āvī, -ātum *vt* to restore, renew, refresh.
redipīscor, -ī *vt* to get back.
reditiō, -ōnis *f* returning.
reditus, -ūs *m* return, returning; (*money*) revenue.
redivīvus *adj* renovated.
redoleō, -ēre, -uī *vi* to give out a smell ♦ *vt* to smell of, smack of.
redomitus *adj* broken in again.
redōnō, -āre *vt* to restore; to give up.
redūcō, -ūcere, -ūxī, -uctum *vt* to draw back; to lead back, bring back; to escort home; to marry again; (*troops*) to withdraw; (*fig*) to restore; (*to a condition*) to make into.
reductiō, -ōnis *f* restoration.
reductor, -ōris *m* man who brings back.
reductus *ppp of* **redūcō** ♦ *adj* secluded, aloof.
reduncus *adj* curved back.
redundantia, -ae *f* extravagance.
redundō, -āre, -āvī, -ātum *vi* to overflow; to abound, be in excess; (*fig*) to stream.
reduvia, -ae *f* hangnail.

redux, -cis *adj* (*gods*) who brings back; (*men*) brought back, returned.
refectus *ppp of* **reficiō**.
refellō, -ere, -ī *vt* to disprove, rebut.
referciō, -cīre, -sī, -tum *vt* to stuff, cram, choke full.
referiō, -īre *vt* to hit back; to reflect.
referō, -ferre, -ttulī, -lātum *vt* to bring back, carry back; to give back, pay back, repay; to repeat, renew; (*authority*) to refer to, trace back to; (*blame, credit*) to ascribe; (*likeness*) to reproduce, resemble; (*memory*) to recall; (*news*) to report, mention; (*opinion*) to reckon amongst; (*record*) to enter; (*senate*) to lay before, move; (*speech*) to reply, say in answer; **grātiam ~** be grateful, requite; **pedem, gradum ~** return; retreat; **ratiōnēs ~** present an account; **sē ~** return.
rēfert, -ferre, -tulit *vi* (*impers*) it is of importance, it matters, it concerns; **meā ~** it matters to me.
refertus *ppp of* **referciō** ♦ *adj* crammed, full.
referveō, -ēre *vi* to boil over.
refervēscō, -ere *vi* to bubble up.
reficiō, -icere, -ēcī, -ectum *vt* to repair, restore; (*body, mind*) to refresh, revive; (*money*) to get back, get in return; (*POL*) to re-elect.
refigō, -gere, -xī, -xum *vt* to unfasten, take down; (*fig*) to annul.
refingō, -ere *vt* to remake.
refīxus *ppp of* **refīgō**.
reflāgitō, -āre *vt* to demand back.
reflātus, -ūs *m* contrary wind.
reflectō, -ctere, -xī, -xum *vt* to bend back, turn back; (*fig*) to bring back ♦ *vi* to give way.
reflexus *ppp of* **reflectō**.
reflō, -āre, -āvī, -ātum *vi* to blow contrary ♦ *vt* to breathe out again.
refluō, -ere *vi* to flow back, overflow.
refluus *adj* ebbing.
reformīdō, -āre *vt* to dread; to shun in fear.
reformō, -āre *vt* to reshape.
refōtus *ppp of* **refoveō**.
refoveō, -ovēre, -ōvī, -ōtum *vt* to refresh, revive.
refrāctāriolus *adj* rather stubborn.
refrāctus *ppp of* **refringō**.
refrāgor, -ārī, -ātus *vi* (*with dat*) to oppose, thwart.
refrēgī *perf of* **refringō**.
refrēnō, -āre, *vt* to curb, restrain.
refricō, -āre, -uī, -ātum *vt* to scratch open; to reopen, renew ♦ *vi* to break out again.
refrigerātiō, -ōnis *f* coolness.
refrigerō, -āre, -āvī, -ātum *vi* to cool, cool off; (*fig*) to flag.
refrīgēscō, -gēscere, -xī *vi* to grow cold; (*fig*) to flag, grow stale.

Noun declensions and verb conjugations are shown on pp xiii to xxv. The present infinitive ending of a verb shows to which conjugation it belongs: **-āre** = 1st; **-ēre** = 2nd; **-ere** = 3rd and **-īre** = 4th. Irregular verbs are shown on p xxvi

refringō, -ingere, -ēgī, -āctum _vt_ to break open; to break off; (_fig_) to break, check.

refrīxī _perf of_ **refrīgēscō**.

refugiō, -ugere, -ūgī _vi_ to run back, flee, shrink ♦ _vt_ to run away from, shun.

refugium, -ī _and_ **iī** _nt_ refuge.

refugus _adj_ fugitive, receding.

refulgeō, -gēre, -sī _vi_ to flash back, reflect light.

refundō, -undere, -ūdī, -ūsum _vt_ to pour back, pour out; (_pass_) to overflow.

refūsus _ppp of_ **refundō**.

refūtātiō, -ōnis _f_ refutation.

refūtātus, -ūs _m_ refutation.

refūtō, -āre, -āvī, -ātum _vt_ to check, repress; to refute, disprove.

rēgālis _adj_ king's, royal, regal.

rēgāliter _adv_ magnificently; tyrannically.

regerō, -rere, -ssī, -stum _vt_ to carry back, throw back.

rēgia, -ae _f_ palace; court; (_camp_) royal tent; (_town_) capital.

rēgiē _adv_ regally; imperiously.

rēgificus _adj_ magnificent.

regignō, -ere _vt_ to reproduce.

Rēgillānus _and_ **ēnsis** _adj see_ **Rēgillus**.

Rēgillus, -ī _m_ Sabine town; lake in Latium (_scene of a Roman victory over the Latins_).

regimen, -inis _nt_ guiding, steering; rudder; rule, command, government; ruler.

rēgīna, -ae _f_ queen, noblewoman.

Rēgīnus _adj see_ **Rēgium**.

regiō, -ōnis _f_ direction, line; boundary line; quarter, region; district, ward, territory; (_fig_) sphere, province; **ē ~ōne** in a straight line; (_with gen_) exactly opposite.

regiōnātim _adv_ by districts.

Rēgium, -ī _and_ **iī** _nt_ town in extreme S. of Italy, (_now_ Reggio).

rēgius _adj_ king's, kingly, royal; princely, magnificent.

reglūtinō, -āre _vt_ to unstick.

rēgnātor, -ōris _m_ ruler.

rēgnātrīx, -īcis _adj_ imperial.

rēgnō, -āre, -āvī, -ātum _vi_ to be king, rule, reign; to be supreme, lord it; (_things_) to prevail, predominate ♦ _vt_ to rule over.

rēgnum, -ī _nt_ kingship, monarchy; sovereignty, supremacy; despotism; kingdom; domain.

regō, -ere, rēxī, rēctum _vt_ to keep straight, guide, steer; to manage, direct; to control, rule, govern; **~ fīnēs** (_law_) mark out the limits.

regredior, -dī, -ssus _vi_ to go back, come back, return; (_MIL_) to retire.

regressus _ppa of_ **regredior**.

regressus, -ūs _m_ return; retreat.

rēgula, -ae _f_ rule, ruler; stick, board; (_fig_) rule, pattern, standard.

rēgulus, -ī _m_ petty king, chieftain; prince.

Rēgulus, -ī _m_ Roman consul taken prisoner by the Carthaginians.

regustō, -āre _vt_ to taste again.

rēiciō, -icere, -iēcī, -iectum _vt_ to throw back, throw over the shoulder, throw off; to drive back, repel; to cast off, reject; to reject with contempt, scorn; (_jurymen_) to challenge, refuse; (_matter for discussion_) to refer; (_time_) to postpone; **sē ~** fling oneself.

rēiectāneus _adj_ to be rejected.

rēiectiō, -ōnis _f_ rejection; (_law_) challenging.

rēiectō, -āre _vt_ to throw back.

rēiectus _ppp of_ **rēiciō**.

relābor, -bī, -psus _vi_ to glide back, sink back, fall back.

relanguēscō, -ēscere, -ī _vi_ to faint; to weaken.

relātiō, -ōnis _f_ (_law_) retorting; (_pl_) magistrate's report; (_RHET_) repetition.

relātor, -ōris _m_ proposer of a motion.

relātus _ppp of_ **referō**.

relātus, -ūs _m_ official report; recital.

relaxātiō, -ōnis _f_ easing.

relaxō, -āre, -āvī, -ātum _vt_ to loosen, open out; (_fig_) to release, ease, relax, cheer.

relēctus _ppp of_ **relegō**.

relēgātiō, -ōnis _f_ banishment.

relēgō, -āre, -āvī, -ātum _vt_ to send away, send out of the way; to banish; (_fig_) to reject; to refer, ascribe.

relegō, -egere, -ēgī, -ēctum _vt_ to gather up; (_place_) to traverse, sail over again; (_speech_) to go over again, reread.

relentēscō, -ere _vi_ to slacken off.

relēvī _perf of_ **relinō**.

relevō, -āre, -āvī, -ātum _vt_ to lift up; to lighten; (_fig_) to relieve, ease, comfort.

relictiō, -ōnis _f_ abandoning.

relictus _ppp of_ **relinquō**.

rēlicuus _etc see_ **reliquus**.

religātiō, -ōnis _f_ tying up.

religiō, -ōnis _f_ religious scruple, reverence, awe; religion; superstition; scruples, conscientiousness; holiness, sanctity (_in anything_); object of veneration, sacred place; religious ceremony, observance.

religiōsē _adv_ devoutly; scrupulously, conscientiously.

religiōsus _adj_ devout, religious; superstitious; involving religious difficulty; scrupulous, conscientious; (_objects_) holy, sacred.

religō, -āre, -āvī, -ātum _vt_ to tie up, fasten behind; (_ship_) to make fast, moor; (_fig_) to bind.

relinō, -inere, -ēvī _vt_ to unseal.

relinquō, -inquere, -īquī, -ictum _vt_ to leave, leave behind; to bequeath; to abandon, forsake; (_argument_) to allow; (_pass_) to remain.

rēliquiae, -ārum _fpl_ leavings, remainder, relics.

reliquus _adj_ remaining, left; (_time_) subsequent, future; (_debt_) outstanding ♦ _nt_ remainder, rest; arrears ♦ _mpl_ the rest; **~um est** it remains, the next point is; **~ī facere**

leave behind, leave over, omit; **in ~um** for
the future.

rell- _etc see_ **rel-**.

relūceō, -cēre, -xī _vi_ to blaze.

relūcēscō, -cēscere, -xī _vi_ to become bright
again.

reluctor, -ārī, -ātus _vi_ to struggle against,
resist.

remaneō, -anēre, -ānsī _vi_ to remain behind;
to remain, continue, endure.

remānō, -āre _vi_ to flow back.

remānsiō, -ōnis _f_ remaining behind.

remedium, -ī _and_ **iī** _nt_ cure, remedy,
medicine.

remēnsus _ppa of_ **remētior**.

remeō, -āre _vi_ to come back, go back, return.

remētior, -tīrī, -nsus _vt_ to measure again; to
go back over.

rēmex, -igis _m_ rower, oarsman.

Rēmī, -ōrum _mpl_ people of Gaul (_in region of
what is now_ Rheims).

rēmigātiō, -ōnis _f_ rowing.

rēmigium, -ī _and_ **iī** _nt_ rowing; oars; oarsmen.

rēmigō, -āre _vi_ to row.

remigrō, -āre _vi_ to move back, return (home).

reminīscor, -ī _vt, vi_ (_usu with gen_) to
remember, call to mind.

remisceō, -scēre, -xtum _vt_ to mix up,
mingle.

remissē _adv_ mildly, gently.

remissiō, -ōnis _f_ release; (_tension_)
slackening, relaxing; (_payment_) remission;
(_mind_) slackness, mildness, relaxation;
(_illness_) abating.

remissus _ppp of_ **remittō** ♦ _adj_ slack; negligent;
mild, indulgent, cheerful.

remittō, -ittere, -īsī, -issum _vt_ to let go back,
send back, release; to slacken, loosen, relax;
to emit, produce; (_mind_) to relax, relieve;
(_notion_) to discard, give up; (_offence, penalty_)
to let off, remit; (_right_) to resign, sacrifice;
(_sound_) to give back ♦ _vi_ to abate.

remixtus _ppp of_ **remisceō**.

remōlior, -īrī, -ītus _vt_ to heave back.

remollēscō, -ere _vi_ to become soft again, be
softened.

remolliō, -īre _vt_ to weaken.

remora, -ae _f_ hindrance.

remorāmina, -um _ntpl_ hindrances.

remordeō, -dēre, -sum _vt_ (_fig_) to worry,
torment.

remoror, -ārī, -ātus _vi_ to linger, stay behind
♦ _vt_ to hinder, delay, defer.

remorsus _ppp of_ **remordeō**.

remōtē _adv_ far.

remōtiō, -ōnis _f_ removing.

remōtus _ppp of_ **removeō** ♦ _adj_ distant, remote;
secluded; (_fig_) far removed, free from.

removeō, -ovēre, -ōvī, -ōtum _vt_ to move
back, withdraw, set aside; to subtract.

remūgiō, -īre _vi_ to bellow in answer, re-echo.

remulceō, -cēre, -sī _vt_ to stroke; (_tail_) to
droop.

remulcum, -ī _nt_ towrope.

remūnerātiō, -ōnis _f_ recompense, reward.

remūneror, -ārī, -ātus _vt_ to repay, reward.

remurmurō, -āre _vi_ to murmur in answer.

rēmus, -ī _m_ oar.

Remus, -ī _m_ brother of Romulus.

renārrō, -āre _vt_ to tell over again.

renāscor, -scī, -tus _vi_ to be born again; to
grow, spring up again.

renātus _ppa of_ **renāscor**.

renāvigō, -āre _vi_ to sail back.

reneō, -ēre _vt_ to unspin, undo.

rēnēs, -um _mpl_ kidneys.

renīdeō, -ēre _vi_ to shine back, be bright; to be
cheerful, smile, laugh.

renīdēscō, -ere _vi_ to reflect the gleam of.

renītor, -ī _vi_ to struggle, resist.

renō, -āre _vi_ to swim back.

rēnō, -ōnis _m_ fur.

renōdō, -āre _vt_ to tie back in a knot.

renovāmen, -inis _nt_ new condition.

renovātiō, -ōnis _f_ renewal; compound
interest.

renovō, -āre, -āvī, -ātum _vt_ to renew,
restore; to repair, revive, refresh; (_speech_)
to repeat; **faenus ~** take compound interest.

renumerō, -āre _vt_ to pay back.

renūntiātiō, -ōnis _f_ report, announcement.

renūntiō, -āre, -āvī, -ātum _vt_ to report, bring
back word; to announce, make an official
statement; (_election_) to declare elected,
return; (_duty_) to refuse, call off, renounce.

renūntius, -ī _and_ **iī** _m_ reporter.

renuō, -ere, -ī _vt, vi_ to deny, decline, refuse.

renūtō, -āre _vi_ to refuse firmly.

reor, rērī, ratus _vi_ to think, suppose.

repāgula, -ōrum _ntpl_ (_door_) bolts, bars.

repandus _adj_ curving back, turned up.

reparābilis _adj_ retrievable.

reparcō, -ere _vi_ to be sparing with, refrain.

reparō, -āre, -āvī, -ātum _vt_ to renew,
recover; to restore, repair; to purchase;
(_mind, body_) to refresh; (_troops_) to recruit.

repastinātiō, -ōnis _f_ digging up again.

repellō, -ellere, -pulī, -ulsum _vt_ to push
back, drive back, repulse; to remove, reject.

rependō, -endere, -endī, -ēnsum _vt_ to
return by weight; to pay, repay; to requite,
compensate.

repēns, -entis _adj_ sudden; new.

repēnsus _ppp of_ **rependō**.

repentē _adv_ suddenly.

repentīnō _adv_ suddenly.

repentīnus _adj_ sudden, hasty; upstart.

repercō _etc see_ **reparcō**.

repercussus _ppp of_ **repercutiō**.

repercussus, -ūs _m_ reflection, echo.

Noun declensions and verb conjugations are shown on pp xiii to xxv. The present infinitive ending of a verb shows
to which conjugation it belongs: **-āre** = 1st; **-ēre** = 2nd; **-ere** = 3rd and **-īre** = 4th. Irregular verbs are shown on p xxvi

repercutiō, -tere, -ssī, -ssum *vt* to make rebound, reflect, echo.

reperiō, -īre, repperī, -tum *vt* to find, find out; to get, procure; to discover, ascertain; to devise, invent.

repertor, -ōris *m* discoverer, inventor, author.

repertus *ppp of* **reperiō** ♦ *ntpl* discoveries.

repetītiō, -ōnis *f* repetition; (RHET) anaphora.

repetītor, -ōris *m* reclaimer.

repetītus *ppp of* **repetō** ♦ *adj*: **altē/longē ~** farfetched.

repetō, -ere, -īvī *and* **iī, -ītum** *vt* to go back to, revisit; to fetch back, take back; (MIL) to attack again; (*action, speech*) to resume, repeat; (*memory*) to recall, think over; (*origin*) to trace, derive; (*right*) to claim, demand back; **rēs ~** demand satisfaction; reclaim one's property; **pecūniae ~undae** extortion.

repetundae, -ārum *fpl* extortion (*by a provincial governor*).

repexus *adj* combed.

repleō, -ēre, -ēvī, -ētum *vt* to fill up, refill; to replenish, make good, complete; to satiate, fill to overflowing.

replētus *adj* full.

replicātiō, -ōnis *f* rolling up.

replicō, -āre *vt* to roll back, unroll, unfold.

rēpō, -ere, -sī, -tum *vi* to creep, crawl.

repōnō, -ōnere, -osuī, -ositum *vt* to put back, replace, restore; to bend back; to put (in the proper place); (*performance*) to repeat; (*something received*) to repay; (*store*) to lay up, put away; (*task*) to lay aside, put down; (*hope*) to place, rest; (*with* **prō**) substitute; **in numerō, in numerum ~** count, reckon among.

reportō, -āre, -āvī, -ātum *vt* to bring back, carry back; (*prize*) to win, carry off; (*words*) to report.

reposcō, -ere *vt* to demand back; to claim, require.

repositus *ppp of* **repōnō** ♦ *adj* remote.

repostor, -ōris *m* restorer.

repostus *etc see* **repositus**.

repōtia, -ōrum *ntpl* second drinking.

repperī *perf of* **reperiō**.

reppulī *perf of* **repellō**.

repraesentātiō, -ōnis *f* vivid presentation; (COMM) cash payment.

repraesentō, -āre, -āvī, -ātum *vt* to exhibit, reproduce; to do at once, hasten; (COMM) to pay cash.

reprehendō, -endere, -endī, -ēnsum *vt* to hold back, catch, restrain; to hold fast, retain; to blame, rebuke, censure; to refute.

reprehēnsiō, -ōnis *f* check; blame, reprimand, refutation.

reprehēnsō, -āre *vt* to keep holding back.

reprehēnsor, -ōris *m* censurer, critic, reviser.

reprehēnsus *ppp of* **reprehendō**.

reprendō *etc see* **reprehendō**.

repressor, -ōris *m* restrainer.

repressus *ppp of* **reprimō**.

reprimō, -imere, -essī, -essum *vt* to keep back, force back; to check, restrain, suppress.

reprōmissiō, -ōnis *f* counterpromise.

reprōmittō, -ittere, -īsī, -issum *vt* to promise in return, engage oneself.

rēptō, -āre *vi* to creep about, crawl along.

repudiātiō, -ōnis *f* rejection.

repudiō, -āre, -āvī, -ātum *vt* to reject, refuse, scorn; (*wife*) to divorce.

repudium, -ī *and* **iī** *nt* divorce; repudiation.

repuerāscō, -ere *vi* to become a child again; to behave like a child.

repugnanter *adv* reluctantly.

repugnantia, -ium *ntpl* contradictions.

repugnō, -āre, -āvī, -ātum *vi* to oppose, resist; to disagree, be inconsistent.

repulsa, -ae *f* refusal, denial, repulse; (*election*) rebuff.

repulsō, -āre *vi* to throb, reverberate.

repulsus *ppp of* **repellō**.

repulsus, -ūs *m* (*light*) reflection; (*sound*) echoing.

repungō, -ere *vt* to prod again.

repūrgō, -āre, -āvī, -ātum *vt* to clear again, cleanse again; to purge away.

reputātiō, -ōnis *f* pondering over.

reputō, -āre, -āvī, -ātum *vt* to count back; to think over, consider.

requiēs, -ētis *f* rest, relaxation, repose.

requiēscō, -scere, -vī, -tum *vi* to rest, find rest; to cease ♦ *vt* to stay.

requiētus *adj* rested, refreshed.

requīritō, -āre *vt* to keep asking after.

requīrō, -rere, -sīvī *and* **siī, -sītum** *vt* to search for, look for; to ask, inquire after; (*with* **ex** *or* **ab**) to question; to need, want, call for; to miss, look in vain for.

requīsītus *ppp of* **requīrō**.

rēs, reī *f* thing, object; circumstance, case, matter, affair; business, transaction; fact, truth, reality; possessions, wealth, money; advantage, interest; (*law*) case; (MIL) campaign, operations; (POL) politics, power, the State; (*writing*) subject matter, story, history; **~ mihi est tēcum** I have to do with you; **~ dīvīna** sacrifice; **~ mīlitāris** war; **~ pūblica** public affairs, politics, the State, republic; **~ rūstica** agriculture; **rem facere** get rich; **rem gerere** wage war, fight; **ad rem** to the point, to the purpose; **in rem** usefully; **ob rem** to the purpose; **ob eam rem** therefore; **ī in malam rem** go to the devil!; **contrā rem pūblicam** unconstitutionally; **ē rē pūblicā** constitutionally; **rē vērā** in fact, actually; **eā rē** for that reason; **tuā rē, ex tuā rē** to your advantage; **ab rē** unhelpfully; **ē rē (nātā)** as things are; **prō rē** according to circumstances; **rēs adversae** failure, adversity; **rēs dubiae** danger; **rēs gestae**

resacrō *etc see* **resecrō**.

resaeviō, -īre *vi* to rage again.

resalūtō, -āre *vt* to greet in return.

resānēscō, -ēscere, -uī *vi* to heal up again.

resarciō, -cīre, -tum *vt* to patch up, repair.

rescindō, -ndere, -dī, -ssum *vt* to cut back, cut open, break down; to open up; (*law, agreement*) to repeal, annul.

rescīscō, -īscere, -īvī *and* **iī, -ītum** *vt* to find out, learn.

rescissus *ppp of* **rescindō**.

rescrībō, -bere, -psī, -ptum *vt* to write back, reply; to rewrite, revise; (*emperors*) to give a decision; (*MIL*) to transfer, re-enlist; (*money*) to place to one's credit, pay back.

rescrīptus *ppp of* **rescrībō** ♦ *nt* imperial rescript.

resecō, -āre, -uī, -tum *vt* to cut back, cut short; to curtail; **ad vīvum** ~ cut to the quick.

resecrō, -āre *vt* to pray again; to free from a curse.

resectus *ppp of* **resecō**.

resecūtus *ppa of* **resequor**.

resēdī *perf of* **resideō**; *perf of* **resīdō**.

resēminō, -āre *vt* to reproduce.

resequor, -quī, -cūtus *vt* to answer.

reserō, -āre, -āvī, -ātum *vt* to unbar, unlock; to disclose.

reservō, -āre, -āvī, -ātum *vt* to keep back, reserve; to preserve, save.

reses, -idis *adj* remaining; inactive; idle; calm.

resideō, -idēre, -ēdī *vi* to remain behind; to be idle, be listless; (*fig*) to remain, rest.

resīdō, -īdere, -ēdī *vi* to sit down, sink down, settle; to subside; (*fig*) to abate, calm down.

residuus *adj* remaining, left over; (*money*) outstanding.

resignō, -āre *vt* to unseal, open; (*fig*) to reveal; (*COMM*) to cancel, pay back.

resiliō, -īre, -uī *vi* to spring back; to recoil, rebound, shrink.

resīmus *adj* turned up.

rēsīna, -ae *f* resin.

rēsīnātus *adj* smeared with resin.

resipiō, -ere *vt* to savour of, smack of.

resipīscō, -īscere, -iī *and* **uī** *vi* to come to one's senses.

resistō, -istere, -titī *vi* to stand still, stop, halt; to resist, oppose; to rise again.

resolūtus *ppp of* **resolvō**.

resolvō, -vere, -vī, -ūtum *vt* to unfasten, loosen, open, release; to melt, dissolve; to relax; (*debt*) to pay up; (*difficulty*) to banish, dispel; (*tax*) to abolish; (*words*) to explain.

resonābilis *adj* answering.

resonō, -āre *vi* to resound, re-echo ♦ *vt* to echo the sound of; to make resound.

resonus *adj* echoing.

resorbeō, -ēre *vt* to suck back, swallow again.

respectō, -āre *vi* to look back; to gaze about, watch ♦ *vt* to look back at, look for; to have regard for.

respectus *ppp of* **respiciō**.

respectus, -ūs *m* looking back; refuge; respect, regard.

respergō, -gere, -sī, -sum *vt* to besprinkle, splash.

respersiō, -ōnis *f* sprinkling.

respersus *ppp of* **respergō**.

respiciō, -icere, -exī, -ectum *vt* to look back at, see behind; (*help*) to look to; (*care*) to have regard for, consider, respect ♦ *vi* to look back, look.

respīrāmen, -inis *nt* windpipe.

respīrātiō, -ōnis *f* breathing; exhalation; taking breath, pause.

respīrātus, -ūs *m* inhaling.

respīrō, -āre, -āvī, -ātum *vt, vi* to breathe, blow back; to breathe again, revive; (*things*) to abate.

resplendeō, -ēre *vi* to flash back, shine brightly.

respondeō, -ondēre, -ondī, -ōnsum *vt* to answer, reply; (*lawyer, priest, oracle*) to advise, give a response; (*law court*) to appear; (*pledge*) to promise in return; (*things*) to correspond, agree, match; **pār parī** ~ return like for like, give tit for tat.

respōnsiō, -ōnis *f* answering; refutation.

respōnsitō, -āre *vi* to give advice.

respōnsō, -āre *vt, vi* to answer back; to defy.

respōnsor, -ōris *m* answerer.

respōnsum, -ī *nt* answer, reply; response, opinion, oracle.

rēspūblica, reīpūblicae *f* public affairs, politics, the State, republic.

respuō, -ere, -ī *vt* to spit out, eject; to reject, refuse.

restagnō, -āre *vi* to overflow; to be flooded.

restaurō, -āre *vt* to repair, rebuild.

resticula, -ae *f* rope, cord.

restinctiō, -ōnis *f* quenching.

restinctus *ppp of* **restinguō**.

restinguō, -guere, -xī, -ctum *vt* to extinguish, quench; (*fig*) to destroy.

restiō, -ōnis *m* rope maker.

restipulātiō, -ōnis *f* counterobligation.

restipulor, -ārī *vt* to stipulate in return.

restis, -is *f* rope.

restitī *perf of* **resistō**; *perf of* **restō**.

restitō, -āre *vi* to stay behind, hesitate.

restituō, -uere, -uī, -ūtum *vt* to replace, restore; to rebuild, renew; to give back, return; (*to a condition*) to reinstate; (*decision*) to quash, reverse; (*character*) to reform.

Noun declensions and verb conjugations are shown on pp xiii to xxv. The present infinitive ending of a verb shows to which conjugation it belongs: -āre = 1st; -ēre = 2nd; -ere = 3rd and -īre = 4th. Irregular verbs are shown on p xxvi

restitūtiō, -ōnis f restoration; reinstating.
restitūtor, -ōris m restorer.
restitūtus ppp of **restituō**.
restō, -āre, -itī vi to stand firm; to resist; to remain, be left; to be in store (for); **quod ~at** for the future.
restrictē adv sparingly; strictly.
restrictus ppp of **restringō ♦** adj tight, short; niggardly; severe.
restringō, -ngere, -nxī, -ctum vt to draw back tightly, bind fast; (teeth) to bare; (fig) to check.
resultō, -āre vi to rebound; to re-echo.
resūmō, -ere, -psī, -ptum vt to take up again, get back, resume.
resupīnō, -āre vt to turn back, throw on one's back.
resupīnus adj lying back, face upwards.
resurgō, -gere, -rēxī, -rēctum vi to rise again, revive.
resuscitō, -āre vt to revive.
retardātiō, -ōnis f hindering.
retardō, -āre, -āvī, -ātum vt to retard, detain, check.
rēte, -is nt net; (fig) snare.
retēctus ppp of **retegō**.
retegō, -egere, -ēxī, -ēctum vt to uncover, open; to reveal.
retemptō, -āre vt to try again.
retendō, -endere, -endī, -entum and ēnsum vt to slacken, relax.
retēnsus ppp of **retendō**.
retentiō, -ōnis f holding back.
retentō etc see **retemptō**.
retentō, -āre vt to keep back, hold fast.
retentus ppp of **retendō**; ppp of **retineō**.
retēxī perf of **retegō**.
retexō, -ere, -uī, -tum vt to unravel; (fig) to break up, cancel; to renew.
rētiārius, -ī and iī m net-fighter.
reticentia, -ae f saying nothing; pause.
reticeō, -ēre, -uī vi to be silent, say nothing ♦ vt to keep secret.
rēticulum, -ī nt small net, hairnet; network bag.
retināculum, -ī nt tether, hawser.
retinēns, -entis pres p of **retineō ♦** adj tenacious, observant.
retinentia, -ae f memory.
retineō, -inēre, -inuī, -entum vt to hold back, detain, restrain; to keep, retain, preserve.
retinniō, -īre vi to ring.
retonō, -āre vi to thunder in answer.
retorqueō, -quēre, -sī, -tum vt to turn back, twist.
retorridus adj dried up, wizened.
retortus ppp of **retorqueō**.
retractātiō, -ōnis f hesitation.
retractō, -āre, -āvī, -ātum vt to rehandle, take up again; to reconsider, revise; to withdraw ♦ vi to draw back, hesitate.
retractus ppp of **retrahō ♦** adj remote.

retrahō, -here, -xī, -ctum vt to draw back, drag back; to withdraw, remove.
retrectō etc see **retractō**.
retribuō, -uere, -uī, -ūtum vt to restore, repay.
retrō adv back, backwards, behind; (time) back, past.
retrōrsum adv backwards, behind; in reverse order.
retrūdō, -dere, -sum vt to push back; to withdraw.
rettulī perf of **referō**.
retundō, -undere, -udī and tudī, -ūsum and ūnsum vt to blunt; (fig) to check, weaken.
retūnsus, retūsus ppp of **retundō ♦** adj blunt, dull.
reus, -ī m the accused, defendant; guarantor, debtor, one responsible; culprit, criminal; **vōtī ~** one who has had a prayer granted.
revalēscō, -ēscere, -uī vi to recover.
revehō, -here, -xī, -ctum vt to carry back, bring back; (pass) to ride, drive, sail back.
revellō, -ellere, -ellī, -ulsum (olsum) vt to pull out, tear off; to remove.
revēlō, -āre vt to unveil, uncover.
reveniō, -enīre, -ēnī, -entum vi to come back, return.
rēvērā adv in fact, actually.
reverendus adj venerable, awe-inspiring.
reverēns, -entis pres p of **revereor ♦** adj respectful, reverent.
reverenter adv respectfully.
reverentia, -ae f respect, reverence, awe.
revereor, -ērī, -itus vt to stand in awe of; to respect, revere.
reversiō (revorsiō), -ōnis f turning back; recurrence.
reversus ppa of **revertor**.
revertō, -ere, -ī; revertor, -tī, -sus vi to turn back, return; to revert.
revexī perf of **revehō**.
revictus ppp of **revincō**.
revinciō, -cīre, -xī, -ctum vt to tie back, bind fast.
revincō, -incere, -īcī, -ictum vt to conquer, repress; (words) to refute, convict.
revinctus ppp of **revinciō**.
revirēscō, -ēscere, -uī vi to grow green again; to be rejuvenated; to grow strong again, flourish again.
revīsō, -ere vt, vi to come back to, revisit.
revīvēscō, -vīscō, -vīscere, -xī vi to come to life again, revive.
revocābilis adj revocable.
revocāmen, -inis nt recall.
revocātiō, -ōnis f recalling; (word) withdrawing.
revocō, -āre, -āvī, -ātum vt to call back, recall; (action) to revoke; (former state) to recover, regain; (growth) to check; (guest) to invite in return; (judgment) to apply, refer; (law) to summon again; (performer) to encore; (troops) to withdraw.

revolō, -āre *vi* to fly back.
revolsus *etc see* **revulsus**.
revolūbilis *adj* that may be rolled back.
revolūtus *ppp of* **revolvō**.
revolvō, -vere, -vī, -ūtum *vt* to roll back, unroll, unwind; (*speech*) to relate, repeat; (*thought*) to think over; (*writing*) to read over; (*pass*) to revolve, return, come round.
revomō, -ere, -uī *vt* to disgorge.
revor- *etc see* **rever-**.
revulsus *ppp of* **revellō**.
rēx, rēgis *m* king; tyrant, despot; leader; patron, rich man.
rēxī *perf of* **regō**.
Rhadamanthus, -ī *m* judge in the lower world.
Rhaetī *etc see* **Raetī**.
Rhamnūs, -ūntis *f* town in Attica (*famous for its statue of Nemesis*).
Rhamnūsis, -ūsidis *f* Nemesis.
Rhamnūsius *adj see n.*
rhapsōdia, -ae *f* a book of Homer.
Rhea, -ae *f* Cybele.
Rhea Silvia, -ae, -ae *f* mother of Romulus and Remus.
Rhēgium *etc see* **Rēgium**.
Rhēnānus *adj* Rhenish.
rhēnō *etc see* **rēnō**.
Rhēnus, -ī *m* Rhine.
Rhēsus, -ī *m* Thracian king (*killed at Troy*).
rhētor, -oris *m* teacher of rhetoric; orator.
rhētorica, -ae *and* **ē, -ēs** *f* art of oratory, rhetoric.
rhētoricē *adv* rhetorically, in an oratorical manner.
rhētoricī, -ōrum *mpl* teachers of rhetoric.
rhētoricus *adj* rhetorical, on rhetoric.
rhīnocerōs, -ōtis *m* rhinoceros.
rhō *nt* (*indecl*) Greek letter rho.
Rhodanus, -ī *m* Rhone.
Rhodius *adj see* **Rhodopē**.
Rhodopē, -ēs *f* mountain range in Thrace.
Rhodopēius *adj* Thracian.
Rhodos (Rhodus), -ī *f* island of Rhodes.
Rhoetēum, -ī *nt* promontory on the Dardanelles (*near Troy*).
Rhoetēus *adj* Trojan.
rhombus, -ī *m* magician's circle; (*fish*) turbot.
rhomphaea, -ae *f* long barbarian javelin.
rhythmicus, -ī *m* teacher of prose rhythm.
rhythmos (-us), -ī *m* rhythm, symmetry.
rīca, -ae *f* sacrificial veil.
rīcinium, -ī *and* **ī ī** *nt* small cloak with hood.
rictum, -ī *nt*, **-us, -ūs** *m* open mouth, gaping jaws.
rīdeō, -dēre, -sī, -sum *vi* to laugh, smile ♦ *vt* to laugh at, smile at; to ridicule
rīdibundus *adj* laughing.
rīdiculāria, -ium *ntpl* jokes.
rīdiculē *adv* jokingly; absurdly.
rīdiculus *adj* amusing, funny; ridiculous, silly

♦ *m* jester ♦ *nt* joke.
rigēns, -entis *pres p of* **rigeō** ♦ *adj* stiff, rigid, frozen.
rigeō, -ēre *vi* to be stiff.
rigēscō, -ēscere, -uī *vi* to stiffen, harden; to bristle.
rigidē *adv* rigorously.
rigidus *adj* stiff, rigid, hard; (*fig*) hardy, strict, inflexible.
rigō, -āre *vt* to water, moisten, bedew; to convey (water).
rigor, -ōris *m* stiffness, hardness; numbness, cold; strictness, severity.
riguī *perf of* **rigēscō**.
riguus *adj* irrigating; watered.
rīma, -ae *f* crack, chink.
rīmor, -ārī, -ātus *vt* to tear open; to search for, probe, examine; to find out.
rīmōsus *adj* cracked, leaky.
ringor, -ī *vi* to snarl.
rīpa, -ae *f* river bank; shore.
Rīphaeī, -ōrum *mpl* mountain range in N. Scythia.
Rīphaeus *adj see* **Rīphaeī**.
rīpula, -ae *f* riverbank.
riscus, -ī *m* trunk, chest.
rīsī *perf of* **rīdeō**.
rīsor, -ōris *m* scoffer.
rīsus, -ūs *m* laughter, laugh; laughing stock.
rīte *adv* with the proper formality *or* ritual; duly, properly, rightly; in the usual manner; fortunately.
rītus, -ūs *m* ritual, ceremony; custom, usage; ~ū after the manner of.
rīvālis, -is *m* rival in love.
rīvālitās, -ātis *f* rivalry in love.
rīvulus, -ī *m* brook.
rīvus, -ī *m* stream, brook; **ē ~ō flūmina māgna facere** ≈ make a mountain of a molehill.
rixa, -ae *f* quarrel, brawl, fight.
rixor, -ārī, -ātus *vi* to quarrel, brawl, squabble.
rōbīginōsus *adj* rusty.
rōbīgō, -inis *f* rust; blight, mould, mildew.
rōboreus *adj* of oak.
rōborō, -āre *vt* to strengthen, invigorate.
rōbur, -oris *nt* oak; hard wood; prison, dungeon (*at Rome*); (*fig*) strength, hardness, vigour; best part, élite, flower.
rōbustus *adj* of oak; strong, hard; robust, mature.
rōdō, -dere, -sī, -sum *vt* to gnaw; (*rust*) to corrode; (*words*) to slander.
rogālis *adj* of a pyre.
rogātiō, -ōnis *f* proposal, motion, bill; request; (*RHET*) question.
rogātiuncula, -ae *f* unimportant bill; question.
rogātor, -ōris *m* proposer; polling clerk.
rogātus, -ūs *m* request.

rogitō, -āre vt to ask for, inquire eagerly.

rogō, -āre, -āvī, -ātum vt to ask, ask for; (*bill*) to propose, move; (*candidate*) to put up for election; **lēgem ~, populum ~** introduce a bill; **magistrātum populum ~** nominate for election to an office; **militēs sacrāmentō ~** administer the oath to the troops; **mālō emere quam rogāre** I'd rather buy it than borrow it.

rogus, -ī m funeral pyre.

Rōma, -ae f Rome.

Rōmānus adj Roman.

Rōmuleus, -us adj of Romulus; Roman.

Rōmulidae, -idārum mpl the Romans.

Rōmulus, -ī m founder and first king of Rome.

rōrāriī, -ōrum mpl skirmishers.

rōridus adj dewy.

rōrifer, -ī adj dew-bringing.

rōrō, -āre vi to distil dew; to drip, trickle ♦ vt to bedew, wet.

rōs, rōris m dew; moisture, water; (*plant*) rosemary; **~ marīnus** rosemary.

rosa, -ae f rose; rose bush.

rosāria, -ōrum ntpl rose garden.

rōscidus adj dewy; wet.

Roscius, -ī m: L. ~ Othō *tribune in 67 BC, whose law reserved theatre seats for the equites;* Q. ~ Gallus *famous actor defended by Cicero;* Sex. ~ *of Ameria, defended by Cicero.*

Roscius, -iānus adj see n.

rosētum, -ī nt rosebed.

roseus adj rosy; of roses.

rōsī perf of **rōdō**.

rōstrātus adj beaked, curved; **columna ~a** column commemorating a naval victory.

rōstrum, -ī nt (*bird*) beak, bill; (*animal*) snout, muzzle; (*ship*) beak, end of prow; (*pl*) orators' platform in the Forum.

rōsus ppp of **rōdō**.

rota, -ae f wheel; potter's wheel, torture wheel; car, disc.

rotō, -āre, -āvī, -ātum vt to turn, whirl, roll; (*pass*) to revolve.

rotundē adv elegantly.

rotundō, -āre vt to round off.

rotundus adj round, circular, spherical; (*style*) well-turned, smooth.

rubefaciō, -facere, -fēcī, -factum vt to redden.

rubēns, -entis pres p of **rubeō** ♦ adj red; blushing.

rubeō, -ēre vi to be red; to blush.

ruber, -rī adj red; **mare ~rum** Red Sea; Persian Gulf; **ōceanus ~** Indian Ocean; **Saxa ~ra** *stone quarries between Rome and Veii.*

rubēscō, -ēscere, -uī vi to redden, blush.

rubēta, -ae f toad.

rubēta, -ōrum ntpl bramble bushes.

rubeus adj of bramble.

Rubicō, -ōnis m *stream marking the frontier between Italy and Gaul.*

rubicundulus adj reddish.

rubicundus adj red, ruddy.

rūbīg- etc see **rōbīg-**.

rubor, -ōris m redness; blush; bashfulness; shame.

rubrīca, -ae f red earth, red ochre.

rubuī perf of **rubēscō**.

rubus, -ī m bramble bush; bramble, blackberry.

ructō, -āre; -or, -ārī vt, vi to belch.

ructus, -us m belching.

rudēns, -entis pres p of **rudō** ♦ m rope; (*pl*) rigging.

Rudiae, -iārum fpl *town in S. Italy* (*birthplace of Ennius*).

rudiārius, -ī and **iī** m retired gladiator.

rudīmentum, -ī nt first attempt, beginning.

Rudīnus adj see **Rudiae**.

rudis adj unwrought, unworked, raw; coarse, rough, badly-made; (*age*) new, young; (*person*) uncultured, unskilled, clumsy; ignorant (of), inexperienced (in).

rudis, -is f stick, rod; foil (*for fighting practice*); (*fig*) discharge.

rudō, -ere, -īvī, -ītum vi to roar, bellow, bray; to creak.

rūdus, -eris nt rubble, rubbish; piece of copper.

rūdus, -eris nt copper coin.

Rūfulī, -ōrum mpl military tribunes (*chosen by the general*).

rūfulus adj red-headed.

rūfus adj red, red-haired.

rūga, -ae f wrinkle, crease.

rūgō, -āre vi to become creased.

rūgōsus adj wrinkled, shrivelled, corrugated.

ruī perf of **ruō**.

ruīna, -ae f fall, downfall; collapse, falling in; debris, ruins; destruction, disaster, ruin (*fig*).

ruīnōsus adj collapsing; ruined.

rumex, -icis f sorrel.

rūmificō, -āre vt to report.

Rūmīna, -ae f *goddess of nursing mothers;* **fīcus ~ālis** the fig tree of Romulus and Remus (*under which the she-wolf suckled them*).

rūminātiō, -ōnis f chewing the cud; (*fig*) ruminating.

rūminō, -āre vt, vi to chew the cud.

rūmor, -ōris m noise, cheering; rumour, hearsay; public opinion; reputation.

rumpia etc see **rhomphaea**.

rumpō, -ere, rūpī, ruptum vt to break, burst tear; to break down, burst through; (*activity*) to interrupt; (*agreement*) to violate, annul; (*delay*) to put an end to; (*voice*) to give vent to; (*way*) to force through.

rūmusculī, -ōrum mpl gossip.

rūna, -ae f dart.

runcō, -āre vi to weed.

ruō, -ere, -ī, -tum vi to fall down, tumble; to rush, run, hurry; to come to ruin ♦ vt to dash down, hurl to the ground; to throw up, turn up.

rūpēs, -is f rock, cliff.

rūpī *perf of* **rumpō**.
ruptor, -ōris *m* violator.
ruptus *ppp of* **rumpō**.
rūricola, -ae *adj* rural, country- (*in cpds*).
rūrigena, -ae *m* countryman.
rūrsus, rūrsum (rūsum) *adv* back, backwards; on the contrary, in return; again.
rūs, rūris *nt* the country, countryside; estate, farm; **rūs** to the country; **rūrī** in the country; **rūre** from the country.
ruscum, -ī *nt* butcher's-broom.
russus *adj* red.
rūsticānus *adj* country- (*in cpds*), rustic.
rūsticātiō, -ōnis *f* country life.
rūsticē *adv* in a countrified manner, awkwardly.
rūsticitās, -ātis *f* country manners, rusticity.
rūsticor, -ārī *vi* to live in the country.
rūsticulus, -ī *m* yokel.
rūsticus *adj* country- (*in cpds*), rural; simple, rough, clownish ♦ *m* countryman.
rūsum *see* **rūrsus**.
rūta, -ae *f* (*herb*) rue; (*fig*) unpleasantness.
ruta caesa *ntpl* minerals and timber on an estate.
rutilō, -āre *vt* to colour red ♦ *vi* to glow red.
rutilus *adj* red, auburn.
rutrum, -ī *nt* spade, shovel, trowel.
rūtula, -ae *f* little piece of rue.
Rutulī, -ōrum *mpl* ancient Latin people.
Rutulus *adj* Rutulian.
Rutupiae, -iārum *fpl* seaport in Kent (*now* Richborough).
Rutupīnus *adj see n.*
rutus *ppp of* **ruō**.

S, s

Saba, -ae *f* town in Arabia Felix.
Sabaeus *adj see n.*
Sabāzia, -iōrum *ntpl* festival of Bacchus.
Sabāzius, -ī *m* Bacchus.
sabbata, -ōrum *ntpl* Sabbath, Jewish holiday.
Sabellus, -ī *m* Sabine, Samnite.
Sabellus, -icus *adj see n.*
Sabīnī, -ōrum *mpl* Sabines (*a people of central Italy*).
Sabīnus *adj* Sabine ♦ *f* Sabine woman ♦ *nt* Sabine estate; Sabine wine; **herba ~a** savin (*a kind of juniper*).
Sabrīna, -ae *f* river Severn.

saburra, -ae *f* sand, ballast.
Sacae, -ārum *mpl* tribe of Scythians.
saccipērium, -ī *and* **iī** *nt* purse-pocket.
saccō, -āre *vt* to strain, filter.
sacculus, -ī *m* little bag, purse.
saccus, -ī *m* bag, purse, wallet.
sacellum, -ī *nt* chapel.
sacer, -rī *adj* sacred, holy; devoted for sacrifice, forfeited; accursed, criminal, infamous; **Mōns ~** hill to which the Roman plebs seceded; **Via ~ra** street from the Forum to the Capitol.
sacerdōs, -ōtis *m/f* priest, priestess.
sacerdōtium, -ī *and* **iī** *nt* priesthood.
sacrāmentum, -ī *nt* deposit made by parties to a lawsuit; civil lawsuit, dispute; (*MIL*) oath of allegiance, engagement.
sacrārium, -ī *and* **iī** *nt* shrine, chapel.
sacrātus *adj* holy, hallowed; **~āta lēx** a law whose violation was punished by devotion to the infernal gods.
sacricola, -ae *m/f* sacrificing priest *or* priestess.
sacrifer, -ī *adj* carrying holy things.
sacrificālis *adj* sacrificial.
sacrificātiō, -ōnis *f* sacrificing.
sacrificium, -ī *and* **iī** *nt* sacrifice.
sacrificō, -āre *vt, vi* to sacrifice.
sacrificulus, -ī *m* sacrificing priest; **rēx ~** high priest.
sacrificus *adj* sacrificial.
sacrilēgium, -ī *and* **iī** *nt* sacrilege.
sacrilegus *adj* sacrilegious; profane, wicked ♦ *m* templerobber.
sacrō, -āre, -āvī, -ātum *vt* to consecrate; to doom, curse; to devote, dedicate; to make inviolable; (*poetry*) to immortalize.
sacrōsanctus *adj* inviolable, sacrosanct.
sacruficō *etc see* **sacrificō**.
sacrum, -rī *nt* holy thing, sacred vessel; shrine; offering, victim; rite; (*pl*) sacrifice, worship, religion; **~ra facere** sacrifice; **inter ~rum saxumque** ≈ with one's back to the wall; **hērēditās sine ~rīs** a gift with no awkward obligations.
saeclum *etc see* **saeculum**.
saeculāris *adj* centenary; (*ECCL*) secular, pagan.
saeculum, -ī *nt* generation, lifetime, age; the age, the times; century; **in ~a** (*ECCL*) for ever.
saepe *adv* often, frequently.
saepe numerō *adv* very often.
saepēs, -is *f* hedge, fence.
saepīmentum, -ī *nt* enclosure.
saepiō, -īre, -sī, -tum *vt* to hedge round, fence in, enclose; (*fig*) to shelter, protect.
saeptus *ppp of* **saepiō** ♦ *nt* fence, wall; stake, pale; (*sheep*) fold; (*Rome*) voting area in the Campus Martius.
saeta, -ae *f* hair, bristle.

saetiger, -ī *adj* bristly.
saetōsus *adj* bristly, hairy.
saevē, -iter *adv* fiercely, cruelly.
saevidicus *adj* furious.
saeviō, -īre, -iī, -ītum *vi* to rage, rave.
saevitia, -ae *f* rage; ferocity, cruelty.
saevus *adj* raging, fierce; cruel, barbarous.
sāga, -ae *f* fortune teller.
sagācitās, -ātis *f* (*dogs*) keen scent; (*mind*) shrewdness.
sagāciter *adv* keenly; shrewdly.
sagātus *adj* wearing a soldier's cloak.
sagāx, -ācis *adj* (*senses*) keen, keen-scented; (*mind*) quick, shrewd.
sagīna, -ae *f* stuffing, fattening; food, rich food; fatted animal.
sagīnō, -are *vt* to cram, fatten; to feed, feast.
sāgiō, -īre *vi* to perceive keenly.
sagitta, -ae *f* arrow.
sagittārius, -ī and iī *m* archer.
sagittifer, -ī *adj* armed with arrows.
sagmen, -inis *nt* tuft of sacred herbs (*used as a mark of inviolability*).
sagulum, -ī *nt* short military cloak.
sagum, -ī *nt* military cloak; woollen mantle.
Saguntīnus *adj see* **Saguntum**.
Saguntum, -ī *nt*, **-us (os), -ī** *f* town in E. Spain.
sāgus *adj* prophetic.
sāl, salis *m* salt; brine, sea; (*fig*) shrewdness, wit, humour, witticism; good taste.
salacō, -ōnis *m* swaggerer.
Salamīnius *adj see* **Salamīs**.
Salamīs, -īnis *f* Greek island near Athens; town in Cyprus.
salapūtium, -ī and iī *nt* manikin.
salārius *adj* salt- (*in cpds*) ♦ *nt* allowance, salary.
salāx, -ācis *adj* lustful, salacious.
salebra, -ae *f* roughness, rut.
Saliāris *adj* of the Salii; sumptuous.
salictum, -ī *nt* willow plantation.
salientēs, -ium *fpl* springs.
salignus *adj* of willow.
Saliī, -ōrum *mpl* priests of Mars.
salillum, -ī *nt* little saltcellar.
salīnae, -ārum *fpl* saltworks.
salīnum, -ī *nt* saltcellar.
saliō, -īre, -uī, -tum *vi* to leap, spring; to throb.
saliunca, -ae *f* Celtic nard.
salīva, -ae *f* saliva, spittle; taste.
salix, -icis *f* willow.
Sallustiānus *adj see* **Sallustius**.
Sallustius, -ī *m* Sallust (*Roman historian*); *his wealthy grand-nephew*.
Salmōneus, -eos *m* son of Aeolus (*punished in Tartarus for imitating lightning*).
Salmōnis, -idis *f* his daughter Tyro.
salsāmentum, -ī *nt* brine, pickle; salted fish.
salsē *adv* wittily.
salsus *adj* salted; salt, briny; (*fig*) witty.
saltātiō, -ōnis *f* dancing, dance.
saltātor, -ōris *m* dancer.

saltātōrius *adj* dancing- (*in cpds*).
saltātrīx, -īcis *f* dancer.
saltātus, -ūs *m* dance.
saltem *adv* at least, at all events; **nōn ~** not even.
saltō, -āre *vt, vi* to dance.
saltuōsus *adj* wooded.
saltus, -ūs *m* leap, bound.
saltus, -ūs *m* woodland pasture, glade; pass, ravine.
salūber *adj see* **salūbris**.
salūbris *adj* health-giving, wholesome; healthy, sound.
salūbritās, -ātis *f* healthiness; health.
salūbriter *adv* wholesomely; beneficially.
saluī *perf of* **saliō**.
salum, -ī *nt* sea, high sea.
salūs, -ūtis *f* health; welfare, life; safety; good wish, greeting; **~ūtem dīcere** greet; bid farewell.
salūtāris *adj* wholesome, healthy; beneficial; **~ littera** letter A (*for absolvō = acquittal*).
salūtāriter *adv* beneficially.
salūtātiō, -ōnis *f* greeting; formal morning visit, levee.
salūtātor, -ōris *m* morning caller; male courtier.
salūtātrīx, -rīcis *f* morning caller; female courtier.
salūtifer, -ī *adj* health-giving.
salūtigerulus *adj* carrying greetings.
salūtō, -āre, -āvī, -ātum *vt* to greet, salute, wish well; to call on, pay respects to.
salvē *adv* well, in good health; all right.
salvē *impv of* **salveō**.
salveō, -ēre *vi* to be well, be in good health; **~ē, ~ētō, ~ēte** hail!, good day!, goodbye!; **~ēre iubeō** I bid good day.
salvus, salvos *adj* safe, alive, intact, well; without violating; all right; **~ sīs** good day to you!; **~a rēs est** all is well; **~ā lēge** without breaking the law.
Samaous *adj see* **Samē**.
Samarobrīva, -ae *f* Belgian town (*now Amiens*).
sambūca, -ae *f* harp.
sambūcistria, -ae *f* harpist.
Samē, -ēs *f* old name of the Greek island Cephallenia.
Samius *adj* Samian ♦ *ntpl* Samian pottery.
Samnīs, -ītis *adj* Samnite.
Samnium, -ī and iī *nt* district of central Italy.
Samos (-us), -ī *f* Aegean island off Asia Minor (*famous for its pottery and as the birthplace of Pythagoras*).
Samothrācēs, -um *mpl* Samothracians.
Samothrācia, -iae *and* **a, -ae** *f* Samothrace (*island in the N. Aegean*).
Samothrācius *adj see n*.
sānābilis *adj* curable.
sānātiō, -ōnis *f* healing.
sanciō, -īre, -xī, -ctum *vt* to make sacred or inviolable; to ordain, ratify; to enact a

punishment against.

sanctimōnia, -ae f sanctity; chastity.

sanctiō, -ōnis f decree, penalty for violating a law.

sanctitās, -ātis f sacredness; integrity, chastity.

sanctitūdō, -inis f sacredness.

sanctō adv solemnly, religiously.

sanctor, -ōris m enacter.

sanctus ppp of **sanciō** ♦ adj sacred, inviolable; holy, venerable; pious, virtuous, chaste.

sandaligerula, -ae f sandalbearer.

sandalium, -ī and **iī** nt sandal, slipper.

sandapila, -ae f common bier.

sandyx, -ycis f scarlet.

sānē adv sensibly; (intensive) very, doubtless; (ironical) to be sure, of course; (concessive) of course, indeed; (in answer) certainly, surely; (with impv) then, if you please; ~ quam very much; haud ~ not so very, not quite.

sanguen etc see **sanguis**.

sanguināns, -āntis adj bloodthirsty.

sanguinārius adj bloodthirsty.

sanguineus adj bloody, of blood; blood-red.

sanguinolentus adj bloody; blood-red; sanguinary.

sanguis, -inis m blood, bloodshed; descent, family; offspring; (fig) strength, life; ~inem dare shed one's blood; ~inem mittere let blood.

saniēs, -em, -ē f diseased blood, matter; venom.

sānitās, -ātis f (body) health, sound condition; (mind) sound sense, sanity; (style) correctness, purity.

sanna, -ae f grimace, mocking.

sannlō, -ōnis m clown.

sānō, -āre, -āvī, -ātum vt to cure, heal; (fig) to remedy, relieve.

Sanquālis avis f osprey.

sānus adj (body) sound, healthy; (mind) sane, sensible; (style) correct; **male ~** mad, inspired; **sānun es?** are you in your senses?

sanxī perf of **sanciō**.

sapa, -ae f new wine.

sapiēns, -entis pres p of **sapiō** ♦ adj wise, discreet ♦ m wise man, philosopher; man of taste.

sapienter adv wisely, sensibly.

sapientia, -ae f wisdom, discernment; philosophy; knowledge.

sapiō, -ere, -īvī and **uī** vi to have a flavour or taste; to have sense, be wise ♦ vt to taste of, smell of, smack of; to understand.

sapor, -ōris m taste, flavour; (food) delicacy; (fig) taste, refinement.

Sapphicus adj see **Sapphō**.

Sapphō, -ūs f famous Greek lyric poetess, native of Lesbos.

sarcina, -ae f bundle, burden; (MIL) pack.

sarcinārius adj baggage- (in cpds).

sarcinātor, -ōris m patcher.

sarcinula, -ae f little pack.

sarciō, -cīre, -sī, -tum vt to patch, mend, repair.

sarcophagus, -ī m sepulchre.

sarculum, -ī nt light hoe.

Sardēs (-is), -ium fpl Sardis (capital of Lydia).

Sardiānus adj see **Sardēs**.

Sardinia, -iniae f island of Sardinia.

sardonyx, -chis f sardonyx.

Sardus, -ous, -iniēnsis adj see **Sardinia**.

sariō, -īre, -īvī and **uī** vt to hoe, weed.

sarīsa, -ae f Macedonian lance.

sarīsophorus, -ī m Macedonian lancer.

Sarmatae, -ārum mpl Sarmatians (a people of S.E. Russia).

Sarmaticus, -is adj see **Sarmatae**.

sarmentum, -ī nt twigs, brushwood.

Sarpēdōn, -onis m king of Lycia.

Sarra, -ae f Tyre.

sarrācum, -ī nt cart.

Sarrānus adj Tyrian.

sarriō etc see **sariō**.

sarsī perf of **sarciō**.

sartāgō, -inis f frying pan.

sartor, -ōris m hoer, weeder.

sartus ppp of **sarciō**.

sat etc see **satis**.

satagō, -ere vi to have one's hands full, be in trouble; to bustle about, fuss.

satelles, -itis m/f attendant, follower; assistant, accomplice.

satiās, -ātis f sufficiency; satiety.

satietās, -ātis f sufficiency; satiety.

satin, satine see **satisne**.

satiō, -āre, -āvī, -ātum vt to satisfy, appease; to fill, saturate; to glut, cloy, disgust.

satiō, -ōnis f sowing, planting; (pl) fields.

satis, sat adj enough, sufficient ♦ adv enough, sufficiently; tolerably, fairly, quite; ~ accipiō take sufficient bail; ~ agō, agitō have one's hands full, be harassed; ~ dō offer sufficient bail; ~ faciō satisfy; give satisfaction, make amends; (creditor) pay.

satisdatiō, -ōnis f giving security.

satisdō see **satis**.

satisfaciō see **satis**.

satisfactiō, -ōnis f amends, apology.

satisne adv quite, really.

satius compar of **satis**: better, preferable.

sator, -ōris m sower, planter; father; promoter.

satrapēs, -is m satrap (Persian governor).

satur, -ī adj filled, sated; (fig) rich.

satura, -ae f mixed dish; medley; (poem) satire; **per ~am** confusingly.

satureia, -ōrum ntpl (plant) savory.

saturitās, -ātis f repletion; fulness, plenty.

Saturnālia, -ium and **iōrum** ntpl festival of

Noun declensions and verb conjugations are shown on pp xiii to xxv. The present infinitive ending of a verb shows to which conjugation it belongs: **-āre** = 1st; **-ēre** = 2nd; **-ere** = 3rd and **-īre** = 4th. Irregular verbs are shown on p xxvi

Saturn in December.

Saturnia, -iae *f* Juno.

Saturnīnus, -ī *m revolutionary tribune in 103 and 100 B.C.*

Saturnius *adj see n.*

Saturnus, -ī *m* Saturn (*god of sowing, ruler of the Golden Age*); the planet Saturn.

saturō, -āre, -āvī, -ātum *vt* to fill, glut, satisfy; to disgust.

satus *ppp of* **serō** ♦ *m* son ♦ *f* daughter ♦ *ntpl* crops.

satus, -ūs *m* sowing, planting; begetting.

satyriscus, -ī *m* little satyr.

satyrus, -ī *m* satyr.

sauciātiō, -ōnis *f* wounding.

sauciō, -āre *vt* to wound, hurt.

saucius *adj* wounded, hurt; ill, stricken.

Sauromatae *etc see* **Sarmatae.**

sāviātiō, -ōnis *f* kissing.

sāviolum, -ī *nt* sweet kiss.

sāvior, -ārī *vt* to kiss.

sāvium, -ī *and* **iī** *nt* kiss.

saxātilis *adj* rock- (*in cpds*).

saxētum, -ī *nt* rocky place.

saxeus *adj* of rock, rocky.

saxificus *adj* petrifying.

saxōsus *adj* rocky, stony.

saxulum, -ī *nt* small rock.

saxum, -ī *nt* rock, boulder; the Tarpeian Rock.

scaber, -rī *adj* rough, scurfy; mangy, itchy.

scabiēs, -em, -ē *f* roughness, scurf; mange, itch.

scabillum, -ī *nt* stool; a castanet played with the foot.

scabō, -ere, scābī *vt* to scratch.

Scaea porta, -ae, -ae *f the west gate of Troy.*

scaena, -ae *f* stage, stage setting; (*fig*) limelight, public life; outward appearance, pretext.

scaenālis *adj* theatrical.

scaenicus *adj* stage- (*in cpds*), theatrical ♦ *m* actor.

Scaevola, -ae *m early Roman who burned his hand off before Porsenna; famous jurist of Cicero's day.*

scaevus *adj* on the left; perverse ♦ *f* omen.

scālae, -ārum *fpl* steps, ladder, stairs.

scalmus -ī *m* tholepin.

scalpellum, -ī *nt* scalpel, lancet.

scalpō, -ere, -sī, -tum *vt* to carve, engrave; to scratch.

scalprum, -ī *nt* knife, penknife; chisel.

scalpurriō, -īre *vi* to scratch.

Scamander, -rī *m* river of Troy (*also called Xanthus*).

scammōnea, -ae *f* (*plant*) scammony.

scamnum, -ī *nt* bench, stool; throne.

scandō, -ere *vt, vi* to climb, mount.

scapha, -ae *f* boat, skiff.

scaphium, -ī *and* **iī** *nt* a boat-shaped cup.

scapulae, -ārum *fpl* shoulder blades;

shoulders.

scāpus, -ī *m* shaft; (*loom*) yarnbeam.

scarus, -ī *m* (*fish*) scar.

scatebra, -ae *f* gushing water.

scateō, -ēre; -ō, -ere *vi* to bubble up, gush out; (*fig*) to abound, swarm.

scatūriginēs, -um *fpl* springs.

scatūriō, -īre *vi* to gush out; (*fig*) to be full of.

scaurus *adj* large-ankled.

scelerātē *adv* wickedly.

scelerātus *adj* desecrated; wicked, infamous, accursed; pernicious.

scelerō, -āre *vt* to desecrate.

scelerōsus *adj* vicious, accursed.

scelestē *adv* wickedly.

scelestus *adj* wicked, villainous, accursed; unlucky.

scelus, -eris *nt* wickedness, crime, sin; (*person*) scoundrel; (*event*) calamity.

scēn- *etc see* **scaen-.**

scēptrifer, -ī *adj* sceptered.

scēptrum, -ī *nt* staff, sceptre; kingship, power.

scēptūchus, -ī *m* sceptre-bearer.

scheda *etc see* **scida.**

schēma, -ae *f* form, figure, style.

Schoenēis, -ēidis *f* Atalanta.

Schoenēius *adj see* **Schoenēis.**

Schoeneus, -eī *m* father of Atalanta.

schoenobatēs, -ae *m* rope dancer.

schola, -ae *f* learned discussion, dissertation, school; sect, followers.

scholasticus *adj* of a school ♦ *m* rhetorician.

scida, -ae *f* sheet of paper.

sciēns, -entis *pres p of* **sciō** ♦ *adj* knowing, purposely; versed in, acquainted with.

scienter *adv* expertly.

scientia, -ae *f* knowledge, skill.

scīlicet *adv* evidently, of course; (*concessive*) no doubt; (*ironical*) I suppose, of course.

scilla *etc see* **squilla.**

scindō, -ndere, -dī, -ssum *vt* to cut open, tear apart, split, break down; to divide, part.

scintilla, -ae *f* spark.

scintillō, -āre *vi* to sparkle.

scintillula, -ae *f* little spark.

sciō, -īre, -īvī, -ītum *vt* to know; to have skill in; (*with infin*) to know how to; **quod ~iam** as far as I know; **~ītō** you may be sure.

Scīpiadēs, -ae *m* Scipio.

scīpiō, -ōnis *m* staff.

Scīpiō, -ōnis *m* famous Roman family name (*esp the conqueror of Hannibal* Africanus); Aemilianus (*destroyer of Carthage and patron of literature*).

scirpeus *adj* rush (*in cpds*) ♦ *f* wickerwork frame.

scirpiculus, -ī *m* rush basket.

scirpus, -ī *m* bulrush.

scīscitor, -ārī, -ātus; -ō, -āre *vt* to inquire; to question.

scīscō, -scere, -vī, -tum *vt* to inquire, learn; (*POL*) to approve, decree, appoint.

scissus *ppp of* **scindō** ♦ *adj* split; (*voice*) harsh.
scītāmenta, -ōrum *ntpl* dainties.
scītē *adv* cleverly, tastefully.
scītor, -ārī, -ātus *vt, vi* to inquire; to consult.
scītulus *adj* neat, smart.
scītum, -ī *nt* decree, statute.
scītus *ppp of* **sciō**; *ppp of* **scīscō** ♦ *adj* clever, shrewd, skilled; (*words*) sensible, witty; (*appearance*) fine, smart.
scītus, -ūs *m* decree.
sciūrus, -ī *m* squirrel.
scīvī *perf of* **sciō**; *perf of* **scīscō**.
scobis, -is *f* sawdust, filings.
scomber, -rī *m* mackerel.
scōpae, -ārum *fpl* broom.
Scopās, -ae *m famous Greek sculptor*.
scopulōsus *adj* rocky.
scopulus, -ī *m* rock, crag, promontory; (*fig*) danger.
scorpiō, -ōnis, -us *and* **os, -ī** *m* scorpion; (*MIL*) a kind of catapult.
scortātor, -ōris *m* fornicator.
scorteus *adj* of leather.
scortor, -ārī *vi* to associate with harlots.
scortum, -ī *nt* harlot, prostitute.
screātor, -ōris *m* one who clears his throat noisily.
screātus, -ūs *m* clearing the throat.
scrība, -ae *m* clerk, writer.
scrībō, -bere, -psī, -ptum *vt* to write, draw; to write down, describe; (*document*) to draw up; (*law*) to designate; (*MIL*) to enlist.
scrīnium, -ī *and* **iī** *nt* book box, lettercase.
scrīptiō, -ōnis *f* writing; composition; text.
scrīptitō, -āre, -āvī, -ātum *vt* to write regularly, compose.
scrīptor, -ōris *m* writer, author; secretary; **rērum ~** historian.
scrīptula, -ōrum *ntpl* lines of a squared board.
scrīptum, -ī *nt* writing, book, work; (*law*) ordinance; **duodecim ~a** Twelve Lines (*a game played on a squared board*).
scrīptūra, -ae *f* writing; composition; document; (*POL*) tax on public pastures; (*will*) provision.
scrīptus *ppp of* **scrībō**.
scrīptus, -ūs *m* clerkship.
scrīpulum, -ī *nt* small weight, scruple.
scrobis, -is *f* ditch, trench; grave.
scrōfa, -ae *f* breeding sow.
scrōfipāscus, -ī *m* pig breeder.
scrūpeus *adj* stony, rough.
scrūpōsus *adj* rocky, jagged.
scrūpulōsus *adj* stony, rough; (*fig*) precise.
scrūpulum *etc see* **scrīpulum**.
scrūpulus, -ī *m* small sharp stone; (*fig*) uneasiness, doubt, scruple.
scrūpus, -ī *m* sharp stone; (*fig*) uneasiness.
scrūta, -ōrum *ntpl* trash.

scrūtor, -ārī, -ātus *vt* to search, probe into, examine; to find out.
sculpō, -ere, -sī, -tum *vt* to carve, engrave.
sculpōneae, -ārum *fpl* clogs.
sculptilis *adj* carved.
sculptor, -ōris *m* sculptor.
sculptus *ppp of* **sculpō**.
scurra, -ae *m* jester; dandy.
scurrīlis *adj* jeering.
scurrīlitās, -ātis *f* scurrility.
scurror, -ārī *vi* to play the fool.
scūtāle, -is *nt* sling strap.
scūtātus *adj* carrying a shield.
scutella, -ae *f* bowl.
scutica, -ae *f* whip.
scutra, -ae *f* flat dish.
scutula, -ae *f* small dish.
scutula *f* wooden roller; secret letter.
scutulāta, -ae *f* a checked garment.
scūtulum, -ī *nt* small shield.
scūtum, -ī *nt* shield.
Scylla, -ae *f* dangerous rock *or* sea monster (*in the Straits of Messina*).
Scyllaeus *adj see* **Scylla**.
scymnus, -ī *m* cub.
scyphus, -ī *m* wine cup.
Scyrius, -ias *adj see* **Scyros**.
Scyros *and* **us, -ī** *f* Aegean island near Euboea.
scytala *see* **scutula**.
Scytha *and* **ēs, -ae** *m* Scythian.
Scythia, -iae *f* Scythia (*country N.E. of the Black Sea*).
Scythicus *adj* Scythian.
Scythis, -idis *f* Scythian woman.
sē *pron* himself, herself, itself, themselves; one another; **apud ~** at home; in his senses; **inter ~** mutually.
sēbum, -ī *nt* tallow, suet, grease.
sēcēdō, -ēdere, -essī, -essum *vi* to withdraw, retire; to revolt, secede.
sēcernō, -ernere, -rēvī, -rētum *vt* to separate, set apart; to dissociate; to distinguish.
sēcessiō, -ōnis *f* withdrawal; secession.
sēcessus, -ūs *m* retirement, solitude; retreat, recess.
sēclūdō, -dere, -sī, -sum *vt* to shut off, seclude; to separate, remove.
sēclūsus *ppp of* **sēclūdō** ♦ *adj* remote.
secō, -āre, -uī, -tum *vt* to cut; to injure; to divide; (*MED*) to operate on; (*motion*) to pass through; (*dispute*) to decide.
sēcrētiō, -ōnis *f* separation.
sēcrētō *adv* apart, in private, in secret.
sēcrētum, -ī *nt* privacy, secrecy; retreat, remote place; secret, mystery.
sēcrētus *ppp of* **sēcernō** ♦ *adj* separate; solitary, remote; secret, private.
secta, -ae *f* path; method, way of life; (*POL*) party; (*PHILOS*) school.

Noun declensions and verb conjugations are shown on pp xiii to xxv. The present infinitive ending of a verb shows to which conjugation it belongs: **-āre** = 1st; **-ēre** = 2nd; **-ere** = 3rd and **-īre** = 4th. Irregular verbs are shown on p xxvi

sectārius *adj* leading.
sectātor, -ōris *m* follower, adherent.
sectilis *adj* cut; for cutting.
sectiō, -ōnis *f* auctioning of confiscated goods.
sector, -ōris *m* cutter; buyer at a public sale.
sector, -ārī, -ātus *vt* to follow regularly, attend; to chase, hunt.
sectūra, -ae *f* digging.
sectus *ppp of* **secō**.
sēcubitus, -ūs *m* lying alone.
sēcubō, -āre, -uī *vi* to sleep by oneself; to live alone.
secuī *perf of* **secō**.
sēcul- *etc see* **saecul-**.
sēcum with himself *etc*.
secundānī, -ōrum *mpl* men of the second legion.
secundārius *adj* second-rate.
secundō *adv* secondly.
secundō, -āre *vt* to favour, make prosper.
secundum *prep* (*place*) behind, along; (*time*) after; (*rank*) next to; (*agreement*) according to, in favour of ♦ *adv* behind.
secundus *adj* following, next, second; inferior; favourable, propitious, fortunate ♦ *fpl* (*play*) subsidiary part; (*fig*) second fiddle ♦ *ntpl* success, good fortune; **~ō flūmine** downstream; **rēs ~ae** prosperity, success.
secūricula, -ae *f* little axe.
secūrifer, -ī *adj* armed with an axe.
secūriger, -ī *adj* armed with an axe.
secūris, -is *f* axe; (*fig*) death blow; (*POL*) authority, supreme power.
secūritās, -ātis *f* freedom from anxiety, composure; negligence; safety, feeling of security.
secūrus *adj* untroubled, unconcerned; carefree, cheerful; careless.
secus *nt* (*indecl*) sex.
secus *adv* otherwise, differently; badly; **nōn ~** even so.
secūtor, -ōris *m* pursuer.
sed *conj* but; but also, but in fact.
sēdātē *adv* calmly.
sēdātiō, -ōnis *f* calming.
sēdātus *ppp of* **sēdō** ♦ *adj* calm, quiet, composed.
sēdecim *num* sixteen.
sēdēcula, -ae *f* low stool.
sedentārius *adj* sitting.
sedeō, -ēre, sēdī, sessum *vi* to sit; (*army*) to be encamped, blockade; (*magistrates*) to be in session; (*clothes*) to suit, fit; (*places*) to be low-lying; (*heavy things*) to settle, subside; (*weapons*) to stick fast; (*inactivity*) to be idle; (*thought*) to be firmly resolved.
sēdēs, -is *f* seat, chair; abode, home; site, ground, foundation.
sēdī *perf of* **sedeō**.
sedīle, -is *nt* seat, chair.
sēditiō, -ōnis *f* insurrection, mutiny.
sēditiōsē *adv* seditiously.

sēditiōsus *adj* mutinous, factious; quarrelsome; troubled.
sēdō, -āre, -āvī, -ātum *vt* to calm, allay, lull.
sēdūcō, -ūcere, -ūxī, -uctum *vt* to take away, withdraw; to divide.
sēductiō, -ōnis *f* taking sides.
sēductus *ppp of* **sēdūcō** ♦ *adj* remote.
sēdulitās, -ātis *f* earnestness, assiduity; officiousness.
sēdulō *adv* busily, diligently; purposely.
sēdulus *adj* busy, diligent, assiduous; officious.
seges, -itis *f* cornfield; crop.
Segesta, -ae *f* town in N.W. Sicily.
Segestānus *adj see* **Segesta**.
segmentātus *adj* flounced.
segmentum, -ī *nt* brocade.
segne, -iter *adv* slowly, lazily.
segnipēs, -edis *adj* slow of foot.
segnis *adj* slow, sluggish, lazy.
segnitia, -ae *and* **ēs, -em, -ē** *f* slowness, sluggishness, sloth.
sēgregō, -āre, -āvī, -ātum *vt* to separate, put apart; to dissociate.
sēiugātus *adj* separated.
sēiugis, -is *m* chariot and six.
sēiūnctim *adv* separately.
sēiūnctiō, -ōnis *f* separation.
sēiūnctus *ppp of* **sēiungō**.
sēiungō, -gere, sēiūnxī, sēiūnctum *vt* to separate, part.
sēlēctiō, -ōnis *f* choice.
sēlēctus *ppp of* **sēligō**.
Seleucus, -ī *m* king of Syria.
sēlībra, -ae *f* half pound.
sēligō, -igere, -ēgī, -ēctum *vt* to choose, select.
sella, -ae *f* seat, chair, stool, sedan chair; **~ curūlis** chair of office for higher magistrates.
sellisternia, -ōrum *ntpl* sacred banquets to goddesses.
sellula, -ae *f* stool; sedan chair.
sellulārius, -ī *and* **iī** *m* mechanic.
sēmanimus *etc see* **sēmianimis**.
semel *adv* once; once for all; first; ever; **~ atque iterum** again and again; **~ aut iterum** once or twice.
Semelē, -ēs *f* mother of Bacchus.
Semelēius *adj see* **Semelē**.
sēmen, -inis *nt* seed; (*plant*) seedling, slip; (*men*) race, child; (*physics*) particle; (*fig*) origin, instigator.
sēmentifer, -ī *adj* fruitful.
sēmentis, -is *f* sowing, planting; young corn.
sēmentīvus *adj* of seed time.
sēmermis *etc see* **sēmiermis**.
sēmēstris *adj* half-yearly, for six months.
sēmēsus *adj* half-eaten.
sēmet *pron* self, selves.
sēmiadapertus *adj* half-open.
sēmianimis, -us *adj* half-dead.
sēmiapertus *adj* half-open.
sēmibōs, -ovis *adj* half-ox.

sēmicaper, -rī *adj* half-goat.
sēmicremātus, sēmicremus *adj* half-burned.
sēmicubitālis *adj* half a cubit long.
sēmideus *adj* half-divine ♦ *m* demigod.
sēmidoctus *adj* half-taught.
sēmiermis, -us *adj* half-armed.
sēmiēsus *adj* half-eaten.
sēmifactus *adj* half-finished.
sēmifer, -ī *adj* half-beast; half-savage.
sēmigermānus *adj* half-German.
sēmigravis *adj* half-overcome.
sēmigrō, -āre *vi* to go away.
sēmihiāns, -antis *adj* half-opened.
sēmihomō, -inis *m* half-man, half-human.
sēmihōra, -ae *f* half an hour.
sēmilacer, -ī *adj* half-mangled.
sēmilautus *adj* half-washed.
sēmilīber, -ī *adj* half-free.
sēmilixa, -ae *m* not much better than a camp follower.
sēmimarīnus *adj* half in the sea.
sēmimās, -āris *m* hermaphrodite ♦ *adj* castrated.
sēmimortuus *adj* half-dead.
sēminārium, -ī *and* **iī** *nt* nursery, seed plot.
sēminātor, -ōris *m* originator.
sēminecis *adj* half-dead.
sēminium, -ī *and* **iī** *nt* procreation; breed.
sēminō, -āre *vt* to sow; to produce; to beget.
sēminūdus *adj* half-naked; almost unarmed.
sēmipāgānus *adj* half-rustic.
sēmiplēnus *adj* half-full, half-manned.
sēmiputātus *adj* half-pruned.
Semīramis, -is *and* **idis** *f* queen of Assyria.
Semīramius *adj see n.*
sēmirāsus *adj* half-shaven.
sēmireductus *adj* half turned back.
sēmirefectus *adj* half-repaired.
sēmirutus *adj* half-demolished, half in ruins.
sēmis, -issis *m* (*coin*) half an as; (*interest*) ½ per cent per month (*i.e. 6 per cent per annum*); (*area*) half an acre.
sēmisepultus *adj* half-buried.
sēmisomnus *adj* half-asleep.
sēmisupīnus *adj* half lying back.
sēmita, -ae *f* path, way.
sēmitālis *adj* of byways.
sēmitārius *adj* frequenting byways.
sēmiūst- *etc see* **sēmūst-**.
sēmivir, -ī *adj* half-man; emasculated; unmanly.
sēmivīvus *adj* half-dead.
sēmodius, -ī *and* **iī** *m* half a peck.
sēmōtus *ppp of* **sēmoveō** ♦ *adj* remote; distinct.
sēmoveō, -ovēre, -ōvī, -ōtum *vt* to put aside, separate.
semper *adv* always, ever, every time.
sempiternus *adj* everlasting, lifelong.

Semprōnius, -ī *m* Roman family name (*esp the Gracchi*).
Semprōnius, -iānus *adj see n.*
sēmūncia, -ae *f* half an ounce; a twenty-fourth.
sēmūnciārius *adj* (*interest*) at the rate of one twenty-fourth.
sēmūstulātus *adj* half-burned.
sēmūstus *adj* half-burned.
senāculum, -ī *nt* open air meeting place (*of the Senate*).
sēnāriolus, -ī *m* little trimeter.
sēnārius, -ī *and* **iī** *m* (iambic) trimeter.
senātor, -ōris *m* senator.
senātōrius *adj* senatorial, in the Senate.
senātus, -ūs *m* Senate; meeting of the Senate.
senātūscōnsultum, -ī *nt* decree of the Senate.
Seneca, -ae *m* Stoic philosopher, tutor of Nero.
senecta, -ae *f* old age.
senectus *adj* old, aged.
senectūs, -ūtis *f* old age; old men.
seneō, -ēre *vi* to be old.
senēscō, -ēscere, -uī *vi* to grow old; (*fig*) to weaken, wane, pine away.
senex, -is (*compar* -**ior**) *adj* old (*over 45*) ♦ *m/f* old man, old woman.
sēnī, -ōrum *adj* six each, in sixes; six; ~ **dēnī** sixteen each.
senīlis *adj* of an old person, senile.
sēniō, -ōnis *m* number six on a dice.
senior *compar of* **senex**.
senium, -ī *and* **iī** *nt* weakness of age, decline; affliction; peevishness.
Senonēs, -um *mpl* tribe of S. Gaul.
sēnsī *perf of* **sentiō**.
sēnsifer, -ī *adj* sensory.
sēnsilis *adj* having sensation.
sēnsim *adv* tentatively, gradually.
sēnsus *ppp of* **sentiō** ♦ *ntpl* thoughts.
sēnsus, -ūs *m* (*body*) feeling, sensation, sense; (*intellect*) understanding, judgment, thought; (*emotion*) sentiment, attitude, frame of mind; (*language*) meaning, purport, sentence; **commūnis** ~ universal human feelings, human sympathy, social instinct.
sententia, -ae *f* opinion, judgment; purpose, will; (*law*) verdict, sentence; (*POL*) vote, decision; (*language*) meaning, sentence, maxim, epigram; **meā** ~**ā** in my opinion; **dē meā** ~**ā** in accordance with my wishes; **ex meā** ~**ā** to my liking; **ex animī meī** ~**ā** to the best of my knowledge and belief; **in** ~**am pedibus īre** support a motion.
sententiola, -ae *f* phrase.
sententiōsē *adv* pointedly.
sententiōsus *adj* pithy.
senticētum, -ī *nt* thornbrake.
sentīna, -ae *f* bilge water; (*fig*) dregs, scum.
sentiō, -īre, sēnsī, sēnsum *vt* (*senses*) to

feel, see, perceive; (*CIRCS*) to experience, undergo; (*mind*) to observe, understand; (*opinion*) to think, judge; (*law*) to vote, decide.

sentis, -is *m* thorn, brier.

sentīscō, -ere *vt* to begin to perceive.

sentus *adj* thorny; untidy.

senuī *perf of* **senēscō**.

seorsum, seorsus *adv* apart, differently.

sēparābilis *adj* separable.

sēparātim *adv* apart, separately.

sēparātiō, -ōnis *f* separation, severing.

sēparātius *adv* less closely.

sēparātus *adj* separate, different.

sēparō, -āre, -āvī, -ātum *vt* to part, separate, divide; to distinguish.

sepeliō, -elīre, -elīvī *and* **eliī, -ultum** *vt* to bury; (*fig*) to overwhelm, overcome.

sēpia, -ae *f* cuttlefish.

Sēplasia, -ae *f* street in Capua where perfumes were sold.

sēpōnō, -ōnere, -osuī, -ositum *vt* to put aside, pick out; to reserve; to banish; to appropriate; to separate.

sēpositus *ppp of* **sēpōnō** ♦ *adj* remote; distinct, choice.

sēpse *pron* oneself.

septem *num* seven.

September, -ris *m* September ♦ *adj* of September.

septemdecim *etc see* **septendecim**.

septemfluus *adj* with seven streams.

septemgeminus *adj* sevenfold.

septemplex, -icis *adj* sevenfold.

septemtriō *etc see* **septentriōnēs**.

septemvirālis *adj* of the septemviri ♦ *mpl* the septemviri.

septemvirātus, -ūs *m* office of septemvir.

septemvirī, -ōrum *mpl* board of seven officials.

septēnārius, -ī *and* **iī** *m* verse of seven feet.

septendecim *num* seventeen.

septēnī, -ōrum *adj* seven each, in sevens.

septentriō, -ōnis *m*, **-ōnēs, -ōnum** *mpl* Great Bear, Little Bear; north; north wind.

septentriōnālis *adj* northern ♦ *ntpl* northern regions.

septiēns, -ēs *adv* seven times.

septimānī, -ōrum *mpl* men of the seventh legion.

septimum *adv* for the seventh time; ~ **decimus** seventeenth.

septimus *adj* seventh.

septingentēsimus *adj* seven hundredth.

septingentī, -ōrum *adj* seven hundred.

septuāgēsimus *adj* seventieth.

septuāgintā *adj* seventy.

septuennis *adj* seven years old.

septumus *adj see* **septimus**.

septūnx, -ūncis *m* seven ounces, seven-twelfths.

sepulcrālis *adj* funeral.

sepulcrētum, -ī *nt* cemetery.

sepulcrum, -ī *nt* grave, tomb.

sepultūra, -ae *f* burial, funeral.

sepultus *ppp of* **sepeliō**.

Sequāna, -ae *f* river Seine.

Sequānī, -ōrum *mpl* people of N. Gaul.

sequāx, -ācis *adj* pursuing, following.

sequens, -entis *pres p of* **sequor** ♦ *adj* following, next.

sequester, -rī *and* **ris** *m* trustee; agent, mediator.

sequestrum, -rī *nt* deposit.

sēquius *compar of* **secus**; otherwise; **nihilō** ~ nonetheless.

sequor, -quī, -cūtus *vt*, *vi* to follow; to accompany, go with; (*time*) to come after, come next, ensue; (*enemy*) to pursue; (*objective*) to make for, aim at; (*pulling*) to come away easily; (*share, gift*) to go to, come to; (*words*) to come naturally.

sera, -ae *f* door bolt, bar.

Serāpēum, -ēī *nt* temple of Serapis.

Serāpis, -is *and* **idis** *m* chief Egyptian god.

serēnitās, -ātis *f* fair weather.

serēnō, -āre *vt* to clear up, brighten up.

serēnus *adj* fair, clear; (*wind*) fair-weather; (*fig*) cheerful, happy ♦ *nt* clear sky, fair weather.

Sērēs, -um *mpl* Chinese.

serēscō, -ere *vi* to dry off.

sēria, -ae *f* tall jar.

sērica, -ōrum *ntpl* silks.

Sēricus *adj* Chinese; silk.

seriēs, -em, -ē *f* row, sequence, succession.

sēriō *adv* in earnest, seriously.

sēriola, -ae *f* small jar.

Serīphius *adj see* **Serīphus**.

Serīphus (-os), -ī *f* Aegean island.

sērius *adj* earnest, serious.

sērius *compar of* **sērō**.

sermō, -ōnis *m* conversation, talk; learned discussion, discourse; common talk, rumour; language, style; every day language, prose; (*pl*) Satires (of Horace).

sermōcinor, -ārī *vi* to converse.

sermunculus, -ī *m* gossip, rumour.

serō, -ere, sēvī, -satum *vt* to sow, plant; (*fig*) to produce, sow the seeds of.

serō, -ere, -tum *vt* to sew, join, wreathe; (*fig*) to compose, devise, engage in.

sērō (*compar* **-ius**) *adv* late; too late.

serpēns, -entis *m/f* snake, serpent; (*constellation*) Draco.

serpentigena, -ae *m* offspring of a serpent.

serpentipēs, -edis *adj* serpent-footed.

serperastra, -ōrum *ntpl* splints.

serpō, -ere, -sī, -tum *vi* to creep, crawl; (*fig*) to spread slowly.

serpyllum, -ī *nt* wild thyme.

serra, -ae *f* saw.

serrācum *etc see* **sarrācum**.

serrātus *adj* serrated, notched.

serrula, -ae *f* small saw.

Sertōriānus *adj see* **Sertōrius**.

Sertōrius, -ī m commander under Marius, who held out against Sulla in Spain.
sertus ppp of **serō** ♦ ntpl garlands.
serum, -ī nt whey, serum.
sērum, -ī nt late hour.
sērus adj late; too late; **~ā nocte** late at night.
serva, -ae f maidservant, slave.
servābilis adj that cannot be saved.
servātor, -ōris m deliverer; watcher.
servātrīx, -īcis f deliverer.
servīlis adj of slaves, servile.
servīliter adv slavishly.
Servīlius, -ī m Roman family name of many consuls.
Servīlius, -ānus adj see n.
serviō, -īre, -īvī and **iī, -ītum** vi to be a slave; (with dat) to serve, be of use to, be good for; (property) to be mortgaged.
servitium, -ī and **iī** nt slavery, servitude; slaves.
servitūdō, -inis f slavery.
servitūs, -ūtis f slavery, service; slaves; (property) liability.
Servius, -ī m sixth king of Rome; famous jurist of Cicero's day.
servō, -āre, -āvī, -ātum vt to save, rescue; to keep, preserve, retain; to store, reserve; to watch, observe, guard; (place) to remain in.
servolus, -ī m young slave.
servos, -ī m see **servus**.
servula, -ae f servant girl.
servulus, -ī m young slave.
servus, -ī m slave, servant ♦ adj slavish, serving; (property) liable to a burden.
sescēnāris adj a year and a half old.
sescēnī, -ōrum adj six hundred each.
sescentēsimus adj six hundredth.
sescentī, -ōrum num six hundred; an indefinitely large number.
sescentiēns, -ēs adv six hundred times.
sēsē etc see **sē**.
seselis, -is f (plant) seseli.
sesqui adv one and a half times.
sesquialter, -ī adj one and a half.
sesquimodius, -ī and **iī** m a peck and a half.
sesquioctāvus adj of nine to eight.
sesquiopus, -eris nt a day and a half's work.
sesquipedālis adj a foot and a half.
sesquipēs, -edis m a foot and a half.
sesquiplāga, -ae f a blow and a half.
sesquiplex, -icis adj one and a half times.
sesquitertius adj of four to three.
sessilis adj for sitting on.
sessiō, -ōnis f sitting; seat; session; loitering.
sessitō, -āre, -āvī vi to sit regularly.
sessiuncula, -ae f small meeting.
sessor, -ōris m spectator; resident.
sēstertium, -ī nt 1000 sesterces; **dēna ~ia** 10,000 sesterces; **centēna mīlia ~ium** 100,000 sesterces; **deciēns ~ium** 1,000,000 sesterces.

sēstertius, -ī and **iī** m sesterce, a silver coin.
Sestius, -ī m tribune defended by Cicero.
Sestius, -iānus adj of a Sestius.
Sestos (-us), -ī f town on Dardanelles (home of Hero).
Sestus adj see **Sestos**.
sēt- etc see **saet-**.
Sētia, -iae f town in S. Latium (famous for wine).
Sētiānus adj see **Sētia**.
sētius compar of **secus**.
seu etc see **sīve**.
sevērē adv sternly, severely.
sevēritās, -ātis f strictness, austerity.
sevērus adj strict, stern; severe, austere; grim, terrible.
sēvī perf of **serō**.
sēvocō, -āre vt to call aside; to withdraw, remove.
sēvum etc see **sēbum**.
sex num six.
sexāgēnārius adj sixty years old.
sexāgēnī, -ōrum adj sixty each.
sexāgēsimus adj sixtieth.
sexāgiēns, -ēs adv sixty times.
sexāgintā num sixty.
sexangulus adj hexagonal.
sexcēn- etc see **sescēn-**.
sexcēnārius adj of six hundred.
sexennis adj six years old, after six years.
sexennium, -ī and **iī** nt six years.
sexiēns, -ēs adv six times.
sexprīmī, -ōrum mpl a provincial town, council.
sextadecimānī, -ōrum mpl men of the sixteenth legion.
sextāns, -antis m a sixth; (coin, weight) a sixth of an as.
sextārius, -ī and **iī** m pint.
Sextīlis, -is m August ♦ adj of August.
sextula, -ae f a sixth of an ounce.
sextum adv for the sixth time.
sextus adj sixth; **~ decimus** sixteenth.
sexus, -ūs m sex.
sī conj if; if only; to see if; **sī forte** in the hope that; **sī iam** assuming for the moment; **sī minus** if not; **sī quandō** whenever; **sī quidem** if indeed; since; **sī quis** if anyone, whoever; **mīrum sī** surprising that; **quod sī** and if, but if.
sībila, -ōrum ntpl whistle, hissing.
sībilō, -āre vi to hiss, whistle ♦ vt to hiss at.
sībilus, -ī m whistle, hissing.
sībilus adj hissing.
Sibulla, Sibylla, -ae f prophetess, Sibyl.
Sibyllīnus adj see **Sibylla**.
sīc adv so, thus, this way, as follows; as one is, as things are; on this condition; yes.
sīca, -ae f dagger.
Sicānī, -ōrum mpl ancient people of Italy

Noun declensions and verb conjugations are shown on pp xiii to xxv. The present infinitive ending of a verb shows to which conjugation it belongs: **-āre** = 1st; **-ēre** = 2nd; **-ere** = 3rd and **-īre** = 4th. Irregular verbs are shown on p xxvi

(*later of Sicily*).

Sicānia, -iae *f* Sicily.

Sicānus, -ius *adj* Sicanian, Sicilian.

sīcārius, -ī *and* **iī** *m* assassin, murderer.

siccē *adv* (*speech*) firmly.

siccitās, -ātis *f* dryness, drought; (*body*) firmness; (*style*) dullness.

siccō, -āre, -āvī, -ātum *vt* to dry; to drain, exhaust; (*sore*) to heal up.

siccoculus *adj* dry-eyed.

siccus *adj* dry; thirsty, sober; (*body*) firm, healthy; (*argument*) solid, sound; (*style*) flat, dull ♦ *nt* dry land.

Sicilia, -ae *f* Sicily.

sicilicula, -ae *f* little sickle.

Siciliēnsis, -s, -dis *adj* Sicilian.

sicine is this how?

sīcubi *adv* if anywhere, wheresoever.

Siculus *adj* Sicilian.

sīcunde *adv* if from anywhere.

sīcut, sīcutī *adv* just as, as in fact; (*comparison*) like, as; (*example*) as for instance; (*with subj*) as if.

Sicyōn, -ōnis *f* town in N. Peloponnese.

Sicyōnius *adj see* **Sicyōn**.

sīdereus *adj* starry; (*fig*) radiant.

Sidicīnī, -ōrum *mpl* people of Campania.

Sidicīnus *adj see n.*

sīdō, -ere, -ī *vi* to sit down, settle; to sink, subside; to stick fast.

Sīdōn, -ōnis *f* famous Phoenician town.

Sīdōnis, -ōnidis *adj* Phoenician ♦ *f* Europa; Dido.

Sīdōnius *adj* Sidonian, Phoenician.

sīdus, -eris *nt* constellation; heavenly body, star; season, climate, weather; destiny; (*pl*) sky; (*fig*) fame, glory.

siem *archaic subj of* **sum.**

Sigambrī *etc see* **Sugambrī**.

Sīgēum, -ī *nt* promontory near Troy.

Sīgēus, -ius *adj* Sigean.

sigilla, -ōrum *ntpl* little figures; seal.

sigillātus *adj* decorated with little figures.

signātor, -ōris *m* witness (to a document).

signifer, -ī *adj* with constellations; ~ **orbis** Zodiac ♦ *m* (MIL) standard-bearer.

significanter *adv* pointedly, tellingly.

significātiō, -ōnis *f* indication, signal, token; sign of approval; (RHET) emphasis; (*word*) meaning.

significō, -āre, -āvī, -ātum *vt* to indicate, show; to betoken, portend; (*word*) to mean.

signō, -āre, -āvī, -ātum *vt* to mark, stamp, print; (*document*) to seal; (*money*) to coin, mint; (*fig*) to impress, designate, note.

signum, -ī *nt* mark, sign, token; (MIL) standard; signal, password; (*art*) design, statue; (*document*) seal; (ASTRO) constellation; **~a cōnferre** join battle; **~a cōnstituere** halt; **~a convertere** wheel about; **~a ferre** move camp; attack; **~a inferre** attack; **~a prōferre** advance; **~a sequī** march in order; **ab ~īs discēdere** leave the ranks; **sub ~īs īre** march

in order.

Sīla, -ae *f* forest in extreme S. Italy

sīlānus, -ī *m* fountain, jet of water.

silēns, -entis *pres p of* **sileō** ♦ *adj* still, silent ♦ *mpl* the dead.

silentium, -ī *and* **iī** *nt* stillness, silence; (*fig*) standstill, inaction.

Sīlēnus, -ī *m* old and drunken companion of Bacchus.

sileō, -ēre, -uī *vi* to be still, be silent; to cease ♦ *vt* to say nothing about.

siler, -is *nt* willow.

silēscō, -ere *vi* to calm down, fall silent.

silex, -icis *m* flint, hard stone; rock.

silicernium, -ī *and* **iī** *nt* funeral feast.

sīlīgō, -inis *f* winter wheat; fine flour.

siliqua, -ae *f* pod, husk; (*pl*) pulse.

sillybus, -ī *m* label bearing a book's title.

Silurēs, -um *mpl* British tribe in S. Wales.

silūrus, -ī *m* sheatfish.

sīlus *adj* snub-nosed.

silva, -ae *f* wood, forest; plantation, shrubbery; (*plant*) flowering stem; (LIT) material.

Silvānus, -ī *m* god of uncultivated land.

silvēscō, -ere *vi* to run to wood.

silvestris *adj* wooded, forest- (*in cpds*); wild; pastoral.

silvicola, -ae *m/f* sylvan.

silvicultrīx, -īcis *adj* living in the woods.

silvifragus *adj* tree-breaking.

silvōsus *adj* woody.

sīmia, -ae *f* ape.

simile, -is *nt* comparison, parallel.

similis *adj* like, similar; ~ **atque** like what; **vērī ~** probable.

similiter *adv* similarly.

similitūdō, -inis *f* likeness, resemblance; imitation; analogy; monotony; (RHET) simile.

sīmiolus, -ī *m* monkey.

simītū *adv* at the same time, together.

sīmius, -ī *and* **iī** *m* ape.

Simoīs, -entis *m* river of Troy.

Simōnidēs, -is *m* Greek lyric poet of Ceos (*famous for dirges*).

Simōnidēus *adj see n.*

simplex, -icis *adj* single, simple; natural, straightforward; (*character*) frank, sincere.

simplicitās, -ātis *f* singleness; frankness, innocence.

simpliciter *adv* simply, naturally; frankly.

simplum, -ī *nt* simple sum.

simpulum, -ī *nt* small ladle; **excitāre flūctūs in ~ō** ≈ raise a storm in a teacup.

simpuvium, -ī *and* **iī** *nt* libation bowl.

simul *adv* at the same time, together, at once; likewise, also; both ... and; **~ ac atque, ut** as soon as ♦ *conj* as soon as.

simulācrum, -ī *nt* likeness, image, portrait, statue; phantom, ghost; (*writing*) symbol; (*fig*) semblance, shadow.

simulāmen, -inis *nt* copy.

simulāns, -antis *pres p of* **simulō** ♦ *adj*

imitative.

simulātē *adv* deceitfully.

simulātiō, -ōnis *f* pretence, shamming, hypocrisy.

simulātor, -ōris *m* imitator; pretender, hypocrite.

simulatque *conj* as soon as.

simulō, -āre, -āvī, -ātum *vt* to imitate, represent; to impersonate; to pretend, counterfeit.

simultās, -ātis *f* feud, quarrel.

sīmulus *adj* snub-nosed.

sīmus *adj* snub-nosed.

sīn *conj* but if; **~ aliter, minus** but if not.

sināpi, -is *nt*, **-is, -is** *f* mustard.

sincērē *adv* honestly.

sincēritās, -ātis *f* integrity.

sincērus *adj* clean, whole, genuine; (*fig*) pure, sound, honest.

sincipitāmentum, -ī *nt* half a head.

sinciput, -itis *nt* half a head; brain.

sine *prep* (*with abl*) without, -less (*in cpds*).

singillātim *adv* singly, one by one.

singulāris *adj* one at a time, single, sole; unique, extraordinary.

singulāriter *adv* separately; extremely.

singulārius *adj* single.

singulī, -ōrum *adj* one each, single, one.

singultim *adv* in sobs.

singultō, -āre *vi* to sob, gasp, gurgle ♦ *vt* to gasp out.

singultus, -ūs *m* sob, gasp, death rattle.

singulus *etc see* **singulī**.

sinister, -rī *adj* left; (*fig*) perverse, unfavourable; (*Roman auspices*) lucky; (*Greek auspices*) unlucky.

sinistra, -rae *f* left hand, left-hand side.

sinistrē *adv* badly.

sinistrōrsus, -um *adv* to the left.

sinō, -ere, sīvī, situm *vt* to let, allow; to let be; **nē dī sīrint** God forbid!

Sinōpē, -ēs *f* Greek colony on the Black Sea.

Sinōpēnsis, -eus *adj see* **Sinōpē**.

Sinuessa, -ae *f* town on the borders of Latium and Campania.

Sinuessānus *adj see* **Sinuessa**.

sinum *etc see* **sīnus**.

sinuō, -āre, -āvī, -ātum *vt* to wind, curve.

sinuōsus *adj* winding, curved.

sinus, -ūs *m* curve, fold; (*fishing*) net; (*GEOG*) bay, gulf, valley; (*hair*) curl; (*ship*) sail; (*toga*) fold, pocket, purse; (*person*) bosom; (*fig*) protection, love, heart, hiding place; **in -ū gaudēre** be secretly glad.

sīnus, -ī *m* large cup.

sīparium, -ī and iī *nt* act curtain.

sīphō, -ōnis *m* siphon; fire engine.

siquandō *adv* if ever.

sīquī, sīquis *pron* if any, if anyone, whoever.

siquidem *adv* if in fact ♦ *conj* since.

sirempse *adj* the same.

Sīrēn, -ēnis *f* Siren.

sīris, sīrit *perf subj of* **sinō**.

Sīrius, -ī *m* Dog Star ♦ *adj* of Sirius.

sirpe, -is *nt* silphium.

sīrus, -ī *m* corn pit.

sīs (*for* sī vīs) *adv* please.

sistō, -ere, stitī, statum *vt* to place, set, plant; (*law*) to produce in court; (*monument*) to set up; (*movement*) to stop, arrest, check ♦ *vi* to stand, rest; (*law*) to appear in court; (*movement*) to stand still, stop, stand firm; **sē ~** appear, present oneself; **tūtum ~** see safe; **vadimōnium ~** duly appear in court; **~ī nōn potest** the situation is desperate.

sistrum, -ī *nt* Egyptian rattle, cymbal.

sisymbrium, -ī and iī *nt* fragrant herb, perhaps mint.

Sīsyphius *adj*, **-idēs, -idae** *m* Ulysses.

Sīsyphus, -ī *m* criminal condemned in Hades to roll a rock repeatedly up a hill.

sitella, -ae *f* lottery urn.

Sīthonis, -idis *adj* Thracian.

Sīthonius *adj* Thracian.

sitīculōsus *adj* thirsty, dry.

sitiēns, -entis *pres p of* **sitiō** ♦ *adj* thirsty, dry; parching; (*fig*) eager.

sitienter *adv* eagerly.

sitiō, -īre *vi* to be thirsty; to be parched ♦ *vt* to thirst for, covet.

sitis, -is *f* thirst; drought.

sittybus *etc see* **sillybus**.

situla, -ae *f* bucket.

situs *ppp of* **sinō** ♦ *adj* situated, lying; founded; (*fig*) dependent.

situs, -ūs *m* situation, site; structure; neglect, squalor, mould; (*mind*) dullness.

sīve *conj* or if; or; whether ... or.

sīvī *perf of* **sinō**.

smaragdus, -ī *m*/*f* emerald.

smīlax, -acis *f* bindweed.

Smintheus, -eī *m* Apollo.

Smyrna, -ae *f* Ionian town in Asia Minor.

Smyrnaeus *adj see* **Smyrna**.

sobol- *etc see* **subol-**.

sobriē *adv* temperately; sensibly.

sobrīna, -ae *f* cousin (*on the mother's side*).

sobrīnus, -ī *m* cousin (*on the mother's side*).

sobrius *adj* sober; temperate, moderate; (*mind*) sane, sensible.

soccus, -ī *m* slipper (*esp the sock worn by actors in comedy*); comedy.

socer, -ī *m* father-in-law.

sociābilis *adj* compatible.

sociālis *adj* of allies, confederate; conjugal.

sociāliter *adv* sociably.

sociennus, -ī *m* friend.

societās, -ātis *f* fellowship, association; alliance.

sociō, -āre, -āvī, -ātum *vt* to unite, associate,

share.

sociofraudus, -ī m deceiver of friends.

socius adj associated, allied ♦ m friend, companion; partner, ally.

sōcordia, -ae f indolence, apathy; folly.

sōcordius adv more carelessly, lazily.

sōcors, -dis adj lazy, apathetic; stupid.

Sōcratēs, -is m famous Athenian philosopher.

Sōcraticus adj of Socrates, Socratic ♦ mpl the followers of Socrates.

socrus, -ūs f mother-in-law.

sodālicium, -ī and **iī** nt fellowship; secret society.

sodālicius adj of fellowship.

sodālis, -is m/f companion, friend; member of a society, accomplice.

sodālitās, -ātis f companionship, friendship; society, club; secret society.

sodālitius etc see **sodālicius**.

sodēs adv please.

sōl, sōlis m sun; sunlight, sun's heat; (poetry) day; (myth) Sun god; **~ oriēns, ~is ortus** east; **~ occidēns, ~is occāsus** west.

sōlāciolum, -ī nt a grain of comfort.

sōlācium, -ī and **iī** nt comfort, consolation, relief.

sōlāmen, -inis nt solace, relief.

sōlāris adj of the sun.

sōlārium, -ī and **iī** nt sundial; clock; balcony, terrace.

sōlātium etc see **sōlācium**.

sōlātor, -ōris m consoler.

soldūriī, -ōrum mpl retainers.

soldus etc see **solidus**.

solea, -ae f sandal, shoe; fetter; (fish) sole.

soleārius, -ī and **iī** m sandal maker.

soleātus adj wearing sandals.

soleō, -ēre, -itus vi to be accustomed, be in the habit, usually do; **ut ~** as usual.

solidē adv for certain.

soliditās, -ātis f solidity.

solidō, -āre vt to make firm, strengthen.

solidus adj solid, firm, dense; whole, complete; (fig) sound, genuine, substantial ♦ nt solid matter, firm ground.

sōliferreum, -ī nt an all-iron javelin.

sōlistimus adj (AUG) most favourable.

sōlitārius adj solitary, lonely.

sōlitūdō, -inis f solitariness, loneliness; destitution; (place) desert.

solitus ppa of **soleō** ♦ adj usual, customary ♦ nt custom; **plūs ~ō** more than usual.

solium, -ī and **iī** nt seat, throne; tub; (fig) rule.

sōlivagus adj going by oneself; single.

sollemne, -is nt religious rite, festival; usage, practice.

sollemnis adj annual, regular; religious, solemn; usual, ordinary.

sollemniter adv solemnly.

sollers, -tis adj skilled, clever, expert; ingenious.

sollerter adv cleverly.

sollertia, -ae f skill, ingenuity.

sollicitātiō, -ōnis f inciting.

sollicitō, -āre, -ātum vt to stir up, disturb; to trouble, distress, molest; to rouse, urge, incite, tempt, tamper with.

sollicitūdō, -inis f uneasiness, anxiety.

sollicitus adj agitated, disturbed; (mind) troubled, worried, alarmed; (things) anxious careful; (cause) disquieting.

solliferreum etc see **sōliferreum**.

sollistimus etc see **sōlistimus**.

soloecismus, -ī m grammatical mistake.

Solōn, -ōnis m famous Athenian lawgiver.

sōlor, -ārī, -ātus vt to comfort, console; to relieve, ease.

sōlstitiālis adj of the summer solstice; midsummer.

sōlstitium, -ī and **iī** nt summer solstice; midsummer, summer heat.

solum, -ī nt ground, floor, bottom; soil, land, country; (foot) sole; (fig) basis; **~ō aequāre** raze to the ground.

sōlum adv only, merely.

sōlus (gen **-īus**, dat **-ī**) see **vicis**; adj only, alone; lonely, forsaken; (place) lonely, deserted.

solūtē adv loosely, freely, carelessly, weakly, fluently.

solūtiō, -ōnis f loosening; payment.

solūtus ppp of **solvō** ♦ adj loose, free; (from distraction) at ease, at leisure, merry; (from obligation) exempt; (from restraint) free, independent, unprejudiced; (moral) lax, weak, insolent; (language) prose, unrhythmical; (speaker) fluent; **ōrātiō ~a, verba ~a** prose.

solvō, -vere, -vī, -ūtum vt to loosen, undo; to free, release, acquit, exempt; to dissolve, break up, separate; to relax, slacken, weaken; to cancel, remove, destroy; to solve, explain; to pay, fulfil; (argument) to refute; (discipline) to undermine; (feelings) to get rid of; (hair) to let down; (letter) to open; (sail) to unfurl; (siege) to raise; (troops) to dismiss ♦ vi to set sail; to pay; **nāvem ~** set sail; **poenās ~** be punished; **praesēns ~** pay cash; **rem ~** pay; **sacrāmentō ~** discharge; **~vendō esse** be solvent.

Solyma, -ōrum ntpl Jerusalem.

Solymus adj of the Jews.

somniculōsē adv sleepily.

somniculōsus adj sleepy.

somnifer, -ī adj soporific; fatal.

somniō, -āre vt to dream, dream about; to talk nonsense.

somnium, -ī and **iī** nt dream; nonsense, fancy.

somnus, -ī m sleep; sloth.

sonābilis adj noisy.

sonipēs, -edis m steed.

sonitus, -ūs m sound, noise.

sonivius adj noisy.

sonō, -āre, -uī, -itum vi to sound, make a noise ♦ vt to utter, speak, celebrate; to sound like.

sonor, -ōris m sound, noise.

sonōrus *adj* noisy, loud.

sōns, sontis *adj* guilty.

sonticus *adj* critical; important.

sonus, -ī *m* sound, noise; (*fig*) tone.

sophistēs, -ae *m* sophist.

Sophoclēs, -is *m* famous Greek tragic poet.

Sophoclēus *adj* of Sophocles, Sophoclean.

sophus *adj* wise.

sōpiō, -īre, -īvī, -ītum *vt* to put to sleep; (*fig*) to calm, lull.

sopor, -ōris *m* sleep; apathy.

sopōrifer, -ī *adj* soporific, drowsy.

sopōrō, -āre *vt* to lull to sleep; to make soporific.

sopōrus *adj* drowsy.

Sōracte, -is *nt* mountain in S. Etruria.

sorbeō, -ēre, -uī *vt* to suck, swallow; (*fig*) to endure.

sorbillō, -āre *vt* to sip.

sorbitiō, -ōnis *f* drink, broth.

sorbum, -ī *nt* service berry.

sorbus, -ī *f* service tree.

sordeō, -ēre *vi* to be dirty, be sordid; to seem shabby; to be of no account.

sordēs, -is *f* dirt, squalor, shabbiness; mourning; meanness; vulgarity; (*people*) rabble.

sordēscō, -ere *vi* to become dirty.

sordidātus *adj* shabbily dressed, in mourning.

sordidē *adv* meanly, vulgarly.

sordidulus *adj* soiled, shabby.

sordidus *adj* dirty, squalid, shabby; in mourning; poor, mean; base, vile.

sōrex, -icis *m* shrewmouse.

sōricīnus *adj* of the shrewmouse.

sōrītēs, -ae *m* chain syllogism.

soror, -ōris *f* sister.

sorōricīda, -ae *m* murderer of a sister.

sorōrius *adj* of a sister.

sors, sortis *f* lot; allotted duty; oracle, prophecy; fate, fortune; (*money*) capital, principal.

sōrsum *etc see* **seōrsum**.

sortilegus *adj* prophetic ♦ *m* soothsayer.

sortior, -īrī, -ītus *vi* to draw *or* cast lots ♦ *vt* to draw lots for, allot, obtain by lot; to distribute, share; to choose; to receive.

sortītiō, -ōnis *f* drawing lots, choosing by lot.

sortītus *ppa of* **sortior** ♦ *adj* assigned, allotted; ~ō by lot.

sortītus, -ūs *m* drawing lots.

Sosius, -ī *m* Roman family name (*esp two brothers Sosii, famous booksellers in Rome*).

sōspes, -itis *adj* safe and sound, unhurt; favourable, lucky.

sōspita, -ae *f* saviour.

sōspitālis *adj* beneficial.

sōspitō, -āre *vt* to preserve, prosper.

sōtēr, -ēris *m* saviour.

spādīx, -īcis *adj* chestnut-brown.

spadō, -ōnis *m* eunuch.

spargō, -gere, -sī, -sum *vt* to throw, scatter, sprinkle; to strew, spot, moisten; to disperse, spread abroad.

sparsus *ppp of* **spargō** ♦ *adj* freckled.

Sparta, -ae, -ē, -ēs *f* famous Greek city.

Spartacus, -ī *m* gladiator who led a revolt against Rome.

Spartānus, -icus *adj* Spartan.

Spartiātēs, -iātae *m* Spartan.

spartum, -ī *nt* Spanish broom.

sparulus, -ī *m* bream.

sparus, -ī *m* hunting spear.

spatha, -ae *f* broadsword.

spatior, -ārī, -ātus *vi* to walk; to spread.

spatiōsē *adv* greatly; after a time.

spatiōsus *adj* roomy, ample, large; (*time*) prolonged.

spatium, -ī *and* **iī** *nt* space, room, extent; (*between points*) distance; (*open space*) square, walk, promenade; (*race*) lap, track, course; (*time*) period, interval; (*opportunity*) time, leisure; (*metre*) quantity.

speciēs, -ēī *f* seeing, sight; appearance, form, outline; (*thing seen*) sight; (*mind*) idea; (*in sleep*) vision, apparition; (*fair show*) beauty, splendour; (*false show*) pretence, pretext; (*classification*) species; **in ~em** for the sake of appearances; like; **per ~em** under the pretence; **sub ~ē** under the cloak.

specillum, -ī *nt* probe.

specimen, -inis *nt* sign, evidence, proof; pattern, ideal.

speciōsē *adv* handsomely.

speciōsus *adj* showy, beautiful; specious, plausible.

spectābilis *adj* visible; notable, remarkable.

spectāculum, spectāculum, -ī *nt* sight, spectacle; public show, play; theatre, seats.

spectāmen, -inis *nt* proof.

spectātiō, -ōnis *f* looking; testing.

spectātor, -ōris *m* onlooker, observer, spectator; critic.

spectātrīx, -īcis *f* observer.

spectātus *ppp of* **spectō** ♦ *adj* tried, proved; worthy, excellent.

spectiō, -ōnis *f* the right to take auspices.

spectō, -āre, -āvī, -ātum *vt* to look at, observe, watch; (*place*) to face; (*aim*) to look to, bear in mind, contemplate, tend towards; (*judging*) to examine, test.

spectrum, -ī *nt* spectre.

specula, -ae *f* watchtower, lookout; height.

spēcula, -ae *f* slight hope.

speculābundus *adj* on the lookout.

speculāris *adj* transparent ♦ *ntpl* window.

speculātor, -ōris *m* explorer, investigator; (*MIL*) spy, scout.

speculātōrius *adj* for spying, scouting ♦ *f* spy

Noun declensions and verb conjugations are shown on pp xiii to xxv. The present infinitive ending of a verb shows to which conjugation it belongs: **-āre** = 1st; **-ēre** = 2nd; **-ere** = 3rd and **-īre** = 4th. Irregular verbs are shown on p xxvi

boat.

speculātrīx, -īcis f watcher.

speculor, -ārī, -ātus vt to spy out, watch for, observe.

speculum, -ī nt mirror.

specus, -ūs m, nt cave; hollow, chasm.

spēlaeum, -ī nt cave, den.

spēlunca, -ae f cave, den.

spērābilis adj to be hoped for.

spērāta, -ātae f bride.

Sperchēis, -idis adj see **Sperchēus**.

Sperchēus (-os), -ī m river in Thessaly.

spernō, -ere, sprēvī, sprētum vt to remove, reject, scorn.

spērō, -āre, -āvī, -ātum vt to hope, hope for, expect; to trust; to look forward to.

spēs, speī f hope, expectation; **praeter spem** unexpectedly; **spē dēiectus** disappointed.

Speusippus, -ī m successor of Plato in the Academy.

sphaera, -ae f ball, globe, sphere.

Sphinx, -ingis f fabulous monster near Thebes.

spīca, -ae f (grain) ear; (plant) tuft; (ASTRO) brightest star in Virgo.

spīceus adj of ears of corn.

spīculum, -ī nt point, sting; dart, arrow.

spīna, -ae f thorn; prickle; fish bone; spine, back; (pl) difficulties, subtleties.

spīnētum, -ī nt thorn hedge.

spīneus adj of thorns.

spīnifer, -ī adj prickly.

spīnōsus adj thorny, prickly; (style) difficult.

spintēr, -ēris nt elastic bracelet.

spīnus, -ī f blackthorn, sloe.

spīra, -ae f coil; twisted band.

spīrābilis adj breathable, life-giving.

spīrāculum, -ī nt vent.

spīrāmentum, -ī nt vent, pore; breathing space.

spīritus, -ūs m breath, breathing; breeze, air; inspiration; character, spirit, courage, arrogance.

spīrō, -āre, -āvī, -ātum vi to breathe, blow; to be alive; to be inspired ♦ vt to emit, exhale; (fig) to breathe, express.

spissātus adj condensed.

spissē adv closely; slowly.

spissēscō, -ere vi to thicken.

spissus adj thick, compact, crowded; slow; (fig) difficult.

splendeō, -ēre vi to be bright, shine; to be illustrious.

splendēscō, -ere vi to become bright.

splendidē adv brilliantly, magnificently, nobly.

splendidus adj bright, brilliant, glittering; (sound) clear; (dress, house) magnificent; (person) illustrious; (appearance) showy.

splendor, -ōris m brightness, lustre; magnificence; clearness; nobility.

spoliātiō, -ōnis f plundering.

spoliātor, -ōris m robber.

spoliātrīx, -īcis f robber.

spoliō, -āre, -āvī, -ātum vt to strip; to rob, plunder.

spolium, -ī and **iī** nt (beast) skin; (enemy) spoils, booty.

sponda, -ae f bed frame; bed, couch.

spondālium, -ī and **iī** nt hymn accompanied by the flute.

spondeō, -ēre, spopondī, spōnsum vt to promise, pledge, vow; (law) to go bail for; (marriage) to betroth.

spondēus, -ī m spondee.

spongia, -ae f sponge; coat of mail.

spōnsa, -ae f fiancée, bride.

spōnsālia, -ium ntpl engagement.

spōnsiō, -ōnis f promise, guarantee; (law) agreement that the loser in a suit pays the winner a sum; bet.

spōnsor, -ōris m guarantor, surety.

spōnsus ppp of **spondeō** ♦ m fiancé, bridegroom ♦ nt agreement, covenant.

spōnsus, -ūs m contract, surety.

sponte f (abl) voluntarily, of one's own accord; unaided, by oneself; spontaneously.

spopondī perf of **spondeō**.

sportella, -ae f fruit basket.

sportula, -ae f small basket; gift to clients, dole.

sprētiō, -ōnis f contempt.

sprētor, -ōris m despiser.

sprētus ppp of **spernō**.

sprēvī perf of **spernō**.

spūma, -ae f foam, froth.

spūmēscō, -ere vi to become frothy.

spūmeus adj foaming, frothy.

spūmifer, -ī adj foaming.

spūmiger, -ī adj foaming.

spūmō, -āre vi to foam, froth.

spūmōsus adj foaming.

spuō, -uere, -uī, -ūtum vi to spit ♦ vt to spit out.

spurcē adv obscenely.

spurcidicus adj obscene.

spurcificus adj obscene.

spurcitia, -ae and **ēs, -ēī** f filth, smut.

spurcō, -āre vt to befoul.

spurcus adj filthy, nasty, foul.

spūtātilicus adj despicable.

spūtātor, -ōris m spitter.

spūtō, -āre vt to spit out.

spūtum, -ī nt spit, spittle.

squāleō, -ēre, -uī vi to be rough, stiff, clotted; to be parched; to be neglected, squalid, filthy; to be in mourning.

squālidē adv rudely.

squālidus adj rough, scaly; neglected, squalid, filthy; (speech) unpolished.

squālor, -ōris m roughness; filth, squalor.

squāma, -ae f scale; scale armour.

squāmeus adj scaly.

squāmifer, -ī adj scaly.

squāmiger, -ī adj scaly ♦ mpl fishes.

squāmōsus adj scaly.

squilla, -ae f prawn, shrimp.

st *interj* sh!

stabilīmentum, -ī *nt* support.

stabiliō, -īre *vt* to make stable; to establish.

stabilis *adj* firm, steady; (*fig*) steadfast, unfailing.

stabilitās, -ātis *f* firmness, steadiness, reliability.

stabulō, -āre *vt* to house, stable ♦ *vi* to have a stall.

stabulum, -ī *nt* stall, stable, steading; lodging, cottage; brothel.

stacta, -ae *f* myrrh oil.

stadium, -ī *and* **iī** *nt* stade, furlong; racetrack.

Stagīra, -ōrum *ntpl* town in Macedonia (*birthplace of Aristotle*).

Stagīrītēs, -ītae *m* Aristotle.

stagnō, -āre *vi* to form pools; to be inundated ♦ *vt* to flood.

stagnum, -ī *nt* standing water, pool, swamp; waters.

stāmen, -inis *nt* warp; thread; (*instrument*) string; (*priest*) fillet.

stāmineus *adj* full of threads.

stata *adj*: **Stata māter** Vesta.

statārius *adj* standing, stationary, steady; calm ♦ *f* refined comedy ♦ *mpl* actors in this comedy.

statēra, -ae *f* scales.

statim *adv* steadily; at once, immediately; ~ **ut** as soon as.

statiō, -ōnis *f* standing still; station, post, residence; (*pl*) sentries; (*NAUT*) anchorage.

Statius, -ī *m* Caecilius (*early writer of comedy*); Papinius (*epic and lyric poet of the Silver Age*).

statīvus *adj* stationary ♦ *ntpl* standing camp.

stator, -ōris *m* attendant, orderly.

Stator, -ōris *m* the Stayer (*epithet of Jupiter*).

statua, -ae *f* statue.

statūmen, -inis *nt* (*ship*) rib.

statuō, -uere, -uī, -ūtum *vt* to set up, place; to bring to a stop; to establish, constitute; to determine, appoint; to decide, settle; to decree, prescribe; (*with infin*) to resolve, propose; (*with acc and infin*) to judge, consider, conclude; (*army*) to draw up; (*monument*) to erect; (*price*) to fix; (*sentence*) to pass; (*tent*) to pitch; (*town*) to build; **condiciōnem** ~ dictate (to); **fīnem** ~ put an end (to); **iūs** ~ lay down a principle; **modum** ~ impose restrictions; **apud animum** ~ make up one's mind; **dē sē** ~ commit suicide; **gravius** ~ **in** deal severely with.

statūra, -ae *f* height, stature.

status *ppp of* **sistō** ♦ *adj* appointed, due.

status, -ūs *m* posture, attitude; position; (*social*) standing, status, circumstances; (*POL*) situation, state, form of government; (*nature*) condition; **reī pūblicae** ~ the political situation; constitution; **dē ~ū movēre** dislodge.

statūtus *ppp of* **statuō**.

stega, -ae *f* deck.

stēliō *see* **stēlliō**.

stēlla, -ae *f* star; ~ **errāns** planet.

stēllāns, -antis *adj* starry.

stēllātus *adj* starred; set in the sky.

stēllifer, -ī *adj* starry.

stēlliger, -ī *adj* starry.

stēlliō, -ōnis *m* newt.

stemma, -tis *nt* pedigree.

stercoreus *adj* filthy.

stercorō, -āre *vt* to manure.

stercus, -oris *nt* dung.

sterilis *adj* barren, sterile; bare, empty; unprofitable, fruitless.

sterilitās, -ātis *f* barrenness.

sternāx, -ācis *adj* bucking.

sternō, -ere, strāvī, strātum *vt* to spread, cover, strew; to smooth, level; to stretch out, extend; to throw to the ground, prostrate; to overthrow; (*bed*) to make; (*horse*) to saddle; (*road*) to pave.

sternūmentum, -ī *nt* sneezing.

sternuō, -ere, -uī *vt, vi* to sneeze.

Steropē, -ēs *f* a Pleiad.

sterquilīnium, -ī *and* **iī, (-um, -ī)** *nt* dung heap.

stertō, -ere, -uī *vi* to snore.

Stēsichorus, -ī *m* Greek lyric poet.

stetī *perf of* **stō**.

Sthenelēius *and* **eis** *and* **ēidis** *adj see n.*

Sthenelus, -ī *m* father of Eurystheus; father of Cycnus.

stigma, -tis *nt* brand.

stigmatiās, -ae *m* branded slave.

stilla, -ae *f* drop.

stillicidium, -ī *and* **iī** *nt* dripping water, rainwater from the eaves.

stillō, -āre, -āvī, -ātum *vi* to drip, trickle ♦ *vt* to let fall in drops, distil.

stilus, -ī *m* stake; pen; (*fig*) writing, composition, style; ~**um vertere** erase.

stimulātiō, -ōnis *f* incentive.

stimulātrīx, -īcis *f* provocative woman.

stimuleus *adj* smarting.

stimulō, -āre, -āvī, -ātum *vt* to goad; to trouble, torment; to rouse, spur on, excite.

stimulus, -ī *m* goad; (*MIL*) stake; (*pain*) sting, pang; (*incentive*) spur, stimulus.

stinguō, -ere *vt* to extinguish.

stīpātiō, -ōnis *f* crowd, retinue.

stīpātor, -ōris *m* attendant; (*pl*) retinue, bodyguard.

stīpendiārius *adj* tributary, liable to a money tax; (*MIL*) receiving pay ♦ *mpl* tributary peoples.

stīpendium, -ī *and* **iī** *nt* tax tribute; soldier's pay; military service, campaign; ~ **merēre**, **merērī** serve; ~ **ēmerērī** complete one's period of service.

Noun declensions and verb conjugations are shown on pp xiii to xxv. The present infinitive ending of a verb shows to which conjugation it belongs: **-āre** = 1st; **-ēre** = 2nd; **-ere** = 3rd and **-īre** = 4th. Irregular verbs are shown on p xxvi

stīpes, -itis *m* log, trunk; tree; (*insult*) blockhead.

stīpō, -āre, -āvī, -ātum *vt* to press, pack together; to cram, stuff full; to crowd round, accompany in a body.

stips, stipis *f* donation, contribution.

stipula, -ae *f* stalk, blade, stubble; reed.

stipulātiō, -ōnis *f* promise, bargain.

stipulātiuncula, -ae *f* slight stipulation.

stipulātus *adj* promised.

stipulor, -ārī *vt, vi* to demand a formal promise, bargain, stipulate.

stīria, -ae *f* icicle.

stirpēs *etc see* **stirps**.

stirpitus *adj* thoroughly.

stirps, -is *f* lower trunk and roots, stock; plant, shoot; family, lineage, progeny; origin; **ab ~e** utterly.

stīva, -ae *f* plough handle.

stlattārius *adj* seaborne.

stō, stāre, stetī, statum *vi* to stand; to remain in position, stand firm; to be conspicuous; (*fig*) to persist, continue; (*battle*) to go on; (*hair*) to stand on end; (*NAUT*) to ride at anchor; (*play*) to be successful; (*price*) to cost; (*with* **ab, cum, prō**) to be on the side of, support; (*with* **in**) to rest, depend on; (*with* **per**) to be the fault of; **stat sententia** one's mind is made up; **per Āfrānium stetit quōminus dīmicārētur** thanks to Afranius there was no battle.

Stōicē *adv* like a Stoic.

Stōicus *adj* Stoic ♦ *m* Stoic philosopher ♦ *ntpl* Stoicism.

stola, -ae *f* long robe (*esp worn by matrons*).

stolidē *adv* stupidly.

stolidus *adj* dull, stupid.

stomachor, -ārī, -ātus *vi* to be vexed, be annoyed.

stomachōsē *adv see adj.*

stomachōsus *adj* angry, irritable.

stomachus, -ī *m* gullet; stomach; taste, liking; dislike, irritation, chagrin.

stōrea (storia), -ae *f* rush mat, rope mat.

strabō, -ōnis *m* squinter.

strāgēs, -is *f* heap, confused mass; havoc, massacre.

strāgulus *adj* covering ♦ *nt* bedspread, rug.

strāmen, -inis *nt* straw, litter.

strāmentum, -ī *nt* straw, thatch; straw bed; covering, rug.

strāmineus *adj* straw-thatched.

strangulō, -āre, -āvī, -ātum *vt* to throttle, choke.

strangūria, -ae *f* difficult discharge of urine.

stratēgēma, -tis *nt* a piece of generalship, stratagem.

stratēgus, -ī *m* commander, president.

stratiōticus *adj* military.

strātum, -ī *nt* coverlet, blanket; bed, couch; horsecloth, saddle; pavement.

strātus *ppp of* **sternō** ♦ *adj* prostrate.

strāvī *perf of* **sternō**.

strēnuē *adv* energetically, quickly.

strēnuitās, -ātis *f* energy, briskness.

strēnuus *adj* brisk, energetic, busy; restless.

strepitō, -āre *vi* to make a noise, rattle, rustle.

strepitus, -ūs *m* din, clatter, crashing, rumbling; sound.

strepō, -ere, -uī *vi* to make a noise, clang, roar, rumble, rustle *etc* ♦ *vt* to bawl out.

striāta, -ae *f* scallop.

strictim *adv* superficially, cursorily.

strictūra, -ae *f* mass of metal.

strictus *ppp of* **stringō** ♦ *adj* close, tight.

strīdeō, -ēre, -ī; -ō, -ere, -ī *vi* to creak, hiss, shriek, whistle.

strīdor, -ōris *m* creaking, hissing, grating.

strīdulus *adj* creaking, hissing, whistling.

strigilis *f* scraper, strigil.

strigō, -āre *vi* to stop, jib.

strigōsus *adj* thin, scraggy; (*style*) insipid.

stringō, -ngere, -nxī, -ctum *vt* to draw together, draw tight; to touch, graze; to cut off, prune, trim; (*sword*) to draw; (*mind*) to affect, pain.

stringor, -ōris *m* twinge.

strix, -igis *f* screech owl.

stropha, -ae *f* trick.

Strophades, -um *fpl* islands off S Greece.

strophiārius, -ī and iī *m* maker of breastbands.

strophium, -ī and iī *nt* breastband; headband.

structor, -ōris *m* mason, carpenter; (*at table*) server, carver.

structūra, -ae *f* construction, structure; works.

structus *ppp of* **struō**.

struēs, -is *f* heap, pile.

struix, -icis *f* heap, pile.

strūma, -ae *f* tumour.

strūmōsus *adj* scrofulous.

struō, -ere, -xī, -ctum *vt* to pile up; to build, erect; to arrange in order; to make, prepare; to cause, contrive, plot.

strūtheus *adj* sparrow- (*in cpds*).

strūthiocamēlus, -ī *m* ostrich.

Strȳmōn, -onis *m* river between Macedonia and Thrace (*now* Struma).

Strȳmonius *adj* Strymonian, Thracian.

studeō, -ēre, -uī *vi* (*usu with dat*) to be keen, be diligent, apply oneself to; to study; (*person*) to be a supporter of.

studiōsē *adv* eagerly, diligently.

studiōsus *adj* (*usu with gen*) keen on, fond of, partial to; studious ♦ *m* student.

studium, -ī and iī *nt* enthusiasm, application, inclination; fondness, affection; party spirit, partisanship; study, literary work.

stultē *adv* foolishly.

stultiloquentia, -ae *f* foolish talk.

stultiloquium, -ī and iī *nt* foolish talk.

stultitia, -ae *f* folly, silliness.

stultividus *adj* simple-sighted.

stultus *adj* foolish, silly ♦ *m* fool.

stupefaciō, -facere, -fēcī, -factum (*pass*
  -fīō, -fierī) *vt* to stun, stupefy.
stupeō, -ēre, -uī *vi* to be stunned, be
  astonished; to be brought to a standstill ♦ *vt*
  to marvel at.
stupēscō, -ere *vi* to become amazed.
stūpeus *etc see* **stuppeus.**
stupiditās, -ātis *f* senselessness.
stupidus *adj* senseless, astounded; dull,
  stupid.
stupor, -ōris *m* numbness, bewilderment;
  dullness, stupidity.
stuppa, -ae *f* tow.
stuppeus *adj* of tow.
stuprō, -āre, -āvī, -ātum *vt* to defile; to
  ravish.
stuprum, -ī *nt* debauchery, unchastity.
sturnus, -ī *m* starling.
Stygius *adj* of the lower world, Stygian.
stylus *etc see* **stilus.**
Stymphalicus, (-ius, -is) *adj* Stymphalian.
Stymphalum, -ī *nt*, **Stymphalus, -ī** *m*
  district of Arcadia (*famous for birds of prey
  killed by Hercules*).
Styx, -ygis *and* **ygos** *f river of Hades.*
Styxius *adj see n.*
suādēla, -ae *f* persuasion.
suādeō, -dēre, -sī, -sum *vi* (*with dat*) to
  advise, urge, recommend.
suāsiō, -ōnis *f* speaking in favour (of a
  proposal); persuasive type of oratory.
suāsor, -ōris *m* adviser; advocate.
suāsus *ppp of* **suādeō.**
suāsus, -ūs *m* advice.
suāveolēns, -entis *adj* fragrant.
suāviātiō *etc see* **sāviātiō.**
suāvidicus *adj* charming.
suāviloquēns, -entis *adj* charming.
suāviloquentia, -ae *f* charm of speech.
suāvior *etc see* **sāvior.**
suāvis *adj* sweet, pleasant, delightful.
suāvitās, -ātis *f* sweetness, pleasantness,
  charm.
suāviter *adv see* **suāvis.**
suāvium *etc see* **sāvium.**
sub *prep* 1. *with abl* (*place*) under, beneath; (*hills,
  walls*) at the foot of, close to; (*time*) during,
  at; (*order*) next to; (*rule*) under, in the reign
  of. 2. *with acc* (*place*) under, along under; (*hills,
  walls*) up to, to; (*time*) up to, just before, just
  after; **~ ictum venīre** come within range; **~
  manum** to hand.
subabsurdē *adv see adj.*
subabsurdus *adj* somewhat absurd.
subaccūsō, -āre *vt* to find some fault with.
subāctiō, -ōnis *f* working (the soil).
subāctus *ppp of* **subigō.**
subadroganter *adv* a little conceitedly.
subagrestis *adj* rather boorish.
subalāris *adj* carried under the arms.

subamārus *adj* rather bitter.
subaquilus *adj* brownish.
subauscultō, -āre *vt, vi* to listen secretly,
  eavesdrop.
subbasilicānus, -ī *m* lounger.
subblandior, -īrī *vi* (*with dat*) to flirt with.
subc- *etc see* **succ-.**
subdidī *perf of* **subdō.**
subdifficilis *adj* rather difficult.
subdiffīdō, -ere *vi* to be a little doubtful.
subditīcius *adj* sham.
subditīvus *adj* sham.
subditus *ppp of* **subdō** ♦ *adj* spurious.
subdō, -ere, -idī, -itum *vt* to put under,
  plunge into; to subdue; to substitute, forge.
subdoceō, -ēre *vt* to teach as an assistant.
subdolē *adv* slily.
subdolus *adj* sly, crafty, underhand.
subdubitō, -āre *vi* to be a little undecided.
subdūcō, -ūcere, -ūxī, -uctum *vt* to pull up,
  raise; to withdraw, remove; to take away
  secretly, steal; (*account*) to balance; (*ship*) to
  haul up, beach; **sē ~** steal away, disappear.
subductiō, -ōnis *f* (*ship*) hauling up; (*thought*)
  reckoning.
subductus *ppp of* **subdūcō.**
subedō, -esse, -ēdī *vt* to wear away
  underneath.
subēgī *perf of* **subigō.**
subeō, -īre, -iī, -itum *vi* to go under, go in; to
  come up to, climb, advance; to come
  immediately after; to come to the
  assistance; to come as a substitute, succeed;
  to come secretly, steal in; to come to mind,
  suggest itself ♦ *vt* to enter, plunge into; to
  climb; to approach, attack; to take the place
  of; to steal into; to submit to, undergo,
  suffer; (*mind*) to occur to.
sūber, -is *nt* cork tree; cork.
subesse *infin of* **subsum.**
subf- *etc see* **suff-.**
subg- *etc see* **sugg-.**
subhorridus *adj* somewhat uncouth.
subiaceō, -ēre, -uī *vi* to lie under, be close
  (to); to be connected (with).
subiciō, -icere, -iēcī, -iectum *vt* to put under,
  bring under; to bring up, throw up; to bring
  near; to submit, subject, expose; to
  subordinate, deal with under; to append, add
  on, answer; to adduce, suggest; to
  substitute; to forge; to suborn; **sē ~** grow up.
subiectē *adv* submissively.
subiectiō, -ōnis *f* laying under; forging.
subiectō, -āre *vt* to lay under, put to; to throw
  up.
subiector, -ōris *m* forger.
subiectus *ppp of* **subiciō** ♦ *adj* neighbouring,
  bordering; subject, exposed.
subigitātiō, -ōnis *f* lewdness.
subigitō, -āre *vt* to behave improperly to.

subigō, -igere, -ēgī, -āctum *vt* to bring up to; to impel, compel; to subdue, conquer; (*animal*) to tame, break in; (*blade*) to sharpen; (*boat*) to row, propel; (*cooking*) to knead; (*earth*) to turn up, dig; (*mind*) to train.

subiī *perf of* **subeō**.

subimpudēns, -entis *adj* rather impertinent.

subinānis *adj* rather empty.

subinde *adv* immediately after; repeatedly.

subīnsulsus *adj* rather insipid.

subinvideō, -ēre *vi* to be a little envious of.

subinvīsus *adj* somewhat odious.

subinvītō, -āre *vt* to invite vaguely.

subīrāscor, -scī, -tus *vi* to be rather angry.

subīrātus *adj* rather angry.

subitārius *adj* sudden, emergency (*in cpds*).

subitō *adv* suddenly.

subitus *ppp of* **subeō** ♦ *adj* sudden, unexpected; (*man*) rash; (*troops*) hastily raised ♦ *nt* surprise, emergency.

subiūnctus *ppp of* **subiungō**.

subiungō, -ungere, -ūnxī, -ūnctum *vt* to harness; to add, affix; to subordinate, subdue.

sublābor, -bī, -psus *vi* to sink down; to glide away.

sublāpsus *ppa of* **sublābor**.

sublātē *adv* loftily.

sublātiō, -ōnis *f* elevation.

sublātus *ppp of* **tollō** ♦ *adj* elated.

sublectō, -āre *vt* to coax.

sublēctus *ppp of* **sublegō**.

sublegō, -egere, -ēgī, -ēctum *vt* to gather up; to substitute; (*child*) to kidnap; (*talk*) to overhear.

sublestus *adj* slight.

sublevātiō, -ōnis *f* alleviation.

sublevō, -āre, -āvī, -ātum *vt* to lift up, hold up; to support, encourage; to lighten, alleviate.

sublica, -ae *f* pile, palisade.

sublicius *adj* on piles.

subligāculum, -ī, subligar, -āris *nt* loincloth.

subligō, -āre *vt* to fasten on.

sublīme *adv* aloft, in the air.

sublīmis *adj* high, raised high, lifted up; (*character*) eminent, aspiring; (*language*) lofty, elevated.

sublīmitās, -ātis *f* loftiness.

sublīmus *etc see* **sublīmis**.

sublingiō, -ōnis *m* scullion.

sublinō, -inere, -ēvī, -itum *vt*: **ōs ~** to fool, bamboozle.

sublitus *ppp of* **sublinō**.

sublūceō, -ēre *vi* to glimmer.

subl,uō, -ere *vt* (*river*) to flow past the foot of.

sublūstris *adj* faintly luminous.

sublūtus *ppp of* **subluō**.

subm- *etc see* **summ-**.

subnātus *adj* growing up underneath.

subnectō, -ctere, -xuī, -xum *vt* to tie under, fasten to.

subnegō, -āre *vt* to half refuse.

subnexus *ppp of* **subnectō**.

subniger, -rī *adj* darkish.

subnīxus *and* **sus** *adj* supported, resting (on); relying (on).

subnuba, -ae *f* rival.

subnūbilus *adj* overcast.

subō, -āre *vi* to be in heat.

subobscēnus *adj* rather indecent.

subobscūrus *adj* somewhat obscure.

subodiōsus *adj* rather odious.

suboffendō, -ere *vi* to give some offence.

subolēs, -is *f* offspring, children.

subolēscō, -ere *vi* to grow up.

subolet, -ēre *vi* (*impers*) there is a faint scent; **~ mihi** I detect, have an inkling.

suborior, -īrī *vi* to spring up in succession.

subōrnō, -āre, -āvī, -ātum *vt* to fit out, equip; to instigate secretly, suborn.

subortus, -ūs *m* rising up repeatedly.

subp- *etc see* **supp-**.

subrancidus *adj* slightly tainted.

subraucus *adj* rather hoarse.

subrēctus *ppp of* **subrigō**.

subrēmigō, -āre *vi* to paddle under (water).

subrēpō, -ere, -sī, -tum *vi* to creep along, steal up to.

subreptus *ppp of* **subripiō**.

subrīdeō, -dēre, -sī *vi* to smile.

subrīdiculē *adv* rather funnily.

subrigō, -igere, -ēxī, -ēctum *vt* to lift, raise.

subringor, -ī *vi* to make a wry face, be rather vexed.

subripiō, -ipere, -ipuī *and* **upuī, -eptum** *vt* to take away secretly, steal.

subrogō, -āre *vt* to propose as successor.

subrōstrānī, -ōrum *mpl* idlers.

subrubeō, -ēre *vi* to blush slightly.

subrūfus *adj* ginger-haired.

subruō, -ere, -ī, -tum *vt* to undermine, demolish.

subrūsticus *adj* rather countrified.

subrutus *ppp of* **subruō**.

subscrībō, -bere, -psī, -ptum *vt* to write underneath; (*document*) to sign, subscribe; (*censor*) to set down; (*law*) to add to an indictment, prosecute; (*fig*) to record; (*with dat*) to assent to, approve.

subscrīptiō, -ōnis *f* inscription underneath; signature; (*censor*) noting down; (*law*) subscription (to an indictment); register.

subscrīptor, -ōris *m* subscriber (to an indictment).

subscrīptus *ppp of* **subscrībō**.

subsecīvus *etc see* **subsicīvus**.

subsecō, -āre, -uī, -ctum *vt* to cut off, clip.

subsēdī *perf of* **subsīdō**.

subsellium, -ī *and* **iī** *nt* bench, seat; (*law*) the bench, the court.

subsentiō, -entīre, -ēnsī *vt* to have an inkling of.

subsequor, -quī, -cūtus *vt, vi* to follow closely; to support; to imitate.

subserviō, -īre *vi* to be a slave; (*fig*) to comply

(with).

subsicīvus *adj* left over; (*time*) spare; (*work*) overtime.

subsidiārius *adj* in reserve ♦ *mpl* reserves.

subsidium, -ī *and* **iī** *nt* reserve ranks, reserve troops; relief, aid, assistance.

subsīdō, -īdere, -ēdī, -essum *vi* to sit down, crouch, squat; to sink down, settle, subside; (*ambush*) to lie in wait; (*residence*) to stay, settle ♦ *vt* to lie in wait for.

subsignānus *adj* special reserve (troops).

subsignō, -āre *vt* to register; to guarantee.

subsiliō, -īre, -uī *vi* to leap up.

subsistō, -istere, -titī *vi* to stand still, make a stand; to stop, halt; to remain, continue, hold out; (*with dat*) to resist ♦ *vt* to withstand.

subsortior, -īrī, -ītus *vt* to choose as a substitute by lot.

subsortītiō, -ōnis *f* choosing of substitutes by lot.

substantia, -ae *f* means, wealth.

substernō, -ernere, -rāvī, -rātum *vt* to scatter under, spread under; (*fig*) to put at one's service.

substitī *perf of* **subsistō**.

substituō, -uere, -uī, -ūtum *vt* to put next; to substitute; (*idea*) to present, imagine.

substitūtus *ppp of* **substituō**.

substō, -āre *vi* to hold out.

substrātus *ppp of* **substernō**.

substrictus *ppp of* **substringō** ♦ *adj* narrow, tight.

substringō, -ngere, -nxī, -ctum *vt* to bind up; to draw close; to check.

substrūctiō, -ōnis *f* foundation.

substruō, -ere, -xī, -ctum *vt* to lay, pave.

subsultō, -āre *vi* to jump up.

subsum, -esse *vi* to be underneath; to be close to, be at hand; (*fig*) to underlie, be latent in.

subsūtus *adj* fringed at the bottom.

subtēmen, -inis *nt* woof; thread.

subter *adv* below, underneath ♦ *prep* (*with acc and abl*) beneath; close up to.

subterdūcō, -cere, -xī *vt* to withdraw secretly.

subterfugiō, -ugere, -ūgī *vt* to escape from, evade.

subterlābor, -ī *vt, vi* to flow past under; to slip away.

subterrāneus *adj* underground.

subtexō, -ere, -uī, -tum *vt* to weave in; to veil, obscure.

subtīlis *adj* slender, fine; (*senses*) delicate, nice; (*judgment*) discriminating, precise; (*style*) plain, direct.

subtīlitās, -ātis *f* fineness; (*judgment*) acuteness, exactness; (*style*) plainness, directness.

subtīliter *adv* finely; accurately; simply.

subtimeō, -ēre *vt* to be a little afraid of.

subtractus *ppp of* **subtrahō**.

subtrahō, -here, -xī, -ctum *vt* to draw away from underneath; to take away secretly; to withdraw, remove.

subtristis *adj* rather sad.

subturpiculus *adj* a little bit mean.

subturpis *adj* rather mean.

subtus *adv* below, underneath.

subtūsus *adj* slightly bruised.

subūcula, -ae *f* shirt, vest.

sūbula, -ae *f* awl.

subulcus, -ī *m* swineherd.

Subūra, -ae *f* a disreputable quarter of Rome.

Subūrānus *adj see* **Subūra**.

suburbānitās, -ātis *f* nearness to Rome.

suburbānus *adj* near Rome ♦ *nt* villa near Rome ♦ *mpl inhabitants of the towns near Rome*.

suburbium, -ī *and* **iī** *nt* suburb.

suburgeō, -ēre *vt* to drive close (to).

subvectiō, -ōnis *f* transport.

subvectō, -āre *vt* to carry up regularly.

subvectus *ppp of* **subvehō**.

subvectus, -ūs *m* transport.

subvehō, -here, -xī, -ctum *vt* to carry up, transport upstream.

subveniō, -enīre, -ēnī, -entum *vi* (*with dat*) to come to the assistance of, relieve, reinforce.

subventō, -āre *vi* (*with dat*) to come quickly to help.

subvereor, -ērī *vi* to be a little afraid.

subversor, -ōris *m* subverter.

subversus *ppp of* **subvertō**.

subvertō, -tere, -tī, -sum *vt* to turn upside down, upset; to overthrow, subvert.

subvexī *perf of* **subvehō**.

subvexus *adj* sloping upwards.

subvolō, -āre *vi* to fly upwards.

subvolvō, -ere *vt* to roll uphill.

subvortō *etc see* **subvertō**.

succavus *adj* hollow underneath.

succēdō, -ēdere, -essī, -essum *vt, vi* (*with dat*) to go under, pass into, take on; (*with dat, acc,* **in**) to go up, climb; (*with dat, acc,* **ad, sub**) to march on, advance to; (*with dat,* **in**) to come to take the place of, relieve; (*with dat,* **in, ad**) to follow after, succeed, succeed to; (*result*) to turn out, be successful.

succendō, -endere, -endī, -ēnsum *vt* to set fire to, kindle; (*fig*) to fire, inflame.

succēnseō *etc see* **suscēnseō**.

succēnsus *ppp of* **succendō**.

succenturiātus *adj* in reserve.

succenturiō, -ōnis *m* under-centurion.

successī *perf of* **succēdō**.

successiō, -ōnis *f* succession.

successor, -ōris *m* successor.

successus *ppp of* **succēdō**.

Noun declensions and verb conjugations are shown on pp xiii to xxv. The present infinitive ending of a verb shows to which conjugation it belongs: **-āre** = 1st; **-ēre** = 2nd; **-ere** = 3rd and **-īre** = 4th. Irregular verbs are shown on p xxvi

successus, -ūs *m* advance uphill; result, success.

succīdia, -ae *f* leg *or* side of meat, flitch.

succīdō, -dere, -dī, -sum *vt* to cut off, mow down.

succidō, -ere, -ī *vi* to sink, give way.

succiduus *adj* sinking, failing.

succinctus *ppp of* **succingō**.

succingō, -gere, -xī, -ctum *vt* to gird up, tuck up; to equip, arm.

succingulum, -ī *nt* girdle.

succinō, -ere *vi* to chime in.

succīsus *ppp of* **succīdō**.

succlāmātiō, -ōnis *f* shouting, barracking.

succlāmō, -āre, -āvī, -ātum *vt* to shout after, interrupt with shouting.

succontumēliōsē *adv* somewhat insolently.

succrēscō, -ere *vi* to grow up (from *or* to).

succrispus *adj* rather curly.

succumbō, -mbere, -buī, -bitum *vi* to fall, sink under; to submit, surrender.

succurrō, -rere, -rī, -sum *vi* to come quickly up; to run to the help of, succour; (*idea*) to occur.

succus *etc see* **sūcus**.

succussus, -ūs *m* shaking.

succustōs, -ōdis *m* assistant keeper.

succutiō, -tere, -ssī, -ssum *vt* to toss up.

sūcidus *adj* juicy, fresh, plump.

sūcinum, -ī *nt* amber.

sūctus *ppp of* **sūgō**.

sucula, -ae *f* winch, windlass.

sucula, -ae *f* piglet; (*pl*) the Hyads.

sūcus, -ī *m* juice, sap; medicine, potion; taste, flavour; (*fig*) strength, vigour, life.

sūdārium, -ī *and* **iī** *nt* handkerchief.

sūdātōrius *adj* for sweating ♦ *nt* sweating bath.

sudis, -is *f* stake, pile, pike, spike.

sūdō, -āre, -āvī, -ātum *vi* to sweat, perspire; to be drenched with; to work hard ♦ *vt* to exude.

sūdor, -ōris *m* sweat, perspiration; moisture; hard work, exertion.

sudus *adj* cloudless, clear ♦ *nt* fine weather.

sueō, -ēre *vi* to be accustomed.

suēscō, -scere, -vī, -tum *vi* to be accustomed ♦ *vt* to accustom.

Suessa, -ae *f* town in Latium.

Suessiōnēs, -um *mpl* people of Gaul (*now* Soissons).

suētus *ppp of* **suēscō** ♦ *adj* accustomed; usual.

Suēvī, -ōrum *mpl* people of N.E. Germany.

sūfes, -etis *m* chief magistrate of Carthage.

suffarcinātus *adj* stuffed full.

suffectus *ppp of* **sufficiō** ♦ *adj* (*consul*) appointed to fill a vacancy during the regular term of office.

sufferō, -re *vt* to support, undergo, endure.

suffes *etc see* **sūfes**.

sufficiō, -icere, -ēcī, -ectum *vt* to dye, tinge; to supply, provide; to appoint in place (of another), substitute ♦ *vi* to be adequate, suffice.

suffīgō, -gere, -xī, -xum *vt* to fasten underneath, nail on.

suffīmen, -inis, suffīmentum, -ī *nt* incense.

suffiō, -īre *vt* to fumigate, perfume.

suffīxus *ppp of* **suffīgō**.

sufflāmen, -inis *nt* brake.

sufflō, -āre *vt* to blow up; to puff up.

suffocō, -āre *vt* to choke, stifle.

suffodiō, -odere, -ōdī, -ossum *vt* to stab; to dig under, undermine.

suffossus *ppp of* **suffodiō**.

suffrāgātiō, -ōnis *f* voting for, support.

suffrāgātor, -ōris *m* voter, supporter.

suffrāgātōrius *adj* supporting a candidate.

suffrāgium, -ī *and* **iī** *nt* vote, ballot; right of suffrage; (*fig*) judgment, approval; ~ **ferre** vote.

suffrāgor, -ārī, -ātus *vi* to vote for; to support, favour.

suffringō, -ere *vt* to break.

suffugiō, -ugere, -ūgī *vt* to run for shelter ♦ *vt* to elude.

suffugium, -ī *and* **iī** *nt* shelter, refuge.

suffulciō, -cīre, -sī, -tum *vt* to prop up, support.

suffundō, -undere, -ūdī, -ūsum *vt* to pour in, to suffuse, fill; to tinge, colour, blush; to overspread.

suffūror, -ārī *vi* to filch.

suffuscus *adj* darkish.

suffūsus *ppp of* **suffundō**.

Sugambrī, -ōrum *mpl* people of N.W. Germany.

suggerō, -rere, -ssī, -stum *vt* to bring up to, supply; to add on, put next.

suggestum, -ī *nt* platform.

suggestus *ppp of* **suggerō**.

suggestus, -ūs *m* platform, stage.

suggrandis *adj* rather large.

suggredior, -dī, -ssus *vi* to come up close, approach ♦ *vt* to attack.

sūgillātiō, -ōnis *f* affronting.

sūgillātus *adj* bruised; insulted.

sūgō, -gere, -xī, -ctum *vt* to suck.

suī *gen of* **sē**.

suī *perf of* **suō**.

suillus *adj* of pigs.

sulcō, -āre *vt* to furrow, plough.

sulcus, -ī *m* furrow; trench; track.

sulfur *etc see* **sulpur**.

Sulla, -ae *m* famous Roman dictator.

Sullānus *adj see n.*

sullāturiō, -īre *vi* to hanker after being a Sulla.

Sulmō, -ōnis *m* town in E. Italy (*birthplace of Ovid*).

Sulmōnēnsis *adj see n.*

sultis *adv* please.

sum, esse, fuī *vi* to be, exist; ~ **ab** belong to; ~ **ad** be designed for; ~ **ex** consist of; **est, sunt** there is, are; **est mihi** I have; **mihi tēcum nīl est** I have nothing to do with you; **est quod** something; there is a reason for; **est ubi**

sometimes; **est ut** it is possible that; **est** (*with gen*) to belong to, be the duty of, be characteristic of; (*with infin*) it is possible, it is permissible; **sunt quī** some; **fuit Ilium** Troy is no more.

sūmen, -inis *nt* udder, teat; sow.

summa, -ae *f* main part, chief point, main issue; gist, summary; sum, amount, the whole; supreme power; **~ rērum** the general interest, the whole responsibility; **~ summārum** the universe; **ad ~am** in short, in fact; in conclusion; **in ~ā** in all; after all.

Summānus, -ī *m* god of nocturnal thunderbolts.

summās, -ātis *adj* high-born, eminent.

summātim *adv* cursorily, summarily.

summātus, -ūs *m* sovereignty.

summē *adv* in the highest degree, extremely.

summergō, -gere, -sī, -sum *vt* to plunge under, sink.

summersus *ppp of* **summergō**.

sumministrō, -āre, -āvī, -ātum *vt* to provide, furnish.

summissē *adv* softly; humbly, modestly.

summissiō, -ōnis *f* lowering.

summissus *ppp of* **summittō** ♦ *adj* low; (*voice*) low, calm; (*character*) mean, grovelling, submissive, humble.

summittō, -ittere, -īsī, -issum *vt* (*growth*) to send up, raise, rear; to despatch, supply; to let down, lower, reduce, moderate; to supersede; to send secretly; **animum ~** submit; **sē ~** condescend.

summolestē *adv* with some annoyance.

summolestus *adj* a little annoying.

summoneō, -ēre, -uī *vt* to drop a hint to.

summorōsus *adj* rather peevish.

summōtor, -ōris *m* clearer.

summōtus *ppp of* **summoveō**.

summoveō, -ovēre, -ōvī, -ōtum *vt* to move away, drive off; to clear away (to make room); to withdraw, remove, banish; (*fig*) to dispel.

summum, -ī *nt* top, surface.

summum *adv* at the most.

summus *adj* highest, the top of, the surface of; last, the end of; (*fig*) utmost, greatest, most important; (*person*) distinguished, excellent ♦ *m* head of the table.

summūtō, -āre *vt* to substitute.

sūmō, -ere, -psī, -ptum *vt* to take, take up; to assume, arrogate; (*action*) to undertake; (*argument*) to assume, take for granted; (*dress*) to put on; (*punishment*) to exact; (*for a purpose*) to use, spend.

sūmptiō, -ōnis *f* assumption.

sūmptuārius *adj* sumptuary.

sūmptuōsē *adv see adj*.

sūmptuōsus *adj* expensive, lavish, extravagant.

sūmptus *ppp of* **sūmō**.

sūmptus, -ūs *m* expense, cost.

Sūnium, -ī *and* **iī** *nt* S.E. promontory of Attica.

suō, suere, suī, sūtum *vt* to sew, stitch, join together.

suōmet, suōpte *emphatic abl of* **suus**.

suovetaurīlia, -ium *ntpl* sacrifice of a pig, sheep and bull.

supellex, -ectilis *f* furniture, goods, outfit.

super *etc adj see* **superus**.

super *adv* above, on the top; besides, moreover; left, remaining ♦ *prep* (*with abl*) upon, above; concerning; besides; (*time*) at; (*with acc*) over, above, on; beyond; besides, over and above.

superā *etc see* **suprā**.

superābilis *adj* surmountable, conquerable.

superaddō, -ere, -itum *vt* to add over and above.

superāns, -antis *pres p of* **superō** ♦ *adj* predominant.

superātor, -ōris *m* conqueror.

superbē *adv* arrogantly, despotically.

superbia, -ae *f* arrogance, insolence, tyranny; pride, lofty spirit.

superbiloquentia, -ae *f* arrogant speech.

superbiō, -īre *vi* to be arrogant, take a pride in; to be superb.

superbus *adj* arrogant, insolent, overbearing; fastidious; superb, magnificent.

supercilium, -ī *and* **iī** *nt* eyebrow; (*hill*) brow, ridge; (*fig*) arrogance.

superēmineō, -ēre *vt* to overtop.

superesse *infin of* **supersum**.

superficiēs, -ēī *f* surface; (*law*) a building (*esp on another's land*).

superfīō, -ierī *vi* to be left over.

superfīxus *adj* fixed on top.

superfluō, -ere *vi* to overflow.

superfuī *perf of* **supersum**.

superfundō, -undere, -ūdī, -ūsum *vt, vi* to pour over, shower; (*pass*) to overflow, spread out.

superfūsus *ppp of* **superfundō**.

supergredior, -dī, -ssus *vt* to surpass.

superiaciō, -iacere, -iēcī, -iectum *and* **iactum** *vt* to throw over, overspread; to overtop; (*fig*) to exaggerate.

superiectus *ppp of* **superiaciō**.

superimmineō, -ēre *vi* to overhang.

superimpendēns, -entis *adj* overhanging.

superimpōnō, -ōnere, -osuī, -ositum *vt* to place on top.

superimpositus *ppp of* **superimpōnō**.

superincidēns, -entis *adj* falling from above.

superincubāns, -antis *adj* lying upon.

superincumbō, -ere *vi* to fling oneself down upon.

superingerō, -ere *vt* to pour down.

superiniciō, -icere, -iēcī, -iectum *vt* to throw upon, put on top.

Noun declensions and verb conjugations are shown on pp xiii to xxv. The present infinitive ending of a verb shows to which conjugation it belongs: **-āre** = 1st; **-ēre** = 2nd; **-ere** = 3rd and **-īre** = 4th. Irregular verbs are shown on p xxvi

superiniectus _ppp of_ **superinicō**.
superīnsternō, -ere _vt_ to lay over.
superior, -ōris _adj_ higher, upper; (_time, order_) preceding, previous, former; (_age_) older; (_battle_) victorious, stronger; (_quality_) superior, greater.
superlātiō, -ōnis _f_ exaggeration.
superlātus _adj_ exaggerated.
supernē _adv_ at the top, from above.
supernus _adj_ upper; celestial.
superō, -āre, -āvī, -ātum _vi_ to rise above, overtop; to have the upper hand; to be in excess, be abundant; to be left over, survive ♦ _vt_ to pass over, surmount, go beyond; to surpass, outdo; (_MIL_) to overcome, conquer; (_NAUT_) to sail past, double.
superobruō, -ere _vt_ to overwhelm.
superpendēns, -entis _adj_ overhanging.
superpōnō, -ōnere, -osuī, -ositum _vt_ to place upon; to put in charge of.
superpositus _ppp of_ **superpōnō**.
superscandō, -ere _vt_ to climb over.
supersedeō, -edēre, -ēdī, -essum _vi_ to forbear, desist from.
superstes, -itis _adj_ standing over; surviving.
superstitiō, -ōnis _f_ awful fear, superstition.
superstitiōsē _adv_ superstitiously; scrupulously.
superstitiōsus _adj_ superstitious; prophetic.
superstō, -āre _vt, vi_ to stand over, stand on.
superstrātus _adj_ spread over.
superstruō, -ere, -xī, -ctum _vt_ to build on top.
supersum, -esse, -fuī _vi_ to be left, remain; to survive; to be in abundance, be sufficient; to be in excess.
supertegō, -ere _vt_ to cover over.
superurgēns, -entis _adj_ pressing from above.
superus (_compar_ **-ior**, _superl_ **suprēmus**, **summus**) _adj_ upper, above ♦ _mpl_ the gods above; the living ♦ _ntpl_ the heavenly bodies; higher places; **mare ~um** Adriatic Sea.
supervacāneus _adj_ extra, superfluous.
supervacuus _adj_ superfluous, pointless.
supervādō, -ere _vt_ to climb over, surmount.
supervehor, -hī, -ctus _vt_ to ride past, sail past.
superveniō, -enīre, -ēnī, -entum _vt_ to overtake, come on top of ♦ _vi_ to come on the scene, arrive unexpectedly.
superventus, -ūs _m_ arrival.
supervolitō, -āre _vt_ to fly over.
supervolō, -āre _vt, vi_ to fly over.
supīnō, -āre, -āvī, -ātum _vt_ to upturn, lay on its back.
supīnus _adj_ lying back, face up; sloping, on a slope; backwards; (_mind_) indolent, careless.
suppāctus _ppp of_ **suppingō**.
suppaenitet, -ēre _vt impers_ to be a little sorry.
suppalpor, -ārī _vi_ to coax gently.
suppār, -aris _adj_ nearly equal.
supparasītor, -ārī _vi_ to flatter gently.

supparus, -ī _m_, **supparum, -ī** _nt_ woman's linen garment; topsail.
suppeditātiō, -ōnis _f_ abundance.
suppeditō, -āre, -āvī, -ātum _vi_ to be at hand, be in full supply, be sufficient; to be rich in ♦ _vt_ to supply, furnish.
suppēdō, -ere _vi_ to break wind quietly.
suppetiae, -ārum _fpl_ assistance.
suppetior, -ārī, -ātus _vi_ to come to the assistance of.
suppetō, -ere, -īvī, _and_ iī, -ītum _vi_ to be available, be in store; to be equal to, suffice for.
suppīlō, -āre _vt_ to steal.
suppingō, -ingere, -āctum _vt_ to fasten underneath.
supplantō, -āre _vt_ to trip up.
supplēmentum, -ī _nt_ full complement; reinforcements.
suppleō, -ēre _vt_ to fill up, make good, make up to the full complement.
supplex, -icis _adj_ suppliant, in entreaty.
supplicātiō, -ōnis _f_ day of prayer, public thanksgiving.
suppliciter _adv_ in supplication.
supplicium, -ī _and_ iī _nt_ prayer, entreaty; sacrifice; punishment, execution, suffering; **~iō afficere** execute.
supplicō, -āre, -āvī, -ātum _vi_ (_with dat_) to entreat, pray to, worship.
supplōdō, -dere, -sī _vt_ to stamp.
supplōsiō, -ōnis _f_ stamping.
suppōnō, -ōnere, -osuī, -ositum _vt_ to put under, apply; to subject; to add on; to substitute, falsify.
supportō, -āre _vt_ to bring up, transport.
suppositīcius _adj_ spurious.
suppositiō, -ōnis _f_ substitution.
suppositus _ppp of_ **suppōnō**.
supposuī _perf of_ **suppōnō**.
suppressiō, -ōnis _f_ embezzlement.
suppressus _ppp of_ **supprimō** ♦ _adj_ (_voice_) low.
supprimō, -imere, -essī, -essum _vt_ to sink; to restrain, detain, put a stop to; to keep secret, suppress.
supprōmus, -ī _m_ underbutler.
suppudet, -ēre _vt_ (_impers_) to be a little ashamed.
suppūrō, -āre _vi_ to fester.
suppus _adj_ head downwards.
supputō, -āre _vt_ to count up.
suprā _adv_ above, up on top; (_time_) earlier, previously; (_amount_) more; **~ quam** beyond what ♦ _prep_ (_with acc_) over, above; beyond; (_time_) before; (_amount_) more than, over.
suprāscandō, -ere _vt_ to surmount.
suprēmum _adv_ for the last time.
suprēmus _adj_ highest; last, latest; greatest; supreme ♦ _ntpl_ moment of death; funeral rites; testament.
sūra, -ae _f_ calf (of the leg).
sūrculus, -ī _m_ twig, shoot; graft, slip.
surdaster, -rī _adj_ rather deaf.

surditās, -ātis f deafness.
surdus adj deaf; silent.
surēna, -ae m grand vizier (of the Parthians).
surgō, -ere, surrēxī, surrēctum vi to rise, get up, stand up; to arise, spring up, grow.
surpere etc = **surripere** etc.
surr- etc see **subr-**.
surrēxī perf of **surgō**.
surrupticius adj stolen.
surrupuī perf of **subripiō**.
sūrsum, sūrsus adv upwards, up, high up; ~ **deōrsum** up and down.
sūs, suis m/f pig, boar, hog, sow.
Sūsa, -ōrum ntpl ancient Persian capital.
suscēnseō, -ēre, -uī vi to be angry, be irritated.
susceptiō, -ōnis f undertaking.
susceptus ppp of **suscipiō**.
suscipiō, -ipere, -ēpī, -eptum vt to take up, undertake; to receive, catch; (child) to acknowledge; to beget; to take under one's protection.
suscitō, -āre, -āvī, -ātum vt to lift, raise; to stir, rouse, awaken; to encourage, excite.
suspectō, -āre vt, vi to look up at, watch; to suspect, mistrust.
suspectus ppp of **suspiciō** ♦ adj suspected, suspicious.
suspectus, -ūs m looking up; esteem.
suspendium, -ī and iī nt hanging.
suspendō, -endere, -endī, -ēnsum vt to hang, hang up; (death) to hang; (building) to support; (mind) to keep in suspense; (movement) to check, interrupt; (pass) to depend.
suspēnsus ppp of **suspendō** ♦ adj raised, hanging, poised; with a light touch; (fig) in suspense, uncertain, anxious; dependent; ~ō **gradū** on tiptoe.
suspicāx, -ācis adj suspicious.
suspiciō, -icere, -exī, -ectum vt to look up at, look up to; to admire, respect; to mistrust.
suspiciō, -ōnis f mistrust, suspicion.
suspiciōsē adv suspiciously.
suspiciōsus adj suspicious.
suspicor, -ārī, -ātus vt to suspect; to surmise, suppose.
suspīrātus, -ūs m sigh.
suspīritus, -ūs m deep breath, difficult breathing; sigh.
suspīrium, -ī and iī nt deep breath, sigh.
suspīrō, -āre, -āvī, -ātum vi to sigh ♦ vt to sigh for; to exclaim with a sigh.
susque dēque adv up and down.
sustentāculum, -ī nt prop.
sustentātiō, -ōnis f forbearance.
sustentō, -āre, -āvī, -ātum vt to hold up, support; (fig) to uphold, uplift; (food, means) to sustain, support; (enemy) to check, hold; (trouble) to suffer; (event) to hold back,

postpone.
sustineō, -inēre, -inuī, -entum vt to hold up, support; to check, control; (fig) to uphold, maintain; (food, means) to sustain, support; (trouble) to bear, suffer, withstand; (event) to put off.
sustollō, -ere vt to lift up, raise; to destroy.
sustulī perf of **tollō**.
susurrātor, -ōris m whisperer.
susurrō, -āre vt, vi to murmur, buzz, whisper.
susurrus, -ūs m murmuring, whispering.
susurrus adj whispering.
sūtēla, -ae f trick.
sūtilis adj sewn.
sūtor, -ōris m shoemaker; ~ **nē suprā crepidam** ≈ let the cobbler stick to his last.
sūtōrius adj shoemaker's; ex-cobbler.
sūtrīnus adj shoemaker's.
sūtūra, -ae f seam.
sūtus ppp of **suō**.
suus adj his, her, its, their; one's own, proper, due, right ♦ mpl one's own troops, friends, followers etc ♦ nt one's own property.
Sybaris, -is f town in S. Italy (noted for its debauchery).
Sybarīta, -ītae m Sybarite.
Sychaeus, -ī m husband of Dido.
sȳcophanta, -ae m slanderer, cheat, sycophant.
sȳcophantia, -ae f deceit.
sȳcophantiōsē adv deceitfully.
sȳcophantor, -ārī, vi to cheat.
Syēnē, -ēs f town in S. Egypt (now Assuan).
syllaba, -ae f syllable.
syllabātim adv syllable by syllable.
symbola, -ae f contribution.
symbolus, -ī m token, symbol.
symphōnia, -ae f concord, harmony.
symphōniacus adj choir (in cpds).
Symplēgades, -um fpl clashing rocks in the Black Sea.
synedrus, -ī m senator (in Macedonia).
Synephēbī, -ōrum mpl Youths Together (comedy by Caecilius).
syngrapha, -ae f promissory note.
syngraphus, -ī m written contract; passport, pass.
Synnada, -ōrum ntpl town in Phrygia (famous for marble).
Synnadēnsis adj see n.
synodūs, -ontis m bream.
synthesis, -is f dinner service; suit of clothes; dressinggown.
Syphāx, -ācis m king of Numidia.
Syrācūsae, -ārum fpl Syracuse.
Syrācūsānus, Syrācūsānius, Syrācosius adj Syracusan.
Syria, -iae f country at the E. end of the Mediterranean.
Syrius, -us and iacus, -iscus adj Syrian.

syrma, -ae *f* robe with a train; (*fig*) tragedy.
Syrtis, -is *f* Gulf of Sidra in N. Africa; sandbank.

T, t

tabella, -ae *f* small board, sill; writing tablet, voting tablet, votive tablet; picture; (*pl*) writing, records, dispatches.
tabellārius *adj* about voting ♦ *m* courier.
tābeō, -ēre *vi* to waste away; to be wet.
taberna, -ae *f* cottage; shop; inn; (*circus*) stalls.
tabernāculum, -ī *nt* tent; ~ **capere** choose a site (for auspices).
tabernāriī, -ōrum *mpl* shopkeepers.
tābēs, -is *f* wasting away, decaying, melting; putrefaction; plague, disease.
tābēscō, -ēscere, -uī *vi* to waste away, melt, decay; (*fig*) to pine, languish.
tābidulus *adj* consuming.
tābidus *adj* melting, decaying; pining; corrupting, infectious.
tābificus *adj* melting, wasting.
tabula, -ae *f* board, plank; writing tablet; votive tablet; map; picture; auction; (*pl*) account books, records, lists, will; ~ **Sullae** Sulla's proscriptions; **XII ~ae** Twelve Tables of Roman laws; **~ae novae** cancellation of debts.
tabulārium, -ī *and* **iī** *nt* archives.
tabulātiō, -ōnis *f* flooring, storey.
tabulātum, -ī *nt* flooring, storey; (*trees*) layer, row.
tābum, -ī *nt* decaying matter; disease, plague.
taceō, -ēre, -uī, -itum *vi* to be silent, say nothing; to be still, be hushed ♦ *vt* to say nothing about, not speak of.
tacitē *adv* silently; secretly.
taciturnitās, -ātis *f* silence, taciturnity.
taciturnus *adj* silent, quiet.
tacitus *ppp of* **taceō** ♦ *adj* silent, mute, quiet; secret, unmentioned; tacit, implied; **per ~um** quietly.
Tacitus, -ī *m* famous Roman historian.
tāctilis *adj* tangible.
tāctiō, -ōnis *f* touching; sense of touch.
tāctus *ppp of* **tangō**.
tāctus, -ūs *m* touch, handling, sense of touch; influence.
taeda, -ae *f* pitch pine, pinewood; torch; plank; (*fig*) wedding.
taedet, -ēre, -uit *and* **taesum est** *vt* (*impers*) to be weary (of), loathe.
taedifer, -ī *adj* torch-bearing.
taedium, -ī *and* **iī** *nt* weariness, loathing.

Taenaridēs, -idae *m* Spartan (*esp Hyacinthus*).
Taenarius, -is *adj* of Taenarus; Spartan.
Taenarum (-on), -ī *nt*, **Taenarus (-os), -ī** *m/f* town and promontory in S. Greece (*now* Matapan); the lower world.
taenia, -ae *f* hairband, ribbon.
taesum est *perf of* **taedet**.
taeter, -rī *adj* foul, hideous, repulsive.
taetrē *adv* hideously.
taetricus *see* **tetricus**.
tagāx, -ācis *adj* light-fingered.
Tagus, -ī *m* river of Lusitania (*now* Tagus).
tālāris *adj* reaching to the ankles ♦ *ntpl* winged sandals; a garment reaching to the ankles.
tālārius *adj* of dice.
Talāsius, -ī *and* **iī** *m* god of weddings; wedding cry.
tālea, -ae *f* rod, stake.
talentum, -ī *nt* talent, *a Greek weight about 25.4kg*; a large sum of money (*esp the Attic talent of 60 minae*).
tāliō, -ōnis *f* retaliation in kind.
tālis *adj* such; the following.
talpa, -ae *f* mole.
tālus, -ī *m* ankle; heel; (*pl*) knuckle bones, oblong dice.
tam *adv* so, so much, so very.
tamdiū *adv* so long, as long.
tamen *adv* however, nevertheless, all the same.
Tāmesis, -is *and* **a, -ae** *m* Thames.
tametsī *conj* although.
tamquam *adv* as, just as, just like ♦ *conj* as if.
Tanagra, -ae *f* town in Boeotia.
Tanais, -is *m* river in Sarmatia (*now* Don).
Tanaquil, -ilis *f* wife of the elder Tarquin.
tandem *adv* at last, at length, finally; (*question*) just.
tangō, -ere, tetigī, tāctum *vt* to touch, handle; (*food*) to taste; (*with force*) to hit, strike; (*with liquid*) to sprinkle; (*mind*) to affect, move; (*place*) to reach; to border on; (*task*) to take in hand; (*by trick*) to take in, fool; (*in words*) to touch on, mention; **dē caelō tāctus** struck by lightning.
tanquam *see* **tamquam**.
Tantaleus *adj*, **-idēs, -idae** *m* Pelops, Atreus, Thyestes *or* Agamemnon.
Tantalis, -idis *f* Niobe *or* Hermione.
Tantalus, -ī *m* father of Pelops (*condemned to hunger and thirst in Tartarus, or to the threat of an overhanging rock*).
tantillus *adj* so little, so small.
tantisper *adv* so long, just for a moment.
tantopere *adv* so much.
tantulus *adj* so little, so small.
tantum *adv* so much, so, as; only, merely; ~ **modo** only; ~ **nōn** all but, almost; ~ **quod** only just.
tantummodo *adv* only.
tantundem *adv* just as much, just so much.
tantus *adj* so great; so little ♦ *nt* so much; so little; **~ī esse** be worth so much, be so dear,

be so important; **~ō** so much, so far; (*with compar*) so much the; **~ō opere** so much; **in ~um** to such an extent; **tria ~a** three times as much.

tantusdem *adj* just so great.

tapēta, -ae *m*, **-ia, -ium** *ntpl* carpet, tapestry, hangings.

Taprobanē, -ēs *f* Ceylon.

tardē *adv* slowly, tardily.

tardēscō, -ere *vi* to become slow, falter.

tardipēs, -edis *adj* limping.

tarditās, -ātis *f* slowness, tardiness; (*mind*) dullness.

tardiusculus *adj* rather slow.

tardō, -āre, -āvī, -ātum *vt* to retard, impede ♦ *vi* to delay, go slow.

tardus *adj* slow, tardy, late; (*mind*) dull; (*speech*) deliberate.

Tarentīnus *adj* Tarentine.

Tarentum, -ī *nt* town in S. Italy (*now Taranto*).

tarmes, -itis *m* woodworm.

Tarpēius *adj* Tarpeian; **mōns ~** the Tarpeian *Rock on the Capitoline Hill from which criminals were thrown.*

tarpezīta, -ae *m* banker.

Tarquiniēnsis *adj* of Tarquinii.

Tarquiniī, -iōrum *mpl* ancient town in Etruria.

Tarquinius *adj* of Tarquin.

Tarquinius, -ī *m* Tarquin (*esp Priscus, the fifth king of Rome, and Superbus, the last king*).

Tarracīna, -ae *f*, **-ae, -ārum** *fpl* town in Latium.

Tarracō, -ōnis *f* town in Spain (*now Tarragona*).

Tarracōnēnsis *adj see n.*

Tarsēnsis *adj see n.*

Tarsus, -ī *f* capital of Cilicia.

Tartareus *adj* infernal.

Tartarus (-os), -ī *m*, **-a, -ōrum** *ntpl* Tartarus, the lower world (*esp the part reserved for criminals*).

tat *interj* hallo there!

Tatius, -ī *m* Sabine king (*who ruled jointly with Romulus*).

Tatius *adj see n.*

Taum, -ī *nt* Firth of Tay.

taureus *adj* bull's ♦ *f* whip of bull's hide.

Taurī, -ōrum *mpl* Thracians of the Crimea.

Tauricus *adj see n.*

tauriformis *adj* bull-shaped.

Taurīnī, -ōrum *mpl* people of N. Italy (*now Turin*).

taurīnus *adj* bull's.

Tauromenītānus *adj see n.*

Tauromenium, -ī *and* **iī** *nt* town in E. Sicily.

taurus, -ī *m* bull.

Taurus, -ī *m* mountain range in S.E. Asia Minor.

taxātiō, -ōnis *f* valuing.

taxeus *adj* of yews.

taxillus, -ī *m* small dice.

taxō, -āre *vt* to value, estimate.

taxus, -ī *f* yew.

Tāygeta, -ōrum *ntpl*, **Tāygetus, -ī** *m* mountain *range in S. Greece.*

Tāygetē, -ēs *f* a Pleiad.

tē *acc and abl of* **tū.**

-te *suffix for* **tū.**

Teānēnsis *adj see n.*

Teānum, -ī *nt* town in Apulia; town in Campania.

techina, -ae *f* trick.

Tecmessa, -ae *f* wife of Ajax.

tēctor, -ōris *m* plasterer.

tēctōriolum, -ī *nt* a little plaster.

tēctōrium, -ī *and* **iī** *nt* plaster, stucco.

tēctōrius *adj* of a plasterer.

tēctum, -ī *nt* roof, ceiling, canopy; house, dwelling, shelter.

tēctus *ppp of* **tegō** ♦ *adj* hidden; secret, reserved, close.

tēcum with you.

Tegea, -ae *f* town in Arcadia.

Tegeaeus *adj* Arcadian ♦ *m* the god Pan ♦ *f* Atalanta.

Tegeātae, -ātārum *mpl* Tegeans.

teges, -etis *f* mat.

tegillum, -ī *nt* hood, cowl.

tegimen, -inis *nt* covering.

tegimentum, -ī *nt* covering.

tegm- *etc see* **tegim-.**

tegō, -ere, tēxī, tēctum *vt* to cover; to hide, conceal; to protect, defend; to bury; **latus ~** walk by the side of.

tēgula, -ae *f* tile; (*pl*) tiled roof.

tegum- *etc see* **tegim.**

Tēius *adj* of Teos.

tēla, -ae *f* web; warp; yarnbeam, loom; (*fig*) plan.

Telamōn, -ōnis *m* father of Ajax.

Tēlegonus, -ī *m* son of Ulysses and Circe.

Tēlemachus, -ī *m* son of Ulysses and Penelope.

Tēlephus, -ī *m* king of Mysia (*wounded by Achilles' spear*).

tellūs, -ūris *f* the earth; earth, ground; land, country.

tēlum, -ī *nt* weapon, missile; javelin, sword; (*fig*) shaft, dart.

temerārius *adj* accidental; rash, thoughtless.

temerē *adv* by chance, at random; rashly, thoughtlessly; **nōn ~** not for nothing; not easily; hardly ever.

temeritās, -ātis *f* chance; rashness, thoughtlessness.

temerō, -āre, -āvī, -ātum *vt* to desecrate, disgrace.

tēmētum, -ī *nt* wine, alcohol.

temnō, -ere *vt* to slight, despise.

tēmō, -ōnis *m* beam (of plough *or* carriage); cart; (*ASTRO*) the Plough.

Tempē *ntpl* famous valley in Thessaly.

temperāmentum, -ī *nt* moderation,

compromise.

temperāns, -antis *pres p of* **temperō** ♦ *adj* moderate, temperate.

temperanter *adv* with moderation.

temperantia, -ae *f* moderation, self-control.

temperātē *adv* with moderation.

temperātiō, -ōnis *f* proper mixture, composition, constitution; organizing power.

temperātor, -ōris *m* organizer.

temperātus *ppp of* **temperō** ♦ *adj* moderate, sober.

temperī *adv* in time, at the right time.

temperiēs, -ēī *f* due proportion; temperature, mildness.

temperō, -āre, -āvī, -ātum *vt* to mix in due proportion, blend, temper; to regulate, moderate, tune; to govern, rule ♦ *vi* to be moderate, forbear, abstain; (*with dat*) to spare, be lenient to.

tempestās, -ātis *f* time, season, period; weather; storm; (*fig*) storm, shower.

tempestīvē *adv* at the right time, appropriately.

tempestīvitās , -ātis *f* seasonableness.

tempestīvus *adj* timely, seasonable, appropriate; ripe, mature; early.

templum, -ī *nt* space marked off for taking auspices; open space, region, quarter; sanctuary; temple.

temporārius *adj* for the time, temporary.

temptābundus *adj* making repeated attempts.

temptāmentum, -ī *nt* trial, attempt, proof.

temptāmina, -um *ntpl* attempts, essays.

temptātiō, -ōnis *f* trial, proof; attack.

temptātor, -ōris *m* assailant.

temptō, -āre, -āvī, -ātum *vt* to feel, test by touching; to make an attempt on, attack; to try, essay, attempt; to try to influence, tamper with, tempt, incite; **vēnās ~** feel the pulse.

tempus, -oris *nt* time; right time, opportunity; danger, emergency, circumstance; (*head*) temple; (*verse*) unit of metre; (*verb*) tense; **~ore** at the right time, in time; **ad ~us** at the right time; for the moment; **ante ~us** too soon; **ex ~ore** on the spur of the moment; to suit the circumstances; **in ~ore** in time; **in ~us** temporarily; **per ~us** just in time; **prō ~ore** to suit the occasion.

tēmulentus *adj* intoxicated.

tenācitās, -ātis *f* firm grip; stinginess.

tenāciter *adv* tightly, firmly.

tenāx, -ācis *adj* gripping, tenacious; sticky; (*fig*) firm, persistent; stubborn; stingy.

tendicula, -ae *f* little snare.

tendō, -ere, tetendī, tentum *and* **tēnsum** *vt* to stretch, spread; to strain; (*arrow*) to aim, shoot; (*bow*) to bend; (*course*) to direct; (*lyre*) to tune; (*tent*) to pitch; (*time*) to prolong; (*trap*) to lay ♦ *vi* to encamp; to go, proceed; to

aim, tend; (*with infin*) to endeavour, exert oneself.

tenebrae, -ārum *fpl* darkness, night; unconsciousness, death, blindness; (*place*) dungeon, haunt, the lower world; (*fig*) ignorance, obscurity.

tenebricōsus *adj* gloomy.

tenebrōsus *adj* dark, gloomy.

Tenedius *adj see n.*

Tenedos (-us), -ī *f Aegean island near Troy.*

tenellulus *adj* dainty little.

teneō, -ēre, -uī *vt* to hold, keep; to possess, occupy, be the master of; to attain, acquire; (*argument*) to maintain, insist; (*category*) to comprise; (*goal*) to make for; (*interest*) to fascinate; (*law*) to bind, be binding on; (*mind*) to grasp, understand, remember; (*movement*) to hold back, restrain ♦ *vi* to hold on, last, persist; (*rumour*) to prevail; **cursum ~** keep on one's course; **sē ~** remain; to refrain.

tener, -ī *adj* tender, delicate; young, weak; effeminate; (*poet*) erotic.

tenerāscō, -ere *vi* to grow weak.

tenerē *adv* softly.

teneritās, -ātis *f* weakness.

tenor, -ōris *m* steady course; **ūnō ~ōre** without a break, uniformly.

tēnsa, -ae *f carriage bearing the images of the gods in procession.*

tēnsus *ppp of* **tendō** ♦ *adj* strained.

tentā- *etc see* **temptā-**.

tentīgō, -inis *f* lust.

tentō *etc see* **temptō**.

tentōrium, -ī *and* **iī** *nt* tent.

tentus *ppp of* **tendō**.

tenuiculus *adj* paltry.

tenuis *adj* thin, fine; small, shallow; (*air*) rarefied; (*water*) clear; (*condition*) poor, mean, insignificant; (*style*) refined, direct, precise.

tenuitās, -ātis *f* thinness, fineness; poverty, insignificance; (*style*) precision.

tenuiter *adv* thinly; poorly; with precision; superficially.

tenuō, -āre, -āvī, -ātum *vt* to make thin, attenuate, rarefy; to lessen, reduce.

tenus *prep* (*with gen or abl*) as far as, up to, down to; **verbō ~** in name, nominally.

Teos, -ī *f town on coast of Asia Minor* (*birthplace of Anacreon*).

tepefaciō, -facere, -fēcī, -factum *vt* to warm.

tepeō, -ēre *vi* to be warm, be lukewarm; (*fig*) to be in love.

tepēscō, -ēscere, -uī *vi* to grow warm; to become lukewarm, cool off.

tepidus *adj* warm, lukewarm.

tepor, -ōris *m* warmth; coolness.

ter *adv* three times, thrice.

terdeciēns *and* **ēs** *adv* thirteen times.

terebinthus, -ī *f* turpentine tree.

terebra, -ae *f* gimlet.

terebrō, -āre vt to bore.

terēdō, -inis f grub.

Terentia, -iae f Cicero's wife.

Terentius, -ī m Roman family name (*esp the comic poet Terence*).

Terentius, -iānus adj see n.

teres, -etis adj rounded (*esp cylindrical*), smooth, shapely; (*fig*) polished, elegant.

Tēreus, -eī and **eos** m king of Thrace (*husband of Procne, father of Itys*).

tergeminus adj threefold, triple.

tergeō, -gēre, -sī, -sum vt to wipe off, scour, clean; to rub up, burnish.

tergīnum, -ī nt rawhide.

tergiversātiō, -ōnis f refusal, subterfuge.

tergiversor, -ārī, -ātus vi to hedge, boggle, be evasive.

tergō etc see **tergeō**.

tergum, -ī nt back; rear; (*land*) ridge; (*water*) surface; (*meat*) chine; (*fig*) hide, leather, anything made of leather; **~a vertere** take to flight; **ā ~ō** behind, in the rear.

tergus, -oris see **tergum**.

termes, -itis m branch.

Terminālia, -ium ntpl Festival of the god of Boundaries.

terminātiō, -ōnis f decision; (*words*) clausula.

terminō, -āre, -āvī, -ātum vt to set bounds to, limit; to define, determine; to end.

terminus, -ī m boundary line, limit, bound; god of boundaries.

ternī, -ōrum adj three each; three.

terō, -ere, -trīvī, trītum vt to rub, crush, grind; to smooth, sharpen; to wear away, use up; (*road*) to frequent; (*time*) to waste; (*word*) to make commonplace.

Terpsichorē, -ēs f Muse of dancing.

terra, -ae f dry land, earth, ground, soil; land, country; **orbis ~ārum** the world; **ubi ~ārum** where in the world.

terrēnus adj of earth; terrestrial, land- (*in cpds*) ♦ nt land.

terreō, -ēre, -uī, -itum vt to frighten, terrify; to scare away; to deter.

terrestris adj earthly, on earth, land- (*in cpds*).

terribilis adj terrifying, dreadful.

terricula, -ōrum ntpl scare, bogy.

terrificō, -āre vt to terrify.

terrificus adj alarming, formidable.

terrigena, -ae m earth-born.

terriloquus adj alarming.

territō, -āre vt to frighten, intimidate.

territōrium, -ī and **iī** nt territory.

territus adj terrified.

terror, -ōris m fright, alarm, terror; a terror.

tersī perf of **tergeō**.

tersus ppp of **tergeō** ♦ adj clean; neat, terse.

tertiadecimānī, -ōrum mpl men of the thirteenth legion.

tertiānus adj recurring every second day ♦ f a

fever ♦ mpl men of the third legion.

tertiō adv for the third time; thirdly.

tertium adv for the third time.

tertius adj third; **~ decimus (decumus)** thirteenth.

terūncius, -ī and **iī** m quarter-as; a fourth; (*fig*) farthing.

tesqua (tesca), -ōrum ntpl waste ground, desert.

tessella, -ae f cube of mosaic stone.

tessera, -ae f cube, dice; (MIL) password; token (*for mutual recognition of friends*); ticket (*for doles*).

tesserārius, -ī and **iī** m officer of the watch.

testa, -ae f brick, tile; (*earthenware*) pot, jug, sherd; (*fish*) shell, shellfish.

testāmentārius adj testamentary ♦ m forger of wills.

testāmentum, -ī nt will, testament.

testātiō, -ōnis f calling to witness.

testātus ppa of **testor** ♦ adj public.

testiculus, -ī m testicle.

testificātiō, -ōnis f giving evidence, evidence.

testificor, -ārī, -ātus vt to give evidence, vouch for; to make public, bring to light; to call to witness.

testimōnium, -ī and **iī** nt evidence, testimony; proof.

testis, -is m/f witness; eyewitness.

testis, -is m testicle.

testor, -ārī, -ātus vt to give evidence, testify; to prove, vouch for; to call to witness, appeal to ♦ vi to make a will.

testū (*abl -ū*) nt earthenware lid, pot.

testūdineus adj of tortoiseshell, tortoise- (*in cpds*).

testūdō, -inis f tortoise; tortoiseshell; lyre, lute; (MIL) shelter for besiegers, covering of shields; (*building*) vault.

testum, -i nt earthenware lid, pot.

tēte emphatic acc of **tū**.

tetendī perf of **tendō**.

tēter etc see **taeter**.

Tēthys, -os f sea goddess; the sea.

tetigī perf of **tangō**.

tetrachmum, tetradrachmum, -ī nt four drachmas.

tetraō, -ōnis m blackcock, grouse or capercailzie.

tetrarchēs, -ae m tetrarch, ruler.

tetrarchia, -ae f tetrarchy.

tetricus adj gloomy, sour.

tetulī archaic perf of **ferō**.

Teucer, -rī m son of Telamon of Salamis; son-in-law of Dardanus.

Teucrī, -rōrum mpl Trojans.

Teucria, -riae f Troy.

Teutonī, -ōrum and **es, -um** mpl Teutons (*a German people*).

Noun declensions and verb conjugations are shown on pp xiii to xxv. The present infinitive ending of a verb shows to which conjugation it belongs: **-āre** = 1st; **-ēre** = 2nd; **-ere** = 3rd and **-īre** = 4th. Irregular verbs are shown on p xxvi

Teutonicus *adj* Teutonic, German.
tēxī *perf of* **tegō.**
texō, -ere, -uī, -tum *vt* to weave; to plait; to build, make; (*fig*) to compose, contrive.
textilis *adj* woven ♦ *nt* fabric.
textor, -ōris *m* weaver.
textrīnum, -ī *nt* weaving; shipyard.
textūra, -ae *f* web, fabric.
textus *ppp of* **texō** ♦ *nt* web, fabric.
textus, -ūs *m* texture.
texuī *perf of* **texō.**
Thāis, -idis *f an Athenian courtesan.*
thalamus, -ī *m* room, bedroom; marriage bed; marriage.
thalassicus *adj* sea-green.
thalassinus *adj* sea-green.
Thalēs, -is *and* **ētis** *m* early Greek philosopher (*one of the seven wise men*).
Thalia, -ae *f* Muse of comedy.
thallus, -ī *m* green bough.
Thamyrās, -ae *m* blinded Thracian poet.
Thapsitānus *adj see* **Thapsus.**
Thapsus (-os), -ī *f* town in N. Africa (*scene of Caesar's victory*).
Thasius *adj see* **Thasus.**
Thasus (-os), -ī *f* Greek island in N. Aegean.
Thaumantias, -dis *f* Iris.
theātrālis *adj* of the theatre, in the theatre.
theātrum, -ī *nt* theatre; audience; (*fig*) theatre, stage.
Thēbae, -ārum *fpl* Thebes (*capital of Boeotia*); town in Upper Egypt.
Thēbais, -aidis *f* Theban woman; *epic poem by Statius.*
Thēbānus *adj* Theban.
thēca, -ae *f* case, envelope.
Themis, -dis *f* goddess of justice.
Themistoclēs, -ī *and* **is** *m* famous Athenian statesman.
Themistoclēus *adj see* **Themistoclēs.**
thēnsaurārius *adj* of treasure.
thēnsaurus *see* **thēsaurus.**
theologus, -ī *m* theologian.
Theophrastus, -ī *m* Greek philosopher (*successor to Aristotle*).
Theopompēus, -īnus *adj see n.*
Theopompus, -ī *m* Greek historian.
thermae, -ārum *fpl* warm baths.
Thermōdōn, -ontis *m* river of Pontus (*where the Amazons lived*).
Thermōdontēus, -ontiacus *adj* Amazonian.
thermopōlium *nt* restaurant serving warm drinks.
thermopōtō, -āre *vt* to refresh with warm drinks.
Thermopylae, -ārum *fpl* famous Greek pass defended by Leonidas.
thēsaurus, -ī *m* treasure, store; storehouse, treasury.
Thēseus, -eī *and* **eos** *m* Greek hero (*king of Athens*).
Thēseus, -ēius *adj*, **-īdēs, -īdae** *m* Hippolytus; (*pl*) Athenians.

Thespiae, -ārum *fpl* Boeotian town near Helicon.
Thespiēnsis *and* **as, -adis** *adj* Thespian.
Thespis, -is *m* traditional founder of Greek tragedy.
Thessalia, -iae *f* Thessaly (*district of N. Greece*).
Thessalicus, -us *and* **is, -idis** *adj* Thessalian.
Thetis, -idis *and* **idos** *f* sea nymph (*mother of Achilles*); the sea.
thiasus, -ī *m* Bacchic dance.
Thoantēus *adj see n.*
Thoās, -antis *m* king of Crimea (*killed by Orestes*); king of Lemnos (*father of Hypsipyle*).
tholus, -ī *m* rotunda.
thōrāx, -ācis *m* breastplate.
Thrāca, -ae, (-ē, -ēs), (-ia, -iae) *f* Thrace.
Thracius, (Thrēicius) *adj* Thracian.
Thrasea, -ae *m* Stoic philosopher under Nero.
Thrasymachus, -ī *m* Greek sophist.
Thrāx, -ācis *m* Thracian; *kind of gladiator.*
Thrēssa, -ae, (Thrēissa, -ae) *f* Thracian woman.
Thrēx, -ēcis *m* kind of gladiator.
Thūcydidēs, -is *m* famous Greek historian.
Thūcydidius *adj* Thucydidean.
Thūlē, -ēs *f* island in the extreme N. (*perhaps Shetland*).
thunnus *see* **thynnus.**
thūr, -is *nt =* **tūs, tūris.**
Thūriī, -iōrum *mpl* town in S. Italy.
Thūrīnus *adj see n.*
thūs *see* **tūs.**
thȳa (thȳia), -ae *f* citrus tree.
Thybris, -is *and* **idis** *m* river Tiber.
Thyestēs, -ae *m* brother of Atreus (*whose son's flesh he served up to him to eat*).
Thyestēus *adj*, **-iadēs, -iadae** *m* Aegisthus.
Thyias (Thȳas), -adis *f* Bacchante.
Thȳlē *see* **Thūlē.**
thymbra, -ae *f* savory.
thymum, -ī *nt* garden thyme.
Thȳnia, -iae *f* Bithynia.
thynnus, -ī *m* tunnyfish.
Thȳnus, (-iacus), (-ias) *adj* Bithynian.
Thyōneus, -eī *m* Bacchus.
thyrsus, -ī *m* Bacchic wand.
tiāra, -ae *f*, **-ās, -ae** *m* turban.
Tiberiānus *adj see n.*
Tiberīnus, -īnis *adj*, **-īnus, -īnī** *m* Tiber.
Tiberis (Tibris), -is *m* river Tiber.
Tiberius, -ī *m* Roman praenomen (*esp the second emperor*).
tibi *dat of* **tū.**
tībia, -ae *f* shinbone; pipe, flute.
tībīcen, -inis *m* flute player; pillar.
tībīcina, -ae *f* flute player.
tībīcinium, -ī *and* **iī** *nt* flute playing.
Tibullus, -ī *m* Latin elegiac poet.
Tībur, -is *nt* town on the river Anio (*now Tivoli*).
Tīburs, -tis, (-tīnus), (-nus) *adj* Tiburtine.
Tīcīnus, -ī *m* tributary of the river Po.

Tigellīnus, -ī *m* favourite of Nero.
tigillum, -ī *nt* small log, small beam.
tignārius *adj* working in wood; **faber ~** carpenter.
tignum, -ī *nt* timber, trunk, log.
Tigrānēs, -is *m* king of Armenia.
tigris, -is *and* **idis** *f* tiger.
tīlia, -ae *f* lime tree.
Tīmaeus, -ī *m* Sicilian historian; Pythagorean philosopher; a dialogue of Plato.
timefactus *adj* frightened.
timeō, -ēre, -uī *vt, vi* to fear, be afraid.
timidē *adv* timidly.
timiditās, -ātis *f* timidity, cowardice.
timidus *adj* timid, cowardly.
timor, -ōris *m* fear, alarm; a terror.
tinctilis *adj* dipped in.
tinctus *ppp of* **tingō**.
tinea, -ae *f* moth, bookworm.
tingō, -gere, -xī, -ctum *vt* to dip, soak; to dye, colour; (fig) to imbue.
tinnīmentum, -ī *nt* ringing noise.
tinniō, -īre *vt, vi* to ring, tinkle.
tinnītus, -ūs *m* ringing, jingle.
tinnulus *adj* ringing, jingling.
tintinnābulum, -ī *nt* bell.
tintinō, -āre *vi* to ring.
tīnus, -ī *m* a shrub, laurustinus.
tinxī *perf of* **tingō**.
Tīphys, -os *m* helmsman of the Argo.
tippula, -ae *f* water spider.
Tīresiās, -ae *m* blind soothsayer of Thebes.
Tīridātēs, -ae *m* king of Armenia.
tīrō, -ōnis *m* recruit, beginner.
tīrōcinium, -ī *and* **iī** *nt* first campaign; recruits; (fig) first attempt, inexperience.
Tīrōniānus *adj see* **Tīrō**.
tīrunculus, -ī *m* young beginner.
Tīryns, -this *f* ancient town in S.E. Greece (home of Hercules).
Tīrynthius *adj* of Tiryns, of Hercules ♦ *m* Hercules.
tis *archaic gen of* **tū**.
Tīsiphonē, -ēs *f* a Fury.
Tīsiphonēus *adj* guilty.
Tītān, -ānis, (-ānus, -ānī) *m* Titan (an ancient race of gods); the sun.
Tītānius, (-āniacus), (-ānis) *adj see n.*
Tīthōnius *adj see n.*
Tīthōnus, -ī *m* consort of Aurora (granted immortality without youth).
tītillātiō, -ōnis *f* tickling.
tītillō, -āre *vt* to tickle.
titubanter *adv* falteringly.
titubātiō, -ōnis *f* staggering.
titubō, -āre *vi* to stagger, totter; to stammer; to waver, falter.
titulus, -ī *m* inscription, label, notice; title of honour; fame; pretext.

Tityos, -ī *m* giant punished in Tartarus.
Tmōlus, -ī *m* mountain in Lydia.
toculiō, -ōnis *m* usurer.
tōfus, -ī *m* tufa.
toga, -ae *f* toga (dress of the Roman citizen); (fig) peace; **~ candida** dress of election candidates; **~ picta** ceremonial dress of a victor in triumph; **~ praetexta** purple-edged toga of magistrates and children; **~ pūra, virīlis** plain toga of manhood.
togātus *adj* wearing the toga ♦ *m* Roman citizen; client ♦ *f* drama on a Roman theme.
togula, -ae *f* small toga.
tolerābilis *adj* bearable, tolerable; patient.
tolerābiliter *adv* patiently.
tolerāns, -antis *pres p of* **tolerō** ♦ *adj* patient.
toleranter *adv* patiently.
tolerantia, -ae *f* endurance.
tolerātiō, -ōnis *f* enduring.
tolerātus *adj* tolerable.
tolerō, -āre, -āvī, -ātum *vt* to bear, endure; to support, sustain.
tollēnō, -ōnis *m* crane, derrick, lift.
tollō, -ere, sustulī, sublātum *vt* to lift, raise; to take away, remove; to do away with, abolish, destroy; (anchor) to weigh; (child) to acknowledge, bring up; (mind) to elevate, excite, cheer; (passenger) to take on board; **signa ~** decamp.
Tolōsa, -ae *f* Toulouse.
Tolōsānus *adj see* **Tolōsa**.
tolūtim *adv* at a trot.
tomāculum, -ī *nt* sausage.
tōmentum, -ī *nt* stuffing, padding.
Tomis, -is *f* town on the Black Sea (to which Ovid was exiled).
Tomītānus *adj see* **Tomis**.
Tonāns, -antis *m* Thunderer (epithet of Jupiter).
tondeō, -ēre, totondī, tōnsum *vt* to shear, clip, shave; to crop, reap, mow; to graze, browse on; (fig) to fleece, rob.
tonitrālis *adj* thunderous.
tonitrus, -ūs *m*, **-ua, -uōrum** *ntpl* thunder.
tonō, -āre, -uī *vi* to thunder ♦ *vt* to thunder out.
tōnsa, -ae *f* oar.
tōnsillae, -ārum *fpl* tonsils.
tōnsor, -ōris *m* barber.
tōnsōrius *adj* for shaving.
tōnstrīcula, -ae *f* barber girl.
tōnstrīna, -ae *f* barber's shop.
tōnstrix, -īcis *f* woman barber.
tōnsūra, -ae *f* shearing, clipping.
tōnsus *ppp of* **tondeō**.
tōnsus, -ūs *m* coiffure.
tōphus *see* **tōfus**.
topiārius *adj* of ornamental gardening ♦ *m* topiarist ♦ *f* topiary.
topicē, -ēs *f* the art of finding topics.

Noun declensions and verb conjugations are shown on pp xiii to xxv. The present infinitive ending of a verb shows to which conjugation it belongs: **-āre** = 1st; **-ēre** = 2nd; **-ere** = 3rd and **-īre** = 4th. Irregular verbs are shown on p xxvi

toral, -ālis _nt_ valance.
torcular, -āris _and_ **um, -ī** _nt_ press.
toreuma, -tis _nt_ embossed work, relief.
tormentum, -ī _nt_ windlass, torsion catapult, artillery; shot; rack, torture; (_fig_) torment, anguish.
tormina, -um _ntpl_ colic.
torminōsus _adj_ subject to colic.
tornō, -āre, -āvī, -ātum _vt_ to turn (in a lathe), round off.
tornus, -ī _m_ lathe.
torōsus _adj_ muscular.
torpēdō, -inis _f_ numbness, lethargy; (_fish_) electric ray.
torpeō, -ēre _vi_ to be stiff, be numb; to be stupefied.
torpēscō, -ēscere, -uī _vi_ to grow stiff, numb, listless.
torpidus _adj_ benumbed.
torpor, -ōris _m_ numbness, torpor, listlessness.
torquātus _adj_ wearing a neckchain.
Torquātus, -ī _m_ surname of Manlius.
torqueō, -quēre, -sī, -tum _vt_ to turn, twist, bend, wind; (_missile_) to whirl, hurl, brandish; (_body_) to rack, torture; (_mind_) to torment.
torquēs _and_ **is, -is** _m/f_ neckchain, necklace, collar.
torrēns, -entis _pres p of_ **torreō ♦** _adj_ scorching, hot; rushing, rapid **♦** _m_ torrent.
torreō, -ēre, -uī, tostum _vt_ to parch, scorch, roast.
torrēscō, -ere _vi_ to become parched.
torridus _adj_ parched, dried up; frostbitten.
torris, -is _m_ brand, firebrand.
torsī _perf of_ **torqueō**.
tortē _adv_ awry.
tortilis _adj_ twisted, winding.
tortor, -ārī _vi_ to writhe.
tortor, -ōris _m_ torturer, executioner.
tortuōsus _adj_ winding; (_fig_) complicated.
tortus _ppp of_ **torqueō ♦** _adj_ crooked; complicated.
tortus, -ūs _m_ twisting, writhing.
torulus, -ī _m_ tuft (of hair).
torus, -ī _m_ knot, bulge; muscle, brawn; couch, bed; (_earth_) bank, mound; (_language_) ornament.
torvitās, -ātis _f_ wildness, grimness.
torvus _adj_ wild, grim, fierce.
tostus _ppp of_ **torreō**.
tot _adj_ (_indecl_) so many, as many.
totidem _adj_ (_indecl_) just as many, the same number of.
totiēns, totiēs _adv_ so often, as often.
totondī _perf of_ **tondeō**.
tōtus (_gen_ **-īus**, _dat_ **-ī**) _adj_ entire, the whole, all; entirely, completely taken up with; **ex ~ō** totally; **in ~ō** on the whole.
toxicum, -ī _nt_ poison.
trabālis _adj_ for beams; **clāvus ~** large nail.
trabea, -ae _f_ ceremonial robe.
trabeātus _adj_ wearing a ceremonial robe.

trabs, -abis _f_ beam, timber; tree; ship; roof.
Trāchīn, -īnis _f_ town in Thessaly (_where Hercules cremated himself_).
Trāchīnius _adj see_ **Trāchīn**.
tractābilis _adj_ manageable, tractable.
tractātiō, -ōnis _f_ handling, treatment.
tractātus, -ūs _m_ handling.
tractim _adv_ slowly, little by little.
tractō, -āre, -āvī, -ātum _vt_ to maul; to handle, deal with, manage; (_activity_) to conduct, perform; (_person_) to treat; (_subject_) to discuss, consider.
tractus _ppp of_ **trahō ♦** _adj_ fluent.
tractus, -ūs _m_ dragging, pulling, drawing; train, track; (_place_) extent, region, district; (_movement_) course; (_time_) lapse; (_word_) drawling.
trādidī _perf of_ **trādō**.
trāditiō, -ōnis _f_ surrender; handing down.
trāditor, -ōris _m_ traitor.
trāditus _ppp of_ **trādō**.
trādō, -ere, -idī, -itum _vt_ to hand over, deliver, surrender; to commit, entrust; to betray; to bequeath, hand down; (_narrative_) to relate, record; (_teaching_) to propound; **sē ~** surrender, devote oneself.
trādūcō (trānsdūcō), -ūcere, -ūxī, -uctum _vt_ to bring across, lead over, transport across; to transfer; to parade, make an exhibition of (in public); (_time_) to pass, spend.
trāductiō, -ōnis _f_ transference; (_time_) passage; (_word_) metonymy.
trāductor, -ōris _m_ transferrer.
trāductus _ppp of_ **trādūcō**.
trādux, -ucis _m_ vine layer.
tragicē _adv_ dramatically.
tragicōmoedia, -ae _f_ tragicomedy.
tragicus _adj_ of tragedy, tragic; in the tragic manner, lofty; terrible, tragic **♦** _m_ writer of tragedy.
tragoedia, -ae _f_ tragedy; (_fig_) bombast.
tragoedus, -ī _m_ tragic actor.
trāgula, -ae _f_ kind of javelin.
trahea, -ae _f_ sledge.
trahō, -here, -xī, -ctum _vt_ to draw, drag, pull, take with one; to pull out, lengthen; to draw together, contract; to carry off, plunder; (_liquid_) to drink, draw; (_money_) to squander; (_wool_) to spin; (_fig_) to attract; (_appearance_) to take on; (_consequence_) to derive, get; (_praise, blame_) to ascribe, refer; (_thought_) to ponder; (_time_) to spin out.
trāiciō, -icere, -iēcī, -iectum _vt_ to throw across, shoot across; (_troops_) to get across, transport; (_with weapon_) to pierce, stab; (_river, etc_) to cross; (_fig_) to transfer **♦** _vi_ to cross.
trāiectiō, -ōnis _f_ crossing, passage; (_fig_) transferring; (_RHET_) exaggeration; (_words_) transposition.
trāiectus _ppp of_ **trāiciō**.
trāiectus, -ūs _m_ crossing, passage.

trālāt- *etc see* **trānslāt-**.

Trallēs, -ium *fpl town in Lydia*.

Tralliānus *adj see n*.

trālūceō *etc see* **trānslūceō**.

trāma, -ae *f* woof, web.

trāmes, -itis *m* footpath, path.

trāmittō *etc see* **trānsmittō**.

trānatō *etc see* **trānsnatō**.

trānō, -āre, -āvī, -ātum *vt, vi* to swim across; (*air*) to fly through.

tranquillē *adv* quietly.

tranquillitās, -ātis *f* quietness, calm; (*fig*) peace, quiet.

tranquillō, -āre *vt* to calm.

tranquillus *adj* quiet, calm ♦ *nt* calm sea.

trāns *prep* (*with acc*) across, over, beyond.

trānsabeō, -īre, -iī *vt* to pierce.

trānsāctor, -ōris *m* manager.

trānsāctus *ppp of* **trānsigō**.

trānsadigō, -ere *vt* to drive through, pierce.

Trānsalpīnus *adj* Transalpine.

trānscendō (trānsscendō), -endere, -endī, -ēnsum *vt, vi* to pass over, surmount; to overstep, surpass, transgress.

trānscrībō (transscrībō), -bere, -psī, -ptum *vt* to copy out; (*fig*) to make over, transfer.

trānscurrō, -rere, -rī, -sum *vt, vi* to run across, run past, traverse.

trānscursus, -ūs *m* running through; (*speech*) cursory remark.

trānsd- *etc see* **trād-**.

trānsēgī *perf of* **trānsigō**.

trānsenna, -ae *f* net, snare; trellis, latticework.

trānseō, -īre, -iī, -itum *vt, vi* to pass over, cross over; to pass along *or* through; to pass by; to outstrip, surpass, overstep; (*change*) to turn into; (*speech*) to mention briefly, leave out, pass on; (*time*) to pass, pass away.

trānsferō, -ferre, -tulī, -lātum *vt* to bring across, transport, transfer; (*change*) to transform; (*language*) to translate; (*RHET*) to use figuratively; (*time*) to postpone; (*writing*) to copy.

trānsfīgō, -gere, -xī, -xum *vt* to pierce; to thrust through.

trānsfīxus *ppp of* **trānsfīgō**.

trānsfodiō, -odere, -ōdī, -ossum *vt* to run through, stab.

trānsfōrmis *adj* changed in shape.

trānsfōrmō, -āre *vt* to change in shape.

trānsfossus *ppp of* **trānsfodiō**.

trānsfuga, -ae *m/f* deserter.

trānsfugiō, -ugere, -ūgī *vi* to desert, come over.

trānsfugium, -ī *and* **iī** *nt* desertion.

trānsfundō, -undere, -ūdī, -ūsum *vt* to decant, transfuse.

trānsfūsiō, -ōnis *f* transmigration.

trānsfūsus *ppp of* **trānsfundō**.

trānsgredior, -dī, -ssus *vt, vi* to step across, cross over, cross; to pass on; to exceed.

trānsgressiō, -ōnis *f* passage; (*words*) transposition.

trānsgressus *ppa of* **trānsgredior**.

trānsgressus, -ūs *m* crossing.

trānsiciō *etc see* **trāiciō**.

trānsigō, -igere, -ēgī, -āctum *vt* to carry through, complete, finish; (*difference*) to settle; (*time*) to pass, spend; (*with cum*) to put an end to; (*with weapon*) to stab.

trānsiī *perf of* **trānseō**.

trānsiliō, trānssiliō, -īre, -uī *vi* to jump across ♦ *vt* to leap over; (*fig*) to skip, disregard; to exceed.

trānsitiō, -ōnis *f* passage; desertion; (*disease*) infection.

trānsitō, -āre *vi* to pass through.

trānsitus *ppp of* **trānseō**.

trānsitus, -ūs *m* passing over, passage; desertion; passing by; transition.

trānslātīcius, trālātīcius *adj* traditional, customary, common.

trānslātiō, trālātiō, -ōnis *f* transporting, transferring; (*language*) metaphor.

trānslātīvus *adj* transferable.

trānslātor, -ōris *m* transferrer.

trānslātus *ppp of* **trānsferō**.

trānslegō, -ere *vt* to read through.

trānslūceō, -ēre *vi* to be reflected; to shine through.

trānsmarīnus *adj* overseas.

trānsmeō, -āre *vi* to cross.

trānsmigrō, -āre *vi* to emigrate.

trānsmissiō, -ōnis *f* crossing.

trānsmissus *ppp of* **trānsmittō**.

trānsmissus, -ūs *m* crossing.

trānsmittō, -ittere, -īsī, -issum *vt* to send across, put across; to let pass through; to transfer, entrust, devote; to give up, pass over; (*place*) to cross over, go through, pass ♦ *vi* to cross.

trānsmontānus *adj* beyond the mountains.

trānsmoveō, -ovēre, -ōvī, -ōtum *vt* to move, transfer.

trānsmūtō, -āre *vt* to shift.

trānsnatō, trānatō, -āre *vi* to swim across ♦ *vt* to swim.

trānsnō *etc see* **trānō**.

Trānspadānus *adj* north of the Po.

trānspectus, -ūs *m* view.

trānspiciō, -ere *vt* to look through.

trānspōnō, -ōnere, -osuī, -ositum *vt* to transfer.

trānsportō, -āre *vt* to carry across, transport, remove.

trānspositus *ppp of* **trānspōnō**.

Trānsrhēnānus *adj* east of the Rhine.

trānss- *etc see* **trāns-**.

Noun declensions and verb conjugations are shown on pp xiii to xxv. The present infinitive ending of a verb shows to which conjugation it belongs: **-āre** = 1st; **-ēre** = 2nd; **-ere** = 3rd and **-īre** = 4th. Irregular verbs are shown on p xxvi

Trānstiberīnus *adj* across the Tiber.
trānstineō, -ēre *vi* to get through.
trānstrum, -ī *nt* thwart.
trānstulī *perf of* **trānsferō**.
trānsultō, -āre *vi* to jump across.
trānsūtus *adj* pierced.
trānsvectiō, -ōnis *f* crossing.
trānsvectus *ppp of* **trānsvehō**.
trānsvehō, -here, -xī, -ctum *vt* to carry across, transport.
trānsvehor, -hī, -ctus *vi* to cross, pass over; (*parade*) to ride past; (*time*) to elapse.
trānsverberō, -āre *vt* to pierce through, wound.
trānsversus (trāversus) *adj* lying across, crosswise, transverse; **digitum ~um** a finger's breadth; **dē ~ō** unexpectedly; **ex ~ō** sideways.
trānsvolitō, -āre *vt* to fly through.
trānsvolō, -āre *vt, vi* to fly across, fly through; to move rapidly across; to fly past, disregard.
trānsvorsus *etc see* **trānsversus**.
trapētus, -ī *m* olive mill, oil mill.
trapezīta *etc see* **tarpezīta**.
Trapezūs, -ūntis *f* Black Sea town (*now* Trebizond).
Trasumennus (Trasimēnus), -ī *m* lake in Etruria (*where Hannibal defeated the Romans*).
trāv- *see* **trānsv-**.
trāvectiō *etc see* **trānsvectiō**.
traxī *perf of* **trahō**.
trecēnī, -ōrum *adj* three hundred each.
trecentēsimus *adj* three-hundredth.
trecentī, -ōrum *num* three hundred.
trecentiēns, -ēs *adv* three hundred times.
trechedīpna, -ōrum *ntpl* dinner shoes (of parasites).
tredecim *num* thirteen.
tremebundus *adj* trembling.
tremefaciō, -facere, -fēcī, -factum *vt* to shake.
tremendus *adj* formidable, terrible.
tremēscō (tremīscō), -ere *vi* to begin to shake ♦ *vt* to be afraid of.
tremō, -ere, -uī *vi* to tremble, quake, quiver ♦ *vt* to tremble at, dread.
tremor, -ōris *m* shaking, quiver, tremor; earthquake.
tremulus *adj* trembling, shivering.
trepidanter *adv* with agitation.
trepidātiō, -ōnis *f* agitation, alarm, consternation.
trepidē *adv* hastily, in confusion.
trepidō, -āre, -āvī, -ātum *vi* to be agitated, bustle about, hurry; to be alarmed; to flicker, quiver ♦ *vt* to start at.
trepidus *adj* restless, anxious, alarmed; alarming, perilous.
trēs, trium *num* three.
trēssis, -is *m* three asses.
trēsvirī, triumvirōrum *mpl* three commissioners, triumvirs.

Trēverī, -ōrum *mpl* people of E. Gaul (*about what is now* Trèves).
Trēvericus *adj see n.*
triangulum, -ī *nt* triangle.
triangulus *adj* triangular.
triāriī, -ōrum *mpl* the third line (*in Roman battle order*), the reserves.
tribuārius *adj* of the tribes.
tribūlis, -is *m* fellow tribesman.
tribulum, -ī *nt* threshing sledge.
tribulus, -ī *m* star thistle.
tribūnal, -ālis *nt* platform; judgment seat; camp platform, cenotaph.
tribūnātus, -ūs *m* tribuneship, rank of tribune.
tribūnicius *adj* of a tribune ♦ *m* ex-tribune.
tribūnus, -ī *m* tribune; **~ plēbis** tribune of the people, a magistrate who defended the rights of the plebeians; **~ mīlitum** *or* **mīlitāris** military tribune, an officer under the legatus; **~ī aerāriī** paymasters.
tribuō, -uere, -uī, -ūtum *vt* to assign, allot; to give, bestow, pay; to concede, allow; to ascribe, attribute; (*subject*) to divide; (*time*) to devote.
tribus, -ūs *m* tribe.
tribūtārius *adj*: **~ae tabellae** letters of credit.
tribūtim *adv* by tribes.
tribūtiō, -ōnis *f* distribution.
tribūtum, -ī *nt* contribution, tribute, tax.
tribūtus *ppp of* **tribuō**.
tribūtus *adj* arranged by tribes.
trīcae, -ārum *fpl* nonsense; tricks, vexations.
trīcēnī, -ōrum *adj* thirty each, in thirties.
triceps, -ipitis *adj* three-headed.
trīcēsimus *adj* thirtieth.
trichila, -ae *f* arbour, summerhouse.
trīciēns, -ēs *adv* thirty times.
trīclīnium, -ī *and* **iī** *nt* dining couch; dining room.
trīcō, -ōnis *m* mischief-maker.
trīcor, -ārī *vi* to make mischief, play tricks.
tricorpor, -is *adj* three-bodied.
tricuspis, -idis *adj* three-pointed.
tridēns, -entis *adj* three-pronged ♦ *m* trident.
tridentifer, -ī *adj* trident-wielding.
tridentiger, -i *adj* trident-wielding.
triduum, -ī *nt* three days.
triennia, -ium *ntpl* a triennial festival.
triennium, -ī *and* **iī** *nt* three years.
triēns, -entis *m* a third; (*coin*) a third of an as; (*measure*) a third of a pint.
trientābulum, -ī *nt* land given by the State as a third of a debt.
trientius *adj* sold for a third.
triērarchus, -ī *m* captain of a trireme.
triēris, -is *f* trireme.
trietēricus *adj* triennial ♦ *ntpl* festival of Bacchus.
trietēris, -idis *f* three years; a triennial festival.
trifāriam *adv* in three parts, in three places.
trifaux, -aucis *adj* three-throated.

trifidus *adj* three-forked.

triformis *adj* triple.

trifūr, -ūris *m* archthief.

trifurcifer, -ī *m* hardened criminal.

trigeminus *adj* threefold, triple ♦ *mpl* triplets.

trigintā *num* thirty.

trigōn, -ōnis *m* a ball game.

trilībris *adj* three-pound.

trilinguis *adj* three-tongued.

trilīx, -icis *adj* three-ply, three-stranded.

trimēstris *adj* of three months.

trimetrus, -ī *m* trimeter.

trimus *adj* three years old.

Trīnacria, -iae *f* Sicily.

Trīnacrius, -is, -idis *adj* Sicilian.

trīnī, -ōrum *adj* three each, in threes; triple.

Trinobantēs, -um *mpl* British tribe in East Anglia.

trinōdis *adj* three-knotted.

triōbolus, -ī *m* half-a-drachma.

Triōnēs, -um *mpl* the Plough; the Little Bear.

tripartītō *adv* in *or* into three parts.

tripartītus, tripertītus *adj* divided into three parts.

tripectorus *adj* three-bodied.

tripedālis *adj* three-foot.

tripert- *etc see* **tripart-**.

tripēs, -edis *adj* three-legged.

triplex, -icis *adj* triple, threefold ♦ *nt* three times as much ♦ *mpl* three-leaved writing tablet.

triplus *adj* triple.

Triptolemus, -ī *m* inventor of agriculture, judge in Hades.

tripudiō, -āre *vi* to dance.

tripudium, -ī and iī *nt* ceremonial dance, dance; a favourable omen (*when the sacred chickens ate greedily*).

tripūs, -odis *f* tripod; the Delphic oracle.

triquetrus *adj* triangular; Sicilian.

trirēmis *adj* with three banks of oars ♦ *f* trireme.

trīs *etc see* **trēs**.

triscurria, -ōrum *ntpl* sheer fooling.

trīstē *adv* sadly; severely.

trīstī = **trīvistī**.

trīsticulus *adj* rather sad.

trīstificus *adj* ominous.

trīstimōnia, -ae *f* sadness.

trīstis *adj* sad, glum, melancholy; gloomy, sombre, dismal; (*taste*) bitter; (*smell*) offensive; (*temper*) severe, sullen, ill-humoured.

trīstitia, -ae *f* sadness, sorrow, melancholy; moroseness, severity.

trīstitiēs, -ēī *f* sorrow.

trisulcus *adj* three-forked.

tritavus, -ī *m* great-great-great-grandfather.

trīticeus *adj* of wheat, wheaten.

trīticum, -ī *nt* wheat.

Trītōn, -ōnis *m* sea god (*son of Neptune*); African lake (*where Minerva was born*).

Trītōnius, -ōniacus, -ōnis *adj* of Lake Triton, of Minerva ♦ *f* Minerva.

trītūra, -ae *f* threshing.

trītus *ppp of* **terō** ♦ *adj* well-worn; (*judgment*) expert; (*language*) commonplace, trite.

trītus, -ūs *m* rubbing, friction.

triumphālis *adj* triumphal ♦ *ntpl* insignia of a triumph.

triumphō, -āre, -āvī, -ātum *vi* to celebrate a triumph; to triumph, exult ♦ *vt* to triumph over, win by conquest.

triumphus, -ī *m* triumphal procession, victory parade; triumph, victory.

triumvir, -ī *m* commissioner, triumvir; mayor (*of a provincial town*).

triumvirālis *adj* triumviral.

triumvirātus, -ūs *m* office of triumvir, triumvirate.

triumvirī, -ōrum *mpl* three commissioners, triumvirs.

trivenēfica, -ae *f* old witch.

trīvī *perf of* **terō**.

Trivia, -ae *f* Diana.

triviālis *adj* common, popular.

trivium, -ī and iī *nt* crossroads; public street.

trivius *adj* of the crossroads.

Trōas, -adis *f* the district of Troy, Troad; Trojan woman ♦ *adj* Trojan.

trochaeus, -ī *m* trochee; tribrach.

trochlea, -ae *f* block and tackle.

trochus, -ī *m* hoop.

Trōglodytae, -ārum *mpl* cave dwellers of Ethiopia.

Trōia, -ae *f* Troy.

Trōilus, -ī *m* son of Priam.

Trōiugena, -ae *m/f* Trojan; Roman.

Trōius and ānus and cus *adj* Trojan.

tropaeum, -ī *nt* victory memorial, trophy; victory; memorial, token.

Trōs, -ōis *m* king of Phrygia; Trojan.

trucīdātiō, -ōnis *f* butchery.

trucīdō, -āre, -āvī, -ātum *vt* to slaughter, massacre.

truculentē *adv see* **truculentus**.

truculentia, -ae *f* ferocity, inclemency.

truculentus *adj* ferocious, grim, wild.

trudis, -is *f* pike.

trūdō, -dere, -sī, -sum *vt* to push, thrust, drive; (*buds*) to put forth.

trulla, -ae *f* ladle, scoop; washbasin.

truncō, -āre, -āvī, -ātum *vt* to lop off, maim, mutilate.

truncus, -ī *m* (*tree*) trunk, bole; (*human*) trunk, body; (*abuse*) blockhead ♦ *adj* maimed, broken, stripped (of); defective.

trūsī *perf of* **trūdō**.

trūsitō, -āre *vt* to keep pushing.

trūsus *ppp of* **trūdō**.

trutina, -ae _f_ balance, scales.

trux, -ucis _adj_ savage, grim, wild.

trygōnus, -ī _m_ stingray.

tū _pron_ you, thou.

tuātim _adv_ in your usual fashion.

tuba, -ae _f_ trumpet, war trumpet.

tūber, -is _nt_ swelling, lump; (_food_) truffle.

tuber, -is _f_ kind of apple tree.

tubicen, -inis _m_ trumpeter.

tubilūstria, -ōrum _ntpl_ festival of trumpets.

tuburcinor, -ārī _vi_ to gobble up, guzzle.

tubus, -ī _m_ pipe.

tuditō, -āre _vt_ to strike repeatedly.

tueor, -ērī, -itus _and_ **tūtus** _vt_ to see, watch, look; to guard, protect, keep.

tugurium, -ī _and_ **iī** _nt_ hut, cottage.

tuitiō, -ōnis _f_ defence.

tuitus _ppa of_ **tueor.**

tulī _perf of_ **ferō.**

Tulliānum, -ī _nt_ State dungeon of Rome.

Tulliānus _adj see_ **Tullius.**

Tulliola, -ae _f_ little Tullia (_Cicero's daughter_).

Tullius, -ī _and_ **iī** _m_ Roman family name (_esp the sixth king_); _the orator Cicero._

Tullus, -ī _m_ third king of Rome.

tum _adv_ (_time_) then, at that time; (_sequence_) then, next ♦ _conj_ moreover, besides; ~ ... ~ at one time ... at another; ~ ... **cum** at the time when, whenever; **cum** ... ~ not only ... but; ~ **dēmum** only then; ~ **ipsum** even then; ~ **māximē** just then; ~ **vērō** then more than ever.

tumefaciō, -facere, -fēcī, -factum _vt_ to make swell; (_fig_) to puff up.

tumeō, -ēre _vi_ to swell, be swollen; (_emotion_) to be excited; (_pride_) to be puffed up; (_language_) to be turgid.

tumēscō, -ēscere, -uī _vi_ to begin to swell, swell up.

tumidus _adj_ swollen, swelling; (_emotion_) excited, enraged; (_pride_) puffed up; (_language_) bombastic.

tumor, -ōris _m_ swelling, bulge; hillock; (_fig_) commotion, excitement.

tumulō, -āre _vt_ to bury.

tumulōsus _adj_ hilly.

tumultuārius _adj_ hasty; (_troops_) emergency.

tumultuātiō, -ōnis _f_ commotion.

tumultuō, -āre, -or, -ārī _vi_ to make a commotion, be in an uproar.

tumultuōsē _adv see_ **tumultuōsus.**

tumultuōsus _adj_ uproarious, excited, turbulent.

tumultus, -ūs _m_ commotion, uproar, disturbance; (_MIL_) rising, revolt, civil war; (_weather_) storm; (_mind_) disorder.

tumulus, -ī _m_ mound, hill; burial mound, barrow.

tunc _adv_ (_time_) then, at that time; (_sequence_) then, next; ~ **dēmum** only then; ~ **quoque** then too; even so.

tundō, -ere, tutudī, tūnsum _and_ **tūsum** _vt_ to beat, thump, hammer; (_grain_) to pound;

(_speech_) to din, importune.

Tūnēs, -ētis _m_ Tunis.

tunica, -ae _f_ tunic; (_fig_) skin, husk.

tunicātus _adj_ wearing a tunic.

tunicula, -ae _f_ little tunic.

tūnsus _ppp of_ **tundō.**

tuor _etc see_ **tueor.**

turba, -ae _f_ disorder, riot, disturbance; brawl, quarrel; crowd, mob, troop, number.

turbāmenta, -ōrum _ntpl_ propaganda.

turbātē _adv_ in confusion.

turbātiō, -ōnis _f_ confusion.

turbātor, -ōris _m_ agitator.

turbātus _ppp of_ **turbō** ♦ _adj_ troubled, disorderly.

turbellae, -ārum _fpl_ stir, row.

turben _etc see_ **turbō.**

turbidē _adv_ in disorder.

turbidus _adj_ confused, wild, boisterous; (_water_) troubled, muddy; (_fig_) disorderly, troubled, alarmed, dangerous.

turbineus _adj_ conical.

turbō, -āre, -āvī, -ātum _vt_ to disturb, throw into confusion; (_water_) to trouble, make muddy.

turbō, -inis _m_ whirl, spiral, rotation; reel, whorl, spindle; (_toy_) top; (_wind_) tornado, whirlwind; (_fig_) storm.

turbulentē _and_ **er** _adv_ wildly.

turbulentus _adj_ agitated, confused, boisterous, stormy; troublemaking, seditious.

turdus, -ī _m_ thrush.

tūreus _adj_ of incense.

turgeō, -gēre, -sī _vi_ to swell, be swollen; (_speech_) to be bombastic.

turgēscō, -ere _vi_ to swell up, begin to swell; (_fig_) to become enraged.

turgidulus _adj_ poor swollen.

turgidus _adj_ swollen, distended; bombastic.

tūribulum, -ī _nt_ censer.

tūricremus _adj_ incense-burning.

tūrifer, -ī _adj_ incense-producing.

tūrilegus _adj_ incense-gathering.

turma, -ae _f_ troop, squadron (_of cavalry_); crowd.

turmālis _adj_ of a troop; equestrian.

turmātim _adv_ troop by troop.

Turnus, -ī _m_ Rutulian king (_chief opponent of Aeneas_).

turpiculus _adj_ ugly little; slightly indecent.

turpificātus _adj_ debased.

turpilucricupidus _adj_ fond of filthy lucre.

turpis _adj_ ugly, deformed, unsightly; base, disgraceful ♦ _nt_ disgrace.

turpiter _adv_ repulsively; shamefully.

turpitūdō, -inis _f_ deformity; disgrace, infamy.

turpō, -āre _vt_ to disfigure, soil.

turriger, -ī _adj_ turreted.

turris, -is _f_ tower, turret; siege tower; (_elephant_) howdah; (_fig_) mansion.

turrītus _adj_ turreted; castellated; towering.

U, u

tursī *perf of* **turgeō.**
turtur, -is *m* turtledove.
tūs, tūris *nt* incense, frankincense.
Tusculānēnsis *adj* at Tusculum.
Tusculānum, -ānī *nt* villa at Tusculum (*esp Cicero's*).
Tusculānus *adj* Tusculan.
tūsculum, -ī *nt* a little incense.
Tusculum, -ī *nt* Latin town near Rome.
Tusculus *adj* Tusculan.
Tuscus *adj* Etruscan.
tussiō, -īre *vi* to cough, have a cough.
tussis, -is *f* cough.
tūsus *ppp of* **tundō.**
tūtāmen, -inis *nt* defence.
tūtāmentum, -ī *nt* protection.
tūte *emphatic form of* **tū.**
tūte *adv* safely, in safety.
tūtēla, -ae *f* keeping, charge, protection; (*of minors*) guardianship, wardship; (*person*) watcher, guardian; ward, charge.
tūtemet *emphatic form of* **tū.**
tūtor, -ārī, -ātus, -ō, -āre *vt* to watch, guard, protect; to guard against.
tūtor, -ōris *m* protector; (*law*) guardian.
tutudī *perf of* **tundō.**
tūtus *ppp of* **tueō** ♦ *adj* safe, secure; cautious ♦ *nt* safety.
tuus *adj* your, yours, thy, thine; your own, your proper; of you.
Tȳdeus, -eī *and* **eos** *m* father of Diomede.
Tȳdidēs, -īdae *m* Diomede.
tympanotrība, -ae *m* timbrel player.
tympanum (typanum), -ī *nt* drum, timbrel (*esp of the priests of Cybele*); (*mechanism*) wheel.
Tyndareus, -eī *m* king of Sparta (*husband of Leda*).
Tyndaridae, -idārum *mpl* Castor and Pollux.
Tyndaris, -idis *f* Helen; Clytemnestra.
Typhoeus, -eos *m* giant under Etna.
Typhōius, -is *adj see n.*
typus, -ī *m* figure.
tyrannicē *adv see* **tyrannicus.**
tyrannicīda, -ae *m* tyrannicide.
tyrannicus *adj* tyrannical.
tyrannis, -idis *f* despotism, tyranny.
tyrannoctonus, -ī *m* tyrannicide.
tyrannus, -ī *m* ruler, king; despot, tyrant.
Tyrās, -ae *m* river Dniester.
Tyrius *adj* Tyrian, Phoenician, Carthaginian; purple.
tyrotarichos, -ī *m* dish of salt fish and cheese.
Tyrrhēnia, -iae *f* Etruria.
Tyrrhēnus *adj* Etruscan, Tyrrhenian.
Tyrtaeus, -ī *m* Spartan war poet.
Tyrus (-os), -ī *f* Tyre (*famous Phoenician seaport*).

ūber, -is *nt* breast, teat; (*fig*) richness.
ūber, -is *adj* fertile, plentiful, rich (in); (*language*) full, copious.
ūberius (*superl* **-rime**) *compar adj* more fully, more copiously.
ūbertās, -ātis *f* richness, plenty, fertility.
ūbertim *adv* copiously.
ubī *adv* (*interrog*) where; (*relat*) where, in which, with whom; when
ubīcumque *adv* wherever; everywhere.
Ubiī, -ōrum *mpl* German tribe on the lower Rhine.
ubīnam *adv* where (in fact)?
ubīquāque *adv* everywhere.
ubīque *adv* everywhere, anywhere.
ubiubī *adv* wherever.
ubīvīs *adv* anywhere.
ūdus *adj* wet, damp.
ulcerō, -āre *vt* to make sore, wound.
ulcerōsus *adj* full of sores; wounded.
ulcīscor, -ī, ultus *vt* to take vengeance on, punish; to take vengeance for, avenge.
ulcus, -eris *nt* sore, ulcer; ~ **tangere** touch on a delicate subject.
ūlīgō, -inis *f* moisture, marshiness.
Ulixēs, -is *m* Ulysses, Odysseus (*king of Ithaca, hero of Homer's Odyssey*).
ullus (*gen* **-īus**, *dat* **-ī**) *adj* any.
ulmeus *adj* of elm.
ulmus, -ī *f* elm; (*pl*) elm rods.
ulna, -ae *f* elbow; arm; (*measure*) ell.
ulterior, -ōris *compar adj* farther, beyond, more remote.
ulterius *compar of* **ultrā.**
ultimus *superl adj* farthest, most remote, the end of; (*time*) earliest, latest, last; (*degree*) extreme, greatest, lowest ♦ *ntpl* the end; ~**um** for the last time; **ad ~um** finally.
ultiō, -ōnis *f* vengeance, revenge.
ultor, -ōris *m* avenger, punisher.
ultrō *adv* beyond, farther, besides ♦ *prep* (*with acc*) beyond, on the far side of; (*time*) past; (*degree*) over and above.
ultrīx, -icis *adj* avenging.
ultrō *adv* on the other side, away; besides; of one's own accord, unasked, voluntarily.
ultrō tribūta *ntpl* State expenditure for public works.
ultus *ppa of* **ulcīscor.**
ulula, -ae *f* screech owl.
ululātus, -ūs *m* wailing, shrieking, yells, whoops.

Noun declensions and verb conjugations are shown on pp xiii to xxv. The present infinitive ending of a verb shows to which conjugation it belongs: **-āre** = 1st; **-ēre** = 2nd; **-ere** = 3rd and **-īre** = 4th. Irregular verbs are shown on p xxvi

ululō, -āre, -āvī, -ātum *vi* to shriek, yell, howl
♦ *vt* to cry out to.

ulva, -ae *f* sedge.

umbella, -ae *f* parasol.

Umber, -rī *adj* Umbrian ♦ *m* Umbrian dog.

umbilīcus, -ī *m* navel; (*fig*) centre; (*book*)
roller end; (*sea*) cockle *or* pebble.

umbō, -ōnis *m* boss (*of a shield*); shield; elbow.

umbra, -ae *f* shadow, shade; (*dead*) ghost;
(*diner*) uninvited guest; (*fish*) grayling;
(*painting*) shade; (*place*) shelter, school,
study; (*unreality*) semblance, mere shadow.

umbrāculum, -ī *nt* arbour; school; parasol.

umbrāticola, -ae *m* lounger.

umbrāticus *adj* fond of idling; in retirement.

umbrātilis *adj* in retirement, private,
academic.

Umbria, -riae *f* Umbria (*district of central Italy*).

umbrifer, -ī *adj* shady.

umbrō, -āre *vt* to shade.

umbrōsus *adj* shady.

ūmectō, -āre *vt* to wet, water.

ūmectus *adj* damp, wet.

ūmeō, -ēre *vi* to be damp, be wet.

umerus, -ī *m* upper arm, shoulder.

ūmēscō, -ere *vi* to become damp, get wet.

ūmidē *adv* with damp.

ūmidulus *adj* dampish.

ūmidus *adj* wet, damp, dank, moist.

ūmor, -ōris *m* liquid, fluid, moisture.

umquam, unquam *adv* ever, at any time.

ūnā *adv* together.

ūnanimāns, -antis *adj* in full agreement.

ūnanimitās, -ātis *f* concord.

ūnanimus *adj* of one accord, harmonious.

ūncia, -ae *f* a twelfth; (*weight*) ounce; (*length*)
inch.

ūnciārius *adj* of a twelfth; (*interest*) 8⅓ per
cent.

ūnciātim *adv* little by little.

uncīnātus *adj* barbed.

ūnciola, -ae *f* a mere twelfth.

ūnctiō, -ōnis *f* anointing.

ūnctitō, -āre *vt* to anoint regularly.

ūnctiusculus *adj* rather too unctuous.

ūnctor, -ōris *m* anointer.

ūnctūra, -ae *f* anointing (*of the dead*).

ūnctus *ppp of* **ungō** ♦ *adj* oiled; greasy,
resinous; (*fig*) rich, sumptuous ♦ *nt*
sumptuous dinner.

uncus, -ī *m* hook, grappling-iron.

uncus *adj* hooked, crooked, barbed.

unda, -ae *f* wave, water; (*fig*) stream, surge.

unde *adv* from where, whence; from whom,
from which; ~ **petitur** the defendant; ~ **unde**
from wherever; somehow or other.

ūndeciēns *and* **ēs** *adv* eleven times.

ūndecim *num* eleven.

ūndecimus *adj* eleventh.

undecumque *adv* from wherever.

ūndēnī, -ōrum *adj* eleven each, eleven.

ūndēnōnāgintā *num* eighty-nine.

ūndeoctōgintā *num* seventy-nine.

ūndēquadrāgintā *num* thirty-nine.

ūndēquīnquāgēsimus *adj* forty-ninth.

ūndēquīnquāgintā *num* forty-nine.

ūndēsexāgintā *num* fifty-nine.

ūndētrīcēsimus *adj* twenty-ninth.

ūndēvīcēsimānī, -ōrum *mpl* men of the
nineteenth legion.

ūndēvīcēsimus *adj* nineteenth.

ūndēvīginti *num* nineteen.

undique *adv* from every side, on all sides,
everywhere; completely.

undisonus *adj* sea-roaring.

undō, -āre *vi* to surge; (*fig*) to roll, undulate.

undōsus *adj* billowy.

ūnetvīcēsimānī, -ōrum *mpl* men of the twenty-
first legion.

ūnetvīcēsimus *adj* twenty-first.

ungō (unguō), -gere, ūnxī, ūnctum *vt* to
anoint, smear, grease.

unguen, -inis *nt* fat, grease, ointment.

unguentārius, -ī *and* **iī** *m* perfumer.

unguentātus *adj* perfumed.

unguentum, -ī *nt* ointment, perfume.

unguiculus, -ī *m* fingernail.

unguis, -is *m* nail (*of finger or toe*); claw, talon,
hoof; **ad ~em** with perfect finish;
trānsversum ~em a hair's breadth; **dē tenerō
~ī** from earliest childhood.

ungula, -ae *f* hoof, talon, claw.

unguō *etc see* **ungō**.

ūnicē *adv* solely, extraordinarily.

ūnicolor, -ōris *adj* all one colour.

ūnicus *adj* one and only, sole; unparalleled,
unique.

ūnifōrmis *adj* simple.

ūnigena, -ae *adj* only-begotten; of the same
parentage.

ūnimanus *adj* with only one hand.

ūniō, -ōnis *m* a single large pearl.

ūniter *adv* together in one.

ūniversālis *adj* general.

ūniversē *adv* in general.

ūniversitās, -ātis *f* the whole; the universe.

ūniversus *adj* all taken together, entire,
general ♦ *mpl* the community as a whole ♦ *nt*
the universe; **in ~um** in general.

unquam *etc see* **umquam**.

ūnus *num* one ♦ *adj* sole, single, only; one and
the same; the outstanding one; an
individual; ~ **et alter** one or two; ~ **quisque**
every single one; **nēmō ~** not a single one; **ad
~um** to a man.

ūnxī *perf of* **ungō**.

ūpiliō, -ōnis *m* shepherd.

upupa, -ae *f* hoopoe; crowbar.

Ūrania, -ae *and* **ē, -ēs** *f* Muse of astronomy.

urbānē *adv* wittily; politely, elegantly.

urbānitās, -ātis *f* city life; refinement,
politeness; wit.

urbānus *adj* town (*in cpds*), city (*in cpds*);
refined, polite; witty, humorous;
impertinent ♦ *m* townsman.

urbicapus, -ī *m* taker of cities.

urbs, urbis f city; Rome.
urceolus, -ī m jug.
urceus, -ī m pitcher, ewer.
ūrēdō, -inis f blight.
urgeō, -gēre, -sī vt, vi to force on, push forward; to press hard on, pursue closely; to crowd, hem in; to burden, oppress; (*argument*) to press, urge; (*work, etc*) to urge on, ply hard, follow up.
ūrīna, -ae f urine.
ūrīnātor, -ōris m diver.
urna, -ae f water jar, urn; voting urn, lottery urn, cinerary urn, money jar.
urnula, -ae f small urn.
ūrō, -ere, ūssī, ūstum vt to burn; to scorch, parch; (*cold*) to nip; (*MED*) to cauterize; (*rubbing*) to chafe, hurt; (*passion*) to fire, inflame; (*vexation*) to annoy, oppress.
ursa, -ae f she-bear, bear; (*ASTRO*) Great Bear, Lesser Bear.
ursī perf of **urgeō**.
ursīnus adj bear's.
ursus, -ī m bear.
urtīca, -ae f nettle.
ūrus, -ī m wild ox.
Usipetēs, -etum, (-iī, -iōrum) mpl German tribe on the Rhine.
ūsitātē adv in the usual manner.
ūsitātus adj usual, familiar.
uspiam adv anywhere, somewhere.
usquam adv anywhere; in any way, at all.
usque adv all the way (to, from), right on, right up to; (*time*) all the time, as long as, continuously; (*degree*) even, as much as; ~ **quāque** everywhere; every moment, on every occasion.
ūssī perf of **ūrō**.
ūstor, -ōris m cremator.
ūstulō, -āre vt to burn.
ūstus ppp of **ūrō**.
ūsūcapiō, -apere, -ēpī, -aptum vt to acquire ownership of, take over.
ūsūcapiō, -ōnis f ownership by use or possession.
ūsūra, -ae f use, enjoyment; interest, usury.
ūsūrārius adj for use and enjoyment; paying interest.
ūsurpātiō, -ōnis f making use (of).
ūsurpō, -āre, -āvī, -ātum vt to make use of, employ, exercise; (*law*) to take possession of, enter upon; (*senses*) to perceive, make contact with; (*word*) to call by, speak of.
ūsus ppa of **ūtor**.
ūsus, -ūs m use, enjoyment, practice; experience, skill; usage, custom; intercourse, familiarity; usefulness, benefit, advantage; need, necessity; ~ **est**, **venit** there is need (of); ~**uī esse, ex** ~**ū esse** be of use, be of service; ~**ū venīre** happen; ~ **et frūctus** use and enjoyment, usufruct.

ut, utī adv how; (*relat*) as; (*explaining*) considering how, according as; (*place*) where; ~ **in ōrātōre** for an orator ♦ conj 1. with *indic*: (*manner*) as; (*concessive*) while, though; (*time*) when, as soon as. 2. with *subj*: (*expressing the idea of a verb*) that, to; (*purpose*) so that, to; (*causal*) seeing that; (*concessive*) granted that, although; (*result*) that, so that; (*fear*) that not; ~ ... **ita** while ... nevertheless; ~ **nōn** without; ~ **quī** seeing that I, he, *etc*; ~ **quisque māximē** the more.
utcumque (utcunque) adv however; whenever; one way or another.
ūtēnsilis adj of use ♦ ntpl necessaries.
ūter, -ris m bag, skin, bottle.
uter (*gen* -**rius**, *dat* -**rī**), -**ra**, -**rum** pron which (of two), the one that; one or the other.
utercumque, utracumque, utrumcumque pron whichever (of two).
uterlibet, utralibet, utrumlibet pron whichever (of the two) you please, either one.
uterque, utraque, utrumque pron each (of two), either, both.
uterum, -ī nt, **uterus, -ī** m womb; child; belly.
utervīs, utravīs, utrumvīs pron whichever (of two) you please; either.
ūtī infin of **ūtor**.
utī etc see **ut**.
ūtibilis adj useful, serviceable.
Utica, -ae f town near Carthage (*where Cato committed suicide*).
Uticēnsis adj see n.
ūtilis adj useful, expedient, profitable; fit (for).
ūtilitās, -ātis f usefulness, expediency, advantage.
ūtiliter adv usefully, advantageously.
utinam adv I wish!, would that!, if only!
utique adv at least, by all means, especially.
ūtor, ūtī, ūsus vi (with abl) to use, employ; to possess, enjoy; to practise, experience; (*person*) to be on intimate terms with, find; **ūtendum rogāre** borrow.
utpote adv inasmuch as, as being.
ūtrārius, -ī and **iī** m watercarrier.
ūtriculārius, -ī and **iī** m bagpiper.
utrimque (utrinque) adv on both sides, on either side.
utrō adv in which direction.
utrobīque see **utrubīque**.
utrōque adv in both directions, both ways.
utrubī adv on which side.
utrubīque adv on both sides, on either side.
utrum adv whether.
utut adv however.
ūva, -ae f grape, bunch of grapes; vine; cluster.
ūvēscō, -ere vi to become wet.
ūvidulus adj moist.
ūvidus adj wet, damp; drunken.

Noun declensions and verb conjugations are shown on pp xiii to xxv. The present infinitive ending of a verb shows to which conjugation it belongs: -**āre** = 1st; -**ēre** = 2nd; -**ere** = 3rd and -**īre** = 4th. Irregular verbs are shown on p xxvi

uxor, -ōris f wife.
uxorcula, -ae f little wife.
uxōrius adj of a wife; fond of his wife.

V, v

vacāns, -antis pres p of vacō ♦ adj unoccupied; (woman) single.
vacātiō, -ōnis f freedom, exemption; exemption from military service; payment for exemption from service.
vacca, -ae f cow.
vaccīnium, -ī and iī nt hyacinth.
vaccula, -ae f heifer.
vacēfiō, -ierī vi to become empty.
vacillō, -āre vi to stagger, totter; to waver, be unreliable.
vacīvē adv at leisure.
vacīvitās, -ātis f want.
vacīvus adj empty, free.
vacō, -āre, -āvī, -ātum vi to be empty, vacant, unoccupied; to be free, aloof (from); to have time for, devote one's time to; ~at there is time.
vacuātus adj empty.
vacuēfaciō, -facere, -fēcī, -factum vt to empty, clear.
vacuitās, -ātis f freedom, exemption; vacancy.
vacuus adj empty, void, wanting; vacant; free (from), clear; disengaged, at leisure; (value) worthless; (woman) single ♦ nt void, space.
vadimōnium, -ī and iī nt bail, security; ~ sistere appear in court; ~ dēserere default.
vādō, -ere vi to go, go on, make one's way.
vador, -ārī, -ātus vt to bind over by bail.
vadōsus adj shallow.
vadum, -ī nt shoal, shallow, ford; water, sea; bottom.
vae interj woe!, alas!
vafer, -rī adj crafty, subtle.
vafrē adv artfully.
vagē adv far afield.
vāgīna, -ae f sheath, scabbard; (grain) husk.
vāgiō, -īre vi to cry.
vāgītus, -ūs m crying, bleating.
vagor, -ārī, -ātus vi to wander, rove, go far afield; (fig) to spread.
vāgor, -ōris m cry.
vagus adj wandering, unsettled; (fig) fickle, wavering, vague.
vah interj (expressing surprise, joy, anger) oh!, ah!
valdē adv greatly, intensely; very.
valē, valēte interj goodbye, farewell.

valēns, -entis pres p of valeō ♦ adj strong, powerful, vigorous; well, healthy.
valenter adv strongly.
valentulus adj strong.
valeō, -ēre, -uī, -itum vi to be strong; to be able, have the power (to); to be well, fit, healthy; (fig) to be powerful, effective, valid; (force) to prevail; (money) to be worth; (word) to mean; ~ apud have influence over, carry weight with; ~ēre iubeō say goodbye to; ~ē dīcō say goodbye; ~eās away with you!
valēscō, -ere vi to grow strong, thrive.
valētūdinārium, -ī and iī nt hospital.
valētūdō, -inis f state of health, health; illness.
valgus adj bow-legged.
validē adv powerfully, very.
validus adj strong, powerful, able; sound, healthy; effective.
vallāris adj (decoration) for scaling a rampart.
vallēs, vallis, -is f valley.
vallō, -āre, -āvī, -ātum vt to palisade, entrench, fortify.
vallum, -ī nt rampart, palisade, entrenchment.
vallus, -ī m stake; palisade, rampart; (comb) tooth.
valvae, -ārum fpl folding door.
vānēscō, -ere vi to disappear, pass away.
vānidicus, -ī m liar.
vāniloquentia, -ae f idle talk.
vāniloquus adj untruthful; boastful.
vānitās, -ātis f emptiness; falsehood, worthlessness, fickleness; vanity.
vānitūdō, -inis f falsehood.
vannus, -ī f winnowing fan.
vānus adj empty; idle, useless, groundless; false, untruthful, unreliable; conceited.
vapidus adj spoilt, corrupt.
vapor, -ōris m steam, vapour; heat.
vapōrārium, -ī and iī nt steam pipe.
vapōrō, -āre vt to steam, fumigate, heat ♦ vi to burn.
vappa, -ae f wine that has gone flat; (person) good-for-nothing.
vāpulō, -āre vi to be flogged, beaten; to be defeated.
variantia, -ae f diversity.
variātiō, -ōnis f difference.
vāricō, -āre vi to straddle.
vāricōsus adj varicose.
vāricus adj with feet wide apart.
variē adv diversely, with varying success.
varietās, -ātis f difference, diversity.
variō, -āre, -āvī, -ātum vt to diversify, variegate; to make different, change, vary ♦ vi to change colour; to differ, vary.
varius adj coloured, spotted, variegated; diverse, changeable, various; (ability) versatile; (character) fickle.
Varius, -ī m epic poet (friend of Vergil and Horace).
varix, -icis f varicose vein.

Varrō, -ōnis m consul defeated at Cannae; antiquarian writer of Cicero's day.

Varrōniānus adj see **Varrō**.

vārus adj knock-kneed; crooked; contrary.

vas, vadis m surety, bail.

vās, vāsis (pl **vāsa, -ōrum**) nt vessel, dish; utensil, implement; (MIL) baggage.

vāsārium, -ī and **iī** nt furnishing allowance (of a governor).

vasculārius, -ī and **iī** m metalworker.

vasculum, -ī nt small dish.

vastātiō, -ōnis f ravaging.

vastātor, -ōris m ravager.

vastē adv (size) enormously; (speech) coarsely.

vastificus adj ravaging.

vastitās, -ātis f desolation, desert; devastation, destruction.

vastitiēs, -ēī f ruin.

vastō, -āre, -āvī, -ātum vt to make desolate, denude; to lay waste, ravage.

vastus adj empty, desolate, uncultivated; ravaged, devastated; (appearance) uncouth, rude; (size) enormous, vast.

vāsum etc see **vās**.

vātēs, -is m/f prophet, prophetess; poet, bard.

Vāticānus adj Vatican (hill on right bank of Tiber).

vāticinātiō, -ōnis f prophesying, prediction.

vāticinātor, -ōris m prophet.

vāticinor, -ārī, -ātus vt, vi to prophesy; to celebrate in verse; to rave, rant.

vāticinus adj prophetic.

-ve conj or; either ... or.

vēcordia, -ae f senselessness; insanity.

vēcors, -dis adj senseless, foolish, mad.

vectīgal, -ālis nt tax; honorarium (to a magistrate); income.

vectiō, -ōnis f transport.

vectis, -is m lever, crowbar; (door) bolt, bar.

Vectis, -is f Isle of Wight.

vectō, -āre vt to carry; (pass) to ride.

vector, -ōris m carrier; passenger, rider.

vectōrius adj transport (in cpds).

vectūra, -ae f transport; (payment) carriage, fare.

vectus ppp of **vehō**.

Vediovis, -is = **Vēiovis**.

vegetus adj lively, sprightly.

vēgrandis adj small.

vehemēns, -entis adj impetuous, violent; powerful, strong.

vehementer adv violently, eagerly; powerfully, very much.

vehementia, -ae f vehemence.

vehiculum, -ī nt carriage, cart; (sea) vessel.

vehō, -here, -xī, -ctum vt to carry, convey; (pass) to ride, sail, drive.

Vēiēns, -entis, (-entānus), (-us) adj see **Vēiī**.

Vēiī, -ōrum mpl ancient town in S. Etruria.

Vēiovis, -is m ancient Roman god (anti-Jupiter).

vel conj or, or perhaps; or rather; or else; either ... or ♦ adv even, if you like; perhaps; for instance; ~ **māximus** the very greatest.

Vēlābrum, -ī nt low ground between Capitol and Palatine hills.

vēlāmen, -inis nt covering, garment.

vēlāmentum, -ī nt curtain; (pl) draped olive branches carried by suppliants.

vēlārium, -ī and **iī** nt awning.

vēlātī, -ōrum mpl supernumerary troops.

vēles, -itis m light-armed soldier, skirmisher.

vēlifer, -ī adj carrying sail.

vēlificātiō, -ōnis f sailing.

vēlificō, -āre vi to sail ♦ vt to sail through.

vēlificor, -ārī vi to sail; (with dat) to make an effort to obtain.

Velīnus, -ī m a Sabine lake.

vēlitāris adj of the light-armed troops.

vēlitātiō, -ōnis f skirmishing.

vēlitēs pl of **vēles**.

vēlitor, -ārī vi to skirmish.

vēlivolus adj sail-winged.

velle infin of **volō**.

vellicō, -āre vt to pinch, pluck, twitch; (speech) to taunt, disparage.

vellō, -ere, vellī and **vulsī, vulsum** vt to pluck, pull, pick; to pluck out, tear up.

vellus, -eris nt fleece, pelt; wool; fleecy clouds.

vēlō, -āre, -āvī, -ātum vt to cover up, clothe, veil; (fig) to conceal.

vēlōcitās, -ātis f speed, rapidity.

vēlōciter adv rapidly.

vēlōx, -ōcis adj fast, quick, rapid.

vēlum, -ī nt sail; curtain, awning; **rēmīs ~īsque** with might and main; ~**a dare** set sail.

velut, velutī adv as, just as; for instance; just as if.

vēmēns etc see **vehemēns**.

vēna, -ae f vein, artery; vein of metal; water course; (fig) innermost nature of feelings, talent, strength; ~**ās temptāre** feel the pulse; ~**ās tenēre** have one's finger on the pulse (of).

vēnābulum, -ī nt hunting spear.

Venāfrānus adj see n.

Venāfrum, -ī nt Samnite town famous for olive oil.

vēnālicius adj for sale ♦ m slave dealer.

vēnālis adj for sale; bribable ♦ m slave offered for sale.

vēnāticus adj hunting (in cpds).

vēnātiō, -ōnis f hunting; a hunt; public show of fighting wild beasts; game.

vēnātor, -ōris m hunter.

vēnātōrius adj hunter's.

vēnātrīx, -īcis f huntress.

vēnātūra, -ae f hunting.

vēnātus, -ūs m hunting.

vēndibilis adj saleable; (fig) popular.

---

vēnditātiō, -ōnis f showing off, advertising.

vēnditātor, -ōris m braggart.

vēnditiō, -ōnis f sale.

vēnditō, -āre vt to try to sell; to praise up, advertise; **sē ~** ingratiate oneself (with).

vēnditor, -ōris m seller.

vēndō (pass **vēneō**), **-ere, -idī, -itum** vt to sell; to betray; to praise up.

venēficium, -ī and **iī** nt poisoning; sorcery.

venēficus adj poisonous; magic ♦ m sorcerer ♦ f sorceress.

venēnātus adj poisonous; magic.

venēnifer, -ī adj poisonous.

venēnō, -āre vt to poison.

venēnum, -ī nt drug, potion; dye; poison; magic charm; (fig) mischief; charm.

vēneō, -īre, -iī, -itum vi to be sold.

venerābilis adj honoured, venerable.

venerābundus adj reverent.

venerātiō, -ōnis f respect, reverence.

venerātor, -ōris m reverencer.

Venereus, Venerius adj of Venus ♦ m highest throw at dice.

veneror, -ārī, -ātus vt to worship, revere, pray to; to honour, respect; to ask for, entreat.

Venetia, -iae f district of the Veneti.

Veneticus adj see n.

Venetus adj Venetian; (colour) blue.

vēnī perf of **veniō**.

venia, -ae f indulgence, favour, kindness; permission, leave; pardon, forgiveness; **bonā tuā ~ā** by your leave; **bonā ~ā audīre** give a fair hearing.

vēniī perf of **vēneō**.

veniō, -īre, vēnī, ventum vi to come; (fig) to fall into, incur, go as far as; **in amīcitiam ~** make friends (with); **in spem ~** entertain hopes.

vēnor, -ārī, -ātus vt, vi to hunt, chase.

venter, -ris m stomach, belly; womb, unborn child.

ventilātor, -ōris m juggler.

ventilō, -āre vt to fan, wave, agitate.

ventiō, -ōnis f coming.

ventitō, -āre vi to keep coming, come regularly.

ventōsus adj windy; like the wind; fickle; conceited.

ventriculus, -ī m belly; (heart) ventricle.

ventriōsus adj pot-bellied.

ventulus, -ī m breeze.

ventus, -ī m wind.

vēnūcula, -ae f kind of grape.

vēnum, vēnō for sale.

vēnumdō (vēnundō), -āre, -edī, -atum vt to sell, put up for sale.

venus, -eris f charm, beauty; love, mating.

Venus, -eris f goddess of love; planet Venus; highest throw at dice.

Venusia, -iae f town in Apulia (birthplace of Horace).

Venusīnus adj see **Venusia**.

venustās, -ātis f charm, beauty.

venustē adv charmingly.

venustulus adj charming little.

venustus adj charming, attractive, beautiful.

vēpallidus adj very pale.

veprēcula, -ae f little brier bush.

veprēs, -is m thornbush, bramblebush.

vēr, vēris nt spring; **~ sacrum** offerings of firstlings.

vērātrum, -ī nt hellebore.

vērāx, -ācis adj truthful.

verbēna, -ae f vervain; (pl) sacred boughs carried by heralds or priests.

verber, -is nt lash, scourge; (missile) strap; (pl) flogging, strokes.

verberābilis adj deserving a flogging.

verberātiō, -ōnis f punishment.

verbereus adj deserving a flogging.

verberō, -āre, -āvī, -ātum vt to flog, beat, lash.

verberō, -ōnis m scoundrel.

verbōsē adv verbosely.

verbōsus adj wordy.

verbum, -ī nt word; saying; expression; (GRAM) verb; (pl) language, talk; **~ ē (dē, prō) ~ō** literally; **ad ~um** word for word; **~ī causa (grātiā)** for instance; **~ō** orally; briefly; **~a dare** cheat, fool; **~a facere** talk; **meīs ~īs** in my name.

vērē adv really, truly, correctly.

verēcundē adv see adj.

verēcundia, -ae f modesty, shyness; reverence, dread; shame.

verēcundor, -ārī vi to be bashful, feel shy.

verēcundus adj modest, shy, bashful.

verendus adj venerable.

vereor, -ērī, -itus vt, vi to fear, be afraid; to revere, respect.

verētrum, -ī nt the private parts.

Vergiliae, -ārum fpl the Pleiads.

Vergilius, -ī m Vergil, Virgil (famous epic poet).

vergō, -ere vt to turn, incline ♦ vi to turn, incline, decline; (place) to face.

vēridicus adj truthful.

vērī similis adj probable.

vērī similitūdō, -inis f probability.

vēritās, -ātis f truth, truthfulness; reality, real life; (character) integrity; (language) etymology.

veritus ppa of **vereor**.

vermiculātus adj inlaid with wavy lines, mosaic.

vermiculus, -ī m grub.

vermina, -um ntpl stomach pains.

vermis, -is m worm.

verna, -ae f slave born in his master's home.

vernāculus adj of home-born slaves; native.

vernīlis adj slavish; (remark) smart.

vernīliter adv slavishly.

vernō, -āre vi to bloom, be spring-like; to be young.

vernula, -ae f young home-born slave; native.

vērnus adj of spring.

vērō adv in fact, assuredly; (confirming) certainly, yes; (climax) indeed; (adversative) but in fact; **minimē ~** certainly not.

Vērōna, -ae f town in N. Italy (birthplace of Catullus).

Vērōnēnsis adj see **Vērōna**.

verpus, -ī m circumcised man.

verrēs, -is m boar.

Verrēs, -is m praetor prosecuted by Cicero.

verrīnus adj boar's, pork (in cpds).

Verrius and īnus adj see n.

verrō, -rere, -rī, -sum vt to sweep, scour; to sweep away, carry off.

verrūca, -ae f wart; (fig) slight blemish.

verrūcōsus adj warty.

verruncō, -āre vi to turn out successfully.

versābundus adj rotating.

versātilis adj revolving; versatile.

versicolor, -ōris adj of changing or various colours.

versiculus, -ī m short line; (pl) unpretentious verses.

versificātor, -ōris m versifier.

versipellis adj of changed appearance; crafty ♦ m werewolf.

versō, -āre, -āvī, -ātum vt to keep turning, wind, twist; (fig) to upset, disturb, ruin; (mind) to ponder, consider.

versor, -ārī, -ātus vi to live, be, be situated; to be engaged (in), be busy (with).

versum adv turned, in the direction.

versūra, -ae f borrowing to pay a debt; loan.

versus ppp of **vertō** ♦ adv turned, in the direction.

versus, -ūs m line, row; verse; (dance) step.

versūtē adv craftily.

versūtiae, -ārum fpl tricks.

versūtiloquus adj sly.

versūtus adj clever; crafty, deceitful.

vertex, -icis m whirlpool, eddy; whirlwind; crown of the head, head; top, summit; (sky) pole.

verticōsus adj eddying, swirling.

vertīgō, -inis f turning round; dizziness.

vertō, -tere, -tī, -sum vt to turn; to turn over, invert; to turn round; to turn into, change, exchange; (cause) to ascribe, impute; (language) to translate; (war) to overthrow, destroy; (pass) to be (in), be engaged (in) ♦ vi to turn; to change; to turn out; **in fugam ~** put to flight; **terga ~** flee; **solum ~** emigrate; **vitiō ~** blame; **annō ~tente** in the course of a year.

Vertumnus, -ī m god of seasons.

verū, -ūs nt spit; javelin.

vērum adv truly, yes; but actually; but, yet; **~ tamen** nevertheless.

vērum, -ī nt truth, reality; right; **~ī similis** probable.

vērus adj true, real, actual; truthful; right, reasonable.

verūtum, -ī nt javelin.

verūtus adj armed with the javelin.

vervēx, -ēcis m wether.

vēsānia, -ae f madness.

vēsāniēns, -entis adj raging.

vēsānus adj mad, insane; furious, raging.

vescor, -ī vi (with abl) to feed, eat; to enjoy.

vescus adj little, feeble; corroding.

vēsīca, -ae f bladder; purse; football.

vēsīcula, -ae f small bladder, blister.

vespa, -ae f wasp.

Vespasiānus, -ī m Roman emperor.

vesper, -is and ī m evening; supper; evening star; west; **~e, ~ī** in the evening.

vespera, -ae f evening.

vesperāscō, -ere vi to become evening, get late.

vespertiliō, -ōnis m bat.

vespertīnus adj evening (in cpds), in the evening; western.

vesperūgō, -inis f evening star.

Vesta, -ae f Roman goddess of the hearth.

Vestālis adj Vestal ♦ f virgin priestess of Vesta.

vester, -rī adj your, yours.

vestibulum, -ī nt forecourt, entrance.

vestīgium, -ī and iī nt footstep, footprint, track; (fig) trace, sign, vestige; (time) moment, instant; **ē ~iō** instantly.

vestīgō, -āre, -āvī, -ātum vt to track, trace, search for, discover.

vestīmentum, -ī nt clothes.

vestiō, -īre, -iī, -ītum vt to clothe, dress; to cover, adorn.

vestispica, -ae f wardrobe woman.

vestis, -is f clothes, dress; coverlet, tapestry, blanket; (snake) slough; **~em mūtāre** change one's clothes; go into mourning.

vestispica etc see **vestipica**.

vestītus, -ūs m clothes, dress; covering; **mūtāre ~um** go into mourning; **redīre ad suum ~um** come out of mourning.

Vesuvius, -ī m the volcano Vesuvius.

veterānus adj veteran.

veterāscō, -scere, -vī vi to grow old.

veterātor, -ōris m expert, old hand; sly fox.

veterātōriē adv see **veterātōrius**.

veterātōrius adj crafty.

veterīnus adj of burden ♦ f and ntpl beasts of burden.

veternōsus adj lethargic, drowsy.

veternus, -ī m lethargy, drowsiness.

vetitus ppp of **vetō** ♦ nt prohibition.

vetō, -āre, -uī, -itum vt to forbid, prohibit, oppose; (tribune) to protest.

vetulus adj little old, poor old.

vetus, -eris adj old, former ♦ mpl the ancients ♦ fpl the old shops (in the Forum) ♦ ntpl antiquity, tradition.

vetustās, -ātis f age, long standing; antiquity;

great age, future age.

vetustus *adj* old, ancient; old-fashioned.

vexāmen, -inis *nt* shaking.

vexātiō, -ōnis *f* shaking; trouble, distress.

vexātor, -ōris *m* troubler, opponent.

vexī *perf of* **vehō**.

vexillārius, -ī *and* **iī** *m* standard-bearer, ensign; (*pl*) special reserve of veterans.

vexillum, -ī *nt* standard, flag; company, troop; **~ prōpōnere** hoist the signal for battle.

vexō, -āre, -āvī, -ātum *vt* to shake, toss, trouble, distress, injure, attack.

via, -ae *f* road, street; way; journey, march; passage; (*fig*) way, method, fashion; the right way; **~ā** properly; **inter ~ās** on the way.

viālis *adj* of the highways.

viārius *adj* for the upkeep of roads.

viāticātus *adj* provided with travelling money.

viāticus *adj* for a journey ♦ *nt* travelling allowance; (MIL) prizemoney, savings.

viātor, -ōris *m* traveller; (*law*) summoner.

vībīx, -īcis *f* weal.

vibrō, -āre, -āvī, -ātum *vt* to wave, shake, brandish, hurl, launch ♦ *vi* to shake, quiver, vibrate; to shimmer, sparkle.

vīburnum, -ī *nt* wayfaring-tree *or* guelder rose.

vīcānus *adj* village (*in cpds*) ♦ *mpl* villagers.

Vica Pota, -ae, -ae *f* goddess of victory.

vicārius *adj* substituted ♦ *m* substitute, proxy; underslave.

vīcātim *adv* from street to street; in villages.

vice (*with gen*) on account of; like.

vicem in turn; (*with gen*) instead of; on account of; like; **tuam ~** on your account.

vīcēnārius *adj* of twenty.

vīcēnī, -ōrum *adj* twenty each, in twenties.

vicēs *pl of* **vicis**.

vīcēsimānī, -ōrum *mpl* men of the twentieth legion.

vīcēsimārius *adj* derived from the 5 per cent tax.

vīcēsimus *adj* twentieth ♦ *f* a 5 per cent tax.

vīcī *perf of* **vincō**.

vicia, -ae *f* vetch.

viciēns *and* **ēs** *adv* twenty times.

vīcīnālis *adj* neighbouring.

vīcīnia, -ae *f* neighbourhood, nearness.

vīcīnitās, -ātis *f* neighbourhood, nearness.

vīcīnus *adj* neighbouring, nearby; similar, kindred ♦ *m/f* neighbour ♦ *nt* neighbourhood.

vicis *gen* (*acc* **-em**, *abl* **-e**) *f* interchange, alternation, succession; recompense; retaliation; fortune, changing conditions; duty, function, place; **in ~em** in turn, mutually.

vicissim *adv* in turn, again.

vicissitūdō, -inis *f* interchange, alternation.

victima, -ae *f* victim, sacrifice.

victimārius, -ī *and* **iī** *m* assistant at sacrifices.

victitō, -āre *vi* to live, subsist.

victor, -ōris *m* conqueror, victor, winner ♦ *adj*

victorious.

victōria, -ae *f* victory.

victōriātus, -ūs *m* silver coin stamped with Victory.

Victōriola, -ae *f* little statue of Victory.

victrīx, -īcis *f* conqueror ♦ *adj* victorious.

victus *ppp of* **vincō**.

vīctus, -ūs *m* sustenance, livelihood; way of life.

vīculus, -ī *m* hamlet.

vīcus, -ī *m* (*city*) quarter, street; (*country*) village, estate.

vidēlicet *adv* clearly, evidently; (*ironical*) of course; (*explaining*) namely.

videō, -ēre, vīdī, vīsum *vt* to see, look at; (*mind*) to observe, be aware, know; to consider, think over; to see to, look out for; to live to see; (*pass*) to seem, appear; to seem right, be thought proper; **mē ~ē** rely on me; **vīderit** let him see to it; **mihi ~eor esse** I think I am; **sī** (**tibi**) **vidētur** if you like.

viduāta *adj* widowed.

viduitās, -ātis *f* bereavement, want; widowhood.

vīdulus, -ī *m* trunk, box.

viduō, -āre *vt* to bereave.

viduus *adj* bereft, bereaved; unmarried; (*with abl*) without ♦ *f* widow; spinster.

Vienna, -ae *f* town in Gaul on the Rhone.

viētus *adj* shrivelled.

vigeō, -ēre, -uī *vi* to thrive, flourish.

vigēscō, -ere *vi* to begin to flourish, become lively.

vigēsimus *etc see* **vīcēsimus**.

vigil, -is *adj* awake, watching, alert ♦ *m* watchman, sentinel; (*pl*) the watch, police.

vigilāns, -antis *pres p of* **vigilō** ♦ *adj* watchful.

vigilanter *adv* vigilantly.

vigilantia, -ae *f* wakefulness; vigilance.

vigilāx, -ācis *adj* watchful.

vigilia, -ae *f* lying awake, sleeplessness; keeping watch, guard; a watch; the watch, sentries; vigil; vigilance.

vigilō, -āre, -āvī, -ātum *vi* to remain awake; to keep watch; to be vigilant ♦ *vt* to spend awake, make while awake at night.

vīgintī *num* twenty.

vīgintīvirātus, -ūs *m* membership of a board of twenty.

vīgintīvirī, -ōrum *mpl* a board *or* commission of twenty men.

vigor, -ōris *m* energy, vigour.

vīlica, -ae *f* wife of a steward.

vīlicō, -āre *vi* to be an overseer.

vīlicus, -ī *m* overseer, manager of an estate, steward.

vīlis *adj* cheap; worthless, poor, mean, common.

vīlitās, -ātis *f* cheapness, low price; worthlessness.

vīliter *adv* cheaply.

vīlla, -ae *f* country house, villa.

vīllic- *etc see* **vīlic-**.

villōsus *adj* hairy, shaggy.

vīllula, -ae *f* small villa.

vīllum, -ī *nt* a drop of wine.

vīllus, -ī *m* hair, fleece; (*cloth*) nap.

vīmen, -inis *nt* osier; basket.

vīmentum, -ī *nt* osier.

Vīminālis *adj* Viminal (*hill of Rome*).

vīmineus *adj* of osiers, wicker.

vīnāceus *adj* grape (*in cpds*).

Vīnālia, -ium *ntpl* Wine festival.

vīnārius *adj* of wine, wine (*in cpds*) ♦ *m* vintner ♦ *nt* wine flask.

vincibilis *adj* easily won.

vinciō, -īre, -xī, -ctum *vt* to bind, fetter; to encircle; (*fig*) to confine, restrain, envelop, attach.

vinclum *nt see* **vinculum.**

vincō, -ere, vīcī, victum *vt* to conquer, defeat, subdue; to win, prevail, be successful; (*fig*) to surpass, excel; (*argument*) to convince, refute, prove conclusively; (*life*) to outlive.

vinctus *ppp of* **vinciō.**

vinculum, -ī *nt* bond, fetter, chain; (*pl*) prison.

vīndēmia, -ae *f* vintage grape harvest.

vīndēmiātor, -ōris *m* vintager.

vīndēmiola, -ae *f* small vintage.

Vīndēmitor, -ōris *m* the Vintager (*a star in Virgo*).

vindex, -icis *m* champion, protector; liberator; avenger ♦ *adj* avenging.

vindicātiō, -ōnis *f* punishment of offences.

vindiciae, -ārum *fpl* legal claim; ~**ās ab lībertāte in servitūtem dare** condemn a free man to slavery.

vindicō, -āre, -āvī, -ātum *vt* to lay claim to; to claim, appropriate; to liberate, protect, champion; to avenge, punish; **in lībertātem ~** emancipate.

vindicta, -ae *f* rod used in manumitting a slave; defence, deliverance; revenge, punishment.

vīnea, -ae *f* vineyard; vine; (MIL) penthouse (for besiegers).

vīnētum, -ī *nt* vineyard.

vīnitor, -ōris *m* vine-dresser.

vinnulus *adj* delightful.

vīnolentia, -ae *f* wine drinking.

vīnolentus *adj* drunk.

vīnōsus *adj* fond of wine, drunken.

vīnum, -ī *nt* wine.

vinxī *perf of* **vinciō.**

viola, -ae *f* violet; stock.

violābilis *adj* vulnerable.

violāceus *adj* violet.

violārium, -ī *and* **iī** *nt* violet bed.

violārius, -ī *and* **iī** *m* dyer of violet.

violātiō, -ōnis *f* desecration.

violātor, -ōris *m* violator, desecrator.

violēns, -entis *adj* raging, vehement.

violenter *adv* violently, furiously.

violentia, -ae *f* violence, impetuosity.

violentus *adj* violent, impetuous, boisterous.

violō, -āre, -āvī, -ātum *vt* to do violence to, outrage, violate; (*agreement*) to break.

vīpera, -ae *f* viper, adder, snake.

vīpereus *adj* snake's, serpent's.

vīperīnus *adj* snake's, serpent's.

vir, virī *m* man; grown man; brave man, hero; husband; (MIL) footsoldier.

virāgō, -inis *f* heroine, warrior maid.

virecta, -ōrum *ntpl* grassy sward.

vireō, -ēre, -uī *vi* to be green; (*fig*) to be fresh, flourish.

vīrēs *pl of* **vīs.**

virēscō, -ere *vi* to grow green.

virga, -ae *f* twig; graft; rod, staff, walking stick, wand; (*colour*) stripe.

virgātor, -ōris *m* flogger.

virgātus *adj* made of osiers; striped.

virgētum, -ī *nt* thicket of osiers.

virgeus *adj* of brushwood.

virgidēmia, -ae *f* crop of flogging.

virginālis *adj* maidenly, of maids.

virginārius *adj* of maids.

virgineus *adj* maidenly, virgin, of virgins.

virginitās, -ātis *f* maidenhood.

virgō, -inis *f* maid, virgin; young woman, girl; constellation Virgo; a Roman aqueduct.

virgula, -ae *f* wand.

virgulta, -ōrum *ntpl* thicket, shrubbery; cuttings, slips.

virguncula, -ae *f* little girl.

viridāns, -antis *adj* green.

viridārium, -ī *and* **iī** *nt* plantation, garden.

viridis *adj* green; fresh, young, youthful ♦ *ntpl* greenery.

viriditās, -ātis *f* verdure, greenness; freshness.

viridor, -ārī *vi* to become green.

virīlis *adj* male, masculine; man's, adult; manly, brave, bold; ~ **pars** one's individual part *or* duty; **prō ~ī parte, portiōne** to the best of one's ability.

virīlitās, -ātis *f* manhood.

virīliter *adv* manfully.

virītim *adv* individually, separately.

vīrōsus *adj* slimy; rank.

virtūs, -ūtis *f* manhood, full powers; strength, courage, ability, worth; (MIL) valour, prowess, heroism; (*moral*) virtue; (*things*) excellence, worth.

vīrus, -ī *nt* slime; poison; offensive smell; salt taste.

vīs (*acc* **vim,** *abl* **vī,** *pl* **vīrēs**) *f* power, force, strength; violence, assault; quantity, amount; (*mind*) energy, vigour; (*word*) meaning, import; (*pl*) strength; (MIL) troops; **per vim** forcibly; **dē vī damnārī** be convicted

---

Noun declensions and verb conjugations are shown on pp xiii to xxv. The present infinitive ending of a verb shows to which conjugation it belongs: **-āre** = 1st; **-ēre** = 2nd; **-ere** = 3rd and **-īre** = 4th. Irregular verbs are shown on p xxvi

of assault; **prō vīribus** with all one's might.

vīs 2nd pers of **volō**.

viscātus adj limed.

viscerātiō, -ōnis f public distribution of meat.

viscō, -āre vt to make sticky.

viscum, -ī nt mistletoe; bird lime.

viscus, -eris (usu pl **-era, -erum**) nt internal organs; flesh; womb, child; (fig) heart, bowels.

vīsendus adj worth seeing.

vīsiō, -ōnis f apparition; idea.

vīsitō, -āre vt to see often; to visit.

vīsō, -ere, -ī, -um vt to look at, survey; to see to; to go and see, visit.

Visurgis, -is m river Weser.

vīsus ppp of **videō** ♦ nt vision.

vīsus, -ūs m sight, the faculty of seeing; a sight, vision.

vīta, -ae f life, livelihood; way of life; career, biography.

vītābilis adj undesirable.

vītābundus adj avoiding, taking evasive action.

vītālis adj of life, vital ♦ nt subsistence ♦ ntpl vitals.

vītāliter adv with life.

vītātiō, -ōnis f avoidance.

Vitellius, -ī m Roman emperor in AD 69.

Vitellius, -iānus adj see n.

vitellus, -ī m little calf; (egg) yolk.

vīteus adj of the vine.

vīticula, -ae f little vine.

vītigenus adj produced from the vine.

vitilēna, -ae f procuress.

vitiō, -āre, -āvī, -ātum vt to spoil, corrupt, violate; to falsify.

vitiōsē adv badly, defectively.

vitiōsitās, -ātis f vice.

vitiōsus adj faulty, corrupt; wicked, depraved; ~ **cōnsul** a consul whose election had a religious flaw in it.

vītis, -is f vine; vine branch; centurion's staff, centurionship.

vītisator, -ōris m vine planter.

vitium, -ī and **iī** nt fault, flaw, defect; (moral) failing, offence, vice; (religion) flaw in the auspices.

vītō, -āre, -āvī, -ātum vt to avoid, evade, shun.

vītor, -ōris m basket maker, cooper.

vitreus adj of glass; glassy ♦ ntpl glassware.

vītricus, -ī m stepfather.

vitrum, -ī nt glass; woad.

vitta, -ae f headband, sacrificial fillet.

vittātus adj wearing a fillet.

vitula, -ae f (of cow) calf.

vitulīnus adj of veal ♦ f veal.

vitulor, -ārī vi to hold a celebration.

vitulus, -ī m calf; foal; ~ **marīnus** seal.

vituperābilis adj blameworthy.

vituperātiō, -ōnis f blame, censure; scandalous conduct.

vituperātor, -ōris m critic.

vituperō, -āre vt to find fault with, disparage; (omen) to spoil.

vīvārium, -ī and **iī** nt fishpond, game preserve.

vīvātus adj animated.

vīvāx, -ācis adj long-lived; lasting; (sulphur) inflammable.

vīvēscō, -ere vi to grow, become active.

vīvidus adj full of life; (art) true to life, vivid; (mind) lively.

vīvirādīx, -īcis f a rooted cutting, layer.

vīvīscō etc see **vīvēscō**.

vīvō, -vere, -xī, -ctum vi to live, be alive; to enjoy life; (fame) to last, be remembered; (with abl) to live on; ~**ve** farewell!; ~**xērunt** they are dead.

vīvus adj alive, living; (light) burning; (rock) natural; (water) running; ~**ō vīdentīque** before his very eyes; **mē** ~**ō** as long as I live, in my lifetime; **ad** ~**um resecāre** cut to the quick; **dē** ~**ō dētrahere** take out of capital.

vix adv with difficulty, hardly, scarcely.

vixdum adv hardly, as yet.

vīxī perf of **vīvō**.

vocābulum, -ī nt name, designation; (GRAM) noun.

vōcālis adj speaking, singing, tuneful ♦ f vowel.

vocāmen, -inis nt name.

vocātiō, -ōnis f invitation; (law) summons.

vocātus, -ūs m summons, call.

vōciferātiō, -ōnis f loud cry, outcry.

vōciferor, -ārī vt to cry out loud, shout.

vocitō, -āre, -āvī, -ātum vt to usually call; to shout.

vocīvus etc see **vacīvus**.

vocō, -āre, -āvī, -ātum vt to call, summon; to call, name; (gods) to call upon; (guest) to invite; (MIL) to challenge; (fig) to bring (into some condition or plight); ~ **dē** name after; ~**in dubium** ~ call in question; **in iūdicium** ~ call to account.

vōcula, -ae f weak voice; soft tone; gossip.

volaema ntpl kind of large pear.

Volaterrae, -ārum fpl old Etruscan town (now Volterra).

Volaterrānus adj see n.

volāticus adj winged; fleeting, inconstant.

volātilis adj winged; swift; fleeting.

volātus, -ūs m flight.

Volcānius adj see n.

Volcānus, -ī m Vulcan (god of fire); fire.

volēns, -entis pres p of **volō** ♦ adj willing, glad, favourable; **mihi** ~**entī est** it is acceptable to me.

volg- etc see **vulg-**.

volitō, -āre vi to fly about, flutter; to hurry, move quickly; (fig) to hover, soar; to get excited.

voln- etc see **vuln-**.

volō, -āre, -āvī, -ātum vi to fly; to speed.

volō, velle, voluī vt to wish, want; to be

willing; to will, purpose, determine;
(*opinion*) to hold, maintain; (*word, action*) to
mean; ~ **dīcere** I mean; **bene** ~ like; **male** ~
dislike; **ōrātum tē** ~ I beg you; **paucīs tē** ~ a
word with you!; **numquid vīs?** (*before leaving*)
is there anything else?; **quid sibi vult?** what
does he mean?; what is he driving at?; **velim
faciās** please do it; **vellem fēcissēs** I wish you
had done it.

volōnēs, -um *mpl* volunteers.

volpēs *etc see* **vulpēs.**

Volscī, -ōrum *mpl people in S. Latium.*

Volscus *adj* Volscian.

volsella, -ae *f* tweezers.

volsus *ppp of* **vellō.**

volt, voltis *older forms of* **vult, vultis.**

Voltumna, -ae *f patron goddess of Etruria.*

voltus *etc see* **vultus.**

volūbilis *adj* spinning, revolving; (*fortune*)
fickle; (*speech*) fluent.

volubilitās, -ātis *f* whirling motion;
roundness; fluency; inconstancy.

volūbiliter *adv* fluently.

volucer, -ris *adj* winged; flying, swift; fleeting.

volucris, -is *f* bird; insect.

volūmen, -inis *nt* roll, book; coil, eddy, fold.

voluntārius *adj* voluntary ♦ *mpl* volunteers.

voluntās, -ātis *f* will, wish, inclination;
attitude, goodwill; last will, testament; **suā
~āte** of one's own accord; **ad ~ātem** with the
consent (of).

volup *adv* agreeably, to one's satisfaction.

voluptābilis *adj* agreeable.

voluptās, -ātis *f* pleasure, enjoyment; (*pl*)
entertainments, sports.

voluptuārius *adj* pleasureable, agreeable;
voluptuous.

volūtābrum, -ī *nt* wallowing place.

volūtātiō, -ōnis *f* wallowing.

volūtō, -āre *vt* to roll about, turn over; (*mind*)
to occupy, engross; (*thought*) to ponder,
think over; (*pass*) to wallow, flounder.

volūtus *ppp of* **volvō.**

volva, -ae *f* womb; (*dish*) sow's womb.

volvō, -vere, -vī, -ūtum *vt* to roll, turn round;
to roll along; (*air*) to breathe; (*book*) to open;
(*circle*) to form; (*thought*) to ponder, reflect
on; (*time*) to roll on; (*trouble*) to undergo;
(*pass*) to roll, revolve ♦ *vi* to revolve, elapse.

vōmer, -eris *m* ploughshare.

vomica, -ae *f* sore, ulcer, abscess, boil.

vōmis *etc see* **vōmer.**

vomitiō, -ōnis *f* vomiting.

vomitus, -ūs *m* vomiting, vomit.

vomō, -ere, -uī, -itum *vt* to vomit, throw up;

to emit, discharge.

vorāgō, -inis *f* abyss, chasm, depth.

vorāx, -ācis *adj* greedy, ravenous; consuming.

vorō, -āre, -āvī, -ātum *vt* to swallow, devour;
(*sea*) to swallow up; (*reading*) to devour.

vors-, vort- *etc see* **vers-, vert-** *etc.*

vōs *pron* you.

Vosegus, -ī *m* Vosges mountains.

voster *etc see* **vester.**

vōtīvus *adj* votive, promised in a vow.

votō *etc see* **vetō.**

vōtum, -ī *nt* vow, prayer; votive offering;
wish, longing; **~ī damnārī** have one's prayer
granted.

vōtus *ppp of* **voveō.**

voveō, -ēre, vōvī, vōtum *vt* to vow, promise
solemnly; to dedicate; to wish.

vōx, vōcis *f* voice; sound, cry, call; word,
saying, expression; accent; **unā vōce**
unanimously.

Vulcānus *see* **Volcānus.**

vulgāris *adj* common, general.

vulgāriter *adv* in the common fashion.

vulgātor, -ōris *m* betrayer.

vulgātus *adj* common; generally known,
notorious.

vulgivagus *adj* roving; inconstant.

vulgō *adv* publicly, commonly, usually,
everywhere.

vulgō, -āre, -āvī, -ātum *vt* to make common,
spread; to publish, divulge, broadcast; to
prostitute; to level down.

vulgus, -ī *nt* (*occ m*) the mass of the people,
the public; crowd, herd; rabble, populace.

vulnerātiō, -ōnis *f* wounding, injury.

vulnerō, -āre, -āvī, -ātum *vt* to wound, hurt;
to damage.

vulnificus *adj* wounding, dangerous.

vulnus, -eris *nt* wound, injury; (*things*)
damage, hole; (*fig*) blow, misfortune, pain.

vulpēcula, -ae *f* little fox.

vulpēs, -is *f* fox; (*fig*) cunning.

vulsī *perf of* **vellō.**

vulsus *ppp of* **vellō.**

vulticulus, -ī *m* a mere look (from).

vultum *etc see* **vultus.**

vultuōsus *adj* affected.

vultur, -is *m* vulture.

vulturius, -ī *and* **iī** *m* vulture, bird of prey;
(*dice*) an unlucky throw.

Vulturnus, -ī *m river in Campania.*

vultus, -ūs *m* look, expression (*esp* in the
eyes); face; (*things*) appearance.

vulva *etc see* **volva.**

Noun declensions and verb conjugations are shown on pp xiii to xxv. The present infinitive ending of a verb shows
to which conjugation it belongs: **-āre** = 1st; **-ēre** = 2nd; **-ere** = 3rd and **-īre** = 4th. Irregular verbs are shown on p xxvi

X, x

Xanthippē, -ēs f wife of Socrates.
Xanthus, -ī m river of Troy (identified with Scamander); river of Lycia.
xenium, -ī and **iī** nt present.

Xenocratēs, -is m disciple of Plato.
Xenophanēs, -is m early Greek philosopher.
Xenophōn, -ontis m famous Greek historian.
Xenophontēus adj see n.
xērampelinae, -ārum fpl dark-coloured clothes.
Xerxēs, -is m Persian king defeated at Salamis.
xiphiās, -ae m swordfish.
xystum, -ī nt, **xystus, -ī** m open colonnade, walk, avenue.

Z, z

Zacynthius adj see n.
Zacynthus (-os), -ī f island off W. Greece (now Zante).
Zama, -ae f town in Numidia (where Scipio defeated Hannibal).
Zamēnsis adj see n.
zāmia, -ae f harm.
Zanclaeus and **ēius** adj see n.
Zanclē, -ēs f old name of Messana.
zēlotypus adj jealous.

Zēnō and **ōn, -ōnis** m founder of Stoicism; a philosopher of Elea; an Epicurean teacher of Cicero.
Zephyrītis, -idis f Arsinoe (queen of Egypt).
Zephyrus, -ī m west wind, zephyr; wind.
Zēthus, -ī m brother of Amphion.
Zeuxis, -is and **idis** m famous Greek painter.
zmaragdus etc see **smaragdus**.
Zmyrna etc see **Smyrna**.
zōdiacus, -ī m zodiac.
zōna, -ae f belt, girdle; (GEOG) zone; (ASTRO) Orion's Belt.
zōnārius adj of belts; sector ~ cutpurse ♦ m belt maker.
zōnula, -ae f little belt.
zōthēca, -ae f private room.
zōthēcula, -ae f cubicle.

ROMAN LIFE AND CULTURE

KEY EVENTS IN ROMAN HISTORY

B.C.

753	Foundation of Rome. Romulus became first king.
600-510	Rome ruled by Etruscan kings.
510	Expulsion of Tarquin and republic established.
507	Consecration of Temple of Jupiter on Capitol.
451	Code of Twelve Tables laid basis of Roman law.
390	Gauls sacked Rome.
367	Lex Liciniae Sextiae; plebeians allowed to be consul.
354	Treaty with Samnites.
343-341	First Samnite war; Romans occupied northern Campania.
340-338	Latin War; separate treaties made with Latins.
327-304	Second Samnite war; Rome increased influence in southern Italy.
321	Samnites defeated Romans at Caudine Forks; truce.
312	Appian Way, first Roman road, built.
298-290	Third Samnite war; Rome now all-powerful in southern Italy.
287	Hortensian Law; People's Assembly became a law-making body.
282-272	Wars with Tarentum and King Pyrrhus of Epirus.
270	Whole peninsula under Roman power.
264-241	First Punic war; Rome defended Greek cities in Sicily.
260	Fleet built; first naval victory at Mylae against Carthaginians.
241	Roman victory over Carthage secured Sicily, source of corn supply.
226	River Ebro treaty; Carthage should not cross into northern Spain.
218-201	Second Punic war against Hannibal.
216	Rome defeated at Battle of Cannae.
214-205	First Macedonian war with Philip V.
202	Scipio defeated Hannibal at Zama.
201	Peace concluded with Carthage; Rome now controlled the western Mediterranean.
200-196	Second Macedonian war; freedom of Greece proclaimed.
172-168	Third Macedonian war; Perseus crushed at Pydna.
148	Macedonia became a Roman province.
146	Carthage destroyed; Corinth destroyed.
133	Tiberius Gracchus became tribune; his assassination caused class conflict.
123-122	Gaius Gracchus carried out political/economic reforms.
121	Gaius was killed.
111-105	Marius and Sulla conducted war against Jugurtha of Numidia.
91-89	Social war between Rome and allies.
89-85	War with Mithridates VI of Pontus.
83-82	Civil war between Sulla and Marius; Sulla captured Rome.
81-79	Sulla, dictator, restored constitution, introduced reforms.
78	Death of Sulla.

77-72	Pompey fought Sertorius in Spain.
73-71	Spartacus' slave revolt.
70	Pompey and Crassus joint consuls; tribunes restored.
67	End of war against Mithridates; pirates controlled by Pompey.
63	Cicero suppressed Catiline's conspiracy.
60	First Triumvirate (Caesar, Pompey, Crassus) was formed.
58-51	Caesar conquered Gaul.
53	Battle of Carrhae; Rome defeated by Parthians; Crassus killed.
49	Caesar crossed Rubicon; civil war with Pompey began.
48	Pompey defeated by Caesar at Pharsalus; Caesar became dictator.
44	Caesar assassinated; Antony sought revenge against conspirators.
43	Second Triumvirate (Antony, Octavian, Lepidus).
42	Battle of Philippi; Triumvirate defeated Brutus and Cassius.
41-40	Antony and Octavian divided territory.
33-32	Rupture between Antony and Octavian.
31	Battle of Actium; Octavian defeated Antony and Cleopatra at sea.
27	Octavian returned powers to Senate; received name Augustus.
18	Julian laws promoted morality, condemned adultery, regulated divorce.
12	Augustus became Pontifex Maximus, head of state religion.
2	Augustus became 'pater patriae', father of his country; apex of his power.

A.D.

4	Tiberius adopted as Augustus' heir.
6	Annexation of Judaea.
9	Varus' three legions destroyed in Germany.
14	Death of Augustus.
14-37	Tiberius emperor; efficient administrator but unpopular.
14-16	Germanicus' successful campaign in Germany.
19	Germanicus died mysteriously; funeral at Antioch.
21-22	Sefanus organized Praetorian Guard.
26-31	Sefanus powerful in Rome; executed in 31.
37-41	Caligula emperor; cruel and tyrannical, was murdered by a tribune.
41-54	Claudius emperor; conquered Britain; showed political judgement.
57-68	Nero emperor; great fire (64); Christians persecuted.
68-69	Year of four emperors - Galba, Otho, Vitellius, Vespasian.
69-79	Vespasian began Flavian dynasty. Colosseum built.
70	Titus, Vespasian's son, captured Jerusalem, destroyed the Temple.
79-81	Titus emperor. Vesuvius erupted (79), Pompeii destroyed.
81-96	Domitian emperor. Border built in Germany; period ended in terror.
96-98	Nerva emperor after Domitian's assassination.
98-117	Trajan emperor - conqueror of Dacia and Parthian empire.
117-138	Hadrian, cultured traveller, soldier and administrator of empire.
122	Hadrian's Wall built between Solway and Tyne.
138-161	Antoninus Pius emperor; orderly, peaceful rule.
141-143	Antonine's Wall built between Forth and Clyde.
161-180	Marcus Aurelius emperor; Commodus, his son, shared power (177-180).

162	War with Parthia.
175-180	War against Germans on the Danube.
180-192	Commodus emperor.
193-211	Septimius Severus became emperor after crisis; died in Britain. Authorized special benefits for army.
211-217	Deterioration under criminal rule of Caracalla.
212	All free men of the empire became citizens.
284-305	Diocletian and Maximian co-emperors, empire divided into 12 dioceses. Prices imposed throughout empire.
303	Christians persecuted by Diocletian.
312	Constantine's victory at Milvian Bridge gave him Rome.
313	Edict of Milan ended persecution of Christians.
324	Constantine became sole emperor.
325	Council of Nicaea made Christianity religion of the empire.
330	Constantine made Byzantium seat of government; renamed it Constantinople.
337	Constantine died a Christian, trying to reorganize the empire.
379-395	Emperor Theodosius kept empire formally intact.
410	Alaric and Goths captured and destroyed Rome.

GOVERNMENT AND ADMINISTRATION

Republic

There was no written constitution. The Republic evolved from the struggle between the Senate and the People - Senatus Populusque Romanus - SPQR.

The Senate (Senatus)
This was the governing body, largely in the hands of the nobles (nobiles) or patricians (patricii).

- it prepared proposals to bring before the people
- it passed decrees (senatus consulta)
- it dealt with emergencies
- it controlled finances and building contracts
- it appointed magistrates to provinces
- it directed foreign relations
- it supervised state religion

The People (Populus)
The resolutions of the people, plebiscita, could have the force of law, but the Senate was allowed greater control. There were four assemblies:

- comitia curiata   formal duties
- comitia centuriata   elected magistrates
- comitia tributa   elected lesser magistrates
- concilium plebis   passed plebiscita

The Knights (Equites)
A third element, or class, emerged (originally from Rome's cavalry) to engage in trade and finance. These businessmen acquired more political influence and became wealthy. By the time of Cicero, they could enter the Senate. Cicero tried to reconcile the three classes, **senatores**, **equites** and **plebs** by his **concordia ordinum** (harmony of the classes).

Magistrates (Magistratus)
A magistrate was an official elected annually by the people. Offices were held in a strict order - **cursus honorum**. After ten years' military service, a young man could begin on the lowest rung of the ladder as follows:

Age	Office	Number	Duties
28	**Quaestor**	(8)	• administered finance maintained public records
30	**Aedile**	(4)	• maintained roads, water supply organized games and festivals
33(39)	**Praetor**	(6)	• civil judge could introduce laws
39(43)	**Consul**	(2)	• commanded army conducted elections presided over Senate carried out its decrees

Other magistrates:

Tribune (10)		• defended plebs' rights
(tribunus plebis)		had right of veto
Censor (2)		• conducted census (every 5 years)
		conducted purification
		revised roll of senators
Dictator (1)		• ruled in crisis (maximum of 6 months)
		conducted military and domestic
		matters

Imperium (supreme power) was held by consuls and praetors and dictators.
Potestas (power to enforce laws) was held by all magistrates.
Lictores (lictors *or* officials) carried **fasces** (bundles of rods) in front of consuls, praetors and dictators as a sign of their authority.

ORGANIZATION OF THE ARMY

Empire

At the time of Augustus there were 28 **legions** (later 25), each legion consisting of approximately 5000 infantrymen, trained for close combat. It was organized as follows:

Legio	Legion	5000 men
10 Cohortes	Cohorts	500 men
6 Centuriae	Centuries	80/100 men

Officers	
Legatus	legionary commander
6 **Tribuni Militum**	tribunes
60 **Centuriones**	centurions (from ranks), in charge of centuries

Recruitment	Citizens
Length of service	20/25 years
Duties	Offensive in important battles, repelling invasion *etc*
Pay	250/300 denarii per day
On retirement	Land or cash bounty

Additional **auxiliary forces** were recruited to help the legions. Particularly necessary were cavalry, drawn from all parts of the Empire, slingers, bowmen, etc. Infantrymen were often recruited locally and formed cohorts of about 500 men.

Auxilia	Auxiliaries	
Ala	Cavalry unit	500 men approx.
16 Turmae	turmae	32 men
Cohors	Infantry unit	500 men

Officers	
Decurio	Decurion (cavalry officer)

Recruitment	Non-citizens
Length of service	25 years
Duties	Frontier skirmishes, occupation, assisting legions

| **Pay** | 100 denarii per day |
| **On retirement** | Citizenship for self/family |

The **Praetorian Guard** was the Emperor's special bodyguard. Three cohorts were based in Rome, six more in nearby towns.

| **Praetorium** | Praetorian Guard | 4500 men |
| **9 Cohortes** | cohorts | 500 men |

Officers	
2 Praefecti Praetorio	praetorian prefects
Recruitment	Citizens (Italy)
Length of service	16 years
Duties	Preserving emperor's power and safety
Pay	1000 denarii per day
On retirement	5000 denarii

FAMILY TREE

	tritavus m tritavia	
(great-great-great-great-grandfather)	(great-great-great-great-grandmother)	

tritavus m **tritavia**
(great-great-great-great-grandfather) | (great-great-great-great-grandmother)

patruus máximus (great-great-granduncle)	amita máxima (great-great-grandaunt)	atavus (great-great-great-grandfather)	m	atavia (great-great-great-grandmother)	avunculus máximus (great-great-granduncle)	mátertera máxima (great-great-grandaunt)
patruus máior (great-granduncle)	amita máior (great-grandaunt)	abavus (great-great-grandfather)	m	abavia (great-great-grandmother)	avunculus máior (great-granduncle)	mátertera máior (great-grandaunt)
patruus mágnus (granduncle)	amita mágna (grandaunt)	proavus (great-grandfather)	m	proavia (great-grandmother)	avunculus mágnus (granduncle)	mátertera mágna (grandaunt)
patruus (uncle)	amita (aunt)	avus (grandfather)	m	avia (grandmother)	avunculus mágnus (granduncle)	mátertera mágna (grandaunt)

noverca (step-mother)	m	pater (father)	m	máter (mother)	m	vítricus (step-father)	avunculus (uncle)	mátertera (aunt)	prósocer m prósocrus (grandfather-in-law) (grandmother-in-law)
									socer m socrus (father-in-law) (mother-in-law)

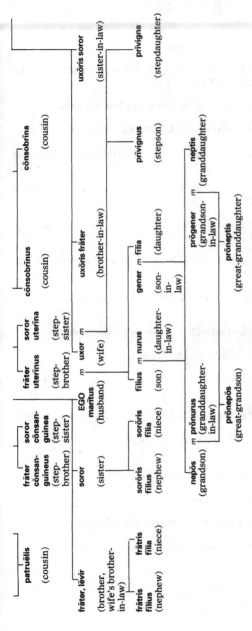

Note: *This is the Family Tree of the man designated* **EGO** *in the fourth generation from the end.*

MAJOR WRITERS

ENNIUS (Quintus Ennius: b 239 B.C.) **Annales**.

PLAUTUS (Titus Maccus *or* Maccius Plautus: b 254 B.C.) **Amphitruo**; the **Aulularia**; the **Menaechmi** and **Miles Gloriosus**.

TERENCE (Publius Terentius Afer) **Andria**; **Mother-in-law**; **Phormio**.

LUCRETIUS (Titus Lucretius Carus: 94 - 55 B.C.) **De Rerum Natura**.

CATULLUS (Gaius Valerius Catullus: c.84 - c.54 B.C.) Lyric poetry; **Ave atque vale**.

CICERO (Marcus Tullius Cicero: b 106 B.C.) **Pro Caelio**; **De Legibus**; the **Tusculan Disputations**; **De Officiis**; **Philippics**.

JULIUS CAESAR (Gaius Iulius Caesar: b c.102 B.C. and assassinated in 44 B.C.) **Bellum Gallicum**; **Bellum Civile**.

SALLUST (Gaius Sallustius Crispus: 86 - 35 B.C.) **Bellum Catilinae**; **Bellum Iugurthinum**.

VIRGIL (Publius Vergilius Maro: 70 - 19 B.C.) **Eclogues**; **Georgics**; the Aeneid.

HORACE (Quintus Horatius Flaccus: b 65 A.D.) **Satires**; **Odes**; **Epistles**.

LIVY (Titus Livius: 59 B.C. - 17 A.D.) **Ab Urbe Condita**.

OVID (Publius Ovidius Naso: 43 B.C. - 17 A.D.) the **Heroides, Ars Amatoria**; the **Metamorphoses**; **Tristia**.

SENECA (Lucius Annaeus Seneca: 4 B.C. - 65 A.D.) **Dialogi**; **Epistolae Morales**.

QUINTILIAN (Marcus Fabius Quintilianus: c.35 - c.95 A.D.) **Institutio Oratorio**.

MARTIAL (Marcus Valerius Martialis: 40 - 104 A.D.) the **Epigrams**.

JUVENAL (Decimus Iunius Iuvenalis) **Satires**.

TACITUS (Cornelius Tacitus) **Agricola**; **Germania**; **Histories**; the **Annals**.

PLINY (Gaius Plinius Secundus: b 61 *or* 62 A.D.) **Letters**.

GEOGRAPHICAL NAMES

The following list of geographical names and their adjectives includes both ancient and medieval Latin forms. The former are printed in Roman type, the latter in Italics. Medieval place names tend to have a variety of Latin forms, but only one has been selected in each case; occasionally both the ancient and the medieval forms have been given. Modern names which have a ready-made Latin form (*e.g.* America) have been omitted, and many names not included in this selection can be easily Latinized on the analogy of those which do appear.

Aachen	*Aquīsgrānum nt*	*adj Aquīsgrānēnsis*
Aberdeen	*Aberdōnia f*	*adj Aberdōnēnsis*
Abergavenny	Gobannium *nt*	
Aberystwith	*Aberistyvium nt*	
Adige, *River*	Athesis *m*	
Adriatic	Mare superum *nt*	*adj* Hadriāticus
Aegean	Mare Aegaeum *nt*	*adj* Aegaeus
Afghanistan	Ariāna *f*	*adj* Ariānus
Africa	Libya *f*,	*adj* Libycus,
	Africa *f*	Africānus
Agrigento	Agrigentum *nt*	*adj* Agrigentīnus
Aisne, *River*	Axona *m*	
Aix-en-Provence	Aquae Sextiae *fpl*	*adj Aquēnsis*
Aix-la-Chapelle	*Aquīsgrānum nt*	*adj Aquisgrānēnsis*
Aix-Les-Bains	Aquae Grātiānae *fpl*	
Ajaccio	*Adiacium nt*	*adj Adiacēnsis*
Aldborough	Isurium (*nt*)	
	Brigantum	
Alexandria	Alexandrēa,	
	Alexandrīa *f*	*adj* Alexandrīnus
Algiers	*Algerium nt*	*adj Algerīnus*
Alps	Alpēs *fpl*	*adj* Alpīnus
Alsace	*Alsatia f*	
Amalfi	Amalphis *f*	*adj Amalphītānus*
Ambleside	Galava *f*	
Amiens	*Ambiānum nt*	*adj Ambiānēnsis*
Amsterdam	*Amstelodamum nt*	*adj Amstelodamēnsis*
Ancaster	Causennae *fpl*	
Angers	*Andegāvum nt*	*adj* Andegāvēnsis
Anglesey	Mona *f*	
Aniene, *River*	Aniō *m*	*adj* Aniēnus
Anjou	Andegāvēnsis ager *m*	
Ankara	Ancyra *f*	*adj* Ancyrānus
Antibes	Antipolis *f*	*adj* Antipolītānus
Antioch	Antiochīa *f*	*adj* Antiochēnus
Antwerp	*Antwerpium nt*	*adj Antwerpiēnsis*
Anzio	Antium *nt*	*adj* Antiās, Antiānus
Aosta	Augusta Praetōria *f*	
Apennines	Mōns Apennīnus *m*	

Aragon	Aragōnia f	
Archangel	Archangelopolis f	
Ardennes	Arduenna f	
Arezzo	Ārētium nt	adj Ārētīnus
Argenteuil	Argentōlium nt	
Argyll	Argadia f	
Arles	Arelās f	adj Arelātēnsis
Armagh	Armācha f	adj Armāchānus
Arno, River	Arnus m	adj Arniēnsis
Arras	Atrebatēs mpl	adj Atrebatēnsis
Artois	Atrebatēs mpl	
Assisi	Assīsium nt	adj Assīsiēnsis
Athens	Athēnae fpl	adj Athēniēnsis
Atlantic	Mare Atlanticum nt	
Augsburg	Augusta (f) Vindelicōrum	adj Augustānus
Autun	Augustodūnum nt	adj Augustodūnēnsis
Auvergne	Arvernī mpl	adj Arvernus
Aventine	Aventīnus m	
Avignon	Aveniō f	adj Aveniōnēnsis
Avon, River	Auvona m	
Babylon	Babylōn f	adj Babylōnius
Baden-Baden	Aquae Aurēliae fpl	
Balearic Islands	Baliārēs Insulae fpl	adj Baliāricus
Balkh	Bactra ntpl	adj Bactriānus
Baltic	Balticum Mare nt	
Bangor	Bangertium nt	adj Bangertiēnsis
Barcelona	Barcinō f	adj Barcinōnēnsis
Bari	Bārium nt	adj Bārēnsis
Basle	Basilēa f	adj Basilēēnsis
Basques	Vascōnēs mpl	adj Vasconicus
Bath	Aquae (fpl) Sulis	
Bayeux	Augustodūrum nt	
Bayreuth	Barūthum nt	
Beauvais	Bellovacī mpl	adj Bellovacēnsis
Beirut	Bērȳtus f	adj Bērȳtius
Belgium	Belgae mpl	adj Belgicus
Bergen	Bergae fpl	
Berlin	Berolīnum nt	adj Berolīnēnsis
Berne	Vērona f	
Berwick	Barvīcum nt	
Besançon	Vesontiō m	adj Bisuntīnus
Black Sea	Pontus (Euxīnus) m	adj Ponticus
Bobbio	Bobbium nt	adj Bobbiēnsis
Bohemia	Boiohaemī mpl	
Bologna	Bonōnia f	adj Bonōniēnsis
Bonn	Bonna f	
Bordeaux	Burdigala f	adj Burdigalēnsis
Boulogne	Bonōnia f	adj Bononiēnsis
Bourges	Avāricum nt	adj Avāricēnsis
Brabant	Brabantia f	
Braganza	Brigantia f	adj Brigantiēnsis

Brancaster	Branodūnum *nt*	
Brandenburg	Brandenburgia *f*	*adj* Brandenburgēnsis
Bremen	Brēma *f*	*adj* Brēmēnsis
Breslau	Bratislavia *f*	*adj* Bratislaviēnsis
Brindisi	Brundisium *nt*	*adj* Brundisīnus
Bristol	Bristolium *nt*	*adj* Bristoliēnsis
Britain	Britannia *f*	*adj* Britannicus
Brittany	Armoricae *fpl*	
Bruges	Brugae *fpl*	*adj* Brugēnsis
Brunswick	Brunsvīcum *nt*	*adj* Brunsvīcēnsis
Brussels	Bruxellae *fpl*	*adj* Bruxellēnsis
Bucharest	Bucarestum *nt*	*adj* Bucarestiēnsis
Burgos	Burgī *mpl*	*adj* Burgitānus
Burgundy	Burgundiōnēs *mpl*	
Cadiz	Gādēs *fpl*	*adj* Gāditānus
Caen	Cadomum *nt*	*adj* Cadomēnsis
Caerleon	Isca *f*	
Caermarthen	Maridūnum *nt*	
Caernarvon	Segontium *nt*	
Caerwent	Venta (*f*) Silurum	
Cagliari	Caralis *f*	*adj* Caralītānus
Cairo	Cairus *f*	
Calais	Calētum *nt*	*adj* Calētanus
Cambrai	Camerācum *nt*	*adj* Camerācēnsis
Cambridge	Cantabrigia *f*	*adj* Cantabrigiēnsis
Campagna	Campānia *f*	*adj* Campānus
Cannes	Canoē *f*	
Canterbury	Durovernum *nt*,	*adj* Cantuāriēnsis
	Cantuāria *f*	
Capri	Capreae *fpl*	*adj* Capreēnsis
Cardigan	Ceretica *f*	
Carlisle	Luguvallium *nt*	
Cartagena	Carthāgō Nova *f*	
Carthage	Carthāgō *f*	*adj* Carthāginiēnsis
Caspian Sea	Mare Caspium *nt*	
Cevennes	Gebenna *f*	*adj* Gebennicus
Ceylon	Tāprobanē *f*	
Champagne	Campānia *f*	*adj* Campānicus
Chartres	Carnūtēs *mpl*	*adj* Carnōtēnus
Chelmsford	Caesaromagus *m*	
Cherbourg	Caesaris burgus *m*	
Chester	Deva *f*	
Chichester	Rēgnum *nt*	
China	Sēres *mpl*	*adj* Sēricus
Cirencester	Corinium (*nt*)	
	Dobunōrum	
Clairvaux	Clāra Vallis *f*	*adj* Clāravallēnsis
Clermont	Nemossus *f*	
Cluny	Clīniacum *nt*	*adj* Clīniacēnsis
Clyde, River	Clōta *f*	
Colchester	Camulodūnum *nt*	
Cologne	Colōnia Agrippīna *f*	*adj* Colōniēnsis

Como, _Lake_	Lārius _m_	_adj_ Lārius
Constance, _Lake_	Lacus Brigantīnus _m_	
Copenhagen	_Hafnia f_	
Corbridge	Corstopitum _nt_	
Cordoba	Corduba _f_	_adj_ Cordubēnsis
Corfu	Corcȳra _f_	_adj_ Corcȳraeus
Corinth	Corinthus _f_	_adj_ Corinthius
Cork	Corcagia _f_	_adj_ Corcagiēnsis
Cornwall	Cornubia _f_	
Cracow	_Cracovia f_	_adj_ Cracoviēnsis
Crete	Crēta _f_	_adj_ Crētēnsis, Crēticus
Cumberland	_Cumbria f_	
Cyprus	Cyprus _f_	_adj_ Cyprius
Cyrene	Cȳrēnae _fpl_	_adj_ Cȳrēnaicus
Damascus	Damascus _f_	_adj_ Damascēnus
Danube, _River_	_(lower)_ Ister _m_,	
	(upper) Dānuvius _m_	
Dardanelles	Hellēspontus _m_	_adj_ Hellēspontius
Dee, _River_	Deva _f_	
Denmark	Dānia _f_	_adj_ Dānicus
Derby	_Derventiō m_	
Devon	_Devōnia f_	
Dijon	Diviō _f_	_adj Diviōnēnsis_
Dneiper, _River_	Borysthenēs _m_	
Dneister, _River_	Danaster _m_	
Don, _River_ (Russian)	Tanais _m_	
Doncaster	Dānum _nt_	
Dorchester	Durnovāria _f_	
Douro, _River_	Durius _m_	
Dover	Dubrī _mpl_	
Dover, _Straits of_	Fretum Gallicum _nt_	
Dresden	_Dresda f_	_adj Dresdēnsis_
Dublin	_Dublīnum nt_	_adj Dublīnēnsis_
Dumbarton	_Britannodūnum nt_	
Dundee	_Taodūnum nt_	
Dunstable	Durocobrīvae _fpl_	
Durham	_Dunelmum nt_	_adj Dunelmēnsis_
Ebro, _River_	Hibērus _m_	
Eden, _River_	Itūna _f_	
Edinburgh	_Edinburgum nt_	_adj Edinburgēnsis_
Egypt	Aegyptus _f_	_adj_ Aegyptius
Elba	Ilva _f_	
Elbe, _River_	Albis _m_	
England	Anglia _f_	_adj_ Anglicus
Etna	Aetna _f_	_adj_ Aetnaeus
Europe	Eurōpa	_adj_ Eurōpaeus
Exeter	Isca (f) Dumnoniōrum	
Fiesole	Faesulae _fpl_	_adj_ Faesulānus
Flanders	Menapiī _mpl_	
Florence	Flōrentia _f_	_adj_ Flōrentīnus
Fontainebleau	_Bellofontānum nt_	
Forth, _River_	Bodotria _f_	

France	Gallia *f*	*adj* Gallicus
Frankfurt	*Francofurtum nt*	
Frejus	Forum (*nt*) Iūliī	*adj* Foroiūliēnsis
Friesland	Frīsiī *mpl*	*adj* Frīsius
Gallipoli	*Callipolis f*	*adj* Callipolitānus
Galloway	*Gallovidia f*	
Ganges	Gangēs *m*	*adj* Gangēticus
Garda, *Lake*	Bēnācus *m*	
Garonne, *River*	Garumna *f*	
Gaul	Gallia *f*	*adj* Gallicus
Gdansk	*Gedānum m*	
Geneva	Genāva *f*	*adj* Genāvēnsis
Geneva, *Lake*	Lemannus lacus *m*	
Genoa	Genua *f*	*adj* Genuēnsis
Germany	Germānia *f*	*adj* Germānicus
Ghent	*Gandavum nt*	*adj* Gandavēnsis
Gibraltar	Calpē *f*	*adj* Calpētānus
Gibraltar, *Straits of*	Fretum Gāditānum *nt*	
Glasgow	*Glasgua f*	*adj* Glasguēnsis
Gloucester	Glēvum *nt*	
Gothenburg	*Gothoburgum nt*	
Graz	*Graecium nt*	
Greece	Graecia *f*	*adj* Graecus
Greenwich	*Grenovicum nt*	
Grenoble	Grātiānopolis *f*	
Groningen	*Groninga f*	
Guadalquivir, *River*	Baetis *m*	
Guadiana, *River*	Anas *m*	
Guernsey	*Sarnia f*	
Hague, *The*	Haga (*f*) Comitis	
Halle	*Halla f*	*adj* Hallēnsis
Hamadān	Ecbatana *ntpl*	
Hamburg	*Hamburgum nt*	*adj* Hamburgēnsis
Hanover	*Hannovera f*	
Harwich	*Harvīcum nt*	
Havre	Grātiae Portus *m*	
Hebrides	Ebūdae Insulae *fpl*	
Hexham	Axelodūnum *nt*	
Holland	Batāvī *mpl*	*adj* Batāvus
Ibiza	Ebusus *f*	*adj* Ebusitānus
Ilkley	*Olicāna f*	
Inn, *River*	Aenus *m*	
Ipswich	*Gippevicum nt*	
Ireland	Hibernia *f*	*adj* Hibernicus
Isar, *River*	Isara *f*	
Istanbul	Bȳzantium *nt*	*adj* Bȳzantīnus
Italy	Italia *f*	*adj* Italicus
Jersey	Caesarea *f*	
Jerusalem	Hierosolyma *ntpl*	*adj* Hierosolymītānus
Jutland	Chersonnēsus Cimbrica *f*	
Karlsbad	*Aquae Carolīnae fpl*	

Kent	Cantium *nt*	
Kiel	*Chilonium nt*	
Koblenz	Cōnfluentēs *mpl*	
Lancaster	*Lancastria f*	
Lanchester	Longovicium *nt*	
Land's End	Bolerium Prōmunturium *nt*	
Lausanne	Lausōnium *nt*	*adj* Lausōniēnsis
Lebanon	Libanus *m*	
Leeds	*Ledesia f*	
Leicester	Ratae (*fpl*) Coritānōrum	
Leiden	Lugdūnum (*nt*) Batāvōrum	
Leipsig	*Lipsia f*	*adj* Lipsiēnsis
Lērida	Ilerda *f*	*adj* Ilerdēnsis
Lichfield	*Etocētum nt*	
Limoges	Augustorītum *nt*	
Lincoln	Lindum *nt*	
Lisbon	Olisīpō *m*	*adj* Olisīpōnēnsis
Lizard Point	Damnonium Prōmunturium *nt*	
Loire, *River*	Liger *m*	*adj* Ligericus
Lombardy	*Langobardia f*	
London	Londinium *nt*	*adj* Londiniēnsis
Lorraine	*Lōthāringia f*	
Lucerne	*Lūceria f*	*adj* Lūcernēnsis
Lund	Londinium (*nt*) Gothōrum	
Lyons	Lugdūnum *nt*	*adj* Lugdūnēnsis
Madrid	*Matrītum nt*	*adj Matrītēnsis*
Maggiore, *Lake*	Verbannus *m*	
Main, *River*	Moenus *m*	
Mainz	Mogontiacum *nt*	
Majorca	Baliāris Māior *f*	
Malta	Melita *f*	
Man, *Isle of*	Monapia *f*	
Manchester	*Mancunium nt*	
Marmara, *Sea of*	Propontis *f*	
Marne, *River*	*Māterna f*	
Marseilles	Massilia *f*	*adj* Massiliēnsis
Matapan	Taenarum *nt*	*adj* Taenarius
Mediterranean	Mare internum *nt*	
Melun	Melodūnum *nt*	
Mērida	Ēmerita *f*	*adj* Ēmeritēnsis
Messina	Messāna *f*	*adj* Messānius
Metz	Dīvodūrum *nt*	
Meuse, *River*	Mosa *f*	
Milan	Mediōlānum *nt*	*adj* Mediōlānēnsis
Minorca	Baliāris Minor *f*	
Modena	Mutina *f*	*adj* Mutinēnsis
Mons	Montēs *mpl*	
Monte Cassino	Casīnum *nt*	*adj* Casīnās
Moray	*Moravia f*	

Morocco	Maurētānia *f*	*adj* Maurus
Moscow	*Moscovia f*	
Moselle, *River*	Mosella *f*	
Munich	*Monacum nt*	*adj Monacēnsis*
Nantes	Namnētēs *mpl*	
Naples	Neāpolis *f*	*adj* Neāpolītānus
Neckar, *River*	Nīcer *m*	
Newcastle	Pōns (*m*) Aeliī,	*adj Novocastrēnsis*
	Novum Castrum *nt*	
Nice	Nīcaea *f*	*adj* Nicaeēnsis
Nile, *River*	Nīlus *m*	*adj* Nīlōticus
Nîmes	Nemausus *f*	*adj* Nemausēnsis
Norway	*Norvēgia f*	*adj Norvēgiānus*
Norwich	*Nordovīcum nt*	
Oder, *River*	Viadrus *m*	
Oporto	Portus Calēnsis *m*	
Orange	Arausiō *f*	
Orkneys	Orcades *fpl*	
Orléans	*Aurēliānum nt*	*adj Aurēliānēnsis*
Oudenarde	*Aldenarda f*	
Oxford	*Oxonia f*	*adj Oxoniēnsis*
Padua	Patavium *nt*	*adj* Patavīnus
Palermo	Panormus *m*	*adj* Panormitānus
Paris	Lutetia *f*, Parīsiī *mpl*	*adj* Parīsiēnsis
Patras	Patrae *fpl*	*adj* Patrēnsis
Persian Gulf	Mare Rubrum *nt*	
Piacenza	Placentia *f*	*adj* Placentīnus
Po, *River*	Padus	*adj* Padānus
Poitiers	Limōnum *nt*	
Poland	*Polōnia f*	
Portsmouth	Māgnus Portus *m*	
Portugal	Lūsitānia *f*	
Pozzuoli	Puteolī *mpl*	*adj* Puteolānus
Prague	*Prāga f*	*adj Prāgēnsis*
Provence	Prōvincia *f*	
Pyrenees	Pȳrēnaeī montēs *mpl*	
Red Sea	Sinus Arābicus *m*	
Rheims	Dūrocortorum *nt*	
Rhine, *River*	Rhēnus *m*	*adj* Rhēnānus
Rhodes	Rhodos *f*	*adj* Rhodius
Rhône, *River*	Rhodanus *m*	
Richborough	Rutupiae *fpl*	*adj* Rutupīnus
Rimini	Arīminum	*adj* Arīminēnsis
Rochester	Dūrobrīvae *fpl*	
Rome	Rōma *f*	*adj* Rōmānus
Rotterdam	*Roterodamum nt*	*adj Roterodamēnsis*
Rouen	*Rothomagus f*	*adj Rothomagēnsis*
Saar, *River*	*Sangona f*	
Salisbury	Sarisberia *f*	
Salzburg	*Iuvāvum nt*	*adj Salisburgēnsis*
Saône, *River*	Arar *m*	

Savoy	Sabaudia f	
Scheldt, River	Scaldis m	
Schleswig	Slesvīcum nt	
Scilly Isles	Cassiterides fpl	
Scotland	Calēdonia f	adj Calēdonius
Seine, River	Sēquana f	
Severn, River	Sabrīna f	
Seville	Hīspalis f	adj Hispalēnsis
Shrewsbury	Salōpia f	
Sicily	Sicilia f	adj Siculus
Sidra, Gulf of	Syrtis (māior) f	
Silchester	Callēva (f) Atrebatum	
Soissons	Augusta (f) Suessiōnum	
Solway Firth	Itūna (f) aestuārium	
Somme, River	Samara f	
Spain	Hispānia f	adj Hispānus
St. Albans	Verulamium nt	
St. Andrews	Andreopolis f	
St. Bernard	(Great) Mōns Pennīnus m, (Little) Alpis Grāia f	
St. Gallen	Sangallēnse coenobium nt	adj Sangallēnsis
St. Gotthard	Alpēs summae fpl	
St. Moritz	Agaunum nt	adj Agaunēnsis
Strasbourg	Argentorātus f	adj Argentorātēnsis
Swabia	Suēvia f	adj Suēvicus
Sweden	Suēcia f	adj Suēcicus
Switzerland	Helvētia f	adj Helvēticus
Syracuse	Syrācūsae fpl	adj Syrācūsānus
Tangier	Tingī f	adj Tingitānus
Taranto	Tarentum nt	adj Tarentīnus
Tarragona	Tarracō f	adj Tarracōnēnsis
Tay, River	Taus m	
Thames, River	Tamesis m	
Thebes	Thēbae fpl	adj Thēbānus
Tiber, River	Tiberis m	adj Tiberīnus
Tivoli	Tībur nt	adj Tīburtīnus
Toledo	Tolētum nt	adj Tolētānus
Toulon	Tolōna f	adj Tolōnēnsis
Toulouse	Tolōsa f	adj Tolōsānus
Tours	Caesarodūnum nt	
Trèves, Trier	Augusta (f) Treverōrum	
Trieste	Tergeste nt	adj Tergestīnus
Tripoli	Tripolis f	adj Tripolitānus
Tunis	Tūnēs f	adj Tūnētānus
Turin	Augusta (f) Taurīnōrum	adj Taurīnus
Tuscany	Etrūria f	adj Etrūscus
Tyrrhenian Sea	Mare īnferum nt	
Utrecht	Ultrāiectum nt	adj Ultrāiectēnsis
Vardar, River	Axius m	
Venice	Venetī mpl, Venetiae fpl	adj Venetus
Verdun	Virodūnum nt	adj Virodūnēnsis

Versailles	*Versāliae fpl*	*adj* *Versāliēnsis*
Vichy	Aquae (*fpl*) Sōlis	
Vienna	*Vindobona f*	*adj* *Vindobenēnsis*
Vosges	Vosegus *m*	
Wales	*Cambria f*	
Wallsend	Segedūnum *nt*	
Warsaw	*Varsavia f*	*adj* *Varsaviēnsis*
Wash, *The*	Metaris (*m*) aestuārium	
Wear, *River*	Vedra *f*	
Weser, *River*	Visurgis *m*	
Westminster	*Westmonastērium nt*	*adj* *Westmonastēriēnsis*
Wiesbaden	Mattiacum *nt*	*adj* Mattiacus
Wight, *Isle of*	Vectis *f*	
Winchester	Venta (*f*) Belgārum	
Worcester	Vigornia *f*	
Worms	*Vormatia f*	
Wroxeter	Viroconium *nt*	
York	Eburācum *nt*	*adj* Eburācēnsis
Zuider Zee	Flēvō *m*	
Zurich	*Turicum nt*	*adj* Tigurīnus

NUMERALS

	Cardinal		Ordinal	
1	ūnus	I	prīmus	1st
2	duo	II	secundus, alter	2nd
3	trēs	III	tertius	3rd
4	quattuor	IV	quārtus	4th
5	quīnque	V	quīntus	5th
6	sex	VI	sextus	6th
7	septem	VII	septimus	7th
8	octō	VIII	octāvus	8th
9	novem	IX	nōnus	9th
10	decem	X	decimus	10th
11	undecim	XI	undecimus	11th
12	duodecim	XII	duodecimus	12th
13	tredecim	XIII	tertius decimus	13th
14	quattuordecim	XIV	quārtus decimus	14th
15	quīndecim	XV	quīntus decimus	15th
16	sēdecim	XVI	sextus decimus	16th
17	septendecim	XVII	septimus decimus	17th
18	duodēvīgintī	XVIII	duodēvīcēsimus	18th
19	ūndēvīgintī	XIX	ūndēvīcēsimus	19th
20	vīgintī	XX	vīcēsimus	20th
21	vīgintī ūnus	XXI	vīcēsimus prīmus	21st
28	duodētrīgintā	XXVIII	duodētrīcēsimus	28th
29	ūndētrīgintā	XXIX	ūndētrīcēsimus	29th
30	trīgintā	XXX	trīcēsimus	30th
40	quadrāgintā	XL	quadrāgēsimus	40th
50	quīnquāgintā	L	quīnquāgēsimus	50th
60	sexāgintā	LX	sexāgēsimus	60th
70	septuāgintā	LXX	septuāgēsimus	70th
80	octōgintā	LXXX	octōgēsimus	80th
90	nōnāgintā	XC	nōnāgēsimus	90th
100	centum	C	centēsimus	100th
101	centum et ūnus	CI	centēsimus prīmus	101st
122	centum vīgintī duo	CXXII	centēsimus vīcēsimus alter	122nd
200	ducentī	CC	ducentēsimus	200th
300	trecentī	CCC	trecentēsimus	300th
400	quadringentī	CCCC	quadringentēsimus	400th
500	quīngentī	D	quīngentēsimus	500th
600	sēscentī	DC	sēscentēsimus	600th
700	septingentī	DCC	septingentēsimus	700th
800	octingentī	DCCC	octingentēsimus	800th
900	nōngentī	DCCCC	nōngentēsimus	900th
1000	mīlle	M	mīllēsimus	1000th
1001	mīlle et ūnus	MI	mīllēsimus prīmus	1001st
1102	mīlle centum duo	MCII	mīllēsimus centēsimus alter	1102nd
3000	tria mīlia	MMM	ter mīllēsimus	3000th
5000	quīnque mīlia	IƆCC	quīnquiēs mīllēsimus	5000th
10,000	decem mīlia	CCIƆƆ	deciēs mīllēsimus	10,000th
100,000	centum mīlia	CCCIƆƆƆ	centiēs mīllēsimus	100,000th
1,000,000	deciēs centēna mīlia	CCCCIƆƆƆƆ	deciēs centiēs mīllēsimus	1,000,000th

NUMERALS

	Distributive		Adverb	
1	singulī	I	semel	1st
2	bīnī	II	bis	2nd
3	ternī (trīnī)	III	ter	3rd
4	quaternī	IV	quater	4th
5	quīnī	V	quīnquiēs	5th
6	sēnī	VI	sexiēs	6th
7	septēnī	VII	septiēs	7th
8	octōnī	VIII	octiēs	8th
9	novēnī	IX	noviēs	9th
10	dēnī	X	deciēs	10th
11	undēnī	XI	undeciēs	11th
12	duodēnī	XII	duodeciēs	12th
13	ternī dēnī	XIII	ter deciēs	13th
14	quaternī dēnī	XIV	quattuordeciēs	14th
15	quīnī dēnī	XV	quīndeciēs	15th
16	sēnī dēnī	XVI	sēdeciēs	16th
17	septēnī dēnī	XVII	septiēs deciēs	17th
18	duodēvīcēnī	XVIII	duodēvīciēs	18th
19	ūndēvīcēnī	XIX	ūndēvīciēs	19th
20	vīcēnī	XX	vīciēs	20th
21	vīcēnī singulī	XXI	semel et vīciēs	21st
28	duodētrīcēnī	XXVIII	duodētrīciēs	28th
29	ūndētrīcēnī	XXIX	ūndētrīciēs	29th
30	trīcēnī	XXX	trīciēs	30th
40	quadrāgēnī	XL	quadrāgiēs	40th
50	quīnquāgēnī	L	quīnquāgiēs	50th
60	sexāgēnī	LX	sexāgiēs	60th
70	septuāgēnī	LXX	septuāgiēs	70th
80	octōgēnī	LXXX	octōgiēs	80th
90	nōnagēnī	XC	nōnāgiēs	90th
100	centēnī	C	centiēs	100th
101	centēnī singulī	CI	semel et centiēs	101st
122	centēnī vīcēnī bīnī	CXXII	centiēs vīciēs bis	122nd
200	ducēnī	CC	ducentiēs	200th
300	trecēnī	CCC	trecentiēs	300th
400	quadringēnī	CCCC	quadringentiēs	400th
500	quīngēnī	D	quīngentiēs	500th
600	sexcēnī	DC	sexcentiēs	600th
700	septingēnī	DCC	septingentiēs	700th
800	octingēnī	DCCC	octingentiēs	800th
900	nōngēnī	DCCCC	nōngentiēs	900th
1000	singula mīlia	M	mīlliēs	1000th
1001	singula mīlia singulī	MI	semel et mīlliēs	1001st
1102	singula mīlia centēnī bīnī	MCII	mīlliēs centiēs bis	1102nd
3000	trīna mīlia	MMM	ter mīlliēs	3000th
5000	quīna mīlia	IƆƆ	quīnquiēs mīlliēs	5000th
10,000	dēna mīlia	CCIƆƆ	deciēs mīlliēs	10,000th
100,000	centēna mīlia	CCCIƆƆƆ	centiēs mīlliēs	100,000th
1,000,000	deciēs centēna mīlia	CCCCIƆƆƆƆ	mīlliēs mīlliēs	1,000,000th

DATES

MONTHS

Three days of the month have special names:

Kalendae the 1st.

Nōnae the 5th of most months, but the 7th of March, May, July and October.

> "In March, July, October, May,
> The Nones are on the 7th day."

Idūs the 13th of most months, but the 15th of March, May, July and October.

If the date is one of these three days, it is expressed in the ablative, with the adjective of the month in agreement, *e.g.*

1st January, **Kalendīs Iānuāriīs**, usually abbreviated **Kal. Ian.**

The day immediately before any of these three is expressed by **prīdiē** with the accusative, *e.g.*

4th February, **prīdiē Nōnās Februāriās**, usually abbreviated **prid. Non. Feb.**

All other dates are expressed as so many days before the next named day, and in reckoning the interval both the date and the named day are counted, *e.g.* the 11th is the 5th day before the 15th.

The formula is all in the accusative, begining with the words **ante diem**, *e.g.* 11th March, **ante diem quīntum Idūs Martiās**, usually abbreviated **a.d. V Id. Mar.**

The following selection of dates for April and May should be a sufficient guide to the dates of any month in the year:—

APRIL		MAY
Kal. Apr.	1	Kal. Mai.
a.d IV Non. Apr.	2	a.d. VI Non. Mai.
a.d. III Non. Apr.	3	a.d. V Non. Mai.
prid. Non. Apr.	4	a.d. IV Non. Mai.
Non. Apr.	5	a.d. III Non. Mai.
a.d. VIII Id. Apr.	6	prid. Non. Mai.
a.d. VII Id. Apr.	7	Non. Mai.
a.d. VI Id. Apr.	8	a.d. VIII Id. Mai.
a.d. V Id. Apr.	9	a.d. VII Id. Mai.
a.d. IV Id. Apr.	10	a.d. VI Id. Mai.
a.d. III Id. Apr.	11	a.d. V Id. Mai.
prid. Id. Apr.	12	a.d. IV Id. Mai.
Id. Apr.	13	a.d. III Id. Mai.
a.d. XVIII Kal. Mai.	14	prid. Id. Mai.
a.d. XVII Kal. Mai.	15	Id. Mai.
a.d. XVI Kal. Mai.	16	a.d. XVII Kal. Iun.

a.d. XV Kal. Mai.	**17**	a.d. XVI Kal. Iun.
a.d. XII Kal. Mai.	**20**	a.d. XIII Kal. Iun.
a.d. VII Kal. Mai.	**25**	a.d. VIII Kal. Iun.
prid. Kal. Mai.	**30**	a.d. III Kal. Iun.
—	**31**	prid. Kal. Iun.

YEARS

A year is denoted either by giving the names of the consuls or by reckoning the number of years from the traditional date of the foundation of Rome, 753 B.C. (A date B.C. should be subtracted from 754, a date A.D. should be added to 753.)

E.g. "In the year 218 B.C.," *either* P. Cornelio Scipione Ti. Sempronio Longo coss. *or* a. u. c. DXXXVI.

MEASURES

Length

12 ūnciae = 1 pēs
5 pedēs = 1 passus
125 passūs = 1 stadium
8 stadia = mīlle passūs

The Roman mile was about 1.48 km.

Area

100 pedēs quadrātī = 1 scrīpulum
144 scrīpula = 1 āctus quadrātus
2 āctūs quadrātī = 1 iugerum
2 iugera = 1 hērēdium
100 hērēdia = 1 centuria

The **iugerum** was about 2529.28 square metres.

Capacity

	4 cochleāria =	1 cyathus
	12 cyathī =	1 sextārius
(*liquid*)	6 sextāriī =	1 congius
	8 congiī =	1 amphora
	20 amphorae =	1 culleus
(*dry*)	8 sextāriī =	1 sēmodius
	2 sēmodiī =	1 modius

The **sextārius** was about half a litre, the **modius** about 9 litres.

Weight

4 scrīpula = 1 sextula
6 sextulae = 1 ūncia
12 ūnciae = 1 lībra

The Roman lb. was about 326 gr, and the **ūncia** was therefore about 27 gr. The twelfths of the **lībra** have the following names, which are also used to denote fractions generally, *e.g.* **hērēs ex triente**, heir to a third of an estate.

¹⁄₁₂ ūncia	⁵⁄₁₂ quīncūnx	¾ dōdrāns
⅙ sextāns	½ sēmis	⅚ dextāns
¼ quadrāns	⁷⁄₁₂ septūnx	¹¹⁄₁₂ deūnx
⅓ triēns	⅔ bēs	

MONEY

Roman

2½ assēs	= 1 sēstertius (*or* nummus)
4 sēstertii	= 1 dēnārius
25 dēnārii	= 1 aureus

The sesterce is represented by a symbol for 2½, properly **II S(ēmis)**, usually standardized in the form HS. The *ntpl* **sēstertia** with the distributive numeral denotes thousands of sesterces, and the numeral adverb with the *gen pl* **sēstertium** (understanding **centēna milia**) means hundred thousands, *e.g.*

10,000 sesterces	= dēna sēstertia	= HS X̄
1,000,000 "	= deciēs sēstertium	= HS IX̄I

Greek

100 drachumae	= 1 mina
60 minae	= 1 talentum

LATIN VERSE

QUANTITY

Both vowels and syllables in Latin may be described as long or short. A long vowel or syllable is one on which the voice dwells for a longer time than on a short one, in much the same way as a minim is long compared with a crotchet in musical notation.

A syllable is long if the vowel in it is either long in itself or followed by two or more consonants. The letter x counts as a double consonant, the letter h not at all, and the following pairs of consonants occurring in the same word after a short vowel do not necessarily make the syllable long:

br, cr, dr, fr, gr, pr, tr; fl, gl, pl.

A syllable is short if its vowel is a short one and not followed by two or more consonants (except for the groups noted in the preceding paragraph).

Examples: In **dūcō** both the vowels are long ("by nature") and therefore the two syllables are long.

In **deus** both the vowels are short, neither is followed by more than one consonant, and therefore the two syllables are short; but if a word beginning with a consonant follows, then the syllable **-us** will become long.

In **adsunt** both the vowels are short, but they are both followed by two consonants, and the two syllables are therefore "long by position".

This long or short characteristic of Latin vowels and syllables is called "quantity." To determine the quantities of vowels no general rules can be given, and some of them are now not known for certain. The vowel quantities of words will have to be learned when the words are learned, or else looked up when the need arises. In final syllables, however, there is a certain regularity to be found, and the following table shows the commonest of these:

ENDING

	Long	Short
-a	1st decl abl sing 1st conj impv sing numerals and most adverbs	1st decl nom and voc sing all nom and acc ntpl **ita, quia**
-e	5th decl abl sing 2nd conj impv sing most adverbs Greek nouns	all other noun and verb endings **bene, male** enclitics

-i	*all endings, except*		**quasi, nisi:** *and sometimes* **mihi, tibi, sibi, ibi, ubi**
-o	*all endings, except*		*sometimes iambic words, esp* **cito, duo, ego, homo, modo, puto, rogo, scio**
-u	*all endings*		
-as	*all endings, except*		*Greek nouns*
-es	*all endings, except*		*3rd decl nom sing with short* **-e-** *in stem* **es** (be) *and compounds* **penes**
-is	*1st and 2nd decl dat and abl pl 3rd decl acc pl 4th conj 2nd pers sing* **vis, sis, velis**		*all others*
-os	*all endings, except*		*2nd decl nom sing* **os** (bone) **compos, impos**
-us	*3rd decl nom sing with long* **-u-** *in stem 4th decl gen sing and nom and acc pl*		*all others*

METRES

Latin Verse is a pattern of long and short syllables, grouped together in "feet" or in lyric lines.

FEET

The commonest Feet employed in Latin metres are:

Anapaest	(short—short—long)	˘ ˘ —
Dactyl	(long—short—short)	— ˘ ˘
Iambus	(short—long)	˘ —
Proceleusmatic	(short—short—short—short)	˘ ˘ ˘ ˘
Spondee	(long—long)	— —
Tribrach	(short—short—short)	˘ ˘ ˘
Trochee	(long—short)	— ˘

CAESURA AND DIAERESIS

The longer lines usually have a regular break near the middle, occurring either in the middle of a foot (**Caesura**) or at the end of a foot (**Diaeresis**). This break need not imply a pause in the sense of the words, but merely the end of a word, provided that it does not go too closely with the word following, as in the case of a preposition before a noun. See examples on pages 4–9 where the caesura is marked †, and the diaeresis //.

ELISION

A vowel or a vowel followed by **m** at the end of a word ("open vowel") is regularly elided before a vowel at the beginning of the next word in the same line. In reciting, the elided syllable should not be dropped entirely, but slurred into the following vowel. An open vowel at the end of a line does not elide before a vowel at the beginning of the next line.

FINAL SYLLABLES

Where the metre requires the final syllable in a line to be long, this syllable may in fact be a short one. This position in the line is commonly called a **syllaba anceps**, and marked down as being either long or short. It is perhaps better to regard this syllable, when the vowel is short, as long by position, since metrical length is a matter of duration, and the end of a line calls naturally for a slight pause in reading, even if the sense runs on to the next line. In the metrical schemes which follow, a long final syllable should be understood in this sense: it may in itself be a short one.

Latin metres fall into three fairly distinct categories, associated with three different genres of verse: 1. *Dactylic*
2. *Iambic and Trochaic*
3. *Lyric*

DACTYLIC VERSE

The Dactylic metres are the **Hexameter** and the **Pentameter**. The Hexameter is the medium of epic, didactic and pastoral poetry, of satires and epistles, and other examples of occasional verse. In conjunction with the Pentameter it forms the **Elegiac Couplet**, the metre most commonly used for love poetry, occasional pieces, and the epigram.

Dactylic Hexameter

The first four feet may be either **dactyls** or **spondees**, the 5th is regularly a dactyl, the 6th always a spondee. In Virgil and later poets the last word is either disyllabic or trisyllabic. A **Caesura** normally occurs in either the 3rd or the 4th foot, and pastoral poetry often has the **"Bucolic Diaeresis"** at the end of the 4th foot. In Virgilian and later usage there is a tendency for words and feet to overlap in the first four feet and to coincide in the last two. Similarly in the first part of the line the metrical ictus and the normal accent of the spoken word tend to fall on different syllables, whereas they regularly coincide in the last two feet.

Example:

Clāss(em) āp|teñt tăcĭ|tī⁺ sŏcĭ|ōsqu(e) ād | lītŏră| tōrquēnt

(*Virgil, Aen.* 4, 289)

Occasional lines will be found in the poets, which deliberately violate the above rules for the sake of obtaining some special effect,

pēr cō|nūbĭă| nōstrā,⁺ pĕr|⌐īncēp|tōs hў̆mĕ|nāeōs

(*Aen.* 4, 316)

The above echoes Greek hexameter, where the final word is Greek and has four syllables, and the caesura comes between the two short syllables of the dactyl in the 3rd foot:

cūm sŏcĭ|⌐īs nā|tōquĕ⁺ pĕ|nātĭbŭs| ēt māg|nīs dīs

(*Aen.* 3, 12)

Note the solemn, archaic touch, suggesting a line of Ennius, where the 5th foot is a spondee, and the last word is monosyllabic.

pārtŭrĭ|ent mōn|tēs,† nā|scētūr| rĭdĭcŭ|lŭs mūs

(Hor, A. P. 139)

The monosyllabic ending, above, creates a comic effect.

Dactylic Pentameter

This line has two equal parts of 2½ feet each. The two feet in the first part may be either **dactyls** or **spondees**, those in the second part are always dactylic. The two half-feet are long (though the final syllable may be a short one), and there is always a diaeresis between the two parts of the line. In Ovid and later poets the last word in the line is regularly disyllabic.

Example:

Aēnē|ān ănĭ|mō // nōxquĕ dĭ|ēsquĕ rĕ|fērt

(Ovid, Her. 7, 26)

SCANSION

The following procedure may assist beginners to scan a normal hexameter or pentameter correctly:—

1. Mark off elisions.
2. Mark the first syllable long, and (Hexameter) the last five dactyl and spondee, or (Pentameter) the last seven syllables, two dactyls and a long syllable.
3. Mark all diphthongs long.
4. Mark all syllables that are long by position, omitting any doubtful cases.
5. Mark any other syllables known to be long.
6. Mark any syllables known to be short.
7. Fill in the few (if any) remaining syllables, and identify the principal caesura.
8. Read the line aloud.

IAMBIC AND TROCHAIC VERSE

The Iambic and Trochaic metres occur mainly in dramatic verse, but some are found elsewhere, as in the lyrics of Catullus and Horace. The principal Iambic metres are the **Senarius**, the **Septenarius**, and the **Octonarius**; the principal Trochaic metres are the Septenarius and Octonarius.

Iambic Senarius

Basically this line consists of six iambic feet, but in practice such a line is very rare.

Example:

> Phăsēl|lŭs īl|lĕ quēm| vĭ dē|tĭs, hōs|pĭ tēs

> (*Cat.* 4, 1)

In drama the last foot is always iambic, and the 5th regularly a spondee. The **spondee** is also very common in the first four feet, the **dactyl** and the **tribrach** are frequent, occasionally the **anapaest** is found, and, more rarely, the **proceleusmatic**. There is usually a **caesura** in either the third or the fourth foot.

Example:

> Ĭn hāc| hă bĭ tās|sĕ plătē|ā dĭc|tūmst Chrȳ|sĭdēm

> (*Ter, And.* 796)

Iambic Septenarius

This line consists of seven and a half feet, basically iambic, but allowing the same variations as in the Senarius. The 4th foot is regularly an Iambus, and is usually followed by a diaeresis: this is an aid to identifying the line.

Example:

> N(am) īdcĭr|c(o) āccēr|sōr nūp|tĭ ās| quōd m(i) ād|părā|rī sēn|sĭt

> (*Ter, And.* 690)

Iambic Octonarius

This line has eight iambic feet, with the same variations as in the other iambic lines. The 4th and 8th feet are regularly iambic, and a diaeresis follows the 4th foot.

Example:

> Cūrā|bĭ tūr.| sēd pătĕr| ădēst.| că vĕt(e) ēs|sĕ trĭs|tēm sēn|tĭ āt

> (*Ter, And.* 403)

Trochaic Septenarius

Apart from drama, this line is common in popular verses, and comes into its own in later Latin poetry. It consists of seven and a half **trochees**, but in practice only the seventh foot is regularly trochaic, while the others may be **spondee, dactyl, tribrach**, or (more rarely) **anapaest**. There is usually a **diaeresis** after the 4th foot.

Example:

> Crās ă|mēt quī| nūnqu(am) ă|māvĭt,| quĭqu(e) ă| māvīt| crās ă|mēt
>
>   (*Pervigilium Veneris*)

Trochaic Octonarius

This is a line of eight trochees, allowing the same variations as above. There is a diaeresis after the 4th foot.

Example:

> Prōin tū| sōllĭ cĭ|tūdĭn|(em) īstām| fālsām| quāe t(e) ēx|crŭcĭ ăt| mīttās
>
>   (*Ter, Heaut.* 177)

LYRIC VERSE

In most lyric metres the line is not to be subdivided into feet, but is itself the unit of scansion, and has a fixed number of syllables. The commonest, which are those used by Catullus and Horace, are the **Hendecasyllabic**, the **Asclepiads**, the **Glyconic** and the **Pherecratic**, which occur either singly or in combinations to form either couplets or stanzas of four lines. Beside these groupings there are the **Alcaic** and **Sapphic** stanzas. Elisions occur much more rarely than in the other metres.

Hendecasyllabic

This is Catullus's favourite line. It consists of eleven syllables in the following pattern:

$$- - - \;\; \breve{\;}\breve{\;}\_ \;\; \breve{\;}\_ \;\; \breve{\;}\_\_$$

Either the first or the second syllable may occasionally be short, and there is usually a caesura after the 5th syllable.

Example:

> Vīvāmŭs, mĕă Lēsbĭ(a), ātqu(e) ămēmūs
>
>   (*Cat.* 5, 1)

Asclepiads

There are two Asclepiad lines, of which the **Lesser** is by far the commoner. It has twelve syllables, in the following pattern with a caesura after the 6th syllable:

$$- - - \smile \smile - \| - \smile \smile - \smile -$$

Māecēnās, ătăvīs⁺ ēdĭtĕ rēgĭbūs

(Hor, Od. I, 1, 1)

The **Greater Asclepiad** is formed by adding a **choriambus** $- \smile \smile -$ after the 6th syllable with a **diaeresis** both before and after it.

Example:

Nūllām, Vārĕ, săcrā vītĕ prĭūs sēvĕrĭs ārbŏrēm

(Hor, Od. I, 18, 1)

Glyconic

The **Glyconic** occurs by itself in Catullus, but more usually it is found in combination with the **Lesser Asclepiad** or the **Pherecratic**. It consists of eight syllables ($- - - \smile \smile - \smile -$), so that it is like a Lesser Asclepiad minus the **choriambus**. It has no regular caesura.

Example:

Dōnēc grātŭs ĕrām tĭbī

(Hor. Od. III, 9, 1)

Pherecratic

The **Pherecratic** is a Glyconic minus the second last (short) syllable. It is found only in combination with other lines.

Example:

Sūspēndĭssĕ pŏtēntī

(Hor, Od. I, 5, 11)

Alcaic Stanza

The **Alcaic stanza** has four lines, of which the first two have the same pattern
$--\smile---\smile-\smile--$. In these there is a regular **caesura** after the 5th syllable. The
third line is $--\smile---\smile--$ and the 4th $-\smile\smile-\smile\smile-\smile--$. Neither of the last two
lines has a regular break in it.

Example:

> Nūnc ēst bĭbēndūm,[†] nūnc pĕdĕ lībĕrō
> pūlsāndă tēllūs,[†] nūnc Sălĭărĭbūs
>   ōrnārĕ pūlvīnār dĕōrūm
>   tēmpŭs ĕrāt dăpĭbūs, sŏdālēs.

(*Hor, Od. I.* 37, 1-4)

Sapphic Stanza

The **Sapphic stanza** also has four lines, of which the first three are the same:
$-\smile---\smile\smile-\smile--$. As in the Alcaic there is a **caesura** after the 5th syllable. The
last line is a short **Adonic** $-\smile\smile--$

Example:

> Īntĕgēr vītāe[†] scĕlĕrīsquĕ pūrūs
> nōn ĕgēt Māurĭs[†] iăcŭlīs nĕqu(e) ārcū
> nēc vĕnēnātīs[†] grăvĭdā săgĭttīs,
>   Fūscĕ, phărētrā.

(*Hor, Od. I.* 22, 1-4)

LATIN PHRASES USED IN ENGLISH

What follows is a list of some of the Latin phrases used in English today.

ab initio	from the beginning.
ab ovo	(lit: from the egg) from the beginning.
absit omen	(lit: may the (evil) omen be absent) may the presentiment not become real or take place.
ab urbe condita	(used in dates) from the foundation of the city (*i.e. from the foundation of Rome in 753 B.C.*).
A.D.	abbr for **anno Domini**.
ad hoc	(lit: for this) for a particular purpose only: **an ad hoc committee; an ad hoc decision.**
ad hominem	(lit: according to the person) 1 directed against a person rather than against his or her arguments. 2 based on or appealing to emotion rather than reason.
ad infinitum	without end; endlessly; to infinity.
ad interim	for the meantime; for the present: **ad interim measures.**
ad-lib	(abbr for **ad libitum**) ♦ *adj* improvised; impromptu ♦ *adv* without restraint; freely; as one pleases ♦ *vb* to improvise and deliver without preparation.
ad libitum	(lit: according to pleasure) as one pleases.
ad majorem Dei gloriam	for the greater glory of God (*the Jesuit motto*).
ad nauseam	(lit: to (the point of) nausea) to a disgusting extent.
ad rem	(lit: to the matter) to the point; without digression: **to reply ad rem; an ad rem discussion.**
advocatus diaboli	devil's advocate.
ad valorem	(lit: according to value) in proportion to the estimated value of the goods taxed.
aet.	(abbr for **aetatis**) at the age of.
Agnus Dei	Lamb of God.
alma mater	(lit: nurturing mother) one's former university, college or school.
alter ego	(lit: other self) 1 a second self. 2 a very close and intimate friend.
a.m.	abbr for **ante meridiem**.
AMDG	abbr for **ad majorem Dei gloriam**.
amor patriae	love of one's country; patriotism.
an.	(abbr for **anno**) in the year.
anno Domini	in the year of our Lord.
anno urbis conditae	in the year of the foundation of the city (*i.e. of Rome in 753 B.C., used in dates*)
anno regni	in the year of the reign (of).

annus mirabilis	(lit: wonderful year) a year of wonders.
antebellum	(lit: before the war) of or during the period before a war, especially the American Civil War.
ante meridiem	before noon.
ante-mortem	before death (*esp in legal or medical contexts*).
a.p.	(abbr for **ante prandium**) before a meal (*in prescriptions*).
apparatus criticus	(lit: critical apparatus) textual notes (*list of variant readings, etc., relating to a document, especially in a scholarly edition of a text*).
aq.	abbr for **aqua**.
aqua vitae	(lit: water of life) brandy.
a.r.	abbr for **anno regni**.
arbiter elegantiae *or* elegantiarum	judge in a matter of taste.
arcus senilis	(lit: senile bow) opaque circle around the cornea of eye (*often seen in elderly people*).
argumentum ad hominem	(lit: argument according to the person: Logic) **1** fallacious argument that attacks not an opponent's beliefs but his motives or character. **2** argument tha shows an opponent's statement to be inconsistent w his other beliefs.
ars longa vita brevis	art is long, life is short.
AUC	abbr for: **1 ab urbe condita. 2 anno urbis conditae**.
aut vincere aut mori	death or victory.
aurora australis	the southern lights.
aurora borealis	the northern lights.
ave	**1** hail! **2** farewell!
ave atque vale	hail and farewell!
Ave Maria	Hail Mary.
beatae memoriae	of blessed memory.
Beata Virgo	the Blessed Virgin.
Beata Virgo Maria	the Blessed Virgin Mary.
b.i.d	(abbr for **bis in die**) twice a day (*in prescriptions*).
bis dat, qui cito dat	the person who gives promptly gives twice.
BV	abbr for **Beata Virgo**.
c, ca	abbr for **circa**.
camera obscura	(lit: dark chamber) camera obscura.
carpe diem	(lit: seize the day) enjoy the pleasures of the momer without concern for the future.
casus belli	(lit: occasion of war) **1** an event or act used to justif war. **2** the immediate cause of a quarrel.
caveat emptor	let the buyer beware.
cetera desunt	the rest is missing.

eris paribus	other things being equal.
ca	around.
dex Juris Canonici	(lit: book of canon law) the official code of canon law (*in the Roman Catholic Church*).
gito, ergo sum	I think, therefore I am (*the basis of Descartes' philosophy*).
npos mentis	of sound mind; sane.
am populo	in the presence of the people; openly.
pus delicti	(lit: the body of the crime: LAW) the body of facts that constitute an offence.
rpus Juris Canonici	(lit: body of canon law) the official compilation of canon law (*in the Roman Catholic Church*).
rpus Juris Civilis	(lit: body of civil law) the body of Roman or civil law.
rigenda	things to be corrected.
pus vile	(lit: worthless body) person or thing fit only to be the object of an experiment.
pa	1 (*LAW*) an act of neglect. 2 (*gen*) a fault; sin; guilt.
n grano salis	with a grain of salt; not too literally.
n laude	(*chiefly US*) with praise (*the lowest of three designations for above-average achievement in examinations*).
riculum vitae	(lit: the course of one's life) curriculum vitae.
facto	*adv* in fact ♦ *adj* existing in fact.
gustibus non est isputandum	there is no arguing about tastes.
jure	according to law; by right; legally.
mortuis nil nisi onum	say nothing but good of the dead.
novo	anew.
o gratias	thanks be to God.
o Optimo Maximo	to God, the best, the Greatest.
o volente	God willing.
profundis	out of the depths of misery or dejection.
s ex machina	(lit: the god from the machine) 1 (*in ancient Greek and Roman drama*) a god introduced into a play to resolve the plot. 2 any unlikely or artificial device serving this purpose.
s Irae	(lit: the day of wrath) 1 a famous Latin hymn of the 13th century, describing the Last Judgment. It is used in the Mass for the dead. 2 a musical setting of this hymn, usually part of a setting of the Requiem.
jecta membra	the scattered remains.
M	abbr for **Deo Optimo Maximo**.
matis personae	(lit: the persons of the drama) the list of characters in a drama.

Ecce Homo	behold the man (*the words of Pontius Pilate to Christ* *accusers* [*John 19:5*]).
editio princeps	(lit: the first edition) the first printed edition of a wc
e.g., eg	abbr for **exempli gratia**.
emeritus	retired from office.
e pluribus unum	one out of many (*motto of USA*).
ER	1 (abbr for **Elizabeth Regina**) Queen Elizabeth; 2 (a for **Eduardus Rex**) King Edward.
errare est humanum	to err is human.
erratum (*pl* **errata**)	error.
et seq.	(abbr for **et sequens**) and the following.
et seqq.	(abbr for **et sequentia**) and those that follow.
ex	(lit: out of, from) 1 (*FINANCE*) not participating in; excluding; without: **ex bonus; ex dividend; ex right** 2 (*COMMERCE*) without charge to the buyer until removed from: **ex quay; ex ship; ex works**.
ex cathedra	(lit: from the chair) 1 with authority. 2 defined by tl pope as infallibly true, to be accepted by all Roman Catholics.
exeat	(lit: let him or her go out) formal leave of absence.
exempli gratia	for example.
exeunt	they go out (*used as a stage direction*).
exeunt omnes	they all go out (*used as a stage direction*).
exit	he or she goes out (*used as a stage direction*).
ex libris	(lit: from the books (of)) from the collection or libr of.
ex officio	by right of position or office.
ex parte	(*LAW*) on behalf of one side or party only (*of an application in a judicial proceeding*): **an ex parte injunction**.
ex post facto	having retrospective effect: **an ex post facto law**.
ex silentio	(lit: from silence) based on a lack of evidence to th contrary (*of a theory, assumption etc*).
extempore	(lit: instantaneously) without planning or preparat impromptu.
ex voto	*adv, adj* in accordance with a vow ♦ *n* offering ma fulfilment of a vow.
facile princeps	(lit: easily first) an obvious leader.
fecit (*abbr* **fec**)	(he or she) made it (*used formerly on works of art n to the artist's name*).
felo de se	suicide.
festina lente	more haste, less speed.
fiat lux	let there be light.
Fidei Defensor	defender of the faith.

us Achates	(lit: faithful Achates) faithful friend or companion (_the name of the faithful companion of Aeneas in Virgil's Aeneid_).
ruit	(he or she) flourished (_used to indicate the period when a historical figure, whose birth and death dates are unknown, was most active_).
ns et origo	the source and origin.
nius loci	(lit: genius of the place) 1 the guardian spirit of a place. 2 the special atmosphere of a particular place.
oria in Excelsis Deo	(lit: glory to God in the highest) 1 the Greater Doxology, beginning in Latin with these words. 2 a musical setting of this.
oria Patri	(lit: glory to the father) 1 the Lesser Doxology, beginning in Latin with these words. 2 a musical setting of this.
nc illae lacrimae	hence those tears.
J	(abbr for **hic jacet**) here lies (_on gravestones_).
JS	(abbr for **hic jacet sepultus**) here lies buried (_on gravestones_).
rrible dictu	horrible to relate.
d.	abbr for **ibidem**.
dem	in the same place (_in annotations, bibliographies, etc., when referring to a book, article, chapter, or page previously cited_).
est	that is (to say); in other words.
m	the same (_used to refer to an article, chapter, etc., previously cited_).
.	abbr for **id est**.
1.	abbr for **ignotus**.
10ratio elenchi	(lit: an ignorance of proof: _Logic_) 1 a purported refutation of a proposition that does not in fact prove it false but merely establishes a related but strictly irrelevant proposition. 2 the fallacy of arguing in this way.
10tum per ignotius	(lit: the unknown by means of the more unknown) an explanation that is obscurer than the thing to be explained.
10tus	unknown.
fatuus	will o' the wisp.
1p.	1 (abbr for **Imperator**) Emperor; 2 (abbr for **Imperatrix**) Empress.
absentia	in one's absence; in the absence of: **he was condemned in absentia.**
aeternum	forever; eternally.
articulo mortis	at the point of death.

in camera	(lit: in the chamber) in private.
in extenso	at full length.
in extremis	(lit: in the furthest reaches) **1** in extremity; in dire straits. **2** at the point of death.
infra	below.
infra dig	(abbr for **infra dignitatem**) beneath one's dignity.
in loco parentis	in place of a parent (*said of a person acting in a paren capacity*).
in medias res	(lit: into the midst of things) in or into the middle of events or a narrative.
in memoriam	in memory of; as a memorial to (*used in obituaries, epitaphs etc*).
in perpetuum	for ever.
in personam	(lit: against the person) directed against a specific person or persons (*LAW: of a judicial act*).
in propria persona	in person; personally.
in rem	(lit: against the matter) directed against property rather than against a specific person (*LAW: of a judici act*).
in rerum natura	in the nature of things.
INRI	(lit: Jesus of Nazareth, King of the Jews) abbr for **Ie Nazarenus Rex Iudaeorum** (*the inscription placed ov Christ's head during the Crucifixion*).
in situ	(lit: in position) in the natural, original, or appropria position.
inter alia	among other things.
inter alios	among other people.
inter vivos	(*LAW*) between living people: **an inter vivos gift**.
in toto	totally; entirely; completely.
in utero	within the womb.
in vacuo	in a vacuum.
in vino veritas	in wine there is truth.
in vitro	(lit: in glass) made to occur outside the body of the organism in an artificial environment (*of biological processes or reactions*): **in vitro fertilization**.
in vivo	(lit: in a living (thing)) occurring or carried out in th living organism (*of biological processes or experiments*).
ipse dixit	(lit: he himself said it) an arbitrary and unsupporte assertion.
ipsissima verba	the very words.
ipso facto	by the fact itself.
i.q.	(lit: the same as) abbr for **idem quod**.
lapsus linguae	a slip of the tongue.
lc	(abbr for **(in) loco citato**) in the place cited.

loci	the law of the place.
non scripta	the unwritten law; common law.
scripta	the written law; statute law.
talionis	the law of revenge or retaliation.
cit.	(abbr for **(in) loco citato**) in the place cited (*in textual annotation*).
gna cum laude	(chiefly US) with great praise (*the second of three designations for above-average achievement in examinations*).
gnum opus	a great work of art or literature (*especially the greatest single work of an artist*).
la fide	undertaken in bad faith.
re clausum	(lit: closed sea: LAW) a sea coming under the jurisdiction of one nation and closed to all others.
re liberum	(lit: free sea: LAW) a sea open to navigation by shipping of all nations.
re nostrum	(lit: our sea) the Mediterranean.
ter	mother (*often used facetiously*).
ter dolorosa	(lit: sorrowful mother) the Virgin Mary sorrowing for the dead Christ (*especially as depicted in art*).
terfamilias	(lit: mother of family) the mother of a family or the female head of a family.
teria medica	(lit: medical matter) 1 the branch of medical science concerned with the study of drugs used in the treatment of disease. 2 the drugs used in the treatment of disease.
a culpa	(lit: my fault) an acknowledgement of guilt.
mento mori	(lit: remember you must die) an object, such as a skull, intended to remind people of the inevitability of death.
ns sana in corpore no	a healthy mind in a healthy body.
ns rea	(lit: guilty mind: LAW) a criminal intention or knowledge that an act is wrong.
les gloriosus	a braggart soldier (*especially as a stock figure in comedy*).
rabile dictu	wonderful to relate.
ttimus	(lit: we send) a warrant of commitment to prison or a command to a jailer directing him to hold someone in prison.
dus operandi	procedure; method of operating; manner of working.
dus ponens	(lit: mood that affirms) the principle that whenever a conditional statement and its antecedent are given to be true its consequent may be validly inferred.

modus tollens	(lit: mood that denies) the principle that whenever a conditional statement and the negation of its consequent are given to be true, the negation of its antecedent may be validly inferred.
modus vivendi	(lit: way of living) a working arrangement between conflicting interests; practical compromise.
motu proprio	(lit: of his own accord) an administrative papal bull
multum in parvo	much in a small space.
mutatis mutandis	with the necessary changes.
NB, N.B., nb, n.b.	(abbr for **nota bene**) note well.
nem. con.	(abbr for **nemine contradicente**) no-one contradicti unanimously.
nemo me impune lacessit	no-one provokes me with impunity.
ne plus ultra	(lit: not more beyond) the extreme or perfect point state.
nihil	nil; nothing.
nihil obstat	there is no obstacle.
nil desperandum	(lit: nothing to be despaired of) never despair.
nisi prius	(lit: unless previously) 1 *in England* (a) a direction th a case be brought up to Westminster for trial befor single judge and jury. (b) the writ giving this direct 2 *in the US* a court where civil actions are tried by a single judge sitting with a jury as distinguished fro an appellate court.
nolens volens	whether willing or unwilling.
noli me tangere	(lit: do not touch me) a warning against interfering with or against touching a person or thing.
nolle prosequi	(lit: do not pursue) an entry made on the court reco when the plaintiff in a civil suit or prosecutor in a criminal prosecution undertakes not to continue th action or prosecution.
nolo contendere	(lit: I do not wish to contend) a plea made by a defendant to a criminal charge having the same eff in those proceedings as a plea of guilty but not precluding him from denying the charge in a subsequent action.
non compos mentis	(lit: not in control of one's mind) mentally incapabl managing one's own affairs; of unsound mind; insa
non prosequitur	(lit: he does not proceed) a judgment in favour of a defendant when the plaintiff failed to take the necessary steps in an action within the time allowe
non sequitur	(lit: it does not follow) 1 (*gen*) a statement having li or no relevance to what preceded it. 2 (*Logic*) a conclusion that does not follow from the premises.
nulli secundus	second to none.

men	(lit: divine power) 1 (*especially in ancient Roman religion*) a deity or spirit presiding over a thing or place. 2 a guiding principle, force, or spirit.
nc Dimittis	(lit: now let depart) 1 the Canticle of Simeon (*Luke 2:29-32*). 2 a musical setting of this.
	1 abbr for **obiit**. 2 (abbr for **obiter**) incidentally; in passing.
iit	he or she died (*on gravestones*).
ter dictum	(lit: something said in passing) 1 (*LAW*) an observation by a judge on some point of law not directly in issue in the case before him and thus neither requiring his decision nor serving as a precedent, but nevertheless of persuasive authority. 2 any comment, remark, or observation made in passing.
scurum per obscurius	(lit: the obscure by means of the more obscure) an explanation that is obscurer than the thing to be explained.
nium-gatherum	(often facetious) a miscellaneous collection; assortment.
us probandi	(*LAW*) the burden of proof.
. cit.	(abbr of **opere citato**) in the work cited.
us anglicanum	(lit: English work) fine embroidery (*especially of church vestments*).
a pro nobis	pray for us.
empora! O mores!	oh the times! oh the customs!
.	abbr of **per annum**.
ce	by leave of; with due deference to (*used to acknowledge politely someone who disagrees with the speaker or writer*).
ri passu	with equal speed or progress; equably (*often used to refer to the right of creditors to receive assets from the same source without one taking precedence*).
ssim	here and there; throughout (*used to indicate that what is referred to occurs frequently in the work cited*).
terfamilias	(lit: father of the family) 1 the male head of a household. 2 the head of a household having authority over its members.
x vobiscum	peace be with you.
ccavi	(lit: I have sinned) a confession of guilt.
culium	(lit: property) property that a father or master allowed his child or slave to hold as his own.
r annum	every year; year by year.
r ardua ad astra	through difficulties to the stars (*motto of the RAF*).
r capita	(lit: according to heads) of or for each person.
r contra	on the contrary.

per diem	(lit: for the day) **1** every day; by the day. **2** an allowa for daily expenses, usually those incurred while working.
per mensem	every month; by the month.
per pro	(abbr for **per procurationem**) by delegation to; thro the agency of (*used when signing documents on beh of someone else*).
persona grata	an acceptable person (*especially a diplomat acceptab to the government of the country to which he is sent*)
persona non grata	unacceptable or unwelcome person.
petitio principii	(lit: an assumption at the beginning: *Logic*) a form o fallacious reasoning in which the conclusion has be assumed in the premises; begging the question.
pia mater	(lit: pious mother) the innermost of the three membranes that cover the brain and spinal cord.
pinxit	(he or she) painted this (*used formerly on works of a next to the artist's name*).
p.m., P.M., pm, PM	abbr. for **1** post meridiem **2** postmortem.
post-bellum	(lit: after war) of or during the period after a war, especially the American Civil War.
post hoc	(lit: after this: *Logic*) the fallacy of assuming that temporal succession is evidence of causal relation.
post hoc, ergo propter hoc	after this, therefore because of this (*a fallacy of reasoning*).
post meridiem	after noon.
postmortem	(lit: after death) *n* **1** dissection and examination of a dead body to determine the cause of death. **2** analys or study of a recently completed event ♦ *adj* occurr after death.
pp	abbr for **1** per pro. **2** post prandium after a meal (*in prescriptions*).
PPS	(lit: after postscript; abbr for **post postscriptum**) additional postscript.
pr	(abbr for: **per rectum**) through the rectum (*in prescriptions*).
prima facie	at a first view.
primum mobile	(lit: first moving (thing)) prime mover.
primus inter pares	first among equals.
prn	(abbr for **pro re nata**) as the situation demands, as needed (*in prescriptions*).
pro forma	(lit: for form's sake) **1** prescribing a set form or procedure. **2** performed in a set manner.
pro patria	for one's country.
pro rata	in proportion.
pro tempore	for the time being.
proxime accessit	(lit: he or she came next) the runner-up.

q.e.	(abbr for **quod est**) which is.
QED	abbr for **quod erat demonstrandum**.
QEF	abbr for **quod erat faciendum**.
quid pro quo	(lit: something for something) 1 a reciprocal exchange. 2 something given in compensation, especially an advantage or object given in exchange for another.
quis custodiet ipsos custodes?	who will guard the guards?
q.l.	(abbr for **quantum libet**) as much as you please (*in prescriptions*).
qm	(abbr for **quaque mane**) every morning (*in prescriptions*).
qn	(abbr for **quaque nocte**) every night (*in prescriptions*).
quod erat demonstrandum	which was to be proved.
quod erat faciendum	which was to be done.
quot homines, tot sententiæ	there are as many opinions as there are people.
quo vadis?	whither goest thou?
qqv	(abbr for **quae vide**) which (*words, items etc*) see (*denoting a cross reference to more than one item*).
qs	(abbr for **quantum sufficit**) as much as will suffice (*in prescriptions*).
qv	(abbr for **quod vide**) which (*word, item etc*) see (*denoting a cross reference*).
rara avis	(lit: rare bird) an unusual, uncommon or exceptional person or thing.
reductio ad absurdum	(lit: reduction to the absurd) 1 a method of disproving a proposition by showing that its inevitable consequences would be absurd. 2 a method of indirectly proving a proposition by assuming its negation to be true and showing that this leads to an absurdity. 3 application of a principle or a proposed principle to an instance in which it is absurd.
requiescat	(lit: may he or she rest) a prayer for the repose of the souls of the dead.
requiescat in pace	may he or she rest in peace.
res gestae	(lit: things done) 1 things done or accomplished; achievements. 2 (*LAW*) incidental facts and circumstances that are admissible in evidence because they introduce or explain the matter in issue.
res ipsa loquitur	(*LAW*) the thing or matter speaks for itself.
res judicata	(*LAW*) a matter already adjudicated upon that cannot be raised again.
res publica	(lit: the public thing) the state, republic, or commonwealth.

resurgam	I shall rise again.
RI	1 (abbr for **Regina et Imperatrix**) Queen and Empre 2 (abbr for **Rex et Imperator**) King and Emperor.
rigor mortis	(lit: rigidity of death) the stiffness of joints and muscular rigidity of a dead body.
RIP	abbr for **requiescat** or **requiescant in pace**.
risus sardonicus	(lit: sardonic laugh) fixed contraction of the facial muscles resulting in a peculiar distorted grin, caus especially by tetanus.
sanctum sanctorum	(lit: holy of holies) 1 (*Bible*) the holy of holies. 2 (*ofte facetious*) an especially private place.
sartor resartus	the tailor patched.
schola cantorum	(lit: school of singers) a choir or choir school maintained by a church.
scire facias	(lit: cause (him) to know) 1 (*LAW, rare*) a judicial wri founded upon some record, such as a judgement, letters patent, etc., requiring the person against wh it is brought to show cause why the record should n be enforced or annulled. 2 a proceeding begun by th issue of such a writ.
semper fidelis	always faithful.
semper idem	always the same.
seq.	(abbr for **sequens**) the following (one).
seqq.	(abbr for **sequentia**) the following (ones).
seriatim	in order.
sic	thus (*often used to call attention to some quoted mistake*).
sic itur ad astra	such is the way to the stars.
sic transit gloria mundi	so passes the glory of the world.
si monumentum requiris, circumspice	if you seek (his) monument, look around you (*inscription on the architect Sir Christopher Wren's t in St Paul's Cathedral*).
sine die	without a day.
sine prole	(*LAW*) without issue.
sine qua non	(lit: without which not) an indispensable condition requirement.
sl	(abbr for **sine loco**) without place (*of publication*).
sp	abbr for **sine prole**.
spiritus asper	rough breathing.
spiritus lenis	smooth breathing.
SPQR	(abbr for **Senatus Populusque Romanus**) the Senat and People of Rome.
sq.	(abbr for **sequens**) the following (one).
sqq.	(abbr for **sequentia**) the following (ones).

Stabat Mater	(lit: the mother was standing) **1** a Latin hymn, probably of the 13th century, commemorating the sorrows of the Virgin Mary at the crucifixion and used in the Mass and various other services. **2** a musical setting of this hymn.
status quo	(lit: the state in which) the existing state of affairs.
stet	let it stand.
sub judice	before a court of law or a judge; under judicial consideration.
sub rosa	(lit: under the rose) secretly.
sub voce	under the word.
sui generis	(lit: of its own kind) unique.
sui juris	(lit: of one's own right) (*LAW*) of full age and not under disability; legally competent to manage one's own affairs; independent.
summa cum laude	(*chiefly U.S.*) with the utmost praise (*the highest of three designations for above-average achievement in examinations. In Britain it is sometimes used to designate a first-class honours degree*).
summum bonum	the principle of goodness in which all moral values are included or from which they are derived; highest or supreme good.
suo jure	(*chiefly LAW*) in one's own right.
suo loco	(*chiefly LAW*) in a person or thing's own or rightful place.
supra	above.
sursum corda	lift up your hearts (to God).
SV	abbr for **sub voce**.
tabula rasa	(lit: a scraped tablet) **1** the mind in its uninformed original state. **2** an opportunity for a fresh start; clean slate.
taedium vitae	(lit: weariness of life) the feeling that life is boring and dull.
Te Deum	(lit: Thee, God) **1** an ancient Latin hymn in rhythmic prose, sung or recited at matins in the Roman Catholic Church and in English translation at morning prayer in the Church of England and used by both churches as an expression of thanksgiving on special occasions. **2** a musical setting of this hymn. **3** a service of thanksgiving in which the recital of this hymn forms a central part.
te igitur	(lit: Thee, therefore: *Roman Catholic Church*) the first prayer of the canon of the Mass.
tempore	in the time of.
tempus fugit	time flies.
terminus ad quem	(lit: the end to which) the aim or terminal point.
terminus a quo	(lit: the end from which) the starting point; beginning.

terra firma	the solid earth; firm ground.
terra incognita	an unexplored or unknown land, region or area for study.
tertium quid	a third something.
t.i.d.	(abbr for **ter in die**) three times a day (*in prescriptio*
tu quoque	you likewise (*a retort made by a person accused of a crime implying that the accuser is also guilty of the sa crime*).
uberrima fides	utmost good faith.
ubique	everywhere.
ubi supra	where (mentioned or cited) above.
ultima Thule	(lit: the most distant Thule) 1 the utmost boundary o limit. 2 a remote goal or aim.
ultra vires	beyond one's powers.
una voce	with one voice.
urbi et orbi	(*Roman Catholic Church*) to the city and the world (a *phrase qualifying the solemn papal blessing*).
ut dict.	(abbr for **ut dictum**) as directed.
ut infra	as below.
ut supra	as above.
v.	abbr for 1 **verso**. 2 **versus**. 3 **vide**.
vade in pace	go in peace.
vade mecum	(lit: go with me) a handbook or other aid carried on t person for immediate use when needed.
væe victis	woe to the conquered!
vale	farewell!
veni, vidi, vici	I came, I saw, I conquered.
venire facias	(lit: you must make come: *LAW*) a writ directing a sheriff to summon suitable persons to form a jury.
verbatim et litteratim	word for word and letter for letter.
verb. sap.	(abbr for **verbum sapienti sat est**) a word is enough the wise.
verso	1 the back of a sheet of printed paper. 2 the side of a coin opposite to the obverse; reverse.
versus	1 against; in opposition to. 2 as opposed to; in contra with.
via	by way of.
via media	a middle course.
vice	in the place of; instead of; as a substitute for.
vice versa	the other way round.
vide	see.
videlicet	namely; to wit.

vi et armis   (lit: by force and arms) a kind of trespass accompanied by force and violence.

VIR   (abbr for **Victoria Imperatrix Regina**) Victoria, Empress and Queen.

virginibus puerisque   for maidens and youths.

vis inertiæ   the power of inertia.

viva voce   (lit: with living voice) *adv, adj* by word of mouth ♦ *n* an oral examination.

viz.   abbr for **videlicet**.

vl   (abbr for **varia lecto**) variant reading.

vollente Deo   God willing.

vox populi   the voice of the people; popular or public opinion.

vox populi, vox Dei   the voice of the people is the voice of God.

VR   (abbr for **Victoria Regina**) Queen Queen Victoria.

VRI   (abbr for **Victoria Regina et Imperatrix**) Victoria, Queen and Empress.

English-Latin

A, a

a, an *art not translated*; (*a certain*) quīdam; **twice a day** bis in diē; **four acres a man** quaterna in singulōs iūgera.

aback *adv*: **taken ~** dēprehēnsus.

abaft *adv* in puppī ♦ *prep* post, pōne.

abandon *vt* relinquere; (*wilfully*) dērelinquere, dēserere; (*to danger*) ōbicere; (*to pleasure*) dēdere; (*plan*) abicere; **~ hope** spem abicere.

abandoned *adj* perditus.

abase *vt* dēprimere; **~ oneself** sē prōsternere.

abash *vt* perturbāre; rubōrem incutere (*dat*).

abate *vt* minuere, imminuere; (*a portion*) remittere ♦ *vi* (*fever*) dēcēdere; (*passion*) dēfervēscere; (*price*) laxāre; (*storm*) cadere.

abatement *n* remissiō *f*, dēminūtiō *f*.

abbess *n* abbātissa *f*.

abbey *n* abbātia *f*.

abbot *n* abbās *m*.

abbreviate *vt* imminuere.

abbreviation *n* (*writing*) nota *f*.

abdicate *vt* sē abdicāre (*abl*).

abdication *n* abdicātiō *f*.

abduct *vt* abripere.

abduction *n* raptus *m*.

aberration *n* error *m*.

abet *vt* adiuvāre, adesse (*dat*), favēre (*dat*).

abettor *n* adiūtor *m*, minister *m*, fautor *m*, socius *m*.

abeyance *n*: **in ~** intermissus; **be in ~** iacēre.

abhor *vt* ōdisse, invīsum habēre.

abhorrence *n* odium *nt*.

abhorrent *adj*: **~ to** aliēnus ab.

abide *vi* (*dwell*) habitāre; (*tarry*) commorārī; (*last*) dūrāre; **~ by** *vt fus* stāre (*abl*), perstāre in (*abl*).

abiding *adj* perpetuus, diūturnus.

ability *n* (*to do*) facultās *f*, potestās *f*; (*physical*) vīrēs *fpl*; (*mental*) ingenium *nt*; **to the best of my ~** prō meā parte, prō virīlī parte.

abject *adj* abiectus, contemptus; (*downcast*) dēmissus.

abjectly *adv* humiliter, dēmissē.

abjure *vt* ēiūrāre.

ablative *n* ablātīvus *m*.

ablaze *adj* flāgrāns, ardēns.

able *adj* perītus, doctus; **be ~** posse, valēre.

able-bodied *adj* rōbustus.

ablution *n* lavātiō *f*.

ably *adv* perītē, doctē.

abnegation *n* abstinentia *f*.

abnormal *adj* inūsitātus; (*excess*) immodicus.

abnormally *adv* inūsitātē, praeter mōrem.

aboard *adv* in nāvī; **go ~** nāvem cōnscendere; **put ~** impōnere.

abode *n* domicilium *nt*, sēdēs *f*.

abolish *vt* tollere, ē mediō tollere, abolēre; (*law*) abrogāre.

abolition *n* dissolūtiō *f*; (*law*) abrogātiō *f*.

abominable *adj* dētestābilis, nefārius.

abominably *adv* nefāriē, foedē.

abominate *vt* dētestārī.

abomination *n* odium *nt*; (*thing*) nefas *nt*.

aboriginal *adj* prīscus.

aborigines *n* aborīginēs *mpl*.

abortion *n* abortus *m*.

abortive *adj* abortīvus; (*fig*) inritus; **be ~** ad inritum redigī.

abound *vi* abundāre, superesse; **~ in** abundāre (*abl*), adfluere (*abl*).

abounding *adj* abundāns, adfluēns, cōpiōsus ab.

about *adv* (*place*) *usu expressed by cpd verbs*; (*number*) circiter, ferē, fermē ♦ *prep* (*place*) circā, circum (*acc*); (*number*) circā, ad (*acc*); (*time*) sub (*acc*); (*concerning*) dē (*abl*); **~ to die** moritūrus; **I am ~ to go** in eō est ut eam.

above *adv* suprā; **from ~** dēsuper; **over and ~** īnsuper ♦ *prep* suprā (*acc*); (*motion*) super (*acc*); (*rest*) super (*abl*); **be ~** (*conduct*) indignārī.

abreast *adv* (*ships*) aequātīs prōrīs; **walk ~ of** latus tegere (*dat*).

abridge *vt* contrahere, compendī facere.

abridgement *n* epitomē *f*.

abroad *adv* peregrē; (*out of doors*) forīs; **be ~** peregrīnārī; **from ~** peregrē.

abrogate *vt* dissolvere; (*law*) abrogāre.

abrupt *adj* subitus, repentīnus; (*speech*) concīsus.

abscess *n* vomica *f*.

abscond *vi* aufugere.

absence *n* absentia *f*; **in my ~** mē absente; **leave of ~** commeātus *m*.

absent *adj* absēns; **be ~** abesse; **~ oneself** *vi* deesse, nōn adesse.

absent-minded *adj* immemor, parum attentus.

absolute *adj* absolūtus, perfectus; (*not limited*) īnfīnītus; (*not relative*) simplex; **~ power** rēgnum *nt*, dominātus *m*; **~ ruler** rēx.

absolutely *adv* absolūtē, omnīnō.

absolution *n* venia *f*.

absolve *vt* absolvere, exsolvere; (*from punishment*) condōnāre.

absorb *vt* bibere, absorbēre; (*fig*) distringere; **I am ~ed in** tōtus sum in (*abl*).

absorbent *adj* bibulus.

abstain *vi* abstinēre, sē abstinēre; (*from violence*) temperāre.

abstemious *adj* sobrius.

abstinence *n* abstinentia *f*, continentia *f*.

abstinent *adj* abstinēns, sobrius.

abstract *adj* mente perceptus, cōgitātiōne comprehēnsus ♦ *n* epitomē *f* ♦ *vt* abstrahere, dēmere.

abstraction *n* (*idea*) nōtiō *f*; (*inattention*) animus parum attentus.

abstruse *adj* reconditus, obscūrus, abstrūsus.

absurd *adj* ineptus, absurdus.

absurdity *n* ineptiae *fpl*, insulsitās *f*.

absurdly *adv* ineptē, absurdē.

abundance *n* cōpia *f*, abundantia *f*; **there is ~ of** abundē est (*gen*).

abundant *adj* cōpiōsus, abundāns, largus; **be ~** abundāre.

abundantly *adv* abundē, abundanter, adfātim.

abuse *vt* abūtī (*abl*); (*words*) maledīcere (*dat*) ♦ *n* probra *ntpl*, maledicta *ntpl*, convīcium *f*, contumēlia *f*.

abusive *adj* maledicus, contumēliōsus.

abut *vi* adiacēre; **~ting on** cōnfīnis (*dat*), fīnitimus (*dat*).

abysmal *adj* profundus.

abyss *n* profundum *nt*, vorāgō *f*; (*water*) gurges *m*; (*fig*) barathrum *nt*.

academic *adj* scholasticus; (*style*) umbrātilis; (*sect*) Acadēmicus.

academy *n* schola *f*; (*Plato's*) Acadēmīa *f*.

accede *vi* adsentīrī; **~ to** accipere.

accelerate *vt*, *vi* adcelerāre, festīnāre; (*process*) mātūrāre.

accent *n* vōx *f*; (*intonation*) sonus *m*; (*mark*) apex *m* ♦ *vt* (*syllable*) acuere; (*word*) sonum admovēre (*dat*).

accentuate *vt* exprimere.

accept *vt* accipere.

acceptable *adj* acceptus, grātus, probābilis; **be ~** placēre.

acceptation *n* significātiō *f*.

access *n* aditus *m*; (*addition*) accessiō *f*; (*illness*) impetus *m*.

accessary *n* socius *m*, particeps *m*.

accessible *adj* (*person*) adfābilis, facilis; **be ~** (*place*) patēre; (*person*) facilem sē praebēre.

accession *n* (*addition*) accessiō *f*; (*king's*) initium rēgnī.

accident *n* cāsus *m*, calamitās *f*.

accidental *adj* fortuītus.

accidentally *adv* cāsū, fortuītō.

acclaim *vt* adclāmāre.

acclamation *n* clāmor *m*, studium *nt*.

acclimatize *vt* aliēnō caelō adsuēfacere.

accommodate *vt* accommodāre, aptāre; (*lodging*) hospitium parāre (*dat*); **~ oneself to** mōrigerārī (*dat*).

accommodating *adj* facilis.

accommodation *n* hospitium *nt*.

accompany *vt* comitārī; (*courtesy*) prōsequī; (*to Forum*) dēdūcere; (*music*) concinere (*dat*).

accomplice *n* socius *m*, particeps *m*, cōnscius *m*.

accomplish *vt* efficere, perficere, patrāre.

accomplished *adj* doctus, perītus.

accomplishment *n* effectus *m*, perfectiō *f*, fīnis *m*; **~s** *pl* artēs *fpl*.

accord *vi* inter sē congruere, cōnsentīre ♦ *vt* dare, praebēre, praestāre ♦ *n* cōnsēnsus *m*, concordia *f*; (*music*) concentus *m*; **of one's own ~** suā sponte, ultrō; **with one ~** unā vōce.

accordance *n*: **in ~ with** ex, ē (*abl*), secundum (*acc*).

according *adv*: **~ to** ex, ē (*abl*), secundum (*acc*); (*proportion*) prō (*abl*); **~ as** prōut.

accordingly *adv* itaque, igitur, ergō.

accost *vt* appellāre, adloquī, compellāre.

account *n* ratiō *f*; (*story*) nārrātiō *f*, expositiō *f*; **on ~ of** ob (*acc*); propter (*acc*), causā (*gen*); **be of no ~** (*person*) nihilī aestimārī, nēquam esse; **on that ~** idcircō ideō; **on your ~** tuā grātiā, tuō nōmine; **give an ~** ratiōnem reddere; **present an ~** ratiōnem referre; **take ~ of** ratiōnem habēre (*gen*); **put down to my ~** mihī expēnsum ferre; **the ~s balance** ratiō cōnstat/convenit.

account *vi*: **~ for** ratiōnēs reddere, adferre (*cūr*); **that ~s for it** haec causa est; (*PROV*) hinc illae lacrimae.

accountant *n* ā ratiōnibus, ratiōcinātor *m*.

accountable *adj* reus; **I am ~ for** mihi ratiō reddenda est (*gen*).

account book *n* tabulae *fpl*; cōdex acceptī et expēnsī.

accoutred *adj* īnstructus, ōrnātus.

accoutrements *n* ōrnāmenta *ntpl*, arma *ntpl*.

accredited *adj* pūblicā auctōritate missus.

accretion *n* accessiō *f*.

accrue *vi* (*addition*) cēdere; (*advantage*) redundāre.

accumulate *vt* cumulāre, congerere, coacervāre ♦ *vi* crēscere, cumulārī.

accumulation *n* cumulus *m*, acervus *m*.

accuracy *n* cūra *f*; (*writing*) subtīlitās *f*.

accurate *adj* (*work*) exāctus, subtīlis; (*worker*) dīligēns.

accurately *adv* subtīliter, ad amussim, dīligenter.

accursed *adj* sacer; (*fig*) exsecrātus, scelestus.

accusation *n* (*act*) accūsātiō *f*; (*charge*) crīmen *nt*; (*unfair*) īnsimulātiō *f*; (*false*) calumnia *f*; **bring an ~ against** accūsāre; (*to a magistrate*) nōmen dēferre (*gen*).

accusative *n* (*case*) accūsātīvus *m*.

accuse *vt* accūsāre, crīminārī, reum facere; (*falsely*) īnsimulāre; **the ~d** reus; (*said by prosecutor*) iste.

accuser *n* accūsātor *m*; (*civil suit*) petītor *m*; (*informer*) dēlātor *m*.

accustom *vt* adsuēfacere; **~ oneself** adsuēscere, consuēscere.

accustomed *adj* adsuētus; **be ~** solēre; **become ~** adsuēscere, consuēscere.

ace *n* ūniō *f*; **I was within an ~ of going** minimum āfuit quin īrem.

acerbity *n* acerbitās *f*.

ache *n* dolor *m* ♦ *vi* dolēre.

achieve *vt* cōnficere, patrāre; (*win*) cōnsequī, adsequī.

achievement *n* factum *nt*, rēs gesta.

acid *adj* acidus.

acknowledge *vt* (*fact*) agnōscere; (*fault*) fatērī, cōnfitērī; (*child*) tollere; (*service*) grātiās agere prō (*abl*); **I have to ~ your letter of 1st March** accēpī litterās tuās Kal. Mart. datās.

acknowledgement *n* cōnfessiō *f*; grātia *f*.

acme *n* fastīgium *nt*, flōs *m*.

aconite *n* aconītum *nt*.

acorn *n* glāns *f*.

acoustics *n* rēs audītōria *f*.

acquaint *vt* certiōrem facere, docēre; **~ oneself with** cognōscere; **~ed with** gnārus (*gen*), perītus (*gen*).

acquaintance *n* (*with fact*) cognitiō *f*, scientia *f*; (*with person*) familiāritās *f*, ūsus *m*; (*person*) nōtus *m*, familiāris *m*.

acquiesce *vi* (*assent*) adquiēscere; (*submit*) aequō animō patī.

acquiescence *n*: **with your ~** tē nōn adversante, pāce tuā.

acquire *vt* adquīrere, adipīscī, cōnsequī; nancīscī.

acquirements *n* artēs *fpl*.

acquisition *n* (*act*) comparātiō *f*, quaestus *m*; (*thing*) quaesītum *nt*.

acquisitive *adj* quaestuōsus.

acquit *vt* absolvere; **~ oneself** sē praestāre, officiō fungī.

acquittal *n* absolūtiō *f*.

acre *n* iūgerum *nt*.

acrid *adj* asper, ācer.

acrimonious *adj* acerbus, truculentus.

acrimony *n* acerbitās *f*.

acrobat *n* fūnambulus *m*.

acropolis *n* arx *f*.

across *adv* trānsversus ♦ *prep* trāns (*acc*).

act *n* factum *nt*, facinus *nt*; (*play*) āctus *m*; (*POL*) āctum *nt*, senātūs cōnsultum *nt*, dēcrētum *nt*; **I was in the ~ of saying** in eō erat ut dīcerem; **caught in the ~** dēprehēnsus ♦ *vi* facere, agere; (*conduct*) sē gerere; (*stage*) histriōnem esse, partēs agere; (*pretence*) simulāre ♦ *vt*: **~ a part** partēs agere, persōnam sustinēre; **~ the part of** agere; **~ as** esse, munere fungī (*gen*); **~ upon** (*instructions*) exsequī.

action *n* (*doing*) āctiō *f*; (*deed*) factum *nt*, facinus *nt*; (*legal*) āctiō *f*, līs *f*; (*MIL*) proelium *nt*; (*of play*) āctiō *f*; (*of speaker*) gestus *m*; **bring an ~ against** lītem intendere, āctiōnem īnstituere (*dat*); **be in ~** agere, rem gerere;

(*MIL*) pugnāre, in aciē dīmicāre; **man of ~** vir strēnuus.

active *adj* impiger, strēnuus, sēdulus, nāvus.

actively *adv* impigrē, strēnuē, nāviter.

activity *n* (*motion*) mōtus *m*; (*energy*) industria *f*, sēdulitās *f*.

actor *n* histriō *m*; (*in comedy*) cōmoedus *m*; (*in tragedy*) tragoedus *m*.

actress *n* mīma *f*.

actual *adj* vērus, ipse.

actually *adv* rē vērā.

actuate *vt* movēre, incitāre.

acumen *n* acūmen *nt*, ingenī aciēs, argūtiae *fpl*.

acute *adj* acūtus, ācer; (*pain*) ācer; (*speech*) argūtus, subtīlis.

acutely *adv* acūtē, ācriter, argūtē.

acuteness *n* (*mind*) acūmen *nt*, aciēs *f*, subtīlitās *f*.

adage *n* prōverbium *nt*.

adamant *n* adamās *m* ♦ *adj* obstinātus.

adamantine *adj* adamantinus.

adapt *vt* accommodāre.

adaptable *adj* flexibilis, facile accommodandus.

adaptation *n* accommodātiō *f*.

add *vt* addere, adicere, adiungere; **be ~ed** accēdere.

adder *n* vīpera *f*.

addicted *adj* dēditus.

addition *n* adiūnctiō *f*, accessiō *f*; additāmentum *nt*, incrēmentum *nt*; **in ~** īnsuper, praetereā; **in ~ to** praeter (*acc*).

additional *adj* novus, adiūnctus.

addled *adj* (*egg*) inritus; (*brain*) inānis.

address *vt* compellāre, alloquī; (*crowd*) cōntiōnem habēre apud (*acc*); (*letter*) īnscrībere; **~ oneself** (*to action*) accingī ♦ *n* adloquium *nt*; (*public*) cōntiō *f*, ōrātiō *f*; (*letter*) īnscrīptiō *f*.

adduce *vt* (*argument*) adferre; (*witness*) prōdūcere.

adept *adj* perītus.

adequate *adj* idōneus, dignus, pār; **be ~** sufficere.

adequately *adv* satis, ut pār est.

adhere *vi* haerēre, adhaerēre; **~ to** inhaerēre (*dat*), inhaerēscere in (*abl*); (*agreement*) manēre, stāre in (*abl*).

adherent *n* adsectātor *m*; (*of party*) fautor *m*; (*of person*) cliēns *m*.

adhesive *adj* tenax.

adieu *interj* valē, valēte; **bid ~ to** valēre iubēre.

adjacent *adj* fīnitimus, vīcīnus; **be ~ to** adiacēre (*dat*).

adjoin *vi* adiacēre (*dat*).

adjoining *adj* fīnitimus, adiūnctus; proximus.

adjourn *vt* (*short time*) differre; (*longer time*) prōferre; (*case*) ampliāre ♦ *vi* rem differre, prōferre.

adjournment *n* dīlātiō *f*, prōlātiō *f*.

adjudge *vt* addīcere, adiūdicāre.

adjudicate *vi* dēcernere.

adjudicator *n* arbiter *m*.
adjunct *n* appendix *f*, accessiō *f*.
adjure *vt* obtestārī, obsecrāre.
adjust *vt* (*adapt*) accommodāre; (*put in order*) compōnere.
adjutant *n* (MIL) optiō *m*; (*civil*) adiūtor *m*.
administer *vt* administrāre, gerere; (*justice*) reddere; (*oath to*) iūreiūrandō adigere; (*medicine*) dare, adhibēre.
administration *n* administrātiō *f*.
administrator *n* administrātor *m*, prōcūrātor *m*.
admirable *adj* admīrābilis, ēgregius.
admirably *adv* ēgregiē.
admiral *n* praefectus classis; ~'s ship nāvis praetōria.
admiralty *n* praefectī classium.
admiration *n* admīrātiō *f*, laus *f*.
admire *vt* admīrārī; mirārī.
admirer *n* laudātor *m*; amātor *m*.
admissible *adj* aequus.
admission *n* (*entrance*) aditus *m*; (*of guilt etc*) cōnfessiō *f*.
admit *vt* (*let in*) admittere, recipere, accipere; (*to membership*) adscīscere; (*argument*) concēdere; (*fault*) fatērī; ~ of patī, recipere.
admittedly *adv* sānē.
admonish *vt* admonēre, commonēre, hortārī.
admonition *n* admonitiō *f*.
ado *n* negōtium *nt*; **make much ~ about nothing** fluctūs in simpulō excitāre; **without more ~** prōtinus, sine morā.
adolescence *n* prīma adulēscentia *f*.
adolescent *adj* adulēscēns ♦ *n* adulēscentulus *m*.
adopt *vt* (*person*) adoptāre; (*custom*) adscīscere; ~ **a plan** consilium capere.
adoption *n* (*person*) adoptiō *f*; (*custom*) adsūmptiō *f*; **by ~** adoptīvus.
adoptive *adj* adoptīvus.
adorable *adj* amābilis, venustus.
adorably *adv* venustē.
adoration *n* (*of gods*) cultus *m*; (*of kings*) venerātiō *f*; (*love*) amor *m*.
adore *vt* (*worship*) venerārī; (*love*) adamāre.
adorn *vt* ōrnāre, exōrnāre, decorāre.
adornment *n* ōrnāmentum *nt*, decus *nt*; ōrnātus *m*.
adrift *adj* fluctuāns; **be ~** fluctuāre.
adroit *adj* sollers, callidus.
adroitly *adv* callidē, scītē.
adroitness *n* sollertia *f*, calliditās *f*.
adulation *n* adūlātiō *f*, adsentātiō *f*.
adulatory *adj* blandus.
adult *adj* adultus.
adulterate *vt* corrumpere, adulterāre.
adulterer *n* adulter *m*.
adulteress *n* adultera *f*.
adulterous *adj* incestus.
adultery *n* adulterium *nt*; **commit ~** adulterāre.
adults *npl* pūberēs *mpl*.
adumbrate *vt* adumbrāre.
advance *vt* prōmovēre; (*a cause*) fovēre;

(*money*) crēdere; (*opinion*) dīcere; (*to honours*) prōvehere; (*time*) mātūrāre ♦ *vi* prōcēdere, prōgredī, adventāre; (MIL) signa prōferre, pedem īnferre; (*progress*) prōficere; (*walk*) incēdere; ~ **to the attack** signa īnferre ♦ *n* prōgressus *m*, prōcessus *m*; (*attack*) impetus *m*; (*money*) mūtuae pecūniae; **in ~** mātūrius; **fix in ~** praefīnīre; **get in ~** praecipere.
advanced *adj* prōvectus; **well ~** (*task*) adfectus.
advancement *n* (POL) honōs *m*.
advantage *n* (*benefit*) commodum *nt*, bonum *nt*, ūsus *m*; (*of place or time*) opportūnitās *f*; (*profit*) fructus *m*; (*superiority*) praestantia *f*; **it is an ~** bono est; **be of ~ to** prōdesse (*dat*), ūsuī esse (*dat*); **to your ~** in rem tuam; **it is to your ~** tibi expedit, tuā interest; **take ~ of** (CIRCS) ūtī; (*person*) dēcipere, fallere; **have an ~ over** praestāre (*dat*); **be seen to ~** māximē placēre.
advantageous *adj* ūtilis, opportūnus.
advantageously *adv* ūtiliter, opportūnē.
advent *n* adventus *m*.
adventitious *adj* fortuītus.
adventure *n* (*exploit*) facinus memorābile *nt*; (*hazard*) perīculum *nt*.
adventurer *n* vir audāx *m*; (*social*) parasītus *m*.
adventurous *adj* audāx.
adversary *n* adversārius *m*, hostis *m*.
adverse *adj* adversus, contrārius, inimīcus.
adversely *adv* contrāriē, inimīcē, male.
adversity *n* rēs adversae *fpl*, calamitās *f*.
advert *vi*: ~ **to** attingere.
advertise *vt* prōscrībere; vēnditāre.
advertisement *n* prōscrīptiō *f*, libellus *m*.
advice *n* cōnsilium *nt*; (POL) auctōritās *f*; (*legal*) respōnsum *nt*; **ask ~ of** cōnsulere; **on the ~ of Sulla** auctōre Sullā.
advisable *adj* ūtilis, operae pretium.
advise *vt* monēre, suādēre (*dat*), cēnsēre (*dat*); ~ **against** dissuādēre.
advisedly *adv* cōnsultō.
adviser *n* auctor *m*, suāsor *m*.
advocacy *n* patrōcinium *nt*.
advocate *n* patrōnus *m*, causidicus *m*; (*supporter*) auctor *m*; **be an ~** causam dīcere ♦ *vt* suādēre, cēnsēre.
adze *n* ascia *f*.
aedile *n* aedīlis *m*.
aedile's *adj* aedīlicius.
aedileship *n* aedīlitās *f*.
aegis *n* aegis *f*; (*fig*) praesidium *nt*.
Aeneid *n* Aenēis *f*.
aerial *adj* āerius.
aesthetic *adj* pulchritūdinis amāns, artificiōsus.
afar *adv* procul; **from ~** procul.
affability *n* cōmitās *f*, facilitās *f*, bonitās *f*.
affable *adj* cōmis, facilis, commodus.
affably *adv* cōmiter.
affair *n* negōtium *nt*, rēs *f*.
affect *vt* afficere, movēre, commovēre;

(*concern*) attingere; (*pretence*) simulāre.
affectation n simulātiō f; (*RHET*) adfectātiō f; (*in diction*) īnsolentia f; quaesīta ntpl.
affected adj (*style*) molestus, pūtidus.
affectedly adv pūtidē.
affecting adj miserābilis.
affection n amor m, cāritās f, studium nt; (*family*) pietās f.
affectionate adj amāns, pius.
affectionately adv amanter, piē.
affiance vt spondēre.
affidavit n testimōnium nt.
affinity n affīnitās f, cognātiō f.
affirm vt adfirmāre, adsevērāre.
affirmation n adfirmātiō f.
affirmative adj: **I reply in the ~** āiō.
affix vt adfīgere, adiungere.
afflict vt adflīctāre, angere, vexāre; afflīgere.
affliction n miseria f, dolor m, rēs adversae fpl.
affluence n cōpia f, opēs fpl.
affluent adj dīves, opulentus, locuplēs.
afford vt praebēre, dare; **I cannot ~** rēs mihi nōn suppetit ad.
affray n rixa f, pugna f.
affright vt terrēre ♦ n terror m, pavor m.
affront vt offendere, contumēliam dīcere (*dat*) ♦ n iniūria f, contumēlia f.
afield adv forīs; **far ~** peregrē.
afloat adj natāns; **be ~** natāre.
afoot adv pedibus; **be ~** gerī.
aforesaid adj suprā dictus.
afraid adj timidus; **be ~ of** timēre, metuere; verērī.
afresh adv dēnuō, dē integrō.
Africa n Africa f.
aft adv in puppī, puppim versus.
after adj posterior ♦ adv post (*acc*), posteā; **the day ~** postrīdiē ♦ conj postquam; **the day ~** postrīdiē quam ♦ prep post (*acc*); (*in rank*) secundum (*acc*); (*in imitation*) ad (*acc*), dē (*abl*); **~ all** tamen, dēnique; **~ reading the book** librō lēctō; **one thing ~ another** aliud ex aliō; **immediately ~** statim ab.
aftermath n ēventus m.
afternoon n: **in the ~** post merīdiem ♦ adj postmerīdiānus.
afterthought n posterior cōgitātiō f.
afterwards adv post, posteā, deinde.
again adv rūrsus, iterum; **~ and ~** etiam atque etiam, identidem; **once ~** dēnuō; (*new point in a speech*) quid?
against prep contrā (*acc*), adversus (*acc*), in (*acc*); **~ the stream** adversō flūmine; **~ one's will** invitus.
agape adj hiāns.
age n (*life*) aetās f; (*epoch*) aetās f, saeculum nt; **old ~** senectūs f; **he is of ~** suī iūris est; **he is eight years of ~** octō annōs nātus est, nōnum annum agit; **of the same ~** aequālis.
aged adj senex, aetāte prōvectus; (*things*) antīquus.
agency n opera f; **through the ~ of** per (*acc*).
agent n āctor m, prōcūrātor m; (*in crime*)

minister m.
aggrandize vt augēre, amplificāre.
aggrandizement n amplificātiō f.
aggravate vt (*wound*) exulcerāre; (*distress*) augēre; **become ~d** ingravēscere.
aggravating adj molestus.
aggregate n summa f.
aggression n incursiō f, iniūria f.
aggressive adj ferōx.
aggressiveness n ferōcitās f.
aggressor n oppugnātor m.
aggrieved adj īrātus; **be ~** indignārī.
aghast adj attonitus, stupefactus; **stand ~** obstupēscere.
agile adj pernix, vēlōx.
agility n pernīcitās f.
agitate vt agitāre; (*mind*) commovēre, perturbāre.
agitation n commōtiō f, perturbātiō f, trepidātiō f; (*POL*) tumultus m.
agitator n turbātor m, concitātor m.
aglow adj fervidus ♦ adv: **be ~** fervēre.
ago adv abhinc (*acc*); **three days ~** abhinc trēs diēs; **long ~** antīquitus, iamprīdem, iamdūdum; **a short time ~** dūdum.
agog adj sollicitus, ērēctus.
agonize vt cruciāre, torquēre.
agonizing adj horribilis.
agony n cruciātus m, dolor m.
agrarian adj agrārius; **~ party** agrāriī mpl.
agree vi (*together*) cōnsentīre, congruere; (*with*) adsentīrī (*dat*), sentīre cum; (*bargain*) pacīscī; (*facts*) cōnstāre, convenīre; (*food*) facilem esse ad concoquendum; **~ upon** cōnstituere, compōnere; **it is agreed** constat (inter omnes).
agreeable adj grātus, commodus, acceptus.
agreeableness n dulcēdō f, iūcunditās f.
agreeably adv iūcundē.
agreement n (*together*) cōnsēnsus m, concordia f; (*with*) adsēnsus m; (*pact*) pactiō f, conventum nt, foedus nt; **according to ~** compāctō, ex compositō; **be in ~** cōnsentīre, congruere.
agricultural adj rūsticus, agrestis.
agriculture n rēs rūstica f, agrī cultūra f.
aground adv: **be ~** sīdere; **run ~** in lītus ēicī, offendere.
ague n horror m, febris f.
ahead adv ante; **go ~** anteīre, praeīre; **go-~** adj impiger; **ships in line ~** agmen nāvium.
aid vt adiuvāre, succurrere (*dat*), subvenīre (*dat*) ♦ n auxilium nt, subsidium nt.
aide-de-camp n optiō m.
ail vt dolēre ♦ vi aegrōtāre, labōrāre, languēre.
ailing adj aeger, īnfirmus.
ailment n morbus m, valētūdō f.
aim vt intendere; **~ at** petere; (*fig*) adfectāre, spectāre, sequī; (*with verb*) id agere ut ♦ n fīnis m, prōpositum nt.
aimless adj inānis, vānus.
aimlessly adv sine ratiōne.
aimlessness n vānitās f.

air n āēr m; (*breeze*) aura f; (*look*) vultus m, speciēs f; (*tune*) modus m; **in the open** ~ sub dīvō; ~**s fastus** m; **give oneself** ~**s** sē iactāre.
airily adv hilarē.
airy adj (*of air*) āerius; (*light*) tenuis; (*place*) apertus; (*manner*) hilaris.
aisle n āla f.
ajar adj sēmiapertus.
akin adj cōnsanguineus, cognātus.
alacrity n alacritās f.
alarm n terror m, formīdō f, trepidātiō f; (*sound*) clāmor m; **sound an** ~ ad arma conclāmāre; **give the** ~ increpāre; **be in a state of** ~ trepidāre ♦ vt terrēre, perterrēre, perturbāre.
alarming adj formīdolōsus.
alas interj heu.
albeit conj etsī, etiamsī.
alcove n zōthēca f.
alder n alnus f.
alderman n decuriō m.
ale n cervīsia f.
alehouse n caupōna f, taberna f.
alert adj prōmptus, alacer, vegetus.
alertness n alacritās f.
alien adj externus; ~ **to** abhorrēns ab ♦ n peregrīnus m.
alienate vt aliēnāre, abaliēnāre, āvertere, āvocāre.
alienation n aliēnātiō f.
alight vi (*from horse*) dēscendere, dēsilīre; (*bird*) īnsīdere.
alight adj: **be** ~ ārdēre; **set** ~ accendere.
alike adj pār, similis ♦ adv aequē, pariter.
alive adj vīvus; **be** ~ vīvere.
all adj omnis; (*together*) ūniversus, cūnctus; (*whole*) tōtus; ~ **but** paene; ~ **for** studiōsus (*gen*); ~ **in** cōnfectus; ~ **of** tōtus; ~ **over with** āctum dē (*abl*); ~ **the best men** optimus quisque; ~ **the more** eō plūs, tantō plūs; **at** ~ ullō modō, quid; **it is** ~ **up with** actum est de (*abl*); **not at** ~ haudquāquam ♦ n fortūnae fpl.
allay vt sēdāre, mītigāre, lēnīre.
allegation n adfirmātiō f; (*charge*) īnsimulātiō f.
allege vt adfirmāre, praetendere; (*in excuse*) excūsāre.
allegiance n fidēs f; **owe** ~ **to** in fidē esse (*gen*); **swear** ~ **to** in verba iūrāre (*gen*).
allegory n allēgoria f, immūtāta ōrātiō f.
alleviate vt mītigāre, adlevāre, sublevāre.
alleviation n levātiō f, levāmentum nt.
alley n (*garden*) xystus m; (*town*) angiportus m.
alliance n societās f, foedus nt.
allied adj foederātus, socius; (*friends*) coniūnctus.
alligator n crocodīlus m.
allocate vt adsignāre, impertīre.
allot vt adsignāre, distribuere; **be** ~**ted** obtingere.
allotment n (*land*) adsignātiō f.
allow vt sinere, permittere (*dat*), concēdere (*dat*), patī; (*admit*) fatērī, concēdere;

(*approve*) comprobāre; **it is** ~**ed** licet (*dat* + *infin*); ~ **for** vt fus ratiōnem habēre (*gen*).
allowance n venia f, indulgentia f; (*pay*) stīpendium nt; (*food*) cibāria ntpl; (*for travel*) viāticum nt; **make** ~ **for** indulgēre (*dat*), ignōscere (*dat*), excūsāre.
alloy n admixtum nt.
all right adj rēctē; **it is** ~ bene est.
allude vi: ~ **to** dēsignāre, attingere, significāre.
allure vt adlicere, pellicere.
allurement n blanditia f, blandīmentum nt, illecebra f.
alluring adj blandus.
alluringly adv blandē.
allusion n mentiō f, indicium nt.
alluvial adj: ~ **land** adluviō f.
ally n socius m ♦ vt sociāre, coniungere.
almanac n fāstī mpl.
almighty adj omnipotēns.
almond n (*nut*) amygdalum nt; (*tree*) amygdala f.
almost adv paene, ferē, fermē, propemodum.
alms n stipem (*no nom*) f.
aloe n aloē f.
aloft adj sublīmis ♦ adv sublīmē.
alone adj sōlus, sōlitārius, ūnus ♦ adv sōlum.
along prep secundum (*acc*), praeter (*acc*) ♦ adv porrō; **all** ~ iamdūdum, ab initiō; ~ **with** unā cum (*abl*).
alongside adv: **bring** ~ adpellere; **come** ~ ad crepīdinem accēdere.
aloof adv procul; **stand** ~ sē removēre ♦ adj sēmōtus.
aloofness n sōlitūdō f, sēcessus m.
aloud adv clārē, māgnā vōce.
alphabet n elementa ntpl.
Alps n Alpēs fpl.
already adv iam.
also adv etiam, et, quoque; īdem.
altar n āra f.
alter vt mūtāre, commūtāre; (*order*) invertere.
alteration n mūtātiō f, commūtātiō f.
altercation n altercātiō f, iūrgium nt.
alternate adj alternus ♦ vt variāre.
alternately adv invicem.
alternation n vicem (*no nom*) f, vicissitūdō f.
alternative adj alter, alius ♦ n optiō f.
although conj quamquam (*indic*), etsī/etiamsī (+ *cond clause*); quamvīs (+ *subj*).
altitude n altitūdō f.
altogether adv omnīnō; (*emphasis*) plānē, prōrsus.
altruism n beneficentia f.
alum n alūmen nt.
always adv semper.
amalgamate vt miscēre, coniungere.
amalgamation n coniūnctiō f, temperātiō f.
amanuensis n librārius m.
amass vt cumulāre, coacervāre.
amateur n idiōta m.
amatory adj amātōrius.
amaze vt obstupefacere; attonāre; **be** ~**d**

obstupēscere.
amazement *n* stupor *m*; **in ~** attonitus, stupefactus.
ambassador *n* lēgātus *m*.
amber *n* sūcinum *nt*.
ambidextrous *adj* utrīusque manūs compos.
ambiguity *n* ambiguitās *f*; (*RHET*) amphibolia *f*.
ambiguous *adj* ambiguus, anceps, dubius.
ambiguously *adv* ambiguē.
ambition *n* glōria *f*, laudis studium.
ambitious *adj* glōriae cupidus, laudis avidus.
amble *vi* ambulāre.
ambrosia *n* ambrosia *f*.
ambrosial *adj* ambrosius.
ambuscade *n* īnsidiae *fpl*.
ambush *n* īnsidiae *fpl* ♦ *vt* īnsidiārī (*dat*).
ameliorate *vt* corrigere, meliōrem reddere.
amelioration *n* prōfectus *m*.
amenable *adj* facilis, docilis.
amend *vt* corrigere, ēmendāre.
amendment *n* ēmendātiō *f*.
amends *n* (*apology*) satisfactiō *f*; **make ~ for** expiāre; **make ~ to** satisfacere (*dat*).
amenity *n* (*scenery*) amoenitās *f*; (*comfort*) commodum *nt*.
amethyst *n* amethystus *f*.
amiability *n* benignitās *f*, suāvitās *f*.
amiable *adj* benignus, suāvis.
amiably *adv* benignē, suāviter.
amicable *adj* amīcus, cōmis.
amicably *adv* amīcē, cōmiter.
amid, amidst *prep* inter (*acc*).
amiss *adv* perperam, secus, incommodē; **take ~** aegrē ferre.
amity *n* amīcitia *f*.
ammunition *n* tēla *ntpl*.
amnesty *n* venia *f*.
among, amongst *prep* inter (*acc*), apud (*acc*).
amorous *adj* amātōrius, amāns.
amorously *adv* cum amōre.
amount *vi*: **~ to** efficere; (*fig*) esse ♦ *n* summa *f*.
amours *n* amōrēs *mpl*.
amphibious *adj* anceps.
amphitheatre *n* amphitheātrum *nt*.
ample *adj* amplus, satis.
amplification *n* amplificātiō *f*.
amplify *vt* amplificāre.
amplitude *n* amplitūdō *f*, cōpia *f*.
amputate *vt* secāre, amputāre.
amuck *adv*: **run ~** bacchārī.
amulet *n* amulētum *nt*.
amuse *vt* dēlectāre, oblectāre.
amusement *n* oblectāmentum *nt*, dēlectātiō *f*; **for ~** animī causā.
amusing *adj* rīdiculus, facētus.
an *indef art see* **a**.
anaemic *adj* exsanguis.
analogous *adj* similis.
analogy *n* prōportiō *f*, comparātiō *f*.
analyse *vt* excutere, perscrūtārī.
analysis *n* explicātiō *f*.
anapaest *n* anapaestus *m*.

anarchical *adj* sēditiōsus.
anarchy *n* reī pūblicae perturbātiō, lēgēs nullae *fpl*, licentia *f*.
anathema *n* exsecrātiō *f*; (*object*) pestis *f*.
ancestor *n* proavus *m*; **~s** *pl* māiōrēs *mpl*.
ancestral *adj* patrius.
ancestry *n* genus *nt*, orīgō *f*.
anchor *n* ancora *f*; **lie at ~** in ancorīs stāre; **weigh ~** ancoram tollere ♦ *vi* ancoram iacere.
anchorage *n* statiō *f*.
ancient *adj* antīquus, prīscus, vetustus; **~ history, ~ world** antīquitās *f*; **from/in ~ times** antīquitus; **the ~s** veterēs.
and *conj* et, atque, ac, -que; **~ ... not** nec, neque; **~ so** itaque.
anecdote *n* fābella *f*.
anent *prep* dē (*abl*).
anew *adv* dēnuō, ab integrō.
angel *n* angelus *m*.
angelic *adj* angelicus; (*fig*) dīvīnus, eximius.
anger *n* īra *f* ♦ *vt* inrītāre.
angle *n* angulus *m* ♦ *vi* hāmō piscārī.
angler *n* piscātor *m*.
Anglesey *n* Mona *f*.
angrily *adv* īrātē.
angry *adj* īrātus; **be ~** īrāscī (*dat*).
anguish *n* cruciātus *m*, dolor *m*; (*mind*) angor *m*.
angular *adj* angulātus.
animal *n* animal *nt*; (*domestic*) pecus *f*; (*wild*) fera *f*.
animate *vt* animāre.
animated *adj* excitātus, vegetus.
animation *n* ārdor *m*, alacritās *f*.
animosity *n* invidia *f*, inimīcitia *f*.
ankle *n* tālus *m*.
annalist *n* annālium scrīptor.
annals *n* annālēs *mpl*.
annex *vt* addere.
annexation *n* adiectiō *f*.
annihilate *vt* dēlēre, extinguere, perimere.
annihilation *n* exstinctiō *f*, interneciō *f*.
anniversary *n* diēs anniversārius; (*public*) sollemne *nt*.
annotate *vt* adnotāre.
annotation *n* adnotātiō *f*.
announce *vt* nūntiāre; (*officially*) dēnūntiāre, prōnūntiāre; (*election result*) renūntiāre.
announcement *n* (*official*) dēnūntiātiō *f*; (*news*) nūntius *m*.
announcer *n* nūntius *m*.
annoy *vt* inrītāre, vexāre; **be ~ed with** aegrē ferre.
annoyance *n* molestia *f*, vexātiō *f*; (*felt*) dolor *m*.
annoying *adj* molestus.
annual *adj* annuus, anniversārius.
annually *adv* quotannīs.
annuity *n* annua *ntpl*.
annul *vt* abrogāre, dissolvere, tollere.
annulment *n* abrogātiō *f*.
anoint *vt* ungere, illinere.

anomalous *adj* novus.
anomaly *n* novitās *f*.
anon *adv* mox.
anonymous *adj* incertī auctōris.
anonymously *adv* sine nōmine.
another *adj* alius; (*second*) alter; **of** ~ aliēnus; **one after** ~ alius ex aliō; **one** ~ inter sē, alius alium; **in** ~ **place** alibī; **to** ~ **place** aliō; **in** ~ **way** aliter; **at** ~ **time** aliās.
answer *vt* respondēre (*dat*); (*by letter*) rescrībere (*dat*); (*agree*) respondēre, congruere; ~ **a charge** crīmen dēfendere; ~ **for** *vt fus* (*surety*) praestāre; (*account*) ratiōnem referre; (*substitute*) īnstar esse (*gen*) ♦ *n* respōnsum *nt*; (*to a charge*) dēfēnsiō *f*, ~ **to the name of** vocārī; **give an** ~ respondēre.
answerable *adj* reus; **I am** ~ **for** ... ratiō mihī reddenda est ... (*gen*).
ant *n* formīca *f*.
antagonism *n* simultās *f*, inimīcitia *f*.
antagonist *n* adversārius *m*, hostis *m*.
antarctic *adj* antarcticus.
antecedent *adj* antecēdēns, prior.
antediluvian *adj* prīscus, horridus, Deucaliōnēus.
antelope *n* dorcas *f*.
anterior *adj* prior.
anteroom *n* vestibulum *nt*.
anthology *n* excerpta *ntpl*; **make an** ~ excerpere.
anthropology *n* rēs hūmānae *fpl*.
anticipate *vt* (*expect*) exspectāre; (*forestall*) antevenīre, occupāre, (*in thought*) animō praecipere.
anticipation *n* exspectātiō *f*, spēs *f*; praesūmptiō *f*.
antics *n* gestus *m*, ineptiae *fpl*.
anticyclo..e *n* serēnitās *f*.
antidote *n* remedium *nt*, medicāmen *nt*.
antipathy *n* fastīdium *nt*, odium *nt*; (*things*) repugnantia *f*.
antiphonal *adj* alternus.
antiphony *n* alterna *ntpl*.
antipodes *n* contrāria pars terrae.
antiquarian *adj* historicus.
antiquary *n* antīquārius *m*.
antiquated *adj* prīscus, obsolētus.
antique *adj* antīquus, prīscus.
antiquity *n* antīquitās *f*, vetustās *f*, veterēs *mpl*.
antithesis *n* contentiō *f*, contrārium *nt*.
antlers *n* cornua *ntpl*.
anvil *n* incūs *f*.
anxiety *n* sollicitūdō *f*, metus *m*, cūra *f*; anxietās *f*.
anxious *adj* sollicitus, anxius; avidus; cupidus.
any *adj* ullus; (*interrog*) ecquī; (*after* sī, nisī, num, nē) quī; (*indef*) quīvīs, quīlibet; **hardly** ~ nullus ferē; ~ **further** longius; ~ **longer** (*of time*) diutius.
anybody *pron* aliquis; (*indef*) quīvīs, quīlibet;

(*after* sī, nisī, num, nē) quis; (*interrog*) ecquis, numquis; (*after neg*) quisquam; **hardly** ~ nēmō ferē.
anyhow *adv* ullō modō, quōquō modō.
anyone *pron see* **anybody**.
anything *pron* aliquid; quidvīs, quidlibet; (*interrog*) ecquid, numquid; (*after neg*) quicquam; (*after* sī, nisī, num, nē) quid; **hardly** ~ nihil ferē.
anywhere *adv* usquam, ubīvīs.
apace *adv* citō, celeriter.
apart *adv* seōrsum, sēparātim ♦ *adj* dīversus; **be six feet** ~ sex pedēs distāre; **set** ~ sēpōnere; **stand** ~ distāre; **joking** ~ remōtō iocō; ~ **from** praeter (*acc*).
apartment *n* cubiculum *nt*, conclāve *nt*.
apathetic *adj* lentus, languidus, ignāvus.
apathy *n* lentitūdō *f*, languor *m*, ignāvia *f*.
ape *n* sīmia *f* ♦ *vt* imitārī.
aperture *n* hiātus *m*, forāmen *nt*, rīma *f*.
apex *n* fastīgium *nt*.
aphorism *n* sententia *f*.
apiary *n* alveārium *nt*.
apiece *adv* in singulōs; **two** ~ bīnī.
aplomb *n* cōnfīdentia *f*.
apocryphal *adj* commentīcius.
apologetic *adj* cōnfitēns, veniam petēns.
apologize *vi* veniam petere, sē excūsāre.
apology *n* excūsātiō *f*.
apoplectic *adj* apoplēcticus.
apoplexy *n* apoplēxis *f*.
apostle *n* apostolus *m*.
apothecary *n* medicāmentārius *m*.
appal *vt* perterrēre, cōnsternere.
appalling *adj* dīrus.
apparatus *n* īnstrūmenta *ntpl*, ōrnāmenta *ntpl*.
apparel *n* vestis *f*, vestīmenta *ntpl*.
apparent *adj* manifestus, apertus, ēvidēns.
apparently *adv* speciē, ut vidētur.
apparition *n* vīsum *nt*, speciēs *f*.
appeal *vi* (*to magistrate*) appellāre; (*to people*) prōvocāre ad; (*to gods*) invocāre, testārī; (*to senses*) placēre (*dat*) ♦ *n* appellātiō *f*, prōvocātiō *f*, testātiō *f*.
appear *vi* (*in sight*) appārēre; (*in court*) sistī; (*in public*) prōdīre; (*at a place*) adesse, advenīre; (*seem*) vidērī.
appearance *n* (*coming*) adventus *m*; (*look*) aspectus *m*, faciēs *f*; (*semblance*) speciēs *f*; (*thing*) vīsum *nt*; **for the sake of ~s** in speciem; (*formula*) dicis causā; **make one's** ~ prōcēdere, prōdīre.
appeasable *adj* plācābilis.
appease *vt* plācāre, lēnīre, mītigāre, sēdāre.
appeasement *n* plācātiō *f*; (*of enemy*) pācificātiō *f*.
appellant *n* appellātor *m*.
appellation *n* nōmen *nt*.
append *vt* adiungere, subicere.
appendage *n* appendix *f*, adiūnctum *nt*.
appertain *vi* pertinēre.
appetite *n* adpetītus *m*; (*for food*) fāmēs *f*.
applaud *vt* plaudere; (*fig*) laudāre.

applause n plausus m; (fig) adsēnsiō f, adprobātiō f.

apple n pōmum nt; mālum nt; ~ **tree** mālus f; ~ **of my eye** ocellus meus; **upset the ~ cart** plaustrum percellere.

appliance n māchina f, īnstrūmentum nt.

applicable adj aptus, commodus; **be ~** pertinēre.

applicant n petītor m.

application n (work) industria f; (mental) intentiō f; (asking) petītiō f; (MED) fōmentum nt.

apply vt adhibēre, admovēre; (use) ūtī (abl); ~ **oneself to** sē adplicāre, incumbere in (acc) ♦ vi pertinēre; (to a person) adīre (acc); (for office) petere.

appoint vt (magistrate) creāre, facere, cōnstituere; (commander) praeficere; (guardian, heir) īnstituere; (time) dīcere, statuere; (for a purpose) dēstināre; (to office) creāre.

appointment n cōnstitūtum nt; (duty) mandātum nt; (office) magistrātus m; **have an ~ with** cōnstitūtum habēre cum; **keep an ~** ad cōnstitūtum venīre.

apportion vt dispertīre, dīvīdere; (land) adsignāre.

apposite adj aptus, appositus.

appraisal n aestimātiō f.

appraise vt aestimāre.

appreciable adj haud exiguus.

appreciate vt aestimāre.

appreciation n aestimātiō f.

apprehend vt (person) comprehendere; (idea) intellegere, mente comprehendere; (fear) metuere, timēre.

apprehension n comprehēnsiō f; metus m, formīdō f.

apprehensive adj anxius, sollicitus; **be ~ of** metuere.

apprentice n discipulus m, tīrō m.

apprenticeship n tīrōcinium nt.

apprise vt docēre, certiōrem facere.

approach vt appropinquāre ad (acc), accēdere ad; (person) adīre ♦ vi (time) adpropinquāre; (season) appetere ♦ n (act) accessus m, aditus m; (time) adpropinquātiō f; (way) aditus m; **make ~es to** adīre ad, ambīre, petere.

approachable adj (place) patēns; (person) facilis.

approbation n adprobātiō f, adsēnsiō f.

appropriate adj aptus, idōneus, proprius ♦ vt adscīscere, adsūmere.

appropriately adv aptē, commodē.

approval n adprobātiō f, adsēnsus m, favor m.

approve vt, vi adprobāre, comprobāre; adsentīrī (dat); (law) scīscere.

approved adj probātus, spectātus.

approximate adj propinquus ♦ vi: ~ **to** accēdere ad.

approximately adv prope, propemodum; (number) ad (acc).

appurtenances n īnstrūmenta ntpl, apparātus m.

apricot n armēniacum nt; ~ **tree** n armēniaca f.

April n mēnsis Aprīlis m; **of ~** Aprīlis.

apron n operīmentum nt.

apropos of prep quod attinet ad.

apse n apsis f.

apt adj aptus, idōneus; (pupil) docilis, prōmptus; ~ **to** prōnus, prōclīvis ad; **be ~ to** solēre.

aptitude n ingenium nt, facultās f.

aptly adv aptē.

aquarium n piscīna f.

aquatic adj aquātilis.

aqueduct n aquae ductus m.

aquiline adj (nose) aduncus.

arable land n arvum nt.

arbiter n arbiter m.

arbitrarily adv ad libīdinem, licenter.

arbitrary adj libīdinōsus (act); (ruler) superbus.

arbitrate vi dīiūdicāre, disceptāre.

arbitration n arbitrium nt, dīiūdicātiō f.

arbitrator n arbiter m, disceptātor m.

arbour n umbrāculum nt.

arbutus n arbutus f.

arc n arcus m.

arcade n porticus f.

arch n fornix m, arcus m ♦ vt arcuāre ♦ adj lascīvus, vafer.

archaeologist n antīquitātis investīgātor m.

archaeology n antīquitātis investīgātiō f.

archaic adj prīscus.

archaism n verbum obsolētum nt.

archbishop n archiepiscopus m.

arched adj fornicātus.

archer n sagittārius m.

archery n sagittāriōrum ars f.

architect n architectus m.

architecture n architectūra f.

architrave n epistylium nt.

archives n tabulae (pūblicae) fpl.

arctic adj arcticus, septentriōnālis ♦ n septentriōnēs mpl.

ardent adj ārdēns, fervidus, vehemēns.

ardently adv ārdenter, ācriter, vehementer.

ardour n ārdor m, fervor m.

arduous adj difficilis, arduus.

area n regiō f; (MATH) superficiēs f.

arena n harēna f.

argonaut n argonauta m.

argosy n onerāria f.

argue vi (discuss) disserere, disceptāre; (dispute) ambigere; disputāre; (reason) argūmentārī ♦ vt (prove) arguere.

argument n (discussion) contrōversia f, disputātiō f; (reason) ratiō f; (proof, theme) argūmentum nt.

argumentation n argūmentātiō f.

argumentative adj lītigiōsus.

aria n canticum nt.

arid adj āridus, siccus.

aright adv rectē, vērē.

arise vi orīrī, coorīrī, exsistere; ~ **from** nāscī ex, proficīscī ab.

aristocracy n optimātēs mpl, nōbilēs mpl; (*govt*) optimātium dominātus m.

aristocrat n optimās m.

aristocratic adj patricius, generōsus.

arithmetic n numerī mpl, arithmētica ntpl.

ark n arca f.

arm n bracchium nt; (*upper*) lacertus m; (*sea*) sinus m; (*weapon*) tēlum nt ♦ vt armāre ♦ vi arma capere.

armament n bellī apparātus m; cōpiae fpl.

armed adj (*men*) armātus; **light-~ troops** levis armātūra f, vēlitēs mpl.

armistice n indutiae fpl.

armlet n armilla f.

armour n arma ntpl; (*kind of*) armātūra f.

armourer n (armōrum) faber m.

armoury n armāmentārium nt.

armpit n āla f.

arms npl (MIL) arma ntpl; **by force of ~** vī et armīs; **under ~** in armīs.

army n exercitus m; (*in battle*) aciēs f; (*on march*) agmen nt.

aroma n odor m.

aromatic adj frāgrāns.

around adv circum (acc), circā (acc) ♦ prep circum (acc).

arouse vt suscitāre, ērigere, excitāre.

arraign vt accūsāre.

arrange vt (*in order*) compōnere, ōrdināre, dīgerere, dispōnere; (*agree*) pacīscī; **~ a truce** indūtias compōnere.

arrangement n ōrdō m, collocātiō f, dispositiō f; pactum nt, cōnstitūtum nt.

arrant adj summus.

array n vestis f, habitus m; (MIL) aciēs f ♦ vt vestīre, exōrnāre; (MIL) īnstruere.

arrears n residuae pecūniae fpl, reliqua ntpl.

arrest vt comprehendere, adripere; (*attention*) in sē convertere; (*movement*) morārī, tardāre ♦ n comprehēnsiō f.

arrival n adventus m.

arrive vi advenīre (ad + acc), pervenīre (ad + acc).

arrogance n superbia f, adrogantia f, fastus m.

arrogant adj superbus, adrogāns.

arrogantly adv superbē, adroganter.

arrogate vt adrogāre.

arrow n sagitta f.

arsenal n armāmentārium nt.

arson n incēnsiōnis crīmen nt.

art n ars f, artificium nt; **fine ~s** ingenuae artēs.

artery n artēria f.

artful adj callidus, vafer, astūtus.

artfully adv callidē, astūtē.

artfulness n astūtia f, dolus m.

artichoke n cinara f.

article n rēs f, merx f; (*clause*) caput nt; (*term*) condiciō f.

articulate adj explānātus, distinctus ♦ vi explānāre, exprimere.

articulately adv explānātē, clārē.

articulation n prōnūntiātiō f.

artifice n ars f, artificium nt, dolus m.

artificer n artifex m, opifex m, faber m.

artificial adj (*work*) artificiōsus; (*appearance*) fūcātus.

artificially adv arte, manū.

artillery n tormenta ntpl.

artisan n faber m, opifex m.

artist n artifex m; pictor m.

artistic adj artificiōsus, ēlegāns.

artistically adv artificiōsē, ēleganter.

artless adj (*work*) inconditus; (*person*) simplex.

artlessly adv inconditē; simpliciter, sine dolō.

artlessness n simplicitās f.

as adv (*before adj, adv*) tam; (*after* **aequus, īdem, similis**) ac, atque; (*correlative*) quam, quālis, quantus ♦ conj (*compar*) ut (+ indic), sīcut, velut, quemadmodum; (*cause*) cum (+ indic), quōniam, quippe quī; (*time*) dum, ut ♦ relat pron quī, quae, quod (+ subj); **~ being** utpote; **~ follows** ita; **~ for** quod attinet ad; **~ if** quasī, tamquam si, velut; (= *while*) usu expressed by pres part; **~ it were** ut ita dīcam; **~ yet** adhūc; **~ soon ~** simul ac/atque (+ perf indic); **~ . . . as possible** quam (+ superl).

as n (*coin*) as m.

ascend vt, vi ascendere.

ascendancy n praestantia f, auctōritās f.

ascendant adj surgēns, potēns; **be in the ~** praestāre.

ascent n ascēnsus m; (*slope*) clīvus m.

ascertain vt comperīre, cognōscere.

ascetic adj nimis abstinēns, austērus.

asceticism n dūritia f.

ascribe vt adscrībere, attribuere, adsignāre.

ash n (*tree*) fraxinus f ♦ adj fraxineus.

ashamed adj: **I am ~** pudet mē; **~ of** pudet (+ acc of person, + gen of thing).

ashen adj pallidus.

ashes n cinis m.

ashore adv (*motion*) in lītus; (*rest*) in lītore; **go ~** ēgredī.

Asia n Asia f.

aside adv sēparatim, sē- (*in cpd*).

ask vt (*question*) rogāre, quaerere; (*request*) petere, poscere; (*beg, entreat*) orāre; **~ for** vt fus petere; rogāre; scīscitārī; percontārī.

askance adv oblīquē; **look ~ at** līmīs oculīs aspicere, invidēre (dat).

askew adv prāvē.

aslant adv oblīquē.

asleep adj sōpītus; **be ~** dormīre; **fall ~** obdormīre, somnum inīre.

asp n aspis f.

asparagus n asparagus m.

aspect n (*place*) aspectus m; (*person*) vultus m; (CIRCS) status m; **have a southern ~** ad merīdiem spectāre; **there is another ~ to the matter** aliter sē rēs habet.

aspen n pōpulus f.

asperity n acerbitās f.

asperse vt maledīcere (dat), calumniārī.

aspersion n calumnia f; **cast ~s on** calumniārī, īnfamiā aspergere.

asphalt n bitūmen nt.

asphyxia n strangulātiō f.
asphyxiate vt strangulāre.
aspirant n petītor m.
aspirate n (GRAM) aspīrātiō f.
aspiration n spēs f; (POL) ambitiō f.
aspire vi: ~ **to** adfectāre, petere, spērāre.
ass n asinus m, asellus m; (fig) stultus.
assail vt oppugnāre, adorīrī, aggredī.
assailable adj expugnābilis.
assailant n oppugnātor m.
assassin n sīcārius m, percussor m.
assassinate vt interficere, occīdere, iugulāre.
assassination n caedēs f, parricidium nt.
assault vt oppugnāre, adorīrī, aggredī;
    (speech) invehī in (acc) ♦ n impetus m,
    oppugnātiō f; (personal) vīs f.
assay vt (metal) spectāre; temptāre, cōnārī.
assemble vt convocāre, congregāre, cōgere ♦
    vi convenīre, congregārī.
assembly n coetus m, conventus m; (plebs)
    concilium nt; (Roman people) comitia ntpl;
    (troops) cōntiō f; (things) congeriēs f.
assent vi adsentīrī, adnuere ♦ n adsēnsus m.
assert vt adfirmāre, adsevērāre, dīcere.
assertion n adfirmātiō f, adsevērātiō f, dictum
    nt, sententia f.
assess vt cēnsēre, aestimāre; ~ **damages**
    lītem aestimāre.
assessment n cēnsus m, aestimātiō f.
assessor n cēnsor m; (assistant) cōnsessor m.
assets n bona ntpl.
assiduity n dīligentia f, sēdulitās f, industria f.
assiduous adj dīligēns, sēdulus, industrius.
assign vt tribuere, attribuere; (land)
    adsignāre; (in writing) perscrībere; (task)
    dēlēgāre; (reason) adferre.
assignation n cōnstitūtum nt.
assignment n adsignātiō f, perscrīptiō f; (task)
    mūnus nt, pēnsum nt.
assimilate vt aequāre; (food) concoquere;
    (knowledge) concipere.
assist vt adiuvāre, succurrere (dat), adesse
    (dat).
assistance n auxilium nt, opem (no nom) f;
    come to the ~ of subvenīre (dat); **be of ~ to**
    auxiliō esse (dat).
assistant n adiūtor m, minister m.
assize n conventus m; **hold ~s** conventūs
    agere.
associate vt cōnsociāre, coniungere ♦ vi rem
    inter sē cōnsociāre; ~ **with** familiāriter ūtī
    (abl) ♦ n socius m, sodālis m.
association n societās f; (club) sodālitās f.
assort vt dīgerere, dispōnere ♦ vi congruere.
assortment n (of goods) variae mercēs fpl.
assuage vt lēnīre, mītigāre, sēdāre.
assume vt (for oneself) adsūmere, adrogāre;
    (hypothesis) pōnere; (office) inīre.
assumption n (hypothesis) sūmptiō f, positum
    nt.
assurance n (given) fidēs f, pignus nt; (felt)
    fīdūcia f; (boldness) cōnfīdentia f.
assure vt cōnfirmāre, prōmittere (dat).

assured adj (person) fīdēns; (fact) explōrātus,
    certus.
assuredly adv certō, certē, profectō, sānē.
astern adv ā puppī; (movement) retrō; ~ **of**
    post.
asthma n anhēlitus m.
astonish vt obstupefacere; attonāre.
astonished adj attonitus, stupefactus; **be ~ed**
    at admīrārī.
astonishing adj mīrificus, mīrus.
astonishment n stupor m, admīrātiō f.
astound vt obstupefacere.
astray adj vagus; **go ~** errāre, aberrāre,
    deerrāre.
astride adj vāricus.
astrologer n Chaldaeus m, mathēmaticus m.
astrology n Chaldaeōrum dīvīnātiō f.
astronomer n astrologus m.
astronomy n astrologia f.
astute adj callidus, vafer.
astuteness n calliditās f.
asunder adv sēparātim, dis- (in cpd).
asylum n asȳlum nt.
at prep in (abl), ad (acc); (time) usu expressed by
    abl; (towns, small islands) loc; ~ **the house of**
    apud (acc); ~ **all events** saltem; see also **dawn,**
    hand, house etc.
atheism n deōs esse negāre.
atheist n atheos m; **be an ~** deōs esse negāre.
Athenian adj Atheniensis.
Athens n Athenae fpl; **at/from ~** Athenis; **to ~**
    Athenas.
athirst adj sitiens; (fig) avidus.
athlete n athlēta m.
athletic adj rōbustus, lacertōsus.
athletics n athlētica ntpl.
athwart prep trāns (acc).
atlas n orbis terrārum dēscrīptiō f.
atmosphere n āēr m.
atom n atomus f, corpus indīviduum nt.
atone vi: ~ **for** expiāre.
atonement n expiātiō f, piāculum nt.
atrocious adj immānis, nefārius, scelestus.
atrociously adv nefāriē, scelestē.
atrociousness n immānitās f.
atrocity n nefas nt, scelus nt, flāgitium nt.
atrophy n marcēscere.
attach vt adiungere, adfīgere, illigāre; (word)
    subicere; ~**ed to** amāns (gen).
attachment n vinculum nt; amor m, studium
    nt.
attack vt oppugnāre, adorīrī, aggredī;
    impetum facere in (acc); (speech) īnsequī,
    invehī in (acc); (disease) ingruere in (acc) ♦ n
    impetus m, oppugnātiō f, incursus m.
attacker n oppugnātor m.
attain vt adsequī, adipīscī, cōnsequī; ~ **to**
    pervenīre ad.
attainable adj impetrābilis, in prōmptū.
attainder n: **bill of ~** prīvilēgium nt.
attainment n adeptiō f.
attainments npl doctrīna f, ērudītiō f.
attaint vt māiestātis condemnāre.

attempt *vt* cōnārī, temptāre; (*with effort*) mōlīrī ♦ *n* cōnātus *m*, inceptum *nt*; (*risk*) perīculum *nt*; **first ~s** rudīmenta *ntpl*.

attend *vt* (*meeting*) adesse (*dat*), interesse (*dat*); (*person*) prōsequī, comitārī; (*master*) appārēre (*dat*); (*invalid*) cūrāre ♦ *vi* animum advertere, animum attendere; **~ to** (*task*) adcūrāre; **~ upon** prōsequī, adsectārī; **~ the lectures of** audīre; **not ~** aliud agere; **~ first to** praevertere (*dat*); **well ~ed** frequēns; **thinly ~ed** īnfrequēns.

attendance *n* (*courtesy*) adsectātiō *f*; (*MED*) cūrātiō *f*; (*service*) apparitiō *f*; **constant ~** adsiduitās *f*; **full ~** frequentia *f*; **poor ~** īnfrequentia *f*; **dance ~ on** haerēre (*dat*).

attendant *n* famulus *m*, minister *m*; (*on candidate*) sectātor *m*; (*on nobleman*) adsectātor *m*; (*on magistrate*) apparitor *m*.

attention *n* animadversiō *f*, animī attentiō *f*; (*to work*) cūra *f*; (*respect*) observantia *f*; **attract ~** digitō mōnstrārī; **call ~ to** indicāre; **pay ~ to** animadvertere, observāre; ratiōnem habēre (*gen*); **~ !** hōc age!

attentive *adj* intentus; (*to work*) dīligēns.

attentively *adv* intentē, dīligenter.

attenuate *vt* attenuāre.

attest *vt* cōnfirmāre, testārī.

attestation *n* testificātiō *f*.

attestor *n* testis *m*.

attic *n* cēnāculum *nt*.

attire *vt* vestīre ♦ *n* vestis *f*, habitus *m*.

attitude *n* (*body*) gestus *m*, status *m*, habitus *m*; (*mind*) ratiō *f*.

attorney *n* āctor *m*; advocātus *m*.

attract *vt* trahere, attrahere, adlicere.

attraction *n* vīs attrahendī; illecebra *f*, invītāmentum *nt*.

attractive *adj* suāvis, venustus, lepidus.

attractively *adv* suāviter, vēnustē, lepidē.

attractiveness *n* venustās *f*, lepōs *m*.

attribute *vt* tribuere, attribuere, adsignāre ♦ *n* proprium *nt*.

attrition *n* attrītus *m*.

attune *vt* modulārī.

auburn *adj* flāvus.

auction *n* auctiō *f*; (*public*) hasta *f*; **hold an ~** auctiōnem facere; **sell by ~** sub hastā vēndere.

auctioneer *n* praecō *m*.

audacious *adj* audāx; protervus.

audaciously *adv* audācter, protervē.

audacity *n* audācia *f*, temeritās *f*.

audible *adj*: **be ~** exaudīrī posse.

audibly *adv* clārā vōce.

audience *n* audītōrēs *mpl*; (*interview*) aditus *m*; **give an ~ to** admittere.

audit *vt* īnspicere ♦ *n* ratiōnum īnspectiō *f*.

auditorium *n* cavea *f*.

auditory *adj* audītōrius.

auger *n* terebra *f*.

augment *vt* augēre, adaugēre ♦ *vi* crēscere, augērī.

augmentation *n* incrēmentum *nt*.

augur *n* augur *m*; **~'s staff** lituus *m* ♦ *vi* augurārī; (*fig*) portendere.

augural *adj* augurālis.

augurship *n* augurātus *m*.

augury *n* augurium *nt*, auspicium *nt*; ōmen *nt*; **take ~ies** augurārī; **after taking ~ies** augurātō.

august *adj* augustus.

August *n* mēnsis Augustus, Sextīlis; **of ~** Sextīlis.

aunt *n* (*paternal*) amita *f*; (*maternal*) mātertera *f*.

auspices *n* auspicium *nt*; **take ~** auspicārī; **after taking ~** auspicātō; **without taking ~** inauspicātō.

auspicious *adj* faustus, fēlīx.

auspiciously *adv* fēlīciter, prosperē.

austere *adj* austērus, sevērus, dūrus.

austerely *adv* sevērē.

austerity *n* sevēritās *f*, dūritia *f*.

authentic *adj* vērus, certus.

authenticate *vt* recognōscere.

authenticity *n* auctōritās *f*, fidēs *f*.

author *n* auctor *m*, inventor *m*; scrīptor *m*.

authoress *n* auctor *f*.

authoritative *adj* fīdus; imperiōsus.

authority *n* auctōritās *f*, potestās *f*, iūs *nt*; (*MIL*) imperium *nt*; (*LIT*) auctor *m*, scrīptor *m*; **enforce ~** iūs suum exsequī; **have great ~** multum pollēre; **on Caesar's ~** auctōre Caesare; **an ~ on** perītus (*gen*).

authorize *vt* potestātem facere (*dat*), mandāre; (*law*) sancīre.

autobiography *n* dē vītā suā scrīptus liber *m*.

autocracy *n* imperium singulāre *nt*, tyrannis *f*.

autocrat *n* tyrannus *m*, dominus *m*.

autocratic *adj* imperiōsus.

autograph *n* manus *f*, chīrographum *nt*.

automatic *adj* necessārius.

automatically *adv* necessāriō.

autonomous *adj* līber.

autonomy *n* lībertās *f*.

Autumn *n* auctumnus *m*.

autumnal *adj* auctumnālis.

auxiliaries *npl* auxilia *ntpl*, auxiliāriī *mpl*.

auxiliary *adj* auxiliāris ♦ *n* adiūtor *m*; **~ forces** auxilia *ntpl*; novae copiae *fpl*.

avail *vi* valēre ♦ *vt* prōdesse (*dat*); **~ oneself of** ūtī (*abl*) ♦ *n* ūsus *m*; **of no ~** frustrā.

available *adj* ad manum, in prōmptū.

avalanche *n* montis ruīna *f*.

avarice *n* avāritia *f*, cupiditās *f*.

avaricious *adj* avārus, cupidus.

avariciously *adv* avārē.

avenge *vt* ulcīscī (+ *abl*), vindicāre.

avenger *n* ultor *m*, vindex *m*.

avenue *n* xystus *m*; (*fig*) aditus *m*, iānua *f*.

aver *vt* adfirmāre, adsevērāre.

average *n* medium *nt*; **on the ~** ferē.

averse *adj* āversus (ab); **be ~ to** abhorrēre ab.

aversion *n* odium *nt*, fastīdium *nt*.

avert *vt* arcēre, dēpellere; (*by prayer*) dēprecārī.

aviary n aviārium nt.
avid adj avidus.
avidity n aviditās f.
avidly adv avidē.
avoid vt vītāre, fugere, dēclīnāre; (battle) dētrectāre.
avoidance n fuga f, dēclīnātiō f.
avow vt fatērī, cōnfitērī.
avowal n cōnfessiō f.
avowed adj apertus.
avowedly adv apertē, palam.
await vt exspectāre; (future) manēre.
awake vt suscitāre, exsuscitāre ♦ vi expergīscī ♦ adj vigil.
awaken vt exsuscitāre.
award vt tribuere; (law) adiūdicāre ♦ n (decision) arbitrium nt, iūdicium nt; (thing) praemium nt.
aware adj gnārus ♦ adj conscius (gen); be ~ scīre; become ~ of percipere.
away adv ā-, ab- (in cpd); be ~ abesse ab (abl); far ~ procul, longē; make ~ with dē mediō tollere.
awe n formīdō f, reverentia f, rēligiō f; stand in ~ of verērī; (gods) venerārī.
awe-struck adj stupidus.
awful adj terribilis, formīdolōsus, dīrus.
awfully adv formīdolōsē.
awhile adv aliquamdiū, aliquantisper, parumper.
awkward adj incallidus, inconcinnus; (to handle) inhabilis; (fig) molestus.
awkwardly adv incallidē, imperītē.
awkwardness n imperītia f, īnscītia f.
awl n sūbula f.
awning n vēlum nt.
awry adj prāvus, dissidēns.
axe n secūris f.
axiom n prōnūntiātum nt, sententia f.
axiomatic adj ēvidēns, manifestus.
axis n axis m.
axle n axis m.
aye adv semper; for ~ in aeternum.
azure adj caeruleus.

B, b

baa vi bālāre ♦ n bālātus m.
babble vi garrīre, blaterāre.
babbler n garrulus m.
babbling adj garrulus.
babe n īnfāns m/f.
babel n dissonae vōcēs fpl.
baboon n sīmia f.
baby n īnfāns m/f.
Bacchanalian adj Bacchicus.
Bacchante n Baccha f.

bachelor n caelebs m; (degree) baccalaureus m.
back n tergum nt; (animal) dorsum nt; (head) occipitium nt; at one's ~ ā tergō; behind one's ~ (fig) clam (acc); put one's ~ up stomachum movēre (dat); turn one's ~ on sē āvertere ab ♦ adj āversus, postīcus ♦ adv retrō, retrōrsum, re- (in cpds) ♦ vt obsecundāre (dat), adesse (dat); ~ water inhibēre rēmīs, inhibēre nāvem ♦ vi: ~ out of dētrectāre, dēfugere.
backbite vt obtrectāre (dat), maledīcere (dat).
backbone n spīna f.
backdoor n postīcum nt.
backer n fautor m.
background n recessus m, umbra f.
backing n fidēs f, favor m.
backslide vi dēscīscere.
backward adj āversus; (slow) tardus; (late) sērus.
backwardness n tardītās f, pigritia f.
backwards adv retrō, retrōrsum.
bacon n lārdum nt.
bad adj malus, prāvus, improbus, turpis; go ~ corrumpī; be ~ for obesse (dat), nocēre (dat).
badge n īnsigne nt, īnfula f.
badger n mēles f ♦ vt sollicitāre.
badly adv male, prāvē, improbē, turpiter.
badness n prāvitās f, nēquitia f, improbitās f.
baffle vt ēlūdere, fallere, frustrārī.
bag n saccus m, folliculus m; hand~ mantica f.
bagatelle n nūgae fpl, floccus m.
baggage n impedīmenta ntpl, vāsa ntpl, sarcinae fpl; ~ train impedīmenta ntpl; without ~ expedītus.
bail n vadimōnium nt; (person) vas m; become ~ for spondēre prō (abl); accept ~ for vadārī; keep one's ~ vadimōnium obīre ♦ vt spondēre prō (abl).
bailiff n (POL) apparitor m; (private) vīlicus m.
bait n esca f, illecebra f ♦ vt lacessere.
bake vt coquere, torrēre.
bakehouse n pistrīna f.
baker n pistor m.
bakery n pistrīna f.
balance n (scales) lībra f, trutina f; (equilibrium) lībrāmentum nt; (money) reliqua ntpl ♦ vt lībrāre; (fig) compēnsāre; the account ~s ratiō cōnstat.
balance sheet n ratiō acceptī et expēnsī.
balcony n podium nt, Maeniānum nt.
bald adj calvus; (style) āridus, iēiūnus.
baldness n calvitium nt; (style) iēiūnitās f.
bale n fascis m; ~ out vt exhaurīre.
baleful adj fūnestus, perniciōsus, tristis.
balk n tignum nt ♦ vt frustrārī, dēcipere.
ball n globus m; (play) pila f; (wool) glomus nt; (dance) saltātiō f.
ballad n carmen nt.
ballast n saburra f.
ballet n saltātiō f.
ballot n suffrāgium nt.
ballot box urna f.
balm n unguentum nt; (fig) sōlātium nt.
balmy adj lēnis, suāvis.

balsam n balsamum nt.
balustrade n cancellī mpl.
bamboozle vt cōnfundere.
ban vt interdīcere (dat), vetāre ♦ n interdictum nt.
banal adj trītus.
banana n ariēna f; (tree) pāla f.
band n vinculum nt, redimīculum nt; (head) īnfula f; (men) caterva f, manus f, grex f ♦ vi: ~ **together** cōnsociārī.
bandage n fascia f, īnfula f ♦ vt obligāre, adligāre.
bandbox n: **out of a ~** (fig) dē capsulā.
bandeau n redimīculum nt.
bandit n latrō m.
bandy vt iactāre; ~ **words** altercārī ♦ adj vārus.
bane n venēnum nt, pestis f, perniciēs f.
baneful adj perniciōsus, pestifer.
bang vt pulsāre ♦ n fragor m.
bangle n armilla f.
banish vt pellere, expellere, ēicere; (law) aquā et ignī interdīcere (dat); (temporarily) relēgāre; (feeling) abstergēre.
banishment n (act) aquae et ignis interdictiō f; relēgātiō f; (state) exsilium nt, fuga f.
bank n (earth) agger m; (river) rīpa f; (money) argentāria f.
banker n argentārius m; (public) mēnsārius m.
bankrupt adj: **be ~** solvendō nōn esse; **declare oneself ~** bonam cōpiam ēiūrāre; **go ~** dēcoquere ♦ n dēcoctor m.
banner n vexillum nt.
banquet n cēna f, epulae fpl; convīvium nt; (religious) daps f ♦ vi epulārī.
banter n cavillātiō f ♦ vi cavillārī.
baptism n baptisma nt.
baptize vt baptizāre.
bar n (door) sera f; (gate) claustrum nt; (metal) later m; (wood) asser m; (lever) vectis m; (obstacle) impedīmentum nt; (law-court) cancellī mpl; (barristers) advocātī mpl; (profession) forum nt; **of the ~** forēnsis; **practise at the ~** causās agere.
bar vt (door) obserāre; (way) obstāre (dat), interclūdere, prohibēre; (exception) excipere, exclūdere.
barb n aculeus m, dēns m, hāmus m.
barbarian n barbarus m ♦ adj barbarus.
barbarism n barbaria f.
barbarity n saevitia f, ferōcia f, immānitās f, inhūmānitās f.
barbarous adj barbarus, saevus, immānis, inhūmānus.
barbarously adv barbarē, inhūmānē.
barbed adj hāmātus.
barber n tōnsor m; ~'**s shop** tōnstrīna f.
bard n vātēs m/f; (Gallic) bardus m.
bare adj nūdus; (mere) merus; **lay ~** nūdāre, aperīre, dētegere ♦ vt nūdāre.
barefaced adj impudēns.
barefoot adj nūdis pedibus.
bare-headed adj capite aperto.
barely adv vix.

bargain n pactum nt, foedus nt; **make a ~** pacīscī; **make a bad ~** male emere; **into the ~** grātiīs ♦ vi pacīscī.
barge n linter f.
bark n cortex m; (dog) lātrātus m; (ship) nāvis f, ratis f ♦ vi lātrāre.
barking n latrātus m.
barley n hordeum nt; **of ~** hordeāceus.
barn n horreum nt.
barrack vt obstrepere (dat).
barracks n castra ntpl.
barrel n cūpa f; ligneum vās nt.
barren adj sterilis.
barrenness n sterilitās f.
barricade n claustrum nt, mūnīmentum nt ♦ vt obsaepīre, obstruere; ~ **off** intersaepīre.
barrier n impedīmentum nt; (racecourse) carcer m.
barrister n advocātus m, patrōnus m, causidicus m.
barrow n ferculum nt; (mound) tumulus m.
barter vt mūtāre ♦ vi mercēs mūtāre ♦ n mūtātiō f, commercium nt.
base adj turpis, vīlis; (birth) humilis, ignōbilis; (coin) adulterīnus.
base n fundāmentum nt; (statue) basis f; (hill) rādīcēs fpl; (MIL) castra ntpl.
baseless adj falsus, inānis.
basely adv turpiter.
basement n basis f; (storey) īmum tabulātum nt.
baseness n turpitūdō f.
bashful adj pudīcus, verēcundus.
bashfulness n pudor m, verēcundia f.
basic adj prīmus.
basin n alveolus m, pelvis f; **wash~** aquālis m.
basis n fundāmentum nt.
bask vi aprīcārī.
basket n corbis f, fiscus m; (for bread) canistrum nt; (for wool) quasillum nt.
basking n aprīcātiō f.
bas-relief n toreuma nt.
bass adj (voice) gravis.
bastard adj nothus.
bastion n prōpugnāculum nt.
bat n vespertīliō m; (games) clāva f.
batch n numerus m.
Bath n Aquae Sulis fpl.
bath n balneum nt; (utensil) lābrum nt, lavātiō f; **Turkish ~** Lacōnicum nt; **cold ~** frīgidārium nt; **hot ~** calidārium nt; ~ **superintendent** balneātor m ♦ vt lavāre.
bathe vt lavāre ♦ vi lavārī, perluī.
bathroom n balneāria ntpl.
baths n (public ~) balneae fpl.
batman n cālō m.
baton n virga f, scīpiō m.
battalion n cohors f.
batter vt quassāre, pulsāre, verberāre.
battering ram n ariēs m.
battery n (assault) vīs f.
battle n pugna f, proelium nt, certāmen nt; **a ~ was fought** pugnatum est; **pitched ~** iūstum

proelium; **line of ~** aciēs *f*; **drawn ~** anceps proelium ♦ *vi* pugnāre, contendere; **~ order** aciēs *f*.

battle-axe *n* bipennis *f*.

battlefield, battle-line *n* aciēs *f*.

battlement *n* pinna *f*.

bawl *vt* vōciferārī, clāmitāre.

bay *n* (*sea*) sinus *m*; (*tree*) laurus *f*, laurea *f*; **of ~** laureus; **at ~** interclūsus ♦ *adj* (*colour*) spādīx ♦ *vi* (*dog*) lātrāre.

be *vi* esse; (*CIRCS*) versārī; (*condition*) sē habēre; **~ at** adesse (*dat*); **~ amongst** interesse (*dat*); **~ in** inesse (*dat*); **consul-to–~** cōnsul dēsignātus; **how are you?** quid agis?; **so ~ it** estō; *see also* **absent, here** etc.

beach *n* lītus *nt*, acta *f* ♦ *vt* (*ship*) subdūcere.

beacon *n* ignis *m*.

bead *n* pilula *f*.

beadle *n* apparitor *m*.

beak *n* rōstrum *nt*.

beaked *adj* rōstrātus.

beaker *n* cantharus *m*, scyphus *m*.

beam *n* (*wood*) trabs *f*, tignum *nt*; (*balance*) iugum *nt*; (*light*) radius *m*; (*ship*) latus *nt*; **on the ~** ā latere ♦ *vi* fulgēre; (*person*) adrīdēre.

beaming *adj* hilaris.

bean *n* faba *f*.

bear *n* ursus *m*, ursa *f*; **Great B~** septentriōnēs *mpl*, Arctos *f*; **Little B~** septentriō minor *m*, Cynosūra *f*; **~'s** ursīnus ♦ *vt* (*carry*) ferre, portāre; (*endure*) ferre, tolerāre, patī; (*produce*) ferre, fundere; (*child*) parere; **~ down upon** appropinquāre; **~ off** ferre; **~ out** *vt* arguere; **~ up** *vi*: **~ up under** obsistere (*dat*), sustinēre; **~ upon** innītī (*dat*); (*refer*) pertinēre ad; **~ with** *vt fus* indulgēre (*dat*); **~ oneself** sē gerere; **I cannot ~ to** addūcī nōn possum ut.

bearable *adj* tolerābilis.

beard *n* barba *f* ♦ *vt* ultrō lacessere.

bearded *adj* barbātus.

beardless *adj* imberbis.

bearer *n* bāiulus *m*; (*letter*) tabellārius *m*; (*litter*) lectīcārius *m*; (*news*) nūntius *m*.

bearing *n* (*person*) gestus *m*, vultus *m*; (*direction*) regiō *f*; **have no ~ on** nihil pertinēre ad; **I have lost my ~s** ubi sim nesciō.

beast *n* bestia *f*; (*large*) bēlua *f*; (*wild*) fera *f*; (*domestic*) pecus *f*.

beastliness *n* foedītās *f*, stuprum *nt*.

beastly *adj* foedus.

beast of burden *n* iūmentum *nt*.

beat *n* ictus *m*; (*heart*) palpitātiō *f*; (*music*) percussiō *f*; (*oars, pulse*) pulsus *m*.

beat *vt* ferīre, percutere, pulsāre; (*the body in grief*) plangere; (*punish*) caedere; (*whip*) verberāre; (*conquer*) vincere, superāre ♦ *vi* palpitāre, micāre; **~ back** repellere; **~ in** perfringere; **~ out** excutere; (*metal*) extundere; **~ a retreat** receptuī canere; **~ about the bush** circuitiōne ūtī; **be ~en** vāpulāre; **dead ~** cōnfectus.

beating *n* verbera *ntpl*; (*defeat*) clādēs *f*; (*time*) percussiō *f*; **get a ~** vāpulāre.

beatitude *n* beātitūdō *f*, fēlīcitās *f*.

beau *n* nitidus homō *m*; (*lover*) amāns *m*.

beauteous *adj* pulcher, fōrmōsus.

beautiful *adj* pulcher, formōsus; (*looks*) decōrus; (*scenery*) amoenus.

beautifully *adv* pulchrē.

beautify *vt* exōrnāre, decorāre.

beauty *n* fōrma *f*, pulchritūdō *f*, amoenitās *f*.

beaver *n* castor *m*, fiber *m*; (*helmet*) buccula *f*.

becalmed *adj* ventō dēstitūtus.

because *conj* quod, quia, quōniam (+ *indic*), quippe quī; **~ of** propter (*acc*).

beck *n* nūtus *m*.

beckon *vt* innuere, vocāre.

become *vi* fierī; **what will ~ of me?** quid me fīet? ♦ *vt* decēre, convenīre in (*acc*).

becoming *adj* decēns, decōrus.

becomingly *adv* decōrē, convenienter.

bed *n* cubīle *nt*, lectus *m*, lectulus *m*; **go to ~** cubitum īre; **make a ~** lectum sternere; **be ~ridden** lectō tenērī; **camp ~** grabātus *m*; **flower~** pulvīnus *m*; **marriage ~** lectus geniālis *m*; **river~** alveus *m*.

bedaub *vt* illinere, oblinere.

bedclothes *n* strāgula *ntpl*.

bedding *n* strāgula *ntpl*.

bedeck *vt* ōrnāre, exōrnāre.

bedew *vt* inrōrāre.

bedim *vt* obscūrāre.

bedpost *n* fulcrum *nt*.

bedraggled *adj* sordidus, madidus.

bedroom *n* cubiculum *nt*.

bedstead *n* sponda *f*.

bee *n* apis *f*; **queen ~** rēx *m*.

beech *n* fāgus *f* ♦ *adj* fāginus.

beef *n* būbula *f*.

beehive *n* alvus *f*.

beekeeper *n* apiārius *m*.

beer *n* cervīsia *f*, fermentum *nt*.

beet *n* bēta *f*.

beetle *n* (*insect*) scarabaeus *m*; (*implement*) fistūca *f*.

beetling *adj* imminēns, mināx.

befall *vi*, *vt* accidere, ēvenīre (*dat*); (*good*) contingere (*dat*).

befit *vt* decēre, convenīre in (*acc*).

before *adv* ante, anteā, antehāc ♦ *prep* ante (*acc*); (*place*) prō (*abl*); (*presence*) apud (*acc*), cōram (*abl*) ♦ *conj* antequam, priusquam.

beforehand *adv* ante, anteā, prae (*in cpd*).

befoul *vt* inquināre, foedāre.

befriend *vt* favēre (*dat*), adiuvāre; (*in trouble*) adesse (*dat*).

beg *vt* ōrāre, obsecrāre, precārī, poscere ab, petere ab; **~ for** petere ♦ *vi* mendīcāre.

beget *vt* gignere, prōcreāre, generāre.

begetter *n* generātor *m*, creātor *m*.

beggar *m* mendīcus *m*.

beggarly *adj* mendīcus, indigēns.

beggary *n* mendīcitās *f*, indigentia *f*.

begin *vi*, *vt* incipere, coepisse; (*speech*)

exōrdīrī; (*plan*) īnstituere, incohāre; (*time*) inīre; ~ **with** incipere ab.

beginning *n* initium *nt*, prīncipium *nt*, exōrdium *nt*, inceptiō *f*; (*learning*) rudīmenta *ntpl*, elementa *ntpl*; (*origin*) orīgō *f*, fōns *m*; **at the ~ of spring** ineunte vēre.

begone *interj* apage, tē āmovē.

begotten *adj* genitus, nātus.

begrudge *vt* invidēre (*dat*).

beguile *vt* dēcipere, fallere.

behalf *n*: **on ~ of** prō (*abl*); **on my ~** meō nōmine.

behave *vi* sē gerere, sē praebēre (*with adj*); **well ~d** bene mōrātus.

behaviour *n* mōrēs *mpl*.

behead *vt* dētruncāre, secūrī percutere.

behest *n* iūssum *nt*.

behind *adv* pōne, post, ā tergō ♦ *prep* post (*acc*), pōne (*acc*).

behindhand *adv* sērō; **be ~** parum prōficere.

behold *vt* aspicere, cōnspicere, intuērī ♦ *interj* ecce, ēn.

beholden *adj* obnoxius, obstrictus, obligātus.

behoof *n* ūsus *m*.

behove *vt* oportēre.

being *n* (*life*) animātiō *f*; (*nature*) nātūra *f*; (*person*) homō *m/f*.

bejewelled *adj* gemmeus, gemmātus.

belabour *vt* verberāre, caedere.

belated *adj* sērus.

belch *vi* ructāre, ēructāre.

beldam *n* anus *f*.

beleaguer *vt* obsidēre, circumsedēre.

belie *vt* abhorrēre ab, repugnāre.

belief *n* fidēs *f*, opīniō *f*; (*opinion*) sententia *f*; **to the best of my ~** ex animī meī sententiā; **past ~ incrēdibilis.**

believe *vt*, *vi* (*thing*) crēdere; (*person*) crēdere (*dat*); (*suppose*) crēdere, putāre, arbitrārī, opīnārī; **~ in gods** deōs esse crēdere; **make ~** simulāre.

believer *n* deōrum cultor *m*; Christiānus *m*.

belike *adv* fortasse.

belittle *vt* obtrectāre.

bell *n* tintinnābulum *nt*; (*public*) campāna *f*.

belle *n* fōrmōsa *f*, pulchra *f*.

belles-lettres *n* litterae *fpl*.

bellicose *adj* ferōx.

belligerent *adj* bellī particeps.

bellow *vi* rūdere, mūgīre ♦ *n* mūgītus *m*.

bellows *n* follis *m*.

belly *n* abdōmen *nt*, venter *m*; (*sail*) sinus *m* ♦ *vi* tumēre.

belong *vi* esse (*gen*), proprium esse (*gen*), inesse (*dat*); (*concern*) attinēre, pertinēre.

belongings *n* bona *ntpl*.

beloved *adj* cārus, dīlectus, grātus.

below *adv* īnfrā, subter ♦ *adj* īnferus ♦ *prep* īnfrā (*acc*), sub (*abl*, *acc*).

belt *n* zōna *f*; (*sword*) balteus *m*.

bemoan *vt* dēplōrāre, lāmentārī.

bemused *adj* stupefactus, stupidus.

bench *n* subsellium *nt*; (*rowing*) trānstrum *nt*;

(*law*) iūdicēs *mpl*; **seat on the ~** iūdicātus *m*.

bend *vt* flectere, curvāre, inclīnāre; (*bow*) intendere; (*course*) tendere, flectere; (*mind*) intendere ♦ *vi* sē īnflectere; (*person*) sē dēmittere; **~ back** reflectere; **~ down** *vi* dēflectere; sē dēmittere ♦ *n* flexus *m*, ānfrāctus *m*.

beneath *adv* subter ♦ *prep* sub (*acc or abl*).

benediction *n* bonae precēs *fpl*.

benedictory *adj* faustus.

benefaction *n* beneficium *nt*, dōnum *nt*.

benefactor *n* patrōnus *m*; **be a ~** bene merērī (dē).

beneficence *n* beneficentia *f*, līberālitās *f*.

beneficent *adj* beneficus.

beneficial *adj* ūtilis, salūbris.

benefit *n* beneficium *nt*; (*derived*) fructus *m*; **have the ~ of** fruī (*abl*) ♦ *vt* prōdesse (*dat*), usuī esse (*dat*).

benevolence *n* benevolentia *f*, benignitās *f*.

benevolent *adj* benevolus, benignus.

benevolently *adv* benevolē, benignē.

benighted *adj* nocte oppressus; (*fig*) ignārus, indoctus.

benign *adj* benignus, cōmis.

bent *n* (*mind*) inclīnātiō *f*, ingenium *nt* ♦ *adj* curvus, flexus; (*mind*) attentus; **be ~ on** studēre (*dat*).

benumb *vt* stupefacere.

benumbed *adj* stupefactus, torpidus; **be ~** torpēre.

bequeath *vt* lēgāre.

bequest *n* lēgātum *nt*.

bereave *vt* orbāre, prīvāre.

bereavement *n* damnum *nt*.

bereft *adj* orbus, orbātus, prīvātus.

berry *n* bāca *f*.

berth *n* statiō *f*; **give a wide ~ to** dēvītāre.

beryl *n* bēryllus *m*.

beseech *vt* implōrāre, ōrāre, obsecrāre.

beset *vt* obsidēre, circumsedēre.

beside *prep* ad (*acc*), apud (*acc*); (*close*) iuxtā (*acc*); **~ the point** nihil ad rem; **be ~ oneself** nōn esse apud sē.

besides *adv* praetereā, accēdit quod; (*in addition*) īnsuper ♦ *prep* praeter (*acc*).

besiege *vt* obsidēre, circumsedēre.

besieger *n* obsessor *m*.

besmear *vt* illinere.

besmirch *vt* maculāre.

besom *n* scōpae *fpl*.

besotted *adj* stupidus.

bespatter *vt* aspergere.

bespeak *vt* (*order*) imperāre; (*denote*) significāre.

besprinkle *vt* aspergere.

best *adj* optimus; **the ~ part** māior pars ♦ *n* flōs *m*, rōbur *nt*; **do one's ~** prō virīlī parte agere; **do one's ~ to** operam dare ut; **have the ~ of it** vincere; **make the ~ of (a situation)** aequō animō accipere; **to the ~ of one's ability** prō virīlī parte; **to the ~ of my knowledge** quod sciam ♦ *adv* optimē.

bestial *adj* foedus.
bestir *vt* movēre; ~ **oneself** expergīscī.
bestow *vt* dōnāre, tribuere, dare, cōnferre.
bestride *vt* (*horse*) sedēre in (*abl*).
bet *n* pignus *nt* ♦ *vt* oppōnere ♦ *vi* pignore
   contendere.
betake *vt* cōnferre, recipere; ~ **o.s.** sē
   cōnferre.
bethink *vt*: ~ **oneself** sē colligere; ~ **oneself of**
   respicere.
betide *vi* accidere, ēvenīre.
betoken *vt* significāre; (*foretell*) portendere.
betray *vt* prōdere, trādere; (*feelings*) arguere;
   without ~ing one's trust salvā fidē.
betrayal *n* prōditiō *f*.
betrayer *n* prōditor *m*; (*informer*) index *m*.
betroth *vt* spondēre, dēspondēre.
betrothal *n* spōnsālia *ntpl*.
better *adj* melior; **it is ~ to** praestat (*infin*); **get
   the ~ of** vincere, superāre; **I am ~** (*in health*)
   melius est mihī; **I had ~ go** praestat īre; **get ~**
   convalēscere; **think ~ of** sententiam mūtāre
   dē ♦ *adv* melius ♦ *vt* corrigere; ~ **oneself**
   prōficere.
betterment *n* prōfectus *m*.
between *prep* inter (*acc*).
beverage *n* pōtiō *f*.
bevy *n* manus *f*, grex *f*.
bewail *vt* dēflēre, lāmentārī, dēplōrāre.
beware *vt* cavēre.
bewilder *vt* cōnfundere, perturbāre.
bewildered *adj* attonitus.
bewilderment *n* perturbātiō *f*, admīrātiō *f*.
bewitch *vt* fascināre; (*fig*) dēlēnīre.
beyond *adv* ultrā, suprā ♦ *prep* ultrā (*acc*),
   extrā (*acc*); (*motion*) trāns (*acc*); (*amount*)
   ultrā, suprā (*acc*); **go/pass ~** excēdere,
   ēgredī.
bezel *n* pāla *f*.
bias *n* inclīnātiō *f*; (*party*) favor *m* ♦ *vt*
   inclīnāre.
biassed *adj* prōpēnsior.
bibber *n* pōtor *m*, pōtātor *m*.
Bible *n* litterae sacrae *fpl*.
bibulous *adj* bibulus.
bicephalous *adj* biceps.
bicker *vi* altercārī, iūrgāre.
bid *vt* iubēre; (*guest*) vocāre, invītāre ♦ *vi* (*at
   auction*) licērī; ~ **for** licērī; ~ **good day**
   salvēre iubēre; **he ~s fair to make progress**
   spēs est eum prōfecturum esse.
biddable *adj* docilis.
bidding *n* iussum *nt*; (*auction*) licitātiō *f*.
bide *vt* manēre, opperīrī.
biennial *adj* biennālis.
bier *n* ferculum *nt*.
bifurcate *vi* sē scindere.
bifurcation *n* (*road*) trivium *nt*.
big *adj* māgnus, grandis, amplus; (*with child*)
   gravida; **very ~** permāgnus; **talk ~** glōriārī.
bight *n* sinus *m*.
bigness *n* māgnitūdō *f*, amplitūdō *f*.
bigot *n* nimis obstinātus fautor *m*.

bigoted *adj* contumāx.
bigotry *n* contumācia *f*, nimia obstinātiō *f*.
bile *n* bīlis *f*, fel *nt*.
bilgewater *n* sentīna *f*.
bilk *vt* fraudāre.
bill *n* (*bird*) rōstrum *nt*; (*implement*) falx *f*; (*law*)
   rogātiō *f*, lēx *f*; (*money*) syngrapha *f*; (*notice*)
   libellus *m*, titulus *m*; **introduce a ~** populum
   rogāre, lēgem ferre; **carry a ~** lēgem
   perferre.
billet *n* hospitium *nt* ♦ *vt* in hospitia dīvidere.
billhook *n* falx *f*.
billow *n* fluctus *m*.
billowy *adj* undōsus.
billy goat *n* caper *m*.
bin *n* lacus *m*.
bind *vt* adligāre, dēligāre, vincīre; (*by oath*)
   adigere; (*by obligation*) obligāre,
   obstringere; (*wound*) obligāre; ~ **fast**
   dēvincīre; ~ **together** conligāre; ~ **over** *vt*
   vadārī.
binding *n* compāgēs *f* ♦ *adj* (*law*) ratus; **it is ~
   on** oportet.
bindweed *n* convolvulus *m*.
biographer *n* vītae nārrātor *m*.
biography *n* vīta *f*.
bipartite *adj* bipartītus.
biped *n* bipēs *m*.
birch *n* bētula *f*; (*flogging*) virgae ulmeae *fpl*.
bird *n* avis *f*; **~s of a feather** parēs cum paribus
   facillimē congregantur; **kill two ~s with one
   stone** ūnō saltū duōs aprōs capere, dē eādem
   fidēliā duōs parietēs dealbāre; **~'s-eye view
   of** dēspectus in (*acc*).
birdcatcher *n* auceps *m*.
birdlime *n* viscum *nt*.
birth *n* (*act*) partus *m*; (*origin*) genus *nt*; **low ~**
   ignōbilitās *f*; **high ~** nōbilitās *f*; **by ~** nātū,
   ortū.
birthday *n* nātālis *m*.
birthday party *n* nātālicia *ntpl*.
birthplace *n* locus nātālis *m*; (*fig*) incūnābula
   ntpl.
birthright *n* patrimōnium *nt*.
bisect *vt* dīvidere.
bishop *n* epīscopus *m*.
bison *n* ūrus *m*.
bit *n* pars *f*; (*food*) frustum *nt*; (*broken off*)
   fragmentum *nt*; (*horse*) frēnum *nt*; ~ **by ~**
   minūtātim; **a ~** *adv* aliquantulum; **a ~ sad**
   tristior.
bitch *n* canis *f*.
bite *vt* mordēre; (*frost*) ūrere ♦ *n* morsus *m*;
   with a ~ mordicus.
biting *adj* mordāx.
bitter *adj* (*taste*) acerbus, amārus; (*words*)
   asper.
bitterly *adv* acerbē, asperē.
bittern *n* būtiō *m*, ardea *f*.
bitterness *n* acerbitās *f*.
bitumen *n* bitūmen *nt*.
bivouac *n* excubiae *fpl* ♦ *vi* excubāre.
bizarre *adj* īnsolēns.

blab vt, vi garrīre, effūtīre.
black adj (dull) āter; (glossy) niger; (dirt)
sordidus; (eye) līvidus; (looks) trux; ~ **and**
blue līvidus; ♦ n ātrum nt, nigrum nt; **dressed**
in ~ ātrātus; (in mourning) sordidātus.
blackberry n mōrum nt.
blackbird n merula f.
blacken vt nigrāre, nigrum reddere;
(character) īnfāmāre, obtrectāre (dat).
blackguard n scelestus, scelerātus m.
blacking n ātrāmentum nt.
blacklist n prōscrīptiō f.
black magic n magicae artēs fpl.
blackmail n minae fpl ♦ vt minīs cōgere.
black mark n nota f.
blacksmith n faber m.
bladder n vēsīca f.
blade n (grass) herba f; (oar) palma f; (sword)
lāmina f.
blame vt reprehendere, culpāre; **I am to** ~
reus sum ♦ n reprehēnsiō f, culpa f.
blameless adj innocēns.
blamelessly adv innocenter.
blamelessness n innocentia f, integritās f.
blameworthy adj accūsābilis, nocēns.
blanch vi exalbēscere, pallēscere.
bland adj mītis, lēnis.
blandishment n blanditiae fpl.
blank adj vacuus, pūrus; (look) stolidus.
blanket n lōdīx f; **wet** ~ nimium sevērus.
blare vi canere, strīdere ♦ n clangor m, strīdor
m.
blarney n lēnōcinium nt.
blaspheme vi maledīcere.
blasphemous adj maledicus, impius.
blasphemy n maledicta ntpl, impietās f.
blast n flātus m, īnflātus m ♦ vt disicere,
discutere; (crops) rōbīgine adficere.
blatant adj raucus.
blaze n flamma f, ignis m, fulgor m ♦ vi
flāgrāre, ārdēre, fulgēre; ~ **up** exārdēscere
♦ vt: ~ **abroad** pervulgāre.
blazon vt prōmulgāre.
bleach vt candidum reddere.
bleak adj dēsertus, tristis, inamoenus.
bleary-eyed adj lippus.
bleat vi bālāre ♦ n bālātus m.
bleed vi sanguinem fundere ♦ vt sanguinem
mittere (dat); **my heart** ~**s** animus mihī dolet.
bleeding adj crūdus, sanguineus ♦ n sanguinis
missiō f.
blemish n macula f, vitium nt ♦ vt maculāre,
foedāre.
blend vt miscēre, immiscēre, admiscēre ♦ n
coniūnctiō f.
bless vt beāre; laudāre; (ECCL) benedīcere; ~
with augēre (abl); ~ **my soul!** ita mē dī ament!
blessed adj beātus, fortūnātus; (emperors)
dīvus.
blessing n (thing) commodum nt, bonum nt;
(ECCL) benedictiō f.
blight n rōbīgō f, ūrēdō f ♦ vt rōbīgine adficere;
(fig) nocēre (dat).

blind adj caecus; (in one eye) luscus; (fig)
ignārus, stultus; (alley) nōn pervius; (forces)
necessārius; **turn a** ~ **eye to** cōnīvēre in (abl)
♦ vt excaecāre, caecāre; (fig) occaecāre;
(with light) praestringere.
blindfold adj capite obvolūtō.
blindly adv temerē.
blindness n caecitās f; (fig) temeritās f,
īnsipientia f.
blink vi nictāre.
bliss n fēlīcitās f, laetitia f.
blissful adj fēlīx, beātus, laetus.
blissfully adv fēlīciter, beātē.
blister n pustula f.
blithe adj hilaris, laetus.
blithely adv hilare, laetē.
blizzard n hiems f.
bloated adj tumidus, turgidus.
blob n gutta f, particula f.
block n (wood) stīpes m, caudex m; (stone)
massa f; (houses) īnsula f; ~ **letter** quadrāta
littera; **stumbling** ~ offēnsiō f.
block vt claudere, obstruere, interclūdere; ~
the way obstāre.
blockade n obsidiō f; **raise a** ~ obsidiōnem
solvere ♦ vt obsidēre, interclūdere.
blockhead n caudex m, bārō m, truncus m.
blockhouse n castellum nt.
blond adj flāvus.
blood n sanguis m; (shed) cruor m; (murder)
caedēs f; (kin) genus nt; **let** ~ sanguinem
mittere; **staunch** ~ sanguinem supprimere;
bad ~ simultās f; **in cold** ~ cōnsultō; **own flesh**
and ~ cōnsanguineus.
bloodless adj exsanguis; (victory) incruentus.
bloodshed n caedēs f.
bloodshot adj sanguineus.
bloodstained adj cruentus.
bloodsucker n hirūdō f.
bloodthirsty adj sanguinārius.
blood vessel n vēna f.
bloody adj cruentus.
bloom n flōs m; **in** ~ flōrēns ♦ vi flōrēre,
flōrēscere, vigēre.
blossom n flōs m ♦ vi efflōrēscere, flōrēre.
blot n macula f; (erasure) litūra f ♦ vt maculāre;
~ **out** dēlēre, oblitterāre.
blotch n macula f.
blotched adj maculōsus.
blow vt, vi (wind) flāre; (breath) adflāre,
anhēlāre; (instrument) canere; (flower)
efflōrēscere; (nose) ēmungere; ~ **out** vi
exstinguere; ~ **over** vi (storm) cadere; (fig)
abīre; ~ **up** vi īnflāre; (destroy) discutere,
disturbāre ♦ n ictus m; (on the cheek) alapa f;
(fig) plāga f; (misfortune) calamitās f; **aim a** ~
at petere; **come to** ~**s** ad manūs venīre.
blowy adj ventōsus.
bludgeon n fustis m.
blue adj caeruleus; **black and** ~ līvidus; **true** ~
fīdissimus; ~ **blood** nōbilitās f.
bluff n rūpēs f, prōmunturium nt ♦ adj

inurbānus ♦ *vt* fallere, dēcipere, verba dare (*dat*), impōnere (*dat*).

blunder *vi* errāre, offendere ♦ *n* error *m*, errātum *nt*; (*in writing*) mendum *nt*.

blunt *adj* hebes; (*manners*) horridus, rūsticus, inurbānus; **be ~** hebēre ♦ *vt* hebetāre, obtundere, retundere.

bluntly *adv* līberius, plānē et apertē.

blur *n* macula *f* ♦ *vt* obscūrāre.

blurt *vt*: **~ out** ēmittere.

blush *vi* rubēre, ērubēscere ♦ *n* rubor *m*.

bluster *vi* dēclāmitāre, lātrāre.

boa *n* boa *f*.

Boadicea *n* Boudicca *f*.

boar *n* verrēs *m*; (*wild*) aper *m*.

board *n* tabula *f*; (*table*) mēnsa *f*; (*food*) vīctus *m*; (*committee*) concilium *nt*; (*judicial*) quaestiō *f*; (*of ten men*) decemvirī *mpl*; (*gaming*) abacus *m*, alveus *m*; **on ~** in nāvī; **go on ~** in nāvem cōnscendere; **go by the ~** intercidere, perīre; **above ~** sine fraude ♦ *vt* (*building*) contabulāre; (*ship*) cōnscendere; (*person*) vīctum praebēre (*dat*) ♦ *vi*: **~ with** dēvertere ad.

boarder *n* hospes *m*.

boast *vi* glōriārī, sē iactāre; **~ of** glōriārī dē (*abl*) ♦ *n* glōria *f*, glōriātiō *f*, iactātiō *f*.

boastful *adj* glōriōsus.

boastfully *adv* glōriōsē.

boasting *n* glōriātiō *f* ♦ *adj* glōriōsus.

boat *n* linter *f*, scapha *f*, cymba *f*; (*ship*) nāvis *f*; **be in the same ~** (*fig*) in eādem nāvī esse.

boatman *n* nauta *m*.

boatswain *n* hortātor *m*.

bobbin *n* fūsus *m*.

bode *vt* portendere, praesāgīre.

bodiless *adj* sine corpore.

bodily *adj* corporeus.

bodkin *n* acus *f*.

body *n* corpus *nt*; (*dead*) cadāver *nt*; (*small*) corpusculum *nt*; (*person*) homō *m/f*; (*of people*) globus *m*, numerus *m*; (*of troops*) manus *f*, caterva *f*; (*of cavalry*) turma *f*; (*of officials*) collēgium *nt*; (*heavenly*) astrum *nt*; **in a ~** ūniversī, frequentēs.

bodyguard *n* custōs *m*, stīpātōrēs *mpl*; (*emperor's*) praetōriānī *mpl*.

bog *n* palūs *f*.

bogey *n* mōnstrum *nt*.

boggle *vi* tergiversārī, haesitāre.

boggy *adj* palūster.

bogus *adj* falsus, fictus.

Bohemian *adj* līberior, solūtior, libīdinōsus.

boil *vt* coquere; (*liquid*) fervefacere; **~ down** dēcoquere ♦ *vi* fervēre, effervēscere; (*sea*) exaestuāre; (*passion*) exārdēscere, aestuāre; **~ over** effervēscere ♦ *n* (*MED*) fūrunculus *m*.

boiler *n* cortīna *f*.

boiling *adj* (*hot*) fervēns.

boisterous *adj* (*person*) turbulentus, vehemēns; (*sea*) turbidus, agitātus; (*weather*) procellōsus, violentus.

boisterously *adv* turbidē, turbulentē.

boisterousness *n* tumultus *m*, violentia *f*.

bold *adj* audāx, fortis, intrepidus; (*impudent*) impudēns, protervus; (*language*) līber; (*headland*) prōminēns; **make ~** audēre.

boldly *adv* audācter, fortiter, intrepidē; impudenter.

boldness *n* audācia *f*, cōnfīdentia *f*; impudentia *f*, petulantia *f*; (*speech*) lībertās *f*.

bolster *n* pulvīnus *m* ♦ *vt*: **~ up** sustinēre, cōnfirmāre.

bolt *n* (*door*) claustrum *nt*, pessulus *m*, sera *f*; (*missile*) tēlum *nt*, sagitta *f*; (*lightning*) fulmen *nt*; **make a ~ for it** sē prōripere, aufugere; **a ~ from the blue** rēs subita, rēs inopīnāta ♦ *vi* (*door*) obserāre, obdere.

bombard *vt* tormentīs verberāre; (*fig*) lacessere.

bombast *n* ampullae *fpl*.

bombastic *adj* tumidus, īnflātus; **be ~** ampullārī.

bond *n* vinculum *nt*, catēna *f*, compes *f*; (*of union*) cōpula *f*, iugum *nt*, nōdus *m*; (*document*) syngrapha *f*; (*agreement*) foedus *nt* ♦ *adj* servus, addictus.

bondage *n* servitūs *f*, famulātus *m*.

bone *n* os *nt*; (*fish*) spīna *f* ♦ *vt* exossāre.

boneless *adj* exos.

bonfire *n* ignis festus *m*.

bonhomie *n* festīvitās *f*.

bon mot *n* dictum *nt*, sententia *f*.

bonny *adj* pulcher, bellus.

bony *adj* osseus.

boo *vt* explōdere.

book *n* liber *m*; (*small*) libellus *m*; (*scroll*) volūmen *nt*; (*modern form*) cōdex *m*; **~s** (*COMM*) ratiōnēs *fpl*, tabulae *fpl*; **bring to ~** in iūdicium vocāre.

bookbinder *n* glūtinātor *m*.

bookcase *n* librārium *nt*, pēgma *nt*.

bookish *adj* litterārum studiōsus.

book-keeper *n* āctuārius *m*.

bookseller *n* librārius *m*, bibliopōla *m*.

bookshop *n* bibliothēca *f*, librāria taberna *f*.

bookworm *n* tinea *f*.

boom *n* (*spar*) longurius *m*; (*harbour*) ōbex *m/f* ♦ *vi* resonāre.

boon *n* bonum *nt*, beneficium *nt*, dōnum *nt* ♦ *adj* festīvus; **~ companion** sodālis *m*, compōtor *m*.

boor *n* agrestis *m*, rūsticus *m*.

boorish *adj* agrestis, rūsticus, inurbānus.

boorishly *adv* rūsticē.

boost *vt* efferre; (*wares*) vēnditāre.

boot *n* calceus *m*; (*MIL*) caliga *f*; (*rustic*) pērō *m*; (*tragic*) cothurnus *m* ♦ *vi* prōdesse; **to ~** īnsuper, praetereā.

booted *adj* calceātus, caligātus.

booth *n* taberna *f*.

bootless *adj* inūtilis, vānus.

bootlessly *adv* frustrā.

booty *n* praeda *f*, spolia *ntpl*.

border *n* ōra *f*, margō *f*; (*country*) fīnis *m*; (*dress*) limbus *m* ♦ *vt* praetexere, margināre;

fīnīre ♦ *vi*: ~ **on** adiacēre (*dat*), imminēre (*dat*), attingere; (*fig*) fīnitimum esse (*dat*).
bordering *adj* fīnitimus.
bore *vt* perforāre, perterebrāre; (*person*) obtundere, fatīgāre; ~ **out** exterebrāre ♦ *n* terebra *f*; (*hole*) forāmen *nt*; (*person*) homō importūnus *m*, ineptus *m*.
boredom *n* lassitūdō *f*.
borer *n* terebra *f*.
born *adj* nātus; **be** ~ nāscī.
borough *n* mūnicipium *nt*.
borrow *vt* mūtuārī.
borrowed *adj* mūtuus; (*fig*) aliēnus.
borrowing *n* mūtuātiō *f*; (*to pay a debt*) versūra *f*.
bosky *adj* nemorōsus.
bosom *n* sinus *m*; (*fig*) gremium *nt*; ~ **friend** familiāris *m/f*, sodālis *m*; **be a ~ friend of** ab latere esse (*gen*).
boss *n* bulla *f*; (*shield*) umbō *m*.
botanist *n* herbārius *m*.
botany *n* herbāria *f*.
botch *vt* male sarcīre, male gerere.
both *pron* ambō, uterque (*gen* **utriusque**, *each of two*) ♦ *adv*: ~ . . . **and** et . . . et, cum . . . tum.
bother *n* negōtium *nt* ♦ *vt* vexāre, molestus esse (*dat*) ♦ *vi* operam dare.
bothersome *adj* molestus.
bottle *n* lagoena *f*, amphora *f* ♦ *vt* (*wine*) diffundere.
bottom *n* fundus *m*; (*ground*) solum *nt*; (*ship*) carīna *f*; **the ~ of** īmus; **be at the ~ of** (*cause*) auctōrem esse; **go to the ~** pessum īre, perīre; **send to the ~** pessum dare; **from the ~** funditus, ab īnfimō.
bottomless *adj* profundus, fundō carēns.
bottommost *adj* īnfimus.
bough *n* rāmus *m*.
boulder *n* saxum *nt*.
boulevard *n* platea *f*.
bounce *vi* salīre, resultāre.
bound *n* fīnis *m*, modus *m*, terminus *m*; (*leap*) saltus *m*; **set ~s to** modum facere (*dat*) ♦ *vt* fīnīre, dēfīnīre, termināre ♦ *vi* salīre, saltāre ♦ *adj* adligātus, obligātus, obstrictus; **be ~ to** (*duty*) dēbēre; **it is ~ to happen** necesse est ēveniat; **be ~ for** tendere in (*acc*); **be storm~** tempestāte tenērī.
boundaries *npl* fīnēs *mpl*.
boundary *n* fīnis *m*; (*of fields*) terminus *m*; (*fortified*) līmes *m*; ~ **stone** terminus *m*.
boundless *adj* immēnsus, īnfīnītus.
boundlessness *n* īnfīnitās *f*, immēnsum *nt*.
bounteous *adj see* **bountiful**.
bounteously *adv* largē, līberāliter, cōpiōsē.
bountiful *adj* largus, līberālis, benignus.
bounty *n* largitās *f*, līberālitās *f*; (*store*) cōpia *f*.
bouquet *n* corollārium *nt*; (*of wine*) flōs *m*.
bourn *n* fīnis *m*.
bout *n* certāmen *nt*; (*drinking*) cōmissātiō *f*.
bovine *adj* būbulus; (*fig*) stolidus.
bow *n* arcus *m*; (*ship*) prōra *f*; (*courtesy*) salūtātiō *f*; **have two strings to one's ~**

duplicī spē ūtī; **rain~** arcus *m* ♦ *vi* flectere, inclīnāre ♦ *vi* caput dēmittere.
bowels *n* alvus *f*; (*fig*) viscera *ntpl*.
bower *n* umbrāculum *nt*, trichila *f*.
bowl *n* (*cooking*) catīnus *m*; (*drinking*) calix *m*; (*mixing wine*) crātēra *f*; (*ball*) pila *f* ♦ *vt* volvere; ~ **over** prōruere.
bow-legged *adj* valgus.
bowler *n* (*game*) dator *m*.
bowstring *n* nervus *m*.
box *n* arca *f*, capsa *f*; (*for clothes*) cista *f*; (*for medicine*) pyxis *f*; (*for perfume*) alabaster *m*; (*tree*) buxus *f*; (*wood*) buxum *nt*; (*blow on ears*) alapa *f* ♦ *vt* inclūdere; ~ **the ears of** alapam dūcere (*dat*), colaphōs īnfringere (*dat*) ♦ *vi* (*fight*) pugnīs certāre.
boxer *n* pugil *m*.
boxing *n* pugilātiō *f*.
boxing glove *n* caestus *m*.
boy *n* puer *m*; **become a ~ again** repuerāscere.
boycott *vt* repudiāre.
boyhood *n* pueritia *f*; **from ~** ā puerō.
boyish *adj* puerīlis.
boyishly *adv* puerīliter.
brace *n* (*building*) fībula *f*; (*strap*) fascia *f*; (*pair*) pār *nt* ♦ *vt* adligāre; (*strengthen*) firmāre.
bracelet *n* armilla *f*.
bracing *adj* (*air*) salūbris.
bracken *n* filix *f*.
bracket *n* uncus *m*.
brackish *adj* amārus.
bradawl *n* terebra *f*.
brag *vi* glōriārī, sē iactāre.
braggart *n* glōriōsus *m*.
braid *vt* nectere.
brain *n* cerebrum *nt*; ingenium *nt*.
brainless *adj* sōcors, stultus.
brainy *adj* ingeniōsus.
brake *n* (*wood*) dūmētum *nt*; (*on wheel*) sufflāmen *nt*.
bramble *n* rubus *m*.
bran *n* furfur *nt*.
branch *n* rāmus *m*; (*kind*) genus *nt* ♦ *vi*: ~ **out** rāmōs porrigere.
branching *adj* rāmōsus.
brand *n* (*fire*) torris *m*, fax *f*; (*mark*) nota *f*; (*sword*) ēnsis *m*; (*variety*) genus *nt* ♦ *vt* (*mark*) inūrere; (*stigma*) notāre; ~ **new** recēns.
brandish *vt* vibrāre.
brass *n* orichalcum *nt*.
bravado *n* ferōcitās *f*; **out of ~** per speciem ferōcitātis.
brave *adj* fortis, ācer ♦ *vt* adīre, patī.
bravely *adv* fortiter, ācriter.
bravery *n* fortitūdō *f*, virtūs *f*.
bravo *interj* bene, euge, macte.
brawl *n* rixa *f*, iūrgium *nt* ♦ *vi* rixārī.
brawn *n* lacertī *mpl*.
brawny *adj* lacertōsus, rōbūstus.
bray *vi* rūdere.
brazen *adj* aēneus; (*fig*) impudēns.
brazier *n* foculus *m*.
breach *n* (*in wall*) ruīna *f*; (*of friendship*)

dissēnsiō f ♦ vt perfringere; ~ **of trust** mala fidēs; **commit a ~ of promise** prōmissīs nōn stāre.
breach of the peace n iūrgium nt, tumultus m.
bread n pānis m.
breadth n lātitūdō f; **in ~** in lātitūdinem (acc).
break vt frangere, perfringere; ~ **down** vt īnfringere, dīruere; ~ **in** vt (animal) domāre; ~ **into pieces** dīrumpere; ~ **off** vt abrumpere, dēfringere; (action) dīrimere; ~ **open** effringere, solvere; ~ **through** vt fus interrumpere; ~ **up** vt dissolvere, interrumpere; ~ **one's word** fidem fallere, violāre; **without ~ing the law** salvīs lēgibus ♦ vi rumpī, frangī; (day) illūcēscere; (strength) dēficere; ~ **off** vi dēsinere; ~ **into** intrāre; ~ **out** vi ērumpere; (sore) recrūdēscere; (trouble) exārdēscere; ~ **up** vi dīlābī, dissolvī; (meeting) dīmittī; ~ **through** vi inrumpere; ~ **with** dissidēre ab ♦ n intermissiō f, intervallum nt.
breakable adj fragilis.
breakage n frāctum nt.
breakdown n (activity) mora f; (health) dēbilitās f.
breaker n fluctus m.
breakfast n iēntāculum nt, prandium nt ♦ vi ientāre, prandēre.
breakwater n mōlēs f.
bream n sparulus m.
breast n pectus nt; (woman's) mamma f; **make a clean ~ of** cōnfitērī.
breastplate n lōrīca f.
breastwork n lōrīca f, pluteus m.
breath n spīritus m, anima f; (bad) hālitus m; (quick) anhēlitus m; (of wind) aura f, adflātus m; **below one's ~** mussitāns; **catch one's ~** obstipēscere; **hold one's ~** animam comprimere, continēre; **take a ~** spīritum dūcere; **take one's ~ away** exanimāre; **waste one's ~** operam perdere; **out of ~** exanimātus.
breathable adj spīrābilis.
breathe vt, vi spīrāre, hālāre; (quickly) anhēlāre; ~ **again** respīrāre; ~ **in** vt, vi spīritum dūcere; ~ **out** vt, vi exspīrāre, exhālāre; ~ **upon** īnspīrāre (dat), adflāre (dat); ~ **one's last** animam agere, efflāre.
breathing n hālitus m, respīrātiō f.
breathing space n respīrātiō f.
breathless adj exanimātus.
breeches n brācae fpl.
breed n genus nt ♦ vt generāre, prōcreāre; (raise) ēducāre, alere; (fig) adferre, efficere; **well-bred** generōsus.
breeder n (animal) mātrix f; (man) generātor m; (fig) nūtrix f.
breeding n (act) fētūra f; (manners) mōrēs mpl; **good ~** hūmānitās f.
breeze n aura f, flātus m.
breezy adj ventōsus; (manner) hilaris.
brevity n brevitās f.
brew vt coquere ♦ vi (fig) parārī, imminēre.

bribe vt corrumpere ♦ vi largīrī ♦ n pecūnia f, mercēs f.
briber n corruptor m, largītor m.
bribery n ambitus m, largītiō f.
brick n later m ♦ adj latericius.
brickwork n latericium nt.
bridal adj nūptiālis; (bed) geniālis ♦ n nūptiae fpl.
bride n nūpta f.
bridegroom m marītus m.
bridge n pōns m ♦ vt pontem impōnere (dat).
bridle n frēnum nt ♦ vt frēnāre, īnfrēnāre.
brief adj brevis; **to be ~** nē longum sit, nē multa.
briefly adv breviter, paucīs verbīs.
briefness n brevitās f.
brier n veprēs m, sentis m.
brig n liburna f.
brigade n legiō f; (cavalry) turma f.
brigadier n lēgātus m.
brigand n latrō m, praedō m.
brigandage n latrōcinium nt.
bright adj clārus, lūculentus; (sky) serēnus; (intellect) ingeniōsus; (manner) hilaris, laetus; **be ~** lūcēre, splendēre.
brighten vt illūstrāre; laetificāre ♦ vi lūcēscere; (person) hilarem fierī.
brightly adv clārē.
brightness n fulgor m, candor m; (sky) serēnitās f.
brilliance n splendor m, fulgor m; (style) nitor m, lūmen nt, īnsignia ntpl.
brilliant adj clārus, illūstris, splendidus; (fig) īnsignis, praeclārus, lūculentus.
brilliantly adv splendidē, praeclārē, lūculentē.
brim n lābrum nt, margō f; **fill to the ~** explēre.
brimstone n sulfur nt.
brindled adj varius.
brine n salsāmentum nt.
bring vt ferre; (person) dūcere; (charge) intendere; (to a place) adferre, addūcere, advehere, dēferre; (to a destination) perdūcere; (to a worse state) redigere; ~ **about** vt efficere; ~ **before** dēferre ad, referre ad; ~ **back** vt (thing) referre; (person) redūcere; ~ **down** vt dēdūcere, dēferre; ~ **forth** (from store) dēprōmere; (child) parere; (crops) ferre, ēdere; ~ **forward** vt (for discussion) iactāre, iacere; (reason) adferre; ~ **home** (bride) dēdūcere; (in triumph) dēportāre; ~ **home to** pervincere; ~ **in** vt invehere, indūcere, intrōdūcere; (import) importāre; (revenue) reddere; ~ **off** vt (success) reportāre; ~ **on** īnferre, importāre; (stage) indūcere; ~ **out** vt efferre; (book) ēdere; (play) dare; (talent) ēlicere; ~ **over** perdūcere, trādūcere; ~ **to bear** adferre; ~ **to light** nūdāre, dētegere; ~ **to pass** perficere, peragere; ~ **to shore** ad litus appellere; ~ **together** contrahere, cōgere; (enemies) conciliāre; ~ **up** vt (child) ēducāre, tollere; (troops) admovēre; (topic) prōferre; ~ **upon oneself** sibī cōnscīscere, sibī contrahere.

brink n ōra f, margō f.
briny adj salsus.
brisk adj alacer, vegetus, ācer.
briskly adv ācriter.
briskness n alacritās f.
bristle n sēta f ♦ vi horrēre, horrēscere.
bristly adj horridus, hirsūtus.
Britain n Brittania f.
Britons n Brittani mpl.
brittle adj fragilis.
broach vt (topic) in medium prōferre.
broad adj lātus; (accent) lātus; (joke)
inurbānus; (daylight) multus.
broadcast vt dissēmināre.
broaden vt dīlātāre.
broadly adv lātē.
broadsword n gladius m.
brocade n Attalica ntpl.
brochure n libellus m.
brogue n pērō m.
broil n rixa f, iūrgium nt ♦ vt torrēre.
broiling adj torridus.
broken adj frāctus; (fig) cōnfectus; (speech)
īnfrāctus.
broken-hearted adj dolōre cōnfectus.
broker n īnstitor m.
bronze n aes nt ♦ adj aēneus, aerātus.
brooch n fibula f.
brood n fētus m; (fig) gēns f ♦ vi incubāre (dat);
(fig) incubāre (dat), fovēre; ~ **over** meditārī.
brook n rīvus m ♦ vt ferre, patī.
brooklet n rīvulus m.
broom n (plant) genista f; (brush) scōpae fpl.
broth n iūs nt.
brother n frāter m; (full) germānus m; ~ **and
sister** marītus mpl.
brotherhood n frāternitās f.
brother-in-law n lēvir m, uxōris frāter m,
sorōris marītus m.
brotherly adj frāternus.
brow n frōns f; (eye) supercilium nt; (hill)
dorsum nt.
browbeat vt obiūrgāre, exagitāre.
brown adj fulvus, spādīx; (skin) adūstus.
browse vi pāscī, dēpāscī.
bruise vt atterere, frangere, contundere ♦ n
vulnus nt.
bruit vt pervulgāre.
brunt n vīs f; **bear the ~ of** exhaurīre.
brush n pēniculus m; (artist's) pēnicillus m;
(quarrel) rixa f ♦ vt verrere, dētergēre; (teeth)
dēfricāre; ~ **aside** vt aspernārī, neglegere; ~
up vt (fig) excolere.
brushwood n virgulta ntpl; (for cutting)
sarmenta ntpl.
brusque adj parum cōmis.
brutal adj atrōx, saevus, inhūmānus.
brutality n atrōcitās f, saevitia f.
brutally adv atrōciter, inhūmānē.
brute n bēlua f, bestia f.
brutish adj stolidus.
bubble n bulla f ♦ vi bullāre; ~ **over**
effervēscere; ~ **up** scatēre.

buccaneer n praedō m, pīrāta m.
buck n cervus m ♦ vi exsultāre.
bucket n situla f, fidēlia f.
buckle n fibula f ♦ vt fibulā nectere; ~ **to**
accingī.
buckler n parma f.
buckram n carbasus m.
bucolic adj agrestis.
bucolics n būcolica ntpl.
bud n gemma f, flōsculus m ♦ vi gemmāre.
budge vi movērī, cēdere.
budget n pūblicae pecūniae ratiō f ♦ vi: ~ **for**
prōvidēre (dat).
buff adj lūteus.
buffalo n ūrus m.
buffet n (blow) alapa f; (fig) plāga f; (sideboard)
abacus m ♦ vt iactāre, tundere.
buffoon n scurra m, balatrō m.
buffoonery n scurrilitās f.
bug n cīmex m.
bugbear n terricula ntpl, terror m.
bugle n būcina f.
bugler n būcinātor m.
build vt aedificāre, struere; (bridge) facere;
(road) mūnīre; ~ **on** vt (add) adstruere;
(hopes) pōnere; ~ **on sand in aquā**
fundāmenta pōnere; ~ **up** vt exstruere; (to
block) inaedificāre; (knowledge) īnstruere; ~
castles in the air spem inānem pāscere ♦ n
statūra f.
builder n aedificātor m, structor m.
building n (act) aedificātiō f; (structure)
aedificium nt.
bulb n bulbus m.
bulge vi tumēre, tumēscere, prōminēre ♦ vi
tuberculum nt; (of land) locus prōminēns m.
bulk n māgnitūdō f, amplitūdō f; (mass) mōlēs
f; (most) plērīque, māior pars.
bulky adj amplus, grandis.
bull n taurus m; ~**'s** taurīnus; **take the ~ by the
horns** rem fortiter adgredī.
bulldog n Molossus m.
bullet n glāns f.
bulletin n libellus m.
bullion n aurum īnfectum nt, argentum
īnfectum nt.
bullock n iuvencus m.
bully n obiūrgātor m, patruus m ♦ vt obiūrgāre,
exagitāre.
bulrush n scirpus m.
bulwark n prōpugnāculum nt; (fig) arx f.
bump n (swelling) tuber nt, tuberculum nt;
(knock) ictus m ♦ vi: ~ **against** offendere.
bumper n plēnum pōculum nt ♦ adj plēnus,
māximus.
bumpkin n rūsticus m.
bumptious adj adrogāns.
bunch n fasciculus m; (of berries) racēmus m.
bundle n fascis m; (of hay) manipulus m ♦ vt
obligāre.
bung n obtūrāmentum nt ♦ vt obtūrāre.
bungle vt male gerere.
bunk n lectus m, lectulus m.

buoy n cortex m ♦ vt sublevāre.
buoyancy n levitās f.
buoyant adj levis; (fig) hilaris.
bur n lappa f.
burden n onus nt; **beast of ~** iūmentum nt ♦ vt
onerāre; **be a ~** oneri esse.
burdensome adj gravis, molestus.
bureau n scrīnium nt.
burgeon vi gemmāre.
burgess n mūniceps m.
burgh n mūnicipium nt.
burgher n mūniceps m.
burglar n fūr m.
burglary n fūrtum nt.
burial n fūnes nt, humātiō f, sepultūra f.
burin n caelum nt.
burlesque n imitātiō f ♦ vt per iocum imitārī.
burly adj crassus.
burn vt incendere, ūrere; (to ashes) cremāre ♦
vi ārdēre, flāgrāre; **~ up** ambūrere,
combūrere, exūrere; **be ~ed down**
dēflāgrāre; **~ out** vi exstinguī; **~ the midnight
oil** lūcubrāre ♦ n (MED) ambūstum nt.
burning adj igneus.
burnish vt polīre.
burrow n cuniculus m ♦ vi dēfodere.
burst vt rumpere, dīrumpere ♦ vi rumpī,
dīrumpī; **~ in** inrumpere; **~ into tears** in
lacrimās effundī; **~ open** refringere; **~ out**
ērumpere, prōrumpere; **~ out laughing**
cachinnum tollere; **~ through** perrumpere
per (acc); **~ upon** offerrī (dat), invādere ♦ n
ēruptiō f; (noise) fragor m; **~ of applause**
clāmōrēs mpl; **with a ~ of speed** citātō gradū,
citātō equō.
bury vt sepelīre, humare; (ceremony) efferre;
(hiding) condere; (things) dēfodere; (fig)
obruere; **~ the hatchet** amīcitiam
reconciliāre.
bush n frutex m; dūmus m; **beat about the ~**
circuitiōne ūtī.
bushel n medimnus m.
bushy adj fruticōsus; (thick) dēnsus; (hair)
hirsūtus.
busily adv strēnuē, impigrē.
business n negōtium nt; (occupation) ars f,
quaestus f; (public life) forum nt; (matter) rēs
f; **it is your ~** tuum est; **make it one's ~ to** id
agere ut; **you have no ~ to** nōn tē decet
(infin); **mind one's own ~** suum negōtium
agere; **~ days** diēs fāstī mpl.
businessman negōtiātor m.
buskin n cothurnus m.
bust n imāgō f.
bustle vi trepidāre, festīnāre; **~ about**
discurrere.
busy adj negōtiōsus, occupātus; (active)
operōsus, impiger, strēnuus; **~ in** occupātus
(abl); **~ on** intentus (dat); **keep ~** vt exercēre;
~ oneself with pertractāre, studēre (dat).
busybody n: **be a ~** aliēnīs negōtīs sē
immiscēre.
but conj sed, at; (2nd place) autem, tamen ♦ adv

modo ♦ prep praeter (acc); **nothing ~** nihil
nisī; **~ that, ~ what** quīn; **not ~ what**
nihilōminus.
butcher n lanius m ♦ vt trucīdāre.
butcher's shop n laniēna f.
butchery n strāgēs f, occīdiō f.
butler n prōmus m.
butt n (cask) cadus m; (of ridicule) lūdibrium nt
♦ vi arietāre; **~ in** interpellāre.
butter n būtyrum nt.
butterfly n pāpiliō m.
buttock n clūnis m/f.
button n bulla f.
buttonhole vt (fig) dētinēre, prēnsāre.
buttress n antērides fpl ♦ vt fulcīre.
buxom adj nitidus.
buy vt emere; **~ provisions** obsonāre; **~ back** vt
redimere; **~ off** vt redimere; **~ up** vt coemere.
buyer n emptor m; (at auctions) manceps m.
buzz n strīdor m, susurrus m ♦ vi strīdere,
susurrāre.
buzzard n būteō m.
by prep (near) ad (acc), apud (acc); prope (acc);
(along) secundum (acc); (past) praeter (acc);
(agent) ā, ab (abl); (instrument) abl; (time) ante
(acc); (oath) per (acc) ♦ adv prope, iuxtā; **~
and ~** mox; **be ~** adesse, adstāre; **~ force of
arms** vī et armīs; **~ land and sea** terrī
marique.
bygone adj praeteritus.
bystander n arbiter m; pl circumstantēs mpl.
byway n dēverticulum nt, trāmes m, sēmita f.
byword n prōverbium nt.

C, c

cabal n factiō f.
cabbage n brassica f, caulis m.
cabin n casa f; (ship) cubiculum nt.
cabinet n armārium nt.
cable n fūnis m; (anchor) ancorāle nt.
cache n thēsaurus m.
cachet n nota f.
cackle vi strepere n ♦ strepitus m, clangor m.
cacophonous adj dissonus.
cacophony n vōcēs dissonae fpl.
cadaverous adj cadāverōsus.
cadence n clausula numerōsa f, numerus m.
cadet n (son) nātū minor; (MIL) contubernālis
m.
cage n cavea f ♦ vt inclūdere.
caitiff n ignāvus m.
cajole vt blandīrī, dēlēnīre.
cake n placenta f.
calamitous adj exitiōsus, calamitōsus.

calamity n calamitās f, malum nt; (MIL) clādēs f.
calculate vt ratiōnem dūcere, inīre.
calculation n ratiō f.
calculator n ratiōcinātor m.
calendar n fāstī mpl.
calends n Kalendae fpl.
calf n (animal) vitulus m, vitula f; (leg) sūra f.
calibre n (fig) ingenium nt, auctōritās f.
call vt vocāre; (name) appellāre, nōmināre; (aloud) clāmāre; (to a place) advocāre, convocāre; ~ **aside** sēvocāre; ~ **down** (curse) dētestārī; ~ **for** vt fus postulāre, requīrere; ~ **forth** ēvocāre, excīre, ēlicere; ~ **in** vt advocāre; ~ **together** convocāre; ~ **on** vt fus (for help) implōrāre; (visit) salūtāre; ~ **off** vt āvocāre, revocāre; ~ **out** vi exclāmāre; ~ **up** vt (dead) excitāre, ēlicere; (MIL) ēvocāre ♦ n vōx f, clāmor m; (summons) invītātiō f; (visit) salūtātiō f.
caller n salūtātor m.
calling n ars f, quaestus m.
callous adj dūrus; **become** ~ obdūrēscere.
callow adj rudis.
calm adj tranquillus, placidus; (mind) aequus ♦ vi: ~ **down** (fig) dēfervēscere ♦ vt sēdāre, tranquillāre ♦ n tranquillitās f; **dead** ~ (at sea) malacia f.
calmly adv tranquillē, placidē; aequō animō.
calumniate vt obtrectāre, crīminārī; (falsely) calumniārī.
calumniator n obtrectātor m.
calumny n opprobria ntpl, obtrectātiō f.
calve vi parere.
cambric n linteum nt.
camel n camēlus m.
camouflage n dissimulātiō f ♦ vt dissimulāre.
camp n castra ntpl; **summer** ~ aestīva ntpl; **winter** ~ hīberna ntpl; **in** ~ sub pellibus; **pitch** ~ castra pōnere; **strike** ~ castra movēre ♦ adj castrēnsis ♦ vi tendere.
campaign n stīpendium nt, bellum nt; (rapid) expedītiō f ♦ vi bellum gerere, stīpendium merēre.
campaigner n mīles m; **old** ~ veterānus m; (fig) veterātor m.
campbed n grabātus m.
camp followers n lixae mpl.
can n hirnea f.
can vi posse (+ infin); (know how) scīre.
canaille n vulgus nt, plebs f.
canal n fossa nāvigābilis f, eurīpus m.
cancel vt indūcere, abrogāre.
cancellation n (writing) litūra f; (law) abrogātiō f.
cancer n cancer m; (fig) carcinōma nt, ulcus nt.
cancerous adj (fig) ulcerōsus.
candelabrum n candēlābrum nt.
candid adj ingenuus, apertus, līber, simplex.
candidate n petītor m; **be a** ~ **for** petere.
candidature n petītiō f.
candidly adv ingenuē.
candle n candēla f.
candlestick n candēlābrum nt.

candour n ingenuitās f, simplicitās f, lībertās f.
cane n (reed) harundō f; (for walking, punishing) virga f ♦ vt verberāre.
canine adj canīnus.
canister n capsula f.
canker n (plants) rōbigō f; (fig) aerūgō f, carcinōma nt ♦ vt corrumpere.
Cannae n Cannae fpl.
cannibal n anthrōpophagus m.
cannon n tormentum nt.
cannot nōn posse, nequīre; **I** ~ **help but** ... facere nōn possum quīn ... (subj), nōn possum nōn ... (infin).
canny adj prūdens, prōvidus, cautus, circumspectus.
canoe n linter f.
canon n nōrma f, rēgula f; (ECCL) canonicus m.
canopy n aulaeum nt.
cant n fūcus m, fūcāta verba ntpl ♦ vt oblīquāre.
cantankerous adj importūnus.
cantankerousness n importūnitās f.
canter n lēnis cursus m ♦ vi lēniter currere.
canticle n canticum nt.
canto n carmen nt.
canton n pāgus m.
canvas n carbasus m, linteum nt ♦ adj carbaseus; **under** ~ sub pellibus.
canvass vi ambīre ♦ vt prēnsāre, circumīre.
canvassing n ambitus m, ambitiō f.
cap n pilleus m; (priest's) galērus m, apex m.
capability n facultās f, potestās f.
capable adj capāx, doctus, perītus.
capably adv bene, doctē.
capacious adj capāx, amplus.
capacity n capācitās f, amplitūdō f; (mind) ingenium nt.
caparison n ephippium nt.
cape n (GEOG) prōmunturium nt; (dress) chlamys f.
caper vi saltāre; (animal) lascīvīre ♦ n saltus m.
capering n lascivia f.
capital adj (chief) praecipuus, prīnceps; (excellent) ēgregius; (law) capitālis; **convict of a** ~ **offence** capitis damnāre ♦ n (town) caput nt; (money) sors f; (class) negōtiātorēs mpl; **make** ~ **out of** ūtī (abl).
capitalist n faenerātor m.
capital punishment n capitis supplicium nt.
capitation tax n capitum exāctiō f.
Capitol n Capitolium nt.
capitulate vi sē dēdere; **troops who have** ~**d** dēditīciī mpl.
capitulation n dēditiō f.
capon n capō m.
caprice n libīdō f, incōnstantia f.
capricious adj incōnstāns, levis.
capriciously adv incōnstanter, leviter.
capriciousness n incōnstantia f, libīdō f.
capsize vt ēvertere ♦ vi ēvertī.
captain m dux m, praefectus m, prīnceps m;

(_MIL_) centuriō m; (_naval_) nāvarchus m; (_of merchant ship_) magister m ♦ vt praeesse (_dat_), dūcere.
captaincy n centuriātus m.
caption n caput nt.
captious adj mōrōsus; (_question_) captiōsus.
captiously adv mōrōsē.
captiousness n mōrōsitās f.
captivate vt capere, dēlēnīre, adlicere.
captive n captīvus m.
captivity n captīvitās f, vincula ntpl.
captor n (_by storm_) expugnātor m; victor m.
capture n (_by storm_) expugnātiō f ♦ vt capere.
car n currus m.
caravan n commeātus m.
carbuncle n (_MED_) fūrunculus m; (_stone_) acaustus m.
carcass n cadāver nt.
card n charta f; (_ticket_) tessera f; (_wool_) pecten nt ♦ vt pectere.
cardamom n amōmum nt.
cardinal adj praecipuus; ~ **point** cardō m ♦ n (_ECCL_) cardīnālis.
care n cūra f; (_anxiety_) sollicitūdō f; (_attention_) dīligentia f; (_charge_) custōdia f; **take ~** cavēre; **take ~ of** cūrāre ♦ vi cūrāre; ~ **for** vt fus (_look after_) cūrāre; (_like_) amāre; **I don't ~** nīl moror; **I couldn't care less about ...** floccī nōn faciō ..., pendō; **I don't ~ about** mittō, nihil moror; **for all I ~** per mē.
career n curriculum nt; (_POL_) cursus honōrum; (_completed_) rēs gestae fpl ♦ vi ruere, volāre.
carefree adj sēcūrus.
careful adj (_cautious_) cautus; (_attentive_) dīligēns, attentus; (_work_) accūrātus.
carefully adv cautē; dīligenter, attentē; accūrātē.
careless adj incautus, neglegēns.
carelessly adv incautē, neglegenter.
carelessness n incūria f, neglegentia f.
caress vt fovēre, blandīrī ♦ n blandīmentum nt, amplexus m.
cargo n onus nt.
caricature n (_picture_) gryllus m; (_fig_) imāgō dētorta f ♦ vt dētorquēre.
carmine n coccum nt ♦ adj coccineus.
carnage n strāgēs f, caedēs f.
carnal adj corporeus; (_pleasure_) libīdinōsus.
carnival n fēriae fpl.
carol n carmen nt ♦ vi cantāre.
carouse vi perpōtāre, cōmissārī ♦ n cōmissātiō f.
carp vi obtrectāre; ~ **at** carpere, rōdere.
carpenter n faber m, lignārius m.
carpet n tapēte nt.
carriage n (_conveying_) vectūra f; (_vehicle_) vehiculum nt; (_for journeys_) raeda f, petorritum nt; (_for town_) carpentum nt, pīlentum nt; (_deportment_) gestus m, incessus m; ~ **and pair** bīgae fpl; ~ **and four** quadrīgae fpl.
carrier n vector m; (_porter_) bāiulus m; **letter ~** tabellārius m.

carrion n cadāver nt.
carrot n carōta f.
carry vt portāre, vehere, ferre, gerere; (_law_) perferre; (_by assault_) expugnāre; ~ **away** auferre, āvehere; (_by force_) rapere; (_with emotion_) efferre; ~ **all before one** ēvincere; ~ **along** (_building_) dūcere; ~ **back** reportāre; revehere, referre; ~ **down** dēportāre, dēvehere; ~ **in** invehere, intrōferre; ~ **off** auferre, asportāre, āvehere; (_by force_) abripere, ēripere; (_prize_) ferre, reportāre; (_success_) bene gerere; ~ **on** vt gerere; (_profession_) exercēre; ~ **out** vi efferre, ēgerere, ēvehere; (_task_) exsequī; ~ **out an undertaking** rem suscipere; ~ **over** trānsportāre, trānsferre; ~ **the day** vincere; ~ **one's point** pervincere; ~ **through** perferre; ~ **to** adferre, advehere; ~ **up** subvehere ♦ vi (_sound_) audīrī; ~ **on** vi pergere; (_flirt_) lascīvīre.
cart n plaustrum nt; carrus nt; **put the ~ before the horse** praeposterum dīcere ♦ vt plaustrō vehere.
Carthage n Carthāgō, Carthāginis f.
Carthaginian adj Carthāginiēnsis; Pūnicus; **the ~s** Poenī mpl.
carthorse n iūmentum nt.
carve vt sculpere; (_on surface_) caelāre; (_meat_) secāre; ~ **out** exsculpere.
carver n caelātor m.
carving n caelātūra f.
cascade n cataracta m.
case n (_instance_) exemplum nt, rēs f; (_legal_) āctiō f, līs f, causa f; (_plight_) tempus nt; (_GRAM_) cāsus m; (_receptacle_) thēca f, involucrum nt; **in ~** sī; (_to prevent_) nē; **in any ~** utut est rēs; **in that ~** ergō; **such is the ~** sīc sē rēs habet; **civil ~** causa prīvāta; **criminal ~** causa pūblica; **win a ~** causam, lītem obtinēre; **lose a ~** causam, lītem āmittere.
casement n fenestra f.
cash n nummī mpl; (_ready_) numerātum nt, praesēns pecūnia f; **pay ~** ex arcā absolvere, repraesentāre.
cash box n arca f.
cashier n dispēnsātor m ♦ vt (_MIL_) exauctōrāre.
cash payment n repraesentātiō f.
cask n cūpa f.
casket n arcula f, pyxis f.
casque n galea f, cassis f.
cast vt iacere; (_account_) inīre; (_eyes_) conicere; (_lots_) conicere; (_covering_) exuere; (_metal_) fundere; ~ **ashore** ēicere; ~ **away** prōicere; ~ **down** dēicere; (_humble_) abicere; ~ **in one's teeth** exprobrāre; ~ **lots** sortīrī; ~ **off** vi abicere, exuere; ~ **out** prōicere, ēicere, pellere ♦ n iactus m; (_moulding_) typus m, fōrma f; **with a ~ in the eye** paetus f.
castanet n crotalum nt.
castaway n ēiectus m.
caste n ōrdō m.
castigate vt animadvertere, castīgāre.
castigation n animadversiō f, castīgātiō f.

castle n arx f, castellum nt.
castrate vt castrāre.
casual adj fortuītus; (person) neglegēns.
casually adv temerē.
casualty n īnfortūnium nt; pl: **casualties** occīsī mpl.
casuist n sophistēs m.
cat n fēlēs f.
cataclysm n dīluvium nt, ruīna f.
catalogue n index m.
catapult n catapulta f, ballista f.
cataract n cataracta f.
catarrh n gravēdō f; **liable to** ~ gravēdinōsus.
catastrophe n calamitās f, ruīna f.
catastrophic adj calamitōsus, exitiōsus.
catch vt capere, dēprehendere, excipere; (disease) contrahere, nancīscī; (fire) concipere, comprehendere; (meaning) intellegere; ~ **at** captāre; ~ **out** vi dēprehendere; ~ **up with** adsequī; ~ **birds** aucupārī; ~ **fish** piscārī ♦ n bolus m.
categorical adj (statement) plānus.
categorically adv sine exceptiōne.
category n numerus m, genus nt.
cater vi obsōnāre.
cateran n praedātor m.
caterer n obsōnātor m.
caterpillar n ērūca f.
caterwaul vi ululāre.
catgut n chorda f.
catharsis n pūrgātiō f.
cathedral n aedēs f.
catholic adj generālis.
catkin n iūlus m.
cattle n (collectively) pecus nt; (singly) pecus f; (for plough) armenta ntpl.
cattle breeder n pecuārius m.
cattle market n forum boārium nt.
cattle thief n abāctor m.
cauldron n cortīna f.
cause n causa f; (person) auctor m; (law) causa f; (party) partēs fpl; **give** ~ **for** māteriam dare (gen); **make common** ~ **with** facere cum, stāre ab; **plead a** ~ causam dīcere; **in the** ~ **of** prō (abl); **without** ~ iniūriā ♦ vt efficere ut (+ subj), facere, facessere (with ut); cūrāre (with gerundive); (feelings) movēre, inicere, ciēre.
causeless adj vānus, sine causā.
causeway n agger m.
caustic adj (fig) mordāx.
cauterize vt adūrere.
caution n (wariness) cautiō f, prūdentia f; (warning) monitum nt ♦ vt monēre, admonēre.
cautious adj cautus, prōvidus, prūdens.
cautiously adv cautē, prūdenter.
cavalcade n pompa f.
cavalier n eques m ♦ adj adrogāns.
cavalierly adv adroganter.
cavalry n equitēs mpl, equitātus m ♦ adj equester; **troop of** ~ turma f.
cavalryman n eques m.

cave n spēlunca f, caverna f; antrum nt; ~ **in** vi concidere, conlābī.
cavern n spēlunca f, caverna f.
cavil vi cavillārī; ~ **at** carpere, cavillārī ♦ n captiō f, cavillātiō f.
cavity n caverna f, cavum nt.
cavort vi saltāre.
caw vi cornīcārī.
cease vi dēsinere, dēsistere.
ceaseless adj adsiduus, perpetuus.
ceaselessly adv adsiduē, perpetuō.
cedar n cedrus f ♦ adj cedrinus.
cede vt cēdere, concēdere.
ceiling n tēctum nt; (panelled) lacūnar nt, laqueārium nt.
celebrate vt (rite) celebrāre, agitāre; (in crowds) frequentāre; (person, theme) laudāre, celebrāre, dīcere.
celebrated adj praeclārus, illūstris, nōtus; **the** ~ **ille.**
celebration n celebrātiō f; (rite) sollemne nt.
celebrity n celebritās f, fāma f; (person) vir illūstris.
celerity n celeritās f, vēlōcitās f.
celery n apium nt.
celestial adj caelestis; dīvīnus.
celibacy n caelibātus m.
celibate n caelebs m.
cell n cella f.
cellar n cella f.
cement n ferrūmen nt ♦ vt coagmentāre.
cemetery n sepulchrētum nt.
cenotaph n tumulus honōrārius, tumulus inānis m.
censer n tūribulum nt, acerra f.
censor n cēnsor m ♦ vt cēnsēre.
censorious adj cēnsōrius, obtrectātor.
censorship n cēnsūra f.
censure n reprehēnsiō f, animadversiō f; (censor's) nota f ♦ vt reprehendere, animadvertere, increpāre; notāre.
census n cēnsus m.
cent n: **one per** ~ centēsima f; **12 per** ~ **per annum** centēsima f (ie monthly).
centaur n centaurus m.
centaury n (plant) centaurēum nt.
centenarian n centum annōs nātus m, nāta f.
centenary n centēsimus annus m.
centesimal adj centēsimus.
central adj medius.
centralize vt in ūnum locum cōnferre; (power) ad ūnum dēferre.
centre n centrum nt, media pars f; **the** ~ **of** medius.
centuple adj centuplex.
centurion n centuriō m.
century n (MIL) centuria f; (time) saeculum nt.
ceramic adj fictilis.
cereal n frūmentum nt.
ceremonial adj sollemnis ♦ n rītus m.
ceremonious adj (rite) sollemnis; (person) officiōsus.
ceremoniously adv sollemniter; officiōsē.

ceremony n caerimōnia f, rītus m; (*politeness*) officium nt; (*pomp*) apparātus m; **master of ceremonies** dēsignātor m.

cerise n coccum nt ♦ adj coccineus.

certain adj (*sure*) certus; (*future*) explōrātus; **a ~** quīdam, quaedam, quoddam; **be ~** (*know*) prō certō scīre/habēre.

certainly adv certē, certō, sine dubiō; (*yes*) ita, māximē; (*concessive*) quidem.

certainty n (*thing*) certum nt; (*belief*) fidēs f; **for a ~** prō certō, explōrātē; **regard as a ~** prō explōrātō habēre.

certificate n testimōnium nt.

certify vt (*writing*) recognōscere; (*fact*) adfirmāre, testificārī.

cessation n fīnis m; (*from labour*) quiēs f; (*temporary*) intermissiō f; (*of hostilities*) indutiae fpl.

chafe vt ūrere; (*fig*) inrītāre ♦ vi stomachārī.

chaff n palea f ♦ vt lūdere.

chaffinch n fringilla f.

chagrin n dolor m, stomachus m ♦ vt stomachum facere (*dat*), sollicitāre.

chain n catēna f; (*for neck*) torquis m; (*sequence*) seriēs f; **~s** pl vincula ntpl ♦ vt vincīre.

chair n sella f; (*of office*) sella curūlis f; (*sedan*) sella gestātōria f, lectīca f; (*teacher's*) cathedra f.

chairman n (*at meeting*) magister m; (*of debate*) disceptātor m.

chalet n casa f.

chalice n calix m.

chalk n crēta f.

chalky adj crētōsus.

challenge n prōvocātiō f ♦ vt prōvocāre, lacessere; (*statement*) in dubium vocāre; (*fig*) invītāre, dēposcere.

challenger n prōvocātor m.

chamber n conclāve nt; (*bed*) cubiculum nt; (*bridal*) thalamus m; (*parliament*) cūria f.

chamberlain n cubiculārius m.

chambermaid n serva f, ancilla f.

chameleon n chamaeleōn f.

chamois n rūpicapra f.

champ vt mandere.

champion n prōpugnātor m, patrōnus m; (*winner*) victor m ♦ vt favēre (*dat*), adesse (*dat*).

chance n fors f, fortūna f, cāsus m; (*opportunity*) occāsiō f; potestās f, facultās f; (*prospect*) spēs f; **game of ~** ālea f; **by ~** cāsū, fortuītō; **have an eye to the main ~** forō ūtī; **on the ~ of** sī forte ♦ adj fortuītus ♦ vi accidere, ēvenīre; **it chanced that ...** accidit ut ... (+ subj); **~ upon** vt fus incidere in, invenīre ♦ vt periclitārī.

chancel n absis f.

chancellor n cancellārius m.

chancy adj dubius, perīculōsus.

chandelier n candēlābrum nt.

chandler n candēlārum propōla m.

change n mūtātiō f, commūtātiō f, permūtātiō f; (*POL*) rēs novae fpl; (*alternation*) vicēs fpl, vicissitūdō f; (*money*) nummī minōrēs mpl ♦ vt mūtāre, commūtāre, permūtāre ♦ vi mūtārī; **~ hands** abaliēnarī; **~ places** ōrdinem permūtāre, inter sē loca permūtāre.

changeable adj incōnstāns, mūtābilis.

changeableness n incōnstantia f, mūtābilitās f.

changeful adj varius.

changeless adj cōnstāns, immūtābilis.

changeling adj subditus m.

channel n canālis m; (*sea*) fretum nt; (*irrigation*) rīvus m; (*groove*) sulcus m.

chant vt cantāre, canere ♦ n cantus m.

chaos n chaos nt; (*fig*) perturbātiō f.

chaotic adj perturbātus.

chap n rīma f; (*man*) homō m.

chapel n sacellum nt, aedicula f.

chaplain n diāconus m.

chaplet n corōna f, sertum nt.

chaps n (*animal*) mālae fpl.

chapter n caput nt.

char vt ambūrere.

character n (*inborn*) indolēs f, ingenium nt, nātūra f; (*moral*) mōrēs mpl; (*reputation*) existimātiō f; (*kind*) genus nt; (*mark*) signum nt, littera f; (*THEAT*) persōna f, partēs fpl; **sustain a ~** persōnam gerere; **I know his ~** sciō quālis sit.

characteristic adj proprius ♦ n proprium nt.

characteristically adv suō mōre.

characterize vt dēscrībere; proprium esse (*gen*).

charcoal n carbō m.

charge n (*law*) accūsātiō f, crīmen nt; (*MIL*) impetus m, dēcursus m; (*cost*) impēnsa f; (*task*) mandātum nt, onus nt; (*trust*) cūra f, tūtēla f; **bring a ~ against** lītem intendere (*dat*); **entertain a ~ against** nōmen recipere (*gen*); **give in ~** in custōdiam trādere; **put in ~ of** praeficere (*acc, dat*); **be in ~ of** praeesse (*dat*) ♦ vt (*law*) accūsāre; (*falsely*) īnsimulāre; (*MIL*) incurrere in (*acc*), signa īnferre in (*acc*), impetum facere in (*acc*); (*duty*) mandāre; (*cost*) ferre, īnferre; (*empty space*) complēre; (*trust*) committere; (*speech*) hortārī; **~ to the account of** expēnsum ferre (*dat*).

chargeable adj obnoxius.

charger n (*dish*) lānx f; (*horse*) equus m.

charily adv cautē, parcē.

chariot n currus m; (*races*) quadrīgae fpl; (*war*) essedum nt.

charioteer n aurīga m; (*war*) essedārius m.

charitable adj benevolus, benignus.

charitably adv benevolē, benignē.

charity n amor m, benignitās f; līberālitās f.

charlatan n planus m.

charm n (*spell*) carmen nt; (*amulet*) bulla f; (*fig*) blanditiae fpl, dulcēdō f, illecebra f; (*beauty*) venus f, lepōs m ♦ vt (*magic*) fascināre; (*delight*) dēlectāre, dēlēnīre.

charming adj venustus, lepidus; (*speech*) blandus; (*scenery*) amoenus.

charmingly *adv* venustē, blandē.

chart *n* tabula *f*.

charter *n* diplōma *nt* ♦ *vt* condūcere.

chary *adj* (*cautious*) cautus; (*sparing*) parcus.

chase *vt* fugāre; (*hunt*) vēnārī; (*pursue*) persequī, īnsequī; (*engrave*) caelāre; ~ **away** pellere, abigere ♦ *n* vēnātus *m*, vēnātiō *f*; (*pursuit*) īnsectātiō *f*.

chaser *n* (*in metal*) caelātor *m*.

chasm *n* hiātus *m*.

chaste *adj* castus, pudīcus; (*style*) pūrus.

chasten *vt* castīgāre, corrigere.

chastener *n* castīgātor *m*, corrēctor *m*.

chastise *vt* castīgāre, animadvertere.

chastisement *n* castīgātiō *f*, poena *f*.

chastity *n* castitās *f*, pudīcitia *f*.

chat *vi* colloquī, sermōcinārī ♦ *n* sermō *m*, colloquium *nt*.

chatelaine *n* domina *f*.

chattels *n* bona *ntpl*, rēs mancipī.

chatter *vi* garrīre; (*teeth*) crepitāre ♦ *n* garrulitās *f*, loquācitās *f*.

chatterbox *n* lingulāca *m/f*.

chatterer *n* garrulus *m*, loquāx *m*.

chattering *adj* garrulus, loquāx ♦ *n* garrulitās *f*, loquācitās *f*; (*teeth*) crepitus *m*.

cheap *adj* vīlis; **hold** ~ parvī aestimāre; **buy** ~ bene emere.

cheapen *vt* pretium minuere (*gen*).

cheaply *adv* vīliter, parvō pretiō.

cheapness *n* vīlitās *f*.

cheat *vt* dēcipere, fraudāre, dēfraudāre, frustrārī ♦ *n* fraudātor *m*.

check *vt* cohibēre, coercēre; (*movement*) impedīre, inhibēre; (*rebuke*) reprehendere; (*test*) probāre ♦ *n* impedīmentum *nt*, mora *f*; (*MIL*) offēnsiō *f*; (*rebuke*) reprehēnsiō *f*; (*test*) probātiō *f*; (*ticket*) tessera *f*.

checkmate *n* incitae calcēs *fpl* ♦ *vt* ad incitās redigere.

cheek *n* gena *f*; (*impudence*) ōs *nt*; ~ **s** *pl* mālae *fpl*; **how have you the ~ to say?** quō ōre dīcis?

cheekbone *n* maxilla *f*.

cheeky *adj* impudēns.

cheep *vi* pīpilāre.

cheer *vt* hilarāre, exhilarāre; hortārī; (*in sorrow*) cōnsōlārī ♦ *vi* clāmāre, adclāmāre; ~ **up!** bonō animō es! ♦ *n* (*shout*) clāmor *m*, plausus *m*; (*food*) hospitium *nt*; (*mind*) animus *m*.

cheerful *adj* alacer, hilaris, laetus.

cheerfully *adv* hilare, laetē.

cheerfulness *n* hilaritās *f*.

cheerily *adv* hilare.

cheerless *adj* tristis, maestus.

cheerlessly *adv* triste.

cheery *adj* hilaris.

cheese *n* cāseus *m*.

chef *n* coquus *m*.

cheque *n* perscrīptiō *f*, syngrapha *f*.

chequer *vt* variāre.

chequered *adj* varius; (*mosaic*) tessellātus.

cherish *vt* fovēre, colere.

cherry *n* (*fruit*) cerasum *nt*; (*tree*) cerasus *f*.

chess *n* latrunculī *mpl*.

chessboard *n* abacus *m*.

chest *n* (*box*) arca *f*, arcula *f*; (*body*) pectus *nt*; ~ **of drawers** armārium *nt*.

chestnut *n* castanea *f* ♦ *adj* (*colour*) spādīx.

chevalier *n* eques *m*.

chevaux-de-frise *n* ēricius *m*.

chew *vt* mandere.

chic *adj* expolītus, concinnus.

chicanery *n* (*law*) calumnia *f*; (*fig*) dolus *m*.

chick *n* pullus *m*.

chicken *n* pullus *m*; **don't count your ~s before they're hatched** adhūc tua messis in herbā est.

chicken-hearted *adj* timidus, ignāvus.

chick-pea *n* cicer *nt*.

chide *vt* reprehendere, increpāre, obiūrgāre.

chief *n* prīnceps *m*, dux *m* ♦ *adj* praecipuus, prīmus; ~ **point** caput *nt*.

chief command *n* summa imperiī.

chiefly *adv* in prīmīs, praesertim, potissimum.

chieftain *n* prīnceps *m*, rēgulus *m*.

chilblain *n* perniō *m*.

child *n* īnfāns *m/f*; **puer** *m*, puerulus *m*, puella *f*; fīlius *m*, fīlia *f*; ~ **'s play** lūdus *m*.

childbed *n* puerperium *nt*.

childbirth *n* partus *m*.

childhood *n* pueritia *f*; **from** ~ ā puerō.

childish *adj* puerīlis.

childishly *adv* puerīliter.

childless *adj* orbus.

childlessness *n* orbitās *f*.

childlike *adj* puerīlis.

children *npl* līberī *mpl*.

chill *n* frīgus *nt* ♦ *adj* frīgidus ♦ *vt* refrīgerāre.

chilly *adj* frīgidus, frīgidior.

chime *vi* sonāre, canere; ~ **in** interpellāre; (*fig*) cōnsonāre ♦ *n* sonus *m*.

chimera *n* chimaera *f*; (*fig*) somnium *nt*.

chimerical *adj* commentīcius.

chimney *n* camīnus *m*.

chin *n* mentum *nt*.

china *n* fictilia *ntpl*.

chink *n* rīma *f*; (*sound*) tinnītus *m* ♦ *vi* crepāre, tinnīre.

chip *n* assula *f*, fragmentum *nt* ♦ *vt* dolāre.

chirp *vi* pīpilāre.

chirpy *adj* hilaris.

chisel *n* scalprum *nt*, scalpellum *nt* ♦ *vt* sculpere.

chit *n* (*child*) pūsiō *m*, puerulus *m*.

chitchat *n* sermunculī *mpl*.

chitterlings *n* hillae *fpl*.

chivalrous *adj* generōsus.

chivalry *n* virtūs *f*; (*men*) iuventūs *f*; (*class*) equitēs *mpl*.

chive *n* caepe *nt*.

chock *n* cuneus *m*.

chock-full *adj* refertus.

choice *n* dēlēctus *m*, ēlēctiō *f*; (*of alternatives*) optiō *f* ♦ *adj* lēctus, eximius, exquīsītus.

choiceness *n* ēlegantia *f*, praestantia *f*.

choir n chorus m.
choke vt suffocāre; (emotion) reprimere; (passage) obstruere.
choler n bīlis f; (anger) īra f, stomachus m.
choleric adj īrācundus.
choose vt legere, ēligere, dēligere; (alternative) optāre; (for office) dēsignāre; (with infin) velle, mālle.
chop vt concīdere; ~ **off** praecīdere ♦ n (meat) offa f.
chopper n secūris f.
choppy adj (sea) asper.
choral adj symphōniacus.
chord n (string) nervus m, chorda f.
chortle vi cachinnāre.
chorus n (singers) chorus m; (song) concentus m, symphōnia f; **in ~** unā vōce.
christen vt baptizāre.
Christian adj Christiānus.
Christianity n Christiānismus m.
chronic adj inveterātus; **become ~** inveterāscere.
chronicle n annālēs mpl, ācta pūblica ntpl ♦ vt in annālēs referre.
chronicler n annālium scrīptor m.
chronological adj: **in ~ order** servātō temporum ōrdine; **make a ~ error** temporibus errāre.
chronology n temporum ratiō f, temporum ōrdō m.
chronometer n hōrologium nt.
chubby adj pinguis.
chuck vt conicere; **~ out** extrūdere.
chuckle vi rīdēre ♦ n rīsus m.
chum n sodālis m.
church n ecclēsia f.
churl n rūsticus m.
churlish adj difficilis, importūnus; avārus.
churlishly adv rūsticē, avārē.
churlishness n mōrōsitās f, avāritia f.
chute n (motion) lāpsus m; (place) dēclīve nt.
cicada n cicāda f.
cincture n cingulum nt.
cinder n cinis m.
cipher n numerus m, nihil nt; (code) notae fpl; **in ~** per notās.
circle n orbis m, circulus m, gȳrus m; **form a ~** in orbem cōnsistere ♦ vi sē circumagere, circumīre.
circlet n īnfula f.
circuit n ambitus m, circuitus m; (assizes) conventus m.
circuitous adj longus; **a ~ route** circuitus m; (speech) ambāgēs fpl.
circular adj rotundus.
circulate vt (news) pervulgāre ♦ vi circumagī; (news) circumferrī, percrēbrēscere.
circulation n ambitus m; **be in ~** in manibus esse; **go out of ~** obsolēscere.
circumcise vt circumcīdere.
circumference n ambitus m.
circumlocution n ambāgēs fpl, circuitiō f.
circumnavigate vt circumvehī.

circumscribe vt circumscrībere; (restrict) coercēre, fīnīre.
circumspect adj cautus, prūdēns.
circumspection n cautiō f, prūdentia f, circumspectiō f.
circumspectly adv cautē, prūdenter.
circumstance n rēs f; **~s** rērum status m; (wealth) rēs f; **as ~s arise** ē rē nātā; **under the ~s** cum haec ita sint, essent; **under no ~s** nēquāquam.
circumstantial adj adventīcius; (detailed) accūrātus; **~ evidence** coniectūra f.
circumstantially adv accūrātē, subtīliter.
circumvallation n circummūnītiō f.
circumvent vt circumvenīre, fallere.
circus n circus m.
cistern n lacus m, cisterna f.
citadel n arx f.
citation n (law) vocātiō f; (mention) commemorātiō f.
cite vt in iūs vocāre; (quote) commemorāre, prōferre.
citizen n cīvis m/f; (of provincial town) mūniceps m; **fellow ~** cīvis m/f; **Roman ~s** Quirītēs mpl ♦ adj cīvīlis, cīvicus.
citizenship n cīvitās f; **deprived of ~** capite dēminūtus; **loss of ~** capitis dēminūtiō f.
citron n (fruit) citrum nt; (tree) citrus f.
city n urbs f, oppidum nt.
civic adj cīvīlis, cīvicus.
civil adj (of citizens) cīvīlis; (war) cīvilis, intestīnus, domesticus; (manners) urbānus, cōmis, officiōsus; (lawsuit) prīvātus.
civilian n togātus m.
civility n urbānitās f, cōmitās f; (act) officium nt.
civilization n exculta hominum vīta f, cultus atque hūmānitās.
civilize vt excolere, expolīre, ad hūmānum cultum dēdūcere.
civil war n bellum cīvīle, bellum domesticum, bellum intestīnum.
clad adj vestītus.
claim vt (for oneself) adrogāre, adserere; (something due) poscere, postulāre, vindicāre; (at law) petere; (statement) adfirmāre ♦ n postulātiō f, postulātum nt; (at law) petītiō f, vindiciae fpl.
claimant n petītor m.
clam n chāma f.
clamber vi scandere.
clammy adj ūmidus, lentus.
clamorous adj vōciferāns.
clamour n strepitus m, clāmōrēs mpl ♦ vi: ~ **against** obstrepere (dat).
clamp n cōnfībula f.
clan n gēns f.
clandestine adj fūrtīvus.
clandestinely adv clam, fūrtim.
clang n clangor m, crepitus m ♦ vi increpāre.
clangour n clangor m.
clank n crepitus m ♦ vi crepitāre.
clansman n gentīlis m.

clap vi plaudere, applaudere; ~ **eyes on**
cōnspicere; ~ **in prison** in vincula conicere
♦ n plausus m; (thunder) fragor m.
clapper n plausor m.
claptrap n iactātiō f.
claque n plausōrēs mpl, operae fpl.
clarify vt pūrgāre; (knowledge) illūstrāre ♦ vi
liquēre.
clarinet n tībia f.
clarion n lituus m, cornū nt.
clarity n perspicuitās f.
clash n concursus m; (sound) strepitus m,
crepitus m; (fig) discrepantia f ♦ vi
concurrere; (sound) increpāre; (fig)
discrepāre ♦ vt cōnflīgere.
clasp n fībula f; (embrace) amplexus m ♦ vt
implicāre; amplectī, complectī; ~ **together**
interiungere.
class n (POL) ōrdō m, classis f; (kind) genus nt;
(school) classis f ♦ vt dēscrībere; ~ **as in**
numerō (gen pl) referre, repōnere, habēre.
classic n scrīptor classicus m.
classical adj classicus; ~ **literature** litterae
Graecae et Rōmānae.
classics npl scrīptōrēs Graecī et Rōmānī.
classify vt dēscrībere, in ōrdinem redigere.
class-mate n condiscipulus m.
clatter n crepitus m ♦ vi increpāre.
clause n (GRAM) incīsum nt, membrum nt; (law)
caput nt; (will) ēlogium nt; **in short** ~**s** incīsim.
claw n unguis m, ungula f ♦ vt (unguibus)
lacerāre.
clay n argilla f; **made of** ~ fictilis.
clayey adj argillāceus.
claymore n gladius m.
clean adj mundus; (fig) pūrus, castus; ~ **slate**
novae tabulae fpl; **make a** ~ **sweep of** omnia
tollere; **show a** ~ **pair of heels** sē in pedēs
conicere; **my hands are** ~ innocēns sum ♦ adv
prōrsus, tōtus ♦ vt pūrgāre.
cleanliness n munditia f.
cleanly adj mundus, nitidus ♦ adv mundē,
pūrē.
cleanse vt pūrgāre, abluere, dētergēre.
clear adj clārus; (liquid) limpidus; (space)
apertus, pūrus; (sound) clārus; (weather)
serēnus; (fact) manifestus, perspicuus;
(language) illūstris, dīlūcidus; (conscience)
rēctus, innocēns; **it is** ~ liquet; ~ **of** līber (abl),
expers (gen); **be** ~ **about** rēctē intellegere;
keep ~ **of** ēvītāre; **the coast is** ~ arbitrī
absunt ♦ vt (of obstacles) expedīre, pūrgāre;
(of a charge) absolvere; (self) pūrgāre; (profit)
lucrārī; ~ **away** āmovēre, tollere; ~ **off** vt
(debt) solvere, exsolvere ♦ vi facessere; ~
out ēluere, dētergēre; ~ **up** vt (difficulty)
illūstrāre, ēnōdāre, explicāre ♦ vi (weather)
disserēnāscere.
clearance n pūrgātiō f; (space) intervallum nt.
clearing n (in forest) lūcus m.
clearly adv clārē; manifestē, apertē,
perspicuē; (with clause) vidēlicet.
clearness n clāritās f; (weather) serēnitās f;

(mind) acūmen nt; (style) perspicuitās f.
clear-sighted adj sagāx, perspicāx.
cleavage n discidium nt.
cleave vt (out) findere, discindere ♦ vi (cling): ~
to haerēre (dat), adhaerēre (dat).
cleaver n dolabra f.
cleft n cliēns m/f, hiātus m ♦ adj fissus, discissus.
clemency n clēmentia f, indulgentia f; **with** ~
clēmenter.
clement adj clēmēns, misericors.
clench vt (nail) retundere; (hand) comprimere.
clerk n scrība m; (of court) lēctor m.
clever adj callidus, ingeniōsus, doctus, astūtus.
cleverly adv doctē, callidē, ingeniōsē.
cleverness n calliditās f, sollertia f.
clew n glomus m.
cliché n verbum trītum nt.
client n cliēns m/f; (lawyer's) cōnsultor m; **body
of** ~**s** clientēla f.
clientele n clientēla f.
cliff n rūpēs f, scopulus m.
climate n caelum nt.
climax n (RHET) gradātiō f; (fig) culmen nt.
climb vt, vi scandere, ascendere; ~ **down**
dēscendere ♦ n ascēnsus m.
climber n scandēns m.
clime n caelum nt, plāga f.
clinch vt cōnfirmāre.
cling vi adhaerēre; ~ **together** cohaerere.
clink vi tinnīre ♦ n tinnītus m.
clip vt tondēre; praecīdere.
clippers n forfex f.
clique n factiō f.
cloak n (rain) lacerna f; (travel) paenula f; (MIL)
sagum nt; palūdāmentum nt; (Greek) pallium
nt; (fig) involūcrum nt; (pretext) speciēs f ♦ vt
tegere, dissimulāre.
clock n hōrologium nt; (sun) sōlārium nt;
(water) clepsydra f; **ten o'** ~ quarta hōra.
clockwise adv dextrōvorsum, dextrōrsum.
clod n glaeba f.
clog n (shoe) sculpōnea f; (fig) impedīmentum
nt ♦ vt impedīre.
cloister n porticus f.
cloistered adj (fig) umbrātilis.
close adj (shut) clausus; (tight) artus; (narrow)
angustus; (near) propinquus; (compact)
refertus, dēnsus; (stingy) parcus; (secret)
obscūrus; (weather) crassus; ~ **together**
dēnsus, refertus; **at** ~ **quarters** comminus; **be**
~ **at hand** īnstāre; **keep** ~ **to** adhaerēre; ~ **to**
prope (acc), iuxtā (acc) ♦ adv prope, iuxtā ♦ n
angiportus m.
close vt claudere, operīre; (finish) perficere,
fīnīre, conclūdere, termināre; (ranks)
dēnsāre ♦ vi claudī; conclūdī, termināri;
(time) exīre; (wound) coīre; (speech)
perōrāre; ~ **with** (fight) manum cōnserere,
signa cōnferre; (deal) paciscī; (offer)
accipere ♦ n fīnis m, terminus m; (action)
exitus m; (sentence) conclūsiō f; **at the** ~ **of
summer** aestāte exeunte.
closely adv prope; (attending) attentē;

(*associating*) coniūnctē; **follow ~** īnstāre (*dat*).
closeness n propinquitās f; (*weather*) gravitās f, crassitūdō f; (*with money*) parsimōnia f; (*friends*) coniūnctiō f; (*manner*) cautiō f.
closet n cubiculum nt, cella f ♦ vt inclūdere.
clot n (*blood*) concrētus sanguis m ♦ vi concrēscere.
cloth n textile nt; (*piece*) pannus m; (*linen*) linteum nt; (*covering*) strāgulum nt.
clothe vt vestīre.
clothes n vestis f, vestītus m, vestīmenta ntpl.
clothier n vestiārius m.
clothing n vestis f, vestītus m, vestīmenta ntpl.
clotted adj concrētus.
cloud n nūbēs f; (*storm*) nimbus m; (*dust*) globus m; (*disfavour*) invidia f ♦ vt nūbibus obdūcere; (*fig*) obscūrāre.
clouded adj obnūbilus.
cloudiness n nūbilum nt.
cloudless adj pūrus, serēnus.
cloudy adj obnūbilus.
clout n pannus m.
clover n trifolium nt.
cloven adj (*hoof*) bifidus.
clown n (*boor*) rūsticus m; (*comic*) scurra m.
clownish adj rūsticus, inurbānus.
clownishness n rūsticitās f.
cloy vt satiāre.
cloying adj pūtidus.
club n (*stick*) fustis m, clāva f; (*society*) sodālitās f; **~ together** vi in commūne cōnsulere, pecūniās cōnferre.
club-footed adj scaurus.
cluck vi singultīre ♦ n singultus m.
clue n indicium nt, vestīgium nt.
clump n massa f; (*earth*) glaeba f; (*trees*) arbustum nt; (*willows*) salictum nt.
clumsily adv ineptē, inēleganter; inconditē, īnfabrē.
clumsiness n īnscītia f.
clumsy adj (*person*) inconcinnus, ineptus; (*thing*) inhabilis; (*work*) inconditus.
cluster n cumulus m; (*grapes*) racēmus m; (*people*) corōna f ♦ vi congregārī.
clutch vt prehendere, adripere; **~ at** captāre nt, comprehēnsiō f; **from one's ~es** ē manibus; **in one's ~es** in potestāte.
clutter n turba f ♦ vt impedīre, obstruere.
coach n currus m, raeda f, pīlentum nt; (*trainer*) magister m ♦ vt ēdocēre, praecipere (*dat*).
coachman n aurīga m, raedārius m.
coagulate vt cōgere ♦ vi concrēscere.
coagulation n concrētiō f.
coal n carbō m; **carry ~s to Newcastle** in silvam ligna ferre.
coalesce vi coīre, coalēscere.
coalition n coitiō f, cōnspīrātiō f.
coarse adj (*quality*) crassus; (*manners*) rūsticus, inurbānus; (*speech*) īnfacētus.
coarsely adv inurbānē, inēleganter.
coarseness n crassitūdō f; rūsticitās f.
coast n lītus nt, ōra maritima f ♦ vi: **~ along** legere, praetervehī.

coastal adj lītorālis, maritimus.
coastline n lītus nt.
coat n pallium nt; (*animals*) pellis f ♦ vt indūcere, inlinere.
coating n corium nt.
coax vt blandīrī, dēlēnīre.
coaxing adj blandus ♦ n blanditiae fpl.
cob n (*horse*) mannus m; (*swan*) cygnus m.
cobble n lapis m ♦ vt sarcīre.
cobbler n sūtor m.
cobweb n arāneum nt.
cock n gallus m, gallus gallīnāceus m; (*other birds*) mās m; (*tap*) epitonium nt; (*hay*) acervus m.
cockatrice n basiliscus m.
cockchafer n scarabaeus m.
cockcrow n gallī cantus m ♦ vt ērigere.
cockerel n pullus m.
cockroach n blatta f.
cocksure adj cōnfīdēns.
cod n callarias m.
coddle vt indulgēre (*dat*), permulcēre.
code n fōrmula f; (*secret*) notae fpl.
codicil n cōdicillī mpl.
codify vt in ōrdinem redigere.
coequal adj aequālis.
coerce vt cōgere.
coercion n vīs f.
coffer n arca f, cista f; (*public*) fiscus m.
coffin n arca f.
cog n dēns m.
cogency n vīs f, pondus nt.
cogent adj gravis, validus.
cogitate vi cōgitāre, meditārī.
cogitation n cōgitātiō f; meditātiō f.
cognate adj cognātus.
cognition n cognitiō f.
cognizance n cognitiō f; **take ~ of** cognōscere.
cognizant adj gnārus.
cohabit vi cōnsuēscere.
cohabitation n cōnsuētūdō f.
coheir n cohērēs m/f.
cohere vi cohaerēre; (*statement*) congruere.
coherence n coniūnctiō f; (*fig*) convenientia f.
coherent adj congruēns.
cohesion n coagmentātiō f.
cohesive adj tenāx.
cohort n cohors f.
coil n spīra f ♦ vt glomerāre.
coin n nummus m ♦ vt cūdere; (*fig*) fingere.
coinage n monēta f; (*fig*) fictum nt.
coincide vi concurrere; (*opinion*) cōnsentīre.
coincidence n concursus m; cōnsēnsus m; **by a ~** cāsū.
coincidental adj fortuītus.
coiner n (*of money*) signātor m.
col n iugum nt.
colander n cōlum nt.
cold adj frīgidus; (*icy*) gelidus; **very ~** perfrīgidus; **be, feel ~** algēre, frīgēre; **get ~** algēscere, frīgēscere ♦ n frīgus nt; (*felt*) algor m; (*malady*) gravēdō f; **catch ~** algēscere, frīgus colligere; **catch a ~**

gravēdinem contrahere; **have a ~** gravēdine labōrāre.

coldish adj frīgidulus, frīgidior.

coldly adv (manner) sine studiō.

coldness n frīgus nt, algor m.

cold water n frīgida f.

colic n tormina ntpl.

collar n collāre nt.

collarbone n iugulum nt.

collate vt cōnferre, comparāre.

collateral adj adiūnctus; (evidence) cōnsentāneus.

collation n collātiō f; (meal) prandium nt, merenda f.

colleague n collēga m.

collect vt colligere, cōgere, congerere; (persons) congregāre, convocāre; (taxes) exigere; (something due) recipere; **~ oneself** animum colligere; **cool and ~ed** aequō animō ♦ vi convenīre, congregārī.

collection n (persons) coetus m, conventus m; (things) congeriēs f; (money) exāctiō f.

collective adj commūnis.

collectively adv commūniter.

collector n (of taxes) exāctor m.

college n collēgium nt.

collide vi concurrere, cōnflīctārī.

collier n carbōnārius m.

collision n concursus m.

collocation n collocātiō f.

collop n offa f.

colloquial adj cottīdiānus.

colloquy n sermō m, colloquium nt.

collude vi praevāricārī.

collusion n praevāricātiō f.

collusive adj praevāricātor.

colonel n lēgātus m.

colonial adj colōnicus ♦ n colōnus m.

colonist n colōnus m.

colonization n dēductiō f.

colonize vt colōniam dēdūcere, cōnstituere in (acc).

colonnade n porticus f.

colony n colōnia f.

colossal adj ingēns, vastus.

colossus n colossus m.

colour n color m; (paint) pigmentum nt; (artificial) fūcus m; (complexion) color m; (pretext) speciēs f; **take on a ~** colōrem dūcere; **under ~ of** per speciem (gen); **local ~** māteria dē regiōne sūmpta ♦ vt colōrāre; (dye) īnficere, fūcāre; (fig) praetendere (dat) ♦ vi rubēre, ērubēscere.

colourable adj speciōsus.

coloured adj (naturally) colōrātus; (artificially) fūcātus.

colourful adj fūcōsus, varius.

colouring n pigmentum nt; (dye) fūcus m.

colourless adj perlūcidus; (person) pallidus; (fig) īnsulsus.

colours n (MIL) signum nt, vexillum nt; (POL) partēs fpl; **sail under false ~** aliēnō nōmine ūtī; **with flying ~** māximā cum gloriā.

colour sergeant n signifer m.

colt n equuleus m, equulus m.

coltsfoot n farfarus m.

column n columna f; (MIL) agmen nt.

coma n sopor m.

comb n pecten m; (bird) crista f; (loom) pecten m; (honey) favus m ♦ vt pectere.

combat n pugna f, proelium nt, certāmen nt ♦ vi pugnāre, dīmicāre, certāre ♦ vt pugnāre cum (abl), obsistere (dat).

combatant n pugnātor m ♦ adj pugnāns; **non ~** imbellis.

combative adj ferōx, pugnāx.

combination n coniūnctiō f, cōnfūsiō f; (persons) cōnspīrātiō f; (illegal) coniūrātiō f.

combine vt coniungere, iungere ♦ vi coīre, coniungī ♦ n societās f.

combustible adj ignī obnoxius.

combustion n dēflāgrātiō f, incendium nt.

come vi venīre, advenīre; (after a journey) dēvenīre; (interj) age!; **how ~s it that ...?**; quī fit ut ...?; **~ across** vi invenīre, offendere; **~ after** sequī, excipere, succēdere (dat); **~ again** revenīre, redīre; **~ away** vi abscēdere; (when pulled) sequī; **~ back** vi revenīre, redīre; regredī; **~ between** intervenīre, intercēdere; **~ down** vi dēvenīre, dēscendere; (from the past) trādī, prōdī; **~ forward** vi prōcēdere, prōdīre; **~ from** vi (origin) dēfluere; **~ in** vi inīre, introīre; ingredī; (revenue) redīre; **~ near** accēdere ad (acc), appropinquāre (dat); **~ nearer and nearer** adventāre; **~ of** vi (family) ortum esse ab, ex (abl); **~ off** vi ēvādere, discēdere; **~ on** vi prōcēdere; (progress) prōficere; (interj) age, agite; **~ on the scene** intervenīre, supervenīre, adesse; **~ out** vi exīre, ēgredī; (hair, teeth) cadere; (flower) flōrēscere; (book) ēdī; **~ over** vi trānsīre; (feeling) subīre, occupāre; **~ to** vi advenīre ad, in (acc); (person) adīre; (amount) efficere; **~ to the help of** subvenīre (dat); succurrere (dat); **~ to nought** ad nihilum recidere; **~ to pass** ēvenīre, fierī; **~ together** convenīre, coīre; **~ up** vi subīre, succēdere; (growth) prōvenīre; **~ upon** vt fus invenīre; **he is coming to** animus eī redit.

comedian n (actor) cōmoedus m; (writer) cōmicus m.

comedienne n mīma f.

comedy n cōmoedia f.

comeliness n decor m, decōrum nt.

comely adj decōrus, pulcher.

comestibles n vīctus m.

comet n comētēs m.

comfort vt sōlārī, cōnsōlārī, adlevāre ♦ n sōlācium nt, cōnsōlātiō f.

comfortable adj commodus; **make oneself ~** corpus cūrāre.

comfortably adv commodē.

comforter n cōnsōlātor m.

comfortless adj incommodus; **be ~** sōlātiō carēre.

comforts npl commoda ntpl.

comic adj cōmicus; facētus ♦ n scurra m.

comical *adj* facētus, rīdiculus.
coming *adj* futūrus ♦ *n* adventus *m*.
comity *n* cōmitās *f*.
command *vt* iubēre (+ *acc and infin*), imperāre
  (*dat and* **ut** *+subj*); dūcere; (*feelings*) regere;
  (*resources*) fruī (*abl*); (*view*) prōspectāre ♦ *n*
  (*MIL*) imperium *nt*; (*sphere*) prōvincia *f*; (*order*)
  imperium *nt*, iussum *nt*, mandātum *nt*; **be in ~**
  (of) praeesse (*dat*); **put in ~ of** praeficere
  (*dat*); **~ of language** fācundia *f*.
commandant *n* praefectus *m*.
commandeer *vt* pūblicāre.
commander *n* dux *m*, praefectus *m*.
commander in chief *n* imperātor *m*.
commandment *n* mandātum *nt*.
commemorate *vt* celebrāre, memoriae
  trādere.
commemoration *n* celebrātiō *f*.
commence *vt* incipere, exōrdīrī, initium
  facere (*gen*).
commencement *n* initium *nt*, exōrdium *nt*,
  prīncipium *nt*.
commend *vt* laudāre; (*recommend*)
  commendāre; (*entrust*) mandāre; **~ oneself** sē
  probāre.
commendable *adj* laudābilis, probābilis.
commendation *n* laus *f*, commendātiō *f*.
commendatory *adj* commendātīcius.
commensurable *adj* pār.
commensurate *adj* congruēns, conveniēns.
comment *vi* dīcere, scrībere; **~ on**
  interpretārī; (*with notes*) adnotāre ♦ *n*
  dictum *nt*, sententia *f*.
commentary *n* commentāriī *mpl*.
commentator *n* interpres *m*.
commerce *n* mercātūra *f*, commercium *nt*;
  engage in ~ mercātūrās facere, negōtiārī.
commercial dealings *n* commercium *nt*.
commercial traveller *n* īnstitor *m*.
commination *n* minae *fpl*.
comminatory *adj* mināx.
commingle *vt* intermiscēre.
commiserate *vt* miserērī (*gen*).
commiseration *n* misericordia *f*; (*RHET*)
  commiserātiō *f*.
commissariat *n* rēs frūmentāria *f*,
  commeātus *m*; (*staff*) frūmentāriī *mpl*.
commissary *n* lēgātus *m*; reī frūmentāriae
  praefectus *m*.
commission *n* (*charge*) mandātum *nt*;
  (*persons*) triumvirī *mpl*, decemvirī *mpl*, etc;
  (*abroad*) lēgātiō *f*; **get a ~** (*MIL*) tribūnum fierī;
  standing ~ (*law*) quaestiō perpetua *f* ♦ *vt*
  mandāre, adlēgāre.
commissioner *n* lēgātus *m*; **three ~s** triumvirī
  mpl; **ten ~s** decemvirī *mpl*.
commit *vt* (*charge*) committere, mandāre;
  (*crime*) admittere; (*to prison*) conicere; (*to an*
  undertaking) obligāre, obstringere; **~ to**
  memory memoriae trādere; **~ to writing**
  litterīs mandāre; **~ an error** errāre; **~ a theft**
  fūrtum facere; *see also* **suicide**.
commitment *n* mūnus *nt*, officium *nt*.

committee *n* dēlēctī *mpl*.
commodious *adj* capāx.
commodity *n* merx *f*, rēs *f*.
commodore *n* praefectus classis *m*.
common *adj* (*for all*) commūnis; (*ordinary*)
  vulgāris, cottīdiānus; (*repeated*) frequēns,
  crēber; (*inferior*) nēquam ♦ *n* compāscuus
  ager *m*, prātum *nt*; **~ man** homō plēbēius *m*; **~**
  soldier gregārius mīles *m*.
commonalty *n* plēbs *f*.
commoner *n* homō plēbēius *m*.
common law *n* mōs māiōrum *m*.
commonly *adv* ferē, vulgō.
common people *n* plēbs *f*, vulgus *nt*.
commonplace *n* trītum prōverbium *nt*; (*RHET*)
  locus commūnis *m* ♦ *adj* vulgāris, trītus.
commons *n* plēbs *f*; (*food*) diāria *ntpl*.
common sense *n* prūdentia *f*.
commonwealth *n* cīvitās *f*, rēs pūblica *f*.
commotion *n* perturbātiō *f*, tumultus *m*;
  cause a ~ tumultuārī.
communal *adj* commūnis.
commune *n* pāgus *m* ♦ *vi* colloquī, sermōnēs
  cōnferre.
communicate *vt* commūnicāre; (*information*)
  nūntiāre, patefacere ♦ *vi*: **~ with**
  commūnicāre (*dat*), commercium habēre
  (*gen*), agere cum (*abl*).
communication *n* (*dealings*) commercium *nt*;
  (*information*) litterae *fpl*, nūntius *m*; (*passage*)
  commeātus *m*; **cut off the ~s of** interclūdere.
communicative *adj* loquāx.
communion *n* societās *f*.
communiqué *n* litterae *fpl*, praedicātiō *f*.
communism *n* bonōrum aequātiō *f*.
community *n* cīvitās *f*, commūne *nt*;
  (*participation*) commūniō *f*.
commutation *n* mūtātiō *f*.
commute *vt* mūtāre, commūtāre.
compact *n* foedus *nt*, conventum *nt* ♦ *adj*
  dēnsus ♦ *vt* dēnsāre.
companion *n* socius *m*, comes *m/f*; (*intimate*)
  sodālis *m*; (*at school*) condiscipulus *m*; (*in*
  army) commīlitō *m*, contubernālis *m*.
companionable *adj* facilis, commodus.
companionship *n* sodālitās *f*, cōnsuētūdō *f*;
  (*MIL*) contubernium *nt*.
company *n* societās *f*, cōnsuētūdō *f*;
  (*gathering*) coetus *m*, conventus *m*; (*guests*)
  cēnantēs *mpl*; (*commercial*) societās *f*;
  (*magistrates*) collēgium *nt*; (*MIL*) manipulus *m*;
  (*THEAT*) grex *m*, caterva *f*; **~ of ten** decuria *f*.
comparable *adj* comparābilis, similis.
comparative *adj* māgnus, sī cum aliīs
  cōnfertur.
comparatively *adv* ut in tālī tempore, ut in eā
  regiōne, ut est captus hominum; **~ few**
  perpaucī, nullus ferē.
compare *vt* comparāre, cōnferre; **~d with** ad
  (*acc*).
comparison *n* comparātiō *f*, collātiō *f*; (*RHET*)
  similitūdō *f*; **in ~ with** prō (*abl*).
compartment *n* cella *f*, pars *f*.

compass *n* ambitus *m*, spatium *nt*, modus *m*;
pair of ~es circinus *m* ♦ *vt* circumdare,
cingere; (*attain*) cōnsequī.
compassion *n* misericordia *f*.
compassionate *adj* misericors, clēmēns.
compassionately *adv* clēmenter.
compatibility *n* convenientia *f*.
compatible *adj* congruēns, conveniēns; **be ~**
congruere.
compatibly *adv* congruenter, convenienter.
compatriot *n* cīvis *m*, populāris *m*.
compeer *n* pār *m*; aequālis *m*.
compel *vt* cōgere.
compendious *adj* brevis.
compendiously *adv* summātim.
compendium *n* epitomē *f*.
compensate *vt* compēnsāre, satisfacere
(*dat*).
compensation *n* compēnsātiō *f*; pretium *nt*,
poena *f*.
compete *vi* certāre, contendere.
competence *n* facultās *f*; (*law*) iūs *nt*; (*money*)
quod sufficit.
competent *adj* perītus, satis doctus, capāx;
(*witness*) locuplēs; **it is ~** licet.
competition *n* certāmen *nt*, contentiō *f*.
competitor *n* competītor *m*, aemulus *m*.
compilation *n* collectānea *ntpl*, liber *m*.
compile *vt* compōnere.
compiler *n* scrīptor *m*.
complacency *n* amor suī *m*.
complacent *adj* suī contentus.
complain *vi* querī, conquerī; **~ of** (*person*)
nōmen dēferre (*gen*).
complainant *n* accūsātor *m*, petītor *m*.
complaint *n* questus *m*, querimōnia *f*; (*law*)
crīmen *nt*; (*MED*) morbus *m*, valētūdō *f*.
complaisance *n* cōmitās *f*, obsequium *nt*,
indulgentia *f*.
complaisant *adj* cōmis, officiōsus, facilis.
complement *n* complēmentum *nt*; numerus
suus *m*; **make up the ~ of** complēre.
complete *vt* (*amount, time*) complēre, explēre;
(*work*) cōnficere, perficere, absolvere,
peragere ♦ *adj* perfectus, absolūtus, integer;
(*victory*) iūstus; (*amount*) explētus.
completely *adv* funditus, omnīnō, absolūtē,
plānē; penitus.
completeness *n* integritās *f*; (*perfection*)
perfectiō *f*.
completion *n* (*process*) absolūtiō *f*, cōnfectiō *f*;
(*end*) fīnis *m*; **bring to ~** absolvere.
complex *adj* implicātus, multiplex.
complexion *n* color *m*.
complexity *n* implicātiō *f*.
compliance *n* accommodātiō *f*, obsequium *nt*,
obtemperātiō *f*.
compliant *adj* obsequēns, facilis.
complicate *vt* implicāre, impedīre.
complicated *adj* implicātus, involūtus,
impedītus.
complication *n* implicātiō *f*.
complicity *n* cōnscientia *f*.

compliment *n* blandīmentum *nt*, honōs *m* ♦ *vt*
blandīrī, laudāre; **~ on** grātulārī (*dat*) dē
(*abl*).
complimentary *adj* honōrificus, blandus.
compliments *npl* (*as greeting*) salūs *f*.
comply *vi* obsequī (*dat*), obtemperāre (*dat*);
mōrem gerere (*dat*), mōrigerārī (*dat*).
component *n* elementum *nt*, pars *f*.
comport *vt* gerere.
compose *vt* (*art*) compōnere, condere,
pangere; (*whole*) efficere, cōnflāre; (*quarrel*)
compōnere, dīrimere; (*disturbance*) sēdāre;
be ~d of cōnsistere ex (*abl*), cōnstāre ex
(*abl*).
composed *adj* tranquillus, placidus.
composer *n* auctor *m*, scrīptor *m*.
composite *adj* multiplex.
composition *n* (*process*) compositiō *f*,
scrīptūra *f*; (*product*) opus *nt*, poēma *nt*,
carmen *nt*; (*quality*) structūra *f*.
composure *n* sēcūritās *f*, aequus animus *m*;
(*face*) tranquillitās *f*.
compound *vt* miscēre; (*words*) duplicāre,
iungere ♦ *vi* (*agree*) pacīscī ♦ *adj* compositus
♦ *n* (*word*) iūnctum verbum *nt*; (*area*)
saeptum *nt*.
compound interest *n* anatocismus *m*.
comprehend *vt* intellegere, comprehendere;
(*include*) continēre, complectī.
comprehensible *adj* perspicuus.
comprehension *n* intellegentia *f*,
comprehēnsiō *f*.
comprehensive *adj* capāx; **be ~** lātē patēre,
multa complectī.
compress *vt* comprimere, coartāre ♦ *n*
fōmentum *nt*.
compression *n* compressus *m*.
comprise *vt* continēre, complectī,
comprehendere.
compromise *n* (*by one side*) accommodātiō *f*;
(*by both sides*) comprōmissum *nt* ♦ *vi*
comprōmittere ♦ *vt* implicāre, in
suspiciōnem vocāre; **be ~d** in suspiciōnem
venīre.
comptroller *n* moderātor *m*.
compulsion *n* necessitās *f*, vīs *f*; **under ~**
coāctus.
compulsory *adj* necesse, lēge imperātus; **use
~ measures** vim adhibēre.
compunction *n* paenitentia *f*.
computation *n* ratiō *f*.
compute *vt* computāre, ratiōnem dūcere.
comrade *n* socius *m*, contubernālis *m*.
comradeship *n* contubernium *nt*.
concatenation *n* seriēs *f*.
concave *adj* concavus.
conceal *vt* cēlāre, abdere, abscondere; (*fact*)
dissimulāre.
concealment *n* occultātiō *f*; (*place*) latebrae
fpl; (*of facts*) dissimulātiō *f*; **in ~** abditus,
occultus; **be in ~** latēre, latitāre; **go into ~**
dēlitēscere.
concede *vt* concēdere.
conceit *n* (*idea*) nōtiō *f*; (*wit*) facētiae *fpl*; (*pride*

superbia _f_, adrogantia _f_, vānitās _f_.
conceited _adj_ glōriōsus, adrogāns.
conceitedness _n_ adrogantia _f_, vānitās _f_.
conceive _vt_ concipere, comprehendere, intellegere.
concentrate _vt_ (_in one place_) cōgere, congregāre; (_attention_) intendere, dēfīgere.
concentrated _adj_ dēnsus.
concentration _n_ animī intentiō _f_.
concept _n_ nōtiō _f_.
conception _n_ conceptus _m_; (_mind_) intellegentia _f_, īnfōrmātiō _f_; (_idea_) nōtiō _f_, cōgitātiō _f_, cōnsilium _nt_.
concern _vt_ (_refer_) attinēre ad (_acc_), interesse (_gen_); (_worry_) sollicitāre; **it ~s me** meā rēfert, meā interest; **as far as I am ~ed** per mē ♦ _n_ rēs _f_, negōtium _nt_; (_importance_) mōmentum _nt_; (_worry_) sollicitūdō _f_, cūra _f_; (_regret_) dolor _m_.
concerned _adj_ sollicitus, anxius; **be ~** dolēre; **be ~ about** molestē ferre.
concerning _prep_ dē (_abl_).
concernment _n_ sollicitūdō _f_.
concert _n_ (_music_) concentus _m_; (_agreement_) cōnsēnsus _m_; **in ~** ex compositō, ūnō animō ♦ _vt_ compōnere; (_plan_) inīre.
concession _n_ concessiō _f_; **by the ~ of** concessū (_gen_); **make a ~** concēdere, tribuere.
conciliate _vt_ conciliāre.
conciliation _n_ conciliātiō _f_.
conciliator _n_ arbiter _m_.
conciliatory _adj_ pācificus.
concise _adj_ brevis; (_style_) dēnsus.
concisely _adv_ breviter.
conciseness _n_ brevitās _f_.
conclave _n_ sēcrētus cōnsessus _m_.
conclude _vt_ (_end_) termināre, fīnīre, cōnficere; (_settle_) facere, compōnere, pangere; (_infer_) īnferre, colligere.
conclusion _n_ (_end_) fīnis _m_; (_of action_) exitus _m_; (_of speech_) perōrātiō _f_; (_inference_) coniectūra _f_; (_decision_) placitum _nt_, sententia _f_; **in ~** dēnique; **try ~s with** contendere cum.
conclusive _adj_ certus, manifestus, gravis.
conclusively _adv_ sine dubiō.
concoct _vt_ coquere; (_fig_) cōnflāre.
concoction _n_ (_fig_) māchinātiō _f_.
concomitant _adj_ adiūnctus.
concord _n_ concordia _f_; (_music_) harmonia _f_.
concordant _adj_ concors.
concordat _n_ pactum _nt_, foedus _nt_.
concourse _n_ frequentia _f_, celebrātiō _f_; (_moving_) concursus _m_.
concrete _adj_ concrētus; **in the ~** rē.
concretion _n_ concrētiō _f_.
concubine _n_ concubīna _f_.
concupiscence _n_ libīdō _f_.
concur _vi_ (_time_) concurrere; (_opinion_) cōnsentīre, adsentīre.
concurrence _n_ (_time_) concursus _m_; (_opinion_) cōnsēnsus _m_.
concurrent _adj_ (_time_) aequālis; (_opinion_) cōnsentāneus; **be ~** concurrere, cōnsentīre.

concurrently _adv_ simul, ūnā.
concussion _n_ ictus _m_.
condemn _vt_ damnāre, condemnāre; (_disapprove_) improbāre; **~ to death** capitis damnāre; **~ for treason** dē māiestāte damnāre.
condemnation _n_ damnātiō _f_; condemnātiō _f_.
condemnatory _adj_ damnātōrius.
condense _vt_ dēnsāre; (_words_) premere.
condescend _vi_ dēscendere, sē submittere.
condescending _adj_ cōmis.
condescension _n_ cōmitās _f_.
condiment _n_ condīmentum _nt_.
condition _n_ (_of body_) habitus _m_; (_external_) status _m_, condiciō _f_, rēs _f_; (_in society_) locus _m_, fortūna _f_; (_of agreement_) condiciō _f_, lēx _f_; **~s of sale** mancipī lēx _f_; **on ~ that** eā condicione ut (_subj_); **in ~** (_animals_) nitidus ♦ _vt_ fōrmāre, regere.
conditional _adj_: **the assistance is ~ on** eā condiciōne succurritur ut (_subj_).
conditionally _adv_ sub condiciōne.
conditioned _adj_ (_character_) mōrātus.
condole _vi_: **~ with** cōnsōlārī.
condolence _n_ cōnsōlātiō _f_.
condonation _n_ venia _f_.
condone _vt_ condōnāre, ignōscere (_dat_).
conduce _vi_ condūcere (ad), prōficere (ad).
conducive _adj_ ūtilis, accommodātus.
conduct _vt_ dūcere; (_escort_) dēdūcere; (_to a place_) addūcere, perdūcere; (_business_) gerere, administrāre; (_self_) gerere ♦ _n_ mōrēs _mpl_; (_past_) vīta _f_, facta _ntpl_; (_business_) administrātiō _f_; **safe ~** praesidium _nt_.
conductor _m_ dux _m_, ductor _m_.
conduit _n_ canālis _m_, aquae ductus _m_.
cone _n_ cōnus _m_.
coney _n_ cunīculus _m_.
confabulate _vi_ colloquī.
confection _n_ cuppēdō _f_.
confectioner _n_ cuppēdinārius _m_.
confectionery _n_ dulcia _ntpl_.
confederacy _n_ foederātae cīvitātēs _fpl_, societās _f_.
confederate _adj_ foederātus ♦ _n_ socius _m_ ♦ _vi_ coniūrāre, foedus facere.
confederation _n_ societās _f_.
confer _vt_ cōnferre, tribuere ♦ _vi_ colloquī, sermōnem cōnferre; **~ about** agere dē (_abl_).
conference _n_ colloquium _nt_, congressus _m_.
conferment _n_ dōnātiō _f_.
confess _vt_ fatērī, cōnfitērī.
confessedly _adv_ manifestō.
confession _n_ cōnfessiō _f_.
confidant _n_ cōnscius _m_.
confide _vi_ fīdere (_dat_), cōnfīdere (_dat_) ♦ _vt_ crēdere, committere.
confidence _n_ fidēs _f_, fīdūcia _f_; **have ~ in** fīdere (_dat_), cōnfīdere (_dat_); **inspire ~ in** fidem facere (_dat_); **tell in ~** tūtīs auribus dēpōnere.
confident _adj_ fīdens; **~ in** frētus (_abl_); **be ~ that** certō scīre, prō certō habēre.
confidential _adj_ arcānus, intimus.

confidentially *adv* inter nōs.
confidently *adv* fīdenter.
confiding *adj* crēdulus.
configuration *n* figūra *f*, fōrma *f*.
confine *vt* (*prison*) inclūdere, in vincula conicere; (*limit*) termināre, circumscrībere; (*restrain*) coercēre, cohibēre; (*to bed*) dētinēre; **be ~d** (*women*) parturīre.
confinement *n* custōdia *f*, vincula *ntpl*, inclūsiō *f*; (*women*) puerperium *nt*.
confines *n* fīnēs *mpl*.
confirm *vt* (*strength*) corrōborāre, firmāre; (*decision*) sancīre, ratum facere; (*fact*) adfirmāre, comprobāre.
confirmation *n* cōnfirmātiō *f*, adfirmātiō *f*.
confirmed *adj* ratus.
confiscate *vt* pūblicāre.
confiscation *n* pūblicātiō *f*.
conflagration *n* incendium *nt*, dēflāgrātiō *f*.
conflict *n* (*physical*) concursus *m*; (*hostile*) certāmen *nt*, proelium *nt*; (*verbal*) contentiō *f*, contrōversia *f*; (*contradiction*) repugnantia *f*, discrepantia *f* ♦ *vi* inter sē repugnāre.
conflicting *adj* contrārius.
confluence *n* cōnfluēns *m*.
confluent *adj* cōnfluēns.
conform *vt* accommodāre ♦ *vi* sē cōnfōrmāre (ad), obsequī (*dat*), mōrem gerere (*dat*).
conformable *adj* accommodātus, conveniēns.
conformably *adv* convenienter.
conformation *n* structūra *f*, confōrmātiō *f*.
conformity *n* convenientia *f*, cōnsēnsus *m*.
confound *vt* (*mix*) cōnfundere, permiscēre; (*amaze*) obstupefacere; (*thwart*) frustrārī; (*suppress*) opprimere, obruere; **~ you!** dī tē perduint.
confounded *adj* miser, sacer, nefandus.
confoundedly *adv* mīrum quantum nefāriē.
confraternity *n* frāternitās *f*.
confront *vt* sē oppōnere (*dat*), obviam īre (*dat*), sē cōram offerre.
confuse *vt* permiscēre, perturbāre.
confused *adj* perturbātus.
confusedly *adv* perturbātē, prōmiscuē.
confusion *n* perturbātiō *f*; (*shame*) rubor *m*.
confutation *n* refūtātiō *f*.
confute *vt* refūtāre, redarguere, convincere.
congé *n* commeātus *m*.
congeal *vt* congelāre, dūrāre ♦ *vi* concrēscere.
congealed *adj* concrētus.
congenial *adj* concors, congruēns, iūcundus.
congeniality *n* concordia *f*, mōrum similitūdō *f*.
congenital *adj* nātīvus.
conger *n* conger *m*.
congested *adj* refertus, dēnsus; (*with people*) frequentissimus.
congestion *n* congeriēs *f*; frequentia *f*.
conglomerate *vt* glomerāre.
conglomeration *n* congeriēs *f*, cumulus *m*.
congratulate *vt* grātulārī (*dat*).
congratulation *n* grātulātiō *f*.

congratulatory *adj* grātulābundus.
congregate *vt* congregāre, cōgere ♦ *vi* convenīre, congregārī.
congregation *n* conventus *m*, coetus *m*.
congress *n* conventus *m*, cōnsessus *m*, concilium *nt*; senātus *m*.
congruence *n* convenientia *f*.
congruent *adj* conveniēns, congruēns.
congruently *adv* convenienter, congruenter.
congruous *adj* see **congruent**.
conical *adj* turbinātus.
coniferous *adj* cōnifer.
conjectural *adj* opīnābilis.
conjecturally *adv* coniectūrā.
conjecture *n* coniectūra *f* ♦ *vt* conicere, augurārī.
conjoin *vt* coniungere.
conjoint *adj* coniūnctus.
conjointly *adv* coniūnctē, ūnā.
conjugal *adj* coniugālis.
conjugate *vt* dēclīnāre.
conjugation *n* (*GRAM*) dēclīnātiō *f*.
conjunct *adj* coniūnctus.
conjunction *n* coniūnctiō *f*, concursus *m*.
conjure *vt* (*entreat*) obtestārī, obsecrāre; (*spirits*) ēlicere, ciēre ♦ *vi* praestigiīs ūtī.
conjurer *n* praestigiātor *m*.
conjuring *n* praestigiae *fpl*.
connate *adj* innātus, nātūrā īnsitus.
connect *vt* iungere, coniungere, cōpulāre, connectere.
connected *adj* coniūnctus; (*unbroken*) continēns; (*by marriage*) adfīnis; **be ~ed with** contingere; **be closely ~ed with** inhaerēre (*dat*), cohaerēre cum (*abl*).
connectedly *adv* coniūnctē, continenter.
connection *n* coniūnctiō *f*, contextus *m*, seriēs *f*; (*kin*) necessitūdō *f*; (*by marriage*) adfīnitās *f*; **~ between ... and ...** ratiō (*gen*) ... cum ... (*abl*); **I have no ~ with you** nīl mihī tēcum est.
connivance *n* venia *f*, dissimulātiō *f*.
connive *vi* conīvēre in (*abl*), dissimulāre.
connoisseur *n* intellegēns *m*.
connotation *n* vīs *f*, significātiō *f*.
connote *vt* significāre.
connubial *adj* coniugālis.
conquer *vt* vincere, superāre.
conquerable *adj* superābilis, expugnābilis.
conqueror *n* victor *m*.
conquest *n* victōria *f*; (*town*) expugnātiō *f*; (*prize*) praemium *nt*, praeda *f*; **the ~ of Greece** Graecia capta.
conscience *n* cōnscientia *f*; **guilty ~** mala cōnscientia; **have a clear ~** nullīus culpae sibī cōnscium esse; **have no ~** nullam rēligiōnem habēre.
conscientious *adj* probus, rēligiōsus.
conscientiously *adv* bonā fidē, rēligiōsē.
conscientiousness *n* fidēs *f*, rēligiō *f*.
conscious *adj* sibī cōnscius; (*aware*) gnārus; (*physically*) mentis compos; **be ~** sentīre.
consciously *adv* sciēns.
consciousness *n* animus *m*; (*of action*)

cōnscientia *f*; **he lost ~** animus eum relīquit.
conscript *n* tīrō *m* ♦ *vt* cōnscrībere.
conscription *n* dēlēctus *m*; (*of wealth*)
pūblicātiō *f*.
consecrate *vt* dēdicāre, cōnsecrāre; (*self*)
dēvovēre.
consecrated *adj* sacer.
consecration *n* dēdicātiō *f*, cōnsecrātiō *f*;
(*self*) dēvōtiō *f*.
consecutive *adj* dēinceps, continuus.
consecutively *adv* dēinceps, ōrdine.
consensus *n* cōnsēnsus *m*.
consent *vi* adsentīre (*dat*), adnuere (*infin*);
(*together*) cōnsentīre ♦ *n* (*one side*) adsēnsus
m; (*all*) cōnsēnsus *m*; **by common ~** omnium
cōnsēnsū.
consequence *n* ēventus *m*, exitus *m*; (*logic*)
conclūsiō *f*; (*importance*) mōmentum *nt*,
auctōritās *f*; **it is of ~ interest; what will be
the ~ of?** quō ēvādet?
consequent *adj* cōnsequēns.
consequential *adj* cōnsentāneus; (*person*)
adrogāns.
consequently *adv* itaque, igitur, prōptereā.
conservation *n* cōnservātiō *f*.
conservative *adj* reī pūblicae cōnservandae
studiōsus; (*estimate*) mediōcris; **~ party**
optimātēs *mpl*.
conservator *n* custōs *m*, cōnservātor *m*.
conserve *vt* cōnservāre, servāre.
consider *vt* cōnsīderāre, contemplārī; (*reflect*)
sēcum volūtāre, meditari, dēlīberāre,
cōgitāre; (*deem*) habēre, dūcere; (*respect*)
respicere, observāre.
considerable *adj* aliquantus, nōnnullus;
(*person*) illūstris.
considerably *adv* aliquantum; (*with compar*)
aliquantō, multō.
considerate *adj* hūmānus, benignus.
considerately *adv* hūmānē, benignē.
consideration *n* cōnsīderātiō *f*, contemplātiō
f, dēlīberātiō *f*; (*respect*) respectus *m*, ratiō *f*;
(*importance*) mōmentum *nt*; (*reason*) ratiō *f*;
(*pay*) pretium *nt*; **for a ~** mercēde, datā
mercēde; **in ~ of** propter (*acc*), prō (*abl*); **on
no ~** nēquāquam; **with ~** cōnsultō; **without ~**
temerē; **take into ~** ad cōnsilium dēferre;
show ~ for respectum habēre (*gen*).
considered *adj* (*reasons*) exquīsītus.
considering *prep* prō (*abl*), propter (*acc*) ♦ *conj*
ut, quōniam.
consign *vt* mandāre, committere.
consist *vi* cōnstāre; **~ in** cōnstāre ex (*abl*),
continērī (*abl*), positum esse in (*abl*); **~ with**
congruere (*dat*), convenīre (*dat*).
consistence *n* firmitās *f*.
consistency *n* cōnstantia *f*.
consistent *adj* cōnstāns; (*with*) cōnsentāneus,
cōngruens; (*of movement*) aequābilis; **be ~**
cohaerēre.
consistently *adv* cōnstanter.
consolable *adj* cōnsōlābilis.
consolation *n* cōnsōlātiō *f*; (*thing*) sōlācium *nt*.

consolatory *adj* cōnsōlātōrius.
console *vt* cōnsōlārī.
consoler *n* cōnsōlātor *m*.
consolidate *vt* (*liquid*) cōgere; (*strength*)
corrōborāre; (*gains*) obtinēre ♦ *vi*
concrēscere.
consolidation *n* concrētiō *f*; cōnfirmātiō *f*.
consonance *n* concentus *m*.
consonant *adj* cōnsonus, haud absonus ♦ *n*
cōnsonāns *f*.
consort *n* cōnsors *m/f*, socius *m*; (*married*)
coniunx *m/f* ♦ *vi*: **~ with** familiāriter ūtī (*abl*),
coniūnctissimē vīvere cum (*abl*).
conspectus *n* summārium *nt*.
conspicuous *adj* ēminēns, īnsignis,
manifestus; **be ~** ēminēre.
conspicuously *adv* manifestō, palam, ante
oculōs.
conspiracy *n* coniūrātiō *f*.
conspirator *n* coniūrātus *m*.
conspire *vi* coniūrāre; (*for good*) cōnspīrāre.
constable *n* lictor *m*.
constancy *n* cōnstantia *f*, firmitās *f*; **with ~**
cōnstanter.
constant *adj* cōnstāns; (*faithful*) fīdus, fidēlis;
(*continuous*) adsiduus.
constantly *adv* adsiduē, saepe, crēbrō.
constellation *n* sīdus *nt*.
consternation *n* trepidātiō *f*, pavor *m*; **throw
into ~** perterrēre, cōnsternere.
constituency *n* suffrāgātōrēs *mpl*.
constituent *adj*: **~ part** elementum *nt* ♦ *n*
(*voter*) suffrāgātor *m*.
constitute *vt* creāre, cōnstituere; esse.
constitution *n* nātūra *f*, status *m*; (*body*)
habitus *m*; (*POL*) cīvitātis fōrma *f*, reī pūblicae
status *m*, lēgēs *fpl*.
constitutional *adj* lēgitimus, iūstus.
constitutionally *adv* ē rē pūblicā.
constrain *vt* cōgere.
constraint *n* vīs *f*; **under ~** coāctus; **without ~**
suā sponte.
constrict *vt* comprimere, cōnstringere.
constriction *n* contractiō *f*.
construct *vt* aedificāre, exstruere.
construction *n* aedificātiō *f*; (*method*)
structūra *f*; (*meaning*) interpretātiō *f*; **put a
wrong ~ on** in malam partem interpretārī.
construe *vt* interpretārī.
consul *n* cōnsul *m*; **~ elect** cōnsul dēsignātus;
ex ~ cōnsulāris *m*.
consular *adj* cōnsulāris.
consulship *n* cōnsulātus *m*; **stand for the ~**
cōnsulātum petere; **hold the ~** cōnsulātum
gerere; **in my ~** mē cōnsule.
consult *vt* cōnsulere; **~ the interests of**
cōnsulere (*dat*) ♦ *vi* dēlīberāre, cōnsiliārī.
consultation *n* (*asking*) cōnsultātiō *f*;
(*discussion*) dēlīberātiō *f*.
consume *vt* cōnsūmere, absūmere; (*food*)
edere.
consumer *n* cōnsūmptor *m*.
consummate *adj* summus, perfectus ♦ *vt*

perficere, absolvere.
consummation n absolūtiō f; fīnis m, ēventus m.
consumption n cōnsūmptiō f; (disease) tābēs f, phthisis f.
consumptive adj pulmōnārius.
contact n tāctus m, contāgiō f; **come in ~ with** contingere.
contagion n contāgiō f.
contagious adj tābificus; **be ~** contāgiīs vulgārī.
contain vt capere, continēre; (self) cohibēre.
container n vās nt.
contaminate vt contāmināre, īnficere.
contamination n contāgiō f, lābēs f.
contemplate vt contemplārī, intuērī; (action) in animō habēre; (prospect) spectāre.
contemplation n contemplātiō f; (thought) cōgitātiō f.
contemplative adj cōgitāns, meditāns; **in a ~ mood** cōgitātiōnī dēditus.
contemporaneous adj aequālis.
contemporaneously adv simul.
contemporary adj aequālis.
contempt n contemptiō f; **be an object of ~** contemptuī esse; **treat with ~** contemptum habēre, conculcāre.
contemptible adj contemnendus, abiectus, vīlis.
contemptuous adj fastīdiōsus.
contemptuously adv contemptim, fastīdiōsē.
contend vi certāre, contendere; (in battle) dīmicāre, pugnāre; (in words) adfirmāre, adsevērāre.
contending adj contrārius.
content adj contentus ♦ n aequus animus m ♦ vt placēre (dat), satisfacere (dat); **be ~ed** satis habēre.
contentedly adv aequō animō.
contention n certāmen nt; contrōversia f; (opinion) sententia f.
contentious adj pugnāx, lītigiōsus.
contentiously adv pugnāciter.
contentiousness n contrōversiae studium nt.
contentment n aequus animus m.
contents n quod inest, quae insunt; (of speech) argūmentum nt.
conterminous adj adfīnis.
contest n certāmen nt, contentiō f ♦ vt (law) lēge agere dē (abl); (office) petere; (dispute) repugnāre (dat), resistere (dat).
contestable adj contrōversus.
contestant n petītor m, aemulus m.
context n contextus m.
contiguity n vīcīnia f, propinquitās f.
contiguous adj vīcīnus, adiacēns; **be ~ to** adiacēre (dat), contingere.
continence n continentia f, abstinentia f.
continent adj continēns, abstinēns ♦ n continēns f.
continently adv continenter, abstinenter.
contingency n cāsus m, rēs f.
contingent adj fortuītus ♦ n (MIL) numerus m.

continual adj adsiduus, perpetuus.
continually adv adsiduē, semper.
continuance n perpetuitās f, adsiduitās f.
continuation n continuātiō f; (of a command) prōrogātiō f; (of a story) reliqua pars f.
continue vt continuāre; (time) prōdūcere; (command) prōrogāre ♦ vi (action) pergere; (time) manēre; (endurance) perstāre, dūrāre; **~ to** imperf indic.
continuity n continuātiō f; (of speech) perpetuitās f.
continuous adj continuus, continēns, perpetuus.
continuously adv perpetuō, continenter.
contort vt contorquēre, dētorquēre.
contortion n distortiō f.
contour n fōrma f.
contraband adj interdictus, vetitus.
contract n pactum nt, mandātum nt, conventum nt; (POL) foedus nt; **trial for a breach of ~** mandātī iūdicium nt ♦ vt (narrow) contrahere, addūcere; (short) dēminuere; (illness) contrahere; (agreement) pacīscī; (for work) locāre; (to do work) condūcere ♦ vi pacīscī.
contraction n contractiō f; (word) compendium nt.
contractor n redemptor m, conductor m.
contradict vt (person) contrādīcere (dat), refrāgārī (dat); (statement) īnfitiās īre (dat); (self) repugnāre (dat).
contradiction n repugnantia f, īnfitiae fpl.
contradictory adj repugnāns, contrārius; **be ~** inter sē repugnāre.
contradistinction n oppositiō f.
contraption n māchina f.
contrariety n repugnantia f.
contrariwise adv ē contrāriō.
contrary adj contrārius, adversus; (person) difficilis, mōrōsus; **~ to** contrā (acc), praeter (acc); **~ to expectations** praeter opīniōnem ♦ n contrārium nt; **on the ~** ē contrāriō, contrā; (retort) immo.
contrast n discrepantia f ♦ vt comparāre, oppōnere ♦ vi discrepāre.
contravene vt (law) violāre; (statement) contrādīcere (dat).
contravention n violātiō f.
contribute vt cōnferre, adferre, contribuere. ♦ vi: **~ towards** cōnferre ad (acc), adiuvāre; **~ to the cost** impēnsās cōnferre.
contribution n conlātiō f; (money) stipem (no nom) f.
contributor n quī cōnfert.
contributory adj adiūnctus.
contrite adj paenitēns.
contrition n paenitentia f.
contrivance n māchinātiō f, excōgitātiō f; (thing) māchina f; (idea) cōnsilium nt; (deceit) dolus m.
contrive vt māchinārī, excōgitāre, struere; (to do) efficere ut.
contriver n māchinātor m, artifex m, auctor m.

control n (*restraint*) frēnum nt; (*power*)
moderātiō f, potestās f, imperium nt; **have ~
of** praeesse (*dat*); **out of ~** impotēns ♦ vt
moderārī (*dat*), imperāre (*dat*).

controller n moderātor m.

controversial adj concertātōrius.

controversy n contrōversia f, disceptātiō f.

controvert vt redarguere, impugnāre, in
dubium vocāre.

contumacious adj contumāx, pervicāx.

contumaciously adv contumāciter,
pervicāciter.

contumacy n contumācia f, pervicācia f.

contusion n sūgillātiō f.

conundrum n aenigma nt.

convalesce vi convalēscere.

convalescence n melior valētūdō f.

convalescent adj convalēscēns.

convene vt convocāre.

convenience n opportūnitās f, commoditās f;
(*thing*) commodum nt; **at your ~** commodō
tuō.

convenient adj idōneus, commodus,
opportūnus; **be ~** convenīre; **very ~**
percommodus.

conveniently adv opportūnē, commodē.

convention n (*meeting*) conventus m;
(*agreement*) conventum nt; (*custom*) mōs m,
iūsta ntpl.

conventional adj iūstus, solitus.

conventionality n mōs m, cōnsuētūdō f.

converge vi in medium vergere, in eundem
locum tendere.

conversant adj perītus, doctus, exercitātus;
be ~ with versārī in (*abl*).

conversation n sermō m, colloquium nt.

converse n sermō m, colloquium nt; (*opposite*)
contrārium nt ♦ vi colloquī, sermōnem
cōnferre ♦ adj contrārius.

conversely adv ē contrāriō, contrā.

conversion n mūtātiō f; (*moral*) mōrum
ēmendātiō f.

convert vt mūtāre, convertere; (*to an opinion*)
dēdūcere ♦ n discipulus m.

convertible adj commūtābilis.

convex adj convexus.

convexity n convexum nt.

convey vt vehere, portāre, convehere;
(*property*) abaliēnāre; (*knowledge*)
commūnicāre; (*meaning*) significāre; **~
across** trānsmittere, trādūcere,
trānsvehere; **~ away** auferre, āvehere; **~
down** dēvehere, dēportāre; **~ into**
importāre, invehere; **~ to** advehere, adferre;
~ up subvehere.

conveyance n vehiculum nt; (*property*)
abaliēnātiō f.

convict vt (*prove guilty*) convincere; (*sentence*)
damnāre ♦ n reus m.

conviction n (*law*) damnātiō f; (*argument*)
persuāsiō f; (*belief*) fidēs f; **carry ~** fidem
facere; **have a ~** persuāsum habēre.

convince vt persuādēre (*dat*); **I am firmly ~d**
mihi persuāsum habeō.

convincing adj (*argument*) gravis; (*evidence*)
manifestus.

convincingly adv manifestō.

convivial adj convīvālis, festīvus.

conviviality n festīvitās f.

convocation n conventus m.

convoke vt convocāre.

convolution n spīra f.

convoy n praesidium nt ♦ vt prōsequī.

convulse vt agitāre; **be ~d with laughter** sē in
cachinnōs effundere.

convulsion n (MED) convulsiō f; (POL) tumultus
m.

convulsive adj spasticus.

coo vi gemere.

cook vt coquere ♦ n coquus m.

cookery n ars coquīnāria f.

cool adj frīgidus; (*conduct*) impudens; (*mind*)
impavidus, lentus ♦ n frīgus nt ♦ vt
refrīgerāre; (*passion*) restinguere, sēdāre ♦
vi refrīgēscere, refrīgerārī, dēfervēscere.

coolly adv aequō animō; impudenter.

coolness n frīgus nt; (*mind*) aequus animus m;
impudentia f.

coop n hara f; (*barrel*) cūpa f ♦ vt inclūdere.

co-operate vi operam cōnferre; **~ with**
adiuvāre, socius esse (*gen*).

co-operation n cōnsociātiō f; auxilium nt,
opera f.

co-operative adj (*person*) officiōsus.

co-operator n socius m.

co-opt vt cooptāre.

coot n fulica f.

copartner n socius m.

copartnership n societās f.

cope vi: **~ with** contendere cum (*abl*); **able to ~
with** pār (*dat*); **unable to ~ with** impār (*dat*).

copier n librārius m.

coping n fastīgium nt.

copious adj cōpiōsus, largus, plēnus,
abundāns.

copiously adv cōpiōsē, abundanter.

copiousness n cōpia f, ūbertās f.

copper n aes nt ♦ adj aēneus.

coppersmith n faber aerārius m.

coppice, copse n dūmētum nt, virgultum
nt.

copy n exemplar nt ♦ vt imitārī; (*writing*)
exscrībere, trānscrībere.

copyist n librārius m.

coracle n linter f.

coral n cūrālium nt.

cord n fūniculus m.

cordage n fūnēs mpl.

cordial adj cōmis, festīvus, amīcus; (*greetings*)
multus.

cordiality n cōmitās f, studium nt.

cordially adv cōmiter, libenter, ex animō.

cordon n corōna f.

core n (*fig*) nucleus m.

cork n sūber nt; (*bark*) cortex m.

corn n frūmentum nt ♦ adj frūmentārius; (*on

the foot) clāvus *m*; **price of ~** annōna *f*.
corndealer *n* frūmentārius *m*.
cornfield *n* seges *f*.
cornel *n* (*tree*) cornus *f*.
corner *n* angulus *m*.
cornet *n* cornū *nt*.
cornice *n* corōna *f*.
coronet *n* diadēma *nt*.
corporal *adj* corporeus.
corporal punishment *n* verbera *ntpl*.
corporation *n* collēgium *nt*; (*civic*)
magistrātūs *mpl*.
corporeal *adj* corporeus.
corps *n* manus *f*.
corpse *n* cadāver *nt*.
corpulence *n* obēsum corpus *nt*.
corpulent *adj* obēsus, pinguis.
corpuscle *n* corpusculum *nt*.
corral *n* praesēpe *nt*.
correct *vt* corrigere, ēmendāre; (*person*)
castīgāre ♦ *adj* vērus; (*language*) integer;
(*style*) ēmendātus.
correction *n* ēmendātiō *f*; (*moral*) corrēctiō *f*;
(*punishment*) castīgātiō *f*.
correctly *adv* bene, vērē.
correctness *n* (*fact*) vēritās *f*; (*language*)
integritās *f*; (*moral*) probitās *f*.
corrector *n* ēmendātor *m*, corrēctor *m*.
correspond *vi* (*agree*) respondēre (*dat*),
congruere (*dat*); (*by letter*) inter sē scrībere.
correspondence *n* similitūdō *f*; epistulae *fpl*.
correspondent *n* epistulārum scrīptor *m*.
corresponding *adj* pār.
correspondingly *adv* pariter.
corridor *n* porticus *f*.
corrigible *adj* ēmendābilis.
corroborate *vt* cōnfirmāre.
corroboration *n* cōnfirmātiō *f*.
corrode *vt* ērōdere, edere.
corrosive *adj* edāx.
corrugate *vt* rūgāre.
corrugated *adj* rūgōsus.
corrupt *vt* corrumpere, dēprāvāre; (*text*)
vitiāre ♦ *adj* corruptus, vitiātus; (*person*)
prāvus, vēnālis; (*text*) vitiātus.
corrupter *n* corruptor *m*.
corruptible *adj* (*matter*) dissolūbilis; (*person*)
vēnālis.
corruption *n* (*of matter*) corruptiō *f*; (*moral*)
corruptēla *f*, dēprāvātiō *f*; (*bribery*) ambitus
m.
corsair *n* pīrāta *m*.
cortège *n* pompa *f*.
coruscate *vi* fulgēre.
coruscation *n* fulgor *m*.
Corybant *n* Corybas *m*.
Corybantic *adj* Corybantius.
cosmetic *n* medicāmen *nt*.
cosmic *adj* mundānus.
cosmopolitan *adj* mundānus.
cosmos *n* mundus *m*.
cost *vt* emī, stāre (*dat*); **it ~ me** dear māgnō
mihi stetit, male ēmī; **it ~ me a talent** talentō

mihi stetit, talentō ēmī; **it ~ me my freedom**
lībertātem perdidi ♦ *n* pretium *nt*, impēnsa *f*;
~ of living annōna *f*; **to your ~** incommodō tuō,
dētrīmentō tuō; **at the ~ of one's reputation**
violātā fāmā, nōn salvā existimātiōne; **I sell**
at ~ price quantī ēmī vēndō.
costliness *n* sūmptus *m*; cāritās *f*.
costly *adj* cārus; (*furnishings*) lautus,
sūmptuōsus.
costume *n* habitus *m*.
cosy *adj* commodus.
cot *n* lectulus *m*.
cote *n* columbārium *nt*.
cottage *n* casa *f*, tugurium *nt*.
cottager *n* rūsticus *m*.
cotton *n* (*tree*) gossympinus *f*; (*cloth*) xylinum
nt.
couch *n* lectus *m* ♦ *vi* recumbere ♦ *vt* (*lance*)
intendere; (*words*) exprimere, reddere.
cough *n* tussis *f* ♦ *vi* tussīre.
council *n* concilium *nt*; (*small*) cōnsilium *nt*.
councillor *n* (*town*) dēcuriō *m*.
counsel *n* (*debate*) cōnsultātiō *f*; (*advice*)
cōnsilium *nt*; (*law*) advocātus *m*, patrōnus *m*;
take ~ cōnsiliārī, dēlīberāre; **take ~ of**
cōnsulere ♦ *vt* suādēre (*dat*), monēre.
counsellor *n* cōnsiliārius *m*.
count *vt* numerāre, computāre; **~ as** dūcere,
habēre; **~ amongst** pōnere in (*abl*); **~ up**
ēnumerāre; **~ upon** cōnfīdere (*dat*); **be ~ed**
among in numerō esse (*gen*) ♦ *vi* aestimārī,
habērī ♦ *n* ratiō *f*; (*in indictment*) caput *nt*;
(*title*) comes *m*.
countenance *n* faciēs *f*, vultus *m*, ōs *nt*; (*fig*)
favor *m*; **put out of ~** conturbāre ♦ *vt* favēre
(*dat*), indulgēre (*dat*).
counter *n* (*for counting*) calculus *m*; (*for play*)
tessera *f*; (*shop*) mēnsa *f* ♦ *adj* contrārius ♦
adv contrā, obviam ♦ *vt* obsistere (*dat*),
respondēre (*dat*).
counteract *vt* obsistere (*dat*), adversārī (*dat*);
(*malady*) medērī (*dat*).
counterattack *vt* in vicem oppugnāre,
adgredī.
counterattraction *n* altera illecebra *f*.
counterbalance *vt* compēnsāre, exaequāre.
counterclockwise *adv* sinistrōrsus.
counterfeit *adj* falsus, fūcātus, adsimulātus,
fictus ♦ *vt* fingere, simulāre, imitārī.
countermand *vt* renūntiāre.
counterpane *n* lōdīx *f*, strāgulum *nt*.
counterpart *n* pār *m/f/nt*.
counterpoise *n* aequum pondus *nt* ♦ *vt*
compēnsāre, exaequāre.
countersign *n* (MIL) tessera *f*.
counting table *n* abacus *m*.
countless *adj* innumerābilis.
countrified *adj* agrestis, rūsticus.
country *n* (*region*) regiō *f*, terra *f*; (*territory*)
fīnēs *mpl*; (*native*) patria *f*; (*not town*) rūs *nt*;
(*open*) agrī *mpl*; **of our ~** nostrās; **live in the ~**
rūsticārī; **living in the ~** rūsticātiō *f*.

country house n vīlla f.

countryman n agricola m; **fellow ~** populāris m, cīvis m.

countryside n agrī mpl, rus nt.

couple n pār nt; **a ~ of** duo ♦ vt cōpulare, coniungere.

couplet n distichon nt.

courage n fortitūdō f, animus m; (MIL) virtūs f; **have the ~ to** audēre; **lose ~** animōs dēmittere; **take ~** bonō animō esse.

courageous adj fortis, ācer; audāx.

courageously adv fortiter, ācriter.

courier n tabellārius m.

course n (movement) cursus m; (route) iter nt; (sequence) seriēs f; (career) dēcursus; (for races) stadium nt, circus m; (of dinner) ferculum nt; (of stones) ōrdō m; (of water) lāpsus m; **of ~** certē, sānē, scīlicet; **as a matter of ~** continuō; **in due ~** mox; **in the ~ of** inter (acc), in (abl); **keep on one's ~** cursum tenēre; **be driven off one's ~**dēicī; **second ~** secunda mēnsa.

court n (space) āreа f; (of house) ātrium nt; (of king) aula f; (suite) cohors f, comitēs mpl; (law) iūdicium nt, iūdicēs mpl; **pay ~ to** ambīre, īnservīre (dat); **hold a ~** forum agere; **bring into ~** in iūs vocāre ♦ vt colere, ambīre; (danger) sē offerre (dat); (woman) petere.

courteous adj cōmis, urbānus, hūmānus.

courteously adv cōmiter, urbānē.

courtesan n meretrīx f.

courtesy n (quality) cōmitās f, hūmānitās f; (act) officium m.

courtier n aulicus m; **~s** pl aula f.

courtly adj officiōsus.

cousin n cōnsobrīnus m, cōnsobrīna f.

cove n sinus m.

covenant n foedus nt, pactum nt ♦ vi pacīscī.

cover vt tegere, operīre; (hide) vēlāre; (march) claudere; **~ over** obdūcere; **~ up** vi obtegere ♦ n integumentum nt, operculum nt; (shelter) latebrae fpl, suffugium nt; (pretence) speciēs f; **under ~ of** sub (abl), sub speciē (gen); **take ~** dēlitēscere.

covering n integumentum nt, involucrum nt, operculum nt; (of couch) strāgulum nt.

coverlet n lōdīx f.

covert adj occultus; (language) oblīquus ♦ n latebra f, perfugium nt; (thicket) dūmētum nt.

covertly adv occultē, sēcrētō.

covet vt concupīscere, expetere.

covetous adj avidus, cupidus.

covetously adv avidē, cupidē.

covetousness n aviditās f, cupiditās f.

covey n grex f.

cow n vacca f ♦ vt terrēre.

coward n ignāvus m.

cowardice n ignāvia f.

cowardly adj ignāvus.

cower vi subsīdere.

cowherd m bubulcus m.

cowl n cucullus m.

coxswain n rēctor m.

coy adj pudens, verēcundus.

coyly adv pudenter, modestē.

coyness n pudor m, verēcundia f.

cozen vt fallere, dēcipere.

crab n cancer m.

crabbed adj mōrōsus, difficilis.

crack n (chink) rīma f; (sound) crepitus m ♦ vt findere, frangere; (whip) crepitāre (abl) ♦ vi (open) fatīscere; (sound) crepāre, crepitāre.

crackle vi crepitāre.

crackling n crepitus m.

cradle n cūnae fpl; (fig) incūnābula ntpl.

craft n ars f; (deceit) dolus m; (boat) nāvigium nt.

craftily adv callidē, sollerter; dolōsē.

craftsman n artifex m, faber m.

craftsmanship n ars f, artificium nt.

crafty adj callidus, sollers; dolōsus.

crag n rūpēs f, scopulus m.

cram vt farcīre, refercīre; (with food) sagīnāre.

cramp n convulsiō f; (tool) cōnfībula f ♦ vt coercēre, coartāre.

crane n (bird) grus f; (machine) māchina f, trochlea f.

crank n uncus m; (person) ineptus m.

crannied adj rīmōsus.

cranny n rīma f.

crash n (fall) ruīna f; (noise) fragor m ♦ vi ruere; strepere.

crass adj crassus; **~ stupidity** mera stultitia.

crate n crātēs fpl.

crater n crātēr m.

cravat n fōcāle nt.

crave vt (desire) concupīscere, adpetere, exoptāre; (request) ōrāre, obsecrāre.

craven adj ignāvus.

craving n cupīdō f, dēsīderium nt, adpetītiō f.

crawl vi (animal) serpere; (person) rēpere.

crayfish n commarus m.

craze n libīdō f ♦ vt mentem aliēnāre.

craziness n dēmentia f.

crazy adj dēmēns, fatuus.

creak vi crepāre.

creaking n crepitus m.

cream n spūma lactis f; (fig) flōs m.

crease n rūga f ♦ vt rūgāre.

create vt creāre, facere, gignere.

creation n (process) fabricātiō f; (result) opus nt; (human) hominēs mpl.

creative adj (nature) creātrīx; (mind) inventor, inventrīx.

creator n creātor m, auctor m, opifex m.

creature n animal nt; (person) homō m/f.

credence n fidēs f.

credentials n litterae commendātīciae fpl; (fig) auctōritās f.

credibility n fidēs f; (source) auctōritās f.

credible adj crēdibilis; (witness) locuplēs.

credit n (belief) fidēs f; (repute) existimātiō f; (character) auctōritās f, grātia f; (COMM) fidēs f; **be a ~ to** decus esse (gen); **it is to your ~** tibī laudī est; **give ~ for** laudem tribuere (gen);

have ~ fidē stāre ♦ *vt* crēdere (*dat*); (*with money*) acceptum referre (*dat*).
creditable *adj* honestus, laudābilis.
creditably *adv* honestē, cum laude.
creditor *n* crēditor *m*.
credulity *n* crēdulitās *f*.
credulous *adj* crēdulus.
creed *n* dogma *nt*.
creek *n* sinus *m*.
creel *n* vīdulus *m*.
creep *vi* (*animal*) serpere; (*person*) rēpere; (*flesh*) horrēre.
cremate *vt* cremāre.
crescent *n* lūna *f*.
crescent-shaped *adj* lūnātus.
cress *n* nasturtium *nt*.
crest *n* crista *f*.
crested *adj* cristātus.
crestfallen *adj* dēmissus.
crevasse *n* hiātus *m*.
crevice *n* rīma *f*.
crew *n* nautae *mpl*, rēmigēs *mpl*, grex *f*, turba *f*.
crib *n* (*cot*) lectulus *m*; (*manger*) praesēpe *nt*.
cricket *n* gryllus *m*.
crier *n* praecō *m*.
crime *n* scelus *nt*, facinus *nt*, flāgitium *nt*.
criminal *adj* scelestus, facinorōsus, flāgitiōsus ♦ *n* reus *m*.
criminality *n* scelus *nt*.
criminally *adv* scelestē, flāgitiōsē.
crimson *n* coccum *nt* ♦ *adj* coccineus.
cringe *vi* adūlārī, adsentārī.
crinkle *n* rūga *f*.
cripple *vt* dēbilitāre, mūtilāre; (*fig*) frangere ♦ *adj* claudus.
crisis *n* discrīmen *nt*.
crisp *adj* fragilis; (*manner*) alacer; (*hair*) crispus.
crisscross *adj* in quīncūncem dispositus.
criterion *n* index *m*, indicium *nt*; **take as a ~** referre ad (*acc*).
critic *n* iūdex *m*; (*literary*) criticus, grammaticus *m*; (*adverse*) castīgātor *m*.
critical *adj* (*mind*) accūrātus, ēlegāns; (*blame*) cēnsōrius, sevērus; (*danger*) perīculōsus, dubius; **~ moment** discrīmen *nt*.
critically *adv* accūrātē, ēleganter; sevērē; cum perīculō.
criticism *n* iūdicium *nt*; (*adverse*) reprehēnsiō *f*.
criticize *vt* iūdicāre; reprehendere, castīgāre.
croak *vi* (*raven*) crōcīre; (*frog*) coaxāre.
croaking *n* cantus *m* ♦ *adj* raucus.
crock *n* olla *f*.
crockery *n* fictilia *ntpl*.
crocodile *n* crocodīlus *m*; **weep ~ tears** lacrimās cōnfingere.
crocus *n* crocus *m*.
croft *n* agellus *m*.
crone *n* anus *f*.
crony *n* sodālis *m*.
crook *n* pedum *nt* ♦ *vt* incurvāre.
crooked *adj* incurvus, aduncus; (*deformed*)

prāvus; (*winding*) flexuōsus; (*morally*) perversus.
crookedly *adv* perversē, prāvē.
crookedness *n* prāvitās *f*.
croon *vt, vi* cantāre.
crop *n* (*grain*) seges *f*, messis *f*; (*tree*) fructus *m*; (*bird*) ingluviēs *f* ♦ *vt* (*reap*) metere; (*graze*) carpere, tondēre; **~ up** *vi* intervenīre.
cross *n* (*mark*) decussis *m*; (*torture*) crux *f* ♦ *adj* trānsversus, oblīquus; (*person*) acerbus, īrātus ♦ *vt* trānsīre; (*water*) trāicere; (*mountain*) trānscendere; superāre; (*enemy*) obstāre (*dat*), frustrārī; **~ out** *vt* (*writing*) expungere ♦ *vi* trānsīre; **~ over** (*on foot*) trānsgredī; (*by sea*) trānsmittere.
crossbar *n* iugum *nt*.
crossbow *n* scorpiō *m*.
cross-examination *n* interrogātiō *f*.
cross-examine *vt* interrogāre, percontārī.
cross-grained *adj* (*fig*) mōrōsus.
crossing *n* trānsitus *m*; (*on water*) trāiectus *m*.
cross purpose *n*: **be at ~s** dīversa spectāre.
cross-question *vt* interrogāre.
crossroads *n* quadrivium *nt*.
crosswise *adv* ex trānsversō; **divide ~** decussāre.
crotchety *adj* mōrōsus, difficilis.
crouch *vi* subsīdere, sē submittere.
crow *n* cornīx *f*; **as the ~ flies** rēctā regiōne ♦ *vi* cantāre; (*fig*) exsultāre, gestīre.
crowbar *n* vectis *m*.
crowd *n* turba *f*, concursus *m*, frequentia *f*; (*small*) grex *m*; multitūdō *f*; **in ~s** gregātim ♦ *vi* frequentāre, celebrāre ♦ *vt* (*place*) complēre; (*person*) stīpāre.
crowded *adj* frequēns.
crown *n* corōna *f*; (*royal*) diadēma *nt*; (*of head*) vertex *m*; (*fig*) apex *m*, flōs *m*; **the ~ of** summus ♦ *vt* corōnāre; (*fig*) cumulāre, fastīgium impōnere (*dat*).
crucial *adj* gravissimus, māximī mōmentī; **~ moment** discrīmen *nt*.
crucifixion *n* crucis supplicium *nt*.
crucify *vt* crucī suffīgere.
crude *adj* crūdus; (*style*) dūrus, inconcinnus.
crudely *adv* dūrē, asperē.
crudity *n* asperitās *f*.
cruel *adj* crūdēlis, saevus, atrōx.
cruelly *adv* crūdēliter, atrōciter.
cruelty *n* crūdēlitās *f*, saevitia *f*, atrōcitās *f*.
cruise *n* nāvigātiō *f* ♦ *vi* nāvigāre.
cruiser *n* speculātōria nāvis *f*.
crumb *n* mīca *f*.
crumble *vi* corruere, putrem fierī ♦ *vt* putrefacere, friāre.
crumbling *adj* putris.
crumple *vt* rūgāre.
crunch *vt* dentibus frangere.
crupper *n* postilēna *f*.
crush *vt* frangere, contundere, obterere; (*fig*) adflīgere, opprimere, obruere ♦ *n* turba *f*, frequentia *f*.
crust *n* crusta *f*; (*bread*) frustum *nt*.

crusty adj (fig) stomachōsus.
crutch n baculum nt.
cry vt, vi clāmāre, clāmitāre; (weep) flēre; (infant) vāgīre; ~ **down** dētrectāre; ~ **out** exclāmāre, vōciferārī; ~ **out against** adclāmāre, reclāmāre; ~ **up** laudāre, vēnditāre ♦ n clāmor m, vōx f; (child's) vāgītus m; (of grief) plōrātus m.
cryptic adj arcānus.
crystal n crystallum nt ♦ adj crystallinus.
cub n catulus m.
cube n cubus m.
cubit n cubitum nt.
cuckoo n coccyx m.
cucumber n cucumis m.
cud n: **chew the** ~ rūminārī.
cudgel n fustis m ♦ vt verberāre.
cue n signum nt, indicium nt.
cuff n (blow) alapa f.
cuirass n lōrīca f.
culinary adj coquīnārius.
cull vt legere, carpere, dēlībāre.
culminate vi ad summum fastīgium venīre.
culmination n fastīgium nt.
culpability n culpa f, noxa f.
culpable adj nocēns.
culprit n reus m.
cultivate vt (land) colere, subigere; (mind) excolere; (interest) fovēre, studēre (dat).
cultivation n cultus m, cultūra f.
cultivator n cultor m, agricola m.
cultural adj hūmānior.
culture n hūmānitās f, bonae artēs fpl.
cultured adj doctus, litterātus.
culvert n cloāca f.
cumber vt impedīre, obesse (dat); (load) onerāre.
cumbersome adj molestus, gravis.
cumulative adj alius ex aliō; **be** ~ cumulārī.
cuneiform adj cuneātus.
cunning adj callidus, astūtus ♦ n ars f, astūtia f, calliditās f.
cunningly adv callidē, astūtē.
cup n pōculum nt; **drink the** ~ **of** (fig) exanclāre, exhaurīre; **in one's** ~**s** ēbrius, pōtus.
cupboard n armārium nt.
Cupid n Cupīdō m, Amor m.
cupidity n avāritia f.
cupola n tholus m.
cupping glass n cucurbita f.
cur n canis m.
curable adj sānābilis.
curative adj salūbris.
curator n custōs m.
curb vt frēnāre, īnfrēnāre; (fig) coercēre, cohibēre ♦ n frēnum nt.
curdle vt cōgere ♦ vi concrēscere.
curds n concrētum lac nt.
cure vt sānāre, medērī (dat) ♦ n remedium nt; (process) sānātiō f.
curio n dēliciae fpl.
curiosity n studium nt; (thing) mīrāculum nt.
curious adj (inquisitive) cūriōsus, cupidus;

(artistic) ēlābōrātus; (strange) mīrus, novus.
curiously adv cūriōsē; summā arte; mīrum in modum.
curl n (natural) cirrus m; (artificial) cincinnus m ♦ vt (hair) crispāre ♦ vi (smoke) volvī.
curling irons n calamistrī mpl.
curly adj crispus.
currency n (coin) monēta f; (use) ūsus m; **gain** ~ (rumour) percrēbrēscere.
current adj vulgātus, ūsitātus; (time) hīc ♦ n flūmen nt; **with the** ~ secundō flūmine; **against the** ~ adversō flūmine.
currently adv vulgō.
curriculum n īnstitūtiō f.
curry vt (favour) aucupārī.
curse n exsecrātiō f, maledictum nt; (formula) exsecrābile carmen nt; (fig) pestis f; ~**s** (interj) malum! ♦ vt exsecrārī, maledīcere (dat).
cursed adj exsecrātus, sacer; scelestus.
cursorily adv breviter, strictim.
cursory adj brevis.
curt adj brevis.
curtail vt minuere, contrahere.
curtailment n dēminūtiō f, contractiō f.
curtain n aulaeum nt ♦ vt vēlāre.
curule adj curūlis.
curve n flexus m, arcus m ♦ vt flectere, incurvāre, arcuāre.
cushion n pulvīnus m.
custodian n custōs m.
custody n custōdia f, tūtēla f; (prison) carcer m; **hold in** ~ custōdīre.
custom n mōs m, cōnsuētūdō f; (national) īnstitūtum nt; ~**s** pl portōria ntpl.
customarily adv plērumque, dē mōre, vulgō.
customary adj solitus, ūsitātus; (rite) sollemnis; **it is** ~ mōs est.
customer n emptor m.
customs officer n portitor m.
cut vt secāre, caedere, scindere; (corn) metere; (branch) amputāre; (acquaintance) āversārī; (hair) dētondēre; ~ **away** abscindere, resecāre; ~ **down** rescindere, caedere, succīdere; ~ **into** incīdere; ~ **off** vt abscīdere, praecīdere; (exclude) exclūdere; (intercept) interclūdere, intercipere; (head) abscindere; ~ **out** vt excīdere, exsecāre; (omit) ōmittere; ~ **out for** aptus ad, nātus ad (acc); ~ **round** circumcīdere; ~ **short** praecīdere; (speech) incīdere, interrumpere; ~ **through** intercīdere; ~ **up** vt concīdere ♦ n vulnus nt.
cutlass n gladius m.
cutlery n cultrī mpl.
cutter n sector m; (boat) lembus m.
cutthroat n sīcārius m.
cutting n (plant) propāgō f ♦ adj acūtus; (fig) acerbus, mordāx.
cuttlefish n sēpia f.
cyclamen n baccar nt.
cycle n orbis m.
cyclone n turbō f.

cylinder *n* cylindrus *m*.
cymbal *n* cymbalum *nt*.
cynic *n* (*PHILOS*) cynicus *m*.
cynical *adj* mordāx, acerbus.
cynically *adv* mordāciter, acerbē.
cynicism *n* acerbitās *f*.
cynosure *n* cynosūra *f*.
cypress *n* cypressus *f*.

D, d

dabble *vi*: ~ **in** gustāre, leviter attingere.
dactyl *n* dactylus *m*.
dactylic *adj* dactylicus.
dagger *n* sīca *f*, pugiō *f*.
daily *adj* diūrnus, cottīdiānus ♦ *adv* cottīdiē, in diēs.
daintily *adv* molliter, concinnē; fastīdiōsē.
daintiness *n* munditia *f*, concinnitās *f*; (*squeamish*) fastīdium *nt*.
dainty *adj* mundus, concinnus, mollis; fastīdiōsus ♦ *npl*: **dainties** cuppēdia *ntpl*.
dais *n* suggestus *m*.
daisy *n* bellis *f*.
dale *n* vallis *f*.
dalliance *n* lascīvia *f*.
dally *vi* lūdere; morārī.
dam *n* mōlēs *f*, agger *m*; (*animal*) māter *f* ♦ *vt* obstruere, exaggerāre.
damage *n* damnum *nt*, dētrīmentum *nt*, malum *nt*; (*inflicted*) iniūria *f*; (*law*) damnum *nt*; **assess ~s** lītem aestimāre ♦ *vt* laedere, nocēre (*dat*); (*by evidence*) laedere; (*reputation*) violāre.
damageable *adj* fragilis.
dame *n* mātrōna *f*, domina *f*.
damn *vt* damnāre, exsecrārī.
damnable *adj* dētestābilis, improbus.
damnably *adv* improbē.
damnation *n* malum *nt*.
damp *adj* ūmidus ♦ *n* ūmor *m* ♦ *vt* madefacere; (*enthusiasm*) restinguere, dēmittere.
damsel *n* puella *f*, virgō *f*.
damson *n* Damascēnum *nt*.
dance *vi* saltāre ♦ *n* saltātiō *f*; (*religious*) tripudium *nt*.
dancer *n* saltātor *m*, saltātrīx *f*.
dandruff *n* porrīgō *f*.
dandy *n* dēlicātus *m*.
danger *n* perīculum *nt*, discrīmen *nt*.
dangerous *adj* perīculōsus, dubius; (*in attack*) īnfestus.
dangerously *adv* perīculōsē.
dangle *vt* suspendere ♦ *vi* pendēre.

dank *adj* ūmidus.
dapper *adj* concinnus, nitidus.
dapple *vt* variāre, distinguere.
dappled *adj* maculōsus, distinctus.
dare *vt* audēre; (*challenge*) prōvocāre; **I ~ say** haud sciō an.
daring *n* audācia *f* ♦ *adj* audāx.
daringly *adv* audācter.
dark *adj* obscūrus, opācus; (*colour*) fuscus, āter; (*fig*) obscūrus; **it is getting ~** advesperāscit; **keep ~** silēre ♦ *n* tenebrae *fpl*; (*mist*) cālīgō *f*; **keep in the ~** cēlāre.
darken *vt* obscūrāre, occaecāre.
darkish *adj* subobscūrus.
darkling *adj* obscūrus.
darkness *n* tenebrae *fpl*; (*mist*) cālīgō *f*.
darksome *adj* obscūrus.
darling *adj* cārus, dīlēctus ♦ *n* dēliciae *fpl*, voluptās *f*.
darn *vt* resarcīre.
darnel *n* lolium *nt*.
dart *n* tēlum *nt*; iaculum *nt* ♦ *vi* ēmicāre, sē conicere ♦ *vt* iaculārī, iacere.
dash *vt* adflīgere; (*hope*) frangere; **~ against** illīdere, incutere; **~ down** dēturbāre; **~ out** ēlīdere; **~ to pieces** discutere; **~ to the ground** prōsternere ♦ *vi* currere, sē incitāre, ruere ♦ *n* impetus *m*; (*quality*) ferōcia *f*.
dashing *adj* ferōx, animōsus.
dastardly *adj* ignāvus.
date *n* (*fruit*) palmula *f*; (*time*) tempus *nt*, diēs *m*; **out of ~** obsolētus; **become out of ~** exolēscere; **to ~** adhūc; **be up to ~** praesentī mōre ūtī ♦ *vt* (*letter*) diem adscrībere; (*past event*) repetere ♦ *vi* initium capere.
dative *n* datīvus *m*.
daub *vt* inlinere.
daughter *n* fīlia *f*; (*little*) fīliola *f*.
daughter-in-law *n* nurus *f*.
daunt *vt* terrēre, perterrēre.
dauntless *adj* impavidus, intrepidus.
dauntlessly *adv* impavidē, intrepidē.
dawdle *vi* cessāre, cunctārī.
dawdler *n* cunctātor *m*.
dawn *n* aurōra *f*, dīlūculum *nt*; (*fig*) orīgō *f*; **prima lux** *f*; **at ~** prīmā lūce ♦ *vi* dīlūcēscere; **day ~s** diēs illūcēscit; **it ~s upon me** mente concipiō.
day *n* diēs *m/f*; (*period*) aetās *f*; **~ about** alternīs diēbus; **~ by ~** in diēs; cotīdiē; **by ~** *adj* diūrnus ♦ *adv* interdiū; **during the ~** interdiū; **every ~** cotīdiē; **from ~ to ~** in diēs, diem dē diē; **late in the ~** multō diē; **next ~** postrīdiē; **one ~/some ~** ōlim; **the ~ after** *adv* postrīdiē ♦ *conj* postrīdiē quam; **the ~ after tomorrow** perendiē; **the ~ before** *adv* prīdiē ♦ *conj* prīdiē quam; **the ~ before yesterday** nūdius tertius; **the present ~** haec aetās; **time of ~** hōra; **twice a ~** bis (in) diē; **~s of old** praeteritum tempus; **~s to come** posteritās; **better ~s rēs** prosperae; **evil ~s rēs** adversae; **three ~s** trīduum *nt*; **two ~s** biduum *nt*; **win**

the ~ vincere.
daybook n adversāria ntpl.
daybreak n aurōra f, prīma lūx f.
daylight n diēs m; **(become)** ~ illūcēscere.
daystar n lūcifer m.
daytime n diēs m; **in the** ~ interdiū.
daze vt obstupefacere ♦ n stupor m.
dazzle vt praestringere.
dazzling adj splendidus, nitēns.
deacon n diāconus m.
deaconess n diāconissa f.
dead adj mortuus; (in battle) occīsus; (LIT) frīgidus; (place) iners, sōlitarius; (senses) hebes; ~ **of night** nox intempesta f; **be** ~ to nōn sentīre; **in** ~ **earnest** sēriō ac vērō; **rise from the** ~ revīvīscere ♦ adv prōrsus, omnīnō.
dead beat adj cōnfectus.
dead body n cadāver m.
dead calm n malacia f.
dead certainty n rēs certissima.
deaden vt (senses) hebetāre, obtundere; (pain) restinguere.
deadlock n incitae fpl; **reach a** ~ ad incitās redigī.
dead loss n mera iactūra.
deadly adj fūnestus, exitiōsus, exitiābilis; (enmity) implācābilis; (pain) acerbissimus.
dead weight n mōlēs f.
deaf adj surdus; **become** ~ obsurdēscere; **be** ~ **to** nōn audīre, obdūrēscere contrā.
deafen vt (with noise) obtundere.
deafness n surditās f.
deal n (amount) cōpia f; **a good** ~ aliquantum nt, bona pars f; (wood) abiēs f ♦ adj abiēgnus ♦ vt (blow) dare, īnflīgere; (share) dīvidere, partīrī ♦ vi agere, negōtiārī; ~ **with** vt fus (person) agere cum (abl); (matter) tractāre.
dealer n (wholesale) negōtiātor m, mercātor m; (retail) caupō m.
dealings n commercium nt, negōtium nt, rēs f.
dean n decānus m.
dear adj (love) cārus, grātus; (cost) cārus, pretiōsus; **my** ~ **Quintus** mī Quīnte; (beginning of letter from Marcus) Marcus Quintō salūtem; ~ **me!** (sorrow) hei!; (surprise) ehem!; **buy** ~ male emere; **sell** ~ bene vēndere.
dearly adv (love) valdē, ārdenter; (value) magnī.
dearness n cāritās f.
dearth n inopia f, pēnūria f.
death n mors f; (natural) obitus m; (violent) nex f, interitus m; **condemn to** ~ capitis damnāre; **put to** ~ interficere; **give the** ~ **blow to** interimere.
deathbed n: **on one's** ~ moriēns, moribundus.
deathless adj immortālis.
deathly adj pallidus.
debar vt prohibēre, exclūdere.
debase vt dēprāvāre, corrumpere; (coin) adulterāre; (self) prōsternere, dēmittere.
debasement n dēdecus nt; (coin) adulterium

nt.
debatable adj ambiguus, dubius.
debate vt disputāre, disceptāre ♦ n contrōversia f, disceptātiō f, altercātiō f.
debater n disputātor m.
debauch vt corrumpere, pellicere ♦ n cōmissātiō f.
debauched adj perditus, prāvus.
debauchee n cōmissātor m.
debaucher n corruptor m.
debauchery n luxuria f, stuprum nt.
debilitate vt dēbilitāre.
debility n īnfirmitās f.
debit n expēnsum nt ♦ vt in expēnsum referre.
debonair adj urbānus, cōmis.
debouch vi exīre.
debris n rūdus nt.
debt n aes aliēnum nt; (booked) nōmen nt; (fig) dēbitum nt; **be in** ~ in aere aliēnō esse; **pay off** ~ aes aliēnum persolvere; **run up** ~ aes aliēnum contrahere; **collect** ~s nōmina exigere; **abolition of** ~s novae tabulae fpl.
debtor n dēbitor m.
decade n decem annī mpl.
decadence n occāsus m.
decadent adj dēgener, dēterior.
decamp vi (MIL) castra movēre; (fig) discēdere, aufugere.
decant vt dēfundere, diffundere.
decanter n lagoena f.
decapitate vt dētruncāre.
decay vi dīlābī, perīre, putrēscere; (fig) tābēscere, senēscere ♦ n ruīna f, lāpsus m; (fig) occāsus m, dēfectiō f.
deceased adj mortuus.
deceit n fraus f, fallācia f, dolus m.
deceitful adj fallāx, fraudulentus, dolōsus.
deceitfully adv fallāciter, dolōsē.
deceive vt dēcipere, fallere, circumvenīre, fraudāre.
deceiver n fraudātor m.
December n mēnsis December m; **of** ~ December.
decemvir n decemvir m; **of the** ~s decemvirālis.
decemvirate n decemvirātus m.
decency n honestum nt, decōrum nt, pudor m.
decent adj honestus, pudēns.
decently adv honestē, pudenter.
deception n fraus f, fallācia f.
deceptive adj fallāx, fraudulentus.
decide vt, vi (dispute) dīiūdicāre, dēcernere, dīrimere; ~ **to do** statuere, cōnstituere (infin); **I have** ~d mihī certum est; ~ **the issue** dēcernere.
decided adj certus, firmus.
decidedly adv certē, plānē.
deciduous adj cadūcus.
decimate vt decimum quemque occīdere.
decipher vt expedīre, ēnōdāre.
decision n (of judge) iūdicium nt; (of council) dēcrētum nt; (of senate) auctōritās f; (of referee) arbitrium nt; (personal) sententia f;

(_quality_) cōnstantia _f._
decisive _adj_ certus; ~ **moment** discrīmen _nt._
decisively _adv_ sine dubiō.
deck _vt_ ōrnāre, exōrnāre ♦ _n_
(_ship_) pōns _m_; **with a** ~ cōnstrātus.
decked _adj_ ōrnātus; (_ship_) cōnstrātus.
declaim _vt, vi_ dēclāmāre, prōnūntiāre.
declamation _n_ dēclāmātiō _f._
declamatory _adj_ dēclāmātōrius.
declaration _n_ adfirmātiō _f_, adsevērātiō _f_;
(_formal_) prōfessiō _f_; (_of war_) dēnūntiātiō _f._
declare _vt_ affirmāre, adsevērāre; (_secret_)
aperīre, expōnere; (_proclamation_)
dēnūntiāre, ēdīcere; (_property in census_)
dēdicāre; (_war_) indīcere.
declension _n_ dēclīnātiō _f._
declination _n_ dēclīnātiō _f._
decline _n_ (_slope_) dēclīve _nt_, dēiectus _m_; (_of age_)
senium _nt_; (_of power_) dēfectiō _f_; (_of nation_)
occāsus _m_ ♦ _vi_ inclīnāre, occidere; (_fig_)
ruere, dēlābī, dēgenerāre ♦ _vt_ dētrectāre,
recūsare; (_GRAM_) dēclīnāre.
decode _vt_ expedīre, ēnōdāre.
decompose _vt_ dissolvere ♦ _vi_ putrēscere.
decomposed _adj_ putridus.
decomposition _n_ dissolūtiō _f._
decorate _vt_ ōrnāre, decorāre.
decoration _n_ ōrnāmentum _nt_; (_medal_) īnsigne
_nt._
decorous _adj_ pudēns, modestus, decōrus.
decorously _adv_ pudenter, modestē.
decorum _n_ pudor _m_, honestum _nt._
decoy _n_ illecebra _f_ ♦ _vt_ adlicere, inescāre.
decrease _n_ dēminūtiō _f_, dēcessiō _f_ ♦ _vt_
dēminuere, extenuāre ♦ _vi_ dēcrēscere.
decree _n_ (_of magistrate_) dēcrētum _nt_, ēdictum
_nt_; (_of senate_) cōnsultum _nt_, auctōritās _f_; (_of
people_) scītum _nt_ ♦ _vt_ ēdīcere, dēcernere;
(_people_) scīscere, iubēre; **the senate** ~**s**
placet senātuī.
decrepit _adj_ īnfirmus, dēbilis, dēcrepitus.
decrepitude _n_ īnfirmitās _f_, dēbilitās _f._
decry _vt_ obtrectāre, reprehendere.
decurion _n_ decuriō _m._
dedicate _vt_ dēdicāre, cōnsecrāre; (_life_)
dēvovēre.
dedication _n_ dēdicātiō _f_; dēvōtiō _f._
dedicatory _adj_ commendātīcius.
deduce _vt_ colligere, conclūdere.
deduct _vt_ dēmere, dētrahere.
deduction _n_ (_inference_) conclūsiō _f_,
cōnsequēns _nt_; (_subtraction_) dēductiō _f_,
dēminūtiō _f._
deed _n_, factum _nt_, facinus _nt_; gestum _nt_; (_legal_)
tabulae _fpl_; ~**s** _pl_ rēs gestae _fpl._
deem _vt_ dūcere, cēnsēre, habēre.
deep _adj_ altus, profundus; (_discussion_)
abstrūsus; (_sleep_) artus; (_sound_) gravis;
(_width_) lātus; **three** ~ (_MIL_) ternī in
lātitūdinem ♦ _n_ altum _nt._
deepen _vt_ dēfodere, altiōrem reddere; (_fig_)
augēre ♦ _vi_ altiōrem fierī; (_fig_) crēscere.
deepest _adj_ īmus.

deeply _adv_ altē, graviter; (_inside_) penitus; **very**
~ valdē, vehementer.
deep-seated _adj_ (_fig_) inveterātus.
deer _n_ cervus _m_, cerva _f_; (_fallow_) dāma _f._
deface _vt_ dēfōrmāre, foedāre.
defaced _adj_ dēfōrmis.
defacement _n_ dēfōrmitās _f._
defalcation _n_ peculātus _m._
defamation _n_ calumnia _f_, opprobrium _nt._
defamatory _adj_ contumēliōsus, probrōsus.
defame _vt_ īnfāmāre, obtrectāre, calumniārī.
default _vi_ dēesse; (_money_) nōn solvere ♦ _n_
dēfectiō _f_, culpa _f_; **let judgment go by** ~
vadimōnium dēserere, nōn respondēre.
defaulter _n_ reus _m._
defeat _vt_ vincere, superāre; (_completely_)
dēvincere; (_plan_) frustrārī, disicere ♦ _n_
clādēs _f_; (_at election_) repulsa _f_, offēnsiō _f_; (_of
plan_) frustrātiō _f._
defeatism _n_ patientia _f._
defeatist _n_ imbellis _m._
defect _n_ vitium _nt._
defection _n_ dēfectiō _f_, sēditiō _f._
defective _adj_ mancus, vitiōsus.
defence _n_ praesidium _nt_, tūtēla _f_; patrōcinium
_nt_; (_speech_) dēfēnsiō _f_; **speak in** ~ dēfendere.
defenceless _adj_ inermis, indēfēnsus; **leave** ~
nūdāre.
defences _npl_ mūnīmenta _ntpl_, mūnītiōnēs _fpl._
defend _vt_ dēfendere, tuērī, custōdīre.
defendant _n_ reus _m._
defender _n_ dēfēnsor _m_, prōpugnātor _m_; (_law_)
patrōnus _m._
defensible _adj_ iūstus.
defensive _adj_ dēfēnsiōnis causā; **be on the** ~
sē dēfendere.
defensively _adv_ dēfendendō.
defer _vt_ differre, prōlātāre ♦ _vi_ mōrem gerere
(_dat_); **I** ~ **to you in this** hōc tibī tribuō.
deference _n_ obsequium _nt_, observantia _f_;
show ~ **to** observāre, īnservīre (_dat_).
deferential _adj_ observāns, officiōsus.
deferment _n_ dīlatiō _f_, prōlātiō _f._
defiance _n_ ferōcia _f_, minae _fpl._
defiant _adj_ ferōx, mināx.
defiantly _adv_ ferōciter, mināciter.
deficiency _n_ vitium _nt_; (_lack_) pēnūria _f_, inopia
_f._
deficient _adj_ vitiōsus, inops; **be** ~ dēesse,
dēficere.
deficit _n_ lacūna _f._
defile _n_ faucēs _fpl_, angustiae _fpl_ ♦ _vt_ inquināre,
contāmināre.
defilement _n_ sordēs _f_, foeditās _f._
define _vt_ (_limits_) fīnīre, dēfīnīre, termināre;
(_meaning_) explicāre.
definite _adj_ certus, dēfīnītus.
definitely _adv_ dēfīnītē; prōrsus.
definition _n_ dēfīnītiō _f_, explicātiō _f._
definitive _adj_ dēfīnītīvus.
deflate _vt_ laxāre.
deflect _vt_ dēdūcere, dēclīnāre ♦ _vi_ dēflectere,
dēgredī.

deflection n dēclīnātiō f, flexus m.
deform vt dēfōrmāre.
deformed adj dēfōrmis, distortus.
deformity n dēfōrmitās f, prāvitās f.
defraud vt fraudāre, dēfraudāre.
defrauder n fraudātor m.
defray vt solvere, suppeditāre.
deft adj habilis.
deftly adv habiliter.
defunct adj mortuus.
defy vt contemnere, spernere, adversārī (dat);
(challenge) prōvocāre, lacessere.
degeneracy n dēprāvātiō f.
degenerate adj dēgener ♦ vi dēgenerāre,
dēscīscere.
degradation n īnfāmia f, ignōminia f, nota f.
degrade vt notāre, abicere; (from office)
movēre.
degrading adj turpis, indignus.
degree n gradus; (social) locus m; **in some ~**
aliquā ex parte; **by ~s** gradātim, sēnsim.
deification n apotheōsis f.
deified adj (emperor) dīvus.
deify vt cōnsecrāre, inter deōs referre.
deign vi dignārī.
deity n deus m.
dejected adj adflīctus, dēmissus.
dejectedly adv animō dēmissō.
dejection n maestitia f.
delay vt dēmorārī, dētinēre, retardāre ♦ vi
cunctārī, cessāre ♦ n mora f, cunctātiō f.
delayer n morātor m, cunctātor m.
delectable adj iūcundus, amoenus.
delegate vt lēgāre, mandāre, committere ♦ n
lēgātus m.
delegation n lēgātiō f, lēgātī mpl.
delete vt dēlēre.
deleterious adj perniciōsus, noxius.
deletion n (writing) litūra f.
deliberate vi dēlīberāre, cōnsulere ♦ adj (act)
cōnsīderātus; (intention) certus; (manner)
cōnsīderātus; (speech) lentus.
deliberately adv dē industriā.
deliberation n dēlīberātiō f.
deliberative adj dēlīberātīvus.
delicacy n (judgment) subtīlitās f, ēlegantia f;
(manners) mollitia f, luxus m; (health)
valētūdō f; (food) cuppēdia ntpl.
delicate adj mollis; (health) īnfīrmus; (shape)
gracilis; (feelings) hūmānus.
delicately adv molliter; hūmānē.
delicious adj suāvis, lautus.
delight n voluptās f, gaudium nt, dēlectātiō f ♦
vt dēlectāre, oblectāre, iuvāre ♦ vi gaudēre,
dēlectārī.
delightful adj iūcundus, dulcis, festīvus;
(scenery) amoenus.
delightfully adv iūcundē, suāviter.
delimitation n dēfīnītiō f.
delineate vt dēscrībere, dēpingere.
delineation n dēscrīptiō f.
delinquency n culpa f, dēlictum nt, noxa f.
delinquent n nocēns m/f, reus m.

delirious adj dēlīrus, āmēns, furiōsus; **be ~**
furere, dēlīrāre.
delirium n furor m, āmentia f.
deliver vt (from) līberāre, exsolvere, ēripere;
(blow) intendere; (message) referre; (speech)
habēre; **~ to** dēferre, trādere, dare; **~ up**
dēdere, trādere; **be ~ed of** parere.
deliverance n līberātiō f.
deliverer n līberātor m.
delivery n (of things due) trāditiō f; (of speech)
āctiō f, prōnūntiātiō f; (of child) partus m.
dell n convallis f.
Delphi n Delphī mpl.
delude vt dēcipere, frustrārī, dēlūdere.
deluge n ēluviō f ♦ vt inundāre.
delusion n error m, fraus f.
delusive adj fallāx, inānis.
delve vt fodere.
demagogue n plēbicola m.
demand vt poscere, postulāre, imperāre;
(urgently) flāgitāre, poscere; (thing due)
exigere; (answer) quaerere; **~ back** repetere
♦ n postulātiō f, postulātum nt.
demarcation n līmes m.
demean vt (self) dēmittere.
demeanour n gestus m, mōs m, habitus m.
demented adj dēmēns, furiōsus.
demerit n culpa f, vitium nt.
demesne n fundus m.
demigod n hērōs m.
demise n obitus m ♦ vt lēgāre.
democracy n cīvitās populāris f.
democrat n homō populāris m/f.
democratic adj populāris.
demolish vt dēmōlīrī, dīruere, dēstruere;
(argument) discutere.
demolition n ruīna f, ēversiō f.
demon n daemōn m.
demonstrate vt (show) mōnstrāre, ostendere,
indicāre; (prove) dēmōnstrāre.
demonstration n exemplum nt; (proof)
dēmōnstrātiō f.
demonstrative adj (manner) vehemēns; (RHET)
dēmōnstrātīvus.
demoralization n corruptiō f, dēprāvātiō f.
demoralize vt corrumpere, dēprāvāre,
labefactāre.
demote vt locō movēre.
demur vi gravārī, recūsāre ♦ n mora f,
dubitātiō f.
demure adj modestus, verēcundus.
demurely adv modestē, verēcundē.
demureness n modestia f, verēcundia f,
pudor m.
demurrer n (law) exceptiō f.
den n latibulum nt, latebra f; (of vice) lustrum
nt.
denarius n dēnārius m.
denial n īnfitiātiō f, negātiō f.
denigrate vt obtrectāre, calumniārī.
denizen n incola m/f.
denominate vt nōmināre, appellāre.
denomination n nōmen nt; (religious) secta f.

denote *vt* notāre, significāre.
denouement *n* exitus *m*.
denounce *vt* dēferre, incūsāre.
denouncer *n* dēlātor *m*.
dense *adj* dēnsus; (*crowd*) frequēns; (*person*) stolidus.
density *n* crassitūdō *f*; (*crowd*) frequentia *f*.
dent *n* nota *f*.
dentate *adj* dentātus.
denture *n* dentēs *mpl*.
denudation *n* spoliātiō *f*.
denude *vt* spoliāre, nūdāre.
denunciation *n* (*report*) indicium *nt*, dēlātiō *f*; (*threat*) minae *fpl*.
deny *vt* īnfitiārī, īnfitiās īre, negāre, abnuere; (*on oath*) abiūrāre; ~ **oneself** genium dēfraudāre.
depart *vi* discēdere (*abl*), abīre, exīre, ēgredī.
department *n* (*district*) regiō *f*, pars *f*; (*duty*) prōvincia *f*, mūnus *nt*.
departure *n* discessus *m*, abitus *m*, dīgressus *m*, exitus *m*; (*change*) mūtātiō *f*; (*death*) obitus *m*.
depend *vi* pendēre; (*be dependent*) pendēre ex (*abl*), nītī (*abl*); (*rely*) fīdere, cōnfīdere; ~**ing on** frētus (*abl*).
dependable *adj* fīdus.
dependant *n* cliēns *m/f*.
dependence *n* clientēla *f*; (*reliance*) fīdūcia *f*.
dependency *n* prōvincia *f*.
dependent *adj* subiectus, obnoxius.
depict *vt* dēscrībere, dēpingere; (*to the life*) expingere.
deplete *vt* dēminuere.
depletion *n* dēminūtiō *f*.
deplorable *adj* turpis, nefandus, pessimus.
deplorably *adv* turpiter, pessimē, miserē.
deplore *vt* dēplōrāre, dēfīere, conquerī.
deploy *vt* explicāre; instruere, dispōnere.
depopulate *vt* vastāre, nūdāre.
depopulation *n* vastātiō *f*, sōlitūdō *f*.
deport *vt* (*banish*) dēportāre; (*self*) gerere.
deportation *n* exsilium *nt*.
deportment *n* gestus *m*, habitus *m*.
depose *vt* dēmovēre, dēpellere; (*evidence*) testārī.
deposit *n* fīdūcia *f*, dēpositum *nt* ♦ *vt* dēpōnere, mandāre.
depositary *n* sequester *m*.
deposition *n* (*law*) testimōnium *nt*, indicium *nt*.
depository *n* apothēca *f*.
depot *n* (*for arms*) armāmentārium *nt*; (*for trade*) emporium *nt*.
deprave *vt* dēprāvāre, corrumpere.
depraved *adj* prāvus.
depravity *n* dēprāvātiō *f*, turpitūdō *f*.
deprecate *vt* abōminārī, dēprecārī.
deprecation *n* dēprecātiō *f*.
depreciate *vt* obtrectāre, dētrectāre.
depreciation *n* obtrectātiō *f*; (*price*) vīlitās *f*.
depredation *n* praedātiō *f*, dīreptiō *f*.
depress *vt* dēprimere; (*mind*) adflīgere,

frangere; **be ~ed** iacēre, animum dēspondēre.
depressing *adj* maestus, tristis.
depression *n* (*place*) cavum *nt*; (*mind*) tristitia *f*, sollicitūdō *f*.
deprivation *n* prīvātiō *f*, spoliātiō *f*.
deprive *vt* prīvāre, spoliāre.
depth *n* altitūdō *f*; (*place*) profundum *nt*, gurges *m*.
deputation *n* lēgātiō *f*, lēgātī *mpl*.
depute *vt* lēgāre, mandāre.
deputy *n* lēgātus *m*; (*substitute*) vicārius *m*.
derange *vt* conturbāre.
deranged *adj* īnsānus, mente captus.
derangement *n* perturbātiō *f*; (*mind*) īnsānia *f*, dēmentia *f*.
derelict *adj* dēsertus.
dereliction *n* (*of duty*) neglegentia *f*.
deride *vt* dērīdēre, inlūdere.
derision *n* rīsus *m*, irrīsiō *f*.
derisive *adj* mordāx.
derivation *n* orīgō *f*.
derive *vt* dūcere, trahere; (*advantage*) capere, parāre; (*pleasure*) dēcerpere, percipere; **be ~d** dēfluere.
derogate *vi* dērogāre, dētrahere; ~ **from** imminuere, obtrectāre.
derogation *n* imminūtiō *f*, obtrectātiō *f*.
derogatory *adj* indignus; ~ **remarks** obtrectātiō *f*.
derrick *n* trochlea *f*.
descant *vt* disserere ♦ *n* cantus *m*.
descend *vi* dēscendere; (*water*) dēlābī; (*from heaven*) dēlābī; (*by inheritance*) pervenīre, prōdī; (*morally*) dēlābī, sē dēmittere; **be ~ed from** orīrī ex (*abl*).
descendant *n* prōgeniēs *f*; ~**s** *pl* minōrēs *mpl*, posterī *mpl*.
descent *n* dēscensus *m*; (*slope*) clīvus *m*, dēiectus *m*; (*birth*) genus *nt*; (*hostile*) dēcursus *m*, incursiō *f*; **make a ~ upon** inrumpere in (*acc*), incursāre in (*acc*).
describe *vt* dēscrībere; (*tell*) nārrāre; (*portray*) dēpingere, exprimere.
description *n* dēscrīptiō *f*; (*tale*) nārrātiō *f*; (*kind*) genus *nt*.
descry *vt* cernere, cōnspicere, prōspectāre.
desecrate *vt* prōfānāre, exaugurāre.
desecration *n* exaugurātiō *f*, violātiō *f*.
desert *vt* dēserere, dērelinquere, dēstituere ♦ *vi* dēscīscere, dēficere ♦ *adj* dēsertus, sōlitārius ♦ *n* (*place*) sōlitūdō *f*, loca dēserta *ntpl*; (*merit*) meritum *nt*.
deserted *adj* dēsertus.
deserter *n* dēsertor *m*; (*MIL*) trānsfuga *m*.
desertion *n* dēfectiō *f*, trānsfugium *nt*.
deserve *vt* merērī; dignus esse quī (+ *subj*); ~ **well of** bene merērī dē (*abl*).
deserved *adj* meritus.
deservedly *adv* meritō.
deserving *adj* dignus.
desiccate *vt* siccāre.
design *n* (*drawing*) adumbrātiō *f*; (*plan*)

cōnsilium *nt*, prōpositum *nt*; **by ~** cōnsultō ♦
vt adumbrāre; in animō habēre.
designate *vt* dēsignāre, mōnstrāre; (*as heir*)
scrībere; (*as official*) dēsignāre ♦ *adj*
dēsignātus.
designation *n* nōmen *nt*, titulus *m*.
designedly *adv* dē industriā, cōnsultō.
designer *n* auctor *m*, inventor *m*.
designing *adj* vafer, dolōsus.
desirable *adj* optābilis, expetendus, grātus.
desire *n* cupīditās *f*; studium *nt*; (*uncontrolled*)
libīdō *f*; (*natural*) adpetītiō *f* ♦ *vt* cupere;
(*much*) exoptāre, expetere; (*command*)
iubēre.
desirous *adj* cupidus, avidus, studiōsus.
desist *vi* dēsistere.
desk *n* scrīnium *nt*.
desolate *adj* dēsertus, sōlitārius; (*place*)
vastus ♦ *vt* vastāre.
desolation *n* sōlitūdō *f*, vastitās *f*; (*process*)
vastātiō *f*.
despair *vi* dēspērāre dē (*abl*), animum
dēspondēre ♦ *n* dēspērātiō *f*.
despairingly *adv* dēspēranter.
despatch *see* dispatch.
desperado *n* homō dēspērātus *m*.
desperate *adj* (*hopeless*) dēspērātus; (*wicked*)
perditus; (*dangerous*) perīculōsus.
desperately *adv* dēspēranter.
desperation *n* dēspērātiō *f*.
despicable *adj* dēspectus, abiectus, turpis.
despicably *adv* turpiter.
despise *vt* contemnere, dēspicere, spernere.
despiser *n* contemptor *m*.
despite *n* malevolentia *f*, odium *nt*.
despoil *vt* spoliāre, nūdāre.
despoiler *n* spoliātor *m*, praedātor *m*.
despond *vi* animum dēspondēre, dēspērāre.
despondency *n* dēspērātiō *f*.
despondent *adj* abiectus, adflīctus, dēmissus;
be ~ animum dēspondēre.
despondently *adv* animō dēmissō.
despot *n* dominus *m*, rēx *m*.
despotic *adj* imperiōsus, superbus.
despotically *adv* superbē.
despotism *n* dominātiō *f*, superbia *f*, rēgnum
nt.
dessert *n* secunda mēnsa *f*.
destination *n* fīnis *m*.
destine *vt* dēstināre, dēsignāre; **~d to be**
futūrus.
destiny *n* fātum *nt*; **of ~** fātālis.
destitute *adj* inops, pauper, prīvātus; **~ of**
expers (*gen*).
destitution *n* inopia *f*, egestās *f*.
destroy *vt* dēlēre, ēvertere, dīrimere,
perdere.
destroyer *n* ēversor *m*.
destructible *adj* fragilis.
destruction *n* exitium *nt*, ēversiō *f*, excidium
nt.
destructive *adj* exitiābilis, perniciōsus.
destructively *adv* perniciōsē.

desuetude *n* dēsuētūdō *f*.
desultorily *adv* carptim.
desultory *adj* varius, incōnstāns.
detach *vt* abiungere, sēiungere, āmovēre,
sēparāre.
detachment *n* (MIL) manus *f*, cohors *f*; (*mind*)
integer animus *m*, līber animus.
detail *n*: **~s** *pl* singula *ntpl*; **in ~** singillātim ♦ *vt*
exsequī.
detain *vt* dēmorārī, dētinēre, distinēre,
morārī.
detect *vt* dēprehendere, patefacere.
detection *n* dēprehēnsiō *f*.
detective *n* inquīsītor *m*.
detention *n* retentiō *f*; (*prison*) vincula *ntpl*.
deter *vt* dēterrēre, absterrēre, impedīre.
deteriorate *vi* dēgenerāre.
deterioration *n* dēprāvātiō *f*, lāpsus *m*.
determinate *adj* certus, fīnītus.
determination *n* obstinātiō *f*, cōnstantia *f*;
(*intention*) prōpositum *nt*, sententia *f*.
determine *vt* (*fix*) fīnīre; (*decide*) statuere,
cōnstituere.
determined *adj* obstinātus; (*thing*) certus; **I
am ~ to** mihī certum est (*infin*).
determinedly *adv* cōnstanter.
deterrent *n*: **act as a ~ to** dēterrēre.
detest *vt* ōdisse, dētēstārī.
detestable *adj* dētēstābilis, odiōsus.
detestation *n* odium *nt*, invidia *f*.
dethrone *vt* rēgnō dēpellere.
detour *n* circuitus *m*; **make a ~** iter flectere;
(MIL) agmen circumdūcere.
detract *vi*: **~ from** dērogāre, dētrahere.
detraction *n* obtrectātiō *f*.
detractor *n* obtrectātor *m*, invidus *m*.
detriment *n* damnum *nt*, dētrīmentum *nt*.
detrimental *adj* damnōsus; **be ~ to** dētrīmentō
esse (*dat*).
devastate *vt* vastāre, populārī.
devastation *n* vastātiō *f*, populātiō *f*; (*state*)
vastitās *f*.
develop *vt* ēvolvere, explicāre; (*person*)
ēducāre, alere ♦ *vi* crēscere; **~ into** ēvādere
in (*acc*).
development *n* explicātiō *f*; (*of men*) ēducātiō
f; (*of resources*) cultus *m*; (*of events*) exitus *m*.
deviate *vi* dēcēdere dē viā, aberrāre,
dēclīnāre; (*speech*) dēgredī.
deviation *n* dēclīnātiō *f*; (*from truth*) error *m*;
(*in speech*) dīgressus *m*.
device *n* (*plan*) cōnsilium *nt*; (*machine*)
māchina *f*; (*emblem*) īnsigne *nt*.
devil *n* diabolus *m*; **go to the ~** abī in malam
crucem!; **talk of the ~** lupus in fābulā!
devilish *adj* scelestus, impius.
devil-may-care *adj* praeceps, lascīvus.
devilment *n* malitia *f*.
devilry *n* magicae artēs *fpl*.
devious *adj* dēvius, errābundus.
devise *vt* excōgitāre, commentārī, fingere.
devoid *adj* vacuus, expers; **be ~ of** carēre (*abl*).
devolve *vi* obtingere, obvenīre ♦ *vt* dēferre,

committere.
devote *vt* dēdicāre; (*attention*) dēdere,
trādere; (*life*) dēvovēre.
devoted *adj* dēditus, studiōsus; (*victim*)
dēvōtus, sacer; **be ~ to** studēre (*dat*),
incumbere (*dat*).
devotee *n* cultor *m*.
devotion *n* amor *m*, studium *nt*; rēligiō *f*.
devour *vt* dēvorāre, cōnsūmere; (*fig*) haurīre.
devout *adj* pius, rēligiōsus.
devoutly *adv* piē, rēligiōsē.
dew *n* rōs *m*.
dewy *adj* rōscidus.
dexterity *n* ars *f*, sollertia *f*.
dexterous *adj* sollers, habilis.
dexterously *adv* sollerter, habiliter.
diabolical *adj* scelestus, nefārius.
diadem *n* diadēma *nt*.
diagnose *vt* discernere, diiūdicāre.
diagnosis *n* iūdicium *nt*.
diagonal *adj* oblīquus.
diagram *n* fōrma *f*.
dial *n* sōlārium *nt*.
dialect *n* dialectus *f*, sermō *m*.
dialectic *n* ars disserendī *f*, dialecticē *f* ♦ *adj*
dialecticus.
dialectician *n* dialecticus *m*.
dialogue *n* dialogus *m*, colloquium *nt*.
diameter *n* diametros *f*.
diamond *n* adamās *m*.
diaphanous *adj* perlūcidus.
diaphragm *n* praecordia *ntpl*.
diary *n* ephēmeris *f*.
diatribe *n* convīcium *nt*.
dice *n* tālus *m*, tessera *f*; **game of ~** ālea *f*.
dictate *vt* dictāre ♦ *n* praeceptum *nt*; **~s of**
nature nātūrae iūdicia *ntpl*.
dictation *n* dictāta *ntpl*; (*fig*) arbitrium *nt*.
dictator *n* dictātor *m*; **~'s** dictātōrius.
dictatorial *adj* imperiōsus, superbus.
dictatorship *n* dictātūra *f*.
diction *n* (*enunciation*) ēlocūtiō *f*; (*words*) ōrātiō
f.
dictionary *n* verbōrum thēsaurus *m*.
die *n* signum *nt*; **the ~ is cast** iacta ālea est ♦ *vi*
morī, perīre, obīre; (*in battle*) cadere,
occumbere; **~ off** dēmorī; **~ out** ēmorī; **be**
dying to exoptāre.
diet *n* (*food*) diaeta *f*; (*meeting*) conventus *m*.
differ *vi* differre, discrepāre, dissentīre.
difference *n* discrepantia *f*, dissimilitūdō *f*; (*of*
opinion) dissēnsiō *f*; **there is a ~** interest.
different *adj* dīversus, varius, dissimilis; **~**
from alius ... ac; **in ~ directions** dīversī; **they**
say ~ things alius aliud dīcit.
differentiate *vt* discernere.
differently *adv* dīversē, variē, alius aliter; **~**
from aliter ... ac.
difficult *adj* difficilis, arduus; **very ~**
perdifficilis, perarduus.
difficulty *n* difficultās *f*, labor *m*, negōtium *nt*;
with ~ difficulter, aegrē, vix; **be in ~**
labōrāre.

diffidence *n* diffīdentia *f*; (*shyness*) pudor *m*;
with ~ modestē.
diffident *adj* diffīdēns; (*shy*) modestus,
verēcundus.
diffidently *adv* modestē.
diffuse *vt* diffundere, dispergere; **be ~d**
diffluere ♦ *adj* fūsus, diffūsus, cōpiōsus.
diffusely *adv* diffūsē, cōpiōsē.
diffuseness *n* cōpia *f*.
dig *vt* fodere; dūcere; (*nudge*) fodicāre; **~ up** *vt*
effodere, ēruere.
digest *vt* coquere, concoquere ♦ *n*
summārium *nt*.
digestion *n* concoctiō *f*; **with a bad ~** crūdus.
digger *n* fossor *m*.
dignified *adj* gravis, augustus.
dignify *vt* honōrāre, honestāre.
dignity *n* gravitās *f*, māiestās *f*, amplitūdō *f*.
digress *vi* dēvertere, dīgredī, dēclīnāre.
digression *n* dēclīnātiō *f*, dīgressus *m*.
dike *n* (*ditch*) fossa *f*; (*mound*) agger *m*.
dilapidated *adj* ruīnōsus.
dilapidation *n* ruīna *f*.
dilate *vt* dīlātāre; (*speech*) plūra dīcere.
dilatorily *adv* tardē, cunctanter.
dilatoriness *n* mora *f*, cunctātiō *f*.
dilatory *adj* tardus, lentus, segnis.
dilemma *n* nōdus *m*, angustiae *fpl*; **be in a ~**
haerēre; **be on the horns of a ~** auribus
tenēre lupum.
diligence *n* dīligentia *f*, industria *f*, cūra *f*.
diligent *adj* dīligēns, industrius, sēdulus.
diligently *adv* dīligenter, sēdulō.
dill *n* anēthum *nt*.
dilly-dally *vi* cessāre.
dilute *vt* dīluere, temperāre.
dim *adj* obscūrus; (*fig*) hebes ♦ *vt* obscūrāre;
hebetāre.
dimension *n* modus *m*; **~s** *pl* amplitūdō *f*,
māgnitūdō *f*.
diminish *vt* minuere, imminuere, extenuāre,
īnfringere ♦ *vi* dēcrēscere.
diminution *n* imminūtiō *f*, dēminūtiō *f*.
diminutive *adj* parvulus, exiguus ♦ *n* (*word*)
dēminūtum *nt*.
diminutiveness *n* exiguitās *f*.
dimly *adv* obscūrē.
dimness *n* tenebrae *fpl*, cālīgō *f*.
dimple *n* gelasīnus *m*.
din *n* fragor *m*, strepitus *m*; **make a ~** strepere
♦ *vt* obtundere.
dine *vi* cēnāre.
diner *n* convīva *m*.
dinghy *n* scapha *f*.
dingy *adj* sordidus; (*colour*) fuscus.
dining room *n* cēnātiō *f*.
dinner *n* cēna *f*.
dinner party *n* convīvium *nt*.
dint *n* ictus *m*; **by ~ of** per (*acc*).
dip *vt* imbuere, mergere ♦ *vi* mergī; **~ into**
(*study*) perstringere.
diploma *n* diplōma *nt*.
diplomacy *n* (*embassy*) lēgātiō *f*; (*tact*)

iūdicium *nt*, sagācitās *f*.
diplomat *n* lēgātus *m*.
diplomatic *adj* sagāx, circumspectus.
diptych *n* tabellae *fpl*.
dire *adj* dīrus, horridus.
direct *vt* regere, dīrigere; (*attention*)
attendere, admovēre, advertere; (*course*)
tendere; (*business*) administrāre, moderārī;
(*letter*) īnscrībere; (*order*) imperāre (*dat*),
iubēre; (*to a place*) viam mōnstrāre (*dat*);
(*weapon*) intendere ♦ *adj* rēctus, dīrēctus;
(*person*) simplex; (*language*) apertus ♦ *adv*
rēctā.
direction *n* (*of going*) cursus *m*, iter *nt*; (*of
looking*) pars *f*, regiō *f*; (*control*) administrātiō
f, regimen *nt*; (*order*) praeceptum *nt*, iussum
nt; **in the ~ of Rome** Rōmam versus; **in all ~s**
passim, undique; **in both ~s** utrōque.
directly *adv* (*place*) rēctā; (*time*) prōtinus,
continuō, statim; (*language*) apertē ♦ *conj*
simulac.
directness *n* (*fig*) simplicitās *f*.
director *n* dux *m*, gubernātor *m*, moderātor *m*.
dirge *n* nēnia *f*.
dirk *n* pūgiō *m*.
dirt *n* sordēs *f*; (*mud*) lūtum *nt*.
dirty *adj* sordidus, foedus; (*speech*) inquinātus
♦ *vt* foedāre, inquināre.
disability *n* vitium *nt*.
disable *vt* dēbilitāre, imminuere.
disabled *adj* mutilus, dēbilis.
disabuse *vt* errōrem dēmere (*dat*).
disaccustom *vt* dēsuēfacere.
disadvantage *n* incommodum *nt*,
dētrīmentum *nt*; **it is a ~** dētrīmentō est.
disadvantageous *adj* incommodus, inīquus.
disadvantageously *adv* incommodē.
disaffected *adj* aliēnātus, sēditiōsus.
disaffection *n* aliēnātiō *f*, sēditiō *f*.
disagree *vi* discrepāre, dissentīre, dissidēre.
disagreeable *adj* molestus, incommodus,
iniūcundus.
disagreeably *adv* molestē, incommodē.
disagreement *n* discordia *f*, dissēnsiō *f*,
discrepantia *f*.
disallow *vt* improbāre, abnuere, vetāre.
disappear *vi* dēperīre, perīre, abīre,
diffugere, ēvānēscere.
disappearance *n* dēcessiō *f*, fuga *f*.
disappoint *vt* dēcipere, spē dēicere, frustrārī;
be ~ed in a hope ā spē dēcidere, dē spē dēicī.
disappointment *n* frustrātiō *f*, malum *nt*.
disapprobation *n* reprehēnsiō *f*, improbātiō *f*.
disapproval *n* improbātiō *f*.
disapprove *vt, vi* improbāre, reprehendere.
disarm *vt* exarmāre, dearmāre; (*fig*) mītigāre.
disarrange *vt* turbāre, cōnfundere.
disarranged *adj* incompositus.
disarrangement *n* turbātiō *f*.
disarray *n* perturbātiō *f* ♦ *vt* perturbāre.
disaster *n* calamitās *f*, cāsus *m*; (*MIL*) clādēs *f*.
disastrous *adj* īnfēlīx, exitiōsus, calamitōsus.
disavow *vt* diffitērī, īnfitiārī.

disavowal *n* īnfitiātiō *f*.
disband *vt* dīmittere.
disbelief *n* diffīdentia *f*, suspiciō *f*.
disbelieve *vt* diffīdere (*dat*).
disburden *vt* exonerāre.
disburse *vt* ērogāre, expendere.
disbursement *n* impēnsa *f*.
disc *n* orbis *m*.
discard *vt* mittere, pōnere, prōicere.
discern *vt* cōnspicere, dīspicere, cernere; (*fig*)
intellegere.
discernment *n* iūdicium *nt*, intellegentia *f*,
sagācitās *f*.
discharge *vt* (*load*) exonerāre; (*debt*)
exsolvere; (*duty*) fungī (*abl*), exsequī;
(*officer*) exauctōrāre; (*troops*) missōs facere,
dīmittere; (*weapon*) iacere, iaculārī;
(*prisoner*) absolvere; (*from body*) ēdere,
reddere ♦ *vi* (*river*) effundī, īnfluere ♦ *n*
(*bodily*) dēfluxiō *f*; (*MIL*) missiō *f*, dīmissiō *f*; (*of
a duty*) perfūnctiō *f*.
disciple *n* discipulus *m*.
discipline *n* (*MIL*) modestia *f*; (*punishment*)
castīgātiō *f*; (*study*) disciplīna *f* ♦ *vt* coercēre,
castīgāre.
disciplined *adj* modestus.
disclaim *vt* renūntiāre, repudiāre, rēicere.
disclaimer *n* repudiātiō *f*.
disclose *vt* aperīre, patefacere, indicāre.
disclosure *n* indicium *nt*.
discoloration *n* dēcolōrātiō *f*.
discolour *vt* dēcolōrāre.
discoloured *adj* dēcolor.
discomfit *vt* vincere, conturbāre,
dēprehendere.
discomfiture *n* clādēs *f*; (*POL*) repulsa *f*.
discomfort *n* molestia *f*, incommodum *nt*.
disconcert *vt* conturbāre, percellere.
disconcerting *adj* molestus.
disconnect *vt* abiungere, sēiungere.
disconnected *adj* dissolūtus, abruptus.
disconnectedly *adv* dissolūtē.
disconsolate *adj* maestus, dēmissus.
disconsolately *adv* animō dēmissō.
discontent *n* offēnsiō *f*, fastīdium *nt*, taedium
nt.
discontented *adj* invidus, fastīdiōsus, parum
contentus.
discontentedly *adv* invītus, inīquō animō.
discontinuance *n* intermissiō *f*.
discontinue *vt* intermittere ♦ *vi* dēsistere,
dēsinere.
discord *n* discordia *f*; (*music*) dissonum *nt*.
discordance *n* discrepantia *f*, dissēnsiō *f*.
discordant *adj* discors, discrepāns; (*music*)
dissonus, absonus.
discount *vt* dētrahere; (*fig*) praetermittere ♦
n dēcessiō *f*; **be at a ~** iacēre.
discountenance *vt* improbāre.
discourage *vt* dēhortārī, dēterrēre; **be ~d**
animum dēmittere, animō dēficere.
discouragement *n* animī abiectiō *f*; (*cause*)
incommodum *nt*.

discourse *n* sermō *m*; (*lecture*) ōrātiō *f* ♦ *vi* conloquī, disserere, disputāre.
discourteous *adj* inurbānus, asper, inhūmānus.
discourteously *adv* inhūmānē, rūsticē.
discourtesy *n* inhūmānitās *f*, acerbitās *f*.
discover *vt* (*find*) invenīre, reperīre; (*detect*) dēprehendere; (*reveal*) aperīre, patefacere; (*learn*) cognōscere.
discoverer *n* inventor *m*.
discovery *n* inventum *nt*.
discredit *vt* notāre, fidem imminuere (*gen*) ♦ *n* invidia *f*, lābēs *f*; **be in ~** iacēre.
discreditable *adj* inhonestus, turpis.
discreditably *adv* inhonestē, turpiter.
discreet *adj* prūdēns, sagāx, cautus.
discreetly *adv* prūdenter, sagāciter, cautē.
discrepancy *n* discrepantia *f*, dissēnsiō *f*.
discretion *n* prūdentia *f*; (*tact*) iūdicium *nt*; (*power*) arbitrium *nt*, arbitrātus *m*; **at your ~** arbitrātū tuō; **surrender at ~** in dēditiōnem venīre, sine ullā pactiōne sē tradere; **years of ~** adulta aetās *f*.
discretionary *adj* līber.
discriminate *vt*, *vi* discernere, internōscere, distinguere.
discriminating *adj* perspicāx, sagāx.
discrimination *n* discrīmen *nt*, iūdicium *nt*.
discursive *adj* vagus, loquāx; **be ~** excurrere.
discuss *vt* agere, disputāre, disceptāre dē (*abl*); **~ terms of peace** dē pāce agere.
discussion *n* disceptātiō *f*, disputātiō *f*.
disdain *vt* contemnere, aspernārī, fastīdīre ♦ *n* contemptiō *f*, fastīdium *nt*.
disdainful *adj* fastīdiōsus, superbus.
disdainfully *adv* fastīdiōsē, superbē.
disease *n* morbus *m*; pestilentia *f*.
diseased *adj* aeger, aegrōtus.
disembark *vi* ē nave ēgredī ♦ *vt* mīlitēs ē nāve expōnere.
disembarkation *n* ēgressus *m*.
disembodied *adj* sine corpore.
disembowel *vt* exenterāre.
disencumber *vt* exonerāre.
disengage *vt* expedīre, līberāre; (*mind*) abstrahere, abdūcere.
disengaged *adj* vacuus, ōtiōsus.
disentangle *vt* expedīre, explicāre, exsolvere.
disfavour *n* invidia *f*.
disfigure *vt* dēfōrmāre, foedāre.
disfigured *adj* dēfōrmis.
disfigurement *n* dēfōrmātiō *f*.
disfranchise *vt* cīvitātem adimere (*dat*).
disfranchised *adj* capite dēminūtus.
disfranchisement *n* capitis dēminūtiō *f*.
disgorge *vt* ēvomere.
disgrace *n* dēdecus *nt*, ignōminia *f*, īnfāmia *f* ♦ *vt* dēdecorāre, dēdecorī esse (*dat*).
disgraceful *adj* ignōminiōsus, flāgitiōsus, turpis; **~ thing** flāgitium *nt*.
disgracefully *adv* turpiter, flāgitiōsē.
disgruntled *adj* mōrōsus, invidus.

disguise *n* integumentum *nt*; (*fig*) speciēs *f*, simulātiō *f*; **in ~** mūtātā veste ♦ *vt* obtegere, involvere; (*fact*) dissimulāre; **~ oneself** vestem mūtāre.
disgust *vt* displicēre (*dat*), fastīdium movēre (*dat*); **be ~ed** stomachārī; **I am ~ed** mē taedet, mē piget ♦ *n* fastīdium *nt*, taedium *nt*.
disgusting *adj* taeter, foedus, dēfōrmis.
disgustingly *adv* foedē.
dish *n* lanx *f*; (*course*) ferculum *nt*.
dishearten *vt* percellere; **be ~ed** animō dēficere, animum dēmittere.
dishevelled *adj* solūtus, passus.
dishonest *adj* perfidus, inīquus, improbus.
dishonestly *adv* improbē, dolō malō.
dishonesty *n* mala fidēs *f*, perfidia *f*, fraus *f*.
dishonour *n* dēdecus *nt*, ignōminia *f*, turpitūdō *f* ♦ *vt* dēdecorāre.
dishonourable *adj* ignōminiōsus, indecōrus, turpis.
dishonourably *adv* turpiter, inhonestē.
disillusion *vt* errōrem adimere (*dat*).
disinclination *n* odium *nt*.
disinclined *adj* invītus, āversus.
disinfect *vt* pūrgāre.
disingenuous *adj* dolōsus, fallāx.
disingenuously *adv* dolōsē.
disinherit *vt* abdicāre, exhērēdāre.
disinherited *adj* exhērēs.
disintegrate *vt* dissolvere ♦ *vi* dīlābī, dissolvī.
disinter *vt* effodere, ēruere.
disinterested *adj* grātuītus, favōris expers.
disinterestedly *adv* sine favōre.
disinterestedness *n* innocentia *f*, integritās *f*.
disjoin *vt* sēiungere.
disjointed *adj* parum cohaerēns.
disk *n* orbis *m*.
dislike *n* odium *nt*, offēnsiō *f*, invidia *f* ♦ *vt* ōdisse; **I ~** mihī displicet, mē piget (*gen*).
dislocate *vt* extorquēre.
dislocated *adj* luxus.
dislodge *vt* dēmovēre, dēicere, dēpellere, dētrūdere.
disloyal *adj* īnfīdus, īnfidēlis; (*to gods, kin, country*) impius.
disloyally *adv* īnfidēliter.
disloyalty *n* perfidia *f*, īnfidēlitās *f*; impietās *f*.
dismal *adj* fūnestus, maestus.
dismally *adv* miserē.
dismantle *vt* nūdāre; (*building*) dīruere.
dismay *n* pavor *m*, formīdō *f* ♦ *vt* terrēre, perturbāre.
dismember *vt* discerpere.
dismiss *vt* dīmittere; (*troops*) missōs facere; (*from service*) exauctōrāre; (*fear*) mittere, pōnere.
dismissal *n* missiō *f*, dīmissiō *f*.
dismount *vi* dēgredī, (ex equō) dēscendere.
disobedience *n* contumācia *f*.
disobedient *adj* contumāx.
disobediently *adv* contrā iūssa.
disobey *vt* nōn pārēre (*dat*), aspernārī.

disoblige vt displicēre (dat), offendere.
disobliging adj inofficiōsus, difficilis.
disobligingly adv contrā officium.
disorder n turba f, cōnfūsiō f; (MED) morbus m; (POL) mōtus m, tumultus m ♦ vt turbāre, miscēre, sollicitāre.
disorderly adj immodestus, inōrdinātus, incompositus; (POL) turbulentus, sēditiōsus; **in a ~ manner** nūllō ōrdine, temerē.
disorganize vt dissolvere, perturbāre.
disown vt (statement) īnfitiārī; (thing) abnuere, repudiāre; (heir) abdicāre.
disparage vt obtrectāre, dētrectāre.
disparagement n obtrectātiō f, probrum nt.
disparager n obtrectātor m, dētrectātor m.
disparate adj dispār.
disparity n discrepantia f, dissimilitūdō f.
dispassionate adj studiī expers.
dispassionately adv sine īrā et studiō.
dispatch vt mittere, dīmittere; (finish) absolvere, perficere; (kill) interficere ♦ n (letter) litterae fpl; (speed) celeritās f.
dispel vt dispellere, discutere.
dispensation n (distribution) partītiō f; (exemption) venia f; (of heaven) sors f; **by divine ~** dīvīnitus.
dispense vt dispertīrī, dīvidere ♦ vi: **~ with** ōmittere, praetermittere, repudiāre.
dispersal n dīmissiō f, diffugium nt.
disperse vt dispergere, dissipāre, dīsicere ♦ vi diffugere, dīlābī.
dispirited adj dēmissō animō; **be ~** animō dēficere, animum dēmittere.
displace vt locō movēre.
display n ostentātiō f, iactātiō f; **for ~** per speciem ♦ vt exhibēre, ostendere, praestāre, sē ferre.
displease vt displicēre (dat), offendere; **be ~d** aegrē ferre, stomachārī, indignārī.
displeasing adj ingrātus, odiōsus.
displeasure n invidia f, offēnsiō f, odium nt.
disport vt: **~ oneself** lūdere.
disposal n (sale) vēnditiō f; (power) arbitrium nt.
dispose vt (troops) dispōnere; (mind) inclīnāre, addūcere ♦ vi: **~ of** abaliēnāre, vēndere; (get rid) tollere; (argument) refellere.
disposed adj adfectus, inclīnātus, prōnus; **well ~** benevolus, bonō animō.
disposition n animus m, affectiō f, ingenium nt, nātūra f; (of troops) dispositiō f.
dispossess vt dētrūdere, spoliāre.
disproportion n inconcinnitās f.
disproportionate adj impār, inconcinnus.
disproportionately adv inaequāliter.
disprove vt refūtāre, redarguere, refellere.
disputable adj dubius, ambiguus.
disputation n disputātiō f.
dispute n altercātiō f, contrōversia f; (violent) iūrgium nt; **beyond ~** certissimus ♦ vi altercārī, certāre, rixārī ♦ vt negāre, in

dubium vocāre.
disqualification n impedīmentum nt.
disqualify vt impedīre.
disquiet n sollicitūdō f ♦ vt sollicitāre.
disquisition n disputātiō f.
disregard n neglegentia f, contemptiō f ♦ vt neglegere, contemnere, ōmittere.
disrepair n vitium nt; **in ~** male sartus.
disreputable adj inhonestus, īnfāmis.
disrepute n īnfāmia f.
disrespect n neglegentia f, contumācia f.
disrespectful adj contumāx, īnsolēns.
disrespectfully adv īnsolenter.
disrobe vt nūdāre, vestem exuere (dat) ♦ vi vestem exuere.
disrupt vt dīrumpere, dīvellere.
disruption n discidium nt.
dissatisfaction n molestia f, aegritūdō f, dolor m.
dissatisfied adj parum contentus; **I am ~ with** ... mē taedet (gen) ....
dissect vt incīdere; (fig) investīgāre.
dissemble vt, vi dissimulāre; mentīrī.
dissembler n simulātor m.
disseminate vt dīvulgāre, dissēmināre.
dissension n discordia f, dissēnsiō f; (violent) iūrgium nt.
dissent vi dissentīre, dissidēre ♦ n dissēnsiō f.
dissertation n disputātiō f.
disservice n iniūria f, incommodum nt.
dissimilar adj dispār, dissimilis.
dissimilarity n discrepantia f, dissimilitūdō f.
dissident adj discors.
dissimulation n dissimulātiō f.
dissipate vt dissipāre, diffundere, disperdere.
dissipated adj dissolūtus, lascīvus, luxuriōsus.
dissipation n dissipātiō f; (vice) luxuria f, licentia f.
dissociate vt dissociāre, sēiungere.
dissociation n sēparātiō f, discidium nt.
dissoluble adj dissolūbilis.
dissolute adj dissolūtus, perditus, libīdinōsus.
dissolutely adv libīdinōsē, luxuriōsē.
dissoluteness n luxuria f.
dissolution n dissolūtiō f, discidium nt.
dissolve vt dissolvere; (ice) liquefacere; (meeting) dīmittere; (contract) dīrimere ♦ vi liquēscere; (fig) solvī.
dissonance n dissonum nt.
dissonant adj dissonus.
dissuade vt dissuādēre (dat), dēhortārī.
dissuasion n dissuāsiō f.
distaff n colus f.
distance n intervallum nt, spatium nt; (long way) longinquitās f; **at a ~** (far) longē; (within sight) procul; (fight) ēminus; **at a ~ of** ... spatiō (gen) ...; **within striking ~** intrā iactum tēlī.
distant adj longinquus; (measure) distāns; (person) parum familiāris; **be ~** abesse (abl).

distaste n fastīdium nt.
distasteful adj molestus, iniūcundus.
distemper n morbus m.
distend vt distendere.
distil vt, vi stillāre.
distinct adj (different) dīversus; (separate) distinctus; (clear) clārus, argūtus; (marked) distinctus; (sure) certus; (well-drawn) expressus.
distinction n discrīmen nt; (dissimilarity) discrepantia f; (public status) amplitūdō f; (honour) honōs m, decus nt; (mark) īnsigne nt; **there is a ~ interest; without ~** prōmiscuē.
distinctive adj proprius, īnsignītus.
distinctively adv propriē, īnsignītē.
distinctly adv clārē, distinctē, certē, expressē.
distinguish vt distinguere, internōscere, dīiūdicāre, discernere; (honour) decorāre, ōrnāre; **~ oneself** ēminēre.
distinguished adj īnsignis, praeclārus, ēgregius, amplissimus.
distort vt dētorquēre; (fig) dēprāvāre.
distorted adj distortus.
distortion n distortiō f; dēprāvātiō f.
distract vt distrahere, distinēre, āvocāre; (mind) aliēnāre.
distracted adj āmēns, īnsānus.
distraction n (state) indīligentia f; (cause) invītāmentum nt; (madness) furor m, dēmentia f; **to ~** efflīctim.
distraught adj āmēns, dēmēns.
distress n labor m, dolor m, aegrimōnia f, aerumna f; **be in ~** labōrāre ♦ vt adflīgere, sollicitāre.
distressed adj adflīctus, sollicitus; **be ~ at** rem aegrē ferre.
distressing adj tristis, miser, acerbus.
distribute vt distribuere, dīvidere, dispertīre.
distribution n partītiō f, distribūtiō f.
district n regiō f, pars f.
distrust n diffīdentia f ♦ vt diffīdere (dat), nōn crēdere (dat).
distrustful adj diffīdēns.
distrustfully adv diffīdenter.
disturb vt perturbāre, conturbāre; commovēre; (mind) sollicitāre.
disturbance n turba f, perturbātiō f; (POL) mōtus m, tumultus m.
disturber n turbātor m.
disunion n discordia f, discidium nt.
disunite vt dissociāre, sēiungere.
disuse n dēsuētūdō f; **fall into ~** obsolēscere.
disused adj dēsuētus, obsolētus.
disyllabic adj disyllabus.
ditch n fossa f, scrobis m.
dithyrambic adj dithyrambicus.
dittany n dictamnum nt.
ditty n carmen nt, cantilēna f.
diurnal adj diūrnus.
divan n lectus m, lectulus m.
dive vi dēmergī.
diver n ūrīnātor m.

diverge vi dēvertere, dīgredī; (road) sē scindere; (opinions) discrepāre.
divergence n dīgressiō f; discrepantia f.
divers adj complūrēs.
diverse adj varius, dīversus.
diversify vt variāre.
diversion n (of water) dērīvātiō f; (of thought) āvocātiō f; (to amuse) oblectāmentum nt; **create a ~** (MIL) hostēs dīstringere; **for a ~** animī causā.
diversity n varietās f, discrepantia f.
divert vt dēflectere, āvertere; (attention) āvocāre, abstrahere; (water) dērīvāre; (to amuse) oblectāre, placēre (dat).
diverting adj iūcundus; (remark) facētus.
divest vt exuere, nūdāre; **~ oneself of** (fig) pōnere, mittere.
divide vt dīvidere; (troops) dīdūcere; **~ among** partīrī, distribuere; **~ from** sēparāre ab, sēiungere ab; **~ out** dispertīrī, dīvidere ♦ vi discēdere, sē scindere; (senate) in sententiam īre; **be ~d** (opinions) discrepāre.
divination n dīvīnātiō f; (from birds) augurium nt; (from entrails) haruspicium nt.
divine vt dīvīnāre ♦ vt dīvīnāre, augurārī, hariolārī; **by ~ intervention** dīvīnitus.
divinely adv dīvīnē.
diviner n dīvīnus m, augur m, haruspex m.
divinity n (status) dīvīnitās f; (god) deus m, dea f.
divisible adj dīviduus.
division n (process) dīvīsiō f, partītiō f; (variance) discordia f, dissēnsiō f; (section) pars f; (grade) classis f; (of army) legiō f; (of time) discrīmen nt; (in senate) discessiō f.
divorce n dīvortium nt, repudium nt ♦ vt (wife) nūntium mittere (dat); (things) dīvellere, sēparāre.
divulge vt aperīre, patefacere, ēvulgāre, ēdere.
dizziness n vertīgō f.
dizzy adj vertīginōsus; (fig) attonitus.
do vt facere, agere; (duty) fungī (abl); (wrong) admittere; **~ away with** vt fus tollere; (kill) interimere; **~ one's best to** id agere ut (subj); **~ without** repudiāre; **~ not ...** nolī/nolīte (+ infin); **how ~ you ~?** quid agis?; **I have nothing to ~ with you** mihī tēcum nihil est commercī; **it has nothing to ~ with me** nihil est ad mē; **that will ~** iam satis est; **be done** fierī; **have done with** dēfungī (abl).
docile adj docilis.
docility n docilitās f.
dock n (ships) nāvāle nt; (law) cancellī mpl ♦ vt praecīdere.
dockyard n nāvālia ntpl.
doctor n medicus m; (UNIV) doctor m ♦ vt cūrāre.
doctrine n dogma nt, dēcrētum nt; (system) ratiō f.
document n litterae fpl, tabula f.
dodge vt dēclīnāre, ēvādere ♦ n dolus m.
doe n cerva f.

doer n āctor m, auctor m.
doff vt exuere.
dog n canis m/f; ~ **star** Canīcula f; ~'s canīnus ♦ vt īnsequī, īnstāre (dat).
dogged adj pertināx.
doggedly adv pertināciter.
dogma n dogma nt, praeceptum nt.
dogmatic adj adrogāns.
dogmatically adv adroganter.
doing n factum nt.
dole n sportula f ♦ vt: ~ **out** dispertīrī, dīvidere.
doleful adj lūgubris, flēbilis, maestus.
dolefully adv flēbiliter.
dolefulness n maestitia f, miseria f.
doll n pūpa f.
dolorous adj lūgubris, maestus.
dolour n maestitia f, dolor m.
dolphin n delphīnus m.
dolt n stīpes m, caudex m.
domain n ager m; (king's) rēgnum nt.
dome n tholus m, testūdō f.
domestic adj domesticus, familiāris; (animal) mānsuētus ♦ n famulus m, servus m, famula f, ancilla f; ~**s** pl familia f.
domesticate vt mānsuēfacere.
domesticated adj mānsuētus.
domesticity n larēs suī mpl.
domicile n domicilium nt, domus f.
dominant adj superior, praepotēns.
dominate vt domināri in (acc), imperāre (dat); (view) dēspectāre.
domination n dominātiō f, dominātus m.
domineer vi domināri, rēgnāre.
dominion n imperium nt, rēgnum nt.
don vt induere ♦ n scholasticus m.
donate vt dōnāre.
donation n dōnum nt.
donkey n asellus m.
donor n dōnātor m.
doom n fātum nt ♦ vt damnāre.
door n (front) iānua f; (back) postīcum nt; (double) forēs fpl; **folding ~s** valvae fpl; **out of ~s** forīs; (to) forās; **next ~ to** iuxtā (acc).
doorkeeper n iānitor m.
doorpost n postis m.
doorway n ōstium nt.
dormant adj sōpītus; **lie ~** iacēre.
dormitory n cubiculum nt.
dormouse n glīs m.
dose n pōculum nt.
dot n pūnctum nt.
dotage n senium nt.
dotard n senex dēlīrus m.
dote vi dēsipere; ~ **upon** dēamāre.
doting adj dēsipiēns, peramāns.
dotingly adv perditē.
double adj duplex; (amount) duplus; (meaning) ambiguus ♦ n duplum nt ♦ vt duplicāre; (promontory) superāre; (fold) complicāre ♦ vi duplicārī; (MIL) currere.
double-dealer n fraudātor m.
double-dealing adj fallāx, dolōsus ♦ n fraus

f, dolus m.
doublet n tunica f.
doubly adv bis, dupliciter.
doubt n dubium nt; (hesitancy) dubitātiō f; (distrust) suspiciō f; **give one the benefit of the ~** innocentem habēre; **no ~** sānē; **I do not ~ that** ... non dubito quīn ... (+ subj); **there is no ~ that** nōn dubium est quīn (subj) ♦ vt dubitāre; (distrust) diffīdere (dat), suspicārī.
doubtful adj dubius, incertus; (result) anceps; (word) ambiguus.
doubtfully adv dubiē; (hesitation) dubitanter.
doubtless adv scīlicet, nīmīrum.
doughty adj fortis, strēnuus.
dove n columba f.
dovecote n columbārium nt.
dowdy adj inconcinnus.
dower n dōs f ♦ vt dōtāre.
dowerless adj indōtātus.
down n plūmae fpl, lānūgō f; (thistle) pappus m.
down adv deōrsum; **be ~** iacēre; ~ **with!** perea(n)t; **up and ~** sūrsum deōrsum ♦ prep dē (abl); ~ **from** dē (abl).
downcast adj dēmissus, maestus.
downfall n ruīna f; (fig) occāsus m.
downhearted adj dēmissus, frāctus animī.
downhill adj dēclīvis; (fig) prōclīvis ♦ adv in praeceps.
downpour n imber m.
downright adj dīrēctus; (intensive) merus.
downstream adv secundō flūmine.
downtrodden adj subiectus, oppressus.
downward adj dēclīvis, prōclīvis.
downwards adv deōrsum.
downy adj plūmeus.
dowry n dōs f.
doyen n pater m.
doze vi dormītāre.
dozen n duodecim.
drab adj sordidior.
drachma n drachma f.
draft n (writing) exemplum nt; (MIL) dīlēctus m; (money) syngrapha f; (literary) silva f ♦ vt scrībere; (MIL) mittere.
drag vt trahere ♦ vi (time) trahī; ~ **on** vi (war) prōdūcere ♦ n harpagō m; (fig) impedīmentum nt.
dragnet n ēverriculum nt.
dragon n drācō m.
dragoon n eques m.
drain n cloāca f ♦ vt (water) dērīvāre; (land) siccāre; (drink) exhaurīre; (resources) exhaurīre.
drainage n dērīvātiō f.
drake n anas m.
drama n fābula f; **the ~** scaena f.
dramatic adj scaenicus.
dramatist n fābulārum scrīptor m.
dramatize vt ad scaenam compōnere.
drape vt vēlāre.
drapery n vestīmenta ntpl.
drastic adj vehemēns, efficāx.
draught n (air) aura f; (drink) haustus m; (net)

bolus *m.*
draughts *n* latrunculī *mpl.*
draw *vt* dūcere, trahere; (*bow*) addūcere;
(*inference*) colligere; (*picture*) scrībere,
pingere; (*sword*) stringere, dēstringere;
(*tooth*) eximere; (*water*) haurīre; ~ **aside**
sēdūcere; ~ **away** āvocāre; ~ **back** *vt*
retrahere ♦ *vi* recēdere; ~ **near**
adpropinquāre; ~ **off** dētrahere; (*water*)
dērīvāre; ~ **out** *vi* ēdūcere; (*lengthen*)
prōdūcere; ~ **over** obdūcere; ~ **taut**
addūcere; ~ **together** contrahere; ~ **up** *vt* (MIL)
īnstruere; (*document*) scrībere.
drawback *n* scrūpulus *m*; **this was the only ~**
hōc ūnum dēfuit.
drawing *n* dēscrīptiō *f*; (*art*) graphicē *f.*
drawing room *n* sellāria *f.*
drawings *npl* līneāmenta *ntpl.*
drawl *vi* lentē dīcere.
drawling *adj* lentus in dīcendō.
dray *n* plaustrum *nt.*
dread *n* formīdō *f*, pavor *m*, horror *m* ♦ *adj*
dīrus ♦ *vt* expavēscere, extimēscere,
formīdāre.
dreadful *adj* terribilis, horribilis,
formīdolōsus, dīrus.
dreadfully *adv* vehementer, atrōciter.
dream *n* somnium *nt* ♦ *vt*, *vi* somniāre.
dreamy *adj* somniculōsus.
dreariness *n* (*place*) vastitās *f*; (*mind*) tristitia
f.
dreary *adj* (*place*) vastus; (*person*) tristis.
dregs *n* faex *f*; (*of oil*) amurca *f*; **drain to the ~**
exhaurīre.
drench *vt* perfundere.
dress *n* vestis *f*, vestītus *m*, vestīmenta *ntpl*;
(*style*) habitus *m* ♦ *vt* vestīre; (*wound*) cūrāre;
(*tree*) amputāre ♦ *vi* induī; ~ **up** *vi* vestum
induere.
dressing *n* (MED) fōmentum *nt.*
drift *n* (*motion*) mōtus *m*; (*snow*) agger *m*;
(*language*) vīs *f*; **I see the ~ of your speech**
videō quōrsum ōrātiō tua tendat ♦ *vi* fluitāre;
(*fig*) lābī, ferrī.
drill *n* terebra *f*; (MIL) exercitātiō *f* ♦ *vt* (*hole*)
terebrāre; (MIL) exercēre; (*pupil*) īnstruere.
drink *vt*, *vi* bibere, pōtāre; ~ **a health**
propīnāre, Graecō mōre bibere; ~ **deep of**
exhaurīre; ~ **in** haurīre; ~ **up** ēpōtāre ♦ *n*
pōtiō *f.*
drinkable *adj* pōtulentus.
drinker *n* pōtor *m.*
drinking bout *n* pōtātiō *f.*
drip *vi* stillāre, dēstillāre.
drive *vt* agere; (*force*) cōgere; ~ **away** abigere;
(*fig*) pellere, prōpulsāre; ~ **back** repellere; ~
home dēfīgere; ~ **in/into** īnfīgere in (*acc*);
(*flock*) cōgere in (*acc*); ~ **off** dēpellere; ~ **out**
exigere, expellere, exturbāre; ~ **through**
trānsfīgere ♦ *vi* vehī; ~ **away** āvehī; ~ **back**
revehī; ~ **in** invehī; ~ **on** *vt* impellere; ~ **round**
circumvehī; ~ **past** praetervehī; **what are**
you driving at? quōrsum tua spectat ōrātiō?

♦ *n* gestātiō *f.*
drivel *vi* dēlīrāre.
drivelling *adj* dēlīrus, ineptus ♦ *n* ineptiae *fpl.*
driver *n* aurīga *m*; rēctor *m.*
drizzle *vi* rōrāre.
droll *adj* facētus, ioculāris.
drollery *n* facētiae *fpl.*
dromedary *n* dromas *m.*
drone *n* (*bee*) fūcus *m*; (*sound*) bombus *m* ♦ *vi*
fremere.
droop *vi* dēmittī; (*flower*) languēscere; (*mind*)
animum dēmittere.
drooping *adj* languidus.
drop *n* gutta *f* ♦ *vi* cadere; (*liquid*) stillāre ♦ *vt*
mittere; (*anchor*) iacere; (*hint*) ēmittere;
(*liquid*) īnstillāre; (*work*) dēsistere ab (*abl*) ♦
vi: ~ **behind** cessāre; ~ **in** *vi* vīsere,
supervenīre; ~ **out** excidere.
dross *n* scōria *f*; (*fig*) faex *f.*
drought *n* siccitās *f.*
drouth *n* sitis *f.*
drove *n* grex *f.*
drover *n* bubulcus *m.*
drown *vt* mergere, obruere; (*noise*) obscūrāre
♦ *vi* aquā perīre.
drowse *vi* dormītāre.
drowsily *adv* somniculōsē.
drowsiness *n* sopor *m.*
drowsy *adj* sēmisomnus, somniculōsus.
drub *vt* pulsāre, verberāre.
drudge *n* mediastīnus *m* ♦ *vi* labōrāre.
drudgery *n* labor *m.*
drug *n* medicāmentum *nt* ♦ *vt* medicāre.
Druids *n* Druidae, Druidēs *mpl.*
drum *n* tympanum *nt*; (*container*) urna *f.*
drummer *n* tympanista *m.*
drunk *adj* pōtus, ēbrius, tēmulentus.
drunkard *n* ēbriōsus *m.*
drunken *adj* ēbriōsus, tēmulentus.
drunkenness *n* ēbrietās *f.*
dry *adj* siccus, āridus; (*thirst*) sitiēns; (*speech*)
āridus, frīgidus; (*joke*) facētus; **be ~** ārēre ♦
vt siccāre ♦ *vi* ārēscere; ~ **up** exārēscere.
dryad *n* dryas *f.*
dry rot *n* rōbīgō *f.*
dual *adj* duplex.
duality *n* duplex nātūra *f.*
dubiety *n* dubium *nt.*
dubious *adj* dubius, incertus; (*meaning*)
ambiguus.
dubiously *adv* dubiē; ambiguē.
duck *n* anas *f* ♦ *vt* dēmergere ♦ *vi* dēmergī, sē
dēmittere.
duckling *n* anaticula *f.*
duct *n* ductus *m.*
dudgeon *n* dolor *m*, stomachus *m.*
due *adj* dēbitus, meritus, iūstus; **be ~** dēbērī; **it**
is ~ to me that … not per mē stat quōminus
(+ *subj*); **be ~ to** orīrī ex, fierī (*abl*) ♦ *n* iūs *nt*,
dēbitum *nt*; (*tax*) vectīgal *nt*; (*harbour*)
portōrium *nt*; **give every man his ~** suum
cuīque tribuere ♦ *adv* rēctā; ~ **to** ob (+ *acc*);
propter (+ *acc*).

duel n certāmen nt.
dug n über nt.
duke n dux m.
dulcet adj dulcis.
dull adj hebes; (weather) subnūbilus; (language) frīgidus; (mind) tardus; **be** ~ hebēre; **become** ~ hebēscere ♦ vt hebetāre, obtundere, retundere.
dullard n stolidus m.
dulness n (mind) tarditās f, stultitia f.
duly adv rītē, ut pār est.
dumb adj mūtus; **be struck** ~ obmūtēscere.
dun n flāgitātor m ♦ vt flāgitāre ♦ adj fuscus.
dunce n bārō m.
dune n tumulus m.
dung n fimus m.
dungeon n carcer m, rōbur nt.
dupe vt dēlūdere, fallere ♦ n crēdulus m.
duplicate n exemplar nt ♦ vt duplicāre.
duplicity n fraus f, perfidia f.
durability n firmitās f, firmitūdō f.
durable adj firmus, perpetuus.
durably adv firmē.
duration n spatium nt; (long) diūturnitās f.
duress n vīs f.
during prep inter (acc), per (acc).
dusk n crepusculum nt, vesper m; **at** ~ prīmā nocte, prīmīs tenebrīs.
dusky adj fuscus.
dust n pulvis m; **throw** ~ **in the eyes of** tenebrās offundere (dat) ♦ vt dētergēre.
dusty adj pulverulentus.
dutiful adj pius, officiōsus.
dutifully adv piē, officiōsē.
dutifulness n pietās f.
duty n (moral) officium nt; (task) mūnus nt; (tax) vectīgal nt; **be on** ~ (MIL) statiōnem agere, excubāre; **do one's** ~ officiō fungī; **do** ~ **for** (pers) in locum sufficī (gen); (thing) adhibērī prō (abl); **it is my** ~ dēbeō, mē oportet, meum est; **it is the** ~ **of a commander** ducis est; **sense of** ~ pietās f.
duty call n salūtātiō f.
duty-free adj immūnis.
dwarf n nānus m.
dwell vi habitāre; ~ **in** incolere; ~ **upon** (theme) commorārī in (abl).
dweller n incola m.
dwelling n domus f, domicilium nt; (place) sēdēs f.
dwindle vi dēcrēscere, extenuārī.
dye n fūcus m, color m ♦ vt īnficere, fūcāre.
dyer n īnfector m.
dying adj moribundus, moriēns.
dynasty n domus (rēgia) f.
dyspepsia n crūditās f.

E, e

each adj & pron quisque; (of two) uterque; ~ **other** inter sē; **one** ~ singulī; ~ **year** quotannīs.
eager adj avidus, cupidus, alācer; ~ **for** avidus (+ gen).
eagerly adv avidē, cupidē, ācriter.
eagerness n cupīdō f, ārdor m, studium nt; alacritās f.
eagle n aquila f.
ear n auris f; (of corn) spīca f; **give** ~ aurem praebēre, auscultāre; **go in at one** ~ **and out at the other** surdīs auribus nārrārī; **prick up one's** ~**s** aurēs ērigere; **with long** ~**s** aurītus.
earl n comes m.
earlier adv ante; anteā.
early adj (in season) mātūrus; (in day) mātūtīnus; (at beginning) prīmus; (in history) antīquus ♦ adv (in day) māne; (before time) mātūrē, temperī; ~ **in life** ab ineunte aetāte.
earn vt merērī, cōnsequī; ~ **a living** vīctum quaerere, quaestum facere.
earnest adj (serious) sērius; (eager) ācer, sēdulus ♦ n pignus nt; (money) arrabō m; **in** ~ sēdulō, ēnīxē.
earnestly adv sēriō, graviter, sēdulō.
earnestness n gravitās f, studium nt.
earnings n quaestus m.
earring n elenchus m.
earth n (planet) tellūs f; (inhabited) orbis terrārum m; (land) terra f; (soil) solum nt, humus f; (fox's) latibulum nt; **where on** ~? ubī gentium?; **of the** ~ terrestris.
earthen adj (ware) fictilis; (mound) terrēnus.
earthenware n fictilia ntpl ♦ adj fictilis.
earthly adj terrestris.
earthquake n terrae mōtus m.
earthwork n agger m.
earthy adj terrēnus.
ease n facilitās f; (leisure) ōtium nt; **at** ~ ōtiōsus; (in mind) sēcūrus; **ill at** ~ sollicitus ♦ vt laxāre, relevāre; (pain) mītigāre.
easily adv facile; (gladly) libenter; (at leisure) ōtiōsē; **not** ~ nōn temerē.
easiness n facilitās f.
east n Oriēns m, sōlis ortus m; ~ **wind** eurus m.
Easter n Pascha f.
easterly, eastern adj orientālis.
eastward adv ad orientem.
easy adj facilis; (manner) adfābilis, facilis; (mind) sēcūrus; (speech) expedītus; (discipline) remissus; ~ **circumstances** dīvitiae fpl, abundantia f.
eat vt edere; cōnsūmere; vescī (abl); ~ **away** rōdere; ~ **up** exedere.
eatable adj esculentus.
eating n cibus m.

eaves *n* suggrunda *f*.
eavesdropper *n* sermōnis auceps *m*.
ebb *n* dēcessus *m*, recessus *m*; **at ~tide**
minuente aestū; **be at a low ~** (*fig*) iacēre ♦ *vi*
recēdere.
ebony *n* ebenus *f*.
ebullient *adj* fervēns.
ebullition *n* fervor *m*.
eccentric *adj* īnsolēns.
eccentricity *n* īnsolentia *f*.
echo *n* imāgō *f* ♦ *vt, vi* resonāre.
eclipse *n* dēfectus *m*, dēfectiō *f* ♦ *vt* obscūrāre;
be ~d dēficere, labōrāre.
eclogue *n* ecloga *f*.
economic *adj* quaestuōsus, sine iactūrā.
economical *adj* (*person*) frūgī, parcus.
economically *adv* nullā iactūrā factā.
economics *n* reī familiāris dispēnsātiō *f*.
economize *vi* parcere.
economy *n* frūgālitās *f*.
ecstasy *n* alacritās *f*, furor *m*.
ecstatic *adj* gaudiō ēlātus.
eddy *n* vertex *m* ♦ *vi* volūtārī.
edge *n* ōra *f*, margō *f*; (*of dish*) labrum *nt*; (*of
blade*) aciēs *f*; **take the ~ off** obtundere; **on ~**
(*fig*) suspēnsō animō ♦ *vt* (*garment*)
praetexere; (*blade*) acuere ♦ *vi*: **~ in sē**
īnsinuāre.
edging *n* limbus *m*.
edible *adj* esculentus.
edict *n* ēdictum *nt*, dēcrētum *nt*.
edification *n* ērudītiō *f*.
edifice *n* aedificium *nt*.
edify *vt* ērudīre.
edit *vt* recognōscere, recēnsēre.
edition *n* ēditiō *f*.
educate *vt* ērudīre, īnfōrmāre; **~ in** īnstituere
ad (*acc*).
education *n* doctrīna *f*; (*process*) īnstitūtiō *f*.
eel *n* anguilla *f*.
eerie *adj* mōnstruōsus.
efface *vt* dēlēre, tollere.
effect *n* (*result*) ēventus *m*; (*impression*) vīs *f*,
effectus *m*; (*show*) iactātiō *f*; **~s** *pl* bona *ntpl*;
for ~ iactātiōnis causā; **in ~** rē vērā; **to this ~**
in hanc sententiam; **without ~** inritus ♦ *vt*
efficere, facere, patrāre.
effective *adj* valēns, validus; (*RHET*) gravis,
ōrnātus.
effectively *adv* validē, graviter, ōrnātē.
effectiveness *n* vīs *f*.
effectual *adj* efficāx, idōneus.
effectually *adv* efficāciter.
effectuate *vt* efficere, cōnsequī.
effeminacy *n* mollitiēs *f*.
effeminate *adj* mollis, effēminātus.
effeminately *adv* molliter, effēminātē.
effervesce *vi* effervēscere.
effete *adj* effētus.
efficacious *adj* efficāx.
efficaciously *adv* efficāciter.
efficacy *n* vīs *f*.
efficiency *n* virtūs *f*, perītia *f*.

efficient *adj* capāx, perītus; (*logic*) efficiēns.
efficiently *adv* perītē, bene.
effigy *n* simulācrum *nt*, effigiēs *f*.
effloresce *vi* flōrēscere.
efflorescence *n* (*fig*) flōs *m*.
effluvium *n* hālitus *m*.
effort *n* opera *f*, cōnātus *m*; (*of mind*) intentiō *f*;
make an ~ ēnītī.
effrontery *n* audācia *f*, impudentia *f*.
effusive *adj* officiōsus.
egg *n* ōvum *nt*; **lay an ~** ōvum parere ♦ *vt*
impellere, īnstīgāre.
egoism *n* amor suī *m*.
egoist *n* suī amāns *m*.
egotism *n* iactātiō *f*.
egotist *n* glōriōsus *m*.
egregious *adj* singulāris.
egress *n* exitus *m*.
eight *num* octō; **~ each** octōnī; **~ times** octiēns.
eighteen *num* duodēvīgintī.
eighteenth *adj* duodēvīcēsimus.
eighth *adj* octāvus.
eight hundred *num* octingentī.
eight hundredth *adj* octingentēsimus.
eightieth *adj* octōgēsimus.
eighty *num* octōgintā; **~ each** octōgēnī; **~ times**
octōgiēns.
either *pron* alteruter, uterlibet, utervīs ♦ *conj*
aut, vel; **~ ... or** aut ... aut; vel ... vel.
ejaculation *n* clāmor *m*.
eject *vt* ēicere, expellere.
ejection *n* expulsiō *f*.
eke *vt*: **eke out** parcendō prōdūcere.
elaborate *vt* ēlabōrāre ♦ *adj* ēlabōrātus,
exquīsītus.
elaborately *adv* summō labōre, exquīsītē.
elan *n* ferōcia *f*.
elapse *vi* abīre, intercēdere; **allow to ~**
intermittere; **a year has ~d since** annus est
cum (*indic*).
elated *adj* ēlātus; **be ~** efferrī.
elation *n* laetitia *f*.
elbow *n* cubitum *nt*.
elder *adj* nātū māior, senior ♦ *n* (*tree*)
sambūcus *f*.
elderly *adj* aetāte prōvectus.
elders *npl* patrēs *mpl*.
eldest *adj* nātū māximus.
elecampane *n* inula *f*.
elect *vt* ēligere, dēligere; (*magistrate*) creāre;
(*colleague*) cooptāre ♦ *adj* dēsignātus;
(*special*) lēctus.
election *n* (*POL*) comitia *ntpl*.
electioneering *n* ambitiō *f*.
elector *n* suffrāgātor *m*.
elegance *n* ēlegantia *f*, lepōs *m*, munditia *f*,
concinnitās *f*.
elegant *adj* ēlegāns, concinnus, nitidus.
elegantly *adv* ēleganter, concinnē.
elegiac *adj*: **~ verse** elegī *mpl*, versūs alternī
mpl.
elegy *n* elegīa *f*.
element *n* elementum *nt*; **~s** *pl* initia *ntpl*,

prīncipia *ntpl*; **out of one's** ~ peregrīnus.
elementary *adj* prīmus.
elephant *n* elephantus *m*, elephas *m*.
elevate *vt* efferre, ērigere.
elevated *adj* ēditus, altus.
elevation *n* altitūdō *f*; (*style*) ēlātiō *f*.
eleven *num* ūndecim; ~ **each** ūndēnī; ~ **times**
    ūndeciēns.
eleventh *adj* ūndecimus.
elf *n* deus *m*.
elicit *vt* ēlicere; (*with effort*) ēruere.
elide *vt* ēlīdere.
eligible *adj* idōneus, aptus.
eliminate *vt* tollere, āmovēre.
elite *n* flōs *m*, rōbur *nt*.
elk *n* alcēs *f*.
ell *n* ulna *f*.
ellipse *n* (*RHET*) dētractiō *f*; (*oval*) ōvum *nt*.
elm *n* ulmus *f* ♦ *adj* ulmeus.
elocution *n* prōnūntiātiō *f*.
elongate *vt* prōdūcere.
elope *vi* aufugere.
eloquence *n* ēloquentia *f*; (*natural*) fācundia *f*,
    dīcendī vīs *f*.
eloquent *adj* ēloquēns; (*natural*) fācundus;
    (*fluent*) disertus.
eloquently *adv* fācundē, disertē.
else *adv* aliōquī, aliter ♦ *adj* alius; **or** ~ aliōquī;
    who ~ quis alius.
elsewhere *adv* alibī; ~ **to** aliō.
elucidate *vt* ēnōdāre, illūstrāre.
elucidation *n* ēnōdātiō *f*, explicātiō *f*.
elude *vt* ēvītāre, frustrārī, fallere.
elusive *adj* fallāx.
emaciated *adj* macer.
emaciation *n* maciēs *f*.
emanate *vi* mānāre; (*fig*) ēmānāre, orīrī.
emanation *n* exhālātiō *f*.
emancipate *vt* ēmancipāre, manū mittere,
    līberāre.
emancipation *n* lībertās *f*.
emasculate *vt* ēnervāre, dēlumbāre.
embalm *vt* condīre.
embankment *n* agger *m*, mōlēs *f*.
embargo *n* interdictum *nt*.
embark *vi* cōnscendere, nāvem cōnscendere;
    ~ **upon** (*fig*) ingredī ♦ *vt* impōnere.
embarkation *n* cōnscēnsiō *f*.
embarrass *vt* (*by confusing*) perturbāre; (*by
    obstructing*) impedīre; (*by revealing*)
    dēprehendere; **be** ~**ed** haerēre.
embarrassing *adj* incommodus,
    intempestīvus.
embarrassment *n* (*in speech*) haesitātiō *f*; (*in
    mind*) sollicitūdō *f*; (*in business*) angustiae *fpl*,
    difficultās *f*; (*cause*) molestia *f*,
    impedīmentum *nt*.
embassy *n* lēgātiō *f*.
embedded *adj* dēfīxus.
embellish *vt* adōrnāre, exōrnāre, decorāre.
embellishment *n* decus *nt*, exōrnātiō *f*,
    ōrnāmentum *nt*.
embers *n* cinis *m*, favilla *f*.

embezzle *vt* peculārī, dēpeculārī.
embezzlement *n* peculātus *m*.
embezzler *n* peculātor *m*.
embitter *vt* exacerbāre.
emblazon *vt* īnsignīre.
emblem *n* īnsigne *nt*.
embodiment *n* exemplar *nt*.
embody *vt* repraesentāre; (*MIL*) cōnscrībere.
embolden *vt* cōnfirmāre; ~ **the hearts of**
    animōs cōnfirmāre.
emboss *vt* imprimere, caelāre.
embrace *vt* amplectī, complectī; (*items*)
    continēre, comprehendere; (*party*) sequī;
    (*opportunity*) adripere ♦ *nt* amplexus *m*,
    complexus *m*.
embroider *vt* acū pingere.
embroidery *n* vestis picta *f*.
embroil *vt* miscēre, implicāre.
emend *vt* ēmendāre, corrigere.
emendation *n* ēmendātiō *f*, corrēctiō *f*.
emerald *n* smaragdus *m*.
emerge *vi* ēmergere, exsistere; ēgredī.
emergency *n* tempus *nt*, discrīmen *nt* ♦ *adj*
    subitārius.
emigrate *vi* migrāre, ēmigrāre.
emigration *n* migrātiō *f*.
eminence *n* (*ground*) tumulus *m*, locus ēditus
    m; (*rank*) praestantia *f*, amplitūdō *f*.
eminent *adj* ēgregius, ēminēns, īnsignis,
    amplus.
eminently *adv* ēgregiē, prae cēterīs, in
    prīmīs.
emissary *n* lēgātus *m*.
emit *vt* ēmittere.
emolument *n* lucrum *nt*, ēmolumentum *nt*.
emotion *n* animī mōtus *m*, commōtiō *f*,
    adfectus *m*.
emotional *adj* (*person*) mōbilis; (*speech*)
    flexanimus.
emperor *n* prīnceps *m*, imperātor *m*.
emphasis *n* pondus *nt*; (*words*) impressiō *f*.
emphasize *vt* exprimere.
emphatic *adj* gravis.
emphatically *adv* adsevēranter, vehementer.
empire *n* imperium *nt*.
employ *vt* ūtī (*abl*); (*for purpose*) adhibēre;
    (*person*) exercēre.
employed *adj* occupātus.
employees *npl* operae *fpl*.
employer *n* redemptor *m*.
employment *n* (*act*) ūsus *m*; (*work*) quaestus
    m.
empower *vt* permittere (*dat*), potestātem
    facere (*dat*).
emptiness *n* inānitās *f*.
empty *adj* inānis, vacuus; (*fig*) vānus, inritus ♦
    vt exhaurīre, exinānīre ♦ *vi* (*river*) īnfluere.
emulate *vt* aemulārī.
emulation *n* aemulātiō *f*.
emulous *adj* aemulus.
emulously *adv* certātim.
enable *vt* potestātem facere (*dat*); efficere
    ut (*subj*).

enact vt dēcernere, ēdīcere, scīscere; (part) agere.

enactment n dēcrētum nt, lēx f.

enamoured adj amāns; **be ~ of** dēamāre.

encamp vi castra pōnere, tendere.

encampment n castra ntpl.

encase vt inclūdere.

enchant vt fascināre; (fig) dēlectāre.

enchantment n fascinātiō f; blandīmentum nt.

enchantress n sāga f.

encircle vt cingere, circumdare, amplectī.

enclose vt inclūdere, saepīre.

enclosure n saeptum nt, māceria f.

encompass vt cingere, circumdare, amplectī.

encounter vt obviam īre (dat), occurrere (dat); (in battle) concurrere cum (abl), congredī cum ♦ n occursus m, concursus m.

encourage vt cōnfirmāre, (co)hortārī, sublevāre, favēre (dat).

encouragement n hortātiō f, favor m, auxilium nt.

encroach vi invādere; **~ upon** occupāre; (fig) imminuere.

encrust vt incrustāre.

encumber vt impedīre, onerāre.

encumbrance n impedīmentum nt, onus nt.

end n fīnis m; (aim) prōpositum nt; (of action) ēventus m, exitus m; (of speech) perōrātiō f; **~ to ~** continuī; **at a loose ~** vacuus, ōtiōsus; **for two days on ~** biduum continenter; **in the ~** dēnique; **the ~ of** extrēmus; (time) exāctus; **put an ~ to** fīnem facere (dat), fīnem impōnere (dat); **to the ~ that** eō cōnsiliō ut (subj); **to what ~?** quō?, quōrsum? ♦ vt fīnīre, cōnficere; (mutual dealings) dīrimere ♦ vi dēsinere; (event) ēvādere; (sentence) cadere; (speech) perōrāre; (time) exīre; **~ up as** ēvādere; **~ with** dēsinere in (acc).

endanger vt perīclitārī, in discrīmen addūcere.

endear vt dēvincīre.

endearing adj blandus.

endearment n blanditiae fpl.

endeavour vt cōnārī, ēnītī ♦ n cōnātus m.

ending n fīnis m, exitus m.

endive n intubum nt.

endless adj īnfīnītus; (time) aeternus, perpetuus.

endlessly adv sine fīne, īnfīnītē.

endorse vt ratum facere.

endow vt dōnāre, īnstruere.

endowed adj praeditus (+ abl).

endowment n dōnum nt.

endurance n patientia f.

endure vi dūrāre, permanēre ♦ vt ferre, tolerāre, patī.

enemy n (public) hostis m, hostēs mpl; (private) inimīcus m; **greatest ~** inimīcissimus m; **~ territory** hosticum nt.

energetic adj impiger, nāvus, strēnuus; (style) nervōsus.

energetically adv impigrē, nāviter, strēnuē.

energy n impigritās f, vigor m, incitātiō f; (mind) contentiō f; (style) nervī mpl.

enervate vt ēnervāre, ēmollīre.

enervation n languor m.

enfeeble vt īnfirmāre, dēbilitāre.

enfold vt involvere, complectī.

enforce vt (law) exsequī; (argument) cōnfirmāre.

enfranchise vt cīvitāte dōnāre; (slave) manū mittere.

engage vt (affection) dēvincīre; (attention) distinēre, occupāre; (enemy) manum cōnserere cum (abl); (hire) condūcere; (promise) spondēre, recipere; **~ the enemy** proelium cum hostibus committere; **be ~d in** versārī in (abl) ♦ vi: **~ in** ingredī, suscipere.

engagement n (COMM) occupātiō f; (MIL) pugna f, certāmen nt; (agreement) spōnsiō f; **keep an ~** fidem praestāre; **break an ~** fidem fallere; **I have an ~ at your house** prōmīsī ad tē.

engaging adj blandus.

engender vt ingenerāre, ingignere.

engine n māchina f.

engineer n māchinātor m ♦ vt mōlīrī.

engraft vt īnserere.

engrave vt īnsculpere, incīdere, caelāre.

engraver n sculptor m, caelātor m.

engraving n sculptūra f, caelātūra f.

engross vt dīstringere, occupāre; **~ed in** tōtus in (abl).

engulf vt dēvorāre, obruere.

enhance vt amplificāre, augēre, exaggerāre.

enigma n aenigma nt, ambāgēs fpl.

enigmatic adj ambiguus, obscūrus.

enigmatically adv per ambāgēs, ambiguē.

enjoin vt imperāre (dat), iniungere (dat).

enjoy vt fruī (abl); (advantage) ūtī (abl); (pleasure) percipere, dēcerpere; **~ oneself** dēlectārī, geniō indulgēre.

enjoyable adj iūcundus.

enjoyment n frūctus m; dēlectātiō f, voluptās f.

enlarge vt augēre, amplificāre, dīlātāre; (territory) prōpāgāre; **~ upon** amplificāre.

enlargement n amplificātiō f, prōlātiō f.

enlighten vt inlūstrāre; docēre, ērudīre.

enlightenment n ērudītiō f, hūmānitās f.

enlist vt scrībere, cōnscrībere; (sympathy) conciliāre ♦ vi nōmen dare.

enliven vt excitāre.

enmesh vt impedīre, implicāre.

enmity n inimīcitia f, simultās f.

ennoble vt honestāre, excolere.

ennui n taedium nt.

enormity n immānitās f; (deed) scelus nt, nefās nt.

enormous adj immānis, ingēns.

enormously adv immēnsum.

enough adj satis (indecl gen) ♦ adv satis; **more than ~** satis superque; **I have had ~ of ...** mē taedet (gen) ....

enquire vi quaerere, percontārī; **~ into**

cognōscere, inquīrere in (acc).
enquiry n percontātiō f; (legal) quaestiō f.
enrage vt inrītāre, incendere.
enrapture vt dēlectāre.
enrich vt dītāre, locuplētāre; ~ **with** augēre (abl).
enrol vt adscrībere, conscrībere ♦ vi nōmen dare.
enshrine vt dēdicāre; (fig) sacrāre.
enshroud vt involvere.
ensign n signum nt, īnsigne nt; (officer) signifer m.
enslave vt in servitūtem redigere.
enslavement n servitūs f.
ensnare vt dēcipere, inlaqueāre, inrētīre.
ensue vi īnsequī.
ensure vt praestāre; ~ **that** efficere ut (subj).
entail vt adferre.
entangle vt impedīre, implicāre, inrētīre.
entanglement n implicātiō f.
enter vi inīre, ingredī, intrāre; (riding) invehī; ~ **into** introīre in (acc); ~ **upon** inīre, ingredī ♦ vt (place) intrare; (account) ferre, indūcere; (mind) subīre.
enterprise n inceptum nt; (character) prōmptus animus m.
enterprising adj prōmptus, strēnuus.
entertain vt (guest) invītāre, excipere; (state of mind) habēre, concipere; (to amuse) oblectāre.
entertainer n acroāma nt.
entertainment n hospitium nt; oblectāmentum nt; acroāma nt.
enthral vt capere.
enthusiasm n studium nt, fervor m; ~ **for** studium nt (+ gen).
enthusiastic adj studiōsus, fervidus.
enthusiastically adv summō studiō.
entice vt inlicere, ēlicere, invītāre.
enticement n illecebra f, lēnōcinium nt.
entire adj integer, tōtus, ūniversus.
entirely adv omnīnō, funditus, penitus.
entitle vt (book) īnscrībere; **be ~d to** merērī, dignum esse quī (subj), iūs habēre (gen).
entity n rēs f.
entomb vt humāre, sepelīre.
entrails n intestīna ntpl, exta ntpl.
entrance n aditus m, introitus m; (act) ingressiō f; (of house) vestibulum nt; (of harbour) ōstium nt.
entrance vt fascināre, cōnsōpīre, capere.
entreat vt implōrāre, obsecrāre; (successfully) exōrāre.
entreaty n precēs fpl.
entrenchment n mūnītiō f.
entrust vt committere, crēdere, mandāre; (for keeping) dēpōnere.
entry n introitus m, aditus m; **make an ~** (book) in tabulās referre.
entwine vt implicāre, involvere.
enumerate vt numerāre, dīnumerāre.
enunciate vt ēdīcere; (word) exprimere.
envelop vt implicāre, involvere.

envelope n involucrum nt.
enviable adj beātus.
envious adj invidus, invidiōsus.
enviously adv invidiōsē.
environment n vīcīnia f; **our ~** ea in quibus versāmur.
envoy n lēgātus m.
envy n invidia f ♦ vt invidēre (dat).
enwrap vt involvere.
ephemeral adj brevis.
ephor n ephorus m.
epic adj epicus ♦ n epos nt.
epicure n dēlicātus m.
epigram n sententia f; (poem) epigramma nt.
epilepsy n morbus comitiālis m.
epilogue n epilogus m.
episode n ēventum nt.
epistle n epistula f, litterae fpl.
epitaph n epigramma nt, titulus m.
epithet n adsūmptum nt.
epitome n epitomē f.
epoch n saeculum nt.
equable adj aequālis; (temper) aequus.
equal adj aequus, pār; **be ~ to** aequāre; (task) sufficere (dat) ♦ n pār m/f ♦ vt aequāre, adaequāre.
equality n aequālitās f.
equalize vt adaequāre, exaequāre.
equally adv aequē, pariter.
equanimity n aequus animus m.
equate vt aequāre.
equator n aequinoctiālis circulus m.
equestrian adj equester.
equidistant adj: **be ~** aequō spatiō abesse, idem distāre.
equilibrium n lībrāmentum nt.
equine adj equīnus.
equinoctial adj aequinoctiālis.
equinox n aequinoctium nt.
equip vt armāre, īnstruere, ōrnāre.
equipment n arma ntpl, īnstrūmenta ntpl, adparātus m.
equipoise n lībrāmentum nt.
equitable adj aequus, iūstus.
equitably adv iūstē, aequē.
equity n aequum nt, aequitās f.
equivalent adj pār, īdem īnstar (gen).
equivocal adj anceps, ambiguus.
equivocally adv ambiguē.
equivocate vi tergiversārī.
era n saeculum nt.
eradicate vt ēvellere, exstirpāre.
erase vt dēlēre, indūcere.
erasure n litūra f.
ere conj priusquam.
erect vt ērigere; (building) exstruere; (statute) pōnere ♦ adj ērēctus.
erection n (process) exstructiō f; (product) aedificium nt.
erode vt rōdere.
erotic adj amātōrius.
err vi errāre, peccāre.
errand n mandātum nt.

errant *adj* vagus.
erratic *adj* incōnstāns.
erroneous *adj* falsus.
erroneously *adv* falsō, perperam.
error *n* error *m*; (*moral*) peccātum *nt*; (*writing*) mendum *nt*.
erudite *adj* doctus.
erudition *n* doctrīna *f*, ērudītiō *f*.
erupt *vi* ērumpere.
eruption *n* ēruptiō *f*.
escapade *n* ausum *nt*.
escape *vi* effugere, ēvādere ♦ *vt* fugere, ēvītāre; (*memory*) excidere ex (*abl*); ~ **the notice of** fallere, praeterīre ♦ *n* effugium *nt*, fuga *f*; **way of** ~ effugium *nt*.
eschew *vt* vītāre.
escort *n* praesidium *nt*; (*private*) dēductor *m* ♦ *vt* comitārī, prōsequī; (*out of respect*) dēdūcere.
especial *adj* praecipuus.
especially *adv* praecipuē, praesertim, māximē, in prīmīs.
espionage *n* inquīsītiō *f*.
espouse *vt* (*wife*) dūcere; (*cause*) fovēre.
espy *vt* cōnspicere, cōnspicārī.
essay *n* cōnātus *m*; (*test*) perīculum *nt*; (*literary*) libellus *m* ♦ *vt* cōnārī, incipere.
essence *n* vīs *f*, nātūra *f*.
essential *adj* necesse, necessārius.
essentially *adv* necessāriō.
establish *vt* īnstituere, condere; (*firmly*) stabilīre.
established *adj* firmus, certus; **be** ~ cōnstāre; **become** ~ (*custom*) inveterāscere.
establishment *n* (*act*) cōnstitūtiō *f*; (*domestic*) familia *f*.
estate *n* fundus *m*, rūs *nt*; (*in money*) rēs *f*; (*rank*) ōrdō *m*.
esteem *vt* aestimāre, respicere ♦ *n* grātia *f*, opīniō *f*.
estimable *adj* optimus.
estimate *vt* aestimāre, ratiōnem inīre (*gen*) ♦ *n* aestimātiō *f*, iūdicium *nt*.
estimation *n* opīniō *f*, sententia *f*.
estrange *vt* aliēnāre, abaliēnāre.
estrangement *n* aliēnātiō *f*, discidium *nt*.
estuary *n* aestuārium *nt*.
eternal *adj* aeternus, perennis.
eternally *adv* semper, aeternum.
eternity *n* aeternitās *f*.
etesian winds *n* etēsiae *fpl*.
ether *n* (*sky*) aethēr *m*.
ethereal *adj* aetherius, caelestis.
ethic, ethical *adj* mōrālis.
ethics *n* mōrēs *mpl*, officia *ntpl*.
Etruscan *n* Etruscus *m* ♦ *adj like* **bonus.**
etymology *n* verbōrum notātiō *f*.
eulogist *n* laudātor *m*.
eulogize *vt* laudāre, conlaudāre.
eulogy *n* laudātiō *f*.
eunuch *n* eunūchus *m*.
euphony *n* sonus *m*.
evacuate *vt* (*place*) exinānīre; (*people*)

dēdūcere.
evacuation *n* discessiō *f*.
evade *vt* dēclīnāre, dēvītāre, ēlūdere.
evaporate *vt* exhālāre ♦ *vi* exhālārī.
evaporation *n* exhālātiō *f*.
evasion *n* tergiversātiō *f*.
evasive *adj* ambiguus.
eve *n* vesper *m*; (*before festival*) pervigilium *nt*; **on the** ~ **of** prīdiē (*gen*).
even *adj* aequus, aequālis; (*number*) pār ♦ *adv* et, etiam; (*tentative*) vel; ~ **if** etsī, etiamsī; tametsī; ~ **more** etiam magis; ~ **so** nihilōminus; ~ **yet** etiamnum; **not** ~ ... nē quidem ♦ *vt* aequāre.
evening *n* vesper *m* ♦ *adj* vespertīnus; ~ **is drawing on** invesperāscit; **in the** ~ vesperī.
evening star *n* Vesper *m*, Hesperus *m*.
evenly *adv* aequāliter, aequābiliter.
evenness *n* aequālitās *f*, aequābilitās *f*.
event *n* ēventum *nt*; (*outcome*) ēventus *m*.
eventide *n* vespertīnum tempus *nt*.
eventuality *n* cāsus *m*.
eventually *adv* mox, aliquandō, tandem.
ever *adv* unquam; (*after* sī, nisī, num, nē) quandō; (*always*) semper; (*after interrog*) -nam, tandem; ~ **so** nimium, nimium quantum; **best** ~ omnium optimus; **for** ~ in aeternum.
everlasting *adj* aeternus, perpetuus, immortālis.
evermore *adv* semper, in aeternum.
every *adj* quisque, omnis; ~ **four years** quīntō quōque annō; ~ **now and then** interdum; **in** ~ **direction** passim; undique; ~ **other day** alternis diebus; ~ **day** cottīdiē ♦ *adj* cottīdiānus.
everybody *pron* quisque, omnēs *mpl*; ~ **agrees** inter omnēs cōnstat; ~ **knows** nēmō est quīn sciat.
everyday *adj* cottīdiānus.
everyone *pron see* **everybody.**
everything omnia *ntpl*; **your health is** ~ **to me** meā māximē interest tē valēre.
everywhere *adv* ubīque, passim.
evict *vt* dēicere, dētrūdere.
eviction *n* dēiectiō *f*.
evidence *n* testimōnium *nt*, indicium *nt*; (*person*) testis *m/f*; (*proof*) argūmentum *nt*; **on the** ~ **of** fidē (*gen*); **collect** ~ **against** inquīrere in (*acc*); **turn King's** ~ indicium profitērī.
evident *adj* manifestus, ēvidēns, clārus; **it is** ~ appāret.
evidently *adv* manifestō, clārē.
evil *adj* malus, improbus, scelerātus.
evildoer *n* scelerātus *m*, maleficus *m*.
evil eye *n* fascinum *nt*, malum *nt*, improbitās *f*.
evil-minded *adj* malevolus.
evince *vt* praestāre.
evoke *vt* ēvocāre, ēlicere.
evolution *n* seriēs *f*, prōgressus *m*; (*MIL*) dēcursus *m*, dēcursiō *f*.
evolve *vt* explicāre, ēvolvere ♦ *vi* crēscere.
ewe *n* ovis *f*.
ewer *n* hydria *f*.
exacerbate *vt* exacerbāre, exasperāre.

exact *vt* exigere ♦ *adj* accūrātus; (*person*) dīligēns; (*number*) exāctus.
exaction *n* exāctiō *f*.
exactly *adv* accūrātē; (*reply*) ita prōrsus; ~ **as** perinde que.
exactness *n* cūra *f*, dīligentia *f*.
exaggerate *vt* augēre, in māius extollere.
exalt *vt* efferre, extollere; laudāre.
exaltation *n* ēlātiō *f*.
examination *n* inquīsītiō *f*, scrūtātiō *f*; (*of witness*) interrogātiō *f*; (*test*) probātiō *f*.
examine *vt* investīgāre, scrūtārī; īnspicere; (*witness*) interrogāre; (*case*) quaerere dē (*abl*); (*candidate*) probāre.
examiner *n* scrūtātor *m*.
example *n* exemplum *nt*, documentum *nt*; **for ~** exemplī grātiā; **make an ~ of** animadvertere in (*acc*); **I am an ~** exemplō sum.
exasperate *vt* exacerbāre, inrītāre.
exasperation *n* inrītātiō *f*.
excavate *vt* fodere.
excavation *n* fossiō *f*.
excavator *n* fossor *m*.
exceed *vt* excēdere, superāre.
exceedingly *adv* nimis, valdē, nimium quantum.
excel *vt* praestāre (*dat*), exsuperāre ♦ *vi* excellere.
excellence *n* praestantia *f*, virtūs *f*.
excellent *adj* ēgregius, praestāns, optimus.
excellently *adv* ēgregiē, praeclārē.
except *vt* excipere ♦ *prep* praeter (*acc*) ♦ *adv* nisī ♦ *conj* praeterquam, nisī quod.
exception *n* exceptiō *f*; **make an ~ of** excipere; **take ~ to** gravārī quod; **with the ~ of** praeter (*acc*).
exceptional *adj* ēgregius, eximius.
exceptionally *adv* ēgregiē, eximiē.
excerpt *vt* excerpere ♦ *n* excerptum *nt*.
excess *n* immoderātiō *f*, intemperantia *f* ♦ *adj* supervacāneus; **be in ~** superesse.
excessive *adj* immoderātus, immodestus, nimius.
excessively *adv* immodicē, nimis.
exchange *vt* mūtāre, permūtāre ♦ *n* permūtātiō *f*; (*of currencies*) collybus *m*.
exchequer *n* aerārium *nt*; (*emperor's*) fiscus *m*.
excise *n* vectīgālia *ntpl* ♦ *vt* excīdere.
excision *n* excīsiō *f*.
excitable *adj* mōbilis.
excite *vt* excitāre, concitāre; (*to action*) incitāre, incendere; (*to hope*) ērigere, exacuere; (*emotion*) movēre, commovēre.
excitement *n* commōtiō *f*.
exclaim *vt* exclāmāre; ~ **against** adclāmāre (*dat*).
exclamation *n* clāmor *m*, exclāmātiō *f*.
exclude *vt* exclūdere.
exclusion *n* exclūsiō *f*.
exclusive *adj* proprius.
exclusively *adv* sōlum.
excogitate *vt* excōgitāre.
excrescence *n* tūber *nt*.

excruciating *adj* acerbissimus.
exculpate *vt* pūrgāre, absolvere.
excursion *n* iter *nt*; (MIL) excursiō *f*.
excuse *n* excūsātiō *f*; (*false*) speciēs *f* ♦ *vt* excūsāre, ignōscere (*dat*); (*something due*) remittere; **plead in ~** excūsāre; **put forward as an ~** praetendere.
execrable *adj* dētestābilis, sacer, nefārius.
execrate *vt* dētestārī, exsecrārī.
execration *n* dētestātiō *f*, exsecrātiō *f*.
execute *vt* efficere, patrāre, exsequī; suppliciō afficere; (*behead*) secūrī percutere.
execution *n* effectus *m*; (*penalty*) supplicium *nt*, mors *f*.
executioner *n* carnifex *m*.
exemplar *n* exemplum *nt*.
exempt *adj* immūnis, līber ♦ *vt* līberāre.
exemption *n* (*from tax*) immūnitās *f*; (*from service*) vacātiō *f*.
exercise *n* exercitātiō *f*, ūsus *m*; (*school*) dictāta *ntpl* ♦ *vt* exercēre, ūtī (*abl*); (*mind*) acuere.
exert *vt* extendere, intendere, ūtī (*abl*); ~ **oneself** mōlīrī, ēnītī, sē intendere.
exertion *n* mōlīmentum *nt*; (*mind*) intentiō *f*.
exhalation *n* exhālātiō *f*, vapor *m*.
exhale *vt* exhālāre, exspīrāre.
exhaust *vt* exhaurīre; (*tire*) dēfatīgāre, cōnficere.
exhaustion *n* dēfatīgātiō *f*.
exhaustive *adj* plēnus.
exhibit *vt* exhibēre, ostendere, expōnere; (*on stage*) ēdere.
exhibition *n* expositiō *f*, ostentātiō *f*.
exhilarate *vt* exhilarāre.
exhort *vt* hortārī, cohortārī.
exhortation *n* hortātiō *f*, hortāmen *nt*.
exhume *vt* ēruere.
exigency *n* necessitās *f*.
exile *n* exsilium *nt*, fuga *f*; (*temporary*) relēgātiō *f*; (*person*) exsul *m*; **live in ~** exsulāre ♦ *vt* in exsilium pellere, dēportāre; (*temporarily*) relēgāre.
exist *vi* esse.
existence *n* vīta *f*.
exit *n* exitus *m*, ēgressus *m*.
exodus *n* discessus *m*.
exonerate *vt* absolvere.
exorbitant *adj* nimius, immoderātus.
exotic *adj* peregrīnus.
expand *vt* extendere, dīlātāre.
expanse *n* spatium *nt*, lātitūdō *f*.
expatiate *vi*: ~ **upon** amplificāre.
expatriate *vt* extermināre ♦ *n* extorris *m*.
expect *vt* exspectāre, spērāre.
expectancy, expectation *n* spēs *f*, exspectātiō *f*, opīniō *f*.
expediency *n* ūtile *nt*, ūtilitās *f*.
expedient *adj* ūtilis, commodus; **it is ~** expedit ♦ *n* modus *m*, ratiō *f*.
expediently *adv* commodē.
expedite *vt* mātūrāre.

expedition n (MIL) expedītiō f.
expeditious adj prōmptus, celer.
expeditiously adv celeriter.
expel vt pellere, expellere, ēicere.
expend vt impendere, expendere.
expenditure n impēnsae fpl, sūmptus m.
expense n impēnsae fpl, impendia ntpl; **at my ~**
meō sūmptū; **at the public ~** dē pūblicō.
expensive adj cārus, pretiōsus; (furnishings)
lautus.
expensively adv sūmptuōsē, māgnō pretiō.
experience n ūsus m, experientia f ♦ vt
experīrī, patī.
experienced adj perītus, expertus (+ gen).
experiment n experīmentum nt ♦ vi: **~ with**
experīrī.
expert adj perītus, sciēns.
expertly adv perītē, scienter.
expertness n perītia f.
expiate vt expiāre, lūere.
expiatio n (act) expiātiō f; (penalty) piāculum
nt.
expiatory adj piāculāris.
expiration n (breath) exspīrātiō f; (time) exitus
m.
expire vi exspīrāre; (die) animam agere,
animam efflāre; (time) exīre.
expiry n exitus m, fīnis m.
explain vt explicāre, expōnere, explānāre,
interpretārī; (lucidly) ēnōdāre; (in detail)
ēdisserere.
explanation n explicātiō f, ēnōdātiō f,
interpretātiō f.
explicit adj expressus, apertus.
explicitly adv apertē.
explode vt discutere ♦ vi dīrumpī.
exploit n factum nt, ausum nt; **~s** pl rēs gestae
fpl ♦ vt ūtī (abl), fruī (abl).
explore vt, vi explōrāre, scrūtārī.
explorer n explōrātor m.
explosion n fragor m.
exponent n interpres m, auctor m.
export vt exportāre ♦ n exportātiō f.
exportation n exportātiō f.
expose vt dētegere, dēnūdāre, patefacere;
(child) expōnere; (to danger) obicere; (MIL)
nūdāre; (for sale) prōpōnere; **~ o.s.** sē
obicere.
exposed adj apertus, obnoxius.
exposition n explicātiō f, interpretātiō f.
expostulate vi expostulāre, conquerī.
expostulation n expostulātiō f.
exposure n (of child) expositiō f; (of guilt)
dēprehēnsiō f; (to hardship) patientia f.
expound vt expōnere, interpretārī.
expounder n interpres m.
express vt (in words) exprimere, dēclārāre,
ēloquī; (in art) effingere ♦ adj expressus;
(speed) celerrimus.
expression n significātiō f; (word) vōx f,
verbum nt; (face) vultus m.
expressive adj significāns; **~ of** index (gen); **be**
very ~ māximam vim habēre.

expressively adv significanter.
expressiveness n vīs f.
expressly adv plānē.
expulsion n expulsiō f, ēiectiō f.
expurgate vt pūrgāre.
exquisite adj ēlegāns, exquīsītus, eximius;
(judgment) subtīlis.
exquisitely adv ēleganter, exquīsītē.
ex-service adj ēmeritus.
extant adj superstes; **be ~** exstāre.
extempore adv ex tempore, subitō ♦ adj
extemporālis.
extemporize vi subita dīcere.
extend vt extendere, dīlātāre; (hand)
porrigere; (line) dūcere; (office) prōrogāre;
(territory) propāgāre ♦ vi patēre, porrigī; **~**
into incurrere in (acc).
extension n prōductiō f, prōlātiō f; (of office)
prōrogātiō f; (of territory) propāgātiō f; (extra)
incrēmentum nt.
extensive adj effūsus, amplus, lātus.
extensively adv lātē.
extent n spatium nt, amplitūdō f; **to a large ~**
māgnā ex parte; **to some ~** aliquā ex parte;
to this ~ hāctenus; **to such an ~** adeō.
extenuate vt levāre, mītigāre.
exterior adj externus, exterior ♦ n speciēs f.
exterminate vt occīdiōne occīdere,
interimere.
extermination n occīdiō f, interneciō f.
external adj externus.
externally adv extrīnsecus.
extinct adj mortuus; (custom) obsolētus.
extinction n exstinctiō f, interitus m.
extinguish vt exstinguere, restinguere.
extinguisher n exstinctor m.
extirpate vt exstirpāre, excīdere.
extol vt laudāre, laudibus efferre.
extort vt extorquēre, exprimere.
extortion n (offence) rēs repetundae fpl.
extortionate adj inīquus, rapāx.
extra adv īnsuper, praetereā ♦ adj additus.
extract vt excerpere, extrahere ♦ n: **make ~s**
excerpere.
extraction n ēvulsiō f; (descent) genus nt.
extraneous adj adventīcius, aliēnus.
extraordinarily adv mīrificē, eximiē.
extraordinary adj extraōrdinārius; (strange)
mīrus, novus; (outstanding) eximius,
īnsignis.
extravagance n intemperantia f; (language)
immoderātiō f, luxuria f; (spending) sūmptus
m.
extravagant adj immoderātus, immodestus;
(spending) sūmptuōsus, prōdigus.
extreme adj extrēmus, ultimus.
extremely adv valdē, vehementer.
extremity n extrēmum nt, fīnis m; (distress)
angustiae fpl; **the ~ of** extrēmus.
extricate vt expedīre, absolvere; **~ oneself**
ēmergere.
exuberance n ūbertās f, luxuria f.
exuberant adj ūber, laetus, luxuriōsus.

exuberantly *adv* übertim.
exude *vt* exsūdāre ♦ *vi* mānāre.
exult *vi* exsultārī, laetārī, gestīre.
exultant *adj* laetus.
exultantly *adv* laetē.
exultation *n* laetitia *f*.
eye *n* oculus *m*; (*needle*) forāmen *nt*; **cast ~s on** oculōs conicere in (*acc*); **have an ~ to** spectāre; **in your ~s** iūdice tē; **keep one's ~s on** oculōs dēfigere in (*abl*); **lose an ~** alterō oculō capī; **see ~ to ~** cōnsentīre; **set ~s on** cōnspicere; **shut one's ~s to** cōnīvēre in (*abl*); **take one's ~s off** oculōs dēicere ab (*abl*); **up to the ~s in** tōtus in (*abl*); **with a cast in the ~** paetus; **with sore ~s** lippus; **sore ~s** lippitūdō *f*; **with one's own ~s** cōram; **with one's ~s open** sciēns ♦ *vt* intuērī, aspicere.
eyeball *n* pūpula *f*.
eyebrow *n* supercilium *nt*.
eyelash *n* palpebrae pilus *m*.
eyelid *n* palpebra *f*.
eyeshot *n* oculōrum coniectus *m*.
eyesight *n* aciēs *f*, oculī *mpl*.
eyesore *n* turpe *nt*; **it is an ~ to me** oculī meī dolent.
eye tooth *n* dēns canīnus *m*.
eyewash *n* sycophantia *f*.
eyewitness *n* arbiter *m*; **be an ~ of** interesse (*dat*).

F, f

fable *n* fābula *f*, apologus *m*.
fabled *adj* fābulōsus.
fabric *n* (*built*) structūra *f*; (*woven*) textile *nt*.
fabricate *vt* fabricārī; (*fig*) comminīscī, fingere.
fabricated *adj* commentīcius.
fabrication *n* (*process*) fabricātiō *f*; (*thing*) commentum *nt*.
fabricator *n* auctor *m*.
fabulous *adj* commentīcius, fictus.
fabulously *adv* incrēdibiliter.
facade *n* frōns *f*.
face *n* faciēs *f*, ōs *nt*; (*aspect*) aspectus *m*; (*impudence*) ōs *nt*; **~ to ~** cōram; **how shall I have the ~ to go back?** quō ōre redībō?; **on the ~ of it** ad speciem, prīmō aspectū; **put a bold ~ on** fortēm sē praebēre; **save ~** factum pūrgāre; **set one's ~ against** adversārī (*dat*) ♦ *vt* spectāre ad (*acc*); (*danger*) obviam īre (*dat*), sē oppōnere (*dat*) ♦ *vi* (*place*) spectāre, vergere; **~ about** (*MIL*) signa convertere.
facetious *adj* facētus, salsus.

facetiously *adv* facētē, salsē.
facetiousness *n* facētiae *fpl*, salēs *mpl*.
facile *adj* facilis.
facilitate *vt* expedīre.
facilities *npl* opportūnitās *f*.
facility *n* facilitās *f*.
facing *adj* adversus ♦ *prep* exadversus (*acc*).
facsimile *n* exemplār *nt*.
fact *n* rēs *f*, vērum *nt*; **as a matter of ~** enimvērō; **the ~ that** quod; **in ~** rē vērā ♦ *conj* etenim; (*climax*) dēnique.
faction *n* factiō *f*.
factious *adj* factiōsus, sēditiōsus.
factiously *adv* sēditiōsē.
factor *n* prōcūrātor *m*.
factory *n* officīna *f*.
faculty *n* facultās *f*, vīs *f*.
fad *n* libīdō *f*.
fade *vi* dēflōrēscere, marcēscere.
faded *adj* marcidus.
faggot *n* sarmentum *nt*.
fail *vi* dēficere, dēesse; (*fig*) cadere, dēcidere; (*in business*) forō cēdere; **~ to** nōn posse; **~ to come** nōn venīre ♦ *vt* dēficere, dēstituere.
failing *n* culpa *f*, vitium *nt*.
failure *n* (*of supply*) dēfectiō *f*; (*in action*) offēnsiō *f*; (*at election*) repulsa *f*.
fain *adv* libenter.
faint *adj* (*body*) languidus, dēfessus; (*impression*) hebes, levis; (*courage*) timidus; (*colour*) pallidus; **be ~** languēre; hebēre ♦ *vi* intermorī, animō linquī; **I feel ~** animō male est.
faint-hearted *adj* animo dēmissus; timidus.
faintly *adv* languidē; leviter.
faintness *n* dēfectiō *f*, languor *m*; levitās *f*.
fair *adj* (*appearance*) pulcher, fōrmōsus; (*hair*) flāvus; (*skin*) candidus; (*weather*) serēnus; (*wind*) secundus; (*copy*) pūrus; (*dealings*) aequus; (*speech*) speciōsus, blandus; (*ability*) mediocris; (*reputation*) bonus ♦ *n* nūndinae *fpl*; **~ and square** sine fūcō ac fallāciīs.
fairly *adv* iūre, iūstē; mediocriter.
fairness *n* aequitās *f*.
fair play *n* aequum et bonum *nt*.
fairy *n* nympha *f*.
faith *n* fidēs *f*; **in good ~** bonā fidē.
faithful *adj* fidēlis, fīdus.
faithfully *adv* fidēliter.
faithfulness *n* fidēlitās *f*.
faithless *adj* īnfidēlis, īnfīdus, perfidus.
faithlessly *adv* īnfidēliter.
faithlessness *n* īnfidēlitās *f*.
fake *vt* simulāre.
falchion *n* falx *f*.
falcon *n* falcō *m*.
fall *vi* cadere; (*gently*) lābī; (*morally*) prōlābī; (*dead*) concidere, occidere; (*fortress*) expugnārī, capī; **~ at** accidere; **~ away** dēficere, dēscīscere; **~ back** recidere; (*MIL*) pedem referre; **~ between** intercidere; **~ behind** cessāre; **~ by the way** intercidere; **~ down** dēcidere, dēlābī; (*building*) ruere,

corruere; ~ **due** cadere; ~ **flat** sē
prōsternere; (*speech*) frīgēre; ~ **forward**
prōlābī; ~ **foul of** incurrere in (*acc*); ~
headlong sē praecipitāre; ~ **in, into** incidere;
~ **in with** occurrere (*dat*); ~ **off** dēcidere; (*fig*)
dēscīscere; ~ **on** incumbere in (*acc*), incidere
in (*acc*); ~ **out** excidere; (*event*) ēvenīre;
(*hair*) dēfluere; ~ **short of** deesse ad; ~ **to** (*by
lot*) obtingere, obvenīre (*dat*); ~ **to the
ground** (*case*) iacēre; ~ **upon** invādere,
ingruere in (*acc*); (*one's neck*) in collum
invādere ♦ *n* cāsus *m*; (*building*) ruīna *f*;
(*moral*) lāpsus *m*; (*season*) autumnus *m*; **the ~
of Capua** Capua capta.
fallacious *adj* captiōsus, fallāx.
fallaciously *adv* fallāciter.
fallacy *n* captiō *f*.
fallible *adj*: **be ~** errāre solēre.
fallow *adj* (*land*) novālis ♦ *n* novāle *nt*; **lie ~**
cessāre.
false *adj* falsus, fictus.
falsehood *n* falsum *nt*, mendācium *nt*; **tell a ~**
mentīrī.
falsely *adv* falsō.
falsify *vt* vitiāre, interlinere.
falter *vi* (*speech*) haesitāre; (*gait*) titubāre.
faltering *adj* (*speech*) īnfrāctus; (*gait*) titubāns
♦ *n* haesitātiō *f*.
fame *n* fāma *f*, glōria *f*, nōmen *nt*.
famed *adj* illūstris, praeclārus.
familiar *adj* (*friend*) intimus; (*fact*) nōtus;
(*manner*) cōmis; ~ **spirit** genius *m*; **be ~ with**
nōvisse; **be on ~ terms with** familiāriter ūtī
(*abl*).
familiarity *n* ūsus *m*, cōnsuētūdō *f*.
familiarize *vt* adsuēfacere.
familiarly *adv* familiāriter.
family *n* domus *f*, gēns *f* ♦ *adj* domesticus,
familiāris; ~ **property** rēs familiāris *f*.
famine *n* famēs *f*.
famished *adj* famēlicus.
famous *adj* illūstris, praeclārus, nōbilis; **make
~** nōbilitāre; **the ~** ille.
fan *n* flābellum *nt*; (*winnowing*) vannus *f* ♦ *vt*
ventilāre; ~ **the flames of** (*fig*) īnflammāre.
fanatic *n* (*religious*) fānāticus *m*.
fanciful *adj* (*person*) incōnstāns; (*idea*)
commentīcius.
fancy *n* (*faculty*) mēns *f*; (*idea*) opīnātiō *f*;
(*caprice*) libīdō *f*; **take a ~ to** amāre incipere;
~ **oneself** sē amāre ♦ *vt* animō fingere,
imāginārī, sibi prōpōnere; ~ **you thinking ...!**
tē crēdere ...! ♦ *adj* dēlicātus.
fancy-free *adj* sēcūrus, vacuus.
fang *n* dēns *m*.
fantastic *adj* commentīcius, mōnstruōsus.
fantasy *n* imāginātiō *f*; (*contemptuous*)
somnium *nt*.
far *adj* longinquus ♦ *adv* longē, procul; (*with
compar*) multō; **be ~ from** longē abesse ab; **be
not ~ from doing** haud multum abest quin
(+*subj*); **by ~** longē; **how ~?** quātenus?,
quoūsque?; **so ~** hāctenus, eātenus; (*limited*)

quādam tenus; **thus ~** hāctenus; ~ **and wide**
lātē; ~ **be it from me to say** equidem dīcere
nōlim; ~ **from thinking ... I** adeō nōn crēdō ...
ut; **as ~ as** *prep* tenus (*abl*) ♦ *adv* ūsque ♦ *conj*
quātenus; (*know*) quod.
farce *n* mīmus *m*.
farcical *adj* rīdiculus.
fare *vi* sē habēre, agere ♦ *n* vectūra *f*; (*boat*)
naulum *nt*; (*food*) cibus *m*.
farewell *interj* valē, valēte; **say ~ to** valēre
iubēre.
far-fetched *adj* quaesītus, arcessītus, altē
repetītus.
farm *n* fundus *m*, praedium *nt* ♦ *vt* (*soil*) colere;
(*taxes*) redimere; ~ **out** locāre.
farmer *n* agricola *m*; (*of taxes*) pūblicānus *m*.
farming *n* agrīcultūra *f*.
farrow *vt* parere ♦ *n* fētus *m*.
far-sighted *adj* prōvidus, prūdēns.
farther *adv* longius, ultrā ♦ *adj* ulterior.
farthest *adj* ultimus, extrēmus ♦ *adv*
longissimē.
fasces *n* fascēs *mpl*.
fascinate *vt* dēlēnīre, capere.
fascination *n* dulcēdō *f*, dēlēnīmenta *ntpl*,
lēnōcinia *ntpl*.
fashion *n* mōs *m*, ūsus *m*; (*manner*) modus *m*,
ratiō *f*; (*shape*) fōrma *f* ♦ *vt* fingere, fōrmāre;
after the ~ of rītū (*gen*); **come into ~** in
mōrem venīre; **go out of ~** obsolēscere.
fashionable *adj* ēlegāns; **it is ~** mōris est.
fashionably *adv* ēleganter.
fast *adj* (*firm*) firmus; (*quick*) celer; **make ~**
dēligāre ♦ *adv* firmē; celeriter; **be ~ asleep**
artē dormīre ♦ *vi* iēiūnus esse, cibō
abstinēre ♦ *n* iēiūnium *nt*.
fasten *vt* fīgere, ligāre; ~ **down** dēfīgere; ~ **on**
inligāre; ~ **to** adligāre; ~ **together** conligāre,
cōnfīgere.
fastening *n* iūnctūra *f*.
fastidious *adj* dēlicātus, ēlegāns.
fastidiously *adv* fastīdiōsē.
fastidiousness *n* fastīdium *nt*.
fasting *n* iēiūnium *nt*, inedia *f* ♦ *adj* iēiūnus.
fastness *n* arx *f*, castellum *nt*.
fat *adj* pinguis, opīmus, obēsus; **grow ~**
pinguēscere ♦ *n* adeps *m/f*.
fatal *adj* (*deadly*) fūnestus, exitiābilis; (*fated*)
fātālis.
fatality *n* fātum *nt*, cāsus *m*.
fatally *adv*: **be ~ wounded** vulnere perīre.
fate *n* fātum *nt*, fortūna *f*, sors *f*.
fated *adj* fātālis.
fateful *adj* fātālis; fūnestus.
Fates *npl* (*goddesses*) Parcae *fpl*.
father *n* pater *m*; (*fig*) auctor *m* ♦ *vt* gignere; ~
upon addīcere, tribuere.
father-in-law *n* socer *m*.
fatherland *n* patria *f*.
fatherless *adj* orbus.
fatherly *adj* paternus.
fathom *n* sex pedēs *mpl* ♦ *vt* (*fig*) exputāre.
fathomless *adj* profundus.

fatigue n fatīgātiō f, dēfatīgātiō f ♦ vt fatīgāre, dēfatīgāre.
fatness n pinguitūdō f.
fatten vt sagīnāre.
fatty adj pinguis.
fatuity n īnsulsitās f, ineptiae fpl.
fatuous adj fatuus, īnsulsus, ineptus.
fault n culpa f, vitium nt; (written) mendum nt; **count as a** ~ vitiō vertere; **find** ~ **with** incūsāre; **it is not your** ~ **that** ... nōn per tē stat quōminus (subj).
faultily adv vitiōsē, mendōsē.
faultiness n vitium nt.
faultless adj ēmendātus, integer.
faultlessly adv ēmendātē.
faulty adj vitiōsus, mendōsus.
faun n faunus m.
fauna n animālia ntpl.
favour n grātia f, favor m; (done) beneficium nt; **win** ~ **with** grātiam inīre apud; **by your** ~ bonā veniā tuā ♦ vt favēre (dat), indulgēre (dat).
favourable adj faustus, prosperus, secundus.
favourably adv faustē, fēlīciter, benignē.
favourite adj dīlectus, grātissimus ♦ n dēliciae fpl.
favouritism n indulgentia f, studium nt.
fawn n hinnuleus m ♦ adj (colour) gilvus ♦ vi: ~ **upon** adūlārī.
fawning adj blandus ♦ n adūlātiō f.
fear n timor m, metus m, formīdō f ♦ vt timēre, metuere, formīdāre, verērī; **fearing that** veritus ne (+ imperf subj).
fearful adj timidus; horrendus, terribilis, formīdolōsus.
fearfully adv timidē; formīdolōsē.
fearless adj impavidus, intrepidus.
fearlessly adv impavidē, intrepidē.
fearlessness n fīdentia f, audācia f.
fearsome adj formīdolōsus.
feasible adj: **it is** ~ fierī potest.
feast n epulae fpl; (private) convīvium nt; (public) epulum nt; (religious) daps f; (festival) festus diēs m ♦ vi epulārī, convīvārī; (fig) pāscī ♦ vt: ~ **one's eyes on** oculōs pāscere (abl).
feat n factum nt, facinus nt.
feather n penna f; (downy) plūma f; **birds of a** ~ **flock together** parēs cum paribus facillimē congregantur.
feathered adj pennātus.
feathery adj plūmeus.
feature n līneāmentum nt; (fig) proprium nt.
February n mēnsis Februārius m; **of** ~ Februārius.
federal adj sociālis, foederātus.
federate vi societātem facere.
federated adj foederātus.
federation n societās f, foederātae cīvitātēs fpl.
fee n honōs m, mercēs f.
feeble adj imbēcillus, īnfirmus, dēbilis.
feebleness n imbēcillitās f, īnfirmitās f.
feebly adv infirmē.

feed vt alere, pāscere ♦ vi pāscī; ~ **on** vescī (abl) ♦ n pābulum nt.
feel vt sentīre; (with hand) tractāre, tangere; (emotion) capere, adficī (abl); (opinion) cēnsēre, sentīre; ~ **one's way** pedetemptim prōgredī ♦ vi sentīre; **I** ~ **glad** gaudeō; ~ **sure** prō certō habēre.
feeling n sēnsus m, tāctus m; (mind) animus m, adfectus m; (pity) misericordia f; **good** ~ voluntās f; **bad** ~ invidia f.
feign vt simulāre, fingere.
feignedly adv simulātē, fictē.
feint n simulātiō f.
felicitate vt grātulārī (dat).
felicitation n grātulātiō f.
felicitous adj fēlīx, aptus.
felicity n fēlīcitās f.
feline adj fēlīnus.
fell vt (tree) succīdere; (enemy) sternere, caedere ♦ adj dīrus, crūdēlis, atrōx ♦ n mōns m; (skin) pellis f.
fellow n socius m, aequālis m; (contemptuous) homō m.
fellow citizen n cīvis m/f.
fellow countryman n cīvis m/f, populāris m/f.
fellow feeling n misericordia f.
fellowship n societās f, sodālitās f.
fellow slave n cōnservus m.
fellow soldier n commīlitō m.
fellow student n condiscipulus m.
felon n nocēns m.
felonious adj scelestus, scelerātus.
felony n scelus nt, noxa f.
felt n coāctum nt.
female adj muliebris ♦ n fēmina f.
feminine adj muliebris.
fen n palūs f.
fence n saepēs f; **sit on the** ~ quiēscere, medium sē gerere ♦ vt saepīre; ~ **off** intersaepīre ♦ vi bātuere, rudibus lūdere.
fencing n rudium lūdus m; ~ **master** lānista m.
fend vt arcēre ♦ vi prōvidēre.
fennel n ferula f.
fenny adj palūster.
ferment n fermentum nt; (fig) aestus m ♦ vt fermentāre; (fig) excitāre, accendere ♦ vi fervēre.
fermentation n fervor m.
fern n filix f.
ferocious adj ferōx, saevus, truculentus.
ferociously adv truculentē.
ferocity n ferōcitās f, saevitia f.
ferret n viverra m ♦ vt: ~ **out** rīmārī, ēruere.
ferry n trāiectus m; (boat) cymba f, pontō m ♦ vt trānsvehere.
ferryman n portitor m.
fertile adj fertīlis, fēcundus.
fertility n fertīlitās f, fēcunditās f.
fertilize vt fēcundāre, laetificāre.
fervent adj fervidus, ārdēns.
fervently adv ārdenter.
fervid adj fervidus.
fervour n ārdor m, fervor m.

festal *adj* festus.
fester *vi* exulcerārī.
festival *n* diēs festus *m*, sollemne *nt*.
festive *adj* (*time*) festus; (*person*) festīvus.
festivity *n* hilaritās *f*; (*event*) sollemne *nt*.
festoon *n* sertum *nt* ♦ *vt* corōnāre.
fetch *vt* arcessere, addūcere; (*price*) vēnīre (*gen*); ~ **out** dēprōmere; ~ **water** aquārī.
fetching *adj* lepidus, blandus.
fetid *adj* foetidus, pūtidus.
fetter *n* compēs *f*, vinculum *nt* ♦ *vt* compedēs inicere (*dat*), vincīre; (*fig*) impedīre.
fettle *n* habitus *m*, animus *m*.
feud *n* simultās *f*, inimīcitia *f*.
fever *n* febris *f*.
feverish *adj* febrīculōsus; (*fig*) sollicitus.
few *adj* paucī; **very** ~ perpaucī; **how** ~? quotus quisque?
fewness *n* paucitās *f*.
fiancé *n* spōnsus *m*.
fiasco *n* calamitās *f*; **be a** ~ frīgēre.
fiat *n* ēdictum *nt*.
fibre *n* fibra *f*.
fickle *adj* incōnstāns, levis, mōbilis.
fickleness *n* incōnstantia *f*, levitās *f*, mōbilitās *f*.
fiction *n* fābula *f*, commentum *nt*.
fictitious *adj* fictus, falsus, commentīcius; (*character*) persōnātus.
fictitiously *adv* fictē.
fidelity *n* fidēlitās *f*, fidēs *f*.
fidget *vi* sollicitārī.
field *n* ager *m*; (*ploughed*) arvum *nt*; (*of grain*) seges *f*; (MIL) campus *m*, aciēs *f*; (*scope*) campus *m*, locus *m*; **in the** ~ (MIL) mīlitiae; **hold the** ~ vincere, praevalēre; ~ **of vision** cōnspectus *m*.
fiend *n* diabolus *m*.
fiendish *adj* nefārius, improbus.
fierce *adj* saevus, ācer, atrōx; (*look*) torvus.
fiercely *adv* ācriter, atrōciter, saevē.
fierceness *n* saevitia *f*, atrōcitās *f*.
fieriness *n* ārdor *m*, fervor *m*.
fiery *adj* igneus, flammeus; (*fig*) ārdēns, fervidus.
fife *n* tībia *f*.
fifteen *num* quīndecim; ~ **each** quīndēnī; ~ **times** quīndeciēns.
fifteenth *adj* quīntus decimus.
fifth *adj* quīntus ♦ *n* quīnta pars *f*.
fiftieth *adj* quīnquāgēsimus.
fifty *num* quīnquāgintā.
fig *n* fīcus *f*; (*tree*) fīcus *f*; **of** ~ fīculnus; **not care a** ~ **for** floccī nōn facere.
fight *n* pugna *f*, proelium *nt* ♦ *vi* pugnāre, dīmicāre; ~ **it out** dēcernere, dēcertāre; ~ **to the end** dēpugnāre ♦ *vt* (*battle*) committere; (*enemy*) pugnāre cum (*abl*).
fighter *n* pugnātor *m*.
fighting *n* dīmicātiō *f*.
figment *n* commentum *nt*.
figurative *adj* trānslātus; **in** ~ **language** trānslātīs per similitūdinem verbīs; **use** ~**ly** trānsferre.
figure *n* figūra *f*, fōrma *f*; (*in art*) signum *nt*; (*of speech*) figūra *f*, trānslātiō *f*; (*pl, on pottery*) sigilla *ntpl* ♦ *vt* figūrāre, fōrmāre; (*art*) fingere, effingere; ~ **to oneself** sibi prōpōnere.
figured *adj* sigillātus.
figurehead *n* (*of ship*) īnsigne *nt*.
filament *n* fibra *f*.
filch *vt* fūrārī, surripere.
file *n* (*tool*) līma *f*; (*line*) ōrdō *m*, agmen *nt*; (*of papers*) fasciculus *m*; ~**s** *pl* tabulae *fpl*; **in single** ~ simplicī ōrdine; **the rank and** ~ gregāriī mīlitēs ♦ *vt* līmāre.
filial *adj* pius.
filigree *n* diatrēta *ntpl*.
fill *vt* implēre, explēre, complēre; (*office*) fungī (*abl*); ~ **up** supplēre.
fillet *n* īnfula *f*, vitta *f* ♦ *vt* (*fish*) exossāre.
fillip *n* stimulus *m*.
filly *n* equula *f*.
film *n* membrāna *f*.
filter *n* cōlum *nt* ♦ *vt* dēliquāre ♦ *vi* percōlārī.
filth *n* sordēs *f*, caenum *nt*.
filthily *adv* foedē, inquinātē.
filthiness *n* foeditās *f*, impūritās *f*.
filthy *adj* foedus, impūrus; (*speech*) inquinātus.
fin *n* pinna *f*.
final *adj* ultimus, postrēmus, extrēmus.
finally *adv* dēnique, tandem, postrēmō.
finance *n* rēs nummāria *f*; (*state*) vectīgālia *ntpl*.
financial *adj* aerārius.
financier *n* faenerātor *m*.
finch *n* fringilla *f*.
find *vt* invenīre, reperīre; (*supplies*) parāre; (*verdict*) iūdicāre; (*pleasure*) capere; ~ **fault with** incūsāre; ~ **guilty** damnāre; ~ **out** comperīre, cognōscere.
finder *n* inventor *m*.
finding *n* iūdicium *nt*, sententia *f*.
fine *n* (*law*) multa *f*, damnum *nt*; **in** ~ dēnique ♦ *vt* multāre ♦ *adj* (*thin*) tenuis, subtīlis; (*refined*) ēlegāns, mundus, decōrus; (*beautiful*) pulcher, venustus; (*showy*) speciōsus; (*of weather*) serēnus.
finely *adv* pulchrē, ēleganter, subtīliter.
fineness *n* tenuitās *f*; ēlegantia *f*; pulchritūdō *f*; speciēs *f*; serēnitās *f*.
finery *n* ōrnātus *m*, munditiae *fpl*.
finesse *n* astūtia *f*, ars *f*, argūtiae *fpl*.
finger *n* digitus *m*; **a** ~**'s breadth** trānsversus digitus; **not lift a** ~ (*in effort*) nē manum quidem vertere ♦ *vt* pertractāre.
fingertips *npl* extrēmī digitī.
finish *n* fīnis *m*; (*art*) perfectiō *f* ♦ *vt* fīnīre, perficere; (*with art*) perficere, expolīre ♦ *vi* dēsinere; ~ **off** transigere, peragere, absolvere.
finishing post *n* mēta *f*.
finishing touch *n* manus extrēma.
finite *adj* circumscrīptus.

ir n abiēs f; of ~ abiēgnus.
ire n ignis m; (conflagration) incendium nt; (in
hearth) focus m; (fig) ārdor m, calor m,
impetus m; be on ~ ārdēre, flagrāre; catch ~
flammam concipere, ignem comprehendere;
set on ~ accendere, incendere ♦ vt
incendere; (fig) īnflammāre; (missile)
iaculārī.
firebrand n fax f.
fire brigade n vigilēs mpl.
fireplace n focus m.
fireside n focus m.
firewood n lignum nt.
firm n societās f ♦ adj firmus, stabilis; (mind)
cōnstāns; stand ~ perstāre.
firmament n caelum nt.
firmly adv firmē, cōnstanter.
firmness n firmitās f, firmitūdō f; cōnstantia f.
first adj prīmus, prīnceps; (of two) prior ♦ adv
prīmum; at ~ prīmō, prīncipiō; at ~ hand
ipse, ab ipsō; come in ~ vincere; give ~ aid to
ad tempus medērī (dat); I was the ~ to see
prīmus vīdī.
first-class adj classicus.
first fruits npl prīmitiae fpl.
firstly adv prīmum.
first-rate adj eximius, lūculentus.
firth n aestuārium nt, fretum nt.
fiscal adj vectīgālis, aerārius.
fish n piscis m ♦ vi piscārī; (fig) expiscārī.
fisher, fisherman n piscātor m.
fishing n piscātus m ♦ adj piscātōrius.
fishing-rod n harundō f.
fish market n forum piscārium nt.
fishmonger n piscārius m.
fish pond n piscīna f.
fissile adj fissilis.
fissure n rīma f.
fist n pugnus m.
fit n (MED) convulsiō f; (of anger, illness) impetus
m; by ~s and starts temerē, carptim ♦ vt
aptāre, accommodāre; (dress) sedēre (dat); ~
out armāre, īnstruere ♦ adj aptus, idōneus,
dignus; I see ~ to mihi vidētur; ~ for aptus ad
(+ acc).
fitful adj dubius, incōnstāns.
fitfully adv incōnstanter.
fitly adv dignē, aptē.
fitness n convenientia f.
fitting n adparātus m, īnstrūmentum nt ♦ adj
idōneus, dignus; it is ~ convenit, decet.
fittingly adv dignē, convenienter.
five num quīnque; ~ each quīnī; ~ times
quīnquiēns; ~ years quīnquennium nt,
lūstrum nt; ~ sixths quīnque partēs.
five hundred num quīngentī; ~ each quīngēnī;
~ times quīngentiēns.
five hundredth adj quīngentēsimus.
fix vt fīgere; (time) dīcere, cōnstituere;
(decision) statuere ♦ n angustiae fpl; put in a ~
dēprehendere.
fixed adj fixus; (attention) intentus; (decision)
certus; (star) inerrāns; be firmly ~ in īnsidēre

(dat).
fixedly adv intentē.
fixity n stabilitās f; (of purpose) cōnstantia f.
fixtures npl adfīxa ntpl.
flabbergast vt obstupefacere.
flabbiness n mollitia f.
flabby adj flaccidus, mollis.
flag n vexillum nt; ~ officer praefectus classis
m ♦ vi flaccēre, flaccēscere, languēscere.
flagellate vt verberāre.
flagon n lagoena f.
flagrant adj manifestus; flāgitiōsus.
flagrantly adv flāgitiōsē.
flagship n nāvis imperātōria f.
flail n fūstis m.
flair n iūdicium nt.
flake n squāma f; ~s pl (snow) nix f.
flame n flamma f ♦ vi flagrāre, exārdēscere.
flaming adj flammeus.
flamingo n phoenīcopterus m.
flank n latus nt; cornū m; on the ~ ab latere, ad
latus ♦ vt latus tegere (gen).
flap n flābellum nt; (dress) lacinia f ♦ vt
plaudere (abl).
flare n flamma f, fulgor m ♦ vi exārdēscere,
flagrāre.
flash n fulgor m; (lightning) fulgur nt; (time)
mōmentum nt ♦ vi fulgēre; (motion) micāre.
flashy adj speciōsus.
flask n ampulla f.
flat adj plānus; (ground) aequus; (on back)
supīnus; (on face) prōnus; (music) gravis;
(style) āridus, frīgidus; fall ~ (fig) frīgēre ♦ n
(land) plānitiēs f; (sea) vadum nt; (house)
tabulātum nt.
flatly adv prōrsus.
flatness n plānitiēs f.
flatten vt aequāre, complānāre.
flatter vt adūlārī (dat), adsentārī (dat), blandīrī
(dat).
flatterer n adsentātor m.
flattering adj blandus.
flatteringly adv blandē.
flattery n adūlātiō f, adsentātiō f, blanditiae fpl.
flatulence n īnflātiō f.
flatulent adj īnflātus.
flaunt vt iactāre ♦ vi iactāre, glōriārī.
flaunting n iactātiō f ♦ adj glōriōsus.
flauntingly adv glōriōsē.
flautist n tībīcen m.
flavour n gustātus m, sapor m ♦ vt imbuere,
condīre.
flavouring n condītiō f.
flavourless adj īnsulsus.
flaw n vitium nt.
flawless adj ēmendātus.
flax n līnum nt.
flaxen adj flāvus.
flay vt dēglūbere.
flea n pūlex m.
fleck n macula f ♦ vt variāre.
fledged adj pennātus.
flee vi fugere, effugere; (for refuge) cōnfugere.

fleece *n* vellus *nt* ♦ *vt* tondēre; (*fig*) spoliāre.
fleecy *adj* lāneus.
fleet *n* classis *f* ♦ *adj* vēlōx, celer.
fleeting *adj* fugāx.
fleetness *n* vēlōcitās *f*, celeritās *f*.
flesh *n* cārō *f*; (*fig*) corpus *nt*; **in the ~** vīvus; **one's own ~ and blood** cōnsanguineus; **put on ~** pinguēscere.
fleshiness *n* corpus *nt*.
fleshliness *n* libīdō *f*.
fleshly *adj* libīdinōsus.
fleshy *adj* pinguis.
flexibility *n* lentitia *f*.
flexible *adj* flexibilis, lentus.
flicker *vi* coruscāre.
flickering *adj* tremulus.
flight *n* (*flying*) volātus *m*; (*fleeing*) fuga *f*; (*steps*) scāla *f*; **put to ~** fugāre, in fugam conicere; **take to ~** sē in fugam dare, terga vertere.
flightiness *n* mōbilitās *f*.
flighty *adj* mōbilis, incōnstāns.
flimsy *adj* tenuis, pertenuis.
flinch *vi* recēdere.
fling *vt* iacere, conicere; (*missile*) intorquēre; **~ away** abicere, prōicere; **~ open** patefacere; **~ in one's teeth** obicere (*dat*); **~ to the ground** prōsternere ♦ *vi* sē incitāre ♦ *n* iactus *m*.
flint *n* silex *m*.
flinty *adj* siliceus.
flippancy *n* lascīvia *f*.
flippant *adj* lascīvus, protervus.
flippantly *adv* petulanter.
flirt *vi* lūdere, lascīvīre ♦ *n* lascīvus *m*, lascīva *f*.
flit *vi* volitāre.
flitch *n* succīdia *f*.
float *vi* innāre, fluitāre; (*in air*) volitāre; **~ down** dēfluere.
flock *n* grex *m*; (*wool*) floccus *m* ♦ *vi* concurrere, congregārī, cōnfluere; **~ in** adfluere.
flog *vt* verberāre, virgīs caedere.
flogging *n* verbera *ntpl*.
flood *n* (*deluge*) ēluviō *f*; (*river*) torrēns *m*; (*tide*) accessus *m*; (*fig*) flūmen *nt* ♦ *vt* inundāre.
floodgate *n* cataracta *f*.
floor *n* solum *nt*; (*paved*) pavīmentum *nt*; (*storey*) tabulātum *nt*; (*threshing*) ārea *f* ♦ *vt* contabulāre; **be ~ed** (*in argument*) iacēre.
flora *n* herbae *fpl*.
floral *adj* flōreus.
florid *adj* flōridus.
flotilla *n* classicula *f*.
flounce *vi* sē conicere ♦ *n* īnstita *f*.
flounder *vi* volutāre; (*in speech*) haesitāre.
flour *n* fārīna *f*.
flourish *vi* flōrēre, vigēre ♦ *vt* vibrāre, iactāre ♦ *n* (*RHET*) calamistrī *mpl*; (*music*) clangor *m*.
flout *vt* aspernārī, inlūdere (*dat*).
flow *vi* fluere, mānāre; (*tide*) accēdere; **~ back** recēdere; **~ between** interfluere; **~ down**

dēfluere; **~ into** īnfluere in (*acc*); **~ out** prōfluere, ēmānāre; **~ past** praeterfluere; **~ through** permānāre; **~ together** cōnfluere; **~ towards** adfluere ♦ *n* flūmen *nt*, cursus *m*; (*tide*) accessus *m*; (*words*) flūmen *nt*.
flower *n* flōs *m*, flōsculus *m* ♦ *vi* flōrēre, flōrēscere.
floweret *n* flōsculus *m*.
flowery *adj* flōridus.
flowing *adj* prōfluēns; **~ with** abundāns (*abl*).
flowingly *adv* prōfluenter.
flown *adj* īnflātus.
fluctuate *vi* aestuāre, fluctuāre.
fluctuating *adj* incōnstāns, incertus.
fluctuation *n* aestus *m*, dubitātiō *f*.
fluency *n* fācundia *f*, verbōrum cōpia *f*.
fluent *adj* disertus, prōfluēns.
fluently *adv* disertē, prōfluenter.
fluid *adj* liquidus ♦ *n* liquor *m*.
fluidity *n* liquor *m*.
fluke *n* (*anchor*) dēns *m*; (*luck*) fortuītum *nt*.
flurry *n* trepidātiō *f* ♦ *vt* sollicitāre, turbāre.
flush *n* rubor *m*; **in the first ~ of victory** victōriā ēlātus ♦ *vi* ērubēscere ♦ *adj* (*full*) abundāns; (*level*) aequus.
fluster *n* trepidātiō *f* ♦ *vt* turbāre, sollicitāre.
flute *n* tībia *f*; **play the ~** tībiā canere.
fluted *adj* striātus.
flutter *n* tremor *m*; (*fig*) trepidātiō *f* ♦ *vi* (*heart*) palpitāre; (*mind*) trepidāre; (*bird*) volitāre.
fluvial *adj* fluviātilis.
flux *n* fluxus *m*; **be in a state of ~** fluere.
fly *n* musca *f* ♦ *vi* volāre; (*flee*) fugere; **~ apart** dissilīre; **~ at** involāre in (*acc*); **~ away** āvolāre; **~ from** fugere; **~ in the face of** obviam īre (*dat*); **~ out** ēvolāre; **~ to** advolāre ad (*acc*); **~ up** ēvolāre, subvolāre; **let ~ at** immittere in (*acc*).
flying *adj* volucer, volātilis; (*time*) fugāx.
foal *n* equuleus *m*, equulus *m* ♦ *vt* parere.
foam *n* spūma *f* ♦ *vi* spūmāre; (*with rage*) saevīre.
foaming *adj* spūmeus.
focus *vt* (*mind*) intendere.
fodder *n* pābulum *nt*.
foe *n* hostis *m*; (*private*) inimīcus *m*.
fog *n* cālīgō *f*, nebula *f*.
foggy *adj* cālīginōsus, nebulōsus.
foible *n* vitium *nt*.
foil *n* (*metal*) lāmina *f*; (*sword*) rudis *f* ♦ *vt* ēlūdere, ad inritum redigere.
foist *vt* inculcāre, interpōnere.
fold *n* sinus *m*; (*sheep*) ovīle *nt* ♦ *vt* plicāre, complicāre; (*hands*) comprimere; (*sheep*) inclūdere; **~ back** replicāre; **~ over** plicāre; **~ together** complicāre; **~ up in** involvere in (*abl*).
folding doors *npl* valvae *fpl*.
foliage *n* frondēs *fpl*.
folk *n* hominēs *mpl* ♦ *adj* patrius.
follow *vt* sequī; (*calling*) facere; (*candidate*) adsectārī; (*enemy*) īnsequī; (*example*) imitārī; (*instructions*) pārēre (*dat*);

(*predecessor*) succēdere (*dat*); (*road*)
pergere; (*speaker*) intellegere; ~ **closely**
īnsequī; ~ **hard on the heels of** īnsequī,
īnsistere (*dat*), īnstāre (*dat*); ~ **out** exsequī; ~
to the grave exsequī; ~ **up** subsequī,
īnsistere (*dat*) ♦ *vi* (*time*) īnsequī; (*inference*)
sequī; **as ~s** ita, in hunc modum.

follower *n* comes *m*; (*of candidate*) adsectātor
m; (*of model*) imitātor *m*; (*of teacher*) audītor
m.

following *adj* tālis; īnsequēns, proximus,
posterus; **on the ~ day** postrīdiē, posterō diē,
proximō diē ♦ *n* adsectātōrēs *mpl*.

folly *n* stultitia *f*, dēmentia *f*, īnsipientia *f*.

foment *vt* fovēre; (*fig*) augēre.

fond *adj* amāns, studiōsus; ineptus; **be ~ of**
amāre.

fondle *vt* fovēre, mulcēre.

fondly *adv* amanter; ineptē.

food *n* cibus *m*; (*fig*) pābulum *nt*.

fool *n* stultus *m*, ineptus *m*; (*jester*) scurra *m*;
make a ~ of ludibriō habēre; **play the ~**
dēsipere ♦ *vt* dēcipere, lūdere; ~ **away**
disperdere ♦ *vi* dēsipere.

foolery *n* ineptiae *fpl*, nūgae *fpl*.

foolhardy *adj* temerārius.

foolish *adj* stultus, ineptus, īnsipiēns.

foolishly *adv* stultē, ineptē.

foolishness *n* stultitia *f*, īnsipientia *f*.

foot *n* pēs *m*; (*MIL*) peditātus *m*; **a ~ long** pedālis;
on ~ pedes; **set ~ on** īnsistere (*dat*); **set on ~**
īnstituere; **the ~ of** īmus ♦ *vt* (*bill*) solvere.

football *n* follis *m*.

footing *n* locus *m*, status *m*; **keep one's ~**
īnsistere; **on an equal ~** ex aequō.

footman *n* pedisequus *m*.

footpad *n* grassātor *m*.

footpath *n* sēmita *f*, trāmes *m*.

footprint *n* vestīgium *nt*.

foot soldier *n* pedes *m*.

footstep *n* vestīgium *nt*; **follow in the ~s of**
vestīgiīs ingredī (*gen*).

foppish *adj* dēlicātus.

for *prep* (*advantage*) *dat*; (*duration*) *acc*; (*after
noun*) *gen*; (*price*) *abl*; (*behalf*) prō (*abl*); (*cause*)
propter (*acc*), causā (*gen*); (*after neg*) prae
(*abl*); (*feelings*) ergā (*acc*); (*lieu*) prō (*abl*);
(*purpose*) ad, in (*acc*); (*time fixed*) in (*acc*) ♦
conj namque; nam (*1st word*), enim (*2nd
word*); (*with pron*) quippe quī; ~ **a long time**
diū; ~ **some time** aliquamdiū.

forage *n* pābulum *nt* ♦ *vi* pābulārī, frūmentārī.

forager *n* pābulātor *m*, frūmentātor *m*.

foraging *n* pābulātiō *f*, frūmentātiō *f*.

forasmuch as *conj* quoniam.

foray *n* incursiō *f*.

forbear *vi* parcere (*dat*), supersedēre (*infin*).

forbearance *n* venia *f*, indulgentia *f*.

forbears *n* māiōrēs *mpl*.

forbid *vt* vetāre (+ *acc and infin*), interdīcere
(*dat and quominus and subj*); **Heaven ~!** dī
meliōra!

forbidding *adj* tristis.

force *n* vīs *f*; (*band of men*) manus *m*; **by ~ of
arms** vī et armīs ♦ *vt* cōgere, impellere;
(*way*) rumpere, mōlīrī; (*growth*) festīnāre; ~
an engagement hostes proeliārī cogere; ~
down dētrūdere; ~ **out** extrūdere, expellere,
exturbāre; ~ **upon** inculcāre; ~ **a way in**
intrōrumpere, inrumpere.

forced *adj* (*march*) māgnus; (*style*) quaesītus; ~
march māgnum iter.

forceful *adj* validus.

forceps *n* forceps *m/f*.

forces *npl* (*MIL*) cōpiae *fpl*.

forcible *adj* validus; (*fig*) gravis.

forcibly *adv* vī, violenter; (*fig*) graviter.

ford *n* vadum *nt* ♦ *vt* vadō trānsīre.

fore *adj* prior; **to the ~** praestō ♦ *adv*: ~ **and aft**
in longitūdinem.

forearm *n* bracchium *nt* ♦ *vt*: **be ~ed**
praecavēre.

forebode *vt* ōminārī, portendere; prasentīre.

foreboding *n* praesēnsiō *f*; ōmen *nt*.

forecast *n* praedictiō *f* ♦ *vt* praedīcere,
prōvidēre.

forecourt *n* vestibulum *nt*.

forefathers *n* māiōrēs *mpl*.

forefinger *n* index *m*.

foreground *n* ēminentia *ntpl*.

forehead *n* frōns *f*.

foreign *adj* peregrīnus, externus; (*goods*)
adventīcius; ~ **to** aliēnus ab; ~ **ways**
peregrīnitās *f*.

foreigner *n* peregrīnus *m*, advena *m*.

foreknow *vt* praenōscere.

foreknowledge *n* prōvidentia *f*.

foreland *n* prōmunturium *nt*.

foremost *adj* prīmus, prīnceps.

forenoon *n* antemerīdiānum tempus *nt*.

forensic *adj* forēnsis.

forerunner *n* praenūntius *m*.

foresee *vt* praevidēre.

foreshadow *vt* praemonēre.

foresight *n* prōvidentia *f*.

forest *n* silva *f*.

forestall *vt* occupāre, antevenīre.

forester *n* silvicola *m*.

foretaste *vt* praegustāre.

foretell *vt* praedīcere, vāticinārī.

forethought *n* prōvidentia *f*.

forewarn *vt* praemonēre.

foreword *n* praefātiō *f*.

forfeit *n* multa *f*, damnum *nt* ♦ *vt* āmittere,
perdere, multārī (*abl*); (*bail*) dēserere.

forfeiture *n* damnum *nt*.

forgather *vi* congregārī, convenīre.

forge *n* fornāx *f* ♦ *vt* fabricārī, excūdere;
(*document*) subicere; (*will*) suppōnere;
(*signature*) imitārī; (*money*) adulterīnōs
nummōs percutere.

forged *adj* falsus, adulterīnus, commentīcius.

forger *n* (*of will*) subiector *m*.

forgery *n* falsum *nt*, commentum *nt*.

forget *vt* oblīvīscī (*gen*); (*thing learnt*)
dēdiscere; **be forgotten** memoriā cadere, ex

animō effluere.
forgetful *adj* immemor; (*by habit*) oblīviōsus.
forgetfulness n oblīviō f.
forgive *vt* ignōscere (*dat*), veniam dare (*dat*).
forgiveness n venia f.
forgo *vt* dīmittere, renūntiāre; (*rights*)
dēcēdere dē iūre.
fork n furca f; (*small*) furcula f; (*road*) trivium
nt.
forlorn *adj* inops, dēstitūtus, exspēs.
form n fōrma f, figūra f; (*of procedure*) fōrmula
f; (*condition*) vigor m; (*etiquette*) mōs m; (*seat*)
scamnum *nt*; (*school*) schola f; (*hare's*)
latibulum *nt* ♦ *vt* fōrmāre, fingere, efficere;
(*MIL*) īnstruere; (*plan*) inīre, capere.
formal *adj* iūstus; (*rite*) sollemnis.
formality n iūsta *ntpl*, rītus m; **as a ~** dicis
causā; **with due ~** rītē.
formally *adv* rītē.
formation n fōrma f, figūra f; (*process*)
cōnfōrmātiō f; **in ~** (*MIL*) īnstructus.
former *adj* prior, prīstinus, vetus; **the ~** ille.
formerly *adv* anteā, ōlim, quondam.
formidable *adj* formīdolōsus.
formidably *adv* formīdolōsē.
formula n fōrmula f; (*dictated*) praefātiō f.
formulate *vt* compōnere.
forsake *vt* dērelinquere, dēstituere, dēserere.
forswear *vt* pēierāre, abiūrāre.
fort n castellum *nt*.
forth *adv* forās; (*time*) posthāc.
forthwith *adv* extemplō, statim, prōtinus.
fortieth *adj* quadragēsimus.
fortification n (*process*) mūnītiō f; (*place*)
mūnīmentum *nt*, arx f.
fortify *vt* mūnīre, ēmūnīre, commūnīre; (*fig*)
cōnfīrmāre.
fortitude n fortitūdō f.
fortnight n quīndecim diēs *mpl*.
fortnightly *adv* quīntō decimō quōque diē.
fortress n arx f, castellum *nt*.
fortuitous *adj* fortuītus.
fortuitously *adv* fortuītō, cāsū.
fortunate *adj* fēlīx, fortūnātus.
fortunately *adv* fēlīciter, bene.
fortune n fortūna f, fors f; (*wealth*) rēs f,
dīvitiae *fpl*; **good ~** fēlīcitās f, secundae rēs
fpl; **bad ~** adversae rēs *fpl*; **make one's ~** rem
facere, rem quaerere; **tell ~s** hariolārī.
fortune-hunter n captātor m.
fortune-teller n hariolus m, sāga f.
forty *num* quadrāgintā; **~ each** quadrāgēnī; **~
times** quadrāgiēns.
forum n forum *nt*.
forward *adj* (*person*) protervus, audāx; (*fruit*)
praecox ♦ *adv* porrō, ante; **bring ~** prōferre;
come ~ prōdīre ♦ *vt* (*letter*) perferre; (*cause*)
adiuvāre, favēre (*dat*).
forwardness n audācia f, alacritās f.
forwards *adv* porrō, prōrsus; **backwards and ~**
rursum prōrsum, hūc illūc.
fosse n fossa f.
foster *vt* alere, nūtrīre; (*fig*) fovēre.

foster child n alumnus m, alumna f.
foster father n altor m, ēducātor m.
foster mother n altrīx f, nūtrīx f.
foul *adj* foedus; (*speech*) inquinātus; **fall ~ of**
inruere in (*acc*).
foully *adv* foedē, inquinātē.
foul-mouthed *adj* maledicus.
foulness n foedītās f.
found *vt* condere, fundāre, īnstituere; (*metal*)
fundere.
foundation n fundāmenta *ntpl*.
founder n fundātor m, conditor m ♦ *vi*
submergī, naufragium facere.
foundling n expositīcia f.
fount n fōns m.
fountain n fōns m.
fountainhead n fōns m, orīgō f.
four *num* quattuor (*indecl*); **~ each** quaternī; **~
times** quater; **~ days** quadriduum *nt*; **~ years**
quadriennium *nt*.
fourfold *adj* quadruplex ♦ *adv* quadrifāriam.
four hundred *num* quadringentī; **~ each**
quadringēnī; **~ times** quadringentiēns.
four hundredth *adj* quadringentēsimus.
fourteen *num* quattuordecim; **~ each** quaternī
dēnī; **~ times** quater deciēns.
fourteenth *adj* quartus decimus.
fourth *adj* quartus ♦ *n* quadrāns m; **three ~s**
dōdrāns m, trēs partēs *fpl*.
fowl n avis f; gallīna f.
fowler n auceps m.
fox n vulpes f; **~'s** vulpīnus.
foxy *adj* astūtus, vafer.
fracas n rīxa f.
fraction n pars f.
fractious *adj* difficilis.
fracture n frāctum os *nt* ♦ *vt* frangere.
fragile *adj* fragilis.
fragility n fragilitās f.
fragment n fragmentum *nt*.
fragrance n odor m.
fragrant *adj* suāvis.
fragrantly *adv* suāviter.
frail *adj* fragilis, īnfirmus, dēbilis.
frailty n dēbilitās f; (*moral*) error m.
frame *vt* fabricārī, fingere, effingere;
(*document*) compōnere ♦ *n* fōrma f; (*of mind*)
adfectiō f, habitus m; **in a ~ of mind** animātus.
framer n fabricātor m, opifex m; (*of law*) lātor m
framework n compāgēs f.
franchise n suffrāgium *nt*, cīvitās f.
frank *adj* ingenuus, apertus; (*speech*) līber.
frankincense n tūs *nt*.
frankly *adv* ingenuē, apertē; līberē.
frankness n ingenuitās f; (*speech*) lībertās f.
frantic *adj* furēns, furiōsus, dēlīrus.
frantically *adv* furenter.
fraternal *adj* frāternus.
fraternally *adv* frāternē.
fraternity n frāternitās f; (*society*) sodālitās f;
(*guild*) collēgium *nt*.
fraternize *vi* amīcitiam iungere.
fratricide n frātricīda m; (*act*) frātris

parricīdium *nt.*
fraud *n* fraus *f,* dolus *m,* falsum *nt;* (*criminal*) dolus malus *m.*
fraudulence *n* fraus *f.*
fraudulent *adj* fraudulentus, dolōsus.
fraudulently *adv* dolōsē, dolō malō.
fraught *adj* plēnus.
fray *n* pugna *f,* rīxa *f* ♦ *vt* terere.
freak *n* mōnstrum *nt;* (*caprice*) libīdō *f.*
freckle *n* lentīgō *f.*
freckly *adj* lentīginōsus.
free *adj* līber; (*disengaged*) vacuus; (*generous*) līberālis; (*from cost*) grātuītus; (*from duty*) immūnis; (*from encumbrance*) expedītus; **be ~ from** vacāre (*abl*); **I am still ~ to** integrum est mihī (*infin*); **set ~** absolvere, līberāre; (*slave*) manū mittere ♦ *adv* grātīs, grātuītō ♦ *vt* līberāre, expedīre, exsolvere.
freebooter *n* praedō *m.*
freeborn *adj* ingenuus.
freedman *n* lībertus *m.*
freedom *n* lībertās *f;* (*from duty*) immūnitās *f.*
freehold *n* praedium līberum *nt* ♦ *adj* immūnis.
freely *adv* līberē; (*lavishly*) cōpiōsē, largē; (*frankly*) apertē; (*voluntarily*) ultrō, suā sponte.
freeman *n* cīvis *m.*
free will *n* voluntās *f;* **of one's own ~** suā sponte.
freeze *vt* gelāre, glaciāre ♦ *vi* concrēscere.
freezing *adj* gelidus; **it is ~** gelat.
freight *n* vectūra *f;* (*cargo*) onus *nt* ♦ *vt* onerāre.
freighter *n* nāvis onerāria *f.*
frenzied *adj* furēns, furiōsus, fānāticus.
frenzy *n* furor *m,* īnsania *f.*
frequency *n* adsiduitās *f.*
frequent *adj* frequēns, crēber ♦ *vt* frequentāre, commeāre in (*acc*).
frequently *adv* saepe, saepenumerō, frequenter.
fresh *adj* (*new*) recēns, novus; (*vigorous*) integer; (*water*) dulcis; (*wind*) ācer.
freshen *vt* renovāre ♦ *vi* (*wind*) incrēbrēscere.
freshly *adv* recenter.
freshman *n* tīrō *m.*
freshness *n* novitās *f,* viriditās *f.*
fret *vi* maerēre, angī ♦ *vt* sollicitāre.
fretful *adj* mōrōsus, querulus.
fretfulness *n* mōrōsitās *f.*
fretted *adj* laqueātus.
friable *adj* puter.
friction *n* trītus *m.*
friend *n* amīcus *m,* familiāris *m/f,* hospes *m,* sodālis *m;* **make ~s with** sē cōnferre ad amīcitiam (*gen*).
friendless *adj* sine amīcīs.
friendliness *n* cōmitās *f,* officium *nt.*
friendly *adj* cōmis, facilis, benīgnus; **on ~ terms** familiāriter.
friendship *n* amīcitia *f,* familiāritās *f.*

frigate *n* liburna *f.*
fright *n* horror *m,* pavor *m,* terror *m;* **take ~** extimēscere, expavēscere.
frighten *vt* terrēre, exterrēre, perterrēre; **~ away** absterrēre; **~ off** dēterrēre; **~ the life out of** exanimāre.
frightful *adj* horribilis, immānis; (*look*) taeter.
frightfully *adv* foedē.
frigid *adj* frīgidus.
frigidity *n* frīgus *nt.*
frill *n* fimbriae *fpl;* (*RHET*) calamistrī *mpl.*
fringe *n* fimbriae *fpl.*
frisk *vi* lascīvīre, exsultāre.
frisky *adj* lascīvus.
fritter *vt:* **~ away** dissipāre; (*time*) extrahere.
frivolity *n* levitās *f.*
frivolous *adj* levis, inānis.
frivolously *adv* ināniter.
fro *adv:* **to and ~** hūc illūc.
frock *n* stola *f.*
frog *n* rāna *f.*
frolic *n* lūdus *m* ♦ *vi* lūdere, lascīvīre.
frolicsome *adj* lascīvus, hilaris.
from *prep* ab (*abl*), ā (*before consonants*); (*out*) ē, ex (*abl*); (*cause*) propter (*acc*); (*prevention*) quōminus, quīn; **~ all directions** undique.
front *n* frōns *f;* **in ~** ā fronte, adversus; **in ~ of** prō (+ *abl*).
frontier *n* līmes *m,* cōnfīnia *ntpl;* **~s** fīnes *mpl.*
front line *n* prima aciēs.
frost *n* gelū *nt.*
frostbitten *adj:* **be ~** vī frīgoris ambūrī.
frosty *adj* gelidus, glaciālis.
froth *n* spūma *f* ♦ *vi* spūmās agere.
frothy *adj* spūmeus.
froward *adj* contumāx.
frown *n* frontis contractiō *f* ♦ *vi* frontem contrahere.
frozen *adj* glaciālis.
fructify *vt* fēcundāre.
frugal *adj* parcus, frūgī.
frugality *n* frūgālitās *f,* parsimōnia *f.*
frugally *adv* parcē, frūgāliter.
fruit *n* frūctus *m;* (*tree*) māla *ntpl;* (*berry*) bāca *f;* (*fig*) frūctus *m;* **~s** *pl* (*of earth*) frūgēs *fpl.*
fruiterer *n* pōmārius *m.*
fruitful *adj* fēcundus, frūctuōsus.
fruitfully *adv* ferāciter.
fruitfulness *n* fēcunditās *f,* ūbertās *f.*
fruition *n* frūctus *m.*
fruitless *adj* inūtilis, vānus.
fruitlessly *adv* nēquīquam, frustrā.
fruit tree *n* pōmum *nt.*
frustrate *vt* frustrārī, ad inritum redigere.
frustration *n* frustrātiō *f.*
fry *vt* frīgere.
frying pan *n* sartāgō *f;* **out of the ~ into the fire** incidit in Scyllam quī vult vītāre Charybdim.
fuel *n* fōmes *m.*
fugitive *adj* fugitīvus ♦ *n* fugitīvus *m,* trānsfuga *m;* (*from abroad*) extorris *m.*
fulfil *vt* (*duty*) explēre, implēre; (*promise*)

praestāre; (*order*) exsequī, perficere.
fulfilment n absolūtiō f.
full adj plēnus (+ *abl*), refertus, explētus;
(*entire*) integer; (*amount*) solidus; (*brother*)
germānus; (*measure*) iūstus; (*meeting*)
frequēns; (*style*) cōpiōsus; **at ~ length**
porrēctus; **at ~ speed** citātō gradū, citātō
equō.
fuller n fullō m.
full-grown adj adultus.
full moon n lūna plēna.
fullness n (*style*) cōpia f; (*time*) mātūritās f.
fully adv plēnē, penitus, funditus.
fulminate vi intonāre.
fulsome adj fastīdiōsus, pūtidus.
fumble vi haesitāre.
fume n fūmus m, hālitus m ♦ vi stomachārī.
fumigate vt suffīre.
fun n iocus m, lūdus m; **for ~** animī causā; **make
~ of** inlūdere, dēlūdere, lūdibriō habēre.
function n officium nt, mūnus nt.
fund n cōpia f.
fundamental adj prīmus ♦ n prīncipium nt,
elementum nt.
funds npl sors f, pecūniae fpl.
funeral n fūnus nt, exsequiae fpl ♦ adj fūnebris.
funeral pile n rogus m.
funeral pyre n rogus m.
funeral rites npl exsequiae fpl, īnferiae fpl.
funereal adj fūnebria, lūgubris.
funnel n īnfundibulum nt.
funny adj ioculāris, rīdiculus.
fur n pellis m.
furbelow n īnstita f.
furbish vt expolīre; **~ up** interpolāre.
Furies npl Furiae fpl.
furious adj saevus, vehemēns, perīrātus.
furiously adv furenter, saevē, vehementer.
furl vt (*sail*) legere.
furlong n stadium nt.
furlough n commeātus m.
furnace n fornāx f.
furnish vt praebēre, suppeditāre; (*equip*)
īnstruere, ōrnāre.
furniture n supellex f.
furrow n sulcus m ♦ vt sulcāre.
furry adj villōsus.
further adj ulterior ♦ adv ultrā, porrō; amplius
♦ vt adiuvāre, cōnsulere (*dat*).
furtherance n prōgressus m; (*means*)
īnstrūmentum nt.
furthermore adv praetereā, porrō.
furthest adj ultimus ♦ adv longissimē.
furtive adj fūrtīvus, clandestīnus.
furtively adv clam, fūrtim.
fury n furor m, saevitia f; īra f.
fuse vt fundere; (*together*) coniungere.
fusion n coniūnctiō f.
fuss n importūnitās f, querimōnia f ♦ vi
conquerī, sollicitārī.
fussy adj importūnus, incommodus.
fusty adj mūcidus.
futile adj inānis, inūtilis, futtilis.

futility n vānitās f, futtilitās f.
future adj futūrus, posterus ♦ n posterum nt,
reliquum nt; **in ~** posthāc; **for the ~** in
posterum.
futurity n posterum tempus nt, posteritās f.

G, g

gabble vi garrīre.
gable n fastīgium nt.
gadfly n tabānus m.
gag vt ōs praeligāre (*dat*), ōs obvolvere (*dat*).
gage n pignus nt.
gaiety n laetitia f, hilaritās f, festīvitās f.
gaily adv hilare, festīve.
gain n lucrum nt, quaestus m ♦ vt comparāre;
adipīscī; (*profit*) lucrārī; (*thing*) parāre,
cōnsequī, capere; (*case*) vincere; (*place*)
pervenīre ad; (*possession of*) potīrī (*gen*);
(*victory*) reportāre; **~ over** conciliāre; **~
ground** incrēbrēscere; **~ possession of**
potior (+ *abl*); **~ the upper hand** rem obtinēre.
gainful adj quaestuōsus.
gainsay vt contrādīcere (*dat*).
gait n incessus m, ingressiō f.
gaiters n ocreae fpl.
gala n diēs festus m.
galaxy n circulus lacteus m.
gale n ventus m.
gall n fel nt, bīlis m ♦ vt ūrere.
gallant adj fortis, audāx; (*courteous*)
officiōsus.
gallantly adv fortiter; officiōsē.
gallantry n virtūs f; urbānitās f.
gall bladder n fel nt.
gallery n porticus f.
galley n nāvis āctuāria f; (*cook's*) culīna f.
galling adj amārus, mordāx.
gallon n congius m.
gallop n cursus m; **at the ~** citātō equō,
admissō equō ♦ vi admissō equō currere.
gallows n īnfēlīx arbor m, furca f.
gallows bird n furcifer m.
galore adv adfatim.
gamble n ālea f ♦ vi āleā lūdere.
gambler n āleātor m.
gambling n ālea f.
gambol n lūsus m ♦ vi lūdere, lascīvīre,
exsultāre.
game n lūdus m; (*with dice*) ālea f; (*hunt*)
praeda f; **play the ~** rēctē facere; **public ~s**
lūdī mpl; **Olympic ~s** Olympia npl; **the ~'s up**
āctum est ♦ adj animōsus.
gamester n āleātor m.
gammon n perna f.
gander n ānser m.

gang n grex m, caterva f.
gangster n grassātor m.
gangway n forus m.
gaol n carcer m.
gaoler n custōs m.
gap n hiātus m, lacūna f.
gape vi hiāre, inhiāre; (opening) dēhiscere.
garb n habitus m, amictus m ♦ vt amicīre.
garbage n quisquiliae fpl.
garden n hortus m; (public) hortī mpl.
gardener n hortulānus m; (ornamental)
  topiārius m.
gardening n hortī cultūra f; (ornamental)
  topiāria f.
gargle vi gargarissāre.
garish adj speciōsus, fūcātus.
garland n sertum nt, corōna f ♦ vt corōnāre.
garlic n ālium nt.
garment n vestis f, vestīmentum nt.
garnish vt ōrnāre, decorāre.
garret n cēnāculum nt.
garrison n praesidium nt, dēfēnsōrēs mpl ♦ vt
  praesidiō mūnīre, praesidium collocāre in
  (abl).
garrotte vt laqueō gulam frangere (dat).
garrulity n garrulitās f.
garrulous adj garrulus, loquāx.
gas n vapor m.
gash n vulnus nt ♦ vt caedere, lacerāre.
gasp n anhēlitus m, singultus m ♦ vi anhēlāre.
gastronomy n gula f.
gate n porta f.
gather vt colligere, cōgere; (fruit) legere;
  (inference) colligere, conicere ♦ vi
  congregārī.
gathering n conventus m, coetus m.
gauche adj inconcinnus, illepidus.
gaudily adv splendidē, speciōsē.
gaudy adj speciōsus, fūcātus, lautus.
gauge n modulus m ♦ vt mētīrī.
Gaul n Gallia f; (person) Gallus m.
gaunt adj macer.
gauntlet n manica f.
gauze n Coa ntpl.
gay adj hilaris, festīvus, laetus.
gaze vi intuērī; ~ **at** intuērī, adspectāre,
  contemplārī.
gazelle n oryx m.
gazette n ācta diūrna ntpl, ācta pūblica ntpl.
gear n īnstrūmenta ntpl; (ship's) armāmenta
  ntpl.
gelding n cantērius m.
gelid adj gelidus.
gem n gemma f.
gender n genus nt.
genealogical adj dē stirpe.
genealogical table n stemma nt.
genealogist n geneālogus m.
genealogy n geneālogia f.
general adj generālis, ūniversus; (usual)
  vulgāris, commūnis; **in** ~ omnīnō ♦ n dux m,
  imperātor m; ~'s tent praetōrium nt.
generalissimo n imperātor m.

generality n vulgus nt, plērīque mpl.
generalize vi ūnīversē loquī.
generally adv ferē, plērumque; (discuss)
  īnfīnītē.
generalship n ductus m.
generate vt gignere, generāre.
generation n aetās f, saeculum nt.
generic adj generālis.
generically adv genere.
generosity n līberālitās f, largitās f.
generous adj līberālis, largus, benīgnus.
generously adv līberāliter, largē, benīgnē.
genesis n orīgō f, prīncipium nt.
genial adj cōmis, hilaris.
geniality n cōmitās f, hilaritās f.
genially adv cōmiter, hilare.
genitive n genitīvus m.
genius n (deity) genius m; (talent) ingenium nt,
  indolēs f; **of** ~ ingeniōsus.
genre n genus nt.
genteel adj urbānus, polītus.
gentility n urbānitās f, ēlegantia f.
gentle adj (birth) ingenuus; (manner) hūmānus,
  indulgēns, mītis; (slope) lēnis, mollis; (thing)
  placidus, lēnis.
gentleman n vir m, ingenuus m, vir honestus
  m.
gentlemanly adj ingenuus, līberālis,
  honestus.
gentleness n hūmānitās f, indulgentia f,
  lēnitās f.
gentlewoman n ingenua f, mulier honesta f.
gently adv lēniter, molliter, placidē.
gentry n ingenuī mpl, optimātēs mpl;
  (contempt) hominēs mpl.
genuine adj vērus, germānus, sincērus.
genuinely adv germānē, sincērē.
genuineness n fidēs f.
geographical adj geōgraphicus; ~ **position**
  situs m.
geography n geōgraphia f.
geometrical adj geōmetricus.
geometry n geōmetria f.
Georgics n Geōrgica ntpl.
germ n germen nt, sēmen nt.
germane adj adfīnis.
germinate vi gemmāre.
gesticulate vi sē iactāre, gestū ūtī.
gesticulation n gestus m.
gesture n gestus m, mōtus m.
get vt adipīscī, nancīscī, parāre; (malady)
  contrahere; (request) impetrāre; (return)
  capere; (reward) ferre; ~ **sth done** cūrāre
  (with gerundive); ~ **sb to do** persuādēre (dat),
  addūcere; ~ **by heart** ēdiscere; ~ **in** repōnere;
  ~ **the better of** superāre; **go and** ~ arcessere
  ♦ vi fierī; ~ **about** (rumour) palam fierī,
  percrēbrēscere; ~ **away** effugere; ~ **at**
  (intent) spectāre; ~ **behind** cessāre; ~ **off**
  absolvī; ~ **on** prōficere; ~ **out** effugere,
  ēvādere; ~ **out of hand** lascīvīre; ~ **out of the**
  way dē viā dēcēdere; ~ **ready** parāre; ~ **rid of**
  abicere, tollere; ~ **to** pervenīre ad;

~ **to know** cognōscere; ~ **together** congregārī; ~ **up** exsurgere.

get-up n ōrnātus m.

ghastliness n pallor m.

ghastly adj pallidus; (sight) taeter.

ghost n larva f, īdōlon nt; ~**s** pl mānēs mpl; **give up the** ~ animam agere, efflāre.

giant n Gigas m.

gibberish n barbaricus sermō m.

gibbet n furca f.

gibe vi inrīdēre.

giddiness n vertīgō f.

giddy adj vertīginōsus; (fig) levis.

gift n dōnum nt; (small) mūnusculum nt; ~**s** pl (mind) ingenium nt.

gifted adj ingeniōsus.

gig n cisium nt.

gigantic adj ingēns, immānis.

gild vt inaurāre.

gill n (measure) quartārius m; (fish) branchia f.

gilt adj aurātus.

gimlet n terebra f.

gin n pedica f, laqueus m.

ginger n zingiberī nt.

gingerly adv pedetemptim.

giraffe n camēlopardālis f.

gird vt circumdāre; ~ **on** accingere; ~ **oneself** cingī; ~ **up** succingere.

girder n tignum nt.

girdle n cingulus m ♦ vt cingere.

girl n puella f, virgō f.

girlhood n aetās puellāris f.

girlish adj puellāris.

girth n ambitus m, amplitūdō f.

gist n firmāmentum nt.

give vt dare, dōnāre, tribuere; (thing due) reddere; ~ **away** largīrī; (bride) in matrimōnium collocāre; (secret) prōdere; ~ **back** reddere, restituere; ~ **birth (to)** pārēre; ~ **in** (name) profitērī; ~ **off** ēmittere; ~ **out** (orders) ēdere; (sound) ēmittere; ~ **thanks** gratias agere; ~ **up** dēdere, trādere; (hope of) dēspērāre; (rights) dēcēdere dē, renūntiāre; ~ **way** cēdere; (MIL) inclīnāre ♦ vi labāre; ~ **in** sē victum fatērī; (MIL) manūs dare; ~ **out** (fail) dēficere; (pretend) ferre; ~ **up** dēsistere; ~ **way** cēdere.

giver n dator m.

glacial adj glaciālis.

glad adj laetus, alacer, hilaris; **be** ~ gaudēre.

gladden vt exhilarāre, oblectāre.

glade n saltus m.

gladiator n gladiātor m.

gladiatorial adj gladiātōrius; **present a** ~ **show** gladiātōrēs dare.

gladly adv laetē, libenter.

gladness n laetitia f, alacritās f, gaudium nt.

glamorous adj venustus.

glamour n venustās f.

glance n aspectus m ♦ vi oculōs conicere; ~ **at** aspicere; (fig) attingere, perstringere; ~ **off** stringere.

glare n fulgor m ♦ vi fulgēre; ~ **at** torvīs oculīs intuērī.

glaring adj (look) torvus; (fault) manifestus; **be** ~ ante pedēs positum esse.

glass n vitrum nt; (mirror) speculum nt.

glassy adj vitreus.

glaze vt vitrō obdūcere.

gleam n fulgor m, lūx f ♦ vi fulgēre, lūcēre.

gleaming adj splendidus, nitidus.

glean vi spīcās legere.

gleaning n spīcilegium nt.

glebe n fundus m.

glee n hilaritās f, gaudium nt.

gleeful adj hilaris, festīvus, laetus.

gleefully adv hilare, laetē.

glen n vallis f.

glib adj prōfluēns, fācundus.

glibly adv prōfluenter.

glide n lāpsus m ♦ vi lābī; ~ **away** ēlābī.

glimmer vi sublūcēre ♦ n: **a** ~ **of hope** spēcula f.

glimpse n aspectus m ♦ vt cōnspicārī.

glint vi renīdēre.

glisten vi fulgēre, nitēre.

glitter vi micāre.

gloaming n crepusculum nt.

gloat vi: ~ **over** inhiāre, animō haurīre, oculōs pāscere (abl).

globe n globus m, sphaera f; (inhabited) orbis terrārum m.

globular adj globōsus.

globule n globulus m, pilula f.

gloom n tenebrae fpl; tristitia f.

gloomy adj tenebricōsus; tristis, dēmissus.

glorify vt illūstrāre, extollere, laudāre.

glorious adj illūstris, praeclārus, splendidus.

gloriously adv praeclārē, splendidē.

glory n laus f, glōria f, decus nt ♦ vi glōriārī, sē iactāre.

gloss n nitor m ♦ vt: ~ **over** (fig) dissimulāre.

glossy adj nitidus.

glove n manica f.

glow n (light) lūmen nt; (heat) ārdor m; (passion) calor m ♦ vi lūcēre, ārdēre, calēre, candēre.

glowing adj candēns, ārdēns, calidus.

glue n glūten nt ♦ vt glūtināre.

glum adj tristis, maestus.

glut vt explēre, saturāre ♦ n satietās f, abundantia f.

glutton n gāneō m, helluō m.

gluttonous adj edāx, vorāx, avidus.

gluttony n gula f, edācitās f.

gnarled adj nōdōsus.

gnash vt, vi frendere; ~ **one's teeth** dentibus frendere.

gnat n culex m.

gnaw vt rōdere; ~ **away** ērōdere.

gnawing adj mordāx.

go vi īre, vādere; (depart) abīre, discēdere; (event) ēvādere; (mechanism) movērī; ~ **about** incipere, adgredī; ~ **after** īnsequī; ~ **away** abīre, discēdere; ~ **back** redīre, regredī; ~ **before** anteīre, praeīre; ~ **by** praeterīre; (*rule*) sequī, ūtī (*abl*); ~ **down** dēscendere; (*storm*) cadere; (*star*) occidere; ~ **for** petere; ~ **forward** prōgredī; ~ **in** intrāre, ingredī; ~ **in for** (*profession*) facere, exercēre; ~ **off** abīre; ~ **on** pergere; (*event*) agī; ~ **out** exīre, ēgredī; (*fire*) extinguī; ~ **over** trānsīre; (*to enemy*) dēscīscere; (*preparation*) meditārī; (*reading*) legere; (*work done*) retractāre; ~ **round** circumīre, ambīre; ~ **through** percurrere; penetrāre; (*suffer*) perferre; ~ **to** adīre, petere; ~ **up** ascendere; ~ **to the help of** subvenīre (+ *dat*); ~ **to meet** obviam īre; ~ **with** comitārī; ~ **without** carēre (*abl*), sē abstinēre (*abl*) ♦ *n* vīs *f*, ācrimōnia *f*.

goad *n* stimulus *m* ♦ *vt* irrītāre; pungere; (*fig*) stimulāre.

go-ahead *adj* impiger.

goal *n* fīnis *m*, mēta *f*.

goat *n* caper *m*, capra *f*.

gobble *vt* dēvorāre.

go-between *n* internūntius *m*, internūntia *f*; (*bribery*) sequester *m*.

goblet *n* pōculum *nt*, scyphus *m*.

god *n* deus *m*.

goddess *n* dea *f*.

godhead *n* dīvīnitās *f*, nūmen *nt*.

godless *adj* impius.

godlike *adj* dīvīnus.

godliness *n* pietās *f*, rēligiō *f*.

godly *adj* pius.

godsend *n* quasi caelō dēmissus.

going *n* itiō *f*; (*way*) iter *nt*; (*departure*) profectiō *f*, discessus *m*.

goitre *n* strūma *nt*.

gold *n* aurum *nt* ♦ *adj* aureus.

golden *adj* aureus; (*hair*) flāvus.

gold leaf *n* bractea *f*.

goldmine *n* aurāria *f*.

goldsmith *n* aurārius *m*, aurifex *m*.

good *adj* bonus, probus; (*fit*) idōneus, aptus; (*considerable*) magnus; ~ **day!** salvē, salvēte!; ~ **looks** fōrma *f*, pulchritūdō *f*; ~ **nature** facilitās *f*, cōmitās *f* ♦ *n* bonum *nt*, commodum *nt*; **do** ~ **to** prōdesse (*dat*); **make** ~ supplēre, praestāre; **seem** ~ vidērī; ♦ *interj* bene.

goodbye *interj* valē, valēte; **say** ~ **to** valēre iubēre.

good-for-nothing *adj* nēquam.

good-humoured *adj* cōmis.

good-looking *adj* pulcher.

goodly *adj* pulcher; (*size*) amplus.

good nature *n* facilitās *f*, cōmitās *f*.

good-natured *adj* facilis, benīgnus, benevolus.

goodness *n* bonitās *f*; (*character*) virtūs *f*, probitās *f*, pietās *f*.

goods *npl* bona *ntpl*, rēs *f*; (*for sale*) merx *f*.

good-tempered *adj* mītis, lēnis.

goodwill *n* benevolentia *f*, favor *m*, grātia *f*.

goose *n* ānser *m/f*.

goose flesh *n* horror *m*.

gore *n* cruor *m* ♦ *vt* cornibus cōnfodere.

gorge *n* faucēs *fpl*, gula *f*; (GEOG) angustiae *fpl* ♦ *vt*: ~ **oneself** sē ingurgitāre.

gorgeous *adj* lautus, splendidus.

gorgeously *adv* lautē, splendidē.

gorgeousness *n* lautitia *f*.

gormandize *vi* helluārī.

gory *adj* cruentus.

gospel *n* ēvangelium *nt*.

gossip *n* (*talk*) sermunculus *m*, rūmusculus *m*, fāma *f*; (*person*) lingulāca *f* ♦ *vi* garrīre.

gouge *vt* ēruere.

gourd *n* cucurbita *f*.

gourmand *n* helluō *m*, gāneō *m*.

gout *n* podagra *f*, articulāris morbus *m*.

gouty *adj* arthrīticus.

govern *vt* (*subjects*) regere; (*state*) administrāre, gubernāre; (*emotion*) moderārī (*dat*), cohibēre.

governess *n* ēducātrīx *f*.

government *n* gubernātiō *f*, administrātiō *f*; (*men*) magistrātūs *mpl*.

governor *n* gubernātor *m*, moderātor *m*; (*province*) prōcōnsul *m*, prōcūrātor *m*.

gown *n* (*men*) toga *f*; (*women*) stola *f*.

grab *vt* adripere, corripere.

grace *n* grātia *f*, lepōs *m*, decor *m*; (*favour*) grātia *f*, venia *f*; (*of gods*) pāx *f*; **be in the good** ~**s of** in grātiā esse apud (*acc*); **with a bad** ~ invītus ♦ *vt* decorāre, ōrnāre.

graceful *adj* decōrus, venustus, lepidus.

gracefully *adv* venustē, lepidē.

graceless *adj* illepidus, impudēns.

gracious *adj* benīgnus, prōpitius, misericors.

graciously *adv* benīgnē, līberāliter.

graciousness *n* benīgnitās *f*, līberālitās *f*.

gradation *n* gradus *m*.

grade *n* gradus *m*.

gradient *n* clīvus *m*.

gradual *adj* lēnis.

gradually *adv* gradātim, sēnsim, paulātim.

graft *n* surculus *m*; (POL) ambitus *m* ♦ *vt* īnserere.

grafting *n* īnsitiō *f*.

grain *n* frūmentum *nt*; (*seed*) grānum *nt*; **against the** ~ invītā Minervā.

grammar *n* grammatica *f*.

grammarian *n* grammaticus *m*.

granary *n* horreum *nt*.

grand *adj* (*person*) amplus, illūstris, ēgregius; (*way of life*) lautus, māgnificus; (*language*) grandis, sublīmis.

granddaughter *n* neptis *f*; **great** ~ prōneptis *f*.

grandeur *n* māiestās *f*, māgnificentia *f*; (*style*) granditās *f*.

grandfather *n* avus *m*; **great** ~ proavus *m*; **great-great-** ~ abavus *m*; **of a** ~ avītus.

grandiloquence *n* māgniloquentia *f*.

grandiloquent *adj* grandiloquus, tumidus.

grandiose *adj* māgnificus.

grandmother *n* avia *f*; **great** ~ proavia *f*.

grandson *n* nepōs *m*; **great** ~ prōnepōs *m*.

grant *vt* dare, concēdere, tribuere; (*admit*)
fatērī ♦ *n* concessiō *f*.
grape *n* ūva *f*.
graphic *adj* expressus; **give a ~ account of** ante
oculōs ponere, oculīs subicere.
grapnel *n* manus ferrea *f*, harpagō *f*.
grapple *vi* luctārī.[7]
grappling iron *n* manus ferrea *f*.
grasp *vt* prēnsāre, comprehendere; (*with
mind*) complectī, adsequī, percipere,
intellegere; **~ at** captāre, adpetere ♦ *n*
manus *f*, comprehēnsiō *f*; (*mind*) captus *m*.
grasping *adj* avārus, rapāx.
grass *n* herba *f*.
grasshopper *n* gryllus *m*.
grassy *adj* herbōsus; herbidus.
grate *n* focus *m* ♦ *vt* atterere; **~ upon**
offendere.
grateful *adj* grātus; **feel ~** grātiam habēre.
gratefully *adv* grātē.
gratification *n* voluptās *f*.
gratify *vt* mōrem gerere (*dat*), mōrigerārī
(*dat*), grātificārī (*dat*).
gratifying *adj* iūcundus.
gratis *adv* grātuītō, grātīs.
gratitude *n* grātia *f*; **show ~** grātiam referre.
gratuitous *adj* grātuītus.
gratuitously *adv* grātuītō.
gratuity *n* stips *f*; (*MIL*) dōnātīvum *nt*.
grave *n* sepulchrum *nt* ♦ *adj* gravis, austērus ♦
vt scalpere.
gravel *n* glārea *f*.
gravely *adv* graviter, sevērē.
gravitate *vi* vergere.
gravity *n* (*person*) sevēritās *f*, tristitia *f*; (*CIRCS*)
gravitās *f*, mōmentum *nt*; (*physics*) nūtus *m*;
by force of ~ nūtū suō.
gray *adj* rāvus; (*hair*) cānus.
graze *vi* pāscī ♦ *vt* (*cattle*) pāscere; (*by touch*)
stringere.
grazing *n* pāstus *m*.
grease *n* arvīna *f* ♦ *vt* ungere.
greasy *adj* pinguis, ūnctus.
great *adj* māgnus, grandis, ingēns, amplus;
(*fame*) īnsignis, praeclārus; **as ~ as ... tantus
... quantus; ~ deal** plūrimum; **~ many**
plūrimī; **how ~** quantus; **very ~** permāgnus.
greatcoat *n* lacerna *f*.
greatest *adj* māximus.
greatly *adv* multum, māgnopere.
greave *n* ocrea *f*.
greed *n* avāritia *f*.
greedily *adv* avārē, cupidē.
greedy *adj* avārus, cupidus; avidus.
Greek *adj* Graecus.
green *adj* viridis; (*unripe*) crūdus; **be ~** virēre.
greenness *n* viriditās *f*.
greens *n* olus *nt*.
greet *vt* salūtāre.
greeting *n* salūs *f*, salūtātiō *f*.
grey *adj* rāvus; (*hair*) cānus.
greyhound *n* vertagus *m*.
grief *n* dolor *m*, maeror *m*, lūctus *m*; **come to ~**

perīre.
grievance *n* querimōnia *f*; iniūria *f*.
grieve *vi* dolēre, maerēre, lūgēre.
grievous *adj* tristis, lūctuōsus; molestus,
gravis, acerbus.
grievously *adv* graviter, valdē.
grim *adj* trux, truculentus; atrōx.
grimace *n* ōris dēprāvātiō *f*; **make a ~** ōs dūcere
grime *n* sordēs *f*, lutum *nt*.
grimy *adj* sordidus, lutulentus.
grin *n* rīsus *m* ♦ *vi* adrīdēre.
grind *vt* contundere; (*corn*) molere; (*blade*)
acuere; **~ down** (*fig*) opprimere.
grindstone *n* cōs *f*.
grip *vt* comprehendere, arripere ♦ *n*
comprehēnsiō *f*; **come to ~s with** in
complexum venīre (*gen*).
gripe *n* tormina *ntpl*.
grisly *adj* horridus, dīrus.
grist *n* (*fig*) ēmolumentum *nt*.
grit *n* harēna *f*.
groan *n* gemitus *m* ♦ *vi* gemere, ingemere.
groin *n* inguen *nt*.
groom *n* agāsō *m*.
groove *n* canālis *m*, stria *f*.
grope *vi* praetentāre.
gross *adj* crassus, pinguis; (*morally*) turpis,
foedus.
grossly *adv* foedē, turpiter; (*very*) valdē.
grossness *n* crassitūdō *f*; turpitūdō *f*.
grotto *n* spēlunca *f*, antrum *nt*.
ground *n* (*bottom*) solum *nt*; (*earth*) terra *f*,
humus *f*; (*cause*) ratiō *f*, causa *f*; (*sediment*)
faex *f*; **on the ~** humī; **on the ~s that** quod (+
subj); **to the ~** humum; **gain ~** prōficere;
(*rumour*) incrēbrēscere; **lose ~** cēdere; (*MIL*)
inclīnāre ♦ *vt* īnstituere ♦ *vi* (*ship*) sīdere.
grounding *n* īnstitūtiō *f*.
groundless *adj* vānus, inānis.
groundlessly *adv* frustrā, temerē.
grounds *n* faex *f*; (*property*) praedium *nt*;
(*reason*) causa *f*; **I have good ~ for doing** nōn
sine causā faciō, iūstīs dē causīs faciō.
groundwork *n* fundāmentum *nt*.
group *n* globus *m*, circulus *m* ♦ *vt* dispōnere.
grouse *n* (*bird*) tetraō *m*; (*complaint*) querēla *f*
♦ *vi* querī.
grove *n* nemus *nt*, lūcus *m*.
grovel *vi* serpere, sē prōsternere, sē
advolvere.
grovelling *adj* humilis, abiectus.
grow *vi* crēscere, glīscere; (*spread*)
percrēbrēscere; (*become*) fierī; **~ old**
(con)senēscere; **~ up** adolēscere, pūbēscere
let ~ (*hair*) prōmittere ♦ *vt* (*crops*) colere;
(*beard*) dēmittere.
growl *n* fremitus *m* ♦ *vi* fremere.
grown-up *adj* adultus, grandis.
growth *n* incrēmentum *nt*, auctus *m*.
grub *n* vermiculus *m*.
grudge *n* invidia *f* ♦ *vt* invidēre (*dat*); (*thing*)
gravārī.
grudgingly *adv* invītus, gravātē.

gruesome *adj* taeter.
gruff *adj* acerbus, asper.
grumble *vi* querī, mussāre ♦ *n* querēla *f.*
grumpy *adj* mōrōsus, querulus.
grunt *n* grunnītus *m* ♦ *vi* grunnīre.
guarantee *n* (*money*) spōnsiō *f*; (*promise*) fidēs *f*; (*person*) praes *m* ♦ *vt* spondēre, praestāre.
guarantor *n* spōnsor *m.*
guard *n* custōdia *f*, praesidium *nt*; (*person*) custōs *m*; **on ~ in** statiōne; **be on one's ~** cavēre; **keep ~** statiōnem agere; **off one's ~** imprūdēns, inopīnāns; **be taken off one's ~** dē gradū dēicī ♦ *vt* custōdīre, dēfendere; (*keep*) cōnservāre; **~ against** cavēre.
guarded *adj* cautus.
guardedly *adv* cautē.
guardhouse *n* custōdia *f.*
guardian *n* custōs *m*; (*of minors*) tūtor *m.*
guardianship *n* custōdia *f*, tūtēla *f.*
guardian spirit *n* genius *m.*
gudgeon *n* gōbius *m.*
guerdon *n* praemium *nt*, mercēs *f.*
guess *n* coniectūra *f* ♦ *vt* dīvīnāre, conicere.
guest *n* hospes *m*, hospita *f*; (*at dinner*) convīva *m*; **uninvited ~** umbra *f*; **~'s** hospitālis.
guffaw *n* cachinnus *m* ♦ *vi* cachinnāre.
guidance *n* moderātiō *f*; **under the ~ of God** dūcente deō.
guide *n* dux *m*, ductor *m*; (*in policy*) auctor *m* ♦ *vt* dūcere; (*steer*) regere; (*control*) moderārī.
guild *n* collēgium *nt.*
guile *n* dolus *m*, fraus *f.*
guileful *adj* dolōsus, fraudulentus.
guilefully *adv* dolosē.
guileless *adj* simplex, innocēns.
guilelessly *adv* sine fraude.
guilt *n* culpa *f*, scelus *nt.*
guiltless *adj* innocēns, īnsōns.
guiltlessly *adv* integrē.
guilty *adj* nocēns, sōns; **find ~** damnāre.
guise *n* speciēs *f.*
guitar *n* fidēs *fpl*; **play the ~** fidibus canere.
gulf *n* sinus *m*; (*chasm*) hiātus *m.*
gull *n* mergus *m* ♦ *vt* dēcipere.
gullet *n* gula *f*, guttur *nt.*
gullible *adj* crēdulus.
gulp *vt* dēvorāre, haurīre.
gum *n* gummī *nt*; (*mouth*) gingīva *f.*
gumption *n* prūdentia *f.*
gurgle *vi* singultāre.
gush *vi* sē prōfundere, ēmicāre ♦ *n* scatūrīginēs *fpl.*
gust *n* flāmen *nt*, impetus *m.*
gusto *n* studium *nt.*
gusty *adj* ventōsus.
gut *n* intestīnum *nt* ♦ *vt* exenterāre; (*fig*) extergēre.
gutter *n* canālis *m.*
guzzle *vi* sē ingurgitāre.
gymnasium *n* gymnasium *nt*, palaestra *f*; **head of a ~** gymnasiarchus *m.*
gymnastic *adj* gymnicus; **~s** *pl* palaestra *f.*
gyrate *vi* volvī.

H, h

habit *n* mōs *m*, cōnsuētūdō *f*; (*dress*) habitus *m*, vestītus *m*; **be in the ~ of** solēre.
habitable *adj* habitābilis.
habitation *n* domus *f*, domicilium *nt*; (*place*) sēdēs *f.*
habitual *adj* ūsitātus.
habitually *adv* ex mōre, persaepe.
habituate *vt* adsuēfacere, īnsuēscere.
hack *vt* caedere, concīdere ♦ *n* (*horse*) caballus *m.*
hackneyed *adj* trītus.
Hades *n* īnferī *mpl.*
haft *n* manubrium *nt.*
hag *n* anus *f.*
haggard *adj* ferus.
haggle *vi* altercārī.
hail *n* grandō *f* ♦ *vi*: **it ~s** grandinat ♦ *vt* salūtāre, adclāmāre ♦ *interj* avē, avēte; salvē, salvēte; **I ~ from Rome** Rōma mihi patria est.
hair *n* capillus *m*; crīnis *m*; (*single*) pīlus *m*; (*animals*) sēta *f*, villus *nt*; **deviate a ~'s breadth from** trānsversum digitum discēdere ab; **split ~s** cavillārī.
hairdresser *n* tōnsor *m.*
hairless *adj* (*head*) calvus; (*body*) glaber.
hairpin *n* crīnāle *nt.*
hairsplitting *adj* captiōsus ♦ *n* cavillātiō *f.*
hairy *adj* pīlōsus.
halberd *n* bipennis *f.*
halcyon *n* alcēdō *f*; **~ days** alcēdōnia *ntpl.*
hale *adj* validus, rōbustus ♦ *vt* trahere, rapere.
half *n* dīmidium *nt*, dīmidia pars *f* ♦ *adj* dīmidius, dīmidiātus; **~ as much again** sesquī; **well begun is ~ done** dīmidium factī quī coepit habet.
half-asleep *adj* sēmisomnus.
half-baked *adj* (*fig*) rudis.
half-dead *adj* sēmianimis, sēmivīvus.
half-full *adj* sēmiplēnus.
half-hearted *adj* incūriōsus, sōcors.
half-heartedly *adv* sine studiō.
half-hour *n* sēmihōra *f.*
half-moon *n* lūna dīmidiāta *f.*
half-open *adj* sēmiapertus.
half pound *n* sēlībra *f.*
half-way *adj* medius; **~ up the hill** in mediō colle.
half-yearly *adj* sēmestris.
hall *n* ātrium *nt*; (*public*) exedra *f.*
hallo *interj* heus.

hallow *vt* sacrāre.
hallucination *n* error *m*, somnium *nt*.
halo *n* corōna *f*.
halt *vi* īnsistere, cōnsistere ♦ *vt* sistere ♦ *n*:
come to a ~ cōnsistere, agmen cōnstituere ♦
adj claudus.
halter *n* capistrum *nt*; (*fig*) laqueus *m*.
halve *vt* bipartīre.
ham *n* perna *f*.
hamlet *n* vīcus *m*.
hammer *n* malleus *m* ♦ *vt* tundere; ~ **out**
excūdere.
hamper *n* corbis *f* ♦ *vt* impedīre; (*with debt*)
obstringere.
hamstring *vt* poplitem succīdere (*dat*).
hand *n* manus *f*; **left** ~ laeva *f*, sinistra *f*; **right** ~
dextra *f*; **an old** ~ veterātor *m*; **at** ~ praestō,
ad manum; **be at** ~ adesse; **at first** ~ ipse; **at**
second ~ ab aliō; **on the one** ~ ... **on the other**
et ... et, quidem ... at; **near at** ~ in expedītō,
inibī; **the matter in** ~ quod nunc īnstat, quae
in manibus sunt; **get out of** ~ lascīvīre; **have**
a ~ **in** interesse (*dat*); **have one's** ~**s full** satis
agere; **lay** ~**s on** manum adferre, inicere
(*dat*); **live from** ~ **to mouth** ad hōram vīvere;
pass from ~ **to** ~ per manūs trādere; **take in** ~
suscipere; ~**s** *pl* (*workmen*) operae *fpl* ♦ *vt*
trādere, porrigere; ~ **down** trādere,
prōdere; ~ **over** dēferre, reddere.
handbill *n* libellus *m*.
handbook *n* ars *f*.
handcuffs *n* manicae *fpl*.
handful *n* manipulus *m*.
handicap *n* impedīmentum *nt*.
handicraft *n* artificium *nt*, ars operōsa *f*.
handily *adv* habiliter.
handiness *n* habilitās *f*; commoditās *f*.
handiwork *n* opus *nt*, manus *f*.
handkerchief *n* sūdārium *nt*.
handle *n* (*cup*) ānsa *f*; (*knife*) manubrium *nt*;
(*fig*) ānsa *f*, occāsiō *f* ♦ *vt* tractāre.
handling *n* tractātiō *f*.
handmaid *n* famula *f*.
handsome *adj* fōrmōsus, pulcher; (*gift*)
līberālis.
handsomely *adv* pulchrē; līberāliter.
handsomeness *n* pulchritūdō *f*, fōrma *f*.
hand-to-hand *adv*: **fight** ~ manum cōnserere,
comminus pugnāre.
handwriting *n* manus *f*.
handy *adj* (*to use*) habilis; (*near*) praestō.
hang *vt* suspendere; (*head*) dēmittere; (*wall*)
vestīre ♦ *vi* pendēre; ~ **back** gravārī,
dubitāre; ~ **down** dēpendēre; ~ **on to** haerēre
(*dat*); ~ **over** imminēre (*dat*), impendēre (*dat*);
go and be ~**ed** abī in malam crucem!
hanger-on *n* cliēns *m/f*, assecla *m/f*.
hanging *n* (*death*) suspendium *nt*; ~**s** *pl* aulaea
ntpl ♦ *adj* pendulus.
hangman *n* carnifex *m*.
hanker *vi*: ~ **after** appetere, exoptāre.
hap *n* fors *f*.
haphazard *adj* fortuītus.

hapless *adj* miser, īnfēlīx.
haply *adv* fortasse.
happen *vi* accidere, ēvenīre, contingere;
(*become*) fierī; **as usually** ~**s** ut fit; ~ **upon**
incidere in (*acc*); **it** ~**s that** accidit ut
(*+subj*).
happily *adv* fēlīciter, beātē, bene.
happiness *n* fēlīcitās *f*.
happy *adj* fēlīx, beātus; laetus; (*in some*
respect) fortūnātus.
harangue *n* cōntiō *f* ♦ *vt* cōntiōnārī apud (+
acc), hortārī.
harass *vt* vexāre, lacessere, exagitāre,
sollicitāre.
harassing *adj* molestus.
harbinger *n* praenūntius *m*.
harbour *n* portus *m* ♦ *vt* recipere.
harbour dues *n* portōria *ntpl*.
hard *adj* dūrus; (*circs*) asper, inīquus; (*task*)
difficilis, arduus; ~ **of hearing** surdaster;
grow ~ dūrēscere ♦ *adv* sēdulō, valdē; ~ **by**
prope, iuxtā; **I am** ~ **put to it to do** aegerrimē
faciō.
hard cash *n* praesēns pecūnia *f*.
harden *vt* dūrāre ♦ *vi* dūrēscere; (*fig*)
obdūrēscere; **become** ~**ed** obdūrēscere.
hard-fought *adj* atrōx.
hard-hearted *adj* crūdēlis, dūrus, inhūmānus.
hardihood *n* audācia *f*.
hardily *adv* sevērē.
hardiness *n* rōbur *nt*; dūritia *f*.
hardly *adv* vix, aegrē; (*severely*) dūriter,
acerbē; ~ **any** nullus ferē.
hardness *n* dūritia *f*; (*fig*) asperitās *f*, inīquitās
f; (*difficulty*) difficultās *f*; ~ **of hearing** surditās
f.
hard-pressed *adj*: **be** ~ labōrāre.
hardship *n* labor *m*, malum *nt*, iniūria *f*.
hard-working *adj* industrius, nāvus, sēdulus.
hardy *adj* dūrus, rōbustus, sevērus.
hare *n* lepus *m*.
hark *interj* auscultā, auscultāte ♦ *vi*: ~ **back to**
repetere.
harm *n* iniūria *f*, damnum *nt*, malum *nt*,
dētrīmentum *nt*; **come to** ~ dētrīmentum
capere, accipere ♦ *vt* laedere, nocēre (*dat*).
harmful *adj* damnōsus, noxius.
harmfully *adv* male.
harmless *adj* innocēns.
harmlessly *adv* innocenter; (*escape*) salvus,
incolumis, inviolātus.
harmonious *adj* cōnsonus, canōrus; (*fig*)
concors; (*things*) congruēns.
harmoniously *adv* modulātē; concorditer;
convenienter.
harmonize *vi* concinere, cōnsentīre,
congruere.
harmony *n* concentus *m*; (*fig*) concordia *f*,
cōnsēnsus *m*.
harness *n* arma *ntpl* ♦ *vt* īnfrēnāre, iungere.
harp *n* fidēs *fpl*; **play the** ~ fidibus canere ♦ *vi*: ~
on (*fig*) cantāre, dictitāre; **be always** ~**ing on**
the same thing cantilēnam eandem canere.

harpist n fidicen m, fidicina f.
harpoon n iaculum nt.
harpy n Harpyia f.
harrow n rāstrum nt ♦ vt occāre.
harrower n occātor m.
harrowing adj horrendus.
harry vt vexāre, dīriperē.
harsh adj dūrus, acerbus, asper; (person) inclēmēns, sevērus.
harshly adv acerbē, asperē; sevērē.
harshness n acerbitās f, asperitās f; crūdēlitās f.
hart n cervus m.
harvest n messis f ♦ vt metere, dēmetere.
harvester n messor m.
hash n farrāgō f ♦ vt comminuere.
haste n festīnātiō f, properātiō f; **in ~** festīnanter; **in hot ~** incitātus; **make ~** festīnāre.
hasten vt mātūrāre, adcelerāre ♦ vi festīnāre, properāre, mātūrāre.
hastily adv properē, raptim; temerē, incōnsulte; īrācundē.
hastiness n temeritās f; (temper) īrācundia f.
hasty adj properus, celer; (action) incōnsultus, temerārius; (temper) īrācundus, ācer; **over ~** praeproperus.
hat n petasus m.
hatch vt exclūdere, parere.
hatchet n dolābra f.
hate n odium nt, invidia f ♦ vt ōdisse.
hated adj: **to be ~ (by sb)** odiō esse (+ dat).
hateful adj odiōsus, invīsus.
hatefully adv odiōsē.
hatred n odium nt.
haughtily adv adroganter, superbē, insolenter.
haughtiness n fastus m, adrogantia f, superbia f.
haughty adj adrogāns, superbus, īnsolēns.
haul vt trahere ♦ n bolus m.
haulage n vectūra f.
haulm n culmus m.
haunch n femur nt.
haunt vt frequentāre ♦ n locus m; (animals) lustrum nt.
have vt habēre, tenēre; (get done) cūrāre (gerundive); **I ~ a house** est mihī domus; **I ~ to go** mihī abeundum est; **~ it out with** rem dēcernere cum; **~ on** gerere, gestāre, indui; **I had better go** melius est īre, praestat īre; **I had rather go** mālim, māllem.
haven n portus m; (fig) perfugium nt.
havoc n exitium nt, vastātiō f, ruīna f.
hawk n accipiter m ♦ vt (wares) circumferre.
hawker n īnstitor m.
hay n faenum nt; **make ~ while the sun shines** forō ūtī.
hazard n perīculum nt, discrīmen nt, ālea f ♦ vt perīclitārī, in āleam dare.
hazardous adj perīculōsus.
haze n nebula f.
hazel n corylus f.
hazy adj nebulōsus; (fig) incertus.

he pron hic, ille, is.
head n caput nt; (person) dux m, prīnceps m; (composition) caput nt; (mind) animus m, ingenium nt; **~ over heels** cernuus; **off one's ~** dēmēns; **be at the ~ of** dūcere, praeesse (dat); **come to a ~** caput facere; (fig) in discrīmen addūcī; **give one his ~** indulgēre (dat), habēnās immittere (dat); **keep one's ~** praesentī animō ūtī; **lose one's ~** suī compotem nōn esse; **shake one's ~** abnuere ♦ vt dūcere, praeesse (dat); **~ off** intercipere ♦ vi (in a direction) tendere.
headache n capitis dolor m.
headfirst adj praeceps.
heading n caput nt.
headland n prōmunturium nt.
headlong adj praeceps ♦ adv in praeceps; **rush ~** sē praecipitāre.
headquarters n (MIL) praetōrium nt.
headship n prīncipātus m.
headsman n carnifex m.
headstrong adj impotēns, pervicāx.
headway n prōfectus m.
heady adj incōnsultus; (wine) vehemēns.
heal vt sānāre, medērī (dat) ♦ vi sānēscere; **~ over** obdūcī.
healer n medicus m.
healing adj salūbris.
health n valētūdō f, salūs f; **state of ~** valētūdō f; **ill ~** valētūdō f; **be in good ~** valēre; **drink the ~ of** propīnāre (dat).
healthful adj salūbris.
healthiness n sānitās f.
healthy adj sānus, integer; (conditions) salūber.
heap n acervus m, cumulus m; **in ~s** acervātim ♦ vt acervāre; **~ together** congerere; **~ up** adcumulāre, coacervāre, congerere.
hear vt audīre; (case) cognōscere; **~ clearly** exaudīre; **~ in secret** inaudīre.
hearer n audītor m.
hearing n (sense) audītus m; (act) audītiō f; (of case) cognitiō f; **get a ~** sibī audientiam facere; **hard of ~** surdaster; **without a ~** indictā causā.
hearken vi auscultāre.
hearsay n fāma f, rūmor m.
heart n cor nt; (emotion) animus m, pectus nt; (courage) animus m; (interior) viscera ntpl; **by ~** memoriā, memoriter; **learn by ~** ēdiscere; **the ~ of the matter** rēs ipsa; **lose ~** animum dēspondēre; **take to ~** graviter ferre.
heartache n dolor m, angor m.
heartbroken adj animī frāctus, aeger; **be ~** animō labōrāre.
heartburning n invidia f.
heartfelt adj sincērus.
hearth n focus m; **~ and home** ārae et focī.
heartily adv vehementer, valdē.
heartiness n studium nt, vigor m.
heartless adj dūrus, inhūmānus, crūdēlis.
heartlessly adv inhūmānē.
heartlessness n inhūmānitās f, crūdēlitās f.
hearty adj studiōsus, vehemēns; (health)

rōbustus; (*feeling*) sincērus.

heat *n* ārdor *m*, calor *m*; (*emotion*) ārdor *m*, aestus *m*; (*race*) missus *m* ♦ *vt* calefacere, fervefacere; (*fig*) accendere; **become ~ed** incalēscere.

heatedly *adv* ferventer, ārdenter.

heath *n* inculta loca *ntpl*.

heathcock *n* attagēn *m*.

heathen *n* pāgānus *m*.

heather *n* erīcē *f*.

heave *vt* tollere; (*missile*) conicere; (*sigh*) dūcere ♦ *vi* tumēre, fluctuāre.

heaven *n* caelum *nt*, dī *mpl*; **~ forbid!** dī meliōra; **from ~** dīvīnitus; **in ~'s name** prō deum fidem!; **be in seventh ~** digitō caelum attingere.

heavenly *adj* caelestis, dīvīnus.

heavily *adv* graviter.

heaviness *n* gravitās *f*, pondus *nt*; (*of spirit*) maestitia *f*.

heavy *adj* gravis; (*air*) crassus; (*spirit*) maestus; (*shower*) māgnus, dēnsus.

heckle *vt* interpellāre.

heckler *n* interpellātor *m*.

hectic *adj* violēns, ācer, fervidus.

hector *vt* obstrepere (*dat*).

hedge *n* saepēs *f* ♦ *vt* saepīre; **~ off** intersaepīre ♦ *vi* tergiversārī.

hedgehog *n* echīnus *m*, ēricius *m*.

heed *vt* cūrāre, respicere ♦ *n* cūra *f*, opera *f*; **pay ~** animum attendere; **take ~** cavēre.

heedful *adj* attentus, cautus, dīligēns.

heedfully *adv* attentē, cautē.

heedfulness *n* cūra *f*, dīligentia *f*.

heedless *adj* incautus, immemor, neglegēns.

heedlessly *adv* incautē, neglegenter, temerē.

heedlessness *n* neglegentia *f*.

heel *n* calx *f*; **take to one's ~s** sē in pedēs conicere ♦ *vi* sē inclīnāre.

hegemony *n* prīncipātus *m*.

heifer *n* būcula *f*.

height *n* altitūdō *f*; (*person*) prōcēritās *f*; (*hill*) collis *m*, iugum *nt*; (*fig*) fastīgium *nt*; **the ~ of** summus.

heighten *vt* augēre, exaggerāre.

heinous *adj* atrōx, nefārius.

heinously *adv* atrōciter, nefāriē.

heinousness *n* atrōcitās *f*.

heir *n* hērēs *m*; **sole ~** hērēs ex asse.

heiress *n* hērēs *f*.

heirship *n* hērēditās *f*.

hell *n* Tartarus *m*, Īnfernī *mpl*.

hellish *adj* īnfernus, scelestus.

helm *n* gubernāculum *nt*, clāvus *m*.

helmet *n* galea *f*.

helmsman *n* gubernātor *m*.

helots *n* Hīlōtae *mpl*.

help *n* auxilium *nt*, subsidium *nt*; **I am a ~** auxiliō sum ♦ *vt* iuvāre (+ *acc*), auxiliārī, subvenīre (*dat*), succurrere (*dat*) ♦ *vi* prōdesse; **I cannot ~** facere nōn possum quīn (*subj*); **it can't be ~ed** fierī nōn potest aliter; **so ~ me God** ita me dī ament.

helper *n* adiūtor *m*, adiūtrix *f*.

helpful *adj* ūtilis; **be ~ to** auxiliō esse (*dat*).

helpless *adj* inops.

helplessness *n* inopia *f*.

hem *n* ōra *f*, limbus *m* ♦ *vt*: **~ in** interclūdere, circumsedēre.

hemlock *n* cicūta *f*.

hemp *n* cannabis *f*.

hen *n* gallīna *f*.

hence *adv* hinc; (*consequence*) igitur, ideō.

henceforth, henceforward *adv* dehinc, posthāc, ex hōc tempore.

her *adj* suus, ēius.

herald *n* praecō *m*; (*POL*) fētiālis *m* ♦ *vt* praenūntiāre.

herb *n* herba *f*, olus *nt*.

herbage *n* herbae *fpl*.

herd *n* pecus *nt*; grex *f*, armentum *nt* ♦ *vi* congregārī.

herdsman *n* pāstor *m*.

here *adv* hīc; **be ~** adesse; **~ and there** passim; **here ... there** alibī ... alibī; **from ~** hinc; **~ is ... ecce** (*acc*) ....

hereabouts *adv* hīc ferē.

hereafter *adv* posthāc, posteā.

hereat *adv* hīc.

hereby *adv* ex hōc, hinc.

hereditary *adj* hērēditārius, patrius.

heredity *n* genus *nt*.

herein *adv* hīc.

hereinafter *adv* īnfrā.

hereof *adv* ēius reī.

hereupon *adv* hīc, quō factō.

herewith *adv* cum hōc, ūnā.

heritable *adj* hērēditārius.

heritage *n* hērēditās *f*.

hermaphrodite *n* androgynus *m*.

hermit *n* homō sōlitārius *m*.

hero *n* vir fortissimus *m*; (*demigod*) hērōs *m*.

heroic *adj* fortissimus, māgnanimus; (*epic*) hērōicus; (*verse*) hērōus.

heroically *adv* fortissimē, audācissimē.

heroism *n* virtūs *f*, fortitūdō *f*.

heron *n* ardea *f*.

hers *pron* suus, ēius.

herself *pron* ipsa *f*; (*reflexive*) sē.

hesitancy *n* dubitātiō *f*.

hesitant *adj* incertus, dubius.

hesitate *vi* dubitāre, haesitāre.

hesitating *adj* dubius.

hesitatingly *adv* cunctanter.

hesitation *n* dubitātiō *f*; **with ~** dubitanter.

heterogeneous *adj* dīversus, aliēnigenus.

hew *vt* dolāre, caedere; **~ down** excīdere, interscindere.

hexameter *n* hexameter *m*.

heyday *n* flōs *m*.

hiatus *n* hiātus *m*.

hiccup *n* singultus *m* ♦ *vi* singultīre.

hide *vt* cēlāre, abdere, abscondere, occultāre; **~ away** abstrūdere; **~ from** cēlāre (*acc*) ♦ *vi* sē abdere, latēre; **~ away** dēlitēscere ♦ *n* pellis *f*, corium *nt*.

hideous _adj_ foedus, dēfōrmis, turpis.
hideously _adv_ foedē.
hideousness _n_ foeditās _f_, dēfōrmitās _f_.
hiding _n_ (_place_) latebra _f_.
hierarchy _n_ ōrdinēs _mpl_.
high _adj_ altus, excelsus; (_ground_) ēditus; (_pitch_) acūtus; (_rank_) amplus; (_price_) cārus; (_tide_) māximus; (_wind_) māgnus; ~ **living** luxuria _f_; ~ **treason** māiestās _f_; ~ **and mighty** superbus; **on** ~ sublīmis ♦ _adv_ altē.
highborn _adj_ nōbilis, generōsus.
high-class _adj_ (_goods_) lautus.
high-flown _adj_ īnflātus, tumidus.
high-handed _adj_ superbus, īnsolēns.
high-handedly _adv_ superbē, licenter.
high-handedness _n_ licentia _f_, superbia _f_.
highland _adj_ montānus.
highlander _n_ montānus _m_.
highlands _npl_ montāna _ntpl_.
highly _adv_ (_value_) māgnī; (_intensity_) valdē.
highly-strung _adj_ trepidus.
high-minded _adj_ generōsus.
high-spirited _adj_ ferōx, animōsus.
highway _n_ via _f_.
highwayman _n_ grassātor _m_, latrō _m_.
hilarious _adj_ festīvus, hilaris.
hilariously _adv_ festīvē, hilare.
hilarity _n_ festīvitās _f_, hilaritās _f_.
hill _n_ collis _m_, mōns _m_; (_slope_) clīvus _m_.
hillock _n_ tumulus _m_.
hilly _adj_ montuōsus, clīvōsus.
hilt _n_ manubrium _nt_, capulus _m_.
himself _pron_ ipse; (_reflexive_) sē.
hind _n_ cerva _f_.
hinder _vt_ impedīre, obstāre (_dat_), morārī.
hindmost _adj_ postrēmus; (_in column_) novissimus.
hindrance _n_ impedīmentum _nt_, mora _f_.
hinge _n_ cardō _f_.
hint _n_ indicium _nt_, suspiciō _f_; **throw out a** ~ inicere ♦ _vt_ subicere, significāre.
hip _n_ coxendīx _f_.
hippodrome _n_ spatium _nt_.
hire _vt_ condūcere; ~ **out** locāre ♦ _n_ conductiō _f_, locātiō _f_; (_wages_) mercēs _f_.
hired _adj_ mercennārius, conductus.
hireling _n_ mercennārius _m_.
hirsute _adj_ hirsūtus.
his _adj_ suus, ēius.
hiss _vi_ sībilāre ♦ _vt_: ~ **off stage** explōdere, exsībilāre ♦ _n_ sībilus _m_.
historian _n_ historicus _m_, rērum scrīptor _m_.
historical _adj_ historicus.
history _n_ historia _f_; **the** ~ **of Rome** rēs Rōmānae _fpl_; **since the beginning of** ~ post hominum memoriam; **ancient** ~ antīquitās _f_.
histrionic _adj_ scaenicus.
hit _n_ ictus _m_, plāga _f_; **a** ~**l** (_in duel_) habet! ♦ _vt_ ferīre, icere, percutere; ~ **against** offendere; ~ **upon** invenīre.
hitch _n_ mora _f_ ♦ _vt_ implicāre; ~ **up** succingere.
hither _adv_ hūc; ~ **and thither** hūc illūc ♦ _adj_ citerior.

hitherto _adv_ adhūc, hāctenus, hūcusque.
hive _n_ alveārium _nt_.
hoar _adj_ cānus ♦ _n_ pruīna _f_.
hoard _n_ thēsaurus _m_, acervus _m_ ♦ _vt_ condere, recondere.
hoarfrost _n_ pruīna _f_.
hoarse _adj_ raucus, fuscus.
hoarsely _adv_ raucā vōce.
hoary _adj_ cānus.
hoax _n_ fraus _f_, fallācia _f_, lūdus _m_ ♦ _vt_ dēcipere, fallere.
hobble _vi_ claudicāre.
hobby _n_ studium _nt_.
hob-nob _vi_ familiāriter ūtī (_abl_).
hocus-pocus _n_ trīcae _fpl_.
hoe _n_ sarculum _nt_ ♦ _vt_ sarrīre.
hog _n_ sūs _m_, porcus _m_; ~'**s** porcīnus.
hogshead _n_ dōlium _nt_.
hoist _vt_ tollere; (_sail_) vēla dare.
hold _n_ (_grasp_) comprehēnsiō _f_; (_power_) potestās _f_; (_ship_) alveus _m_; **gain a** ~ **over** obstringere, sibi dēvincīre; **get** ~ **of** potīrī (_abl_); **keep** ~ **of** retinēre; **lose** ~ **of** ōmittere; **take** ~ **of** prehendere, comprehendere ♦ _vt_ tenēre, habēre; (_possession_) possidēre; (_office_) gerere, fungī (_abl_); (_capacity_) capere; (_meeting_) habēre; ~ **a meeting** concilium habēre; ~ **one's own with** parem esse (_dat_); ~ **over** differre, prōlātāre; ~ **water** (_fig_) stāre ♦ _vi_ manēre, dūrāre; (_opinion_) dūcere, existimāre, adfirmāre; ~ **back** _vt_ retinēre, inhibēre ♦ _vi_ gravārī, dubitāre; ~ **cheap** parvī facere; ~ **fast** _vt_ retinere, amplectī ♦ _vi_ haerēre; ~ **good** valēre; ~ **out** _vt_ porrigere, extendere; (_hope_) ostendere ♦ _vi_ dūrāre, perstāre; ~ **together** cohaerēre; ~ **up** tollere; (_falling_) sustinēre; (_movement_) obstāre (_dat_), morārī; ~ **with** adsentīre (_dat_).
holdfast _n_ fībula _f_.
holding _n_ (_land_) agellus _m_.
hole _n_ forāmen _nt_, cavum _nt_; **make a** ~ **in** pertundere, perforāre.
holiday _n_ ōtium _nt_; festus diēs _m_; **on** ~ fēriātus; ~**s** _pl_ fēriae _fpl_.
holily _adv_ sānctē.
holiness _n_ sānctitās _f_.
hollow _adj_ cavus, concavus; (_fig_) inānis, vānus ♦ _n_ cavum _nt_, caverna _f_ ♦ _vt_ excavāre.
hollowness _n_ (_fig_) vānitās _f_.
holly _n_ aquifolium _nt_.
holy _adj_ sānctus.
homage _n_ observantia _f_, venerātiō _f_; **pay** ~ **to** venerārī, colere.
home _n_ domus _f_; (_town, country_) patria _f_; **at** ~ domī; **from** ~ domō ♦ _adj_ domesticus ♦ _adv_ domum.
homeless _adj_ profugus.
homely _adj_ simplex, rūsticus; (_speech_) plēbēius.
homestead _n_ fundus _m_.
homewards _adv_ domum.
homicide _n_ (_act_) homicīdium _nt_, caedēs _f_;

(*person*) homicīda *m*.
homily *n* sermō *m*.
homogeneous *adj* aequābilis.
homologous *adj* cōnsimilis.
hone *n* cōs *f* ♦ *vt* acuere.
honest *adj* probus, frūgī, integer.
honestly *adv* probē, integrē.
honesty *n* probitās *f*, fidēs *f*.
honey *n* mel *nt*.
honeycomb *n* favus *m*.
honeyed *adj* mellītus, mulsus.
honorarium *n* stips *f*.
honorary *adj* honōrārius.
honour *n* honōs *m*; (*repute*) honestās *f*;
existimātiō *f*; (*chastity*) pudor *m*; (*trust*) fidēs *f*;
(*rank*) dignitās *f*; (*award*) decus *nt*, īnsigne *nt*;
(*respect*) observantia *f* ♦ *vt* honōrāre,
decorāre; (*respect*) observāre, colere; **do ~ to**
honestāre.
honourable *adj* honestus, probus; (*rank*)
illūstris, praeclārus.
honourably *adv* honestē.
hood *n* cucullus *m*.
hoodwink *vt* verba dare (*dat*).
hoof *n* ungula *f*.
hook *n* uncus *m*, hāmus *m* ♦ *vt* hāmō capere.
hooked *adj* aduncus, hāmātus.
hoop *n* circulus *m*; (*toy*) trochus *m*.
hoot *vi* obstrepere; **~ off** (*stage*) explōdere.
hop *n* saltus *m*; **catch on the ~** in ipsō articulō
opprimere ♦ *vi* salīre.
hope *n* spēs *f*; **in the ~ that** sī forte; **give up ~**
spem dēpōnere, dēspērāre; **past ~**
dēspērātus; **entertain ~s** spem habēre ♦ *vt*
spērāre.
hopeful *adj* bonae speī; **be ~** aliquam spem
habēre.
hopefully *adv* nōn sine spē.
hopeless *adj* dēspērātus.
hopelessly *adv* dēspēranter.
hopelessness *n* dēspērātiō *f*.
horde *n* multitūdō *f*.
horizon *n* fīniēns *m*.
horizontal *adj* aequus, lībrātus.
horizontally *adv* ad lībram.
horn *n* cornū *nt*; (*shepherd's*) būcina *f*.
horned *adj* corniger.
hornet *n* crabrō *m*; **stir up a ~'s nest** crabrōnēs
inrītāre.
horny *adj* corneus.
horoscope *n* sīdus nātālicium *nt*.
horrible *adj* horrendus, horribilis, dīrus,
foedus.
horribly *adv* foedē.
horrid *adj* horribilis.
horrify *vt* terrēre, perterrēre.
horror *n* horror *m*, terror *m*; odium *nt*.
horse *n* equus *m*; (*cavalry*) equitēs *mpl*; **flog a
dead ~** asellum currere docēre; **spur a
willing ~** currentem incitāre; **~'s** equīnus.
horseback *n*: **ride on ~back** in equō vehī; **fight
on ~back** ex equō pugnāre.
horseman *n* eques *m*.

horseradish *n* armoracia *f*.
horse soldier *n* eques *m*.
horticulture *n* hortōrum cultus *m*.
hospitable *adj* hospitālis.
hospitably *adv* hospitāliter.
hospital *n* valētūdinārium *nt*.
hospitality *n* hospitālitās *f*, hospitium *nt*.
host *n* hospes *m*; (*inn*) caupō *m*; (*number*)
multitūdō *f*; (*MIL*) exercitus *m*.
hostage *n* obses *m/f*.
hostelry *n* taberna *f*, dēversōrium *nt*.
hostile *adj* hostīlis, īnfēnsus, inimīcus;
īnfestus; **in a ~ manner** īnfēnsē, hostīliter,
inimīcē.
hostility *n* inimīcitia *f*; **hostilities** *pl* bellum *nt*.
hot *adj* calidus, fervidus, aestuōsus; (*boiling*)
fervēns; (*fig*) ārdēns; **be ~** calēre, fervēre,
ārdēre; **get ~** calēscere.
hotch-potch *n* farrāgō *f*.
hotel *n* dēversōrium *nt*.
hot-headed *adj* ārdēns, temerārius, praeceps.
hotly *adv* ārdenter, ācriter.
hot-tempered *adj* īrācundus.
hot water *n* calida *f*.
hound *n* canis *m* ♦ *vt* īnstāre (*dat*).
hour *n* hōra *f*.
hourly *adv* in hōrās.
house *n* domus *f*, aedēs *fpl*; (*country*) vīlla *f*;
(*family*) domus *f*, gēns *f*; **at the ~ of** apud (*acc*);
full ~ frequēns senātus, frequēns theātrum
♦ *vt* hospitiō accipere, recipere; (*things*)
condere.
household *n* familia *f*, domus *f* ♦ *adj*
familiāris, domesticus.
householder *n* paterfamiliās *m*, dominus *m*.
housekeeping *n* reī familiāris cūra *f*.
housemaid *n* ancilla *f*.
housetop *n* fastīgium *nt*.
housewife *n* māterfamiliās *f*, domina *f*.
housing *n* hospitium *nt*; (*horse*) ōrnāmenta
ntpl.
hovel *n* gurgustium *nt*.
hover *vi* pendēre; (*fig*) impendēre.
how *adv* (*interrog*) quemadmodum; quōmodō,
quō pactō; (*excl*) quam; **~ great/big/large**
quantus; **~ long** (*time*) quamdiū; **~ many** quot
~ much quantum; **~ often** quotiēns.
howbeit *adv* tamen.
however *adv* tamen; autem, nihilōminus;
utcumque, quōquō modō; **~ much** quamvīs,
quantumvīs; **~ great** quantuscumque.
howl *n* ululātus *m* ♦ *vi* ululāre; (*wind*) fremere.
howsoever *adv* utcumque.
hub *n* axis *m*.
hubbub *n* tumultus *m*.
huckster *n* īnstitor *m*, propōla *m*.
huddle *n* turba *f* ♦ *vi* congregārī.
hue *n* color *m*; **~ and cry** clāmor *m*.
huff *n* offēnsiō *f* ♦ *vt* offendere.
hug *n* complexus *m* ♦ *vt* complectī.
huge *adj* ingēns, immānis, immēnsus, vastus.
hugely *adv* vehementer.
hugeness *n* immānitās *f*.

hulk n alveus m.
hull n alveus m.
hum n murmur nt, fremitus m ♦ vi
murmurāre, fremere.
human adj hūmānus.
human being n homō m/f.
humane adj hūmānus, misericors.
humanely adv hūmānē, hūmāniter.
humanism n litterae fpl.
humanist n homō litterātus m.
humanity n hūmānitās f; misericordia f.
humanize vt excolere.
humanly adv hūmānitus.
human nature n hūmānitās f.
humble adj humilis, modestus ♦ vt dēprimere;
(oneself) summittere.
humbleness n humilitās f.
humbly adv summissē, modestē.
humbug n trīcae fpl.
humdrum adj vulgāris; (style) pedester.
humid adj ūmidus, madidus; **be ~** madēre.
humidity n ūmor m.
humiliate vt dēprimere, dēdecorāre.
humiliation n dēdecus nt.
humility n modestia f, animus summissus m.
humorist n homō facētus m.
humorous adj facētus, ioculāris, rīdiculus.
humorously adv facētē.
humour n facētiae fpl; (disposition) ingenium
nt; (mood) libīdō f; **be in a bad ~** sibī
displicēre ♦ vt indulgēre (dat), mōrem
gerere (dat), mōrigerārī (dat).
hump n gibbus m.
hunchback n gibber m.
hundred num centum; **~ each** centēnī; **~ times**
centiēns.
hundredth adj centēsimus.
hundredweight n centumpondium nt.
hunger n famēs f ♦ vi ēsurīre.
hungrily adv avidē.
hungry adj ēsuriēns, ieiūnus, avidus; **be ~**
ēsurīre.
hunt n vēnātiō f, vēnātus m ♦ vt vēnārī,
indāgāre, exagitāre.
hunter n vēnātor m.
hunting n vēnātiō f; (fig) aucupium nt.
hunting spear n vēnābulum nt.
huntress n vēnātrix f.
huntsman n vēnātor m.
hurdle n crātēs f; (obstacle) obex m/f.
hurl vt conicere, ingerere, iaculārī, iācere.
hurly-burly n turba f, tumultus m.
hurrah interj euax, iō.
hurricane n procella f.
hurried adj praeproperus, praeceps, trepidus.
hurriedly adv properātō, cursim, festīnanter.
hurry vt adcelerāre, mātūrāre ♦ vi festīnāre,
properāre; **~ along** vt rapere; **~ away** vi
discēdere, properāre; **~ about** vi discurrere;
~ on vt mātūrāre; **~ up** vi properāre ♦ n
festīnātiō f; **in a ~** festīnanter, raptim.
hurt n iniūria f, damnum nt; vulnus nt ♦ vt
laedere, nocēre (dat); **it ~s** dolet.

hurtful adj nocēns, damnōsus.
hurtfully adv nocenter, damnōsē.
hurtle vi volāre; sē praecipitāre.
husband n vir m, marītus m ♦ vt parcere (dat).
husbandry n agrī cultūra f; (economy)
parsimōnia f.
hush n silentium nt ♦ vt silentium facere (dat),
lēnīre ♦ vi tacēre, silēre; **~ up** comprimere,
cēlāre ♦ interj st!
hushed adj tacitus.
husk n folliculus m, siliqua f ♦ vt dēglūbāre.
husky adj fuscus, raucus.
hustle vt trūdere, īnstāre (dat).
hut n casa f, tugurium nt.
hutch n cavea f.
hyacinth n hyacinthus m.
hybrid n hibrida m/f.
hydra n hydra f.
hyena n hyaena f.
hygiene n salūbritās f.
hygienic adj salūbris.
hymeneal adj nūptiālis.
hymn n carmen nt ♦ vt canere.
hyperbole n superlātiō f.
hypercritical adj Aristarchus m.
hypocaust n hypocaustum nt.
hypocrisy n simulātiō f, dissimulātiō f.
hypocrite n simulātor m, dissimulātor m.
hypocritical adj simulātus, fictus.
hypothesis n positum nt, sūmptiō f,
coniectūra f.
hypothetical adj sūmptus.

I, i

I pron ego.
iambic adj iambēus.
iambus n iambus m.
ice n glaciēs f.
icicle n stīria f.
icon n simulacrum nt.
icy adj glaciālis, gelidus.
idea n nōtiō f, nōtitia f, imāgō f; (Platonic) fōrma
f; (expressed) sententia f; **conceive the ~ of**
īnfōrmāre; **with the ~ that** eō consiliō ut (+
subj).
ideal adj animō comprehēnsus; (perfect)
perfectus, optimus ♦ n specimen nt, speciēs
f, exemplar nt.
identical adj īdem, cōnsimilis.
identify vt agnōscere.
identity n: **establish the ~ of** cognōscere quis
sit.
Ides n Idūs fpl.
idiocy n animī imbēcillitās f.

idiom n proprium nt, sermō m.
idiomatic adj proprius.
idiomatically adv sermōne suō, sermōne propriō.
idiosyncrasy n proprium nt, libīdō f.
idiot n excors m.
idiotic adj fatuus, stultus.
idiotically adv stultē, ineptē.
idle adj ignāvus, dēses, iners; (*unoccupied*) ōtiōsus, vacuus; (*useless*) inānis, vānus; **be ~** cessāre, dēsidēre; **lie ~** (*money*) iacēre ♦ vi cessāre.
idleness n ignāvia f, dēsidia f, inertia f; ōtium nt.
idler n cessātor m.
idly adv ignāvē; ōtiōsē; frustrā, nēquīquam.
idol n simulacrum nt; (*person*) dēliciae fpl.
idolater n falsōrum deōrum cultor m.
idolatry n falsōrum deōrum cultus m.
idolize vt venerārī.
idyll n carmen Theocrītēum nt.
if conj sī; (*interrog*) num, utrum; **~ anyone** sī quis; **~ ever** sī quandō; **~ not** nisī; **~ only** dum, dummodo; **~ ... or** sīve ... sīve; **as ~** quasi, velut; **but ~** sīn, quodsī; **even ~** etiamsī.
igneous adj igneus.
ignite vt accendere, incendere ♦ vi ignem concipere.
ignoble adj (*birth*) ignōbilis; (*repute*) illīberālis, turpis.
ignominious adj ignōminiōsus, īnfāmis, turpis.
ignominiously adv turpiter.
ignominy n ignōminia f, īnfāmia f, dēdecus nt.
ignoramus n idiōta m, indoctus m.
ignorance n īnscītia f, ignōrātiō f.
ignorant adj ignārus, indoctus; (*of something*) īnscītus, rudis; (*unaware*) īnscius; **be ~ of** nescīre, ignōrāre.
ingorantly adv īnscienter, īnscītē, indoctē.
ignore vt praetermittere.
ilex n īlex f.
Iliad n Ilias f.
ill adj aeger, aegrōtus, invalidus; (*evil*) malus; **be ~** aegrōtāre; **fall ~** in morbum incidere; **~ at ease** sollicitus ♦ adv male, improbē ♦ n malum nt, incommodum nt, aerumna f, damnum nt.
ill-advised adj incōnsultus.
ill-bred adj agrestis, inurbānus.
ill-disposed adj malevolus, invidus.
illegal adj illicitus, vetitus.
illegally adv contrā lēgēs.
ill-fated adj īnfēlīx.
ill-favoured adj turpis.
ill-gotten adj male partus.
ill-health n valētūdō f.
illicit adj vetitus.
illimitable adj īnfīnītus.
illiteracy n litterārum īnscītia f.
illiterate adj illitterātus, inērudītus.
ill-natured adj malevolus, malignus.
illness n morbus m, valētūdō f.

illogical adj absurdus.
ill-omened adj dīrus, īnfaustus.
ill-starred adj īnfēlīx.
ill-tempered adj īrācundus, amārus, stomachōsus.
ill-timed adj immātūrus, intempestīvus.
ill-treat vt malefacere (*dat*).
illuminate vt illūmināre, illūstrāre.
illumination n lūmina ntpl.
illusion n error m, somnium nt.
illusive, illusory adj fallāx.
illustrate vt illūstrāre; (*with instances*) exemplō cōnfirmāre.
illustration n exemplum nt.
illustrious adj illūstris, īnsignis, praeclārus.
illustriously adv praeclārē.
ill will n invidia f.
image n imāgō f, effigiēs f; (*idol*) simulacrum nt; (*verbal*) figūra f, similitūdō f.
imagery n figūrae fpl.
imaginary adj commentīcius, fictus.
imagination n cōgitātiō f, opīnātiō f.
imaginative adj ingeniōsus.
imagine vt animō fingere, animum indūcere, ante oculōs pōnere; (*think*) opīnārī, arbitrārī.
imbecile adj animō imbēcillus, fatuus, mente captus.
imbecility n animī imbēcillitās f.
imbibe vt adbibere; (*fig*) imbuī (*abl*).
imbrue vt īnficere.
imbue vt imbuere, īnficere, tingere.
imitable adj imitābilis.
imitate vt imitārī.
imitation n imitātiō f; (*copy*) imāgō f.
imitator n imitātor m, imitātrix f, aemulātor m.
immaculate adj integer, ēmendātus.
immaculately adv integrē, sine vitiō.
immaterial adj indifferēns.
immature adj immātūrus.
immeasurable adj immēnsus, īnfīnītus.
immediate adj īnstāns, praesēns; (*neighbour*) proximus.
immediately adv statim, extemplō, cōnfestim.
immemorial adj antīquissimus; **from time ~** post hominum memoriam.
immense adj immēnsus, immānis, ingēns, vastus.
immensely adv vehementer.
immensity n immēnsum nt, māgnitūdō f.
immerse vt immergere, mergere.
immigrant n advena m.
immigrate vi migrāre.
imminent adj īnstāns, praesēns; **be ~** imminēre, impendēre.
immobile adj fīxus, immōbilis.
immoderate adj immoderātus, immodestus.
immoderately adv immoderātē, immodestē.
immodest adj impudīcus, inverēcundus.
immolate vt immolāre.
immoral adj prāvus, corruptus, turpis.
immorality n corruptī mōrēs mpl, turpitūdō f.

immorally adv prāvē, turpiter.
immortal adj immortālis, aeternus.
immortality n immortālitās f.
immortalize vt in astra tollere.
immortally adv aeternum.
immovable adj fīxus, immōbilis.
immune adj immūnis, vacuus.
immunity n immūnitās f, vacātiō f.
immure vt inclūdere.
immutability n immūtābilitās f.
immutable adj immūtābilis.
imp n puer improbus m.
impact n ictus m, incussus m.
impair vt imminuere, corrumpere.
impale vt induere, īnfīgere.
impalpable adj tenuissimus.
impart vt impertīre, commūnicāre; (courage)
  addere.
impartial adj aequus, medius.
impartiality n aequābilitās f.
impartially adv sine favōre.
impassable adj invius; (mountains)
  inexsuperābilis; (fig) inexplicābilis.
impasse n mora f, incitae fpl.
impassioned adj ārdēns, fervidus.
impassive adj rigidus, sēnsū carēns.
impatience n aviditās f; (of anything)
  impatientia f.
impatient adj trepidus, avidus; impatiēns.
impatiently adv aegrē.
impeach vt diem dīcere (dat), accūsāre.
impeachment n accūsātiō f, crīmen nt.
impeccable adj ēmendātus.
impecunious adj pauper.
impede vt impedīre, obstāre (dat).
impediment n impedīmentum nt.
impel vt impellere, incitāre.
impend vi impendēre, imminēre, īnstāre.
impenetrable adj impenetrābilis; (country)
  invius, impervius.
impenitent adj: I am ~ nīl mē paenitet.
imperative adj necessārius.
imperceptible adj tenuissimus, obscurus.
imperceptibly adv sēnsim.
imperfect adj imperfectus, vitiōsus.
imperfection n vitium nt.
imperfectly adv vitiōsē.
imperial adj imperātōrius, rēgius.
imperil vt in discrīmen addūcere, labefactāre.
imperious adj imperiōsus, superbus.
imperiously adv superbē.
imperishable adj immortālis, aeternus.
impersonate vt partēs agere (gen).
impertinence n importūnitās f, protervitās f.
impertinent adj importūnus, protervus,
  ineptus.
impertinently adv importūnē, ineptē,
  protervē.
imperturbable adj immōtus, gravis.
impervious adj impervius, impenetrābilis.
impetuosity n ārdor m, violentia f, vīs f.
impetuous adj violēns, fervidus, effrēnātus.
impetuously adv effrēnātē.

impetus n impetus m.
impiety n impietās f.
impinge vi incidere.
impious adj impius, profānus; it is ~ nefas est.
impiously adv impiē.
impish adj improbus.
implacable adj implācābilis, inexōrābilis,
  dūrus.
implacably adv dūrē.
implant vt īnserere, ingignere.
implement n īnstrūmentum nt ♦ vt implēre,
  exsequī.
implicate vt implicāre, impedīre.
implication n indicium nt.
implicit adj tacitus; absolūtus.
implicitly adv absconditē; (trust) omnīnō,
  summā fidē.
implore vt implōrāre, obsecrāre.
imply vt significāre, continēre; be ~ied inesse.
impolite adj inurbānus, illepidus.
impolitely adv inurbānē.
impolitic adj incōnsultus, imprūdēns.
imponderable adj levissimus.
import vt importāre, invehere; (mean) velle ♦
  n significātiō f.
importance n gravitās f, mōmentum nt; (rank)
  dignitās f, amplitūdō f, auctōritās f; it is of
  great ~ to me meā māgnī rēfert.
important adj gravis, māgnī mōmentī; it is ~
  interest (+ gen) rēfert; more ~, most ~
  antīquior, antīquissimus.
importation n invectiō f.
imports npl importātīcia ntpl.
importunate adj molestus.
importune vt flāgitāre, īnstāre (dat).
impose vt impōnere; (by order) indīcere,
  iniungere; ~ upon illūdere, fraudāre, abūtī
  (abl).
imposing adj māgnificus, lautus.
imposition n fraus f; (tax) tribūtum nt.
impossible adj: it is ~ fierī nōn potest.
impost n tribūtum nt, vectīgal nt.
impostor n planus m, fraudātor m.
imposture n fraus f, fallācia f.
impotence n īnfirmitās f.
impotent adj īnfirmus, dēbilis; (with rage)
  impotēns.
impotently adv frustrā; (rage) impotenter.
impound vt inclūdere; (confiscate) pūblicāre.
impoverish vt in inopiam redigere.
impracticable adj: be ~ fierī nōn posse.
imprecate vt exsecrārī.
imprecation n exsecrātiō f.
impregnable adj inexpugnābilis.
impregnate vt imbuere, īnficere.
impress vt imprimere; (on mind) īnfīgere;
  (person) permovēre; (MIL) invītum scrībere.
impression n (copy) exemplar nt; (mark)
  signum nt; (feeling) impulsiō f; (belief)
  opīnātiō f; make an ~ of exprimere; make an
  ~ on commovēre; have the ~ opīnārī.
impressionable adj crēdulus.
impressive adj gravis.

impressively *adv* graviter.
impressiveness *n* gravitās *f*.
imprint *n* impressiō *f*, signum *nt* ♦ *vt*
imprimere; (*on mind*) īnfīgere, inūrere.
imprison *vt* inclūdere, in vincula conicere.
imprisonment *n* custōdia *f*, vincula *ntpl*.
improbable *adj* incrēdibilis, haud vērīsimilis.
impromptu *adv* ex tempore.
improper *adj* indecōrus, ineptus.
improperly *adv* prāvē, perperam.
impropriety *n* culpa *f*, offēnsa *f*.
improve *vt* ēmendāre, corrigere; (*mind*)
excolere ♦ *vi* prōficere, meliōrem fierī.
improvement *n* ēmendātiō *f*, prōfectus *m*.
improvident *adj* imprōvidus; (*with money*)
prōdigus.
improvidently *adv* imprōvidē; prōdigē.
improvise *vt* ex tempore compōnere,
excōgitāre.
imprudence *n* imprūdentia *f*.
imprudent *adj* imprūdēns.
imprudently *adv* imprūdenter.
impudence *n* impudentia *f*, audācia *f*.
impudent *adj* impudēns, audāx.
impudently *adv* impudenter, protervē.
impugn *vt* impugnāre, in dubium vocāre.
impulse *n* impetus *m*, impulsus *m*.
impulsive *adj* praeceps, violentus.
impulsively *adv* impetū quōdam animī.
impulsiveness *n* impetus *m*, violentia *f*.
impunity *n* impūnitās *f*; **with ~** impūne.
impure *adj* impūrus, incestus, inquinātus.
impurely *adv* impūrē, incestē, inquinātē.
impurity *n* impūritās *f*, sordēs *fpl*.
imputation *n* crīmen *nt*.
impute *vt* attribuere, adsignāre; **~ as a fault**
vitiō vertere.
in *prep* in (*abl*); (*with motion*) in (*acc*); (*authors*)
apud (*acc*); (*time*) *abl*; **~ doing this** dum hoc
faciō; **~ my youth** adulēscēns; **~ that** quod ♦
adv (*rest*) intrā; (*motion*) intrō.
inaccessible *adj* inaccessus.
inaccuracy *n* neglegentia *f*, incūria *f*; (*error*)
mendum *nt*.
inaccurate *adj* parum dīligēns, neglegēns.
inaccurately *adv* neglegenter.
inaction *n* inertia *f*.
inactive *adj* iners, quiētus; **be ~** cessāre.
inactivity *n* inertia *f*, ōtium *nt*.
inadequate *adj* impār, parum idōneus.
inadequately *adv* parum.
inadvertency *n* imprūdentia *f*.
inadvertent *adj* imprūdēns.
inadvertently *adv* imprūdenter.
inane *adj* inānis, vānus; ineptus, stultus.
inanely *adv* ineptē.
inanimate *adj* inanimus.
inanity *n* ineptiae *fpl*, stultitia *f*.
inapplicable *adj*: **be ~** nōn valēre.
inappropriate *adj* aliēnus, parum aptus.
inarticulate *adj* īnfāns.
inartistic *adj* sine arte, dūrus, inēlegāns.
inasmuch as *conj* quōniam, cum (*subj*).

inattention *n* incūria *f*, neglegentia *f*.
inattentive *adj* neglegēns.
inattentively *adv* neglegenter.
inaudible *adj*: **be ~** audīrī nōn posse.
inaugurate *vt* inaugurāre, cōnsecrāre.
inauguration *n* cōnsecrātiō *f*.
inauspicious *adj* īnfaustus, īnfēlix.
inauspiciously *adv* malīs ōminibus.
inborn *adj* innātus.
incalculable *adj* inaestimābilis.
incantation *n* carmen *nt*.
incapable *adj* inhabilis, indocilis; **be ~** nōn
posse.
incapacitate *vt* dēbilitāre.
incapacity *n* inertia *f*, īnscītia *f*.
incarcerate *vt* inclūdere, in vincula conicere.
incarnate *adj* hūmānā speciē indūtus.
incautious *adj* incautus, temerārius.
incautiously *adv* incautē.
incendiary *adj* incendiārius.
incense *n* tūs *nt* ♦ *vt* inrītāre, stomachum
movēre (*dat*); **be ~d** stomachārī.
incentive *n* incitāmentum *nt*, stimulus *m*.
inception *n* initium *nt*, exōrdium *nt*.
incessant *adj* adsiduus.
incessantly *adv* adsiduē.
incest *n* incestus *m*.
inch *n* digitus *m*, ūncia *f*.
incident *n* ēventum *nt*, cāsus *m*, rēs *f*.
incidental *adj* fortuītus.
incidentally *adv* cāsū.
incipient *adj* prīmus.
incisive *adj* ācer.
incite *vt* īnstīgāre, impellere, hortārī,
incitāre.
incitement *n* invītāmentum *nt*, stimulus *m*.
inciter *n* īnstimulātor *m*.
incivility *n* importūnitās *f*, inhūmānitās *f*.
inclemency *n* (*weather*) intemperiēs *f*.
inclement *adj* asper, tristis.
inclination *n* inclīnātiō *f*, animus *m*, libīdō *f*;
(*slope*) clīvus *m*.
incline *vt* inclīnāre; (*person*) indūcere ♦ *vi*
inclīnāre, incumbere; **~ towards sē**
adclīnāre ♦ *n* adclīvitās *f*, clīvus *m*.
inclined *adj* inclīnātus, prōpēnsus; **I am ~ to**
think haud sciō an.
include *vt* inclūdere, continēre, complectī.
incognito *adv* clam.
incoherent *adj* interruptus; **be ~** nōn
cohaerēre.
income *n* fructus *m*, mercēs *f*.
incommensurate *adj* dispār.
incommode *vt* molestiam adferre (*dat*).
incomparable *adj* singulāris, eximius.
incompatibility *n* discrepantia *f*, repugnantia
f.
incompatible *adj* īnsociābilis, repugnāns; **be**
~ with dissidēre ab, repugnāre (*dat*).
incompetence *n* inertia *f*, īnscītia *f*.
incompetent *adj* iners, īnscītus.
incomplete *adj* imperfectus.
incomprehensible *adj* incrēdibilis.

inconceivable *adj* incrēdibilis.

inconclusive *adj* inānis.

incongruous *adj* absonus, aliēnus.

inconsiderable *adj* exiguus.

inconsiderate *adj* imprōvidus, incōnsultus.

inconsistency *n* discrepantia *f*, incōnstantia *f*.

inconsistent *adj* incōnstāns; **be ~** discrepāre; **be ~ with** abhorrēre ab, repugnāre (*dat*).

inconsistently *adv* incōnstanter.

inconsolable *adj* nōn cōnsōlābilis.

inconspicuous *adj* obscūrus; **be ~** latēre.

inconstancy *n* incōnstantia *f*, levitās *f*.

inconstant *adj* incōnstāns, levis, mōbilis.

inconstantly *adv* incōnstanter.

incontestable *adj* certus.

incontinence *n* incontinentia *f*.

incontinent *adj* intemperāns.

inconvenience *n* incommodum *nt* ♦ *vt* incommodāre.

inconvenient *adj* incommodus.

inconveniently *adv* incommodē.

incorporate *vt* īnserere, adiungere.

incorrect *adj* falsus; **be ~** nōn cōnstāre.

incorrectly *adv* falsō, perperam.

incorrigible *adj* improbus, perditus.

incorruptibility *n* integritās *f*.

incorruptible *adj* incorruptus.

increase *n* incrēmentum *nt*, additāmentum *nt*, auctus *m* ♦ *vt* augēre, amplificāre ♦ *vi* crēscere, incrēscere.

increasingly *adv* magis magisque.

incredible *adj* incrēdibilis.

incredibly *adv* incrēdibiliter.

incredulous *adj* incrēdulus.

increment *n* incrēmentum *nt*.

incriminate *vt* crīminārī.

inculcate *vt* inculcāre, īnfīgere.

incumbent *adj*: **it is ~ on** oportet.

incur *vt* subīre; (*guilt*) admittere.

incurable *adj* īnsānābilis.

incursion *n* incursiō *f*.

indebted *adj* obnoxius; **be ~** dēbēre.

indecency *n* obscēnitās *f*.

indecent *adj* obscēnus, impudīcus.

indecently *adv* obscēnē.

indecision *n* dubitātiō *f*.

indecisive *adj* anceps, dubius; **the battle is ~** ancipitī Marte pugnātur.

indecisively *adv* incertō ēventū.

indecorous *adj* indecōrus.

indeed *adv* profectō, sānē; (*concessive*) quidem; (*interrog*) itane vērō?; (*reply*) certē, vērō; (*with pron*) dēmum; (*with adj, adv, conj*) adeō.

indefatigable *adj* impiger.

indefensible *adj*: **be ~** dēfendī nōn posse; (*belief*) tenērī nōn posse; (*offence*) excūsārī nōn posse.

indefinite *adj* incertus, ambiguus, īnfīnītus.

indefinitely *adv* ambiguē; (*time*) in incertum.

indelicate *adj* pūtidus, indecōrus.

independence *n* lībertās *f*.

independent *adj* līber, suī iūris.

indescribable *adj* inēnārrābilis.

indestructible *adj* perennis.

indeterminate *adj* incertus.

index *n* index *m*.

indicate *vt* indicāre, significāre.

indication *n* indicium *nt*, signum *nt*.

indict *vt* diem dīcere (*dat*), accūsāre, nōmen dēferre (*gen*).

indictment *n* accūsātiō *f*.

indifference *n* neglegentia *f*, languor *m*.

indifferent *adj* (*manner*) neglegēns, frīgidus, sēcūrus; (*quality*) mediocris.

indifferently *adv* neglegenter; mediocriter; (*without distinction*) promiscuē, sine discrīmine.

indigence *n* indigentia *f*, egestās *f*.

indigenous *adj* indigena.

indigent *adj* indigēns, egēnus.

indigestible *adj* crūdus.

indigestion *n* crūditās *f*.

indignant *adj* indignābundus, īrātus; **be ~** indignārī.

indignantly *adv* īrātē.

indignation *n* indignātiō *f*, dolor *m*.

indignity *n* contumēlia *f*, indignitās *f*.

indigo *n* Indicum *nt*.

indirect *adj* oblīquus.

indirectly *adv* oblīquē, per ambāgēs.

indirectness *n* ambāgēs *fpl*.

indiscipline *n* lascīvia *f*, licentia *f*.

indiscreet *adj* incōnsultus, imprūdēns.

indiscreetly *adv* incōnsultē, imprūdenter.

indiscretion *n* imprūdentia *f*; (*act*) culpa *f*.

indiscriminate *adj* prōmiscuus.

indiscriminately *adv* prōmiscuē, sine discrīmine.

indispensable *adj* necesse, necessārius.

indisposed *adj* īnfīrmus, aegrōtus, (*will*) āversus, aliēnātus; **be ~** aegrōtāre; abhorrēre, aliēnārī.

indisposition *n* īnfīrmitās *f*, valētūdō *f*.

indisputable *adj* certus, manifestus.

indisputably *adv* certē, sine dubiō.

indissoluble *adj* indissolūbilis.

indistinct *adj* obscūrus, obtūsus; (*speaker*) balbus.

indistinctly *adv* obscūrē; **pronounce ~** opprimere; **speak ~** balbutīre.

individual *adj* proprius ♦ *n* homō *m/f*, prīvātus *m*; **~s** *pl* singulī *mpl*.

individuality *n* proprium *nt*.

individually *adv* singulātim, prīvātim.

indivisible *adj* indīviduus.

indolence *n* dēsidia *f*, ignāvia *f*, inertia *f*.

indolent *adj* dēses, ignāvus, iners.

indolently *adv* ignāvē.

indomitable *adj* indomitus.

indoor *adj* umbrātilis.

indoors *adv* intus; (*motion*) intrā.

indubitable *adj* certus.

indubitably *adv* sine dubiō.

induce *vt* indūcere, addūcere, persuādēre (*dat*).

inducement *n* illecebra *f*, praemium *nt*.
induction *n* (*logic*) inductiō *f*.
indulge *vt* indulgēre (*dat*).
indulgence *n* indulgentia *f*, venia *f*; (*favour*) grātia *f*.
indulgent *adj* indulgēns, lēnis.
indulgently *adv* indulgenter.
industrious *adj* industrius, impiger, dīligēns.
industriously *adv* industriē.
industry *n* industria *f*, dīligentia *f*, labor *m*.
inebriated *adj* ēbrius.
inebriation *n* ēbrietās *f*.
ineffable *adj* eximius.
ineffective *adj* inūtilis, invalidus.
ineffectively *adv* ināniter.
ineffectual *adj* inritus.
inefficient *adj* īnscītus, parum strēnuus.
inelegant *adj* inēlegāns, inconcinnus.
inelegantly *adv* inēleganter.
inept *adj* ineptus.
ineptly *adv* ineptē.
inequality *n* dissimilitūdō *f*, inīquitās *f*.
inert *adj* iners, sōcors, immōbilis.
inertia *n* inertia *f*.
inertly *adv* tardē, lentē.
inestimable *adj* inaestimābilis.
inevitable *adj* necessārius.
inevitably *adv* necessāriō.
inexact *adj* parum subtīlis.
inexhaustible *adj* perennis.
inexorable *adj* inexōrābilis.
inexpediency *n* inūtilitās *f*, incommodum *nt*.
inexpedient *adj* inūtilis; **it is ~** nōn expedit.
inexpensive *adj* vīlis.
inexperience *n* imperītia *f*, īnscītia *f*.
inexperienced *adj* imperītus, rudis, īnscītus.
inexpert *adj* imperītus.
inexpiable *adj* inexpiābilis.
inexplicable *adj* inexplicābilis, inēnōdābilis.
inexpressible *adj* inēnārrābilis.
inextricable *adj* inexplicābilis.
infallible *adj* certus, errōris expers.
infamous *adj* īnfāmis, flāgitiōsus.
infamously *adv* flāgitiōsē.
infamy *n* īnfāmia *f*, flāgitium *nt*, dēdecus *nt*.
infancy *n* īnfantia *f*; (*fig*) incūnābula *ntpl*.
infant *n* īnfāns *m/f*.
infantile *adj* puerīlis.
infantry *n* peditēs *mpl*, peditātus *m*.
infantryman *n* pedes *m*.
infatuate *vt* īnfatuāre.
infatuated *adj* dēmēns.
infatuation *n* dēmentia *f*.
infect *vt* īnficere.
infection *n* contāgiō *f*.
infer *vt* īnferre, colligere.
inference *n* conclūsiō *f*.
inferior *adj* (*position*) īnferior; (*quality*) dēterior.
infernal *adj* īnfernus.
infest *vt* frequentāre.
infidel *adj* impius.
infidelity *n* perfidia *f*, īnfidēlitās *f*.

infiltrate *vi* sē īnsinuāre.
infinite *adj* īnfīnītus, immēnsus.
infinitely *adv* longē, immēnsum.
infinitesimal *adj* minimus.
infinity *n* īnfīnitās *f*.
infirm *adj* īnfirmus, invalidus.
infirmary *n* valētūdinārium *nt*.
infirmity *n* morbus *m*.
inflame *vt* accendere, incendere, īnflammāre. **be ~d** exārdēscere.
inflammation *n* (*MED*) īnflātiō *f*.
inflate *vt* īnflāre.
inflated *adj* (*fig*) īnflātus, tumidus.
inflexible *adj* rigidus.
inflexion *n* (*GRAM*) flexūra *f*; (*voice*) flexiō *f*.
inflict *vt* īnflīgere, incutere; (*burden*) impōnere; (*penalty*) sūmere; **be ~ed with** labōrāre ex.
infliction *n* poena *f*; malum *nt*.
influence *n* (*physical*) impulsiō *f*, mōmentum *nt*; (*moral*) auctōritās *f*; (*partial*) grātia *f*; **have ~** valēre; **have great ~ with** plūrimum posse apud; **under the ~ of** īnstinctus (*abl*) ♦ *vt* impellere, movēre, addūcere.
influential *adj* gravis, potēns; grātiōsus.
influenza *n* gravēdō *f*.
inform *vt* docēre, certiōrem facere; **~ against** nōmen dēferre (*gen*).
informant *n* index *m*, auctor *m*.
information *n* indicium *nt*, nūntius *m*.
informer *n* index *m*, dēlātor *m*; **turn ~** indicium profitērī.
infrequent *adj* rārus.
infrequently *adv* rārō.
infringe *vt* violāre, imminuere.
infringement *n* violātiō *f*.
infuriate *vt* efferāre.
infuriated *adj* furibundus.
infuse *vt* īnfundere; (*fig*) inicere.
ingenious *adj* ingeniōsus, callidus; (*thing*) artificiōsus.
ingeniously *adv* callidē, summā arte.
ingenuity *n* ars *f*, artificium *nt*, acūmen *nt*.
ingenuous *adj* ingenuus, simplex.
ingenuously *adv* ingenuē, simpliciter.
ingenuousness *n* ingenuitās *f*.
ingle *n* focus *m*.
inglorious *adj* inglōrius, ignōbilis, inhonestus.
ingloriously *adv* sine glōriā, inhonestē.
ingot *n* later *m*.
ingrained *adj* īnsitus.
ingratiate *vt*: **~ oneself with** grātiam inīre ab, sē īnsinuāre in familiāritātem (*gen*); **~ oneself into** sē īnsinuāre in (*acc*).
ingratitude *n* ingrātus animus *m*.
ingredient *n* pars *f*.
inhabit *vt* incolere, habitāre in (*abl*).
inhabitable *adj* habitābilis.
inhabitant *n* incola *m/f*.
inhale *vt* haurīre.
inharmonious *adj* dissonus.
inherent *adj* īnsitus; **be ~ in** inhaerēre (*dat*), inesse (*dat*).

inherently *adv* nātūrā.
inherit *vt* excipere.
inheritance *n* hērēditās *f*, patrimōnium *nt*;
　divide an ~ herctum ciēre; come into an ~
　hērēditātem adīre.
inheritor *n* hērēs *m/f*.
inhibit *vt* prohibēre, inhibēre.
inhospitable *adj* inhospitālis.
inhuman *adj* inhūmānus, immānis, crūdēlis.
inhumanity *n* inhūmānitās *f*, crūdēlitās *f*.
inhumanly *adv* inhūmānē, crūdēliter.
inimical *adj* inimīcus.
inimitable *adj* singulāris, eximius.
iniquitous *adj* inīquus, improbus, nefārius.
iniquity *n* scelus *nt*, flāgitium *nt*.
initial *adj* prīmus.
initiate *vt* initiāre; (*with knowledge*) imbuere.
initiative *n* initium *nt*; **take the ~** initium
　capere, facere; occupāre (*inf*).
inject *vt* inicere.
injudicious *adj* incōnsultus, imprūdēns.
injunction *n* iussum *nt*, praeceptum *nt*.
injure *vt* laedere, nocēre (*dat*).
injurious *adj* damnōsus, nocēns.
injury *n* iniūria *f*, damnum *nt*; (*bodily*) vulnus
　nt.
injustice *n* iniūria *f*, inīquitās *f*.
ink *n* ātrāmentum *nt*.
inkling *n* audītiō *f*, suspiciō *f*.
inland *adj* mediterrāneus; **further ~** interior.
inlay *vt* īnserere.
inlet *n* sinus *m*, aestuārium *nt*.
inly *adv* penitus.
inmate *n* inquilīnus *m*.
inmost *adj* intimus.
inn *n* dēversōrium *nt*; caupōna *f*, taberna *f*.
innate *adj* innātus, īnsitus.
inner *adj* interior.
innermost *adj* intimus.
innkeeper *n* caupō *m*.
innocence *n* innocentia *f*.
innocent *adj* innocēns, īnsōns; (*character*)
　integer, castus.
innocently *adv* innocenter, integrē, castē.
innocuous *adj* innoxius.
innovate *vt* novāre.
innovation *n* novum *nt*, nova rēs *f*.
innovator *n* novārum rērum auctor *m*.
innuendo *n* verbum inversum *nt*.
innumerable *adj* innumerābilis.
inoffensive *adj* innocēns.
inoffensively *adv* innocenter.
inopportune *adj* intempestīvus.
inopportunely *adv* intempestīvē.
inordinate *adj* immodicus, immoderātus.
inordinately *adv* immoderātē.
inquest *n* quaestiō *f*; **hold an ~ on** quaerere dē.
inquire *vi* exquīrere, rogāre; **~ into** inquīrere
　in (*acc*), investīgāre.
inquiry *n* quaestiō *f*, investīgātiō *f*; (*asking*)
　interrogātiō *f*; **make ~** exquīrere; **make ~ies**
　about inquīrere in (*acc*); **hold an ~ on**
　quaerere dē, quaestiōnem īnstituere dē.

inquisition *n* inquīsītiō *f*.
inquisitive *adj* cūriōsus.
inquisitiveness *n* cūriōsitās *f*.
inquisitor *n* inquīsītor *m*.
inroad *n* incursiō *f*, impressiō *f*; **make an ~**
　incursāre.
insane *adj* īnsānus, mente captus; **be ~**
　īnsānīre.
insanity *n* īnsānia *f*, dēmentia *f*.
insatiable *adj* īnsatiābilis, inexplēbilis,
　īnsaturābilis.
insatiably *adv* īnsaturābiliter.
inscribe *vt* īnscrībere.
inscription *n* epigramma *nt*; (*written*)
　īnscrīptiō *f*.
inscrutable *adj* obscūrus.
insect *n* bestiola *f*.
insecure *adj* īnstabilis, intūtus.
insecurity *n* perīcula *ntpl*.
insensate *adj* ineptus, stultus.
insensible *adj* torpidus; (*fig*) dūrus.
insensitive *adj* dūrus.
inseparable *adj* coniūnctus; **be the ~**
　companion of ab latere esse (*gen*).
inseparably *adv* coniūnctē.
insert *vt* īnserere, immittere, interpōnere.
insertion *n* interpositiō *f*.
inshore *adv* prope lītus.
inside *adv* intus; (*motion*) intrō ♦ *adj* interior ♦
　n pars *f* interior ♦ *prep* intrā (*acc*); **get right ~**
　sē īnsinuāre in (*acc*); **turn ~ out** excutere; **on**
　the ~ interior.
insidious *adj* īnsidiōsus, subdolus.
insidiously *adv* īnsidiōsē.
insight *n* intellegentia *f*, cognitiō *f*.
insignia *n* īnsignia *ntpl*.
insignificance *n* levitās *f*.
insignificant *adj* levis, exiguus, nullīus
　mōmentī; (*position*) humilis.
insincere *adj* simulātus, fūcōsus.
insincerely *adv* simulātē.
insincerity *n* simulātiō *f*, fraus *f*.
insinuate *vt* īnsinuāre; (*hint*) significāre ♦ *vi*
　sē īnsinuāre.
insinuating *adj* blandus.
insinuation *n* ambigua verba *ntpl*.
insipid *adj* īnsulsus, frīgidus.
insipidity *n* īnsulsitās *f*.
insist *vi* īnstāre; **~ on** postulāre.
insistence *n* pertinācia *f*.
insistent *adj* pertināx.
insolence *n* īnsolentia *f*, contumācia *f*,
　superbia *f*.
insolent *adj* īnsolēns, contumāx, superbus.
insolently *adv* īnsolenter.
insoluble *adj* inexplicābilis.
insolvency *n* reī familiāris naufragium *nt*.
insolvent *adj*: **be ~** solvendō nōn esse.
inspect *vt* īnspicere; (MIL) recēnsēre.
inspection *n* cognitiō *f*; (MIL) recēnsiō *f*.
inspector *n* cūrātor *m*.
inspiration *n* adflātus *m*, īnstinctus *m*.
inspire *vt* īnstinguere, incendere.

instability n mōbilitās f.
install vt inaugurāre.
instalment n pēnsiō f.
instance n exemplum nt; **for** ~ exemplī causā, grātiā; **at the** ~ admonitū; **at my** ~ mē auctōre ♦ vt memorāre.
instant adj īnstāns, praesēns ♦ n temporis pūnctum nt, mōmentum nt.
instantaneous adj praesēns.
instantaneously adv continuō, īlicō.
instantly adv īlicō, extemplō.
instead of prep prō (abl), locō (gen); (with verb) nōn ... sed.
instigate vt īnstīgāre, impellere.
instigation n impulsus m, stimulus m; auctōritās f; **at my** ~ mē auctōre.
instigator n īnstimulātor m, auctor m.
instil vt imbuere, adspīrāre, inicere.
instinct n nātūra f, ingenium nt, sēnsus m.
instinctive adj nātūrālis.
instinctively adv nātūrā, ingeniō suō.
institute vt īnstituere, inaugurāre.
institution n īnstitūtum nt; societās f.
instruct vt docēre, īnstituere, īnstruere; ērudīre; (order) praecipere (dat).
instruction n doctrīna f, disciplīna f; praeceptum nt; **give ~s** dēnūntiāre, praecipere.
instructor n doctor m, praeceptor m.
instructress n magistra f.
instrument n īnstrūmentum nt; (music) fidēs fpl; (legal) tabulae fpl.
instrumental adj ūtilis.
instrumentalist n fidicen m, fidicina f.
instrumentality n opera f.
insubordinate adj turbulentus, sēditiōsus.
insubordination n intemperantia f, licentia f.
insufferable adj intolerandus, intolerābilis.
insufficiency n inopia f.
insufficient adj minor; **be** ~ nōn sufficere.
insufficiently adv parum.
insulate vt sēgregāre.
insult n iniūria f, contumēlia f, probrum nt ♦ vt maledīcere (dat), contumēliam impōnere (dat).
insulting adj contumēliōsus.
insultingly adv contumēliōsē.
insuperable adj inexsuperābilis.
insupportable adj intolerandus, intolerābilis.
insurance n cautiō f.
insure vi cavēre.
insurgent n rebellis m.
insurmountable adj inexsuperābilis.
insurrection n mōtus m, sēditiō f.
intact adj integer, intāctus, incolumis.
integrity n integritās f, innocentia f, fidēs f.
intellect n ingenium nt, mēns f, animus m.
intellectual adj ingeniōsus.
intelligence n intellegentia f, acūmen nt; (MIL) nūntius m.
intelligent adj ingeniōsus, sapiēns, argūtus.
intelligently adv ingeniōsē, sapienter, satis acūtē.

intelligible adj perspicuus, apertus.
intemperance n intemperantia f, licentia f.
intemperate adj intemperāns, intemperātus.
intemperately adv intemperanter.
intend vt (with inf) in animō habēre, velle; (with object) dēstināre.
intense adj ācer, nimius.
intensely adv valdē, nimium.
intensify vt augēre, amplificāre; **be ~ied** ingravēscere.
intensity n vīs f.
intensive adj ācer, multus, adsiduus.
intensively adv summō studiō.
intent adj ērēctus, intentus; **be** ~ **on animum** intendere in (acc) ♦ n cōnsilium nt; **with** ~ cōnsultō.
intention n cōnsilium nt, prōpositum nt; **it is my** ~ **mihī** in animō est; **with the** ~ **of eā** mente, eō cōnsiliō ut (subj).
intentionally adv cōnsultō, dē industriā.
inter vt humāre.
intercalary adj intercalāris.
intercalate vt intercalāre.
intercede vi intercēdere, dēprecārī.
intercept vt excipere, intercipere; (cut off) interclūdere.
intercession n dēprecātiō f; (tribune's) intercessiō f.
intercessor n dēprecātor m.
interchange vt permūtāre ♦ n permūtātiō f, vicissitūdō f.
intercourse n commercium nt, ūsus m, cōnsuētūdō f.
interdict n interdictum nt ♦ vt interdīcere (dat), vetāre.
interest n (advantage) commodum nt; (study) studium nt; (money) faenus nt, ūsūra f; **compound** ~ anatocismus m; **rate of** ~ faenus nt; ~ **at 12 per cent (per annum)** centēsimae fpl; **it is of** ~ interest; **it is in my ~s** meā interest; **consult the ~s of** cōnsulere (dat); **take an** ~ **in animum** intendere (dat) ♦ vt dēlectāre, capere; (audience) tenēre; ~ **oneself in** studēre (dat).
interested adj attentus; (for gain) ambitiōsus.
interesting adj iūcundus, novus.
interfere vi intervenīre: (with) sē interpōnere (dat), sē admiscēre ad; (hinder) officere (dat).
interference n interventus m, intercessiō f.
interim n: **in the** ~ interim, intereā.
interior adj interior ♦ n pars interior f; (country) interiōra ntpl.
interject vt exclāmāre.
interjection n interiectiō f.
interlace vt intexere.
interlard vt variāre.
interlock vt implicāre.
interloper n interpellātor m.
interlude n embolium nt.
intermarriage n cōnūbium nt.
intermediary adj medius ♦ n internūntius m.
intermediate adj medius.
interment n humātiō f.

interminable *adj* sempiternus, longus.
intermingle *vt* intermiscēre ♦ *vi* sē
immiscēre.
intermission *n* intercapēdō *f*, intermissiō *f*.
intermittent *adj* interruptus.
intermittently *adv* interdum.
intern *vt* inclūdere.
internal *adj* internus; (*POL*) domesticus.
internally *adv* intus, domī.
international *adj*: ~ law iūs gentium.
internecine *adj* internecīvus.
interplay *n* vicēs *fpl*.
interpolate *vt* interpolāre.
interpose *vt* interpōnere ♦ *vi* intercēdere.
interposition *n* intercessiō *f*.
interpret *vt* interpretārī.
interpretation *n* interpretātiō *f*.
interpreter *n* interpres *m/f*.
interrogate *vt* interrogāre, percontārī.
interrogation *n* interrogātiō *f*, percontātiō *f*.
interrupt *vt* (*action*) intercipere; (*speaker*)
interpellāre; (*talk*) dirimere; (*continuity*)
intermittere.
interrupter *n* interpellātor *m*.
interruption *n* interpellātiō *f*; intermissiō *f*.
intersect *vt* dīvidere, secāre.
intersperse *vt* distinguere.
interstice *n* rīma *f*.
intertwine *vt* intexere, implicāre.
interval *n* intervallum *nt*, spatium *nt*; **after an ~**
spatiō interpositō; **after an ~ of a year** annō
interiectō; **at ~s** interdum; **at frequent ~s**
identidem; **leave an ~** intermittere.
intervene *vt* intercēdere, intervenīre.
intervention *n* intercēssiō *f*, interventus *m*; **by
the ~ of** intercursū (*gen*).
interview *n* colloquium *nt*, aditus *m* ♦ *vt*
convenīre.
interweave *vt* implicāre, intexere.
intestate *adj* intestātus ♦ *adv* intestātō.
intestine *adj* intestīnus; (*POL*) domesticus ♦ *npl*
intestīna *ntpl*; (*victim's*) exta *ntpl*.
intimacy *n* familiāritās *f*.
intimate *adj* familiāris; **be an ~ friend of** ab
latere esse (*gen*); **a very ~ friend**
perfamiliāris *m/f* ♦ *vt* dēnūntiāre.
intimately *adv* familiāriter.
intimation *n* dēnūntiātiō *f*; (*hint*) indicium *nt*.
intimidate *vt* minārī (*dat*), terrōrem inicere
(*dat*).
intimidation *n* metus *m*, minae *fpl*.
into *prep* in (*acc*), intrā (*acc*).
intolerable *adj* intolerandus, intolerābilis.
intolerably *adv* intoleranter.
intolerance *n* impatientia *f*.
intolerant *adj* impatiēns, intolerāns.
intonation *n* sonus *m*, flexiō *f*.
intone *vt* cantāre.
intoxicate *vt* ēbrium reddere.
intoxicated *adj* ēbrius.
intoxication *n* ēbrietās *f*.
intractable *adj* indocilis, difficilis.
intransigent *adj* obstinātus.

intrepid *adj* intrepidus, impavidus.
intrepidity *n* audācia *f*, fortitūdō *f*.
intricacy *n* implicātiō *f*.
intricate *adj* implicātus, involūtus.
intricately *adv* implicitē.
intrigue *n* factiō *f*, artēs *fpl*, fallācia *f* ♦ *vi*
māchinārī, fallāciīs ūtī.
intriguing *adj* factiōsus; blandus.
intrinsic *adj* vērus, innātus.
intrinsically *adv* per sē.
introduce *vt* indūcere, īnferre, importāre;
(*acquaintance*) commendāre; (*custom*)
īnstituere.
introduction *n* exōrdium *nt*, prooemium *nt*; (*of
person*) commendātiō *f*; **letter of ~** litterae
commendātīciae *fpl*.
intrude *vi* sē interpōnere, intervenīre.
intruder *n* interpellātor *m*, advena *m*; (*fig*)
aliēnus *m*.
intrusion *n* interpellātiō *f*.
intuition *n* sēnsus *m*, cognitiō *f*.
inundate *vt* inundāre.
inundation *n* ēluviō *f*.
inure *vt* dūrāre, adsuēfacere.
invade *vt* invādere.
invalid *adj* aeger, dēbilis; (*null*) inritus.
invalidate *vt* īnfīrmāre.
invaluable *adj* inaestimābilis.
invariable *adj* cōnstāns, immūtābilis.
invariably *adv* semper.
invasion *n* incursiō *f*.
invective *n* convīcium *nt*.
inveigh *vi*: ~ **against** invehī in (*acc*), īnsectārī.
inveigle *vt* illicere, pellicere.
invent *vt* fingere, comminīscī, invenīre.
invention *n* inventum *nt*; (*faculty*) inventiō *f*.
inventor *n* inventor *m*, auctor *m*.
inverse *adj* inversus.
inversely *adv* inversō ōrdine.
invert *vt* invertere.
invest *vt* (*in office*) inaugurāre; (*MIL*) obsidēre,
circumsedēre; (*money*) locāre.
investigate *vt* investīgāre, indāgāre; (*case*)
cognōscere.
investigation *n* investīgātiō *f*, indāgātiō *f*;
(*case*) cognitiō *f*.
investment *n* (*MIL*) obsessiō *f*; (*money*) locāta
pecūnia *f*.
inveterate *adj* inveterātus, vetus; **become ~**
inveterāscere.
invidious *adj* invidiōsus.
invidiously *adv* invidiōsē.
invigorate *vt* recreāre, reficere.
invincible *adj* invictus.
inviolable *adj* inviolātus; (*person*)
sacrōsanctus.
inviolably *adv* inviolātē.
inviolate *adj* integer.
invisible *adj* caecus; **be ~** vidērī nōn posse.
invitation *n* invītātiō *f*; **at the ~ of** invītātū
(*gen*).
invite *vt* invītāre, vocāre.
inviting *adj* suāvis, blandus.

invitingly adv blandē, suāviter.
invocation n testātiō f.
invoke vt invocāre, testārī.
involuntarily adv īnscienter, invītus.
involuntary adj coāctus.
involve vt implicāre, involvere; **be ~d in** inligārī (abl).
invulnerable adj inviolābilis; **be ~** vulnerārī nōn posse.
inward adj interior.
inwardly adv intus.
inwards adv intrōrsus.
inweave vt intexere.
inwrought adj intextus.
irascibility n īrācundia f.
irascible adj īrācundus.
irate adj īrātus.
ire n īra f.
iris n hyacinthus m.
irk vt incommodāre; **I am ~ed** mē piget.
irksome adj molestus.
irksomeness n molestia f.
iron n ferrum nt; **of ~** ferreus ♦ adj ferreus.
ironical adj inversus.
ironically adv inversīs verbīs.
iron mine n ferrāria f.
ironmonger n negōtiātor ferrārius m.
ironmongery n ferrāmenta ntpl.
iron ore n ferrum īnfectum nt.
iron-tipped adj ferrātus.
irony n illūsiō f, verbōrum inversiō f, dissimulātiō f.
irradiate vt illūstrāre.
irrational adj absurdus, ratiōnis expers; (animal) brūtus.
irrationally adv absurdē, sine ratiōne.
irreconcilable adj repugnāns, īnsociābilis.
irrefutable adj certus, invictus.
irregular adj incompositus; (ground) inaequālis; (meeting) extraōrdinārius; (troops) tumultuārius.
irregularity n inaequālitās f; (conduct) prāvitās f, licentia f; (election) vitium nt.
irregularly adv nullō ōrdine; (elected) vitiō.
irrelevant adj aliēnus.
irreligion n impietās f.
irreligious adj impius.
irremediable adj īnsānābilis.
irreparable adj inrevocābilis.
irreproachable adj integer, innocēns.
irresistible adj invictus.
irresolute adj dubius, anceps.
irresolutely adv dubitanter.
irresolution n dubitātiō f.
irresponsibility n licentia f.
irresponsible adj lascīvus, levis.
irretrievable adj inrevocābilis.
irreverence n impietās f.
irreverent adj impius.
irreverently adv impiē.
irrevocable adj inrevocābilis.
irrigate vt inrigāre.
irrigation n inrigātiō f.

irritability n īrācundia f.
irritable adj īrācundus.
irritate vt inrītāre, stomachum movēre (dat).
irritation n īrācundia f, stomachus m.
island n īnsula f.
islander n īnsulānus m.
isle n īnsula f.
isolate vt sēgregāre, sēparāre.
isolation n sōlitūdō f.
issue n (result) ēventus m, exitus m; (children) prōlēs f; (question) rēs f; (book) ēditiō f; **decide the ~** dēcernere, dēcertāre; **the point at ~** quā dē rē agitur ♦ vt distribuere; (book) ēdere; (announcement) prōmulgāre; (coin) ērogāre ♦ vi ēgredī, ēmānāre; (result) ēvādere, ēvenīre.
isthmus n isthmus m.
it pron hōc, id.
itch n (disease) scabiēs f; (fig) cacoēthes nt ♦ vi prūrīre.
item n nōmen nt, rēs f.
iterate vt iterāre.
itinerant adj vāgus, circumforāneus.
itinerary n iter nt.
its adj suus, ēius.
itself pron ipse, ipsa, ipsum.
ivory n ebur nt ♦ adj eburneus.
ivy n hedera f.

J, j

jabber vi blaterāre.
jackdaw n grāculus m.
jaded adj dēfessus, fatīgātus.
jagged adj serrātus.
jail n carcer m.
jailer n custōs m, carcerārius m.
jam vt comprimere; (way) obstruere.
jamb n postis m.
jangle vi crepitāre; rixārī.
janitor n iānitor m.
January n mēnsis Iānuārius m; **of ~** Iānuārius.
jar n urna f; (for wine) amphora f; (for water) hydria f; (sound) offēnsa f; (quarrel) rixa f ♦ vi offendere.
jasper n iaspis f.
jaundice n morbus arquātus.
jaundiced adj ictericus.
jaunt n: **take a ~** excurrere.
jauntily adv hilare, festīvē.
jauntiness n hilaritās f.
jaunty adj hilaris, festīvus.
javelin n iaculum nt, pīlum nt; **throw the ~** iaculārī.
jaw n māla f; **~s** pl faucēs fpl.

jay n grāculus m.
jealous adj invidus; **be ~ of** invidēre (dat).
jealousy n invidia f.
jeer n irrīsiō f ♦ vi irrīdēre; **~ at** illūdere.
jejune adj iēiūnus, exīlis.
jeopardize vt in perīculum addūcere.
jeopardy n perīculum nt.
jerk n subitus mōtus m.
jest n iocus m.
jester n scurra m.
jet n (mineral) gagātēs m; (of water) saltus m ♦ vi salīre.
jetsam n ēiectāmenta ntpl.
jettison vt ēicere.
jetty n mōlēs f.
Jew n Iūdaeus.
jewel n gemma f.
Jewish adj Iūdaicus.
jig n tripudium nt.
jilt vt repudiāre.
jingle n nēnia f ♦ vi crepitāre, tinnīre.
job n opus nt.
jocose adj see **jocular**.
jocular adj facētus, ioculāris.
jocularity n facētiae fpl.
jocularly adv facētē, per iocum.
jocund adj hilaris, festīvus.
jog vt fodicāre; (fig) stimulāre ♦ vi ambulāre.
join vt iungere, coniungere, cōpulāre ♦ vi coniungī, sē coniungere; **~ in** interesse (dat), sē immiscēre (dat); **~ battle with** proelium committere (+ abl).
joiner n faber m.
joint adj commūnis ♦ n commissūra f; (of body) articulus m, nōdus m; **~ by ~** articulātim.
jointed adj geniculātus.
joint-heir n cohērēs m/f.
jointly adv ūnā, coniūnctē.
joist n tignum nt.
joke n iocus m ♦ vi iocārī, lūdere.
joking n iocus m; **~ apart** remōtō iocō.
jokingly adv per iocum.
jollity n hilaritās f, festīvitās f.
jolly adj hilaris, festīvus.
jolt vt iactāre.
jolting n iactātiō f.
jostle vt agitāre, offendere.
jot n minimum nt; **not a ~** nihil; **not care a ~** nōn floccī facere.
journal n ācta diūrna ntpl.
journey n iter nt.
journeyman n opifex m.
Jove n Iuppiter m.
jovial adj hilaris.
joviality n hilaritās f.
jovially adv hilare.
jowl n māla f; **cheek by ~** iuxtā.
joy n gaudium nt, laetitia f, alacritās f.
joyful adj laetus, hilaris.
joyfully adv laetē, hilare.
joyfulness n gaudium nt, laetitia f.
joyless adj tristis, maestus.

joyous adj see **joyful**.
joyously adv see **joyfully**.
jubilant adj laetus, gaudiō exsultāns.
judge n iūdex m, arbiter m ♦ vt iūdicāre; (think) exīstimāre, cēnsēre; **~ between** dīiūdicāre.
judgeship n iūdicātus m.
judgment n iūdicium nt, arbitrium nt; (opinion) sententia f; (punishment) poena f; (wisdom) iūdicium nt; **in my ~** meō animō, meō arbitrātū; **pass ~ on** statuere dē; **sit in ~** iūdicium exercēre.
judgment seat n tribūnal nt.
judicature n iūrisdictiō f; (men) iūdicēs mpl.
judicial adj iūdiciālis; (law) iūdiciārius.
judiciary n iūdicēs mpl.
judicious adj prūdēns, cōnsīderātus.
judiciously adv prūdenter.
jug n hydria f, urceus m.
juggler n praestīgiātor m.
juggling n praestīgiae fpl.
juice n liquor m, sūcus m.
juicy adj sūcī plēnus.
July n mēnsis Quīnctīlis, Iūlius m; **of ~** Quīnctīlis, Iūlius.
jumble n congeriēs f ♦ vt cōnfundere.
jump n saltus m ♦ vi salīre; **~ across** trānsilīre; **~ at** (opportunity) captāre, adripere, amplectī; **~ down** dēsilīre; **~ on to** īnsilīre in (acc).
junction n coniūnctiō f.
juncture n tempus nt.
June n mēnsis Iūnius; **of ~** Iūnius.
junior adj iūnior, nātū minor.
juniper n iūniperus f.
Juno n Iūnō, Iūnōnis f.
Jupiter n Iuppiter, Iovis m.
juridical adj iūdiciārius.
jurisconsult n iūriscōnsultus m.
jurisdiction n iūrisdictiō f, diciō f; **exercise ~** iūs dīcere.
jurisprudence n iūrisprūdentia f.
jurist n iūriscōnsultus m.
juror n iūdex m.
jury n iūdicēs mpl.
just adj iūstus, aequus ♦ adv (exactly) prōrsus; (only) modo; (time) commodum, modo; (with adv) dēmum, dēnique; (with pron) adeō dēmum, ipse; **~ as** (comparison) aequē ac, perinde ac, quemadmodum; sīcut; **~ before** (time) cum māximē, sub (acc); **~ now** modo, nunc; **~ so** ita prōrsus, sānē; **only ~** vix.
justice n iūstitia f, aequitās f, iūs nt; (person) praetor m; **administer ~** iūs reddere.
justiciary n praetor m.
justifiable adj iūstus.
justifiably adv iūre.
justification n pūrgātiō f, excūsātiō f.
justify vt excūsāre, pūrgāre.
justly adv iūstē, aequē; iūre, meritō.
jut vi prōminēre, excurrere.
jutting adj prōiectus.
juvenile adj iuvenīlis, puerīlis.

K, k

keel n carīna f.
keen adj ācer; (*mind*) acūtus, argūtus; (*sense*) sagāx; (*pain*) acerbus; **I am ~ on** studeō.
keenly adv ācriter, sagāciter, acūtē, acerbē.
keenness n (*scent*) sagācitās f; (*sight*) aciēs f; (*pain*) acerbitās f; (*eagerness*) studium nt, ārdor m.
keep vt servāre, tenēre, habēre; (*celebrate*) agere, celebrāre; (*guard*) custōdīre; (*obey*) observāre; (*preserve*) cōnservāre; (*rear*) alere, pāscere; (*store*) condere; **~ apart** distinēre; **~ away** arcēre; **~ back** dētinēre, reservāre; **~ down** comprimere; (*exuberance*) dēpāscere; **~ in** cohibēre, claudere; **~ in with** grātiam sequī (*gen*); **~ off** arcēre, dēfendere; **~ one's word** fidem praestāre; **~ one's hands off** manūs abstinēre; **~ house** domī sē retinēre; **~ secret** cēlāre; **~ together** continēre; **~ up** sustinēre, cōnservāre; **~ up with** subsequī; **~ waiting** dēmorārī ♦ vi dūrāre, manēre ♦ n arx f.
keeper n custōs m.
keeping n custōdia f; **in ~ with** prō (*abl*); **be in ~ with** convenīre (*dat*).
keg n cadus m.
ken n cōnspectus m.
kennel n stabulum nt.
kerb n crepīdō f.
kernel n grānum nt, nucleus m.
kettle n lebēs f.
key n clāvis f; (*fig*) claustra ntpl, iānua f; **~ position** cardō m.
kick vi calcitrāre ♦ vt calce ferīre.
kid n haedus m.
kidnap vt surripere.
kidnapper n plagiārius m.
kidney n rēn m.
kidney bean n phasēlus m.
kid's adj haedīnus.
kill vt interficere, interimere; (*in battle*) occīdere; (*murder*) necāre, iugulāre; (*time*) perdere.
killer n interfector m.
kiln n fornāx f.
kin n cognātī mpl, propinquī mpl; **next of ~** proximī mpl.
kind adj bonus, benīgnus, benevolus ♦ n genus nt; **of such a ~** tālis; **what ~ of** quālis ♦ adj cōmis.
kindle vt incendere, succendere, īnflammāre.
kindliness n cōmitās f, hūmānitās f.
kindling n (*fuel*) fōmes m.
kindly adv benīgnē.
kindness n benīgnitās f, benevolentia f; (*act*) beneficium nt, officium nt, grātia f.

kindred n necessitūdō f, cognātiō f; propinquī mpl, cognātī mpl ♦ adj cognātus, adfīnis.
king n rēx m.
kingdom n rēgnum nt.
kingfisher n alcēdō f.
kingly adj rēgius, rēgālis.
kingship n rēgnum nt.
kink n vitium nt.
kinsfolk n cognātī mpl, necessāriī mpl.
kinsman n cognātus m, propinquus m, necessārius m.
kinswoman n cognāta f, propinqua f, necessāria f.
kismet n fātum nt.
kiss n ōsculum nt ♦ vt ōsculārī.
kit n (*MIL*) sarcina f.
kitchen n culīna f.
kitchen garden n hortus m.
kite n mīluus m.
kite's adj mīluīnus.
knack n callidītās f, artificium nt; **have the ~ of** callēre.
knapsack n sarcina f.
knave n veterātor m.
knavish adj improbus.
knavishly adv improbē.
knead vt depsere, subigere.
knee n genū nt.
kneel vi genibus nītī.
knife n culter m; (*surgeon's*) scalprum nt.
knight n eques m ♦ vt in ōrdinem equestrem recipere.
knighthood n ōrdō equester m.
knightly adj equester.
knit vt texere; (*brow*) contrahere.
knob n bulla f.
knock vt ferīre, percutere; **~ at** pulsāre; **~ against** offendere; **~ down** dēicere, adflīgere; (*at auction*) addīcere; **~ off** dēcutere; (*work*) dēsistere ab; **~ out** ēlīdere, excutere; (*unconscious*) exanimāre; (*fig*) dēvincere; **~ up** suscitāre ♦ n pulsus m, ictus m.
knock-kneed adj vārus.
knoll n tumulus m.
knot n nōdus m ♦ vt nectere.
knotty adj nōdōsus; **~ point** nōdus m.
know vt scīre; (*person*) nōvisse; **~ all about** explōrātum habēre; **~ again** agnōscere; **~ how to** scīre; **not ~** ignōrāre, nescīre; **let me ~** fac sciam, fac mē certiōrem; **get to ~** cognōscere ♦ n **in the ~** cōnscius.
knowing adj prūdēns, callidus.
knowingly adv cōnsultō, sciēns.
knowledge n scientia f, doctrīna f; (*practical*) experientia f; (*of something*) cognitiō f.
knowledgeable adj gnārus, doctus.
known adj nōtus; **make ~** dēclārāre.
knuckle n articulus m.
knuckle bone n tālus m.
kotow vi adulārī.
kudos n glōria f, laus f.

L, l

label n titulus m ♦ vt titulō īnscrībere.
laboratory n officīna f.
laborious adj labōriōsus, operōsus.
laboriously adv operōsē.
laboriousness n labor m.
labour n labor m, opera f; (work done) opus nt; (work allotted) pēnsum nt; (workmen) operae fpl; **be in ~** parturīre ♦ vi labōrāre, ēnītī; **~ at** ēlabōrāre; **~ under a delusion** errōre fallī.
laboured adj adfectātus.
labourer n operārius m; **~s** pl operae fpl.
labyrinth n labyrinthus m.
lace n texta rēticulāta ntpl; (shoe) ligula f ♦ vt nectere.
lacerate vt lacerāre.
laceration n lacerātiō f.
lack n inopia f, dēfectiō f ♦ vt egēre (abl), carēre (abl).
lackey n pedisequus m.
laconic adj brevis.
laconically adv ūnō verbō, paucīs verbīs.
lacuna n lacūna f.
lad n puer m.
ladder n scāla f.
lade vt onerāre.
laden adj onustus, onerātus.
lading n onus nt.
ladle n trulla f.
lady n domina f, mātrōna f, mulier f.
ladylike adj līberālis, honestus.
lag vi cessāre.
lagoon n stagnum nt.
lair n latibulum nt.
lake n lacus m.
lamb n agnus m; (flesh) agnīna f; **ewe ~** agna f.
lame adj claudus; (argument) inānis; **be ~** claudicāre.
lameness n claudicātiō f.
lament n lāmentātiō f, lāmentum nt ♦ vt lūgēre, lāmentārī; (regret) dēplōrāre.
lamentable adj lāmentābilis, miserābilis.
lamentably adv miserābiliter.
lamentation n lāmentātiō f.
lamp n lucerna f, lychnus m.
lampoon n satura f ♦ vt carmine dēstringere.
lance n hasta f, lancea f.
lancer n hastātus m.
lancet n scalpellum nt.
land n terra f; (country) terra f, regiō f; (territory) fīnēs mpl; (native) patria f; (property) praedium nt, ager m; (soil) solum nt ♦ vt expōnere ♦ vi ē nāve ēgredī ♦ adj terrēnus, terrestris.
landfall n adpulsus m.
landing place n ēgressus m.

landlady n caupōna f.
landlord n dominus m; (inn) caupō m.
landmark n lapis m; **be a ~** ēminēre.
landscape n agrōrum prōspectus m.
landslide n terrae lābēs f, lāpsus m.
landwards adv terram versus.
lane n (country) sēmita f; (town) angiportus m.
language n lingua f; (style) ōrātiō f, sermō m; (diction) verba ntpl; **bad ~** maledicta ntpl.
languid adj languidus, remissus.
languidly adv languidē.
languish vi languēre, languēscere; (with disease) tābēscere.
languor n languor m.
lank, lanky adj exīlis, gracilis.
lantern n lanterna f, lucerna f.
lap n gremium nt, sinus m ♦ vt lambere; (cover) involvere.
lapse n (time) lāpsus m; (mistake) errātum nt; **after the ~ of a year** interiectō annō ♦ vi lābī; (agreement) inritum fierī; (property) revertī.
larceny n fūrtum nt.
larch n larix f ♦ adj larignus.
lard n adeps m/f.
larder n cella penāria f.
large adj māgnus, grandis, amplus; **at ~** solūtus; **very ~** permāgnus; **as ~ as ...** tantus ... quantus.
largely adv plērumque.
largesse n largītiō f; (MIL) dōnātīvum nt; (civil) congiārium nt; **give ~** largīrī.
lark n alauda f.
lascivious adj libīdinōsus.
lasciviously adv libīdinōsē.
lasciviousness n libīdō f.
lash n flagellum nt, lōrum nt; (eye) cilium nt ♦ vt verberāre; (tie) adligāre; (with words) castīgāre.
lashing n verbera ntpl.
lass n puella f.
lassitude n languor m.
last adj ultimus, postrēmus, suprēmus; (in line) novissimus; (preceding) proximus; **at ~** tandem, dēmum, dēnique; **for the ~ time** postrēmum ♦ n fōrma f; **let the cobbler stick to his ~** nē sūtor suprā crepidam ♦ vi dūrāre, permanēre.
lasting adj diūtinus, diūturnus.
lastly adv postrēmō, dēnique.
latch n pessulus m.
latchet n corrigia f.
late adj sērus; (date) recēns; (dead) dēmortuus; (emperor) dīvus; **~ at night** multā nocte; **till ~ in the day** ad multum diem ♦ adv sērō; **too ~** sērō; **too ~ to** sērius quam quī (subj); **of ~** nūper.
lately adv nūper.
latent adj occultus, latitāns.
later adj posterior ♦ adv posteā, posthāc, mox.
latest adj novissimus.
lath n tigillum nt.
lathe n tornus m.
lather n spūma f.

Latin *adj* Latīnus; **speak ~** Latīnē loquī; **understand ~** Latīnē scīre; **translate into ~** Latīnē reddere; **in Latin** latinē.
Latinity *n* Latīnitās *f.*
latitude *n* (*GEOG*) caelum *nt*; (*scope*) lībertās *f.*
latter *adj* posterior; **the ~** hīc.
latterly *adv* nūper.
lattice *n* trānsenna *f.*
laud *n* laus *f* ♦ *vt* laudāre.
laudable *adj* laudābilis, laude dignus.
laudatory *adj* honōrificus.
laugh *n* rīsus *m*; (*loud*) cachinnus *m* ♦ *vi* rīdēre, cachinnāre; **~ at** (*joke*) rīdēre; (*person*) dērīdēre; **~ up one's sleeve** in sinū gaudēre.
laughable *adj* rīdiculus.
laughing stock *n* lūdibrium *nt.*
laughter *n* rīsus *m.*
launch *vt* (*missile*) contorquēre; (*ship*) dēdūcere; **~ an attack** impetum dare ♦ *vi*: **~ out into** ingredī in (*acc*) ♦ *n* celōx *f*, lembus *m.*
laureate *adj* laureātus.
laurel *n* laurus *m* ♦ *adj* laureus.
lave *vt* lavāre.
lavish *adj* prōdigus, largus ♦ *vt* largīrī, profundere.
lavishly *adv* prōdigē, effūsē.
lavishness *n* largitās *f.*
law *n* lēx *f*; (*system*) iūs *nt*; (*divine*) fās *nt*; **civil ~** iūs cīvīle; **constitutional ~** iūs pūblicum; **international ~** iūs gentium; **go to ~** lēge agere, lītigāre; **break the ~** lēges violāre; **pass a ~** (*magistrate*) lēgem perferre; (*people*) lēgem iubēre.
law-abiding *adj* bene mōrātus.
law court *n* iūdicium *nt*; (*building*) basilica *f.*
lawful *adj* lēgitimus; (*morally*) fās.
lawfully *adv* lēgitimē, lēge.
lawgiver *n* lēgum scrīptor *m.*
lawless *adj* exlēx.
lawlessly *adv* licenter.
lawlessness *n* licentia *f.*
lawn *n* prātulum *nt.*
law-suit *n* līs *f*, āctiō *f.*
lawyer *n* iūriscōnsultus *m*, causidicus *m.*
lax *adj* dissolūtus, remissus.
laxity *n* dissolūtiō *f.*
lay *vt* pōnere, locāre; (*ambush*) collocāre, tendere; (*disorder*) sēdāre; (*egg*) parere; (*foundation*) iacere; (*hands*) inicere; (*plan*) capere, inīre; (*trap*) tendere; (*wager*) facere; **~ aside** pōnere; (*in store*) repōnere; **~ by** repōnere; **~ down** dēpōnere; (*rule*) statuere; **~ hold of** prehendere, adripere; **~ in** condere; **~ a motion before** referre ad; **~ on** impōnere; **~ open** patefacere; (*to attack*) nūdāre; **~ out** (*money*) impendere, ērogāre; (*camp*) mētārī; **~ siege to** obsidēre; **~ to heart** in pectus dēmittere; **~ up** recondere; **~ upon** iniungere, impōnere; **~ violent hands on** vim adferre, adhibēre (*dat*); **whatever they could ~ hands on** quod cuīque in manum vēnisset; **~ waste** vastāre ♦ *n* carmen *nt*, melos *nt.*

lay *adj* (*ECCL*) lāicus.
layer *n* corium *nt*; (*stones*) ōrdō *m*; (*plant*) propāgō *f.*
layout *n* dēsignātiō *f.*
laze *vi* ōtiārī.
lazily *adv* ignāvē, ōtiōsē.
laziness *n* ignāvia *f*, dēsidia *f*, pigritia *f.*
lazy *adj* ignāvus, dēsidiōsus, piger.
lea *n* prātum *nt.*
lead *vt* dūcere; (*life*) agere; (*wall*) perdūcere; (*water*) dērīvāre; **~ across** trādūcere; **~ around** circumdūcere; **~ astray** in errōrem indūcere; **~ away** abdūcere; **~ back** redūcere; **~ down** dēdūcere; **~ in** intrōdūcere; **~ on** addūcere; **~ out** ēdūcere; **~ over** trādūcere; **~ the way** dūcere, praeīre; **~ up to** tendere ad, spectare ad; **the road ~s ...** via fert ....
lead *n* plumbum *nt* ♦ *adj* plumbeus.
leaden *adj* (*colour*) līvidus.
leader *n* dux *m*, ductor *m.*
leadership *n* ductus *m.*
leading *adj* prīmus, prīnceps, praecipuus.
leaf, *pl* **leaves** *n* folium *nt*, frōns *f*; (*paper*) scheda *f*; **put forth leaves** frondēscere.
leaflet *n* libellus *m.*
leafy *adj* frondōsus.
league *n* foedus *nt*, societās *f*; (*distance*) tria mīlia passuum ♦ *vi* coniūrāre, foedus facere.
leagued *adj* foederātus.
leak *n* rīma *f* ♦ *vi* mānāre, rimās agere.
leaky *adj* rīmōsus.
lean *adj* macer, exīlis, gracilis ♦ *vi* nītī; **~ back** sē reclīnāre; **~ on** innītī in (*abl*), incumbere (*dat*); **~ over** inclīnāre.
leaning *n* prōpēnsiō *f* ♦ *adj* inclīnātus.
leanness *n* gracilitās *f*, maciēs *f.*
leap *n* saltus *m* ♦ *vi* salīre; (*for joy*) exsultāre; **~ down** dēsilīre; **~ on to** īnsilīre in (*acc*).
leap year *n* annus bissextilis *m.*
learn *vt* discere; (*news*) accipere, audīre; (*by heart*) ēdiscere; (*discover*) cognōscere.
learned *adj* doctus, ērudītus, litterātus.
learnedly *adv* doctē.
learner *n* tīrō *m*, discipulus *m.*
learning *n* doctrīna *f*, ērudītiō *f*, litterae *fpl.*
lease *n* (*taken*) conductiō *f*; (*given*) locātiō *f* ♦ *vt* condūcere; locāre.
leash *n* cōpula *f.*
least *adj* minimus ♦ *adv* minimē; **at ~** saltem; **to say the ~** ut levissimē dīcam; **not in the ~** haudquāquam.
leather *n* corium *nt*, alūta *f.*
leathery *adj* lentus.
leave *n* (*of absence*) commeātus *m*; (*permission*) potestās *f*, venia *f*; **ask ~** veniam petere; **give ~** potestātem facere; **obtain ~** impetrāre; **by your ~** pace tuā, bonā tuā veniā ♦ *vt* relinquere, dēserere; (*legacy*) lēgāre; **~ alone** nōn tangere, manum abstinēre ab; **~ behind** relinquere; **~ in the lurch** dēstituere, dērelinquere; **~ off** dēsinere, dēsistere ab;

(*temporarily*) intermittere; (*garment*) pōnere;
~ **out** praetermittere, ōmittere ♦ *vi*
discēdere ab (+ *abl*), abīre.
leaven *n* fermentum *nt*.
leavings *n* rēliquiae *fpl*.
lecherous *adj* salāx.
lecture *n* acroāsis *f*, audītiō *f* ♦ *vi* docēre,
scholam habēre.
lecturer *n* doctor *m*.
lecture room *n* audītōrium *nt*.
ledge *n* līmen *nt*.
ledger *n* cōdex acceptī et expēnsī.
lee *n* pars ā ventō tūta.
leech *n* hirūdō *f*.
leek *n* porrum *nt*.
leer *vi* līmīs oculīs intuērī.
lees *n* faex *f*; (*of oil*) amurca *f*.
left *adj* sinister, laevus ♦ *n* sinistra *f*, laeva *f*; **on
the ~** ā laevā, ad laevam, ā sinistrā.
leg *n* crūs *nt*; (*of table*) pēs *m*.
legacy *n* lēgātum *nt*; ~ **hunter** captātor *m*.
legal *adj* lēgitimus.
legalize *vt* sancīre.
legally *adv* secundum lēgēs, lēge.
legate *n* lēgātus *m*.
legation *n* lēgātiō *f*.
legend *n* fābula *f*; (*inscription*) titulus *m*.
legendary *adj* fābulōsus.
legerdemain *n* praestīgiae *fpl*.
legging *n* ocrea *f*.
legible *adj* clārus.
legion *n* legiō *f*; **men of the 10th ~** decumānī
mpl.
legionary *n* legiōnārius *m*.
legislate *vi* lēgēs scrībere, lēgēs facere.
legislation *n* lēgēs *fpl*, lēgēs scrībendae.
legislator *n* lēgum scrīptor *m*.
legitimate *adj* lēgitimus.
legitimately *adv* lēgitimē.
leisure *n* ōtium *nt*; **at ~** ōtiōsus, vacuus; **have ~
for** vacāre (*dat*).
leisured *adj* ōtiōsus.
leisurely *adj* lentus.
lend *vt* commodāre, mūtuum dare; (*at interest*)
faenerārī; (*ear*) aurēs praebēre, admovēre; ~
a ready ear aurēs patefacere; ~ **assistance**
opem ferre.
length *n* longitūdō *f*; (*time*) diūturnitās *f*; **at ~**
tandem, dēmum, dēnique; (*speech*) cōpiōsē.
lengthen *vt* extendere; (*time*) prōtrahere;
(*sound*) prōdūcere.
lengthwise *adv* in longitūdinem.
lengthy *adj* longus, prōlixus.
leniency *n* clēmentia *f*.
lenient *adj* clēmēns, mītis.
leniently *adv* clēmenter.
lentil *n* lēns *f*.
leonine *adj* leōnīnus.
leopard *n* pardus *m*.
less *adj* minor ♦ *adv* minus; ~ **than** (*num*) intrā
(*acc*); **much ~, still ~** nēdum.
lessee *n* conductor *m*.
lessen *vt* minuere, imminuere, dēminuere ♦

vi dēcrēscere.
lesson *n* documentum *nt*; **be a ~ to** documentō
esse (*dat*); ~**s** *pl* dictāta *ntpl*; **give ~s** scholās
habēre; **give ~s in** docēre.
lessor *n* locātor *m*.
lest *conj* nē (+ *subj*).
let *vt* (*allow*) sinere; (*lease*) locāre; (*imper*) fac;
~ **alone** ōmittere; (*mention*) nē dīcam; ~
blood sanguinem mittere; ~ **down**
dēmittere; ~ **fall** ā manibus mittere; (*word*)
ēmittere; ~ **fly** ēmittere; ~ **go** mittere,
āmittere; (*ship*) solvere; ~ **in** admittere; ~
loose solvere; ~ **off** absolvere, ignōscere
(*dat*); ~ **oneself go** geniō indulgēre; ~ **out**
ēmittere; ~ **slip** āmittere, ōmittere.
lethal *adj* mortifer.
lethargic *adj* veternōsus.
lethargy *n* veternus *m*.
letter *n* epistula *f*, litterae *fpl*; (*of alphabet*)
littera *f*; **the ~ of the law** scrīptum *nt*; **to the ~**
ad praescrīptum; **by ~** per litterās; ~**s**
(*learning*) litterae *fpl*; **man of ~s** scrīptor *m*.
lettered *adj* litterātus.
lettuce *n* lactūca *f*.
levee *n* salūtātiō *f*.
level *adj* aequus, plānus ♦ *n* plānitiēs *f*;
(*instrument*) lībra *f*; **do one's ~ best** prō virīlī
parte agere; **put on a ~ with** exaequāre cum
♦ *vt* aequāre, adaequāre, inaequāre; (*to the
ground*) solō aequāre, sternere; (*weapon*)
intendere.
level-headed *adj* prūdēns.
levelled *adj* (*weapon*) īnfestus.
lever *n* vectis *m*.
levity *n* levitās *f*; (*fun*) iocī *mpl*, facētiae *fpl*.
levy *vt* (*troops*) scrībere; (*tax*) exigere ♦ *n*
dīlectus *m*.
lewd *adj* impudīcus.
lewdness *n* impudīcitia *f*.
liable *adj* obnoxius; **render ~** obligāre.
liaison *n* cōnsuētūdō *f*.
liar *n* mendāx *m*.
libel *n* probrum *nt*, calumnia *f* ♦ *vt* calumniārī.
libellous *adj* probrōsus, fāmōsus.
liberal *adj* līberālis; (*in giving*) largus,
benīgnus; ~ **education** bonae artēs *fpl*.
liberality *n* līberālitās *f*, largitās *f*.
liberally *adv* līberāliter, largē, benīgnē.
liberate *vt* līberāre; (*slave*) manū mittere.
liberation *n* līberātiō *f*.
liberator *n* līberātor *m*.
libertine *n* libīdinōsus *m*.
liberty *n* lībertās *f*; (*excess*) licentia *f*; **I am at ~
to** mihī licet (*inf*); **I am still at ~ to** integrum
est mihī (*inf*); **take a ~ with** licentius ūtī (*abl*),
familiārius sē gerere in (*acc*).
libidinous *adj* libīdinōsus.
librarian *n* librārius *m*.
library *n* bibliothēca *f*.
licence *n* (*permission*) potestās *f*; (*excess*)
licentia *f*.
license *vt* potestātem dare (*dat*).
licentious *adj* dissolūtus.

licentiousness n libīdō f, licentia f.
lick vt lambere; mulcēre.
lictor n lictor m.
lid n operculum nt.
lie n mendācium nt; **give the ~ to** redarguere; **tell a ~** mentīrī ♦ vi mentīrī; (*lie down*) iacēre; (*place*) situm esse; (*consist*) continērī; **as far as in me ~s** quantum in mē est; **~ at anchor** stāre; **~ between** interiacēre; **~ down** cubāre, discumbere; **~ heavy on** premere; **~ hid** latēre; **~ in wait** īnsidiārī; **~ low** dissimulāre; **~ on** incumbere (*dat*); **~ open** patēre; hiāre.
lien n nexus m.
lieu n: **in ~ of** locō (*gen*).
lieutenant n decuriō m; legātus m.
life n vīta f; (*in danger*) salūs f, caput nt; (*biography*) vīta f; (*breath*) anima f; (*RHET*) sanguis m; (*time*) aetās f; **come to ~ again** revīvīscere; **draw to the ~** exprimere; **for ~** aetātem; **matter of ~ and death** capitāle nt; **prime of ~** flōs aetātis; **way of ~** mōrēs mpl.
lifeblood n sanguis m.
life-giving adj almus, vītalis.
lifeguard n custōs m; (*emperor's*) praetōriānus m.
lifeless adj exanimis; (*style*) exsanguis.
lifelike adj expressus.
lifelong adj perpetuus.
lifetime n aetās f.
lift vt tollere, sublevāre; **~ up** efferre, attollere.
light n lūx f, lūmen nt; (*painting*) lūmen nt; **bring to ~** in lūcem prōferre; **see in a favourable ~** in meliōrem partem interpretārī; **throw ~ on** lūmen adhibēre (*dat*) ♦ vt accendere, incendere; (*illuminate*) illūstrāre, illūmināre; **be lit up** collūcēre ♦ vi: **~ upon** invenīre, offendere ♦ adj illūstris; (*movement*) agilis; (*weight*) levis; **grow ~** illūcēscere, dīlūcēscere; **make ~ of** parvī pendere.
light-armed adj expedītus.
lighten vi fulgurāre ♦ vt levāre.
lighter n linter f.
light-fingered adj tagāx.
light-footed adj celer, pernīx.
light-headed adj levis, volāticus.
light-hearted adj hilaris, laetus.
lightly adv leviter; pernīciter.
lightness n levitās f.
lightning n fulgur nt; (*striking*) fulmen nt; **be hit by ~** dē caelō percutī; **of ~** fulgurālis.
like adj similis, pār; **~ this** ad hunc modum ♦ adv similiter, sīcut, rītū (*gen*) ♦ vt amāre; **I ~** mihī placet, mē iuvat; **I ~ to** libet (*inf*); **I don't ~** nīl moror, mihī displicet; **look ~** similem esse, referre.
likelihood n vērī similitūdō f.
likely adj vērī similis ♦ adv sānē.
liken vt comparāre, aequiperāre.
likeness n imāgō f, īnstar nt, similitūdō f.
likewise adv item; (*also*) etiam.
liking n libīdō f, grātia f; **to one's ~** ex

sententiā.
lily n līlium nt.
limb n membrum nt, artus m.
lime n calx f; (*tree*) tilia f.
limelight n celebritās f; **enjoy the ~** mōnstrārī digitō.
limestone n calx f.
limit n fīnis m, terminus m, modus m; **mark the ~s of** dētermināre ♦ vt fīnīre, dēfinīre, termināre; (*restrict*) circumscrībere.
limitation n modus m.
limp adj mollis, flaccidus ♦ vi claudicāre.
limpid adj limpidus.
linden n tilia f.
line n līnea f; (*battle*) aciēs f; (*limit*) modus m; (*outline*) līneāmentum nt; (*writing*) versus m; **in a straight ~** ē regiōne; **~ of march** agmen nt; **read between the ~s** dissimulātā dispicere; **ship of the ~** nāvis longa; **write a ~** pauca scrībere ♦ vt (*street*) saepīre.
lineage n genus nt, stirps f.
lineal adj (*descent*) gentīlis.
lineaments n līneāmenta ntpl, ōris ductūs mpl.
linen n linteum nt ♦ adj linteus.
liner n nāvis f.
linger vi cunctārī, cessāre, dēmorārī.
lingering adj tardus ♦ n cunctātiō f.
linguist n: **be a ~** complūrēs linguās callēre.
link n ānulus m; (*fig*) nexus m, vinculum nt ♦ vt coniungere.
lintel n līmen superum nt.
lion n leō m; **~'s** leōnīnus; **~'s share** māior pars.
lioness n leaena f.
lip n lābrum nt; **be on everyone's ~s** in ōre omnium hominum esse, per omnium ōra ferrī.
lip service n: **pay ~ to** verbō tenus obsequī (*dat*).
liquefy vt liquefacere.
liquid adj liquidus ♦ n liquor m.
liquidate vt persolvere.
liquor n liquor m; vīnum nt.
lisp vi balbūtīre.
lisping adj blaesus.
lissom adj agilis.
list n index m, tabula f; (*ship*) inclīnātiō f ♦ vt scrībere ♦ vi (*lean*) sē inclīnāre; (*listen*) auscultāre; (*wish*) cupere.
listen vi auscultāre; **~ to** auscultāre, audīre.
listener n audītor m, auscultātor m.
listless adj languidus.
listlessness n languor m.
literally adv ad verbum.
literary adj (*man*) litterātus; **~ pursuits** litterae fpl, studia ntpl.
literature n litterae fpl.
lithe adj mollis, agilis.
litigant n lītigātor m.
litigate vi lītigāre.
litigation n līs f.
litigious adj lītigiōsus.
litter n (*carriage*) lectīca f; (*brood*) fētus m; (*straw*) strāmentum nt; (*mess*) strāgēs f ♦ vt

sternere; (*young*) parere.
little *adj* parvus, exiguus; (*time*) brevis; **very ~** perexiguus, minimus; **~ boy** puerulus *m* ♦ *n* paulum *nt*, aliquantulum *nt*; **for a ~** paulisper, parumper; **~ or nothing** vix quicquam ♦ *adv* paulum, nōnnihil; (*with comp*) paulō; **~ by ~** paulātim, sēnsim, gradātim; **think ~ of** parvī aestimāre; **too ~** parum (*+ gen*).
littleness *n* exiguitās *f*.
littoral *n* lītus *nt*.
live *vi* vīvere, vītam agere; (*dwell*) habitāre; **~ down** (*reproach*) ēluere; **~ on** (*food*) vescī (*abl*) ♦ *adj* vīvus.
livelihood *n* vīctus *m*.
liveliness *n* alacritās *f*, hilaritās *f*.
livelong *adj* tōtus.
lively *adj* alacer, hilaris.
liven *vt* exhilarāre.
liver *n* iecur *nt*.
livery *n* vestis famulāris *f*.
livid *adj* līvidus; **be ~** līvēre.
living *adj* vīvus ♦ *n* vīctus *m*; (*earning*) quaestus *m*.
lizard *n* lacerta *f*.
lo *interj* ecce.
load *n* onus *nt* ♦ *vt* onerāre.
loaf *n* pānis *m* ♦ *vi* grassārī.
loafer *n* grassātor *m*.
loam *n* lutum *nt*.
loan *n* mūtuum *nt*, mūtua pecūnia *f*.
loathe *vt* fastīdīre, ōdisse.
loathing *n* fastīdium *nt*.
loathsome *adj* odiōsus, taeter.
lobby *n* vestibulum *nt*.
lobe *n* fibra *f*.
lobster *n* astacus *m*.
local *adj* indigena, locī.
locality *n* locus *m*.
locate *vt* reperīre; **be ~d** situm esse.
location *n* situs *m*.
loch *n* lacus *m*.
lock *n* (*door*) sera *f*; (*hair*) coma *f* ♦ *vt* obserāre.
locomotion *n* mōtus *m*.
locust *n* locusta *f*.
lodge *n* casa *f* ♦ *vi* dēversārī ♦ *vt* īnfīgere; (*complaint*) dēferre.
lodger *n* inquilīnus *m*.
lodging *n* hospitium *nt*, dēversōrium *nt*.
loft *n* cēnāculum *nt*.
loftiness *n* altitūdō *f*, sublīmitās *f*.
lofty *adj* excelsus, sublīmis.
log *n* stīpes *m*; (*fuel*) lignum *nt*.
loggerhead *n*: **be at ~s** rixārī.
logic *n* dialecticē *f*.
logical *adj* dialecticus, ratiōne frētus.
logically *adv* ex ratiōne.
logician *n* dialecticus *m*.
loin *n* lumbus *m*.
loiter *vi* grassārī, cessāre.
loiterer *n* grassātor *m*, cessātor *m*.
loll *vi* recumbere.
lone *adj* sōlus, sōlitārius.
loneliness *n* sōlitūdō *f*.

lonely, lonesome *adj* sōlitārius.
long *adj* longus; (*hair*) prōmissus; (*syllable*) prōductus; (*time*) longus, diūturnus; **in the ~ run** aliquandō; **for a ~ time** diū; **to make a ~ story short** nē longum sit, nē longum faciam ♦ *adv* diū; **~ ago** iamprīdem, iamdūdum; **as ~ as** *conj* dum; **before ~** mox; **for ~** diū; **how ~** quamdiū, quōusque; **I have ~ been wishing** iam prīdem cupiō; **not ~ after** haud multō post; **any ~er** diūtius; (*distance*) longius; **no ~er** nōn iam ♦ *vi*: **~ for** dēsīderāre, exoptāre, expetere; **~ to** gestīre.
longevity *n* vīvācitās *f*.
longing *n* dēsīderium *nt*, cupīdō *f* ♦ *adj* avidus.
longingly *adv* avidē.
longitudinally *adv* in longitūdinem.
long-lived *adj* vīvāx.
long-suffering *adj* patiēns.
long-winded *adj* verbōsus, longus.
longwise *adv* in longitūdinem.
look *n* aspectus *m*; (*expression*) vultus *m* ♦ *vi* aspicere; (*seem*) vidērī, speciem praebēre; **~ about** circumspicere; **~ after** prōvidēre (*dat*), cūrāre; **~ at** spectāre ad (*+ acc*), aspicere, intuērī; (*with mind*) contemplārī; **~ back** respicere; **~ down** dēspectāre; (*fig*) dēspicere; **~ for** quaerere, petere; **~ forward to** exspectāre; **~ here** heus tu, ehodum; **~ into** īnspicere, intrōspicere; **~ out** prōspicere; (*beware*) cavēre; **~ round** circumspicere; **~ through** perspicere; **~ to** ratiōnem habēre (*gen*); (*leader*) spem pōnere in (*abl*); **~ towards** spectāre ad; **~ up** suspicere; **~ up to** suspicere; **~ upon** habēre.
looker-on *n* arbiter *m*.
lookout *n* (*place*) specula *f*; (*man*) vigil *m*, excubiae *fpl*.
looks *npl* speciēs *f*; **good ~** fōrma *f*, pulchritūdō *f*.
loom *n* tēla *f* ♦ *vi* in cōnspectum sē dare.
loop *n* orbis *m*, sinus *m*.
loophole *n* fenestra *f*.
loose *adj* laxus, solūtus, remissus; (*morally*) dissolūtus; **let ~ on** immittere in (*acc*) ♦ *vt* (*undo*) solvere; (*slacken*) laxāre.
loosely *adv* solūtē, remissē.
loosen *vt* (re)solvere; (*structure*) labefacere.
looseness *n* dissolūtiō *f*, dissolūtī mōrēs *mpl*.
loot *n* praeda *f*, rapīna *f*.
lop *vt* amputāre.
lopsided *adj* inaequālis.
loquacious *adj* loquāx.
loquacity *n* loquācitās *f*.
lord *n* dominus *m* ♦ *vi*: **~ it** dominārī.
lordliness *n* superbia *f*.
lordly *adj* superbus; (*rank*) nōbilis.
lordship *n* dominātiō *f*, imperium *nt*.
lore *n* litterae *fpl*, doctrīna *f*.
lose *vt* āmittere, perdere; **~ an eye** alterō oculō capī; **~ heart** animum dēspondēre; **~ one's way** deerrāre ♦ *vi* (*in contest*) vincī.
loss *n* damnum *nt*, dētrīmentum *nt*; **be at a ~** haerēre, haesitāre; **suffer ~** damnum

accipere, facere; ~**es** (*in battle*) caesī *mpl*.
lost *adj* āmissus, absēns; **be** ~ perīre, interīre;
give up for ~ dēplōrāre.
lot *n* sors *f*; **be assigned by** ~ sorte obvenīre;
draw a ~ sortem dūcere; draw ~s for sortīrī;
a ~ **of** multus, plūrimus.
loth *adj* invītus.
lottery *n* sortēs *fpl*; (*fig*) ālea *f*.
lotus *n* lōtos *f*.
loud *adj* clārus, māgnus.
loudly *adv* māgnā vōce.
loudness *n* māgna vōx *f*.
lounge *vi* ōtiārī.
louse *n* pedis *m/f*.
lout *n* agrestis *m*.
lovable *adj* amābilis.
love *n* amor *m*; **be hopelessly in** ~ dēperīre; **fall
in** ~ **with** adamāre ♦ *vt* amāre, dīligere; **I** ~ **to**
mē iuvat (*inf*).
love affair *n* amor *m*.
loveless *adj* amōre carēns.
loveliness *n* grātia *f*, venustās *f*.
lovely *adj* pulcher, amābilis, venustus.
love poem *n* carmen amātōrium *nt*.
lover *n* amāns *m*, amātor *m*.
lovesick *adj* amōre aeger.
loving *adj* amāns.
lovingly *adv* amanter.
low *adj* humilis; (*birth*) ignōbilis; (*price*) vīlis;
(*sound*) gravis; (*spirits*) dēmissus; (*voice*)
dēmissus; **at** ~ **water** aestūs dēcessū; **be** ~
iacēre; **lay** ~ interficere ♦ *vi* mūgīre.
lower *adj* īnferior; **the** ~ **world** īnferī *mpl*; **of
the** ~ **world** īnfernus ♦ *adv* īnferius ♦ *vt*
dēmittere, dēprimere ♦ *vi* (*cloud*) obscūrārī,
minārī.
lowering *adj* mināx.
lowest *adj* īnfimus, īmus.
lowing *n* mūgītus *m*.
lowland *adj* campestris.
lowlands *n* campī *mpl*.
lowliness *n* humilitās *f*.
lowly *adj* humilis, obscūrus.
low-lying *adj* dēmisssus; **be** ~ sedēre.
lowness *n* humilitās *f*; (*spirit*) tristitia *f*.
loyal *adj* fidēlis, fīdus; (*citizen*) bonus.
loyally *adv* fidēliter.
loyalty *n* fidēs *f*, fidēlitās *f*.
lubricate *vt* ungere.
lucid *adj* clārus, perspicuus.
lucidity *n* perspicuitās *f*.
lucidly *adv* clārē, perspicuē.
luck *n* fortūna *f*, fors *f*; **good** ~ fēlicitās *f*; **bad** ~
īnfortūnium *nt*.
luckily *adv* fēlīciter, faustē, prosperē.
luckless *adj* īnfēlīx.
lucky *adj* fēlīx, fortūnātus; (*omen*) faustus.
lucrative *adj* quaestuōsus.
lucre *n* lucrum *nt*, quaestus *m*.
lucubration *n* lūcubrātiō *f*.
ludicrous *adj* rīdiculus.
ludicrously *adv* rīdiculē.
lug *vt* trahere.

luggage *n* impedīmenta *ntpl*, sarcina *f*.
lugubrious *adj* lūgubris, maestus.
lukewarm *adj* tepidus; (*fig*) segnis, neglegēns;
be ~ tepēre.
lukewarmly *adv* segniter, neglegenter.
lukewarmness *n* tepor *m*; (*fig*) neglegentia *f*,
incūria *f*.
lull *vt* sōpīre; (*storm*) sēdāre ♦ *n* intermissiō *f*.
lumber *n* scrūta *ntpl*.
luminary *n* lūmen *nt*, astrum *nt*.
luminous *adj* lūcidus, illūstris.
lump *n* massa *f*; (*on body*) tuber *nt*.
lumpish *adj* hebes, crassus, stolidus.
lunacy *n* īnsānia *f*.
lunar *adj* lūnāris.
lunatic *n* īnsānus *m*.
lunch *n* prandium *nt* ♦ *vi* prandēre.
lung *n* pulmō *m*; *pl* (*ANAT*) latera *ntpl*.
lunge *n* ictus *m* ♦ *vi* prōsilīre.
lurch *n*: **leave in the** ~ dērelinquere, dēstituere
♦ *vi* titubāre.
lure *n* esca *f* ♦ *vt* allicere, illicere, ēlicere.
lurid *adj* lūridus.
lurk *vi* latēre, latitāre, dēlitēscere.
luscious *adj* praedulcis.
lush *adj* luxuriōsus.
lust *n* libīdō *f* ♦ *vi* libīdine flagrāre,
concupīscere.
lustful *adj* libīdinōsus.
lustily *adv* validē, strēnuē.
lustiness *n* vigor *m*, nervī *mpl*.
lustration *n* lūstrum *nt*.
lustre *n* fulgor *m*, splendor *m*.
lustrous *adj* illūstris.
lusty *adj* validus, lacertōsus.
lute *n* cithara *f*, fidēs *fpl*.
lute player *n* citharista *m*, citharistria *f*,
fidicen *m*, fidicina *f*.
luxuriance *n* luxuria *f*.
luxuriant *adj* luxuriōsus.
luxuriate *vi* luxuriārī.
luxuries *pl* lautitiae *fpl*.
luxurious *adj* luxuriōsus, sūmptuōsus, lautus.
luxuriously *adv* sūmptuōsē, lautē.
luxury *n* luxuria *f*, luxus *m*.
lynx *n* lynx *m/f*; ~**-eyed** lyncēus.
lyre *n* lyra *f*, fidēs *fpl*; **play the** ~ fidibus canere.
lyric *adj* lyricus ♦ *n* carmen *nt*.
lyrist *n* fidicen *m*, fidicina *f*.

M, m

mace *n* scīpiō *m*.
machination *n* dolus *m*.
machine *n* māchina *f*.

mackerel n scomber m.

mad adj īnsānus, furiōsus, vēcors, dēmēns; **be ~** īnsānīre, furere.

madam n domina f.

madden vt furiāre, mentem aliēnāre (dat).

madly adv insānē, furiōsē, dēmenter.

madness n īnsānia f, furor m, dēmentia f; (animals) rabiēs f.

maelstrom n vertex m.

magazine n horreum nt, apothēca f.

maggot n vermiculus m.

magic adj magicus ♦ n magicae artēs fpl.

magician n magus m, veneficus m.

magistracy n magistrātus m.

magistrate n magistrātus m.

magnanimity n māgnanimitās f, līberalitās f.

magnanimous adj generōsus, līberālis, māgnanimus.

magnet n magnēs m.

magnificence n māgnificentia f, adparātus m.

magnificent adj māgnificus, amplus, splendidus.

magnificently adv māgnificē, amplē, splendidē.

magnify vt amplificāre, exaggerāre.

magnitude n māgnitūdō f.

magpie n pīca f.

maid n virgō f; (servant) ancilla f.

maiden n virgō f.

maidenhood n virginitās f.

maidenly adj virginālis.

mail n (armour) lōrīca f; (letters) epistulae fpl.

maim vt mutilāre.

maimed adj mancus.

main adj prīnceps, prīmus; **~ point** caput nt ♦ n (sea) altum nt, pelagus nt; **with might and ~** manibus pedibusque, omnibus nervīs.

mainland n continēns f.

mainly adv praecipuē, plērumque.

maintain vt (keep) tenēre, servāre; (keep up) sustinēre; (keep alive) alere, sustentāre; (argue) adfirmāre, dēfendere.

maintenance n (food) alimentum nt.

majestic adj augustus, māgnificus.

majestically adv augustē.

majesty n māiestās f.

major adj māior.

majority n māior pars f, plērīque; **have attained one's ~** suī iūris esse.

make vt facere, fingere; (appointment) creāre; (bed) sternere; (cope) superāre; (compulsion) cōgere; (consequence) efficere; (craft) fabricārī; (harbour) capere; (living) quaerere; (sum) efficere; (with adj) reddere; (with verb) cōgere; **~ away with** tollere, interimere; **~ good** supplēre, resarcīre; **~ light of** parvī facere; **~ one's way** iter facere; **~ much of** māgnī aestimāre, multum tribuere (dat); **~ for** petere; **~ out** arguere; **~ over** dēlēgāre, trānsferre; **~ ready** parāre; **~ a speech** orātiōnem habēre; **~ a truce** indutiās compōnere; **~ war on** bellum inferre; **~ up** (loss) supplēre; (total) efficere; (story)

fingere; **be made** fierī.

make-believe n simulātiō f.

maker n fabricātor m, auctor m.

make-up n medicāmina ntpl.

maladministration n (charge) repetundae fpl.

malady n morbus m.

malcontent adj novārum rērum cupidus.

male adj mās, māsculus.

malefactor n nocēns m, reus m.

malevolence n malevolentia f.

malevolent adj malevolus, malignus.

malevolently adv malignē.

malformation n dēprāvātiō f.

malice n invidia f, malevolentia f; **bear ~ towards** invidēre (dat).

malicious adj invidiōsus, malevolus, malignus.

maliciously adv malignē.

malign adj malignus, invidiōsus ♦ vt obtrectāre.

malignant adj malevolus.

maligner n obtrectātor m.

malignity n malevolentia f.

malleable adj ductilis.

mallet n malleus m.

mallow n malva f.

malpractices n dēlicta ntpl.

maltreat vt laedere, vexāre.

malversation n pecūlātus m.

man n (human being) homō m/f; (male) vir m; (MIL) mīles m; (chess) latrunculus m; **to a ~** omnēs ad ūnum; **~ who** is qui; **old ~** senex m; **young ~** adulēscēns m; **~ of war** nāvis longa f ♦ vt (ship) complēre; (walls) praesidiō firmāre.

manacle n manicae fpl ♦ vt manicās inicere (dat).

manage vt efficere, gerere, gubernāre, administrāre; (horse) moderārī; (with verb) posse.

manageable adj tractābilis, habilis.

management n administrātiō f, cūra f; (finance) dispēnsātiō f.

manager n administrātor m, moderātor m; dispēnsātor m.

mandate n mandātum nt.

mane n iuba f.

manful adj virīlis, fortis.

manfully adv virīliter, fortiter.

manger n praesēpe nt.

mangle vt dīlaniāre, lacerāre.

mangy adj scaber.

manhood n pūbertās f, toga virīlis f.

mania n īnsānia f.

maniac n furiōsus m.

manifest adj manifestus, apertus, clārus ♦ vt dēclārāre, aperīre.

manifestation n speciēs f.

manifestly adv manifestō, apertē.

manifesto n ēdictum nt.

manifold adj multiplex, varius.

manikin n homunciō m, homunculus m.

manipulate vt tractāre.

manipulation *n* tractātiō *f.*
mankind *n* hominēs *mpl*, genus hūmānum *nt.*
manliness *n* virtūs *f.*
manly *adj* fortis, virīlis.
manner *n* modus *m*, ratiō *f*; (*custom*) mōs *m*,
  ūsus *m*; ~s *pl* mōrēs *mpl*; **after the ~ of** rītū,
  mōre (*gen*); **good ~s** hūmānitās *f*, modestia *f.*
mannered *adj* mōrātus.
mannerism *n* mōs *m.*
mannerly *adj* bene mōrātus, urbānus.
manoeuvre *n* (MIL) dēcursus *m*, dēcursiō *f*; (*fig*)
  dolus *m* ♦ *vi* dēcurrere; (*fig*) māchinārī.
manor *n* praedium *nt.*
mansion *n* domus *f.*
manslaughter *n* homicīdium *nt.*
mantle *n* pallium *nt*; (*women's*) palla *f.*
manual *adj*: ~ **labour** opera *f* ♦ *n* libellus *m*, ars
  f.
manufacture *n* fabrica *f* ♦ *vt* fabricārī.
manumission *n* manūmissiō *f.*
manumit *vt* manū mittere, ēmancipāre.
manure *n* fimus *m*, stercus *nt* ♦ *vt* stercorāre.
manuscript *n* liber *m*, cōdex *m.*
many *adj* multī; **as ~ as** tot ... quot; **how ~?**
  quot?; **so ~** tot; **in ~ places** multifāriam; **a**
  good ~ complūrēs; **too ~** nimis multī; **the ~**
  vulgus *nt*; **very ~** permultī, plūrimī.
map *n* tabula *f* ♦ *vt*: ~ **out** dēscrībere,
  dēsignāre.
maple *n* acer *nt* ♦ *adj* acernus.
mar *vt* corrumpere, dēfōrmāre.
marauder *n* praedātor *m*, dēpopulātor *m.*
marble *n* marmor *nt* ♦ *adj* marmoreus.
March *n* mēnsis Martius *m*; **of ~** Martius.
march *n* iter *nt*; **line of ~** agmen *nt*; **by forced**
  ~es māgnīs itineribus; **on the ~** ex itinere, in
  itinere; **quick ~** plēnō gradū; **a regular day's ~**
  iter iūstum *nt* ♦ *vi* contendere, iter facere,
  incēdere, īre; ~ **out** exīre; ~ **on** signa
  prōferre, prōgredī ♦ *vt* dūcere; ~ **out**
  ēdūcere; ~ **in** intrōdūcere.
mare *n* equa *f.*
margin *n* margō *f*; (*fig*) discrīmen *nt.*
marigold *n* caltha *f.*
marine *adj* marīnus ♦ *n* mīles classicus *m.*
mariner *n* nauta *m.*
marital *adj* marītus.
maritime *adj* maritimus.
marjoram *n* amāracus *m.*
mark *n* nota *f*; (*of distinction*) īnsigne *nt*; (*target*)
  scopos *m*; (*trace*) vestīgium *nt*; **nihil the ~**
  nihil ad rem; **it is the ~ of a wise man to**
  sapientis est (*inf*); **be wide of the ~** errāre ♦
  vt notāre, dēsignāre; (*observe*)
  animadvertere, animum attendere; ~ **out**
  (*site*) mētārī, dēsignāre; (*for purpose*)
  dēnotāre.
marked *adj* īnsignis, manifestus.
markedly *adv* manifestō.
marker *n* index *m.*
market *n* macellum *nt*; ~ **day** nūndinae *fpl*; ~
  town emporium *nt*; **cattle ~** forum boārium
  nt; **fish ~** forum piscārium *nt.*

marketable *adj* vēndibilis.
marketplace *n* forum *nt.*
market prices *npl* annōna *f.*
market town *n* emporium *nt.*
marking *n* macula *f.*
maroon *vt* dērelinquere.
marriage *n* mātrimōnium *nt*, coniugium *nt*;
  (*ceremony*) nūptiae *fpl*; **give in ~** collocāre; ~
  bed lectus geniālis *m.*
marriageable *adj* nūbilis.
marrow *n* medulla *f.*
marry *vt* (*a wife*) dūcere, in mātrimōnium
  dūcere; (*a husband*) nūbere (*dat*).
marsh *n* palūs *f.*
marshal *n* imperātor *m* ♦ *vt* īnstruere.
marshy *adj* palūster.
mart *n* forum *nt.*
marten *n* mēlēs *f.*
martial *adj* bellicōsus, ferōx.
martyr *n* dēvōtus *m*; (ECCL) martyr *m/f.*
marvel *n* mīrāculum *nt*, portentum *nt* ♦ *vi*
  mīrārī; ~ **at** admīrārī.
marvellous *adj* mīrus, mīrificus, mīrābilis.
marvellously *adv* mīrē, mīrum quantum.
masculine *adj* mās, virīlis.
mash *n* farrāgō *f* ♦ *vt* commiscēre,
  contundere.
mask *n* persōna *f* ♦ *vt* persōnam induere (*dat*);
  (*fig*) dissimulāre.
mason *n* structor *m.*
masonry *n* lapidēs *mpl*, caementum *nt.*
masquerade *n* simulātiō *f* ♦ *vi* vestem
  mūtāre; ~ **as** speciem sibi induere (*gen*),
  persōnam ferre (*gen*).
mass *n* mōlēs *f*; (*of small things*) congeriēs *f*; (*of*
  people) multitūdō *f*; (ECCL) missa *f*; **the ~es**
  vulgus *nt*, plēbs *f* ♦ *vt* congerere, coacervāre.
massacre *n* strāgēs *f*, caedēs *f*, interneciō *f* ♦
  vt trucīdāre.
massive *adj* ingēns, solidus.
massiveness *n* mōlēs *f*, soliditās *f.*
mast *n* mālus *m.*
master *n* dominus *m*; (*school*) magister *m*; **be ~**
  of dominārī in (*abl*); (*skill*) perītum esse
  (*gen*); **become ~ of** potīrī (*abl*); **be one's own**
  ~ suī iūris esse; **not ~ of** impotēns (*gen*); **a**
  past ~ veterātor *m* ♦ *vt* dēvincere; (*skill*)
  ēdiscere; (*passion*) continēre.
masterful *adj* imperiōsus.
masterly *adj* doctus, perītus.
masterpiece *n* praeclārum opus *nt.*
mastery *n* dominātiō *f*, imperium *nt*,
  arbitrium *nt.*
masticate *vt* mandere.
mastiff *n* Molossus *m.*
mat *n* storea *f.*
match *n* (*person*) pār *m/f*; (*marriage*) nūptiae *fpl*;
  (*contest*) certāmen *nt*; **a ~ for** pār (*dat*); **no ~**
  for impār (*dat*) ♦ *vt* exaequāre, adaequāre ♦
  vi congruere.
matchless *adj* singulāris, ūnicus.
mate *n* socius *m*; (*married*) coniunx *m/f* ♦ *vi*
  coniungī.

material adj corporeus; (*significant*) haud levis
♦ n māteriēs f; (*literary*) silva f.
materialize vi ēvenīre.
materially adv māgnopere.
maternal adj māternus.
mathematical adj mathēmaticus.
mathematician n mathēmaticus m,
geōmetrēs m.
mathematics n ars mathēmatica f, numerī
mpl.
matin adj mātūtīnus.
matricide n (*act*) mātricīdium nt; (*person*)
mātricīda m.
matrimony n mātrimōnium nt.
matrix n fōrma f.
matron n mātrōna f.
matter n māteria f, corpus nt; (*affair*) rēs f; (MED)
pūs nt; **what is the ~ with you?** quid tibī est?
vi: **it ~s** interest, rēfert.
matting n storea f.
mattock n dolābra f.
mattress n culcita f.
mature adj mātūrus; (*age*) adultus ♦ vi
mātūrēscere.
maturity n mātūritās f; (*age*) adulta aetās f.
maul n fistūca f ♦ vt contundere, dīlaniāre.
maw n ingluviēs f.
mawkish adj pūtidus.
mawkishly adv pūtidē.
maxim n dictum nt, praeceptum nt, sententia f.
maximum adj quam māximus, quam
plūrimus.
May n mēnsis Māius m; **of ~** Māius.
may vi posse; **I ~** licet mihī.
mayor n praefectus m.
maze n labyrinthus m.
mead n (*drink*) mulsum nt; (*land*) prātum nt.
meagre adj exīlis, iēiūnus.
meagrely adv exīliter, iēiūnē.
meagreness n exīlitās f.
meal n (*flour*) farīna f; (*repast*) cibus m.
mealy-mouthed adj blandiloquus.
mean adj humilis, abiectus; (*birth*) ignōbilis;
(*average*) medius, mediocris ♦ n modus m,
mediocritās f ♦ vt dīcere, significāre; (*word*)
valēre; (*intent*) velle, in animō habēre.
meander vi sinuōsō cursū fluere.
meaning n significātiō f, vīs f, sententia f;
what is the ~ of? quid sibī vult?, quōrsum
spectat?.
meanly adv abiectē, humiliter.
meanness n humilitās f; (*conduct*) illīberālitās
f, avāritia f.
means n īnstrūmentum nt; (*of doing*) facultās
f; (*wealth*) opēs fpl; **by ~ of** per (acc); **by all ~**
māximē; **by no ~** nūllō modō, haudquāquam;
of small ~ pauper.
meantime, meanwhile adv intereā, interim.
measles n boa f.
measure n modus m, mēnsūra f; (*rhythm*)
numerī mpl; (*plan*) cōnsilium nt; (*law*) rogātiō
f, lēx f; **beyond ~** nimium; **in some ~** aliquā ex
parte; **take ~s** cōnsulere; **take the ~ of** quālis

sit cognōscere; **without ~** immoderātē ♦ vt
mētīrī; **~ out** dīmētīrī; (*land*) mētārī.
measured adj moderātus.
measureless adj īnfīnītus, immēnsus.
measurement n mēnsūra f.
meat n carō f.
mechanic n opifex m, faber m.
mechanical adj mēchanicus.
mechanical device māchinātiō f.
mechanics n māchinālis scientia f.
mechanism n māchinātiō f.
medal n īnsigne nt.
meddle vi sē interpōnere.
meddlesome adj cūriōsus.
Medes n Mīdī mpl.
mediate vi intercēdere; **~ between**
compōnere, conciliāre.
mediator n intercessor m, dēprecātor m.
medical adj medicus.
medicate vt medicāre.
medicinal adj medicus, salūbris.
medicine n (*art*) medicīna f; (*drug*)
medicāmentum nt.
medicine chest n narthēcium nt.
mediocre adj mediocris.
mediocrity n mediocritās f.
meditate vi meditārī, cōgitāre, sēcum
volūtāre.
meditation n cōgitātiō f, meditātiō f.
medium n internūntius m; (*means*) modus m ♦
adj mediocris.
medley n farrāgō f.
meek adj mītis, placidus.
meekly adv summissō animō.
meet adj idōneus, aptus ♦ n conventus m ♦ vi
convenīre ♦ vt obviam īre (dat), occurrere
(dat); (*fig*) obīre; **~ with** invenīre, excipere.
meeting n cōnsilium nt, conventus m.
melancholic adj melancholicus.
melancholy n ātra bīlis f; tristitia f, maestitia f
♦ adj tristis, maestus.
mêlée n turba f, concursus m.
mellow adj mītis; (*wine*) lēnis; **become ~**
mītēscere; **make ~** mītigāre.
mellowness n mātūritās f.
melodious adj canōrus, numerōsus.
melodiously adv numerōsē.
melody n melos nt, modī mpl.
melt vt liquefacere, dissolvere; (*fig*) movēre ♦
vi liquēscere, dissolvī; (*fig*) commovērī; **~
away** dēliquēscere.
member n membrum nt; (*person*) socius m.
membrane n membrāna f.
memento n monumentum nt.
memoir n commentārius m.
memorable adj memorābilis,
commemorābilis.
memorandum n hypomnēma nt.
memorial n monumentum nt.
memorize vt ēdiscere.
memory n memoria f; **from ~** memoriter.
menace n minae fpl ♦ vt minārī, minitārī;
(*things*) imminēre (dat).

menacing *adj* mināx.
menacingly *adv* mināciter.
menage *n* familia *f*.
mend *vt* sarcīre, reficere ♦ *vi* meliōrem fierī; (*health*) convalēscere.
mendacious *adj* mendāx.
mendacity *n* mendācium *nt*.
mendicant *n* mendīcus *m*.
mendicity *n* mendīcitās *f*.
menial *adj* servīlis, famulāris ♦ *n* servus *m*, famulus *m*.
menstrual *adj* mēnstruus.
mensuration *n* mētiendī ratiō *f*.
mental *adj* cōgitātiōnis, mentis.
mentality *n* animī adfectus *m*, mēns *f*.
mentally *adv* cōgitātiōne, mente.
mention *n* mentiō *f* ♦ *vt* memorāre, mentiōnem facere (*gen*); (*casually*) inicere; (*briefly*) attingere; **omit to ~** praetermittere.
mentor *n* auctor *m*, praeceptor *m*.
mercantile *adj* mercātōrius.
mercenary *adj* mercennārius, vēnālis ♦ *n* mercennārius mīles *m*.
merchandise *n* mercēs *fpl*.
merchant *n* mercātor *m*.
merchantman *n* nāvis onerāria *f*.
merchant ship *n* nāvis onerāria *f*.
merciful *adj* misericors, clēmens.
mercifully *adv* clēmenter.
merciless *adj* immisericors, inclēmens, inhūmānus.
mercilessly *adv* inhūmānē.
mercurial *adj* hilaris.
mercy *n* misericordia *f*, clēmentia *f*, venia *f*; **at the ~ of** obnoxius (*dat*), in manū (*gen*).
mere *n* lacus *m* ♦ *adj* merus, ipse.
merely *adv* sōlum, tantum, dumtaxat.
meretricious *adj* meretricius; **~ attractions** lēnōcinia *ntpl*.
merge *vt* cōnfundere ♦ *vi* cōnfundī.
meridian *n* merīdiēs *m* ♦ *adj* merīdiānus.
merit *n* meritum *nt*, virtūs *f* ♦ *vt* merērī.
meritorious *adj* laudābilis.
meritoriously *adv* optimē.
mermaid *n* nympha *f*.
merrily *adv* hilare, festīvē.
merriment *n* hilaritās *f*, festīvitās *f*.
merry *adj* hilaris, festīvus; **make ~** lūdere.
merrymaking *n* lūdus *m*, festīvitās *f*.
mesh *n* macula *f*.
mess *n* (*dirt*) sordēs *f*, squālor *m*; (*trouble*) turba *f*; (*food*) cibus *m*; (*MIL*) contubernālēs *mpl*.
message *n* nūntius *m*.
messenger *n* nūntius *m*.
messmate *n* contubernālis *m*.
metal *n* metallum *nt* ♦ *adj* ferreus, aereus.
metamorphose *vt* mūtāre, trānsfōrmāre.
metamorphosis *n* mūtātiō *f*.
metaphor *n* trānslātiō *f*.
metaphorical *adj* trānslātus.
metaphorically *adv* per trānslātiōnem.
metaphysics *n* dialectica *ntpl*.

mete *vt* mētīrī.
meteor *n* fax caelestis *f*.
meteorology *n* prognōstica *ntpl*.
methinks *vi*: **~ I am** mihī videor esse.
method *n* ratiō *f*, modus *m*.
methodical *adj* dispositus; (*person*) dīligēns.
methodically *adv* dispositē.
meticulous *adj* accūrātus.
meticulously *adv* accūrātē.
meticulousness *n* cūra *f*.
metonymy *n* immūtātiō *f*.
metre *n* numerī *mpl*, modī *mpl*.
metropolis *n* urbs *f*.
mettle *n* ferōcitās *f*, virtūs *f*.
mettlesome *adj* ferōx, animōsus.
mew *n* (*bird*) larus *m*; **~s** *pl* stabula *ntpl* ♦ *vi* vāgīre.
miasma *n* hālitus *m*.
mid *adj* medius ♦ *prep* inter (*acc*).
midday *n* merīdiēs *m* ♦ *adj* merīdiānus.
middle *adj* medius ♦ *n* medium *nt*; **in the ~** medius, in mediō; **~ of** medius.
middling *adj* mediocris.
midge *n* culex *m*.
midget *n* pūmiliō *m/f*.
midland *adj* mediterrāneus.
midnight *n* media nox *f*.
midriff *n* praecordia *ntpl*.
midst *n* medium *nt*; **in the ~** medius; **in the ~ of** inter (*acc*); **through the ~ of** per medium.
midsummer *n* sōlstitium *nt* ♦ *adj* sōlstitiālis.
midway *adv* medius.
midwife *n* obstetrix *f*.
midwinter *n* brūma *f* ♦ *adj* brūmālis.
mien *n* aspectus *m*, vultus *m*.
might *n* vīs *f*, potentia *f*; **with ~ and main** omnibus nervīs, manibus pedibusque.
mightily *adv* valdē, magnopere.
mighty *adj* ingēns, validus.
migrate *vi* abīre, migrāre.
migration *n* peregrīnātiō *f*.
migratory *adj* advena.
mild *adj* mītis, lēnis, clēmēns.
mildew *n* rōbīgō *f*.
mildly *adv* lēniter, clēmenter.
mildness *n* clēmentia *f*, mānsuētūdō *f*; (*weather*) caelī indulgentia *f*.
mile *n* mīlle passūs *mpl*; **~s** *pl* mīlia passuum.
milestone *n* lapis *m*, mīliārium *nt*.
militant *adj* ferōx.
military *adj* mīlitāris ♦ *n* mīlitēs *mpl*.
military service *n* mīlitia *f*.
militate *vi*: **~ against** repugnāre (*dat*), facere contrā (*acc*).
militia *n* mīlitēs *mpl*.
milk *n* lac *nt* ♦ *vt* mulgēre.
milk pail *n* mulctra *f*.
milky *adj* lacteus.
mill *n* pistrīnum *nt*.
milled *adj* (*coin*) serrātus.
millennium *n* mīlle annī *mpl*.
miller *n* pistor *m*.
millet *n* mīlium *nt*.

million *num* deciēs centēna mīlia *ntpl*.
millionaire *n* rēx *m*.
millstone *n* mola *f*, molāris *m*.
mime *n* mīmus *m*.
mimic *n* imitātor *m*, imitātrīx *f* ♦ *vt* imitārī.
mimicry *n* imitātiō *f*.
minatory *adj* mināx.
mince *vt* concīdere; **not ~ words** plānē
apertēque dīcere ♦ *n* minūtal *nt*.
mind *n* mēns *f*, animus *m*, ingenium *nt*;
(*opinion*) sententia *f*; (*memory*) memoria *f*; **be
in one's right ~** mentis suae esse; **be of the
same ~** eadem sentīre; **be out of one's ~**
īnsanīre; **bear in ~** meminisse (*gen*),
memorem esse (*gen*); **call to ~** memoriā
repetere, recordārī; **have a ~ to** libet; **have in
~** in animō habēre; **put one's ~ to** animum
applicāre ad (+ *acc*); **make up one's ~**
animum indūcere, animō obstināre,
statuere; **put in ~ of** admonēre (*gen*); **speak
one's ~** sententiam suam aperīre; **to one's ~**
ex sententiā ♦ *vt* cūrāre, attendere; **~ one's
own business** suum negōtium agere ♦ *vi*
gravārī; **I don't ~** nīl moror; **never ~** mitte.
minded *adj* animātus.
mindful *adj* memor.
mine *n* metallum *nt*; (MIL) cuniculus *m*; (*fig*)
thēsaurus *m* ♦ *vi* fodere; (MIL) cuniculum
agere ♦ *pron* meus.
miner *n* fossor *m*.
mineral *n* metallum *nt*.
mingle *vt* miscēre, commiscēre ♦ *vi* sē
immiscēre.
miniature *n* minima pictūra *f*.
minimize *vt* dētrectāre.
minimum *n* minimum *nt* ♦ *adj* quam minimus.
minion *n* cliēns *m/f*; dēlicātus *m*.
minister *n* administer *m* ♦ *vi* ministrāre,
servīre.
ministry *n* mūnus *nt*, officium *nt*.
minor *adj* minor ♦ *n* pupillus *m*, pupilla *f*.
minority *n* minor pars *f*; **in one's ~** nōndum suī
iūris.
Minotaur *n* Mīnōtaurus *m*.
minstrel *n* fidicen *m*.
minstrelsy *n* cantus *m*.
mint *n* (*plant*) menta *f*; (*money*) Monēta *f* ♦ *vt*
cūdere.
minute *n* temporis mōmentum *nt*.
minute *adj* minūtus, exiguus, subtīlis.
minutely *adv* subtīliter.
minuteness *n* exiguitās *f*, subtīlitas *f*.
minutiae *n* singula *ntpl*.
minx *n* lascīva *f*.
miracle *n* mīrāculum *nt*, mōnstrum *nt*.
miraculous *adj* mīrus, mīrābilis.
miraculously *adv* dīvīnitus.
mirage *n* falsa speciēs *f*.
mire *n* lutum *nt*.
mirror *n* speculum *nt* ♦ *vt* reddere.
mirth *n* hilaritās *f*, laetitia *f*.
mirthful *adj* hilaris, laetus.
mirthfully *adv* hilare, laetē.

miry *adj* lutulentus.
misadventure *n* īnfortūnium *nt*, cāsus *m*.
misapply *vt* abūtī (*abl*); (*words*) invertere.
misapprehend *vt* male intellegere.
misapprehension *n* error *m*.
misappropriate *vt* intervertere.
misbegotten *adj* nothus.
misbehave *vi* male sē gerere.
miscalculate *vi* errāre, fallī.
miscalculation *n* error *m*.
miscall *vt* maledīcere (*dat*).
miscarriage *n* abortus *m*; (*fig*) error *m*.
miscarry *vi* aborīrī; (*fig*) cadere, inritum esse.
miscellaneous *adj* prōmiscuus, varius.
miscellany *n* farrāgō *f*.
mischance *n* īnfortūnium *nt*.
mischief *n* malum *nt*, facinus *nt*, maleficium *nt*;
(*children*) lascīvia *f*.
mischievous *adj* improbus, maleficus;
lascīvus.
misconceive *vt* male intellegere.
misconception *n* error *m*.
misconduct *n* dēlictum *nt*, culpa *f*.
misconstruction *n* prāva interpretātiō *f*.
misconstrue *vt* male interpretārī.
miscreant *n* scelerātus *m*.
misdeed *n* maleficium *nt*, dēlictum *nt*.
misdemeanour *n* peccātum *nt*, culpa *f*.
miser *n* avārus *m*.
miserable *adj* miser, infēlīx; **make oneself ~**
sē cruciāre.
miserably *adv* miserē.
miserliness *n* avāritia *f*.
miserly *adj* avārus.
misery *n* miseria *f*, aerumna *f*.
misfortune *n* malum *nt*, īnfortūnium *nt*,
incommodum *nt*, rēs adversae *fpl*.
misgiving *n* suspiciō *f*, cūra *f*; **have ~s** parum
cōnfīdere.
misgovern *vt* male regere.
misgovernment *n* prāva administrātiō *f*.
misguide *vt* fallere, dēcipere.
misguided *adj* dēmēns.
mishap *n* īnfortūnium *nt*.
misinform *vt* falsa docēre.
misinterpret *vt* male interpretārī.
misinterpretation *n* prāva interpretātiō *f*.
misjudge *vt* male iūdicāre.
mislay *vt* āmittere.
mislead *vt* dēcipere, indūcere, auferre.
mismanage *vt* male gerere.
misnomer *n* falsum nōmen *nt*.
misogyny *n* mulierum odium *nt*.
misplace *vt* in aliēnō locō collocāre.
misplaced *adj* (*fig*) vānus.
misprint *n* mendum *nt*.
mispronounce *vt* prāvē appellāre.
misquote *vt* perperam proferre.
misrepresent *vt* dētorquēre, invertere;
(*person*) calumniārī.
misrepresentation *n* calumnia *f*.
misrule *n* prāva administrātiō *f*.
miss *vt* (*aim*) aberrāre (*abl*); (*loss*) requīrere,

dēsīderāre; (_notice_) praetermittere ♦ _n_ error _m_; (_girl_) virgō _f._
misshapen _adj_ distortus, dēfōrmis.
missile _n_ tēlum _nt._
missing _adj_ absēns; **be ~** dēesse, dēsīderārī.
mission _n_ lēgātiō _f._
missive _n_ litterae _fpl._
misspend _vt_ perdere, dissipāre.
misstatement _n_ falsum _nt_, mendācium _nt._
mist _n_ nebula _f_, cālīgō _f._
mistake _n_ error _m_; (_writing_) mendum _nt_; **full of ~s** mendōsus ♦ _vt_: **~ for** habēre prō (_abl_); **be ~n** errāre, fallī.
mistletoe _n_ viscum _nt._
mistranslate _vt_ prāvē reddere.
mistress _n_ domina _f_; (_school_) magistra _f_; (_lover_) amīca _f._
mistrust _n_ diffīdentia _f_, suspiciō _f_ ♦ _vt_ diffīdere (_dat_).
mistrustful _adj_ diffīdēns.
mistrustfully _adv_ diffīdenter.
misty _adj_ nebulōsus.
misunderstand _vt_ male intellegere ♦ _vi_ errāre.
misunderstanding _n_ error _m_; (_quarrel_) discidium _nt._
misuse _n_ malus ūsus _m_ ♦ _vt_ abūtī (_abl_).
mite _n_ parvulus _m_; (_insect_) vermiculus _m._
mitigate _vt_ mītigāre, lēnīre.
mitigation _n_ mītigātiō _f._
mix _vt_ miscēre; **~ in** admiscēre; **~ together** commiscēre; **get ~ed up with** admiscērī cum, sē interpōnere (_dat_).
mixed _adj_ prōmiscuus.
mixture _n_ (_act_) temperātiō _f_; (_state_) dīversitās _f._
mnemonic _n_ artificium memoriae _nt._
moan _n_ gemitus _m_ ♦ _vi_ gemere.
moat _n_ fossa _f._
mob _n_ vulgus _nt_, turba _f_ ♦ _vt_ circumfundī in (_acc_).
mobile _adj_ mōbilis, agilis.
mobility _n_ mōbilitās _f_, agilitās _f._
mobilize _vt_ (MIL) ēvocāre.
mock _vt_ irrīdēre, lūdibriō habēre, lūdificārī; (_ape_) imitārī; **~ at** inlūdere ♦ _n_ lūdibrium _nt_ ♦ _adj_ simulātus, fictus.
mocker _n_ dērīsor _m._
mockery _n_ lūdibrium _nt_, irrīsus _m._
mode _n_ modus _m_, ratiō _f._
model _n_ exemplar _nt_, exemplum _nt_ ♦ _vt_ fingere.
modeller _n_ fictor _m._
moderate _adj_ (_size_) modicus; (_conduct_) moderātus ♦ _vt_ temperāre; (_emotion_) temperāre (_dat_) ♦ _vi_ mītigārī.
moderately _adv_ modicē, moderātē, mediocriter.
moderation _n_ moderātiō _f_, modus _m_; (_mean_) mediocritās _f._
moderator _n_ praefectus _m._
modern _adj_ recēns.
modernity _n_ haec aetās _f._

modest _adj_ pudīcus, verēcundus.
modestly _adv_ verēcundē, pudenter.
modesty _n_ pudor _m_, verēcundia _f._
modicum _n_ paullulum _nt_, aliquantulum _nt._
modification _n_ mūtātiō _f._
modify _vt_ immūtāre; (_law_) derogāre aliquid dē.
modulate _vt_ (_voice_) īnflectere.
modulation _n_ flexiō _f_, inclīnātiō _f._
moiety _n_ dīmidia pars _f._
moist _adj_ ūmidus.
moisten _vt_ ūmectāre, rigāre.
moisture _n_ ūmor _m._
molar _n_ genuīnus _m._
mole _n_ (_animal_) talpa _f_; (_on skin_) naevus _m_; (_pier_) mōlēs _f._
molecule _n_ corpusculum _nt._
molehill _n_: **make a mountain out of a ~** ē rīvō flūmina māgna facere, arcem facere ē cloācā.
molest _vt_ sollicitāre, vexāre.
molestation _n_ vexātiō _f._
mollify _vt_ mollīre, lēnīre.
molten _adj_ liquefactus.
moment _n_ temporis mōmentum _nt_, temporis pūnctum _nt_; **for a ~** parumper; **in a ~** iam; **without a ~'s delay** nullā interpositā morā; **be of great ~** māgnō mōmentō esse; **it is of ~** interest.
momentary _adj_ brevis.
momentous _adj_ gravis, māgnī mōmentī.
momentum _n_ impetus _m._
monarch _n_ rēx _m_, tyrannus _m._
monarchical _adj_ rēgius.
monarchy _n_ rēgnum _nt._
monastery _n_ monastērium _nt._
monetary _adj_ pecūniārius.
money _n_ pecūnia _f_; (_cash_) nummī _mpl_; **for ~** mercēde; **ready ~** nummī, praesēns pecūnia; **make ~** rem facere, quaestum facere.
moneybag _n_ fiscus _m._
moneyed _adj_ nummātus, pecūniōsus.
moneylender _n_ faenerātor _m._
moneymaking _n_ quaestus _m._
mongoose _n_ ichneumōn _m._
mongrel _n_ hibrida _m._
monitor _n_ admonitor _m._
monk _n_ monachus _m._
monkey _n_ sīmia _f._
monograph _n_ libellus _m._
monologue _n_ ōrātiō _f._
monopolize _vt_ absorbēre, sibī vindicāre.
monopoly _n_ arbitrium _nt._
monosyllabic _adj_ monosyllabus.
monosyllable _n_ monosyllabum _nt._
monotonous _adj_ aequābilis.
monotony _n_ taedium _nt._
monster _n_ mōnstrum _nt_, portentum _nt_, bēlua _f._
monstrosity _n_ mōnstrum _nt._
monstrous _adj_ immānis, mōnstruōsus; improbus.
month _n_ mēnsis _m._
monthly _adj_ mēnstruus.

monument n monumentum nt.
monumental adj ingēns.
mood n adfectiō f, adfectus m, animus m;
(GRAM) modus m; **I am in the ~ for** libet (inf).
moody adj mōrōsus, tristis.
moon n lūna f; **new ~** interlūnium nt.
moonlight n: **by ~** ad lūnam.
moonshine n somnia ntpl.
moonstruck adj lūnāticus.
moor vt religāre ♦ n tesqua ntpl.
moorings n ancorae fpl.
moot n conventus m; **it is a ~ point** discrepat ♦
vt iactāre.
mop n pēniculus m ♦ vt dētergēre.
mope vi maerēre.
moral adj honestus, probus; (opposed to
physical) animī; (PHILOS) mōrālis ♦ n
documentum nt.
morale n animus m; **~ is low** iacet animus.
morality n bonī mōrēs mpl, virtūs f.
moralize vi dē officiīs disserere.
morally adv honestē.
morals npl mōrēs mpl.
morass n palūs f.
moratorium n mora f.
morbid adj aeger.
mordant adj mordāx.
more adj plūs, pluris (in sg + gen, in pl + adj) ♦
adv plūs, magis, amplius; (extra) ultrā; **~ than**
amplius quam; **~ than three feet** amplius trēs
pedēs; **~ and ~** magis magisque; **never ~**
immo; **~ or less** ferē; **no ~** (time) nōn diūtius,
nunquam posteā.
moreover adv tamen, autem, praetereā.
moribund adj moribundus.
morning n māne nt; **early in the ~** bene māne;
this ~ hodiē māne; **good ~** salvē ♦ adj
mātūtīnus.
morning call n salūtātiō f.
morning watch n (NAUT) tertia vigilia f.
moron n sōcors m.
morose adj acerbus, tristis.
moroseness n acerbitās f, tristitia f.
morrow n posterus diēs m; **on the ~** posterō
diē, postrīdiē.
morsel n offa f.
mortal adj mortālis, hūmānus; (wound)
mortifer ♦ n mortālis m/f, homō m/f; **poor ~**
homunculus m.
mortality n mortālitās f; (death) mors f; **the ~**
was high plūrimī periērunt.
mortally adv: **be ~ wounded** mortiferum
vulnus accipere.
mortar n mortārium nt.
mortgage n pignus nt, fīdūcia f ♦ vt obligāre.
mortification n dolor m, angor m.
mortified adj: **be ~ at** aegrē ferre.
mortify vt mordēre, vexāre; (lust) coercēre ♦
vi putrēscere.
mortise vt immittere.
mosaic n emblēma nt, lapillī mpl ♦ adj
tessellātus.
mosquito n culex m.

mosquito net n cōnōpēum nt.
moss n muscus m.
mossy adj muscōsus.
most adj plūrimus, plērusque; **for the ~ part**
māximam partem ♦ adv māximē, plūrimum.
mostly adv plērumque, ferē.
mote n corpusculum nt.
moth n tinea f.
mother n māter f; **of a ~** māternus.
mother-in-law n socrus f.
motherless adj mātre orbus.
motherly adj māternus.
mother tongue n patrius sermō m.
mother wit n Minerva f.
motif n argūmentum nt.
motion n mōtus m; (for law) rogātiō f; (in
debate) sententia f; **propose a ~** ferre; **set in ~**
movēre ♦ vt innuere.
motionless adj immōbilis.
motive n causa f, ratiō f; **I know your ~ in**
asking sciō cūr rogēs.
motley adj versicolor, varius.
mottled adj maculōsus.
motto n sententia f.
mould n fōrma f; (soil) humus f; (fungus)
mūcor m ♦ vt fingere, fōrmāre.
moulder vi putrēscere ♦ n fictor m.
mouldering adj puter.
mouldiness n situs m.
mouldy adj mūcidus.
moult vi pennas exuere.
mound n agger m, tumulus m.
mount n mōns m; (horse) equus m ♦ vt
scandere, cōnscendere, ascendere ♦ vi
ascendere; **~ up** ēscendere.
mountain n mōns m.
mountaineer n montānus m.
mountainous adj montuōsus.
mourn vi maerēre, lūgēre ♦ vt dēflēre,
lūgēre.
mourner n plōrātor m; (hired) praefica f.
mournful adj (cause) lūctuōsus, acerbus;
(sound) lūgubris, maestus.
mournfully adv maestē.
mourning n maeror nt, lūctus m; (dress)
sordēs fpl; **in ~** fūnestus; **be in ~** lūgēre; **put**
on ~ vestem mūtāre, sordēs suscipere;
wearing ~ ātrātus.
mouse n mūs m.
mousetrap n mūscipulum nt.
mouth n ōs nt; (river) ōstium nt.
mouthful n bucca f.
mouthpiece n interpres m.
movable adj mōbilis ♦ npl: **~s** rēs fpl, supellex
f.
move vt movēre; (emotion) commovēre; **~**
backwards and forwards reciprocāre; **~ out**
of the way dēmovēre; **~ up** admovēre ♦ vi
movērī; (residence) dēmigrāre; (proposal)
ferre, cēnsēre; **~ into** immigrāre in (acc); **~**
on prōgredī.
movement n mōtus m; (process) cursus m;
(society) societās f.

mover *n* auctor *m*.
moving *adj* flēbilis, flexanimus.
mow *vt* secāre, dēmetere.
mower *n* faenisex *m*.
much *adj* multus ♦ *adv* multum; (*with compar*)
multō; **as ~ as** tantum quantum; **so ~** tantum;
(*with verbs*) adeo; **~ less** nēdum; **too ~** nimis ♦
n multum *nt*.
muck *n* stercus *nt*.
mud *n* lutum *nt*.
muddle *n* turba *f* ♦ *vt* turbāre.
muffle *vt* involvere; **~ up** obvolvere.
muffled *adj* surdus.
mug *n* pōculum *nt*.
mulberry *n* mōrum *nt*; (*tree*) mōrus *f*.
mule *n* mūlus *m*.
muleteer *n* mūliō *m*.
mulish *adj* obstinātus.
mullet *n* mullus *m*.
multifarious *adj* multiplex, varius.
multiform *adj* multifōrmis.
multiply *vt* multiplicāre ♦ *vi* crēscere.
multitude *n* multitūdō *f*.
multitudinous *adj* crēberrimus.
mumble *vt* (*words*) opprimere ♦ *vi*
murmurāre.
munch *vt* mandūcāre.
mundane *adj* terrestris.
municipal *adj* mūnicipālis.
municipality *n* mūnicipium *nt*.
munificence *n* largitās *f*.
munificent *adj* largus, mūnificus.
munificently *adv* mūnificē.
munitions *n* bellī adparātus *m*.
mural *adj* mūrālis.
murder *n* parricīdium *nt*, caedēs *f*; **charge with
~** inter sīcāriōs accūsāre; **trial for ~** quaestiō
inter sīcāriōs ♦ *vt* interficere, iūgulāre,
necāre.
murderer *n* sīcārius *m*, homicīda *m*, parricīda
m, percussor *m*.
murderess *n* interfectrīx *f*.
murderous *adj* cruentus.
murky *adj* tenebrōsus.
murmur *n* murmur *nt*; (*angry*) fremitus *m* ♦ *vi*
murmurāre; fremere.
murmuring *n* admurmurātiō *f*.
muscle *n* torus *m*.
muscular *adj* lacertōsus.
muse *vi* meditārī ♦ *n* Mūsa *f*.
mushroom *n* fungus *m*, bōlētus *m*.
music *n* (*art*) mūsica *f*; (*sound*) cantus *m*, modī
mpl.
musical *adj* (*person*) mūsicus; (*sound*)
canōrus.
musician *n* mūsicus *m*; (*strings*) fidicen *m*;
(*wind*) tībīcen *m*.
muslin *n* sindōn *f*.
must *n* (*wine*) mustum *nt* ♦ *vi* dēbēre; **I ~ go** mē
oportet īre, mihī eundum est.
mustard *n* sināpi *nt*.
muster *vt* convocāre, cōgere; (*review*)
recēnsēre ♦ *vi* convenīre, coīre ♦ *n*

conventus *m*; (*review*) recēnsiō *f*.
muster roll *n* album *nt*.
mustiness *n* situs *m*.
musty *adj* mūcidus.
mutability *n* incōnstantia *f*.
mutable *adj* incōnstāns, mūtābilis.
mute *adj* mūtus.
mutilate *vt* mūtilāre, truncāre.
mutilated *adj* mūtilus, truncus.
mutilation *n* lacerātiō *f*.
mutineer *n* sēditiōsus *m*.
mutinous *adj* sēditiōsus.
mutiny *n* sēditiō *f* ♦ *vi* sēditiōnem facere.
mutter *vi* mussitāre.
mutton *n* carō ovilla *f*.
mutual *adj* mūtuus.
mutually *adv* mūtuō, inter sē.
muzzle *n* ōs *nt*, rōstrum *nt*; (*guard*) fiscella *f* ♦ *vt*
fiscellā capistrāre.
my *adj* meus.
myriad *n* decem mīlia; (*any large no.*) sēscentī.
myrmidon *n* satelles *m*.
myrrh *n* murra *f*.
myrtle *n* myrtus *f* ♦ *adj* myrteus.
myrtle grove *n* myrtētum *nt*.
myself *pron* ipse, egomet; (*reflexive*) mē.
mysterious *adj* arcānus, occultus.
mysteriously *adv* occultē.
mystery *n* arcānum *nt*; (*rites*) mystēria *ntpl*;
(*fig*) latebra *f*.
mystic *adj* mysticus.
mystical *adj* mysticus.
mystification *n* fraus *f*, ambāgēs *fpl*.
mystify *vt* fraudāre, cōnfundere.
myth *n* fābula *f*.
mythical *adj* fābulōsus.
mythology *n* fābulae *fpl*.

N, n

nabob *n* rēx *m*.
nadir *n* fundus *m*.
nag *n* caballus *m* ♦ *vt* obiūrgitāre.
naiad *n* nāias *f*.
nail *n* clāvus *m*; (*finger*) unguis *m*; **hit the ~ on
the head** rem acū tangere ♦ *vt* clāvīs
adfīgere.
naive *adj* simplex.
naively *adv* simpliciter.
naiveté *n* simplicitās *f*.
naked *adj* nūdus.
nakedly *adv* apertē.
name *n* nōmen *nt*; (*repute*) existimātiō *f*; (*term*)
vocābulum *nt*; **by ~** nōmine; **have a bad ~**
male audīre; **have a good ~** bene audīre; **in**

the ~ of verbīs (*gen*); (*oath*) per ♦ *vt* appellāre, vocāre, nōmināre; (*appoint*) dīcere.

nameless *adj* nōminis expers, sine nōmine.

namely *adv* nempe, dīcō.

namesake *n* gentīlis *m/f*.

nanny goat *n* capra *f*.

nap *n* brevis somnus *m*; (*cloth*) villus *nt*.

napkin *n* linteum *nt*.

narcissus *n* narcissus *m*.

narcotic *adj* somnifer.

nard *n* nardus *f*.

narrate *vt* nārrāre, ēnārrāre.

narration *n* nārrātiō *f*.

narrative *n* fābula *f*.

narrator *n* nārrātor *m*.

narrow *adj* angustus ♦ *vt* coartāre ♦ *vi* coartārī.

narrowly *adv* aegrē, vix.

narrowness *n* angustiae *fpl*.

narrows *n* angustiae *fpl*.

nasal *adj* nārium.

nascent *adj* nāscēns.

nastily *adv* foedē.

nastiness *n* foeditās *f*.

nasty *adj* foedus, taeter, impūrus.

natal *adj* nātālis.

nation *n* populus *m*; (*foreign*) gēns *f*.

national *adj* pūblicus, cīvīlis; (*affairs*) domesticus.

nationality *n* cīvitās *f*.

native *adj* indigena; (*speech*) patrius ♦ *n* incola *m*, indigena *m/f*.

native land *n* patria *f*.

nativity *n* ortus *m*.

natural *adj* nātūrālis; (*innate*) nātīvus, genuīnus, īnsitus.

naturalization *n* cīvitās *f*.

naturalize *vt* cīvitāte dōnāre.

naturalized *adj* (*person*) cīvitāte dōnātus; (*thing*) īnsitus.

naturally *adv* nātūrāliter, secundum nātūram; (*of course*) scīlicet, certē.

nature *n* nātūra *f*; rērum nātūra *f*; (*character*) indolēs *f*, ingenium *nt*; (*species*) genus *nt*; course of ~ nātūra *f*; I know the ~ of sciō quālis sit.

naught *n* nihil *nt*; set at ~ parvī facere.

naughty *adj* improbus.

nausea *n* nausea *f*; (*fig*) fastīdium *nt*.

nauseate *vt* fastīdium movēre (*dat*); be ~d with fastīdīre.

nauseous *adj* taeter.

nautical *adj* nauticus, maritimus.

naval *adj* nāvālis.

navel *n* umbilīcus *m*.

navigable *adj* nāvigābilis.

navigate *vt*, *vi* nāvigāre.

navigation *n* rēs nautica *f*; (*sailing*) nāvigātiō *f*.

navigator *n* nauta *m*, gubernātor *m*.

navy *n* classis *f*, cōpiae nāvālēs *fpl*.

nay *adv* nōn; ~ more immo.

near *adv* prope ♦ *adj* propinquus ♦ *prep* prope (*acc*), ad (*acc*); lie ~ adiacēre (*dat*) ♦ *vt* adpropinquāre (*dat*).

nearby *adj* iuxtā.

nearer *adj* propior.

nearest *adj* proximus.

nearly *adv* paene, prope, fermē.

neat *adj* nitidus, mundus, concinnus; (*wine*) pūrus.

neatly *adv* mundē, concinnē.

neatness *n* munditia *f*.

nebulous *adj* nebulōsus; (*fig*) incertus.

necessaries *n* rēs ad vīvendum necessāriae *fpl*.

necessarily *adv* necessāriō, necesse.

necessary *adj* necessārius, necesse; it is ~ oportet (+ *acc and infin or gerundive of vt*).

necessitate *vt* cōgere (*inf*), efficere ut (*subj*).

necessitous *adj* egēnus, pauper.

necessity *n* necessitās *f*; (*thing*) rēs necessāria *f*; (*want*) paupertās *f*, egestās *f*.

neck *n* collum *nt*.

neckcloth *n* fōcāle *nt*.

necklace *n* monīle *nt*, torquis *m*.

nectar *n* nectar *nt*.

need *n* (*necessity*) necessitās *f*; (*want*) egestās *f*, inopia *f*, indigentia *f*; there is ~ of opus est (*abl*); there is no ~ to nihil est quod, cūr (*subj*) ♦ *vt* egēre (*abl*), carēre, indigēre (*abl*); I ~ opus est mihī (*abl*).

needful *adj* necessārius.

needle *n* acus *f*.

needless *adj* vānus, inūtilis.

needlessly *adv* frustrā, sine causā.

needs *adv* necesse ♦ *npl* necessitātēs *fpl*.

needy *adj* egēns, inops, pauper.

nefarious *adj* nefārius, scelestus.

negation *n* negātiō *f*, īnfitiātiō *f*.

negative *adj* negāns ♦ *n* negātiō *f*; answer in the ~ negāre ♦ *vt* vetāre, contrādīcere (*dat*).

neglect *n* neglegentia *f*, incūria *f*; (*of duty*) dērelictiō *f* ♦ *vt* neglegere, ōmittere.

neglectful *adj* neglegēns, immemor.

negligence *n* neglegentia *f*, incūria *f*.

negligent *adj* neglegēns, indīligēns.

negligently *adv* neglegenter, indīligenter.

negligible *adj* levissimus, minimī mōmentī.

negotiate *vi* agere dē ♦ *vt* (*deal*) peragere; (*difficulty*) superāre.

negotiation *n* āctiō *f*, pactum *nt*.

negotiator *n* lēgātus *m*, conciliātor *m*.

negro *n* Aethiops *m*.

neigh *vi* hinnīre.

neighbour *n* vīcīnus *m*, fīnitimus *m*.

neighbourhood *n* vīcīnia *f*, vīcīnitās *f*.

neighbouring *adj* vīcīnus, fīnitimus, propinquus.

neighbourly *adj* hūmānus, amīcus.

neighing *n* hinnītus *m*.

neither *adv* neque, nec; nēve, neu ♦ *pron* neuter ♦ *adj* neuter, neutra, neutrum (*like alter*); ~ ... nor nec/neque ... nec/neque.

neophyte *n* tīrō *m*.

nephew *n* frātris fīlius *m*, sorōris fīlius *m*.

Nereid *n* Nērēis *f*.
nerve *n* nervus *m*; (*fig*) audācia *f*; **~s** *pl* pavor *m*, trepidātiō *f*; **have the ~ to** audēre ♦ *vt* cōnfirmāre.
nervous *adj* diffīdēns, sollicitus, trepidus.
nervously *adv* trepidē.
nervousness *n* sollicitūdō *f*, diffīdentia *f*.
nest *n* nīdus *m* ♦ *vi* nīdificāre.
nestle *vi* recubāre.
nestling *n* pullus *m*.
net *n* rēte *nt* ♦ *vt* inrētīre.
nether *adj* īnferior.
nethermost *adj* īnfimus, īmus.
netting *n* rēticulum *nt*.
nettle *n* urtīca *f* ♦ *vt* inrītāre, ūrere.
neuter *adj* neuter.
neutral *adj* medius; **be ~** neutrī partī sē adiungere, medium sē gerere.
neutralize *vt* compēnsāre.
never *adv* nunquam.
nevertheless *adv* nihilōminus, at tamen.
new *adj* novus, integer, recēns.
newcomer *n* advena *m/f*.
newfangled *adj* novus, inaudītus.
newly *adv* nūper, modo.
newness *n* novitās *f*.
news *n* nūntius *m*; **what ~?** quid novī?; **~ was brought that** nūntiātum est (+ *acc and infin*).
newspaper *n* ācta diūrna/pūblica *ntpl*.
newt *n* lacerta *f*.
next *adj* proximus; (*time*) īnsequēns ♦ *adv* dēinde, dēinceps; **~ day** postrīdiē; **~ to** iuxtā; **come ~ to** excipere.
nibble *vi* rōdere.
nice *adj* bellus, dulcis; (*exact*) accūrātus; (*particular*) fastīdiōsus.
nicely *adv* bellē, probē.
nicety *n* subtīlitās *f*.
niche *n* aedicula *f*.
nick *n*: **in the ~ of time** in ipsō articulō temporis.
nickname *n* cognōmen *nt*.
niece *n* frātris fīlia *f*, sorōris fīlia *f*.
niggardliness *n* illīberālitās *f*, avāritia *f*.
niggardly *adj* illīberālis, parcus, avārus.
nigh *adv* prope.
night *n* nox *f*; **by ~** noctū; **all ~** pernox; **spend the ~** pernoctāre; **be awake all ~** pervigilāre ♦ *adj* nocturnus.
night bird *n* noctua *f*.
nightfall *n* prīmae tenebrae *fpl*; **at ~** sub noctem.
nightingale *n* luscinia *f*.
nightly *adj* nocturnus ♦ *adv* noctū.
nightmare *n* incubus *m*.
night work *n* lūcubrātiō *f*.
nimble *adj* agilis, pernīx.
nimbleness *n* agilitās *f*, pernīcitās *f*; (*mind*) argūtiae *fpl*.
nimbly *adv* pernīciter.
nine *num* novem; **~ each** novēnī; **~ times** noviēns; **~ days'** novendiālis.
nine hundred *num* nōngentī.
nine hundredth *adj* nōngentēsimus.

nineteen *num* ūndēvigintī; **~ each** ūndēvīcēnī; **~ times** deciēns et noviēns.
nineteenth *adj* ūndēvīcēsimus.
ninetieth *adj* nōnāgēsimus.
ninety *num* nōnāgintā; **~ each** nōnāgēnī; **~ times** nōnāgiēns.
ninth *adj* nōnus.
nip *vt* vellicāre; (*frost*) ūrere.
nippers *n* forceps *m*.
nipple *n* papilla *f*.
no *adv* nōn; (*correcting*) immo; **say ~** negāre ♦ *adj* nullus.
nobility *n* nōbilitās *f*; (*persons*) optimātēs *mpl*, nōbilēs *mpl*.
noble *adj* nōbilis; (*birth*) generōsus; (*appearance*) decōrus.
nobleman *n* prīnceps *m*, optimās *m*.
nobly *adv* nōbiliter, praeclārē.
nobody *n* nēmō *m*.
nocturnal *adj* nocturnus.
nod *n* nūtus *m* ♦ *vi* nūtāre; (*sign*) adnuere; (*sleep*) dormītāre.
noddle *n* caput *nt*.
node *n* nōdus *m*.
noise *n* strepitus *m*, sonitus *m*; (*loud*) fragor *m*; **make a ~** increpāre, strepere ♦ *vt*: **~ abroad** ēvulgāre; **be ~d abroad** percrēbrēscere.
noiseless *adj* tacitus.
noiselessly *adv* tacitē.
noisily *adv* cum strepitū.
noisome *adj* taeter, gravis.
noisy *adj* clāmōsus.
nomadic *adj* vagus.
nomenclature *n* vocābula *ntpl*.
nominally *adv* nōmine, verbō.
nominate *vt* nōmināre, dīcere; (*in writing*) scrībere.
nomination *n* nōminātiō *f*.
nominative *adj* nōminātīvus.
nominee *n* nōminātus *m*.
nonappearance *n* absentia *f*.
nonce *n*: **for the ~** semel.
nonchalance *n* aequus animus *m*.
nonchalantly *adv* aequō animō.
noncombatant *adj* imbellis.
noncommittal *adj* circumspectus.
nondescript *adj* īnsolitus.
none *adj* nullus ♦ *pron* nēmō *m*.
nonentity *n* nihil *nt*, nullus *m*.
nones *n* Nōnae *fpl*.
nonexistent *adj* quī nōn est.
nonplus *vt* ad incitās redigere.
nonresistance *n* patientia *f*.
nonsense *n* nūgae *fpl*, ineptiae *fpl*.
nonsensical *adj* ineptus, absurdus.
nook *n* angulus *m*.
noon *n* merīdiēs *m* ♦ *adj* merīdiānus.
no one *pron* nēmō *m* (*for gen/abl use* **nullus**).
noose *n* laqueus *m*.
nor *adv* neque, nec; nēve, neu.
norm *n* nōrma *f*.
normal *adj* solitus.
normally *adv* plērumque.

north n septentriōnēs *mpl* ♦ *adj* septentriōnālis.
northeast *adv* inter septentriōnēs et orientem.
northerly *adj* septentriōnālis.
northern *adj* septentriōnālis.
North Pole n arctos f.
northwards *adv* ad septentriōnēs versus.
northwest *adv* inter septentriōnēs et occidentem ♦ *adj*: ~ **wind** Cōrus m.
north wind n aquilō m.
nose n nāsus m, nārēs *fpl*; **blow the ~** ēmungere; **lead by the ~** labiīs ductāre ♦ *vi* scrūtārī.
nostril n nāris f.
not *adv* nōn, haud; ~ **at all** haudquāquam; ~ **as if** nōn quod, nōn quō; ~ **but what** nōn quīn; ~ **even** nē ... quidem; ~ **so very** nōn ita; ~ **that** nōn quō; **and ~** neque; **does ~, did ~** (*interrog*) nonne; **if** ... ~ nisi; **that ~** (*purpose*) nē; (*fear*) nē nōn; ~ **long after** haud multō post; ~ **only** ... **but also** non modo/solum ... sed etiam; ~ **yet** nōndum.
notability n vir praeclārus m.
notable *adj* īnsignis, īnsignītus, memorābilis.
notably *adv* īnsignītē.
notary n scrība m.
notation n notae *fpl*.
notch n incīsūra f ♦ *vt* incīdere.
note n (*mark*) nota f; (*comment*) adnotātiō f; (*letter*) litterulae *fpl*; (*sound*) vōx f; **make a ~ of** in commentāriōs referre ♦ *vt* notāre; (*observe*) animadvertere.
notebook n pugillārēs *mpl*.
noted *adj* īnsignis, praeclārus, nōtus.
noteworthy *adj* memorābilis.
nothing n nihil, nīl *nt*; ~ **but** merus, nīl nisi; **come to ~** in inritum cadere; **for ~** frustrā; (*gift*) grātīs, grātuītō; **good for ~** nēquam; **think ~ of** nihilī facere.
notice n (*official*) prōscrīptiō f; (*private*) libellus m; **attract ~** cōnspicī; **escape ~** latēre; **escape the ~ of** fallere; **give ~ of** dēnūntiāre; **take ~ of** animadvertere ♦ *vt* animadvertere, cōnspicere.
noticeable *adj* cōnspicuus, īnsignis.
noticeably *adv* īnsignītē.
notification n dēnūntiātiō f.
notify *vt* (*event*) dēnūntiāre, indicāre; (*person*) renūntiāre (*dat*), certiōrem facere.
notion n nōtiō f, īnfōrmātiō f; suspiciō f.
notoriety n īnfāmia f.
notorious *adj* fāmōsus, īnfāmis; (*thing*) manifestus.
notoriously *adv* manifestō.
notwithstanding *adv* nihilōminus, tamen ♦ *prep*: ~ **the danger** in tantō discrīmine.
nought n nihil, nīl *nt*.
noun n nōmen *nt*.
nourish *vt* alere, nūtrīre.
nourisher n altor m, altrīx f.
nourishment n cibus m, alimenta *ntpl*.
novel *adj* novus, inaudītus ♦ n fābella f.
novelty n rēs nova f; novitās f, īnsolentia f.

November n mēnsis November m; **of ~** November.
novice n tīrō m.
now *adv* nunc; (*past*) iam; ~ **and then** interdum; **just ~** nunc; (*lately*) dūdum, modo; ~ ... ~ modo ... modo ♦ *conj* at, autem.
nowadays *adv* nunc, hodiē.
nowhere *adv* nusquam.
nowise *adv* nūllō modō, haudquāquam.
noxious *adj* nocēns, noxius.
nuance n color m.
nucleus n sēmen *nt*.
nude *adj* nūdus.
nudge *vt* fodicāre.
nudity n nūdātum corpus *nt*.
nugget n massa f.
nuisance n malum *nt*, incommodum *nt*.
null *adj* inritus.
nullify *vt* inritum facere; (*law*) abrogāre.
numb *adj* torpēns, torpidus; **be ~** torpēre; **become ~** torpēscere.
number n numerus m; **a ~ of** complūrēs, aliquot; **a great ~** multitūdō f, frequentia f; **a small ~** īnfrequentia f; **in large ~s** frequentēs ♦ *vt* numerāre, ēnumerāre.
numberless *adj* innumerābilis.
numbness n torpor m.
numerous *adj* frequēns, crēber, plūrimī.
nun n monacha f.
nuptial *adj* nūptiālis.
nuptials n nūptiae *fpl*.
nurse n nūtrīx f ♦ *vt* (*child*) nūtrīre; (*sick*) cūrāre; (*fig*) fovēre.
nursery n (*children*) cubiculum *nt*; (*plants*) sēminārium *nt*.
nursling n alumnus m, alumna f.
nurture n ēducātiō f.
nut n nux f.
nutrition n alimenta *ntpl*.
nutritious *adj* salūbris.
nutshell n putāmen *nt*.
nut tree n nux f.
nymph n nympha f.

O, o

O *interj* ō!
oaf n agrestis m.
oak n quercus f; (*evergreen*) īlex f; (*timber*) rōbur n ♦ *adj* quernus, īlignus, rōboreus; ~ **forest** quercētum *nt*.
oakum n stuppa f.
oar n rēmus m.
oarsman n rēmex m.
oaten *adj* avēnāceus.
oath n iūsiūrandum *nt*; (MIL) sacrāmentum *nt*;

(*imprecation*) exsecrātiō *f*; **false ~ periūrium**
nt; **take an ~ iūrāre; take an ~ of allegiance to**
in verba iūrāre (*gen*).
oats *n* avēna *f*.
obduracy *n* obstinātus animus *m*.
obdurate *adj* obstinātus, pervicāx.
obdurately *adv* obstinātē.
obedience *n* oboedientia *f*, obsequium *nt*.
obedient *adj* oboediēns, obsequēns; **be ~ to**
pārēre (*dat*), obtemperāre (*dat*), obsequī
(*dat*).
obediently *adv* oboedienter.
obeisance *n* obsequium *nt*; **make ~ to** adōrāre.
obelisk *n* obeliscus *m*.
obese *adj* obēsus, pinguis.
obesity *n* obēsitās *f*, pinguitūdō *f*.
obey *vt* pārēre (*dat*), obtemperāre (*dat*),
oboedīre (*dat*); **~ orders** dictō pārēre.
obituary *n* mortēs *fpl*.
object *n* rēs *f*; (*aim*) fīnis *m*, prōpositum *nt*; **be**
an ~ of hate odiō esse; **with what ~** quō
cōnsiliō ♦ *vi* recūsāre, gravārī; **but, it is ~ed**
at enim; ~ to improbāre.
objection *n* recūsātiō *f*, mora *f*; **I have no ~** nīl
moror.
objectionable *adj* invīsus, iniūcundus.
objective *adj* externus ♦ *n* prōpositum *nt*, fīnis
m.
objurgate *vt* obiūrgāre, culpāre.
oblation *n* dōnum *nt*.
obligation *n* (*legal*) dēbitum *nt*; (*moral*)
officium *nt*; **lay under an ~** obligāre,
obstringere.
obligatory *adj* dēbitus, necessārius.
oblige *vt* (*force*) cōgere; (*contract*) obligāre,
obstringere; (*compliance*) mōrem gerere
(*dat*), mōrigerārī (*dat*); **I am ~d to** (*action*)
dēbeō (*inf*); (*person*) amāre, grātiam habēre
(*dat*).
obliging *adj* cōmis, officiōsus.
obligingly *adv* cōmiter, officiōsē.
oblique *adj* oblīquus.
obliquely *adv* oblīquē.
obliquity *n* (*moral*) prāvitās *f*.
obliterate *vt* dēlēre, oblitterāre.
obliteration *n* litūra *f*.
oblivion *n* oblīviō *f*.
oblivious *adj* oblīviōsus, immemor.
oblong *adj* oblongus.
obloquy *n* vītuperātiō *f*, opprobrium *nt*.
obnoxious *adj* invīsus.
obscene *adj* obscaenus, impūrus.
obscenity *n* obscaenitās *f*, impūritās *f*.
obscure *adj* obscūrus, caecus ♦ *vt* obscūrāre,
officere (*dat*).
obscurely *adv* obscūrē; (*speech*) per ambāgēs.
obscurity *n* obscūritās *f*; (*speech*) ambāgēs *fpl*.
obsequies *n* exsequiae *fpl*.
obsequious *adj* officiōsus, ambitiōsus.
obsequiously *adv* officiōsē.
obsequiousness *n* adsentātiō *f*.
observance *n* observantia *f*; (*rite*) rītus *m*.
observant *adj* attentus, dīligēns.

observation *n* observātiō *f*, animadversiō *f*;
(*remark*) dictum *nt*.
observe *vt* animadvertere, contemplārī; (*see*)
cernere, cōnspicere; (*remark*) dīcere; (*adhere*
to) cōnservāre, observāre.
observer *n* spectātor *m*, contemplātor *m*.
obsess *vt* occupāre; **I am ~ed by** tōtus sum in
(*abl*).
obsession *n* studium *nt*.
obsolescent *adj*: **be ~** obsolēscere.
obsolete *adj* obsolētus; **become ~** exolēscere.
obstacle *n* impedīmentum *nt*, mora *f*.
obstinacy *n* pertinācia *f*, obstinātus animus *m*.
obstinate *adj* pertināx, obstinātus.
obstinately *adv* obstinātō animō.
obstreperous *adj* clāmōsus, ferus.
obstruct *vt* impedīre, obstruere, obstāre (*dat*);
(*POL*) intercēdere (*dat*); (*fig*) officere (*dat*).
obstruction *n* impedīmentum *nt*; (*POL*)
intercessiō *f*
obstructionist *n* intercessor *m*.
obtain *vt* adipīscī, nancīscī, cōnsequī;
comparāre; (*by request*) impetrāre ♦ *vi*
tenēre, obtinēre.
obtrude *vi* sē inculcāre ♦ *vt* ingerere.
obtrusive *adj* importūnus, molestus.
obtuse *adj* hebes, stolidus.
obtusely *adv* stolidē.
obtuseness *n* stupor *m*.
obverse *adj* obversus.
obviate *vt* tollere, praevertere.
obvious *adj* ēvidēns, manifestus, apertus; **it is**
~ appāret.
obviously *adv* ēvidenter, apertē, manifestō.
occasion *n* occāsiō *f*, locus *m*; (*reason*) causa *f*
♦ *vt* movēre, facessere, auctōrem esse (*gen*).
occasional *adj* fortuītus.
occasionally *adv* interdum, nōnnunquam.
occidental *adj* occidentālis.
occult *adj* arcānus.
occupancy *n* possessiō *f*.
occupant *n* habitātor *m*, possessor *m*.
occupation *n* quaestus *m*, occupātiō *f*.
occupier *n* possessor *m*.
occupy *vt* possidēre; (*MIL*) occupāre; (*space*)
complēre; (*attention*) distinēre, occupāre.
occur *vi* ēvenīre, accidere; (*to mind*)
occurrere, in mentem venīre *f*.
occurrence *n* ēventum *nt*; rēs *f*.
ocean *n* mare *nt*, ōceanus *m*.
October *n* mēnsis Octōber *m*; **of ~** Octōber.
ocular *adj* oculōrum; **give ~ proof of** ante
oculōs pōnere, videntī dēmōnstrāre.
odd *adj* (*number*) impār; (*moment*) subsecīvus;
(*appearance*) novus, īnsolitus.
oddity *n* novitās *f*; (*person*) homō rīdiculus *m*.
oddly *adv* mīrum in modum.
odds *n* praestantia *f*; **be at ~ with** dissidēre
cum; **the ~ are against us** imparēs sumus; **the**
~ are in our favour superiōrēs sumus.
ode *n* carmen *nt*.
odious *adj* invīsus, odiōsus.
odium *n* invidia *f*.

odorous *adj* odōrātus.
odour *n* odor *m*.
of *prep gen*; (*origin*) ex, dē; (*cause*) *abl*; **all ~ us** nōs omnēs; **the city ~ Rome** urbs Rōma.
off *adv* procul; (*prefix*) ab-; **~ and on** interdum; **~ with you** aufer tē; **come ~** ēvādere; **well ~** beātus; **well ~ for** abundāns (*abl*).
offal *n* quisquiliae *fpl*.
offence *n* offēnsiō *f*; (*legal*) dēlictum *nt*; **commit an ~** dēlinquere.
offend *vt* laedere, offendere; **be ~ed** aegrē ferre ♦ *vi* delinquere; **~ against** peccāre in (*acc*), violāre.
offender *n* reus *m*.
offensive *adj* odiōsus; (*smell*) gravis; (*language*) contumēliōsus; **take the ~** bellum īnferre.
offensively *adv* odiōsē; graviter.
offer *vt* offerre, dare, praebēre; (*hand*) porrigere; (*violence*) adferre; (*honour*) dēferre; (*with verb*) profitērī, pollicērī ♦ *n* condiciō *f*; **~ for sale** venditāre.
offering *n* dōnum *nt*; (*to the dead*) īnferiae *fpl*.
off-hand *adj* neglegēns, incūriōsus.
office *n* (*POL*) magistrātus *m*, mūnus *nt*, honōs *m*; (*kindness*) officium *nt*; (*place*) mēnsa *f*.
officer *n* praefectus *m*; lēgātus *m*.
official *adj* pūblicus ♦ *n* adiūtor *m*, minister *m*.
officially *adv* pūblicē.
officiate *vi* operārī, officiō fungī.
officious *adj* molestus.
officiously *adv* molestē.
officiousness *n* occursātiō *f*.
offing *n*: **in the ~** procul.
offset *vt* compēnsāre.
offspring *n* prōgeniēs *f*, līberī *mpl*; (*animal*) fētus *m*.
often *adv* saepe, saepenumerō; **as ~ as** quotiēns; totiēs ... quotiēs; **how ~?** quotiēns?; **so ~** totiēns; **very ~** persaepe.
ogle *vi*: **~ at** līmīs oculīs intuērī.
ogre *n* mōnstrum *nt*.
oh *interj* (*joy, surprise*) ōh!; (*sorrow*) prō!
oil *n* oleum *nt* ♦ *vt* ungere.
oily *adj* oleōsus.
ointment *n* unguentum *nt*.
old *adj* (*person*) senex; (*thing*) vetus; (*ancient*) antīquus, prīscus; **~ age** senectūs *f*; **be ten years ~** decem annōs habēre; **ten years ~** decem annōs nātus; **two years ~** bīmus; **good ~** antīquus; **good ~ days** antīquitās *f*; **grow ~** senēscere; **of ~** quondam.
olden *adj* prīscus, prīstinus.
older *adj* nātū māior, senior.
oldest *adj* nātū māximus.
old-fashioned *adj* antīquus, obsolētus.
old man *n* senex *m*.
oldness *n* vetustās *f*.
old woman *n* anus *f*.
oligarchy *n* paucōrum dominātiō *f*, optimātium factiō *f*.
olive *n* olea *f*; **~ orchard** olīvētum *nt*.

Olympiad *n* Olympias *f*.
Olympic *adj* Olympicus; **win an ~ victory** Olympia vincere.
Olympic Games *n* Olympia *ntpl*.
omen *n* ōmen *nt*, auspicium *nt*; **announce a bad ~** obnūntiāre; **obtain favourable ~s** litāre.
ominous *adj* īnfaustus, mināx.
omission *n* praetermissiō *f*, neglegentia *f*.
omit *vt* ōmittere, praetermittere.
omnipotence *n* īnfīnīta potestās *f*.
omnipotent *adj* omnipotēns.
on *prep* (*place*) in (*abl*), in- (*prefix*); (*time*) *abl*; (*coast of*) ad (*acc*); (*subject*) dē (*abl*); (*side*) ab (*abl*) ♦ *adv* porrō, usque; **and so ~** ac deinceps; **~ hearing the news** nūntiō acceptō; **~ equal terms** (*in battle*) aequō Marte; **~ the following day** posterō/proximō diē; postrīdiē; **~ this side of** citrā (+ *acc*).
once *adv* semel; (*past*) ōlim, quondam; **at ~** extemplō, statim; (*together*) simul; **for ~** aliquandō; **~ and for all** semel; **~ more** dēnuō, iterum; **~ upon a time** ōlim, quondam.
one *num* ūnus ♦ *pron* quīdam; (*of two*) alter, altera, alterum; **~ and the same** ūnus; **~ another** inter sē, alius alium; **~ or the other** alteruter; **~ day** ōlim; **~ each** singulī; **~ would have thought** crēderēs; **be ~ of** in numerō esse (*gen*); **be at ~** idem sentīre; **it is all ~** nihil interest; **the ~ ... the other** hic, ille; **this is the ~** hōc illud est.
one-eyed *adj* luscus.
oneness *n* ūnitās *f*.
onerous *adj* gravis.
oneself *pron* ipse; (*reflexive*) sē.
one-sided *adj* inaequālis, inīquus.
onion *n* caepe *nt*.
onlooker *n* spectātor *m*.
only *adj* ūnus, sōlus; (*son*) ūnicus ♦ *adv* sōlum, tantum, modo; (*with clause*) nōn nisi, nīl nisi, nihil aliud quam; (*time*) dēmum; **if ~** sī modo; (*wish*) utinam.
onrush *n* incursus *m*.
onset *n* impetus *m*.
onslaught *n* incursus *m*; **make an ~ on** (*words*) invehī in (*acc*).
onto *prep* in (+ *acc*).
onus *n* officium *nt*.
onward, onwards *adv* porrō.
onyx *n* onyx *m*.
ooze *vi* mānāre, stillāre.
opaque *adj* haud perlūcidus.
open *adj* apertus; (*wide*) patēns, hiāns; (*ground*) pūrus, apertus; (*question*) integer; **lie ~** patēre; **stand ~** hiāre; **throw ~** adaperīre, patefacere; **it is ~ to me to** mihī integrum est (*inf*); **while the question is still ~** rē integrā ♦ *vt* aperīre, patefacere; (*book*) ēvolvere; (*letter*) resolvere; (*speech*) exōrdīrī; (*with ceremony*) inaugurāre; (*will*) resignāre ♦ *vi* aperīrī, hiscere; (*sore*) recrūdēscere; **~ out** extendere, pandere; **~ up** (*country*) aperīre.
open air *n*: **in the ~** sub dīvō.

open-handed *adj* largus, mūnificus.
open-handedness *n* largitās *f*.
open-hearted *adj* ingenuus.
opening *n* forāmen *nt*, hiātus *m*; (*ceremony*)
cōnsecrātiō *f*; (*opportunity*) occāsiō *f*, ānsa *f*
♦ *adj* prīmus.
openly *adv* palam, apertē.
open-mouthed *adj*: **stand ~ at** inhiāre.
operate *vi* rem gerere ♦ *vt* movēre.
operation *n* opus *nt*, āctiō *f*; (*MED*) sectiō *f*.
operative *adj* efficāx.
ophthalmia *n* lippitūdō *f*.
opiate *adj* somnifer.
opine *vi* opīnārī, existimāre.
opinion *n* sententia *f*; (*of person*) existimātiō *f*;
public ~ fāma *f*; **in my ~** meō iūdiciō, meō
animō.
opponent *n* adversārius *m*, hostis *m*.
opportune *adj* opportūnus, tempestīvus.
opportunely *adv* opportūnē.
opportunity *n* occāsiō *f*; (*to act*) facultās *f*;
potestās *f*.
oppose *vt* (*barrier*) obicere; (*contrast*)
oppōnere ♦ *vi* adversārī (*dat*), resistere (*dat*),
obstāre (*dat*); **be ~d to** adversārī (*dat*);
(*opinion*) dīversum esse ab.
opposite *adj* (*facing*) adversus; (*contrary*)
contrārius, dīversus ♦ *prep* contrā (*acc*),
adversus (*acc*); **directly ~** ē regiōne (*gen*)
♦ *adv* ex adversō.
opposition *n* repugnantia *f*; (*party*) factiō
adversa *f*.
oppress *vt* opprimere, adflīgere; (*burden*)
premere, onerāre.
oppression *n* iniūria *f*, servitūs *f*.
oppressive *adj* gravis, inīquus; **become more
~** ingravēscere.
oppressor *n* tyrannus *m*.
opprobrious *adj* turpis.
opprobriously *adv* turpiter.
opprobrium *n* dēdecus *nt*, ignōminia *f*.
optical *adj* oculōrum.
optical illusion *n* oculōrum lūdibrium *nt*.
optimism *n* spēs *f*.
option *n* optiō *f*, arbitrium *nt*; **I have no ~** nōn
est arbitriī meī.
optional *adj*: **it is ~ for you** optiō tua est.
opulence *n* opēs *fpl*, cōpia *f*.
opulent *adj* dīves, opulentus.
or *conj* aut, vel, -ve; (*after utrum*) an; **~ else**
aliōquīn; **~ not** (*direct*) annōn; (*indirect*)
necne.
oracle *n* ōrāculum *nt*.
oracular *adj* fātidicus; (*fig*) obscūrus.
oral *adj*: **give an ~ message** vōce nūntiāre.
orally *adv* vōce, verbīs.
oration *n* ōrātiō *f*.
orator *n* ōrātor *m*.
oratorical *adj* ōrātōrius.
oratory *n* ēloquentia *f*, rhētoricē *f*; (*for prayer*)
sacellum *nt*; **of ~** dīcendī, ōrātōrius.
orb *n* orbis *m*.
orbit *n* orbis *m*, ambitus *m*.
orchard *n* pōmārium *nt*.

ordain *vt* ēdīcere, sancīre.
ordeal *n* labor *m*.
order *n* (*arrangement*) ōrdō *m*; (*class*) ōrdō *m*;
(*battle*) aciēs *f*; (*command*) iussum *nt*,
imperium *nt*; (*money*) perscrīptiō *f*; **in ~**
dispositus; (*succession*) deinceps; **in ~ that/to**
ut (+ *subj*); **in ~ that not** nē (+ *subj*); **put in ~**
dispōnere, ōrdināre; **by ~ of** iussū (*gen*); **out
of ~** incompositus; **without ~s from** iniussū
(*gen*) ♦ *vt* (*arrange*) dispōnere, ōrdināre;
(*command*) iubēre (+ *acc and infin*), imperāre
(*dat and ut/nē +subj*).
orderly *adj* ōrdinātus; (*conduct*) modestus ♦ *n*
accēnsus *m*.
ordinance *n* ēdictum *nt*, institūtum *nt*.
ordinarily *adv* plērumque, ferē.
ordinary *adj* ūsitātus, solitus, cottīdiānus.
ordnance *n* tormenta *ntpl*.
ordure *n* stercus *m*.
ore *n* aes *nt*; **iron ~** ferrum īnfectum *nt*.
Oread *n* (*MYTH*) Oreas *f*.
organ *n* (*bodily*) membrum *nt*; (*musical*)
organum *nt*, hydraulus *m*.
organic *adj* nātūrālis.
organically *adv* nātūrā.
organization *n* ōrdinātiō *f*, structūra *f*.
organize *vt* ōrdināre, īnstituere, adparāre.
orgies *n* orgia *ntpl*.
orgy *n* cōmissātiō *f*.
orient *n* oriēns *m*.
oriental *adj* Asiāticus.
orifice *n* ōstium *nt*.
origin *n* orīgō *f*, prīncipium *nt*; (*source*) fōns *m*;
(*birth*) genus *nt*.
original *adj* prīmus, prīstinus; (*LIT*) proprius
♦ *n* exemplar *nt*.
originally *adv* prīncipiō, antīquitus.
originate *vt* īnstituere, auctōrem esse (*gen*)
♦ *vi* exorīrī; **~ in** innāscī in (*abl*), initium
dūcere ab.
originator *n* auctor *m*.
orisons *n* precēs *fpl*.
ornament *n* ōrnāmentum *nt*; (*fig*) decus *nt* ♦ *vt*
ōrnāre, decorāre; **I am ~** ōrnamentō sum.
ornamental *adj* decōrus; **be ~** decorī esse.
ornamentally *adv* ōrnātē.
ornate *adj* ōrnātus.
ornately *adv* ōrnātē.
orphan *n* orbus *m*, orba *f*.
orphaned *adj* orbātus.
orthodox *adj* antīquus.
orthography *n* orthographia *f*.
oscillate *vi* reciprocāre.
osculate *vt* ōsculārī.
osier *n* vīmen *n* ♦ *adj* vīmineus.
osprey *n* haliaeetos *m*.
ostensible *adj* speciōsus.
ostensibly *adv* per speciem.
ostentation *n* iactātiō *f*, ostentātiō *f*.
ostentatious *adj* glōriōsus, ambitiōsus.
ostentatiously *adv* glōriōsē.
ostler *n* agāsō *m*.
ostrich *n* strūthiocamēlus *m*.

other *adj* alius; (*of two*) alter; **one or the ~**
alteruter; **every ~ year** tertiō quōque annō;
on the ~ side of ultrā (+ *acc*); **of ~s** aliēnus.
otherwise *adv* aliter; (*if not*) aliōquī.
otter *n* lutra *f*.
ought *vi* dēbēre (+ *infin or gerundive of vt*); **I ~**
mē oportet; **I ~ to have said** dēbuī dīcere.
ounce *n* ūncia *f*; **two ~s** sextāns *m*; **three ~s**
quadrāns *m*; **four ~s** triēns *m*; **five ~s**
quīncūnx *m*; **six ~s** sēmis *m*; **seven ~s** septūnx
m; **eight ~s** bēs *m*; **nine ~s** dōdrāns *m*; **ten ~s**
dextāns *m*; **eleven ~s** deūnx *m*.
our *adj* noster.
ourselves *pron* ipsī; (*reflexive*) nōs.
oust *vt* extrūdere, ēicere.
out *adv* (*rest*) forīs; (*motion*) forās; **~ of** dē, ē/ex
(*abl*); (*cause*) propter (*acc*); (*beyond*) extrā,
ultrā (*acc*); **be ~** (*book*) in manibus esse;
(*calculation*) errāre; (*fire*) exstinctum esse;
(*secret*) palam esse.
outbreak *n* initium *nt*, ēruptiō *f*.
outburst *n* ēruptiō *f*.
outcast *n* profugus *m*.
outcome *n* ēventus *m*, exitus *m*.
outcry *n* clāmor *m*, adclāmātiō *f*; **raise an ~**
against obstrepere (*dat*).
outdistance *vt* praevertere.
outdo *vt* superāre.
outdoor *adj* sub dīvō.
outer *adj* exterior.
outermost *adj* extrēmus.
outfit *n* īnstrūmenta *ntpl*; vestīmenta *ntpl*.
outflank *vt* circumīre.
outgrow *vt* excēdere ex.
outing *n* excursiō *f*.
outlandish *adj* barbarus.
outlaw *n* prōscrīptus *m* ♦ *vt* prōscrībere, aquā
et ignī interdīcere (*dat*).
outlawry *n* aquae et ignis interdictiō *f*.
outlay *n* impēnsa *f*, sūmptus *m*.
outlet *n* ēmissārium *nt*, exitus *m*.
outline *n* ductus *m*, adumbrātiō *f* ♦ *vt*
adumbrāre.
outlive *vt* superesse (*dat*).
outlook *n* prōspectus *m*.
outlying *adj* longinquus, exterior.
outnumber *vt* numerō superiōrēs esse,
multitūdine superāre.
out-of-doors *adv* forīs.
outpost *n* statiō *f*.
outpouring *n* effūsiō *f*.
output *n* fructus *m*.
outrage *n* flāgitium *nt*, iniūria *f* ♦ *vt* laedere,
violāre.
outrageous *adj* flāgitiōsus, indignus.
outrageously *adv* flāgitiōsē.
outrider *n* praecursor *m*.
outright *adv* penitus, prōrsus; semel.
outrun *vt* praevertere.
outset *n* initium *nt*.
outshine *vt* praelūcēre (*dat*).
outside *adj* externus ♦ *adv* extrā, forīs;
(*motion to*) forās; **~ in** inversus; **from ~**

extrīnsecus ♦ *n* exterior pars *f*; (*show*)
speciēs *f*; **at the ~** summum, ad summum; **on
the ~** extrīnsecus ♦ *prep* extrā (*acc*).
outsider *n* aliēnus *m*; (POL) novus homō *m*.
outskirts *n* suburbānus ager *m*; **on the ~**
suburbānus.
outspoken *adj* līber.
outspokenness *n* lībertās *f*.
outspread *adj* patulus.
outstanding *adj* ēgregius, īnsignis,
singulāris; (*debt*) residuus.
outstep *vt* excēdere.
outstretched *adj* passus, porrēctus, extentus.
outstrip *vt* praevertere.
outvote *vt* suffrāgiīs superāre.
outward *adj* externus; **~ form** speciēs *f* ♦ *adv*
domō, forās.
outweigh *vt* praeponderāre.
outwit *vt* dēcipere, circumvenīre.
outwork *n* prōpugnāculum *nt*, bracchium *nt*.
outworn *adj* exolētus.
oval *adj* ōvātus ♦ *n* ōvum *nt*.
ovation *n* (*triumph*) ovātiō *f*; **receive an ~** cum
laudibus excipī.
oven *n* furnus *m*, fornāx *f*.
over *prep* (*above*) super (*abl*), suprā (*acc*);
(*across*) super (*acc*); (*extent*) per (*acc*); (*time*)
inter (*acc*); **~ and above** super (*acc*), praeter
(*acc*); **all ~** per; **~ against** adversus (*acc*) ♦ *adv*
suprā; (*excess*) nimis; (*done*) cōnfectus; **~**
again dēnuō; **~ and above** īnsuper; **~ and ~**
identidem; **be left ~** superesse, restāre; **it is**
all ~ with āctum est dē.
overall *adj* tōtus ♦ *adv* ubīque, passim.
overawe *vt* formīdinem inicere (*dat*).
overbalance *vi* titubāre.
overbearing *adj* superbus.
overboard *adv* ē nāvī, in mare; **throw ~**
excutere, iactāre.
overbold *adj* importūnus.
overburden *vt* praegravāre.
overcast *adj* nūbilus.
overcoat *n* paenula *f*, lacerna *f*.
overcome *vt* superāre, vincere.
overconfidence *n* cōnfīdentia *f*.
overconfident *adj* cōnfīdēns.
overdo *vt* modum excēdere in (*abl*).
overdone *adj* (*style*) pūtidus.
overdraw *vt* (*style*) exaggerāre.
overdue *adj* (*money*) residuus.
overestimate *vt* māiōris aestimāre.
overflow *n* ēluviō *f* ♦ *vi* abundāre, redundāre
♦ *vt* inundāre.
overgrown *adj* obsitus; **be ~** luxuriāre.
overhang *vt*, *vi* impendēre, imminēre (*dat*).
overhaul *vt* reficere.
overhead *adv* īnsuper.
overhear *vt* excipere, auscultāre.
overjoyed *adj* nimiō gaudiō ēlātus.
overladen *adj* praegravātus.
overland *adv* terrā.
overlap *vt* implicāre.
overlay *vt* indūcere.

overload *vt* (*fig*) obruere.
overlook *vt* (*place*) dēspectāre, imminēre (*dat*); (*knowledge*) ignōrāre; (*notice*) neglegere, praetermittere; (*fault*) ignōscere (*dat*).
overlord *n* dominus *m*.
overmaster *vt* dēvincere.
overmuch *adv* nimis, plūs aequō.
overnight *adj* nocturnus ♦ *adv* noctū.
overpower *vt* superāre, domāre, obruere, opprimere.
overpraise *vt* in māius extollere.
overrate *vt* māiōris aestimāre.
overreach *vt* circumvenīre.
overriding *adj* praecipuus.
overrule *vt* rescindere.
overrun *vt* pervagārī; (*fig*) obsidēre.
oversea *adj* trānsmarīnus.
oversee *vt* praeesse (*dat*).
overseer *n* cūrātor *m*, custōs *m*.
overset *vt* ēvertere.
overshadow *vt* officere (*dat*).
overshoot *vt* excēdere.
oversight *n* neglegentia *f*.
overspread *vt* offendere (*dat*), obdūcere.
overstep *vt* excēdere.
overt *adj* apertus.
overtake *vt* cōnsequī; (*surprise*) opprimere, dēprehendere.
overtax *vt* (*fig*) abūtī (*abl*).
overthrow *vt* ēvertere; (*destroy*) prōflīgāre, dēbellāre ♦ *n* ēversiō *f*, ruīna *f*.
overtly *adv* palam.
overtop *vt* superāre.
overture *n* exōrdium *nt*; **make ~s to** temptāre, agere cum, lēgātōs mittere ad.
overturn *vt* ēvertere.
overweening *adj* superbus, adrogāns, īnsolēns.
overwhelm *vt* obruere, dēmergere, opprimere.
overwhelming *adj* īnsignis, vehementissimus.
overwhelmingly *adv* mīrum quantum.
overwork *vi* plūs aequō labōrāre ♦ *vt* cōnficere ♦ *n* immodicus labor *m*.
overwrought *adj* (*emotion*) ēlātus; (*style*) ēlabōrātus.
owe *vt* dēbēre.
owing *adj*: **be ~** dēbērī; **~ to** (*person*) per; (*cause*) ob/propter (*acc*).
owl *n* būbō *m*; ulula *f*.
own *adj* proprius; **my ~** meus; **have of one's ~** domī habēre; **hold one's ~** parem esse ♦ *vt* possidēre, habēre; (*admit*) fatērī, cōnfitērī.
owner *n* dominus *m*, possessor *m*.
ownership *n* possessiō *f*, mancipium *nt*.
ox *n* bōs *m*.
ox herd *n* bubulcus *m*.
oyster *n* ostrea *f*.

P, p

pace *n* passus *m*; (*speed*) gradus *m*; **keep ~ gradum cōnferre** ♦ *vi* incēdere; **~ up and down** spatiārī, inambulāre.
pacific *adj* pācificus; (*quiet*) placidus.
pacification *n* pācificātiō *f*.
pacifist *n* imbellis *m*.
pacify *vt* (*anger*) plācāre; (*rising*) sēdāre.
pack *n* (*MIL*) sarcina *f*; (*animals*) grex *m*; (*people*) turba *f* ♦ *vt* (*kit*) colligere; (*crowd*) stīpāre; **~ together** coartāre; **~ up** colligere, compōnere ♦ *vi* vāsa colligere; **send ~ing** missum facere ♦ *adj* (*animal*) clītellārius.
package *n* fasciculus *m*, sarcina *f*.
packet *n* fasciculus *m*; (*ship*) nāvis āctuāria *f*.
packhorse *n* iūmentum *nt*.
packsaddle *n* clītellae *fpl*.
pact *n* foedus *nt*, pactum *nt*.
pad *n* pulvillus *m*.
padding *n* tōmentum *nt*.
paddle *n* rēmus *m* ♦ *vi* rēmigāre.
paddock *n* saeptum *nt*.
paean *n* paeān *m*.
pagan *adj* pāgānus.
page *n* (*book*) pāgina *f*; (*boy*) puer *m*.
pageant *n* pompa *f*, spectāculum *nt*.
pageantry *n* adparātus *m*.
pail *n* situla *f*.
pain *n* dolor *m*; **be in ~** dolēre ♦ *vt* dolōre adficere.
painful *adj* acerbus; (*work*) labōriōsus.
painfully *adv* acerbē, labōriōsē.
painless *adj* dolōris expers.
painlessly *adv* sine dolōre.
painlessness *n* indolentia *f*.
pains *npl* opera *f*; **take ~** operam dare; **take ~ with** (*art*) ēlabōrāre.
painstaking *adj* dīligēns, operōsus.
painstakingly *adv* dīligenter, summā cūrā.
paint *n* pigmentum *nt*; (*cosmetic*) fūcus *m* ♦ *vt* pingere; (*red*) fūcāre; (*in words*) dēpingere; (*portrait*) dēpingere.
paintbrush *n* pēnicillus *m*.
painter *n* pictor *m*.
painting *n* pictūra *f*.
pair *n* pār *nt* ♦ *vt* coniungere, compōnere.
palace *n* rēgia *f*.
palatable *adj* suāvis, iūcundus.
palate *n* palātum *nt*.
palatial *adj* rēgius.
palaver *n* colloquium *nt*, sermunculī *mpl*.
pale *n* pālus *m*, vallus *m*; **beyond the ~** extrāneus ♦ *adj* pallidus; **look ~** pallēre; **grow ~** pallēscere; **~ brown** subfuscus; **~ green** subviridis ♦ *vi* pallēscere.
paleness *n* pallor *m*.

palimpsest n palimpsēstus m.
paling n saepēs f.
palisade n (MIL) vallum nt.
palish adj pallidulus.
pall n (funeral) pallium nt ♦ vi taedēre.
pallet n grabātus m.
palliasse n strāmentum nt.
palliate vt extenuāre, excūsāre.
palliation n excūsātiō f.
palliative n lēnīmentum nt.
pallid adj pallidus.
pallor n pallor m.
palm n (hand) palma f; (tree) palma f ♦ vt: ~ off
   impōnere.
palmy adj flōrēns.
palpable adj tractābilis; (fig) manifestus.
palpably adv manifestō, propalam.
palpitate vi palpitāre, micāre.
palpitation n palpitātiō f.
palsied adj membrīs captus.
palsy n paralysis f.
paltry adj vīlis, frīvolus.
pamper vt indulgēre (dat).
pampered adj dēlicātus.
pamphlet n libellus m.
pan n patina f, patella f; (frying) sartāgō f; (of
   balance) lanx f.
pancake n laganum nt.
pander n lēnō m ♦ vi: ~ to lēnōcinārī (dat).
panegyric n laudātiō f.
panegyrist n laudātor m.
panel n (wall) abacus m; (ceiling) lacūnār nt;
   (judges) decuria f.
panelled adj laqueātus.
pang n dolor m.
panic n pavor m ♦ vi trepidāre.
panic-stricken adj pavidus.
panniers n clītellae fpl.
panoply n arma ntpl.
panorama n prōspectus m.
panpipe n fistula f.
pant vi anhēlāre.
panther n panthēra f.
panting n anhēlitus m.
pantomime n mīmus m.
pantry n cella penāria f.
pap n mamma f.
paper n charta f.
papyrus n papyrus f.
par n: on a ~ with pār (dat).
parable n parabolē f.
parade n pompa f; (show) adparātus m ♦ vt
   trādūcere, iactāre ♦ vi pompam dūcere,
   incēdere.
paradox n verba sēcum repugnantia; ~es pl
   paradoxa ntpl.
paragon n exemplar nt, specimen nt.
paragraph n caput nt.
parallel adj parallēlus; (fig) cōnsimilis.
paralyse vt dēbilitāre; (with fear) percellere;
   be ~d torpēre.
paralysis n dēbilitās f; (fig) torpēdō f.
paramount adj prīnceps, summus.

paramour n adulter m.
parapet n lōrīca f.
paraphernalia n adparātus m.
paraphrase vt vertere.
parasite n parasītus m.
parasol n umbella f.
parboiled adj subcrūdus.
parcel n fasciculus m ♦ vt: ~ out distribuere,
   dispertīre.
parch vt torrēre.
parched adj torridus, āridus; be ~ ārēre.
parchment n membrāna f.
pardon n venia f ♦ vt ignōscere (dat); (offence)
   condōnāre.
pardonable adj ignōscendus.
pare vt dēglūbere; (nails) resecāre.
parent n parēns m/f, genitor m, genetrīx f.
parentage n stirps f, genus nt.
parental adj patrius.
parenthesis n interclūsiō f.
parings n praesegmina ntpl.
parish n (ECCL) paroecia f.
parity n aequālitās f.
park n hortī mpl.
parlance n sermō m.
parley n colloquium nt ♦ vi colloquī, agere.
parliament n senātus m; house of ~ cūria f.
parliamentary adj senātōrius.
parlour n exedrium nt.
parlous adj difficilis, perīculōsus.
parochial adj mūnicipālis.
parody n carmen ioculāre nt ♦ vt calumniārī.
parole n fidēs f.
paronomasia n agnōminātiō f.
paroxysm n accessus m.
parricide n (doer) parricīda m; (deed)
   parricīdium nt.
parrot n psittacus m.
parry vt ēlūdere, prōpulsāre.
parsimonious adj parcus.
parsimoniously adv parcē.
parsimony n parsimōnia f, frūgālitās f.
part n pars f; (play) partēs fpl, persōna f; (duty)
   officium nt; ~s loca ntpl; (ability) ingenium nt;
   for my ~ equidem; for the most ~ māximam
   partem; on the ~ of ab; act the ~ of persōnam
   sustinēre, partēs agere; have no ~ in expers
   esse (gen); in ~ partim; it is the ~ of a wise
   man sapientis est; play one's ~ officiō
   satisfacere; take ~ in interesse (dat),
   particeps esse (gen); take in good ~ in bonam
   partem accipere; take someone's ~ adesse
   alicuī, dēfendere aliquem; from all ~s
   undique; in foreign ~s peregrē; in two ~s
   bifāriam; (MIL) bipartītō; in three ~s
   trifāriam; (MIL) tripartītō; of ~s ingeniōsus ♦
   vt dīvidere, sēparāre, dirimere; ~ company
   dīversōs discēdere ♦ vi dīgredī, discēdere;
   (things) dissilīre; ~ with renūntiāre.
partake vi interesse, particeps esse; ~ of
   gustāre.
partial adj (biased) inīquus, studiōsus;
   (incomplete) mancus; be ~ to favēre (dat),

studēre (*dat*); **win a ~ victory** aliquā ex parte
vincere.
partiality *n* favor *m*, studium *nt*.
partially *adv* partim, aliquā ex parte.
participant *n* particeps *m/f*.
participate *vi* interesse, particeps esse.
participation *n* societās *f*.
particle *n* particula *f*.
parti-coloured *adj* versicolor, varius.
particular *adj* (*own*) proprius; (*special*)
praecipuus; (*exact*) dīligēns, accūrātus;
(*fastidious*) fastīdiōsus; **a ~ person** quīdam ♦
n rēs *f*; **with full ~s** subtīliter; **give all the ~s**
omnia exsequī; **in ~** praesertim.
particularity *n* subtīlitās *f*.
particularize *vt* singula exsequī.
particularly *adv* praecipuē, praesertim, in
prīmīs, māximē.
parting *n* dīgressus *m*, discessus *m* ♦ *adj*
ultimus.
partisan *n* fautor *m*, studiōsus *m*.
partisanship *n* studium *nt*.
partition *n* (*act*) partītiō *f*; (*wall*) pariēs *m*;
(*compartment*) loculāmentum *nt* ♦ *vt*
dīvidere.
partly *adv* partim, ex parte.
partner *n* socius *m*; (*in office*) collēga *f*.
partnership *n* societās *f*; **form a ~** societātem
inīre.
partridge *n* perdīx *m/f*.
parturition *n* partus *m*.
party *n* (*POL*) factiō *f*, partēs *fpl*; (*entertainment*)
convīvium *nt*; (*MIL*) manus *f*; (*individual*) homō
m/f; (*associate*) socius *m*, cōnscius *m*.
party spirit *n* studium *nt*.
parvenu *n* novus homō *m*.
pass *n* (*hill*) saltus *m*; (*narrow*) angustiae *fpl*,
faucēs *fpl*; (*crisis*) discrīmen *nt*; (*document*)
diplōma *nt*; (*fighting*) petītiō *f*; **things have
come to such a ~** in eum locum ventum est,
adeō rēs rediit ♦ *vi* īre, praeterīre; (*time*)
trānsīre; (*property*) pervenīre; **~ away** abīre;
(*die*) morī, perīre; (*fig*) dēfluere; **~ by**
praeterīre; **~ for** habērī prō (*abl*); **~ off** abīre;
~ on pergere; **~ over** trānsīre; **come to ~** fierī,
ēvenīre; **let ~** intermittere, praetermittere ♦
vt praeterīre; (*riding*) praetervehī; (*by hand*)
trādere; (*law*) iubēre; (*limit*) excēdere;
(*sentence*) interpōnere, dīcere; (*test*)
satisfacere (*dat*); (*time*) dēgere, agere; **~
accounts** ratiōnēs ratās habēre; **~ the day**
diem cōnsūmere; **~ a law** lēgem ferre; **~ a
decree** dēcernere; **~ off** ferre; **~ over**
praeterīre, mittere; (*fault*) ignōscere (*dat*); **~
round** trādere; **~ through** trānsīre.
passable *adj* (*place*) pervius; (*standard*)
mediocris.
passably *adv* mediocriter.
passage *n* iter *nt*, cursus *m*; (*land*) trānsitus *m*;
(*sea*) trānsmissiō *f*; (*book*) locus *m*; **of ~** (*bird*)
advena.
passenger *n* vector *m*.
passer-by *n* praeteriēns *m*.

passing *n* obitus *m* ♦ *adj* admodum.
passion *n* animī mōtus *m*, permōtiō *f*, ārdor *m*;
(*anger*) īra *f*; (*lust*) libīdō *f*.
passionate *adj* ārdēns, impotēns, ācer;
īrācundus.
passionately *adv* vehementer, ārdenter;
īrācundē; **be ~ in love** amōre ārdēre.
passive *adj* iners.
passiveness *n* inertia *f*, patientia *f*.
passport *n* diplōma *nt*.
password *n* tessera *f*.
past *adj* praeteritus; (*recent*) proximus ♦ *n*
praeterita *ntpl* ♦ *prep* praeter (*acc*); (*beyond*)
ultrā (*acc*).
paste *n* glūten *nt* ♦ *vt* glūtināre.
pastime *n* lūdus *m*, oblectāmentum *nt*.
pastoral *adj* pastōrālis; (*poem*) būcolicus.
pastry *n* crustum *nt*.
pasture *n* pāstus *m*, pāscuum *nt* ♦ *vt* pāscere.
pat *vt* dēmulcēre ♦ *adj* opportūnus.
patch *n* pannus *m* ♦ *vt* resarcīre.
patchwork *n* centō *m*.
pate *n* caput *nt*.
patent *adj* apertus, manifestus ♦ *n*
prīvilēgium *nt*.
patently *adv* manifestō.
paternal *adj* paternus.
path *n* sēmita *f*, trāmes *m*.
pathetic *adj* miserābilis.
pathetically *adv* miserābiliter.
pathfinder *n* explorātor *m*.
pathless *adj* āvius.
pathos *n* misericordia *f*; (*RHET*) dolor *m*.
pathway *n* sēmita *f*.
patience *n* patientia *f*.
patient *adj* patiēns ♦ *n* aeger *m*.
patiently *adv* patienter, aequō animō.
patois *n* sermō *m*.
patrician *adj* patricius ♦ *n* patricius *m*.
patrimony *n* patrimōnium *nt*.
patriot *n* amāns patriae *m*.
patriotic *adj* pius, amāns patriae.
patriotically *adv* prō patriā.
patriotism *n* amor patriae *m*.
patrol *n* excubiae *fpl* ♦ *vi* circumīre.
patron *n* patrōnus *m*, fautor *m*.
patronage *n* patrōcinium *nt*.
patroness *n* patrōna *f*, fautrīx *f*.
patronize *vt* favēre (*dat*), fovēre.
patronymic *n* nōmen *nt*.
patter *vi* crepitāre ♦ *n* crepitus *m*.
pattern *n* exemplar *nt*, exemplum *nt*, nōrma *f*;
(*ideal*) specimen *nt*; (*design*) figūra *f*.
paucity *n* paucitās *f*.
paunch *n* abdōmen *nt*, venter *m*.
pauper *n* pauper *m*.
pause *n* mora *f*, intervallum *nt* ♦ *vi* īnsistere,
intermittere.
pave *vt* sternere; **~ the way** (*fig*) viam mūnīre.
pavement *n* pavīmentum *nt*.
pavilion *n* tentōrium *nt*.
paw *n* pēs *m* ♦ *vt* pede pulsāre.
pawn *n* (*chess*) latrunculus *m*; (*COMM*) pignus *nt*,

fīdūcia *f* ♦ *vt* oppignerāre.
pawnbroker *n* pignerātor *m*.
pay *n* mercēs *f*; (MIL) stīpendium *nt*; (*workman*)
manupretium *nt* ♦ *vt* solvere, pendere; (*debt*)
exsolvere; (*in full*) persolvere; (*honour*)
persolvere; (MIL) stīpendium numerāre (*dat*);
(*penalty*) dare, luere; ~ **down** numerāre; ~ **for**
condūcere; ~ **off** dissolvere, exsolvere; ~ **out**
expendere; (*publicly*) ērogāre; ~ **up**
dēpendere; ~ **a compliment to** laudāre; ~
respects to salūtāre ♦ *vi* respondēre; **it ~s**
expedit.
payable *adj* solvendus.
paymaster *n* (MIL) tribūnus aerārius *m*.
payment *n* solūtiō *f*; (*money*) pēnsiō *f*.
pea *n* pīsum *n*; **like as two ~s** tam similis quam
lac lactī est.
peace *n* pāx *f*; ~ **and quiet** ōtium *nt*; **breach of**
the ~ vīs *f*; **establish** ~ pācem conciliāre; **hold**
one's ~ reticēre; **sue for** ~ pācem petere.
peaceable *adj* imbellis, placidus.
peaceably *adv* placidē.
peaceful *adj* tranquillus, placidus, pācātus.
peacefully *adv* tranquillē.
peacemaker *n* pācificus *m*.
peace-offering *n* piāculum *nt*.
peach *n* Persicum *nt*.
peacock *n* pāvō *m*.
peak *n* apex *m*, vertex *m*.
peal *n* (*bell*) sonitus *m*; (*thunder*) fragor *m* ♦ *vi*
sonāre.
pear *n* pirum *nt*; (*tree*) pirus *f*.
pearl *n* margarīta *f*.
pearly *adj* gemmeus; (*colour*) candidus.
peasant *n* agricola *m*, colōnus *m*.
peasantry *n* agricolae *mpl*.
pebble *n* calculus *m*.
pebbly *adj* lapidōsus.
peccadillo *n* culpa *f*.
peck *n* (*measure*) modius *m* ♦ *vt* vellicāre.
peculate *vi* pecūlārī.
peculation *n* pecūlātus *m*.
peculiar *adj* (*to one*) proprius; (*strange*)
singulāris.
peculiarity *n* proprietās *f*, nota *f*.
peculiarly *adv* praecipuē, praesertim.
pecuniary *adj* pecūniārius.
pedagogue *n* magister *m*.
pedant *n* scholasticus *m*.
pedantic *adj* nimis dīligenter.
pedantically *adv* dīligentior.
pedantry *n* nimia dīligentia *f*.
peddle *vt* circumferre.
pedestal *n* basis *f*.
pedestrian *adj* pedester ♦ *n* pedes *m*.
pedigree *n* stirps *f*, stemma *nt* ♦ *adj* generōsus.
pediment *n* fastīgium *nt*.
pedlar *n* īnstitor *m*, circumforāneus *m*.
peel *n* cortex *m* ♦ *vt* glūbere.
peep *vi* dīspicere ♦ *n* aspectus *m*; **at** ~ **of day**
prīmā lūce.
peer *vi*: ~ **at** intuērī ♦ *n* pār *m*; (*rank*) patricius
m.

peerless *adj* ūnicus, ēgregius.
peevish *adj* stomachōsus, mōrōsus.
peevishly *adv* stomachōsē, mōrōsē.
peevishness *n* stomachus *m*, mōrōsitās *f*.
peg *n* clāvus *m*; **put a round ~ in a square hole**
bovī clītellās impōnere ♦ *vt* clāvīs dēfīgere.
pelf *n* lucrum *nt*.
pellet *n* globulus *m*.
pell-mell *adv* prōmiscuē, turbātē.
pellucid *adj* perlūcidus.
pelt *n* pellis *f* ♦ *vt* petere ♦ *vi* violenter cadere.
pen *n* calamus *m*, stilus *m*; (*cattle*) saeptum *nt* ♦
vt scrībere.
penal *adj* poenālis.
penalize *vt* poenā adficere, multāre.
penalty *n* poena *f*, damnum *nt*; (*fine*) multa *f*;
pay the ~ poenās dare.
penance *n* supplicium *nt*.
pencil *n* graphis *f*.
pending *adj* sub iūdice ♦ *prep* inter (*acc*).
penetrable *adj* pervius.
penetrate *vt* penetrāre.
penetrating *adj* ācer, acūtus; (*mind*)
perspicāx.
penetration *n* (*mind*) acūmen *nt*.
peninsula *n* paenīnsula *f*.
penitence *n* paenitentia *f*.
penitent *adj*: **I am** ~ mē paenitet.
penknife *n* scalpellum *nt*.
penmanship *n* scrīptiō *f*, manus *f*.
pennant *n* vexillum *nt*.
penny *n* dēnārius *m*.
pension *n* annua *ntpl*.
pensioner *n* ēmeritus *m*.
pensive *adj* attentus.
pensiveness *n* cōgitātiō *f*.
pent *adj* inclūsus.
penthouse *n* (MIL) vīnea *f*.
penurious *adj* parcus, avārus, tenāx.
penuriousness *n* parsimōnia *f*, tenācitās *f*.
penury *n* egestās *f*, inopia *f*.
people *n* hominēs *mpl*; (*nation*) populus *m*, gēns
f; **common** ~ plēbs *f* ♦ *vt* frequentāre.
peopled *adj* frequēns.
pepper *n* piper *nt*.
peradventure *adv* fortasse.
perambulate *vi* spatiārī, inambulāre.
perceive *vt* sentīre, percipere, intellegere.
perceptible *adj*: **be** ~ sentīrī posse, audīrī
posse.
perception *n* sēnsus *m*.
perch *n* (*bird's*) pertica *f*; (*fish*) perca *f* ♦ *vi*
īnsīdēre.
perchance *adv* fortasse, forsitan (*subj*).
percolate *vi* permānāre.
percussion *n* ictus *m*.
perdition *n* exitium *nt*.
peregrinate *vi* peregrīnārī.
peregrination *n* peregrīnātiō *f*.
peremptorily *adv* praecīsē, prō imperiō.
peremptory *adj* imperiōsus.
perennial *adj* perennis.
perfect *adj* perfectus, absolūtus; (*entire*)

integer; (*faultless*) ēmendātus ♦ *vt* perficere, absolvere.
perfection *n* perfectiō *f*, absolūtiō *f*.
perfectly *adv* perfectē, ēmendātē; (*quite*) plānē.
perfidious *adj* perfidus, perfidiōsus.
perfidiously *adv* perfidiōsē.
perfidy *n* perfidia *f*.
perforate *vt* perforāre, terebrāre.
perforation *n* forāmen *nt*.
perforce *adv* per vim, necessāriō.
perform *vt* perficere, peragere; (*duty*) exsequī, fungī (*abl*); (*play*) agere.
performance *n* (*process*) exsecūtiō *f*, fūnctiō *f*; (*deed*) factum *nt*; (*stage*) fābula *f*.
performer *n* āctor *m*; (*music*) tībīcen *m*, fidicen *m*; (*stage*) histriō *m*.
perfume *n* odor *m*, unguentum *nt* ♦ *vt* odōrāre.
perfumer *n* unguentārius *m*.
perfumery *n* unguenta *ntpl*.
perfunctorily *adv* neglegenter.
perfunctory *adj* neglegēns.
perhaps *adv* fortasse, forsitan (*subj*), nesciō an (*subj*); (*tentative*) vel; (*interrog*) an.
peril *n* perīculum *m*, discrīmen *nt*.
perilous *adj* perīculōsus.
perilously *adv* perīculōsē.
perimeter *n* ambitus *m*.
period *n* tempus *nt*, spatium *nt*; (*history*) aetās *f*, (*end*) terminus *m*; (*sentence*) complexiō *f*, ambitus *m*.
periodic *adj* (*style*) circumscrīptus.
periodical *adj* status.
periodically *adv* certīs temporibus, identidem.
peripatetic *adj* vagus; (*sect*) peripatēticus.
periphery *n* ambitus *m*.
periphrasis *n* circuitus *m*.
perish *vi* perīre, interīre.
perishable *adj* cadūcus, fragilis, mortālis.
peristyle *n* peristȳlium *nt*.
perjure *vi*: ~ **o.s.** pēierāre.
perjured *adj* periūrus.
perjurer *n* periūrus *m*.
perjury *n* periūrium *nt*; **commit** ~ pēierāre.
permanence *n* cōnstantia *f*, stabilitās *f*.
permanent *adj* stabilis, diūturnus, perpetuus.
permanently *adv* perpetuō.
permeable *adj* penetrābilis.
permeate *vt* penetrāre ♦ *vi* permānāre.
permissible *adj* licitus, concessus; **it is** ~ licet.
permission *n* potestās *f*; **ask** ~ veniam petere; **give** ~ veniam dare, potestātem facere; **by** ~ of permissū (*gen*); **with your kind** ~ bonā tuā veniā; **without your** ~ tē invītō.
permit *vt* sinere, permittere (*dat*); **I am ~ted** licet mihī.
pernicious *adj* perniciōsus, exitiōsus.
perorate *vi* perōrāre.
peroration *n* perōrātiō *f*, epilogus *m*.
perpendicular *adj* dīrēctus.
perpendicularly *adv* ad perpendiculum, ad līneam.

perpetrate *vt* facere, admittere.
perpetual *adj* perpetuus, perennis, sempiternus.
perpetually *adv* perpetuō.
perpetuate *vt* continuāre, perpetuāre.
perpetuity *n* perpetuitās *f*.
perplex *vt* sollicitāre, cōnfundere.
perplexing *adj* ambiguus, perplexus.
perplexity *n* haesitātiō *f*.
perquisite *n* pecūlium *nt*.
persecute *vt* īnsectārī, exagitāre; persequi.
persecution *n* īnsectātiō *f*.
persecutor *n* īnsectātor *m*.
perseverance *n* pesevērantia *f*, cōnstantia *f*.
persevere *vi* persevērāre, perstāre; ~ **in** tenēre.
Persian *n* Persa *m*.
persist *vt* īnstāre, perstāre, persevērāre.
persistence, persistency *n* pertinācia *f*, persevērantia *f*.
persistent *adj* pertināx.
persistently *adv* pertināciter, persevēranter.
person *n* homō *m/f*; (*counted*) caput *nt*; (*character*) persōna *f*; (*body*) corpus *nt*; **in** ~ ipse praesēns.
personage *n* vir *m*.
personal *adj* prīvātus, suus.
personality *n* nātūra *f*; (*person*) vir ēgregius *m*.
personally *adv* ipse, cōram.
personal property *n* pecūlium *nt*.
personate *vt* persōnam gerere (*gen*).
personification *n* prosōpopoeia *f*.
personify *vt* hūmānam nātūram tribuere (*dat*).
personnel *n* membra *ntpl*, sociī *mpl*.
perspective *n* scaenographia *f*.
perspicacious *adj* perspicāx, acūtus.
perspicacity *n* perspicācitās *f*, acūmen *nt*.
perspicuity *n* perspicuitās *f*.
perspicuous *adj* perspicuus.
perspiration *n* sūdor *m*.
perspire *vi* sūdāre.
persuade *vt* persuādēre (*dat*); (*by entreaty*) exōrāre.
persuasion *n* persuāsiō *f*.
persuasive *adj* blandus.
persuasively *adv* blandē.
pert *adj* procāx, protervus.
pertain *vi* pertinēre, attinēre.
pertinacious *adj* pertināx.
pertinaciously *adv* pertināciter.
pertinacity *n* pertinācia *f*.
pertinent *adj* appositus; **be** ~ ad rem pertinēre.
pertinently *adv* appositē.
pertly *adv* procāciter, protervē.
perturb *vt* perturbāre.
perturbation *n* animī perturbātiō *f*, trepidātiō *f*.
peruke *n* capillāmentum *nt*.
perusal *n* perlēctiō *f*.
peruse *vt* perlegere; (*book*) ēvolvere.

pervade vt permānāre per, complēre; (*emotion*) perfundere.
pervasive adj crēber.
perverse adj perversus, prāvus.
perversely adv perversē.
perversion n dēprāvātiō f.
perversity n perversitās f.
pervert vt dēprāvāre; (*words*) dētorquēre; (*person*) corrumpere.
perverter n corruptor m.
pessimism n dēspērātiō f.
pest n pestis f.
pester vt sollicitāre.
pestilence n pestilentia f, pestis f.
pestilential adj pestilēns, nocēns.
pestle n pistillum nt.
pet n dēliciae fpl ♦ vt in dēliciīs habēre, dēlēnīre.
petard n: **be hoist with his own ~** suō sibī gladiō iugulārī.
petition n precēs fpl; (*POL*) libellus m ♦ vt ōrāre.
petrify vt (*fig*) dēfīgere; **be petrified** stupēre, obstupēscere.
pettifogger n lēgulēius m.
pettiness n levitās f.
pettish adj stomachōsus.
petty adj levis, minūtus.
petulance n protervitās f.
petulant adj protervus, petulāns.
petulantly adv petulanter.
pew n subsellium nt.
phalanx n phalanx f.
phantasy n commentīcia ntpl.
phantom n simulacrum nt, īdōlon nt.
phases npl vicēs fpl.
pheasant n phāsiānus m.
phenomenal adj eximius, singulāris.
phenomenon n rēs f, novum nt, spectāculum nt.
philander vi lascīvīre.
philanthropic adj hūmānus, beneficus.
philanthropically adv hūmānē.
philanthropy n hūmānitās f, beneficia ntpl.
Philippic n Philippica f.
philologist n grammaticus m.
philology n grammatica ntpl.
philosopher n philosophus m, sapiēns m.
philosophical adj philosophus; (*temperament*) aequābilis.
philosophize vi philosophārī.
philosophy n philosophia f, sapientia f.
philtre n philtrum nt.
phlegm n pituīta f; (*temper*) lentitūdō f.
phlegmatic adj lentus.
phoenix n phoenīx m.
phrase n locūtiō f; (*GRAM*) incīsum nt.
phraseology n verba ntpl, ōrātiō f.
physic n medicāmentum nt; **~s** pl physica ntpl.
physical adj physicus; (*of body*) corporis.
physician n medicus m.
physicist n physicus m.
physique n corpus nt, vīrēs fpl.

piazza n forum nt.
pick n (*tool*) dolabra f; (*best part*) lēctī mpl, flōs m ♦ vt (*choose*) legere, dēligere; (*pluck*) carpere; **~ out** ēligere, excerpere; **~ up** colligere.
pickaxe n dolabra f.
picked adj ēlēctus, dēlēctus.
picket n (*MIL*) statiō f.
pickle n muria f ♦ vt condīre.
picture n pictūra f, tabula f ♦ vt dēpingere; (*to oneself*) ante oculōs pōnere.
picturesque adj (*scenery*) amoenus.
pie n crustum nt.
piebald adj bicolor, varius.
piece n pars f; (*broken off*) fragmentum nt; (*food*) frustum nt; (*coin*) nummus m; (*play*) fābula f; **break in ~s** comminuere; **fall to ~s** dīlābī; **take to ~s** dissolvere; **tear in ~s** dīlaniāre.
piecemeal adv membrātim, minūtātim.
pied adj maculōsus.
pier n mōlēs f.
pierce vt perfodere, trānsfīgere; (*bore*) perforāre; (*fig*) pungere.
piercing adj acūtus.
piety n pietās f, religiō f.
pig n porcus m, sūs m/f; **buy a ~ in a poke** spem pretiō emere; **~'s** suillus.
pigeon n columba f; **wood ~** palumbēs f.
pig-headed adj pervicāx.
pigment n pigmentum nt.
pigsty n hara f.
pike n dolō m, hasta f.
pikeman n hastātus m.
pile n acervus m, cumulus m; (*funeral*) rogus m; (*building*) mōlēs f; (*post*) sublica f ♦ vt cumulāre, congerere; **~ up** exstruere, adcumulāre, coacervāre.
pile-driver n fistūca f.
pilfer vt fūrārī, surripere.
pilferer n fūr m, fūrunculus m.
pilgrim n peregrīnātor m.
pilgrimage n peregrīnātiō f.
pill n pilula f.
pillage n rapīna f, dēpopulātiō f, expīlātiō f ♦ vt dīripere, dēpopulārī, expīlāre.
pillager n expīlātor m, praedātor m.
pillar n columen nt, columna f.
pillory n furca f.
pillow n pulvīnus nt, culcita f.
pilot n gubernātor m, ductor m ♦ vt regere, gubernāre.
pimp n lēnō m.
pimple n pustula f.
pin n acus f ♦ vt adfīgere.
pincers n forceps m/f.
pinch vt pervellere, vellicāre; (*shoe*) ūrere; (*for room*) coartāre.
pine n pīnus f ♦ vi tābēscere; **~ away** intābēscere; **~ for** dēsīderāre.
pinion n penna f.
pink adj rubicundus.
pinnace n lembus m.

pinnacle n fastīgium nt.
pint n sextārius m.
pioneer n antecursor m.
pious adj pius, religiōsus.
piously adv piē, religiōsē.
pip n grānum nt.
pipe n (*music*) fistula f, tībia f; (*water*) canālis m
♦ vi fistulā canere.
piper n tībīcen m.
pipkin n olla f.
piquancy n sāl m, vīs f.
piquant adj salsus, argūtus.
pique n offēnsio f, dolor m ♦ vt offendere.
piracy n latrōcinium nt.
pirate n pīrāta m praedō m.
piratical adj pīrāticus.
piscatorial adj piscātōrius.
piston n embolus m.
pit n fovea f, fossa f; (THEAT) cavea f.
pitch n pix f; (*sound*) sonus m ♦ vt (*camp*)
pōnere; (*tent*) tendere; (*missile*) conicere.
pitch-black adj piceus.
pitched battle n proelium iustum nt.
pitcher n hydria f.
pitchfork n furca f.
pitch pine n picea f.
piteous adj miserābilis, flēbilis.
piteously adv miserābiliter.
pitfall n fovea f.
pith n medulla f.
pithy adj (*style*) dēnsus; ~ **saying** sententia f.
pitiable adj miserandus.
pitiful adj miser, miserābilis; misericors.
pitifully adv miserē, miserābiliter.
pitiless adj immisericors, immītis.
pitilessly adv crūdēliter.
pittance n (*food*) dēmēnsum nt; (*money*) stips
f.
pity n misericordia f; **take ~ on** miserērī (+acc
of person, gen of things); **it is a ~ that** male
accidit quod ♦ vt miserērī (*gen*); **I ~ me**
miseret (*gen*).
pivot n cardō m.
placability n plācābilitās f.
placable adj plācābilis.
placard n libellus m.
placate vt plācāre.
place n locus m; **in another ~** alibī; **in the first ~**
prīmum; **in ~ of** locō (*gen*), pro (+ *abl*); **to this
~** hūc; **out of ~** intempestīvus; **give ~ to**
cēdere (*dat*); **take ~** fierī, accidere; **take the ~
of** in locum (*gen*) succēdere ♦ vt pōnere,
locāre, collocāre; **~ beside** adpōnere; **~ over**
(*in charge*) praepōnere; **~ round** circumdare;
~ upon impōnere.
placid adj placidus, tranquillus, quiētus.
placidity n tranquillitās f, sedātus animus m.
placidly adv placidē, quiētē.
plagiarism n fūrtum nt.
plagiarize vt fūrārī.
plague n pestilentia f, pestis f.
plain adj (*lucid*) clārus, perspicuus;
(*unadorned*) subtīlis, simplex; (*frank*)
sincērus; (*ugly*) invenustus ♦ n campus m,

plānitiēs f; **of the ~** campester.
plainly adv perspicuē; simpliciter, sincērē.
plainness n perspicuitās f; simplicitās f.
plaint n querella f.
plaintiff n petītor m.
plaintive adj flēbilis, queribundus.
plaintively adv flēbiliter.
plait vt implicāre, nectere.
plan n cōnsilium nt; (*of a work*) fōrma f,
dēsignātiō f; (*of living*) ratiō f; (*intent*)
prōpositum nt; (*drawing*) dēscrīptiō f ♦ vt (*a
work*) dēsignāre, dēscrībere; (*intent*)
cōgitāre, meditārī; cōnsilium capere or
inīre; (*with verb*) in animō habēre (*inf*).
plane n (*surface*) plānitiēs f; (*tree*) platanus f;
(*tool*) runcīna f ♦ adj aequus, plānus ♦ vt
runcīnāre.
planet n stēlla errāns f.
plank n tabula f.
plant n herba f, planta f ♦ vt (*tree*) serere; (*field*)
cōnserere; (*colony*) dēdūcere; (*feet*) pōnere;
~ firmly īnfīgere.
plantation n arbustum nt.
planter n sator m, colōnus m.
plaque n tabula f.
plaster n albārium nt, tectōrium nt; (MED)
emplastrum nt; **~ of Paris** gypsum nt ♦ vt
dealbāre.
plasterer n albārius m.
plastic adj ductilis, fūsilis.
plate n (*dish*) catillus m; (*silver*) argentum nt;
(*layer*) lāmina f ♦ vt indūcere.
platform n suggestus m; rōstrum nt, tribūnal
nt.
platitude n trīta sententia f.
platter n patella f, lanx f.
plaudit n plausus m.
plausibility n vērīsimilitūdō f.
plausible adj speciōsus, vērī similis.
play n lūdus m; (THEAT) fābula f; (*voice*)
inclīnātiō f; (*scope*) campus m; (*hands*) gestus
m; **~ on words** agnōminātiō f; **fair ~** aequum et
bonum ♦ vi lūdere; (*fountain*) scatēre ♦ vt
(*music*) canere; (*instrument*) canere (*abl*);
(*game*) lūdere (*abl*); (*part*) agere; **~ the part of**
agere; **~ a trick on** lūdificārī, impōnere (*dat*).
playbill n ēdictum nt.
player n lūsor m; (*at dice*) āleātor m; (*on flute*)
tībīcen m; (*on lyre*) fidicen m; (*on stage*)
histriō m.
playful adj lascīvus; (*words*) facētus.
playfully adv per lūdum, per iocum.
playfulness n lascīvia f; facētiae fpl.
playground n ārea f.
playmate n collūsor m.
playwright n fābulārum scrīptor m.
plea n causa f; (*in defence*) dēfēnsiō f, excūsātiō
f.
plead vi causam agere, causam ōrāre, causam
dīcere; (*in excuse*) dēprecārī, excūsāre; **~
with** obsecrāre.
pleader n āctor m, causidicus m.
pleasant adj iūcundus, dulcis, grātus; (*place*)

amoenus.

pleasantly adv iūcundē, suāviter.

pleasantry n facētiae fpl, iocus m.

please vt placēre (dat), dēlectāre; **try to ~** īnservīre (dat); **just as you ~** quod commodum est; **if you ~** sīs; **~d with** contentus (abl); **be ~d with oneself** sibī placēre ♦ adv amābō.

pleasing adj grātus, iūcundus, amoenus; **be ~ to cordī esse** (dat).

pleasurable adj iūcundus.

pleasure n voluptās f; (decision) arbitrium nt; **it is my ~ libet; derive ~** voluptātem capere ♦ vt grātificārī (dat).

pleasure grounds n hortī mpl.

pleasure-loving adj dēlicātus.

plebeian adj plēbēius ♦ n: **the ~s** plēbs f.

plebiscite n suffrāgium nt.

plectrum n plēctrum nt.

pledge n pignus nt ♦ vt obligāre; **~ oneself** prōmittere, spondēre; **~ one's word** fidem obligāre, fidem interpōnere.

Pleiads n Plēiadēs fpl.

plenary adj īnfīnītus.

plenipotentiary n lēgātus m.

plenitude n cōpia f, mātūritās f.

plentiful adj cōpiōsus, largus.

plentifully adv cōpiōsē, largē.

plenty n cōpia f, abundantia f; (enough) satis.

pleonasm n redundantia f.

pleurisy n lateris dolor m.

pliable adj flexibilis, mollis, lentus.

pliant adj flexibilis, mollis, lentus.

pliers n forceps m/f.

plight n habitus m, discrīmen nt ♦ vt spondēre.

plod vi labōrāre, operam īnsūmere.

plot n coniūrātiō f, īnsidiae fpl; (land) agellus m; (play) argūmentum nt ♦ vi coniūrāre, mōlīrī.

plotter n coniūrātus m.

plough n arātrum nt ♦ vt arāre; (sea) sulcāre; **~ up exarāre.**

ploughing n arātiō f.

ploughman n arātor m.

ploughshare n vōmer m.

pluck n fortitūdō f ♦ vt carpere, legere; **~ out** ēvellere; **~ up courage** animum recipere, animō adesse.

plucky adj fortis.

plug n obtūrāmentum nt ♦ vt obtūrāre.

plum n prūnum nt; (tree) prūnus f.

plumage n plūmae fpl.

plumb n perpendiculum nt ♦ adj dīrēctus ♦ adv ad perpendiculum ♦ vt (building) ad perpendiculum exigere; (depth) scrūtārī.

plumber n artifex plumbārius m.

plumb line n līnea f, perpendiculum nt.

plume n crista f ♦ vt: **~ oneself on** iactāre, prae sē ferre.

plummet n perpendiculum nt.

plump adj pinguis.

plumpness n nitor m.

plunder n (act) rapīna f; (booty) praeda f ♦ vi praedārī ♦ vt dīripere, expīlāre.

plunderer n praedātor m, spoliātor m.

plundering n rapīna f ♦ adj praedābundus.

plunge vt mergere, dēmergere; (weapon) dēmittere ♦ vi mergī, sē dēmergere.

plural adj plūrālis.

plurality n multitūdō f, plūrēs pl.

ply vt exercēre.

poach vt surripere.

pocket n sinus m.

pocket money n pecūlium nt.

pod n siliqua f.

poem n poēma nt, carmen nt.

poesy n poēsis f.

poet n poēta m.

poetess n poētria f.

poetic adj poēticus.

poetical adj = **poetic.**

poetically adv poēticē.

poetry n (art) poētica f; (poems) poēmata ntpl, carmina ntpl.

poignancy n acerbitās f.

poignant adj acerbus, acūtus.

poignantly adv acerbē, acūtē.

point n (dot) pūnctum nt; (place) locus m; (item) caput nt; (sharp end) aciēs f; (of sword) mucrō m; (of epigram) acūleī mpl; **~ of honour** officium nt; **beside the ~ ab rē; to the ~ ad rem; from this ~ hinc; to that ~ eō; up to this ~ hāctenus, adhūc; without ~** īnsulsus; **in ~ of fact** nempe; **make a ~ of doing** cōnsultō facere; **on the ~ of death** moritūrus; **on the ~ of happening** inibī; **I was on the ~ of saying** in eō erat ut dīcerem; **matters have reached such a ~ eō rēs recidit; come to the ~** ad rem redīre; **the ~ at issue is illud quaeritur; the main ~ cardō m, caput nt; turning ~ articulus temporis m ♦ vt acuere, exacuere; (aim) intendere; (punctuate) distinguere; ~ out indicāre, dēmōnstrāre; ostendere.

point-blank adj simplex ♦ adv praecīsē.

pointed adj acūtus; (criticism) acūleātus; (wit) salsus.

pointedly adv apertē, dīlūcidē.

pointer n index m.

pointless adj īnsulsus, frīgidus.

pointlessly adv īnsulsē.

point of view n iūdicium nt, sententia f.

poise n lībrāmen nt; (fig) urbānitās f ♦ vt lībrāre.

poison n venēnum nt ♦ vt venēnō necāre; (fig) īnficere.

poisoned adj venēnātus.

poisoner n venēficus m.

poisoning n venēficium nt.

poisonous adj noxius.

poke vt trūdere, fodicāre.

polar adj septentriōnālis.

pole n asser m, contus m; (ASTRO) polus m.

poleaxe n bipennis f.

polemic n contrōversia f.

police n lictōrēs mpl; (night) vigilēs mpl.

policy n ratiō f, cōnsilium nt; **honesty is the**

best ~ ea māximē condūcunt quae sunt rēctissima.

polish n (*appearance*) nitor m; (*character*) urbānitās f; (*LIT*) līma f ♦ vt polīre; (*fig*) expolīre.

polished adj polītus, mundus; (*person*) excultus, urbānus; (*style*) līmātus.

polite adj urbānus, hūmānus, cōmis.

politely adv urbānē, cōmiter.

politeness n urbānitās f, hūmānitās f, cōmitās f.

politic adj prūdēns, circumspectus.

political adj cīvīlis, pūblicus; ~ **life** rēs pūblica f.

politician n magistrātus m.

politics n rēs pūblica f; **take up** ~ ad rem pūblicam accēdere.

polity n reī pūblicae fōrma f.

poll n caput nt; (*voting*) comitia ntpl ♦ vi suffrāgia inīre.

poll tax n tribūtum nt in singula capita impositum.

pollute vt inquināre, contāmināre.

pollution n corruptēla f.

poltroon n ignāvus m.

pomegranate n mālum Pūnicum nt.

pomp n adparātus m.

pomposity n māgnificentia f, glōria f.

pompous adj māgnificus, glōriōsus.

pompously adv māgnificē, glōriōsē.

pompousness n māgnificentia f.

pond n stagnum nt, lacūna f.

ponder vi sēcum reputāre ♦ vt animō volūtāre, in mente agitāre.

ponderous adj gravis, ponderōsus.

ponderously adv graviter.

poniard n pugiō m.

pontiff n pontifex m.

pontifical adj pontificālis, pontificius.

pontoon n pontō m.

pony n mannus m.

pooh-pooh vt dērīdēre.

pool n lacūna f, stagnum nt ♦ vt cōnferre.

poop n puppis f.

poor adj pauper, inops; (*meagre*) exīlis; (*inferior*) improbus; (*pitiable*) miser; ~ **little** misellus.

poorly adj aeger, aegrōtus ♦ adv parum, tenuiter.

pop n crepitus m ♦ vi ēmicāre.

pope n pāpa m.

poplar n pōpulus f.

poppy n papāver nt.

populace n vulgus nt, plēbs f.

popular adj grātus, grātiōsus; (*party*) populāris.

popularity n populī favor m, studium nt.

popularly adv vulgō.

populate vt frequentāre.

population n populus m, cīvēs mpl.

populous adj frequēns.

porcelain n fictilia ntpl.

porch n vestibulum nt.

porcupine n hystrīx f.

pore n forāmen nt ♦ vi: ~ **over** scrūtārī, incumbere in (*acc*).

pork n porcīna f.

porous adj rārus.

porridge n puls f.

port n portus m ♦ adj (*side*) laevus, sinister.

portage n vectūra f.

portal n porta f.

portcullis n cataracta f.

portend vt portendere.

portent n mōnstrum nt, portentum nt.

portentous adj mōnstruōsus.

porter n iānitor m; (*carrier*) bāiulus m.

portico n porticus f.

portion n pars f; (*marriage*) dōs f; (*lot*) sors f.

portliness n amplitūdō f.

portly adj amplus, opīmus.

portrait n imāgō f, effigiēs f.

portray vt dēpingere, exprimere, effingere.

pose n status m, habitus m ♦ vt pōnere ♦ vi habitum sūmere.

poser n nōdus m.

posit vt pōnere.

position n (*GEOG*) situs m (*body*) status m, gestus m; (*rank*) dignitās f; (*office*) honōs m; (*MIL*) locus m; **be in a** ~ **to** habēre (*inf*); **take up a** ~ (*MIL*) locum capere.

positive adj certus; **be** ~ **about** adfirmāre.

positively adv certō, adfirmātē, rē vērā.

posse n manus f.

possess vt possidēre, habēre; (*take*) occupāre, potīrī (*abl*).

possession n possessiō f; ~**s** pl bona ntpl, fortūnae fpl; **take** ~ **of** potīrī (*abl*), occupāre, manum inicere (*dat*); (*inheritance*) obīre; (*emotion*) invādere, incēdere (*dat*); **gain** ~ **of** potior (+ *abl*).

possessor n possessor m, dominus m.

possibility n facultās f; **there is a** ~ fierī potest.

possible adj: **it is** ~ fierī potest; **as big as** ~ quam māximus.

possibly adv fortasse.

post n pālus m; (*MIL*) statiō f; (*office*) mūnus nt; (*courier*) tabellārius m; **leave one's** ~ locō cēdere, signa relinquere ♦ vt (*troops*) locāre, collocāre; (*at intervals*) dispōnere; (*letter*) dare, tabellāriō dare; (*entry*) in cōdicem referre; **be** ~**ed** (*MIL*) in statiōne esse.

postage n vectūra f.

poster n libellus m.

posterior adj posterior.

posterity n posterī mpl; (*time*) posteritās f.

postern n postīcum nt.

posthaste adv summā celeritāte.

posthumous adj postumus.

posthumously adv (*born*) patre mortuō; (*published*) auctōre mortuō.

postpone vt differre, prōferre.

postponement n dīlātiō f.

postscript n: **add a** ~ adscrībere, subicere.

postulate vt sūmere ♦ n sūmptiō f.

posture n gestus m, status m.

pot n olla f, matella f.
pot-bellied adj ventriōsus.
potency n vīs f.
potent adj efficāx, valēns.
potentate n dynastēs m, tyrannus m.
potential adj futūrus.
potentiality n facultās f.
potentially adv ut fierī posse vidētur; ~ **an emperor** capāx imperiī.
potently adv efficienter.
potion n pōtiō f.
pot-pourri n farrāgō f.
potsherd n testa f.
pottage n iūs nt.
potter n figulus m; ~'s figulāris.
pottery n fictilia ntpl.
pouch n pēra f, sacculus m.
poultice n fōmentum nt, emplastrum nt.
poultry n gallīnae fpl.
pounce vi involāre, īnsilīre.
pound n lībra f; **five ~s** (weight) **of gold** aurī quīnque pondo ♦ vt conterere; pulsāre.
pour vt fundere; ~ **forth** effundere; ~ **in** īnfundere; ~ **on** superfundere; ~ **out** effundere ♦ vi fundī, fluere; ~ **down** ruere, sē praecipitāre.
pouring adj (rain) effūsus.
poverty n paupertās f, egestās f, inopia f; (style) iēiūnitās f.
powder n pulvis m.
powdery adj pulvereus.
power n potestās f; (strength) vīrēs fpl; (excessive) potentia f; (supreme) imperium nt; (divine) nūmen nt; (legal) auctōritās f; (of father) manus f; **as far as is in my ~** quantum in mē est; **have great ~** multum valēre, posse; **have of ~ attorney** cognitōrem esse; **it is still in my ~ to** integrum est mihī (inf).
powerful adj validus, potēns.
powerfully adv valdē.
powerless adj impotēns, imbēcillus; **be ~** nihil valēre.
powerlessness n imbēcillitas f.
practicable adj in apertō; **be ~** fierī posse.
practical adj (person) habilis.
practical joke n lūdus m.
practical knowledge n ūsus m.
practically adv ferē, paene.
practice n ūsus m, exercitātiō f; (RHET) meditātiō f; (habit) consuētūdō f, mōs m; **corrupt ~s** malae artēs.
practise vt (occupation) exercēre, facere; (custom) factitāre; (RHET) meditārī ♦ vi (MED) medicīnam exercēre; (law) causās agere.
practised adj exercitātus, perītus.
practitioner n (MED) medicus m.
praetor n praetor nt; ~'s praetōrius.
praetorian adj praetōrius.
praetorian guards npl praetōriānī mpl.
praetorship n praetūra f.
praise n laus f ♦ vt laudāre.
praiser n laudātor m.
praiseworthy adj laudābilis, laude dignus.

prance vi exsultāre.
prank n lūdus m.
prate vi garrīre.
prating adj garrulus.
pray vi deōs precārī, deōs venerārī ♦ vt precārī, ōrāre; ~ **for** petere, precārī; ~ **to** adōrāre.
prayer(s) n precēs fpl.
prayerful adj supplex.
preach vt, vi docēre, praedicāre.
preacher n ōrātor m.
preamble n exōrdium nt.
prearranged adj cōnstitūtus.
precarious adj dubius, perīculōsus.
precariousness n discrīmen nt.
precaution n cautiō f, prōvidentia f; **take ~s** cavēre, praecavēre.
precede vt praeīre (dat), anteīre (dat), antecēdere.
precedence n prīmārius locus m; **give ~ to** cēdere (dat); **take ~** (thing) antīquius esse; (person) prīmās agere.
precedent n exemplum nt; (law) praeiūdicium nt; **breach of ~** īnsolentia f; **in defiance of ~** īnsolenter.
preceding adj prior, superior.
precept n praeceptum nt.
preceptor n doctor m, magister m.
precinct n terminus m, templum nt.
precious adj cārus; pretiōsus; (style) pūtidus.
precious stone n gemma f.
precipice n locus praeceps m, rūpēs f.
precipitancy n festīnātiō f.
precipitate vt praecipitāre ♦ adj praeceps; praeproperus.
precipitation n festīnātiō f.
precipitous adj dēruptus, praeceps, praeruptus.
precise adj certus, subtīlis; (person) accūrātus.
precisely adv dēmum.
precision n cūra f.
preclude vt exclūdere, prohibēre.
precocious adj praecox.
precocity n festīnāta mātūritās f.
preconceive vt praecipere; ~**d idea** praeiūdicāta opīniō f.
preconception n praeceptiō f.
preconcerted adj ex compositō factus.
precursor n praenūntius m.
predatory adj praedātōrius.
predecessor n dēcessor m; **my ~** cuī succēdō.
predestination n fātum nt, necessitās f.
predestine vt dēvovēre.
predetermine vt praefīnīre.
predicament n angustiae fpl, discrīmen nt.
predicate n attribūtum nt.
predict vt praedīcere, augurārī.
prediction n praedictiō f.
predilection n amor m, studium nt.
predispose vt inclīnāre, praeparāre.
predisposition n inclīnātiō f.
predominance n potentia f, praestantia f.

predominant *adj* praepotēns, praecipuus.
predominantly *adv* plērumque.
predominate *vi* pollēre, dominārī.
pre-eminence *n* praestantia *f.*
pre-eminent *adj* ēgregius, praecipuus, excellēns.
pre-eminently *adv* ēgregiē, praecipuē, excellenter.
preface *n* prooemium *nt*, praefātiō *f* ♦ *vi* praefārī.
prefect *n* praefectus *m.*
prefecture *n* praefectūra *f.*
prefer *vt* (*charge*) dēferre; (*to office*) anteferre; (*choice*) antepōnere (*acc and dat*), posthabēre (*dat and acc*); (*with verb*) mālle.
preferable *adj* potior.
preferably *adv* potius.
preference *n* favor *m*; **give ~ to** antepōnere, praeoptāre; **in ~ to** potius quam.
preferment *n* honōs *m*, dignitās *f.*
prefix *vt* praetendere ♦ *n* praepositiō *f.*
pregnancy *n* graviditās *f.*
pregnant *adj* gravida.
prejudge *vt* praeiūdicāre.
prejudice *n* praeiūdicāta opīniō *f*; (*harmful*) invidia *f*, incommodum *nt*; **without ~** cum bonā veniā ♦ *vt* obesse (*dat*); **be ~d against** invidēre (*dat*), male opīnārī dē (*abl*).
prejudicial *adj* damnōsus; **be ~ to** obesse (*dat*), nocēre (*dat*), officere (*dat*), dētrīmentō esse (*dat*).
preliminaries *npl* praecurrentia *ntpl.*
preliminary *adj* prīmus ♦ *n* prōlūsiō *f.*
prelude *n* prooemium *nt.*
premature *adj* immātūrus; (*birth*) abortīvus.
prematurely *adv* ante tempus.
premeditate *vt* praecōgitāre, praemeditārī.
premeditated *adj* praemeditātus.
premier *adj* prīnceps, praecipuus.
premise *n* (*major*) prōpositiō *f*; (*minor*) adsūmptiō *f*; **~s** *pl* aedēs *fpl*, domus *f.*
premium *n* praemium *nt*; **be at a ~** male emī.
premonition *n* monitus *m.*
preoccupation *n* sollicitūdō *f.*
preoccupied *adj* sollicitus, districtus.
preordain *vt* praefīnīre.
preparation *n* (*process*) adparātiō *f*, comparātiō *f*; (*product*) adparātus *m*; (*of speech*) meditātiō *f*; **make ~s for** īnstruere, exōrnāre, comparāre.
prepare *vt* parāre, adparāre, comparāre; (*speech*) meditārī; (*with verb*) parāre; **~d for** parātus ad (+ *acc*).
preponderance *n* praestantia *f.*
preponderate *vi* praepollēre, vincere.
preposition *n* praepositiō *f.*
prepossess *vt* commendāre (*dat and acc*), praeoccupāre.
prepossessing *adj* suāvis, iūcundus.
prepossession *n* favor *m.*
preposterous *adj* absurdus.
prerogative *n* iūs *nt.*
presage *n* ōmen *nt* ♦ *vt* ōminārī,
portendere.
prescience *n* prōvidentia *f.*
prescient *adj* prōvidus.
prescribe *vt* imperāre; (*MED*) praescrībere; (*limit*) fīnīre.
prescription *n* (*MED*) compositiō *f*; (*right*) ūsus *m.*
presence *n* praesentia *f*; (*appearance*) aspectus *m*; **~ of mind** praesēns animus *m*; **in the ~ of** cōram (*abl*); apud (*abl*); **in my ~** mē praesente.
present *adj* praesēns, īnstāns; **be ~** adesse; **be ~ at** interesse (*dat*) ♦ *n* praesēns tempus *nt*; (*gift*) dōnum *nt*; **at ~** in praesentī, nunc; **for the ~** in praesēns ♦ *vt* dōnāre, offerre; (*on stage*) indūcere; (*in court*) sistere; **~ itself** occurrere.
presentable *adj* spectābilis.
presentation *n* dōnātiō *f.*
presentiment *n* augurium *nt.*
presently *adv* mox.
preservation *n* cōnservātiō *f.*
preserve *vt* cōnservāre, tuērī; (*food*) condīre.
preside *vi* praesidēre (*dat*).
presidency *n* praefectūra *f.*
president *n* praefectus *m.*
press *n* prēlum *nt* ♦ *vt* premere; (*crowd*) stīpāre; (*urge*) īnstāre (*dat*); **~ for** flāgitāre; **~ hard** (*pursuit*) īnsequī, īnstāre (*dat*), īnsistere (*dat*); **~ out** exprimere; **~ together** comprimere.
pressing *adj* īnstāns, gravis.
pressure *n* pressiō *f*, nīsus *m.*
prestige *n* auctōritās *f*, opīniō *f.*
presumably *adv* sānē.
presume *vt* sūmere, conicere ♦ *vi* audēre, cōnfīdere; **I ~** opīnor, crēdō.
presuming *adj* adrogāns.
presumption *n* coniectūra *f*; (*arrogance*) adrogantia *f*, licentia *f.*
presumptuous *adj* adrogāns, audāx.
presumptuously *adv* adroganter, audacter.
presuppose *vt* praesūmere.
pretence *n* simulātiō *f*, speciēs *f*; **under ~ of** per speciem (*gen*); **under false ~s** dolō malō.
pretend *vt* simulāre, fingere; **~ that ... not** dissimulāre.
pretender *n* captātor *m.*
pretension *n* postulātum *nt*; **make ~s to** affectāre, sibī adrogāre.
pretentious *adj* adrogāns, glōriōsus.
pretext *n* speciēs *f*; **under ~ of** per speciem (*gen*); **on the ~ that** quod + *subj.*
prettily *adv* pulchrē, bellē.
prettiness *n* pulchritūdō *f*, lepōs *m.*
pretty *adj* formōsus, pulcher, bellus ♦ *adv* admodum, satis.
prevail *vi* vincere; (*custom*) tenēre, obtinēre; **~ upon** persuādēre (*dat*); (*by entreaty*) exōrāre.
prevailing *adj* vulgātus.
prevalent *adj* vulgātus; **be ~** obtinēre; **become ~** incrēbrēscere.
prevaricate *vi* tergiversārī.

prevarication n tergiversātiō f.

prevaricator n veterātor m.

prevent vt impedīre (+ **quōminus/quīn** and subj), prohibēre (+ acc and infin).

prevention n impedītiō f.

previous adj prior, superior.

previously adv anteā, antehāc.

prevision n prōvidentia f.

prey n praeda f ♦ vi: ~ **upon** īnsectārī; (fig) vexāre, carpere.

price n pretium nt; (of corn) annōna f; **at a high** ~ māgnī; **at a low** ~ parvī ♦ vt pretium cōnstituere (gen).

priceless adj inaestimābilis.

prick vt pungere; (goad) stimulāre; ~ **up the ears** aurēs adrigere.

prickle n acūleus m.

prickly adj aculeātus, horridus.

pride n superbia f, fastus m; (boasting) glōria f; (object) decus nt; (best part) flōs m ♦ vt: ~ **oneself on** iactāre, prae sē ferre.

priest n sacerdōs m; (especial) flāmen m; **high** ~ pontifex m, antistēs m.

priestess n sacerdōs f; **high** ~ antistita f.

priesthood n sacerdōtium nt, flāminium nt.

prig n homō fastīdiōsus m.

priggish adj fastīdiōsus.

prim adj modestior.

primarily adv prīncipiō, praecipuē.

primary adj prīmus, praecipuus.

prime adj prīmus, ēgregius; ~ **mover** auctor m ♦ n (person) prīnceps m/f; (money) sors f.

principally adv in prīmīs, māximē, māximam partem.

principle n prīncipium nt; (rule) fōrmula f, ratiō f; (character) fidēs f; ~**s** pl īnstitūta ntpl, disciplīna f; **first** ~**s** elementa ntpl, initia ntpl.

print n nota f, signum nt; (foot) vestīgium nt ♦ vt imprimere.

prior adj prior, potior.

priority n: **give** ~ **to** praevertere (dat).

prise vt sublevāre; ~ **open** vectī refringere.

prison n carcer m, vincula ntpl; **put in** ~ in vincula conicere.

prisoner n reus m; (for debt) nexus m; (of war) captīvus m; ~ **at the bar** reus m, rea f; **take** ~ capere.

pristine adj prīscus, prīstinus, vetus.

privacy n sēcrētum nt.

private adj (individual) prīvātus; (home) domesticus; (secluded) sēcrētus ♦ n (MIL) gregārius mīles m.

privately adv clam, sēcrētō.

private property n res familiāris f.

privation n inopia f, egestās f.

privet n ligustrum nt.

privilege n iūs nt, immūnitās f.

privileged adj immūnis.

privy adj sēcrētus; ~ **to** cōnscius (gen).

prize n praemium nt; (captured) praeda f; ~ **money** manubiae fpl ♦ vt māgnī aestimāre.

pro-Athenian adj rērum Athēniēnsium studiōsus.

probability n vērī similitūdō f.

probable adj vērī similis; **more** ~ vērō propior.

probably adv fortasse.

probation n probātiō f.

probationer n tīrō m.

probe vt īnspicere, scrūtārī.

probity n honestās f, integritās f.

problem n quaestiō f; **the** ~ **is** illud quaeritur.

problematical adj dubius, anceps.

procedure n ratiō f, modus m; (law) fōrmula f.

proceed vi pergere, prōcedere, prōgredī; (narrative) īnsequī; ~ **against** persequī, lītem intendere (dat); ~ **from** orīrī, proficīscī ex.

proceedings n ācta ntpl.

proceeds n fructus m, reditus m.

process n ratiō f; (law) āctiō f; **in the** ~ **of time** post aliquod tempus.

procession n pompa f; (fig) agmen nt.

proclaim vt ēdīcere, prōnūntiāre, praedicāre, dēclārāre; ~ **war upon** bellum indīcere + dat.

proclamation n ēdictum nt.

proclivity n prōpēnsiō f.

proconsul n prōcōnsul m.

proconsular adj prōcōnsulāris.

proconsulship n prōcōnsulātus m.

procrastinate vt differre, prōferre ♦ vi cunctārī.

procrastination n prōcrāstinātiō f, mora f.

procreate vt generāre, prōcreāre.

procreation n prōcreātiō f.

procreator n generātor m.

procumbent adj prōnus.

procurator n prōcūrātor m.

procure vt parāre, adipīscī, adquīrere; (by request) impetrāre.

procurer n lēnō m.

prod vt stimulāre.

prodigal adj prōdigus ♦ n nepōs m.

prodigality n effūsiō f.

prodigally adv effūsē.

prodigious adj ingēns, immānis.

prodigy n prōdigium nt, portentum nt; (fig) mīrāculum nt.

produce vt ēdere; (young) parere; (crops) ferre; (play) dare, docēre; (line) prōdūcere; (in court) sistere; (into view) prōferre; (from store) prōmere, dēprōmere ♦ n fructus m; (of earth) frūgēs fpl; (in money) reditus m.

product n opus nt; ~ **of** fructus (gen).

production n opus nt.

productive adj fēcundus, ferāx, fructuōsus.

productivity n fēcunditās f, ūbertās f.

profanation n violātiō f.

profane adj profānus, impius ♦ vt violāre, polluere.

prime adj prīscus.

primeval adj prīscus.

primitive adj prīstinus, incultus.

primordial adj prīscus.

prince n rēgulus m; rēgis fīlius m; prīnceps m.

princely adj rēgālis.

princess n rēgis fīlia f.

principal adj praecipuus, prīnceps, māximus ♦ n (person) prīnceps m/f; (money) sors f.

profanely *adv* impiē.
profanity *n* impietās *f.*
profess *vt* profitērī, prae sē ferre; ~ **to be** profitērī sē.
profession *n* professiō *f;* (*occupation*) ars *f,* haeresis *f.*
professor *n* doctor *m.*
proffer *vt* offerre, pollicērī.
proficiency *n* prōgressus *m,* perītia *f;* **attain** ~ prōficere.
proficient *adj* perītus.
profile *n* ōris līneāmenta *ntpl;* (*portrait*) oblīqua imāgō *f.*
profit *n* lucrum *nt,* ēmolumentum *nt,* fructus *m;* **make a ~ out of** quaestuī habēre ♦ *vt* prōdesse (*dat*) ♦ *vi:* ~ **by** fruī (*abl*), ūtī (*abl*); (*opportunity*) arripere.
profitable *adj* fructuōsus, ūtilis.
profitably *adv* ūtiliter.
profligacy *n* flāgitium *nt,* perditī mōrēs *mpl.*
profligate *adj* perditus, dissolūtus ♦ *n* nepōs *m.*
profound *adj* altus; (*discussion*) abstrūsus.
profoundly *adv* penitus.
profundity *n* altitūdō *f.*
profuse *adj* prōdigus, effūsus.
profusely *adv* effūsē.
profusion *n* abundantia *f,* adfluentia *f;* **in ~** abundē.
progenitor *n* auctor *m.*
progeny *n* prōgeniēs *f,* prōlēs *f.*
prognostic *n* signum *nt.*
prognosticate *vt* ōminārī, augurārī, praedīcere.
prognostication *n* ōmen *nt,* praedictiō *f.*
programme *n* libellus *m.*
progress *n* prōgressus *m;* **make ~** prōficere ♦ *vi* prōgredī.
progression *n* prōgressus *m.*
progressively *adv* gradātim.
prohibit *vt* vetāre, interdīcere (*dat*).
prohibition *n* interdictum *nt.*
project *n* prōpositum *nt* ♦ *vi* ēminēre, exstāre; (*land*) excurrere ♦ *vt* prōicere.
projectile *n* tēlum *nt.*
projecting *adj* ēminēns.
projection *n* ēminentia *f.*
proletarian *adj* plēbēius.
proletariat *n* plēbs *f.*
prolific *adj* fēcundus.
prolix *adj* verbōsus, longus.
prolixity *n* redundantia *f.*
prologue *n* prologus *m.*
prolong *vt* dūcere, prōdūcere; (*office*) prōrogāre.
prolongation *n* (*time*) propāgātiō *f;* (*office*) prōrogātiō *f.*
promenade *n* ambulātiō *f* ♦ *vi* inambulāre, spatiārī.
prominence *n* ēminentia *f.*
prominent *adj* ēminēns, īnsignis; **be ~** ēminēre.
promiscuous *adj* prōmiscuus.

promiscuously *adv* prōmiscuē.
promise *n* prōmissum *nt;* **break a ~** fidem fallere; **keep a ~** fidem praestāre; **make a ~** fidem dare; **a youth of great ~** summae speī adulēscēns ♦ *vt* prōmittere, pollicērī; (*in marriage*) dēspondēre; ~ **in return** reprōmittere ♦ *vi:* ~ **well** bonam spem ostendere.
promising *adj* bonae speī.
promissory note *n* syngrapha *f.*
promontory *n* prōmunturium *nt.*
promote *vt* favēre (*dat*); (*growth*) alere; (*in rank*) prōdūcere.
promoter *n* auctor *m,* fautor *m.*
promotion *n* dignitās *f.*
prompt *adj* alacer, prōmptus ♦ *vt* incitāre, commovēre; (*speaker*) subicere.
prompter *n* monitor *m.*
promptitude *n* alacritās *f,* celeritās *f.*
promptly *adv* extemplō, citō.
promulgate *vt* prōmulgāre, palam facere.
promulgation *n* prōmulgātiō *f.*
prone *adj* prōnus; (*mind*) inclīnātus.
prong *n* dēns *m.*
pronounce *vt* ēloquī, appellāre; (*oath*) interpōnere; (*sentence*) dīcere, prōnūntiāre.
pronounced *adj* manifestus, īnsignis.
pronouncement *n* ōrātiō *f,* adfirmātiō *f.*
pronunciation *n* appellātiō *f.*
proof *n* documentum *nt,* argūmentum *nt;* (*test*) probātiō *f* ♦ *adj* immōtus, impenetrābilis.
prop *n* adminiculum *nt,* firmāmentum *nt* ♦ *vt* fulcīre.
propaganda *n* documenta *ntpl.*
propagate *vt* prōpāgāre.
propagation *n* prōpāgātiō *f.*
propel *vt* incitāre, prōpellere.
propensity *n* inclīnātiō *f.*
proper *adj* idōneus, decēns, decōrus; rēctus; **is ~** decet.
properly *adv* decōrē; rēctē.
property *n* rēs *f,* rēs mancipī, bona *ntpl;* (*estate*) praedium *nt;* (*attribute*) proprium *nt;* (*slave's*) pecūlium *f.*
prophecy *n* vāticinium *nt,* praedictiō *f.*
prophesy *vt* vāticinārī, praedīcere.
prophet *n* vātēs *m,* fātidicus *m.*
prophetess *n* vātēs *f.*
prophetic *adj* dīvīnus, fātidicus.
prophetically *adv* dīvīnitus.
propinquity *n* (*place*) vīcīnitās *f;* (*kin*) propinquitās *f.*
propitiate *vt* plācāre.
propitiation *n* plācātiō *f,* litātiō *f.*
propitious *adj* fēlīx, faustus; (*god*) praesēns.
proportion *n* mēnsūra *f;* **in ~** prō portiōne, prō ratā parte; **in ~ to** prō (*abl*).
proportionately *adv* prō portiōne, prō ratā parte.
proposal *n* condiciō *f.*
propose *vt* prōpōnere; (*motion*) ferre, rogāre; (*penalty*) inrogāre; (*candidate*) rogāre

magistrātum.
proposer n auctor m, lātor m.
proposition n (offer) condiciō f; (plan)
cōnsilium nt, prōpositum nt; (logic)
prōnūntiātum nt.
propound vt expōnere, in medium prōferre.
propraetor n prōpraetor m.
proprietor n dominus m.
propriety n decōrum nt; (conduct) modestia f;
with ~ decenter.
propulsion n impulsus m.
prorogation n prōrogātiō f.
prorogue vt prōrogāre.
prosaic adj pedester.
proscribe vt prōscrībere.
proscription n prōscrīptiō f.
prose n ōrātiō f, ōrātiō solūta f.
prosecute vt (task) exsequī, gerere; (at law)
accūsāre, lītem intendere (dat).
prosecution n exsecūtiō f; (at law) accūsātiō f;
(party) accūsātor m.
prosecutor n accūsātor m.
prosody n numerī mpl.
prospect n prōspectus m; (fig) spēs f ♦ vi
explōrāre.
prospective adj futūrus, spērātus.
prosper vi flōrēre, bonā fortūnā ūtī ♦ vt
fortūnāre.
prosperity n fortūna f, rēs secundae fpl,
fēlīcitās f.
prosperous adj fēlīx, fortūnātus, secundus.
prosperously adv prosperē.
prostrate adj prōstrātus, afflīctus; **lie ~** iacēre
♦ vt prōsternere, dēicere; **~ oneself**
prōcumbere, sē prōicere.
prostration n frāctus animus m.
prosy adj longus.
protagonist n prīmārum partium āctor m.
protect vt tuērī, dēfendere, custōdīre,
prōtegere.
protection n tūtēla f, praesidium nt; (law)
patrōcinium nt; (POL) fidēs f; **put oneself under
the ~ of** in fidem venīre (gen); **take under
one's ~** in fidem recipere.
protector n patrōnus m, dēfēnsor m, custōs m.
protectress n patrōna f.
protégé n cliēns m.
protest n obtestātiō f; (POL) intercessiō f ♦ vi
obtestārī, reclāmāre; (POL) intercēdere.
protestation n adsevērātiō f.
prototype n archetypum nt.
protract vt dūcere, prōdūcere.
protrude vi prōminēre.
protruding adj exsertus.
protuberance n ēminentia f, tūber nt.
protuberant adj ēminēns, turgidus.
proud adj superbus, adrogāns, īnsolēns; **be ~**
superbīre; **be ~ of** iactāre.
proudly adv superbē.
prove vt dēmōnstrāre, arguere, probāre; (test)
experīrī ♦ vi (person) se praebēre; (event)
ēvādere; **~ oneself** sē praebēre, sē praestāre;
not ~n nōn liquet.

proved adj expertus.
provenance n orīgō f.
provender n pābulum nt.
proverb n prōverbium nt.
proverbial adj trītus; **become ~** in prōverbium
venīre.
provide vt parāre, praebēre; **~ for** prōvidēre
(dat); **the law ~s** lēx iubet; **~ against**
praecavēre.
provided that conj dum, dummodo (+ subj).
providence n prōvidentia f; Deus m.
provident adj prōvidus, cautus.
providential adj dīvīnus; secundus.
providentially adv dīvīnitus.
providently adv cautē.
providing conj dum, dummodo.
province n prōvincia f.
provincial adj prōvinciālis; (contemptuous)
oppidānus, mūnicipālis.
provision n parātus m; **make ~ for** prōvidēre
(dat); **make ~** cavēre.
provisionally adv ad tempus.
provisions n cibus m, commeātus m, rēs
frūmentāria f.
proviso n condiciō f; **with this ~** hāc lēge.
provocation n inrītāmentum nt, offēnsiō f.
provocative adj (language) molestus,
invidiōsus.
provoke vt inrītāre, lacessere; (to action)
excitāre.
provoking adj odiōsus, molestus.
provost n praefectus m.
prow n prōra f.
prowess n virtūs f.
prowl vi grassārī, vagārī.
proximate adj proximus.
proximity n propinquitās f, vīcīnia f.
proxy n vicārius m.
prude n fastīdiōsa f.
prudence n prūdentia f.
prudent adj prūdēns, cautus, sagāx.
prudently adv prūdenter, cautē.
prudery n fastīdiōsa quaedam pudīcitia f.
prudish adj fastīdiōsus.
prune vt amputāre.
pruner n putātor m.
pruning hook n falx f.
pry vi inquīrere; **~ into** scrūtārī.
pseudonym n falsum nōmen nt.
psychology n animī ratiō f.
Ptolemy n Ptolemaeus m.
puberty n pūbertās f.
public adj pūblicus; (speech) forēnsis; **~ life** rēs
pūblica f, forum nt; **in ~** forīs; **appear in ~** in
medium prōdīre; **make ~** in mediō pōnere,
forās perferre; **make a ~ case of** in medium
vocāre; **act for the ~ good** in medium
cōnsulere; **be a ~ figure** in lūce versārī,
digitō mōnstrārī ♦ n vulgus nt, hominēs mpl.
publican n (taxes) pūblicānus m; (inn) caupō m.
publication n ēditiō f, prōmulgātiō f; (book)
liber m.
publicity n lūx f, celebritās f.

publicly _adv_ palam; (_by the state_) pūblicē.
public opinion _n_ fāma _f_.
publish _vt_ vulgāre, dīvulgāre; (_book_) ēdere.
pucker _vt_ corrūgāre.
puerile _adj_ puerīlis.
puerility _n_ ineptiae _fpl_.
puff _n_ aura _f_ ♦ _vt_ īnflāre ♦ _vi_ anhēlāre.
puffed up _adj_ īnflātus, tumidus.
pugilism _n_ pugilātus _m_.
pugilist _n_ pugil _m_.
pugnacious _adj_ pugnāx.
pugnacity _n_ ferōcitās _f_.
puissance _n_ potentia _f_, vīrēs _fpl_.
puissant _adj_ potēns.
pull _n_ tractus _m_; (_of gravity_) contentiō _f_ ♦ _vt_
trahere, tractāre; ~ **apart** distrahere; ~ **at**
vellicāre; ~ **away** āvellere; ~ **back** retrahere;
~ **down** dēripere, dētrahere; (_building_)
dēmōlīrī; ~ **off** āvellere; ~ **out** ēvellere,
extrahere; ~ **through** _vi_ pervincere; (_illness_)
convalēscere; ~ **up** (_plant_) ēruere;
(_movement_) coercēre; ~ **to pieces** dīlaniāre.
pullet _n_ pullus gallīnāceus _m_.
pulley _n_ trochlea _f_.
pulmonary _adj_ pulmōneus.
pulp _n_ carō _f_.
pulpit _n_ suggestus _m_.
pulsate _vi_ palpitāre, micāre.
pulse _n_ (_plant_) legūmen _nt_; (_of blood_) vēnae _fpl_;
feel the ~ vēnās temptāre.
pulverize _vt_ contundere.
pumice stone _n_ pūmex _m_.
pummel _vt_ verberāre.
pump _n_ antlia _f_ ♦ _vt_ haurīre; ~ **out** exhaurīre.
pumpkin _n_ cucurbita _f_.
pun _n_ agnōminātiō _f_.
punch _n_ ictus _m_ ♦ _vt_ pertundere, percutere.
punctilious _adj_ rīligiōsus.
punctiliousness _n_ rīligiō _f_.
punctual _adj_ accūrātus, dīligēns.
punctuality _n_ dīligentia _f_.
punctually _adv_ ad hōram, ad tempus.
punctuate _vt_ distinguere.
punctuation _n_ interpūnctiō _f_.
puncture _n_ pūnctiō _f_ ♦ _vt_ pungere.
pundit _n_ scholasticus _m_.
pungency _n_ ācrimōnia _f_; (_in debate_) aculeī _mpl_.
pungent _adj_ ācer, mordāx.
punish _vt_ pūnīre, animadvertere in (_acc_);
poenam sūmere dē (+ _abl_); **be ~ed** poenās
dare.
punishable _adj_ poenā dignus.
punisher _n_ vindex _m_, ultor _m_.
punishment _n_ poena _f_, supplicium _nt_;
(_censors'_) animadversiō _f_; **capital** ~ capitis
supplicium _nt_; **corporal** ~ verbera _ntpl_; **inflict**
~ **on** poenā adficere, poenam capere dē (_abl_),
supplicium sūmere dē (_abl_); **submit to** ~
poenam subīre; **undergo** ~ poenās dare,
pendere, solvere.
punitive _adj_ ulcīscendī causā.
punt _n_ pontō _m_.
puny _adj_ pusillus.

pup _n_ catulus _m_ ♦ _vi_ parere.
pupil _n_ discipulus _m_, discipula _f_; (_eye_) aciēs _f_,
pūpula _f_.
pupillage _n_ tūtēla _f_.
puppet _n_ pūpa _f_.
puppy _n_ catulus _m_.
purblind _adj_ luscus.
purchase _n_ emptiō _f_; (_formal_) mancipium _nt_ ♦
_vt_ emere.
purchaser _n_ emptor _m_; (_at auction_) manceps _m_.
pure _adj_ pūrus, integer; (_morally_) castus;
(_mere_) merus.
purely _adv_ pūrē, integrē; (_solely_) sōlum, nīl
nisi; (_quite_) omnīnō, plānē.
purgation _n_ pūrgātiō _f_.
purge _vt_ pūrgāre, expūrgāre.
purification _n_ lūstrātiō _f_, pūrgātiō _f_.
purify _vt_ pūrgāre, expūrgāre.
purist _n_ fastīdiōsus _m_.
purity _n_ integritās _f_, castitās _f_.
purloin _vt_ surripere, fūrārī.
purple _n_ purpura _f_ ♦ _adj_ purpureus.
purport _n_ sententia _f_; (_of words_) vīs _f_; **what is
the** ~ **of?** quō spectat?, quid vult? ♦ _vt_ velle
spectāre ad.
purpose _n_ prōpositum _nt_, cōnsilium _nt_, mēns _f_;
for that ~ eō; **for the** ~ **of** ad (_acc_), ut (_subj_), eā
mente ut, eō cōnsiliō ut (_subj_); **on** ~ cōnsultō,
dē industriā; **to the** ~ ad rem; **to what** ~?
quō?, quōrsum?; **to no** ~ frustrā, nēquīquam;
without achieving one's ~ rē īnfectā ♦ _vt_ in
animō habēre, velle.
purposeful _adj_ intentus.
purposeless _adj_ inānis.
purposely _adv_ cōnsultō, dē industriā.
purr _n_ murmur _nt_ ♦ _vi_ murmurāre.
purse _n_ marsupium _nt_, crumēna _f_; **privy** ~
fiscus _m_ ♦ _vt_ adstringere.
pursuance _n_ exsecūtiō _f_; **in** ~ **of** secundum
(_acc_).
pursue _vt_ īnsequī, īnsectārī, persequī;
(_closely_) īnstāre (_dat_), īnsistere (_dat_); (_aim_)
petere; (_course_) īnsistere.
pursuer _n_ īnsequēns _m_; (_law_) accūsātor _m_.
pursuit _n_ īnsectātiō _f_; (_hunt_) vēnātiō _f_;
(_ambition_) studium _nt_.
purvey _vt_ parāre; (_food_) obsōnāre.
purveyance _n_ prōcūrātiō _f_.
purveyor _n_ obsōnātor _m_.
purview _n_ prōvincia _f_.
pus _n_ pūs _nt_.
push _n_ pulsus _m_, impetus _m_ ♦ _vt_ impellere,
trūdere, urgēre; ~ **away** āmovēre; ~ **back**
repellere; ~ **down** dēprimere, dētrūdere; ~
forward prōpellere; ~ **in** intrūdere; ~ **on**
incitāre; ~ **through** perrumpere.
pushing _adj_ cōnfīdēns.
pusillanimity _n_ ignāvia _f_, timor _m_.
pusillanimous _adj_ ignāvus, timidus.
pustule _n_ pustula _f_.
put _vt_ (_in a state_) dare; (_in a position_) pōnere; (_in
words_) reddere; (_argument_) pōnere; (_spur_)
subdere; (_to some use_) adhibēre; ~ **an end to**

putrefaction–quick

fīnem facere (*dat*); ~ **a question to**
interrogāre; ~ **against** adpōnere; ~ **among**
intericere; ~ **aside** sēpōnere; ~ **away** pōnere,
dēmovēre; (*store*) repōnere; ~ **back**
repōnere; repellere; ~ **beside** adpōnere; ~
between interpōnere; ~ **by** condere; ~ **down**
dēpōnere; (*revolt*) opprimere; ~ **forth**
extendere; (*growth*) mittere; ~ **forward**
ostentāre; (*plea*) adferre; ~ **in** immittere,
īnserere; (*ship*) adpellere; ~ **off** differre; ~ **on**
impōnere; (*clothes*) induere; (*play*) dare; ~
out ēicere; (*eye*) effodere; (*fire*) exstinguere;
(*money*) pōnere; (*tongue*) exserere; ~ **out of**
the way dēmovēre; ~ **out to sea** in altum
ēvehi, solvere; ~ **over** superimpōnere; ~ **to**
adpōnere; (*flight*) dare in (*acc*), fugāre,
prōflīgāre; in fugam conicere; (*sea*) solvere;
~ **together** cōnferre; ~ **under** subicere; ~ **up**
(*for sale*) prōpōnere; (*lodge*) dēvertere,
dēversārī apud; ~ **up with** ferre, patī; ~ **upon**
impōnere.
putrefaction *n* pūtor *m*.
putrefy *vi* putrēscere.
putrid *adj* putridus.
puzzle *n* nōdus *m* ♦ *vt* impedīre, sollicitāre; **be**
~d haerēre.
puzzling *adj* ambiguus, perplexus.
pygmy *n* pygmaeus *m*.
pyramid *n* pȳramis *f*.
pyramidal *adj* pȳramidātus.
pyre *n* rogus *m*.
Pyrenees *npl* Pyrenaeī (montēs) *mpl*.
python *n* pȳthōn *m*.

Q, q

quack *n* (*doctor*) circulātor *m* ♦ *vi* tetrinnīre.
quadrangle *n* ārea *f*.
quadruped *n* quadrupēs *m/f*.
quadruple *adj* quadruplex.
quaestor *n* quaestor *m*; ~**'s** quaestōrius.
quaestorship *n* quaestūra *f*.
quaff *vt* ēpōtāre, haurīre.
quagmire *n* palūs *f*.
quail *n* (*bird*) coturnīx *f* ♦ *vi* pāvēscere,
trepidāre.
quaint *adj* novus, īnsolitus.
quaintness *n* īnsolentia *f*.
quake *vi* horrēre, horrēscere ♦ *n* (*earth*) mōtus
m.
quaking *n* horror *m*, tremor *m* ♦ *adj* tremulus.
qualification *n* condiciō *f*; (*limitation*) exceptiō
f.
qualified *adj* (*for*) aptus, idōneus, dignus; (*in*)
perītus, doctus.

qualify *vi* prōficere ♦ *vt* temperāre, mītigāre.
qualities *npl* ingenium *nt*.
quality *n* nātūra *f*, vīs *f*; indolēs *f*; (*rank*) locus
m, genus *nt*; **I know the ~ of** sciō quālis sit.
qualm *n* riligiō *f*, scrūpulus *m*.
quandary *n* angustiae *fpl*; **be in a ~** haerēre.
quantity *n* cōpia *f*, numerus *m*; (*metre*) vōcum
mēnsiō *f*; **a large ~** multum *nt*, plūrimum *nt*; **a**
small ~ aliquantulum *nt*.
quarrel *n* dissēnsiō *f*, contrōversia *f*; (*violent*)
rixa *f*, iūrgium *nt* ♦ *vi* rixārī, altercārī.
quarrelsome *adj* pugnāx, lītigiōsus.
quarry *n* lapicīdinae *fpl*, metallum *nt*; (*prey*)
praeda *f* ♦ *vt* excīdere.
quart *n* duō sextāriī *mpl*.
quartan *n* (*fever*) quartāna *f*.
quarter *n* quarta pars *f*, quadrāns *m*; (*sector*)
regiō *f*; (*direction*) pars *f*, regiō *f*; (*respite*)
missiō *f*; **~s** castra *ntpl*; (*billet*) hospitium *nt*;
come to close ~s manum cōnserere; (*armies*)
signa cōnferre; **winter ~s** hīberna *ntpl* ♦ *vt*
quadrifidam dīvidere; (*troops*) in hospitia
dīvidere.
quarterdeck *n* puppis *f*.
quarterly *adj* trimestris ♦ *adv* quartō quōque
mēnse.
quartermaster *n* (*navy*) gubernātor *m*; (*army*)
castrōrum praefectus *m*.
quarterstaff *n* rudis *f*.
quash *vt* comprimere; (*decision*) rescindere.
quatrain *n* tetrastichon *nt*.
quaver *n* tremor *m* ♦ *vi* tremere.
quavering *adj* tremebundus.
quay *n* crepīdō *f*.
queasy *adj* fastīdiōsus.
queen *n* rēgīna *f*; (*bee*) rēx *m*.
queer *adj* īnsolēns, rīdiculus.
quell *vt* opprimere, domāre, dēbellāre.
quench *vt* exstinguere, restinguere; (*thirst*)
sēdāre, explēre.
querulous *adj* querulus, queribundus.
query *n* interrogātiō *f* ♦ *vt* in dubium vocāre ♦
vi rogāre.
quest *n* investīgātiō *f*; **go in ~ of** investīgāre,
anquīrere.
question *n* interrogātiō *f*; (*at issue*) quaestiō *f*,
rēs *f*; (*in doubt*) dubium *nt*; **ask a ~** rogāre,
quaerere, scīscitārī, percontārī; **call in ~** in
dubium vocāre, addubitāre; **out of the ~**
indignus; **be out of the ~** improbārī, fierī nōn
posse; **the ~ is** illud quaeritur; **there is no ~**
that nōn dubium est quīn (*subj*); **without ~**
sine dubiō ♦ *vt* interrogāre; (*closely*)
percontārī; (*doubt*) in dubium vocāre ♦ *vi*
dubitāre.
questionable *adj* incertus, dubius.
questioner *n* percontātor *m*.
questioning *n* interrogātiō *f*.
queue *n* agmen *nt*.
quibble *n* captiō *f* ♦ *vi* cavillārī.
quibbler *n* cavillātor *m*.
quibbling *adj* captiōsus.
quick *adj* (*speed*) celer, vēlōx, citus; (*to act*)

alacer, impiger; (*to perceive*) sagāx; (*with hands*) facilis; (*living*) vīvus; **be ~** properāre, festīnāre; **cut to the ~** ad vīvum resecāre; (*fig*) mordēre.

quicken *vt* adcelerāre; (*with life*) animāre.

quickening *adj* vītālis.

quickly *adv* celeriter, citō; (*haste*) properē; (*mind*) acūtē; **as ~ as possible** quam celerrimē.

quickness *n* celeritās *f*, vēlōcitās *f*; (*to act*) alacritās *f*; (*to perceive*) sagācitās *f*, sollertia *f*.

quicksand *n* syrtis *f*.

quick-tempered *adj* īrācundus.

quick-witted *adj* acūtus, sagāx, perspicāx.

quiescence *n* inertia *f*, ōtium *nt*.

quiescent *adj* iners, ōtiōsus.

quiet *adj* tranquillus, quiētus, placidus; (*silent*) tacitus; **be ~** quiēscere; silēre ♦ *n* quiēs *f*, tranquillitās *f*; silentium *nt*; (*peace*) pāx *f* ♦ *vt* pācāre, compōnere.

quietly *adv* tranquillē, quiētē; tacitē, per silentium; aequō animō.

quietness *n* tranquillitās *f*; silentium *nt*.

quill *n* penna *f*.

quince *n* cydōnium *nt*.

quinquennial *adj* quinquennālis.

quinquereme *n* quinquerēmis *f*.

quintessence *n* flōs *m*, vīs *f*.

quip *n* sāl *m*, facētiae *fpl*.

quirk *n* captiuncula *f*; **~s** *pl* trīcae *fpl*.

quit *vt* relinquere ♦ *adj* līber, solūtus.

quite *adv* admodum, plānē, prōrsus; **not ~** minus, parum; (*time*) nōndum.

quits *n* parēs *mpl*.

quiver *n* pharetra *f* ♦ *vi* tremere, contremere.

quivering *adj* tremebundus, tremulus.

quoit *n* discus *m*.

quota *n* pars *f*, rata pars *f*.

quotation *n* (*act*) commemorātiō *f*; (*passage*) locus *m*.

quote *vt* prōferre, commemorāre.

quoth *vt* inquit.

R, r

rabbit *n* cunīculus *m*.

rabble *n* turba *f*; (*class*) vulgus *nt*, plēbēcula *f*.

rabid *adj* rabidus.

rabidly *adv* rabidē.

race *n* (*descent*) genus *nt*, stirps *f*; (*people*) gēns *f*, nōmen *nt*; (*contest*) certāmen *nt*; (*fig*) cursus *m*, curriculum *nt*; (*water*) flūmen *nt*; **run a ~** cursū certāre; **run the ~** (*fig*) spatium dēcurrere ♦ *vi* certāre, contendere.

racecourse *n* (*foot*) stadium *nt*; (*horse*) spatium *nt*.

racer *n* cursor *m*.

racial *adj* gentīlis.

rack *n* (*torture*) tormentum *nt*; (*shelf*) pluteus *m*; **be on the ~** (*fig*) cruciāri ♦ *vt* torquēre, cruciāre; **~ off** (*wine*) diffundere.

racket *n* (*noise*) strepitus *m*.

racy *adj* (*style*) salsus.

radiance *n* splendor *m*, fulgor *m*.

radiant *adj* splendidus, nitidus.

radiantly *adv* splendidē.

radiate *vi* fulgēre; (*direction*) dīversōs tendere ♦ *vt* ēmittere.

radical *adj* īnsitus, innātus; (*thorough*) tōtus ♦ *n* novārum rērum cupidus *m*.

radically *adv* omnīnō, penitus, funditus.

radish *n* rādīx *f*.

radius *n* radius *m*.

raffish *adj* dissolūtus.

raffle *n* ālea *f* ♦ *vt* āleā vēndere.

raft *n* ratis *f*.

rafter *n* trabs *f*, tignum *nt*.

rag *n* pannus *m*.

rage *n* īra *f*, furor *m*; **be all the ~** in ōre omnium esse; **spend one's ~** exsaevīre ♦ *vi* furere, saevīre; (*furiously*) dēbacchārī.

ragged *adj* pannōsus.

raid *n* excursiō *f*, incursiō *f*, impressiō *f*; **make a ~** excurrere ♦ *vt* incursiōnem facere in (*acc*).

rail *n* longurius *m* ♦ *vt* saepīre ♦ *vi*: **~ at** maledīcere (*dat*), convīcia facere (*dat*).

railing *n* saepēs *f*, cancellī *mpl*.

raillery *n* cavillātiō *f*.

raiment *n* vestis *f*.

rain *n* pluvia *f*, imber *m* ♦ *vi* pluere; **it is raining** pluit.

rainbow *n* arcus *m*.

rainstorm *n* imber *m*.

rainy *adj* pluvius.

raise *vt* tollere, ēlevāre; (*army*) cōgere, cōnscrībere; (*children*) ēducāre; (*cry*) tollere; (*from dead*) excitāre; (*laugh*) movēre; (*money*) cōnflāre; (*price*) augēre; (*siege*) exsolvere; (*structure*) exstruere; (*to higher rank*) ēvehere; **~ up** ērigere, sublevāre.

raisin *n* astaphis *f*.

rajah *n* dynastēs *m*.

rake *n* rastrum *nt*; (*person*) nepōs *m* ♦ *vt* rādere; **~ in** conrādere; **~ up** (*fig*) ēruere.

rakish *adj* dissolūtus.

rally *n* conventus *m* ♦ *vt* (*troops*) in ōrdinem revocāre; (*with words*) hortārī; (*banter*) cavillārī ♦ *vi* sē colligere.

ram *n* ariēs *m*; (*battering*) ariēs *m* ♦ *vt*: **~ down** fistūcāre; **~ home** (*fact*) inculcāre.

ramble *n* errātiō *f* ♦ *vi* vagārī, errāre.

rambling *adj* vagus; (*plant*) errāticus; (*speech*) fluēns.

ramification *n* rāmus *m*.

rammer *n* fistūca *f*.

rampage *vi* saevīre.

rampant *adj* ferōx.

rampart n agger m, vallum nt.

ranch n lātifundium nt.

rancid adj pūtidus.

rancour n odium nt, acerbitās f, invidia f.

random adj fortuītus; **at ~** temerē.

range n ōrdō m, seriēs f; (mountain) iugum nt; (of weapon) iactus m; **within ~** intrā tēlī iactum; **come within ~** sub ictum venīre ♦ vt ōrdināre ♦ vi ēvagārī, pervagārī; (in speech) excurrere.

rank n (line) ōrdō m; (class) ōrdō m; (position) locus m, dignitās f; **~ and file** gregāriī mīlitēs mpl; **keep the ~s** ōrdinēs observāre; **the ~s** (MIL) aciēs, acieī f; **leave the ~s** ōrdine ēgredī, ab signīs discēdere; **reduce to the ~s** in ōrdinem redigere ♦ vt numerāre ♦ vi in numerō habērī.

rank adj luxuriōsus; (smell) gravis, foetidus.

rankle vi exulcerāre.

rankness n luxuriēs f.

ransack vt dīripere, spoliāre.

ransom n redemptiō f, pretium nt ♦ vt redimere.

rant vi latrāre.

ranter n rabula m, latrātor m.

rap n ictus m ♦ vt ferīre.

rapacious adj rapāx, avidus.

rapaciously adv avidē.

rapacity n rapācitās f, aviditās f.

rape n raptus m.

rapid adj rapidus, vēlōx, citus, incitātus.

rapidity n celeritās f, vēlōcitās f, incitātiō f.

rapidly adv rapidē, vēlōciter, citō.

rapine n rapīna f.

rapt adj intentus.

rapture n laetitia f, alacritās f.

rare adj rārus; (occurrence) īnfrequēns; (quality) singulāris.

rarefy vt extenuāre.

rarely adv rārō.

rarity n rāritās f; (thing) rēs īnsolita f.

rascal n furcifer m, scelestus m.

rascally adj improbus.

rash adj temerārius, audāx, incōnsultus, praeceps.

rashly adv temerē, incōnsultē.

rashness n temeritās f, audācia f.

rat n mūs m/f.

rate n (cost) pretium nt; (standard) nōrma f; (tax) vectīgal nt; (speed) celeritās f; **at any ~** (concessive) utique, saltem; (adversative) quamquam, tamen ♦ vt (value) aestimāre; (scold) increpāre, obiūrgāre.

rather adv potius, satius; (somewhat) aliquantum; (with comp) aliquantō; (with verbs) mālō; (correcting) immo; **~ sad** tristior; **I would ~** mālō; **I ~ think** haud sciō an; **~ than** magis quam, potius quam.

ratification n (formal) sānctiō f.

ratify vt ratum facere, sancīre; (law) iubēre.

rating n taxātiō f, aestimātiō f; (navy) nauta m; (scolding) obiūrgātiō f.

ratiocinate vi ratiōcinārī.

ratiocination n ratiōcinātiō f.

ration n dēmēnsum nt.

rational adj animō praeditus; **be ~** sapere.

rationality n ratiō f.

rationally adv ratiōne.

rations npl cibāria ntpl, diāria ntpl.

rattle n crepitus m; (toy) crotalum nt ♦ vi crepitāre, increpāre.

raucous adj raucus.

ravage vt dēpopulārī, vastāre, dīripere.

rave vi furere, īnsānīre; (fig) bacchārī, saevīre.

raven n cornīx f.

ravenous adj rapāx, vorāx.

ravenously adv avidē.

ravine n faucēs fpl, hiātus m.

raving adj furiōsus, īnsānus ♦ n furor m.

ravish vt rapere; (joy) efferre.

raw adj crūdus; (person) rudis, agrestis.

ray n radius m; **the first ~ of hope appeared** prīma spēs adfulsit.

raze vt excīdere, solō aequāre.

razor n novācula f.

reach n (space) spatium nt; (mind) captus m; (weapon) ictus m; **out of ~ of** extrā (acc); **within ~** ad manum ♦ vt advenīre ad (+ acc); attingere; (space) pertinēre ad; (journey) pervenīre ad.

react vi adficī; **~ to** ferre.

reaction n: **what was his ~ to?** quō animō tulit?

read vt legere; (a book) ēvolvere; (aloud) recitāre; **~ over** perlegere.

reader n lēctor m.

readily adv facile, libenter, ultrō.

readiness n facilitās f; **in ~** ad manum, in prōmptū, in expedītō.

reading n lēctiō f.

readjust vt dēnuō accommodāre.

ready adj parātus, prōmptus; (manner) facilis; (money) praesēns; **get, make ~** parāre, expedīre, adōrnāre.

reaffirm vt iterum adfirmāre.

real adj vērus, germānus.

real estate n fundus m, solum nt.

realism n vēritās f.

realistic adj vērī similis.

reality n rēs f, rēs ipsa f, vērum nt; **in ~** rēvērā.

realize vt intellegere, animadvertere; (aim) efficere, peragere; (money) redigere.

really adv vērē, rēvērā, profectō; **~?** itane vērō?

realm n rēgnum nt.

reap vt metere; **~ the reward of** fructum percipere ex.

reaper n messor m.

reappear vi revenīre.

rear vt alere, ēducāre; (structure) exstruere ♦ vi sē ērigere ♦ n tergum nt; (MIL) novissima aciēs f, novissimum agmen nt; **in the ~** ā tergō; **bring up the ~** agmen claudere, agmen cōgere ♦ adj postrēmus, novissimus.

rearguard n novissimum agmen nt,

novissimī *mpl*.

rearrange *vt* ōrdinem mūtāre (*gen*).

reason *n* (*faculty*) mēns *f*, animus *m*, ratiō *f*; (*sanity*) sānitās *f*; (*argument*) ratiō *f*; (*cause*) causa *f*; (*moderation*) modus *m*; **by ~ of** propter (*acc*); **for this ~** idcircō, ideō, proptereā; **in ~** aequus, modicus; **with good ~ iūre**; **without ~** temerē, sine causā; **without good ~** frustrā, iniūriā; **give a ~ for** ratiōnem adferre (*gen*); **I know the ~ for** sciō cūr, quamobrem (*subj*); **there is no ~ for** nōn est cūr, nihil est quod (*subj*); **lose one's ~** īnsānīre ♦ *vi* ratiōcinārī, disserere.

reasonable *adj* aequus, iūstus; (*person*) modestus; (*amount*) modicus.

reasonably *adv* ratiōne, iūstē; modicē.

reasoning *n* ratiō *f*, ratiōcinātiō *f*.

reassemble *vt* colligere, cōgere.

reassert *vt* iterāre.

reassume *vt* recipere.

reassure *vt* firmāre, cōnfirmāre.

rebate *vt* dēdūcere.

rebel *n* rebellis *m* ♦ *adj* sēditiōsus ♦ *vi* rebelliōnem facere, rebellāre, dēscīscere.

rebellion *n* sēditiō *f*, mōtus *m*.

rebellious *adj* sēditiōsus.

rebound *vi* resilīre.

rebuff *n* repulsa *f* ♦ *vt* repellere, āversārī.

rebuild *vt* renovāre, restaurāre.

rebuke *n* reprehēnsiō *f*, obiūrgātiō *f* ♦ *vt* reprehendere, obiūrgāre, increpāre.

rebut *vt* refūtāre, redarguere.

recalcitrant *adj* invītus.

recall *n* revocātiō *f*, reditus *m* ♦ *vt* revocāre; (*from exile*) redūcere; (*to mind*) reminīscī (*gen*), recordārī (*gen*).

recant *vt* retractāre.

recantation *n* receptus *m*.

recapitulate *vt* repetere, summātim dīcere.

recapitulation *n* ēnumerātiō *f*.

recapture *vt* recipere.

recast *vt* reficere, retractāre.

recede *vi* recēdere.

receipt *n* (*act*) acceptiō *f*; (*money*) acceptum *nt*; (*written*) apocha *f*.

receive *vt* accipere, capere; (*in turn*) excipere.

receiver *n* receptor *m*.

recent *adj* recēns.

recently *adv* nūper, recēns.

receptacle *n* receptāculum *nt*.

reception *n* aditus *m*, hospitium *nt*.

receptive *adj* docilis.

recess *n* recessus *m*, angulus *m*; (*holiday*) fēriae *fpl*.

recharge *vt* replēre.

recipe *n* compositiō *f*.

recipient *n* quī accipit.

reciprocal *adj* mūtuus.

reciprocally *adv* mūtuō, inter sē.

reciprocate *vt* referre, reddere.

reciprocity *n* mūtuum *nt*.

recital *n* nārrātiō *f*, ēnumerātiō *f*; (*LIT*) recitātiō *f*.

recitation *n* recitātiō *f*.

recite *vt* recitāre; (*details*) ēnumerāre.

reciter *n* recitātor *m*.

reck *vt* ratiōnem habēre (*gen*).

reckless *adj* temerārius, incautus, praeceps.

recklessly *adv* incautē, temerē.

recklessness *n* temeritās *f*, neglegentia *f*.

reckon *vt* (*count*) computāre, numerāre; (*think*) cēnsēre, dūcere; (*estimate*) aestimāre; **~ on** cōnfīdere (*dat*); **~ up** dīnumerāre; (*cost*) aestimāre; **~ with** contendere cum.

reckoning *n* ratiō *f*.

reclaim *vt* repetere; (*from error*) revocāre.

recline *vi* recumbere; (*at table*) accumbere; (*plur*) discumbere.

recluse *n* homō sōlitārius *m*.

recognition *n* cognitiō *f*.

recognizance *n* vadimōnium *nt*.

recognize *vt* agnōscere; (*approve*) accipere; (*admit*) fatērī.

recoil *vi* resilīre; **~ from** refugere; **~ upon** recidere in (*acc*).

recollect *vt* reminīscī (*gen*).

recollection *n* memoria *f*, recordātiō *f*.

recommence *vt* renovāre, redintegrāre.

recommend *vt* commendāre; (*advise*) suādēre (*dat*).

recommendation *n* commendātiō *f*; (*advice*) cōnsilium *nt*; **letter of ~** litterae commendātīciae.

recompense *vt* remūnerārī, grātiam referre (*dat*) ♦ *n* praemium *nt*, remūnerātiō *f*.

reconcile *vt* compōnere, reconciliāre; **be ~d in** grātiam redīre.

reconciliation *n* reconciliātiō *f*, grātia *f*.

recondite *adj* reconditus, abstrūsus.

recondition *vt* reficere.

reconnaissance *n* explōrātiō *f*.

reconnoitre *vt, vi* explōrāre; **without reconnoitring** inexplōrātō.

reconquer *vt* recipere.

reconsider *vt* reputāre, retractāre.

reconstruct *vt* restituere, renovāre.

reconstruction *n* renovātiō *f*.

record *n* monumentum *nt*; (*LIT*) commentārius *m*; **~s** *pl* tabulae *fpl*, fāstī *mpl*, ācta *ntpl*; **break the ~** priōrēs omnēs superāre ♦ *vt* in commentārium referre; (*history*) perscrībere, nārrāre.

recount *vt* nārrāre, commemorāre.

recourse *n*: **have ~ to** (*for safety*) cōnfugere ad (*as expedient*) dēcurrere ad.

recover *vt* recipere, recuperāre; (*loss*) reparāre; **~ oneself** sē colligere; **~ one's senses** ad sānitātem revertī ♦ *vi* convalēscere.

recovery *n* recuperātiō *f*; (*from illness*) salūs *f*.

recreate *vt* recreāre.

recreation *n* requiēs *f*, remissiō *f*, lūdus *m*.

recriminate *vi* in vicem accūsāre.

recrimination *n* mūtua accūsātiō *f*.

recruit *n* tīrō *m* ♦ *vt* (*MIL*) cōnscrībere; (*strength*) reficere.

recruiting officer n conquīsītor m.
rectify vt corrigere, ēmendāre.
rectitude n probitās f.
recumbent adj supīnus.
recuperate vi convalēscere.
recur vi recurrere, redīre.
recurrence n reditus m, reversiō f.
recurrent adj adsiduus.
red adj ruber.
redden vi ērubēscere ♦ vt rutilāre.
reddish adj subrūfus.
redeem vt redimere, līberāre.
redeemer n līberātor m.
redemption n redemptiō f.
red-haired adj rūfus.
red-handed adj: **catch ~ in** manifestō scelere dēprehendere.
red-hot adj fervēns.
red lead n minium nt.
redness n rubor m.
redolent adj: **be ~ of** redolēre.
redouble vt ingemināre.
redoubt n prōpugnāculum nt.
redoubtable adj īnfestus, formīdolōsus.
redound vi redundāre; **it ~s to my credit** mihī honōrī est.
redress n remedium nt; **demand ~** rēs repetere ♦ vt restituere.
reduce vt minuere, attenuāre; (to a condition) redigere, dēdūcere; (MIL) expugnāre; **~ to the ranks in** ōrdinem cōgere.
reduction n imminūtiō f; (MIL) expugnātiō f.
redundancy n redundantia f.
redundant adj redundāns; **be ~** redundāre.
reduplication n gemīnātiō f.
re-echo vt reddere, referre ♦ vi resonāre.
reed n harundō f.
reedy adj harundineus.
reef n saxa ntpl ♦ vt (sail) subnectere.
reek n fūmus m ♦ vi fūmāre.
reel vi vacillāre, titubāre.
re-enlist vt rescrībere.
re-establish vt restituere.
refashion vt reficere.
refer vt (person) dēlēgāre; (matter) rēicere, remittere ♦ vi: **~ to** spectāre ad; (in speech) attingere, perstringere.
referee n arbiter m.
reference n ratiō f; (in book) locus m.
refine vt excolere, expolīre; (metal) excoquere.
refined adj hūmānus, urbānus, polītus.
refinement n hūmānitās f, cultus m, ēlegantia f.
refit vt reficere.
reflect vt reddere, repercutere ♦ vi meditārī; **~ upon** cōnsīderāre, sēcum reputāre; (blame) reprehendere.
reflection n (of light) repercussus m; (image) imāgō f; (thought) meditātiō f, cōgitātiō f; (blame) reprehēnsiō f; **cast ~s on** maculīs aspergere, vitiō vertere; **with due ~** cōnsīderātē; **without ~** incōnsultē.

reflux n recessus m.
reform n ēmendātiō f ♦ vt (lines) restituere; (error) corrigere, ēmendāre, meliōrem facere ♦ vi sē corrigere.
reformation n corrēctiō f.
reformer n corrēctor m, ēmendātor m.
refract vt īnfringere.
refractory adj contumāx.
refrain vi temperāre, abstinēre (dat), supersedēre (inf).
refresh vt recreāre, renovāre, reficere; (mind) integrāre.
refreshed adj requiētus.
refreshing adj dulcis, iūcundus.
refreshment n cibus m.
refuge n perfugium nt; (secret) latebra f; **take ~ with** perfugere ad (acc); **take ~ in** confugere.
refugee n profugus m.
refulgence n splendor m.
refulgent adj splendidus.
refund vt reddere.
refusal n recūsātiō f, dētrectātiō f.
refuse n pūrgāmenta ntpl; (fig) faex f ♦ vt (request) dēnegāre; (offer) dētrectāre, recūsāre; (with verb) nōlle.
refutation n refūtātiō f, reprehēnsiō f.
refute vt refellere, redarguere, revincere.
regain vt recipere.
regal adj rēgius, rēgālis.
regale vt excipere, dēlectāre; **~ oneself** epulārī.
regalia n īnsignia ntpl.
regally adv rēgāliter.
regard n respectus m, ratiō f; (esteem) grātia f; **with ~ to ad** (acc), quod attinet ad ♦ vt (look) intuērī, spectāre; (deem) habēre, dūcere; **send ~s to** salūtem dīcere (dat).
regarding prep dē (abl).
regardless adj neglegēns, immemor.
regency n interrēgnum nt.
regent n interrēx m.
regicide n (person) rēgis interfector m; (act) rēgis caedēs f.
regime n administrātiō f.
regimen n vīctus m.
regiment n legiō f.
region n regiō f, tractus m.
register n tabulae fpl, album nt ♦ vt in tabulās referre, perscrībere; (emotion) ostendere, sūmere.
registrar n tabulārius m.
registry n tabulārium nt.
regret n dolor m; (for past) dēsīderium nt; (for fault) paenitentia f ♦ vt dolēre; **I ~ mē** paenitet, mē piget (gen).
regretful adj maestus.
regretfully adv dolenter.
regrettable adj īnfēlīx, īnfortūnātus.
regular adj (consistent) cōnstāns; (orderly) ōrdinātus; (habitual) solitus, adsiduus; (proper) iūstus, rēctus.
regularity n moderātiō f, ōrdō m; (consistency) cōnstantia f.

regularly *adv* ōrdine; cōnstanter; iūstē, rēctē.
regulate *vt* ōrdināre, dīrigere; (*control*) moderārī.
regulation *n* lēx *f*, dēcrētum *nt*.
rehabilitate *vt* restituere.
rehearsal *n* meditātiō *f*.
rehearse *vt* meditārī.
reign *n* rēgnum *nt*; (*emperor's*) prīncipātus *m*; in the ~ of Numa rēgnante Numā ♦ *vi* rēgnāre; (*fig*) dominārī.
reimburse *vt* rependere.
rein *n* habēna *f*; give full ~ to habēnās immittere ♦ *vt* īnfrēnāre.
reindeer *n* rēnō *m*.
reinforce *vt* firmāre, cōnfirmāre.
reinforcement *n* subsidium *nt*; ~s *pl* novae cōpiae *fpl*.
reinstate *vt* restituere, redūcere.
reinstatement *n* restitūtiō *f*, reductiō *f*; (*to legal privileges*) postlīminium *nt*.
reinvigorate *vt* recreāre.
reiterate *vt* dictitāre, iterāre.
reiteration *n* iterātiō *f*.
reject *vt* rēicere; (*with scorn*) respuere, aspernārī, repudiāre.
rejection *n* rēiectiō *f*, repulsa *f*.
rejoice *vi* gaudēre, laetārī ♦ *vt* dēlectāre.
rejoicing *n* gaudium *nt*.
rejoin *vt* redīre ad ♦ *vi* respondēre.
rejoinder *n* respōnsum *nt*.
rejuvenate *vt*: be ~d repuerāscere.
rekindle *vt* suscitāre.
relapse *vi* recidere.
relate *vt* (*tell*) nārrāre, commemorāre, expōnere; (*compare*) cōnferre ♦ *vi* pertinēre.
related *adj* propinquus; (*by birth*) cognātus; (*by marriage*) adfīnis; (*fig*) fīnitimus.
relation *n* (*tale*) nārrātiō *f*; (*connection*) ratiō *f*; (*kin*) necessārius *m*, cognātus *m*, adfīnis *m*.
relationship *n* necessitūdō *f*; (*by birth*) cognātiō *f*; (*by marriage*) adfīnitās *f*; (*connection*) vīcīnitās *f*.
relative *adj* cum cēterīs comparātus ♦ *n* propinquus *m*, cognātus *m*, adfīnis *m*, necessārius *m*.
relatively *adv* ex comparātiōne.
relax *vt* laxāre, remittere ♦ *vi* languēscere.
relaxation *n* remissiō *f*, requiēs *f*, lūdus *m*.
relay *n*: ~s of horses dispositī equī *mpl*.
release *vt* solvere, exsolvere, līberāre, expedīre; (*law*) absolvere ♦ *n* missiō *f*, līberātiō *f*.
relegate *vt* relēgāre.
relent *vi* concēdere, plācārī, flectī.
relentless *adj* immisericors, inexōrābilis; (*things*) improbus.
relevant *adj* ad rem.
reliability *n* fīdūcia *f*.
reliable *adj* fīdus.
reliance *n* fīdūcia *f*, fidēs *f*.
reliant *adj* frētus.
relic *n* rēliquiae *fpl*.

relief *n* levātiō *f*, levāmen *nt*, adlevāmentum *nt* (*aid*) subsidium *nt*; (*turn of duty*) vicēs *fpl*; (*art*) ēminentia *f*; (*sculpture*) toreuma *nt*; bas ~ anaglypta *ntpl*; in ~ ēminēns, expressus; throw into ~ exprimere, distinguere.
relieve *vt* levāre, sublevāre; (*aid*) subvenīre (*dat*); (*duty*) succēdere (*dat*), excipere; (*art*) distinguere.
religion *n* religiō *f*, deōrum cultus *m*.
religious *adj* religiōsus, pius; ~ feeling religiō *f*.
religiously *adv* religiōsē.
relinquish *vt* relinquere; (*office*) sē abdicāre (*abl*).
relish *n* sapor *m*; (*sauce*) condīmentum *nt*; (*zest*) studium *nt* ♦ *vt* dēlectārī (*abl*).
reluctance *n*: with ~ invītus.
reluctant *adj* invītus.
reluctantly *adv* invītus, gravātē.
rely *vi* fīdere (*dat*), cōnfīdere (*dat*).
relying *adj* frētus (*abl*).
remain *vi* manēre, morārī; (*left over*) restāre, superesse.
remainder *n* reliquum *nt*.
remaining *adj* reliquus; the ~ cēterī *pl*.
remains *n* rēliquiae *fpl*.
remand *vt* (*law*) ampliāre.
remark *n* dictum *nt* ♦ *vt* dīcere; (*note*) observāre.
remarkable *adj* īnsignis, ēgregius, memorābilis.
remarkably *adv* īnsignītē, ēgregiē.
remediable *adj* sānābilis.
remedy *n* remedium *nt* ♦ *vt* medērī (*dat*), sānāre.
remember *vt* meminisse (*gen*); (*recall*) recordārī (*gen*), reminīscī (*gen*).
remembrance *n* memoria *f*, recordātiō *f*.
remind *vt* admonēre, commonefacere.
reminder *n* admonitiō *f*, admonitum *nt*.
reminiscence *n* recordātiō *f*.
remiss *adj* dissolūtus, neglegēns.
remission *n* venia *f*.
remissness *n* neglegentia *f*.
remit *vt* remittere; (*fault*) ignōscere (*dat*); (*debt*) dōnāre; (*punishment*) condōnāre; (*question*) referre.
remittance *n* pecūnia *f*.
remnant *n* fragmentum *nt*; ~s *pl* rēliquiae *fpl*.
remonstrance *n* obtestātiō *f*, obiūrgātiō *f*.
remonstrate *vi* reclāmāre; ~ with obiūrgāre; ~ about expostulāre.
remorse *n* paenitentia *f*, cōnscientia *f*.
remorseless *adj* immisericors.
remote *adj* remōtus, reconditus.
remotely *adv* procul.
remoteness *n* longinquitās *f*.
removal *n* āmōtiō *f*; (*going*) migrātiō *f*.
remove *vt* āmovēre, dēmere, eximere, removēre; (*out of the way*) dēmovēre ♦ *vi* migrāre, dēmigrāre.
remunerate *vt* remūnerārī.
remuneration *n* mercēs *f*, praemium *nt*.

rend vt scindere, dīvellere.
render vt reddere; (music) interpretārī; (translation) vertere; (thanks) referre.
rendering n interpretātiō f.
rendez-vous n cōnstitūtum nt.
renegade n dēsertor m.
renew vt renovāre, integrāre, īnstaurāre, redintegrāre.
renewal n renovātiō f; (ceremony) īnstaurātiō f.
renounce vt renūntiāre, mittere, repudiāre.
renovate vt renovāre, reficere.
renown n fāma f, glōria f.
renowned adj praeclārus, īnsignis, nōtus.
rent n (tear) fissum nt; (pay) mercēs f ♦ vt (hire) condūcere; (lease) locāre.
renunciation n cessiō f, repudiātiō f.
repair vt reficere, sarcīre ♦ vi sē recipere ♦ n: **keep in good ~** tuērī; **in bad ~** ruīnōsus.
reparable adj ēmendābilis.
reparation n satisfactiō f.
repartee n facētiae fpl, salēs mpl.
repast n cēna f, cibus m.
repay vt remūnerārī, grātiam referre (dat); (money) repōnere.
repayment n solūtiō f.
repeal vt abrogāre ♦ n abrogātiō f.
repeat vt iterāre; (lesson) reddere; (ceremony) īnstaurāre; (performance) referre.
repeatedly adv identidem, etiam atque etiam.
repel vt repellere, dēfendere.
repellent adj iniūcundus.
repent vi: **I ~** mē paenitet (+ gen of thing).
repentance n paenitentia f.
repentant adj paenitēns.
repercussion n ēventus m.
repertory n thēsaurus m.
repetition n iterātiō f.
repine vi conquerī.
replace vt repōnere, restituere; **~ by** substituere.
replacement n supplēmentum nt.
replenish vt replēre, supplēre.
replete adj plēnus.
repletion n satietās f.
replica n apographon nt.
reply vi respondēre ♦ n respōnsum nt.
report n (talk) fāma f, rūmor m; (repute) opīniō f; (account) renūntiātiō f, litterae fpl; (noise) fragor m; **make a ~** renūntiāre ♦ vt referre, dēferre, renūntiāre.
repose n quiēs f, requiēs f ♦ vt repōnere, pōnere ♦ vi quiēscere.
repository n horreum nt.
reprehend vt reprehendere, culpāre.
reprehensible adj accūsābilis, improbus.
reprehension n reprehēnsiō f, culpa f.
represent vt dēscrībere, effingere, exprimere, imitārī; (character) partēs agere (gen), persōnam gerere (gen); (case) prōpōnere; (substitute for) vicārium esse (gen).
representation n imāgō f, imitātiō f; **make ~s to** admonēre.

representative n lēgātus m.
repress vt reprimere, cohibēre.
repression n coercitiō f.
reprieve n mora f, venia f ♦ vt veniam dare (dat).
reprimand vt reprehendere, increpāre ♦ n reprehēnsiō f.
reprisals n ultiō f.
reproach vt exprobāre, obicere (dat) ♦ n exprobrātiō f, probrum nt; (cause) opprobrium nt.
reproachful adj contumēliōsus.
reprobate adj perditus.
reproduce vt propāgāre; (likeness) referre.
reproduction n prōcreātiō f; (likeness) imāgō f.
reproductive adj genitālis.
reproof n reprehēnsiō f, obiūrgātiō f.
reprove vt reprehendere, increpāre, obiūrgāre.
reptile n serpēns f.
republic n lībera rēspūblica f, cīvitās populāris f.
republican adj populāris.
repudiate vt repudiāre.
repudiation n repudiātiō f.
repugnance n fastīdium nt, odium nt.
repugnant adj invīsus, adversus.
repulse n dēpulsiō f; (at election) repulsa f ♦ vt repellere, āversārī, prōpulsāre.
repulsion n repugnantia f.
repulsive adj odiōsus, foedus.
reputable adj honestus.
reputation n fāma f, existimātiō f; (for something) opīniō f (gen); **have a ~** nōmen habēre.
repute n fāma f, existimātiō f; **bad ~** īnfāmia f.
reputed adj: **I am ~ to be** dīcor esse.
request n rogātiō f, postulātum nt; **obtain a ~** impetrāre ♦ vt rogāre, petere; (urgently) dēposcere.
require vt (demand) imperāre, postulāre; (need) egēre (abl); (call for) requīrere.
requirement n postulātum nt, necessārium nt.
requisite adj necessārius.
requisition n postulātiō f ♦ vt imperāre.
requital n grātia f, vicēs fpl.
requite vt grātiam referre (dat), remūnerārī.
rescind vt rescindere, abrogāre.
rescript n rescrīptum nt.
rescue vt ēripere, expedīre, servāre ♦ n salūs f; **come to the ~ of** subvenīre (dat).
research n investīgātiō f.
resemblance n similitūdō f, imāgō f, īnstar nt.
resemble vt similem esse (dat), referre.
resent vt aegrē ferre, indignārī.
resentful adj īrācundus.
resentment n dolor m, indignātiō f.
reservation n (proviso) exceptiō f.
reserve vt servāre; (store) recondere; (in a deal) excipere ♦ nt (MIL) subsidium nt; (disposition) pudor m, reticentia f; (caution) cautiō f; **in ~** in succenturiātus; **without ~**

palam.
reserved *adj* (*place*) adsignātus; (*disposition*)
taciturnus, tēctus.
reservedly *adv* circumspectē.
reserves *npl* subsidia *ntpl*.
reservoir *n* lacus *m*.
reside *vi* habitāre; ~ **in** incolere.
residence *n* domicilium *nt*, domus *f.*
resident *n* incola *m/f.*
residual *adj* reliquus.
residue, residuum *n* reliqua pars *f.*
resign *vt* cēdere; (*office*) abdicāre mē, tē *etc* dē
(+ *abl*); ~ **oneself** acquiēscere ♦ *vi* sē
abdicāre.
resignation *n* abdicātiō *f;* (*state of mind*)
patientia *f,* aequus animus *m.*
resigned *adj* patiēns; **be ~ to** aequō animō
ferre.
resilience *n* mollitia *f.*
resilient *adj* mollis.
resist *vt* resistere (*dat*), adversārī (*dat*),
repugnāre (*dat*).
resistance *n* repugnantia *f;* **offer ~** obsistere
(*dat*).
resistless *adj* invictus.
resolute *adj* fortis, cōnstāns.
resolutely *adv* fortiter, cōnstanter.
resolution *n* (*conduct*) fortitūdō *f,* cōnstantia *f;*
(*decision*) dēcrētum *nt,* sententia *f;* (*into parts*)
sēcrētiō *f.*
resolve *n* fortitūdō *f,* cōnstantia *f* ♦ *vt*
dēcernere, cōnstituere; (*into parts*)
dissolvere; **the senate ~s** placet senātuī.
resonance *n* sonus *m.*
resonant *adj* canōrus.
resort *n* locus celeber *m;* **last ~** ultimum
auxilium *nt* ♦ *vi* frequentāre, ventitāre; (*have
recourse*) dēcurrere, dēscendere, cōnfugere.
resound *vi* resonāre, personāre.
resource *n* subsidium *nt;* (*means*) modus *m;* **~s**
pl opēs *fpl,* cōpiae *fpl.*
resourceful *adj* versūtus, callidus.
resourcefulness *n* calliditās *f,* versūtus
animus *m.*
respect *n* (*esteem*) honōs *m,* observantia *f;*
(*reference*) ratiō *f;* **out of ~** honōris causā; **pay
one's ~s to** salūtāre; **show ~ for** observāre; **in
every ~** ex omnī parte, in omnī genere; **in ~ of**
ad (*acc*), ab (*abl*) ♦ *vt* honōrāre, observāre,
verērī.
respectability *n* honestās *f.*
respectable *adj* honestus, līberālis, frūgī.
respectably *adv* honēstē.
respectful *adj* observāns.
respectfully *adv* reverenter.
respectfulness *n* observantia *f.*
respective *adj* suus (*with* quisque).
respectively *adv* alius ... alius.
respiration *n* respīrātiō *f,* spīritus *m.*
respire *vi* respīrāre.
respite *n* requiēs *f,* intercapēdō *f,* intermissiō
f.
resplendence *n* splendor *m.*

resplendent *adj* splendidus, illūstris.
resplendently *adv* splendidē.
respond *vi* respondēre.
response *n* respōnsum *nt.*
responsibility *n* auctōritās *f,* cūra *f.*
responsible *adj* reus; (*witness*) locuplēs; **be ~
for** praestāre.
responsive *adj* (*pupil*) docilis; (*character*)
facilis.
rest *n* quiēs *f,* ōtium *nt;* (*after toil*) requiēs *f;*
(*remainder*) reliqua pars *f;* **be at ~**
requiēscere; **set at ~** tranquillāre; **the ~ of**
reliquī ♦ *vi* requiēscere, acquiēscere; **~ on**
nītī (*abl*), innītī in (*abl*) ♦ *vt* (*hope*) pōnere in
(*abl*).
rest *n* cēteri *mpl.*
resting place *n* cubīle *nt,* sēdēs *f.*
restitution *n* satisfactiō *f;* **make ~** restituere;
demand ~ rēs repetere.
restive *adj* contumāx.
restless *adj* inquiētus, sollicitus; **be ~**
fluctuārī.
restlessness *n* sollicitūdō *f.*
restoration *n* renovātiō *f;* (*of king*) reductiō *f.*
restore *vt* reddere, restituere; (*to health*)
recreāre; (*to power*) redūcere; (*damage*)
reficere, redintegrāre.
restorer *n* restitūtor *m.*
restrain *vt* coercēre, comprimere, cohibēre.
restraint *n* moderātiō *f,* temperantia *f,* frēnī
mpl; **with ~** abstinenter.
restrict *vt* continēre, circumscrībere.
restricted *adj* artus; **~ to** proprius (*gen*).
restriction *n* modus *m,* fīnis *m;* (*limitation*)
exceptiō *f.*
result *n* ēventus *m,* ēventum *nt,* exitus *m;* **the ~
is that** quō fit ut ♦ *vi* ēvenīre, ēvādere.
resultant *adj* cōnsequēns.
resume *vt* repetere.
resuscitate *vt* excitāre, suscitāre.
retail *vt* dīvēndere, vēndere.
retailer *n* caupō *m.*
retain *vt* retinēre, tenēre, cōnservāre.
retainer *n* satelles *m.*
retake *vt* recipere.
retaliate *vi* ulcīscī.
retaliation *n* ultiō *f.*
retard *vt* retardāre, remorārī.
retention *n* cōnservātiō *f.*
retentive *adj* tenāx.
reticence *n* taciturnitās *f.*
reticent *adj* taciturnus.
reticulated *adj* rēticulātus.
retinue *n* satellitēs *mpl,* comitātus *m.*
retire *vi* recēdere, abscēdere; (*from office*)
abīre; (*from province*) dēcēdere; (*MIL*) pedem
referre, sē recipere.
retired *adj* ēmeritus; (*place*) remōtus.
retirement *n* (*act*) recessus *m,* dēcessus *m;*
(*state*) sōlitūdō *f,* ōtium *nt;* **life of ~** vīta
prīvāta.
retiring *adj* modestus, verēcundus.
retort *vt* respondēre, referre ♦ *n*

respōnsum *nt.*
retouch *vt* retractāre.
retrace *vt* repetere, iterāre.
retract *vt* revocāre, renūntiāre.
retreat *n* (MIL) receptus *m*; (*place*) recessus *m*, sēcessus *m*; **sound the ~** receptuī canere ♦ *vi* sē recipere, pedem referre; regredī.
retrench *vt* minuere, recīdere.
retrenchment *n* parsimōnia *f.*
retribution *n* poena *f.*
retributive *adj* ultor, ultrīx.
retrieve *vt* reparāre, recipere.
retrograde *adj* (*fig*) dēterior.
retrogression *n* regressus *m.*
retrospect *n*: **in ~** respicientī.
retrospective *adj*: **be ~** retrōrsum sē referre.
retrospectively *adv* retrō.
return *n* reditus *m*; (*pay*) remūnerātiō *f*; (*profit*) fructus *m*, pretium *nt*; (*statement*) professiō *f*; **make a ~ of** profitērī; **in ~ for** prō (+ *abl*); **in ~** in vicem, vicissim ♦ *vt* reddere, restituere, referre ♦ *vi* redīre, revenīre, revertī; (*from province*) dēcēdere.
reunion *n* convīvium *nt.*
reunite *vt* reconciliāre.
reveal *vt* aperīre, patefacere.
revel *n* cōmissātiō *f*, bacchātiō *f*; **~s** *pl* orgia *ntpl* ♦ *vi* cōmissārī, bacchārī; **~ in** luxuriārī.
revelation *n* patefactiō *f.*
reveller *n* cōmissātor *m.*
revelry *n* cōmissātiō *f.*
revenge *n* ultiō *f*; **take ~ on** vindicāre in (*acc*) ♦ *vt* ulcīscī.
revengeful *adj* ulcīscendī cupidus.
revenue *n* fructus *m*, reditus *m*, vectīgālia *ntpl.*
reverberate *vi* resonāre.
reverberation *n* repercussus *m.*
revere *vt* venerārī, colere.
reverence *n* venerātiō *f*; (*feeling*) religiō *f*; reverentia *f.*
reverent *adj* religiōsus, pius.
reverently *adv* religiōsē.
reverie *n* meditātiō *f*, somnium *nt.*
reversal *n* abrogātiō *f.*
reverse *adj* contrārius ♦ *n* contrārium *nt*; (MIL) clādēs *f* ♦ *vt* invertere; (*decision*) rescindere.
reversion *n* reditus *m.*
revert *vi* redīre, revertī.
review *n* recognitiō *f*, recēnsiō *f* ♦ *vt* (MIL) recēnsēre.
revile *vt* maledīcere (*dat*).
revise *vt* recognōscere, corrigere; (*LIT*) līmāre.
revision *n* ēmendātiō *f*; (*LIT*) līma *f.*
revisit *vt* revīsere.
revival *n* renovātiō *f.*
revive *vt* recreāre, excitāre ♦ *vi* revīvīscere, renāscī.
revocation *n* revocātiō *f.*
revoke *vt* renūntiāre, īnfectum reddere.
revolt *n* sēditiō *f*, dēfectiō *f* ♦ *vi* dēficere, rebellāre.
revolting *adj* taeter, obscēnus.
revolution *n* (*movement*) conversiō *f*; (*change*)

rēs novae *fpl*; (*revolt*) mōtus *m*; **effect a ~** rēs novāre.
revolutionary *adj* sēditiōsus, novārum rērum cupidus.
revolve *vi* volvī, versārī, convertī ♦ *vt* (*in mind*) volūtāre.
revulsion *n* mūtātiō *f.*
reward *n* praemium *nt*, mercēs *f* ♦ *vt* remūnerārī, compēnsāre.
rhapsody *n* carmen *nt*; (*epic*) rhapsōdia *f.*
rhetoric *n* rhētorica *f*; **of ~** rhētoricus; **exercise in ~** dēclāmātiō *f*; **practise ~** dēclāmāre; **teacher of ~** rhētōr *m.*
rhetorical *adj* rhētoricus, dēclāmātōrius.
rhetorically *adv* rhētoricē.
rhetorician *n* rhētōr *m*, dēclāmātor *m.*
rhinoceros *n* rhīnocerōs *m.*
rhyme *n* homoeoteleuton *nt*; **without ~ or reason** temerē.
rhythm *n* numerus *m*, modus *m.*
rhythmical *adj* numerōsus.
rib *n* costa *f.*
ribald *adj* obscēnus.
ribaldry *n* obscēnitās *f.*
ribbon *n* īnfula *f.*
rice *n* oryza *f.*
rich *adj* dīves, locuplēs; opulentus; (*fertile*) ūber, opīmus; (*food*) pinguis.
riches *n* dīvitiae *fpl*, opēs *fpl.*
richly *adv* opulentē, largē, lautē.
richness *n* ūbertās *f*, cōpia *f.*
rid *vt* līberāre; **get ~ of** dēpōnere, dēmovēre, exuere.
riddle *n* aenigma *nt*; (*sieve*) cribrum *nt* ♦ *vt* (*with wounds*) cōnfodere.
ride *vt* equitāre, vehī; **~ a horse** in equō vehī; **~ at anchor** stāre; **~ away** abequitāre, āvehī; **~ back** revehī; **~ between** interequitāre; **~ down** dēvehī; **~ into** invehī; **~ off** āvehī; **~ out** ēvehī; **~ past** praetervehī; **~ round** circumvehī (*dat*), circumequitāre; **~ up and down** perequitāre; **~ up to** adequitāre ad, advehī ad.
rider *n* eques *m.*
ridge *n* iugum *nt.*
ridicule *n* lūdibrium *nt*, irrīsus *m* ♦ *vt* irrīdēre, illūdere, lūdibriō habēre.
ridiculous *adj* rīdiculus, dērīdiculus.
ridiculously *adv* rīdiculē.
riding *n* equitātiō *f.*
rife *adj* frequēns.
riff-raff *n* faex populī *f.*
rifle *vt* expīlāre, spoliāre.
rift *n* rīma *f.*
rig *vt* (*ship*) armāre, ōrnāre ♦ *n* habitus *m.*
rigging *n* rudentēs *mpl.*
right *adj* rēctus; (*just*) aequus, iūstus; (*true*) rēctus, vērus; (*proper*) lēgitimus, fās; (*hand*) dexter; **it is ~** decet (+ *acc and infin*); **it is not ~** dēdecet (+ *acc and infin*); **you are ~** vēra dīcis; **if I am ~** nisi fallor; **in the ~ place** in locō; **at the ~ time** ad tempus; **at ~ angles** ad parēs angulōs; **on the ~** ā dextrā ♦ *adv* rēctē, bene,

probē; (*justifiably*) iūre; ~ **up to** usque ad
(*+ acc*); ~ **on** rēctā ♦ *n* (*legal*) iūs *nt*; (*moral*) fās
nt ♦ *vt* (*replace*) restituere; (*correct*)
corrigere; (*avenge*) ulcīscī.
righteous *adj* iūstus, sanctus, pius.
righteously *adv* iūstē, sanctē, piē.
righteousness *n* sanctitās *f*, pietās *f*.
rightful *adj* iūstus, lēgitimus.
rightfully *adv* iūstē, lēgitimē.
right hand *n* dextra *f*.
right-hand *adj* dexter; ~ **man** comes *m*.
rightly *adv* rēctē, bene; iūre.
right-minded *adj* sānus.
rigid *adj* rigidus.
rigidity *n* rigor *m*; (*strictness*) sevēritās *f*.
rigidly *adv* rigidē, sevērē.
rigmarole *n* ambāgēs *fpl*.
rigorous *adj* dūrus; (*strict*) sevērus.
rigorously *adv* dūriter, sevērē.
rigour *n* dūritia *f*; sevēritās *f*.
rile *vt* inrītāre, stomachum movēre (*dat*).
rill *n* rīvulus *m*.
rim *n* labrum *nt*.
rime *n* pruīna *f*.
rind *n* cortex *m*.
ring *n* ānulus *m*; (*circle*) orbis *m*; (*of people*)
corōna *f*; (*motion*) gyrus *m* ♦ *vt* circumdare;
(*bell*) movēre ♦ *vi* tinnīre, sonāre.
ringing *n* tinnītus *m* ♦ *adj* canōrus.
ringleader *n* caput *m*, dux *m*.
ringlet *n* cincinnus *m*.
rinse *vt* colluere.
riot *n* tumultus *m*, rixa *f*; **run ~** exsultāre,
luxuriārī, tumultuārī, turbās efficere; (*revel*)
bacchārī.
rioter *n* cōmissātor *m*.
riotous *adj* tumultuōsus, sēditiōsus;
(*debauched*) dissolūtus; ~ **living** cōmissātiō *f*,
luxuria *f*.
riotously *adv* tumultuōsē; luxuriōsē.
rip *vt* scindere.
ripe *adj* mātūrus; **of ~ judgment** animī
mātūrus.
ripen *vt* mātūrāre ♦ *vi* mātūrēscere.
ripeness *n* mātūritās *f*.
ripple *n* unda *f* ♦ *vi* trepidāre.
rise *vi* orīrī, surgere; (*hill*) ascendere; (*wind*)
cōnsurgere; (*passion*) tumēscere; (*voice*)
tollī; (*in size*) crēscere; (*in rank*) ascendere;
(*in revolt*) coorīrī, arma capere; ~ **and fall**
(*tide*) reciprocāre; ~ **in** (*river*) orīrī ex (*abl*); ~ **out**
ēmergere; ~ **up** exsurgere ♦ *n* ascēnsus *m*;
(*slope*) clīvus *m*; (*increase*) incrēmentum *nt*;
(*start*) ortus *m*; **give ~ to** parere.
rising *n* (*sun*) ortus *m*; (*revolt*) mōtus *m* ♦ *adj*
(*ground*) ēditus.
risk *n* perīculum *nt*; **run a ~** perīculum subīre,
ingredī ♦ *vt* perīclitārī, in āleam dare.
risky *adj* perīculōsus.
rite *n* rītus *m*.
ritual *n* caerimōnia *f*.
rival *adj* aemulus ♦ *n* aemulus *m*, rīvālis *m* ♦ *vt*

aemulārī.
rivalry *n* aemulātiō *f*.
river *n* flūmen *nt*, fluvius *m* ♦ *adj* fluviātilis.
riverbed *n* alveus *m*.
riverside *n* rīpa *f*.
rivet *n* clāvus *m* ♦ *vt* (*attention*) dēfīgere.
rivulet *n* rīvulus *m*, rīvus *m*.
road *n* via *f*, iter *nt*; **on the ~** in itinere, ex
itinere; **off the ~** dēvius; **make a ~** viam
mūnīre.
roadstead *n* statiō *f*.
roam *vi* errāre, vagārī; ~ **at large** ēvagārī.
roar *n* fremitus *m* ♦ *vi* fremere.
roast *vt* torrēre ♦ *adj* āssus ♦ *n* āssum *nt*.
rob *vt* spoliāre, exspoliāre, expīlāre; (*of hope*)
dēicere dē.
robber *n* latrō *m*, fūr *m*; (*highway*) grassātor *m*.
robbery *n* latrōcinium *nt*.
robe *n* vestis *f*; (*woman's*) stola *f*; (*of state*)
trabea *f* ♦ *vt* vestīre.
robust *adj* rōbustus, fortis.
robustness *n* rōbur *nt*, firmitās *f*.
rock *n* saxum *nt*; (*steep*) rūpēs *f*, scopulus *m* ♦ *vt*
agitāre ♦ *vi* agitārī, vacillāre.
rocky *adj* saxōsus, scopulōsus.
rod *n* virga *f*; (*fishing*) harundō *f*.
roe *n* (*deer*) capreolus *m*, caprea *f*; (*fish*) ōva *ntp*
rogue *n* veterātor *m*.
roguery *n* nēquitia *f*, scelus *nt*.
roguish *adj* improbus, malus.
role *n* partēs *fpl*.
roll *n* (*book*) volūmen *nt*; (*movement*) gyrus *m*;
(*register*) album *nt*; **call the ~ of** legere;
answer the ~ call ad nōmen respondēre ♦ *vt*
volvere ♦ *vi* volvī, volūtārī; ~ **down** *vt*
dēvolvere ♦ *vi* dēfluere; ~ **over** *vt* prōvolvere
♦ *vi* prōlābī; ~ **up** *vt* convolvere.
roller *n* (*AGR*) cylindrus *m*; (*for moving*)
phalangae *fpl*; (*in book*) umbilīcus *m*.
rollicking *adj* hilaris.
rolling *adj* volūbilis.
Roman *adj* Rōmānus ♦ *n*: **the ~s** Rōmānī *mpl*.
romance *n* fābula *f*; amor *m*.
romantic *adj* fābulōsus; amātōrius.
Rome *n* Rōma *f*; **at ~** Rōmae; **from ~** Rōmā; **to ~**
Rōmam.
romp *vi* lūdere.
roof *n* tēctum *nt*; (*of mouth*) palātum *nt* ♦ *vt*
tegere, integere.
rook *n* corvus *m*.
room *n* conclāve *nt*; camera *f*; (*small*) cella *f*;
(*bed*) cubiculum *nt*; (*dining*) cēnāculum *nt*;
(*dressing*) apodytērium *nt*; (*space*) locus *m*;
make ~ for locum dare (*dat*), cēdere (*dat*).
roominess *n* laxitās *f*.
roomy *adj* capāx.
roost *vi* stabulārī.
rooster *n* gallus gallīnāceus *m*.
root *n* rādīx *f*; **take ~** coalēscere ♦ *vt*: ~ **out**
ērādīcāre.
rooted *adj* (*fig*) dēfixus; **deeply ~** (*custom*)
inveterātus; **be ~ in** īnsidēre (*dat*); **become**
deeply ~ inveterāscere.

rope–rural

rope n fūnis m; (thin) restis f; (ship's) rudēns m;
know the ~s perītum esse.
rose n rosa f.
rosemary n rōs marīnus m.
rostrum n rōstra ntpl, suggestus m.
rosy adj roseus, purpureus.
rot n tābēs f ♦ vi putrēscere, pūtēscere ♦ vt
putrefacere.
rotate vi volvī, sē convertere.
rotation n conversiō f; (succession) ōrdō m,
vicissitūdō f; in ~ ōrdine; move in ~ in orbem
īre.
rote n: by ~ memoriter.
rotten adj putridus.
rotund adj rotundus.
rotundity n rotunditās f.
rouge n fūcus m ♦ vt fūcāre.
rough adj asper; (art) incultus, rudis;
(manners) agrestis, inurbānus; (stone)
impolītus; (treatment) dūrus, sevērus;
(weather) atrōx, procellōsus ♦ vi: ~ it dūram
vītam vīvere.
rough-and-ready adj fortuītus.
rough draft n (LIT) silva f.
roughen vt asperāre, exasperāre.
rough-hew vt dolāre.
roughly adv asperē, dūriter; (with numbers)
circiter.
roughness n asperitās f.
round adj rotundus; (spherical) globōsus;
(cylindrical) teres ♦ n (circle) orbis m; (motion)
gȳrus m; (series) ambitus m; go the ~s (MIL)
vigiliās circumīre ♦ vt (cape) superāre; ~ off
rotundāre; (sentence) concludere; ~ up
compellere ♦ adv circum, circā; go ~ ambīre
♦ prep circum (acc), circā (acc).
roundabout adj: ~ story ambāgēs fpl; ~ route
circuitus m, ānfrāctus m.
roundly adv (speak) apertē, līberē.
rouse vt excīre, excitāre; (courage) adrigere.
rousing adj vehemēns.
rout n fuga f; (crowd) turba f ♦ vt fugāre,
fundere; in fugam conicere; prōflīgāre.
route n cursus m, iter nt.
routine n ūsus m, ōrdō m.
rove vi errāre, vagārī.
rover n vagus m; (sea) pīrāta m.
row n (line) ōrdō m; (noise) turba f, rixa f ♦ vi
(boat) rēmigāre ♦ vt rēmīs incitāre.
rowdy adj turbulentus.
rower n rēmex m.
rowing n rēmigium nt.
royal adj rēgius, rēgālis.
royally adv rēgiē, rēgāliter.
royalty n (power) rēgnum nt; (persons) rēgēs
mpl, domus rēgia f.
rub vt fricāre, terere; ~ away conterere; ~
hard dēfricāre; ~ off dētergēre; ~ out dēlēre;
~ up expolīre.
rubbing n trītus m.
rubbish n quisquiliae fpl; (talk) nūgae fpl.
rubble n rūdus nt.
rubicund adj rubicundus.

rudder n gubernāculum nt, clāvus m.
ruddy adj rubicundus, rutilus.
rude adj (uncivilized) barbarus, dūrus,
inurbānus; (insolent) asper,
importūnus.
rudely adv horridē, rusticē; petulanter.
rudeness n barbariēs f; petulantia f,
importūnitās f.
rudiment n elementum nt, initium nt.
rudimentary adj prīmus, incohātus.
rue n (herb) rūta f ♦ vt: I ~ mē paenitet (gen).
rueful adj maestus.
ruffian n grassātor m.
ruffle vt agitāre; (temper) sollicitāre,
commovēre.
rug n strāgulum nt.
rugged adj horridus, asper.
ruggedness n asperitās f.
ruin n ruīna f; (fig) exitium nt, perniciēs f; go to
~ pessum īre, dīlābī ♦ vt perdere, dēperdere,
pessum dare; (moral) corrumpere,
dēprāvāre; be ~ed perīre.
ruined adj ruīnōsus.
ruinous adj exitiōsus, damnōsus.
rule n (instrument) rēgula f, amussis f;
(principle) nōrma f, lēx f, praeceptum nt;
(government) dominātiō f, imperium nt; ten-
foot ~ decempeda f; as a ~ ferē; lay down ~s
praecipere; make it a ~ to īnstituere (inf); ~
of thumb ūsus m ♦ vt regere, moderārī ♦ vi
rēgnāre, dominārī; (judge) ēdīcere; (custom)
obtinēre; ~ over imperāre (dat).
ruler n (instrument) rēgula f; (person) dominus
m, rēctor m.
ruling n ēdictum nt.
rumble vi mūgīre.
rumbling n mūgītus m.
ruminate vi rūminārī.
rummage vi: ~ through rīmārī.
rumour n fāma f, rūmor m.
rump n clūnis f.
run vi currere; (fluid) fluere, mānāre; (road)
ferre; (time) lābī ♦ n cursus m; ~ about
discurrere, cursāre; ~ across incidere in
(acc); ~ after sectārī; ~ aground offendere; ~
away aufugere, terga vertere; (from) fugere,
dēfugere; ~ down dēcurrere, dēfluere ♦ vt
(in words) obtrectāre; ~ high (fig) glīscere; ~
into incurrere in (acc), īnfluere in (acc); ~ off
with abripere, abdūcere; ~ on pergere; ~ out
(land) excurrere; (time) exīre; (supplies)
dēficere; ~ over vt (with car) obterere; (details)
percurrere; ~ riot luxuriārī; ~ through
(course) dēcurrere; (money) disperdere; ~
short dēficere; ~ up to adcurrere ad; ~ up
against incurrere in (acc); ~ wild lascīvīre ♦
vt gerere, administrāre.
runaway adj fugitīvus.
rung n gradus m.
runner n cursor m.
running n cursus m ♦ adj (water) vīvus.
rupture n (fig) dissidium nt ♦ vt dīrumpere.
rural adj rūsticus, agrestis.

ruse n fraus f, dolus m.
rush n (*plant*) cārex f, iuncus m; (*movement*)
   impetus m ♦ vi currere, sē incitāre, ruere; ~
   forward sē prōripere; prōruere; ~ **in** inruere,
   incurrere; ~ **out** ēvolāre, sē effundere ♦ adj
   iunceus.
russet adj flāvus.
rust n (*iron*) ferrūgō f; (*copper*) aerūgō f ♦ vi
   rōbīginem trahere.
rustic adj rūsticus, agrestis.
rusticate vi rūsticārī ♦ vt relēgāre.
rusticity n mōrēs rūsticī mpl.
rustle vi increpāre, crepitāre ♦ n crepitus m.
rusty adj rōbīginōsus.
rut n orbita f.
ruthless adj inexōrābilis, crūdēlis.
ruthlessly adv crūdēliter.
rye n secāle nt.

S, s

sabbath n sabbata ntpl.
sable adj āter, niger.
sabre n acīnacēs m.
sacerdotal adj sacerdōtālis.
sack n saccus m; (MIL) dīreptiō f ♦ vt dīripere,
   expīlāre; spoliāre.
sackcloth n cilicium nt.
sacred adj sacer, sanctus.
sacredly adv sanctē.
sacredness n sanctitās f.
sacrifice n sacrificium nt, sacrum nt; (*act*)
   immolātiō f; (*victim*) hostia f; (*fig*) iactūra f ♦
   vt immolāre, sacrificāre, mactāre; (*fig*)
   dēvovēre, addīcere ♦ vi sacra facere; (*give
   up*) prōicere.
sacrificer n immolātor m.
sacrilege n sacrilegium nt.
sacrilegious adj sacrilegus.
sacristan n aedituus m.
sacrosanct adj sacrōsanctus.
sad adj maestus, tristis; (*thing*) tristis.
sadden vt dolōre adficere.
saddle n strātum nt ♦ vt sternere; (*fig*)
   impōnere.
saddlebags n clītellae fpl.
sadly adv maestē.
sadness n tristitia f, maestitia f.
safe adj tūtus; (*out of danger*) incolumis,
   salvus; (*to trust*) fīdus. ~ **and sound** salvus ♦
   n armārium nt.
safe-conduct n fidēs pūblica f.
safeguard n cautiō f, prōpugnāculum nt ♦ vt
   dēfendere.
safely adv tūtō, impūne.
safety n salūs f, incolumitās f;

seek ~ **in flight** salutem fugā petere.
saffron n crocus m ♦ adj croceus.
sag vi dēmittī.
sagacious adj prūdēns, sagāx, acūtus.
sagaciously adv prūdenter, sagāciter.
sagacity n prūdentia f, sagācitās f.
sage n sapiēns m; (*herb*) salvia f ♦ adj sapiēns.
sagely adv sapienter.
sail n vēlum nt; **set** ~ vēla dare, nāvem solvere;
   shorten ~ vēla contrahere ♦ vi nāvigāre; ~
   past legere, praetervehī.
sailing n nāvigātiō f.
sailor n nauta m.
sail yard n antenna f.
saint n vir sanctus m.
sainted adj beātus.
saintly adj sanctus.
sake n: **for the** ~ grātiā (*gen*), causā (*gen*),
   propter (*acc*); (*behalf*) prō (*abl*).
salacious adj salāx.
salad n morētum nt.
salamander n salamandra f.
salary n mercēs f.
sale n vēnditiō f; (*formal*) mancipium nt;
   (*auction*) hasta f; **for** ~ vēnālis; **be for** ~
   prōstāre; **offer for** ~ vēnum dare.
saleable adj vēndibilis.
salient adj ēminēns; ~ **points** capita ntpl.
saline adj salsus.
saliva n salīva f.
sallow adj pallidus.
sally n ēruptiō f; (*wit*) facētiae fpl ♦ vi
   ērumpere, excurrere.
salmon n salmō m.
salon n ātrium nt.
salt n sal m ♦ adj salsus.
saltcellar n salīnum nt.
saltpetre n nitrum nt.
salt-pits n salīnae fpl.
salty adj salsus.
salubrious adj salūbris.
salubriously adv salūbriter.
salubriousness n salūbritās f.
salutary adj salūtāris, ūtilis.
salutation n salūs f.
salute vt salūtāre.
salvage vt servāre, ēripere.
salvation n salūs f.
salve n unguentum nt.
salver n scutella f.
same adj īdem; ~ **as** īdem ac; **all the** ~
   nihilōminus; **one and the** ~ūnus et īdem;
   from the ~ **place** indidem; **in the** ~ **place**
   ibīdem; **to the** ~ **place** eōdem; **at the** ~ **time**
   simul, eōdem tempore; (*adversative*) tamen;
   it is all the ~ **to me** meā nōn interest.
Samnites n Samnītēs, Samnītium mpl.
sample n exemplum nt, specimen nt ♦ vt
   gustāre.
sanctify vt cōnsecrāre.
sanctimony n falsa rēligiō f.
sanction n comprobātiō f, auctōritās f ♦ vt
   ratum facere.

sanctity n sanctitās f.

sanctuary n fānum nt, dēlubrum nt; (for men) asÿlum nt.

sand n harēna f.

sandal n (outdoors) crepida f; (indoors) solea f.

sandalled adj crepidātus, soleātus.

sandpit n harēnāria f.

sandstone n tōfus m.

sandy adj harēnōsus; (colour) flāvus.

sane adj sānus.

sangfroid n aequus animus m.

sanguinary adj cruentus.

sanguine adj laetus.

sanitary adj salūbris.

sanity n mēns sāna f.

sap n sūcus m ♦ vt subruere.

sapience n sapientia f.

sapient adj sapiēns.

sapling n surculus m.

sapper n cunīculārius m.

sapphire n sapphīrus f.

sarcasm n aculeī mpl, dicācitās f.

sarcastic adj dicāx, acūleātus.

sardonic adj amārus.

sash n cingulum nt.

satchel n loculus m.

sate vt explēre, satiāre.

satellite n satelles m.

satiate vt explēre, satiāre, saturāre.

satiety n satietās f.

satire n satura f; (pl, of Horace) sermōnēs mpl.

satirical adj acerbus.

satirist n saturārum scrīptor m.

satirize vt perstringere, notāre.

satisfaction n (act) explētiō f; (feeling) voluptās f; (penalty) poena f; **demand** ~ rēs repetere.

satisfactorily adv ex sententiā.

satisfactory adj idōneus, grātus.

satisfied adj: **be** ~ satis habēre, contentum esse.

satisfy vt satisfacere (dat); (desire) explēre.

satrap n satrapēs m.

saturate vt imbuere.

satyr n satyrus m.

sauce n condīmentum nt; (fish) garum nt.

saucer n patella f.

saucily adv petulanter.

saucy adj petulāns.

saunter vi ambulāre.

sausage n tomāculum nt, hīllae fpl.

savage adj ferus, efferātus; (cruel) atrōx, inhūmānus; saevus.

savagely adv ferōciter, inhūmānē.

savagery n ferōcitās f, inhūmānitās f.

savant n vir doctus m.

save vt servāre; ~ **up** reservāre ♦ prep praeter (acc).

saving adj parcus; ~ **clause** exceptiō f ♦ n compendium nt; ~**s** pl peculium nt.

saviour n līberātor m.

savory n thymbra f.

savour n sapor m; (of cooking) nīdor m ♦ vi

sapere; ~ **of** olēre, redolēre.

savoury adj condītus.

saw n (tool) serra f; (saying) prōverbium nt ♦ vt serrā secāre.

sawdust n scobis f.

say vt dīcere; that ... **not** negāre; ~ **no** negāre; **he** ~**s** (quoting) inquit; **he** ~**s yes** āit; **they** ~ ferunt (+ acc and infin).

saying n dictum nt.

scab n (disease) scabiēs f; (over wound) crusta f.

scabbard n vāgīna f.

scabby adj scaber.

scaffold, scaffolding n fala f.

scald vt ūrere.

scale n (balance) lanx f; (fish, etc) squāma f; (gradation) gradūs mpl; (music) diagramma nt ♦ vt scālīs ascendere.

scallop n pecten m.

scalp n capitis cutis f.

scalpel n scalpellum nt.

scamp n verberō m.

scamper vi currere.

scan vt contemplārī; (verse) mētīrī.

scandal n īnfāmia f, opprobrium nt; (talk) calumnia f.

scandalize vt offendere.

scandalous adj flāgitiōsus, turpis.

scansion n syllabārum ēnārrātiō f.

scant adj exiguus, parvus.

scantily adv exiguē, tenuiter.

scantiness n exiguitās f.

scanty adj exiguus, tenuis, exīlis; (number) paucus.

scapegoat n piāculum nt.

scar n cicātrīx f.

scarce adj rārus; **make oneself** ~ sē āmovēre, dē mediō recēdere ♦ adv vix, aegrē.

scarcely adv vix, aegrē; ~ **anyone** nēmō ferē.

scarcity n inopia f, angustiae fpl.

scare n formīdō f ♦ vt terrēre; ~ **away** absterrēre.

scarecrow n formīdō f.

scarf n fōcāle nt.

scarlet n coccum nt ♦ adj coccinus.

scarp n rūpēs f.

scathe n damnum nt.

scatter vt spargere; dispergere, dissipāre; (violently) disicere ♦ vi diffugere.

scatterbrained adj dēsipiēns.

scattered adj rārus.

scene n spectāculum nt; (place) theātrum nt.

scenery n locī faciēs f, speciēs f; (beautiful) amoenitās f.

scent n odor m; (sense) odōrātus m; **keen** ~ sagācitās f ♦ vt odōrārī; (perfume) odōribus perfundere.

scented adj odōrātus.

sceptic n Pyrrhōnēus m.

sceptical adj incrēdulus.

sceptre n scēptrum nt.

schedule n tabulae fpl, ratiō f.

scheme n cōnsilium nt, ratiō f ♦ vt māchinārī,

mōlīrī.

schemer n māchinātor m.

schism n discidium nt, sēcessiō f.

scholar n vir doctus m, litterātus m; (*pupil*) discipulus m.

scholarly adj doctus, litterātus.

scholarship n litterae fpl, doctrīna f.

scholastic adj umbrātilis.

school n (*elementary*) lūdus m; (*advanced*) schola f; (*high*) gymnasium nt; (*sect*) secta f, domus f ♦ vt īnstituere.

schoolboy n discipulus m.

schoolmaster n magister m.

schoolmistress n magistra f.

science n doctrīna f, disciplīna f, ars f.

scimitar n acīnacēs m.

scintillate vi scintillāre.

scion n prōgeniēs f.

Scipio n Scīpiō, Scīpiōnis m.

scissors n forfex f.

scoff vi irrīdēre; ~ **at** dērīdēre.

scoffer n irrīsor m.

scold vt increpāre, obiūrgāre.

scolding n obiūrgātiō f.

scoop n trulla f ♦ vt: ~ **out** excavāre.

scope n (*aim*) fīnis m; (*room*) locus m, campus m; **ample** ~ laxus locus.

scorch vt exūrere, torrēre.

scorched adj torridus.

score n (*mark*) nota f; (*total*) summa f; (*reckoning*) ratiō f; (*number*) vīgintī ♦ vt notāre ♦ vi vincere.

scorn n contemptiō f ♦ vt contemnere, spernere.

scorner n contemptor m.

scornful adj fastīdiōsus.

scornfully adv contemptim.

scorpion n scorpiō m, nepa f.

scot-free adj immūnis, impūnītus.

scoundrel n furcifer m.

scour vt (*clean*) tergēre; (*range*) percurrere.

scourge n flagellum nt; (*fig*) pestis f ♦ vt verberāre, virgīs caedere.

scout n explōrātor m, speculātor m ♦ vi explōrāre, speculārī ♦ vt spernere, repudiāre.

scowl n frontis contractiō f ♦ vi frontem contrahere.

scraggy adj strigōsus.

scramble vi: ~ **for** certātim captāre; ~ **up** scandere.

scrap n frūstum nt.

scrape vt rādere, scabere; ~ **off** abrādere.

scraper n strigilis f.

scratch vt rādere; (*head*) perfricāre; ~ **out** exsculpere, ērādere.

scream n clāmor m, ululātus m ♦ vi clāmāre, ululāre.

screech n ululātus m ♦ vi ululāre.

screen n obex m/f; (*from sun*) umbra f; (*fig*) vēlāmentum nt ♦ vt tegere.

screw n clāvus m; (*of winepress*) cochlea f.

scribble vt properē scrībere.

scribe n scrība m.

script n scrīptum nt; (*handwriting*) manus f.

scroll n volūmen nt.

scrub vt dētergēre, dēfricāre.

scruple n rēligiō f, scrūpulus m.

scrupulous adj rēligiōsus; (*careful*) dīligēns.

scrupulously adv rēligiōsē, dīligenter.

scrupulousness n rēligiō f; dīligentia f.

scrutinize vt scrūtārī, intrōspicere in (acc), excutere.

scrutiny n scrūtātiō f.

scud vi volāre.

scuffle n rixa f.

scull n calvāria f; (*oar*) rēmus m.

scullery n culīna f.

sculptor n fictor m, sculptor m.

sculpture n ars fingendī f; (*product*) statuae fpl ♦ vt sculpere.

scum n spūma f.

scurf n porrīgō f.

scurrility n maledicta ntpl.

scurrilous adj maledicus.

scurvy adj (*fig*) turpis, improbus.

scythe n falx f.

sea n mare nt; aequor nt; **open** ~ altum nt; **put t‹** ~ solvere; **be at** ~ nāvigāre; (*fig*) in errōre versārī ♦ adj marīnus; (*coast*) maritimus.

seaboard n lītus nt.

seafaring adj maritimus, nauticus.

seafight n nāvāle proelium nt.

seagull n larus m.

seal n (*animal*) phōca f; (*stamp*) signum nt ♦ vt signāre; ~ **up** obsignāre.

seam n sūtūra f.

seaman n nauta m.

seamanship n scientia et ūsus nauticārum rērum.

seaport n portus m.

sear vt adūrere, torrēre.

search n investīgātiō f ♦ vi investīgāre, explōrāre ♦ vt excutere, scrūtārī; **in** ~ **of** causā (+ gen); ~ **for** quaerere, exquīrere, investīgāre; ~ **into** inquīrere, anquīrere; ~ **out** explōrāre, indāgāre.

searcher n inquīsītor m.

searching adj acūtus, dīligēns.

seashore n lītus nt.

seasick adj: **be** ~ nauseāre.

seasickness n nausea f.

seaside n mare nt.

season n annī tempus nt, tempestās f; (*right time*) tempus nt, opportūnitās f; **in** ~ tempestīvē ♦ vt condīre.

seasonable adj tempestīvus.

seasonably adv tempestīvē.

seasoned adj (*food*) condītus; (*wood*) dūrātus

seasoning n condīmentum nt.

seat n sēdēs f; (*chair*) sedīle nt; (*home*) domus f domicilium nt; **keep one's** ~ (*riding*) in equō haerēre ♦ vt collocāre; ~ **oneself** īnsidēre.

seated adj: **be** ~ sedēre.

seaweed n alga f.

seaworthy adj ad nāvigandum ūtilis.

secede *vi* sēcēdere.
secession *n* sēcessiō *f*.
seclude *vt* sēclūdere, abstrūdere.
secluded *adj* sēcrētus, remōtus.
seclusion *n* sōlitūdō *f*, sēcrētum *nt*.
second *adj* secundus, alter; **a ~ time** iterum ♦ *n* temporis pūnctum *nt*; (*person*) fautor *m*; **~ sight** hariolātiō *f* ♦ *vt* favēre (*dat*), adesse (*dat*).
secondary *adj* īnferior, dēterior.
seconder *n* fautor *m*.
second-hand *adj* aliēnus, trītus.
secondly *adv* deinde.
secrecy *n* sēcrētum *nt*, silentium *nt*.
secret *adj* secretus; occultus, arcānus; (*stealth*) fūrtīvus ♦ *n* arcānum *nt*; **keep ~** dissimulāre, cēlāre; **in ~** clam; **be ~** latēre.
secretary *n* scrība *m*, ab epistolīs, ā manū.
secrete *vt* cēlāre, abdere.
secretive *adj* tēctus.
secretly *adv* clam, occultē, sēcrētō.
sect *n* secta *f*, schola *f*, domus *f*.
section *n* pars *f*.
sector *n* regiō *f*.
secular *adj* profānus.
secure *adj* tūtus ♦ *vt* (*MIL*) firmāre, ēmūnīre; (*fasten*) religāre; (*obtain*) parāre, nancīscī.
securely *adj* tūtō.
security *n* salūs *f*, impūnitās *f*; (*money*) cautiō *f*, pignus *nt*, spōnsiō *f*; **sense of ~** sēcūritās *f*; **give good ~** satis dare; **on good ~** (*loan*) nōminibus rēctis cautus; **stand ~ for** praedem esse prō (*abl*).
sedan *n* lectīca *f*.
sedate *adj* placidus, temperātus, gravis.
sedately *adv* placidē.
sedateness *n* gravitās *f*.
sedge *n* ulva *f*.
sediment *n* faex *f*.
sedition *n* sēditiō *f*, mōtus *m*.
seditious *adj* sēditiōsus.
seditiously *adv* sēditiōsē.
seduce *vt* illicere, pellicere.
seducer *n* corruptor *m*.
seduction *n* corruptēla *f*.
seductive *adj* blandus.
seductively *adv* blandē.
sedulity *n* dīligentia *f*.
sedulous *adj* dīligēns, sēdulus.
sedulously *adv* dīligenter, sēdulō.
see *vt* vidēre, cernere; (*suddenly*) cōnspicārī; (*performance*) spectāre; (*with mind*) intellegere; **go and ~** vīsere, invīsere; **~ to** vidēre, cōnsulere (*dat*); curare (+ *acc and gerundive*); **~ through** dīspicere; **~ that you are** vidē ut sīs, fac sīs; **~ that you are not** vidē nē sīs, cavē sīs.
seed *n* sēmen *nt*; (*in a plant*) grānum *nt*; (*in fruit*) acinum *nt*; (*fig*) stirps *f*, prōgeniēs *f*.
seedling *n* surculus *m*.
seed-time *n* sēmentis *f*.
seeing that *conj* quōniam, siquidem.
seek *vt* petere, quaerere.

seeker *n* indāgātor *m*.
seem *vi* vidērī.
seeming *adj* speciōsus ♦ *n* speciēs *f*.
seemingly *adv* ut vidētur.
seemly *adj* decēns, decōrus; **it is ~** decet.
seep *vi* mānāre, percōlārī.
seer *n* vātēs *m/f*.
seethe *vi* fervēre.
segregate *vt* sēcernere, sēgregāre.
segregation *n* sēparātiō *f*.
seize *vt* rapere, corripere, adripere, prehendere; (*MIL*) occupāre; (*illness*) adficere; (*emotion*) invādere, occupāre.
seizure *n* ēreptiō *f*, occupātiō *f*.
seldom *adv* rārō.
select *vt* ēligere, excerpere, dēligere ♦ *adj* lēctus, ēlēctus.
selection *n* ēlēctiō *f*, dēlēctus *m*; (*LIT*) ecloga *f*.
self *n* ipse; (*reflexive*) sē; **a second ~** alter īdem.
self-centred *adj* glōriōsus.
self-confidence *n* cōnfīdentia *f*, fidūcia *f*.
self-confident *adj* cōnfīdēns.
self-conscious *adj* pudibundus.
self-control *n* temperantia *f*.
self-denial *n* abstinentia *f*.
self-evident *adj* manifestus; **it is ~** ante pedēs positum est.
self-governing *adj* līber.
self-government *n* lībertās *f*.
self-important *adj* adrogāns.
self-interest *n* ambitiō *f*.
selfish *adj* inhūmānus, avārus; **be ~** suā causā facere.
selfishly *adv* inhūmānē, avārē.
selfishness *n* inhūmānitās *f*, incontinentia *f*, avāritia *f*.
self-made *adj* (*man*) novus.
self-possessed *adj* aequō animō.
self-possession *n* aequus animus *m*.
self-reliant *adj* cōnfīdēns.
self-respect *n* pudor *m*.
self-restraint *n* modestia *f*.
self-sacrifice *n* dēvōtiō *f*.
selfsame *adj* ūnus et īdem.
sell *vt* vēndere; (*in lots*) dīvēndere; **be sold** vēnīre.
seller *n* vēnditor *m*.
selvage *n* limbus *m*.
semblance *n* speciēs *f*, imāgō *f*.
semicircle *n* hēmicyclium *nt*.
senate *n* senātus *m*; **hold a meeting of the ~** senātum habēre; **decree of the ~** senātūs cōnsultum *nt*.
senate house *n* cūria *f*.
senator *n* senātor *m*; (*provincial*) decuriō *m*; **~s** *pl* patrēs *mpl*.
senatorial *adj* senātōrius.
send *vt* mittere; **~ across** trānsmittere; **~ ahead** praemittere; **~ away** dīmittere; **~ back** remittere; **~ for** arcessere; (*doctor*) adhibēre; **~ forth** ēmittere; **~ forward** praemittere; **~ in** immittere, intrōmittere; **~ out** ēmittere; (*in different directions*)

dīmittere; ~ **out of the way** ablēgāre; ~ **up**
submittere.
senile *adj* senīlis.
senility *n* senium *nt*.
senior *adj* nātū māior; (*thing*) prior.
sensation *n* sēnsus *m*; (*event*) rēs nova *f*; **lose ~**
obtorpēscere; **create a ~** hominēs
obstupefacere.
sensational *adj* novus, prōdigiōsus.
sense *n* (*faculty*) sēnsus *m*; (*wisdom*) prūdentia
f; (*meaning*) vis *f*, sententia *f*; **common ~**
prūdentia *f*; **be in one's ~s** apud sē esse,
mentis suae esse; **out of one's ~s** dēmēns;
recover one's ~s resipīscere; **what is the ~ of**
quid sibī vult? ◆ *vt* sentīre.
senseless *adj* absurdus, ineptus, īnsipiēns.
senselessly *adv* īnsipienter.
senselessness *n* īnsipientia *f*.
sensibility *n* sēnsus *m*.
sensible *adj* prūdēns, sapiēns.
sensibly *adv* prūdenter, sapienter.
sensitive *adj* mollis, inrītābilis, patibilis.
sensitiveness *n* mollitia *f*.
sensual *adj* libīdinōsus.
sensuality *n* libīdō *f*, voluptās *f*.
sensually *adv* libīdinōsē.
sentence *n* (*judge*) iūdicium *nt*, sententia *f*;
(*GRAM*) sententia *f*; **pass ~** iūdicāre; **execute ~**
lēge agere ◆ *vt* damnāre; ~ **to death** capitis
damnāre.
sententious *adj* sententiōsus.
sententiously *adv* sententiōsē.
sentient *adj* patibilis.
sentiment *n* (*feeling*) sēnsus *m*; (*opinion*)
sententia *f*; (*emotion*) mollitia *f*.
sentimental *adj* mollis, flēbilis.
sentimentality *n* mollitia *f*.
sentimentally *adv* molliter.
sentries *npl* statiōnēs *fpl*, excubiae *fpl*.
sentry *n* custōs *m*, vigil *m*; **be on ~ duty in**
statiōne esse.
separable *adj* dīviduus, sēparābilis.
separate *vt* sēparāre, dīvidere, disiungere;
(*forcibly*) dīrimere, dīvellere ◆ *vi* dīgredī ◆
adj sēparātus, sēcrētus.
separately *adv* sēparātim, seōrsum.
separation *n* sēparātiō *f*; (*violent*) discidium
nt.
September *n* mēnsis September *m*; **of ~**
September.
sepulchral *adj* fūnebris.
sepulchre *n* sepulcrum *nt*.
sepulture *n* sepultūra *f*.
sequel *n* exitus *m*, quae sequuntur.
sequence *n* seriēs *f*, ōrdō *m*.
sequestered *adj* sēcrētus.
serenade *vt* occentāre.
serene *adj* tranquillus, sēcūrus.
serenely *adv* tranquillē.
serenity *n* sēcūritās *f*.
serf *n* servus *m*.
serfdom *n* servitūs *f*.
sergeant *n* signifer *m*.

series *n* seriēs *f*, ōrdō *m*.
serious *adj* gravis, sērius, sevērus.
seriously *adv* graviter, sēriō, sevērē.
seriousness *n* gravitās *f*.
sermon *n* ōrātiō *f*.
serpent *n* serpēns *f*.
serpentine *adj* tortuōsus.
serrated *adj* serrātus.
serried *adj* cōnfertus.
servant *n* (*domestic*) famulus *m*, famula *f*;
(*public*) minister *m*, ministra *f*; **family ~s**
familia *f*.
servant maid *n* ancilla *f*.
serve *vt* servīre (*dat*); (*food*) ministrāre,
adpōnere; (*interest*) condūcere (*dat*) ◆ *vi* (*MIL*)
stīpendia merēre, mīlitāre; (*suffice*)
sufficere; ~ **as** esse prō (*abl*); ~ **in the cavalry**
equō merēre; ~ **in the infantry** pedibus
merēre; **having ~d one's time** ēmeritus; ~ **a**
sentence poenam subīre; ~ **well** bene merērī
dē (*abl*).
service *n* (*status*) servitium *nt*, famulātus *m*;
(*work*) ministerium *nt*; (*help*) opera *f*; (*by an*
equal) meritum *nt*, beneficium *nt*; (*MIL*) mīlitia
f, stīpendia *ntpl*; **be of ~ to** prōdesse (*dat*),
bene merērī dē; **I am at your ~** adsum tibī;
complete one's ~ stīpendia ēmerērī.
serviceable *adj* ūtilis.
servile *adj* servīlis; (*fig*) abiectus, humilis.
servility *n* adūlātiō *f*.
servitude *n* servitūs *f*.
session *n* conventus *m*; **be in ~** sedēre.
sesterce *n* sēstertius *m*; **10 ~s** decem sēstertiī;
10,000 ~s dēna sēstertia *ntpl*; **1,000,000 ~s**
deciēs sēstertium.
set *vt* pōnere, locāre, statuere, sistere; (*bone*)
condere; (*course*) dīrigere; (*example*) dare;
(*limit*) impōnere; (*mind*) intendere; (*music*)
modulārī; (*sail*) dare; (*sentries*) dispōnere;
(*table*) īnstruere; (*trap*) parāre ◆ *vi* (*ASTRO*)
occidere; ~ **about** incipere; ~ **against**
oppōnere; ~ **apart** sēpōnere; ~ **aside**
sēpōnere; ~ **down** (*writing*) perscrībere; ~
eyes on cōnspicere; ~ **foot on** ingredī; ~ **forth**
expōnere, ēdere; ~ **free** līberāre; ~ **in motion**
movēre; ~ **in order** compōnere, dispōnere; ~
off (*decoration*) distinguere; (*art*) illūmināre;
~ **on** (*to attack*) immittere; ~ **on foot**
īnstituere; ~ **on fire** incendere; ~ **one's heart**
on exoptāre; ~ **out** *vi* proficīscī; ~ **over**
praeficere, impōnere; ~ **up** statuere; (*fig*)
cōnstituere.
set *adj* (*arrangement*) status; (*purpose*) certus;
(*rule*) praescrīptus; (*speech*) compositus; **of ~**
purpose cōnsultō ◆ *n* (*persons*) numerus *m*;
(*things*) congeriēs *f*; (*current*) cursus *m*.
setback *n* repulsa *f*.
settee *n* lectulus *m*.
setting *n* (*ASTRO*) occāsus *m*; (*event*) locus *m*.
settle *n* sella *f* ◆ *vt* statuere; (*annuity*)
praestāre; (*business*) trānsigere; (*colony*)
dēdūcere; (*debt*) exsolvere; (*decision*)
cōnstituere; (*dispute*) dēcīdere, compōnere

♦ vi (abode) cōnsīdere; (agreement) cōnstituere, convenīre; (sediment) dēsīdere; ~ **in** īnsidēre (dat).
settled adj certus, explōrātus.
settlement n (of a colony) dēductiō f; (colony) colōnia f; (of dispute) dēcīsiō f, compositiō f; (to wife) dōs f.
settler n colōnus m.
set to n pugna f.
seven num septem; ~ **each** septēnī; ~ **times** septiēns.
seven hundred num septingentī.
seven hundredth adj septingentēsimus.
seventeen num septendecim.
seventeenth adj septimus decimus.
seventh adj septimus; **for the** ~ **time** septimum.
seventieth adj septuāgēsimus.
seventy num septuāgintā; ~ **each** septuāgēnī; ~ **times** septuāgiēns.
sever vt incīdere, sēparāre, dīvidere.
several adj complūrēs, aliquot.
severally adv singulī.
severe adj gravis, sevērus, dūrus; (style) austērus; (weather) asper; (pain) ācer, gravis.
severely adv graviter, sevērē.
severity n gravitās f, asperitās f, sevēritās f.
sew vt suere; ~ **up** cōnsuere; ~ **up in** īnsuere in (acc).
sewer n cloāca f.
sex n sexus m.
shabbily adv sordidē.
shabbiness n sordēs fpl.
shabby adj sordidus.
shackle n compēs f, vinculum nt ♦ vt impedīre, vincīre.
shade n umbra f; (colour) color m; ~**s** pl mānēs mpl; **put in the** ~ officere (dat) ♦ vt opācāre, umbram adferre (dat).
shadow n umbra f.
shadowy adj obscūrus; (fig) inānis.
shady adj umbrōsus, opācus.
shaft n (missile) tēlum nt, sagitta f; (of spear) hastīle nt; (of cart) tēmō m; (of light) radius m; (excavation) puteus m.
shaggy adj hirsūtus.
shake vt quatere, agitāre; (structure) labefacere, labefactāre; (belief) īnfīrmāre; (resolution) labefactāre, commovēre; ~ **hands with** dextram dare (dat) ♦ vi quatī, agitārī, tremere, horrēscere; ~ **off** dēcutere, excutere; ~ **out** excutere.
shaking n tremor m.
shaky adj īnstābilis, tremebundus.
shall aux vb = fut indic.
shallot n caepa Ascalōnia f.
shallow adj brevis, vadōsus; (fig) levis.
shallowness n vada ntpl; (fig) levitās f.
shallows n brevia ntpl, vada ntpl.
sham adj fictus, falsus, fūcōsus ♦ n simulātiō f, speciēs f ♦ vt simulāre.
shambles n laniēna f.

shame n (feeling) pudor m; (cause) dēdecus nt, ignōminia f; **it** ~**s** pudet (+ acc of person, gen of thing); **it is a** ~ flāgitium est ♦ vt rubōrem incutere (dat) ♦ interj prō pudor!
shamefaced adj verēcundus.
shameful adj ignōminiōsus, turpis.
shamefully adv turpiter.
shameless adj impudēns.
shamelessly adv impudenter.
shamelessness n impudentia f.
shank n crūs nt.
shape n fōrma f, figūra f ♦ vt fōrmāre, fingere; (fig) īnfōrmāre ♦ vi: ~ **well** prōficere.
shapeless adj īnfōrmis, dēfōrmis.
shapelessness n dēfōrmitās f.
shapeliness n fōrma f.
shapely adj fōrmōsus.
shard n testa f.
share n pars f; (plough) vōmer m; **go** ~**s with** inter sē partīrī ♦ vt (give) partīrī, impertīre; (have) commūnicāre, participem esse (gen).
sharer n particeps m/f, socius m.
shark n volpēs marīna f.
sharp adj acūtus; (fig) ācer, acūtus; (bitter) amārus.
sharpen vt acuere; (fig) exacuere.
sharply adv ācriter, acūtē.
sharpness n aciēs f; (mind) acūmen nt, argūtiae fpl; (temper) acerbitās f.
shatter vt quassāre, perfringere, adflīgere; (fig) frangere.
shave vt rādere; ~ **off** abrādere.
shavings n rāmenta ntpl.
she pron haec, ea, illa.
sheaf n manipulus m.
shear vt tondēre, dētondēre.
shears n forficēs fpl.
sheath n vāgīna f.
sheathe vt recondere.
shed vt fundere; (blood) effundere; (one's own) profundere; (tears) effundere; (covering) exuere; ~ **light on** (fig) lūmen adhibēre (dat).
sheen n nitor m.
sheep n ovis f; (flock) pecus nt.
sheepfold n ovīle nt.
sheepish adj pudibundus.
sheepishly adv pudenter.
sheer adj (absolute) merus; (steep) praeruptus.
sheet n (cloth) linteum nt; (metal) lāmina f; (paper) carta f, scheda f; (sail) pēs m; (water) aequor nt.
shelf n pluteus m, pēgma nt.
shell n concha f; (egg) putāmen nt; (tortoise) testa f.
shellfish n conchȳlium nt.
shelter n suffugium nt, tegmen nt; (refuge) perfugium nt, asȳlum nt; (lodging) hospitium nt; (fig) umbra f ♦ vt tegere, dēfendere; (refugee) excipere ♦ vi latēre; ~ **behind** (fig) dēlitēscere in (abl).
sheltered adj (life) umbrātilis.
shelve vt differre ♦ vi sē dēmittere.

shelving *adj* dēclīvis.
shepherd *n* pastor *m*.
shield *n* scūtum *nt*; clipeus *m*; (*small*) parma *f*; (*fig*) praesidium *nt* ♦ *vt* prōtegere, dēfendere.
shift *n* (*change*) mūtātiō *f*; (*expedient*) ars *f*, dolus *m*; **make ~ to** efficere ut; **in ~s** per vicēs ♦ *vt* mūtāre; (*move*) movēre ♦ *vi* mūtārī; discēdere.
shiftless *adj* iners, inops.
shifty *adj* vafer, versūtus.
shilling *n* solidus *m*.
shimmer *vi* micāre ♦ *n* tremulum lūmen *nt*.
shin *n* tībia *f*.
shine *vi* lūcēre, fulgēre; (*reflecting*) nitēre; (*fig*) ēminēre; **~ forth** ēlūcēre, ēnitēre; effulgēre; **~ upon** adfulgēre (*dat*) ♦ *n* nitor *m*.
shingle *n* lapillī *mpl*, glārea *f*.
shining *adj* lūcidus, splendidus; (*fig*) illūstris.
shiny *adj* nitidus.
ship *n* nāvis *f*; **admiral's ~** nāvis praetōria; **decked ~** nāvis tēcta, nāvis cōnstrāta ♦ *vt* (*cargo*) impōnere; (*to a place*) nāvī invehere.
shipowner *n* nāviculārius *m*.
shipping *n* nāvēs *fpl*.
shipwreck *n* naufragium *nt*; **suffer ~** naufragium facere.
shipwrecked *adj* naufragus.
shirk *vt* dēfugere, dētrectāre.
shirt *n* subūcula *f*.
shiver *n* horror *m* ♦ *vi* horrēre, tremere ♦ *vt* perfringere, comminuere.
shivering *n* horror *m*.
shoal *n* (*fish*) exāmen *nt*; (*water*) vadum *nt*; **~s** *pl* brevia *ntpl*.
shock *n* impulsus *m*; (*battle*) concursus *m*, cōnflīctus *m*; (*hair*) caesariēs *f*; (*mind*) offēnsiō *f* ♦ *vt* percutere, offendere.
shocking *adj* atrōx, dētestābilis, flāgitiōsus.
shoddy *adj* vīlis.
shoe *n* calceus *m*.
shoemaker *n* sūtor *m*.
shoot *n* surculus *m*; (*vine*) pampinus *m* ♦ *vi* frondēscere; (*movement*) volāre; **~ up** ēmicāre ♦ *vt* (*missile*) conicere, iaculārī; (*person*) iaculārī, trānsfīgere.
shop *n* taberna *f*.
shore *n* lītus *nt*, ōra *f* ♦ *vt* fulcīre.
short *adj* brevis; (*broken*) curtus; (*amount*) exiguus; **for a ~ time** parumper, paulisper; **~ of** (*number*) intrā (*acc*); **be ~ of** indigēre (*abl*); **cut ~** interpellāre; **in ~** ad summam, dēnique; **very ~** perbrevis; **fall ~ of** nōn pervenīre ad, abesse ab; **run ~** dēficere; **to cut a long story ~** nē multīs morer, nē multa.
shortage *n* inopia *f*.
shortcoming *n* dēlictum *nt*, culpa *f*.
short cut *n* via compendiāria *f*.
shorten *vt* curtāre, imminuere, contrahere; (*sail*) legere.
shorthand *n* notae *fpl*.
shorthand writer *n* āctuārius *m*.
short-lived *adj* brevis.

shortly *adv* (*time*) brevī; (*speak*) breviter; **~ after** paulō post, nec multō post.
shortness *n* brevitās *f*, exiguitās *f*; (*difficulty*) angustiae *fpl*.
short-sighted *adj* (*fig*) imprōvidus, imprūdēns.
short-sightedness *n* imprūdentia *f*.
short-tempered *adj* īrācundus.
shot *n* ictus *m*; (*range*) iactus *m*.
should *vi* (*duty*) dēbēre.
shoulder *n* umerus *m*; (*animal*) armus *m* ♦ *vt* (*burden*) suscipere.
shout *n* clāmor *m*, adclāmātiō *f* ♦ *vt*, *vi* clāmāre, vōciferārī; **~ down** obstrepere (*dat*); **~ out** exclāmāre.
shove *vt* trūdere, impellere.
shovel *n* rutrum *nt*.
show *n* speciēs *f*; (*entertainment*) lūdī *mpl*, spectāculum *nt*; (*stage*) lūdicrum *nt*; **for ~** in speciem; **put on a ~** spectācula dare ♦ *vt* mōnstrāre, indicāre, ostendere, ostentāre; (*point out*) dēmōnstrāre; (*qualities*) praestāre; **~ off** *vi* sē iactāre ♦ *vt* ostentāre.
shower *n* imber *m* ♦ *vt* fundere, conicere.
showery *adj* pluvius.
showiness *n* ostentātiō *f*.
showing off *n* iactātiō *f*.
showy *adj* speciōsus.
shred *n* fragmentum *nt*; **in ~s** minūtātim; **tear to ~s** dīlaniāre ♦ *vt* concīdere.
shrew *n* virāgō *f*.
shrewd *adj* acūtus, ācer, sagāx.
shrewdly *adv* acūtē, sagāciter.
shrewdness *n* acūmen *nt*, sagācitās *f*.
shriek *n* ululātus *m* ♦ *vi* ululāre.
shrill *adj* acūtus, argūtus.
shrine *n* fānum *nt*, dēlubrum *nt*.
shrink *vt* contrahere ♦ *vi* contrahī; **~ from** abhorrēre ab, refugere ab, dētrectāre.
shrivel *vt* corrūgāre ♦ *vi* exārēscere.
shroud *n* integumentum *nt*; **~s** *pl* rudentēs *mpl* ♦ *vt* involvere.
shrub *n* frutex *m*.
shrubbery *n* fruticētum *nt*.
shudder *n* horror *m* ♦ *vi* exhorrēscere; **~ at** horrēre.
shuffle *vt* miscēre ♦ *vi* claudicāre; (*fig*) tergiversārī.
shun *vt* vītāre, ēvītāre, dēfugere.
shut *vt* claudere; (*with cover*) operīre; (*hand*) comprimere; **~ in** inclūdere; **~ off** interclūdere; **~ out** exclūdere; **~ up** inclūdere.
shutter *n* foricula *f*, lūmināre *nt*.
shuttle *n* radius *m*.
shy *adj* timidus, pudibundus, verēcundus.
shyly *adv* timidē, verēcundē.
shyness *n* verēcundia *f*.
sibyl *n* sibylla *f*.
sick *adj* aeger, aegrōtus; **be ~** aegrōtāre; **feel ~** nauseāre; **I am ~ of** mē taedet (*gen*).
sicken *vt* fastīdium movēre (*dat*) ♦ *vi* nauseāre, aegrōtāre.

sickle n falx f.

sickly adj invalidus.

sickness n nausea f; (illness) morbus m, aegritūdō f.

side n latus nt; (direction) pars f; (faction) partēs fpl; (kin) genus nt; **on all ~s** undique; **on both ~s** utrimque; **on one ~** unā ex parte; **on our ~** ā nōbis; **be on the ~ of** stāre ab, sentīre cum; **on the far ~ of** ultrā (acc); **on this ~** hīnc; **on this ~ of** cis (acc), citrā (acc) ♦ vi: **~ with** stāre ab, facere cum.

sideboard n abacus m.

sidelong adj oblīquus.

sideways adv oblīquē, in oblīquum.

sidle vi oblīquō corpore incēdere.

siege n obsidiō f, oppugnātiō f; **lay ~ to** obsidēre.

siege works n opera ntpl.

siesta n merīdiātiō f; **take a ~** merīdiāre.

sieve n crībrum nt.

sigh n suspīrium nt; (loud) gemitus m ♦ vi suspīrāre, gemere.

sight n (sense) vīsus m; (process) aspectus m; (range) cōnspectus m; (thing seen) spectāculum nt, speciēs f; **at ~ ex tempore; at first ~** prīmō aspectū; **in ~** in cōnspectū; **come into ~** in cōnspectum sē dare; **in the ~ of** in oculīs (gen); **catch ~ of** cōnspicere; **lose ~ of** ē cōnspectū āmittere; (fig) oblīvīscī (gen) ♦ vt cōnspicārī.

sightless adj caecus.

sightly adj decōrus.

sign n signum nt, indicium nt; (distinction) īnsigne nt; (mark) nota f; (trace) vestīgium nt; (proof) documentum nt; (portent) ōmen nt; (Zodiac) signum nt; **give a ~** innuere ♦ vi signum dare, innuere ♦ vt subscrībere (dat); (as witness) obsignāre.

signal n signum nt; **give the ~ for retreat** receptuī canere ♦ vi signum dare ♦ adj īnsignis, ēgregius.

signalize vt nōbilitāre.

signally adv ēgregiē.

signature n nōmen nt, manus f, chīrographum nt.

signet n signum nt.

signet ring n ānulus m.

significance n interpretātiō f, significātiō f, vīs f; (importance) pondus nt.

significant adj gravis, clārus.

signification n significātiō f.

signify vt significāre, velle; (omen) portendere; **it does not ~** nōn interest.

silence n silentium nt; **in ~** per silentium ♦ vt comprimere; (argument) refūtāre.

silent adj tacitus; (habit) taciturnus; **be ~** silēre, tacēre; **be ~ about** silēre, tacēre; **become ~** conticēscere.

silently adv tacitē.

silhouette n adumbrātiō f.

silk n bombȳx m; (clothes) sērica ntpl ♦ adj bombȳcinus, sēricus.

silken adj bombȳcinus.

sill n līmen nt.

silliness n stultitia f, ineptiae fpl.

silly adj fatuus, ineptus; stultus; **be ~** dēsipere.

silt n līmus m.

silver n argentum nt ♦ adj argenteus.

silver mine n argentāria f.

silver plate n argentum nt.

silver-plated adj argentātus.

silvery adj argenteus.

similar adj similis.

similarity n similitūdō f.

similarly adv similiter.

simile n similitūdō f.

simmer vi lēniter fervēre.

simper vi molliter subrīdēre.

simple adj simplex; (mind) fatuus; (task) facilis.

simpleton n homō ineptus m.

simplicity n simplicitās f; (mind) stultitia f.

simplify vt faciliōrem reddere.

simply adv simpliciter; (merely) sōlum, tantum.

simulate vt simulāre.

simulation n simulātiō f.

simultaneously adv simul, ūnā, eōdem tempore.

sin n peccātum nt, nefās nt, dēlictum nt ♦ vi peccāre.

since adv abhinc; **long ~** iamdūdum ♦ conj (time) ex quō tempore, postquam; (reason) cum (+ subj), quoniam; **~ he** quippe quī ♦ prep ab (abl), ex (abl), post (acc); **ever ~** usque ab.

sincere adj sincērus, simplex, apertus.

sincerely adv sincērē, ex animō.

sincerity n fidēs f, simplicitās f.

sinew n nervus m.

sinewy adj nervōsus.

sinful adj improbus, impius, incestus.

sinfully adv improbē, impiē.

sing vt canere, cantāre; **~ of** canere.

singe vt adūrere.

singer n cantor m.

singing n cantus m ♦ adj canōrus.

single adj ūnus, sōlus, ūnicus; (unmarried) caelebs ♦ vt: **~ out** ēligere, excerpere.

single-handed adj ūnus.

singly adv singillātim, singulī.

singular adj singulāris; (strange) novus.

singularly adv singulāriter, praecipuē.

sinister adj īnfaustus, malevolus.

sink vi dēsīdere; (in water) dēmergī; **~ in** inlābī, īnsīdere ♦ vt dēprimere, mergere; (well) fodere; (fig) dēmergere.

sinless adj integer, innocēns, castus.

sinner n peccātor m.

sinuous adj sinuōsus.

sip vt gustāre, lībāre.

siphon n siphō m.

sir n (to master) ere; (to equal) vir optime; (title) eques m.

sire n pater m.

siren n sīrēn f.

sirocco n Auster m.
sister n soror f; ~'s sorōrius.
sisterhood n germānitās f; (*society*) sorōrum societās f.
sister-in-law n glōs f.
sisterly adj sorōrius.
sit vi sedēre; ~ **beside** adsidēre (*dat*); ~ **down** cōnsīdere; ~ **on** īnsidēre (*dat*); (*eggs*) incubāre; ~ **at table** accumbere; ~ **up** (*at night*) vigilāre.
site n situs m, locus m; (*for building*) ārea f.
sitting n sessiō f.
situated adj situs.
situation n situs m; (*circs*) status m, condiciō f.
six num sex; ~ **each** sēnī; ~ **or seven** sex septem; ~ **times** sexiēns.
six hundred num sēscentī; ~ **each** sēscēnī; ~ **times** sēscentiēns.
six hundredth adj sēscentēsimus.
sixteen num sēdecim; ~ **each** sēnī dēnī; ~ **times** sēdeciēns.
sixteenth adj sextus decimus.
sixth adj sextus; **for the** ~ **time** sextum.
sixtieth adj sexagēsimus.
sixty num sexāgintā; ~ **each** sexāgēnī; ~ **times** sexāgiēns.
size n māgnitūdō f, amplitūdō f; (*measure*) mēnsūra f, fōrma f.
skate vi per glaciem lābī; ~ **on thin ice** (*fig*) incēdere per ignēs suppositōs cinerī dolōsō.
skein n glomus nt.
skeleton n ossa ntpl.
sketch n adumbrātiō f, dēscrīptiō f ♦ vt adumbrāre, īnfōrmāre.
skewer n verū nt.
skiff n scapha f, lēnunculus m.
skilful adj perītus, doctus, scītus; (*with hands*) habilis.
skilfully adv perītē, doctē; habiliter.
skill n ars f, perītia f, sollertia f.
skilled adj perītus, doctus; ~ **in** perītus (+ gen).
skim vt dēspūmāre; ~ **over** (*fig*) legere, perstringere.
skin n cutis f; (*animal*) pellis f ♦ vt pellem dētrahere (*dat*).
skinflint n avārus m.
skinny adj macer.
skip vi exsultāre ♦ vt praeterīre.
skipper n magister m.
skirmish n leve proelium nt ♦ vi vēlitārī.
skirmisher n vēles m, excursor m.
skirt n īnstita f; (*border*) limbus m ♦ vt contingere (*dat*); (*motion*) legere.
skittish adj lascīvus.
skulk vi latēre, dēlitēscere.
skull n caput nt.
sky n caelum nt; **of the** ~ caelestis.
skylark n alauda f.
slab n tabula f.
slack adj remissus, laxus; (*work*) piger, neglegēns.
slacken vt remittere, dētendere ♦ vi laxārī.
slackness n remissiō f; pigritia f.

slag n scōria f.
slake vt restinguere, sēdāre.
slam vt adflīgere.
slander n maledicta ntpl, obtrectātiō f; (*law*) calumnia f ♦ vt maledīcere (*dat*), īnfāmāre, obtrectāre (*dat*).
slanderer n obtrectātor m.
slanderous adj maledicus.
slang n vulgāria verba ntpl.
slant vi in trānsversum īre.
slanting adj oblīquus, trānsversus.
slantingly adv oblīquē, ex trānsversō.
slap n alapa f ♦ vt palmā ferīre.
slapdash adj praeceps, temerārius.
slash vt caedere ♦ n ictus m.
slate n (*roof*) tēgula f; (*writing*) tabula f ♦ vt increpāre.
slatternly adj sordidus, incōmptus.
slaughter n caedēs f, strāgēs f ♦ vt trucīdāre.
slaughterhouse n laniēna f.
slave n servus m; (*domestic*) famulus m; (*home born*) verna m; **be a** ~ **to** īnservīre (*dat*); **household** ~**s** familia f.
slave girl n ancilla f.
slavery n servitūs f.
slavish adj servīlis.
slavishly adv servīliter.
slay vt interficere, occīdere.
slayer n interfector m.
sleek adj nitidus, pinguis.
sleep n somnus m; **go to** ~ obdormīscere ♦ vi dormīre; ~ **off** vt ēdormīre.
sleeper n dormītor m.
sleepiness n sopor m.
sleepless adj īnsomnis, vigil.
sleeplessness n īnsomnia f.
sleepy adj somniculōsus; **be** ~ dormītāre.
sleeve n manica f.
sleight of hand n praestīgiae fpl.
slender adj gracilis, exīlis.
slenderness n gracilitās f.
slice n frūstum nt ♦ vt secāre.
slide n lāpsus m ♦ vi lābī.
slight adj levis, exiguus, parvus ♦ n neglegentia f ♦ vt neglegere, offendere.
slightingly adv contemptim.
slightly adv leviter, paululum.
slightness n levitās f.
slim adj gracilis.
slime n līmus m.
slimness n gracilitās f.
slimy adj līmōsus, mūcōsus.
sling n funda f ♦ vt mittere, iaculārī.
slinger n funditor m.
slink vi sē subdūcere.
slip n lāpsus m; (*mistake*) offēnsiuncula f; (*plant*) surculus m ♦ vi lābī; ~ **away** ēlābī, dīlābī; ~ **out** ēlābī; (*word*) excidere; **give the** ~ **to** ēlūdere; **let** ~ āmittere, ēmittere; (*opportunity*) ōmittere; **there's many a** ~ **twix the cup and the lip** inter ōs et offam multa interveniunt.
slipper n solea f.

slippery *adj* lūbricus.
slipshod *adj* neglegēns.
slit *n* rīma *f* ♦ *vt* findere, incīdere.
sloe *n* spīnus *m*.
slope *n* dēclīve *nt*, clīvus *m*; (*steep*) dēiectus *m* ♦ *vi* sē dēmittere, vergere.
sloping *adj* dēclīvis, dēvexus; (*up*) adclīvis.
slot *n* rīma *f*.
sloth *n* inertia *f*, segnitia *f*, dēsidia *f*, ignāvia *f*.
slothful *adj* ignāvus, iners, segnis.
slothfully *adv* ignāvē, segniter.
slouch *vi* languidē incēdere.
slough *n* (*skin*) exuviae *fpl*; (*bog*) palūs *f*.
slovenliness *n* ignāvia *f*, sordēs *fpl*.
slovenly *adj* ignāvus, sordidus.
slow *adj* tardus, lentus; (*mind*) hebes.
slowly *adv* tardē, lentē.
slowness *n* tarditās *f*.
sludge *n* līmus *m*.
slug *n* līmāx *f*.
sluggard *n* homō ignāvus *m*.
sluggish *adj* piger, segnis; (*mind*) hebes.
sluggishly *adv* pigrē, segniter.
sluggishness *n* pigritia *f*, inertia *f*.
sluice *n* cataracta *f*.
slumber *n* somnus *m*, sopor *m* ♦ *vi* dormīre.
slump *n* vīlis annōna *f*.
slur *n* nota *f*; **cast ~ on** dētrectāre ♦ *vt*: **~ words** balbūtīre.
sly *adj* astūtus, vafer, callidus; **on the ~** ex opīnātō.
slyly *adv* astūtē, callidē.
slyness *n* astūtia *f*.
smack *n* (*blow*) ictus *m*; (*with hand*) alapa *f*; (*boat*) lēnunculus *m*; (*taste*) sapor *m* ♦ *vt* ferīre ♦ *vi*: **~ of** olēre, redolēre.
small *adj* parvus, exiguus; **how ~** quantulus, quantillus; **so ~** tantulus; **very ~** perexiguus, minimus; **a ~ meeting of** īnfrequēns.
smaller *adj* minor.
smallest *adj* minimus.
smallness *n* exiguitās *f*, brevitās *f*.
small talk *n* sermunculus *m*.
smart *adj* (*action*) ācer, alacer; (*dress*) concinnus, nitidus; (*pace*) vēlōx; (*wit*) facētus, salsus ♦ *n* dolor *m* ♦ *vi* dolēre; (*fig*) ūrī, mordērī.
smartly *adv* ācriter; nitidē; vēlōciter; facētē.
smartness *n* alacritās *f*; (*dress*) nitor *m*; (*wit*) facētiae *fpl*, sollertia *f*.
smash *n* ruīna *f* ♦ *vt* frangere, comminuere.
smattering *n*: **get a ~ of** odōrārī, prīmīs labrīs attingere; **with a ~ of** imbūtus (*abl*).
smear *vt* oblinere, ungere.
smell *n* (*sense*) odōrātus *m*; (*odour*) odor *m*; (*of cooking*) nīdor *m* ♦ *vt* olfacere, odōrārī ♦ *vi* olēre.
smelly *adj* olidus.
smelt *vt* fundere.
smile *n* rīsus *m* ♦ *vi* subrīdēre; **~ at** adrīdēre (*dat*); **~ upon** rīdēre ad; (*fig*) secundum esse (*dat*).
smiling *adj* laetus.

smirk *vi* subrīdēre.
smith *n* faber *m*.
smithy *n* fabrica *f*.
smock *n* tunica *f*.
smoke *n* fūmus *m* ♦ *vi* fūmāre.
smoky *adj* fūmōsus.
smooth *adj* lēvis; (*skin*) glaber; (*talk*) blandus; (*sea*) placidus; (*temper*) aequus; (*voice*) lēvis, teres ♦ *vt* sternere, līmāre.
smoothly *adv* lēviter, lēniter.
smoothness *n* lēvitās *f*, lēnitās *f*.
smother *vt* opprimere, suffocāre.
smoulder *vi* fūmāre.
smudge *n* macula *f*.
smug *adj* suī contentus.
smuggle *vt* fūrtim importāre.
smugness *n* amor suī *m*.
smut *n* fūlīgō *f*.
snack *n* cēnula *f*; **take a ~** gustāre.
snag *n* impedīmentum *nt*, scrūpulus *m*.
snail *n* cochlea *f*.
snake *n* anguis *m*, serpēns *f*.
snaky *adj* vīpereus.
snap *vt* rumpere, praerumpere; **~ the fingers** digitīs concrepāre ♦ *vi* rumpī, dissilīre; **~ at** mordēre; **~ up** corripere.
snare *n* laqueus *m*, plaga *f*, pedica *f* ♦ *vt* inrētīre.
snarl *n* gannītus *m* ♦ *vi* gannīre.
snatch *vt* rapere, ēripere, adripere, corripere; **~ at** captāre.
sneak *n* perfidus *m* ♦ *vi* conrēpere; **~ in sē** īnsinuāre; **~ out** ēlābī.
sneaking *adj* humilis, fūrtīvus.
sneer *n* irrīsiō *f* ♦ *vi* irrīdēre, dērīdēre.
sneeze *n* sternūtāmentum *nt* ♦ *vi* sternuere.
sniff *vt* odōrārī.
snip *vt* praecīdere, secāre.
snob *n* homō ambitiōsus *m*.
snood *n* mitra *f*.
snooze *vi* dormītāre.
snore *vi* stertere.
snoring *n* rhoncus *m*.
snort *n* fremitus *m* ♦ *vi* fremere.
snout *n* rōstrum *nt*.
snow *n* nix *f* ♦ *vi* ningere; **~ed under** nive obrutus; **it is ~ing** ningit.
snowy *adj* nivālis; (*colour*) niveus.
snub *vt* neglegere, praeterīre.
snub-nosed *adj* sīmus.
snuff *n* (*candle*) fungus *m*.
snug *adj* commodus.
snugly *adv* commodē.
so *adv* (*referring back*) sīc; (*referring forward*) ita; (*with adj and adv*) tam; (*with verb*) adeō; (*consequence*) ergō, itaque, igitur; **and ~** itaque; **~ great** tantus; **so-so** sīc; **~ as to** ut; **~ be it** estō; **~ big** tantus; **~ far** usque adeō, adhūc; **~ far as** quod; **~ far from** adeō nōn; **~ little** tantillus; **~ long as** dum; **~ many** tot; **~ much** *adj* tantus ♦ *adv* tantum; (*with compar*) tantō; **~ often** totiēns; **~ that** ut (+ *subj*); **~ that ... not** (*purpose*) nē; (*result*) ut nōn; **and ~ on** deinceps; **not ~ very** haud ita; **say ~** id dīcere.

soak vt imbuere, madefacere.
soaking adj madidus.
soap n sapō m.
soar vi in sublīme ferrī, subvolāre; ~ **above** superāre.
sob n singultus m ◆ vi singultāre.
sober adj sobrius; (conduct) modestus; (mind) sānus.
soberly adv sobriē, modestē.
sobriety n modestia f, continentia f.
so-called adj quī dīcitur.
sociability n facilitās f.
sociable adj facilis, cōmis.
sociably adv faciliter, cōmiter.
social adj sociālis, commūnis.
socialism n populāris ratiō f.
socialist n homō populāris m/f.
society n societās f; (class) optimātēs mpl; (being with) convīctus m; **cultivate the ~ of** adsectārī; **secret ~** sodālitās f.
sod n caespes m, glaeba f.
soda n nitrum nt.
sodden adj madidus.
soever adv -cumque.
sofa n lectus m.
soft adj mollis; (fruit) mītis; (voice) submissus; (character) dēlicātus; (words) blandus.
soften vt mollīre; (body) ēnervāre; (emotion) lēnīre, mītigāre ◆ vi mollēscere, mītēscere.
soft-hearted adj misericors.
softly adv molliter, lēniter; blandē.
softness n mollitia f, mollitiēs f.
soil n solum nt, humus f ◆ vt inquināre, foedāre.
sojourn n commorātiō f, mānsiō f ◆ vi commorārī.
sojourner n hospes m, hospita f.
solace n sōlātium nt, levātiō f ◆ vt sōlārī, cōnsōlārī.
solar adj sōlis.
solder n ferrūmen nt ◆ vt ferrūmināre.
soldier n mīles m; **be a ~** mīlitāre; **common ~** manipulāris m, gregārius mīles m; **fellow ~** commīlitō m; **foot ~** pedes m; **old ~** veterānus m ◆ vi mīlitāre.
soldierly adj mīlitāris.
soldiery n mīles m.
sole adj sōlus, ūnus, ūnicus ◆ n (foot) planta f; (fish) solea f.
solecism n soloecismus m.
solely adv sōlum, tantum, modō.
solemn adj gravis; (religion) sanctus.
solemnity n gravitās f; sanctitās f.
solemnize vt agere.
solemnly adv graviter; rītē.
solicit vt flāgitāre, obsecrāre.
solicitation n flāgitātiō f.
solicitor n advocātus m.
solicitous adj anxius, trepidus.
solicitously adv anxiē, trepidē.
solicitude n cūra f, anxietās f.
solid adj solidus; (metal) pūrus; (food) firmus; (argument) firmus; (character) cōnstāns,

spectātus; **become ~** concrēscere; **make ~** cōgere.
solidarity n societās f.
solidify vt cōgere ◆ vi concrēscere.
solidity n soliditās f.
solidly adv firmē, cōnstanter.
soliloquize vi sēcum loquī.
soliloquy n ūnīus ōrātiō f.
solitary adj sōlus, sōlitārius; (instance) ūnicus; (place) dēsertus.
solitude n sōlitūdō f.
solo n canticum nt.
solstice n (summer) sōlstitium nt; (winter) brūma f.
solstitial adj sōlstitiālis, brūmālis.
soluble adj dissolūbilis.
solution n (of puzzle) ēnōdātiō f.
solve vt ēnōdāre, explicāre.
solvency n solvendī facultās f.
solvent adj: **be ~** solvendō esse.
sombre adj obscūrus; (fig) tristis.
some adj aliquī; (pl) nonnūllī, aliquot; **~ people** sunt quī (+ subj); **~ ... other** alius ... alius; **for ~ time** aliquamdiū; **with ~ reason** nōn sine causā ◆ pron aliquis; (pl) nonnūllī, sunt quī (subj), erant quī (subj).
somebody pron aliquis; **~ or other** nescioquis.
somehow adv quōdammodō, nescio quōmodō.
someone pron aliquis; (negative) quisquam; **~ or other** nescioquis; **~ else** alius.
something pron aliquid; **~ or other** nescioquid; **~ else** aliud.
sometime adv aliquandō; (past) quondam.
sometimes adv interdum, nonnumquam; **~ ... ~** modo ... modo.
somewhat adv aliquantum, nōnnihil, paulum; (with compar) paulō, aliquantō.
somewhere adv alicubi; (to) aliquō; **~ else** alibī; (to) aliō; **from ~** alicunde; **from ~ else** aliunde.
somnolence n somnus m.
somnolent adj sēmisomnus.
son n filius m; **small ~** fīliolus m.
song n carmen nt, cantus m.
son-in-law n gener m.
sonorous adj sonōrus, canōrus.
soon adv mox, brevi, citō; **as ~ as** ut prīmum, cum prīmum (+ fut perf), simul āc/atque (+ perf indic); **as ~ as possible** quam prīmum; **too ~** praemātūrē, ante tempus.
sooner adv prius, mātūrius; (preference) libentius, potius; **~ or later** sērius ōcius; **no ~ said than done** dictum factum.
soonest adv mātūrissimē.
soot n fūlīgō f.
soothe vt dēlēnīre, permulcēre.
soothing adj lēnis, blandus.
soothingly adv blandē.
soothsayer n hariolus m, vātēs m/f, haruspex m.
sooty adj fūmōsus.
sop n offa f; (fig) dēlēnīmentum nt.

sophism–specify

sophism n captiō f.
sophist n sophistēs m.
sophistical adj acūleātus, captiōsus.
sophisticated adj lepidus, urbānus.
sophistry n captiō f.
soporific adj sopōrifer, somnifer.
soprano adj acūtus.
sorcerer n veneficus m.
sorceress n venefica f, saga f.
sorcery n venēficium nt; (means) venēna ntpl,
carmina ntpl.
sordid adj sordidus; (conduct) illīberālis.
sordidly adv sordidē.
sordidness n sordēs fpl; illīberālitās f.
sore adj molestus, gravis, acerbus; **feel ~**
dolēre ♦ n ulcus nt.
sorely adv graviter, vehementer.
sorrel n lapathus f, lapathum nt.
sorrow n dolor m, aegritūdō f; (outward)
maeror m; (for death) lūctus m ♦ vi dolēre,
maerere, lūgēre.
sorrowful adj maestus, tristis.
sorrowfully adv maestē.
sorry adj paenitēns; (poor) miser; **I am ~ for**
(remorse) mē paenitet, mē piget (gen); (pity)
mē miseret (gen).
sort n genus nt; **a ~ of** quīdam; **all ~s of** omnēs;
the ~ of tālis; **this ~ of** huiusmodī; **the**
common ~ plēbs f; **I am not the ~ of man to**
nōn is sum quī (+ subj); **I am out of ~s** mihī
displiceō ♦ vt dīgerere, compōnere; (votes)
diribēre.
sortie n excursiō f, excursus m, ēruptiō f; **make**
a ~ ērumpere, excurrere.
sot n ēbriōsus m.
sottish adj ēbriōsus, tēmulentus.
sottishness n vīnolentia f.
soul n anima f, animus m; (essence) vīs f;
(person) caput nt; **not a ~** nēmō ūnus; **the ~ of**
(fig) medulla f.
soulless adj caecus, dūrus.
sound n sonitus m, sonus m; (articulate) vōx f;
(confused) strepitus m; (loud) fragor m;
(strait) fretum nt ♦ vt (signal) canere;
(instrument) īnflāre; (depth) scrūtārī,
temptāre; (person) animum temptāre (gen) ♦
vi canere, sonāre; (seem) vidērī; **~ a retreat**
receptuī canere ♦ adj sānus, salūbris;
(health) firmus; (sleep) artus; (judgment)
exquīsītus; (argument) vērus; **safe and ~**
salvus, incolumis.
soundly adv (beat) vehementer; (sleep) artē;
(study) penitus, dīligenter.
soundness n sānitās f, integritās f.
soup n iūs nt.
sour adj acerbus, amārus, acidus; **turn ~**
acēscere; (fig) coacēscere ♦ vt (fig)
exacerbāre.
source n fōns m; (river) caput nt; (fig) fōns m,
orīgō f; **have its ~ in** orīrī ex; (fig) proficīscī
ex.
sourness n acerbitās f; (temper) mōrōsitās f.
souse vt immergere.

south n merīdiēs f ♦ adj austrālis ♦ adv ad
merīdiem.
south-east adv inter sōlis ortum et merīdiem.
southerly adj ad merīdiem versus.
southern adj austrālis.
south-west adv inter occāsum sōlis et
merīdiem.
south wind n auster m.
souvenir n monumentum nt.
sovereign n rēx m, rēgīna f ♦ adj prīnceps,
summus.
sovereignty n rēgnum nt, imperium nt,
prīncipātus m; (of the people) māiestās f.
sow n scrōfa f, sūs f.
sow vt serere; (field) cōnserere ♦ vi sementem
facere.
sower n sator m.
sowing n sēmentis f.
spa n aquae fpl.
space n (extension) spatium nt; (not matter)
ināne nt; (room) locus m; (distance)
intervallum nt; (time) spatium nt; **open ~** ārea
f; **leave a ~ of** intermittere ♦ vt: **~ out**
dispōnere.
spacious adj amplus, capāx.
spaciousness n amplitūdō f.
spade n pāla f, rūtrum nt.
span n (measure) palmus m; (extent) spatium nt
♦ vt iungere.
spangle n bractea f.
spangled adj distinctus.
spar n tignum nt.
spare vt parcere (dat); (to give) suppeditāre; **~**
time for vacāre (dat) ♦ adj exīlis; (extra)
subsecīvus.
sparing adj parcus.
sparingly adv parcē.
spark n scintilla f; (fig) igniculus m.
sparkle vi scintillāre, nitēre, micāre.
sparrow n passer m.
sparse adj rārus.
spasm n convulsiō f.
spasmodically adv interdum.
spatter vt aspergere.
spawn n ōva ntpl.
speak vt, vi loquī; (make speech) dīcere,
contiōnārī, ōrātiōnem habēre; **~ out** ēloquī; **~**
to adloquī; (converse) colloquī cum; **~ well of**
bene dīcere (dat); **it ~s for itself** rēs ipsa
loquitur.
speaker n ōrātor m.
speaking n: **art of ~** dīcendī ars f; **practise**
public ~ dēclāmāre ♦ adj: **likeness ~** vīvida
imāgō.
spear n hasta f.
spearman n hastātus m.
special adj praecipuus, proprius.
speciality n proprium nt.
specially adv praecipuē, praesertim.
species n genus nt.
specific adj certus.
specification n dēsignātiō f.
specify vt dēnotāre, dēsignāre.

specimen n exemplar nt, exemplum nt.
specious adj speciōsus.
speciously adv speciōsē.
speciousness n speciēs f.
speck n macula f.
speckled adj maculīs distinctus.
spectacle n spectāculum nt.
spectacular adj spectābilis.
spectator n spectātor m.
spectral adj larvālis.
spectre n larva f.
speculate vi cōgitāre, coniectūrās facere; (comm) forō ūtī.
speculation n cōgitātiō f, coniectūra f; (comm) ālea f.
speculator n contemplātor m; (comm) āleātor m.
speech n ōrātiō f; (language) sermō m, lingua f; (to people or troops) cōntiō f; **make a ~** ōrātiōnem/cōntiōnem habēre.
speechless adj ēlinguis, mūtus.
speed n celeritās f, cursus m, vēlōcitās f; **with all ~** summa celeritate; **at full ~** māgnō cursū, incitātus; (riding) citātō equō ♦ vt adcelerāre, mātūrāre ♦ vi properāre, festīnāre.
speedily adv celeriter, citō.
speedy adj celer, vēlōx, citus.
spell n carmen nt.
spellbound adj: **be ~** obstipēscere.
spelt n far nt.
spend vt impendere, īnsūmere; (public money) ērogāre; (time) agere, cōnsūmere, terere; (strength) effundere; **~ itself** (storm) dēsaevīre; **~ on** īnsūmere (acc & dat).
spendthrift n nepōs m, prōdigus m.
sphere n globus m; (of action) prōvincia f.
spherical adj globōsus.
sphinx n sphinx f.
spice n condīmentum nt; **~s** pl odōrēs mpl ♦ vt condīre.
spicy adj odōrātus; (wit) salsus.
spider n arānea f; **~'s web** arāneum nt.
spike n dēns m, clāvus m.
spikenard n nardus m.
spill vt fundere, profundere ♦ vi redundāre.
spin vt (thread) nēre, dēdūcere; (top) versāre; **~ out** (story) prōdūcere ♦ vi circumagī, versārī.
spindle n fūsus m.
spine n spīna f.
spineless adj ēnervātus.
spinster n virgō f.
spiral adj intortus ♦ n spīra f.
spire n cōnus m.
spirit n (life) anima f; (intelligence) mēns f; (soul) animus m; (vivacity) spīritus m, vigor m, vīs f; (character) ingenium nt; (intention) voluntās f; (of an age) mōrēs mpl; (ghost) anima f; **~s** pl mānēs mpl; **full of ~** alacer, animōsus.
spirited adj animōsus, ācer.
spiritless adj iners, frāctus, timidus.
spiritual adj animī.

spit n verū nt ♦ vi spuere, spūtāre; **~ on** cōnspūtāre; **~ out** exspuere.
spite n invidia f, malevolentia f, līvor m; **in ~ of me** mē invītō; **in ~ of the difficulties** in his angustiīs ♦ vt incommodāre, offendere.
spiteful adj malevolus, malignus, invidus.
spitefully adv malevolē, malignē.
spitefulness n malevolentia f.
spittle n spūtum nt.
splash n fragor m ♦ vt aspergere.
spleen n splēn m; (fig) stomachus m.
splendid adj splendidus, lūculentus; īnsignis; (person) amplus.
splendidly adv splendidē, optimē.
splendour n splendor m, fulgor m; (fig) lautitiī f, adparātus m.
splenetic adj stomachōsus.
splice vt iungere.
splint n ferula f.
splinter n fragmentum nt, assula f ♦ vt findere.
split vt findere ♦ vi dissilīre ♦ adj fissus ♦ n fissum nt; (fig) dissidium nt.
splutter vi balbūtīre.
spoil n praeda f ♦ vt (rob) spoliāre; (mar) corrumpere ♦ vi corrumpī.
spoiler n spoliātor m; corruptor m.
spoils npl spolia ntpl, exuviae fpl.
spoke n radius m; **put a ~ in one's wheel** inicere scrūpulum (dat).
spokesman n interpres m, ōrātor m.
spoliation n spoliātiō f, dīreptiō f.
spondee n spondēus m.
sponge n spongia f.
sponsor n spōnsor m; (fig) auctor m.
spontaneity n impulsus m, voluntās f.
spontaneous adj voluntārius.
spontaneously adv suā sponte, ultrō.
spoon n cochlear nt.
sporadic adj rārus.
sporadically adv passim.
sport n lūdus m; (in Rome) campus m; (fun) iocus m; (ridicule) lūdibrium nt; **make ~ of** illūdere (dat) ♦ vi lūdere.
sportive adj lascīvus.
sportiveness n lascīvia f.
sportsman n vēnātor m.
sportsmanlike adj honestus, generōsus.
spot n macula f; (place) locus m; (dice) pūnctum nt; **on the ~** īlicō ♦ vt maculāre; (see) animadvertere.
spotless adj integer, pūrus; (character) castus.
spotted adj maculōsus.
spouse n coniunx m/f.
spout n (of jug) ōs nt; (pipe) canālis m ♦ vi ēmicāre.
sprain vt intorquēre.
sprawl vi sē fundere.
sprawling adj fūsus.
spray n aspergō f ♦ vt aspergere.
spread vt pandere, extendere; (news) dīvulgāre; (infection) vulgāre ♦ vi patēre; (rumour) mānāre, incrēbrēscere; (feeling) glīscere.

spreadeagle vt dispandere.
spreading adj (tree) patulus.
spree n cōmissātiō f.
sprig n virga f.
sprightliness n alacritās f.
sprightly adj alacer, hilaris.
spring n (season) vēr nt; (water) fōns m; (leap)
saltus m ♦ vi (grow) crēscere, ēnāscī; (leap)
salīre; ~ **from** orīrī ex, proficīscī ex; ~ **on to**
īnsilīre in (acc); ~ **up** exorīrī, exsilīre ♦ vt: ~
a leak rīmās agere; ~ **a surprise on**
admīrātiōnem movēre (dat) ♦ adj vērnus.
springe n laqueus m.
sprinkle vt aspergere; ~ **on** īnspergere (dat).
sprint vi currere.
sprout n surculus m ♦ vi fruticārī.
spruce adj nitidus, concinnus.
sprung adj ortus, oriundus.
spume n spūma f.
spur n calcar nt; ~ **of a hill** prōminēns collis; **on
the** ~ **of the moment** ex tempore ♦ vt
incitāre; ~ **the willing horse** currentem
incitāre; ~ **on** concitāre.
spurious adj falsus, fūcōsus, fictus.
spurn vt spernere, aspernārī, respuere.
spurt vi ēmicāre; (run) sē incitāre ♦ n impetus
m.
spy n speculātor m, explōrātor m ♦ vi speculārī
♦ vt cōnspicere; ~ **out** explōrāre.
squabble n iūrgium nt ♦ vi rixārī.
squad n (MIL) decuria f.
squadron n (cavalry) āla f, turma f; (ships)
classis f.
squalid adj sordidus, dēfōrmis.
squall n procella f.
squally adj procellōsus.
squalor n sordēs fpl, squālor m.
squander vt dissipāre, disperdere, effundere.
squanderer n prōdigus m.
square n quadrātum nt; (town) ārea f ♦ vt
quadrāre; (account) subdūcere ♦ vi cōnstāre,
congruere ♦ adj quadrātus.
squash vt conterere, contundere.
squat vi subsīdere ♦ adj brevis atque obēsus.
squatter n (on land) agripeta m.
squawk vi crōcīre.
squeak n strīdor m ♦ vi strīdere.
squeal n vāgītus m ♦ vi vāgīre.
squeamish adj fastīdiōsus; **feel** ~ nauseāre,
fastīdīre.
squeamishness n fastīdium nt, nausea f.
squeeze vt premere, comprimere; ~ **out**
exprimere.
squint adj perversus ♦ n: **person with a** ~
strabō m ♦ vi strabō esse.
squinter n strabō m.
squinting adj paetus.
squire n armiger m; (landed) dominus m.
squirm vi volūtārī.
squirrel n sciūrus m.
squirt vt ēicere, effundere ♦ vi ēmicāre.
stab n ictus m, vulnus nt ♦ vt fodere, ferīre,
percutere.

stability n stabilitās f, firmitās f, cōnstantia f.
stabilize vt stabilīre, firmāre.
stable adj firmus, stabilis ♦ n stabulum nt,
equīle nt; **shut the** ~ **door after the horse is
stolen** clipeum post vulnera sūmere.
stack n acervus m ♦ vt congerere, cumulāre.
stadium n spatium nt.
staff n scīpiō m, virga f; (augur's) lituus m;
(officers) contubernālēs mpl.
stag n cervus m.
stage n pulpitum nt, proscēnium nt; (theatre)
scēna f, theātrum nt; (scene of action) campus
m; (of journey) iter nt; (of progress) gradus m ♦
adj scēnicus ♦ vt (play) dare, docēre.
stage fright n horror m.
stagger vi titubāre ♦ vt obstupefacere.
stagnant adj iners.
stagnate vi (fig) cessāre, refrīgēscere.
stagnation n cessātiō f, torpor m.
stagy adj scēnicus.
staid adj sevērus, gravis.
stain n macula f, lābēs f; (fig) dēdecus nt,
ignōminia f ♦ vt maculāre, foedāre,
contāmināre; ~ **with** īnficere (abl).
stainless adj pūrus, integer.
stair n scālae fpl, gradus mpl.
staircase n scālae fpl.
stake n pālus m, stīpes m; (pledge) pignus nt; **be
at** ~ agī, in discrīmine esse ♦ vt (wager)
dēpōnere.
stale adj obsolētus, effētus; (wine) vapidus.
stalemate n: **reach a** ~ ad incitās redigī.
stalk n (corn) calamus m; (plant) stīpes m ♦ vi
incēdere ♦ vt vēnārī, īnsidiārī (dat).
stall n (animal) stabulum nt; (seat) subsellium
nt; (shop) taberna f ♦ vt stabulāre.
stallion n equus m.
stalwart adj ingēns, rōbustus, fortis.
stamina n patientia f.
stammer n haesitātiō f ♦ vi balbūtīre.
stammering adj balbus.
stamp n fōrma f; (mark) nota f, signum nt; (of
feet) supplōsiō f ♦ vt imprimere; (coin) ferīre,
signāre; (fig) inūrere; ~ **one's feet** pedem
supplōdere; ~ **out** exstinguere.
stampede n discursus m; (fig) pavor m ♦ vi
discurrere; (fig) expavēscere.
stance n status m.
stanchion n columna f.
stand n (position) statiō f; (platform) suggestus
m; **make a** ~ resistere, restāre ♦ vi stāre;
(remain) manēre; (matters) sē habēre ♦ vt
statuere; (tolerate) ferre, tolerāre; ~ **against**
resistere (dat); ~ **aloof** abstāre; ~ **by** adsistere
(dat); (friend) adesse (dat); (promise)
praestāre; ~ **convicted** manifestum tenērī; ~
down concēdere; ~ **fast** cōnsistere; ~ **one's
ground** in locō perstāre; ~ **for** (office) petere;
(meaning) significāre; (policy) postulāre; ~ **in
awe of** in metū habēre; ~ **in need of** indigēre
(abl); ~ **on** īnsistere in (abl); ~ **on end**
horrēre; ~ **on one's dignity** gravitātem suam
tuērī; ~ **out** ēminēre, exstāre; (against)

resistere (*dat*); (*to sea*) in altum prōvehī; ~
out of the way of dēcēdere (*dat*); ~ over
(*case*) ampliāre; ~ still cōnsistere, īnsistere;
~ to reason sequī; ~ trial reum fierī; ~ up
surgere, cōnsurgere; ~ up for dēfendere,
adesse (*dat*); ~ up to respōnsāre (*dat*).

standard *n* (MIL) signum *nt*; (*measure*) nōrma *f*;
~ author scrīptor classicus *m*; up to ~ iūstus;
judge by the ~ of referre ad.

standard-bearer *n* signifer *m*.

standing *adj* perpetuus ♦ *n* status *m*; (*social*)
locus *m*, ōrdō *m*; of long ~ inveterātus; be of
long ~ inveterāscere.

stand-offish *adj* tēctus.

standstill *n*: be at a ~ haerēre, frīgēre; bring
to a ~ ad incitās redigere; come to a ~
īnsistere.

stanza *n* tetrastichon *nt*.

staple *n* uncus *m* ♦ *adj* praecipuus.

star *n* stēlla *f*, astrum *nt*; sīdus *nt*; shooting ~s
acontiae *fpl*.

starboard *adj* dexter.

starch *n* amylum *nt*.

stare *n* obtūtus *m* ♦ *vi* intentīs oculīs intuērī,
stupēre; ~ at contemplārī.

stark *adj* rigidus; simplex ♦ *adv* plānē, omnīnō.

starling *n* sturnus *m*.

starry *adj* stēllātus.

start *n* initium *nt*; (*movement*) saltus *m*;
(*journey*) profectiō *f*; by fits and ~s carptim;
have a day's ~ on diē antecēdere ♦ *vt*
incipere, īnstituere; (*game*) excitāre;
(*process*) movēre ♦ *vi* (*with fright*) resilīre;
(*journey*) proficīscī; ~ up exsilīre.

starting place *n* carcerēs *mpl*.

startle *vt* excitāre, terrēre.

starvation *n* famēs *f*.

starve *vi* fame cōnficī; (*cold*) frīgēre ♦ *vt* fame
ēnecāre.

starveling *n* famēlicus *m*.

state *n* (*condition*) status *m*, condiciō *f*; (*pomp*)
adparātus *m*; (POL) cīvitās *f*, rēs pūblica *f*; the
~ of affairs is ita sē rēs habet; I know the ~ of
affairs quō in locō rēs sit sciō; of the ~
pūblicus ♦ *adj* pūblicus ♦ *vt* adfirmāre,
expōnere, profitērī; ~ one's case causam
dīcere.

stateliness *n* māiestās *f*, gravitās *f*.

stately *adj* gravis, grandis, nōbilis.

statement *n* adfirmātiō *f*, dictum *nt*; (*witness*)
testimōnium *nt*.

state of health *n* valētūdō *f*.

state of mind *n* adfectiō *f*.

statesman *n* vir reī pūblicae gerendae
perītus *m*, cōnsilī pūblicī auctor *m*.

statesmanlike *adj* prūdēns.

statesmanship *n* cīvīlis prūdentia *f*.

static *adj* stabilis.

station *n* locus *m*; (MIL) statiō *f*; (*social*) locus *m*,
ōrdō *m* ♦ *vt* collocāre, pōnere; (*in different
places*) dispōnere.

stationary *adj* immōtus, statārius, stabilis.

statistics *n* cēnsus *m*.

statuary *n* fictor *m*.

statute *n* statua *f*, signum *nt*, imāgō *f*.

statuette *n* sigillum *nt*.

stature *n* fōrma *f*, statūra *f*.

status *n* locus *m*.

status quo *n*: restore the ~ ad integrum
restituere.

statutable *adj* lēgitimus.

statute *n* lēx *f*.

staunch *vt* (*blood*) sistere ♦ *adj* fīdus,
cōnstāns.

stave *vt* perrumpere, perfringere; ~ off
arcēre.

stay *n* firmāmentum *nt*; (*fig*) columen *nt*;
(*sojourn*) mānsiō *f*, commorātiō *f* ♦ *vt* (*prop*)
fulcīre; (*stop*) dētinēre, dēmorārī ♦ *vi*
manēre, commorārī.

stead *n* locus *m*; stand one in good ~ prōdesse
(*dat*).

steadfast *adj* firmus, stabilis, cōnstāns; ~ at
home tenēre sē domī.

steadfastly *adv* cōnstanter.

steadfastness *n* firmitās *f*, cōnstantia *f*.

steadily *adv* firmē, cōnstanter.

steadiness *n* stabilitās *f*; (*fig*) cōnstantia *f*.

steady *adj* stabilis, firmus; (*fig*) gravis,
cōnstāns.

steak *n* offa *f*.

steal *vt* surripere, fūrārī ♦ *vi*: ~ away sē
subdūcere; ~ over subrēpere (*dat*); ~ into sē
īnsinuāre in (*acc*); ~ a march on occupāre.

stealing *n* fūrtum *nt*.

stealth *n* fūrtum *nt*; by ~ fūrtim, clam.

stealthily *adv* fūrtim, clam.

stealthy *adj* fūrtīvus, clandestīnus.

steam *n* aquae vapor *m*, fūmus *m* ♦ *vi* fūmāre.

steed *n* equus *m*.

steel *n* ferrum *nt*, chalybs *m* ♦ *adj* ferreus ♦ *vt*
dūrāre; ~ oneself obdūrēscere.

steely *adj* ferreus.

steelyard *n* statēra *f*.

steep *adj* arduus, praeceps, praeruptus;
(*slope*) dēclīvis ♦ *vt* imbuere.

steeple *n* turris *f*.

steepness *n* arduum *nt*.

steer *vi* gubernāre, regere, dīrigere ♦ *n*
iuvencus *m*.

steering *n* gubernātiō *f*.

steersman *n* gubernātor *m*; rector *m*.

stellar *adj* stēllārum.

stem *n* stīpes *m*, truncus *m*; (*ship*) prōra *f* ♦ *vt*
adversārī (*dat*); ~ the tide of (*fig*) obsistere
(*dat*).

stench *n* foetor *m*.

stenographer *n* exceptor *m*, āctuārius *m*.

stenography *n* notae *fpl*.

stentorian *adj* (*voice*) ingēns.

step *n* gradus *m*; (*track*) vestīgium *nt*; (*of stair*)
gradus *m*; ~ by ~ gradātim; flight of ~s
gradus *mpl*; take a ~ gradum facere; take ~s
to ratiōnem inīre ut, vidēre ut; march in ~ in
numerum īre; out of ~ extrā numerum ♦ *vi*
gradī, incēdere; ~ aside dēcēdere; ~ back

regredī; ~ **forward** prōdīre; ~ **on** insistere (*dat*).

stepdaughter n prīvīgna f.

stepfather n vītricus m.

stepmother n noverca f.

stepson n prīvīgnus m.

stereotyped adj trītus.

sterile adj sterilis.

sterility n sterilitās f.

sterling adj integer, probus, gravis.

stern adj dūrus, sevērus; (*look*) torvus ♦ n puppis f.

sternly adv sevērē, dūriter.

sternness n sevēritās f.

stew vt coquere.

steward n prōcūrātor m; (*of estate*) vīlicus m.

stewardship n prōcūrātiō f.

stick n (*for beating*) fūstis m; (*for walking*) baculum nt ♦ vi haerēre; ~ **at nothing** ad omnia dēscendere; ~ **fast in** inhaerēre (*dat*), inhaerēscere in (*abl*); ~ **out** ēminēre; ~ **to** adhaerēre (*dat*); ~ **up** ēminēre; ~ **up for** dēfendere ♦ vt (*with glue*) conglūtināre; (*with point*) fīgere; ~ **into** īnfīgere; ~ **top on** praefīgere.

stickler n dīligēns (*gen*).

sticky adj lentus, tenāx.

stiff adj rigidus; (*difficult*) difficilis; **be** ~ rigēre.

stiffen vt rigidum facere ♦ vi rigēre.

stiffly adv rigidē.

stiff-necked adj obstinātus.

stiffness n rigor m.

stifle vt suffocāre; (*fig*) opprimere, restinguere.

stigma n nota f.

stigmatize vt notāre.

stile n saepēs f.

still adj immōtus, tranquillus, quiētus; tacitus ♦ vt lēnīre ♦ adv etiam, adhūc, etiamnum; (*past*) etiam tum; (*with compar*) etiam; (*adversative*) tamen, nihilōminus.

stillness n quiēs f; silentium nt.

stilly adj tacitus.

stilted adj (*language*) īnflātus.

stilts n grallae fpl.

stimulant n stimulus m.

stimulate vt stimulāre, acuere, exacuere, excitāre.

stimulus n stimulus m.

sting n aculeus m; (*wound*) ictus m; (*fig*) aculeus m, morsus m ♦ vt pungere, mordēre.

stingily adv sordidē.

stinginess n avāritia f, sordēs fpl, tenācitās f.

stinging adj (*words*) aculeātus, mordāx.

stingy adj sordidus, tenāx.

stink n foetor m ♦ vi foetere; ~ **of** olēre.

stinking adj foetidus.

stint n modus m; **without** ~ abundē ♦ vt circumscrībere.

stipend n mercēs f.

stipulate vt pacīscī, stipulārī.

stipulation n condiciō f, pactum nt.

stir n tumultus m ♦ vt movēre, agitāre; (*fig*)

commovēre; ~ **up** excitāre, incitāre ♦ vi movērī.

stirring adj impiger, tumultuōsus; (*speech*) ārdēns.

stitch vt suere ♦ n sūtūra f; (*in side*) dolor m.

stock n stirps f, genus nt, gēns f; (*equipment*) īnstrūmenta ntpl; (*supply*) cōpia f; (*investment*) pecūniae fpl; **live~** rēs pecuāria f ♦ vt īnstruere ♦ adj commūnis, trītus.

stockade n vallum nt.

stock dove n palumbēs m/f.

stock in trade n īnstrūmenta ntpl.

stocks n (*ship*) nāvālia ntpl; (*torture*) compedēs fpl.

stock-still adj plānē immōtus.

stocky adj brevis atque obēsus.

stodgy adj crūdus, īnsulsus.

stoic n Stōicus m ♦ adj Stōicus.

stoical adj dūrus, patiēns.

stoically adv patienter.

stoicism n Stōicōrum ratiō f, Stōicōrum disciplīna f.

stoke vt agitāre.

stole n stola f.

stolid adj stolidus.

stolidity n īnsulsitās f.

stolidly adv stolidē.

stomach n stomachus m; venter m ♦ vt patī, tolerāre.

stone n lapis m, saxum nt; (*precious*) gemma f, lapillus m; (*of fruit*) acinum nt; **leave no** ~ **unturned** omnia experīrī; **kill two birds with one** ~ ūnō saltū duōs aprōs capere; **hewn** ~ saxum quadrātum; **unhewn** ~ caementum nt ♦ vt lapidibus percutere ♦ adj lapideus; ~ **blind** plānē caecus; ~ **deaf** plānē surdus.

stonecutter n lapicīda m.

stony adj (*soil*) lapidōsus; (*path*) scrūpōsus; (*feeling*) dūrus, ferreus.

stool n sēdēcula f.

stoop vi sē dēmittere; ~ **to** dēscendere in (*acc*).

stop n mora f; (*punctuation*) pūnctum nt; **come to a** ~ īnsistere; **put a** ~ **to** comprimere, dirimere ♦ vt sistere, inhibēre, fīnīre; (*restrain*) cohibēre; (*hole*) obtūrāre; ~ **up** occlūdere, interclūdere ♦ vi dēsinere, dēsistere; (*motion*) īnsistere.

stopgap n tībīcen m.

stoppage n interclūsiō f, impedīmentum nt.

stopper n obtūrāmentum nt.

store n cōpia f; (*place*) horreum nt; (*for wine*) apothēca f; **be in** ~ **for** manēre; **set great** ~ **by** māgnī aestimāre ♦ vt condere, repōnere; ~ **away** recondere; ~ **up** repōnere, congerere.

storehouse n (*fig*) thēsaurus m.

storekeeper n cellārius m.

storeship n nāvis frūmentāria f.

storey n tabulātum nt.

stork n cicōnia f.

storm n tempestās f, procella f; **take by** ~ expugnāre ♦ vt (MIL) expugnāre ♦ vi saevīre; ~ **at** īnsectārī, invehī in (*acc*).

stormbound adj tempestāte dētentus.
stormer n expugnātor m.
storming n expugnātiō f.
stormy adj turbidus, procellōsus; (fig)
  turbulentus.
story n fābula f, nārrātiō f; (short) fābella f;
  (untrue) mendācium nt.
storyteller n nārrātor m; (liar) mendāx m.
stout adj pinguis; (brave) fortis; (strong)
  validus, rōbustus; (material) firmus.
stouthearted adj māgnanimus.
stoutly adv fortiter.
stove n camīnus m, fornāx f.
stow vt repōnere, condere; ~ **away** vi in nāvī
  dēlitēscere.
straddle vi vāricāre.
straggle vi deerrāre, pālārī.
straggler n pālāns m.
straggling adj dispersus, rārus.
straight adj rēctus, dīrēctus; (fig) apertus,
  vērāx; **in a ~ line** rēctā, ē regiōne; **set ~**
  dīrigere ♦ adv dīrēctō, rēctā.
straighten vt corrigere, extendere.
straightforward adj simplex, dīrēctus; (easy)
  facilis.
straightforwardness n simplicitās f.
straightness n (fig) integritās f.
straightway adv statim, extemplō.
strain n contentiō f; (effort) labor m; (music)
  modī mpl; (breed) genus nt ♦ vt intendere,
  contendere; (injure) nimiā contentiōne
  dēbilitāre; (liquid) dēliquāre, percōlāre ♦ vi
  ēnītī, vīrēs contendere.
strained adj (language) arcessītus.
strainer n cōlum nt.
strait adj angustus ♦ n fretum nt; ~**s** pl
  angustiae fpl.
straiten vt coartāre, contrahere; ~**ed**
  circumstances angustiae fpl.
strait-laced adj tristis, sevērus.
strand n lītus nt; (of rope) fīlum nt ♦ vt (ship)
  ēicere.
strange adj novus, īnsolitus; (foreign)
  peregrīnus; (another's) aliēnus; (ignorant)
  rudis, expers.
strangely adv mīrē, mīrum in modum.
strangeness n novitās f, īnsolentia f.
stranger n (from abroad) advena f; peregrīnus
  m; (visiting) hospes m, hospita f; (not of the
  family) externus m; (unknown) ignōtus m.
strangle vt strangulāre, laqueō gulam
  frangere.
strap n lōrum nt, habēna f.
strapping adj grandis.
stratagem n cōnsilium nt, fallācia f.
strategic adj (action) prūdēns; (position)
  idōneus.
strategist n artis bellicae perītus m.
strategy n ars imperātōria f, cōnsilia ntpl.
straw n (stalk) culmus m; (collective)
  strāmentum nt; **not care a ~ for** floccī nōn
  facere ♦ adj strāmenticius.
strawberry n frāgum nt.

strawberry tree n arbutus m.
stray vt aberrāre, deerrāre; vagārī ♦ adj
  errābundus.
streak n līnea f, macula f; (light) radius m;
  (character) vēna f ♦ vt maculāre.
stream n flūmen nt, fluvius m; **down** ~ secundō
  flūmine; **up** ~ adversō flūmine ♦ vi fluere, sē
  effundere; ~ **into** īnfluere in (acc).
streamlet n rīvus m, rīvulus m.
street n via f, platea f.
strength n vīrēs fpl; (of material) firmitās f; (fig)
  rōbur nt, nervī mpl; (MIL) numerus m; **know
  the enemy's** ~ quot sint hostēs scīre; **on the** ~
  of frētus (abl).
strengthen vt firmāre, corrōborāre; (position)
  mūnīre.
strenuous adj impiger, strēnuus, sēdulus.
strenuously adv impigrē, strēnuē.
strenuousness n industria f.
stress n (words) ictus m; (meaning) vīs f;
  (importance) mōmentum nt; (difficulty) labor
  m; **lay great ~ on** in māgnō discrīmine pōnere
  ♦ vt exprimere.
stretch n spatium nt, tractus m; **at a ~** sine ullā
  intermissiōne ♦ vt tendere, intendere;
  (length) prōdūcere, extendere; (facts) in
  māius crēdere; ~ **a point** indulgēre; ~ **before**
  obtendere; ~ **forth** porrigere; ~ **oneself** (on
  ground) sternī; ~ **out** porrigere, extendere ♦
  vi extendī, patēscere.
strew vt (things) sternere; (place) cōnsternere.
stricken adj saucius.
strict adj (defined) ipse, certus; (severe)
  sevērus, rigidus; (accurate) dīligēns.
strictly adv sevērē; dīligenter; ~ **speaking**
  scīlicet, immo.
strictness n sevēritās f; dīligentia f.
stricture n vītuperātiō f.
stride n passus m; **make great ~s** (fig) multum
  prōficere ♦ vi incēdere, ingentēs gradūs
  ferre.
strident adj asper.
strife n discordia f, pugna f.
strike vt ferīre, percutere; (instrument)
  pellere, pulsāre; (sail) subdūcere; (tent)
  dētendere; (mind) venīre in (acc); (camp)
  movēre; (fear into) incutere in (acc); ~ **against**
  offendere; ~ **out** dēlēre; ~ **up** (music)
  incipere; ~ **a bargain** pacīscī; **be struck**
  vāpulāre ♦ vi (work) cessāre.
striking adj īnsignis, īnsignītus, ēgregius.
strikingly adv īnsignītē.
string n (cord) resticula f; (succession) seriēs f;
  (instrument) nervus m; (bow) nervus m; **have
  two ~s to one's bow** duplicī spē ūtī ♦ vt (bow)
  intendere; (together) coniungere.
stringency n sevēritās f.
stringent adj sevērus.
strip vt nūdāre, spoliāre, dēnūdāre; ~ **off**
  exuere; (leaves) stringere, dēstringere ♦ n
  lacinia f.
stripe n virga f; (on tunic) clāvus m; ~**s** pl
  verbera ntpl.

striped *adj* virgātus.

stripling *n* adulescentulus *m*.

strive *vi* nītī, ēnītī, contendere; (*contend*) certāre.

stroke *n* ictus *m*; (*lightning*) fulmen *nt*; (*oar*) pulsus *m*; (*pen*) līnea *f*; ~ **of luck** fortūna secunda *f* ♦ *vt* mulcēre, dēmulcēre.

stroll *vi* deambulāre, spatiārī.

strong *adj* fortis, validus; (*health*) rōbustus, firmus; (*material*) firmus; (*smell*) gravis; (*resources*) pollēns, potēns; (*feeling*) ācer, māgnus; (*language*) vehemēns, probrōsus; **be** ~ valēre; **be twenty** ~ vīgintī esse numerō.

strongbox *n* arca *f*.

stronghold *n* arx *f*.

strongly *adv* validē, vehementer, fortiter, ācriter, graviter.

strong-minded *adj* pertināx, cōnstāns.

strophe *n* stropha *f*.

structure *n* aedificium *nt*; (*form*) structūra *f*; (*arrangement*) compositiō *f*.

struggle *n* (*effort*) cōnātus *m*; (*fight*) pugna *f*, certāmen *nt* ♦ *vi* nītī; certāre, contendere; (*fight*) luctārī; ~ **upwards** ēnītī.

strut *vi* māgnificē incēdere.

stubble *n* stipula *f*.

stubborn *adj* pertināx, pervicāx.

stubbornly *adv* pertināciter, pervicāciter.

stubbornness *n* pertinācia *f*, pervicācia *f*.

stucco *n* gypsum *nt*.

stud *n* clāvus *m*; (*horses*) equī *mpl*.

studded *adj* distinctus.

student *n* discipulus *m*; **be a** ~ **of** studēre (*dat*).

studied *adj* meditātus, accūrātus; (*language*) exquīsītus.

studio *n* officīna *f*.

studious *adj* litterīs dēditus, litterārum studiōsus; (*careful*) attentus.

studiously *adv* dē industriā.

study *vt* studēre (*dat*); (*prepare*) meditārī; ~ **under** audīre ♦ *n* studium *nt*; (*room*) bibliothēca *f*.

stuff *n* māteria *f*; (*cloth*) textile *nt* ♦ *vt* farcīre, refercīre; (*with food*) sagīnāre.

stuffing *n* sagina *f*; (*of cushion*) tōmentum *nt*.

stultify *vt* ad inritum redigere.

stumble *vi* offendere; ~ **upon** incidere in (*acc*), offendere.

stumbling block *n* offēnsiō *f*.

stump *n* stīpes *m*.

stun *vt* stupefacere; (*fig*) obstupefacere, cōnfundere.

stunned *adj* attonitus.

stunt *vt* corporis auctum inhibēre.

stunted *adj* curtus.

stupefaction *n* stupor *m*.

stupefied *adj*: **be** ~ stupēre, obstupefacere.

stupefy *vt* obstupefacere.

stupendous *adj* mīrus, mīrificus.

stupid *adj* stultus, hebes, ineptus.

stupidity *n* stultitia *f*.

stupidly *adv* stultē, ineptē.

stupor *n* stupor *m*.

sturdily *adv* fortiter.

sturdiness *n* rōbur *nt*, firmitās *f*.

sturdy *adj* fortis, rōbustus.

sturgeon *n* acipēnser *m*.

stutter *vi* balbūtire.

stuttering *adj* balbus.

sty *n* hara *f*.

style *n* (*kind*) genus *nt*, ratiō *f*; (*of dress*) habitus *m*; (*of prose*) ēlocūtiō *f*, ōrātiō *f*; (*pen*) stilus *m* ♦ *vt* appellāre.

stylish *adj* ēlegāns, lautus, expolītus.

stylishly *adv* ēleganter.

suasion *n* suāsiō *f*.

suave *adj* blandus, urbānus.

suavity *n* urbānitās *f*.

subaltern *n* succenturiō *m*.

subdivide *vt* dīvidere.

subdivision *n* pars *f*, mōmentum *nt*.

subdue *vt* subigere, dēvincere, redigere, domāre; (*fig*) cohibēre.

subdued *adj* dēmissus, summissus.

subject *n* (*person*) cīvis *m/f*; (*matter*) rēs *f*; (*theme*) locus *m*, argūmentum *nt* ♦ *adj* subiectus; ~ **to** obnoxius (*dat*) ♦ *vt* subicere; obnoxium reddere.

subjection *n* servitūs *f*.

subjective *adj* proprius.

subject matter *n* māteria *f*.

subjoin *vt* subicere, subiungere.

subjugate *vt* subigere, dēbellāre, domāre.

sublime *adj* sublīmis, ēlātus, excelsus.

sublimely *adv* excelsē.

sublimity *n* altitūdō *f*, ēlātiō *f*.

submarine *adj* submersus.

submerge *vt* dēmergere; (*flood*) inundāre ♦ *vi* sē dēmergere.

submersed *adj* submersus.

submission *n* obsequium *nt*, servitium *nt*; (*fig*) patientia *f*.

submissive *adj* submissus, docilis, obtemperāns.

submissively *adv* submissē, oboedienter, patienter.

submit *vi* sē dēdere; ~ **to** pārēre (*dat*), obtemperāre (*dat*), patī, subīre ♦ *vt* (*proposal*) referre.

subordinate *adj* subiectus, secundus ♦ *vt* subiungere, subicere.

suborn *vt* subicere, subōrnāre.

subpoena *vt* testimōnium dēnūntiāre (*dat*).

subscribe *vt* (*name*) subscrībere; (*money*) cōnferre.

subscription *n* collātiō *f*.

subsequent *adj* sequēns, posterior.

subsequently *adv* posteā, mox.

subserve *vt* subvenīre (*dat*), commodāre.

subservience *n* obsequium *nt*.

subservient *adj* obsequēns; (*thing*) ūtilis, commodus.

subside *vi* dēsīdere, resīdere; (*fever*) dēcēdere; (*wind*) cadere; (*passion*) dēfervēscere.

subsidence *n* lābēs *f*.

subsidiary *adj* subiectus, secundus.
subsidize *vt* pecūniās suppeditāre (*dat*).
subsidy *n* pecūniae *fpl*, vectīgal *nt*.
subsist *vi* cōnstāre, sustentārī.
subsistence *n* vīctus *m*.
substance *n* (*matter*) rēs *f*, corpus *nt*; (*essence*) nātūra *f*; (*gist*) summa *f*; (*reality*) rēs *f*; (*wealth*) opēs *fpl*.
substantial *adj* solidus; (*real*) vērus; (*important*) gravis; (*rich*) opulentus, dīves.
substantially *adv* rē; māgnā ex parte.
substantiate *vt* cōnfirmāre.
substitute *vt* subicere, repōnere, substituere ♦ *n* vicārius *m*.
substratum *n* fundāmentum *nt*.
subterfuge *n* latebra *f*, perfugium *nt*.
subterranean *adj* subterrāneus.
subtle *adj* (*fine*) subtīlis; (*shrewd*) acūtus, astūtus.
subtlety *n* subtīlitās *f*; acūmen *nt*, astūtia *f*.
subtly *adv* subtīliter; acūtē, astūtē.
subtract *vt* dētrahere, dēmere; (*money*) dēdūcere.
subtraction *n* dētractiō *f*, dēductiō *f*.
suburb *n* suburbium *nt*.
suburban *adj* suburbānus.
subvention *n* pecūniae *fpl*.
subversion *n* ēversiō *f*, ruīna *f*.
subversive *adj* sēditiōsus.
subvert *vt* ēvertere, subruere.
subverter *n* ēversor *m*.
succeed *vi* (*person*) rem bene gerere; (*activity*) prosperē ēvenīre; ~ **in obtaining** impetrāre ♦ *vt* īnsequī, excipere, succēdere (*dat*).
success *n* bonus ēventus *m*, rēs bene gesta *f*.
successful *adj* fēlīx; (*thing*) secundus; **be ~** rem bene gerere; (*play*) stāre.
successfully *adv* fēlīciter, prosperē, bene.
succession *n* (*coming next*) successiō *f*; (*line*) seriēs *f*, ōrdō *m*; **alternate ~** vicissitūdō *f*; **in ~** deinceps, ex ōrdine.
successive *adj* continuus, perpetuus.
successively *adv* deinceps, ex ōrdine; (*alternately*) vicissim.
successor *n* successor *m*.
succinct *adj* brevis, pressus.
succinctly *adv* breviter, pressē.
succour *n* auxilium *nt*, subsidium *nt* ♦ *vt* subvenīre (*dat*), succurrere (*dat*), opem ferre (*dat*).
succulence *n* sūcus *m*.
succulent *adj* sūcidus.
succumb *vi* succumbere, dēficere.
such *adj* tālis, ēiusmodī, hūiusmodī; (*size*) tantus; **at ~ a time** id temporis; ~ **great** tantus.
suchlike *adj* hūiusmodī, ēiusdem generis.
suck *vt* sūgere; ~ **in** sorbēre; ~ **up** exsorbēre, ēbibere.
sucker *n* surculus *m*.
sucking *adj* (*child*) lactēns.
suckle *vt* nūtrīcārī, mammam dare (*dat*).
suckling *n* lactēns *m/f*.

sudden *adj* subitus, repentīnus.
suddenly *adv* subitō, repente.
sue *vt* in iūs vocāre, lītem intendere (*dat*); ~ **for** rogāre, petere, ōrāre.
suffer *vt* patī, ferre, tolerāre; (*injury*) accipere; (*loss*) facere; (*permit*) patī, sinere ♦ *vi* dolōre afficī; ~ **defeat** clādem accipere; ~ **from** labōrāre ex, afficī (*abl*); ~ **for** poenās dare (*gen*).
sufferable *adj* tolerābilis.
sufferance *n* patientia *f*, tolerantia *f*.
suffering *n* dolor *m*.
suffice *vi* sufficere, suppetere.
sufficiency *n* satis.
sufficient *adj* idōneus, satis (*gen*).
sufficiently *adv* satis.
suffocate *vt* suffocāre.
suffrage *n* suffrāgium *nt*.
suffuse *vt* suffundere.
sugar *n* saccharon *nt*.
suggest *vt* admonēre, inicere, subicere; ~ **itself** occurrere.
suggestion *n* admonitiō *f*; **at the ~ of** admonitū (*gen*); **at my ~** mē auctōre.
suicidal *adj* fūnestus.
suicide *n* mors voluntāria *f*; **commit ~** mortem sibī cōnscīscere.
suit *n* (*law*) līs *f*, āctiō *f*; (*clothes*) vestītus *m* ♦ *vt* convenīre (*dat*), congruere (*dat*); (*dress*) sedēre (*dat*), decēre; **it ~s** decet; **to ~ me** dē meā sententiā.
suitability *n* convenientia *f*.
suitable *adj* aptus (+ *acc*), idōneus (+ *acc*).
suitably *adv* aptē, decenter.
suite *n* comitēs *mpl*, comitātus *m*.
suitor *n* procus *m*, amāns *m*.
sulk *vi* aegrē ferre, mōrōsum esse.
sulky *adj* mōrōsus, tristis.
sullen *adj* tristis, mōrōsus.
sullenness *n* mōrōsitās *f*.
sully *vt* īnfuscāre, contāmināre.
sulphur *n* sulfur *nt*.
sultriness *n* aestus *m*.
sultry *adj* aestuōsus.
sum *n* summa *f*; ~ **of money** pecūnia *f* ♦ *vt* subdūcere, computāre; ~ **up** summātim dēscrībere; **to ~ up** ūnō verbō, quid plūra?
summarily *adv* strictim, summātim; sine morā.
summarize *vt* summātim dēscrībere.
summary *n* summārium *nt*, epitomē *f* ♦ *adj* subitus, praesēns.
summer *n* aestās *f* ♦ *adj* aestīvus; **of ~** aestīvus.
summit *n* vertex *m*, culmen *nt*; (*fig*) fastīgium *nt*; **the ~ of** summus.
summon *vt* arcessere; (*meeting*) convocāre; (*witness*) citāre; ~ **up courage** animum sūmere.
summons *n* (*law*) vocātiō *f* ♦ *vt* in iūs vocāre, diem dīcere (*dat*).
sumptuary *adj* sūmptuārius.
sumptuous *adj* sūmptuōsus, adparātus,

māgnificus, lautus.

sumptuously adv sūmptuōsē, māgnificē.

sun n sōl m ♦ vt: ~ **oneself** aprīcārī.

sunbeam n radius m.

sunburnt adj adūstus.

sunder vt sēparāre, dīvidere.

sundial n sōlārium nt.

sundry adj dīversī, complūrēs.

sunlight n sōl m.

sunlit adj aprīcus.

sunny adj aprīcus, serēnus.

sunrise n sōlis ortus m.

sunset n sōlis occāsus m.

sunshade n umbella f.

sunshine n sōl m.

sup vi cēnāre.

superabundance n abundantia f.

superabundant adj nimius.

superabundantly adv satis superque.

superannuated adj ēmeritus.

superb adj māgnificus.

superbly adv māgnificē.

supercilious adj adrogāns, superbus.

superciliously adv adroganter, superbē.

superciliousness n adrogantia f, fastus m.

supererogation n: of ~ ultrō factus.

superficial adj levis; **acquire a ~ knowledge of** prīmīs labrīs gustare.

superficiality n levitās f.

superficially adv leviter, strictim.

superfluity n abundantia f.

superfluous adj supervacāneus, nimius; **be ~** redundāre.

superhuman adj dīvīnus, hūmānō māior.

superimpose vt superimpōnere.

superintend vt prōcūrāre, praeesse (dat).

superintendence n cūra f.

superintendent n cūrātor m, praefectus m.

superior adj melior, amplior; **be ~** praestāre, superāre ♦ n prīnceps m, praefectus m.

superiority n praestantia f; **have the ~** superāre; (in numbers) plūrēs esse.

superlative adj ēgregius, optimus.

supernatural adj dīvīnus.

supernaturally adv dīvīnitus.

supernumerary adj adscrīptīcius; **~ soldiers** accēnsī mpl.

superscription n titulus m.

supersede vt succēdere (dat), in locum succēdere (gen); **~ gold with silver** prō aurō argentum suppōnere.

superstition n rēligiō f, superstitiō f.

superstitious adj rēligiōsus, superstitiōsus.

supervene vi īnsequī, succēdere.

supervise vt prōcūrāre.

supervision n cūra f.

supervisor n cūrātor m.

supine adj supīnus; (fig) neglegēns, segnis.

supinely adv segniter.

supper n cēna f; **after ~** cēnātus.

supperless adj iēiūnus.

supplant vt praevertere.

supple adj flexibilis, mollis.

supplement n appendix f ♦ vt amplificāre.

supplementary adj additus.

suppleness n mollitia f.

suppliant n supplex m/f.

supplicate vt supplicāre, obsecrāre.

supplication n precēs fpl.

supplies npl commeātus m.

supply n cōpia f ♦ vt suppeditāre, praebēre; (loss) supplēre.

support n firmāmentum nt; (help) subsidium nt, adiūmentum nt; (food) alimenta ntpl; (of party) favor m; (of needy) patrōcinium nt; **I ~** subsidiō sum (dat); **lend ~ to rumours** alimenta rūmōribus addere ♦ vt fulcīre; (living) sustinēre, sustentāre; (with help) adiuvāre, opem ferre (dat); (at law) adesse (dat).

supportable adj tolerābilis.

supporter n fautor m; (at trial) advocātus m; (of proposal) auctor m.

supporting cast n adiūtōrēs mpl.

suppose vi (assume) pōnere; (think) existimāre, opīnārī, crēdere; **~ it is true** fac vērum esse.

supposedly adv ut fāma est.

supposing conj sī; (for the sake of argument) sī iam.

supposition n opīniō f; **on this ~** hōc positō.

supposititious adj subditus, subditīvus.

suppress vt opprimere, comprimere; (knowledge) cēlāre, reticēre; (feelings) coercēre, reprimere.

suppression n (of fact) reticentia f.

supremacy n imperium nt, dominātus m, prīncipātus m.

supreme adj summus; **be ~** dominārī; **~ command** imperium nt.

supremely adv ūnicē, plānē.

sure adj certus; (fact) explōrātus; (friend) fīdus; **be ~ of** compertum habēre; **feel ~** persuāsum habēre, haud scīre an; prō certō habēre; **make ~ of** (fact) comperīre; (action) efficere ut; **to be ~** quidem; **~ enough** rē vērā.

surely adv certō, certē, nonne; (tentative) scīlicet, sānē; **~ you do not think?** num putās?; **~ not** num.

surety n (person) vās m, praes m, spōnsor m; (deposit) fīdūcia f; **be ~ for** spondēre prō.

surf n fluctus m.

surface n superficiēs f; **~ of the water** summa aqua.

surfeit n satietās f ♦ vt satiāre, explēre.

surge n aestus m, fluctus m ♦ vi tumēscere.

surgeon n chīrūrgus m.

surgery n chīrūrgia f.

surlily adv mōrōsē.

surliness n mōrōsitās f.

surly adj mōrōsus, difficilis.

surmise n coniectūra f ♦ vi suspicārī, conicere, augurārī.

surmount vt superāre.

surmountable adj superābilis.

surname n cognōmen nt.

surpass vt excellere, exsuperāre, antecēdere.

surpassing *adj* excellēns.
surplus *n* reliquum *nt*; (*money*) pecūniae residuae *fpl*.
surprise *n* admīrātiō *f*; (*cause*) rēs inopīnāta *f*; **take by ~** dēprehendere ♦ *adj* subitus ♦ *vt* dēprehendere; (*MIL*) opprimere; **be ~d** dēmīrārī; **be ~d at** admīrārī.
surprising *adj* mīrus, mīrābilis.
surprisingly *adv* mīrē, mīrābiliter.
surrender *vt* dēdere, trādere, concēdere ♦ *vi* sē dēdere; **~ unconditionally to** sē suaque omnia potestātī permittere (*gen*) ♦ *n* dēditiō *f*; (*legal*) cessiō *f*; **unconditional ~** permissiō *f*.
surreptitious *adj* fūrtīvus.
surreptitiously *adv* fūrtim, clam; **get in ~** inrēpere in (*acc*).
surround *vt* circumdare, cingere, circumvenīre, circumfundere.
surrounding *adj* circumiectus; **~s** *n* vīcīnia *f*.
survey *vt* contemplārī, cōnsīderāre; (*land*) mētārī ♦ *n* contemplātiō *f*; (*land*) mēnsūra *f*.
surveyor *n* fīnītor *m*, agrīmēnsor *m*, mētātor *m*.
survival *n* salūs *f*.
survive *vt* superāre ♦ *vt* superesse (*dat*).
survivor *n* superstes *m/f*.
susceptibility *n* mollitia *f*.
susceptible *adj* mollis.
suspect *vt* suspicārī; **be ~ed** in suspiciōnem venīre.
suspend *vt* suspendere; (*activity*) differre; (*person*) locō movēre; **be ~ed** pendēre.
suspense *n* dubitātiō *f*; **be in ~** animī pendēre, haerēre.
suspicion *n* suspiciō *f*; **direct ~ to** suspiciōnem adiungere ad.
suspicious *adj* (*suspecting*) suspiciōsus; (*suspected*) dubius, anceps.
sustain *vt* (*weight*) sustinēre; (*life*) alere, sustentāre; (*hardship*) ferre, sustinēre; (*the part of*) agere.
sustenance *n* alimentum *nt*, vīctus *m*.
sutler *n* lixa *m*.
suzerain *n* dominus *m*.
swaddling clothes *n* incūnābula *ntpl*.
swagger *vi* sē iactāre.
swaggerer *n* homō glōriōsus *m*.
swallow *n* hirundō *f* ♦ *vt* dēvorāre; **~ up** absorbēre.
swamp *n* palūs *f* ♦ *vt* opprimere.
swampy *adj* ūlīginōsus.
swan *n* cycnus *m*; **~'s** cycnēus.
swank *vi* sē iactāre.
sward *n* caespes *m*.
swarm *n* exāmen *nt*; (*fig*) nūbēs *f* ♦ *vi*: **~ round** circumfundī.
swarthy *adj* fuscus, aquilus.
swathe *vt* conligāre.
sway *n* dīciō *f*, imperium *nt*; **bring under one's ~** suae dīciōnis facere ♦ *vt* regere ♦ *vi* vacillāre.
swear *vi* iūrāre; **~ allegiance to** iūrāre in verba (*gen*).

sweat *n* sūdor *m* ♦ *vi* sūdāre.
sweep *vt* verrere; **~ away** rapere; **~ out** ēverrere.
sweet *adj* dulcis, suāvis.
sweeten *vt* dulcem reddere.
sweetheart *n* dēliciae *fpl*.
sweetly *adv* dulciter, suāviter.
sweetness *n* dulcitūdō *f*, suāvitās *f*.
sweet-tempered *adj* suāvis, cōmis.
swell *n* tumor *m* ♦ *vi* tumēre, tumēscere; (*fig*) glīscere ♦ *vt* inflāre.
swelling *adj* tumidus ♦ *n* tumor *m*.
swelter *vi* aestū labōrāre.
swerve *vi* dēclīnāre, dēvertere ♦ *n* dēclīnātiō *f*.
swift *adj* celer, vēlōx, incitātus.
swiftly *adv* celeriter, vēlōciter.
swiftness *n* celeritās *f*, vēlōcitās *f*.
swill *vt* (*rinse*) colluere; (*drink*) ēpōtāre.
swim *vi* nāre, innāre; (*place*) natāre; **~ across** trānāre; **~ ashore** ēnāre; **~ to** adnāre.
swimming *n* natātiō *f*.
swindle *vt* circumvenīre, verba dare (*dat*) ♦ *n* fraus *f*.
swine *n* sūs *m/f*.
swineherd *n* subulcus *m*.
swing *n* (*motion*) oscillātiō *f* ♦ *vi* oscillāre ♦ *vt* lībrāre.
swinish *adj* obscēnus.
swirl *n* vertex *m* ♦ *vi* volūtārī.
switch *n* virga *f* ♦ *vt* flectere, torquēre.
swivel *n* cardō *f*.
swollen *adj* tumidus, turgidus, īnflātus.
swoon *n* dēfectiō *f* ♦ *vi* intermorī.
swoop *n* impetus *m* ♦ *vi* lābī; **~ down on** involāre in (*acc*).
sword *n* gladius *m*; **put to the ~** occīdere; **with fire and ~** ferrō ignīque.
swordsman *n* gladiātor *m*.
sworn *adj* iūrātus.
sybarite *n* dēlicātus *m*.
sycophancy *n* adsentātiō *f*, adūlātiō *f*.
sycophant *n* adsentātor *m*, adūlātor *m*.
syllable *n* syllaba *f*.
syllogism *n* ratiōcinātiō *f*.
sylvan *adj* silvestris.
symbol *n* signum *nt*, īnsigne *nt*.
symmetrical *adj* concinnus, aequus.
symmetry *n* concinnitās *f*, aequitās *f*.
sympathetic *adj* concors, misericors.
sympathetically *adv* misericorditer.
sympathize *vi* cōnsentīre; **~ with** miserērī (*gen*).
sympathy *n* concordia *f*, cōnsēnsus *m*; misericordia *f*.
symphony *n* concentus *m*.
symptom *n* signum *nt*, indicium *nt*.
syndicate *n* societās *f*.
synonym *n* verbum idem dēclārāns *nt*.
synonymous *adj* idem dēclārāns.
synopsis *n* summārium *nt*.
syringe *n* clystēr *m*.
system *n* ratiō *f*, fōrmula *f*; (*PHILOS*) disciplīna *f*.

systematic adj ōrdinātus, cōnstāns.
systematically adv ratiōne, ōrdine.
systematize vt in ōrdinem redigere.

T, t

tabernacle n tabernāculum nt.
table n mēnsa f; (inscribed) tabula f; (list) index m; **at ~** inter cēnam; **turn the ~s on** pār parī referre.
tablet n tabula f, tabella f.
taboo n rēligiō f.
tabulate vt in ōrdinem redigere.
tacit adj tacitus.
tacitly adv tacitē.
taciturn adj taciturnus.
taciturnity n taciturnitās f.
tack n clāvulus m; (of sail) pēs m ♦ vt: **~ on** adsuere ♦ vi (ship) reciprocārī, nāvem flectere.
tackle n armāmenta ntpl ♦ vt adgredī.
tact n iūdicium nt, commūnis sēnsus m, hūmānitās f.
tactful adj prūdēns, hūmānus.
tactfully adv prūdenter, hūmāniter.
tactician n reī mīlitāris perītus m.
tactics n rēs mīlitāris f, bellī ratiō f.
tactless adj ineptus.
tactlessly adv ineptē.
tadpole n rānunculus m.
tag n appendicula f.
tail n cauda f; **turn ~** terga vertere.
tailor n vestītor m.
taint n lābēs f, vitium nt ♦ vt inquināre, contāmināre, īnficere.
take vt capere, sūmere; (auspices) habēre; (disease) contrahere; (experience) ferre; (fire) concipere; (meaning) accipere, interpretārī; (in the act) dēprehendere; (person) dūcere; **~ after** similem esse (dat, gen); **~ across** trānsportāre; **~ arms** arma sūmere; **~ away** dēmere, auferre, adimere, abdūcere; **~ back** recipere; **~ by storm** expugnāre; **~ care that** curāre ut/ne (+ subj); **~ down** dētrahere; (in writing) exscrībere; **~ for** habēre prō; **~ hold of** prehendere; **~ in** (as guest) recipere; (information) percipere, comprehendere; (with deceit) dēcipere; **~ in hand** incipere, suscipere; **~ off** dēmere; (clothes) exuere; **~ on** suscipere; **~ out** eximere, extrahere; (from store) prōmere; **~ over** excipere; **~ place** fierī, accidere; **~ prisoner** capere; **~ refuge in** cōnfugere ad (+ infin); **~ the field** in aciem dēscendere; **~ to** sē dēdere (dat), amāre; **~ to oneself** suscipere; **~ up** sūmere,

tollere; (task) incipere, adgredī ad; (in turn) excipere; (room) occupāre; **~ upon oneself** recipere, sibī sūmere.
taking adj grātus ♦ n (MIL) expugnātiō f.
tale n fābula f, fābella f.
talent n (money) talentum nt; (ability) ingenium nt, indolēs f.
talented adj ingeniōsus.
talk n sermō m; (with another) colloquium nt; **common ~** fāma f; **be the ~ of the town** in ōre omnium esse ♦ vi loquī; (to one) colloquī cum; **~ down to** ad intellectum audientis dēscendere; **~ over** cōnferre, disserere dē.
talkative adj loquāx.
talkativeness n loquācitās f.
tall adj prōcērus, grandis.
tallness n prōcēritās f.
tallow n sēbum nt.
tally n tessera f ♦ vi congruere.
talon n unguis m.
tamarisk n myrīca f.
tambourine n tympanum nt.
tame vt domāre, mānsuēfacere ♦ adj mānsuētus; (character) ignāvus; (language) īnsulsus, frīgidus.
tamely adv ignāvē, lentē.
tameness n mānsuētūdō f; (fig) lentitūdō f.
tamer n domitor m.
tamper vi: **~ with** (person) sollicitāre; (writing) interpolāre.
tan vt imbuere.
tang n sapor m.
tangible adj tāctilis.
tangle n nōdus m ♦ vt implicāre.
tank n lacus m.
tanned adj (by sun) adūstus.
tanner n coriārius m.
tantalize vt lūdere.
tantamount adj pār, īdem.
tantrum n īra f.
tap n epitonium nt; (touch) plāga f ♦ vt (cask) relinere; (hit) ferīre.
tape n taenia f.
taper n cēreus m ♦ vi fastīgārī.
tapestry n aulaea ntpl.
tar n pix f.
tardily adv tardē, lentē.
tardiness n tarditās f, segnitia f.
tardy adj tardus, lentus.
tare n lolium nt.
targe n parma f.
target n scopus m.
tariff n portōrium nt.
tarn n lacus m.
tarnish vt īnfuscāre, inquināre ♦ vi īnfuscārī.
tarry vi morārī, commorārī, cunctārī.
tart adj acidus, asper ♦ n scriblīta f.
tartly adv acerbē.
tartness n asperitās f.
task n pēnsum nt, opus nt, negōtium nt; **take to ~** obiūrgāre.
taskmaster n dominus m.
tassel n fimbriae fpl.

taste n (*sense*) gustātus m; (*flavour*) sapor m; (*artistic*) iūdicium nt, ēlegantia f; (*for rhetoric*) aurēs fpl; **of ~** doctus; **in good ~** ēlegāns ♦ vt gustāre, dēgustāre ♦ vi sapere; **~ of** resipere.
tasteful adj ēlegāns.
tastefully adv ēleganter.
tastefulness n ēlegantia f.
tasteless adj īnsulsus, inēlegāns.
tastelessly adv īnsulsē, inēleganter.
tastelessness n īnsulsitās f.
taster n praegustātor m.
tasty adj dulcis.
tattered adj pannōsus.
tatters n pannī mpl.
tattoo vt compungere.
taunt n convīcium nt, probrum nt ♦ vt exprobrāre, obicere (*dat of pers, acc of charge*).
taunting adj contumēliōsus.
tauntingly adv contumēliōsē.
taut adj intentus; **draw ~** addūcere.
tavern n taberna f, hospitium nt.
tawdry adj vīlis.
tawny adj fulvus.
tax n vectīgal nt, tribūtum nt; **a 5 per cent ~** vīcēsima f; **free from ~** immūnis ♦ vt vectīgal impōnere (*dat*); (*strength*) contendere; **~ with** (*charge*) obicere (*acc & dat*), īnsimulāre.
taxable adj vectīgālis.
taxation n vectīgālia ntpl.
tax collector n exāctor m.
tax farmer n pūblicānus m.
taxpayer n assiduus m.
teach vt docēre, ērudīre, īnstituere; (*thoroughly*) ēdocēre; (*pass*) discere; **~ your grandmother** sūs Minervam.
teachable adj docilis.
teacher n magister m, magistra f, doctor m; (PHILOS) praeceptor m; (*of literature*) grammaticus m; (*of rhetoric*) rhētor m.
teaching n doctrīna f, disciplīna f.
team n (*animals*) iugum nt.
tear n lacrima f; **shed ~s** lacrimās effundere ♦ vt scindere; **~ down** revellere; **~ in pieces** dīlaniāre, discerpere, lacerāre; **~ off** abscindere, dēripere; **~ open** rescindere; **~ out** ēvellere; **~ up** convellere.
tearful adj flēbilis.
tease vt lūdere, inrītāre.
teat n mamma f.
technical adj (*term*) proprius.
technique n ars f.
tedious adj longus, lentus, odiōsus.
tediously adv molestē.
tedium n taedium nt, molestia f.
teem vi abundāre.
teeming adj fēcundus, refertus.
teens n: **in one's ~** adulescentulus.
teethe vi dentīre.
tell vt (*story*) nārrāre; (*person*) dīcere (*dat*); (*number*) ēnumerāre; (*inform*) certiōrem facere; (*difference*) intellegere; (*order*) iubēre (+ acc and infin), imperāre (+ ut/ne and subj);

~ the truth vēra dīcere; **~ lies** mentior ♦ vi valēre; **~ the difference between** discernere; **I cannot ~** nesciō.
telling adj validus.
temerity n temeritās f.
temper n animus m, ingenium nt; (*bad*) īra f, īrācundia f; (*of metal*) temperātiō f ♦ vt temperāre; (*fig*) moderārī (*dat*).
temperament n animī habitus m, animus m.
temperamental adj incōnstāns.
temperance n temperantia f, continentia f.
temperate adj temperātus, moderātus, sobrius.
temperately adv moderātē.
temperature n calor m, frīgus nt; **mild ~** temperiēs f.
tempest n tempestās f, procella f.
tempestuous adj procellōsus.
temple n templum nt, aedēs f; (*head*) tempus nt.
temporal adj hūmānus, profānus.
temporarily adv ad tempus.
temporary adj brevis.
temporize vi temporis causā facere, tergiversārī.
tempt vt sollicitāre, pellicere, invītāre.
temptation n illecebra f.
tempter n impulsor m.
ten num decem; **~ each** dēnī; **~ times** deciēns.
tenable adj inexpugnābilis, stabilis, certus.
tenacious adj tenāx, firmus.
tenaciously adv tenāciter.
tenacity n tenācitās f.
tenant n inquilīnus m, habitātor m; (*on land*) colōnus m.
tenantry n colōnī mpl.
tend vi spectāre, pertinēre ♦ vt cūrāre, colere.
tendency n inclīnātiō f, voluntās f.
tender adj tener, mollis ♦ vt dēferre, offerre.
tenderhearted adj misericors.
tenderly adv indulgenter.
tenderness n indulgentia f, mollitia f.
tendon n nervus m.
tendril n clāviculus m.
tenement n habitātiō f; **block of ~s** īnsula f.
tenet n dogma nt, dēcrētum nt.
tennis court n sphaeristērium nt.
tenor n (*course*) tenor m; (*purport*) sententia f.
tense adj intentus ♦ n tempus nt.
tension n intentiō f.
tent n tabernāculum nt; (*general's*) praetōrium nt.
tentacle n bracchium nt.
tentatively adv experiendō.
tenterhooks n: **on ~** animī suspēnsus.
tenth adj decimus; **for the ~ time** decimum; **men of the ~ legion** decumānī mpl.
tenuous adj rārus.
tenure n possessiō f.
tepid adj tepidus; **be ~** tepēre.
tergiversation n tergiversātiō f.
term n (*limit*) terminus m; (*period*) spatium nt; (*word*) verbum nt ♦ vt appellāre, nuncupāre.

terminate vt termināre, fīnīre ♦ vi dēsinere; (*words*) cadere.
termination n fīnis m, terminus m.
terminology n vocābula ntpl.
terms npl condiciō f, lēx f; **propose ~** condiciōnem ferre; **be on good ~ in grātiā** esse; **we come to ~** inter nōs convenit.
terrain n ager m.
terrestrial adj terrestris.
terrible adj terribilis, horribilis, horrendus.
terribly adv horrendum in modum.
terrific adj formīdolōsus; vehemēns.
terrify vt terrēre, perterrēre, exterrēre.
terrifying adj formīdolōsus.
territory n ager m, fīnēs mpl.
terror n terror m, formīdō f, pavor m; **object of ~** terror m; **be a ~ to** terrōrī esse (*dat*).
terrorize vt metum inicere (*dat*).
terse adj pressus, brevis.
tersely adv pressē.
terseness n brevitās f.
tessellated adj tessellātus.
test n experīmentum nt, probātiō f; (*standard*) obrussa f; **put to the ~** experīrī, perīclitārī; **stand the ~** spectārī ♦ vt experīrī, probāre, spectāre.
testament n testāmentum nt.
testamentary adj testāmentārius.
testator n testātor m.
testify vt testificārī.
testifying n testificātiō f.
testily adv stomachōsē.
testimonial n laudātiō f.
testimony n testimōnium nt.
testy adj difficilis, stomachōsus.
tether n retināculum nt, vinculum nt ♦ vt religāre.
tetrarch n tetrarchēs m.
tetrarchy n tetrarchia f.
text n verba ntpl.
textbook n ars f.
textile adj textilis.
textual adj verbōrum.
texture n textus m.
than conj quam abl; **other ~** alius ac.
thank vt grātiās agere (*dat*); **~ you** bene facis; **no, ~ you** benīgnē.
thankful adj grātus.
thankfully adv grātē.
thankfulness n grātia f.
thankless adj ingrātus.
thanklessly adv ingrātē.
thanks n grātiae fpl, grātēs fpl; **return ~** grātiās agere, grātēs persolvere; **~ to you** operā tuā, beneficiō tuō; **it is ~ to sb that ... not** per aliquem stat quominus (+ subj).
thanksgiving n grātulātiō f; (*public*) supplicātiō f.
that pron (*demonstrative*) ille; (*relat*) quī ♦ conj (*statement*) acc & infin; (*command, purpose, result*) ut; (*fearing*) nē; (*emotion*) quod; **oh ~** utinam.
thatch n culmus m, strāmenta ntpl ♦ vt tegere,

integere.
thaw vt dissolvere ♦ vi liquēscere, tābēscere.
the art not expressed; (*emphatic*) ille; (*with compar*) quō ... eō.
theatre n theātrum nt.
theatrical adj scēnicus.
theft n fūrtum nt.
their adj eōrum; (*ref to subject*) suus.
theme n māteria f, argūmentum nt.
themselves pron ipsī; (*reflexive*) sē.
then adv (*time*) tum, tunc; (*succession*) deinde, tum, posteā; (*consequence*) igitur, ergō; **now and ~** interdum; **only ~** tum dēmum.
thence adv inde.
thenceforth adv inde, posteā, ex eō tempore.
theologian n theologus m.
theology n theologia f.
theorem n prōpositum nt.
theoretical adj contemplātīvus.
theory n ratiō f; **~ and practice** ratiō atque ūsus.
there adv ibī, illīc; (*thither*) eō, illūc; **from ~** inde, illinc; **here and ~** passim; **~ is** est; (*interj*) ecce.
thereabout(s) adv circā, circiter, prope.
thereafter adv deinde, posteā.
thereby adv eā rē, hōc factō.
therefore adv itaque, igitur, ergō, idcircō.
therein adv inibī, in eō.
thereof adv ēius, ēius reī.
thereon adv īnsuper, in eō.
thereupon adv deinde, statim, inde, quo facto.
therewith adv cum eō.
thesis n prōpositum nt.
thews n nervī mpl.
they pron iī, hī, illī.
thick adj dēnsus; (*air*) crassus.
thicken vt dēnsāre ♦ vi concrēscere.
thickening n concrētiō f.
thicket n dūmētum nt.
thickheaded adj stupidus, hebes.
thickly adv dēnsē; **~ populated** frequēns.
thickness n crassitūdō f.
thickset adj brevis atque obēsus.
thick-skinned adj: **be ~** callēre; **become ~** occallēscere.
thief n fūr m.
thieve vt fūrārī, surripere.
thievery n fūrtum nt.
thievish adj fūrāx.
thigh n femur nt.
thin adj exīlis, gracilis, tenuis; (*attendance*) īnfrequēns ♦ vt attenuāre, extenuāre; **~ out** rārefacere; **~ down** dīluere.
thine adj tuus.
thing n rēs f; **as ~s are** nunc, cum haec ita sint.
think vi cōgitāre; (*opinion*) putāre, existimāre, arbitrārī, rērī, crēdere; **as I ~** meā sententiā; **~ about** cōgitāre dē; **~ highly of** magnī aestimāre; **~ nothing of** nihilī facere; **~ out** excōgitāre; **~ over** reputāre, in mente agitāre.
thinker n philosophus m.

thinking _adj_ sapiēns ♦ _n_ cōgitātiō _f_; **~ that** ratus, arbitratus.

thinly _adv_ exīliter, tenuiter; rārē.

thinness _n_ exīlitās _f_, gracilitās _f_; (_person_) maciēs _f_; (_number_) exiguitās _f_, īnfrequentia _f_; (_air_) tenuitās _f_.

thin-skinned _adj_ inrītābilis.

third _adj_ tertius; **for the ~ time** tertium ♦ _n_ tertia pars _f_, triēns _m_; **two ~s** duae partēs, bēs _m_.

thirdly _adv_ tertiō.

thirst _n_ sitis _f_ ♦ _vi_ sitīre; **~ for** sitīre.

thirstily _adv_ sitienter.

thirsty _adj_ sitiēns.

thirteen _num_ tredecim; **~ each** ternī dēnī; **~ times** terdeciēns.

thirteenth _adj_ tertius decimus.

thirtieth _adj_ trīcēsimus.

thirty _num_ trīgintā; **~ each** trīcēnī; **~ times** trīciēns.

this _pron_ hīc.

thistle _n_ carduus _m_.

thither _adv_ eō, illūc.

thole _n_ scalmus _nt_.

thong _n_ lōrum _nt_, habēna _f_.

thorn _n_ spīna _f_, sentis _m_.

thorny _adj_ spīnōsus.

thorough _adj_ absolūtus, germānus; (_work_) accūrātus.

thoroughbred _adj_ generōsus.

thoroughfare _n_ via _f_.

thoroughly _adv_ penitus, omnīnō, funditus.

thoroughness _n_ cūra _f_, diligentia _f_.

thou _pron_ tū.

though _conj_ etsī, etiamsī, quamvīs (+ _subj_), quamquam all (+ _indic_).

thought _n_ (_faculty_) cōgitātiō _f_, mēns _f_, animus _m_; (_an idea_) cōgitātum _nt_, nōtiō _f_; (_design_) cōnsilium _nt_, prōpositum _nt_; (_expressed_) sententia _f_; (_heed_) cautiō _f_, prōvidentia _f_; (_RHET_) inventiō _f_; **second ~s** posteriōrēs cōgitātiōnēs.

thoughtful _adj_ cōgitābundus; prōvidus.

thoughtfully _adv_ prōvidē.

thoughtless _adj_ incōnsīderātus, incōnsultus, imprōvidus, immemor.

thoughtlessly _adv_ temerē, incōnsultē.

thoughtlessness _n_ incōnsīderantia _f_, imprūdentia _f_.

thousand _num_ mīlle; **~s** _pl_ mīlia (+ _gen_) _ntpl_; **~ each** mīllēnī; **~ times** mīlliēns; **three ~** tria mīlia.

thousandth _adj_ mīllēsimus.

thrall _n_ servus _m_.

thraldom _n_ servitūs _f_.

thrash _vt_ verberāre.

thrashing _n_ verbera _ntpl_.

thread _n_ fīlum _nt_; **hang by a ~** (_fig_) fīlō pendēre ♦ _vt_: **~ one's way** sē īnsinuāre.

threadbare _adj_ trītus, obsolētus.

threat _n_ minae _fpl_, minātiō _f_.

threaten _vt_ minārī (_dat of pers_), dēnūntiāre ♦ _vi_ imminēre, impendēre.

threatening _adj_ mināx, imminēns.

threateningly _adv_ mināciter.

three _num_ trēs; **~ each** ternī; **~ times** ter; **~ days** triduum _nt_; **~ years** triennium _nt_; **~ quarters** trēs partēs _fpl_, dōdrāns _m_.

three-cornered _adj_ triangulus, triquetrus.

threefold _adj_ triplex.

three hundred _num_ trecentī; **~ each** trecēnī; **~ times** trecentiēns.

three hundredth _adj_ trecentēsimus.

three-legged _adj_ tripēs.

three-quarters _n_ dōdrāns _m_, trēs partēs _fpl_.

thresh _vt_ terere, exterere.

threshing floor _n_ ārea _f_.

threshold _n_ līmen _nt_.

thrice _adv_ ter.

thrift _n_ frūgālitās _f_, parsimōnia _f_.

thriftily _adv_ frūgāliter.

thrifty _adj_ parcus, frūgī.

thrill _n_ horror _m_ ♦ _vt_ percellere, percutere ♦ _vi_ trepidāre.

thrilling _adj_ mīrābilis.

thrive _vi_ vigēre, valēre, crēscere.

thriving _adj_ valēns, vegetus; (_crops_) laetus.

throat _n_ faucēs _fpl_, guttur _nt_; **cut the ~ of** iugulāre.

throaty _adj_ gravis, raucus.

throb _vi_ palpitāre, micāre ♦ _n_ pulsus _m_.

throe _n_ dolor _m_; **be in the ~s of** labōrāre ex.

throne _n_ solium _nt_; (_power_) rēgnum _nt_.

throng _n_ multitūdō _f_, frequentia _f_ ♦ _vt_ celebrāre; **~ round** stīpāre, circumfundī (_dat_).

throttle _vt_ strangulāre.

through _prep_ per (_acc_); (_cause_) propter (_acc_), _abl_ ♦ _adv_: **~ and ~** penitus; **carry ~** exsequī, peragere; **go ~** trānsīre; **run ~** percurrere; **be ~ with** perfūnctum esse (_abl_).

throughout _adv_ penitus, omnīnō ♦ _prep_ per (_acc_).

throw _n_ iactus _m_, coniectus _m_ ♦ _vt_ iacere, conicere; **~ about** iactāre; **~ across** trāicere; **~ away** abicere; (_something precious_) prōicere; **~ back** rēicere; **~ down** dēturbāre, dēicere; **~ into** inicere; **~ into confusion** perturbāre; **~ off** excutere, exsolvere; **~ open** patefacere; **~ out** ēicere, prōicere; **~ over** inicere; (_fig_) dēstituere; **~ overboard** iactūram facere (_gen_); **~ to** (_danger_) obicere; **~ up** ēicere; (_building_) exstruere; **~ a bridge over** pontem inicere (_dat_), pontem faciendum cūrāre in (_abl_); **~ light on** (_fig_) lūmen adhibēre (_dat_); **~ a rider** equitem excutere.

throwing _n_ coniectiō _f_, iactus _m_.

thrum _n_ līcium _nt_.

thrush _n_ turdus _m_.

thrust _vt_ trūdere, pellere, impingere; **~ at** petere; **~ away** dētrūdere; **~ forward** prōtrūdere; **~ home** dēfīgere; **~ into** īnfīgere, impingere; **~ out** extrūdere.

thud _n_ gravis sonitus _m_.

thug _n_ percussor _m_, sīcārius _m_.

thumb n pollex m; **have under one's ~** in
potestāte suā habēre.
thump n plāga f ♦ vt tundere, pulsāre.
thunder n tonitrus m ♦ vi tonāre, intonāre; **it
~s** tonāt.
thunderbolt n fulmen nt.
thunderer n tonāns m.
thunderstruck adj attonitus.
thus adv (referring back) sīc; (referring forward)
ita; **~ far** hāctenus.
thwack vt verberāre.
thwart vt obstāre (dat), officere (dat),
remorārī, frustrārī ♦ n (boat's) trānstrum nt.
thy adj tuus.
thyme n thymum nt; (wild) serpyllum nt.
tiara n diadēma nt.
ticket n tessera f.
tickle vt titillāre.
tickling n titillātiō f.
ticklish adj lūbricus.
tidal adj: **~ waters** aestuārium nt.
tide n aestus m; (time) tempus nt; **ebb ~** aestūs
recessus m; **flood ~** aestūs accessus m; **turn
of the ~** commūtātiō aestūs; **the ~ will turn**
(fig) circumagētur hīc orbis.
tidily adv concinnē, mundē.
tidiness n concinnitās f, munditia f.
tidings n nūntius m.
tidy adj concinnus, mundus.
tie n (bond) vinculum nt, cōpula f; (kin)
necessitūdō f ♦ vt ligāre; (knot) nectere; **~
fast** dēvincīre, cōnstringere; **~ on** illigāre; **~
to** adligāre; **~ together** colligāre; **~ up**
adligāre; (wound) obligāre.
tier n ōrdō m.
tiff n dissēnsiō f.
tiger n tigris m, more usu f.
tight adj strictus, astrictus, intentus; (close)
artus; **draw ~** intendere, addūcere.
tighten vt adstringere, contendere.
tightly adv artē, angustē.
tightrope n extentus fūnis; **~ walker** n
fūnambulus m.
tigress n tigris f.
tile n tegula f, imbrex f, later nt.
till conj dum, dōnec ♦ prep usque ad (acc), in
(acc); **not ~** dēmum ♦ n arca f ♦ vt colere.
tillage n cultus m.
tiller n (AGR) cultor m; (ship) clāvus m,
gubernāculum nt.
tilt vt inclīnāre.
tilth n cultus m, arvum nt.
timber n (for building) māteria f; (firewood)
lignum nt.
timbrel n tympanum nt.
time n tempus nt; (lifetime) aetās f; (interval)
intervallum nt, spatium nt; (of day) hōra f;
(leisure) ōtium nt; (rhythm) numerus m;
another ~ aliās; **at ~s** aliquandō, interdum; **at
all ~s** semper; **at any ~** umquam; **at one ~ . . .
at another** aliās . . . aliās; **at that ~** tunc, id
temporis; **at the right ~** ad tempus, mātūrē,
tempestīvē; **at the same ~** simul; tamen; **at

the wrong ~** intempestīvē; **beating ~**
percussiō f; **convenient ~** opportūnitās f; **for a
~** aliquantisper, parumper; **for a long ~** diū;
for some ~ aliquamdiū; **for the ~ being** ad
tempus; **from ~ to ~** interdum, identidem;
have a good ~ geniō indulgēre; **have ~ for**
vacāre (dat); **in ~** ad tempus, tempore; **in a
short ~** brevī; **in good ~** tempestīvus; **in the ~
of** apud (acc); **keep ~** (marching) gradum
cōnferre; (music) modulārī; **many ~s** saepe,
saepenumerō; **pass, spend ~** tempus sūmere,
dēgere; **several ~s** aliquotiēns; **some ~**
aliquandō; **waste ~** tempus terere; **what is
the ~?** quota hōra est?; **~ expired** ēmeritus.
time-honoured adj antīquus.
timeliness n opportūnitās f.
timely adj opportūnus, tempestīvus, mātūrus.
timid adj timidus.
timidity n timiditās f.
timidly adv timidē.
timorous adj timidus.
timorously adv timidē.
tin n stannum nt, plumbum album nt ♦ adj
stanneus.
tincture n color m, sapor m ♦ vt īnficere.
tinder n fōmes m.
tinge vt imbuere, īnficere, tingere.
tingle vi horrēre.
tingling n horror m.
tinkle vi tinnīre ♦ n tinnītus m.
tinsel n bractea f; (fig) speciēs f, fūcus m.
tint n color m ♦ vt colōrāre.
tiny adj minūtus, pusillus, perexiguus.
tip n apex m, cacūmen nt, extrēmum nt; **the ~ of**
prīmus, extrēmus ♦ vt praefīgere; **~ over**
invertere.
tipple vi pōtāre.
tippler n pōtor m, ēbrius m.
tipsy adj tēmulentus.
tiptoes n: **on ~** suspēnsō gradū.
tirade n obiūrgātiō f, dēclāmātiō f.
tire vt fatīgāre; **~ out** dēfatīgāre ♦ vi dēfetīscī,
fatīgārī; **I ~ of** mē taedet (gen); **it ~s** taedet (+
acc of person, gen of thing).
tired adj (dē)fessus, lassus; **~ out** dēfessus; **I
am ~ of** mē taedet.
tiresome adj molestus, difficilis.
tiring adj labōriōsus, operōsus.
tiro n tīrō m, rudis m.
tissue n textus m.
tit n: **give ~ for tat** pār parī respondēre.
Titan n Tītān m.
titanic adj immānis.
titbit n cuppēdium nt.
tithe n decuma f.
tithe gatherer n decumānus m.
titillate vt titillāre.
titillation n titillātiō f.
title n (book) īnscrīptiō f, index m; (inscription)
titulus m; (person) nōmen nt, appellātiō f;
(claim) iūs nt, vindiciae fpl; **assert one's ~ to**
vindicāre; **give a ~ to** īnscrībere.
titled adj nōbilis.

title deed n auctōritās f.
titter n rīsus m ♦ vi rīdēre.
tittle-tattle n sermunculus m.
titular adj nōmine.
to prep ad (acc), in (acc); (attitude) ergā (acc); (giving) dat; (towns, small islands, domus, rūs) acc ♦ conj (purpose) ut ♦ adv: **come ~** animum recipere; **~ and fro** hūc illūc.
toad n būfō m.
toady n adsentātor m, parasītus m ♦ vt adsentārī (dat).
toadyism n adsentātiō f.
toast n: **drink a ~** propīnāre ♦ vt torrēre; (drink) propīnāre (dat).
today adv hodiē; **~'s** hodiernus.
toe n digitus m; **big ~** pollex m.
toga n toga f.
together adv ūnā, simul; **bring ~** cōgere, congerere; **come ~** convenīre, congregārī; **put ~** cōnferre, compōnere.
toil n labor m; (snare) rēte nt ♦ vi labōrāre; **~ at** ēlabōrāre in (abl).
toilet n (lady's) cultus m.
toilsome adj labōriōsus, operōsus.
toil-worn adj labōre cōnfectus.
token n īnsigne nt, signum nt, indicium nt.
tolerable adj tolerābilis, patibilis; (quality) mediocris; (size) modicus.
tolerably adv satis, mediocriter.
tolerance n patientia f, tolerantia f.
tolerant adj indulgēns, tolerāns.
tolerantly adv indulgenter.
tolerate vt tolerāre, ferre, indulgēre (dat).
toleration n patientia f; (freedom) lībertās f.
toll n vectīgal nt; (harbour) portōrium nt.
toll collector n exāctor m; portitor m.
tomb n sepulcrum nt.
tombstone n lapis m.
tome n liber m.
tomorrow adv crās; **~'s** crāstinus; **the day after ~** perendiē; **put off till ~** in crāstinum differre.
tone n sonus m, vōx f; (painting) color m.
tongs n forceps m/f.
tongue n lingua f; (shoe) ligula f; **on the tip of one's ~** in prīmōribus labrīs.
tongue-tied adj ēlinguis, īnfāns.
tonnage n amphorae fpl.
tonsils n tōnsillae fpl.
tonsure n rāsūra f.
too adv (also) etiam, īnsuper, quoque; (excess) nimis ♦ compar adj: **~ far** extrā modum; **~ much** nimium; **~ long** nimium diū; **~ great to** māior quam quī (subj); **~ late** sērius; **~ little** parum (+ gen).
tool n īnstrūmentum nt; (AGR) ferrāmentum nt; (person) minister m.
tooth n dēns m; **~ and nail** tōtō corpore atque omnibus ungulīs; **cast in one's teeth** exprobrāre, obicere; **cut teeth** dentīre; **in the teeth of** obviam (dat), adversus (acc); **with the teeth** mordicus.
toothache n dentium dolor m.

toothed adj dentātus.
toothless adj ēdentulus.
toothpick n dentiscalpium nt.
toothsome adj suāvis, dulcis.
top n vertex m, fastīgium nt; (tree) cacūmen nt; (toy) turbō m; **from ~ to toe** ab īmīs unguibus usque ad verticem summum; **the ~ of** summus ♦ vt exsuperāre; **~ up** supplēre ♦ adj superior, summus.
tope vi pōtāre.
toper n pōtor m.
topiary adj topiārius. ♦ n topiārium opus nt.
topic n rēs f; (RHET) locus m; **~ of conversation** sermō m.
topical adj hodiernus.
topmost adj summus.
topography n dēscrīptiō f.
topple vi titubāre; **~ over** prōlābī.
topsail n dolō m.
topsyturvy adv praeposterē; **turn ~** sūrsum deōrsum versāre, permiscēre.
tor n mōns m.
torch n fax f, lampas f.
torment n cruciātus m; (mind) angor m ♦ vt cruciāre; (mind) discruciāre, excruciāre, angere.
tormentor n tortor m.
tornado n turbō m.
torpid adj torpēns; **be ~** torpēre; **grow ~** obtorpēscere.
torpor n torpor m, inertia f.
torrent n torrēns m.
torrid adj torridus.
torsion n tortus m.
torso n truncus m.
tortoise n testūdō f.
tortoiseshell n testūdō f.
tortuous adj flexuōsus.
torture n cruciātus m, supplicium nt; **instrument of ~** tormentum nt ♦ vt torquēre, cruciāre, excruciāre.
torturer n tortor m, carnifex m.
toss n iactus m ♦ vt iactāre, excutere; **~ about** agitāre; **be ~ed** (at sea) fluitāre.
total adj tōtus, ūniversus ♦ n summa f.
totality n ūniversitās f.
totally adv omnīnō, plānē.
totter vi lābāre, titubāre; **make ~** labefactāre.
tottering n titubātiō f.
touch n tāctus m; **a ~ of** aliquantulum (gen); **finishing ~** manus extrēma f ♦ vt tangere, attingere; (feelings) movēre, tangere ♦ vi inter sē contingere; **~ at** nāvem appellere ad; **~ on** (topic) attingere, perstringere; **~ up** expolīre.
touch-and-go adj anceps ♦ n discrīmen nt.
touching adj (place) contiguus; (emotion) flexanimus ♦ prep quod attinet ad (acc).
touchstone n (fig) obrussa f.
touchy adj inrītābilis, stomachōsus.
tough adj dūrus.
toughen vt dūrāre.
toughness n dūritia f.

tour n iter nt; (*abroad*) peregrīnātiō f.
tourist n viātor m, peregrīnātor m.
tournament n certāmen nt.
tow n stuppa f; **of ~** stuppeus ♦ vt adnexum trahere, remulcō trahere.
toward(s) prep ad (acc), versus (*after noun, acc*); (*feelings*) in (acc), ergā (acc); (*time*) sub (acc).
towel n mantēle nt.
tower n turris f ♦ vi ēminēre.
towered adj turrītus.
town n urbs f, oppidum nt; **country ~** mūnicipium nt ♦ adj urbānus.
town councillor n decuriō m.
townsman n oppidānus m.
townspeople npl oppidānī mpl.
towrope n remulcum nt.
toy n crepundia ntpl ♦ vi lūdere.
trace n vestīgium nt, indicium nt ♦ vt investīgāre; (*draw*) dēscrībere; **~ out** dēsignāre.
track n (*mark*) vestīgium nt; (*path*) callis m, sēmita f; (*of wheel*) orbita f; (*of ship*) cursus m ♦ vt investīgāre, indāgāre.
trackless adj invius.
tract n (*country*) tractus m, regiō f; (*book*) libellus m.
tractable adj tractābilis, facilis, docilis.
trade n mercātūra f, mercātus m; (*a business*) ars f, quaestus m; **freedom of ~** commercium nt ♦ vi mercātūrās facere, negōtiārī; **~ in** vēndere, vēnditāre.
trader n mercātor m, negōtiātor m.
tradesman n opifex m.
tradition n fāma f, mōs māiōrum m, memoria f.
traditional adj ā māiōribus trāditus, patrius.
traditionally adv mōre māiōrum.
traduce vt calumniārī, obtrectāre (*dat*).
traducer n calumniātor m, obtrectātor m.
traffic n commercium nt; (*on road*) vehicula ntpl ♦ vi mercātūrās facere; **~ in** vēndere, vēnditāre.
tragedian n (*author*) tragoedus m; (*actor*) āctor tragicus m.
tragedy n tragoedia f; (*fig*) calamitās f, malum nt.
tragic adj tragicus; (*fig*) tristis.
tragically adv tragicē; male.
tragicomedy n tragicocōmoedia f.
trail n vestīgia ntpl ♦ vt trahere ♦ vi trahī.
train n (*line*) agmen nt, ōrdō m; (*of dress*) īnstita f; (*army*) impedīmenta ntpl; (*followers*) comitēs mpl, satellitēs mpl, cohors f ♦ vt īnstituere, īnstruere, docēre, adsuēfacere; exercēre; (*weapon*) dīrigere.
trainer n (*sport*) lanista m, aliptēs m.
training n disciplīna f, īnstitūtiō f; (*practice*) exercitātiō f.
trait n līneāmentum nt.
traitor n prōditor m.
traitorous adj perfidus, perfidiōsus.
traitorously adv perfidiōsē.

trammel vt impedīre.
tramp n (*man*) planus m; (*of feet*) pulsus m ♦ vi gradī.
trample vi: **~ on** obterere, prōterere, prōculcāre.
trance n stupor m; (*prophetic*) furor m.
tranquil adj tranquillus, placidus, quiētus, sēdātus.
tranquility n tranquillitās f, quiēs f, pāx f.
tranquillize vt pācāre, sēdāre.
tranquilly adv tranquillē, placidē, tranquillō animō.
transact vt agere, gerere, trānsigere.
transaction n rēs f, negōtium nt.
transactor n āctor m.
transalpine adj trānsalpīnus.
transcend vt superāre, excēdere.
transcendence n praestantia f.
transcendent adj eximius, ēgregius, excellēns.
transcendental adj dīvīnus.
transcendentally adv eximiē, ēgregiē, ūnicē.
transcribe vt dēscrībere, trānscrībere.
transcriber n librārius m.
transcript n exemplar nt, exemplum nt.
transfer n trānslātiō f; (*of property*) aliēnātiō f ♦ vt trānsferre; (*troops*) trādūcere; (*property*) abaliēnāre; (*duty*) dēlēgāre.
transference n trānslātiō f.
transfigure vt trānsfōrmāre.
transfix vt trānsfīgere, trāicere, trānsfodere; (*mind*) obstupefacere; **be ~ed** stupēre, stupēscere.
transform vt commūtāre, vertere.
transformation n commūtātiō f.
transgress vt violāre, perfringere ♦ vi dēlinquere.
transgression n dēlictum nt.
transgressor n violātor m.
transience n brevitās f.
transient adj fluxus, cadūcus, brevis.
transit n trānsitus m.
transition n mūtātiō f; (*speech*) trānsitus m.
transitory adj brevis, fluxus.
translate vt vertere, reddere; **~ into Latin** Latīnē reddere.
translation n: **a Latin ~ of Homer** Latīnē redditus Homērus.
translator n interpres m.
translucent adj perlūcidus.
transmarine adj trānsmarīnus.
transmission n missiō f.
transmit vt mittere; (*legacy*) trādere, prōdere.
transmutable adj mūtābilis.
transmutation n mūtātiō f.
transmute vt mūtāre, commūtāre.
transom n trabs f.
transparency n perlūcida nātūra f.
transparent adj perlūcidus; (*fig*) perspicuus.
transparently adv perspicuē.
transpire vi (*get known*) ēmānāre, dīvulgārī; (*happen*) ēvenīre.
transplant vt trānsferre.

transport n vectūra f; (*ship*) nāvis onerāria f; (*emotion*) ēlātiō f, summa laetitia f ♦ vt trānsportāre, trānsvehere, trānsmittere; **be ~ed** (*fig*) efferrī, gestīre.
transportation n vectūra f.
transpose vt invertere; (*words*) trāicere.
transposition n (*words*) trāiectiō f.
transverse adj trānsversus, oblīquus.
transversely adv in trānsversum, oblīquē.
trap n laqueus m; (*fig*) īnsidiae fpl ♦ vt dēcipere, excipere; (*fig*) inlaqueāre.
trappings n ōrnāmenta ntpl, īnsignia ntpl; (*horse's*) phalerae fpl.
trash n nūgae fpl.
trashy adj vīlis.
Trasimene n Trasimēnus m.
travail n labor m, sūdor m; (*woman's*) puerperium nt ♦ vi labōrāre, sūdāre; parturīre.
travel n itinera ntpl; (*foreign*) peregrīnātiō f ♦ vi iter facere; (*abroad*) peregrīnārī; **~ through** peragrāre; **~ to** contendere ad, in (*acc*), proficīscī in (*acc*).
traveller n viātor m; (*abroad*) peregrīnātor m.
traverse vt peragrāre, lūstrāre; **~ a great distance** multa mīlia passuum iter facere.
travesty n perversa imitātiō f ♦ vt perversē imitārī.
tray n ferculum nt.
treacherous adj perfidus, perfidiōsus; (*ground*) lūbricus.
treacherously adv perfidiōsē.
treachery n perfidia f.
tread vi incēdere, ingredī; **~ on** īnsistere (*dat*) ♦ n gradus m, incessus m.
treadle n (*loom*) īnsilia ntpl.
treadmill n pistrīnum nt.
treason n māiestās f, perduelliō f; **be charged with ~** māiestātis accūsārī; **be guilty of high ~ against** māiestātem minuere, laedere (*gen*).
treasonable adj perfidus, perfidiōsus.
treasure n gāza f, thēsaurus m; (*person*) dēliciae fpl ♦ vt māximī aestimāre, dīligere, fovēre; **~ up** condere, congerere.
treasure house n thēsaurus m.
treasurer n aerāriī praefectus m; (*royal*) dioecētēs m.
treasury n aerārium nt; (*emperor's*) fiscus m.
treat n convīvium nt; dēlectātiō f ♦ vt (*in any way*) ūtī (*abl*), habēre, tractāre, accipere; (*patient*) cūrāre; (*topic*) tractāre; (*with hospitality*) invītāre; **~ with** agere cum; **~ as a friend** amīcī locō habēre.
treatise n liber m.
treatment n tractātiō f; (MED) cūrātiō f.
treaty n foedus nt; **make a ~** foedus ferīre.
treble adj triplus; (*voice*) acūtus ♦ n acūtus sonus m ♦ vt triplicāre.
tree n arbor f.
trek vi migrāre ♦ n migrātiō f.
trellis n cancellī mpl.
tremble vi tremere, horrēre.

trembling n tremor m, horror m ♦ adj tremulus.
tremendous adj immānis, ingēns, vastus.
tremendously adv immāne quantum.
tremor n tremor m.
tremulous adj tremulus.
trench n fossa f.
trenchant adj ācer.
trenchantly adv ācriter.
trend n inclīnātiō f ♦ vi vergere.
trepidation n trepidātiō f.
trespass n dēlictum nt ♦ vi dēlinquere; **~ on** (*property*) invādere in (*acc*); (*patience, time, etc*) abūtī (*abl*).
trespasser n quī iniussū dominī ingreditur.
tress n crīnis m.
trial n (*essay*) experientia f; (*test*) probātiō f; (*law*) iūdicium nt, quaestiō f; (*trouble*) labor m aerumna f; **make ~ of** experīrī, perīculum facere (*gen*); **be brought to ~** in iūdicium venīre; **put on ~** in iūdicium vocāre; **hold a ~ on** quaestiōnem habēre dē (*abl*).
triangle n triangulum nt.
triangular adj triangulus, triquetrus.
tribe n tribus m; gēns f; (*barbarian*) nātiō f.
tribulation n aerumna f.
tribunal n iūdicium nt.
tribune n tribūnus m; (*platform*) rōstra ntpl.
tribuneship, tribunate n tribūnātus m.
tribunician adj tribūnicius.
tributary adj vectīgālis ♦ n: **be a ~ of** (*river*) īnfluere in (*acc*).
tribute n tribūtum nt, vectīgal nt; (*verbal*) laudātiō f; **pay a ~ to** laudāre.
trice n: **in a ~** mōmentō temporis.
trick n dolus m, fallācia f, fraus f, īnsidiae fpl, ars f; (*conjurer's*) praestīgiae fpl; (*habit*) mōs m ♦ vt fallere, dēcipere, ēlūdere; (*with words*) verba dare (*dat*); **~ out** ōrnāre, distinguere.
trickery n dolus m, fraus f, fallāciae fpl.
trickle n guttae fpl ♦ vi mānāre, dēstillāre.
trickster n fraudātor m, veterātor m.
tricky adj lūbricus, difficilis.
trident n tridēns m, fuscina f.
tried adj probātus, spectātus.
triennial adj trietēricus.
triennially adv quartō quōque annō.
trifle n nūgae fpl, paululum nt ♦ vi lūdere, nūgārī; **~ with** lūdere.
trifling adj levis, exiguus.
triflingly adv leviter.
trig adj lepidus, concinnus.
trigger n manulea f.
trim adj nitidus, concinnus ♦ vt putāre, tondēre; (*lamp*) oleum īnstillāre (*dat*) ♦ vi temporibus servīre.
trimly adv concinnē.
trimness n nitor m, munditia f.
trinket n crepundia ntpl.
trip n iter nt ♦ vt supplantāre ♦ vi lābī, titubāre; **~ along** currere; **~ over** incurrere in (*acc*).
tripartite adj tripartītus.

tripe n omāsum nt.
triple adj triplex, triplus ♦ vt triplicāre.
triply adv trifāriam.
tripod n tripus m.
trireme n trirēmis f.
trite adj trītus.
triumph n triumphus m; (victory) victōria f ♦ vi triumphāre; vincere; ~ **over** dēvincere.
triumphal adj triumphālis.
triumphant adj victor; laetus.
triumvir n triumvir m.
triumvirate n triumvirātus m.
trivial adj levis, tenuis.
triviality n nūgae fpl.
trochaic adj trochaicus.
trochee n trochaeus m.
Trojan n Trōiānus m.
troop n grex f, caterva f; (cavalry) turma f ♦ vi cōnfluere, congregārī.
trooper n eques m.
troops npl cōpiae fpl.
trope n figūra f, trānslātiō f.
trophy n tropaeum nt; **set up a** ~ tropaeum pōnere.
tropic n sōlstitiālis orbis m; ~**s** pl loca fervida ntpl.
tropical adj tropicus.
trot vi tolūtim īre.
troth n fidēs f.
trouble n incommodum nt, malum nt, molestia f, labor m; (effort) opera f, negōtium nt; (disturbance) turba f, tumultus m; **take the** ~ **to** operam dare ut; **be worth the** ~ operae pretium esse ♦ vt (disturb) turbāre; (make uneasy) sollicitāre, exagitāre; (annoy) incommodāre, molestiam exhibēre (dat); ~ **oneself about** cūrāre, respicere; **be ~d with** labōrāre ex.
troubler n turbātor m.
troublesome adj molestus, incommodus, difficilis.
troublesomeness n molestia f.
troublous adj turbidus, turbulentus.
trough n alveus m.
trounce vt castīgāre.
troupe n grex f, caterva f.
trousered adj brācātus.
trousers n brācae fpl.
trow vi opīnārī.
truant adj tardus ♦ n cessātor m; **play** ~ cessāre, nōn compārēre.
truce n indutiae fpl.
truck n carrus m; **have no** ~ **with** nihil commercī habēre cum.
truckle vi adsentārī.
truculence n ferōcia f, asperitās f.
truculent adj truculentus, ferōx.
truculently adv ferōciter.
trudge vi rēpere, pedibus incēdere.
true adj vērus; (genuine) germānus, vērus; (loyal) fīdus, fidēlis; (exact) rēctus, iūstus.
truism n verbum trītum nt.
truly adv rēvērā, profectō, vērē.

trumpery n nūgae fpl ♦ adj vīlis.
trumpet n tuba f, būcina f.
trumpeter n būcinātor m, tubicen m.
trump up vt ēmentīrī, cōnfingere.
truncate vt praecīdere.
truncheon n fustis m, scīpiō m.
trundle vt volvere.
trunk n truncus m; (elephant's) manus f; (box) cista f.
truss n fascia f ♦ vt colligāre.
trust n fidēs f, fīdūcia f; **breach of** ~ mala fidēs; **held in** ~ fīdūciārius; **put** ~ **in** fidem habēre (dat) ♦ vt cōnfīdere (dat), crēdere (dat); (entrust) committere, concrēdere.
trustee n tūtor m.
trusteeship n tūtēla f.
trustful adj crēdulus, fīdēns.
trustfully adv fīdenter.
trustily adv fidēliter.
trustiness n fidēs f, fidēlitās f.
trusting adj fīdēns.
trustingly adv fīdenter.
trustworthily adv fidēliter.
trustworthiness n fidēs f, integritās f.
trustworthy adj fīdus, certus; (witness) locuplēs; (authority) certus, bonus.
trusty adj fīdus, fidēlis.
truth n vēritās f, vērum nt; **in** ~ rē vērā.
truthful adj vērāx.
truthfully adv vērē.
truthfulness n fidēs f.
try vt (attempt) cōnārī, (test) experīrī, temptāre; (harass) exercēre; (judge) iūdicāre, cognōscere; ~ **for** petere, quaerere.
trying adj molestus.
tub n alveus m, cūpa f.
tubby adj obēsus.
tube n fistula f.
tufa n tōfus m.
tuft n crista f.
tug vt trahere, tractāre.
tuition n īnstitūtiō f.
tumble vi concidere, corruere, prōlābī ♦ n cāsus m.
tumbledown adj ruīnōsus.
tumbler n pōculum nt.
tumid adj tumidus, īnflātus.
tumour n tūber nt.
tumult n tumultus m, turba f; (fig) perturbātiō f.
tumultuous adj tumultuōsus, turbidus.
tumultuously adv tumultuōsē.
tumulus n tumulus m.
tun n dolium nt.
tune n modī mpl, carmen nt; **keep in** ~ concentum servāre; **out of** ~ absonus, dissonus; (strings) incontentus ♦ vt (strings) intendere.
tuneful adj canōrus.
tunefully adv numerōsē.
tunic n tunica f; **wearing a** ~ tunicātus.
tunnel n cunīculus m.
tunny n thunnus m.

turban n mitra f, mitella f.
turbid adj turbidus.
turbot n rhombus m.
turbulence n tumultus m.
turbulent adj turbulentus, turbidus.
turbulently adv turbulentē, turbidē.
turf n caespes m.
turgid adj turgidus, īnflātus.
turgidity n (RHET) ampullae fpl.
turgidly adv īnflātē.
turmoil n turba f, tumultus m; (mind)
  perturbātiō f.
turn n (motion) conversiō f; (bend) flexus m,
  ānfrāctus m; (change) commūtātiō f,
  vicissitūdō f; (walk) spatium nt; (of mind)
  adfectus m; (of language) sententia f,
  cōnfōrmātiō f; ~ of events mutātiō rērum f;
  bad ~ iniūria f; good ~ beneficium nt; ~ of the
  scale mōmentum nt; take a ~ for the worse in
  pēiōrem partem vertī; in ~s invicem,
  vicissim, alternī; in one's ~ locō ōrdine ♦ vt
  vertere, convertere, flectere; (change)
  vertere, mūtāre; (direct) intendere, dīrigere;
  (translate) vertere, reddere; (on a lathe)
  tornāre; ~ the edge of retundere; ~ the head
  mentem exturbāre; ~ the laugh against
  rīsum convertere in (acc); ~ the scale (fig)
  mōmentum habēre; ~ the stomach nauseam
  facere; ~ to account ūtī (abl), in rem suam
  convertere ♦ vi versārī, circumagī; (change)
  vertere, mūtārī; (crisis) pendēre; (direction)
  convertī; (scale) prōpendēre; ~ king's/
  queen's evidence indicium profitērī; ~
  against vt aliēnāre ab ♦ vi dēscīscere ab; ~
  around (se) circumvertere; ~ aside vt
  dēflectere, dēclīnāre ♦ vi dēvertere, sē
  dēclīnāre; ~ away vt āvertere, dēpellere ♦ vi
  āversārī, discēdere; ~ back vi revertī; ~
  down vt invertere; (proposal) rēicere; ~ into
  vi vertere in (acc), mūtārī in (acc); ~ out vt
  ēicere, expellere ♦ vi cadere, ēvenīre,
  ēvādere; ~ outside in excutere; ~ over vt
  ēvertere; (book) ēvolvere; (in mind) volūtāre,
  agitāre; ~ round vt circumagere ♦ vi
  convertī; ~ up vt retorquēre; (earth) versāre;
  (nose) corrūgāre ♦ vi adesse, intervenire; ~
  upside down invertere.
turncoat n trānsfuga m.
turning n flexus m, ānfrāctus m.
turning point n discrīmen nt, mēta f.
turnip n rāpum nt.
turpitude n turpitūdō f.
turquoise n callais f ♦ adj callainus.
turret n turris f.
turreted adj turrītus.
turtle n testūdō f; turn ~ invertī.
turtle dove n turtur m.
tusk n dēns m.
tussle n luctātiō f ♦ vi luctārī.
tutelage n tūtēla f.
tutelary adj praeses.
tutor n praeceptor m, magister m ♦ vt docēre,
  praecipere (dat).

tutorship n tūtēla f.
twaddle n nūgae fpl.
twang n sonus m ♦ vi increpāre.
tweak vi vellicāre.
tweezers n forceps m/f, volsella f.
twelfth adj duodecimus ♦ n duodecima pars f,
  ūncia f; eleven ~s deūnx m; five ~s quīncūnx
  m; seven ~s septūnx m.
twelve num duodecim; ~ each duodēnī; ~ times
  duodeciēns.
twelvemonth n annus m.
twentieth adj vīcēsimus ♦ n vīcēsima pars f;
  (tax) vīcēsima f.
twenty num vīgintī; ~ each vīcēnī; ~ times
  vīciēns.
twice adv bis; ~ as much duplus, bis tantō; ~ a
  day bis diē, bis in diē.
twig n virga f, rāmulus m.
twilight n (morning) dīlūculum nt; (evening)
  crepusculum nt.
twin adj geminus ♦ n geminus m, gemina f.
twine n resticula f ♦ vt nectere, implicāre,
  contexere ♦ vi sē implicāre; ~ round
  complectī.
twinge n dolor m.
twinkle vi micāre.
twirl vt intorquēre, contorquēre ♦ vi
  circumagī.
twist vt torquēre, intorquēre ♦ vi torquērī.
twit vt obicere (dat).
twitch vt vellicāre ♦ vi micāre.
twitter vi pīpilāre.
two num duo; ~ each bīnī; ~ days biduum nt; ~
  years biennium nt; ~ years old bīmus; ~ by ~
  bīnī; ~ feet long bipedālis; in ~ parts
  bifāriam, bipartītō.
two-coloured adj bicolor.
two-edged adj anceps.
twofold adj duplex, anceps.
two-footed adj bipēs.
two-headed adj biceps.
two-horned adj bicornis.
two hundred num ducentī; ~ each ducēnī; ~
  times ducentiēns.
two hundredth adj ducentēsimus.
two-oared adj birēmis.
two-pronged adj bidēns, bifurcus.
two-way adj bivius.
type n (pattern) exemplar nt; (kind) genus
  nt.
typhoon n turbō m.
typical adj proprius, solitus.
typically adv dē mōre, ut mōs est.
typify vt exprimere.
tyrannical adj superbus, crūdēlis.
tyrannically adv superbē, crūdēliter.
tyrannize vi dominārī, rēgnāre.
tyrannous adj see tyrannical
tyrannously adv see tyrannically.
tyranny n dominātiō f, rēgnum nt.
tyrant n rēx m, crūdēlis dominus m; (Greek)
  tyrannus m.
tyro n tīrō m, rudis m.

U, u

ubiquitous *adj* omnibus locīs praesēns.
ubiquity *n* ūniversa praesentia *f*.
udder *n* über *nt*.
ugliness *n* foed…tās *f*, dēfōrmitās *f*, turpitūdō *f*.
ugly *adj* foedus, dēfōrmis, turpis.
ulcer *n* ulcus *nt*, vomica *f*.
ulcerate *vi* ulcerārī.
ulcerous *adj* ulcerōsus.
ulterior *adj* ulterior.
ultimate *adj* ultimus, extrēmus.
ultimately *adv* tandem, ad ultimum.
umbrage *n* offēnsiō *f*; **take ~ at** indignē ferre, patī.
umbrageous *adj* umbrōsus.
umbrella *n* umbella *f*.
umpire *n* arbiter *m*, disceptātor *m*.
unabashed *adj* intrepidus, impudēns.
unabated *adj* integer.
unable *adj* impotēns; **be ~** nōn posse, nequīre.
unacceptable *adj* ingrātus.
unaccompanied *adj* sōlus.
unaccomplished *adj* īnfectus, imperfectus; (*person*) indoctus.
unaccountable *adj* inexplicābilis.
unaccountably *adv* sine causā, repentē.
unaccustomed *adj* īnsuētus, īnsolitus.
unacquainted *adj* ignārus (*gen*), imperītus (*gen*).
unadorned *adj* inōrnātus, incōmptus; (*speech*) nūdus, ēnucleātus.
unadulterated *adj* sincērus, integer.
unadvisedly *adv* imprūdenter, incōnsultē.
unaffected *adj* simplex, candidus.
unaffectedly *adv* simpliciter.
unaided *adj* sine auxiliō, nūdus.
unalienable *adj* proprius.
unalloyed *adj* pūrus.
unalterable *adj* immūtābilis.
unaltered *adj* immūtātus.
unambiguous *adj* apertus, certus.
unambitious *adj* humilis, modestus.
unanimity *n* cōnsēnsiō *f*, ūnanimitās *f*.
unanimous *adj* concors, ūnanimus; **be ~** idem omnēs sentīre.
unanimously *adv* ūnā vōce, omnium cōnsēnsū.
unanswerable *adj* necessārius.
unanswerably *adv* sine contrōversiā.
unappreciative *adj* ingrātus.
unapproachable *adj* inaccessus; (*person*) difficilis.
unarmed *adj* inermis.
unasked *adj* ultrō, suā sponte.
unassailable *adj* inexpugnābilis.
unassailed *adj* intāctus, incolumis.

unassuming *adj* modestus, dēmissus; **~ manners** modestia *f*.
unassumingly *adv* modestē.
unattached *adj* līber.
unattempted *adj* intentātus; **leave ~** praetermittere.
unattended *adj* sōlus, sine comitibus.
unattractive *adj* invenustus.
unauthentic *adj* incertō auctōre.
unavailing *adj* inūtilis, inānis.
unavenged *adj* inultus.
unavoidable *adj* necessārius.
unavoidably *adv* necessāriō.
unaware *adj* īnscius, ignārus.
unawares *adv* inopīnātō, dē imprōvīsō; incautus.
unbalanced *adj* turbātus.
unbar *vt* reserāre.
unbearable *adj* intolerābilis, intolerandus.
unbearably *adv* intoleranter.
unbeaten *adj* invictus.
unbecoming *adj* indecōrus, inhonestus; **it is ~** dēdecet.
unbeknown *adj* ignōtus.
unbelief *n* diffīdentia *f*.
unbelievable *adj* incrēdibilis.
unbelievably *adv* incrēdibiliter.
unbelieving *adj* incrēdulus.
unbend *vt* remittere, laxāre ♦ *vi* animum remittere, aliquid dē sevēritāte remittere.
unbending *adj* inexōrābilis, sevērus.
unbiassed *adj* integer, incorruptus, aequus.
unbidden *adj* ultrō, sponte.
unbind *vt* solvere, resolvere.
unblemished *adj* pūrus, integer.
unblushing *adj* impudēns.
unblushingly *adv* impudenter.
unbolt *vt* reserāre.
unborn *adj* nōndum nātus.
unbosom *vt* patefacere, effundere.
unbound *adj* solūtus.
unbounded *adj* īnfīnītus, immēnsus.
unbridled *adj* īnfrēnātus; (*fig*) effrēnātus, indomitus, impotēns.
unbroken *adj* integer; (*animal*) intractātus; (*friendship*) inviolātus; (*series*) perpetuus, continuus.
unburden *vt* exonerāre; **~ oneself of** aperīre, patefacere.
unburied *adj* inhumātus, īnsepultus.
unbusinesslike *adj* iners.
uncalled-for *adj* supervacāneus.
uncanny *adj* mīrus, mōnstruōsus.
uncared-for *adj* neglectus.
unceasing *adj* perpetuus, adsiduus.
unceasingly *adv* perpetuō, adsiduē.
unceremonious *adj* agrestis, inurbānus.
unceremoniously *adv* inurbānē.
uncertain *adj* incertus, dubius, anceps; **be ~** dubitāre, pendēre.
uncertainly *adv* incertē, dubitanter.
uncertainty *n* incertum *nt*; (*state*) dubitātiō *f*.
unchangeable *adj* immūtābilis; (*person*)

cōnstāns.
unchanged *adj* immūtātus, īdem; **remain ~**
permanēre.
uncharitable *adj* inhūmānus, malignus.
uncharitableness *n* inhūmānitās *f*.
uncharitably *adv* inhūmānē, malignē.
unchaste *adj* impudīcus, libīdinōsus.
unchastely *adv* impudīcē.
unchastity *n* incestus *m*, libīdō *f*.
unchecked *adj* līber, indomitus.
uncivil *adj* inurbānus, importūnus,
inhūmānus.
uncivilized *adj* barbarus, incultus, ferus.
uncivilly *adv* inurbānē.
uncle *n* (*paternal*) patruus *m*; (*maternal*)
avunculus *m*.
unclean *adj* immundus; (*fig*) impūrus,
obscēnus.
uncleanly *adv* impūrē.
uncleanness *n* sordēs *fpl*; (*fig*) impūritās *f*,
obscēnitās *f*.
unclose *vt* aperīre.
unclothe *vt* nūdāre, vestem dētrahere (*dat*).
unclothed *adj* nūdus.
unclouded *adj* serēnus.
uncoil *vt* explicāre, ēvolvere.
uncomely *adj* dēfōrmis, turpis.
uncomfortable *adj* incommodus, molestus.
uncomfortably *adv* incommodē.
uncommitted *adj* vacuus.
uncommon *adj* rārus, īnsolitus, inūsitātus;
(*eminent*) ēgregius, singulāris, eximius.
uncommonly *adv* rārō; ēgregiē, ūnicē.
uncommonness *n* īnsolentia *f*.
uncommunicative *adj* tēctus, taciturnus.
uncomplaining *adj* patiēns.
uncompleted *adj* imperfectus.
uncompromising *adj* dūrus, rigidus.
unconcern *n* sēcūritās *f*.
unconcerned *adj* sēcūrus, ōtiōsus.
unconcernedly *adv* lentē.
uncondemned *adj* indemnātus.
unconditional *adj* absolūtus.
unconditionally *adv* nullā condiciōne.
uncongenial *adj* ingrātus.
unconnected *adj* sēparātus, disiūnctus;
(*style*) dissolūtus.
unconquerable *adj* invictus.
unconquered *adj* invictus.
unconscionable *adj* improbus.
unconscionably *adv* improbē.
unconscious *adj*: **~ of** īnscius (*gen*), ignārus
(*gen*); **become ~** sōpīrī, animō linquī.
unconsciousness *n* sopor *m*.
unconsecrated *adj* profānus.
unconsidered *adj* neglectus.
unconstitutional *adj* illicitus.
unconstitutionally *adv* contrā lēgēs, contrā
rem pūblicam.
uncontaminated *adj* pūrus, incorruptus,
integer.
uncontrollable *adj* impotēns, effrēnātus.
uncontrollably *adv* effrēnātē.

uncontrolled *adj* līber, solūtus.
unconventional *adj* īnsolitus, solūtus.
unconvicted *adj* indemnātus.
unconvincing *adj* incrēdibilis, nōn vērī
similis.
uncooked *adj* crūdus.
uncorrupted *adj* incorruptus, integer.
uncouple *vt* disiungere.
uncouth *adj* horridus, agrestis, inurbānus.
uncouthly *adv* inurbānē.
uncouthness *n* inhūmānitās *f*, rūsticitās *f*.
uncover *vt* dētegere, aperīre, nūdāre.
uncritical *adj* indoctus, crēdulus.
uncultivated *adj* incultus; (*fig*) agrestis,
rūsticus, impolītus.
uncultured *adj* agrestis, rudis.
uncut *adj* intōnsus.
undamaged *adj* integer, inviolātus.
undaunted *adj* intrepidus, fortis.
undecayed *adj* incorruptus.
undeceive *vt* errōrem tollere (*dat*), errōrem
ēripere (*dat*).
undecided *adj* dubius, anceps; (*case*) integer.
undecked *adj* (*ship*) apertus.
undefended *adj* indēfēnsus, nūdus.
undefiled *adj* integer, incontāminātus.
undemonstrative *adj* taciturnus.
undeniable *adj* certus.
undeniably *adv* sine dubiō.
undependable *adj* inconstāns, mōbilis.
under *adv* īnfrā, subter ♦ *prep* sub (*abl*), īnfrā
(*acc*); (*number*) intrā (*acc*); (*motion*) sub (*acc*);
~ arms in armīs; **~ colour** (pretext of) speciē
(*gen*), per speciem (*gen*); **~ my leadership** mē
duce; **~ the circumstances** cum haec ita sint;
labour ~ labōrāre ex; **~ the eyes of** in
cōnspectū (+ *gen*); **~ the leadership of** *abl* +
duce.
underage *adj* impūbēs.
undercurrent *n*: **an ~ of** lātens.
underestimate *vt* minōris aestimāre.
undergarment *n* subūcula *f*.
undergo *vt* subīre, patī, ferre.
underground *adj* subterrāneus ♦ *adv* sub
terrā.
undergrowth *n* virgulta *ntpl*.
underhand *adj* clandestīnus, fūrtīvus ♦ *adv*
clam, fūrtim.
underline *vt* subscrībere.
underling *n* minister *m*, satelles *m/f*.
undermine *vt* subruere; (*fig*) labefacere,
labefactāre.
undermost *adj* īnfimus.
underneath *adv* īnfrā ♦ *prep* sub (*abl*), īnfrā
(*acc*); (*motion*) sub (*acc*).
underprop *vt* fulcīre.
underrate *vt* obtrectāre, extenuāre, minōris
aestimāre.
understand *vt* intellegere, comprehendere;
(*be told*) accipere, comperīre; (*in a sense*)
interpretārī; **~ Latin** Latīnē scīre.
understandable *adj* crēdibilis.
understanding *adj* sapiēns, perītus ♦ *n*

intellegentia *f*; (*faculty*) mēns *f*, intellectus *m*; (*agreement*) cōnsēnsus *m*; (*condition*) condiciō *f*.

undertake *vt* suscipere, sūmere, adīre ad; (*business*) condūcere; (*case*) agere, dēfendere; (*promise*) recipere, spondēre.

undertaker *n* dissignātor *m*.

undertaking *n* inceptum *nt*, inceptiō *f*.

undervalue *vt* minōris aestimāre.

underwood *n* virgulta *ntpl*.

underworld *n* Īnferī *mpl*.

undeserved *adj* immeritus, iniūstus.

undeservedly *adv* immeritō, indignē.

undeserving *adj* indignus.

undesigned *adj* fortuītus.

undesignedly *adv* fortuītō, temerē.

undesirable *adj* odiōsus, ingrātus.

undeterred *adj* immōtus.

undeveloped *adj* immātūrus.

undeviating *adj* dīrēctus.

undigested *adj* crūdus.

undignified *adj* levis, inhonestus.

undiminished *adj* integer.

undiscernible *adj* invīsus, obscūrus.

undisciplined *adj* lascīvus, immoderātus; (*MIL*) inexercitātus.

undiscovered *adj* ignōtus.

undisguised *adj* apertus.

undisguisedly *adv* palam, apertē.

undismayed *adj* impavidus, intrepidus.

undisputed *adj* certus.

undistinguished *adj* ignōbilis, inglōrius.

undisturbed *adj* tranquillus, placidus.

undo *vt* (*knot*) expedīre, resolvere; (*sewing*) dissuere; (*fig*) īnfectum reddere.

undoing *n* ruīna *f*.

undone *adj* īnfectus; (*ruined*) perditus; **be ~** perīre, disperīre; **hopelessly ~** dēperditus.

undoubted *adj* certus.

undoubtedly *adv* sine dubiō, plānē.

undress *vt* exuere, vestem dētrahere (*dat*).

undressed *adj* nūdus.

undue *adj* nimius, immoderātus, inīquus.

undulate *vi* fluctuāre.

undulation *n* spīra *f*.

unduly *adv* nimis, plūs aequō.

undutiful *adj* impius.

undutifully *adv* impiē.

undutifulness *n* impietās *f*.

undying *adj* immortālis, aeternus.

unearth *vt* ēruere, dētegere.

unearthly *adj* mōnstruōsus, dīvīnus, hūmānō māior.

uneasily *adv* aegrē.

uneasiness *n* sollicitūdō *f*, perturbātiō *f*.

uneasy *adj* sollicitus, anxius, inquiētus.

uneducated *adj* illitterātus, indoctus, rudis; **be ~** litterās nescīre.

unemployed *adj* ōtiōsus.

unemployment *n* cessātiō *f*.

unencumbered *adj* expedītus, līber.

unending *adj* perpetuus, sempiternus.

unendowed *adj* indōtātus.

unendurable *adj* intolerandus, intolerābilis.

unenjoyable *adj* iniūcundus, molestus.

unenlightened *adj* rudis, inērudītus.

unenterprising *adj* iners.

unenviable *adj* nōn invidendus.

unequal *adj* impār, dispār.

unequalled *adj* ūnicus, singulāris.

unequally *adv* inaequāliter, inīquē.

unequivocal *adj* apertus, plānus.

unerring *adj* certus.

unerringly *adv* certē.

unessential *adj* adventīcius, supervacāneus.

uneven *adj* impār; (*surface*) asper, inīquus, inaequābilis.

unevenly *adv* inīquē, inaequāliter.

unevenness *n* inīquitās *f*, asperitās *f*.

unexamined *adj* (*case*) incognitus.

unexampled *adj* inaudītus, ūnicus, singulāris.

unexceptionable *adj* ēmendātus; (*authority*) certissimus.

unexpected *adj* imprōvīsus, inopīnātus, īnspērātus.

unexpectedly *adv* dē imprōvīsō, ex īnspērātō, inopīnātō, necopīnātō.

unexplored *adj* inexplōrātus.

unfading *adj* perennis, vīvus.

unfailing *adj* perennis, certus, perpetuus.

unfailingly *adv* semper.

unfair *adj* inīquus, iniūstus.

unfairly *adv* inīquē, iniūstē.

unfairness *n* inīquitās *f*, iniūstitia *f*.

unfaithful *adj* īnfidēlis, īnfīdus, perfidus.

unfaithfully *adv* īnfidēliter.

unfaithfulness *n* īnfidēlitās *f*.

unfamiliar *adj* novus, ignōtus, īnsolēns; (*sight*) invīsitātus.

unfamiliarity *n* īnsolentia *f*.

unfashionable *adj* obsolētus.

unfasten *vt* solvere, refīgere.

unfathomable *adj* īnfīnītus, profundus.

unfavourable *adj* inīquus, adversus, importūnus.

unfavourably *adv* inīquē, male; **be ~ disposed** āversō animō esse.

unfed *adj* iēiūnus.

unfeeling *adj* dūrus, crūdēlis, ferreus.

unfeelingly *adv* crūdēliter.

unfeigned *adj* sincērus, vērus, simplex.

unfeignedly *adv* sincērē, vērē.

unfilial *adj* impius.

unfinished *adj* īnfectus, imperfectus.

unfit *adj* inūtilis, incommodus, aliēnus.

unfix *vt* refīgere.

unflinching *adj* impavidus, firmus.

unfold *vt* explicāre, ēvolvere; (*story*) expōnere, ēnārrāre.

unfolding *n* explicātiō *f*.

unforeseen *adj* imprōvīsus.

unforgettable *adj* memorābilis.

unforgiving *adj* implācābilis.

unformed *adj* īnfōrmis.

unfortified *adj* immūnītus, nūdus.

unfortunate *adj* īnfēlīx, īnfortūnātus.
unfortunately *adv* īnfēlīciter, male; ~ **you did not come** male accidit quod nōn vēnistī.
unfounded *adj* inānis, vānus.
unfrequented *adj* dēsertus.
unfriendliness *n* inimīcitia *f*.
unfriendly *adj* inimīcus, malevolus; **in an ~ manner** inimīcē.
unfruitful *adj* sterilis; (*fig*) inānis, vānus.
unfruitfulness *n* sterilitās *f*.
unfulfilled *adj* īnfectus, inritus.
unfurl *vt* explicāre, pandere.
unfurnished *adj* nūdus.
ungainly *adj* agrestis, rūsticus.
ungallant *adj* inurbānus, parum cōmis.
ungenerous *adj* illīberālis; ~ **conduct** illīberālitās *f*.
ungentlemanly *adj* illīberālis.
ungirt *adj* discinctus.
ungodliness *n* impietās *f*.
ungodly *adj* impius.
ungovernable *adj* impotēns, indomitus.
ungovernableness *n* impotentia *f*.
ungraceful *adj* inconcinnus, inēlegāns.
ungracefully *adv* inēleganter.
ungracious *adj* inhūmānus, petulāns, importūnus.
ungraciously *adv* acerbē.
ungrammatical *adj* barbarus; **be ~** soloecismum facere.
ungrateful *adj* ingrātus.
ungrudging *adj* largus, nōn invītus.
ungrudgingly *adv* sine invidiā.
unguarded *adj* intūtus; (*word*) incautus, incōnsultus.
unguardedly *adv* temerē, incōnsultē.
unguent *n* unguentum *nt*.
unhallowed *adj* profānus, impius.
unhand *vt* mittere.
unhandy *adj* inhabilis.
unhappily *adv* īnfēlīciter, miserē.
unhappiness *n* miseria *f*, tristitia *f*, maestitia *f*.
unhappy *adj* īnfēlix, miser, tristis.
unharmed *adj* incolumis, integer, salvus.
unharness *vt* disiungere.
unhealthiness *n* valētūdō *f*; (*climate*) gravitās *f*.
unhealthy *adj* invalidus, aeger; (*climate*) gravis, pestilens.
unheard *adj* inaudītus; (*law*) indictā causā.
unheard-of *adj* inaudītus.
unheeded *adj* neglectus.
unheeding *adj* immemor, sēcūrus.
unhelpful *adj* difficilis, invītus.
unhesitating *adj* audāx, prōmptus.
unhesitatingly *adv* sine dubitātiōne.
unhewn *adj* rudis.
unhindered *adj* expedītus.
unhinged *adj* mente captus.
unhistorical *adj* fictus, commentīcius.
unholiness *n* impietās *f*.
unholy *adj* impius.

unhonoured *adj* inhonōrātus.
unhoped-for *adj* īnspērātus.
unhorse *vt* excutere, equō dēicere.
unhurt *adj* integer, incolumis.
unicorn *n* monocerōs *m*.
uniform *adj* aequābilis, aequālis ♦ *n* īnsignia *ntpl*; (*MIL*) sagum *nt*; **in ~** sagātus; **put on ~** saga sūmere.
uniformity *n* aequābilitās *f*, cōnstantia *f*.
uniformly *adv* aequābiliter, ūnō tenōre.
unify *vt* coniungere.
unimaginative *adj* hebes, stolidus.
unimpaired *adj* integer, incolumis, illībātus.
unimpeachable *adj* (*character*) integer; (*style*) ēmendātus.
unimportant *adj* levis, nullīus mōmentī.
uninformed *adj* indoctus, ignārus.
uninhabitable *adj* inhabitābilis.
uninhabited *adj* dēsertus.
uninitiated *adj* profānus; (*fig*) rudis.
uninjured *adj* integer, incolumis.
unintelligent *adj* īnsipiēns, tardus, excors.
unintelligible *adj* obscūrus.
unintelligibly *adv* obscūrē.
unintentionally *adv* imprūdēns, temerē.
uninteresting *adj* frīgidus, āridus.
uninterrupted *adj* continuus, perpetuus.
uninterruptedly *adv* continenter, sine ullā intermissiōne.
uninvited *adj* invocātus; ~ **guest** umbra *f*.
uninviting *adj* iniūcundus, invenustus.
union *n* coniūnctiō *f*; (*social*) cōnsociātiō *f*, societās *f*; (*POL*) foederātae cīvitātēs *fpl*; (*agreement*) concordia *f*, cōnsēnsus *m*; (*marriage*) coniugium *nt*.
unique *adj* ūnicus, ēgregius, singulāris.
unison *n* concentus *m*; (*fig*) concordia *f*, cōnsēnsus *m*.
unit *n* ūniō *f*.
unite *vt* coniungere, cōnsociāre, cōpulāre ♦ *v* coīre; cōnsentīre, cōnspīrāre; (*rivers*) cōnfluere.
unity *n* (*concord*) concordia *f*, cōnsēnsus *m*.
universal *adj* ūniversus, commūnis.
universally *adv* ūniversus, omnis; (*place*) ubīque.
universe *n* mundus *m*, rērum nātūra *f*.
university *n* academīa *f*.
unjust *adj* iniūstus, inīquus.
unjustifiable *adj* indignus, inexcūsābilis.
unjustly *adv* iniūstē, iniūriā.
unkempt *adj* horridus.
unkind *adj* inhūmānus, inīquus.
unkindly *adv* inhūmānē, asperē.
unkindness *n* inhūmānitās *f*.
unknowingly *adv* imprūdēns, īnscius.
unknown *adj* ignōtus, incognitus; (*fame*) obscūrus.
unlawful *adj* vetitus, iniūriōsus.
unlawfully *adv* iniūriōsē, iniūriā.
unlearn *vt* dēdiscere.
unlearned *adj* indoctus, inērudītus.
unless *conj* nisī.

unlettered *adj* illiterātus.
unlike *adj* dissimilis (+ *gen or dat*), dispār.
unlikely *adj* nōn vērīsimilis.
unlimited *adj* īnfīnītus, immēnsus.
unload *vt* exonerāre, deonerāre; (*from ship*)
  expōnere.
unlock *vt* reserāre, reclūdere.
unlooked-for *adj* īnspērātus, inexpectātus.
unloose *vt* solvere, exsolvere.
unlovely *adj* invenustus.
unluckily *adv* īnfēlīciter.
unlucky *adj* īnfēlīx, īnfortūnātus; (*day*) āter.
unmake *vt* īnfectum reddere.
unman *vt* mollīre, frangere, dēbilitāre.
unmanageable *adj* inhabilis.
unmanly *adj* mollis, ēnervātus, muliebris.
unmannerliness *n* importūnitās *f*,
  inhūmānitās *f*.
unmannerly *adj* importūnus, inhūmānus.
unmarried *adj* (*man*) caelebs; (*woman*) vidua.
unmask *vt* nūdāre, dētegere.
unmatched *adj* ūnicus, singulāris.
unmeaning *adj* inānis.
unmeasured *adj* īnfīnītus, immoderātus.
unmeet *adj* parum idōneus.
unmelodious *adj* absonus, absurdus.
unmentionable *adj* īnfandus.
unmentioned *adj* indictus; **leave ~** ōmittere.
unmerciful *adj* immisericors, inclēmēns.
unmercifully *adv* inclēmenter.
unmerited *adj* immeritus, indignus.
unmindful *adj* immemor.
unmistakable *adj* certus, manifestus.
unmistakably *adv* sine dubiō, certē.
unmitigated *adj* merus.
unmixed *adj* pūrus.
unmolested *adj* intāctus.
unmoor *vt* solvere.
unmoved *adj* immōtus.
unmusical *adj* absonus, absurdus.
unmutilated *adj* integer.
unnatural *adj* (*event*) mōnstruōsus; (*feelings*)
  impius, inhūmānus; (*style*) arcessītus,
  pūtidus.
unnaturally *adv* contrā nātūram; impiē,
  inhūmānē; pūtidē.
unnavigable *adj* innāvigābilis.
unnecessarily *adv* nimis.
unnecessary *adj* inūtilis, supervacāneus.
unnerve *vt* dēbilitāre, frangere.
unnoticed *adj*: **be ~** latēre, fallere.
unnumbered *adj* innumerus.
unobjectionable *adj* honestus, culpae expers.
unobservant *adj* tardus.
unobserved *adj*: **be ~** latēre, fallere.
unobstructed *adj* apertus, pūrus.
unobtrusive *adj* verēcundus; **be ~** fallere.
unobtrusiveness *n* verēcundia *f*.
unoccupied *adj* vacuus, ōtiōsus.
unoffending *adj* innocēns.
unofficial *adj* prīvātus.
unorthodox *adj* abnōrmis.
unostentatious *adj* modestus, verēcundus.

unostentatiously *adv* nullā iactātiōne.
unpaid *adj* (*services*) grātuītus; (*money*)
  dēbitus.
unpalatable *adj* amārus; (*fig*) iniūcundus,
  īnsuāvis.
unparalleled *adj* ūnicus, inaudītus.
unpardonable *adj* inexcūsābilis.
unpatriotic *adj* impius.
unpitying *adj* immisericors, ferreus.
unpleasant *adj* iniūcundus, ingrātus,
  īnsuāvis, gravis, molestus.
unpleasantly *adv* iniūcundē, ingrātē,
  graviter.
unpleasantness *n* iniūcunditās *f*, molestia *f*.
unpleasing *adj* ingrātus, invenustus.
unploughed *adj* inarātus.
unpoetical *adj* pedester.
unpolished *adj* impolītus; (*person*) incultus,
  agrestis, inurbānus; (*style*) inconditus, rudis.
unpopular *adj* invidiōsus, invīsus.
unpopularity *n* invidia *f*, odium *nt*.
unpractised *adj* inexercitātus, imperītus.
unprecedented *adj* īnsolēns, novus,
  inaudītus.
unprejudiced *adj* integer, aequus.
unpremeditated *adj* repentīnus, subitus.
unprepared *adj* imparātus.
unprepossessing *adj* invenustus, illepidus.
unpretentious *adj* modestus, verēcundus.
unprincipled *adj* improbus, levis, prāvus.
unproductive *adj* īnfēcundus, sterilis.
unprofitable *adj* inūtilis, vānus.
unprofitably *adv* frustrā, ab rē.
unpropitious *adj* īnfēlīx, adversus.
unpropitiously *adv* malīs ōminibus.
unprotected *adj* indēfēnsus, intūtus, nūdus.
unprovoked *adj* ultrō (*adv*).
unpunished *adj* impūnītus ♦ *adv* impūne.
unqualified *adj* nōn idōneus; (*unrestricted*)
  absolūtus.
unquestionable *adj* certus.
unquestionably *adv* facile, certē.
unquestioning *adj* crēdulus.
unravel *vt* retexere; (*fig*) ēnōdāre, explicāre.
unready *adj* imparātus.
unreal *adj* falsus, vānus.
unreality *n* vānitās *f*.
unreasonable *adj* inīquus, importūnus.
unreasonableness *n* inīquitās *f*.
unreasonably *adv* inīquē.
unreasoning *adj* stolidus, temerārius.
unreclaimed *adj* (*land*) incultus.
unrefined *adj* impolītus, inurbānus, rudis.
unregistered *adj* incēnsus.
unrelated *adj* aliēnus.
unrelenting *adj* implācābilis, inexōrābilis.
unreliable *adj* incertus, levis.
unreliably *adv* leviter.
unrelieved *adj* perpetuus, adsiduus.
unremitting *adj* adsiduus.
unrequited *adj* inultus, inānis.
unreservedly *adv* apertē, sine ullā
  exceptiōne.

unresponsive *adj* hebes.
unrest *n* inquiēs *f*, sollicitūdō *f*.
unrestrained *adj* līber, impotēns, effrēnātus, immoderātus.
unrestricted *adj* līber, absolūtus.
unrevenged *adj* inultus.
unrewarded *adj* inhonōrātus.
unrewarding *adj* ingrātus, vānus.
unrighteous *adj* iniūstus, impius.
unrighteously *adv* iniūstē, impiē.
unrighteousness *n* impietās *f*.
unripe *adj* immātūrus, crūdus.
unrivalled *adj* ēgregius, singulāris, ūnicus.
unroll *vt* ēvolvere, explicāre.
unromantic *adj* pedester.
unruffled *adj* immōtus, tranquillus.
unruliness *n* licentia *f*, impotentia *f*.
unruly *adj* effrēnātus, impotēns, immoderātus.
unsafe *adj* perīculōsus, dubius; (*structure*) īnstābilis.
unsaid *adj* indictus.
unsatisfactorily *adv* nōn ex sententiā, male.
unsatisfactory *adj* parum idōneus, malus.
unsatisfied *adj* parum contenus.
unsavoury *adj* īnsuāvis, taeter.
unscathed *adj* incolumis, integer.
unschooled *adj* indoctus, inērudītus.
unscrupulous *adj* improbus, impudēns.
unscrupulously *adv* improbē, impudenter.
unscrupulousness *n* improbitās *f*, impudentia *f*.
unseal *vt* resignāre, solvere.
unseasonable *adj* intempestīvus, importūnus.
unseasonableness *n* incommoditās *f*.
unseasonably *adv* intempestīvē, importūnē.
unseasoned *adj* (*food*) nōn condītus; (*wood*) viridis.
unseat *vt* (*rider*) excutere.
unseaworthy *adj* īnfirmus.
unseeing *adj* caecus.
unseemly *adj* indecōrus.
unseen *adj* invīsus; (*ever before*) invīsitātus.
unselfish *adj* innocēns, probus, līberālis.
unselfishly *adv* līberāliter.
unselfishness *n* innocentia *f*, līberālitās *f*.
unserviceable *adj* inūtilis.
unsettle *vt* ad incertum revocāre, turbāre, sollicitāre.
unsettled *adj* incertus, dubius; (*mind*) sollicitus, suspēnsus; (*times*) turbidus.
unsew *vt* dissuere.
unshackle *vt* expedīre, solvere.
unshaken *adj* immōtus, firmus, stabilis.
unshapely *adj* dēfōrmis.
unshaven *adj* intōnsus.
unsheathe *vt* dēstringere, stringere.
unshod *adj* nūdis pedibus.
unshorn *adj* intōnsus.
unsightliness *n* dēfōrmitās *f*, turpitūdō *f*.
unsightly *adj* foedus, dēfōrmis.
unskilful *adj* indoctus, īnscītus, incallidus.

unskilfully *adv* indoctē, īnscītē, incallide.
unskilfulness *n* īnscītia *f*, imperītia *f*.
unskilled *adj* imperītus, indoctus; ~ **in** imperitus (+ *gen*).
unslaked *adj* (*lime*) vīvus; (*thirst*) inexplētus.
unsociable *adj* īnsociābilis, difficilis.
unsoiled *adj* integer, pūrus.
unsolicited *adj* voluntārius ♦ *adv* ultrō.
unsophisticated *adj* simplex, ingenuus.
unsound *adj* īnfirmus; (*mind*) īnsānus; (*opinion*) falsus, perversus.
unsoundness *n* īnfirmitās *f*; īnsānitās *f*; prāvitās *f*.
unsparing *adj* inclēmēns, immisericors; (*lavish*) prōdigus.
unsparingly *adv* inclēmenter; prōdigē.
unspeakable *adj* īnfandus, incrēdibilis.
unspeakably *adv* incrēdibiliter.
unspoilt *adj* integer.
unspoken *adj* indictus, tacitus.
unspotted *adj* integer, pūrus.
unstable *adj* īnstabilis; (*fig*) incōnstāns, levis.
unstained *adj* pūrus, incorruptus, integer.
unstatesmanlike *adj* illīberālis.
unsteadily *adv* incōnstanter; **walk** ~ titubāre.
unsteadiness *n* (*fig*) incōnstantia *f*.
unsteady *adj* īnstabilis; (*fig*) incōnstāns.
unstitch *vt* dissuere.
unstring *vt* retendere.
unstudied *adj* simplex.
unsubdued *adj* invictus.
unsubstantial *adj* levis, inānis.
unsuccessful *adj* īnfēlīx; (*effort*) inritus; **be** ~ offendere; **I am** ~ mihī nōn succēdit.
unsuccessfully *adv* īnfēlīciter, rē īnfectā.
unsuitable *adj* incommodus, aliēnus, importūnus; **it is** ~ dēdecet.
unsuitableness *n* incommoditās *f*.
unsuitably *adv* incommodē, ineptē.
unsuited *adj* parum idōneus.
unsullied *adj* pūrus, incorruptus.
unsure *adj* incertus, dubius.
unsurpassable *adj* inexsuperābilis.
unsurpassed *adj* ūnicus, singulāris.
unsuspected *adj* latēns, nōn suspectus; **be** ~ latēre, in suspiciōnem nōn venīre.
unsuspecting *adj* imprōvidus, imprūdēns.
unsuspicious *adj* nōn suspicāx, crēdulus.
unswerving *adj* cōnstāns.
unsworn *adj* iniūrātus.
unsymmetrical *adj* inaequālis.
untainted *adj* incorruptus, integer.
untamable *adj* indomitus.
untamed *adj* indomitus, ferus.
untaught *adj* indoctus, rudis.
unteach *vt* dēdocēre.
unteachable *adj* indocilis.
untenable *adj* inānis, īnfirmus.
unthankful *adj* ingrātus.
unthankfully *adv* ingrātē.
unthankfulness *n* ingrātus animus *m*.
unthinkable *adj* incrēdibilis.
unthinking *adj* incōnsīderātus, imprōvidus.

unthriftily *adv* prōdigē.
unthrifty *adj* prōdigus, profūsus.
untidily *adv* neglegenter.
untidiness *n* neglegentia *f*.
untidy *adj* neglegēns, inconcinnus, squālidus.
untie *vt* solvere.
until *conj* dum, dōnec ♦ *prep* usque ad (*acc*), in (*acc*); ~ **now** adhūc.
untilled *adj* incultus.
untimely *adj* intempestīvus, immātūrus, importūnus.
untiring *adj* impiger; (*effort*) adsiduus.
unto *prep* ad (*acc*), in (*acc*).
untold *adj* innumerus.
untouched *adj* intāctus, integer.
untoward *adj* adversus, malus.
untrained *adj* inexercitātus, imperītus, rudis.
untried *adj* intemptātus, inexpertus; (*trial*) incognitus.
untrodden *adj* āvius.
untroubled *adj* tranquillus, placidus, quiētus; (*mind*) sēcūrus.
untrue *adj* falsus, fictus; (*disloyal*) īnfīdus, īnfīdēlis.
untrustworthy *adj* īnfīdus, mōbilis.
untruth *n* mendācium *nt*, falsum *nt*.
untruthful *adj* mendāx, falsus.
untruthfully *adv* falsō, falsē.
untuneful *adj* absonus.
unturned *adj*: **leave no stone** ~ nihil intemptātum relinquere, omnia experīrī.
untutored *adj* indoctus, incultus.
unused *adj* (*person*) īnsuētus, īnsolitus; (*thing*) integer.
unusual *adj* īnsolitus, inūsitātus, īnsolēns, novus.
unusually *adv* īnsolenter, praeter cōnsuētūdinem.
unusualness *n* īnsolentia *f*, novitās *f*.
unutterable *adj* īnfandus, inēnārrābilis.
unvarnished *adj* (*fig*) simplex, nūdus.
unveil *vt* (*fig*) aperīre, patefacere.
unversed *adj* ignārus (*gen*), imperītus (*gen*).
unwanted *adj* supervacāneus.
unwarily *adv* imprudenter, incautē, incōnsultē.
unwariness *n* imprūdentia *f*.
unwarlike *adj* imbellis.
unwarrantable *adj* inīquus, iniūstus.
unwarrantably *adv* iniūriā.
unwary *adj* imprūdēns, incautus, incōnsultus.
unwavering *adj* stabilis, immōtus.
unwearied, unwearying *adj* indēfessus, adsiduus.
unweave *vt* retexere.
unwedded *adj* (*man*) caelebs; (*woman*) vidua.
unwelcome *adj* ingrātus.
unwell *adj* aeger, aegrōtus.
unwept *adj* indēflētus.
unwholesome *adj* pestilēns, gravis.
unwieldy *adj* inhabilis.
unwilling *adj* invītus; **be** ~ nolle.
unwillingly *adv* invītus.

unwind *vt* ēvolvere, retexere.
unwise *adj* stultus, īnsipiēns, imprūdēns.
unwisely *adv* īnsipienter, imprūdenter.
unwittingly *adv* imprūdēns, īnsciēns.
unwonted *adj* īnsolitus, inūsitātus.
unworthily *adv* indignē.
unworthiness *n* indignitās *f*.
unworthy *adj* indignus (+ *abl*).
unwounded *adj* intāctus, integer.
unwrap *vt* ēvolvere, explicāre.
unwritten *adj* nōn scrīptus; ~ **law** mōs *m*.
unwrought *adj* īnfectus, rudis.
unyielding *adj* dūrus, firmus, inexōrābilis.
unyoke *vt* disiungere.
up *adv* sūrsum; ~ **and down** sūrsum deōrsum; ~ **to** usque ad (*acc*), tenus (*abl, after noun*); **bring** ~ subvehere; (*child*) ēducāre; **climb** ~ ēscendere; **come** ~ **to** aequāre; **lift** ~ ērigere, sublevāre; **from childhood** ~ ā puerō; **it is all** ~ **with** āctum est dē; **well** ~ **in** gnārus (*gen*), perītus (*gen*); **what is he** ~ **to?** quid struit? ♦ *prep* (*motion*) in (*acc*) ♦ *n*: ~**s and downs** (*fig*) vicissitūdinēs *fpl*.
upbraid *vt* exprobrāre (*dat pers, acc charge*); obicere (*dat and acc*), increpāre, castīgāre.
upbringing *n* ēducātiō *f*.
upheaval *n* ēversiō *f*.
upheave *vt* ēvertere.
uphill *adj* acclīvis ♦ *adv* adversō colle, in adversum collem.
uphold *vt* sustinēre, tuērī, servāre.
upholstery *n* supellex *f*.
upkeep *n* impēnsa *f*.
upland *adj* montānus.
uplift *vt* extollere, sublevāre.
upon *prep* in (*abl*), super (*abl*); (*motion*) in (*acc*), super (*acc*); (*dependence*) ex (*abl*); ~ **this** quō factō.
upper *adj* superior; **gain the** ~ **hand** superāre, vincere.
uppermost *adj* suprēmus, summus.
uppish *adj* superbus.
upright *adj* rēctus, ērēctus; (*character*) integer, probus, honestus.
uprightly *adv* rēctē; integrē.
uprightness *n* integritās *f*.
upriver *adj, adv* adversō flūmine.
uproar *n* tumultus *m*; clāmor *m*.
uproarious *adj* tumultuōsus.
uproariously *adv* tumultuōsē.
uproot *vt* ērādīcāre, exstirpāre, ēruere.
upset *vt* ēvertere, invertere, subvertere; ~ **the apple cart** plaustrum percellere ♦ *adj* (*fig*) perturbātus.
upshot *n* ēventus *m*.
upside-down *adv*: **turn** ~ ēvertere, invertere; (*fig*) miscēre.
upstart *n* novus homō *m* ♦ *adj* repentīnus.
upstream *adj, adv* adversō flūmine.
upward(s) *adv* sūrsum; ~ **of** (*number*) amplius.
urban *adj* urbānus, oppidānus.
urbane *adj* urbānus, cōmis.
urbanely *adv* urbānē, cōmiter.

urbanity n urbānitās f.

urchin n (boy) puerulus m; (animal) echīnus m.

urge vt urgēre, impellere; (speech) hortārī, incitāre; (advice) suādēre; (request) sollicitāre; ~ **on** incitāre ♦ n impulsus m; dēsīderium nt.

urgency n necessitās f.

urgent adj praesēns, gravis; **be** ~ instāre.

urgently adv graviter.

urn n urna f.

usage n mōs m, īnstitūtum nt, ūsus m.

use n ūsus m; (custom) mōs m, cōnsuētūdō f; **be of** ~ ūsuī esse, prōdesse, condūcere; **out of** ~ desuētus; **go out of** ~ exolēscere; **in common** ~ ūsitātus; **it's no** ~ nīl agis, nīl agimus ♦ vt ūtī (abl); (improperly) abūtī; (for a purpose) adhibēre; (word) ūsurpāre; ~ **up** cōnsūmere, exhaurīre; **~d to** adsuētus (dat); solēre (+ infin); **I ~d to do** faciebam.

useful adj ūtilis; **be** ~ ūsuī esse.

usefully adv ūtiliter.

usefulness n ūtilitās f.

useless adj inūtilis; (thing) inānis, inritus; **be** ~ nihil valēre.

uselessly adv inūtiliter, frustrā.

uselessness n inānitās f.

usher n (court) apparitor m; (theatre) dēsignātor m ♦ vt: ~ **in** indūcere, intrōdūcere.

usual adj ūsitātus, solitus; **as** ~ ut adsolet, ut fert cōnsuētūdō, ex cōnsuētūdine; **out of the** ~ īnsolitus, extrā ōrdinem.

usually adv ferē, plērumque; **he** ~ **comes** venīre solet.

usufruct n ūsus et frūctus m.

usurer n faenerātor m.

usurp vt occupāre, invādere in (acc), ūsurpāre.

usurpation n occupātō f.

usury n faenerātiō f, ūsūra f; **practise** ~ faenerārī.

utensil n īnstrūmentum nt, vās nt.

utility n ūtilitās f, commodum nt.

utilize vt ūtī (abl); (for a purpose) adhibēre.

utmost adj extrēmus, summus; **at the** ~ summum; **do one's** ~ omnibus vīribus contendere.

utter adj tōtus, extrēmus, summus ♦ vt ēmittere, ēdere, ēloquī, prōnūntiāre.

utterance n dictum nt; (process) prōnūntiātiō f.

utterly adv funditus, omnīnō, penitus.

uttermost adj extrēmus, ultimus.

V, v

vacancy n inānitās f; (office) vacuitās f; **there is a** ~ locus vacat; **elect to fill a** ~ sufficere.

vacant adj inānis, vacuus; **be** ~ vacāre.

vacate vt vacuum facere.

vacation n fēriae fpl.

vacillate vi vacillāre, dubitāre.

vacillation n dubitātiō f.

vacuity n inānitās f.

vacuous adj vacuus.

vacuum n ināne nt.

vagabond n grassātor m ♦ adj vagus.

vagary n libīdō f.

vagrancy n errātiō f.

vagrant n grassātor m, vagus m.

vague adj incertus, dubius.

vaguely adv incertē.

vain n vānus, inānis, inritus; (person) glōriōsus; **in** ~ frustrā.

vainglorious adj glōriōsus.

vainglory n glōria f, iactantia f.

vainly adv frustrā, nēquīquam.

vale n vallis f.

valet n cubiculārius m.

valiant adj fortis, ācer.

valiantly adv fortiter, ācriter.

valid adj ratus; (argument) gravis, firmus.

validity n vīs f, auctōritās f.

valley n vallis f.

valorous adj fortis.

valour n virtūs f.

valuable adj pretiōsus.

valuation n aestimātiō f.

value n pretium nt; (fig) vīs f, honor m ♦ vt aestimāre; (esteem) dīligere; ~ **highly** māgnī aestimāre; ~ **little** parvī aestimāre, parvī facere.

valueless adj vīlis, minimī pretī.

valuer n aestimātor m.

van n (in battle) prīma aciēs f; (on march) prīmum agmen nt.

vanguard n prīmum agmen nt.

vanish vi diffugere, ēvānēscere, dīlābī.

vanity n (unreality) vānitās f; (conceit) glōria f.

vanquish vt vincere, superāre, dēvincere.

vanquisher n victor m.

vantage n (ground) locus superior m.

vapid adj vapidus, īnsulsus.

vapidly adv īnsulsē.

vaporous adj nebulōsus.

vapour n vapor m, nebula f; (from earth) exhālātiō f.

variable adj varius, mūtābilis.

variableness n mūtābilitās f, incōnstantia f.

variance n discordia f, dissēnsiō f, discrepantia f; **at** ~ discors; **be at** ~ dissidēre

inter sē discrepāre; **set at** ~ aliēnāre.
variant *adj* varius.
variation *n* varietās *f*, vicissitūdō *f*.
variegate *vt* variāre.
variegated *adj* varius.
variety *n* varietās *f*; (*number*) multitūdō *f*;
(*kind*) genus *nt*; **a** ~ **of** dīversī.
various *adj* varius, dīversus.
variously *adv* variē.
varlet *n* verberō *m*.
varnish *n* pigmentum *nt*; (*fig*) fūcus *m*.
varnished *adj* (*fig*) fūcātus.
vary *vt* variāre, mūtāre; (*decorate*) distinguere
♦ *vi* mūtārī.
vase *n* vās *nt*.
vassal *n* ambāctus *m*; (*fig*) cliēns *m*.
vast *adj* vastus, immānis, ingēns, immēnsus.
vastly *adv* valdē.
vastness *n* māgnitūdō *f*, immēnsitās *f*.
vat *n* cūpa *f*.
vault *n* (ARCH) fornix *f*; (*jump*) saltus *m* ♦ *vi*
salīre.
vaulted *adj* fornicātus.
vaunt *vt* iactāre, ostentāre ♦ *vi* sē iactāre,
glōriārī.
vaunting *n* ostentātiō *f*, glōria *f* ♦ *adj*
glōriōsus.
veal *n* vitulīna *f*.
vedette *n* excursor *m*.
veer *vi* sē vertere, flectī.
vegetable *n* holus *nt*.
vehemence *n* vīs *f*, violentia *f*; (*passion*) ārdor
m, impetus *m*.
vehement *adj* vehemēns, violentus, ācer.
vehemently *adv* vehementer, ācriter.
vehicle *n* vehiculum *nt*.
Veii *n* Veiī, Vēiōrum *mpl*.
veil *n* rīca *f*; (*bridal*) flammeum *nt*; (*fig*)
integumentum *nt* ♦ *vt* vēlāre, tegere.
vein *n* vēna *f*.
vellum *n* membrāna *f*.
velocity *n* celeritās *f*, vēlōcitās *f*.
venal *adj* vēnālis.
vend *vt* vēndere.
vendetta *n* simultās *f*.
vendor *n* caupō *m*.
veneer *n* (*fig*) speciēs *f*, fūcus *m*.
venerable *adj* gravis, augustus.
venerate *vt* colere, venerārī.
veneration *n* venerātiō *f*, cultus *m*.
venerator *n* cultor *m*.
vengeance *n* ultiō *f*, poena *f*; **take** ~ **on** ulcīscī,
vindicāre in (*acc*); **take** ~ **for** ulcīscī,
vindicāre.
vengeful *adj* ultor.
venial *adj* ignōscendus.
venison *n* dāma *f*, ferīna *f*.
venom *n* venēnum *nt*; (*fig*) vīrus *nt*.
venomous *adj* venēnātus.
vent *n* spīrāculum *nt*; (*outlet*) exitus *m*; **give** ~
to profundere, ēmittere ♦ *vt* ēmittere;
(*feelings on*) profundere in (*acc*), ērumpere
in (*acc*).

ventilate *vt* perflāre; (*opinion*) in medium
prōferre, vulgāre.
ventilation *n* perflāre.
venture *n* perīculum *nt*; (*gamble*) ālea *f*; **at a** ~
temerē ♦ *vi* audēre ♦ *vt* perīclitārī, in āleam
dare.
venturesome *adj* audāx, temerārius.
venturesomeness *n* audācia *f*, temeritās *f*.
veracious *adj* vērāx, vēridicus.
veracity *n* vēritās *f*, fidēs *f*.
verb *n* verbum *nt*.
verbally *adv* per colloquia; (*translate*) ad
verbum, verbum prō verbō.
verbatim *adv* ad verbum, totidem verbīs.
verbiage *n* verba *ntpl*.
verbose *adj* verbōsus.
verbosity *n* loquendī prōfluentia *f*.
verdant *adj* viridis.
verdict *n* sententia *f*, iūdicium *nt*; **deliver a** ~
sententiam prōnūntiāre; **give a** ~ **in favour of**
causam adiūdicāre (*dat*).
verdigris *n* aerūgō *f*.
verdure *n* viriditās *f*.
verge *n* ōra *f*; **the** ~ **of** extrēmus; **on the** ~ **of**
(*fig*) prope (*acc*) ♦ *vi* vergere.
verification *n* cōnfirmātiō *f*.
verify *vt* cōnfirmāre, comprobāre.
verily *adv* profectō, certē.
verisimilitude *n* vērī similitūdō *f*.
veritable *adj* vērus.
veritably *adv* vērē.
verity *n* vēritās *f*.
vermilion *n* sandīx *f*.
vermin *n* bestiolae *fpl*.
vernacular *adj* patrius ♦ *n* patrius sermō *m*.
vernal *adj* vērnus.
versatile *adj* versūtus, varius.
versatility *n* versātile ingenium *nt*.
verse *n* (*line*) versus *m*; (*poetry*) versus *mpl*,
carmina *ntpl*.
versed *adj* īnstructus, perītus, exercitātus.
versification *n* ars versūs faciendī.
versify *vt* versū inclūdere ♦ *vi* versūs facere.
version *n* (*of story*) fōrma *f*; **give a Latin** ~ **of**
Latīnē reddere.
vertex *n* vertex *m*, fastīgium *nt*.
vertical *adj* rēctus, dīrēctus.
vertically *adv* ad līneam, rēctā līneā, ad
perpendiculum.
vertigo *n* vertīgō *f*.
vervain *n* verbēna *f*.
verve *n* ācrimōnia *f*.
very *adj* ipse ♦ *adv* admodum, valdē,
vehementer ♦ *superl*: **at that** ~ **moment** tum
māximē; **not** ~ nōn ita.
vessel *n* (*receptacle*) vās *nt*; (*ship*) nāvigium *nt*.
vest *n* subūcula *f* ♦ *vt*: ~ **power in** imperium
dēferre (*dat*); ~**ed interests** nummī locātī *mpl*.
vestal *adj* vestālis ♦ *n* virgō vestālis *f*.
vestibule *n* vestibulum *nt*.
vestige *n* vestīgium *nt*, indicium *nt*.
vestment *n* vestīmentum *nt*.
vesture *n* vestis *f*.

vetch n vicia f.
veteran adj veterānus ♦ n (MIL) veterānus m; (fig) veterātor m.
veto n interdictum nt; (tribune's) intercessiō f ♦ vt interdīcere (dat); (tribune) intercēdere (dat).
vex vt vexāre, sollicitāre, stomachum movēre (dat); **be ~ed** aegrē ferre, stomachārī.
vexation n (caused) molestia f; (felt) dolor m, stomachus m.
vexatious adj odiōsus, molestus.
vexatiously adv molestē.
vexed adj īrātus; (question) anceps.
via prep per (acc).
viaduct n pōns m.
viands n cibus m.
vibrate vi vībrāre, tremere.
vibration n tremor m.
vicarious adj vicārius.
vice n (general) prāvitās f, perditī mōrēs mpl; (particular) vitium nt, flāgitium nt; (clamp) fībula f.
viceroy n prōcūrātor m.
vicinity n vīcīnia f, vīcīnitās f.
vicious adj prāvus, vitiōsus, flāgitiōsus; (temper) contumāx.
viciously adv flāgitiōsē; contumāciter.
vicissitude n vicissitūdō f; **~s** pl vicēs fpl.
victim n victima f, hostia f; (fig) piāculum nt; (exploited) praeda f; **be the ~ of** labōrāre ex; **fall a ~ to** morī (abl); (trickery) circumvenīrī (abl).
victimize vt nocēre (dat), circumvenīre.
victor n victor m.
victorious adj victor m, victrīx f; **be ~** vincere.
victory n victōria f; **win a ~** victōriam reportāre; **win a ~ over** vincere, superāre.
victory message n laureātae litterae fpl.
victory parade n triumphus m.
victual vt rem frūmentāriam suppeditāre (dat).
victualler n caupō m; (MIL) frūmentārius m.
victuals n cibus m; (MIL) frūmentum nt, commeātus m.
vie vi certāre, contendere; **~ with** aemulārī.
view n cōnspectus m; (from far) prōspectus m; (from high) dēspectus m; (opinion) sententia f; **exposed to ~** in mediō; **entertain a ~** sentīre; **in ~ of** propter (acc); **in my ~** meā sententiā, meō iūdiciō; **end in ~** prōpositum nt; **have in ~** spectāre; **point of ~** iūdicium nt; **with a ~ to** eō cōnsiliō ut ♦ vt īnspicere, spectāre, intuērī.
vigil n pervigilium nt; **keep a ~** vigilāre.
vigilance n vigilantia f, dīligentia f.
vigilant adj vigilāns, dīligēns.
vigilantly adv vigilanter, dīligenter.
vigorous adj ācer, vegetus, integer; (style) nervōsus.
vigorously adv ācriter, strēnuē.
vigour n vīs f, nervī mpl, integritās f.
vile adj turpis, impūrus, abiectus.
vilely adv turpiter, impūrē.

vileness n turpitūdō f, impūritās f.
vilification n obtrectātiō f, calumnia f.
vilify vt obtrectāre, calumniārī, maledīcere (dat).
villa n vīlla f.
village n pāgus m, vīcus m; **in every ~** pāgātim.
villager n pāgānus m, vīcānus m.
villain n furcifer m, scelerātus m.
villainous adj scelestus, scelerātus, nēquam.
villainously adv scelestē.
villainy n scelus nt, nēquitia f.
vindicate vt (right) vindicāre; (action) pūrgāre (belief) arguere; (person) dēfendere, prōpugnāre prō (abl).
vindication n dēfēnsiō f, pūrgātiō f.
vindicator n dēfēnsor m, prōpugnātor m.
vindictive adj ultor, ulcīscendī cupidus.
vine n vītis f; **wild ~** labrusca f.
vinedresser n vīnitor m.
vinegar n acētum nt.
vineyard n vīnea f, vīnētum nt.
vintage n vindēmia f.
vintner n vīnārius m.
violate vt violāre.
violation n violātiō f.
violator n violātor m.
violence n violentia f, vīs f, iniūria f; **do ~ to** violāre; **offer ~ to** vim īnferre (dat).
violent adj violentus, vehemēns; (passion) ācer, impotēns; **~ death** nex f.
violently adv vehementer, per vim.
violet n viola f.
viper n vīpera f.
viperous adj (fig) malignus.
virgin n virgō f ♦ adj virginālis.
virginity n virginitās f.
virile adj virīlis.
virility n virtūs f.
virtually adv rē vērā, ferē.
virtue n virtūs f, honestum nt; (woman's) pudīcitia f; (power) vis f, potestās f; **by ~ of** ex (abl).
virtuous adj honestus, probus, integer.
virtuously adv honestē.
virulence n vīs f, vīrus nt.
virulent adj acerbus.
virus n vīrus nt.
visage n ōs n, faciēs f.
vis-à-vis prep exadversus (acc).
viscosity n lentor m.
viscous adj lentus, tenāx.
visible adj ēvidēns, cōnspicuus, manifestus; **be ~** appārēre.
visibly adv manifestō.
vision n (sense) vīsus m; (power) aspectus m; (apparition) vīsum nt, vīsiō f; (whim) somnium nt.
visionary adj vānus ♦ n somniāns m.
visit n adventus m; (formal) salūtātiō f; (long) commorātiō f; **pay a ~ to** invīsere ♦ vt vīsere; **~ occasionally** intervīsere; **go to ~** invīsere.
visitation n (to inspect) recēnsiō f; (to punish) animadversiō f.

visitor n hospes m, hospita f; (formal) salūtātor m.

visor n buccula f.

vista n prōspectus m.

visual adj oculōrum.

visualize vt animō cernere, ante oculōs pōnere.

visually adv oculīs.

vital adj (of life) vītālis; (essential) necessārius, māximī mōmentī.

vitality n vīs f; (style) sanguis m.

vitally adv praecipuē, imprīmīs.

vitals n viscera ntpl.

vitiate vt corrumpere, vitiāre.

vitreous adj vitreus.

vitrify vt in vitrum excoquere.

vituperate vt vituperāre, obiūrgāre.

vituperation n vituperātiō f, maledicta ntpl.

vituperative adj maledicus.

vivacious adj alacer, vegetus, hilaris.

vivaciously adv hilare.

vivacity n alacritās f, hilaritās f.

vivid adj vīvidus, ācer.

vividly adv ācriter.

vivify vt animāre.

vixen n vulpēs f.

vocabulary n verbōrum cōpia f.

vocal adj: ~ music vōcis cantus m.

vocation n officium nt, mūnus nt.

vociferate vt, vi vōciferārī, clāmāre.

vociferation n vōciferātiō f, clāmor m.

vociferous adj vōciferāns.

vociferously adv māgnīs clāmōribus.

vogue n mōs m; **be in ~** flōrēre, in honōre esse.

voice n vōx f ♦ vt exprimere, ēloquī.

void adj inānis, vacuus; ~ **of** expers (gen); **null and ~** inritus ♦ n ināne nt ♦ vt ēvomere, ēmittere.

volatile adj levis, mōbilis.

volatility n levitās f.

volition n voluntās f.

volley n imber m.

volubility n volūbilitās f.

voluble adj volūbilis.

volume n (book) liber m; (mass) mōlēs f; (of sound) māgnitūdō f.

voluminous adj cōpiōsus.

voluntarily adv ultrō, suā sponte.

voluntary adj voluntārius; (unpaid) grātuītus.

volunteer n (MIL) ēvocātus m ♦ vt ultrō offerre ♦ vi (MIL) nōmen dare.

voluptuary n dēlicātus m, homō voluptārius m.

voluptuous adj voluptārius, mollis, dēlicātus, luxuriōsus.

voluptuously adv molliter, dēlicātē, luxuriōsē.

voluptuousness n luxuria f, libīdō f.

vomit vt vomere, ēvomere; ~ **up** ēvomere.

voracious adj vorāx, edāx.

voraciously adv avidē.

voracity n edācitās f, gula f.

vortex n vertex m, turbō m.

votary n cultor m.

vote n suffrāgium nt; (opinion) sententia f; ~ **for** (candidate) suffrāgārī (dat); (senator's motion) discēdere in sententiam (gen) ♦ vi (election) suffrāgium ferre; (judge) sententiam ferre; (senator) cēnsēre; **take a ~** (senate) discessiōnem facere ♦ vt (senate) dēcernere; ~ **against** (bill) antīquāre.

voter n suffrāgātor m.

votive adj vōtīvus.

vouch vi spondēre; ~ **for** praestāre, testificārī.

voucher n (person) auctor m; (document) auctōritās f.

vouchsafe vt concēdere.

vow n vōtum nt; (promise) fidēs f ♦ vt vovēre; (promise) spondēre.

vowel n vōcālis f.

voyage n nāvigātiō f, cursus m ♦ vi nāvigāre.

vulgar adj (common) vulgāris; (low) plēbēius, sordidus, īnsulsus.

vulgarity n sordēs fpl, īnsulsitās f.

vulgarly adv vulgō; īnsulsē.

vulnerable adj nūdus; (fig) obnoxius; **be ~** vulnerārī posse.

vulture n vultur m; (fig) vulturius m.

W, w

wad n massa f.

wade vi per vada īre; ~ **across** vadō trānsīre.

waft vt ferre, vehere.

wag n facētus homō m, ioculātor m ♦ vt movēre, mōtāre, agitāre ♦ vi movērī, agitārī.

wage n mercēs f; (pl) mercēs f, manupretium nt; (fig) pretium nt, praemium nt ♦ vt gerere; ~ **war on** bellum īnferre (dat)/gerere.

wager n spōnsiō f ♦ vi spōnsiōnem facere ♦ vt dēpōnere, oppōnere.

waggery n facētiae fpl.

waggish adj facētus, rīdiculus.

waggle vt agitāre, mōtāre.

wagon n plaustrum nt, carrus m.

waif n inops m/f.

wail n ēiulātus m ♦ vi ēiulāre, dēplōrāre, lāmentārī.

wailing n plōrātus m, lāmentātiō f.

waist n medium corpus nt; **hold by the ~** medium tenēre.

wait n: **have a long ~** diū exspectāre; **lie in ~** īnsidiārī ♦ vi manēre, opperīrī, exspectāre; ~ **for** exspectāre; ~ **upon** (accompany) adsectārī, dēdūcere; (serve) famulārī (dat); (visit) salūtāre.

waiter n famulus m, minister m.

waive *vt* dēpōnere, remittere.
wake *vt* excitāre, suscitāre ♦ *vi* expergīscī.
wake *n* vestīgia *ntpl*; **in the ~** pōne, ā tergō;
follow in the ~ of vestīgiīs instāre (*gen*).
wakeful *adj* vigil.
wakefulness *n* vigilantia *f*.
waken *vt* excitāre ♦ *vi* expergīscī.
walk *n* (*act*) ambulātiō *f*, deambulātiō *f*; (*gait*)
incessus *m*; (*place*) ambulātiō *f*, xystus *m*; **~ of**
life status *m*; **go for a ~** spatiārī, deambulāre
♦ *vi* ambulāre, īre, gradī; (*with dignity*)
incēdere; **~ about** inambulāre; **~ out** ēgredī.
wall *n* mūrus *m*; (*indoors*) pariēs *m*; (*afield*)
māceria *f*; **~s** *pl* (*of town*) moenia *ntpl* ♦ *vt*
mūnīre, saepīre; **~ up** inaedificāre.
wallet *n* pēra *f*.
wallow *vi* volūtārī.
walnut *n* iūglāns *f*.
wan *adj* pallidus.
wand *n* virga *f*.
wander *vi* errāre, vagārī; (*in mind*) ālūcinārī;
~ over pervagārī.
wanderer *n* errō *m*, vagus *m*.
wandering *adj* errābundus, vagus ♦ *n* errātiō
f, error *m*.
wane *vi* dēcrēscere, senēscere.
want *n* inopia *f*, indigentia *f*, egestās *f*, pēnūria
f; (*craving*) dēsīderium *nt*; **in ~** inops; **be in ~**
egēre ♦ *vt* (*lack*) carēre (*abl*), egēre (*abl*),
indigēre (*abl*); (*miss*) dēsīderāre; (*wish*)
velle.
wanting *adj* (*missing*) absēns; (*defective*)
vitiōsus, parum idōneus; **be ~** deesse,
dēficere ♦ *prep* sine (*abl*).
wanton *adj* lascīvus, libīdinōsus ♦ *vi*
lascīvīre.
wantonly *adv* lascīvē, libīdinōsē.
war *n* bellum *nt*; **regular ~** iūstum bellum;
fortunes of ~ fortūna bellī; **outbreak of ~**
exortum bellum; **be at ~ with** bellum gerere
cum; **declare ~** bellum indīcere; **discontinue**
~ bellum dēpōnere; **end ~** (*by agreement*)
compōnere; (*by victory*) cōnficere; **enter ~**
bellum suscipere; **give the command of a ~**
bellum mandāre; **make ~** bellum īnferre;
prolong a ~ bellum trahere; **provoke ~**
bellum movēre; **wage ~** bellum gerere;
wage ~ on bellum īnferre (*dat*) ♦ *vi* bellāre.
warble *vi* canere, cantāre.
warbling *adj* garrulus, canōrus ♦ *n* cantus *m*.
war cry *n* clāmor *m*.
ward *n* custōdia *f*; (*person*) pupillus *m*, pupilla
f; (*of town*) regiō *f* ♦ *vt*: **~ off** arcēre,
dēfendere, prōpulsāre.
warden *n* praefectus *m*.
warder *n* custōs *m*.
wardrobe *n* vestiārium *nt*.
wardship *n* tūtēla *f*.
warehouse *n* apothēca *f*.
wares *n* merx *f*, mercēs *fpl*.
warfare *n* bellum *nt*.
warily *adv* prōvidenter, cautē.
wariness *n* circumspectiō *f*, cautiō *f*.

warlike *adj* ferōx, bellicōsus.
warm *adj* calidus; (*fig*) ācer, studiōsus; **be ~**
calēre; **become ~** calefierī, incalēscere; **keep**
~ fovēre; **~ baths** thermae *fpl* ♦ *vt* calefacere
tepefacere, fovēre ♦ *vi* calefierī.
warmly *adv* (*fig*) ferventer, studiōsē.
warmth *n* calor *m*.
warn *vt* monēre, admonēre.
warning *n* (*act*) monitiō *f*; (*particular*) monitum
nt; (*lesson*) documentum *nt*, exemplum *nt*.
warp *n* stāmina *ntpl* ♦ *vt* dēprāvāre, īnflectere
warped *adj* (*fig*) prāvus.
warrant *n* auctōritās *f* ♦ *vt* praestāre.
warranty *n* cautiō *f*.
warrior *n* bellātor *m*, bellatrīx *f*, mīles *m*.
warship *n* nāvis longa *f*.
wart *n* verrūca *f*.
wary *adj* prōvidus, cautus, prūdēns.
wash *vt* lavāre; (*of rivers, sea*) adluere; **~ away**
dīluere; **~ clean** abluere; **~ out** (*fig*) ēluere ♦
vi lavārī.
washbasin *n* aquālis *m*.
washing *n* lavātiō *f*.
wasp *n* vespa *f*.
waspish *adj* acerbus, stomachōsus.
waste *n* dētrīmentum *nt*, intertrīmentum *nt*;
(*extravagance*) effūsiō *f*; (*of time*) iactūra *f*;
(*land*) sōlitūdō *f*, vastitās *f* ♦ *adj* dēsertus,
vastus; **lay ~** vastāre, populārī ♦ *vt*
cōnsūmere, perdere, dissipāre; (*time*)
terere, absūmere; (*with disease*) absūmere ♦
vi: **~ away** tābēscere, intābēscere.
wasteful *adj* prōdigus, profūsus; (*destructive*)
damnōsus, perniciōsus.
wastefully *adv* prōdigē.
wasting *n* tābēs *f*.
wastrel *n* nebulō *m*.
watch *n* (*being awake*) vigilia *f*; (*sentry*) statiō *f*,
excubiae *fpl*; **keep ~** excubāre; **keep ~ on,**
over custōdīre, invigilāre (*dat*); **set ~** vigiliās
dispōnere; **at the third ~** ad tertiam būcinam
♦ *vt* (*guard*) custōdīre; (*observe*) intuērī,
observāre, spectāre ad (+ *acc*); **~ for**
observāre, exspectāre; (*enemy*) īnsidiārī
(*dat*); **~ closely** adservāre.
watcher *n* custōs *m*.
watchful *adj* vigilāns.
watchfully *adv* vigilanter.
watchfulness *n* vigilantia *f*.
watchman *n* custōs *m*, vigil *m*.
watchtower *n* specula *f*.
watchword *n* tessera *f*, signum *nt*.
water *n* aqua *f*; **deep ~** gurges *m*; **fresh ~** aqua
dulcis; **high ~** māximus aestus; **running ~**
aqua prōfluēns; **still ~** stagnum *nt*; **fetch ~**
aquārī; **fetching ~** aquātiō *f*; **cold ~** frīgida *f*;
hot ~ calida *f*; **troubled ~s** (*fig*) turbidae rēs ♦
vt (*land*) inrigāre; (*animal*) adaquāre.
water carrier *n* aquātor *m*; (*Zodiac*) Aquārius
m.
water clock *n* clepsydra *f*.
waterfall *n* cataracta *f*.
watering *n* aquātiō *f*; **~ place** *n* (*spa*) aquae *fpl*.

water pipe n fistula f.
watershed n aquārum dīvortium nt.
water snake n hydrus m.
water spout n prēstēr m.
watery adj aquōsus, ūmidus.
wattle n crātēs f.
wave n unda f, fluctus m ♦ vt agitāre, iactāre ♦ vi fluctuāre.
waver vi dubitāre, fluctuārī, nūtāre, vacillāre, labāre, inclināre.
wavering adj dubius, incōnstāns ♦ n dubitātiō f, fluctuātiō f.
wavy adj undātus; (hair) crispus.
wax n cēra f ♦ vt cērāre ♦ vi crēscere.
waxen adj cēreus.
waxy adj cērōsus.
way n via f; (route) iter nt; (method) modus m, ratiō f; (habit) mōs m; (ship's) impetus m; **all the ~ to, from** usque ad, ab; **by the ~** (parenthesis) etenim; **get in the ~ of** intervenīre (dat), impedīre; **get under ~** nāvem solvere; **give ~** (structure) labāre; (MIL) cēdere; **give ~ to** indulgēre (dat); **go out of one's ~ to do** ultrō facere; **have one's ~** imperāre; **in a ~** quōdam modō; **in this ~** ad hunc modum; **it is not my ~ to** nōn meum est (infin); **lose one's ~** deerrāre; **make ~** dē viā dēcēdere; **make ~ for** cēdere (dat); **make one's ~ into** sē īnsinuāre in (acc); **on the ~** inter viam, in itinere; **out of the ~** āvius, dēvius; (fig) reconditus; **pave the ~ for** praeparāre; **put out of the ~** tollere; **right of ~** iter; **stand in the ~ of** obstāre (dat); **that ~** illāc; **this ~** hāc; **~s and means** opēs fpl, reditūs mpl.
wayfarer n viātor m.
waylay vt īnsidiārī (dat).
wayward adj protervus, incōnstāns, levis.
waywardness n libīdō f, levitās f.
we pron nōs.
weak adj dēbilis, īnfirmus, imbēcillus; (health) invalidus; (argument) levis, tenuis; (senses) hebes.
weaken vt dēbilitāre, īnfirmāre; (resistance) frangere, labefactāre ♦ vi imminuī, labāre.
weakling n imbēcillus m.
weakly adj invalidus, aeger ♦ adv īnfirmē.
weak-minded adj mollis.
weakness n dēbilitās f, īnfirmitās f; (of argument) levitās f; (of mind) mollitia f, imbēcillitās f; (flaw) vitium nt; **have a ~ for** delectārī (abl).
weal n salūs f, rēs f; (mark of blow) vībex f; **the common ~** rēs pūblica f.
wealth n dīvitiae fpl, opēs fpl; **a ~ of** cōpia f, abundantia f.
wealthy adj dīves, opulentus, locuplēs, beātus; **make ~** locuplētāre, dītāre; **very ~** praedīves.
wean vt lacte dēpellere; (fig) dēdocēre.
weapon n tēlum nt.
wear n (dress) habitus m; **~ and tear** intertrīmentum nt ♦ vt gerere, gestāre; (rub)

terere, conterere; **~ out** cōnficere ♦ vi dūrāre; **~ off** minuī.
wearily adv cum lassitūdine, languidē.
weariness n fatīgātiō f, lassitūdō f; (of) taedium nt.
wearisome adj molestus, operōsus, labōriōsus.
weary adj lassus, fessus, dēfessus, fatīgātus ♦ vt fatīgāre; **I am weary of** me taedet (+ gen).
weasel n mustēla f.
weather n tempestās f, caelum nt; **fine ~** serēnitās f ♦ vt superāre.
weather-beaten adj tempestāte dūrātus.
weave vt texere.
weaver n textor m, textrix f.
web n (on loom) tēla f; (spider's) arāneum nt.
wed vt (a wife) dūcere; (a husband) nūbere (dat).
wedding n nūptiae fpl.
wedge n cuneus m ♦ vt cuneāre.
wedlock n mātrimōnium nt.
weed n inūtilis herba f ♦ vt runcāre.
weedy adj exīlis.
week n hebdomas f.
ween vt arbitrārī, putāre.
weep vi flēre, lacrimārī; **~ for** dēflēre, dēplōrāre.
weeping n flētus m, lacrimae fpl.
weevil n curculiō m.
weft n subtēmen nt; (web) tēla f.
weigh vt pendere, exāmināre; (anchor) tollere; (thought) ponderāre; **~ down** dēgravāre, opprimere; **~ out** expendere ♦ vi pendere.
weight n pondus nt; (influence) auctōritās f, mōmentum nt; (burden) onus nt; **have great ~** (fig) multum valēre; **he is worth his ~ in gold** aurō contrā cōnstat.
weightily adv graviter.
weightiness n gravitās f.
weighty adj gravis.
weir n mōlēs f.
weird adj mōnstruōsus ♦ n fātum nt.
welcome adj grātus, exspectātus, acceptus ♦ n salūtātiō f ♦ vt excipere, salvēre iubēre ♦ interj salvē, salvēte.
welfare n salūs f.
well n puteus m; (spring) fōns m ♦ vi scatēre ♦ adj salvus, sānus, valēns; **be ~** valēre ♦ adv bene, probē; (transition) age ♦ interj (concession) estō; (surprise) heia; **~ and good** estō; **~ begun is half done** dīmidium factī quī coepit habet; **~ done!** probē!; **~ met** opportūnē venis; **~ on in years** aetāte prōvectus; **all is ~** bene habet; **as ~** etiam; **as ~ as** cum ... tum, et ... et; **let ~ alone** quiēta nōn movēre; **take ~** in bonam partem accipere; **wish ~** favēre (dat); **you may ~ say** iūre dīcis; **you might as ~ say** illud potius dīcās.
well-advised adj prūdēns.
well-behaved adj modestus.
wellbeing n salūs f.
well-bred adj generōsus, līberālis.

well-disposed *adj* benevolus, amīcus.
well-informed *adj* ērudītus.
well-judged *adj* ēlegāns.
well-knit *adj* dēnsus.
well-known *adj* nōtus, nōbilis; (*saying*) trītus.
well-nigh *adv* paene.
well-off *adj* beātus, fortūnātus; **you are ~** bene est tibī.
well-read *adj* litterātus.
well-timed *adj* opportūnus.
well-to-do *adj* beātus, dīves.
well-tried *adj* probātus.
well-turned *adj* rotundus.
well-versed *adj* perītus, expertus.
well-wisher *n* amīcus *m*, benevolēns *m*.
well-worn *adj* trītus.
welter *n* turba *f* ♦ *vi* miscērī, turbārī; (*wallow*) volūtārī.
wench *n* muliercula *f*.
wend *vt*: **~ one's way** īre, sē ferre.
west *n* occidēns *m*, sōlis occāsus *m* ♦ *adj* occidentālis.
westerly, western *adj* occidentālis.
westwards *adv* ad occidentem.
west wind *n* Favōnius *m*.
wet *adj* ūmidus, madidus; **be ~** madēre; **~ weather** pluvia *f* ♦ *vt* madefacere.
wether *n* vervēx *m*.
wet nurse *n* nūtrīx *f*.
whack *n* ictus *m*, plāga *f* ♦ *vt* pulsāre, verberāre.
whale *n* bālaena *f*.
wharf *n* crepīdō *f*.
what *pron* (*interrog*) quid; (*adj*) quī; (*relat*) id quod, ea quae; **~ kind of?** qualis.
whatever, whatsoever *pron* quidquid, quodcumque; (*adj*) quīcumque.
wheat *n* trīticum *nt*.
wheaten *adj* trīticeus.
wheedle *vt* blandīrī, pellicere.
wheedling *adj* blandus ♦ *n* blanditiae *fpl*.
wheel *n* rota *f* ♦ *vt* flectere, circumagere ♦ *vi* sē flectere, circumagī.
wheelbarrow *n* pabō *m*.
wheeze *vi* anhēlāre.
whelm *vt* obruere.
whelp *n* catulus *m*.
when *adv* (*interrog*) quandō, quō tempore ♦ *conj* (*time*) cum (+ *subj*), ubī (+ *indic*).
whence *adv* unde.
whenever *conj* quotiēns, utcumque, quandocumque, cum (+ *perf/pluperf indic*); (*as soon as*) simul āc.
where *adv* ubī; (*to*) quō; **~ ... from** unde; **~ to** quo (*interrog and relat*).
whereabouts *n* locus *m*; **your ~** quō in locō sīs.
whereas *conj* quōniam; (*contrast*) *not expressed*.
whereby *adv* quō pāctō, quō.
wherefore *adv* (*interrog*) quārē, cūr; (*relat*) quamobrem, quāpropter.
wherein *adv* in quō, in quā.
whereof *adv* cūius, cūius reī.

whereon *adv* in quō, in quā.
whereupon *adv* quō factō.
wherever *conj* ubiubī, quācumque.
wherewith *adv* quī, cum quō.
wherry *n* linter *f*.
whet *vt* acuere; (*fig*) exacuere.
whether *conj* (*interrog*) utrum; (*single question*) num; (*condition*) sīve, seu; **~ ... or** utrum ... an (*in indir question*); (*in cond clauses*) seu (sive) ... seu (sive); **~ ... not** utrum ... necne (*in indir question*).
whetstone *n* cōs *f*.
whey *n* serum *nt*.
which *pron* (*interrog*) quis; (*of two*) uter; (*relat*) quī ♦ *adj* quī; (*of two*) uter.
whichever *pron* quisquis, quīcumque; (*of two*) utercumque.
whiff *n* odor *m*.
while *n* spatium *nt*, tempus *nt*; **for a ~** parumper; **a little ~** paulisper; **a long ~** diū; **it is worth ~** expedit, operae pretium est; **once in a ~** interdum ♦ *conj* dum + *pres indic* (= *during the time that*); + *imperf indic* (= *all the time that*) ♦ *vt*: **~ away** dēgere, fallere.
whilst *conj* dum.
whim *n* libīdō *f*, arbitrium *nt*.
whimper *n* vāgītus *m* ♦ *vi* vāgīre.
whimsical *adj* facētus, īnsolēns.
whimsically *adv* facētē.
whimsy *n* dēliciae *fpl*, facētiae *fpl*.
whine *n* quīritātiō *f* ♦ *vi* quīritāre.
whinny *n* hinnītus *m* ♦ *vi* hinnīre.
whip *n* flagellum *nt*, flagrum *nt* ♦ *vt* flagellāre, verberare.
whirl *n* turbō *m* ♦ *vt* intorquēre contorquēre ♦ *vi* contorquērī.
whirlpool *n* vertex *m*, vōragō *f*.
whirlwind *n* turbō *m*.
whisper *n* susurrus *m* ♦ *vt, vi* susurrāre, īnsusurrāre; **~ to** ad aurem admonēre, in aurem dīcere.
whistle *n* (*instrument*) fistula *f*; (*sound*) sībilus *m* ♦ *vi* sībilāre.
white *adj* albus; (*shining*) candidus; (*complexion*) pallidus; (*hair*) cānus; **turn ~** exalbēscere ♦ *n* album *nt*; (*egg*) albūmen *nt*.
white-hot *adj*: **to be ~** excandēscere.
whiten *vt* dealbāre ♦ *vi* albēscere.
whiteness *n* candor *m*.
whitewash *n* albārium *nt* ♦ *vt* dealbāre.
whither *adv* quō; **~soever** quōcumque.
whitish *adj* albulus.
whizz *n* strīdor *m* ♦ *vi* strīdere, increpāre.
who *pron* quis; (*relat*) quī.
whoever *pron* quisquis, quīcumque.
whole *adj* tōtus, cūnctus; (*unhurt*) integer, incolumis; (*healthy*) sānus ♦ *n* tōtum *nt*, summa *f*, ūniversitās *f*; **on the ~** plērumque.
wholehearted *adj* studiōsissimus.
wholeheartedly *adv* ex animō.
wholesale *adj* māgnus, cōpiōsus; **~ business** negōtiātiō *f*; **~ dealer** mercātor *m*, negōtiātor *m*.

wholesome adj salūtāris, salūbris.
wholesomeness n salūbritās f.
wholly adv omnīnō, tōtus.
whoop n ululātus m ♦ vi ululāre.
whose pron cūius.
why adv cūr, quārē, quamobrem, qua de causa.
wick n mergulus m.
wicked adj improbus, scelestus; (to gods, kin, country) impius.
wickedly adv improbē, scelestē, impiē.
wickedness n improbitās f, scelus nt, impietās f.
wicker adj vīmineus ♦ n vīmen nt.
wide adj lātus, amplus; **be ~ of** aberrāre ab ♦ adv lātē; **far and ~** longē lātēque.
widely adv lātē; (among people) vulgō.
widen vt laxāre, dilātāre.
widespread adj effūsus, vulgātus.
widow n vidua f.
widowed adj viduus, orbus.
widower n viduus m.
widowhood n viduitās f.
width n lātitūdō f, amplitūdō f.
wield vt tractāre, gestāre, ūtī (abl).
wife n uxor f.
wifely adj uxōrius.
wig n capillāmentum nt.
wild adj ferus, indomitus, saevus; (plant) agrestis; (land) incultus; (temper) furibundus, impotens, āmēns; (shot) temerārius; **~ state** feritās f.
wild beast n fera f.
wilderness n sōlitūdō f, loca dēserta ntpl.
wildly adv saevē.
wildness n feritās f.
wile n dolus m, ars f, fraus f.
wilful adj pervicāx, contumāx; (action) cōnsultus.
wilfully adv contumāciter; cōnsultō.
wilfulness n pervicācia f, libīdō f.
wilily adv astūtē, vafrē.
wiliness n astūtia f.
will n (faculty) voluntās f, animus m; (intent) cōnsilium nt; (decision) arbitrium nt; (of gods) nūtus m; (document) testāmentum nt; **~ and pleasure** libīdō f; **against one's ~** invītus; **at ~** ad libīdinem suam; **good ~** studium nt; **ill ~** invidia f; **with a ~** summō studiō; **without making a ~** intestātus, intestātō ♦ vt velle, fut; (legacy) lēgāre; **as you ~** ut libet.
willing adj libēns, parātus; **be ~** velle; **not be ~** nōlle.
willingly adv libenter.
willingness n voluntās f.
willow n salix f ♦ adj salignus.
willowy adj gracilis.
wilt vi flaccēscere.
wily adj astūtus, vafer, callidus.
wimple n mitra f.
win vt ferre, obtinēre, adipisci; (after effort) auferre; (victory) reportāre; (fame) cōnsequī, adsequī; (friends) sibī conciliāre; **~ the day**

vincere; **~ over** dēlēnīre, conciliāre ♦ vi vincere.
wince vi resilīre.
winch n māchina f, sucula f.
wind n ventus m; (north) aquilō m; (south) auster m; (east) eurus m; (west) favōnius m; **I get ~ of** subolet mihī; **run before the ~** ventō sē dare; **take the ~ out of one's sails** suō sibī gladiō iugulāre; **there is something in the ~** nescioquid olet; **which way the ~ blows** quōmodo sē rēs habeat.
wind vt torquēre; **~ round** intorquēre ♦ vi flectī, sinuāre; **~ up** (speech) perōrāre.
windbag n verbōsus m.
winded adj anhēlāns.
windfall n repentīnum bonum nt.
winding adj flexuōsus, tortuōsus ♦ n flexiō f, flexus m; **~s** pl (speech) ambāgēs fpl.
windlass n māchina f, sucula f.
window n fenestra f.
windpipe n aspera artēria f.
windward adj ad ventum conversus ♦ adv: **to ~** ventum versus.
windy adj ventōsus.
wine n vīnum nt; (new) mustum nt; (undiluted) merum nt.
winebibber n vīnōsus m.
wine cellar n apothēca f.
wine merchant n vīnārius m.
wine press n prēlum nt.
wing n āla f, (MIL) cornū nt, āla f; (of bird) penna f; **take ~** ēvolāre; **take under one's ~** patrōnus fierī (gen), clientem habēre, in custōdiam recipere.
winged adj ālātus, pennātus, volucer.
wink n nictus m ♦ vi nictāre; **~ at** cōnīvēre (dat).
winner n victor m.
winning adj blandus, iūcundus.
winningly adv blandē, iūcundē.
winning post n mēta f.
winnings n lucra ntpl.
winnow vt ventilāre; (fig) excutere.
winnowing-fan n vannus f.
winsome adj blandus, suāvis.
winter n hiems f; (mid) brūma f ♦ adj hiemālis, hībernus ♦ vi hībernāre.
winter quarters n hīberna ntpl.
wintry adj hiemālis, hībernus.
wipe vt dētergēre; **~ away** abstergēre; **~ dry** siccāre; **~ off** dētergēre; **~ out** dēlēre; **~ the nose** ēmungere.
wire n fīlum aēneum nt.
wiry adj nervōsus.
wisdom n sapientia f; (in action) prūdentia f; (in judgment) cōnsilium nt.
wise adj sapiēns, prūdēns.
wisely adv sapienter, prūdenter.
wish n optātum nt, vōtum nt; (for something missing) dēsīderium nt; **~es** pl (greeting) salūs f ♦ vt optāre, cupere, velle; **~ for** exoptāre, expetere, dēsīderāre; **~ good-day** salvēre iubēre; **as you ~** ut libet; **I ~ I could** utinam

possim.
wishful *adj* cupidus.
wishing *n* optātiō *f.*
wisp *n* manipulus *m.*
wistful *adj* dēsīderī plenus.
wistfully *adv* cum dēsīderiō.
wistfulness *n* dēsīderium *nt.*
wit *n* (*humour*) facētiae *fpl*, salēs *mpl*; (*intellect*)
argūtiae *fpl*, ingenium *nt*; **caustic ~** dicācitās
f; **be at one's wits' end** valdē haerēre; **be out
of one's ~s** dēlīrāre; **have one's ~s about one**
prūdens esse; **to ~** nempe, dīcō.
witch *n* sāga *f*, strīga *f.*
witchcraft *n* veneficium *nt*, magicae artēs *fpl.*
with *prep* (*person*) cum (*abl*); (*thing*) abl; (*in
company*) apud (*acc*); (*fight*) cum (*abl*), contrā
(*acc*); **be angry ~** īrāscī (*dat*); **begin ~** incipere
ab; **rest ~** esse penes (*acc*); **end ~** dēsinere in
(*acc*); **what do you want ~ me?** quid mē vis?
withdraw *vt* dēdūcere, dētrahere; (*fig*)
āvocāre; (*words*) retractāre ♦ *vi* discēdere,
abscēdere, sē recipere, sē subdūcere.
withdrawal *n* (*MIL*) receptus *m.*
wither *vt* torrēre ♦ *vi* dēflōrēscere.
withered *adj* marcidus.
withhold *vt* abstinēre, retinēre, supprimere.
within *adv* intus, intrā; (*motion*) introˉ ♦ *prep*
intrā (*acc*), in (*abl*).
without *adv* extrā, forīs; **from ~** extrīnsecus;
be ~ vacāre (*abl*), carēre (*abl*) ♦ *prep* sine
(*abl*), expers (*gen*); **I admire ~ fearing** ita
laudō ut nōn timeam; **~ breaking the law**
salvīs lēgibus; **you cannot see ~** admiring
vidēre nōn potes quīn laudēs; **you cannot
appreciate ~ seeing for yourself** aestimāre
nōn potes nisī ipse vīderis; **~ doubt** sine
dubio; **~ the order of** iniūssū (*gen*); **~ striking
a blow** rē integrā.
withstand *vt* resistere (*dat*), obsistere (*dat*);
(*attack*) ferre, sustinēre.
withy *n* vīmen *nt.*
witless *adj* excors, ineptus, stultus.
witness *n* (*person*) testis *m/f*; (*to a document*)
obsignātor *m*; (*spectator*) arbiter *m*; (*evidence*)
testimōnium *nt*; **call as ~** antestārī; **bear ~**
testificārī; **call to ~** testārī ♦ *vt* testificārī;
(*see*) vidēre, intuērī.
witnessing *n* testificātiō *f.*
witticism *n* dictum *nt*; **~s** *pl* facētiae *fpl.*
wittily *adv* facētē, salsē.
wittingly *adv* sciēns.
witty *adj* facētus, argūtus, salsus; (*caustic*)
dicāx.
wizard *n* magus *m*, veneficus *m.*
wizardry *n* magicae artēs *fpl.*
wizened *adj* marcidus.
woad *n* vitrum *nt.*
wobble *vi* titubāre; (*structure*) labāre.
woe *n* luctus *m*, dolor *m*, aerumna *f*; **~s** *pl* mala
ntpl, calamitātēs *fpl*; **~ to** vae (*dat*).
woeful *adj* tristis, maestus, aerumnōsus.
woefully *adv* triste, miserē.
wolf *n* lupus *m*, lupa *f*; **~'s** lupīnus.

woman *n* fēmina *f*, mulier *f*; **old ~** anus *f*;
married ~ mātrōna *f*; **~'s** muliebris.
womanish *adj* muliebris, effēminātus.
womanly *adj* muliebris.
womb *n* uterus *m.*
wonder *n* admīrātiō *f*; (*of a thing*)
admīrābilitās *f*; (*thing*) mīrāculum *nt*, mīrum
nt, portentum *nt* ♦ *vi* mīrārī; **~ at** admīrārī,
dēmīrārī.
wonderful *adj* mīrus, mīrābilis, admīrābilis; **~
to relate** mīrābile dictu.
wonderfully *adv* mīrē, mīrābiliter, mīrum
quantum.
wonderfulness *n* admīrābilitās *f.*
wondering *adj* mīrābundus.
wonderment *n* admīrātiō *f.*
wondrous *adj* mīrus, mīrābilis.
wont *n* mōs *m*, cōnsuētūdō *f.*
wonted *adj* solitus.
woo *vt* petere.
wood *n* silva *f*, nemus *nt*; (*material*) lignum *nt*;
gather ~ lignārī; **touch ~l** absit verbō invidia
♦ *adj* ligneus.
woodcutter *n* lignātor *m.*
wooded *adj* silvestris, saltuōsus.
wooden *adj* ligneus.
woodland *n* silvae *fpl* ♦ *adj* silvestris.
woodman *n* lignātor *m.*
wood nymph *n* dryas *f.*
woodpecker *n* pīcus *m.*
wood pigeon *n* palumbēs *m/f.*
woodwork *n* tigna *ntpl.*
woodworker *n* faber tignārius *m.*
woody *adj* silvestris, silvōsus.
wooer *n* procus *m.*
woof *n* subtēmen *nt.*
wool *n* lāna *f.*
woollen *adj* lāneus.
woolly *adj* lānātus.
word *n* verbum *nt*; (*spoken*) vōx *f*; (*message*)
nūntius *m*; (*promise*) fidēs *f*; (*term*)
vocābulum *nt*; **~ for ~** ad verbum, verbum ē
verbō; **a ~ with you!** paucīs tē volō!; **break
one's ~** fidem fallere; **bring back ~**
renūntiāre; **by ~ of mouth** ōre; **fair ~s**
blanditiae *fpl*; **give one's ~** fidem dare; **have a
~ with** colloquī cum; **have ~s with** iūrgāre
cum; **have a good ~ for** laudāre; **in a ~** ūnō
verbō, dēnique; **keep one's ~** fidem
praestāre; **of few ~s** taciturnus; **take at one's
~** crēdere (*dat*).
wording *n* verba *ntpl.*
wordy *adj* verbōsus.
work *n* (*energy*) labor *m*, opera *f*; (*task*) opus *nt*;
(*thing done*) opus *nt*; (*book*) liber *m*; (*trouble*)
negōtium *nt*; **~s** (*MIL*) opera *ntpl*; (*mechanism*)
māchinātiō *f*; (*place*) officīna *f* ♦ *vi* labōrāre ♦
vt (*men*) exercēre; (*metal*) fabricārī; (*soil*)
subigere; (*results*) efficere; **~ at** ēlabōrāre; **~
in** admiscēre; **~ off** exhaurīre; **~ out**
ēlabōrāre; **~ up** (*emotion*) efferre; **~ one's
way up** prōficere ♦ *vi* gerī.
workaday *adj* cottīdiānus.

workhouse n ergastulum nt.

working n (mechanism) māchinātiō f; (soil) cultus m.

workman n (unskilled) operārius m; (skilled) opifex m, faber m; **workmen** operae fpl.

workmanship n ars f, artificium nt.

workshop n fabrica f, officīna f.

world n (universe) mundus m; (earth) orbis terrārum m; (nature) rērum nātūra f; (mankind) hominēs mpl; (masses) vulgus nt; **of the ~** mundānus; **man of the ~** homō urbānus m; **best in the ~** rērum optimus, omnium optimus; **where in the ~** ubī gentium.

worldliness n quaestūs studium nt.

worldly adj quaestuī dēditus.

worm n vermis m ♦ vi: **~ one's way** sē īnsinuāre.

worm-eaten adj vermiculōsus.

wormwood n absinthium nt.

worn adj trītus.

worried adj sollicitus, anxius.

worry n cūra f, sollicitūdō f ♦ vi sollicitārī ♦ vt vexāre, sollicitāre; (of dogs) lacerāre.

worse adj pēior, dēterior; **grow ~** ingravēscere; **make matters ~** rem exasperāre ♦ adv pēius, dēterius.

worsen vi ingravēscere, dēteriōr fierī.

worship n venerātiō f, deōrum cultus m; (rite) sacra ntpl, rēs dīvīnae fpl ♦ vt adōrāre, venerārī, colere.

worst adj pessimus, dēterrimus; **~ enemy** inimīcissimus m; **endure the ~** ultima patī; vincere.

worsted n lāna f.

worth n (value) pretium nt; (moral) dignitās f, frūgālitās f, virtūs f; (prestige) auctōritās f ♦ adj dignus; **for all one's ~** prō virīlī parte; **how much is it ~?** quanti vēnit?; **it is ~ a lot** multum valet; **it is ~ doing** operae pretium est.

worthily adv dignē, meritō.

worthiness n dignitās f.

worthless adj (person) nēquam; (thing) vīlis, inānis.

worthlessness n levitās f, nēquitia f; vīlitās f.

worthy adj dignus; (person) frūgī, honestus; **~ of** dignus (abl).

wound n vulnus nt ♦ vt vulnerāre; (feelings) offendere.

wounded adj saucius.

wrangle n iūrgium nt, rixa f ♦ vi iūrgāre, rixārī, altercārī.

wrap vt involvere, obvolvere; **~ round** intorquēre; **~ up** involvere.

wrapper n involucrum nt.

wrapping n integumentum nt.

wrath n īra f, īrācundia f.

wrathful adj īrātus.

wrathfully adv īrācundē.

wreak vt: **~ vengeance on** saevīre in (acc), ulcīscī.

wreath n corōna f, sertum nt.

wreathe vt (garland) torquēre; (object) corōnāre.

wreck n naufragium nt ♦ vt frangere; (fig) perdere; **be ~ed** naufragium facere.

wreckage n fragmenta ntpl.

wrecked adj (person) naufragus; (ship) frāctus.

wrecker n perditor m.

wren n rēgulus m.

wrench vt intorquēre, extorquēre; **~ away** ēripere; **~ open** effringere.

wrest vt extorquēre.

wrestle vi luctārī.

wrestler n luctātor m, athlēta m.

wrestling n luctātiō f.

wretch n scelerātus m, nēquam homō m; **poor ~** miser homō m.

wretched adj īnfēlīx, miser; (pitiful) flēbilis.

wretchedly adv miserē.

wretchedness n miseria f; maestitia f.

wriggle vi sē torquēre.

wriggling adj sinuōsus.

wright n faber m.

wring vt torquēre; **~ from** extorquēre.

wrinkle n rūga f ♦ vt corrūgāre.

wrinkled adj rūgōsus.

wrist n prīma palmae pars f.

writ n (legal) auctōritās f.

write vt scrībere; (book) cōnscrībere; **~ off** indūcere; **~ on** īnscrībere (dat); **~ out** exscrībere, dēscrībere; **~ out in full** perscrībere.

writer n (LIT) scrīptor m, auctor m; (clerk) scrība m.

writhe vi torquērī.

writing n (act) scrīptiō f; (result) scrīptum nt.

wrong adj falsus, perversus, prāvus; (unjust) iniūstus, inīquus; **be ~, go ~** errāre ♦ n iniūria f, culpa f, noxa f, malum nt; **do ~** peccāre, dēlinquere; **right and ~** (moral) honesta ac turpia ntpl ♦ vt laedere, nocēre (dat); (by deceit) fraudāre.

wrongdoer n, maleficus m, scelerātus m.

wrongdoing n scelus nt.

wrongful adj iniūstus, iniūriosus, inīquus.

wrongfully adv iniūriā, iniūstē, inīquē.

wrong-headed adj perversus.

wrong-headedness n perversitās f.

wrongly adv falsō, dēprāvātē, male, perperam.

wroth adj īrātus.

wrought adj factus.

wry adj dētortus; **make a ~ face** ōs dūcere.

wryness n prāvitās f.

Y, y

yacht *n* phasēlus *m*.
yard *n* (*court*) ārea *f*; (*measure*) trēs pedēs.
yardarm *n* antenna *f*.
yarn *n* fīlum *nt*; (*story*) fābula *f*.
yawn *n* hiātus *m* ◆ *vi* hiāre, ōscitāre; (*chasm*) dehiscere.
ye *pron* vōs.
yean *vt* parere.
year *n* annus *m*; **every** ~ quotannīs; **for a** ~ **in annum**; **half** ~ sēmēstre spatium *nt*; **this** ~'s hōrnus; **twice a** ~ bis annō; **two** ~**s** biennium *nt*; **three** ~**s** triennium *nt*; **four** ~**s** quadriennium *nt*; **five** ~**s** quinquennium *nt*.
yearly *adj* annuus, anniversārius ◆ *adv* quotannīs.
yearn *vi*: ~ **for** dēsīderāre, exoptāre.
yearning *n* dēsīderium *nt*.
yeast *n* fermentum *nt*.
yell *n* clāmor *m*; (*of pain*) ēiulātiō *f* ◆ *vi* clāmāre, eiulāre.
yellow *adj* flāvus; (*pale*) gilvus; (*deep*) fulvus; (*gold*) luteus; (*saffron*) croceus.
yelp *n* gannītus *m* ◆ *vi* gannīre.
yeoman *n* colōnus *m*.
yes *adv* ita vērō (est), māximē; (*correcting*) immo.
yesterday *adv* herī ◆ *n* hesternus diēs *m*; ~'s hesternus; **the day before** ~ nudius tertius.
yet *adv* (*contrast*) tamen, nihilōminus, attamen; (*time*) adhūc, etiam; (*with compar*) etiam; **and** ~ atquī, quamquam; **as** ~ adhūc; **not** ~ nōndum.
yew *n* taxus *f*.
yield *n* fructus *m* ◆ *vt* (*crops*) ferre, efferre; (*pleasure*) adferre; (*concession*) dare, concēdere; (*surrender*) dēdere ◆ *vi* cēdere; (*surrender*) sē dēdere, sē trādere; ~ **to the**

wishes of mōrem gerere (*dat*), obsequī (*dat*).
yielding *adj* (*person*) facilis, obsequēns; (*thing*) mollis ◆ *n* cessio *f*; dēditiō *f*.
yoke *n* iugum *nt* ◆ *vt* iungere, coniungere.
yokel *n* agrestis *m*.
yolk *n* vitellus *m*.
yonder *adv* illīc ◆ *adj* ille, iste.
yore *n*: **of** ~ quondam, ōlim.
you *pron* tū, vōs.
young *adj* iuvenis, adulēscēns; (*child*) parvus; ~**er** iūnior, nātū minor; ~**est** nātū minimus ◆ *n* fētus *m*, pullus *m*, catulus *m*.
young man *n* iuvenis *m*; adulēscēns *m*.
youngster *n* puer *m*.
your *adj* tuus, vester.
yourself *pron* ipse.
youth *n* (*age*) iuventūs *f*, adulescentia *f*; (*person*) iuvenis *m*, adulēscēns *m*; (*collective*) iuventūs *f*.
youthful *adj* iuvenīlis, puerīlis.
youthfully *adv* iuvenīliter.

Z, z

zeal *n* studium *nt*, ārdor *m*.
zealot *n* studiōsus *m*, fautor *m*.
zealous *adj* studiōsus, ārdēns.
zealously *adv* studiōsē, ārdenter.
zenith *n* vertex *m*.
zephyr *n* Favōnius *m*.
zero *n* nihil *nt*.
zest *n* (*taste*) sapor *m*; (*fig*) gustātus *m*, impetus *m*.
zigzag *n* ānfrāctus *m* ◆ *adj* tortuōsus.
zither *n* cithara *f*.
zodiac *n* signifer orbis *m*.
zone *n* cingulus *m*.

Grammar and Verb Tables

This book is designed to help pupils and students of Latin to understand the grammar of the language. For beginners, the book provides an introduction to and explanation of the basic forms. More advanced students will find it an invaluable guide for reference and revision.

All parts of speech (nouns, pronouns, adjectives etc) are treated separately and clearly explained for the benefit of learners. Differences in usages are illustrated by extensive examples from many Latin authors. *American students and teachers, please note: this book is designed for use by students around the world, many of whom use British case ordering (Nom, Voc, Acc, Gen, Dat, Abl).*

A special section on word order in Latin, one of the greatest problems for students and pupils, has been included to guide the learner through both simple and compound sentences.

For ease of reference, all necessary structures, such as Indirect Statement, Conditional Sentences etc, have been listed under Contents. Each is then explained, for both English and Latin usage, to show the learner how to recognize the structure and translate it into English. Further examples of all structures are provided, for practice.

Handy, practical hints are given in the section on Translation Guidelines, to highlight the more common problems that confront students, and to assist in translation.

The final part of the grammar section lists the many "false friends" or confusable words that often lead students and pupils astray when translating from Latin. This section is of particular importance for examination candidates.

Tables of regular verbs provide information on verb formation and usage, while unique verbs are given in full with their meanings. A special feature of the grammar is a list of the 400 most common verbs, both regular and irregular. Irregular parts of verbs are highlighted and the conjugation number of each listed, so that by referring to the table indicated by this number, any part of the verb may be deduced.

6 CONTENTS

Abbreviations used

abl	ablative	m, masc	masculine
acc	accusative	nt, neut	neuter
adv	adverb	nom	nominative
conj	conjunction	pl	plural
dat	dative	plup	pluperfect
dep	deponent	p(p)	page(s)
f, fem	feminine	prep	preposition
gen	genitive	pron	pronoun
indic	indicative	sing	singular
intrans	intransitive	voc	vocative

NOUNS 7

Nouns

A noun is the name of a person, thing or quality.

Gender

- In Latin, as in English, the gender of nouns, representing persons or living creatures, is decided by meaning. Nouns denoting male people and animals are masculine

vir	a man
Gaius	Gaius
cervus	stag

- Nouns denoting female people and animals are feminine

femina	a woman
Cornelia	Cornelia
cerva	doe/hind

- However, the gender of things or qualities in Latin is decided by the ending of the noun.

  anulus (ring) *masc*
  sapientia (wisdom) *fem*
  barba (beard) *fem*
  gaudium (joy) *nt*

Number

- Nouns may be singular, denoting one, or plural, denoting two or more. This is shown by change of ending

sing	*pl*
terra (land)	terrae
modus (way)	modi
opus (work)	opera

Cases

- There are six cases in Latin, expressing the relationship of the noun to the other words in the sentence.

Nominative
the subject of the verb: **Caesar** died

Vocative
addressing someone/thing: Welcome, **Alexander**

Accusative
the object of the verb: The cat ate **the mouse**

Genitive
belonging to someone/thing: The home **of my friend**

Dative
the indirect object of the verb: I gave the book **to my son**

Ablative
says by, with or from whom/what: This was agreed **by the Senate**

Declensions

- Latin nouns are divided into five groups or declensions by the ending of their stems. Each declension has six cases, both singular and plural, denoted by different endings. The endings of the genitive singular case help to distinguish the different declensions.

	STEMS	GENITIVE SINGULAR
1st Declension	-a	-ae
2nd Declension	-ŏ *or* u	-ī
3rd Declension	-i, u, consonant	-is
4th Declension	-ŭ	-ūs
5th Declension	-ē	-ēi

First Declension

- All nouns end in -a in the nominative case and all are feminine except when the noun indicates a male, *eg* **poēta** (a poet), **agricola** (a farmer), *etc.*

	SINGULAR		PLURAL	
Nom	fēmina	the woman	fēminae	women
Voc	fēmina	o woman	fēminae	o women
Acc	fēminam	the woman	fēminās	women
Gen	fēminae	of the woman	fēminārum	of the women
Dat	fēminae	to/for the woman	fēminīs	to/for the women
Abl	fēminā	by/with/ from the woman	fēminīs	by/with/ from the women

- Note that **dea** (goddess) and **filia** (daughter), have their dative and ablative plurals **deābus** and **filiābus**

Declensions (contd)

Second Declension

- Nouns of the second declension end in -us, or a few in -er or -r. All are masculine. Those few which end in -um are neuter.

	SINGULAR		PLURAL	
		slave		slaves
Nom	servus		servī	
Voc	serve		servī	
Acc	servum		servōs	
Gen	servī		servōrum	
Dat	servō		servīs	
Abl	servō		servīs	

	SINGULAR		PLURAL	
		boy		boys
Nom	puer		puerī	
Voc	puer		puerī	
Acc	puerum		puerōs	
Gen	puerī		puerōrum	
Dat	puerō		puerīs	
Abl	puerō		puerīs	

	SINGULAR		PLURAL	
		war		wars
Nom	bellum		bella	
Voc	bellum		bella	
Acc	bellum		bella	
Gen	bellī		bellōrum	
Dat	bellō		bellīs	
Abl	bellō		bellīs	

- Note that proper names ending in -ius have vocative in -ī, o Vergilī – o Virgil!

- **deus** (god), has an alternative vocative **deus**, and plural forms **dī** in nominative and **dīs** in dative and ablative.

Third Declension

This is the largest group of nouns and may be divided into two broad categories, stems ending in a consonant and those ending in -i. All genders in this declension must be learnt.

Consonant Stems

- ending in -l

consul, -is *m* (consul)

	SINGULAR	PLURAL
Nom	cōnsul	cōnsulēs
Voc	cōnsul	cōnsulēs
Acc	cōnsulem	cōnsulēs
Gen	cōnsulis	cōnsulum
Dat	cōnsulī	cōnsulibus
Abl	cōnsule	cōnsulibus

- ending in -n

legio, -onis *f* (legion)

	SINGULAR	PLURAL
Nom	legiō	legiōnēs
Voc	legiō	legiōnēs
Acc	legiōnem	legiōnēs
Gen	legiōnis	legiōnum
Dat	legiōnī	legiōnibus
Abl	legiōne	legiōnibus

Continued

Declensions (contd)

flumen, -inis *nt* (river)

	SINGULAR	PLURAL
Nom	flūmen	flūmina
Voc	flūmen	flūmina
Acc	flūmen	flūmina
Gen	flūminis	flūminum
Dat	flūminī	flūminibus
Abl	flūmine	flūminibus

● Note that the genitive plural of these nouns ends in -um.

● Stems ending in -i

civis, -is *m/f* (citizen)

	SINGULAR	PLURAL
Nom	cīvis	cīvēs
Voc	cīvis	cīvēs
Acc	cīvem	cīvēs
Gen	cīvis	cīvium
Dat	cīvī	cīvibus
Abl	cīve	cīvibus

● Note that these nouns have genitive plural in -ium.

Neuter Nouns

mare, -is *nt* (sea)

	SINGULAR	PLURAL
Nom	mare	maria
Voc	mare	maria
Acc	mare	maria
Gen	maris	marium
Dat	marī	maribus
Abl	marī	maribus

animal, -is *nt* (animal)

	SINGULAR	PLURAL
Nom	animal	animālia
Voc	animal	animālia
Acc	animal	animālia
Gen	animālis	animālium
Dat	animālī	animālibus
Abl	animālī	animālibus

● Note that the ablative singular of these neuter nouns ends in -I.

● Nominative, vocative and accusative singular endings of neuter nouns are identical.

● Nominative, vocative and accusative plural endings of neuter nouns in **all** declensions end in -**ă**.

Continued

Declensions (contd)

Monosyllabic Consonant Stems

The following have their genitive plural in -ium:

arx, arcis f (citadel) — arcium (of citadels)
gēns, gentis f (race) — gentium (of races)
mōns, montis m (mountain) — montium (of mountains)

nox, noctis f (night) — noctium (of nights)
pōns, pontis m (bridge) — pontium (of bridges)
urbs, urbis f (city) — urbium (of cities)

Fourth Declension

Nouns in this declension end in -us in the nominative singular and are mainly masculine. A few end in -u and are neuter.

exercitus, -ūs *m* (army)

	SINGULAR	PLURAL
Nom	exercitus	exercitūs
Voc	exercitus	exercitūs
Acc	exercitum	exercitūs
Gen	exercitūs	exercituum
Dat	exercituī	exercitibus
Abl	exercitū	exercitibus

genū, -ūs *nt* (knee)

	SINGULAR	PLURAL
Nom	genū	genua
Voc	genū	genua
Acc	genū	genua
Gen	genūs	genuum
Dat	genū	genibus
Abl	genū	genibus

- Note that a few common nouns are feminine, *eg* **domus** (house), **manus** (hand), **Idus** (Ides or 15th of the month).

- The form **domī** (at home) is an old form called locative. **domō** (from home) *abl sing*, **domōs** *acc pl* and **domōrum** *gen pl* are also used besides the fourth declension forms of **domus** (house).

Fifth Declension

There are only a few nouns in this declension. All end in -ēs in the nominative case. Most are masculine, but **diēs** (day) and **merīdiēs** (midday) are feminine.

diēs, -diēī *m* (day)

	SINGULAR	PLURAL
Nom	diēs	diēs
Voc	diēs	diēs
Acc	diem	diēs
Gen	diēī	diērum
Dat	diēī	diēbus
Abl	diē	diēbus

16 NOUNS

Cases

Use Of Cases

Nominative Case

The nominative case is used where:

- the noun is the **subject** of the verb (→**1**)
- the noun is a **complement** (→**2**)
- the noun is in **apposition** to the subject (→**3**)

Accusative Case

The accusative case is used:

- for the **direct object** of the verb (→**4**)
- with verbs of teaching and asking which take accusative of person and thing (→**5**)
- Verbs of naming, making *etc* take two accusatives for the same person or thing (→**6**)
- in exclamations (→**7**)
- to show extent of space (→**8**)
- to show extent of time (→**9**)
- to show motion to a place or country usually with a preposition (→**10**)
- to show motion towards, without a preposition, before names of towns and small islands (→**11**)

    Note also: **domum** (home), **rus** (to the country), **foras** (outside)

- for an object with similar meaning to the verb (*cognate*) (→**12**)

Continued

Examples

1 **Sextus** ridet
Sextus laughs

2 Romulus **rex** factus est
Romulus was made king

3 Marcus Annius, **eques Romanus,** hoc dicit
Marcus Annius, a Roman businessman, says this

4 canis **baculum** petit
the dog fetches the stick

5 **puerum litteras** docebo
I shall teach the boy literature

6 **Ancum Martium regem** populus creavit
The people made Ancus Martius king

7 o **tempora,** o **mores**
what times, what conduct!

8 murus decem **pedes** altus est
the wall is 10 foot high

9 Troia decem **annos** obsessa est
Troy was under siege for 10 years

10 **ad Hispaniam** effugerunt
they escaped to Spain

11 **Athenas** legati missi sunt
Ambassadors were sent to Athens

12 **vitam** bonam **vixit**
he lived a good life

Cases (contd)

Dative Case

- Indirect object (*ie* to or for whom an action is performed) (→**1**)

- used with verbs of obeying (**parēre**), resisting (**resistere**), pleasing (**placēre**), ordering (**imperāre**) *etc* (→**2**)

- verb compounds (beginning **ad-**, **ob-**, **prae-**, **sub-**) denoting helping or hindering take dative (→**3**)

  adesse – come to help
  subvenire – help

- indicates possession (→**4**)

- is used with adjectives meaning "like" (**similis**), "fit" (**aptus**), "near" (**proximus**) (→**5**)

- indicates a purpose (known as *predicative dative*) (→**6**)

- shows the agent of gerund/gerundive (→**7**)

Examples

1 pecuniam **domino** dedit
he gave the money to his master

2 maria terraeque **Deo** parent
land and sea obey God

3 Pompeius **hostibus** obstitit
Pompey opposed the enemy

4 Poppaea amica est **Marciae**
Poppaea is Marcia's friend

5 feles **tigri** similis est
the cat is like a tiger

6 nemo mihi **auxilio** est
there is no-one to help me

7 omnia erant agenda **nobis**
everything had to be done by us

Continued

Cases (contd)

Genitive Case

- Indicates possession (→1)
- Denotes part of a whole (→2)
- Indicates a quality, always with an adjective (→3)
- Is used as a predicate, where a person represents a quality (→4)
- Is used with superlatives (→5)
- Precedes causa and gratia (for the sake of) (→6)
- Is used after certain adjectives (→7)

sciens	(knowing)
inscius	(ignorant of)
cupidus	(desiring)
particeps	(sharing) *etc*

- Is used with verbs of remembering (**memini**) and forgetting (**obliviscor**) (→8)
- Follows verbs of accusing, convicting *etc* (→9)
- Represents value or worth (→10)

Continued

Examples

1 domus **regis**
the king's house

uxor **Augusti**
the wife of Augustus

2 quid **novi**
what news?

plus **cibi**
more food

3 magnae **auctoritatis** es
your reputation is great

4 **stulti est** hoc facere
it is the mark of a fool to do this

5 Indus est **omnium fluminum** maximum
the Indus is the greatest of all rivers

6 tu me **amoris causa** servavisti
you saved me for love's sake

7 Verres, **cupidus pecuniae**, ex hereditate praedatus est
Verres, greedy for money, robbed the estate

8 **mortis** memento
remember death

9 ante **actarum rerum** Antonius accusatus est
Antony was accused of previous offences

10 frumentum **minimi** vendidit
he sold corn at the lowest price

flocci non facio
I don't care at all

Cases (contd)

Ablative Case

- Indicates place, usually with the preposition "in" (→**1**)
  Note, however: **totā Asiā** – throughout Asia
  terrā marīque – by land and sea

- Indicates motion from, or down from a place, usually with prepositions **ex**, **de**, **a(b)** (→**2**)

- Note prepositions are omitted before names of towns, small islands and **domo** (from home), **rure** (from the country), **foris** (from outside) (→**3**)

- Represents time when or within which something happens (→**4**)

- Indicates origin, sometimes with prepositions **in**, **ex**, **a(b)** (→**5**)

- Is used to show material from which something is made (→**6**)

- Indicates manner (how something is done), usually with **cum** when there is no adjective, and without **cum** when there is an adjective (→**7**)

- Is used with verbs of depriving, filling, needing and with **opus est** (→**8**)

- Is used with deponent verbs **utor** (use), **abutor** (abuse), **fungor** (accomplish), **potior** (gain possession of) (→**9**)

- States cause (→**10**)

- To form **ablative absolute**, where a noun in the ablative is combined with a participle or another noun or adjective in the same case, to form an idea independent of the rest of the sentence. This is equivalent to an adverbial clause (→**11**)

1 Milo **in urbe** mansit
   Milo remained in the city

2 **de equo** cecidit
   He fell down from his horse
   praedam **ex urbe ornatissima** sustulit
   He stole booty from the rich city

3 **domo** cucurrerunt servi
   The slaves ran from the house

4 **hac nocte** Agricola obiit
   Agricola died on this night
   decem annis Lacedaimonii non haec confecerunt
   The Spartans did not complete this task within 10 years

5 Romulus et Remus, **Marte nati**
   Romulus and Remus, sons of Mars
   flumina **in Caucaso monte** orta
   Rivers rising in the Caucasus mountains

6 statua **ex auro** facta est
   The statue was made of gold

7 mulieres **cum virtute** vixerunt
   The women lived virtuously
   summa celeritate Poeni regressi sunt
   The Carthaginians retreated at top speed

8 aliquem **vita** privare
   to deprive someone of life
   opus est mihi **divitiis**
   I need wealth

9 **vi** et **armis** usus est
   He used force of arms

10 leo **fame** decessit
   The lion died of hunger

11 **exigua parte aestatis reliqua,** Caesar in Britanniam proficisci contendit
   Although only a little of the summer remained, Caesar hurried to set out for Britain

Adjectives

An adjective adds a quality to the noun. It usually follows the noun but sometimes comes before it for emphasis. The adjective agrees with its noun in number, case and gender.

Gender

vir bonus (*masc*)　a good man
fēmina pulchra (*fem*)　a beautiful woman
bellum longum (*neut*)　a long war

Number

virī bonī (*pl*)　good men
fēminae pulchrae (*pl*)　beautiful women
bella longa (*pl*)　long wars

Case

virō bonō (*dat sing*)　for a good man
fēminās pulchrās (*acc pl*)　beautiful women
bellī longī (*gen sing*)　of a long war

• Adjectives are declined like nouns and usually arranged in two groups:

1 those with endings of the first and second declensions
2 those with endings of the third declension

First and Second Declensions

bonus, bona, bonum (good)

SINGULAR

	Masc	Fem	Neut
Nom	bonus	bona	bonum
Voc	bone	bona	bonum
Acc	bonum	bonam	bonum
Gen	bonī	bonae	bonī
Dat	bonō	bonae	bonō
Abl	bonō	bonā	bonō

PLURAL

	Masc	Fem	Neut
Nom	bonī	bonae	bona
Voc	bonī	bonae	bona
Acc	bonōs	bonās	bona
Gen	bonōrum	bonārum	bonōrum
Dat	bonīs	bonīs	bonīs
Abl	bonīs	bonīs	bonīs

26 ADJECTIVES

Declensions (contd)

miser, misera, miserum (unhappy)

SINGULAR

	Masc	Fem	Neut
Nom	miser	misera	miserum
Voc	miser	misera	miserum
Acc	miserum	miseram	miserum
Gen	miserī	miserae	miserī
Dat	miserō	miserae	miserō
Abl	miserō	miserā	miserō

PLURAL

	Masc	Fem	Neut
Nom	miserī	miserae	misera
Voc	miserī	miserae	misera
Acc	miserōs	miserās	misera
Gen	miserōrum	miserārum	miserōrum
Dat	miserīs	miserīs	miserīs
Abl	miserīs	miserīs	miserīs

- **liber** (free) and **tener** (tender) are declined like **miser**

ADJECTIVES 27

pulcher, pulchra, pulchrum (beautiful)

SINGULAR

	Masc	Fem	Neut
Nom	pulcher	pulchra	pulchrum
Voc	pulcher	pulchra	pulchrum
Acc	pulchrum	pulchram	pulchrum
Gen	pulchrī	pulchrae	pulchrī
Dat	pulchrō	pulchrae	pulchrō
Abl	pulchrō	pulchrā	pulchrō

PLURAL

	Masc	Fem	Neut
Nom	pulchrī	pulchrae	pulchra
Voc	pulchrī	pulchrae	pulchra
Acc	pulchrōs	pulchrās	pulchra
Gen	pulchrōrum	pulchrārum	pulchrōrum
Dat	pulchrīs	pulchrīs	pulchrīs
Abl	pulchrīs	pulchrīs	pulchrīs

- **aeger** (sick), **crēber** (frequent), **integer** (whole), **niger** (black), **piger** (slow) and **sacer** (sacred) are declined like **pulcher**

Declensions (contd)

• The following group of adjectives form their genitive singular in **-ius** and dative singular in **-i**:

alius, -a, -ud	another
alter, altera, alterum	one of two
neuter, neutra, neutrum	neither
nūllus, -a, -um	none
sōlus, -a, -um	alone
tōtus, -a, -um	whole
ūllus, -a, -um	any
ūnus, -a, -um	one
uter, utra, utrum	which of two?

solus (alone)

SINGULAR

	Masc	Fem	Neut
Nom	solus	sola	solum
Acc	solum	solam	solum
Gen	solius	solius	solius
Dat	soli	soli	soli
Abl	solo	sola	solo

PLURAL

	Masc	Fem	Neut
Nom	soli	solae	sola
Acc	solos	solas	sola
Gen	solorum	solarum	solorum
Dat	solis	solis	solis
Abl	solis	solis	solis

Third Declension

Adjectives of the third declension, like nouns, may be divided into two broad types, those with consonant stems and those with vowel stems in **-i**.

Consonant Stems

These have **one** ending in nominative singular.

prūdēns (wise)

SINGULAR

	Masc	Fem	Neut
Nom	prūdēns	prūdēns	prūdēns
Voc	prūdēns	prūdēns	prūdēns
Acc	prūdentem	prūdentem	prūdēns
Gen	prūdentis	prūdentis	prūdentis
Dat	prūdentī	prūdentī	prūdentī
Abl	prūdentī	prūdentī	prūdentī

PLURAL

	Masc	Fem	Neut
Nom	prūdentēs	prūdentēs	prūdentia
Voc	prūdentēs	prūdentēs	prūdentia
Acc	prūdentēs	prūdentēs	prūdentia
Gen	prūdentium	prūdentium	prūdentium
Dat	prūdentibus	prūdentibus	prūdentibus
Abl	prūdentibus	prūdentibus	prūdentibus

• **dīligēns** (careful), **innocēns** (innocent), **potēns** (powerful), **frequēns** (frequent), **ingēns** (huge) are declined like **prūdēns**

Declensions (contd)

amāns (loving)

SINGULAR

	Masc	Fem	Neut
Nom	amāns	amāns	amāns
Voc	amāns	amāns	amāns
Acc	amantem	amantem	amāns
Gen	amantis	amantis	amantis
Dat	amantī	amantī	amantī
Abl	amante	amante	amante

PLURAL

	Masc	Fem	Neut
Nom	amantēs	amantēs	amantia
Voc	amantēs	amantēs	amantia
Acc	amantēs	amantēs	amantia
Gen	amantium	amantium	amantium
Dat	amantibus	amantibus	amantibus
Abl	amantibus	amantibus	amantibus

- All Present participles are declined like **amāns**, although Present participles of the other conjugations end in **-ēns**

- When participles are used as adjectives **-ī** is used instead of **-e** in ablative singular case

fēlix (lucky)

SINGULAR

	Masc	Fem	Neut
Nom	fēlix	fēlix	fēlix
Voc	fēlix	fēlix	fēlix
Acc	fēlicem	fēlicem	fēlix
Gen	fēlicis	fēlicis	fēlicis
Dat	fēlicī	fēlicī	fēlicī
Abl	fēlicī	fēlicī	fēlicī

PLURAL

	Masc	Fem	Neut
Nom	fēlicēs	fēlicēs	fēlicia
Voc	fēlicēs	fēlicēs	fēlicia
Acc	fēlicēs	fēlicēs	fēlicia
Gen	fēlicium	fēlicium	fēlicium
Dat	fēlicibus	fēlicibus	fēlicibus
Abl	fēlicibus	fēlicibus	fēlicibus

audāx (bold) and **ferōx** (fierce) are declined like **fēlix**

- Note that all the above adjectives have the same case endings in all genders except for the neuter accusative singular and the neuter nominative, vocative and accusative plural.

Declensions (contd)

Vowel Stems

The following adjectives have **two** endings in nominative singular, one for masculine and feminine, one for neuter.

fortis, forte (brave)

SINGULAR

	Masc	Fem	Neut
Nom	fortis	fortis	forte
Voc	fortis	fortis	forte
Acc	fortem	fortem	forte
Gen	fortis	fortis	fortis
Dat	fortī	fortī	fortī
Abl	fortī	fortī	fortī

PLURAL

	Masc	Fem	Neut
Nom	fortēs	fortēs	fortia
Voc	fortēs	fortēs	fortia
Acc	fortēs	fortēs	fortia
Gen	fortium	fortium	fortium
Dat	fortibus	fortibus	fortibus
Abl	fortibus	fortibus	fortibus

- **brevis** (short), **facilis** (easy), **gravis** (heavy), **levis** (light), **omnis** (all), **tristis** (sad), **turpis** (disgraceful), **talis** (of such a kind), and **qualis** (of which kind), are declined like **fortis**.

The following adjectives have **three** endings in nominative singular.

ācer, ācris, ācre (sharp)

SINGULAR

	Masc	Fem	Neut
Nom	ācer	ācris	ācre
Voc	ācer	ācris	ācre
Acc	ācrem	ācrem	ācre
Gen	ācris	ācris	ācris
Dat	ācrī	ācrī	ācrī
Abl	ācrī	ācrī	ācrī

PLURAL

	Masc	Fem	Neut
Nom	ācrēs	ācrēs	ācria
Voc	ācrēs	ācrēs	ācria
Acc	ācrēs	ācrēs	ācria
Gen	ācrium	ācrium	ācrium
Dat	ācribus	ācribus	ācribus
Abl	ācribus	ācribus	ācribus

- **alacer** (lively), **equester** (of cavalry), and **volucer** (winged), are declined like **acer**, and **celer** (swift), declines similarly, but keeps **-e-** throughout (*eg* **celer, celeris, celere**)

Use of Adjectives

There are two ways of using adjectives.

- They can be used **attributively**, where the adjective in English comes before the noun: the new car

- An attributive adjective in Latin usually follows its noun but may sometimes come before it with a change of meaning (→**1**)

- They can be used **predicatively**, where the adjective comes after the verb: the car is new (→**2**)

- If an adjective describes two nouns, it agrees in gender with the nearer (→**3**)

- When an adjective describes two subjects of different sex it is often masculine plural (→**4**)

- When an adjective describes two subjects representing things without life it is often neuter plural (→**5**)

Examples

1 res **parvae**
small things
in **parvis rebus**
in unimportant matters
civis **Romanus** sum
I am a Roman citizen

2 Servi erant **fideles**
The slaves were faithful

3 Antonius, vir consilii **magni** et prudentiae
Antony, a man of great wisdom and prudence

4 frater et soror sunt **timidi**
Brother and sister are frightened

5 Calor et ventus per artus **praesentia** erant
Warmth and wind were present in the limbs

Comparative and Superlative

Adjectives also have comparative forms *eg* I am **luckier** than you, and superlative forms *eg* the **noblest** Roman of them all.

Formation

● The comparative is formed by adding **-ior** (*masc* and *fem*) and **-ius** (*neut*) to the consonant stem of the adjective and the superlative by adding **-issimus, -a, -um** to the stem:

POSITIVE		
altus	high	
audāx	bold	
brevis	short	
prūdēns	wise	

COMPARATIVE		
altior	higher	
audācior	bolder	
brevior	shorter	
prūdentior	wiser	

SUPERLATIVE		
altissimus	highest	
audācissimus	boldest	
brevissimus	shortest	
prūdentissimus	wisest	

● If the adjective ends in **-er** (*in masc nom sing*) add **-rimus** to form the superlative.

POSITIVE		
ācer	sharp	
celer	swift	
miser	unhappy	
pulcher	beautiful	

COMPARATIVE		
ācrior	sharper	
celerior	swifter	
miserior	more unhappy	
pulchrior	more beautiful	

SUPERLATIVE		
ācerrimus	sharpest	
celerrimus	swiftest	
miserrimus	most unhappy	
pulcherrimus	most beautiful	

● Six adjectives ending in **-ilis** (*in masc nom sing*) add **-limus** to the stem to form the superlative.

POSITIVE		
facilis	easy	
difficilis	difficult	
similis	like	
dissimilis	unlike	
gracilis	slight	
humilis	low	

COMPARATIVE		
facilior	easier	
difficilior	more difficult	
similior	more like	
dissimilior	more unlike	
gracilior	more slight	
humilior	lower	

SUPERLATIVE		
facillimus	easiest	
difficillimus	most difficult	
simillimus	most like	
dissimillimus	most unlike	
gracillimus	most slight	
humillimus	lowest	

Continued

Comparative and Superlative (contd)

Irregular comparison

- Some adjectives have irregular comparative and superlative forms:

POSITIVE
bonus	good
malus	bad
parvus	small
magnus	big
multus	much
multī	many

COMPARATIVE
melior	better
pēior	worse
minor	smaller
māior	bigger
plūs	more
plūrēs	more

SUPERLATIVE
optimus	best
pessimus	worst
minimus	smallest, least
māximus	biggest
plūrimus	most
plūrimī	most

- Note that all adjectives ending in **-us** preceded by a vowel (except those ending in **-quus**) form comparative and superlative thus:

idōneus	suitable
magis idōneus	more suitable
māximē idōneus	most suitable

but

antīquus	old
antīquior	older
antīquissimus	oldest

- Note the following comparatives and superlatives where there is no positive form:

exterior	outer	**extrēmus**	furthest
inferior	lower	**īnfimus** or **īmus**	lowest
superior	upper, higher	**suprēmus** or **summus**	highest
posterior	later	**postrēmus**	latest

Continued

Comparative and Superlative (contd)

Declension of Comparative and Superlative

• All comparatives decline like adjectives of the third declension.

	SINGULAR		*PLURAL*	
	Masc/Fem	Neut	Masc/Fem	Neut
Nom	altior	altius	altiōrēs	altiōra
Voc	altior	altius	altiōrēs	altiōra
Acc	altiōrem	altius	altiōrēs	altiōra
Gen	altiōris	altiōris	altiōrum	altiōrum
Dat	altiōrī	altiōrī	altiōribus	altiōribus
Abl	altiōre	altiōre	altiōribus	altiōribus

• Note ablative singular in **-e**.

• All superlatives decline like adjectives of first and second declensions (*eg* **bonus, bona, bonum**).

Use

• The comparative is often followed by **quam** (than), or the thing or person compared is given in the ablative case (→**1**)

• Sometimes the comparative can be translated by "rather" or "quite" (→**2**)

• The comparative is often strengthened by "**multo**" (→**3**)

• Sometimes the superlative can be translated by "very", or even as a positive adjective in English (→**4**)

• "**quam**" with the superlative means "as ... as possible" (→**5**)

Examples

1 Marcus est **altior quam soror**
   Marcus est **altior sorore**
   Marcus is taller than his sister

2 Gallus erat **fortior**
   the Gaul was rather brave

3 **multo carior**
   much dearer

4 **vir sapientissimus**
   a very wise man
   integerrima vita
   of virtuous life

5 **quam paucissimi**
   as few people as possible

42 ADVERBS

Adverbs

An adverb modifies a verb, adjective, another adverb or a noun. It answers questions such as "how?", "when?", "why?", "where?", "to what extent?".

Formation

- Some are formed from nouns *eg* **furtim** (stealthily) or pronouns **aliās** (at other times) but most are formed from adjectives.

- Accusative singular neuter of adjectives of extent:

multum	much	**nimium**	too much
paulum	a little	**aliquantum**	somewhat
prīmum	first	**cēterum**	for the rest

- Adjectives in **-us** and **-er** change to **-e**:

altē	highly	**miserē**	wretchedly

- Ablative forms of these adjectives in **-o** or **-a**:

certē *or* **certō**	certainly	**verē**	in truth
dextrā	on the right	**verō**	certainly

- Adjectives of the third declension add **-ter/-iter**:

audācter	boldly	**celeriter**	quickly
prūdenter	wisely		

Position

- An adverb comes before the verb, adjective, adverb or noun that it modifies (→1)

- However adverbs of time often come at the beginning of the sentence (→2)

Examples   ADVERBS 43

1 **vehementer** errabas, Verres
   you were making a big mistake, Verres

   nimium libera respublica
   too free a state

   bis consul
   twice consul

2 **cras mane** putat se venturum esse
   He thinks he will come tomorrow morning

   saepe hoc mecum cogitavi
   I often thought this over by myself

Common Adverbs

• Manner – "how?"

ita	thus	crudeliter	cruelly
sīc	thus	iustē	justly
aliter	otherwise	liberē	freely
fortē	by chance	repentē	suddenly
magnoperē	greatly		

• Time – "when?"

iam, nunc	now	(n)umquam	(n)ever
simul	at the same time	iterum	again
anteā	before	saepe	often
posteā	afterwards	hodiē	today
cōtīdiē	every day	herī	yesterday
diū	for a long time	crās	tomorrow
mox	soon	postrīdiē	next day
interim or -ea	meanwhile	statim	immediately
tum	then		

• Place – "where?"

ubi?	where?	unde?	where from?	quō?	where to?
ibi	there	inde	from there	eō	to there
hīc	here	hinc	from here	hūc	to here
usquam	any-where	nusquam	nowhere		

Others

etiam	also	fortasse	perhaps
quoque	also	consultō	on purpose
quidem	indeed	scilicet	no doubt

Comparison of Adverbs

The comparative form of the adverb is the nominative singular neuter of the comparative adjective. The superlative of the adverb is formed by changing -us of the superlative adjective to -ē.

POSITIVE		COMPARATIVE		SUPERLATIVE	
altē	highly	altius	more highly	altissimē	most highly
audacter	boldly	audacius	more boldly	audacissimē	most boldly
bene	well	melius	better	optimē	best
breviter	briefly	brevius	more briefly	brevissimē	most briefly
diū	for a long time	diūtius	longer	diūtissimē	longest
facile	easily	facilius	more easily	facillimē	most easily
magnoperē	greatly	magis	more	maximē	most
male	badly	peius	worse	pessimē	worst
miserē	wretchedly	miserius	more wretchedly	miserrimē	most wretchedly
multum	much	plūs	more	plūrimum	most
paulum	a little	minus	less	minimē	least
prope	near	propius	nearer	proximē	nearest
saepe	often	saepius	more often	saepissimē	most often

- Notes on use of the comparative adjective may be applied also to the comparative adverb (see p 40).

Examples

rem totam brevius cognoscite
Find out about the whole matter more briefly

magis consilio quam virtute vicit
He won more because of his strategy than his courage

legiones diutius sine consule fuerunt
The legions were too long without a consul

multo plus
much more

optimē
very well

mihi placebat Pomponius maximē vel minimē
I liked Pomponius the most or disliked him the least

optimus quisque id optimē facit
All the best people do it best

quam celerrimē as quickly as possible

Pronouns

Personal Pronouns

The pronouns **ego** (I), **nōs** (we), **tū** (you, *sing*), **vōs** (you, *pl*) decline as follows:

	SINGULAR	
Nom	**ego**	I
Acc	**mē**	me
Gen	**meī**	of me
Dat	**mihi**	to/for me
Abl	**mē**	by/with/from me

	PLURAL	
Nom	**nōs**	we
Acc	**nōs**	us
Gen	**nostrum**	of us
Dat	**nōbis**	to/for us
Abl	**nōbis**	by/with/from us

Nom	**tū**	you
Acc	**tē**	you
Gen	**tuī**	of you
Dat	**tibi**	to/for you
Abl	**tē**	by/with/from you

Nom	**vōs**	you
Acc	**vōs**	you
Gen	**vestrum**	of you
Dat	**vobis**	to/for you
Abl	**vōbis**	by/with/from you

Possessive

meus, -a, -um my   **tuus, -a, -um** your
noster, -ra, -rum our   **vester, -ra, -rum** your

- **nostri** and **vestri** are alternative forms of genitive plural.

- Possessives are sometimes used instead of the genitive of personal pronouns:

odium tuum
hatred of you

- For the third person pronoun, he/she/it, Latin uses **is, ea, id**:

	SINGULAR Masc		Fem		Neut	
Nom	**is**	he	**ea**	she	**id**	it
Acc	**eum**	him	**eam**	her	**id**	it
Gen	**ēius**	of him	**ēius**	of her	**ēius**	of it
Dat	**ei**	to him	**ei**	to her	**ei**	to it
Abl	**eō**	by him	**eā**	by her	**eō**	by it

	PLURAL					
Nom	**ei**	they	**eae**	they	**ea**	they
Acc	**eōs**	them	**eās**	them	**ea**	them
Gen	**eōrum**	of them	**eārum**	of them	**eōrum**	of them
Dat	**eis**	to them	**eis**	to them	**eis**	to them
Abl	**eis**	by them	**eis**	by them	**eis**	by them

Use

- Pronouns as subjects (I, you) are not usually used in Latin. The person of the verb is indicated by the ending (*eg* **misimus** – we sent). **ego, nos** *etc* are used only for emphasis:

ego vulgus odi, **tū** amas
I hate crowds, you love them

- The genitive forms **nostrum** and **vestrum** are used partitively:

multi **nostrum**
many of us
pauci **vestrum**
a few of you

Reflexive Pronouns

	myself	yourself
Acc	mē	tē
Gen	meī	tuī
Dat	mihi	tibi
Abl	mē	tē

	ourselves	yourselves
Acc	nōs	vōs
Gen	nostrum	vestrum
Dat	nōbis	vōbis
Abl	nōbis	vōbis

- These are identical in form to personal pronouns.

	himself/herself/itself/themselves
Acc	sē
Gen	suī
Dat	sibi
Abl	sē

- Reflexive pronouns are used to refer to the subject of the sentence:

quisque **se** amat
everybody loves themselves

me lavo
I wash myself

Determinative Pronouns

- **is** – he/that, **ea** – she, **id** – it: as above
- **idem** (the same)

SINGULAR

	Masc	Fem	Neut
Nom	īdem	eadem	idem
Acc	eundem	eandem	idem
Gen	eiusdem	eiusdem	eiusdem
Dat	eidem	eidem	eidem
Abl	eōdem	eādem	eōdem

PLURAL

	Masc	Fem	Neut
Nom	eīdem	eaedem	eadem
Acc	eōsdem	eāsdem	eadem
Gen	eōrundem	eārundem	eōrundem
Dat	eīsdem	eīsdem	eīsdem
Abl	eīsdem	eīsdem	eīsdem

- **ipse** (himself/herself/itself/themselves)

SINGULAR

	Masc	Fem	Neut
Nom	ipse	ipsa	ipsum
Acc	ipsum	ipsam	ipsum
Gen	ipsīus	ipsīus	ipsīus
Dat	ipsī	ipsī	ipsī
Abl	ipsō	ipsā	ipsō

PLURAL

	Masc	Fem	Neut
Nom	ipsī	ipsae	ipsa
Acc	ipsōs	ipsās	ipsa
Gen	ipsōrum	ipsārum	ipsōrum
Dat	ipsīs	ipsīs	ipsīs
Abl	ipsīs	ipsīs	ipsīs

Demonstrative Pronouns

● **hic** (this/these)

		SINGULAR	
	Masc	Fem	Neut
Nom	hic	haec	hōc
Acc	hunc	hanc	hōc
Gen	hūius	hūius	hūius
Dat	huic	huic	huic
Abl	hōc	hāc	hōc

		PLURAL	
Nom	hae	hae	haec
Acc	hōs	hās	haec
Gen	hōrum	hārum	hōrum
Dat	hīs	hīs	hīs
Abl	hīs	hīs	hīs

● **ille** (that/those)

		SINGULAR	
	Masc	Fem	Neut
Nom	ille	illa	illud
Acc	illum	illam	illud
Gen	illīus	illīus	illīus
Dat	illī	illī	illī
Abl	illō	illā	illō

		PLURAL	
Nom	illī	illae	illa
Acc	illōs	illās	illa
Gen	illōrum	illārum	illōrum
Dat	illīs	illīs	illīs
Abl	illīs	illīs	illīs

● Note that **īdem**, **hīc**, **ille** and all their parts may be adjectives as well as pronouns

---

Examples

1 **eadem** femina
the same woman

hic puer
this boy

tu autem **eadem** ages?
Are you going to do the same things?

2 patria est carior quam **nos ipsi**
Our native land is dearer than ourselves

3 **hac** remota, quomodo **illum** aestimemus?
When she is removed, how are we to judge him?

4 **nos** oportet opus conficere
We must complete the task

5 accusatores dicunt **te ipsam** testem **eius** criminis esse
The prosecutors claim that you yourself are the witness of that crime

6 sed **haec** omitto; ad **illa** quae **me** magis moverunt respondeo
But I pass over these matters; I reply to those which have affected me more deeply

7 pax **vobiscum**
Peace be with you!

8 puella intravit; **ea mihi** litteras dedit
The girl came in; she gave me a letter

Relative Pronouns

SINGULAR

	Masc	Fem	
Nom	quī	quae	who
Acc	quem	quam	whom
Gen	cūius	cūius	whose
Dat	cui	cui	to whom
Abl	quō	quā	by whom

	Neut	
Nom	quod	which/that
Acc	quod	which/that
Gen	cūius	of which
Dat	cui	to which
Abl	quō	by which

PLURAL

	Masc	Fem	
Nom	quī	quae	who
Acc	quōs	quās	whom
Gen	quōrum	quārum	whose
Dat	quibus	quibus	to whom
Abl	quibus	quibus	by whom

	Neut	
Nom	quae	which
Acc	quae	which
Gen	quōrum	of which
Dat	quibus	to which
Abl	quibus	by which

- A relative pronoun attaches a subordinate clause to a word preceding it (its antecedent). It agrees with this word in number and gender but takes its case from its own clause (→**1**)

- **quīdam, quaedam, quoddam** (a certain, somebody) **quīcumque, quaecumque, quodcumque** (whoever/ whatever), decline in the same way as the relative above (→**2**)

1 **iuvenis cuius librum Sextus legit laetus erat**
The young man, whose book Sextus read, was happy

Fortunata, quae erat uxor Trimalchiōnis, saltāre coeperat
Fortunata, who was Trimalchio's wife, had begun to dance

tum duo crotalia protulit quae Fortunātae consideranda dedit
Then she brought out a pair of earrings which she gave to Fortunata to look at

2 **quīdam ex legatis**
a certain ambassador

tu, quīcumque es
you, whoever you are

Interrogative Pronouns

SINGULAR

	Masc		Fem	
Nom	quis	who?	quis/quae	who?
Acc	quem	whom?	quam	whom?
Gen	cūius	whose?	cūius	whose?
Dat	cuī	to whom?	cuī	to whom?
Abl	quō	by whom?	quā	by whom?

	Neut	
Nom	quid	what?
Acc	quid	what?
Gen	cūius	of what?
Dat	cuī	to what?
Abl	quō	by what?

PLURAL

	Masc		Fem	
Nom	quī	who?	quae	who?
Acc	quōs	whom?	quās	whom?
Gen	quōrum	whose?	quārum	whose?
Dat	quibus	to whom?	quibus	to whom?
Abl	quibus	by whom?	quibus	by whom?

	Neut			
Nom	quae	what?	Dat	quibus to what?
Acc	quae	what?	Abl	quibus by what?
Gen	quōrum	of what?		

- The interrogative pronoun is used to ask questions and usually is the first word in the sentence (→1)

- quisquis, quisquis, quidquid (whoever, whatever)
  quisque, quisque, quidque (each)
  quisquam, quisquam, quicquam (anyone, anything)
  aliquis, aliquis, aliquid (someone, something)
  These pronouns decline in the same way as quis above
  (→2)

Examples

1 quae fuit enim causa quamobrem istī mulierī venenum dare vellet Caelius?
What was the reason why Caelius wanted to give that woman poison?

quid agam, iudices?
What am I to do, men of the jury?

quōs ad cenam invitavistī?
Whom did you invite for dinner?

quōrum agrōs Gallī incenderunt?
Whose fields did the Gauls burn?

2 quisque is est
whoever he is

sī quemquam video
if I see anyone

liber alicuius
someone's book

Prepositions

A preposition expresses the relationship of one word to another. Each Latin preposition governs a noun or pronoun in the accusative or ablative case. Some prepositions govern both cases. Some may also be used as adverbs *eg* **prope** (near).

Position

● Prepositions generally come before the noun, or an adjective or equivalent qualifying the noun *eg*

ad villam
to the house

ad Ciceronis villam
to Cicero's house

● **cum** follows a personal pronoun *eg*

mēcum
with me

Prepositions governing the Accusative

On the following pages you will find some of the most frequent uses of prepositions in Latin. In the list below, the broad meaning is given on the left, with examples of usage following. Prepositions are given in alphabetical order.

ad

to/towards (*a place or person*)

oculos ad caelum sustulit
he raised his eyes to heaven

at, in the direction of, with regard to

ad Capuam profectus sum
I set out in the direction of Capua

ad portas
at the gates

ad duo milia occisi
about 2000 were killed

nil ad me attinet
it means nothing to me

adversum (-us)

opposite

sedens adversus te
sitting opposite you

towards

adversus Italiam
towards (*ie* facing) Italy

against

adversum flumen
against the stream

Continued

60 PREPOSITIONS

Prepositions governing the Accusative (contd)

ante

before (*of place and time*), used with ordinal number in dates

ante meridiem
before midday

ante limen
before the doorway

ante diem quintum Kalendas Ianuarias
28th December (*ie* 5th before Kalends of January)

apud

at/near (*usually with persons*)

Crassus apud eum sedet
Crassus is sitting near him

in the writing of

apud Platonem
in Plato's writings

before (*authorities*)

apud pontifices
before the high priests

circum (circa)

around, about (*of place, people*)

circum forum
around the forum

circum Hectorem
around Hector

circa montes
around the mountains

circa decem millia Gallorum
about ten thousand Gauls

PREPOSITIONS 61

contra

against

contra hostes
against the enemy

contra ventos
against the wind

opposite

contra Britanniam
facing Britain

extra

outside of

extra muros
outside the walls

beyond (*of place and time*)

extra iocum
beyond a joke

inter

between

inter oppositos exercitus
between the opposing armies

amans inter se
loving each other

among

inter saucios
among the wounded

inter manus
within reach

during

inter hos annos
during these years

Continued

Prepositions governing the Accusative (contd)

intra

within (*of place and time*)

intra parietes
within the walls

intra quattuor annos
within four years

ob

on account of

quam ob rem
therefore

ob stultitiam
on account of your
foolishness

per

through

per noctem
through the night

by means of

per vos
by means of you

per aetatem periit
he died of old age

per deos iuro
I swear by the gods

---

post

after (*of time and place*)

post urbem conditam
after the foundation of the
city

post tergum
behind your back

praeter

beyond

praeter naturam
beyond nature

besides

**praeter se tres alios
adduxit**
he brought three others
besides himself

except for

praeter paucos
except for a few

prope

near

prope me habitavit
he lived near me

propter

on account of

propter metum mortis
on account of fear of
death

Continued

Prepositions governing the Accusative (contd)

secundum

along (*of place*)	**secundum flumen** along the river
immediately after (*time*)	**secundum quietem** on waking from sleep
according to	**secundum naturam** according to nature

trans

across	**vexillum trans vallum traicere** to take the standard across the rampart
	trans Rhenum across the Rhine

ultra

beyond (*of time, degree etc*)	**ultra vires** beyond one's power

Prepositions governing the Ablative

Those which are spatial represent the idea of rest in a place or motion from a place.

a(b)

from (*of place, people, direction, time*)	**ab arce hostes deiecti sunt** the enemy were driven from the citadel
	a nobis abesse to be distant from us
	a dextrā from the right
	a tertiā horā from the third hour
by (*agent*)	**ab amicis desertus** abandoned by friends

cum

with	**vade mecum** go with me!
	cum curā loqui to speak with care
	cum Augusto coniurare to conspire with Augustus
	summa cum laude with distinction

Continued

Prepositions governing the Ablative (contd)

dē

down from	**dē caelō demittere** to send down from heaven
away from	**de tricliniō exire** to go away from the dining room
about	**cogitare de hāc rē** to think about this matter
	dē industriā on purpose
during or at (of time)	**dē nocte** at night, during the night

ē(x)

out of (from)	**ē carcere effugerunt** they escaped from prison
	ex equis desilire to jump from their horses
	quidam ex Hispania someone from Spain
	statua ex argentō facta a statue made of silver
immediately after	**ex consulatu** immediately after his consulship
from	**ex hōc diē** from that day
	ex aequō equally

pro

for/on behalf of	**pro se quisque** each one for himself/herself
	pro patriā mori to die for one's country
according to	**pro viribus agere** to act according to one's ability
in front of	**pro rostris** in front of the rostrum

sine

without	**sine spē** without hope
	sine pecuniā without money

Prepositions governing Accusative and Ablative

in

with accusative

into	**in hanc urbem venire** to come into the city
till	**in primam lucem dormivit** he slept till dawn
against	**in rem publicam aggredi** to attack the state

with ablative

in	**puella in illā domō laetē vivebat** the girl lived happily in that house
on	**in capite coronam gerebat** he wore a crown on his head
	in animo habere to intend (to have in one's mind)
within (*of time*)	**in omni aetate** within every age
in (*of condition*)	**in parte facilis, in parte difficilis** easy in parts, difficult in others

sub

with accusative

beneath	**sub iugum mittere** to send beneath the yoke (*ie into slavery*)
below (*with verb of motion*)	**sub ipsum murum** just below the wall
before (*of time*)	**sub vesperum** just before nightfall

with ablative

under (*of place and power*)	**sub montibus constituere** to station under the mountains
	sub Nerone under the power of Nero

super

with accusative

over, above (*of place*), in addition	**super capita hostium** over the heads of the enemy
	alii, super alios, advenerunt they arrived one after the other

with ablative

concerning/about	**super his rebus scribam** I shall write about these matters

Numerals

Cardinal and Ordinal Numbers

		CARDINAL	ORDINAL
1	I	ūnus, -a, -um	prīmus, -a, -um
2	II	duo, -ae, -o	secundus, -a, -um
3	III	trēs, tria	tertius, -a, -um
4	IV	quattuor	quartus, -a, -um
5	V	quīnque	quīntus, -a, -um
6	VI	sex	sextus, -a, -um
7	VII	septem	septimus, -a, -um
8	VIII	octō	octāvus, -a, -um
9	IX	novem	nōnus, -a, -um
10	X	decem	decimus, -a, -um
11	XI	ūndecim	ūndecimus, -a, -um
12	XII	duodecim	duodecimus, -a, -um
13	XIII	tredecim	tertius decimus, -a, -um
14	XIV	quattuordecim	quartus decimus, -a, -um
15	XV	quīndecim	quīntus decimus, -a, -um
16	XVI	sēdecim	sextus decimus, -a, -um
17	XVII	septendecim	septimus decimus, -a, -um
18	XVIII	duodēvigintī	duodēvicēsimus, -a, -um
19	XIX	ūndēvigintī	undēvicēsimus, -a, -um
20	XX	vigintī	vicēsimus, -a, -um
21	XXI	vigintī ūnus	vicēsimus prīmus
30	XXX	trigintā	tricēsimus
40	XL	quadrāgintā	quadrāgēsimus
50	L	quīnquāgintā	quīnquāgēsimus
60	LX	sexāgintā	sexāgēsimus
70	LXX	septuāgintā	septuāgēsimus
80	LXXX	octōgintā	octōgēsimus
90	XC	nōnāgintā	nōnāgēsimus
100	C	centum	centēsimus

		CARDINAL	ORDINAL
200	CC	ducentī, -ae, -a	ducentēsimus
300	CCC	trecentī, -ae, -a	trecentēsimus
400	CCCC	quadringentī, -ae, -a	quadringentēsimus
500	D (IↃ)	quīngentī, -ae, -a	quīngentēsimus
600	DC	sescentī, -ae, -a	sescentēsimus
700	DCC	septingentī, -ae, -a	septingentēsimus
800	DCCC	octingentī, -ae, -a	octingentēsimus
900	DCCCC	nōngentī, -ae, -a	nōngentēsimus
1000	M (CIↃ)	mīlle	mīllēsimus
2000	MM	duo mīlia	bis mīllēsimus
1,000,000		deciēs centēna (centum)	mīlia

- Fractions are expressed as follows:

dīmidia pars	1/2	
tertia pars	1/3	
quārta pars	1/4	

Continued

Cardinal and Ordinal Numbers (contd)

- Ordinal numbers (→1) decline like 1st and 2nd declension adjectives

- Cardinal numbers (→2) do not decline except for **ūnus, duo, trēs** and hundreds (**ducentī** etc)

- **ūnus** declines as 1st and 2nd declension adjectives except that the genitive singular ends in -**īus** and the dative in -**ī**

- **duo** (two) declines as follows:

	Masc	Fem	Neut
Nom	**duo**	**duae**	**duo**
Acc	**duōs**	**duās**	**duo**
Gen	**duōrum**	**duārum**	**duōrum**
Dat	**duōbus**	**duābus**	**duōbus**
Abl	**duōbus**	**duābus**	**duōbus**

ambō, -ae, -a (both) declines in the same way

- **trēs** (three) declines as follows:

	Masc	Fem	Neut
Nom	**trēs**	**trēs**	**tria**
Acc	**trēs**	**trēs**	**tria**
Gen	**trium**	**trium**	**trium**
Dat	**tribus**	**tribus**	**tribus**
Abl	**tribus**	**tribus**	**tribus**

- Genitive of hundreds, *eg* **trecentī** ends -**um** (→3)

- **mīlia** (thousands) declines as follows:

Nom	**mīlia**	Dat	**mīlibus**
Acc	**mīlia**	Abl	**mīlibus**
Gen	**mīlium**		

- **mīlle** (thousand) does not decline.

Examples

1 coquus **secundam** mensam parāverat
The cook had prepared the second course

legiōnis **nōnae** militēs magnam partem hostium interfēcērunt
Soldiers of the ninth legion killed a large number of the enemy

2 **decem mīlia** passuum exercitus prōgressus est
The army advanced 10 miles

Cerberus, quī **tria** capita habēbat, in antrō recubuit
Cerberus, who had three heads, crouched in the cave

Stellae **novem** orbēs cōnfēcērunt
The stars completed nine orbits

duodēvīgintī onerāriae nāvēs hūc accēdēbant
Eighteen cargo ships were approaching

Caesar **trecentōs** militēs trans Padānum trāiēcit
Caesar transported three hundred soldiers across the River Po

3 da mī bāsia **mīlle**
Give me a thousand kisses

trecentum mīlitum (*gen*)
of three hundred soldiers

4 **duo mīlia passuum** (*gen*)
2000 paces *or* 2 miles

Distributive Numerals

These are used when repetition is involved as when multi-plying (→1)

1	singulī, -ae, -a	one each
2	bīnī, -ae, -a	two each
3	ternī (trīnī)	
4	quaternī	
5	quīnī	
6	sēnī	
7	septēnī	
8	octōnī	
9	novēnī	
10	dēnī	

Numeral Adverbs

1	semel	once
2	bis	twice
3	ter	
4	quater	
5	quīnquiēs	
6	sexiēs	
7	septiēs	
8	octiēs	
9	noviēs	
10	deciēs	

(→2)

1 **bīnī gladiātōrēs**
(*describing pairs of gladiators*)

bīna castra
two camps

quaternōs dēnāriōs in singulās vīnī amphorās
4 denarii each for a bottle of wine

2 nōn plūs quam **semel**
not more than once

deciēs centēna mīlia sestertium *or* **deciēs** sestertium
1,000,000 sesterces

ter quattuor
twelve (*three times four*)

Dates

- Events of the year were usually recorded by using the names of the consuls holding office that year (→**1**)
- From the late republic the date of the foundation of Rome was established – 753 BC and time was calculated from this date (→**2**)
- The four seasons were: (→**3**)

ver, veris (nt)	spring
aestās, -ātis (f)	summer
autumnus, -i (m)	autumn
hiems, -is (f)	winter

- The months were reformed by Julius Caesar (7 of 31 days, 4 of 30, 1 of 28, and an extra day each leap year). Each month (mensis, -is, m) was identified by the following adjectives:

Iānuārius	January
Februārius	February
Martius	March
Aprīlis	April
Māius	May
Iūnius	June
Iūlius (Quintīlis)	July
Augustus (Sextīlis)	August
September	September
Octōber	October
November	November
December	December

- Three important days each month were:

Kalendae, -ārum (fpl)	Kalends or 1st
Nonae, -ārum (fpl)	Nones or 5th/7th
Idus, -uum (fpl)	Ides or 13th/15th

Continued

1 **Nerone iterum L. Pisone consulibus** pauca memoria digna evenerunt
Few incidents worth recording took place during the year when Nero and Lucius Piso were consuls (AD 57)

Lentulo Gaetulico C. Calvisio consulibus decreta sunt triumphi insignia Poppaeo Sabino
A triumph was voted to Poppaeus Sabinus during the consulship of Lentulus Gaetulicus and Gaius Calvisius

2 **ab urbe condita**
since the foundation of Rome

ante urbem conditam
before the foundation of the city

post urbem conditam
after the foundation of the city

3 ineunte aestate
in the beginning of summer

media aestate
midsummer

iam hieme confecta
when winter was already over

vere ineunte Antonius Tarentum navigavit
At the beginning of spring, Antony sailed to Tarentum

Dates (contd)

- In March, July, October and May, Nones fall on the 7th and Ides on the 15th day (5th and 13th in all other months).

- To refer to these dates, the ablative is used (→1)

- To refer to the day before these dates, use pridiē (→2)

- All other days were reckoned by counting (inclusively) the days before the next main date. "ante diem" + accusative of ordinal numbers and the next main date were used:
9th of February is 5 days before the 13th of February (counting inclusively). 28th April is 4 days before 1st May (→3)

- An easy way to work out such dates is to add one to Nones and Ides and subtract the Latin number. Add two to the number of days in the month before the Kalends, again subtracting the given Latin number. You will then have the date in English.

- The day was divided into twelve hours horae, -arum (fpl). The hours of darkness into four watches of three hours each, vigiliae, -arum (fpl), from 6–9 pm, 9–12 pm, 12–3 am, 3–6 am

- Other ways of expressing time:

primā luce	at dawn
solo orto	at sunrise
solis occasu	at sunset
media nocte	at midnight
noctu, nocte	at night
mane	in the morning
meridie	at midday
sub vesperum	towards evening
vespere	in the evening (→4)

Examples

1 Kalendīs Martiīs
on the 1st of March

Idibus Decembribus
on the 13th of December

Idibus Martiīs Caesar a Bruto interfectus est
Caesar was killed by Brutus on the 15th of March

2 pridie Nonas Ianuarias (Non. Ian.)
4th January

3 ante diem quintum Idus Februarias
9th February

ante diem quartum Kalendas Maias
28th April

4 prima hora
at the first hour (6–7 am)

tertia vigilia
during the third watch (midnight–3 am)

tertia fere vigilia navem solvit
He set sail after midnight (during the third watch)

ipse **hora circiter quarta diei** cum primis navibus Britanniam attigit
He himself reached Britain with the first ships around 10 o'clock in the morning

vespere vinum optimum convivae bibunt
In the evening, the guests drink vintage wine

Word Order

Simple Sentences

Word order in English is stricter than in Latin. The usual English order – subject + verb + object – differentiates the meaning of sentences such as, "The cat caught the mouse" and "The mouse caught the cat". Latin order is more flexible since the endings of words clearly show their function, whatever their position in the sentence.

Compare the following:

feles murem cepit   the cat caught the mouse
murem cepit feles   it was the cat that caught the mouse

The sentences are identical in meaning, although the emphasis is different. This difference in word order often makes it difficult for English translators to unravel long Latin sentences. However there are certain principles to help:

● The normal *grammatical* word order in Latin is:

  Subject first, Predicate after (by Predicate understand "verb")

● Expressions qualifying the subject (*ie* adjectives) must be near the subject

● Expressions qualifying the predicate (*eg* objects, adverbs, prepositional phrases) must be near the verb

Thus the usual word order of a simple sentence is:

(Connecting Word)
Subject
(Adjective)
Object
Adverbs *or* Prepositional Phrases
Predicate (verb) (→**1**)

Continued

Examples

1 at **hostes** magnam virtutem in extrema spe salutis **praestiterunt**
But the enemy showed great courage, finally hoping to save themselves

Ariovistus ad postulata Caesaris pauca **respondit**
Ariovistus briefly replied to Caesar's demands

iste **Hannibal** sic hanc Tertiam **dilexit**
Thus that Hannibal loved this Tertia

Simple Sentences (contd)

- Another principle is *emphasis*, where the words are in an unusual order, *eg* subject last, predicate first (→**1**)

- Questions usually begin with interrogatives (→**2**)

- Adjectives may precede or follow nouns. Check agreement of endings (→**3**)

- Genitives usually follow the governing word (→**4**)

- Words in apposition usually follow one another, although "rex" often comes first (→**5**)

- Adverbs usually come before their verb, adjective or adverb (→**6**)

- Prepositions usually come before their nouns (→**7**) but note, magna **cum** cura (with great care).

- Finally, watch out for the omission of words, particularly parts of **esse** (to be) (→**8**)

Examples

1 horum adventu **redintegratur** | **seditio** (subject last)
On their arrival trouble broke out once more
confecerunt me | **infirmitates** meorum (verb first)
I have been upset by the illnesses of my slaves

2 **quid** hoc loco potes dicere, homo amentissime?
What can you say at this point, you madman?
quis clarior in Graecia Themistocle?
Who (is) more famous in Greece than Themistocles?

3 **bello magno** victus   **magna domus**
conquered in a great war   a large house

4 multi **nostrum**   filius **Augusti**
many of us   Augustus' son

5 Cicero, **consul**
Cicero, the consul
rex Tarquinius
King Tarquinius

6 **vix** cuiquam persuadebatur
hardly anyone could be persuaded
multo carius
much dearer

7 **in** villam
into the house
sub monte
under the mountain

8 **pudor inde et miseratio et patris Agrippae, Augusti avi memoria (est)**
A feeling of pity and shame came over them and they remembered her father Agrippa and her grandfather Augustus

Compound Sentences

A compound sentence is one with a main clause and one or more subordinate clauses. In Latin this is called a **period**, where the most important idea is kept to the end.

- conservate parenti filium, parentem filio, (1), ne aut senectutem iam prope desperatam contempsisse aut adulescentiam plenam spei│maximae non modo non aluisse vos verum etiam perculisse atque adflixisse videamini (2). (Cic. – Pro Caelio 32.80)

1. Main clause
   save a son for his father, a father for his son.

2. Negative purpose clause
   lest you appear either to have cast aside an old man near despair or that you have failed to sustain a young man full of the highest hopes, but have even struck him down and ruined him.

Note that this sentence builds towards a climax at the end. The most important verbs here are **perculisse** and **adflixisse** rather than **videamini** (you may seem). Notice also the rhythm of the last two words. Repetition of similar phrases is common – **parenti filium, parentem filio**. This sentence is a good illustration of an orator's style.

- Historical style is much simpler, often a subordinate clause followed by a main clause:

  cum equites nostri funditoribus sagittariisque flumen transgressi essent (1), cum equitatu proelium commiserunt

1. Subordinate adverbial clause of time
   when our cavalry had crossed the river with slingers and archers

2. Main clause
   they joined battle with the cavalry

- Participle phrase followed by the **main clause** and **subordinate** clause:

  nec patrum cognitionibus satiatus iudiciis (1), adsidebat in cornu tribunalis (2), ne praetorem curuli depelleret (Tac Ann I 75)

1. Participle phrase
   nor was he (the emperor) satisfied with taking part in Senate trials

2. Main clause
   he used to sit in the ordinary lawcourts

3. Subordinate clause of purpose
   in case he pushed the praetor from his curule chair

Many other combinations of clauses are possible. It is important to relate the sentence to its context and to the passage as a whole as Latin sentences are linked logically. It is often helpful when translating a long sentence to pick out subjects and verbs in order to recognize the structure of the clauses and grasp the overall meaning of the sentence.

Simple Sentences

Direct Statement

The basic patterns involved in direct statement have been illustrated under **Word Order** (*see p 80*).

Direct Questions

In Latin a direct question can be expressed as follows by:

● an interrogative pronoun (→**1**)

   quis? (who?), **quid?** (what?), **cur?** (why?)

● adding **-ne** to the first word, where no definite answer is indicated (→**2**)

● **nonne**, when the expected answer is YES (→**3**)

● **num**, when the expected answer is NO (→**4**)

● **utrum ... an(non)**
   -ne ...an(non) } (whether) ... or (not)
   ... an(non)
   in double questions (→**5**)

Continued

Examples

1 **quis est**
    Who is it?

    quid dicit?
    What is he saying?

    cur lacrimas?
    Why are you crying?

2 timesne Verrem?
    Are you scared of Verres?

3 **nonne** cladem audivisti?
    Surely you heard of the defeat?
    or You heard of the defeat, didn't you?

4 **num** heri venisti?
    Surely you didn't come yesterday?
    or You didn't come yesterday, did you?

5 utrum has condiciones accepistis **annon**?
    Have you accepted these conditions or not?

Simple Sentences (contd)

Direct Command

- A direct command in Latin is expressed in the second person by the imperative if positive, by **noli(te)** with the present infinitive if negative (→**1**)

- A direct command in the first or third persons is expressed by the present subjunctive, with **nē** if negative (→**2**)

Wishes

- Wishes are expressed in Latin by **utinam** with the subjunctive, **utinam nē** when negative (→**3**)

- **vellem** may also be used with imperfect or pluperfect subjunctive to express wishes (→**4**)

Examples

1 **venite** mecum
come with me

noli me tangere
don't touch me

2 **vivamus** atque **amemus**
let us live and let us love

ne **fiat** lux
let there not be light

3 **utinam** frater redeat
I wish my brother would return (*future*)

utinam ne vere scriberem
I wish I were not writing the truth (*present*)

utinam brevi moratus esses
I wish you had stayed a little (*past*)

4 **vellem** me ad cenam **invitavisses**
I wish you had invited me to dinner

Compound Sentences

Indirect Statement

"You are making a mistake" is a *direct statement.* "I think that you are making a mistake" is an *indirect statement.*

- The indirect statement is the object clause of "I think". In indirect statement in Latin, the subject of the clause (*eg* te) goes into the accusative case, the verb is an infinitive (errare):

Puto te errare
I think that you are making a mistake

- This pattern is used after verbs of saying, thinking, perceiving, knowing (→**1**)

1			
audire	hear	negare	say ... not
cognoscere	discover	nescire	not to know
credere	believe	putare	think
dicere	say	scire	know
intellegere	understand	sentire	perceive
meminisse	remember	videre	see
narrare	tell		

Continued

Indirect Statement (contd)

Translation

- The *present infinitive* refers to actions happening at the same time and may be translated – is, are, was, were.

- The *perfect infinitive* refers to prior action and may be translated – has, have, had.

- The *future infinitive* refers to future action and may be translated – will, would.

putamus	**te errāre** **te errāvisse** **te errātūrum esse**	
We think		that you are making a mistake that you have made a mistake that you will make a mistake

putabamus	**te errāre** **te errāvisse** **te errātūrum esse**	
We thought		that you were making a mistake that you had made a mistake that you would make a mistake

- Notice that when the main verb is *past* tense, translate the present infinitive – "was, were", the past infinitive – "had", the future infinitive – "would".

- The reflexive pronoun **sē** is used to refer to the subject of the main verb (→**1**)

- Translate **negō** – I say that ... not (→**2**)

- Verbs of promising, hoping, threatening or swearing (*eg* **promittō, pollicĕor, spērō, minor, iuro**) are followed by an accusative and future infinitive (→**3**)

1 senex dixit **se** thesaurum invenisse
The old man said that he had found treasure

2 **negavit** servum domum venturum esse
He said that the slave would not come home

3 **promisi me festinaturum esse**
I promised that I would hurry

sperabat se hoc confecturum esse
He hoped that he could complete this
or He hoped to complete this

Further Examples

creditores existimabant **eum** totam pecuniam **per-didisse**
His creditors thought that he had lost all his money

memini **simulacra** deorum de caelo **percussa esse**
I remember that the gods' statues were struck down from the heavens

vidistine **Catonem** in bibliotheca **sedere**?
Did you see Cato sitting in the library?

iuro **me** pro patria fortiter **pugnaturum esse**
I swear that I shall fight bravely for my country

iam ego credo **vos** verum **dixisse**
I now believe that you spoke the truth

negavit **nihil** umquam pulchrius statua **fuisse**
He said that nothing had ever been more beautiful than that statue

Indirect Question

"Where did he come from?" is a *direct question*. "I asked where he had come from" is an *indirect question*. Latin uses the same interrogative words (**quis** – who, **quid** – what *etc*) and the verb in indirect questions is always subjunctive

> **rogavi unde venisset**
> I asked where he had come from

- Latin uses six different forms of the subjunctive in this construction in a precise sequence depending on the main verb (→**1**)

Examples

1 rogo

	unde veniat	(present)
	unde venerit	(perfect)
	unde venturus sit	(future)

I ask

	where he comes from	(present)
	where he has come from	(perfect)
	where he will come from	(future)

rogavi

	unde veniret	(imperfect)
	unde venisset	(pluperfect)
	unde venturus esset	(future perfect)

I asked

	where he was coming from	(imperfect)
	where he had come from	(pluperfect)
	where he would come from	(future perfect)

Continued

Indirect Question (contd)

Translation

Translation of tenses in indirect question is *easy*, because English uses the same tenses as Latin, as can be seen on page 94.

- The reflexive pronoun **se** is used to refer to the subject of the main verb (→**1**)

- **utrum ... an** (if ... or), **utrum ... necne** (whether ... or not) are also used in indirect questions (→**2**)

- **num** is used to mean "if" in indirect questions (→**3**)

Examples

1 rogavit **quando se visuri essemus**
He asked when we would see him

2 roga **utrum** iverit **an** manserit
Ask whether he went or stayed

roga **utrum** manserit **necne**
Ask whether he stayed or not

rogavit **utrum** Scylla infestior **esset** Charybdis **necne**
He asked whether Charybdis was more dangerous than Scylla or not

3 nescio **num** venturi sint
I don't know if they will come

Further Examples

nescimus **quid facturi simus**
We don't know what we shall do

mirum est **quanta sit Roma**
It is amazing how big Rome is
or The size of Rome is amazing

exploratores cognoverunt **quanti essent** Poeni
Scouts discovered what the numbers of the Carthaginians were

incredibile est **quomodo** talia facere **potuerit**
It is incredible how he was able to do such things

nemo audivit **quid rex constituisset**
No one heard what the king had decided
or No one heard the king's decision

Indirect Command

"Come here" is a *direct command.* "I ordered you to come here" is an *indirect command.* Indirect commands in Latin are expressed by **ut** (when positive) or **nē** (when negative) and have their verbs in the subjunctive (→**1**)

- Latin uses two tenses of the subjunctive, present or imperfect, in this construction. It uses the present subjunctive if the main verb is present or future tense and imperfect subjunctive if the main verb is in the past tense. (→**2**)

Translation

- The English translation of the indirect command is the same, whichever tense is used in Latin – the infinitive (*eg* to come)

- The reflexive **se** is used to refer to the subject of the main verb (→**3**)

- Common verbs introducing indirect command are:

hortor	encourage
moneo	warn
oro	beg
persuadeo	persuade
rogo	ask

- *Only* **iubeo** (to order), **veto** (to tell … not), are usually used with the infinitive in Latin (→**4**)

Examples

1 tibi imperavi **ut** venirēs
I ordered you to come
tibi imperavi **ne** venires
I forbade you to come
milites oravit **ne** in castris diutius **manerent**
He begged his soldiers not to stay in camp any longer
hoc rogo, mi Tiro, **ne** temere **naviges**
I beg you, my dear Tiro, not to sail carelessly

2 tibi **impero ut** venias   *(present)*
I order you to come
tibi imperavi **ut** venires   *(imperfect)*
I ordered you to come
deos precor **ut** nobis **parcant**
I beg the gods to spare us
amicos roga **ut veniant**, operamque **dent**, et messim
hanc nobis **adiuvent**
Ask your friends to come and lend a hand and help
us with this harvest

3 nos oravit ut **sibi** cibum daremus
He begged us to give him food

4 **iubeo** eos navigare
I order them to sail
veto eos navigare
I tell them not to sail
mater me **vetuit** in murum **ascendere**
Mother forbade me to climb on the wall
Antonius eos **iussit** adventum **suum exspectare**
Antony told them to await his arrival

Purpose or Final Clauses

There are two ways of expressing purpose in English:

> I am hurrying to the city to see the games
>
> *or* I am hurrying to the city so that I may see the games

- In Latin **ut** is used with the present or imperfect subjunctive, to express purpose. The present subjunctive is used if the main verb is in the present or future tense and the imperfect subjunctive if the main verb is in the past tense (→**1**)

- Negative purpose clauses are introduced by **ne** which can be translated "so that … not", "in case", "to avoid", "lest" etc (→**2**)

- If there is a comparative adjective or adverb in the Latin sentence **quō** is used instead of **ut** (→**3**)

- The relative **qui, quae, quod** may be used instead of **ut**, if it refers to an object in the main clause (→**4**)

- After negative **ne**, **quis** is used instead of **aliquis** to mean "anyone"

- Note that **se** is used to refer to the subject of the main verb (→**5**)

- **ad** is used with the gerundive to express purpose (→**6**)

- The supine **-um** is used after verbs of motion to express purpose (→**7**)

Examples

1 ad urbem festīnō **ut** ludōs **videam**
I am hurrying to the city to see the games
ad urbem festīnāvī **ut** ludōs **viderem**
I hurried to the city to see the games
filium multō cum fletū complexus, pepulit **ut abīret**
Embracing his son tearfully, he drove him to leave

2 Tiberius hoc recūsāvit **ne** Germanicus imperium **haberet**
Tiberius refused this lest Germanicus had power
pontem rescīderunt **ne** hostes flūmen **transīrent**
They broke down the bridge in case the enemy crossed the river

3 puellae cantābant **quō** laetiōrēs essent **hospitēs**
The girls sang to make their guests happier

4 rex sex mīlitēs delegit **quī** ad Graeciam **proficīscerentur**
The king chose six soldiers to set off for Greece

5 in silvīs **sē** abdidit **ne quis sē** vidēret
He hid in the woods lest anyone should see him
sed **ut** venēnum manifestō comprehendī **posset**, constituī locum iussit, **ut** eō **mitteret** amicos, **quī latērent**, cum vēnisset Licinius, venenumque traderet, comprehenderent
But *so that the poison could be seized openly*, he ordered that a place be appointed, *to send friends there, to hide*. When Licinius came to hand over the poison they could arrest him.

6 Verres ad Siciliam vēnit **ad urbes dīripiendas**
Verres came to Sicily to plunder its cities

7 veniunt **spectātum**
They come to see

Result or Consecutive Clauses

The road is so long that I am tired
It was so hot that we could not work

In both these sentences, a result or consequence is expressed in English by using words such as

so ... that (positive)
so that ... not (negative)

- In Latin the following words are frequently used in the main clause

adeo	to such an extent
ita	thus, so
talis	of such a kind
tam	so
tantus	so great
tot	so many

- In the result clause, **ut** (so that) and **ut ... non** (so that ... not) are used with the present or imperfect subjunctive. Present subjunctive is used where the main verb is in the present and the imperfect subjunctive is used where the main verb is past (→**1**)

- **Note** that **eum** is used to refer to "him" instead of **se** when referring to the subject of the main clause as in the first example (→**1**)

1 Gallus **tam** ferox est **ut** omnes Romani eum **timeant**
The Gaul is so fierce that all the Romans are scared of him

tanta erat tempestas **ut** nautae navem **non solverent**
So great was the storm that the sailors could not set sail

nemo est **adeo** stultus **ut non** discere **possit**
No one is so stupid that he can't learn

tot sententiae erant **ut** nemo **consentiret**
There were so many opinions that no one could agree

tales nos esse putamus **ut** ab omnibus **laudemur**
We think that we are the sort of people to be praised by everyone

Verbs of Fearing

In Latin, verbs of fearing (**timeo**, **metuo**, **paveo**, **vereor**) are followed by **nē**, **nē non** or **ut** with the present and perfect, imperfect and pluperfect subjunctive according to sequence of tenses:

- The present subjunctive represents present and future tenses in English

  I am afraid he is coming
  I am afraid he will come

- The perfect subjunctive represents the past tense in English

  I am afraid that he has come

- When the verb of fearing is in the past tense, imperfect and pluperfect subjunctive are used in Latin instead (→**1**)

- **nē** is used if the fear is expressed in a positive sentence (ie I am afraid he will come). **nē nōn**, **ut** is used if the fear is expressed negatively (ie I am afraid that he won't come) (→**2**)

- As in English, the infinitive can follow a verb of fearing, provided that the subjects of both are the same (→**3**)

Examples

1 veritus sum **ne** veniret
I was afraid he was coming
veritus sum **ne venisset**
I was afraid that he had come

2 **vereor ne** amicus **veniat**
I am afraid lest my friend comes
or lest my friend will come

vereor ne amicus **non veniat**
I am afraid that my friend won't come
vereor ut amicus **venerit**
I am afraid that my friend has not come
verebar ne amicus **non venisset**
I was afraid that my friend had not come

metuo ne virtutis maiorum nostrum **obliviscamur**
I am afraid that we shall forget the courage of our ancestors

paves ne ducas tu illam
You are afraid to marry her
Verres, **veritus ne** servi bellum in Sicilia **facerent**, multos in vincula coniecit
Verres, fearing that slaves might revolt in Sicily, threw many into prison
Romani **verebantur ne** fortiter **non pugnavissent**
The Romans were afraid that they had not fought bravely

3 timeo **abire**
I am afraid to go away
mulier **timebat manere** sola
The woman was scared to remain alone

106 SENTENCES

Conditional Sentences

Compare the following two sentences in English:

(a) If I tell you a lie, you will be angry
(b) If I were to tell you a lie, you would be angry

The first is a *logical statement of fact*, stating what *will* happen, the second is a *hypothesis*, stating what *would* happen.

For the first type of sentence, Latin uses the indicative mood in both main and conditional clauses. For the second type, Latin uses the subjunctive mood in both main and conditional clauses.

Translate type (a) as follows:

si hoc **dicis**, sapiens **es**
if you say this, you are wise

si hoc **dicebas**, sapiens **eras**
if you were saying this, you were wise

si hoc **dixisti**, erravisti
if you said this, then you made a mistake

si hoc **dixeris**, errabis
if you say this, you will make a mistake

Notice that the same tenses in English are used as in Latin except in the last sentence. Latin is more precise – you *will have said* this, before you make a mistake, therefore Latin uses the *future perfect* tense.

Continued

SENTENCES 107

- Consider also the following sentence:

si me **amabis**, mecum **manebis**
If you love me, you will stay with me

Latin uses the *future* tense in both clauses, English uses the *present* tense in the "if" clause. Both actions, "loving" and "remaining" *logically* refer to the *future*.

Translate type (b) as follows:

(*present*)
si hoc **dicas**, **erres**
if you were to say this, you would be making a mistake

(*imperfect*)
si hoc **diceres**, **errares**
if you said (*or* were saying) that, you would be making a mistake

(*pluperfect*)
si hoc **dixisses**, **erravisses**
if you had said that, you would have made a mistake

Notice that both tenses of the subjunctive are the same in the above examples. Sometimes an imperfect may be used in one clause and the pluperfect in the other:

si pudorem **haberes**, Romā **abiisses**
if you had any sense of shame, you would have left Rome

Conditional Sentences (contd)

Negative Conditional Sentences

- **nisi** (unless) is the negative of **si** (if). (→**1**)

- **si non** (if not), is less common and negates *one* word, or is used when the same verb is repeated (→**2**)

Examples

1 **nisi** id statim **feceris**, ego te **tradam** magistratui
Unless you do this immediately, I shall hand you over to the magistrate

nisi utilem **crederem**, non pacem **peterem**
Unless I thought it useful, I would not be seeking peace

2 **si** me **adiuveris**, laeta **ero**; **si** me **non adiuveris**, tristis **ero**
If you help me, I shall be happy; if you don't help me, I shall be sad

si navigatio **non morabitur**, mox te **videbo**
If my sailing is not delayed, I shall see you soon

Further Examples

(b) quis illum sceleratum fuisse **putavisset**, **si tacuisset**?
Who would have thought he was a rascal, if he had kept quiet?

(b) multi **agerent** et **pugnarent si** rei publicae **videretur**
Many would act and fight, if the state decided

(a) **gaudemus si** liberi in horto **ludunt**
We are happy if the children play in the garden

(b) **si quis** in caelum **ascendisset**, pulchritudinem side-rum **conspexisset**
If anyone had gone up to heaven, he would have seen the beauty of the stars

110 SENTENCES

Concessive Clauses

In English, Concessive clauses usually begin with "al-though":

Although he is rich, he is not happy
I shall succeed although it is difficult

● **quamquam** (although) is followed by the indicative (→**1**)

  Note that **tamen** (however) is often used in the main clause in concessive sentences

● **quamvis** (although) is always followed by the subjunctive (→**2**)

● **cum** in the sense "although" is always followed by the subjunctive (→**3**)

● **etsi** (although) takes the indicative or subjunctive according to the same rules as **si** (see p 106). The indicative is more common (→**4**)

Examples   SENTENCES   111

1 medici **quamquam intellegunt**, numquam **tamen** aegris de morbo dicunt
Although doctors know, they never tell their patients about their illness

quamquam Aeneas dicere **volebat**, Dido solo fixos oculos aversa tenebat
Although Aeneas wished to speak, Dido turned away and kept her eyes fixed on the ground

2 **quamvis** frater **esset** molestus, Marcus eum amavit
Although his brother was a nuisance, Marcus loved him

feminae, **quamvis** in periculo **essent**, tamen liberos servaverunt
Although the women were in danger, yet they saved their children

3 **cum non didicissem** geometrias, litteras sciebam
Although I had not learnt geometry, I knew my letters

non poterant, **cum vellent**, Lucium liberare
They were not able, although they wished, to free Lucius

4 **etsi** servus **est**, certe persona est
Although he is a slave, he is a person

etsi victoriam non **reportavissetis**, tamen vos contentos esse oportebat
Although you had not won a victory, yet you should have been content

etsi domi **esset filius iuvenis**, agros ipse colebat
Although he had a young son at home, he cultivated the fields by himself

112 SENTENCES

Causal Clauses

Clauses which begin with the words "because" or "since" and give a reason for something are often called causal clauses in English.

- Causal clauses have their verbs in the indicative when the *actual* cause is stated. They are introduced by **quod**, **quia** (because), and **quoniam** (since) (→**1**)

- **quod** is used with the subjunctive when the cause is only *suggested* (→**2**)

- **non quod** (+*subj*) ... **sed quia** (+*indic*) not because ... but because ..., is used when the first reason is discarded. The true reason is expressed in the indicative (→**3**)

- **cum** (since, as) is always followed by the subjunctive (→**4**)

- **qui** with the subjunctive can be used to mean "since" (→**5**)

Examples

1 non iratus sum **quod** in me **fuisti** asperior
I am not angry because you were too harsh towards me

in crypta Neapolitana vecti, timebamus **quia** longior et obscurior carcere **erat**
Travelling in the Naples tunnel, we were afraid because it was longer and darker than a prison

quoniam ita tu **vis**, ego Puteolos tecum proficiscar
Since you wish this, I shall set off with you to Pozzuoli

2 templa spoliare non poterant **quod** religione im-**pedirentur**
They could not plunder the temples because (they said) they were prevented by religious feelings

3 mater semper maxime laboravit **non quod** necessarium **esset sed quia** honestum esse **videbatur**
Mother always worked very hard, not because it was necessary but because it seemed proper

4 quae **cum** ita **sint**, Catilina, egredere ex urbe!
Since this is so, Catilina, leave the city!

Caesar, **cum** in continente hiemare **constituisset**, ad Galliam rediit
Since Caesar had decided to spend the winter on the mainland, he returned to Gaul

5 sapiens erat **qui** studiis totos annos **dedisset**
He was wise since he had devoted all his years to study

SENTENCES 113

114 SENTENCES

Temporal Clauses

Clauses denoting time are introduced by conjunctions, followed by verbs in the indicative. Some conjunctions, *eg* **cum** (when) may also take the subjunctive. (→**1**)

Conjunctions followed by the indicative:

ut **ubi**	when, as when
cum primum **ubi primum** **ut primum**	as soon as
simul ac **simul atque**	as soon as
quotiens **quamdiu** **ex quo (tempore)**	as often as, whenever as long as, while ever since
postquam **posteaquam**	after (**post** or **postea** may be separated from **quam**)

Continued

Examples   SENTENCES 115

1 **ut** valetudo Germanici Romae **nuntiata est**, magna ira erat
When Germanicus' state of health was announced in Rome, there was great anger

ubi primum classis visa est, **complentur** non modo portus sed moenia ac tecta
As soon as the fleet was seen, not only the harbour but the walls and rooftops were filled (with people)

quod **ubi cognitum est** hostibus, universi nonam legionem nocte aggressi sunt
When this was discovered by the enemy, all of them attacked the ninth legion at night

quotiens proficiscor, pluit
Every time I set out, it rains

manebat **quamdiu poterat**
He stayed as long as he could

septimus annus est, milites, **ex quo** Britanniam **vicistis**
It is seven years, soldiers, since you conquered Britain

postquam vallum **intravit**, portas stationibus **confirmavit**
After entering the fortification, he strengthened the gates with guards

post tertium diem **quam redierat**, mortuus est
He died three days after his return

Temporal Clauses (contd)

Conjunctions which take the indicative or subjunctive:

cum

- **when**   with indicative and often **tum** in the main clause (→**1**)

- **whenever**   with the following pattern of tenses in the indicative: (→**2**)

    + **perfect** followed by **present** tense
    + **future perfect** followed by **future** tense
    + **pluperfect** followed by **imperfect** tense

- **when, as**   with the imperfect or pluperfect subjunctive narrative (→**3**)

dum

- **while**   with indicative

    the present tense is used when **dum** means "during the time that" (→**4**)

- Note that where the same tense (here, the future) is used in both clauses, **dum** means "all the time that". Latin uses future **vivam** more accurately than English "live" (→**5**)

Continued

Examples

1 **cum** tu Romae **eras**, **tum** ego domi eram
   When you were in Rome, I was then at home

2 **cum surrexerat, cadebat**
   Whenever he got up, he fell down

   cum domum **veni**, amicum **visito**
   Whenever I come home, I visit my friend

3 Socrates, **cum** triginta tyranni **essent**, non exibat
   Socrates didn't go out when there were 30 tyrants

   cum id Caesari **nuntiatum esset** ab urbe profectus est
   When that message had been given to Caesar, he set out from the city

4 **dum** haec **geruntur** sex milia hominum ad Rhenum contenderunt
   While this was going on, 6000 men marched to the Rhine

5 **dum vivam**, laeta **ero**
   While I live, I shall be happy

Temporal Clauses (contd)

Clauses which take Indicative or Subjunctive (contd)

dum, donec

- **until**   with subjunctive, often with the sense of purpose or suspense (→**1**)

antequam, priusquam

- **before**   with indicative (→**2**)

- **ante** and **prius**   may be separated from **quam** especially in negative sentences (→**3**)

- **before**   with subjunctive, usually with a sense of purpose or limit (→**4**)

Examples

1   multa Antonio concessit **dum** interfectores patris **ulcisceretur**
He made many concessions to Antony until he could avenge his father's killers

Haterius in periculo erat **donec** Augustam auxilium **oraret**
Haterius was in danger until he begged for Augusta's help

2   **antequam finiam**, hoc dicam
Before I finish, I shall say this

priusquam gallus **cantabit**, ter me negabis
Before the cock crows, you will deny me three times

3   neque **prius** fugere destiterunt **quam** ad castra **pervenerunt**
They didn't stop running away before reaching their camp

4   consul Romam festinavit **antequam** Hannibal eo **perveniret**
The consul hurried to Rome before Hannibal could reach it

ita cassita nidum migravit **priusquam** agricola frumentum **meteret**
And so the lark abandoned her nest before the farmer could reap the corn

120 SENTENCES

Comparative Clauses

- These are adverbial clauses which express likeness, agreement (or the opposite) with what is stated in the main clause. (→1)

- When the comparative clause states a fact (as above) the verb is in the **indicative**. The commonest words of comparison are (→2)

ut (as), **sicut** (just as), **aliter ac, aliter ut** (different from), **idem ac, idem atque, qui** etc (the same as)

- When the comparative clause is purely **imaginary**, the verb is **subjunctive**. The commonest words used with this type of clause are (→3)

velut(si), quasi, tamquam (si) (as if)

SENTENCES 121

Examples

1 eadem dixi ac prius dixeram
I said the same as I had said before

2 **ego ita ero, ut me esse oportet**
I shall be as I should be

sicut lupus agnos rapit, ita mater liberos servat
Just as the wolf snatches the lamb, so the mother saves her children

haud aliter se gerebat ac solebat
He behaved as he usually did
or He behaved no differently from usual

idem abierunt qui venerant
The same men vanished as came

3 **velutsi haec res nihil ad se pertinuisset, tacebat**
He remained silent, as if this thing had nothing to do with him

hic flammae Aetnae minantur quasi ad caelum sublatae sint
Here Aetna's flames threaten, as if raised to the heavens

Cleopatram salutaverunt **tamquam si esset** regina
They greeted Cleopatra as if she were queen

122 SENTENCES

Relative Clauses

- Relative clauses are more common in Latin than in English. They are introduced by the following:

qui, quae, quod	which, who, that
ubi	where, in which
unde	from where, from which

  These relatives come at the beginning of the clause but after prepositions.

- The relative agrees with a word which precedes it – its *antecedent* – in gender and number, but takes its case from its own clause (→**1**)

  qui is masculine plural agreeing with antecedent **Romani**, nominative because it is the subject of **incenderunt**

- **quā** is feminine singular agreeing with **regio**, ablative after preposition in (→**2**)

- **quos** is masculine plural agreeing with **servos**, accusative because it is the object of **iudicavit** (→**3**)

- The relative **quod** refers to a sentence, and **id** is omitted (**id quod** – that which). This is often used in parenthesis, and not attached grammatically to the rest of the sentence

- After **cuius** (of, concerning which) the noun **laudationis** is repeated (→**4**)

- The relative sometimes agrees with the following word, especially with the verb **esse** (→**5**)

Continued

SENTENCES 123

Examples

1 hi sunt Romani **qui** libros incenderunt
These are the Romans who burnt the books

2 haec est regio **in qua** ego sum natus
This is the region in which I was born

3 servos **quos** ipse iudicavit, eos sua sponte liberavit
He willingly freed those slaves whom he himself had judged

4 deinde, **quod** alio loco antea dixi, quae est ista tandem laudatio, **cuius laudationis** legati et principes et publice tibi navem aedificatam, et privatim se ipsos abs te spoliatos esse dixerunt? (**Cicero**, Verres V 58)
Well then, as I said earlier elsewhere, what does that praise consist of, namely that publicly the ambassadors and chief citizens said a ship had been built for you, but privately that they themselves had been robbed by you?

5 iusta gloria **qui** fructus virtutis est, bello quaeritur
True glory, which is the reward of courage, is looked for in war

124 SENTENCES

Relative Clauses (contd)

Use Of Subjunctive In Relative Clauses

- The subjunctive is used in relative clauses dependent on infinitives or subjunctives (→1)

- When **qui** is used with the subjunctive, it may express cause (→2)

  quippe qui is sometimes used with **qui** in this sense

- When **qui** *etc* is used with the present or imperfect subjunctive, it may express purpose (→3)

- **qui** with the subjunctive is used with the following (→4)

  dignus est **qui**   he is worthy of
  idoneus est **qui**   he is fit to
  sunt **qui**   there are people who
  nemo est **qui**   there is no one who

- At the beginning of a sentence, any part of **qui, quae, quod** may be used as a connective (instead of the demonstrative) with the previous sentence. Translate it in English by "this" or "that" (→5)

Examples   SENTENCES 125

1 quis sit **cui** vita talis **placeat?**
    Who is there that likes such a life?

2 multa de mea sententia questus est Caesar (**quippe**)
    qui Ravennae Crassum ante **vidisset**
    Caesar complained a lot about my decision since he
    had seen Crassus at Ravenna previously

3 legatos misit **qui** pacem **peterent**
    He sent ambassadors to ask for peace

4 Sunt **qui** dicere **timeant**
    There are some who are afraid to speak

    nemo **idoneus** aderat **qui responderet**
    There was nobody there capable of replying

5 **quod** cum **audivisset**, soror lacrimas fudit
    When she heard this, my sister shed tears

    quae cum ita **sint**, Vatinium defendam
    Since this is so, I shall defend Vatinius

Negatives

There are several ways of forming a negative in Latin.

non

- This is the common negative in the indicative and usually stands before the verb, although it may be put in front of any word for emphasis (→**1**)

- Two negatives in the same sentence make an affirmative (→**2**)

haud

- This makes a single word negative, usually an adjective or an adverb (→**3**)

- It is also used in expressions such as **haud scio an** (I don't know whether), and **haud dubito** (I don't doubt) (→**4**)

- **haudquaquam** means not at all (→**5**)

Continued

---

1 ante horam tertiam noctis de foro **non discedit**
He didn't leave the forum before nine o'clock at night

Ambarri Caesarem certiorem faciunt se, vastatis agris, **non facile** vim hostium ab oppidis prohibere
The Ambarri informed Caesar that it was **not easy** for them, since their territory was destroyed, to keep the enemy force away from their towns

Caesar **non exspectandum** sibi statuit dum Helvetii pervenirent
Caesar decided **not to wait** till the Swiss arrived

2 non possum non facere
I must do

non sumus ignari
We are well aware

3 **haud magnus**
not great

haud procul
not far away

4 **haud scio an** ire mihi liceat
I don't know whether I am allowed to go

5 homo bonus, **haudquaquam** eloquens
A good man but not at all a good speaker

128 SENTENCES

Negatives (contd)

ne

- This is the negative of the imperative and subjunctive. It is also used in many subordinate clauses where the verb is in the subjunctive (→1)

- Wishes (→2)

- Purpose (→3)

- Indirect command (→4)

- Fearing (→5)

Continued

1 ne diutius **vivamus**
Let us **not** live any longer

2 utinam **ne** id **accidisset**
I wish that it **had not happened**

3 agnus celeriter fugit **ne** lupi se **caperent**
The lamb ran away quickly **in case** the wolves caught it

4 pater mihi imperavit **ne** abirem
Father told me **not to go away**

5 cives metuebant **ne** Tiberius libertatem sibi **non redderet**
The citizens were afraid that Tiberius **would not give** them **back** their freedom

veritus sum **ne** id quod accidit **adveniret**
I was afraid that what did in fact happen **might take place**

Negatives (contd)

Other Negatives

- **neque … neque** neither … nor (→**1**)

- **neque … quisquam** neither anyone *or* and no one

- **neque … quidquam** neither anything *or* and nothing

- **neque … umquam** neither ever *or* and never
- **nemo … umquam** no one ever *or* never anyone

- **nihil … umquam** nothing ever *or* never anything (→**2**)

- Notice the following combinations:

  nonnulli some *but* **nulli … non** all
  nonnihil somewhat *but* **nihil … non** everything (→**3**)

- **non solum … sed etiam** } not only … but also
  non solum … sed quoque } (→**4**)

- Roman authors repeat negatives for effect (→**5**)

1 **neque** illo adit **quisquam neque** eis ipsis **quidquam**
praeter oram maritimam notum est
Neither did anyone approach that place, nor did they
themselves know anything except the coast

2 **neque** post id tempus **umquam** summis nobiscum
copiis hostes contenderunt
And after that the enemy never engaged in battle with
us at full strength

ego **nihil umquam** feci solus
I never did anything alone

3 **nonnulli** amici
some friends

nulli amici **non** venerunt
all my friends came

4 Herennius Pontius, iam gravis annis, **non solum** mi-
litaribus **sed quoque** civilibus muneribus abscesserat
Herennius Pontius, now old, had withdrawn not only
from military but also from civic duties

5 **nihil** audio quod audisse, **nihil** dico quod dixisse paeni-
teat; **nemo** apud me quemquam sinistris sermonibus
carpit, **neminem** ipse reprehendo, **nisi** tamen me cum
parum commode scribo; **nulla** spe, **nullo** timore sol-
licitor, **nullis** rumoribus inquietor; mecum tantum et
cum libellis loquor (**Pliny** Ep 1, 9)
I hear nothing that I would regret having heard, I say
nothing that I would regret having said; at home nobody nags me with vicious remarks, I don't blame
anyone except myself when I write badly; no hope or
fear worries me, no idle talk disturbs me; I speak only
to myself and to my books

Translation Guidelines

Translating from Latin into English can be both a challenge and a pleasure. The word order of both languages is different: word order shows the relationship of words in English, in Latin it is shown by word endings. Sentences are generally shorter in English, structures simpler. Latin sentences often contain more subordinate clauses, sometimes embedded in other clauses, and often build up to form a long periodic sentence. Subject matter is two thousand years distant in time, although many ideas are still familiar to us today. The following guidelines are suggested to help in translation.

Guidelines

- *Establish the context* of the passage to be translated. Read the introduction in English carefully, find out *who* or *what* is being discussed, *when* and *where* the action took place.

- *Read through the whole passage* fairly quickly to gain some general understanding of the passage, however incomplete.

- *Focus on each sentence,* either taking each word as it comes, or establishing subject/verb/object according to your normal approach. Many find it helpful to pick out the verbs and work out the structure of the clauses. Watch for agreement of adjectives with nouns and how prepositional phrases fit in.

- *Watch conjunctions et, sed etc* and connectives such as **tamen** (however), and **igitur** (therefore). These help explain the logic of the passage as a whole.

- *Note punctuation.* It can be helpful in isolating clauses within the sentences, or marking off an ablative absolute.

- *Be open-minded.* Does **cum,** for example, mean "when", "since", or "although"? Don't decide till the whole sentence is worked out.

- *Use dictionaries carefully.* Check words of similar spelling, check endings. Once you have found the right Latin word, check all of its meanings before deciding on the correct translation.

- *Watch out for features of style eg* use of two adjectives with same meaning etc.

- Finally, *check your translation.* Does the narrative or logic of the passage seem consistent? Does your English sound natural? Does it represent the tone or style of the Latin passage? At this stage, fill in any blanks or make corrections.

134 TRANSLATION

Translation Problems

Finding the subject

- Look for a noun with a nominative ending. Check with verb ending for agreement. If there is no nominative, the subject will be indicated by the verb ending. Remember that, in Latin, the subject is continued from the previous sentence unless there is clear indication otherwise (→**1**)

Adjective agreement

- Check which adjective agrees with which noun in number, case and gender. Remember that it may be separated from its noun.

      a   b   b   a

te **flagrantis atrox hora Caniculae** nescit tangere
The blazing Dog Star's fierce daytime heat can't touch you

Passive

- Often it is better to turn a Latin passive verb into an active verb in English (→**2**)

Tense

- English is not so precise as Latin in its use of tenses. Use the tense that seems most natural in English, for example, English past tense for historic present in Latin, or English present tense for Latin future perfect in a conditional clause (→**3**)

Continued

Examples   TRANSLATION 135

1   **consules** et armare plebem et inermem pati **timebant**. **sedabant** tumultum, sedando interdum movebant.
The consuls were afraid both to arm the people and to leave them unarmed. They quelled the riot, but sometimes, in quelling it, they stirred it up again.

2   hoc a tu **demonstrari** et **probari** volo
I wish you to demonstrate and prove this
or I wish this to be demonstrated and proved by you

3   hoc faciam si **potuero** (*future perfect*)
I shall do this if I can (*present*)

Translation Problems (contd)

Ablative absolute

hostibus victis can be translated:

when the enemy had been beaten
after beating the enemy
they beat the enemy and ...
although the enemy were beaten

Choose the version that makes most sense within the context of the passage.

Omission of esse

- Parts of **esse** (to be) are often omitted and have to be supplied in English (→**1**)

Omission of small words (ut, id, eo, hic etc)

- Check that you do not omit to translate these words – they are often very important (→**2**)

Neuter plurals

- **omnia** (everything) and **multa** (many things) are often mistranslated.

Impersonal passives

- It is worthwhile learning these (→**3**)

Continued

Examples

1 sed Germanicus quanto (**erat**) summae spei propior, tanto impensius pro Tiberio niti
But the nearer Germanicus **was** to succeeding, the more strenuously he exerted himself on behalf of Tiberius

2 eo   to there (*adv*), by, with *or* from him (*abl of pronoun*)
id ... quod   that which
hic   this (*pron*), here (*adv*)
fit ... ut   it happens ... that

3 allatum est   it was announced
cognitum est   it was discovered
pugnatum est   a battle was fought
traditum est   it was recorded
visum est   it seemed

Translation Problems (contd)

Similarity of English/Latin Words

A higher percentage of English words are derived from Latin than from any other source. This can be helpful when trying to deduce the meaning of a Latin word, *eg* **portus** (port). But **porta** (gate) may cause confusion. The following examples taken from actual examination scripts provide a cautionary note. The correct translation follows in brackets:

Examples   TRANSLATION   139

prima luce nuntius hic **Ameriam** venit
At dawn the messenger came to America
(*At dawn the messenger came to Ameria*)

sex et quinquaginta **milia passuum** in cisio pervolavit
56 thousand flew past in a chariot
(*He quickly travelled fifty-six miles in a chariot*)

ut mori **mallet**
He would rather be killed by a mallet
(*To prefer to die*)

legati **crediderunt**
The embassy got credit
(*The ambassadors believed*)

False Friends/Confusables

ad (+ *acc*)	to, towards
ab (+ *abl*)	from, by, with
adeo	to such an extent
adeō	I approach
aestās	summer
aestus	heat, tide
aetas	age
aura	breeze
aurēs (*pl*)	ears
aurum	gold
avis	bird
avus	grandfather
cadō	I fall
caedō	I cut, kill
cēdō	I go, yield
campus	plain
castra (*pl*)	camp
cēterum	but
cēterī (*pl*)	the rest
coepī	I began
coēgi	I forced
constituō	I decide
consistō	I stop

Continued

crimen	charge
scelus	crime
cum (*prep*)	with
cum (*conj*)	when, since, although
dominus	master
domus	house
equitēs (*pl*)	horsemen
equus	horse
fama	fame, report
fames	hunger
forte	by chance
fortis	brave (*not strong*)
fugāre	to put to flight
fugere	to flee, escape
hōra	hour
hōrum (*gen pl*)	of these
iaceō	I lie
iaciō	I throw
imperātor	general (*not emperor*)
imperātus	ordered (*past participle*)
inveniō	I find (*not come in*)
invītō	I invite
invītus	unwilling
iter, -ineris	journey
iterum	again
lātus, -a, -um	broad
lātus, -a, -um	brought
lātus, -eris	side

False Friends/Confusables (contd)

līber, -rī	book
līber, -a, -um	free
līberī, -ōrum (pl)	children
lībertus, -ī	freedman
magister, -rī	master
magistrātus	magistrate
malus, -a, -um	bad
mālum, -ī	apple
mālō, malle	I prefer
manus, -ūs	hand, band
mānēs, -ium	spirits of dead
miser, -a, -um	unhappy
mīseram	I had sent (plup of mitto)
morior, -ī	I die
moror, -ārī	I delay
nauta	sailor
nāvis	ship
nēmō	no one
nimium	too much
occāsio	opportunity
occāsus (solis)	setting (of sun)
occidere	to fall, set
occīdere	to kill
opem	help
opera, -ae	work
opus, -eris	task
opus est	it is necessary

Continued

ōra, -ae	coast
ōrō, -āre	I pray, beg
ōs, ōris	face
ōs, ōssis	bone
parcō, -ere	I spare
pareō, -ēre	I obey
pario, -ere	I give birth to
parō, -āre	I prepare
passus, -us	a pace
passus, -a, -um	suffered (past participle of patior)
porta, -ae	gate
portus, -us	port
portō, -āre	I carry
quaerō, -ere	I seek
queror, -ī	I complain
quīdam	a certain (person)
quīdem	indeed
reddō, -ere	I give back
redeō, -īre	I go back
serviō, -īre	I serve
servō, -āre	I save
sōl, -is	sun
soleō, -ēre	I am accustomed
solitus sum	
solum, -ī	soil
sōlus, -a, -um	alone

False Friends/Confusables (contd)

tamen	however
tandem	at last
ut(ī)	in order that, as, when
utī (*dep*)	to use
vallis, -is	valley
vallum, -i	wall, rampart
victor	winner
victus (*past part*)	beaten
vinctus (*past part*)	bound
vīs	force
vīres, -ium	strength
vir, -ī	man
virga, -ae	stick
virgō, -inis	girl
vīta, -ae	life
vītō, -āre	I avoid

VERB TABLES

Conjugations

There are four patterns of regular Latin verbs called conjugations. Each can be identified by the ending of the **present infinitive**:

- First conjugation verbs end in **-āre** (*eg* amāre – to love)
- Second conjugation verbs end in **-ēre** (*eg* habēre – to have)
- Third conjugation verbs end in **-ere** (*eg* mittere – to send)
- Fourth conjugation verbs end in **-īre** (*eg* audīre – to hear)

Each regular verb has three **stems**:

- A **present stem** which is found by cutting off **-re** from the present infinitive (*eg* amāre, habēre, mittere, audīre).

- A **perfect stem** which is formed by adding **-v** to the present stem in the first and fourth conjugations (*eg* amāvī, audīvī), and by adding **-u** to the present stem in the second conjugation (*eg* habuī).

  In the third conjugation there are several possible endings (*eg* scrīpsī, dīxī).

  Some short verbs lengthen the stem vowel (*eg* lēgī), others double the first consonant and vowel (*eg* cucurrī).

- A **supine stem** which is formed by cutting off **-um** from the supine forms (*eg* amātum, habitum, missum, audītum).

148 VERBS

Tenses

These forms of the verb show when an action takes place, in the present, in the past or in the future.

In Latin there are six tenses:

1 Present
2 Imperfect } formed from the **present** stem
3 Future

4 Perfect
5 Pluperfect } formed from the **perfect** stem
6 Future Perfect

Tenses Formed from the Present Stem

The following endings are added to the stem:

	PRESENT	IMPERFECT	FUTURE Conj 1&2	FUTURE Conj 3&4
sing				
1st person	-ō	-bam	-bō	-am
2nd person	-s	-bas	-bis	-ēs
3rd person	-t	-bat	-bit	-et
pl				
1st person	-mus	-bāmus	-bimus	-ēmus
2nd person	-tis	-bātis	-bitis	-ētis
3rd person	-nt	-bant	-bunt	-ent

Note that the above endings show the number and person of the subject of the verb. Subject pronouns are therefore not normally necessary in Latin.

Continued

VERBS 149

Conjugations

	1	2	3	4
INFINITIVE	amāre	habēre	mittere	audīre
PRESENT STEM	amā-	habē-	mitte-	audī-
PRESENT				
	amō	habeō	mittō	audiō
	amās	habēs	mittis	audīs
	amat	habet	mittit	audit
	amāmus	habēmus	mittimus	audīmus
	amātis	habētis	mittitis	audītis
	amant	habent	mittunt	audiunt
IMPERFECT				
	amābam	habēbam	mittēbam	audiēbam
	amābās	habēbās	mittēbās	audiēbās
	amābat	habēbat	mittēbat	audiēbat
	amābāmus	habēbāmus	mittēbāmus	audiēbāmus
	amābātis	habēbātis	mittēbātis	audiēbātis
	amābant	habēbant	mittēbant	audiēbant
FUTURE				
	amābō	habēbō	mittam	audiam
	amābis	habēbis	mittēs	audiēs
	amābit	habēbit	mittet	audiet
	amābimus	habēbimus	mittēmus	audiēmus
	amābitis	habēbitis	mittētis	audiētis
	amābunt	habēbunt	mittent	audient

Tenses (contd)

Use:

The Present

In Latin, the present tense expresses what is going on now and can be translated into English in two ways (*eg* laborat – he works, he is working)

- The present is often used in Latin instead of a past tense to make the action more exciting (→**1**)

- Sometimes the Latin present tense is used to describe an action begun in the past and and still continuing (→**2**)

The Imperfect

- Describes what went on or continued for a time (→**3**)

- Denotes an action repeated in the past (→**4**)

- Is used when an action is intended or interrupted (→**5**)

- Is sometimes translated "had" when used with **iam** (→**6**)

The Future

- Is used in Latin as in English to denote what will or is going to be or to happen (→**7**)

- Is occasionally used as a command (→**8**)

- After "**si**" (if) in conditional sentences, it is sometimes translated as present tense in English (→**9**)

Examples

1 **prima luce Caesar Gallos oppugnat**
Caesar attacked the Gauls at dawn

2 **Alexander iam tres annos regit**
Alexander has been ruling for three years now

3 **pluebat** – it was raining

4 **fortiter pugnabant**
They used to fight bravely
or They kept fighting bravely

5 **Romam intrabam**
I was about to enter Rome

6 **multos iam dies villam habitabat**
He had already lived in the house for many days

7 **hoc faciemus**
We shall do this
or We are going to do this

erit gloria
There will be glory

8 **non me vocabis**
Don't call me

9 **si id credes, errabis**
If you believe this, you will be making a mistake

		Conj	Page
confīrmō, confīrmāre, confīrmāvī, confīrmātum	strengthen	1	
confiteor, confitērī, confessus sum	confess	2	
congredior, congredī, congressus sum	meet	3	
conicio, conicere, coniēcī, coniectum	throw	3	
coniungō, coniungere, coniūnxī, coniūnctum	join	3	
coniūrō, coniūrāre, coniūrāvī, coniūrātum	conspire	1	
conor, conārī, conātus sum	try	1	
consentiō, consentīre, consēnsī, consēnsum	agree	4	
consistō, consistere, constitī, constitum	stop	3	
conspiciō, conspicere, conspexī, conspectum	catch sight of	3	
constō, constāre, constitī	agree	1	
constituō, constituere, constituī, constitūtum	decide	3	
construō, construere, construxī, constructum	construct	3	
consulō, consulere, consuluī, consultum	consult	3	
consūmō, consūmere, consūmpsī, consūmptum	use up	3	
contemnō, contemnere, contempsī, contemptum	despise	3	
contendō, contendere, contendī, contentum	strive/hurry	3	
contingō, contingere, contigī, contactum	touch	3	

		Conj	Page
conveniō, convenīre, convēnī, conventum	meet	4	
corripiō, corripere, corripuī, correptum	seize	3	
crēdō, crēdere, crēdidī, crēditum	believe	3	
crescō, crescere, crēvī, crētum	grow	3	
culpō, culpāre, culpāvī, culpātum	blame	1	
cupiō, cupere, cupīvī, cupītum	desire	1	
cūrō, cūrāre, cūrāvī, cūrātum	look after	3	
currō, currere, cucurrī, cursum	run	1	
custōdiō, custōdīre, custōdīvī, custōditum	guard	4	
damnō, damnāre, damnāvī, damnātum	condemn	1	
dēbeō, dēbēre, dēbuī, dēbitum	have to/owe	2	
dēdō, dēdere, dēdidī, dēditum	hand over/yield	3	
dēdūcō, dēdūcere, dēdūxī, dēductum	bring/escort	3	
dēfendō, dēfendere, dēfendī, dēfensum	defend	3	
dēficiō, dēficere, dēfēcī, dēfectum	revolt/fail	3	
dēiciō, dēicere, dēiēcī, dēiectum	throw down	3	
dēlectō, dēlectāre, dēlectāvī, dēlectatum	delight	1	
dēleō, dēlere, dēlēvī, dēlētum	destroy	2	
dēligō, dēligere, dēlēgī, dēlectum	choose	3	
dēmōnstrō, dēmōnstrāre, dēmōnstrāvī, dēmōnstrātum	show	1	
dēpōnō, dēpōnere, dēposuī, dēpositum	lay down	3	

		Conj Page
descendō, descendere, descendī, descensum	go down	3
dēserō, dēserere, dēseruī, dēsertum	desert	3
dēsiderō, dēsiderāre, dēsiderāvī, dēsiderātum	long for	1
dēsiliō, dēsilīre, dēsiluī, dēsultum	jump down	3
dēsinō, dēsinere, dēsiī, dēsitum	stop/leave off	3
dēsistō, dēsistere, dēstitī	stop/leave off	3
dēspērō, dēspērāre, dēspērāvī, dēspērātum	despair	1
dēstruō, dēstruere, dēstruxī, dēstructum	destroy	3
dīcō, dīcere, dīxī, dictum	tell/say	3
dīligō, dīligere, dīlexī, dīlectum	love	3
dīmittō, dīmittere, dīmīsī, dīmissum	send away	3
discēdō, discēdere, discessī, discessum	go away	3
discō, discere, didicī	learn	3
dīvidō, dīvidere, dīvīsī, dīvīsum	divide	3
dō, dāre, dedī, datum	give	1
doceō, docēre, docuī, doctum	teach	2
doleō, dolēre, doluī, dolitum	grieve	2
dormiō, dormīre, dormīvī, dormītum	sleep	4
dubitō, dubitāre, dubitāvī, dubitātum	doubt	1
dūcō, dūcere, dūxī, ductum	lead	3
edō, edere, ēdī, ēsum	eat	3
efficiō, efficere, effēcī, effectum	complete	3
effugiō, effugere, effūgī	escape	3
ēgredior, ēgredī, ēgressus sum	go out	3
emō, emere, ēmī, emptum	buy	3
eō, īre, īvī, itum	go	210

		Conj Page
errō, errāre, errāvī, errātum	wander/be wrong	1
ērumpō, ērumpere, ērūpī, ēruptum	burst out	3
excitō, excitāre, excitāvī, excitātum	arouse	1
exeō, exīre, exiī, exitum	go out	2
exerceō, exercēre, exercuī, exercitum	exercise/train	2
existimō, existimāre, existimāvī, existimātum	think	1
expellō, expellere, expulī, expulsum	drive out	3
experior, experīrī, expertus sum	try/test	4
exspectō, exspectāre, exspectāvī, exspectātum	wait for	1
exuō, exuere, exuī, exūtum	take off	3
faciō, facere, fēcī, factum	do/make	3
fallō, fallere, fefellī, falsum	deceive	3
faveō, favēre, fāvī, fautum	favour	2
ferō, ferre, tulī, lātum	bring/bear	204
festinō, festīnāre, festīnāvī, festīnātum	hurry	1
fīgō, fīgere, fīxī, fīxum	fix	3
fingō, fingere, finxī, fictum	invent	3
fīō, fierī, factus sum	become/happen	208
flectō, flectere, flexī, flexum	bend	3
fleō, flēre, flēvī, flētum	weep	2
fluō, fluere, flūxī, flūxum	flow	3
frangō, frangere, frēgī, frāctum	break	3
fruor, fruī, frūctus or fruitus sum	enjoy	3
fugiō, fugere, fūgī, fugitum	flee/escape	3
fugō, fugāre, fugāvī, fugātum	put to flight	1
fundō, fundere, fūdī, fūsum	pour	3
fungor, fungī, functus sum	perform	3

		Conj Page
gaudeō, gaudēre, **gāvīsus sum**	be glad	2
gemō, gemere, **gemuī, gemitum**	groan	3
gerō, gerere, **gessī, gestum**	carry on/wear	3
gignō, gignere, **genuī, genitum**	produce	3
habeō, habēre, habuī, habitum	have/keep	2
habitō, habitāre, habitāvī, habitātum	live (in)	1
haereō, haerēre, **haesī, haesum**	stick	2
hauriō, haurīre, **hausī, haustum**	drain away	4
horreō, horrēre, horruī	stand on end	2
hortor, hortārī, hortātus sum	encourage	1
iaceō, iacēre, iacuī	lie down	2
iaciō, iacere, **iēcī, iactum**	throw	3
ignōscō, ignōscere, **ignōvī, ignōtum**	forgive	3
immineō, imminēre	threaten	2
impediō, impedīre, impedīvī, impedītum	hinder	4
impellō, impellere, **impulī, impulsum**	drive on	3
imperō, imperāre, imperāvī, imperātum	order	1
incendō, incendere, **incendī, incēnsum**	burn	3
incipiō, incipere, **coepī, coeptum**	begin	3
incitō, incitāre, incitāvī, incitātum	drive on	1
inclūdō, inclūdere, **inclūsī, inclūsum**	include	3
incolō, incolere, **incoluī**	live (in)	3
inferō, inferre, intulī, illātum	bring against	3
ingredior, ingredī, **ingressus sum**	enter	3

		Conj Page
instituō, instituere, instituī, **institūtum**	set up	3
instruō, instruere, **instrūxī, instrūctum**	set/draw up	3
intellegō, intellegere, **intellēxī, intellēctum**	realize	3
interficiō, interficere, **interfēcī, interfectum**	kill	3
intersum, interesse	be among/be important	(impers)
intrō, intrāre, intrāvī, intrātum	enter	1
inveniō, invenīre, **invēnī, inventum**	come upon/find	4
invītō, invītāre, invītāvī, invītātum	invite	1
irrumpō, irrumpere, **irrūpī, irruptum**	rush into	3
iubeō, iubēre, **iussī, iussum**	order	2
iūdicō, iūdicāre, iūdicāvī, iūdicātum	judge	1
iungō, iungere, **iūnxī, iūnctum**	join	3
iūrō, iūrāre, iūrāvī, iūrātum	swear	1
iuvō, iuvāre, **iūvī, iūtum**	help	1
lābor, lābī, **lāpsus sum**	slip	3
labōrō, labōrāre, labōrāvī, labōrātum	work	1
lacessō, lacessere, lacessīvī, **lacessītum**	harass	3
lacrimō, lacrimāre, lacrimāvī, lacrimātum	weep	1
laedō, laedere, **laesī, laesum**	hurt	3
lateō, latēre, latuī	lie hidden	2
laudō, laudāre, laudāvī, laudātum	praise	1
lavō, lavāre, **lāvī, lautum/lavātum/lōtum**	wash	1
legō, legere, **lēgī, lēctum**	read/choose	3

Principal parts	Meaning	Conj/Page
levō, levāre, levāvī, levātum	lighten	1
līberō, līberāre, līberāvī, līberātum	free	1
licet, licēre, licuit	it is allowed	2
locō, locāre, locāvī, locātum	place	1
loquor, loquī, **locūtus sum**	speak	3
lūdō, lūdere, **lūsī, lūsum**	play	3
lustrō, lustrāre, lustrāvī, lustrātum	purify/scan	1
mālō, mālle, māluī	prefer	*216*
mandō, mandāre, mandāvī, mandātum	command/trust	1
maneō, manēre, **mānsī, mānsum**	remain/stay	2
meminī, meminisse	remember	*219*
mentior, mentīrī, mentītus sum	tell lies	4
metuō, metuere, **metuī**	fear	3
minor, minārī, minātus sum	threaten	1
minuō, minuere, **minuī, minūtum**	lessen	3
miror, mirārī, mirātus sum	wonder (at)	1
misceō, miscēre, **miscuī, mixtum**	mix	2
{ misereor, miserērī, miseritus sum	pity	2
{ miseret, miserēre, miseruit *(eg me miseret tui – I am sorry for you)*		
mittō, mittere, **mīsī, missum**	send	3
mōlior, mōlīrī, mōlītus sum	strive/toil	4
moneō, monēre, monuī, monitum	advise/warn	2
morior, morī, **mortuus sum**	die	3
moror, morārī, morātus sum	delay/loiter	1
moveō, movēre, **mōvī, mōtum**	move	2
mūniō, mūnīre, mūnīvī/mūniī, mūnītum	fortify	4
mūtō, mūtāre, mūtāvī, mūtātum	change	1
nancīscor, nancīscī, **na(n)ctus sum**	obtain	3
nārrō, nārrāre, nārrāvī, nārrātum	tell	1

Principal parts	Meaning	Conj/Page
nāscor, nāscī, **nātus sum**	be born	3
nāvigō, nāvigāre, nāvigāvī, nāvigātum	sail	1
necō, necāre, necāvī, necātum	kill	1
negō, negāre, negāvī, negātum	refuse/deny	1
neglegō, neglegere, **neglēxī, neglēctum**	neglect	3
nesciō, nescīre, nescīvī or iī, nescītum	not to know	4
noceō, nocēre, nocuī, nocitum	harm	2
nōlō, nōlle, nōluī	not to wish/be unwilling	*214*
nōscō, nōscere, **nōvī, nōtum** (in perfect tenses translate as "know")	get to know	3
nūntiō, nūntiāre, nūntiāvī, nūntiātum	announce	1
obeō, obīre, obīvī or iī, obitum	die	*219*
obiciō, obicere, **obiēcī, obiectum**	throw to/oppose	3
oblīvīscor, oblīvīscī, **oblītus sum**	forget	3
obsideō, obsidēre, **obsēdī, obsessum**	besiege	2
obtineō, obtinēre, obtinuī, **obtentum**	hold/obtain	2
occīdō, occidere, **occidī, occāsum**	fall	3
occīdō, occidere, **occidī, occīsum**	kill	3
occupō, occupāre, occupāvī, occupātum	seize	1
occurrō, occurrere, **occurrī, occursum**	meet	3
odī, ōdisse	hate	*219*
offerō, offerre, obtulī, oblātum	present	*219*

		Conj / Page
oportet, oportēre, oportuit	be proper/ought	2
opprimō, opprimere, **oppressī**, **oppressum**	crush	3
oppugnō, oppugnāre, oppugnāvī, oppugnātum	attack	1
optō, optāre, optāvī, optātum	wish	1
orior, orīrī, **ortus sum**	arise	4
orō, orāre, orāvī, orātum	beg/plead	1
ornō, ornāre, ornāvī, ornātum	decorate/equip	1
ostendō, ostendere, ostendī, **ostentum**	show	3
pācō, pācāre, pācāvī, pācātum	pacify	1
paenitet, paenitēre, paenituit	repent of	2
pandō, pandere, **pandī, passum**	spread out	3
parcō, parcere, **pepercī, parsum**	spare	3
pāreō, parēre, paruī	obey	2
pariō, parere, **peperī, partum**	give birth to	3
parō, parāre, parāvī, parātum	prepare	1
pāscō, pāscere, **pāvī, pāstum**	feed	3
patefaciō, patefacere, **patefēcī, patefactum**	open	3
pateō, patēre, patuī	be open	2
patior, patī, **passus sum**	suffer/allow	3
paveō, pavēre, **pāvī**	fear	2
pellō, pellere, **pepulī, pulsum**	drive	3
pendeō, pendēre, **pependī** (*intrans*)	hang	2
pendō, pendere, **pependī, pēnsum**	weigh/pay	3
perdō, perdere, **perdidī, perditum**	lose/destroy	3
pereō, **perīre, periī, peritum**	perish	3
perficiō, perficere, **perfēcī, perfectum**	complete	3

		Conj / Page
pergō, pergere, **perrēxī, perrēctum**	proceed	3
permittō, permittere, **permīsī, permissum**	allow	3
persuadeō, persuadēre, **persuāsī, persuāsum**	persuade	2
pertineō, pertinēre, pertinuī, **pertentum**	concern	2
perturbō, perturbāre, perturbāvī, perturbātum	confuse	1
perveniō, pervenīre, **pervēnī, perventum**	arrive at	4
petō, petere, **petīvī, petītum**	seek/ask	3
placeō, placēre, placuī, placitum	please	2
placet, placēre, placuit	it seems good	2
polliceor, pollicērī, **pollicitus sum**	promise	2
pōnō, pōnere, **posuī, positum**	place/put	3
portō, portāre, portāvī, portātum	carry	1
poscō, poscere, **poposcī**	ask for/demand	3
possum, posse, potuī	to be able	*200*
postulō, postulāre, postulāvī, postulātum	demand	1
potior, potīrī, potītus sum	gain possession of	4
praebeō, praebēre, praebuī, praebitum	show	2
praeficiō, praeficere, **praefēcī, praefectum**	put in command of	3
praestō, praestāre, **praestitī, praestātum**	stand out	1
premō, premere, **pressī, pressum**	press	3
prōcēdō, prōcēdere, **prōcessī, prōcessum**	advance	3

Latin	Meaning	Conj
prōdō, prōdere, prōdidī, prōditum	betray	3
proficīscor, proficīscī, profectus sum	set out	3
prōgredior, prōgredī, progressus sum	advance	3
prohibeō, prohibēre, prohibuī, prohibitum	prevent	2
prōmittō, prōmittere, prōmīsī, prōmissum	promise	3
prōvideō, prōvidēre, prōvīdī, prōvīsum	take precautions	2
pugnō, pugnāre, pugnāvī, pugnātum	fight	1
pūniō, pūnīre, pūnīvī or iī, pūnītum	punish	4
putō, putāre, putāvī, putātum	think	1
quaerō, quaerere, quaesīvī, quaesītum	ask/seek	3
queror, querī, questus sum	complain	3
quiēscō, quiēscere, quiēvī, quiētum	keep quiet	3
rapiō, rapere, rapuī, raptum	snatch/seize	3
recipiō, recipere, recēpī, receptum	receive/recover	3
recūsō, recūsāre, recūsāvī, recūsātum	refuse	1
reddō, reddere, reddidī, redditum	give back/return	3
redeō, redīre, rediī, reditum	come back/return	3
redūcō, redūcere, redūxī, reductum	bring back	3
regō, regere, rēxī, rēctum	rule	3
regredior, regredī, regressus sum	retreat	3
relinquō, relinquere, relīquī, relictum	leave	3

Latin	Meaning	Conj
remittō, remittere, remīsī, remissum	send back	3
reor, rērī, ratus sum	think	2
repellō, repellere, reppulī, repulsum	drive back	3
reperiō, reperīre, repperī, repertum	find	4
resistō, resistere, restitī	resist	3
respiciō, respicere, respexī, respectum	look back	3
respondeō, respondēre, respondī, respōnsum	answer	2
restō, restāre, restitī	remain	1
restituō, restituere, restituī, restitūtum	restore	3
retineō, retinēre, retinuī, retentum	hold back	2
rīdeō, rīdēre, rīsī, rīsum	laugh	2
rogō, rogāre, rogāvī, rogātum	ask	1
rumpō, rumpere, rūpī, ruptum	burst	3
ruō, ruere, ruī, rutum (ruitūrus – fut part)	rush/fall	3
sciō, scīre, scīvī/iī, scītum	know	4
scrībō, scrībere, scrīpsī, scrīptum	write	3
sēcernō, sēcernere, sēcrēvī, sēcrētum	set apart	3
secō, secāre, secuī, sectum	cut	1
sedeō, sedēre, sēdī, sessum	sit	2
sentiō, sentīre, sēnsī, sēnsum	feel/perceive	4
sepeliō, sepelīre, sepelīvī, sepultum	bury	4
sequor, sequī, secūtus sum	follow	3
serō, serere, sēvī, satum	sow	3
serviō, servīre, servīvī, servītum	serve/be a slave	4
servō, servāre, servāvī, servātum	save	1

Principal parts	Meaning	Conj	Page
simulō, simulāre, simulāvī, simulātum	pretend	1	
sinō, sinere, **sīvī, situm**	allow	3	
sistō, sistere, **stitī, statum**	set up	3	
soleō, solēre, **solitus sum**	be used to	2	
sollicitō, sollicitāre, sollicitāvī, sollicitātum	worry	1	
solvō, solvere, **solvī, solūtum**	loosen	3	
sonō, sonāre, **sonuī, sonitum**	sound	1	
spargō, spargere, **sparsī, sparsum**	scatter/sprinkle	3	
spectō, spectāre, spectāvī, spectātum	look at	1	
spērō, spērāre, spērāvī, spērātum	hope	1	
spoliō, spoliāre, spoliāvī, spoliātum	rob/plunder	1	
statuō, statuere, **statuī, statūtum**	set up	3	
sternō, sternere, **strāvī, strātum**	cover/overthrow	3	
stō, stāre, **stetī, stātum**	stand	1	
struō, struere, **strūxī, strūctum**	build	3	
studeō, studēre, studuī	study	2	
suādeō, suādēre, **suāsī, suāsum**	advise	2	
subeō, subīre, subiī, subitum	undergo		
succēdō, succēdere, **successī, successum**	go up/relieve	3	
succurrō, succurrere, succurrī, succursum	help	3	196
sum, esse, fuī, futūrus	take		
sūmō, sūmere, **sūmpsī, sūmptum**	take	3	
superō, superāre, superāvī, superātum	overcome	1	
supersum, superesse, superfuī	survive		
surgō, surgere, **surrēxī, surrēctum**	rise/get up	3	
suscipiō, suscipere, **suscēpī, susceptum**	undertake	3	

Principal parts	Meaning	Conj	Page
suspicor, suspicārī, suspicātus sum	suspect	1	
sustineō, sustinēre, sustinuī, **sustentum**	sustain	2	
taceō, tacēre, tacuī, tacitum	be silent	2	
taedet, taedēre, taeduit, **taesum est**	be tired of	2	
tangō, tangere, **tetigī, tāctum**	touch	3	
tegō, tegere, **tēxī, tēctum**	cover	3	
tendō, tendere, **tetendī, tentum** or **tēnsum**	stretch	3	
teneō, tenēre, tenuī, **tentum**	hold	2	
terreō, terrēre, terruī, territum	terrify	2	
timeō, timēre, timuī	fear	2	
tollō, tollere, **sustulī, sublātum**	raise/remove	3	
tonō, tonāre, tonuī	thunder	1	
torqueō, torquēre, **torsī, tortum**	twist	2	
trādō, trādere, **trādidī, trāditum**	hand over	3	
trahō, trahere, **trāxī, tractum**	drag	3	
traiciō, traicere, **traiēcī, traiectum**	take across	3	
trānseō, trānsīre, trānsiī, trānsitum	cross over	2	
tueor, tuērī, tuitus sum	look at	2	
ulcīscor, ulcīscī, **ultus sum**	punish/avenge	3	
urgeō, urgēre, **ursī**	press/urge	2	
ūrō, ūrere, **ussī, ustum**	burn	3	
ūtor, ūtī, **ūsus sum**	use	3	
valeō, valēre, valuī, valitum	be strong	2	
vastō, vastāre, vastāvī, vastātum	destroy	1	
vehō, vehere, **vēxī, vectum**	carry	3	
vendō, vendere, **vendidī, venditum**	sell	3	
veniō, venīre, **vēnī, ventum**	come	4	
vereor, verērī, veritus sum	fear	2	

The following index lists comprehensively both grammatical terms and key words in English and Latin.